Handbook of Policing

Chris Lewis
51, Langdale Drive,
Nuneaton,
CV11 6EY
Tel 024 7637079.

Handbook of Policing

Edited by Tim Newburn

WILLAN
PUBLISHING

Published by

Willan Publishing
Culmcott House
Mill Street, Uffculme
Cullompton, Devon
EX15 3AT, UK
Tel: +44(0)1884 840337
Fax: +44(0)1884 840251
e-mail: info@willanpublishing.co.uk
website: www.willanpublishing.co.uk

Published simultaneously in the USA and Canada by

Willan Publishing
c/o ISBS, 920 NE 58th Ave, Suite 300,
Portland, Oregon 97213-3786, USA
Tel: +001(0)503 287 3093
Fax: +001(0)503 280 8832
e-mail: info@isbs.com
website: www.isbs.com

First published 2003
Reprinted 2004
ISBN 1-84392-019-0 Paperback
ISBN 1-84392-020-4 Hardback

British Library Cataloguing-in-Publication Data

A catalogue record for this book is available from the British Library.

Typeset by TW Typesetting, Plymouth, Devon
Project management by Deer Park Productions, Tavistock, Devon
Printed and bound by TJ International Ltd, Trecerus Industrial Estate, Padstow,
Cornwall, PL28 8RW

Contents

Acknowledgements

Publisher's
This book has undergone an extensive peer review process, benefiting from informed advice on the text from a range of specialists in different aspects of policing, both practitioners and academics. The editor and publishers are especially grateful to Inspector Martin Wright, West Midlands Police, and Dr Rob C, Mawby, Keele University, who have reviewed all the chapters in this book.

We are also grateful to the following who reviewed one or more chapters of this Handbook, or who provided valued input into the process of refining plans for the overall content and organisation of the book: Peter Ainsworth, Adam Crawford, Howard Davis, David Dixon, Janet Foster, John Grieve, Gordon Hughes, Trevor Jones, Gloria Laycock, Lawrence Lustgarten, Rob C. Mawby, Peter Neyroud, Ken Pease, Robert Reiner, Keith Soothill, Peter Spindler, Kevin Stenson, Nick Tilley, Steve Uglow, Neil Walker, Louise Westmarland, Peter Woods.

Editor's
Putting together this Handbook was an immense task. Thanks are due to all the authors for their contributions and for responding with patience to my promptings. Brian Willan and his colleagues at Willan Publishing provided me with more support and advice in this task than it is usual to expect, or indeed receive, from a publisher. I am immensely grateful to Brian for his help with the project and for contributing so significantly to its development and realisation. My work in this area has benefited hugely from conversations with a large number of friends and colleagues in recent years, including: Ian Blair, Tony Bottoms, Ben Bowling, Janet Chan, Stan Cohen, Adam Crawford, David Dixon, David Downes, Paul Ekblom, Nigel Fielding, Janet Foster, David Garland, Andrew Goldsmith, Roger Graef, John Grieve, Chris Hale, Stephanie Hayman, Frances Heidensohn, Simon Holdaway, Mike Hough, Les Johnston,

Trevor Jones, George Kelling, Nicola Lacey, Gloria Laycock, Mike Levi, Alison Liebling, Ian Loader, Kieran McEvoy, Eugene McLaughlin, Mike Maguire, Lisa Maher, Peter Manning, Steve Mastrofski, Mario Matassa, Rob C. Mawby, Rob I. Mawby, Rod Morgan, Peter Neyroud, Detlef Nogala, Frédéric Ocqueteau, Ken Pease, Coretta Phillips, Phillip Rawlings, Robert Reiner, Declan Roche, Sebastian Roché, Paul Rock, Geoff Pearson, Jill Peay, Maurice Punch, George Rigakos, Bill Saulsbury, Steve Savage, Marty Schwartz, Clifford Shearing, Mike Shiner, Wes Skogan, Nigel South, David Smith, Betsy Stanko, Philip Stenning, Nick Tilley, Steve Uglow, Jaap de Waard, Tank Waddington, Neil Walker, David Wall, Paul Whitehouse, and Paul Wiles. As always my greatest debt is to Mary, Gavin, Robin, Lewis and Owen.

List of abbreviations

ABC	acceptable behaviour contract
ACMA	Authorised Competent Military Authority
ACPO	Association of Chief Police Officers
APA	Association of Police Authorities
APACS	Association for Payment Clearing Services
ASBO	anti-social behaviour order
ATM	automated teller machine
ATOL	Air Travel Organisers' Licensing
BAWP	British Association for Women in Policing
BCS	British Crime Survey
BCU	basic command unit
BSA	Business Software Alliance
BSIA	British Security Industry Association
BTP	British Transport Police
BVPI	Best Value performance indicator
BVPP	Best Value performance plan
C18	Combat 18
CAA	Civil Aviation Authority
CAD	computer-aided dispatch
CAMPS	consultation, adaptation, mobilisation and problem-solving
CCC	Civil Contingencies Committee
CCTV	closed-circuit television
CDA	Crime and Disorder Act 1998
CDIIU	Central Drugs and Illegal Immigration Unit
CDPD	cellular digital packet data
CDRP	Crime and Disorder Reduction Partnership
CHIS	covert human intelligence source

CID	criminal investigation department
CIU	Criminal Intelligence Unit
CPO	crime prevention officer
CPOSA	Chief Police Officers' Staff Association
CPS	Crown Prosecution Service
CPT	child protection team
CSO	community support officer
CSU	community safety unit
DEA	Drug Enforcement Administration
DMSU	divisional mobile support unit
DORA	Defence of the Realm Act
DPPB	District Policing Partnership Board
DTI	Department of Trade and Industry
DTOA	Drug Trafficking Offences Act 1986
DWP	Department of Work and Pensions
ECHR	European Convention on Human Rights
EHO	environmental health officer
ELO	Europol liaison officer
EPA	Emergency Provisions Act 1973
FATF	Financial Action Task Force
FBI	Federal Bureau of Investigation
FIU	financial investigation unit
FLINTS	Forensic Led Intelligence System
FMI	Financial Management Initiative
FSA	Financial Services Authority
GCHQ	Government Communications Headquarters
GIS	geographic information system
GPA	Gay Police Association
HMCIC	Her Majesty's Chief Inspector of Constabulary
HMI	Her Majesty's Inspector of Constabulary
HMIC	Her Majesty's Inspectorate of Constabulary
HOLMES	Home Office Large Major Enquiry System
HR	human resources
IAG	independent advisory group
ICPC	International Criminal Police Commission
ICPO	International Criminal Police Office/International Criminal Police Organisation
ICVS	International Crime Victim Survey
ILP	intelligence-led policing
INHOPE	Internet Hotline Providers in Europe
IPCC	Independent Police Complaints Commission
ISP	Internet service provider
IWF	Internet Watch Foundation
LACOTS	Local Authorities Co-ordinating Body on Food and Trading Standards

LAGPA	Lesbian and Gay Police Association
LAPD	Los Angeles Police Department
LCC	London County Council
LPU	local policing units
LTAF	London Team Against Fraud
MACP	military aid to the civil power
MDP	Ministry of Defence Police
MDT	mobile data terminal
MO	modus operandi
MoD	Ministry of Defence
MoDP	Ministry of Defence Police
MOOTW	military operations other than war
MPD	Metropolitan Police Department
MPS	Metropolitan Police Service
NaCTSO	National Counter Terrorism and Security Office
NBPA	National Black Police Association
NCF	National Competency Framework
NCIS	National Crime Intelligence Service
NCPE	National Centre for Policing Excellence
NCS	National Crime Squad
NCWP	National Centre for Women and Policing
NDIU	National Drugs Intelligence Unit
NDPB	non-departmental public body
NFA	no further action
NHTCU	National Hi-Tech Crime Unit
NIM	National Intelligence Model
NOS	National Occupational Standards
NPM	new public management
NPT	National Police Training
NRC	National Reporting Centre
NSPCA	National Society for the Prevention of Cruelty to Children
NSPIS	National Strategy for Police Information Systems
NUPPO	National Union of Police and Prison Officers
NW	Neighbourhood Watch
OCU	operational command unit
OFA	outside the force area
OSPRE	Objective Structured Performance Related Police Promotion Exam
OSS	one-stop shop
OTE	Organisation for Timeshare in Europe
PACE	Police and Criminal Evidence Act 1984
PAT	problem triangle analysis
PBO	policing by objectives
PCA	Police Complaints Authority
PCCG	police community consultative groups

PCSO	police community support officer
PI	performance indicator
PICTU	Police International Counter Terrorism Unit
PITO	Police Information Technology Organisation
PMC	Police and Magistrates' Courts Bill
PMCA	Police and Magistrates' Courts Act 1994
PNC	Police National Computer
POLSA	police search advisers
POP	problem-oriented policing
PRC	People's Republic of China
PSA	Police Superintendents' Association
PSI	Policy Studies Institute
PSNI	Police Service for Northern Ireland
PSSO	Police Skills and Standards Organisation
PSU	Police Standards Unit
PTA	Prevention of Terrorism Act
RCCP	Royal Commission on Criminal Procedure
RCMP	Royal Canadian Mounted Police
RCS	regional crime squad
RIAA	Record Industry Association of America
RICO	Racketeer Influenced Corrupt Organizations legislation
RIPA	Regulation of Investigatory Powers Act 2000
RJ	restorative justice
RSPCA	Royal Society for the Prevention of Cruelty to Animals
RUC	Royal Ulster Constabulary
SARA	scanning, analysis, response and assessment
SCC	Strategic Command Course
SDEA	Scottish Drug Enforcement Agency
SFO	Serious Fraud Office
SIA	Security Industry Authority
SIO	senior investigating officer
SJC	standing joint committee
SWAT	special weapons and tactics
TCG	Tasking and Co-ordination Group
UBP	unit beat policing
UKAEAC	United Kingdom Atomic Energy Authority Constabulary
VSS	victim statement scheme
VWP	Voluntary Women Patrol
WHOA	Women Halting Online Abuse
WMD	weapons of mass destruction
WPS	Women Police Service
YOT	youth offending team

List of figures, tables and boxes

Figures

Tables

Boxes

Table of statutes

Notes on Contributors

Ben Bowling is Professor of Criminology and Criminal Justice at King's College, London. He has a BA in psychology from Manchester Metropolitan University and a PhD from the LSE. He has held positions of Senior Research Officer in the Home Office, Assistant Professor at John Jay College (City University of New York) and Lecturer in Criminology at Cambridge University. He contributed to the Stephen Lawrence Inquiry and has acted as a consultant to the Metropolitan Police Service, the Commission for Racial Equality and the United Nations. His books include *Young People and Crime* (with J. Graham, Home Office, 1995), *Violent Racism* (Oxford University Press, 1999) and *Racism, Crime and Justice* (with C. Phillips, Longman, 2002).

Simon Byrne is the BCU Commander at Knowsley in Merseyside. Between 2001 and 2003, Knowsley was the site of a Home Office-sponsored project to research and test new ideas to reduce crime. He began his police career in the Metropolitan Police before moving to Merseyside where he has held roles both in uniform and CID at operational and strategic level. In 1998, Simon was seconded to Liverpool City Council to lead the police implementation of the Crime and Disorder Act. He helped establish the Citysafe crime and disorder reduction partnership and the city's anti-social behaviour unit which has since received national acclaim. Following promotion to superintendent he was soon appointed as the Force Crime Reduction Manager where he led the Be Streetsafe campaign to tackle street robbery, introducing new tactics to tackle street crime and anti-social behaviour. In 2002, he was seconded to work in the Policing Bureaucracy Task Force led by Sir David O'Dowd. Simon holds an MA with Distinction from the University of Manchester in police management.

Janet B.L. Chan is currently Head of the School of Social Science and Policy at the University of New South Wales. Her research interest has been in the critical theorising of reforms and innovations in criminal justice, including criminal trial, sentencing, penal policy and policing. She has published extensively in these areas and has also served as research consultant to numerous government bodies in Australia. She is a part-time commissioner of the NSW Law Reform Commission, a panel member of the Criminology Research Council and a member of the NSW Crime Prevention Council. Her recent publications include *Changing Police Culture* (1997); *e-Policing: The Impact of Information Technology on Police Practices* (2001); *Managing Prejudicial Publicity: An Empirical Study of Criminal Jury Trials in New South Wales* (2001); and *Fair Cop: Learning the Art of Policing* (2003).

Nina Cope is currently a strategic researcher in the Metropolitan Police Service where she is responsible for undertaking qualitative research projects and supporting training to enhance the use of criminological research in police practice. She previously worked as a lecturer and researcher at the Universities of Warwick, Cambridge and Surrey, where she contributed to the Diploma and MSc for police officers, which was delivered as part of the Strategic Command Course and conducted research on intelligence-led policing. She has a broad range of research interests in policing and crime, including analysis, youth offending and drugs. She has also undertaken consultancy training with Merseyside and Hertfordshire Police.

Adam Crawford is Professor of Criminology and Criminal Justice at the University of Leeds. He is author of numerous books including *The Local Governance of Crime*; *Crime Prevention and Community Safety*; *Integrating a Victim Perspective within Criminal Justice*; *Crime and Insecurity: The Governance of Safety in Europe*; and *Youth Offending and Restorative Justice* (with T. Newburn). He has worked for the New Zealand Ministry of Justice, the French Ministry of the Interior and the Northern Ireland Office on matters of community safety. He is currently managing a number of research studies exploring the nature of the 'extended police family', including an evaluation of the deployment of police community support officers in West Yorkshire. He is a member of the Leeds Community Safety Partnership and its 'Evaluation' Champion.

Clive Emsley is Professor of History at the Open University, where he also directs a research group focused on the history of policing in Europe. He was educated at the Universities of York and Cambridge. First appointed to the Open University in 1970, he has subsequently taught at the University of Paris VIII and at the University of Calgary, and has held visiting fellowships in Australia and New Zealand. He is an academic adviser to the Police History Society and the Galleries of Justice Museum, and since 1995 he has been President of the International Association for the History of Crime and Criminal Justice. His publications include *The English Police: A Political and Social History* (2nd edn, London, 1996) and *Gendarmes and the State in Nineteenth-century Europe* (Oxford, 1999).

Janet Foster is based in the Sociology Department at the London School of Economics and has extensive experience as a qualitative researcher on crime, community and policing issues. She has also worked with some of Britain's most senior police officers, directing a bespoke programme for the Strategic Command Course between 1997 and 2000, and has also worked with a range of government departments and police forces across Britain and in Europe. Janet is currently researching a book on police leadership and cultural change and recently received (with Tim Newburn) a grant from the Home Office to evaluate the impact of the Stephen Lawrence Inquiry on policing in Britain.

Frances Heidensohn is Professor of Social Policy, University of London, Goldsmiths College. She worked previously in the Civil Service and at the London School of Economics. She has researched and written extensively on women and crime, gender and justice and policing and comparative criminology. Her books include *Women and Crime* (Palgrave/Macmillan, 1996); *Women in Control? The Role of Women in Law Enforcement* (Oxford University Press, 1992); *Gender and Policing* (with J. Brown, Palgrave, 2000); and *Sexual Politics and Social Control* (Open University Press, 2000). She was a key contributor to the founding conference of the Australasian Council of Women and Policing and has maintained her links with them and with other networks. From 1992 to 1999 she was Chair of the Health Authority for the East End and the City of London; she is a Commissioner for Judicial Appointments and a member of the Sentencing Advisory Panel.

Carolyn Hoyle is Lecturer in Criminology at the Centre for Criminological Research and Fellow of Green College, University of Oxford. She is the author of *Negotiating Domestic Violence* (Oxford University Press, 1998); co-author of *Proceed with Caution: An Evaluation of the Thames Valley Police Initiative in Restorative Cautioning* (YPS, 2002); and co-editor of *New Visions of Crime Victims* (Hart Publishing, 2002). She has also written various book chapters, Home Office reports and peer-reviewed articles on restorative justice, victims and domestic violence. She has recently directed two large-scale projects on restorative justice (for the Joseph Rowntree Foundation and the Youth Justice Board) and is currently directing (with Richard Young) studies of restorative justice in the police complaints process (for the Nuffield Foundation) and a restorative cautioning reconviction study (for the Home Office).

Yvonne Jewkes is Senior Lecturer and Director of Undergraduate Studies for Criminology at the University of Hull. She has published extensively in the areas of crime, criminal justice and the mass media, including the transformative impact of new media on criminal and deviant behaviour. Her books include *Dot.cons: Crime, Deviance and Identity on the Internet* (Willan, 2003), which addresses a diverse range of issues including policing and surveillance in cyberspace, identity theft, cyberstalking and prostitution on the Net; *Captive Audience: Media, Masculinity and Power in Prisons* (Willan, 2002); *Criminology: A Reader* (Sage, 2002); and the forthcoming *Media and Crime: A Critical Introduction* (Sage, 2004). She is also a founding editor of the new Sage journal, *Crime, Media, Culture: An International Journal*.

Trevor Jones teaches criminology at the University of Cardiff. His research interests include the relationship between policing and democratic institutions, policing and race relations, and the growth of commercial and other forms of policing. His publications have examined developments in police accountability in England and Wales and in the Netherlands. He jointly conducted (with Tim Newburn) the first national empirical study of the commercial security industry in the UK. Recent work has also included a study of the 1990s reforms of police governance in England and Wales, and an exploration of the relationships between the police and 'hard-to-reach' groups.

Maggy Lee is Lecturer in the Department of Sociology, University of Essex. Before joining the University of Essex in 1996, she worked as a criminal justice researcher at the Institute for the Study of Drug Dependence. Her main areas of research include public and private policing; police cautioning; drug policy and enforcement; juvenile delinquency and youth justice; and migration and human rights. Recent publications include *Youth, Crime and Police Work* (Macmillan, 1998); 'Drugs and policing in Europe: from low streets to high places,' in N. South (ed.) *Drugs – Cultures, Controls and Everyday Life* (Sage, 1999); 'Social wrongs and human rights in late modern Britain,' *Social Justice* (2000, vol. 27); *Crime in Modern Britain* (with Carrabine, Cox and South, Oxford University Press, 2002).

Michael Levi has been Professor of Criminology at Cardiff University since 1991. His books and research reports include *The Phantom Capitalists; Regulating Fraud; The Investigation, Prosecution, and Trial of Serious Fraud*; and (jointly authored) *Money Laundering in the UK: An Appraisal of Suspicion-based Reporting; Investigating, Seizing and Confiscating the Proceeds of Crime*; and *Financial Havens: Banking Secrecy and Money-Laundering* (UN, 1998). His most recent books (with Andy Pithouse), *White-collar Crime and its Victims* and *Reporting White-collar Crime* will be published by Oxford University Press in 2004. He has also edited *Fraud: Organization, Motivation and Control I and II; Reflections on Organised Crime: Patterns and Control*; and *The Corruption of Politics and the Politics of Corruption*. He has carried out several studies of the prevention of payment card fraud and organised crime for the Home Office, and has written on identity and crime risks and on business and crime reduction for the DTI Crime Foresight Panel. He has recently completed a study for the ESRC Future Governance Research initiative – *Controlling the International Money-trail: A Multi-level Cross-national Public Policy Review* – on the shaping of global governance of financial crime and its proceeds since the mid-1980s.

Matt Long studied at postgraduate level at the Institute of Criminology, University of Cambridge. He has been a lecturer at Bramshill for five years. Between 1998 and 2000 he taught police middle managers on the Junior Command Course. For the last three years he has lectured on what was the Accelerated Promotion Course (now the High Potential Development Scheme), including a spell as Acting Head. His research interests are in the domain of public sector performance, particularly the phenomenon of 'naming and shaming', and he is completing a doctorate on Best Value in policing. In 2002 he served as Visiting Professor at John Jay College, the City University of New York.

Mike Maguire is Professor of Criminology and Criminal Justice at Cardiff University. He has managed and conducted research on numerous crime-related topics, especially burglary, victims, policing, prisons, probation and parole. His work on policing includes research (with C. Norris) for the Royal Commission on Criminal Justice examining the conduct and supervision of criminal investigations, several studies of intelligence-led and targeted policing, and a recent evaluation (with T. John) of the implementation of the National Intelligence Model. He has over 100 publications to his name, including co-editing (with R. Morgan and R. Reiner) *The Oxford Handbook of Criminology* (Oxford University Press, 3rd edn, 2002). He also edits a book series for the Open University Press. He was a member of the Parole Board and is currently a member of the Correctional Services Accreditation Panel.

Mario Matassa is currently Research Fellow, Mannheim Centre for Criminology, London School of Economics, having previously worked at the Public Policy Research Unit, Goldsmiths College, the Home Office Policing and Reducing Crime Unit and Leeds University where he completed his PhD on policing in a divided society. In the past four years he has worked as a consultant to the Metropolitan Police Service and has been involved in three major studies of the policing of hate crimes. His recent publications include *Community Safety Structures: An International Literature Review* for the Criminal Justice Review Programme (HMSO, Belfast, with Adam Crawford); and 'Problem-oriented evaluation? Evaluating problem-oriented policing initiatives' (with Tim Newburn), in N. Tilley and K. Bullock (eds) *Crime Reduction and Problem-oriented Policing* (Willan, 2003).

Rob C. Mawby joined Keele University's Criminology Department in September 2003. Prior to this he was Head of the Centre for Public Services Management and Research at Staffordshire University. He is the author of *Policing Images: Policing, Communication and Legitimacy* (2002), and co-author of *Practical Police Management* (1998). He has undertaken consultancy and applied research projects for, among others, the European Commission, the Home Office and the Police Standards Unit. These have focused on diverse aspects of policing, including police accountability and police corruption, police–media relations, the effectiveness of intensive supervision prolific offender projects and the deployment of police drugs-scanning dogs.

Rob I. Mawby is Professor of Criminology and Criminal Justice and Director of the Community Justice Research Centre, University of Plymouth. He is the author of eight books and numerous articles in academic books and journals. His main research interests cover policing, victim issues, crime reduction, and tourism and crime. His research has a particular cross-national emphasis, and he has carried out research on, with or on behalf of the police in a number of countries, as well as locally in Devon and Cornwall, where he was, until recently, chair of Plymouth Mediation. His most recent books include *Policing* *across the World: Issues for the Twenty-first Century* (UCL Press, 1999) and *Burglary* (Willan, 2001).

Tim Newburn is Professor of Criminology and Social Policy and Director of the Mannheim Centre for Criminology at the London School of Economics. He has written and researched widely on issues of crime and justice and, in particular, on policing and security. He has acted as an adviser to the Home Office on various aspects of policing and to the Metropolitan Police on integrity and corruption. His books on policing include *Democracy and Policing* (with Trevor Jones and David Smith, 1994); *Themes in Contemporary Policing* (with William Saulsbury and Joy Mott, 1996); *Policing after the Act* (with Trevor Jones, 1997); *The Future of Policing* (with Rod Morgan, 1997); *Private Security and Public Policing* (with Trevor Jones, 1998); and *Policing, Surveillance and Social Control* (with Stephanie Hayman, 2001). He is currently working on a study of the impact of the Stephen Lawrence Inquiry.

Peter Neyroud is the Chief Constable of Thames Valley Police. He has had a police career for over 23 years in Hampshire, West Mercia and Thames Valley, in roles ranging from beat officer, community and race relations co-ordinator, senior investigator, director of intelligence and assistant chief constable in both support and operational roles. He has held national responsibility for Police Use of Firearms in the UK, for the introduction of the Human Rights Act and for restorative justice. He is the author of several studies on policing, including *Policing, Ethics and Human Rights* (with Alan Beckley) and *Public Participation in Policing* (for the IPPR). He is a Council Member of Justice. He is a dual Swiss-British national.

Ken Pease is Professor of Criminology at Huddersfield University and Visiting Professor of Crime Science at the Jill Dando Institute, University College London. He is a chartered forensic psychologist who has acted as Head of the Home Office's Police Research Group, and has previously held chairs at the Universities of Manchester and Saskatchewan. The Applied Criminology Group at Huddersfield, which he heads, has always been based in an operational police station (currently Kirkburton). He is a former member of the Parole Board.

Coretta Phillips is a Lecturer in Social Policy at the London School of Economics and Political Science, having previously been Principal Research Officer in the Home Office. While there, she undertook an observational study of the arrest and detention process in police stations in England and Wales, and worked with the police and other agencies on a crime prevention initiative to reduce repeat racial victimisation on a London housing estate. Her current research interests focus on issues of ethnicity, racism and criminal justice, and she is currently engaged in a study of minority professional associations in the criminal justice field, including the police. She is author of *Racism, Crime and Justice* (with Ben Bowling, Longman, 2002).

Philip Rawlings is Senior Lecturer, Faculty of Law, University College London. He is the author of several books and papers on policing and the history of crime and criminal justice, including *Policing: A Short History* (Willan, 2002); *Crime and Power: A History of Criminal Justice 1688–1998* (Longman, 1999); and *Drunks, Whores and Idle Apprentices: Criminal Biographies of the Eighteenth Century* (Routledge, 1992). He is also joint author of *Imprisonment: A Concise History* (Croom Helm, 1985).

Robert Reiner is Professor of Criminology in the Law Department, London School of Economics. He is author of *The Blue-coated Worker* (Cambridge University Press, 1978); *The Politics of the Police* (Oxford University Press, 3rd edn, 2000); *Chief Constables* (Oxford University Press, 1991); and editor of (with M. Cross) *Beyond Law and Order* (Macmillan, 1991), (with S. Spencer) *Accountable Policing* (Institute for Public Policy Research, 1993), *Policing* (Dartmouth, 1996) and (with M. Maguire and R. Morgan) *The Oxford Handbook of Criminology* (Oxford University Press, 3nd edn, 2002). He has published over one hundred papers on policing and criminal justice topics. His current research is a study financed by the Economic and Social Research Council, analysing changing media representations of crime and criminal justice since the Second World War.

Andrew Sanders is Professor of Criminal Law and Criminology at the University of Manchester. He is author of *Community Justice* (IPPR, 2001), is co-author (with Richard Young) of *Criminal Justice* (Butterworths, 2nd edn, 2000) and co-author (with Mike McConville and Roger Leng) of *The Case for the Prosecution* (Routledge, 1991). He is currently evaluating (with Roger Evans) provisions for vulnerable and intimidated witnesses arising from Speaking up for Justice. He was a member of the Parole Board for England and Wales from 1995 to 2001, was appointed to the Attorney-General's Advisory Board for HM CPS Inspectorate in January 2001 and is a Life Sentence Commissioner for Northern Ireland.

Nigel South is Professor of Sociology, University of Essex. He has published widely on policing, including (with N. Dorn and K. Murji) the influential *Traffickers: Drug Markets and Law Enforcement* (1992); *Policing for Profit* (Sage, 1988), one of the first studies of private security; articles on police informants; and the chapter on 'Police and policing' in the successful textbook *The New British Politics* (I. Budge *et al.*, 3rd edn, 2003). He has been involved in consultancy and multi-agency collaborations with the police, local government and health services and, with Maggy Lee, developed a BA in Society, Law and Policing for police students. From 1996 to 2003 he was, first, Director of the Health and Social Services Institute and then Head of the Department of Health and Human Sciences at Essex.

Nick Tilley is Professor of Sociology at Nottingham Trent University and Visiting Professor at the Jill Dando Institute of Crime Science, University College London. He was seconded as a consultant to the Home Office Research, Development and Statistics Directorate from 1992 to 2003. He has conducted studies relating, among other things, to the use of forensic science in crime investigation; to the implementation of problem-oriented policing; and to the prevention of a range of crimes including domestic burglary, shootings, crimes against small businesses, crimes at motorway service areas and car crime. The Home Office-funded 'Tilley Award' is made annually to the best examples of crime and disorder problem-solving initiatives submitted by police services and crime and disorder partnerships.

P.A.J. Waddington is Professor of Political Sociology, School of Sociology, Politics and International Relations, the University of Reading. He is author of *Policing Citizens* (UCL Press, 1999), *Liberty and Order* (UCL Press, 1994) and *Strong Arm of the Law* (Clarendon Press, 1991) and numerous articles on a wide range of policing issues. Tank Waddington also writes a weekly column for the magazine, *Police Review*. He headed an international inquiry into the policing of the Boipatong massacre in South Africa (1992) and was recently consulted by the US Department of Defense on the use of non-lethal weapons for riot control purposes.

Neil Walker is Professor of European Law at the European University Institute, Florence, and was previously Professor of Legal and Constitutional Theory at the University of Aberdeen. He has written extensively on the legal and organisational aspects of policing – both domestic and international – including *Policing in a Changing Constitutional Order* (Sweet & Maxwell, 2000). For many years he taught at the Scottish Police Training College at Tulliallan, Fife, and has also lectured at the National Police College, Bramshill. He has given evidence on policing matters to a number of official inquiries, including, on several occasions, to the House of Lords Committee on European Legislation regarding developments in police and criminal justice co-operation. He has on several occasions undertaken research into practical aspects of policing and criminal justice at the request of government departments, including a study of the reform options for Northern Ireland criminal justice system as part of the post-Belfast Agreement Review of the Northern Ireland Criminal Justice System in 2000.

Alan Wright is an independent scholar in the fields of policing and crime investigation. Before entering academia in 1985, he served in the Metropolitan Police for 25 years, mostly in CID, where he worked on the Kray case and on other gang crime and homicide cases. He is a former senior lecturer at the Institute of Criminal Justice Studies, University of Portsmouth, for whom he continues to deliver contract work. He has published widely on policing and is the author of *Policing: An Introduction to Concepts and Practice* (Willan, 2002). He lectures at several universities and is Honorary Research Fellow at the Applied Criminology Group, Huddersfield University. Recent consultancy includes work for the Specialist Crime Directorate (Metropolitan Police) and the City of London Police.

Richard Young is Reader in Criminal Justice and Assistant Director of the Centre for Criminological Research, University of Oxford. With colleagues, he has conducted three research projects on aspects of policing, including an action research study of restorative cautioning in partnership with Thames Valley Police. He has acted as a tutor on the Bramshill Strategic Command Course and lectured on restorative justice for students taking the Diploma and MSt Degree in Applied Criminology and Police Studies offered by Cambridge University. He is currently co-directing a project examining how Hampshire Constabulary and Thames Valley Police handle complaints by members of the public against their officers.

Chapter 1

Introduction: understanding policing

Tim Newburn

Image and reality

We live in complex times. Few doubt the importance of the police in the maintenance of order. Most opinion polls asking questions about security return the finding that the public appetite for 'more bobbies on the beat' remains undimmed. Yet, it is also the case that people are now much more sceptical about the abilities of the police than once would have been the case and are likely to be much more critical about their interactions with police officers. Writing in the interwar years Charles Reith, in his 'orthodox' history of the police, suggested that 'What is astonishing ... is the patience and blindness displayed both by citizens and authority in England over a period of nearly a hundred years, during which they persistently rejected the proposed and *obvious police remedy* for their increasing fears and sufferings' (1938: v, emphasis added). It is rarer now for policing to be viewed as an obvious remedy for the problems that confront us for 'police and policing cannot deliver on the great expectations now placed on them in terms of crime control' (Reiner 2000: 217). Nevertheless, there remains considerable residual faith in this particular state institution.

Public constabularies, in the sense we now know them, are less than two centuries old. Though there has only been concentrated scholarly attention on policing for a small part of that period, the police and policing are now a staple of sociological, criminological and popular discourse. There was considerable resistance to the introduction of the new police in the nineteenth century and, indeed, it was not until the mid-twentieth century that anything like a broad degree of social legitimacy was achieved in the UK. By any standards, the public police service is now a formidable social institution. Its size and its cost, for example, have grown dramatically.

Up until the late 1970s there existed broad agreement between the main political parties on questions of 'law and order'. The end of this bipartisan consensus led to an intense battle over criminal justice generally, and arguably policing most particularly. The Thatcher administration signalled its desire to be perceived to be supportive of the police service by implementing the Edmund Davies pay agreement soon after reaching office in 1979. This led to a very substantial increase in police expenditure – doubling from £1.6 billion in 1979 to £3.4 billion in 1984, though only a six per cent increase in staff levels. Although the pattern has been far from smooth since, expenditure has continued to rise, reaching £7.7 billion by 2000 and anticipated to rise to £9.3 billion during 2003–4. This represents very nearly one half of total government expenditure on the criminal justice system; by comparison, the prison service was expected to cost £2.6 billion in 2003–4 and the probation service £0.6 billion. A significant element of recent increases in expenditure has been devoted to attempts to increase police numbers. While this has by no means always been the focus of increased expenditure historically – as the Edmund Davies increases illustrate – nevertheless, police numbers have themselves increased substantially in recent decades. There were in the region of 50,000 police officers in 1955. This had increased to approximately 80,000 by 1975 and 118,000 by 1995. Total police officer strength stood at 131,548 in September 2002, with a further 4,000 recruits planned during 2003.

In part, this growing expenditure reflects the increased workload facing the police service. Whatever their other shortcomings, one thing that officially recorded crime rates are able to indicate fairly accurately is the number of calls on police time. Quite clearly this has expanded vastly in the postwar period. Notifiable offences recorded by the police, for example, grew from slightly over half a million in the early 1950s to substantially in excess of five million per annum at the beginning of the new century (see Figure 1.1). The most dramatic increase occurred between 1980 and 1992, during which period recorded crime more than doubled.

Figure 1.1 Recorded crime, England and Wales, 1950–2000

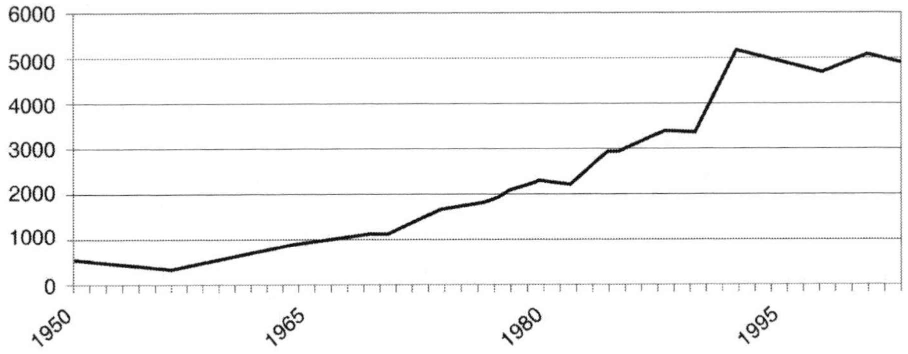

Source: Criminal Statistics England and Wales

There have been times when politicians assumed that increased expenditure on the police would lead, almost mechanically, to greater effectiveness in crime control (see, for example, Baker 1993). While this is no longer the case, and indeed there is considerable scepticism in some quarters about police efficiency and effectiveness, there remains considerable competition between the political parties to be seen to be supportive of the police. Recent years have seen the police service become a much more effective lobbying body. The Association of Chief Police Officers (ACPO), in particular, has become a key player in the politics of crime control and, in the main, home secretaries have been reluctant to take on the police service. One of the clearest ways in which political support can be delivered is through a commitment to provide increased resources and this has been a political stance that, for understandable reasons, the police service has been keen to encourage – and has generally managed to do successfully.

More problematic, however, has been the relationship between the police and the public. During the past 20 years there has been a substantial decline in public satisfaction with the police, with the proportion of people saying that the police do a 'very good' job declining from 43 per cent in 1982 to 24 per cent in 1992 and then again to 20 per cent in 2000 (see Figure 1.2), though overall levels of approval remain relatively high.

Figure 1.2 Public confidence in the police, 1982–2000 (BCS)

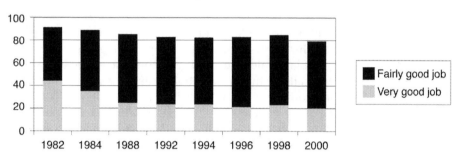

Source: Sims and Myhill (2001)

In part, the continuing faith in the police relates to the important role that they have played, at least up until relatively recent times, as a focus for a particular conception of English identity and social order. More particularly, the police for the bulk of the postwar period have been able to call upon a large degree of support from significant sections of the population not because – or not *entirely* because – of what they do, but because of what they represent. The immediate postwar period, and the fictional figure of PC George Dixon, have come to take on a particular resonance in relation to British policing. Why this supposed 'golden age' has become such a powerful symbol is difficult precisely to fathom but, as Loader (1997: 16) suggests, it is likely not only to be 'about the allure of a seemingly safer and more harmonious era; it is also a means of recalling just how great this medium-sized, multi-cultural, economically-declining, European nation once was'. Rising crime levels, together with a decline in faith in the efficacy of criminal justice generally, and the police in particular, together with a raft of sociopolitical changes to our way of life, have created significant challenges to this symbolic image of policing. Nevertheless, it remains the case that there is an almost endless public fascination with the police as an organisation and with policing as a set of activities.

3

Nowhere can this fascination be seen more clearly than in the changing media representations of policing in postwar Britain. As Reiner (see Chapter 11) and others note, important elements of the shifting nature of policing have been captured in the changing characters and representations in television drama, from the romantic and politically uncontroversial society policed by George Dixon, through the gradual emergence of an increasingly complex world of the 1960s and 1970s (*Z-cars* and subsequently the regional crime squad in *Softly, Softly*), to the acknowledgement, and implicit acceptance, of police rule-breaking by the Flying Squad in *The Sweeney*. In some respects, the multiple representations now available on television – from hard-edged soap opera (*The Bill*[1]) through attempts to recover a 'golden age' (*Heartbeat*) to farce (*Thin Blue Line*) and fly on the wall (*Rail Cops*) – reflect the somewhat fractured and plural nature of contemporary policing, and also the somewhat more problematic relationship between policing and national identity.

In part, such dramatic representations have much to tell us about the realities of policing, though they are also a potent source, reproduction and reinforcement of the myth and mystique that surround policing. As I have already implied, in recent times the police have become much more adept at managing and manipulating images and messages about what they are and what they do. Attempting to understand the changing nature of police representation, and how this relates to the realities of policing 'on the ground', is a central aim of this book. So plentiful, and sometimes so seductive, are the images of policing now available that it is relatively easy to persuade ourselves that we understand and somehow 'know' policing. This handbook focuses on the realities of contemporary policing, exploring the nature and organisation of policing activities, how policing is conducted, the problems and controversies that exist, and the key issues and debates that are likely to shape its possible futures.

Studying policing

In recent decades social scientists and historians have become increasingly preoccupied with policing. The sociopolitical changes of the 1960s permissive era set in train a number of changes in policing, as well as stimulating considerable academic thought on how policing should be theorised and understood. Since that period there has been a very significant expansion in both the sociology *of* the police and sociology *for* the police (Banton 1964). In recent times, in part reflecting the apparently increasingly complex policing division of labour, the sociology of poli*cing* has also grown substantially (Jones and Newburn 1998). At the same time 'law and order' in general, and policing in particular, have also become much more politicised and contested.

Much early work on policing focused on the nature of the police role and of police 'culture'. In particular, work by Banton in the 1960s, Cain in the 1970s and Smith and Gray in the 1980s set the parameters for much that has followed. Banton's observation that the police officer is primarily a 'peace officer' rather than a 'law officer' spending relatively little time enforcing the law compared with 'keeping the peace' had a profound influence on criminological work in this area. Subsequent work also focused on what were primarily functional definitions of police work with Cain (1979), for example, arguing that the police ought to be defined in terms of their key practice – the maintenance of order. Despite criticism, much academic writing continued in this tradition of analysing what policing *is* in terms of what constabularies *do*, and much such work focused on the idea that a considerable portion of police work should be understood in terms other than crime control, or even order maintenance (Punch 1979). In contrast to studies focusing on the 'police function', work by Bittner and others focused on the legal capacity brought by the police to their activities. Starting from the position that neither the public generally, nor the police in particular, succeed particularly well in describing and justifying what it is that the police do, Bittner argued that it is the police's position as the sole agency with access to the state's monopoly of the legitimate use of force which makes them distinctive and accounts for the breadth of their role. As he put it:

> the police are empowered and required to impose or, as the case may be, coerce a provisional solution upon emergent problems without having to brook or defer to opposition of any kind, and that further, their competence to intervene extends to every kind of emergency, without any exceptions whatever. This and this alone is what the existence of the police uniquely provides, and it is on this basis that they may be required to do the work of thief-catchers and of nurses, depending on the occasion (1974: 17).

Bittner's crucial contribution was to identify what was distinctive about the role and contribution of public constabularies.

As I suggested above, much of the early sociology of policing tended not to allow its gaze to stray much beyond the public police. Recent years have seen much greater attention paid to the private security sector and to the range of policing providers that lie somewhere between the 'public' and 'private' spheres (see Shearing and Stenning 1987; South 1988; Johnston 1992; Jones and Newburn 1998), though the bulk of criminological attention continues to be paid to public constabularies – and this is the case for this volume too. The title of this volume – the Handbook of Poli*cing* – is deliberately chosen. Though much space is devoted to the nature and work of the police, wherever relevant, authors have focused attention on other policing bodies. As such, it is very much a child of its time, taking the increasingly complex, fragmented and plural nature of policing as a major focus.

Two other major additions transformed the study of policing during this period. The first was the emergence of a set of critical historians who, in Reiner's (2000) terms, challenged the 'cop-sided view of history' with a revisionist 'lop-sided' account (e.g. Storch 1975). The result is a much richer history of policing arrangements, and one that is able to grasp the extra-ordinary story of increasing police legitimacy during the nineteenth and early twentieth centuries while allowing for the fact that the power of the police is always contested (see, in particular, Reiner 2000: ch. 1). The second development was the emergence of a form of policy-oriented (administrative) criminology focusing in the main on police activity, operations and performance. Much of this was funded by government and was influenced by the dominant research paradigm emerging in the Home Office in particular in the late 1970s and 1980s (see, for example, Heal *et al.* 1985).

Work on the police has continued to expand since that time. Indeed, from a period 30 years ago in which the police service was, perhaps understandably, somewhat nervous about, and on occasion actively resistant to, criminological research, we now find ourselves in a position where most forces have some form of internal research capability, and all forces actively encourage research. The subdiscipline of police studies is now well established within British criminology and beyond. Both professionals within the police service itself and students studying criminology and related subjects are increasingly involved in the study of policing in its broad sense. Courses are proliferating and this shows no sign of diminishing. A number of specialist journals cater for, and facilitate, this market in ideas, and the range of books on policing – including book series – is increasing all the time. It is for this territory that the *Handbook of Policing* is designed.

The volume

This volume aims to provide a broad introduction to policing – attractive to students at all levels and to practitioners – without sacrificing the commitment to high-quality scholarship. The intention in this volume has been to cover all the major aspects of policing – in its broad sense – inviting experts in their particular fields to address key themes in the history, theory and practice of policing. This is a range that is difficult to capture within a single book and, certainly, existing textbooks in this area have only attempted to cover part of this terrain. Thus, the *Handbook of Policing* has a broader focus than has hitherto been possible in a single volume on policing and one of its aims, therefore, is to attempt to provide the core reading for an entire course on policing, supplemented by other books and journals.

Clearly, the amount of criminological attention now paid to the police, and the quantity of research being undertaken, is significantly greater than in previous periods. The handbook seeks to increase awareness of existing research, to provide the means with which to assess the major claims of such work and to outline the social, political and cultural context in which the nature of policing is to be understood. It covers issues of theory, principle and practice, seeks to engage with the major debates about the direction of policing and to explore the latest developments in the field.

As I have suggested above, its other main aim is to bring high-quality scholarship, using experts in particular fields, to each of the topics in the volume. This was an ambitious task and I was extraordinarily fortunate that all the authors who were originally approached to contribute to the volume agreed to do so. They were given a somewhat unenviable task: to attempt to capture, in a relatively short space, the key ideas, arguments and debates in their particular field in a way that would do justice to the complexity of the ideas, while remaining accessible to students. I am enormously grateful to them all for the hard work that has gone into achieving this.

One of the most difficult decisions in planning the volume was deciding where to set the boundaries, and what to leave out. No doubt there will be disagreements about the choices that were eventually made. Were the size of the volume not an issue then there were undoubtedly other chapters that could and would have been included. In addition, there are numerous chapters that covered territory that, arguably, could easily have been the subject of several separate chapters. Similarly, much more attention could have been paid to developments outside England and Wales. Initially, I considered the possibility of a handbook that would be comparative in outlook. However, the complexity of policing arrangements internationally meant, I felt, that it would be impossible to deal with the range of issues the handbook needed to cover in sufficient depth, and with sufficient range, to make for a satisfactory volume. Consequently, the volume focuses primarily on policing in England and Wales. However, there remains a strong comparative element within the book, taking in developments in the USA, Europe and Australia.

The handbook is aimed at students, researchers, teachers and practitioners. In relation to students the handbook is appropriate for both undergraduate and postgraduate studies in criminology and its subdisciplines, as well as sociology, social policy, politics and management. There is also a very considerable practitioner audience consisting of police officers, either at management levels within the police service or likely eventually to reach such levels, together with those working in other organisations, whose work involves crime and policing-related issues. The police service is currently quite well served in terms of specific and targeted training manuals. At a time when policing is under pressure, and to a degree is beginning, to devolve responsibility to local levels, police service staff – both officers and civilians – are increasingly having to manage staff and resources, are devising and implementing policing plans, accounting for budgets and are taking on a set of managerial and administrative duties unknown to their predecessors. As a consequence, the knowledge required by the modern officer is in many respects quite different from what would have been distilled from traditional training programmes.

For the increasing number of highly educated and reflective officers working within an increasingly professionalised service, however, there is no comprehensive and authoritative source on policing they can turn to. This volume, which is ambitious in both scope and approach, seeks to fill these gaps.

That said, the volume is critical in intent. Every effort has been made to think *critically* about the nature of policing and the issues affecting it. In some respects, policing is intrinsically conflictual and controversial. In addition, it has become the site of ever-greater political contestation. This volume reflects both this nature and the content of these debates. Authors write from different perspectives – from critical criminologist to chief constable. As a consequence there is much to be gained from reading chapters in conjunction with each other, contrasting different perspectives and approaches. What links the contributions is a commitment to critical scholarship; a willingness to question and provoke; but, overall, a commitment to examining and evaluating evidence. All the chapters were completed in 2003. They are therefore up to date, drawing on the most recently published writing and research. Recent years have seen a number of important developments:

- The Police Reform Act 2002 has further stimulated the pluralisation of policing.

- Increasing technological sophistication has led to a number of significant potential advances, including DNA profiling and a more general emphasis on the use of intelligence in policing.

- A number of political developments, not the least of which was the terrorist attacks on the Twin Towers and the Pentagon, have had an important impact on international and transnational policing.

- Some significant changes have been made to the nature of the police organisation including both the development of new central police organisations and increasing emphasis on basic command units.

- Recruitment to, and promotion within, the police service has changed with greater emphasis placed on formal educational qualifications – perhaps the most obvious illustration of increasing police professionalism.

- Women officers remain a minority within the police service but, in recent years, have become increasingly visible at ACPO level.

- Training of officers at all ranks is being reorganised and a new training body has been created.

- The Stephen Lawrence Inquiry in particular has drawn attention to the problematic nature of policing and diversity.

- Much greater emphasis is now placed upon partnership or multi-agency working, particularly since the Crime and Disorder Act 1998.

- New structures and new technologies have led to the greater attention being paid to 'new' forms of criminality (such as cybercrime) and to some 'older' forms as well (such as white-collar and organised crime).

- Changing political circumstances have reworked debates around governance and accountability, leading to more emphasis on performance management on the one hand and to a consideration of ethics and human rights on the other.

- The limitations of traditional systems of justice have led to a greater willingness to experiment with new developments (or modernised forms of traditional techniques), such as restorative justice.

The need to understand these issues and related developments makes this project particularly timely. The handbook looks at all these questions and more. This is undoubtedly the most ambitious volume on policing to date, seeking to take stock of the full range of developments and issues in this most important of public services. In staking out its territory, the volume aims to set out the parameters for police studies as an important subdiscipline of criminology and to provide the basis for teaching in this area.

In covering this ground the volume is divided into four major parts. The first considers policing in its comparative and historical context. What are the major models of policing and how did they develop? How is policing best theorised and understood? How was policing organised and arranged before formalised state agencies became the norm in liberal democracies? How has policing developed in the past two centuries? All too often books on criminal justice generally, or policing in particular, avoid much discussion of history and origins. It is simply not possible, however, to make sense of where we are today unless we have a clear sense of how we got here, and how it might and has occurred differently elsewhere. The chapters in the first part of the book explore the development of policing internationally and historically, looking both at policing before the police and policing in its contemporary setting.

The second part of the volume looks at the context within which policing takes place. Policing, as I have alluded to, appears to be becoming increasingly fragmented and complex. Despite this, texts frequently assume that readers come fully equipped with a fairly comprehensive knowledge of structures and systems. This is more often than not a mistake. This volume seeks to describe, to analyse and to explain the contemporary topography of policing. What do international and domestic policing structures look like? How is the police service organised domestically? What do rank structures and organisational hierarchies have to tell us about modern policing? How is policing in its broad sense (the extended family of policing appears to be the currently favoured term) to be understood? How have international and, increasingly, transnational forms of policing developed? What powers are available to the police, how do they exercise them and what might this tell us about the nature of police organisational cultures? And how is policing represented and understood in our media-saturated times?

The third part looks at how the police operate. How do the police analyse and investigate crime? Underneath the rhetoric and claims about the power of ICT, is crime analysis revolutionising policing or are the changes more superficial? What do some of the major models of policing such as 'problem-oriented policing' and 'intelligence-led policing' mean, how widespread are they and what impact do they have on day-to-day policing? What approach do the police take to such issues as crime reduction and community safety, drugs and the policing of the streets? Have responses to terrorism and organised crime changed as a result of globalisation and the growth of transnational policing bodies?

The final part of the handbook examines a range of key themes in contemporary policing. Some of these are debates of relatively long standing – such as that over governance and accountability; others are somewhat newer on the policing scene – such as ethics. However, what these and a number of other chapters in this part share is a common concern with how police behaviour and performance are determined, managed and governed. All public services, including the police, are now subject to an increasingly bureaucratic system of performance management. This, together with some of the higher-profile examples of apparent 'failure', have led to renewed scrutiny of police leadership and the chapters in Part IV explore both the general governance of the police and the more specific questions of what makes for effective management and leadership. As many chapters throughout the volume argue and illustrate, there is an almost inevitable tension between quantitative performance management and a focus on the quality of service being delivered. The treatment of women – by the police, as well as within the organisation – and more recently, the policing of minority ethnic communities, have drawn particular attention to some of these tensions and the way in which they are operationalised. The chapters which focus on these issues put questions about values, attitudes and appropriate conduct centre-stage. This is examined in relation to leadership, to the treatment of staff, to the nature of police–community relations, as well as to the possible reorientation of policing styles through the adoption of restorative justice-influenced practices. Arguably, given the power of the police to exercise potentially violent supervision, it is precisely these questions – of values and ethics – that should dominate both our practical and our normative debates about the future of policing.

Note

1   Which first appeared as a one-off, one-hour TV drama, entitled *Woodentop*.

References

Baker, K. (1993) *The Turbulent Years: My Life in Politics*. London: Faber & Faber.

Banton, M. (1964) *The Policeman in the Community*. London: Tavistock.

Bittner, E. (1974) 'Florence Nightingale in pursuit of Willie Sutton: a theory of the police', in H. Jacob (ed.) *The Potential for Reform of Criminal Justice*. Newbury Park, CA: Sage.

Cain, M. (1979) 'Trends in the sociology of police work', *International Journal of the Sociology of Law*, 7(2): 158.

Heal, K., Tarling, R. and Burrows, J. (1985) *Policing Today*. London: HMSO.

Johnston, L. (1992) *The Rebirth of Private Policing*. London: Routledge.

Johnston, L. (1993) 'Privatization and protection: spatial and sectoral ideologies in British policing and crime prevention', *Modern Law Review*, 56(6): 771–92.

Jones, T. and Newburn, T. (1998) *Private Security and Public Policing*. Oxford: Clarendon Press.

Loader, I. (1997) 'Policing and the social: questions of symbolic power', *British Journal of Sociology*, 48(1): 1–18.

Punch, M. (1979) 'The secret social service', in S. Holdaway (ed.) *The British Police*. London: Edward Arnold.

Reiner, R. (2000) *The Politics of the Police* (3rd edn). Oxford: Oxford University Press.

Reith, C. (1938) *The Police Idea: Its History and Evolution in England in the Eighteenth Century and After*. London: Oxford University Press.

Shearing, C.D. and Stenning, P. (1987) *Private Policing*. London: Sage.

Sims, L. and Myhill, A. (2001) *Policing and the Public: Findings from the 2000 British Crime Survey. Research Findings 136*. London: Home Office.

South, N. (1988) *Policing for Profit*. London: Sage.

Storch, R. (1975) 'The plague of blue locusts: police reform and popular resistance in northern England 1840–57', *International Review of Social History*, 20: 61–90.

Part I

Policing in Comparative and Historical Perspective

Tim Newburn

We cannot possibly understand contemporary policing without reflecting on how it came to be the way we find it now. What are the origins of our current arrangements? Might it have been different and, if so, in what ways and to what extent? Is policing organised differently in different social, political and cultural situations? It is questions of this order that should form the basis of any developed understanding of current issues and trends in policing. All too often, however, relatively little attention is devoted to longer historical developments and concerns. Too frequently, history is treated as if it were either of less importance than the study of contemporary developments or, even where it is viewed as being important, it is its perceived intrinsic value that is valued rather than being viewed as central to the ways in which we make sense of our current arrangements. In constructing this volume, a very deliberate decision was taken that this oversight should not be repeated. We begin from the position that a reasonably developed understanding of the long-term history of the police, and of policing, is a prerequisite for a book that aims to be comprehensive in its treatment of the subject and to give students and other readers a firm basis on which to pursue this subject.

As I have already implied, not only is the starting point for the book the acknowledgement of the importance of historical understanding but also wherever possible this should be comparative too; we should have at least some sense of contrasting histories in other jurisdictions. This is only possible in part in a volume such as this. Thus, though the primary focus of the contributions in this volume is on policing in England and Wales, we have sought to include some sense of comparative developments in a number of key chapters. In particular, the opening chapter in this first part of the book examines the differing models of policing that have developed around the world. Rob Mawby (Chapter 2) discusses the variation in the structure and role of police organisations, distinguishing between Anglo-American systems and those that have developed in continental Europe, colonial societies, communist countries and within different parts of Asia. All police forces are subject to change, and in some respects there appear to be some similarities in lines of development observable in different parts of the world. However, as Mawby rightly warns, 'this should not necessarily be taken as evidence that modern police systems are converging'.

Moving then to policing in Britain, Philip Rawlings's chapter (Chapter 3) is the first of three historical overviews. Rawlings examines 'policing before the police' – the nature, structure and meaning of policing activities before the creation of the 'New Police' in the early nineteenth century. He begins with the communal policing of the Middle Ages, a period characterised by considerable community responsibility for order maintenance via the hue and cry and the system of frankpledge. The three centuries from the mid-thirteenth century onward, he suggests, saw the replacement of community responsibility with the rise of officials drawn from the parish, the county and the Crown. The seventeenth and eighteenth centuries saw the continuation of this process with the professionalisation of the watch and the rise of watchmen and constables and, in the eighteenth century, patrols such as those most famously associated with Bow Street – a process which culminated in the late 1820s with the establishment of the Metropolitan Police.

Clive Emsley (Chapter 4) continues the story picking up around 1829 with the intervention of Robert Peel and the emergence of the 'New Police'. He outlines the contrasting Whig and revisionist histories of the development of the formal state system of policing, taking in the nineteenth century and the first half of the twentieth. According to Emsley, though there was a degree of good fortune attending Peel's legislation to create the Metropolitan Police in 1829, and there was continued scepticism about the French model, anxiety about crime had converted many to the idea that policing required greater organisation and formalisation. Nevertheless, concern both about the threat to liberty and about the suspected military nature of the new police organisation continued. The remainder of the century saw the expansion of this new system of policing to the provinces together with growing formalisation and centralisation. Despite the considerable consolidation that occurred during the first century of the police, as Emsley concludes, by the end of the Second World War there remained more than 100 separate forces in England and Wales. Consequently, there were still many policy-makers and administrators who felt that further amalgamation of forces, and further centralisation of common police services, would be beneficial. In many ways his conclusion anticipates much of what was to follow.

Finally in Part I, Tim Newburn (Chapter 5) takes the narrative from the end of the Second World War, focusing on the very significant developments that have changed the topography of policing from that point to the present day. At the heart of much that has changed in this period, he suggests, is the continuation of the long-term process of centralisation through which the Home Office, and government generally, has extended its power over the police. Simultaneously, however, policing as a set of activities has become exceedingly more complex in recent decades, a mixed economy of provision having emerged. The other major themes he identifies concern the changing role and image of policing, the increasingly problematic relationship between the police and particular minority ethnic communities – highlighted by the Scarman and Stephen Lawrence Inquiries – and the heightened managerialist scrutiny of policing services.

Overall, it appears that policing now finds itself at an important juncture. Crime, though not currently rising, continues to place enormous demands on the police. Public expectations – apparently partly independently of crime levels – continue to rise, though trust appears increasingly problematic. As security becomes increasingly commodified, the police service faces enormous challenges in maintaining what hitherto – for the best part of a century and a half at least – has been a position of considerable authority. Cultural, social, political, economic and technological changes are all having a major impact on what the police do, what they are expected to do and what they are able to do. Part I of the *Handbook of Policing* examines how we reached this position; the remainder explores the nature of policing and the challenges facing it.

Chapter 2

Models of policing

R.I. Mawby

Introduction

The police officer on the streets, the representative of an institution known as 'the police', is a concept that is familiar to most citizens of modern societies. It is a concept that we take for granted, but at the same time one that incorporates numerous inconsistencies and variations. For example, there is a marked difference between 'policing' as a process and 'the police' as an organisation. Policing, a term we might apply to the process of preventing and detecting crime and maintaining order, is an activity that might be engaged in by any number of agencies or individuals (see Chapter 7). It is, on the one hand, widely recognised that members of the public, especially victims, engage in policing in so far as they report crimes to the authorities and help identify the perpetrators. On the other hand, the private sector and agencies like Neighbourhood Watch and its less institutionalised (US) cousin, the Guardian Angels, probation officers enforcing drug-testing orders, social workers engaged in child protection work, street wardens employed by local councils and a myriad of other agencies engaged in partnership work, co-operate in policing societies. The police as an institution, in contrast, is responsible for a range of services, as recent debates surrounding 'core issues' in England and Wales well illustrate (Mawby 2000). Yet the nature and extent of both policing and the police vary between different countries. This chapter focuses on the police as an institution and discusses the extent of this variation and also changes over time.

In focusing on the police, it is essential to define precisely what we mean by the term. Elsewhere, I have suggested that when we consider police systems in different societies we mean by the police an agency that can be distinguished in terms of its *legitimacy*, its *structure* and its *function* (Mawby 1990). Legitimacy implies that the police are granted some degree of monopoly within society by those with the power to so authorise, whether this is an elite within the society, an occupying power or the community as a whole. Structure implies that the police is an organised force, with some degree of specialisation and with a code of practice within which, for example, legitimate use of force is specified. Clearly, however, the extent of organisation or specialisation, and the types of force considered appropriate, will vary. Finally, function implies that the role of the police is concentrated on the maintenance of law and order and the prevention and detection of offences. Again, there will be considerable differences here in terms not only of different definitions of crime but also the balance between law and order, or prevention and detection, and the extent to which other duties are assigned to the police.

The extent to which police systems in different societies do vary is a subject of considerable debate. Writing in 1985, David Bayley argued that while differences between police systems remained, the modern police were distinct from their predecessors in terms of their specialisation, professionalism and publicness. Specialisation in that the modern police were employed exclusively on 'policing' and within the police organisation tended to specialise further; professionalism in that selection and training were ever more important; and public in that policing tended to be carried out by agencies of the state. Even then, however, the distinctiveness of the modern police was more apparent than real. Civilianisation, two-tier police systems and the existence of private and community police alternatives illustrated the continued diversity of police structures, while differences in their functions remained. Indeed, in the light of subsequent developments, particularly an expansion in private police organisations, Bayley and Shearing (1996) argued that by the 1990s a new era of *policing* had emerged, with resultant implications for the nature of police systems.

However, as Jones and Newburn (2002) observe, the Bayley and Shearing argument takes little account of police systems outside the Anglo-American mould and tends to assume a convergence of police systems. In contrast, I would argue that the police systems of different countries have, historically, varied markedly, and while we can identify shifts in policing arrangements in most countries, these are based on changing circumstances that are only occasionally global, and are mainly localised. The following sections use the threefold distinction of structure, function and legitimacy to provide a brief overview of the police in six societal 'groupings'. First, by way of introduction, the focus is on England and Wales. The following six sections then concentrate on five police systems that have been identified and discussed in the literature: continental Europe; colonial societies; communist societies and post-communist police systems; North America; and Far Eastern countries. In each case, variations between countries and changes over time are acknowledged. While clearly there are vast parts of the world that are excluded from this analysis, the main thrust of the chapter is to stress the extent of differences between police systems, the underlying reasons behind these differences and continuing variation in an increasingly global society.

England and Wales

Despite the tendency among some commentators to refer to the British police, in fact the police of England and Wales are quite distinct from their counterparts in Northern Ireland, the Channel Islands, and – to a lesser extent – Scotland. While this section focuses on England and Wales, differences *within* the British Isles should not be ignored (Mawby 1999a).

The modern police system in England and Wales can be traced back to the early nineteenth century. By this time, the locally based 'team' of justices and constables, adequate for enforcing the law in rural areas, was proving inadequate in industrial and more urbanised communities, where rising crime and – significantly – political protest, proved problematic. The police system that emerged reflected these concerns (see Chapters 3 and 4).

First, in terms of function, it was clearly the policy of both government and senior management to focus on the police role in crime control and the maintenance of order, most especially crime prevention through uniformed patrol, while at the same time cultivating the image of the police as also fulfilling a welfare and service order role (Donajgrodzki 1977). The Home Office was concerned that the role should not be extended too far, particularly by making the police (local) government administrators in the way that many continental and colonial forces were (see below), but equally saw it as important to portray the police as a service rather than a force, in part to counteract the quite explicit involvement of the police in riot control and the policing of public protests.

What then of the structure of the new police? Successive Acts through the nineteenth century resulted in three types of police force: the London Metropolitan Police, county forces and borough police. While the Home Office acted to curb the proliferation of small borough forces, the advantage of the new policing arrangement was the balance between central and local government. As a result, despite local variations a degree of conformity existed that was perhaps unique within a localised system. This interpretation of local control is particularly notable in the context of police legitimacy. In no sense were local forces accountable to their local communities. Rather, the new policing structure reconfirmed the power of local elites that had epitomised the old system (Wall 1998), with the Home Office's influence crucial but at least partly covert.

The police of England and Wales thus inherited a broad mandate to provide a service to the public that was wider than an exclusive emphasis on crime control and public order maintenance. Nevertheless research has indicated that an increasing number of public-initiated police contacts are crime related, especially in inner-city areas (Shapland and Vagg 1988; Skogan 1995) and in a time of stretched resources many have argued that police duties should be more closely restricted to crime work. This was the dominant message behind the setting up of the Posen (1994) Inquiry into core policing tasks, which, despite denials, was envisaged as clearing the way towards the privatisation of so-called 'peripheral' police work (Mawby 2000). The conclusions of the inquiry fell short of recommendations to promote wholesale change (Home Office 1995), but the debate itself signalled a marked shift in thinking about the English police (Cassels 1994; Reiner 1994). However while this debate has centred attention on the balance between crime fighting and service roles for the police, perhaps the most notable shift in emphasis on police functions emanates from the role of the police under the Conservative government of Margaret Thatcher, particularly in the early 1980s, where police were clearly used to enforce government policies, notably in breaking the power of the unions, best illustrated in the confrontations during the miners' strike (Fine and Millar 1985). The English police, despite the power of the myth, have never been divorced from politics, and the role of the police in these industrial disputes reaffirmed their role in preserving the status quo, through the maintenance of public order.

Industrial disputes and urban protests in the 1980s also bequeathed dramatic changes in the structure of the police. True, the 'average' police officer patrols armed only with a truncheon, albeit a longer and heavier one than in the past. However, recent years have seen considerable pressure from within the ranks to issue firearms on a routine basis (Waddington 1999). All forces include officers trained and qualified to use firearms, and many deploy armed response teams (Jefferson 1990). Backup squads, normally used in public order situations, specially trained and issued with riot gear, operate as paramilitary units and provide a high-profile range of policing light years from the cosy Dixon of Dock Green imagery of 1950s Britain. Thus while the police of England and Wales remain among a minority in international terms who do not routinely carry firearms, armed police are becoming a more common sight on the mainland, and the question of arming the police is perhaps more openly debated than ever before (Ingleton 1996).

A further key question regarding the structure of the police relates to the balance between local and central control and organisation of policing. Home Office influence towards consistency was evident through the latter half of the nineteenth century, but at the outbreak of the Second World War there remained nearly 200 separate local forces. These were reduced to 43 by the mid-1970s. The 1962 Royal Commission on the Police identified the protection of local police forces' autonomy through the institution of the tripartite structure of accountability: individual chief constables, police authorities and central government. However, it is widely accepted that local government influence on policing has been muted and recent developments have further strengthened the role of central government. These include the role of the National Reporting Centre, notably during the miners' strike, as a mechanism for providing a co-ordination of police planning and policy implementation; the increased influence of central bodies, such as the Audit Commission and Her Majesty's Inspectorate of Constabulary (HMIC), on local forces' policies and practices (Applegate 2003; Loveday and Reid 2003); the creation of the National Criminal Intelligence Service; the expanding role of the national police training college in the approval and training of senior officers; and, with the Police and Magistrates Courts Act 1994, the introduction of central government direct influence on the appointment of a significant minority of Police Authority members (Loveday 1996).

The central/local debate is at the heart of debate over police legitimacy. Police legitimacy is derived from the law and public consent. The Police and Criminal Evidence Act 1984 strengthened legal controls over police powers, with regulations of police procedures and practices that had previously been the subject of common law being brought together and more clearly presented (Reiner 2000; see Chapter 10). Accountability to the public is more ambiguous. On the one hand it may reflect indirect accountability through the medium of elected politicians, at local or national level. On the other hand it may imply direct accountability to citizens 'in general'.

The extended influence of central government raises questions about the level of control local citizens and local communities hold over their police. While it was not local communities but local elites that controlled the police in their formative years, there is clear evidence that the rise of central government influence has undermined local influence on policing. Nevertheless, opportunities for local scrutiny of policing operations and policy have been strengthened in at least four ways, with the introduction of Crime and Disorder Reduction Partnerships (CDRPs), whereby the police and other local agencies are required to produce regular audit and strategy documents (Home Office 2001; Hughes *et al.* 2002), the formation of police consultative committees (Morgan 1992), the establishment of lay visitors schemes whereby designated members of the local community routinely visit prisoners remanded in police cells (Weatheritt and Vieira 1998), and the introduction of Independent Advisory Groups to monitor police racism following the Stephen Lawrence Inquiry These attempts to allay public concern by providing public access to local police management and by providing 'independent' scrutiny of police stations have been bolstered by incorporating police services into the Citizen's Charter, encouraging forces to produce their own force charters and by urging forces routinely to carry out 'consumer' surveys (Bunt and Mawby 1994). While in many ways this enhances local people's say in policing matters, it signals a shift from seeing legitimacy in terms of citizens' rights to a position where the citizen is replaced by the consumer. The question thus becomes one of which members of the public rate as consumers, with a say in policing issues.

Continental Europe

Discussions of an alleged continental European policing system have a long history, and Fosdick's (1969 edition) account of continental police at the beginning of the twentieth century is the first of many attempts to identify key characteristics of the police systems of continental Europe (see, for example, Bayley 1975, 1979). At the same time, most authors have been at pains to distance this model from policing in England and Wales, and indeed early debates over the need for a professional police in England emphasised the undesirability of following the continental route.

None the less, pressures towards harmonisation have emanated from the European Community, supported by European and international law. Trevi, for example, was established in 1975–6 as an intergovernmental co-operative mechanism between member states that established working parties comprised of senior officers from different European police forces to plan joint operations. The Schengen Treaty was first signed in 1962 and subsequently expanded, notably through the 1984 Fontainebleau Declaration. This espoused as its basic principle the desirability of freedom of movement within the EU, but in recognising that this facilitated the movement of illegal goods and services also sought to enhance international police co-operation. The UK has not been a party to Fontainebleau, but in much of Europe the principle of greater co-operation has been accepted, initially through Trevi and later through the Schengen Convention of 1990 and the 1991 Maastricht Treaty.

Ironically, moves to facilitate co-operation have also served to emphasise differences and, on occasions, have led to aggravation, a case in point being German concern over the more liberal Dutch approach to drug control. This suggests that in discussing policing on continental Europe we need to be mindful of the differences between countries, as well as differences between the continent and England and Wales, and also aware that increased co-operation is quite different from harmonisation or convergence.

Traditionally, the police systems on continental Europe, derived as they were from the Roman colonial system, have generally been more centralised and more wide ranging than in England and Wales. In terms of the dimensions described earlier, I have argued that continental police systems may be characterised as (1) structurally more centralised and militaristic; (2) function-ally putting more emphasis on political and administrative tasks; and (3) in terms of legitimacy, being more closely tied to government and less account-able either to public or law (Mawby 1990). Nevertheless, there are marked variations between countries (Mawby 1992).

In terms of structure, for example, Iceland and Switzerland have, respect-ively, district and canton-based systems, and the Netherlands reorganised in 1993 into 25 regional forces (Interpol 1992; Jones 1995). Similarly, in Germany most police are based in the counties (*Länders*). At the other extreme, a few countries, including Sweden and the Irish Republic, have one centralised, national force. What is more characteristic of the traditional continental model, though, is a structure whereby one centralised, militaristic force is counterbal-anced by either a second or by a medley of local city forces. The French, Italian and Spanish police may traditionally be identified most fully with the model: in each case the maintenance of at least two police forces allowing govern-ments to ensure that no one institution achieved too much power. While the police in most continental countries carry firearms, it is also the case that in many countries there is at least one centralised force that evidences significant militaristic qualities. In France, for example, the state police comes under the Ministry of the Interior, whereas the *gendarmerie* is a military force under the Ministry of Defence, with a two-tier entry system, barrack accommodation and impressive armaments. The *carabinieri* operate in much the same way in Italy, as do the *guardia civil* in Spain.

Continental police systems are also distinctive in terms of their roles and responsibilities. Although a welfare orientation is rarely evident, traditionally forces have carried out a wide range of administrative responsibilities, albeit in the case of Germany these were scaled down in the postwar period (Fairchild 1988). Thus in different countries the police have held responsibili-ties for passport control, building regulations, tax collection, milk inspection, alimony supervision and collecting meteorological data!

In the past, continental police systems were also distinguished in terms of their lack of public accountability, being directly responsible to the head of state. While this is less easily reconciled with the liberal democracies of postwar Europe, it is still the case that public accountability is more restricted in countries where the police are more centralised and militaristic. Even here, though, there are exceptions, with Sweden, for example, incorporating a local accountability mechanism within its centralised structure.

The example of Sweden is illustrative of the fluidity of change throughout Europe. Sweden moved towards a national structure in 1965, with the National Police Act 1984 providing the basis of the current centralised framework (Akermo 1986). Elsewhere, however, policing has become more localised in some respects, as illustrated through the extension of local police units in France (Kania 1989; Journes 1993) as well as in Italy and Spain. Other changes include the removal of a range of non-crime responsibilities from the police in France under the Mitterand presidency. However, while it is tempting to see these as indicative of a convergence across Europe there is little evidence of any consistency here. Rather, it appears that governments have used their autonomy to respond to national issues where they arise. For example, in Germany the significance of the national police has faded as border patrols have become less necessary, and the Dutch system, never excessively centralised, was changed due to controversy over area variations in police costs, and is now structured in a way that is more akin to England and Wales.

Overall, there are still marked differences between the police of England and Wales and their counterparts from the continent, as well as considerable differences between the nations of continental Europe. That said, co-operation between European nations, accelerated by developments in the EU, has contributed to a greater degree of interchange between police systems (Benyon *et al.* 1993; Hebenton and Thomas 1995; see Chapter 6).

Colonial societies

A second police system that has been consistently recognised in the literature is the colonial model. In many respects it corresponds to the continental model – not surprising given that much of the administrative and legal structure of European states was based on earlier Roman institutions, where the Romans were themselves colonists. This also serves to remind us that the British were not the only colonists (Igbinovia 1981; Cole 1999). However, while the French transported their centralised, militaristic policing structure across their empire, the British government allegedly created a different type of policing for its empire, one that was more appropriate for the control of a subjugated population. The model it used was the one first established for Ireland (Tobias 1977), where the police could not rely on public consent, and then deployed throughout British-controlled Africa, Asia and the Caribbean.

Again using my model, colonial police may be characterised as (1) structurally more centralised and militaristic (for example, armed and living as units in barracks); (2) in functional terms, giving more priority to public order tasks, but also having a number of administrative responsibilities; and (3) deriving their legitimacy from their colonial masters rather than the indigenous population. There has, however, been considerable debate over the distinctiveness of a colonial model. On the one hand, Brogden (1987) has argued that the differences between British and British colonial policing have been exaggerated. On the other hand, Anderson and Killingray (1991, 1992) claimed that the differences between colonial systems exceeded the similarities.

What is clear is that the British government saw the establishment of a strong police apparatus as central to the establishment of control and legitimacy across its empire. To enforce control, the police were formed according to a militaristic model, although not necessarily armed. Nor was the police system necessarily centralised: in India the provinces or states had their own police forces although the Indian Police Service was responsible for the recruitment, training and deployment of senior ranks; in Nigeria, at least two forces operated in different parts of the country. However, clearly the police acted on behalf of the British government and had little local mandate, frequently operating with draconian powers. A further illustration of the lack of local influence was the common practice of recruiting staff from either the British military or from elsewhere in the Empire, ensuring that the police did not establish close relationships with the indigenous population.

The police were part of the administrative structure, and their roles reflected this. They were involved in ensuring that local government ticked over quietly. While crime control might have been important, especially where it involved ex-patriots as victims, maintaining order and eliminating dissent were pivotal (Arnold 1986). The police were engaged in putting down political protest, including labour disputes, while in Hong Kong guarding against the threat of communism was central to their mandate (Anderson and Killingray 1991).

The fact that the British government experienced similar problems through-out its Empire provided an important push towards conformity. This was strengthened, though, with centralised administration and control through the Colonial Police Service, based in London, central training for officers, the formation of the Inspector General of Colonial Police in 1948 and the practice of transferring senior officers between different countries.

However, just as there were differences in emphasis between different parts of the Empire, so the model shifted at different points in time. In particular, in the conflict building up to independence, which in many cases culminated in armed insurrection, the response of the British government was to accentuate the key features of the model. So, for example, police numbers were increased, central control was strengthened, police arms were improved and links between police and military were enhanced (Anderson and Killingray 1992). That this should happen at a time when the legitimacy of the British government and its police was being challenged is scarcely surprising. What is equally important to stress, though, is that it makes problematic the transition from a colonial police to a postcolonial system of policing by consent. Moreover, given the inevitability of conflict and disorder after independence, the social control functions of the colonial police came to be valued by the new regimes. In consequence, the strategy, as in India (Arnold 1986), seems to have been to replace the (British) officer class but preserve the key aspects of the system. The lesson, here, seems to be that even with significant political change police systems may continue as before.

Communist societies

The claim that there is, or was, a distinctive communist police system has also been the subject of debate. For example, although some, like Shelley (1997), have argued that the system defined and propagated by the USSR was unique, it is plausible to argue that it was in many ways conceived out of the police models of continental Europe. Alternatively, there are clear differences between the police systems of Russia, the 'colonial power' of central/eastern Europe and the People's Republic of China (PRC). As elsewhere, then, the extent to which countries' police systems can be categorised into an ideal type is influenced by a host of variables such as social structure, prevailing culture, the influence of other countries and, in the case of communist countries, the nature of the previous regime and the distinctive form taken by the revolution. This section thus focuses on the (old) USSR and China as exemplars of communist systems up until the 1980s.

If we compare the USSR and China, it is immediately clear that they varied enormously in terms of size, density and levels of urbanisation. For example, the USSR covered an area of about 8.5 million square miles, with a population of 270 million, but despite its low population density some two thirds of the people lived in cities. China, in contrast, with 1,000 million people and a land surface of 3.7 million square miles, was nearly ten times as densely populated, but only a fifth of the population lived in cities. The implications of these differences for social control are clearly profound.

Similarly, the emergence of the communist regime was different. Kowalewski (1981) noted that in the former the revolution of 1917 was all but completed by 1920, leading to minority Bolshevik control of a country where grass-roots support for the new regime was minimal. These conditions therefore paved the way for a highly centralised economy and state, with control exerted through a party elite and where the former Tsarist Secret Police provided a model for the new secret police, the *cheka*. In China, on the other hand, decades of civil war culminated in the creation in 1949 of a rural-based popular government that was dependent upon peasant support and saw the Mass Line as a mechanism for forging conformity. That said, we can assess the extent to which the police systems in each country conformed to a communist model or developed in different ways.

Taking first the functions of the police, it is incontestable that a major role of the police in each country was to deal with crime. However, the extent to which crime control was *the main role* of the police is questionable. In each case the police played a key political role in maintaining the regime.

In the USSR, for example, the *cheka*'s mandate was to control the border and to prevent internal counter-revolutionary activity, a mandate it accepted with such ruthlessness that it was disbanded in 1922, although its replacements – the GPU, MGB and, later, the KGB – were counter-intelligence organisations with considerably more power than the conventional police, the militia (Conquest 1968). Moreover, the latter also played a major part in political control through the regulation of passports and identity cards, through which it had a direct influence on the free movement of the population.

In China the police public security bureau also play a crucial role in surveying where people live and the police are responsible for keeping a register of all families in the neighbourhood and all births, deaths and marriages, and visitors are also required to be registered. Since 1985 the police have also been involved in administering the personal identity card system (Chen 2002).

The political role of the police was not the only way in which the functions of the police were wide-ranging. However, whereas in the USSR the emphasis has been on administrative responsibilities, in China this has incorporated a prioritisation of welfare and social service roles. The household census provided the mechanism for the police to identify need and respond to it. Thus: 'The household registration police are familiar with the needs of widowers, widows and other elderly people in their vicinities. They often help them wash clothes, buy food grain, clean their houses, manage household affairs and get to hospitals when they fall ill' (Yun 1983: 22).

Turning to consider the structure of the police in communist societies, the centralised nature of policing is evident. In the USSR any degree of local autonomy that existed in theory appears to have been purely fictional. In China, each of the three major cities and 29 provinces had its own public security bureau and while attached to the Ministry of Public Security the opportunity for local influence appears slightly greater.

However, the militaristic qualities of the police seemed to vary. At one extreme, the USSR's militia was essentially militaristic, with a rank structure equivalent to the military and recruits drawn from either the party or the armed forces; firearms were carried. In contrast, in China the police seemed to have been more civilianised and, while the emphasis has changed (see below), a recurrent theme was to ensure that the police remained close to the people. Thus, although party members and former members of the rebel forces joined the police in the new PRC, the majority of the police were unarmed and civilian (Wong 2002).

This acknowledgement of party membership is crucial to an understanding of the legitimacy of the police in communist societies. The inter-relationship of party and police was perhaps the most significant feature of the system. In both countries covered here, the police included a disproportionate number of party members, but in addition the party independently exerted considerable influence on police practices.

In the USSR, with an early emphasis on a written constitution, the militia was in theory accountable to the law, although the security forces have traditionally operated above the law. As Solomon (1987) noted, however, the influence of the party on the entire criminal justice system meant that the concept of separation of powers was entirely absent. Similarly, attempts to involve the public in the policing process seemed to result in either additional party control through the creation of police aides (at best) or a complex informer system (at worst).

One of the key distinctions between Soviet and Maoist versions of communism was over the role of law, with Mao seeing law as a conservative force and preferring a dialectic process whereby the system was adjusted according to criticism and counter-criticism. Emphasis was placed on local community groups (controlled by the party) to stand as a corrective to police elitism (Cohen 1966).

Although the above discussion is of different communist systems at one point in time, clearly the emphasis changed as the balance of power shifted and new priorities gained ascendancy. In the USSR, for example, Lenin's preference for apportioning some power to factory committees illustrated an example of locally based crime control that was dismantled in Stalin's ruthless pursuit of a totalitarian central regime, but re-emerged under Khrushchev, with the introduction of Comrades Courts, the Campaign against Parasites and the People's Guard.

Perhaps the most notable shifts, however, were to be found in China. The period of establishment (1949–53) with an emphasis on the Mass Line and prioritisation of a rural economy was supplanted by a period of Soviet influence (1953–57), which itself was rescinded by the Great Leap Forward (1957–61) when the power of the party over the 'professional expert' was re-established. This in turn was superseded by a move towards greater bureaucracy and professionalism during the 1961–64 period, and then a further reaffirmation of the party during the Cultural Revolution (1964–68). There was then a period of uneasy calm, culminating in Mao's death, the removal of the Gang of Four and the gradual move towards a market economy.

While the role of local community groups is still crucial, and indeed is arguably more important than in the past (Chen 2002), in other respects the police in Deng Xiaoping's modern China has changed. Wong (2002), in a wide-ranging review, argues that the police priorities have changed, with greater emphasis on 'crime fighting' and order maintenance and less on political matters or welfare work; that the structure of the police has changed, with the police more centralised and professional; and that the accountability of the police has been transformed, with recruitment of more non-party members, a greater emphasis on the rule of law through the 1995 Law on People's Police of the PRC, and the introduction of a Ministry of Supervision. However, given that economic changes have so far exceeded political changes it remains doubtful exactly how radical recent changes have been.

In Europe, the reform of police systems following the break up of the USSR has also been the subject of debate. On the one hand, it appears that change in Russia and many of its former states has been minimal (Shelley 1999; Beck and Chistyakova 2002). On the other hand, reform in some, but by no means all, of its central/eastern European 'colonies' was accorded priority in the embryonic periods of the new regimes. For this reason, the following section focuses on the emerging police systems of central/eastern Europe, commonly termed 'societies in transition' (Zvekic 1996, 1998).

Central/eastern Europe

The late 1980s saw a dramatic redrawing of the political map of Europe. For this reason alone it would be difficult to ignore discussion of policing in central and eastern Europe. However, there are relatively few accessible data on police systems in central and eastern Europe prior to 1939, and, while currently a considerable amount of evidence is emerging from Hungary and Poland, there are rather fewer from countries such as Albania, Bulgaria and Romania.

The difficulties are compounded by the enormous variations between these societies in transition. Some were part of the former USSR, others had some semblance of separate identity; some of the former, like Estonia, vigorously pursued independence, while others, like Kazakhstan, had it virtually forced upon them. Some have committed themselves to radical economic reforms and await EU membership; others, like Bulgaria and Romania, have been slower to change. Demographic and geographical differences are also marked. Poland has a population of over 38 million and its capital, Warsaw, houses over one and a half million. Estonia's entire population is similar to that of Warsaw. The political status of countries prior to Soviet domination also varied. Some attained a degree of independence in the interwar period; for others, history reveals a cycle of dominance by one conqueror after another (Rothschild 1993).

Social, economic and cultural changes have added to the pressure on criminal justice systems in general and the police in particular. Economic inefficiency, collapse of living standards and social dislocation have bred a criminogenic environment (Anderson 1995) and the rising levels of crime are well illustrated in official statistics. Victim survey data, while being relatively recent, also suggest that from comparatively low rates under communism crime rates in societies in transition may be catching up with those in the west; certainly, public anxiety has increased (Zvekic 1996, 1998; Mawby 1999b).

The police systems of eastern bloc countries in the postwar period were closely modelled on that of the USSR, and thus unsurprisingly incorporated political and administrative responsibilities, a strong centralised secret police and a centralised, militaristic uniformed police. Being accountable to the party, there was little popular mandate (Ward 1984; Cullen 1992; Dános and Tauber 1995; Mawby 1999b). In many postcommunist societies it is frequently referred to as a 'repressive' system.

It is also notable that during the mid-1980s, as these regimes faced more overt public opposition, the repressive political role of the police became *more* pronounced. In Czechoslovakia, Zapletal and Tomin (1995) note that the police were associated with brutality in the period leading up to 1989. In the GDR the police played a key role in protecting the Honiker government in the early 1980s (Cooper 1996). Similarly Jasinski (1995) describes the role of the police in attempting to repress *Solidarity* in Poland in the 1980s.

Given the importance of the police in sustaining the 'old' system, it is scarcely surprising that the new democratic regimes of central and eastern Europe should have prioritised changing them, and in the early days of the new regimes, changes to police systems were considered crucial (Mawby 1999b). However, while the most radical changes occurred in East Germany, where East Germany's police organisation was absorbed into West Germany's, elsewhere changes were less radical. Changes to police *personnel* appear to have been widespread in the early phase of development. But the function, structure and legitimacy of the police have been affected rather less. Some changes *have* taken place but they have perhaps not been as radical as was envisaged at the time of the collapse of communism in central and eastern Europe.

What is also notable though is a marked difference *between* postcommunist societies (Mawby 1996; Zvekic 1996). Nevertheless, local reviews of policing and the results of recent research tend to suggest that changes to police systems in countries in transition have been disappointing. This may in part be due to rising crime, and especially escalating fear of crime, in eastern Europe, leading to public concern that regimes should maintain a strong force.

The link between central/eastern and western Europe and the USA is also important in terms of how the police of postcommunist societies will change. Political alliances with the west, through Interpol, EU membership and joint training operations will draw postcommunist societies closer to the west, and especially closer to western Europe (Tupman 1995) and the USA (Marenin 1998). In the latter case, however, US concern to emphasise the war against crime, and especially the international drug problem, has taken priority over any emphasis upon democratising and decentralising the police.

The impediments to change in eastern Europe bear a striking similarity to those in postcolonial societies. As in the latter, the death throes of the old regimes incorporated a toughening of police systems, while the crime and public disorder problems associated with 'independence' have led to pressures to retain aspects of the old repressive system. Thus, while calls to move to a more community-oriented police have been made in both postcolonial and postcommunist societies, as Table 2.1 demonstrates this has inherent difficulties. In particular, as in South Africa (Brogden and Shearing 1993), an ideal type community policing system is – in terms of function, structure and legitimacy – almost the opposite of what previously existed.

Table 2.1 Aspects of community policing in the context of colonial and eastern European police systems

	Community policing	*Colonial*	*Eastern European*
Function	Welfare	Control	Control
Structure	Localised, civilian	Centralised, militaristic	Centralised, militaristic
Legitimacy	Local people	Colonial power	Central party

North America

Despite the alleged 'Anglo-American' policing tradition and the direct influence of Britain on the Canadian system, from the beginning differences between the USA, Canada and England and Wales have been recognised. Differences between the current police systems of England and Wales, the USA and Canada are best understood in this historical context.

In many ways, the circumstances in which paid police systems developed in Canada and the USA were similar. For example, in both countries the majority of the early settlers lived in townships on the east coast, and modern police forces first featured in these townships. The key difference, however, was the relationship held with the British government. While the USA had attained independence in 1788, before the establishment of paid police in Britain, Canada's independence was ratified in the North America Act 1867.

Before then, early policing was directly influenced by the British government; afterwards, as part of the British Empire, Canada continued to be subject to British influence. In British Canada, paid town forces were established at a similar time to England. However, of perhaps greater significance during the nineteenth century was the policing of the vast, underpopulated areas of rural Canada, where control of the Indian and Inuit populations, protection of the territory from foreign incursions and the need to impose order within the goldfields required distinctive forms of policing, based on the colonial model. This force was seen as ideal for exerting order across the vast territories of Canada, whose sheer scale made law enforcement, public administration and the assertion of sovereignty difficult (Morrison 1985).

This force, originally known as the North-West Mounted Police, extended its influence in the early twentieth century, taking on security and counter-espionage services during the First World War and, in 1919, helping to break the Winnipeg general strike (Horrall 1980). In 1920 it was renamed the Royal Canadian Mounted Police (RCMP) and continued to expand, on the one hand taking on additional responsibilities from federal government, on the other hand extending its services in the provinces. By the 1930s it provided police services in the Yukon and Northwest Territories and for six of the ten provinces; in the postwar period it assumed provincial policing responsibilities in two further provinces and established a foothold in urban policing (Chapman 1978).

In direct contrast, policing and law enforcement in the USA emerged in the aftermath of the struggle for independence and concern that control from Westminster should not be substituted by control from Washington (Sweatman and Cross 1989). Nevertheless, in rural areas with significant public disorder problems and a perceived threat from labourers, aliens and the like, police organisations were formed that showed striking similarities to the colonial model. The establishment of the Pennsylvanian force in 1905, for example, heralded a new wave of state forces designed to 'crush disorders, whether industrial or otherwise, which arose in the foreign-filled districts of the state' (Reppetto 1978: 130).

An appreciation of early policing arrangements in the USA thus has to take account of differences according to the areas being policed. As in Canada, the first examples of paid police forces were found in the cities, where high crime rates, threats to public order and the conflicts engendered by internal and externals migration came to be viewed as unacceptable. City administrators therefore looked elsewhere – initially to England and subsequently to other American cities – for ideas about how to respond to the problems (Monkkonen 1981). The first modern force, established in New York in 1844, for example, was in many respects modelled on the London police (Miller 1977).

Local government interests dictated that these early police carried out a wide variety of administrative and service tasks, rather than concentrating solely on law enforcement (Fosdick 1920: 211–15; Smith 1940; Fogelson 1977; Monkkonen 1981). In other respects, US city police were markedly different from their English cousins. For example, they were almost immediately issued with firearms, but only reluctantly donned uniforms (Miller 1977), the latter being rejected initially as 'un-American', 'undemocratic' and symbolic of the (British) military (Fosdick 1920: 70). Perhaps the most notable distinctions, however, surrounded the community base for US city police, expressed in terms of recruitment policies and control of the police. For example, unlike the

English police, US city police were specifically recruited from their local communities (Miller 1977) and local residency requirements continued well into the twentieth century (Smith 1940; Fogelson 1977).

However the fact that police officers were closely identified with their precincts and the power structure at that local level meant that corruption was an endemic feature of city police (Fogelson 1977). The Lexow Committee of 1895 was one of many inquiries to demonstrate not merely the extensiveness of police corruption but also the impotence of local government to eliminate it. The extent to which corruption was a feature of the political manipulation of the police is illustrated in the way in which control over the police was exercised. Whether the police were controlled by a single commissioner or board of commissioners, the fact that such appointments were temporary and subject – directly or otherwise – to political influence, meant that the police were a political football. On one level this was reflected in a power play between the (usually Democrat controlled) city and the (often Republican controlled) state (Miller 1977). On another level it meant that a change of political control meant not merely a change in police policy but also the replacement of senior officers (Fosdick 1920). In rural areas, political influence on policing was even more direct, with popular elections substituting for the control of colonial governors (Smith 1940).

This plethora of policing arrangements developed in the nineteenth and early twentieth century without any central direction. Indeed the lack of a public national police force meant that on occasions national private police systems were used by central government (Johnston 1999). Early attempts to co-ordinate policing activities were taken on by the International Association of Chiefs of Police which established a national clearing house for criminal identification records in 1896 and initiated a uniform crime-reporting system in 1927. Those responsibilities were subsequently transferred to the Bureau of Investigation, which was renamed the Federal Bureau of Investigation (FBI) (Smith 1940). The creation of the FBI was not however uncontroversial, given popular distrust of central government (Walker 1983).

Thus while in Canada, British colonial policing provided an alternative to local urban policing systems that resulted in the creation of the RCMP as a national, if not monopolistic, public police agency, reaction against colonial dominance in the USA created an atmosphere of suspicion towards central control and the proliferation of local autonomous forces. The different ways in which the police developed in Canada and the USA provide the foundations for the police today.

Underpinning the structure of policing in Canada today is the 1867 constitution, modified in 1982, which established a federal government structure with considerable autonomy delegated to the provinces. This means that policing within each province is a matter for local government to decide, with the result that policing is a combination of metropolitan and provincial forces. But the federal police, the RCMP, provides three sets of services that impinge on this local blueprint. It acts as a federal police force with national responsibilities throughout the country; it maintains the responsibilities for policing the Yukon and Northwest Territories; and it can be subcontracted to provide police services at provincial and municipal level. In Ontario and

Quebec the RCMP's responsibilities are confined to national legislation and policing is provided by metropolitan and – to a lesser extent – provincial forces, but elsewhere the RCMP has a substantial foothold as provider of provincial and metropolitan policing.

In essence then, Canada today has at least two policing systems. In Ontario and Quebec, and in many municipalities elsewhere, policing is provided locally, by provincial government, municipal government or an amalgamation of municipalities. In such cases the role of the police parallels discussion in Britain and the USA. Local accountability, through a variety of police boards and commissions (Stenning 1981; Hann *et al.* 1985) similarly reflects much of the debate elsewhere over unrepresentativeness of membership. On the other hand, the RCMP, with its traditional order-maintenance emphasis and its involvement in a wide range of administrative responsibilities (Weller 1981; Dion 1982; Morrison 1985), appears as a more remote and more militaristic alternative. Moreover with its centralised structure it is clear that local accountability has traditionally been restricted, even where its relationship is a contractual one (Weller 1981), although recently it has established citizens' advisory councils (Bayley 1994).

The situation in the USA is somewhat different. In terms of functions it is commonly agreed that the police of the USA have moved away from their broader welfare mandate and have concentrated more on the crime-fighting role. To a large extent this is associated with moves to reform the community-based early police with their roots in local politics by creating a more 'professional' police, where professionalism is located at the organisational rather than the individual level and becomes bound in with militarism (Fogelson 1977; Walker 1977).

However while some commentators, like McKenzie and Gallagher (1989), see this as a linear development, there is considerable evidence that the police have either maintained or re-established a wider mandate. A variety of studies from the 1960s onwards demonstrated that routine police work involved providing a myriad of services for the public and that 'dealing with crime' is only a small part of the patrolling officer's workload, leading Bayley to assert that the US police spend little of their time preventing crime and more of it 'restoring order and providing general assistance' (Bayley 1994: 18–19). This was probably accentuated as the USA entered the 'community problem-solving era' (Kelling and Moore 1988), with community policing prioritised, at least on a policy level, far more than in England and Wales. Structural changes towards decentralisation, the introduction of foot patrols, closer links with community groups, etc., were thus paralleled by an emphasis upon problem-solving over crime control, crime being recognised as a symptom of community problems rather than the cause (Eck and Spelman 1987; Goldstein 1987; Rosenbaum 1994). Interestingly, while zero-tolerance policing emerged in New York (Kelling and Coles 1996), it appears to have been accepted less enthusiastically elsewhere in the USA than in England and Wales (Burke 1998; Innes 1999).

Clearly developments in policing incorporated both police functions and police structure. The move to rid the police of corruption accentuated the militaristic image of the police, leading Walker (1977: 171) to argue that 'The hierarchical, semi-military organisational form was one of the major fruits of professionalism'. Equally, problem-oriented policing has emphasised decentralisation of command and a more accountable structure (Goldstein 1987).

However, much of the research emphasis has been on urban, especially 'big-city', police rather than rural areas (Maguire *et al.* 1997). Leaving aside the traditionally significant – and growing – private security sector (Johnston 1999), there are, in fact, six levels of public law-enforcement organisation: federal, state, county, city, rural and 'special district' (Walker 1983; Sweatman and Cross 1989).

At the federal level, while no agency has responsibility for policing in general, some 50 agencies have specialist nationwide law-enforcement responsibilities (Sweatman and Cross 1989). Of these perhaps the best known are the FBI and the DEA (Drug Enforcement Administration), with 11,523 and 4,161 full-time operatives respectively (Bureau of Justice Statistics 2002). The former is responsible to the Attorney General and deals with crimes that transcend state boundaries, principally pornography, racketeering, bank robbery, white-collar crime and terrorism. Overall about 10 per cent of police are based in federal government agencies (Maguire and Pastore 1994).

The second level of law enforcement is the state. Forty-nine states have their own police force, in total employing 55,892 full-time sworn officers. The largest force is the California Highway Patrol with about 6,600 full-time officers, the smallest North Dakota Highway Patrol with 127 (Bureau of Justice Statistics 2002). State forces are commonly accountable to state governors.

The third level of law enforcement is the county. Most of the counties in the USA have their own police departments, headed by a sheriff elected to run the department for 2–4 years, who is in turn accountable to the county administrators. In 1999 there were some 3,088 sheriffs departments employing about 185,859 sworn officers, more than three times the number in state forces (Bureau of Justice Statistics 2002).

The fourth level of law enforcement, and the one that has received the most attention from researchers, is the city. There are about 3,220 police forces in cities of over 250,000 population, employing on average 2,465 sworn personnel. The largest force is New York City with over 40,000 officers, the smallest Anaheim with about 400 (Bureau of Justice Statistics 2002).

The fifth level of law enforcement operates at the rural level in the small towns. There are over 13,000 such forces, employing about 438,000 full-time sworn officers, with 46.5 per cent of these agencies located in areas with less than 2,500 people (Bureau of Justice Statistics 2002). As a result, while in terms of personnel the typical US police officer works for a large urban department, the most common police *organisations* are small-town, independent forces.

Finally, separate police forces may be located in 'special districts', providing the police services to particular institutions and/or geographical areas like parks, university campus and military bases (Ostrom *et al.* 1978; Walker 1983).

It is scarcely surprising, given the extent of variation, that police standards also differ considerably. Personnel levels differ markedly, with the largest cities spending more per capita and having more police per population (Bureau of Justice Statistics 2002). The fragmented nature of policing is further illustrated by the difficulty of transferring from one police department to another. Clearly also many police jurisdictions overlap. New York, for example, with the largest city force, is also serviced by five county forces which have jurisdiction in different parts of the city (Sweatman and Cross 1989).

The extent of variation is equally reflected in differing mechanisms for accountability. Thus police chiefs, notably county sheriffs, may be elected and thereby directly accountable, or they may be political or internal appointments accountable to mayors or police boards. The extent of corruption associated with the early police led reformers away from a politically accountable police. Reformers like Fosdick and Vollmer favoured the London Metropolitan Police model whereby police were internally accountable and politics was (allegedly) distanced from police management (Reppetto 1978). Thus Fogelson (1977) argued that attempts during the 1970s to decentralise police organisations, encourage citizen participation and break down professional barriers, and hold the police externally accountable, failed because of fears of a return to earlier levels of corruption. Nevertheless, marked differences in political influence over the police remain. The very different relationship that exists between police and local government in different US cities was illustrated in Ruchelman's (1974) study of police politics in New York, Philadelphia and Chicago in the 1960s. The pervasive nature of police corruption at the time is more widely illustrated in Sherman's (1978) work.

In many respects, the police systems of the USA and Canada have converged. In each case, local forces carry out a range of crime and service-related functions and are accountable to the local political machine, while federal forces have a wider mandate and are less readily accountable. However, although some have argued that the plethora of US police forces have become more centrally co-ordinated through the increasing influence of the FBI (Loveday 1999), the extent of diversity in the USA remains a distinctive feature. In contrast, in Canada the RCMP plays a more explicit and significant role that can be traced back to its colonial heritage.

The Far East

Most policing literature focuses on either western industrial societies or those – like (post) colonial countries – that were influenced by them. Far Eastern examples are less common, with Japan – possibly the most extensively researched of all police systems outside England and North America – the notable exception. In considering policing in the Far East, it is useful to focus on Japan and then briefly consider other examples (Leishman 1999).

Before the opening up of Japan to western influence, social control was based around groups of families, the *gonin gumi*, enforced at a regional level by the feudal system and its samurai warriors. However, the late nineteenth century saw Japan import models of policing from continental Europe (albeit these were reworked within an essentially Japanese model). Thus the fact that the police operated within a culture that was moulded by Confucianism, Buddhism and Taoism, where duty and obligation were central and rights subordinate, suggests both that social control in Japan is more problematic than Bayley (1976), for one, implied (see also Miyazawa 1992) and that Japan's police may share many characteristics with its geographical and cultural neighbours. One good example of control is the pivotal role played by the police prior to the Second World War, leading the US occupying forces in the immediate postwar period to attempt to reduce the power of the police and to impose a local system of policing. Nevertheless, these reforms were short lived and, by the mid-1950s, Japan had reverted to a police system that combined central control with local presence (Aldous 1997).

Indeed, there has been considerable debate over the essential structure of the Japanese police, which incorporates a number of contradictions. For example, they wear firearms but rarely use them, and they are centrally administered through the National Police Agency, but are divided into 47 local prefectures that are predominantly funded from local taxation. On a local level, they operate out of police substations, known as *koban* in the cities and *chuzaisho* in rural areas. While this provides a local presence that is missing in many western societies, the Japanese have been keen to prevent their police displaying divided loyalties, recruiting them from other areas of the country and transferring them regularly.

In terms of function, the police traditionally encompassed a wide range of responsibilities, but many of the administrative ones were dropped in the 1940s. Most notably, though, they embrace a range of welfare responsibilities, including carrying out periodic household surveys, counselling and advising on debt and family relationships.

This, alongside the localised nature of policing, led Bayley (1976) to argue that the Japanese police were held in high esteem by the public and were accountable to the public (Bayley 1983). However, this perspective has been undermined on a number of fronts. First, it is evident that while in theory the police are locally accountable, in practice public safety commissions are conservative bodies that show few teeth. Secondly, the legal system provides the police with considerable opportunity to pressurise suspects, and examples of the police exceeding even this latitude are common (Miyazawa 1989). Finally, the pervasive occupational culture (Bayley 1976) provides insulation from external influence (Miyazawa 1989, 1992). As a result, it is scarcely surprising that the image of the police derived from consumer surveys like the International Crime Victim Survey (ICVS) is less positive than early police studies implied (Kesteren *et al.* 2002).

In turning to compare Japan with its neighbours, a number of factors are worthy of consideration. On the one hand, cultural similarities and the direct influence of Japan during its occupation of, for example, Singapore, Korea and parts of China, suggest that police systems might be similar. On the other hand, differences in the political systems (Leishman 1999) and varying outside influences have encouraged differences in the ways in which systems have developed. Thus, as noted earlier, Mao drew on the Japanese model in moulding the Chinese police system, and also based policing within Confucian ethics, remoulded as communist principles, but the PRC's political system provides a contrasting framework for police accountability, with party involvement more immediate and more challenging than Japan's conservative and weak public safety commissions. Similarly, Singapore inherited many of the features of the Japanese police, most notably in terms of a local police presence and the operation of the police census, but within a more tightly controlled political system (Austin 1987).

South Korea provides another example of where Japanese colonial influence is still evident in modern policing, but where the USA was more than willing to sanction a more distanced and repressive police in the interests of the 'war' against communism. Lee's comparison of Japan and South Korea emphasises the differences but also notes that 'both forces are natural, hierarchical, authoritarian – respected and feared by the vast majority; opposed even hated by politically progressive minorities' (1990: 91).

Japan inherited many of its ideas on modern police systems from continental Europe, but then modified these to match its distinctive culture. It is these modifications, particularly the balance between a local police presence and a centralised control system, that it passed on to its neighbours, but these were in turn adapted to fit different political systems and to meet different disorder priorities. Thus, although it is arguable that there is a distinct Far Eastern police system, again there are considerable variations within the subcontinent.

Discussion

This brief review of police systems across the world illustrates the extent of variation that still exists. Police organisations differ in terms of how they are structured, what roles they carry out and the extent to which and mechanisms through which they are held accountable. On the one hand, I have argued that in addition to police systems in England and Wales and North America we might distinguish police systems in continental Europe, colonial societies, communist countries and the Far East. On the other hand, there are marked differences between countries within each of these categories, even among the small number of examples included here. For example, the ideal type continental police, with a centralised, militaristic and largely unaccountable police, carrying out a wide range of high policing and administrative tasks, may be evident in France, Italy and Spain, but was very different from the police of Scandinavian countries or the Netherlands. And the Soviet model of policing may be readily recognised in the police systems of its European 'colonies', but differs markedly from that in China.

Similarly, all police systems are subject to change. However, although the modern police contrast starkly with the police of newly industrialising societies, and indeed the police in England and Wales (or the USA) today differ from their predecessors of the 1970s or 1980s, this should not necessarily be taken as evidence that modern police systems are converging. True, the global village brings senior police managers and politicians closer to their contemporaries from other countries, and police innovations are more readily transferred from one country to another than was the case even 30 years ago, but the examples of postcommunist and postcolonial countries illustrate the difficulties this entails. The fact that changes to policy or practice in one country were successful is no guarantee that innovations can be successfully implemented, much less operate effectively, in another system. Police systems are closely embedded in the wider structure and culture of their societies. They are resistant to change, even when political systems change, and a change of personnel does not guarantee that the system itself can be transformed. A review of police in different societies, then, both informs us of the distinctions that can still be drawn and introduces us to the complexities of change.

Selected further reading

Most of the academic analysis of police systems across the globe can be assigned to one or more of five categories. First, a number of writers have focused on criminal justice systems in one particular country. Of course, such material is not necessarily comparative, but where academics are writing about non-Anglo-American countries and aiming for a wider audience, it is almost inevitable that they draw international comparisons. Examples of police systems in transition, such as Brogden and Shearing's analysis of South Africa (*Policing for a New South Africa*, 1993) or Aldous' work on postwar Japan (*The Police in Occupation Japan*, 1997) are particularly illuminating.

A second approach is to draw comparisons between two or more countries. Of these, perhaps the best known is Bayley's critique of the Japanese police (*Forces of Order: Policing Modern Japan*, 1991 edition), in which he draws on his experience of the US system. Others include Miller's comparison of the emergence of the modern police in New York and London (*Cops and Bobbies*, 1977).

A third approach that is perhaps a variant on this, is what we might term the global perspective. Here primary or secondary material may be drawn from a number of countries to illustrate similarities in structures or issues facing policy-makers and practitioners. Bayley's *Patterns of Policing* (1985) provides a useful illustration of this approach: on the one hand, he contrasts aspects of policing, such as whether or not the police are organised on a national basis as a centralised institution or on a local level. On the other hand, he identifies what he sees as the key features of modern police systems – public, specialised and professional – and argues that in contemporary society similarities between nations are more notable than differences. In his more recent work (*Police for the Future*, 1994), Bayley focuses almost exclusively on the similarities between police systems. Based on research in Australia, England, Canada, Japan and the USA he argues that the police face a common set of problems related to their roles, and sets out various 'agendas for change'.

A fourth category of international comparison is where authors draw links between countries by focusing on international or multinational agencies. One recent example is debate over police co-operation in Europe – see Anderson *et al.*'s *Policing the European Union* (1995) and Hebenton and Thomas's *Policing Europe* (1995).

Finally, the police systems of a wide range of countries can be covered separately. This endeavour can, however, be approached in a number of different ways. One is to focus on a number of countries separately and to identify the core features of their policing systems in the context of their social and political systems, subsequently classifying them according to a typology – see Findlay and Zvekic's *Alternative Policing Styles* (1993) and Mawby's *Comparative Policing Issues* (1990). The alternative, as adopted here, is to provide a broad-brush approach by considering a range of contrasting systems. Thus Mawby's *Policing across the World* (1999) distinguishes between Anglo-American policing, policing on continental Europe, communist/postcommunist policing, colonial systems and the type of policing that has emerged in the Far East. More detailed discussions of any of these models are also available. For example, the similarities and differences between colonial police systems have been the subject of detailed scrutiny in two volumes edited by Anderson and Killingray – *Policing the Empire* (1991) and *Policing and Decolonisation* (1992).

References

Akermo, K.E. (1986) 'Organisational changes and remodelling of the Swedish police', *Canadian Police College Journal*, 10(4): 245–63.

Aldous, C. (1997) *The Police in Occupation Japan*. London: Routledge.

Anderson, D.M. and Killingray, D. (eds) (1991) *Policing the Empire*. Manchester: Manchester University Press.

Anderson, D.M. and Killingray, D. (eds) (1992) *Policing and Decolonisation*. Manchester: Manchester University Press.

Anderson, M. (1995) 'Police co-operation with eastern Europe in an EC framework', in J.-P. Brodeur (ed.) *Comparison in Policing: An International Perspective*. Aldershot: Avebury, 175–83.

Anderson, M., Boer, M. den, Cullen, P., Gilmore, W., Raab, C. and Walker, N. (1995) *Policing the European Union: Theory, Law and Practice*. New York, NY: Oxford University Press.

Applegate, R.J. (2003) 'Influencing police policy and practice in England and Wales: the local/central debate revisited', *International Journal of Police Science and Management*, forthcoming.

Arnold, D. (1986) *Police Power and Colonial Rule: Madras 1859–1947*. Oxford: Oxford University Press.

Austin, W.T. (1987) 'Crime and custom in an orderly society: the Singapore prototype', *Criminology*, 25: 279–94.

Bayley, D.H. (1975) 'The police and political developments in Europe', in C. Tilley (ed.) *The Formations of Nation States in Europe*. Princetown, NJ: Princetown University Press, 328–79.

Bayley, D.H. (1976) *Forces of Order: Police Behaviour in Japan and the United States*. Berkeley, CA: University of California Press.

Bayley, D.H. (1979) 'Police function, structure and control in western Europe and North America: comparative historical studies', in N. Morris and M. Tonry (eds) *Crime and Justice: An Annual Review of Research*. Chicago, IL: University of Chicago Press, 109–43.

Bayley, D.H. (1983) 'Accountability and control of police', in T. Bennett (ed.) *The Future of Policing*. Cropwood Conference Series 15. Cambridge: Institute of Criminology, 146–62.

Bayley, D.H. (1985) *Patterns of Policing*. New Brunswick, NJ: Princetown University Press.

Bayley, D.H. (1991) *Forces of Order: Policing Modern Japan*. Berkeley, CA: University of California Press.

Bayley, D.H. (1994) *Police for the Future*. New York, NY: Oxford University Press.

Bayley, D. and Shearing, C. (1996) 'The future of policing', *Law and Society Review*, 30(3): 585–606.

Beck, A. and Chistyakova, Y. (2002) 'Crime and policing in post-Soviet societies: bridging the police/public divide', *Policing and Society*, 12(2): 123–37.

Benyon, J., Turnbull, A., Willis, R., Woodward, R. and Beck, A. (1993) *Police Cooperation in Europe: An Investigation*. Leicester: Centre for the Study of Public Order, University of Leicester.

Brogden, M. (1987) 'The emergence of the police: the colonial dimension', *British Journal of Criminology*, 27: 4–14.

Brogden, M. and Shearing, C. (1993) *Policing for a New South Africa*. London: Routledge.

Bunt, P. and Mawby, R.I. (1994) 'Quality of policing', *Public Policy Review*, 2(3): 58–60.

Bureau of Justice Statistics (2002) *Sourcebook of Criminal Justice Statistics Online* (www.albany.edu/sourcebook).

Burke, R.H. (ed.) (1998) *Zero Tolerance Policing*. Leicester: Perpetuity Press.

Cassels, Sir J. (1994) *Independent Committee of Inquiry into the Role and Responsibilities of the Police*. London: Police Foundation.

Chapman, B. (1978) 'The Canadian police: a survey', *Police Studies*, 1(1): 62–72.

Chen, X. (2002) 'Community and policing strategies: a Chinese approach to crime control', *Policing and Society*, 12(1): 1–13.

Cohen, J.A. (1966) 'The criminal process in the People's Republic of China: an introduction', *Harvard Law Review*, 79: 469–533.

Cole, B. (1999) 'Post-colonial systems', in R.I. Mawby (ed.) *Policing across the World: Issues for the Twenty-first Century*. London: UCL Press, 88–108.

Conquest, R. (1968) *The Soviet Police System*. London: Bodley Head.

Cooper, B. (1996) 'The fall of the wall and the East German police', in M. Pagon (ed.) *Policing in Central and Eastern Europe: Comparing Firsthand Knowledge with Experience from the West*. Ljubljana, Slovenia: College of Police and Security Studies, 239–52.

Cullen, P. (1992) *Working Paper II: The German Police and European Co-operation*. Edinburgh: Department of Politics, University of Edinburgh.

Dános, V. and Tauber, I. (1995) 'Relationship between the Hungarian police and society', in L. Shelley and J. Vigh (eds) *Social Changes, Crime and the Police*. Chur, Switzerland: Harwood Academic Publishers, 118–25.

Dion, R. (1982) *Crimes of the Secret Police*. Montreal: Black Rose Books.

Donajgrodzki, A.P. (ed.) (1977) *Social Control in the Nineteenth Century*. London: Croom Helm.

Eck, J.E. and Spelman, W. (1987) ' "Who ya gonna call?" The police as problem-busters', *Crime and Delinquency*, 33: 31–52.

Fairchild, E.S. (1988) *German Police*. Springfield, MA: Charles C. Thomas.

Findlay, M. and Zvekic, U. (eds) (1993) *Alternative Policing Styles: Cross-cultural Perspectives*. Boston, MA: Kluwer.

Fine, B. and Millar, R. (eds) (1985) *Policing the Miners' Strike*. London: Lawrence & Wishart.

Fogelson, R.M. (1977) *Big-city Police*. Cambridge, MA: Harvard University Press.

Fosdick, R.B. (1920) *American Police Systems*. New York, NY: The Century Co.

Fosdick, R.B. (1969) *European Police Systems*. Montelair, NJ: Patterson Smith.

Goldstein, H. (1987) 'Towards community-oriented policing: potential, basic require-ments, and threshold questions', *Crime and Delinquency*, 33: 6–30.

Hann, R.G., McGinnis, J.H., Stenning, P.C. and Farson, A.S. (1985) 'Municipal police governance and accountability in Canada: an empirical study', *Canadian Police College Journal*, 9(1): 1–85.

Hebenton, B. and Thomas, T. (1995) *Policing Europe: Co-operation, Conflict and Control*. London: Macmillan.

Home Office (1995) *Review of Police Core and Ancillary Tasks*. London: HMSO.

Home Office (2001) *Crime and Disorder/Police Partnerships* (www.homeoffice.gov.uk/rds/crimedisorder.html).

Horrall, S.W. (1980) 'The Royal North-West Mounted Police and labour unrest in western Canada', *Canadian Historical Review*, 16: 169–90.

Hughes, G., McLaughlin, E. and Muncie, J. (eds) (2002) *Crime Prevention and Community Safety: New Directions*. London: Sage.

Igbinovia, P.E. (1981) 'The pattern of policing in Africa: the French and British connections', *Police Journal*, April: 123–55.

Ingleton, R. (1996) *Arming the British Police: The Great Debate*. London: Frank Cass.

Innes, M. (1999) 'An iron fist in an iron glove? The zero tolerance policing debate', *Howard Journal*, 38(4): 397–410.

Interpol (1992) 'Netherlands', *Police*, November: 20–1.

Jasinski, J. (1995) 'Crime control in Poland: an overview', in J. Jasinski and A. Siemaszko (eds) *Crime Control in Poland*. Warsaw: Oficyna Naukowa, 6–10.

Jefferson, T. (1990) *The Case against Paramilitary Policing*. Milton Keynes: Open University Press.

Johnston, L. (1999) 'Private policing: uniformity and diversity', in R.I. Mawby (ed.) *Policing across the World: Issues for the Twenty-first Century*. London: UCL Press, 226–38.

Jones, T. (1995) *Policing and Democracy in the Netherlands*. London: Policy Studies Institute.

Jones, T. and Newburn, T. (2002) 'The transformation of policing?', *British Journal of Criminology*, 42: 129–46.

Journes, C. (1993) 'The structure of the French police system: is the French police a national force?', *International Journal of the Sociology of Law*, 21(3): 281–7.

Kania, R.R.E. (1989) 'The French municipal police experiment', *Police Studies*, 12: 125–31.

Kelling, G.L. and Coles, C.M. (1996) *Fixing Broken Windows: Restoring Order and Reducing Crime in our Communities*. New York, NY: Free Press.

Kelling, G.L. and Moore, M.H. (1988) *The Evolving Strategy of Policing. Perspectives on Policing*. Washington, DC: US Department of Justice.

Kesteren, J. van, Mayhew, P. and Nieuwbeerta, P. (2002) *Criminal Victimisation in Seventeen Industrialised Countries: Key Findings from the 2000 International Crime Victims survey* (http://www.minjust.nl/B_ORGAN/WODC/publicaties/Rapporten/pub rapp/ob187.htm).

Kowalewski, D. (1981) 'China and the Soviet Union: a comparative model for analysis', *Studies in Comparative Communism*, 14(4): 279–306.

Lee, S.Y. (1990) 'Morning calm, rising sun: national character and policing in South Korea and in Japan', *Police Studies*, 13: 91–110.

Leishman, F. (1999) 'Policing in Japan: east Asian archetype?', in R.I. Mawby (ed.) *Policing across the World: Issues for the Twenty-first Century*. London: UCL Press, 109–25.

Loveday, B. (1996) 'Business as usual? The new police authorities and the Police and Magistrates' Courts Act', *Local Government Studies*, 22: 22–39.

Loveday, B. (1999) 'Government and accountability of the police', in R.I. Mawby (ed.) *Policing across the World: Issues for the Twenty-first Century*. London: UCL Press, 132–50.

Loveday, B. and Reid, A. (2003) *Going Local: Who Should Run Britain's Police*. London: Policy Exchange.

Maguire, E.R, Kuhns, J.B., Uchida, C.D. and Cox, S.M. (1997) 'Patterns of community policing in nonurban America', *Journal of Research in Crime and Delinquency*, 34(3): 368–94.

Maguire, K. and Pastore, A.L. (1994) *Sourcebook of Criminal Justice Statistics 1994*. Washington, DC: US Department of Justice.

Marenin, O. (1998) 'United States police assistance to emerging democracies', *Policing and Society*, 8: 153–67.

Mawby, R.I. (1990) *Comparative Policing Issues: The British and American Experience in International Perspective*. London: Routledge.

Mawby, R.I. (1992) 'Comparative police systems: searching for a continental model', in K. Bottomley *et al.* (eds) *Criminal Justice: Theory and Practice*. London: British Society of Criminology/ISTD, 108–32.

Mawby, R.I. (1996) 'Comparative research of police practices in England, Germany, Poland and Hungary', in M. Pagon (ed.) *Policing in Central and Eastern Europe:*

Comparing Firsthand Knowledge with Experience from the West. Ljubljanar, Slovemia: College of Police and Security Studies, 473–85.

Mawby, R.I. (1999a) 'Variations on a theme: the development of professional police in the British Isles and North America', in R.I. Mawby (ed.) *Policing across the World: Issues for the Twenty-first Century*. London: UCL Press, 28–58.

Mawby, R.I. (1999b) 'The changing face of policing in central and eastern Europe', *International Journal of Police Science and Management*, 2(3): 199–216.

Mawby, R.I. (ed.) (1999c) *Policing across the World: Issues for the Twenty-first Century*. London: UCL Press.

Mawby, R.I. (2000) 'Core policing: the seductive myth', in F. Leishman *et al.* (eds) *Core Issues in Policing* (2nd edn). London: Longman, 107–23.

McKenzie, I.K. and Gallagher, G.P. (1989) *Behind the Uniform: Policing in Britain and America*. Hemel Hempstead: Harvester-Wheatsheaf.

Miller, W.R. (1977) *Cops and Bobbies: Police Authority in New York and London, 1830–1870*. Chicago, IL: University of Chicago Press.

Miyazawa, S. (1989) 'Scandal and hard reform: implications of a wiretapping case to the control of organisational police crimes in Japan', *Kobe University Law Review*, 23(13): 13–25.

Miyazawa, S. (1992) *Policing in Japan: A Study on Making Crime*. New York, NY: State University of New York Press.

Monkkonen, E. (1981) *Police in Urban America, 1860–1920*. Cambridge, MA: Cambridge University Press.

Morgan, R. (1992) 'Talking about policing', in D. Downes (ed.) *Unravelling Criminal Justice*. London: Macmillan, 165–83.

Morrison, W.R. (1985) *Showing the Flag: The Mounted Police and Canadian Sovereignty in the North, 1894–1925*. Vancouver: University of British Columbia Press.

Ostrom, E., Parks, R.B. and Whitaker, G.P. (1978) *Patterns of Metropolitan Policing*. Cambridge, MA: Ballinger.

Posen, I. (1994) 'What is policing?', *Police Review*, 11 February: 14–15.

Reiner, R. (1994) 'What should the police be doing?', *Policing*, 10(3): 151–7.

Reiner, R. (2000) *The Politics of the Police*. Oxford: Oxford University Press.

Reppetto, T.A. (1978) *The Blue Parade*. New York, NY: Free Press.

Rosenbaum, D.P. (ed.) (1994) *The Challenge of Community Policing*. Thousand Oaks, CA: Sage.

Rothschild, J. (1993) *Return to Diversity: a Political History of East Central Europe since World War II*. New York, NY: Oxford University Press.

Ruchelman, L. (1974) *Police Politics: A Comparative Study of Three Cities*. Cambridge, MA: Ballinger.

Shapland, J. and Vagg, J. (1988) *Policing by the Public*. London: Routledge.

Shelley, L. (1997) *Policing Soviet Society: The Evolution of State Control*. London: Routledge.

Shelley, L. (1999) 'Post-socialist policing: limitations on institutional change', in R.I. Mawby (ed.) *Policing across the World: Issues for the Twenty-first Century*. London: UCL Press, 75–87.

Sherman, L. (1978) *Scandal and Reform: Controlling Police Corruption*. Berkeley, CA: University of California Press.

Skogan, W. (1995) *Contacts between Police and Public: Findings from the 1992 British Crime Survey*. Home Office Research Study 134. London: Home Office.

Smith, B. (1940) *Police Systems in the United States*. New York, NY: Harper & Bros.

Solomon, P.H. (1987) 'The case of the vanishing acquittal: informal norms and the practice of Soviet criminal justice', *Soviet Studies*, 39(4); 531–55.

Stenning, P.C. (1981) 'The role of police boards and commissions as institutions of municipal police governance', in D.C. Shearing (ed.) *Organizational Police Deviance*. Toronto: Butterworths, 49–82.

Sweatman, B. and Cross, A. (1989) 'The police in the United States', *CJ International*, 5(1): 11–18.

Tobias, J.J. (1977) 'The British colonial police: an alternative police style', in P.J. Stead (ed.) *Pioneers in Policing*. Maidenhead: Patterson Smith, 241–61.

Tupman, B. (1995) 'Keeping an eye on eastern Europe', *Policing*, 11: 249–60.

Waddington, P.A.J. (1999) 'Armed and unarmed policing', in R.I. Mawby (ed.) *Policing across the World: Issues for the Twenty-first Century*. London: UCL Press, 151–66.

Walker, S. (1977) *A Critical History of Police Reform*. Lexington, MA: Lexington Books.

Walker, S. (1983) *The Police in America: An Introduction*. New York, NY: McGraw-Hill.

Wall, D. (1998) *The Chief Constables of England and Wales: The Socio-legal History of a Criminal Justice Elite*. Aldershot: Ashgate.

Ward, R.H. (1984) 'Police and criminal justice in Hungary', *Police Studies*, 6: 31–4.

Weatheritt, M. and Vieira, C. (1998) *Lay Visiting to Police Stations. Home Office Research Study* 188. London: Home Office.

Weller, G.R. (1981) 'Politics and the police: the case of the Royal Canadian Mounted Police'. Paper presented by the annual conference of the Political Studies Association, Hull.

Wong, K.C. (2002) 'Policing in the People's Republic of China: the road to reform in the 1990s', *British Journal of Criminology*, 42: 281–316.

Yun, T. (1983) 'The police and the people', *Beijing Review*, 23 May: 22–7.

Zapletal, J. and Tomin, M. (1995) 'Attitudes of the Czechoslovak public towards the police after 1989 in light of empirical investigation', in L. Shelley and J. Vigh (eds) *Social Changes, Crime and the Police*. Chur, Switzerland: Harwood Academic Publishers, 190–4.

Zvekic, U. (1996) 'Policing and attitudes towards police in countries in transition', in M. Pagon (ed.) *Policing in Central and Eastern Europe: Comparing Firsthand Knowledge with Experience from the West*. Ljubljana, Slovenia: College of Police and Security Studies, 45–59.

Zvekic, U. (1998) *Criminal Victimisation in Countries in Transition*. Rome: UNICRI.

Chapter 3

Policing before the police

Philip Rawlings

Communal policing in the Middle Ages (600–1350)

It is difficult today to contemplate Britain without the police. Yet they are a relatively recent phenomenon, and it is not immediately obvious why the state, through these officials, should intervene where there has been wrongdoing – and then generally only wrongdoing designated as criminal. In England during the period before the Conquest of 1066, the evidence suggests that, while the state intervened, it did so in a way which drew on the customary practices of the blood-feud and communal intervention. The codes of law drawn up by Anglo-Saxon kings beginning with Æthelbert (died 616) were expressions of royal authority. Although at first they seem to have been concerned mainly with the codification of customary practice, they also began to rearticulate the rights of the victim and the role of the community – the neighbourhood, village, parish or town – into duties that were owed to the Crown. Over the next few centuries, the victim's right to kill a wrongdoer was restricted and, instead, an expectation was established that offenders would be brought before the courts: for instance, the laws of Æthelbert directed that anyone who 'take revenge before he demand justice' was to provide compensation (Thorpe 1840: 109), while the laws of Ine (died 726) required that the killing of a thief be justified by showing that 'he whom he killed was a thief trying to escape' (Simpson 1981: 74).

The other key aspect of the Anglo-Saxon codes of law was the obligations they placed on the community. Although these duties were given legal force by the state, they originated in the rhythms of conflict and collaboration inherent in any community. For instance, the laws of Athelstan (died 939) directed that a thief who fled 'shall be pursued to his death by all men who are willing to carry out the king's wishes' (Riggs 1963: 46). The hue and cry, as this came to be known, appears to have originated in the normal expectation that this is what neighbours would do. Similarly, the system of frankpledge, which also originated before the Conquest, combined the tendency of a community to exclude strangers with neighbourly curiosity. With a few exceptions, all adult men were required to be members of a tithing, so that strangers were suspect. Each tithing member swore 'I ... will not be a thief nor the fellow of a thief, nor will I conceal a theft nor a thief but will reveal it to those to whom it should be revealed' (Maitland and Baildon 1891: 76).

It may have been that the victim and the community remained central to law enforcement because this reflected customary practice and so lent legitimacy to the new system, but it was also the case that the Crown had neither the inclination nor the resources to intervene itself. In the feudal system power was diffused so that the connection between the Crown and its subjects was not direct but ran through various intermediaries. Furthermore, the immediate threat posed by thieves was to the local community, and local people were likely to be better equipped to identify offenders, even though this might allow powerful criminals to operate with impunity. On the other hand, the Crown did see potential for raising revenue, not just through the penalties imposed on offenders, but also through the fines levied on those who neglected their duties in relation to enforcement. As much as anything, it was this revenue potential that drove the formalisation of these duties and the creation of complex systems of accountability that ran through parish, county and royal officials and courts. Indeed, the law enforcement process at this time could be characterised, not so much as a means of identifying offenders, but more as a set of obligations placed on officials, witnesses, victims and whole communities.

In 1285 the Statute of Winchester purported to reinforce this community-based approach to the prevention of crime and the detection of offenders. The hue and cry was strengthened by a requirement that the community compensate the victim where the hue had been raised following a robbery and the offender had escaped. Town gates were to be closed at night and, in the summer months when drier roads facilitated travel, a watch was to be posted with the authority to arrest strangers 'where they find a Cause for Suspicion'. The town bailiff was to ensure that any resident who gave lodging to a stranger was ready to 'answer for him', typically by giving security for good behaviour. A case from Northampton in 1329 illustrates communal policing or, rather, because for obvious reasons the story is only told from one viewpoint, indicates how this system was expected to work (Sutherland 1983: i, 168–9):

At Heyford on 30 May 1317, Robert fitz Bartholomew of Heyford received certain unknown thieves as guests in his house. The watchmen of the town saw that those thieves were staying up suspiciously late in the night and therefore went to enter the house; when they came to one door Robert and the rest of the thieves went out the other door. The hue and cry were raised at once and the men of the town came to pursue and arrest the aforesaid felons. Among the men of the town came a certain John of Bannebury, who has now died, who pursued the felons, calling upon them to surrender to the king's peace. They would by no means surrender or permit themselves to be judged by the law, nor could those who were pursuing them take them alive. A general fight ensued between the felons and their pursuers, and John of Bannebury cut off the head of the aforesaid Robert. The chattels of the aforesaid Robert are confiscated for flight.

The rise of the official (1350–1688)

Yet, well before John of Bannebury was summarily decapitated, it was feared that crime had continued to rise in spite of the Statute of Winchester. One reason given for this was that the provisions of the statute were being ignored, but the truth seems to have been that key assumptions underpinning communal policing no longer held true.

Communal policing was the progeny of feudalism and, like it, depended on the existence of relatively stable communities. However, by the late thirteenth century the feudal system was in decay: the economy was stagnating while food prices were being forced up by a rise in population coupled with a decline in food production. Then, in the fourteenth century severe famines and the plague of 1348 decimated the population and destroyed many communities. The labour shortage that resulted pushed up wages and encouraged greater mobility. This mobility raised concerns that the economic and political order was being undermined, and it created obvious difficulties for a policing system that depended on an internally coherent community with a stable population. These problems led many in the political elite to swallow their reservations about encouraging the acquisition of power by the Crown and, instead, to support a national strategy that was co-ordinated by justices of the peace appointed by the Crown (Palmer 1993).

To some extent, these events merely accelerated a long-established trend whereby the community's obligations for law enforcement were being shifted into the hands of officials who came from the parish, the county and the Crown. So, for instance, all members of a tithing were required to appear periodically before the sheriff to answer questions about the performance of their functions, but in practice the tithing was represented by a chief pledge or tithingman. There was also nothing new about the Crown seeking to increase its authority at the expense of local power-holders through the appointment of royal officials: some of these officials had been given a permanent place in the counties, such as coroners; some were appointed to deal with temporary crises, such as keepers of the peace; and some were periodically sent to hold local officials and communities accountable for their actions, such as assize judges. Indeed, the extent of the legal reforms implemented by Henry II in the middle of the twelfth century led one historian to conclude that, 'Judicial activity and law continued to be characterized by a considerable degree of local self-government, but in important aspects it was self-government at the king's command' (Hudson 1996: 141).

Nevertheless, the events of the fourteenth century seemed decisive in the shift of policing responsibilities from the community to officials and, just as significantly, they led to the duties of these officials being focused on the regulation of labouring people. In terms of crime control through prevention and detection, there was a deepening split between the fulfilment of procedural obligations, which increasingly came to be something for which officials were held to account, such as the requirement that the constable lead the hue and cry, and the actual detection of offenders, which was, primarily, a matter for victims.

Although the varied nature of medieval local government makes it difficult to generalise, in most communities the main official in terms of law enforcement was the constable, whose office probably derived from that of chief pledge. He served for one year, was unpaid and was elected from the more substantial people in a parish. For obvious reasons, Shakespeare's depiction of the constable as incompetent, lazy and ignorant is likely to remain influential in how we view these officials, but it should be remembered that his characters served dramatic and comic purposes so that, while this portrayal should not be wholly dismissed, nor should it be taken at face value. It is certainly possible to find examples of poor-quality constables, though such complaints seem to have been rare. In her excellent study of the constable in the early modern period, Kent (1986) declared herself 'impressed by the time, effort, and even financial sacrifice that was expected, and so often given'. This was in spite of the fact that their duties had grown relentlessly and in the early seventeenth century included such matters as military organisation, tax collection, the regulation of alehouses, weights and measures, the maintenance of public order, the control of vagrants, environmental pollution, and the arrest and custody of suspects. Moreover, at that time, unpopular taxes and laws regulating popular culture were making the work particularly difficult. Yet few seem to have avoided service, although it is difficult to judge whether this was out of a sense of duty or because they could not afford the fine for refusing to serve, or because they employed a deputy to do most of the work.

Such apparent neglect as there was by some constables in performing their functions may have been symptomatic of the complex position in which they sometimes found themselves. On the one hand, the constable's performance was subject to scrutiny by the justices of the peace, who might themselves be under pressure from central government. On the other hand, the constable depended on maintaining a good relationship with the community, both because without it many aspects of the work would have been difficult to perform and because these people were his neighbours. Moreover, uncertainty about the constable's legal powers laid them open to harassment by litigation, although, presumably, more common was the sort of verbal abuse meted out in the 1660s by William Shepheard who, when angered by the action of Thomas Webb, a Norfolk constable, provided an insight into a world of invective that we seem to have lost: 'I wonder what rogues made you a constable. I could shit a better constable, the devil take you . . . You Goodman Jackanapes, what will you do to me Goodman Constable, Goodman Turd' (Rosenheim 1991: 65). The motive for such attacks varied: in 1583 a constable in Colchester was set upon in an effort to obtain the release of a prisoner (Emmison 1970: 106), and hatred of the taxes imposed by the government of Charles I led to assaults on the constables charged with collecting them. Some constables did not endear themselves to their neighbours by the enthusiasm with which they undertook their duties as, for instance, when Puritan constables set about enforcing laws on popular leisure activities in the late sixteenth and early seventeenth centuries. More broadly, the economic, social, religious and political upheavals of the fourteenth to seventeenth centuries tended to deepen the cultural gap between the more prosperous members of a community from whom the constable came and their poorer neighbours. This often created the sort of divisions within communities from which emerged both the enthusiasm of Puritan constables for their work and the opposition of those who resented these intrusions – although it should be added that the local elite did not necessarily side with the constable in these confrontations. In short, trapped between the justices and their neighbours and, perhaps, possessing clear views of their own, the constable's situation was not easy: as James Gyffon put it in 1626 (Wrightson and Levine 1995: 115):

The Justices will set us by the heels
If we do not as we should
Which if we perform, the townsmen will storm
Some of them hang 's if they could.

The key official in connecting the parish officers to the Crown in the late Middle Ages was the justice of the peace. This office emerged in the midst of the crises in the fourteenth century as a means of controlling wages and prices, but the justices acquired a broad range of judicial and administrative responsibilities and relatively quickly formed an 'elaborate and co-ordinated system which for the first time provided the crown with a permanent judicial presence' (Musson and Ormrod 1999: 74). Although the Crown used its powers of appointment and dismissal to influence opinion among the justices, this did not mean they were mere puppets. Most came from the land-owning gentry and some were members of Parliament so that, while they were doubtless often flattered by the connection with the Crown, their position in the county gave them authority that could not lightly be ignored. Even when the shortage of active justices in the eighteenth century, particularly in towns, led to more appointments from the middling classes, the government did not necessarily find these men more compliant. On the other hand, while the Crown was keen to influence many of the aspects of local administration that came under the control of the justices, their responsibility for the day-to-day routine of law enforcement and order maintenance was of less concern to government or, at most, attracted its attention only spasmodically.

Watchmen and constables in the eighteenth century

All towns were required by the Statute of Winchester to establish a watch and householders were periodically obliged to perform this duty. Aside from guarding the entrances to the town, the watchman's primary function was to patrol the streets and maintain order by, for instance, arresting drunks and prostitutes: watchmen in sixteenth-century Devizes were instructed to challenge those who 'suspiciously walk about the Towne in the nyght' (Cunnington 1925: ii, 1), and little had changed by the eighteenth century when London watchmen were authorised to arrest 'all night walkers, malefactors, rogues, vagabonds, and other disorderly persons whom they shall find disturbing the publick peace, or shall have just cause to suspect of any evil designs' (10 Geo. II, c. 22).

There is some evidence that watch duty was unpopular; so, for instance, in Norfolk John Callin attacked William Child in 1665 when Child told him it was his turn to serve (Rosenheim 1991: 59). Although relatively few refusals were recorded, it is difficult to know whether this was because people undertook the duty, or because they paid the fine or hired a substitute, or because concern about the issue only arose at times of crisis, as in 1665 when the Surrey justices, alarmed at the possibility of the plague spreading from London, fined a large number of people for neglecting their duty (Powell and Jenkinson 1938: 69, 245–6). In any event, in London by the eighteenth century few householders were choosing to serve and, as a result, there was professionalisation of the watch by default. Householders distanced themselves from this function and criticism of the quality and performance of watchmen became common, although the difficulties and dangers of the work, the low pay and the long hours were largely ignored. The burgeoning of the economy and the leisure industry in the eighteenth century also appears to have changed expectations of the watch. People stayed out into the night and many towns facilitated this by street lighting schemes, so that the idea of the watch enforcing an informal curfew no longer seemed appropriate. Instead, the expectation was that the watch would be more active in protecting those whose legitimate business or pleasure took them on to the streets at night (Beattie 2001: 169–225).

During the eighteenth and early nineteenth centuries, and in varying degrees, local authorities across the country sought to improve or to establish watch schemes. As growing economic activity expanded villages into towns, particularly in the North and the Midlands, the local elite often wanted their town to acquire the trappings of civic status and these included a professional watch system. However, reform encountered a number of difficulties: house-holders, who were keen for the watch to be improved, were often less enthusiastic about contributing to the cost; the complex structure of the government in many boroughs could also obstruct reform; and there were struggles between local political and interest groups to gain control over any new watch scheme.

An important breakthrough came in London when the parishes of St James, Piccadilly and St George, Hanover Square, obtained legislation in 1735 under which householders exchanged the duty to serve in the watch for the duty to pay a watch rate (8 Geo. II, c. 15). Other parishes in London followed this example, but the initial enthusiasm had been prompted by a crime panic and this faded with the outbreak of war in 1739 which, it was supposed, would remove into the armed forces the young men responsible for most of the crime. The next surge in reform did not occur until peace came in 1748. However, by the end of the century the establishment of new watch schemes and the reform of existing ones had become commonplace across the country. To some extent, there seems to have been a snowball effect with reform of the watch in one place leading neighbouring communities to introduce changes because of the fear that criminals would migrate from well policed to poorly policed areas. This fear was reinforced by the construction of turnpike roads, which enabled faster travel. At Clapham in Surrey, for instance, a proposal to reform the watch in 1785 was put forward because the village 'is become large and populous, and, from its Vicinity to the Metropolis, the Inhabitants thereof, and also all Persons passing to and from the same in the Night Time, are much exposed to Robberies, and other Outrages' (*Journal of the House of Commons* 1785: xl, 616). Reform did not necessarily stop once a new watch scheme was in place. Many watch committees continued to seek improvements so that, by the early nineteenth century, some places had fairly sophisticated regulations about the qualifications, pay, working methods and discipline of the watchmen, and in many London parishes cover was improved by the appointment of patrol officers with greater freedom to operate than the watchmen, who were confined to a particular area or beat.

The jurisdictional problems with a system based on the parish caused some concerns in London: Stephen Haydon, a watchman, told the Old Bailey in 1741 that, although he had heard the cries of a robbery victim, he had not gone to her assistance because 'it being out of my Parish I durst not venture to go' (*OBSP* July 1741: 4). Unitary schemes were established elsewhere in the country, and some poorer London parishes recognised the advantage in joining their watch schemes together as, for instance, happened in Southwark in 1766. In 1770 John Fielding, the Bow Street magistrate and an adviser to the government in crime, complained to a select committee that the watch in Westminster 'is insufficient, their Duty too hard, and Pay too small' (*Journal of the House of Commons* 1770: xxii, 879), and he attacked the parishes for their parsimony and their failure to co-operate with each other. Yet, while legislation in 1774 brought some uniformity in Westminster in terms of pay, duties and force strength, Fielding's proposal to unify the watch and place it under the control of the Middlesex magistrates – of which he was one – failed, as had similar plans earlier in the century, including one put forward in 1749 by his step-brother, the novelist and Bow Street magistrate, Henry Fielding. Ratepayers remained resolute in their wish to maintain local control and accountability; there was also reluctance among the members of the parish vestries, who controlled the watch, to relinquish their power; and richer parishes with good schemes feared that a unified watch in Westminster would lead to reduced coverage if resources were channelled into poorer areas.

In spite of the reforms, criticism of the watchmen persisted throughout the eighteenth and early nineteenth centuries, although it is sometimes difficult to judge whether this was because they were inefficient or because expectations about what they should achieve had risen. Newspapers delighted in recounting stories of the incompetence of watchmen, such as when the *London Evening Post* (29 February 1772) reported that lead had been stolen from the roof of a London watch-house, and it is not difficult to find confirmation of these stories in parish minutes. John Pizzey, who served in Holborn, London, was rewarded by the watch committee in 1819 for making an arrest, but within 18 months had been dismissed for 'improper conduct'; reinstated following a petition of support from householders on his beat, he was dismissed again three months later for falsely charging a gentleman with assaulting him, which offence he compounded by his defiant attitude to the watch committee when interviewed (St Andrew, Holborn, B/1D21: 21 July 1819–20, June 1821). Yet it is important to recognise that the watch schemes also enjoyed a good deal of support, both in the parishes and in the reports of select committee inquiries. By the nineteenth century, the watch forces in some London parishes, such as Marylebone, were impressive and, indeed, the early Metropolitan Police based its organisation and practices on such forces and drew recruits from them (see Chapter 4). Moreover, in the wake of the creation of the Metropolitan Police, there were angry complaints that local accountability had been lost and that the level of coverage had deteriorated.

Like the watch, the office of constable underwent important changes in the eighteenth century. In many places the distribution of constables was proving inadequate in the light of changing populations: for example, in the City of London in 1663 there was one constable for every 25.5 houses in the Bread Street ward, but only one for every 486.5 houses in Cripplegate Without (Beattie 2001: 114–68). But, as with the watch, efforts to implement reform had to contend with complexities in the structure and politics of local government, so that an apparently uncontroversial proposal to increase the number of constables in the City took decades to achieve. In contrast to the watch, there does seem to have been a greater willingness among householders in the eighteenth century to serve. This may be because of the fine that was imposed for a refusal, but it may have reflected the office's status. Nevertheless, as has been mentioned, the workload was burdensome, and in some places it was customary to hire a deputy; indeed, in Westminster this practice had became so common that legislation was passed in 1756 to formalise the arrangements for their appointment. John Fielding who, generally, supported the professionalisation of policing, praised the 'general good Behaviour, Diligence and Activity' of the Westminster deputies (Reynolds 1998: 46–7), although other commentators expressed concern that they were part of a process by which, as one writer put it in 1829: 'the office has fallen into the hands of the lowest class of retailers and costardmongers, who make up the deficient allowance of their principals by indirect sources of emolument' (Wade 1829: 78).

As well as these local policing schemes based on the constable and the watch, there were other types of public provision. Government employed customs and excise officers for the purposes, among other things, of safeguarding the duties charged on goods and regulating the import and export of certain types of goods. The increasing expenditure of government in the eighteenth century, coupled with the resistance of the gentry to taxes on land, led to the imposition of duties on a wide range of goods, and this, in turn, increased the opportunities for illicit trading and smuggling. On the east and south coasts, there were long traditions of smuggling, and some gangs were well organised, popular and prepared to use violence. This led the government to deploy troops to support the customs and excise officers, as was the case with the campaign in the mid-eighteenth century against the Hawkhurst gang in Sussex (Winslow 1977). Other government departments, such as the Mint and the Post Office, also employed officers to enforce laws relating to their spheres of interest.

In addition, the Bow Street patrols were established in the late eighteenth century. John Fielding used the opportunity of a crime panic that followed the end of the Seven Years War in 1763 to obtain government funding for a force of officers under his direction, which was charged with patrolling the highways leading into London – a task that during previous crises had been undertaken by soldiers. The government withdrew its support for the patrols in the following year on the ground that policing was a matter for the local authorities, although the decision was, doubtless, also influenced by the cost. However, Fielding managed to persuade government to reinstate the funding shortly afterwards. The Bow Street force became permanent with both foot and horse patrols, and by 1829 its numbers had expanded to around 400. These officers wore distinctive uniforms, were armed and, unlike the parish forces, were not confined to particular areas but, instead, could be used to target crime hotspots throughout Westminster.

In 1785 there was an attempt to reorganise policing in London. This was the result of a crime panic that followed the demobilisation of a huge army and navy at the end of the American War of Independence. The panic led the authorities to resort to the traditional response of increasing the number of people hanged and to search for a destination to which convicts might be transported as a replacement for the American colonies, but it also prompted innovation in the form of prison building by local authorities and the proposal by the government of William Pitt that the policing of the metropolis be put into the hands of commissioners. The bill failed because of concerns about cost, the loss of parochial control and the increase in government power, although the decisive issue was the City of London's resentment at what it regarded as an invasion of its privileges. However, in 1792 the Middlesex Justices Act was passed. It did not apply to the City, but for the rest of the metropolis seven police offices were established, each staffed with stipendiary magistrates and a small group of officers and having a jurisdiction that was not confined by parish boundaries.

The state of the watch in London remained an issue of debate, both inside and outside Parliament, in the early nineteenth century, but the implementation of a unitary policing scheme remained unlikely. One criticism was that it would increase the power of central government and that this would threaten liberty: in 1822 a select committee commented that, while such a system might deliver improved crime control, it was 'difficult to reconcile ... with that perfect freedom of action and exemption from interference, which are the great privileges and blessings of society in this country' (Select Committee 1822: 9). Moreover, as has been mentioned, the richer and more politically powerful parishes were largely content with their policing arrangements, which were often well organised and funded, and were also keen to resist any loss of authority or accountability. Yet it was evident that many parishes struggled with the burden of administering and financing an efficient watch.

There was also a general concern about the ability of the watch forces – both in London and elsewhere – to cope with major disturbances. This weakness was exposed by the Gordon Riots in 1780, during which large parts of London were in the hands of the rioters for five days. Yet, although this event remained in the public consciousness well into the nineteenth century, the issue was not addressed because of the continued support for a decentralised policing system. The army could be used to support the civil authorities in the eighteenth century, but this raised a number of difficult issues. The distrust of powerful government meant there was strong opposition to the existence of a large standing army and the use of troops against civilians, but there was also the question of the cost of maintaining an army. Moreover, the magistrates, who had the power to request assistance from the army, had a number of concerns about doing so: the nearest barracks might be at some distance, so the soldiers would arrive too late; there was uncertainty about who could order the soldiers to use force and what force might be used; and it was feared that the presence of soldiers could stir up resentment that might otherwise have been peacefully dissipated. The civil authorities had been criticised for failing to use the army early enough to quell the Gordon Riots, and there were accusations that the troops themselves had been sympathetic to the rioters. At the other extreme, in 1761 the soldiers of the North Yorkshire Militia became known as the Hexham Butchers after charging into a crowd, which had gathered in that market town to protest new methods of conscription, and hacking to death 40 people.

Efforts were made after the Gordon Riots and during the French Wars (1793–1815) to reduce the dependence on soldiers by establishing paramilitary forces composed of part-time volunteers but, drawn, as they tended to be, from the landed and the middling classes, these forces proved difficult to control and, after a charge by one such force turned a peaceful meeting in Manchester into the Peterloo Massacre in 1819, unpopular. On the whole, therefore, the government and local authorities continued to rely on the army. To improve the distribution of troops around the country, a large number of barracks was built and, in 1812, at the height of the industrial protests known as the Luddite disturbances, about 12,000 soldiers were stationed in the Midlands and the North – more than Wellesley (later the Duke of Wellington) took to Portugal. Even so, the uncertainty and indecision about the use of the army remained and were again exposed during the riots in London in support of Queen Caroline in 1820–1. These seem to have caused consternation to one observer in particular, Robert Peel, who became Home Secretary in 1822. However, even if he did contemplate the formation of a civil force that might, among other things, take on riot control, the issue remained politically sensitive and did not feature prominently in his public pronouncements on policing in London.

Alongside these public policing schemes, there was probably an expansion in privately employed watchmen during the eighteenth century. In some prosperous areas neighbours joined together to fund a patrol and, indeed, by the mid-nineteenth century some 150 communities in London were using guarded gates for protection against traffic and thieves (Draper 1984). Some of the hundreds of societies for the prosecution of offenders, which appeared all over the country from the mid-eighteenth century and which drew funding from members, employed patrols to guard the property of their subscribers. Many warehouse owners, dockyard operators and turnpike trustees also operated small forces of watchmen, some of whom were sworn as constables or enjoyed special statutory powers. In Yorkshire worsted manufacturers obtained legislation to outlaw certain working practices and employed inspectors to enforce these laws. But the most famous of these private forces was the Thames River Police, which was established in 1797 and was, initially, funded by dock owners. The role played by these officers in imposing new work practices in the docks led to a riot in October 1798, which resulted in the death of a foreman and the execution of a dockworker. However, not only did the force survive and expand, in 1800 its funding and control passed into the hands of the government, as part of the reform of policing in London that had begun with Pitt's bill of 1785.

The practice of policing: maintaining order

The transformations in the social, economic and political relationships of the fourteenth century not only led to a reorganisation of policing in which officials and the Crown played a greater role but they also provided those officials with an agenda in which the focus was on the regulation of labouring people rather than the detection of offenders.

From the fourteenth century onwards laws on work, vagrancy, poor relief and morality proliferated and encompassed the whole of the labouring population in both their economic and social lives. Their justification can be found in the Statute of Labourers 1351, which was passed in the wake of the plague to deal with, among other things, the rising labour costs that had resulted from the shortage of workers. However, the statute ascribed this shortage, not to the plague, but to the attitudes of workers: '[some] will not serve unless they may receive excessive wages, and some rather willing to beg in idleness, than by labour to get their living'. Working people, it was believed, had to be closely regulated otherwise they would drift into idleness and immorality, and from there to poverty, vagrancy and crime.

Vagrants were seen as symbolising the dangers posed both by the labouring poor and by inefficient regulation (Slack 1988). They were defined in law as those who were engaged in jobs that involved moving around, such as pedlars and jugglers but, more broadly, they were 'all wandering persons and common Labourers being persons able in bodye using loitering and refusing to worcke for . . . reasonable Wages' (39 Eliz. I, c. 4 (1597), s. 2). Vagrants were routinely blamed for the spreading of crime and disease, and were subject to severe punishments, such as whipping. The height of the campaign against vagrancy came in the sixteenth century. In 1596, during a severe economic depression, a series of poor harvests and the demobilisation of large numbers of troops, Edward Hext, a Somerset magistrate, wrote to Elizabeth's chief minister, Lord Burghley, claiming that:

> the Infynyte numbers of the Idle wanderynge people and robbers of the land are the chefest cause of the dearthe, for thowghe they labor not, and yet they spend dobly as myche as the laborer dothe, for they lye idlely in the ale howses daye and nyght eatinge and drynkynge excessively (Tawney and Power 1951: iii, 341–2).

That the government also took this view is suggested by a proclamation issued in 1596 ordering monthly searches for 'pretended soldiers' and appointing provost marshals with wide powers to sweep up vagrants.

Alongside this penal attitude to vagrancy, the Tudors did, however, introduce a system of poor relief. This was, in part, a consequence of the Reformation and involved the parish taking over responsibility for the poor from the church. Yet, although the poor laws provided assistance to the indigent and acknowledged the state's obligation in this regard, they also amounted to a flexible and broad disciplinary regime that had an impact on all labouring people, whether they required assistance or not. A pauper, who was not a vagrant, could be incarcerated in a workhouse or house of correction, or returned to her or his place of settlement (broadly, the place of birth or long residence or, in the case of a married woman, the settlement of her husband). Since settlement defined the responsibility of a parish to provide relief for a pauper, casual workers might be moved on before they could acquire a settlement and pregnant women pressured into marrying someone from another parish, even if no claim for relief had been made.

Alongside provisions on vagrancy and poor relief, there were laws on labour and morality. Labour laws, such as the Statute of Labourers 1351, regulated various aspects of work, including wages, controlled or prohibited attempts by workers to organise strikes or trade unions and gave justices of the peace broad powers to discipline employees. Employers were subject to some regulation, but to a lesser extent than the workforce and the sanctions involved were of a quite different order: for instance, while the apprentice who ran away before the end of an apprenticeship was likely to be imprisoned, the abusive master or mistress was, at worst, only likely to suffer the cancellation of the apprenticeship agreement. Finally, the labouring population was also subject to a maze of legislation on morality, which concentrated on the regulation of popular culture. Once again, the justification for these laws lay in the connections that were made between immorality, crime and poverty. A statute of 1606 declared drunkenness to be:

> the root and foundation of many other enormous sins, as bloodshed, stabbing, murder, swearing, fornication, adultery, and such like, to the great dishonour of God, and of our nation, the overthrow of many good arts and manual trades, the disabling of divers workmen, and the general impoverishing of many good subjects, abusively wasting the good creatures of God (4 Jac. I, c. 5).

Administration of the laws on vagrancy, poor relief, labour and morality was placed into the hands of parish officials under the supervision of the justices of the peace. In practice, this gave the officials fairly wide powers because there was little likelihood of their decisions being challenged. Edward Hext was concerned that this led to lax enforcement, which, in turn, encouraged what he regarded as the natural idleness of the labouring people: he complained 'of Constables and Tythingmen that suffer [vagrants] to wander, and of inhabitants that releve them contrary to the lawe' (Tawney and Power 1951: iii, 344). Yet officials faced problems in carrying out their duties. The law was often obscure or difficult to enforce. For instance, the identification of a pauper's place of settlement was likely to depend on information supplied by that person, which an official would have neither the time nor the resources to verify, even if he were inclined to do so: Amy Moore was arrested in Salisbury for vagrancy three times between 1603 and 1607, and on each occasion was removed to a different place because of the information she gave concerning her settlement (Slack 1975). In any event, even if officials were robust in their general attitude to the poor, some seem to have been more sympathetic when confronted by an individual pauper, or were simply unwilling to spend time enforcing the law: encouraging someone to move to the next parish and even giving him or her a few pence may have seemed the kindest or simplest option. In this context, we can contrast Hext's strident views with those of William Lambarde, a Kent justice, writing in the same year, who, although certainly willing to use the whip against vagrants, was, nevertheless, critical of the harsh policy adopted towards demobilised soldiers:

> what marvel is it if after their return from the wars they do either lead their lives in begging or end them by hanging. Nevertheless we are by many duties most bounden to help and relieve them, considering that they fight for the truth of God and defense of their country; yea, they fight our own war and do serve in our places, enduring cold and hunger when we live at ease and fare well (Read 1962: 183–4).

Another aspect of this issue of enforcement has already been touched on, namely, the relationship between the officials, the communities within which they lived and the justices of the peace. Communities would have agreed on the need for a moral order, but that did not mean there was agreement about its shape or how it was to be maintained. This, in turn, led to conflict around enforcement, or reluctance to use the law, not just because of the cost involved, but also because it placed control over the definition of moral order outside the community. Instead, informal methods would be used to impose order, such as rough music, which involved noisy demonstrations aimed at an individual whose behaviour was regarded as objectionable, 'to make soe notorious an abuse exemplarye whereby others evill disposed might be discoraged from committinge the like' (Reay 1998: 160). Sometimes, however, there seemed no alternative to the law, although it is safe to assume that, like most litigants, a community resorted to the law in the expectation of receiving support for its view. In the 1590s the villagers of Little Onn in Staffordshire petitioned the justices to have William Alcocke bound over to keep the peace. They complained that he did not repair his fences, took fuel from his neighbours' hedges and that:

> he ys so stout and prodigall that he may in no wyse be reprehended for any of these his manifest faultes and suspiciouse lyffe but he thereupon threateneth to kill ... the manner of his lyffe ys so suspicious as wee greatlie doubt hym ... [He] thinketh hym selfe a man Lawlesse and therefore lyvethe without the compasse of all good order (Burne 1932: 25–7).

However, as has been seen in the context of those constables who enthusiastically enforced the laws on morality in the late sixteenth and early seventeenth centuries, communities were often internally divided over these issues: a complaint to the Somerset Quarter Sessions in 1608 about the immorality of John Newman's lifestyle was met by a petition from 26 of his neighbours who provided an unqualified endorsement of his honesty and industriousness (Bates Harbin 1907–8: i, 16).

In the eighteenth century these laws regulating the labouring poor continued to grow, but there does appear to have been a shift in the reasoning behind them and their enforcement. Some continued to view the immorality of the poor in fairly apocalyptic terms. The societies for the reformation of manners were formed in 1690 as voluntary organisations to prosecute offences against morality. However, the initial enthusiasm among the political elite, which was probably not shared by the poor who were the societies' targets, soon evaporated in the face of criticism, part of which Daniel Defoe (1709) rendered into doggerel: 'Your Annual Lists of Criminals appeare/But no Sir *Harry* or Sir *Charles* is there'. By the 1720s the societies had lost most of their support and attempts to revive them later in the century met with only limited success. On the whole, immorality continued to be viewed as a serious problem, but it had also become commonplace to point out, as Defoe had done, that there were anomalies when comparing attitudes towards the morality of the rich and the poor. The differential treatment was justified by arguing that the immorality of the rich had little effect – indeed, there was a view that their indulgences were beneficial to the economy – whereas the immorality of the poor led them into poverty and crime, although it is possible to see in the writings of those, such as Henry Fielding (1988), who dealt with these issues some discomfort at having to make this distinction.

In general, the view of the poor taken by those who debated social policy in the eighteenth century can be contrasted with the opinions that underpinned Tudor policy. While assumptions about the inherent dishonesty, immorality and idleness of the poor continued to hold sway, they were no longer seen as a threat to the political order. Such fears had largely been displaced by concern over the cost of poor relief and by the recognition that, 'Our domestic safety and comfort, our private wealth and prosperity, our national riches, strength, and glory, are dependent upon an industrious and well-order'd Poor' (Potter 1775: 1). This acknowledgement that the poor created wealth in which they did not share was not meant to generate sympathy for them; instead it was regarded as placing them under an obligation to work or to work harder: 'having nothing but their labour to bestow on the society, if they withhold this from it they become useless members; and having nothing but their labour to procure a support for themselves they must of necessity become burdensome' (Fielding 1988: 228). This argument was seen as justifying both the failure to regulate the rich, who were not so central to the economy, and the emphasis on the regulation of the labouring poor, although since parish officials administered this regulation its enforcement remained patchy. However, the poor were not simply regulated by more laws, their opportunities for earning a living outside the discipline of the labour relationship were also reduced. During the eighteenth century, common land, on which the poor might have raised some cattle, came under increasing pressure from land-owners, and non-waged work, such as gleaning, was criminalised. More broadly, there was growing support for the removal of regulations on capital. This meant the withdrawal of legal protections for labouring people and a greater willingness to oppose forms of popular action that had given a voice to the powerless, such as trade unionism in the workplace or the use of riot to influence food prices (Hay and Rogers 1997).

The practice of policing: crime control

The concentration of officials on the regulation of the poor meant that they did not really fill the gap left by the decline in the community's role in the detection of offenders. Suspects were identified in a number of different ways. The *Old Bailey Sessions Paper* for December 1720, to take one session at random, reported 27 trials at the Old Bailey involving convictions for stealing or attempted stealing. There is too little information in five cases to draw any conclusions about the means by which the suspect was identified. In 13 cases, the connection between the defendant and the crime seems to have been made fairly rapidly: in nine of these, at least one defendant was an employee or former employee, and in the other four, at least one defendant was caught near the scene of the crime. In the nine other cases, there was a delay in identifying the suspects; in most of these it is difficult to know how the identification was made, although in four the arrest was made because a pawnbroker or dealer in goods to whom the stolen property had been taken became suspicious.

Since officials were not expected to undertake an active role in detection, it is not surprising to find that a large proportion of the offenders were discovered by the victim or were caught near the scene of the crime. In 1637, William Stevenson reported that, as he walked through the crowds at Scarborough market, he felt the hand of John Watson 'very busie aboute his reight pockett' (Ashcroft 1991: 299). Thomas Armstrong, one of the defendants at the Old Bailey in 1720, was apprehended as he was leaving the public house from which he had stolen property. Mrs Richins, who worked there, confronted Armstrong but, although she 'threw him down', he escaped, only to be pursued and caught by two men, who had heard her cries of 'stop thief'. Employees of the victim had a greater opportunity to steal and were, perhaps, also more likely to be identified as suspects: so, for instance, in another of the cases before the Old Bailey in 1720, the coincidence of Mary Ann de la Fountain disappearing from her employment at the same time as the theft of a silver knife and fork led to her arrest and the discovery of the missing items. Some victims were prepared to engage in fairly prolonged detective work: suspecting that an ex-employee had stolen from his shop in Tower Hill, London, George Arthur went, first, to the man's lodgings in Old Street, then travelled the considerable distance to Bristol and eventually caught up with him in Bath (*OBSP* December 1784: 183–4). Those victims who subscribed to one of the societies for the prosecution of offenders, which appeared in the late eighteenth century, were encouraged to undertake a pursuit because they could claim the expenses incurred (King 1989; Philips 1989).

Of course, it is difficult to discuss those occasions when victims either did nothing or took action outside the criminal justice system. Since a prosecution usually depended on the involvement of the victim, they had a broad discretion to decide on the responses that most suited their interests and these did not necessarily coincide with those of the justice system. A victim might have wished to avoid the cost and inconvenience of a prosecution that would not guarantee the return of stolen property, or might have been reluctant to bring a petty thief to the gallows. If, for instance, a victim of theft identified the offender, there were a number of options, which did not involve prosecution: he or she might pay for the return of the goods, or be content with some compensation or an apology, or just ignore the matter. In 1649, at the height of the civil war, John Dickinson, who was a farmer in North Yorkshire, explained that he reached a settlement with the men who had stolen his sheep 'because . . . it was a dangerous tyme and Elvard was a soldier and may been hee and his partners might have done the said Dickinson some harme' (Ashcroft 1991: 196–7). In the early eighteenth century, Jonathan Wild built a highly profitable business based on mediating between victims and thieves, and he cunningly reduced the effort involved by organising some of the thefts himself; yet, as one of his biographers put it, 'The People who had been robb'd, it may be suppos'd were always willing enough to hear of their Goods again, and very thankful to the Discoverer' (Anon 1725: 8). Legislation may have terminated some of the business practices that Wild had perfected, but many victims continued to place the return of their property above the prosecution of the thief. The eighteenth-century boom in the newspaper trade enabled victims to contact thieves directly by advertising rewards for the return of their property, which was typically described as 'lost', with the added promise of 'no questions asked' (Styles 1989). Although illegal, compromising an offence was commonplace; indeed, in 1750 Horace Walpole, the son of the former prime minister, Robert Walpole, came to an agreement for the return of a watch with James Maclean, 'the gentleman highwayman', who had robbed him in Hyde Park. Even justices of the peace often seem to have regarded mediation between victim and offender as part of their broader role of maintaining local harmony: so, for instance, in 1665 Robert Doughty, a Norfolk justice, persuaded a farmer to drop a prosecution for theft in exchange for compensation from one woman, a day's unpaid work from another and an apology from a third (Rosenheim 1991: 61).

Third parties sometimes became involved in the detection process. By the eighteenth century the hue and cry had lost its role as a means of compelling the community to pursue a suspect but, as the arrest of Thomas Armstrong in 1720 shows, a shout of 'Stop thief!' could still bring assistance from neighbours and bystanders. The involvement of pawnbrokers and those who dealt in second-hand goods in the arrest of thieves came as a result of the tightening of the laws on receiving stolen goods in the eighteenth century. James Washfield, who was convicted at the Old Bailey in 1720, had been arrested when he tried to sell some stolen brass weights to Samuel Wood. For some reason Wood became suspicious and had 'stopt him, and upon hearing a very indifferent character of him, had him before a justice, where he confess'd he stole them'. Then, there were the chance encounters. In 1733, on going to the aid of John Cullington, who had fallen from his horse, John Felt noticed that several bullets had rolled from Cullington's pocket, 'which made me suspect him for a Highwayman, and therefore I secur'd him' (OBSP December 1733: 10). Finally, a significant number of offenders were identified as a result of comrades being persuaded by magistrates to give evidence for the prosecution in exchange for immunity: when James Dalton was arrested in 1728, he quickly offered to appear as a Crown witness against the members of the gang of street robbers which he led.

Constables and watchmen did also detect suspects: responding to the cries of a robbery victim, Moses Bennet, a London watchman, chased and caught

Benjamin Beckenfield (*OBSP* December 1750); and Michael Hollingsworth was arrested in the cellar of the Half Moon in Westminster in 1817 after a watchman noticed an open window (*OBSP* October 1817: 472–3). Watchmen also made arrests as a consequence of stopping someone whose behaviour appeared 'suspicious': William Paine was convicted of stealing a pig in 1740 after being stopped while walking through Bermondsey one night by a watchman who heard a squeak coming from the sack slung over his shoulder (*Surrey Assizes* July 1740: 9). However, in general, the watchmen and constables were concerned with order maintenance, and doubtless many were as unenthusiastic about engaging in detection work as the constable in London who told a robbery victim in 1734 that 'he should be upon Duty that Night, and would look after such Fellows as I had describ'd' (*OBSP* December 1734: pt I, 9). Officers would make an arrest or search premises but, usually, only after a suspect had been identified: in the summer of 1739, Henry Davies suspected that Elizabeth Williams had picked his pocket, so he found out where she lived, obtained a warrant from a magistrate and only then called on the assistance of the constable to make the arrest and search her house (*Surrey Assizes* August 1739: 9).

Some of the more active justices of the peace did advertise for information about a notorious crime or instructed a parish officer to make inquiries into a suspicious person who had been arrested but against whom no specific charge had been laid. However, those justices who engaged in the criminal justice process (which, by the eighteenth century, many did not) tended to confine themselves to their statutory duty. In felony cases, they were required to collect such evidence 'as shall be material to prove the felony'. This involved examining the victim, the suspect and the witnesses and then binding them over to appear at the trial with the objective of ensuring that the prosecution would not be abandoned (2 & 3 Ph. & Mar., c. 10). In theory, the justices were not concerned with any possible defence, but some seem to have considered whether the 'right' person had been arrested by testing the evidence and, as has been seen, it was not uncommon for them to step even further outside their authority by encouraging parties to reach a compromise.

The enthusiasm with which victims and officials pursued a suspect was, doubtless, influenced, not just by the time, effort and expense involved but also by the degree of danger. Crowds could just as easily fight to free a pickpocket, who had been grabbed by a victim, as seek to arrest him or her, and even well armed officers might be reluctant to pursue some suspects. When John Warden, a constable, went to the Black Boy Inn in Lewkener Lane, London, to make an arrest in 1734 he was well aware that this was a dangerous area, so he armed himself and took along a number of colleagues. However, he was forced to abandon his mission because, on entering the inn, he was confronted by 'about thirty shabby Fellows, who begun to mob us, so that we were glad to get away' (*OBSP* December 1734: pt I, 20). Others were less fortunate: a London watchman called Crowder was shot dead in 1750 as he joined in the pursuit of some street robbers (*OBSP* 20 October 1750).

On occasions, local and central government did press officials to take action against crime, but such campaigns were usually short lived and often concerned with what were seen as the underlying causes, which meant the focus tended to fall on the regulation of the labouring poor. Even where officials were charged with pursuing offenders, their efforts might be undermined by other government policies. That this had long been a problem can be seen in the way attempts by the Crown to tackle crime in the fourteenth century were undermined by the enthusiasm of Edward I and his descendants for fighting their neighbours. These wars required a constant supply of soldiers that could only be met from the prisons and, as a result, the judges were routinely confronted by defendants waving royal pardons. The Middle Ages and early modern periods are littered with other short-term campaigns against crime, some directed by local authorities, some by the Crown. However, by the eighteenth century, active intervention in criminal justice policy had started to become a routine part of the state's functions. A crime panic in the late seventeenth century may have triggered this involvement, but it was facilitated and driven by the new constitutional authority that Parliament acquired in the wake of the overthrow of James II in 1688. Members of Parliament were now able to explore their anxieties about crime. A mix of policies emerged: there was a toughening of penalties through the construction of the 'Bloody Code', which involved the extension of capital punishment to more crimes, and through the transportation to America and later Australia of those who had been pardoned or convicted of non-capital crimes; there were also provisions designed to encourage prosecutions by paying the costs of poor prosecutors and by offering rewards to those who obtained the conviction of certain types of offender.

Rewards had been used since the fourteenth century to persuade people to prosecute victimless crimes, such as religious nonconformity, profane swearing and operating an unlicensed alehouse. From the late seventeenth century, this idea was extended to more serious offences with payments as high as £500 for the conviction of those engaged in certain smuggling offences. In addition, victims, their families and local authorities offered rewards in response to particular crimes. These inducements encouraged some people, such as professional constables and watchmen and even offenders, to exploit their connections and engage in thief-taking.

Since payment of the reward depended on conviction, the thief-takers were keen not to leave the gathering of evidence to the magistrate, but to take charge of the process by extracting a confession. Commonly, their interrogations took place in a nearby inn: Charles Shooter, who was described in court as a child, alleged in 1741 that thief-takers had tricked him to confess by getting him drunk (*OBSP* January 1741). If two suspects were taken, the thief-takers might set them in competition against each other with a promise of allowing one to appear as a witness for the Crown and so escape prosecution – a promise they had no power to make and which was often not fulfilled. The testimony of witnesses was also important and, doubtless, many were coached. When Nicholas Sweetman was asked at the Surrey Assizes in 1741 how he could be sure that it had been the accused who had robbed him, he blurted out, 'I was told by a Gentleman who makes it his Business to take up these Sort of People' (Surrey Assizes July 1741: 2–3). Greater care was exercised by the thief-taker who, after a mail robbery in 1721, took two witnesses to Newgate Prison. There, as they told the Old Bailey, both identified

William Wade, who had been arrested on suspicion, but they were careful to add that they had picked from a dozen or more prisoners who had been exercising in the yard, and that the thief-taker had given them no hint and had told them not to confer (*OBSP* July 1721: 7).

A cynic might be a little suspicious at the frequency with which thief-takers themselves were victims of crime or just happened to be passing the scene of a crime in progress. There was also some extra-judicial criticism that rewards encouraged perjury; a claim that seemed to draw substance from cases where thief-takers were convicted of having laid false charges of robbery, such as John Waller in the 1730s and the Macdaniel gang in the 1750s. Moreover, there was good reason to suppose that some thief-takers did not bother to go to the trouble of bringing a prosecution, which might end with a jury failing to produce a conviction of an offence that carried a reward, and, instead, they sought to extort money from people by threatening them with prosecution.

In spite of the notoriety of these practices, the judges seem not to have been impressed by unsupported allegations from defendants about the behaviour of thief-takers. Beattie (2001: 244) seems right in his suggestion that they 'were tolerated because they were useful'. Indeed, some thief-takers appear to have enjoyed close relationships with the more active London magistrates and constables and to have been familiar figures to the judges. The judges did construct certain rules of evidence, such as that confessions should be voluntary, but these, probably, posed few difficulties for thief-takers and could have even worked to their advantage because appearing to conform to them may have improved the chances of obtaining a conviction. What eventually caused problems for the thief-takers was, according to Beattie (2001: 413), that by the 1740s the trade was becoming overstocked and profits squeezed. In addition, as defence lawyers became more common in the late eighteenth century, the evidence of those who stood to earn a reward was subjected to more careful scrutiny (Langbein 2003).

The emergence of a body of thief-takers attached to the magistrates' office at Bow Street may also have played a part in this decline. In the second half of the eighteenth century, Henry and John Fielding were energetic in their pursuit of offenders and in publicising both that work and their ideas. John Fielding devised a plan that involved advertising through newspapers for victims and witnesses to bring information to Bow Street. This information was then distributed to selected London thief-takers and to magistrates throughout the country (Styles 1983). Fielding (1768: vi) believed that this would increase the likelihood of offenders being caught and that 'the Certainty ... of speedy Detection, must deter some at least'. He claimed that this approach was the only way of tackling gang crime, which was causing particular anxiety at the time. Moreover, a national plan that enabled the rapid exchange of information between magistrates offered a means of tackling those offenders who travelled about the country and who drew support from a network of receivers and safe houses.

One difficulty facing the Fieldings was to convince governments to fund their plans. However, crime panics in the late 1740s and the 1760s, together with their skill in using newspapers and pamphlets to publicise their work, helped them to extract some financial support, although obtaining sufficient permanent funding proved more difficult. As an alternative, Fielding found some of the Bow Street thief-takers posts as gaolers or deputy constables, but they also had to rely on rewards or on fees paid by victims and this brought with it some of the stink of the Waller and Macdaniel cases. Another problem was that the plan to control crime through the detection of offenders was something of a departure from the assumptions that had underpinned an important part of criminal justice policy. It was believed that by attaching the death penalty to a large number of offences the Bloody Code allowed the gallows to be used as a means of deterring a broad range of prospective offenders, but this required that only a few carefully selected offenders be executed because otherwise there would be revulsion at the bloodshed, or sympathy for the hanged, or a dilution of the message (Hay 1977). There was, in short, no need for a more efficient system of detection. More generally, Fielding's plan displaced the victim from the centre of crime control by laying emphasis on skill, professionalism, continuity and the need to construct networks for the collection and dissemination of information. On the other hand, the plan was in tune with some other developments in criminal justice policy. For instance, although it was accepted that not all felons should be hanged, there were sustained efforts to establish punishments, such as transportation, that would deal with those who were pardoned; in other words, it was regarded as important that all offenders were punished, which had not previously been the case. This was reinforced by the policies aimed at encouraging prosecutions, such as the payment of costs and rewards. Moreover, Fielding's plan reflected the tendency in policing towards greater professionalism, which has already been discussed in the context of the watch.

Yet, in spite of all these developments, at the beginning of the nineteenth century it was still the case that most suspects were identified in the same ways as they had been in 1720. Even where a thief-taker or a Bow Street officer was involved, they usually depended for their raw information on the victim. However, this reality was already being marginalised by the idea that it was the professional – 'the Bow Street Runner' – who was at the heart of the detection process. This impression had been created by the stress laid on publicity by the Fieldings and had been sustained by other magistrates, who followed their example, and by newspaper proprietors, for whom crime was newsworthy, especially where there was a chase that required the involvement of the Runners.

Conclusion

Up to the late seventeenth century, the state's principal interest in policing had been in order maintenance, which meant the control of the labouring classes. This had been achieved through regulations whose enforcement was left to private citizens acting as watchmen, constables, poor law officers and justices of the peace. Crime control through detection remained a matter for victims and their families and neighbours. By the early nineteenth century the picture had changed. The policing functions of maintaining order on the streets, riot control and detection were still regarded as separate, but there had been important changes in the execution of these tasks.

Everywhere towns followed the example set in London by passing responsibility for street patrols from householders to professional watchmen. Detection was still mainly done by victims, but the lucrative rewards offered for the conviction of certain types of offenders established the trade of thief-taking, and this opened the way for John Fielding's detective bureaucracy at Bow Street. Riot control continued to be the responsibility of local officers, such as the watchmen and constables, but the building of barracks across the country meant local authorities could more readily call on the assistance of soldiers.

These changes were the product of the politicisation of criminal justice. The change in the role of Parliament and the rapid expansion of the newspaper industry and the book trade opened up opportunities for public discussion on a range of domestic issues, including crime. The regulation of the labouring classes remained a significant theme, but more attention was given to addressing crime through changes in punishment and policing. A major premise of this debate was that crime could not be resolved by individuals and amateurs and that, therefore, the state (local and central) had to intervene: this can be seen in all areas of criminal justice, from the Treasury's funding of transportation and rewards for the conviction of offenders to the rebuilding of prisons by towns and the reorganisation of watch forces by parishes.

In practice, individuals remained central to various aspects of policing: victims continued to undertake the bulk of detection work well into the nineteenth century. Yet the debate on crime was dominated by those, like John Fielding, who believed that in a remodelled policing system the role of citizens would be to supply information for officers to collate, interpret and act upon. While ordinary people may have welcomed the marginalisation of their role, the continuation of crime and the fear of victimisation led many to take measures to protect themselves and their property. This led to a surge in crime prevention and private policing from the mid-eighteenth century: a good deal of the work done by thief-takers and the Bow Street officers was private client work but, more significant, were the proliferation of advice on crime prevention, the establishment of hundreds of societies for the prosecution of offenders after the 1740s, the employment of watchmen to guard businesses and neighbourhoods, the growing demand for more sophisticated locks that led to the rapid expansion of the lock-building industry in the Midlands, the use of alarms in houses and so forth. Private security arrangements were, perhaps, regarded as allowing people to re-establish some form of personal control, but they also undermined the debate on policing because they took place outside formal policing structures and, therefore, did not form part of the idea of policing that was being constructed. The difficulties that this exclusion causes to a rational debate on policing have never been properly addressed.

Selected further reading

For overviews of the whole period, see Critchley's *A History of Police in England and Wales, 900–1966* (1967) and Rawlings's *Policing: A Short History* (2002). On the Middle Ages, the definitive study of the early codes of law is Wormald's *The Making of English*

Law (1999), while the administration of criminal justice is discussed in Musson's *Public Order and Law Enforcement* (1995), Musson and Ormrod's *The Evolution of English Justice* (1999) and Summerson's 'The structure of law enforcement in thirteenth century England' (1979); see also the controversial account in Palmer's *English Law in the Age of the Black Death, 1348–1381* (1993). For a discussion of the range of officials in the medieval justice system, see Cam's (1950). Vagrancy and poor relief in the Tudor and Stuart periods are discussed in Beier's *Masterless Men* (1985) and Slack's *Poverty and Policy in Tudor and Stuart England* (1988); see also Rogers' 'Policing the poor in eighteenth-century London: the vagrancy laws and their administration' (1991). Kent's *The English Village Constable, 1580–1642* (1986) is an excellent book concerned with the Tudor and early Stuart period, as is an essay on the dilemmas facing the constable by Wrightson (1980). The puritan regulation of morality is discussed in Underdown's *Revel, Riot and Rebellion* (1987) and, for a case study of the administration of criminal justice in the seventeenth century, see Herrup's *The Common Peace* (1987). On the involvement of victims in the detection of crime, see Gaskill's 'The displacement of providence: policing and prosecution in seventeenth- and eighteenth-century England' (1996), King's 'Prosecution associations and their impact on eighteenth-century Essex' (1989), Philips' 'Good men to associate and bad men to conspire' (1989) and Styles' 'Print and policing' (1989). The work of the watchmen has received relatively scant consideration, although see, Beattie's *Policing and Punishment in London, 1660–1750* (2001), Henderson's *Disorderly Women in Eighteenth-century London* (1999) and Reynolds's *Before the Bobbies* (1989). Watch reform in the eighteenth century is discussed in Reynolds and Beattie, the thief-takers in Beattie, Howson's *Thief-taker General* (1970), Paley's 'Thief-takers in London in the age of the Macdaniel gang, *c.* 1745–1754' (1989) and Wales' 'Thief-takers and their clients in later Stuart London' (2001), and the ideas of Sir John Fielding in Styles' 'Sir John Fielding and the problem of crime investigation in eighteenth-century England' (1983) and Rawlings' 'The idea of policing' (1995). The role of the army in the policing of riots is considered in Hayter's *The Army and the Crowd in Mid-Georgian England* (1978). The *Old Bailey Sessions Paper* is a valuable, if not wholly reliable, resource for the study of crime in the eighteenth century, and by 2004 the publications for the years 1674–1834 will be available in a free-to-all online (www.oldbaileyonline.org) version that is easy to use, allows the reader to choose between the original and a transcription, and has excellent search and statistical facilities as well as a bibliography and links to other sites.

References

Anon (1725) *The True and Genuine Account of the Life and Actions of the Late Jonathan Wild*. London.

Ashcroft, M. (ed.) (1991) *Scarborough Records 1600–1640: A Calendar*. North Yorkshire County Record Office Publications, 47.

Bates Harbin, The Rev. E.H. (ed.) (1907–8) *Quarter Sessions Records for the County of Somerset*. Vols 23 and 24. Somerset Record Society.

Beattie, J.M. (2001) *Policing and Punishment in London 1660–1750: Urban Crime and the Limits of Terror*. Oxford: Oxford University Press.

Beier, A.L. (1985) *Masterless Men: The Vagrancy Problem in England 1560–1640*. London: Methuen.

Burne, S.A.H. (ed.) (1932) *The Staffordshire Quarter Sessions Rolls*. Vol. II: 1590–1593. Kendal: The William Salt Archaeological Society.

Cam, H.M. (1950) in J.F. Willard *et al.* (eds) *The English Government at Work, 1327–1336*. Vol. III. Cambridge, MA: The Medieval Academy of America.

Critchley, T.A. (1967) *A History of Police in England and Wales, 900–1966*. London: Constable.

Cunnington, B.H. (ed.) (1925) *Some Annals of the Borough of Devizes. Being a Series of Extracts from the Corporation Records, 1555 to 1791*. Devizes: George Simpson.

Defoe, D. (1709) *Review*, Edinburgh, 7 April.

Draper, M. (1984) 'Bloomsbury gates and bars: the maintenance of tranquillity on the Bedford estates', *Camden History Review*, 12: 2–4.

Emmison, F.G. (1970) *Elizabethan Life: Disorder*. Chelmsford: Essex County Council.

Fielding, H. (1988) *An Enquiry into the Causes of the Late Increase of Robbers*. Oxford: Oxford University Press.

Fielding, J. (1768) *Extracts from Such of the Penal Laws, as Particularly Relate to the Peace and Good Order of this Metropolis*. London.

Gaskill, M. (1996) 'The displacement of providence: policing and prosecution in seventeenth- and eighteenth-century England', *Continuity and Change*, 11: 347–74.

Hay, D. (1977) 'Property, authority and the criminal law', in D. Hay *et al.* (eds) *Albion's Fatal Tree: Crime and Society in Eighteenth-century England*. Harmondsworth: Penguin Books.

Hay, D. and Rogers, N. (1997) *Eighteenth-century English Society: Shuttles and Swords*. Oxford: Oxford University Press.

Hay, D. and Snyder, F. (eds) (1989) *Policing and Prosecution in Britain 1750–1850*. Oxford: Oxford University Press.

Hay, D. *et al.* (eds) (1977) *Albion's Fatal Tree: Crime and Society in Eighteenth-century England*. Harmondsworth: Penguin Books.

Hayter, T. (1978) *The Army and the Crowd in Mid-Georgian England*. London: Macmillan.

Henderson, T. (1999) *Disorderly Women in Eighteenth-century London: Prostitution and Control in the Metropolis, 1730–1830*. London: Longman.

Herrup, C. (1987) *The Common Peace: Participation and the Criminal Law in Seventeenth-century England*. Cambridge: Cambridge University Press.

Howson, G. (1970) *Thief-taker General: The Rise and Fall of Jonathan Wild*. London: Hutchinson.

Hudson, J. (1996) *The Formation of the English Common Law: Law and Society in England from the Norman Conquest to Magna Carta*. London: Longman.

Kent, J.R. (1986) *The English Village Constable, 1580–1642: A Social and Administrative Study*. Oxford: Clarendon Press.

King, P. (1989) 'Prosecution associations and their impact on eighteenth-century Essex', in D. Hay and F. Snyder (eds) *Policing and Prosecution in Britain 1750–1850*. Oxford: Oxford University Press.

Langbein, J.H. (2003) *The Origins of Adversary Criminal Trial*. Oxford: Oxford University Press.

Maitland, F.W. and Baildon, W.P. (eds) (1891) *The Court Baron: Being Precedents for Use in Seigniorial and Other Local Courts*. Selden Society.

Musson, A. (1995) *Public Order and Law Enforcement: The Local Administration of Criminal Justice, 1294–1350*. Woodbridge: The Boydell Press.

Musson, A. and Ormrod, W.M. (1999) *The Evolution of English Justice: Law, Politics and Society in the Fourteenth Century*. London: Macmillan.

Paley, R. (1989) 'Thief-takers in London in the age of the McDaniel gang, *c.* 1745–1754', in D. Hay and F. Snyder (eds) *Policing and Prosecution in Britain 1750–1850*. Oxford: Oxford University Press.

Palmer, R.C. (1993) *English Law in the Age of the Black Death, 1348–1381: A Transformation of Governance and Law*. London: University of North Carolina Press.

Philips, D. (1989) 'Good men to associate and bad men to conspire: associations for the prosecution of felons in England 1768–1860', in D. Hay and F. Snyder (eds) *Policing and Prosecution in Britain 1750–1850*. Oxford: Oxford University Press.

Potter, R. (1775) *Observations on the Poor Laws, on the Present State of the Poor, and on the Houses of Industry*. London.

Powell, D.L. and Jenkinson, H. (eds) (1938) *Surrey Quarter Sessions Records: Order Book and Sessions Rolls Easter 1663–Epiphany 1666*. Vol. 39. Surrey Record Society.

Rawlings, P.J. (1995) 'The idea of policing: a history', *Policing and Society*, 5: 129–49.

Rawlings, P.J. (2002) *Policing: A Short History*. Cullompton: Willan.

Read, C. (ed.) (1962) *William Lambarde and Local Government: His 'Ephemeris' and Twenty-nine Charges to Juries and Commissions*. Ithaca, NY: Cornell University Press.

Reay, B. (1998) *Popular Cultures in England 1550–1750*. London: Longman.

Reynolds, E.A. (1998) *Before the Bobbies: The Night Watch and Police Reform in Metropolitan London, 1720–1830*. Stanford, CA: Stanford University Press.

Riggs, C.H. (1963) *Criminal Asylum in Anglo-Saxon Law. University of Florida Monographs in Social Studies 18*. Gainesville, FL: University of Florida Press.

Rogers, N. (1991) 'Policing the poor in eighteenth-century London: the vagrancy laws and their administration', *Histoire Sociale*, 47: 127–47.

Rosenheim, J.M. (ed.) (1991) *The Notebook of Robert Doughty 1662–1665*. Vol. 54. Norfolk Record Series.

Select Committee (1822) *Report from the Select Committee on the Police of the Metropolis*. Parliamentary Papers, (440) Vol. IV.

Simpson, A.W.B. (1981) 'The laws of Ethelbert', in M.S. Arnold *et al.* (eds) *On the Law and Customs of England: Essays in Honor of Samuel E. Thorne*. Chapel Hill, NC: University of North Carolina Press.

Slack, P.A. (ed.) (1975) *Poverty in Early Stuart Salisbury*. Vol. 31. Wiltshire Record Society.

Slack, P.A. (1988) *Poverty and Policy in Tudor and Stuart England*. London: Longman.

Styles, J. (1983) 'Sir John Fielding and the problem of crime investigation in eighteenth-century England', *Transactions of the Royal Historical Society* 5th Series, 33: 127–49.

Styles, J. (1989) 'Print and policing: crime advertising in eighteenth-century provincial England', in D. Hay and F. Snyder (eds) *Policing and Prosecution in Britain 1750–1850*. Oxford: Oxford University Press.

Summerson, H.R.T. (1979) 'The structure of law enforcement in thirteenth-century England', *American Journal of Legal History*, 23: 313–27.

Sutherland, D.W. (ed.) (1983) *The Eyre of Northampton 3–4 Edward III A.D. 1329–1330*. Vols 97 and 98. Selden Society.

Tawney, R.H. and Power, E. (1951) *Tudor Economic Documents being Selected Documents Illustrating the Economic and Social History of Tudor England*. London: Longmans, Green & Co.

Thorpe, B. (1840) *Ancient Laws and Institutions of England*. London.

Underdown, D. (1987) *Revel, Riot and Rebellion: Popular Politics and Culture in England, 1603–1660*. Oxford: Oxford University Press.

Wade, J. (1829) *A Treatise on the Police and Crimes of the Metropolis*. London.

Wales, T. (2001) 'Thief-takers and their clients in later Stuart London', in P. Griffiths and M. Jenner (eds) *Londinopolis*. Manchester: Manchester University Press.

Winslow, C. (1977) 'Sussex smugglers', in D. Hay *et al.* (1977) *Albion's Fatal Tree: Crime and Society in Eighteenth-century England*. Harmondsworth: Penguin Books.

Wormald, P. (1999) *The Making of English Law: King Alfred to the Twelfth Century*. Oxford: Blackwell.

Wrightson, K. (1980) in J. Brewer and J. Styles (eds) *An Ungovernable People: The English and their Law in the Seventeenth and Eighteenth Centuries*. London: Hutchinson.

Wrightson, K. and Levine, D. (1995) *Poverty and Piety in an English Village: Terling, 1525–1700*. Oxford: Clarendon Press.

Daily Journal
Journal of the House of Commons
London Evening Post
OBSP (Old Bailey Sessions Paper)
Surrey Assizes, *The Proceedings on the King's Common of the Peace, and Oyer and Terminer, and Gaol-delivery of the County Gaol, Held for the County of Surry* (also titled *The Proceedings of the Assizes for the County of Surry*).

Holborn Public Library, parish records of St Andrew, Holborn.

Chapter 4

The birth and development of the police

Clive Emsley

Introduction

The year 1829 is commonly seen as the one in which the 'New Police' were established in England. The traditional Whig histories, accounts infused with the idea of social progress pushed forward by far-sighted men, assumed that London's Metropolitan Police were a significant advance on what had existed before and, in support of their arguments, they quoted early nineteenth-century police reformers who maintained as much. In the perception of these histories late Georgian and early Victorian British society sought to be consensual but was threatened by mob violence and rising crime committed by individuals who, as 'criminals', were separate from the majority within society. The 'New Police' were a neutral government's solution to these threats (Reith 1938, 1943; Critchley 1978; Ascoli 1979). The Whig histories also assumed the gradual spread of policing through parliamentary legislation was a further illustration of the success, superiority and public acceptance of the Metropolitan model. Charles Reith, the doyen of the Whig police historians, even argued that British success in two world wars during the twentieth century was, at least in part, due to a superior policing system – a 'kin' police as opposed to a state-directed *gendarmerie* (Reith 1952: 20, 244). From the late 1960s revisionist historians started to challenge this view. They began from a perception of late Georgian and early Victorian society as divided internally, primarily by class conflict. In the revisionist view, the New Police were an instrument for controlling and disciplining a burgeoning, and increasingly self-confident and non-deferential, working class (Storch 1975, 1976).

There is no easy resolution to the dichotomy between consensual and conflicting views of society. It is something that has always been at the heart of policing as well as of police history. Nor is it something that this chapter can seek to resolve. The chapter has much more modest aims: divided into three sections it seeks simply to provide a chronological account of how the police institution developed from the early nineteenth to the mid-twentieth centuries. It has two main emphases. First, it draws attention to the British insistence throughout the period that their police were different from those on continental Europe – an insistence that can probably best be explained by ignorance, prejudice or a combination of the two. Secondly, it describes a steady current of centralisation, not part of a conspiracy, but something generally perceived by the legislative, governmental and legal elite as in the best interests of society as a whole and of the police institution in particular.

Origins and early years

The statement that a 'new' police was established in London in 1829 assumes that an 'old' police had previously existed. The latter had been a mixture of parish constables, watchmen and an increasing number of 'professional' detectives. The police established by Peel in 1829 were, essentially, centrally controlled, uniformed watchmen with a rigid work discipline geared for supervising the streets and, in theory, for preventing rather than detecting crime. In many respects, and whatever the police reformers and Whig historians maintained, they were not so much 'new' as a significant refinement and centralisation of the old London watches.

The recent detailed research on the watch system of eighteenth and early nineteenth-century London has drawn attention to the improvements made under various local Acts of Parliament (Reynolds 1998; Beattie 2001). By the 1820s several parishes had watch organisations made up of fit, relatively young men, not the old decrepit 'Charlies' of the Whig histories. The problem was that some parishes were wealthier than others, and while the wealthy could afford an efficient watch, their less well-to-do neighbouring parishes might be far less fortunate. Parochial division was a further problem highlighted by Sir Robert Peel, the Home Secretary, to Parliament in April 1829: 'The chief requisites of an efficient police were unity of design and responsibility of agents – both of which were not only not ensured by the present parochial watch-house system, but were actually prevented by it' (*Parliamentary Debates* 1829: xxi, col. 872). As Home Secretary Peel was determined to reform the criminal justice system and he saw improved policing as part and parcel of this. In the aftermath of the Napoleonic Wars there were anxieties about rising crime, about offenders escaping prosecution because victims could not afford the costs of criminal prosecutions or because victims and jurors were reluctant to see thieves exposed to a lottery in courts in which the death penalty was the statutory punishment for most felonies. In the mid-1820s Peel recast the criminal code and extended the financial assistance for poor prosecutors. As Chief Secretary for Ireland between 1812 and 1818 he had experience of developing a police institution. But he was also well aware that while the English might countenance a police force in Ireland, their perception of their own liberty and their hostility to things French made them very wary of any institution that smacked of a military presence or a political surveillance of the population.

In 1828 a parliamentary select committee set up by Peel and chaired by T.G.B. Escourt, Peel's fellow member for Oxford University, presented conclusions favourable to the creation of a centralised police organisation for London. Peel introduced his Metropolitan Police Bill in April the following year and it had a relatively trouble-free passage through Parliament. This was due partly to good management, partly to good fortune and partly also to the probability that, concerns about the French model apart, anxiety about crime had won new converts to the idea of a centralised police organisation. Peel persuaded Parliament to let the bill be scrutinised by the same select committee that had expressed itself sympathetic to reform in 1828. He forestalled the opposition of the powerful City of London by omitting its square-mile jurisdiction from his bill. The potential opposition of the London parishes was fortuitously silenced by their own problems in defending themselves against charges of corruption and exclusivity. Finally, the furore over another bill concerning Catholic emancipation possibly diverted some parliamentary and public opposition. The bill was passed in June (10 Geo. IV c. 44) and the first Metropolitan Police constables took to the London streets in September.

According to the instructions issued for the new police their principal task was 'the prevention of crime'. The assumption was that by the regular patrolling of his beat and the careful checking of doors and windows, especially at night, the patrolling police constable would deter thieves. But the constable could also apprehend any individual about whom he had 'reasonable suspicion' as well as vagrants, prostitutes and 'all idle and disorderly persons'. The latter powers had existed for the old parish watchmen under a variety of statutes and had been consolidated by the Vagrancy Act 1824. The instructions also delineated those tasks of the old parish constables that now fell to the police constables: powers to arrest or to take an individual's name and address for a future summons in such matters as careless driving, gaming, street nuisances, and keeping pubs, coffee and tea shops open after the regulatory hours. Within weeks of their first deployment the new police were also being used in groups to clear the streets of Saturday night's hung-over human detritus, before the respectable walked to church for the Sunday morning service. In addition to the prevention of crime, it seems clear that, from very early on, the new police were seen as a means to establish and to maintain a new threshold of order and respectability on the public highways.

A uniform was perceived as necessary for the new Metropolitan Police so as to demonstrate that the men were not engaged in a 'system of espionage' which, it was believed, was the essential role of the police in France during both the old regime and under Napoleon. France also had an armed, military police institution that patrolled the main roads – the *gendarmerie*. Since the Glorious Revolution of 1688 'freeborn Englishmen' had been concerned about any attempt to police them regularly by means of the army, or to use troops to prevent what they considered to be legitimate protest. Peel, and the two men whom he appointed as commissioners of the Metropolitan Police – the soldier, Colonel Charles Rowan, and the lawyer, Richard Mayne – set out to ensure that their new policemen did not look military. They wore top hats and blue uniform long-tailed coats; both very different from the plumed shakos and scarlet, short-tailed coats of the British infantry. The ordinary police constable carried a wooden baton as his only normal armament. The fact that the men belonged to an hierarchical, drilled and fiercely disciplined organisation was glossed over in the assertions that the New Police were not military. However there were complaints in the ranks about the drilling and ferocious discipline, some of which was reported in the press, and some radicals referred to the police by an anglicised corruption of the word *gendarmes* into 'Jenny Darbies'.

Hostility to the Metropolitan Police in its early years was not confined to its supposed threats to English liberties or to its suspected military nature. London parishes intensely disliked having to fund a police institution over which they had no control. Moreover some parishes found themselves having to pay more for the new police when their streets were now patrolled by fewer police constables than when they had previously had watchmen. Some responded by demanding a degree of control over the police in their area, by lowering the value of house rentals to frustrate the new precepting system or simply by withholding money. The government ignored the demands for local control but, in 1833, introduced legislation by which a quarter of police expenses up to £60,000 were met out of the Consolidated Fund (Palmer 1988: 305–8; Paley 1989). This softened, but did not silence the complaints, and protest about having to fund a police over which they had no control was an issue that was to recur within local government in London throughout the nineteenth and twentieth centuries.

For its first ten years the Metropolitan Police functioned alongside the constables working for the stipendiary magistrates in the old police offices established in 1792. These constables appear to have conducted investigations and to have detected offenders, though their modus operandi and their efficiency await historical investigation. Some offenders were stupid enough to attempt thefts in full view of patrolling Metropolitan Police constables. But even though it was also recognised that the uniformed police constable might only temporarily delay an offence being committed and might not be the best person to take a thief, Rowan and Mayne were not keen to establish a plain-clothed detective force. For one thing they appear to have been reluctant to offer any opportunity for accusations to be levelled that their men were acting as spies; for another, they appear to have been anxious that, whereas the uniformed constable on a regular beat could easily be supervised by his superiors, a plain-clothed constable working on his own initiative was far more difficult to keep track of and observe. In 1842, however, three years after the closure of the old police offices, the Metropolitan Police established its own detective force.

Even before the creation of the Metropolitan Police, new structures were being developed in the provinces, and for much the same reasons: there was concern about crime; there were also concerns for the development and maintenance of a new threshold of order. Lord Grey's government considered plans for a national police organisation at the time of the Great Reform Bill, but their enthusiasm appears to have died as the popular agitation demanding parliamentary reform subsided (Philips and Storch 1994). Thereafter while single-minded Benthamite police reformers, like the individuals who made up the Royal Commission on a Rural Constabulary that met from 1836 to 1839, were keen for a single centralised organisation, central government appears to have accepted that the supervision of police institutions should, with the exception of the Metropolitan Police in London, be the responsibility of local government. Thus the Municipal Corporations Act 1835 (5 & 6 Wm. IV c. 76) required the new elected councils of corporate boroughs to establish watch committees whose task was to provide and supervise a body of police appropriate for their community. The county police legislation of 1839 and 1840 (2 & 3 Vict. c. 93; 3 & 4 Vict. c. 88) enabled counties to establish police forces if they so wished. While the chief constables of the counties were to have more autonomy than their borough counterparts and, unlike their borough counterparts, required the approval of the Home Secretary for their appointment, the new county police came within the remit of the traditional rulers of the counties – the benches of magistrates. Alongside the enabling legislation of 1839 the government, alarmed by local bickering in three urban areas where Chartism appeared a significant force, itself established police forces under chief constables appointed directly by the Home Office. These centralised forces for Birmingham, Bolton and Manchester, however, were handed over to local control after three years.

There were several models available for the new provincial police and, for a variety of reasons, the Metropolitan one was not always favoured. In Gloucestershire the new constabulary was based firmly on the Irish model with the men deployed in fours in small barracks across the county. Several counties, like Gloucestershire, chose their chief constables from the senior ranks in Ireland. Others looked to the Metropolitan Police for their senior officers. Northamptonshire selected a former Bow Street Runner. In some boroughs the former watchmen were put in uniforms and now called policemen; while a few of the smaller boroughs did not even bother to implement the police requirements of the Municipal Corporations Act. Hostility to the police continued in both boroughs and counties throughout the 1840s and early 1850s, and this was not simply the hostility of political radicals. There was considerable concern over the cost of the police and whether they were providing value for money. In 1842 there was a petitioning campaign across much of the country urging the abolition or, at least, the reduction of police forces; the common complaint was that, even though they had to pay for them, many rural districts rarely saw a patrolling constable. In Lancashire, most notably, the campaign led to the quarter sessions voting a reduction in the county force from 502 to 355 men (Emsley 1996: 45–6). Several counties steadfastly refused to take up the provisions of the 1839 and 1840 legislation. They preferred to develop the old police system; the Parish Constables Acts of 1842 and 1850 (5 & 6 Vict. c. 109; 13 & 14 Vict. c. 20) enabled them to do this with professional superintending constables. Often recruited from the new police forces, a superintending constable was placed in a subdivision of a county and charged with co-ordinating and supervising the traditional parish constables.

During the 1840s central government left county quarter sessions and borough watch committees to develop policing as they saw fit. But it became interested in policing matters once again at the beginning of the 1850s. Lord Palmerston as Home Secretary in 1853–4 was in favour of making the provisions of the 1839 legislation mandatory. A House of Commons select committee was established in 1853. It was packed with supporters of the idea of rationalising the county police system and appears to have ensured that the majority of its witnesses would be men critical of the superintending constables system. The committee's report duly recommended that a uniform system of policing be established across the whole country, that at the very least the smaller borough forces be amalgamated with the counties and that a government grant be provided for the county forces. The bill, which was drafted in the wake of the report, went rather further than the report in proposing the amalgamation with larger county forces of the five smallest county forces and of all borough forces in towns with a population of less than 20,000. It promised also to establish a system of government inspection. But it made no provision for any government grant. The bill provoked outrage, particularly in the boroughs. Borough representatives flocked to London to protest, and Palmerston was forced to withdraw his bill. In February 1855 Palmerston became Prime Minister, and the new Home Secretary, Sir George Grey, came up with a new police bill which carefully drew the sting of local objections to its predecessor (Philips and Storch 1999).

The County and Borough Police Act 1856 (19 & 20 Vict. c. 69) required all counties to establish police forces under the direction of the county benches. It also prompted hitherto recalcitrant boroughs to comply with the 1835 legislation and to appoint a watch committee that would establish and supervise a police force – though the number that had previously failed to establish forces has probably been overestimated as a result of the failure of various boroughs to supply details to the Home Office (Wall 1998: 33). The plans to amalgamate smaller forces with their larger neighbours were dropped, but the proposal for a Treasury grant was adopted. Henceforth efficient forces were to receive one quarter of their costs for pay and clothing from central government. Efficiency was to be decided by a system of inspection with a team of inspectors of constabulary making annual reports to Parliament. A similar Act, passed in the following year, brought a similar structure to policing in Scotland. This was far from the scale of centralisation that the Benthamite police reformers such as Edwin Chadwick advocated, but it was a significant step towards central government involvement in provincial policing, and it was further than other European states had gone in their supervision of provincial police organisations. The British might still insist that they had no centralised police, and nothing like the military *gendarmeries* of continental Europe – with reference to the latter, and excluding the situation in Ireland, they were right. But the administrative and organisational structure of the Metropolitan Police was much like that of capital city and state police on continental Europe. At the same time, municipal policing on the continent was much like that in England, but even in centralised France and Imperial Germany it lacked the uniform supervision of a national inspectorate (Emsley 1999).

Early nineteenth-century police reformers had different perspectives. The aspirations of men like Chadwick, one of the three commissioners of the 1836 Royal Commission on a Rural Constabulary, were never met. In the circumstances of the times they could not be met. No government could countenance the cost of a centralised police and there was a wariness and a reluctance to impose any sort of centralised system – a system that the English believed, quite wrongly, to exist across continental Europe. Pragmatic and influential politicians like Peel, however, were keen for reform, and recognised the possibilities of what could be done. It is significant too that the Whig government of Melbourne profited from Peel's support in 1839, and the reforms of the early 1850s built on a similar coalition of Peelite conservatives and Whig/Liberals.

Consolidation

In the early 1850s London's Metropolitan Police basked in the success of the Great Exhibition. Thousands of visitors had poured into London, but order had been maintained while thefts from the visitors appeared to have been kept to a minimum. In addition, England with its boasted civilian police had escaped the revolutionary upheavals of 1848. Disorders associated with Chartism paled into insignificance besides the pitched battles on the streets of Berlin, Paris, Rome, Vienna and other cities. The relative social peace in England over the following few decades enabled the new police structures to consolidate without major, massive deployments for the maintenance of public order. There were occasional instances of loud criticism when the police appeared to fail in preventing offences or in apprehending criminal offenders, notably the garrotting panic of 1862 and the murders accredited to Jack the Ripper in 1888. There was similar criticism when the police failed to control disorder, or when their action in such control seemed excessive, such as the turbulent Reform Bill agitation around Hyde Park in 1866 and the events of Bloody Sunday in Trafalgar Square in 1887. But by and large the press were complimentary. The 'Bobby' became acknowledged as a minor, but key support to the constitutional structure; and, arguably, his comic appearance in Gilbert and Sullivan's *The Pirates of Penzance* was indicative of this.

The image of the Bobby was largely based on the London experience. Many of the traditional histories have implied that London was the model that other forces sought to copy, though the administrative and command structures remained very different. In the boroughs the watch committees had the power of appointment and dismissal and they were the bodies responsible for discipline. In some instances the committees appear to have delegated many of their duties to their head constables. But the committees often met one or more times a week and, as representatives of elected town councils, they were conscious of the demands of their constituents and the level of the local rates. A dominance of Tory brewers and publicans, or a majority of temperance reformers on the committee, provided the most obvious examples of instances in which local politicians could influence police policy and behaviour. In some boroughs the police were regarded above all as servants of the municipality; they could be expected to collect market tolls or to act as mace bearers on civic occasions. In the counties the police committees of magistrates enjoyed much less authority over their chief constables, and this looser authority continued following the local government reforms of 1888 (51 & 52 Vict. c. 41). This legislation introduced an elective element into the supervision of the county constabularies by the replacement of committees of magistrates by standing joint committees (SJCs) composed of an equal number of magistrates and elected county councillors. It was these committees which now appointed the chief constables of counties, subject to Home Office approval, and which precepted the county councils for police costs. But the SJCs never met with the frequency of borough watch committees, nor did they have the watch committees' powers over their police and, as a result, the greater autonomy of the county chief constables remained. Arguments that the Metropolitan Police should be brought under the supervision of the new London County Council (LCC), created at the same time as the local government reforms, were vigorously opposed by the government on the grounds that the force had 'imperial' tasks – protecting the monarch, Parliament and public buildings. Fears were also expressed about the potential threat to central government from the police should the LCC ever have a majority of socialists and radicals (Emsley 1996: 86).

Many of the provincial forces subscribed to the idea of 'the prevention of crime' as their first duty. Nevertheless officers found themselves taking on a variety of duties that could not always be immediately related to this aim. Burgeoning cities were developing traffic problems that were handed over to the police to resolve; and the police were commonly charged with the licensing and regulation of cabs. Following the Education Act 1870 some men were appointed as school attendance officers with the duty of ensuring that working-class children attended school, and that parents who kept their children away were served with a summons. Some suggestions of new roles for the police were discouraged by central government, notably the idea, popular with a few ex-military chief constables, that the police might be trained as military auxiliaries and equipped with rifles and cannon in case of invasion. The assumptions about the inter-relationship between vagrancy and crime, however, encouraged the use of police as Poor Law relieving officers, but while some of the new inspectors of constabulary encouraged this, others saw the task as taking up too much time and deflecting police officers from their proper duties.

The inspectors of constabulary introduced a degree of uniformity across the provincial police institutions by defining what activities were proper for the police and what constituted police efficiency. Initially a few boroughs were resistant to their recommendations and even refused to accept the Treasury grant. But to local politicians dependent on a local electorate, the value of the grant eventually proved stronger than civic pride, especially when, in 1874, it was increased from one quarter to one half the cost of pay and clothing. Other pressures, internal and external to the police institutions, also made for increased centralisation and greater uniformity.

Police officers were drawn from the unskilled or semi-skilled working class. The pay was not high, though it was regular and not subject to the ups and downs of the trade cycle. There were also official perks such as the uniform, medical assistance that, in some forces, was extended to a man's family, and, very rare for a Victorian working-class occupation, a pension or some sort of gratuity at the end of a man's service. The pension was properly formalised and guaranteed by the Police Act 1890 (53 & 54 Vict. c. 45) to any man who retired after having served for 25 years or who was forced to retire on medical grounds after 15. But there were also drawbacks to the job. The discipline was harsh. Patrolling an urban beat at the regulation pace of two and a half miles an hour, while it might be enlivened by the occasional incident, was generally gruelling and monotonous. Trudging country lanes was no better. Much of the patrolling was done at night and it had to be done whatever the weather. Beat sergeants checked the men regularly in urban areas, and country policemen had to make conference points at set times to meet fellow constables or sergeants. The police officer was meant to demonstrate his respectability the whole time, and this extended to his family. When a man wanted to marry he needed permission, and his future wife commonly had her respectability investigated. Moreover, unlike other wives in the unskilled and semi-skilled working class, many, possibly most, of the police forces forbade their men's wives from taking employment. This could have a severe impact on the overall family budget and create difficulties in maintaining the required respectability. At times economic pressures, harsh discipline and general dissatisfaction provoked industrial action in individual forces. However the development of a trade press for the police helped to foster a national awareness among officers. *The Police Service Advertiser*, first published in 1864, declared itself to be 'A Journal for the Police and Constabulary Forces of Great Britain and the Colonies'. The paper's editorials and letter columns discussed wage rates and conditions of service. It also provided advice on legal questions and on aspects of the policeman's job. The *Advertiser* was relatively short lived. Its more well-known successor, *Police Review and Parade Gossip*, began publication in 1893. By the outbreak of the First World War the *Police Review* had conducted several vigorous and high-profile campaigns on behalf of officers who considered themselves to have been poorly or wrongfully treated by their superiors. And while it had eventually come out in opposition to the idea, the *Review* had also been deeply involved in debates about the justification for a police trades union.

While internal processes linked with a trade press brought police officers to an awareness of themselves as a national body, the Home Office continued to urge centralisation, rationalisation and greater uniformity. The Municipal Corporations (New Charters) Act 1877 (40 & 41 Vict. C. 69) prohibited the formation of police forces in any new boroughs with a population of fewer than 20,000 – the same figure as that suggested in Palmerston's aborted bill nearly a quarter of a century before. Seven years later a bill was introduced that would have removed the existing Treasury grant from any borough with a population of fewer than 20,000, effectively forcing it to amalgamate with a neighbour. The bill failed, but the local government reform legislation of 1888 effectively abolished the forces of boroughs with populations under 10,000. The mandatory pension enforced by the 1890 Act removed one of the key instruments by which watch committees could ultimately force compliance on a head constable. The bright young men brought into the Home Office as a result of the introduction of open competition for places forced the pace in these changes. Notable here was Edward Troup who joined the Home Office in 1880 and held the post of Permanent Under-Secretary of State from 1908 to 1922. In an essay published some years after his retirement Troup made it clear that, in his opinion, local autonomy in policing matters was too extensive, particularly when it involved 'ignorant or meddling watch committees in the smaller boroughs' (Troup 1928: 15).

The Police Act 1890 also recommended that forces enter into agreement with each other to provide mutual aid in cases of popular disturbance. Assistance had been provided on an ad hoc basis at least since the middle of the nineteenth century with men from one force supporting another confronted with an election riot or with the potential of industrial disorder. Few formal agreements for such aid appear to have been made in the immediate aftermath of the 1890 Act, but the industrial unrest in the decade immediately before the First World War saw such aid provided on numerous occasions. This unrest also highlighted the general difficulties inherent in policing such disputes as the boundaries of peaceful picketing were becoming unclear, and some particular issues relating to the command and control of local police in disputes were attaining national importance. In south Wales in 1910, within a few months of each other, borough police were required to act in contradictory ways. A strike in the Newport docks witnessed a police chief and his watch committee refusing to protect 'blackleg' labour on the grounds that their first duty was to preserve the public peace. Shortly afterwards a lockout in Swansea was the occasion of police baton charges, on the orders of the head constable and in defence of the interests of the employers. The baton charges were ordered without consulting the watch committee who would appear to have preferred the sort of approach used in Newport. The south Wales coal strike of 1910–11 and the nationwide rail strike of the summer of 1911 witnessed an interventionist Home Secretary, Winston Churchill, dispatching police and troops around the country to maintain the peace and ensure essential services. There is some debate about the overall impact of these actions, yet many of them point towards a growing separation of chief police officers from their local government committees and a growing tendency of central government, in the form of the Home Office, to link directly with the police rather than negotiating with police committees (Morgan 1987; Weinberger 1991).

The English boasted that they had no political police, but in comparison with countries such as France where royalists, Bonapartists, Jacobins and socialists all had alternative constitutions, alternative governments and often some experience of government, they had very little need of political police. There had been some relatively low-profile surveillance of Chartists as well as of refugees from the continental revolutions. It was the fear of Irish terrorism, particularly with the Fenian bombing campaigns of 1867–8 and 1881–5, that prompted the creation of the Metropolitan Police Special Branch. By the turn of the century the Special Branch was investigating foreign anarchists, socialists, suffragettes and any others that its political masters, and sometimes its own officers, deemed a threat to the British way of life (Porter 1987). Special Branch remained a section of the Metropolitan Police but political surveillance spread into the provinces especially with the spy scares in the period shortly before the First World War. It was at this point that Vernon Kell, the future head of MI5 then preparing a secret register of aliens, got into contact with provincial police chiefs. Nevertheless, as late as April 1914, the Home

Secretary could still respond sharply to an MP's question with the statement that, while there was indeed a Special Branch responsible to the Commissioner of the Metropolitan Police, 'there is no "political" branch of the Criminal Investigation Department' (*Parliamentary Debates* 1914: lxi, col. 1874).

New challenges and standardisation

In the first half of the twentieth century two world wars and concerns about industrial unrest served further to separate local police from local authority. War and shifting perceptions of gender combined to foster the development of women police, while technological change, in the shape of the motor car telephone and wireless communications, began to impact both on police relations with the public and on methods of policing.

The First World War put enormous pressures on the police. First, police numbers were depleted initially with the recall of reservists to the colours and then with the departure of volunteers for the military. Recruitment was halted. At the same time a reduced and ageing workforce found itself burdened by additional wartime tasks such as the protection of vulnerable points, the pursuit of deserters, the investigation of 'misconduct' on the part of women who were in receipt of a separation allowance because their husbands were in the forces and the enforcement of a variety of new requirements under the Defence of the Realm Regulations. Special constables were recruited to assist and the right of retirement of regular police officers was restricted. But the wartime pressures still meant that beats and hours were lengthened and that the guaranteed weekly rest day, established by Act of Parliament as recently as 1910, was circumscribed in various ways by different forces. Wartime inflation had a deleterious effect on police pay. There was concern in both central and local government that a significant pay increase could create problems with the return of peace. But the decisions to solve the problem by awarding non-pensionable war bonuses from time to time did little to alleviate either the financial problems of police families or the growing disaffection that provided ready recruits for the emerging National Union of Police and Prison Officers (NUPPO). In August 1918 the dismissal from the Metropolitan Police of an ex-guardsman and Boer War veteran for his union activities precipitated a strike among the Metropolitan and City of London Police forces. The authorities caved in making a scapegoat of the Metropolitan Police Commissioner, Sir Edward Henry, reinstating the dismissed constable and promising a pay rise, a war bonus and a widow's pension scheme.

From an early stage of the war there was disquiet that large military encampments and the traditional garrison towns and seaports now bloated with new recruits would act as magnets for prostitutes and encourage weak young women to 'fall'. There was also anxiety about the large numbers of young women, now outside the usual supervision of their families, having been recruited to staff the munitions factories. These concerns led, for the first time, to the use of women police. Male officers alone had been responsible for the supervision of prostitutes before the war and while, even with the Contagious Diseases Acts, in force between 1864 and 1886, the British had never established the kind of morals police that had been present on continental Europe, this supervision had commonly led to accusations of corruption, high-handedness and insensitivity. Since the late nineteenth century the searching and supervision of women in police stations had usually been entrusted to a police matron, often the wife of the station sergeant. The Voluntary Women Patrols (VWP), which began in the early months of the war, were organised by the National Union of Women Workers, a voluntary body dedicated to social work. These patrols were rather more popular with the authorities than the Women Police Volunteers (known as the Women Police Service (WPS) from February 1915) established by former militant suffragettes and morality campaigners, who wore uniforms and sought the status and powers of male police officers. In 1916 the Metropolitan Police Commissioner contracted 40 VWP personnel as full-time members of his force. In October 1918 the new Commissioner, General Sir Nevil Macready, announced the formation of the Metropolitan Police Women Patrols, again drawing principally on the VWP, much to the annoyance of the more aggressive leadership of the WPS (Carrier 1988; Douglas 1999).

The exigencies of war provided new occasions for watch committees and SJCs to be bypassed as chief constables linked with central government agencies. Concerns about German spies, then about Bolshevik subversion strengthened the ties between the secret security agencies and the police; even local members of the Independent Labour Party or of local trades councils found their way on to lists of suspects. The country was divided into special administrative areas each under the command of an Authorised Competent Military Authority (ACMA). The several chief constables in such an area were subordinate to the ACMA with reference to his powers under the emergency wartime regulations. Early in 1918 the Home Office divided the country into eight districts and established the District Conference system whereby all the chief constables in the district met regularly; the eight districts, in turn, appointed members to a central committee to confer with the Home Office and the military. Indirectly, the police strike of August 1918 brought about further standardisation of the police service across the country.

The success of the strike by police officers in London in 1918, together with the ambiguous statement of the Prime Minister, Lloyd George, that he could not recognise the police union during wartime, encouraged recruitment to the NUPPO, especially among provincial officers. In the new year a committee, chaired by Lord Desborough, appointed in the aftermath of the strike to inquire into the police service in England, Wales and Scotland, began taking evidence on police pay and conditions, with much of the evidence being presented by NUPPO members. The Desborough Committee's report, presented in the early summer, rejected nationalisation as alien to the British constitution in which, it claimed, law and order was the task of local authority. It also feared that nationalisation would prejudice the unique relationship between the public and the police. However, with reference to conditions of service and pay, the committee recommended standardisation across the country. It also stressed that police pay needed a boost beyond that given to the London police in the wake of the strike and rapidly copied elsewhere; police pay, the committee explained, compared unfavourably with other occupations, even unskilled ones. Finally, the committee suggested that there should be some formal body with 'the right to confer' over such matters as pay and conditions of service (Desborough 1919 and 1920).

The government was keen to accept the recommendations rapidly. It was also keen to see off the NUPPO and it set out to use the improved pay and conditions resulting from Desborough, together with the promise of 'the right to confer', as means to this end. The union, fearing for its survival, called a second strike in August 1919. Officers struck in London, Liverpool and Birmingham; in the latter two cities the men had long been dissatisfied with their superiors and their conditions. But the strike was a disaster. All those who took industrial action were dismissed and were never reinstated. The union was destroyed and union membership prohibited (Klein 2001). A Police Federation was established with the right to confer, but not the right to strike. Finally, while some local authorities expressed concern about the effect of the police pay award on local budgets and the sense of paying men of the same rank the same rate in widely differing economic and social conditions, uniformity in pay and conditions was established across the country.

Industrial unrest in the years following the war, together with fears of what such unrest might herald, ensured that the Home Office maintained its close links with, and direct lines to, chief constables. At the same time statements from the Home Office and various legal authorities were increasingly stressing the police officer was primarily a servant of the Crown rather than a servant of local government. Justice McCardie's celebrated, but legally questionable ruling in the case of *Fisher* v. *Oldham Corporation* in 1930, confirmed this official line. The ruling subsequently became a significant plank underpinning the limitations placed on police committees with reference to what are considered police operational decisions (Lustgarten 1986: 56–61; Emsley 1996: 163–4; see Chapter 24).

There was a succession of scandals during the 1920s largely concerning arbitrary and high-handed behaviour by police officers. The most celebrated of these occurred in 1928 with the arrest of a leading economics expert, Sir Leo Chiozza Money, for indecency with a young woman in Hyde Park. The scandals resulted in the creation of a Royal Commission on Police Powers and Procedures which met in the winter of 1928–9. The commission's deliberations coincided with revelations of corruption and the taking of bribes by a police sergeant involved with the investigation of vice in central London. The trial of Sergeant Goddard resulted in a conviction and in subsequent years the scale of corruption was revealed to have been far more extensive than the prosecution of one man might suggest. Nevertheless the royal commission, while acknowledging that even the police force contained a few 'rotten apples', gave the institution a clean bill of health (Emsley 2001).

There is a consensus that the Desborough award combined with the economic depression of the interwar years to bring recruits to the police of a slightly higher social background that had previously been the case. Even so, the rigid discipline remained, alterations to police practice and procedures could be very slow and the determination to maintain local independence was allowed to work against efficiency. Some forces still did not have detective departments and the Departmental Committee on Detective Work and

Procedures that reported in 1938 concluded that those that did exist were, in general, lagging seriously behind many of their counterparts on continental Europe and in North America. Some forces, initially as a result of the determination of a particular chief constable, sought to employ new technology and various scientific aids for policing. Yet tight control on the purse strings by watch committees and SJCs could act as a check to such developments, and if a progressive municipality pressed ahead with wireless communications the overall value could be limited if surrounding counties refused to follow suit. The development of the family car began to bring police officers into confrontation with members of the middle class for the first time, but investment in motor vehicles for the police and in training to deal specifically with motoring offences was slow. Rationalisation and standardisation in these areas tended to be driven from the centre usually by the Home Office. Thus it was, in the aftermath of the Road Traffic Act 1930, that the Home Office made it clear that it expected all but the smallest forces to establish motor patrols. Seven years later the Home Secretary announced an experimental motor patrol scheme for London, Essex and Lancashire, popularly known as 'the courtesy cops'. And throughout the 1930s the Home Office fostered the development of what became known as 'common police services', namely wireless depots and forensic science laboratories that might be used by all forces.

The threat of a new war also ensured the strengthening of links between central government and the police. Discussions about the possibility of war and the likely role and responsibilities of the police had begun at the end of the 1920s and a committee had been established to prepare war instructions for the police in 1933. In consequence, the police were much better prepared for the exigencies of war in 1939 than they had been 25 years earlier. As with the previous conflict, it was the pressures of war that forced the pace of change, and particularly with reference to the greater acceptance of women officers and the abolition of the smaller forces.

The preparations for war included the organisation of large numbers of auxiliary police who would be able to replace men called up for military service and carry out the additional tasks necessitated by the war emergency. The experiment of using women police during the First World War had not led to any great advance during peacetime. Indeed, the Parliamentary Committee on the Employment of Women on Police Duties that met in 1920 reported that 142 of the 241 chief constables in England, Wales and Scotland were opposed to women police. In 1939 there were only 226 women police officers in England and Wales, and all but a hundred of these were serving in London. Their duties were largely restricted to dealing with women and children. The range of duties of attested women officers did not change during the Second World War, but the number of women officers was more than doubled. In addition, more than 3,000 auxiliary women police, of whom about a tenth were fully and formally sworn in with all the duties of a constable, were recruited principally to carry out clerical tasks, to work in canteens and to drive police vehicles. Some forces had to be pressurised by the Home Office into accepting women even for the latter responsibilities. Nevertheless, by the end of the war the number of chief constables prepared to accept women police had increased significantly, even if women officers continued to be restricted to the gendered roles of the care of juvenile and women offenders and family liaison. The rank and file also began to accept them, if grudgingly, with the Police Federation agreeing to the admission of women members in 1948.

As part and parcel of its suggestions for rationalisation the Desborough Committee had recommended the amalgamation with the surrounding county force of all separate police in boroughs with a population of 50,000 or less. No action was taken on this proposal and frequent suggestions throughout the interwar years that the smaller forces be amalgamated with their larger neighbours were similarly left to lie on the table. It would seem that the fears of upsetting both local pride and the traditions of laissez-faire liberalism continued to act as a check on central government in this respect. The demands of war, however, finally encouraged ministers and their civil servants to move. Centralised direction was assumed, following a procedure already developed during the General Strike of 1926, with the country being divided into 11 districts each under a civil commissioner who was responsible for supervising and co-ordinating civil defence and the activities of central and local government agencies. The assumption was also that fewer police forces would facilitate command and control, especially in the event of invasion. As a consequence a wave of amalgamations were enforced during 1942, particularly in the south and south east. Assurances were given that the amalgamations were for the duration of the war; however peace and the election of a Labour government brought the Police Act 1946 (9 & 10 Geo. VI c. 46) which confirmed the wartime changes and made provision for others. By the end of 1947 the 180 prewar forces in England and Wales had been reduced to 131 and, while representatives of local government were unhappy with events, the barriers to future amalgamations had been significantly breached.

The problems of an ageing, depleted workforce dissatisfied over pay were not as acute in 1945 as they had been at the close of the First World War. But there were difficulties and, over the first years of peace, many of these were aggravated. Men returning to the police after war service, or newly recruited after war service, often resented individuals who appeared to owe their senior rank simply to the fact that they had not been in the military during the war years and had consequently been promoted because there was no one else. They also resented the continuance of oppressive discipline and pettifogging regulations which, in some forces, still required that a man's fiancée be interviewed and investigated for her respectability and that still forbade a man's wife from taking up paid employment. The proportionately higher pay rates of the interwar years were rapidly eaten away by high industrial wages and inflation. The government introduced new and improved pay scales in April 1945, and awarded a further increase in pay the following year. But police personnel leached away and in May 1948 a committee was established under Lord Oaksey to investigate police conditions of service. The Police Federation hoped that the Oaksey Committee would come up with a report as favourable to the police as that of the Desborough Committee. In some ways it did, praising police officers for their qualities and for dealing with ever greater and more complex tasks. But on the crucial issue of pay, while the federation was hoping for increases of between one third and one half, Oaksey took note of the government's recent statement on incomes, costs and prices, and recommended only 15 per cent (Oaksey 1949).

The Oaksey Committee drew attention to the monotony of police work. For most officers the job still involved patrolling a beat on foot and a high proportion of patrolling was still done at night. According to evidence presented to the committee, outside London 80 per cent of constables spent the whole of their first ten years of service on beat duty. However, the committee was also given details of an experimental system established in Aberdeen to cope with the personnel shortage. Here beats had been combined and put under the supervision of a small squad, commanded by a sergeant, and linked with police cars equipped with two-way radios. A working party of the committee studied the scheme in depth. It was sceptical about its overall value and suspected that the improved morale of the officers involved might be only temporary. However it also found no evidence to substantiate the fears of traditionalists that such a significant reorganisation of the beat system and the greater use of cars by police would be bad for police–public relations.

While, in the decade following the war, police morale remained low and personnel retention continued to be a problem, police relations with the public appeared to be good. In 1950 the feature film *The Blue Lamp* was premiered. The film was in the tradition of the wartime eulogies of the armed services – *In Which We Serve* (the navy, 1942), *The Way Ahead* (the army, 1944), *The Way to the Stars* (the airforce, 1945). It fitted also with a new series of Ealing films putting an emphasis on community in English life. In Police Constable George Dixon, shot dead in the film but resurrected a few years later for a long-running television series (*Dixon of Dock Green*), *The Blue Lamp* introduced a character that was to become a benchmark for the police in future years (see Chapter 11). Honest, upright, cool and calm, and uvuncular with the public, with young tearaways and with 'villains' alike, Dixon was an ideal type. He fitted what *The Times*, in its review of the film, called 'an indulgent tradition' of the English police officer. Probably some men like Dixon had existed, and some had sought and continued to seek to follow such a pattern of behaviour. But even by 1950 Dixon was fast becoming an anachronism as forces increasingly looked to technological solutions, such as the Aberdeen system, to resolve their personnel problems as forces recognised that more and more of the population were leaving the pavements for the convenience of the family car. Moreover, with more than 100 separate forces still existing in England and Wales, there were still Home Office administrators, and others, who considered that more amalgamations and further centralisation of common police services would benefit both police personnel and the country at large.

Selected further reading

Critchley's *A History of Police in England and Wales* (1978) is a comprehensive and, by far, the most perceptive of the more traditional Whig histories. Emsley's *The English Police: A Political and Social History* (1996) is a general history that summarises recent research and current debates and that draws upon several largely unexplored provincial police archives, as well as the better known parliamentary and Metropolitan Police records. Philips's and Storch's *Policing Provincial England 1829–1856: The Politics of Reform* (1999) is an important, exhaustively researched reassessment of the emergence of police institutions in the provinces of Victorian England. Shpayer-Makov's *The Making of a Policeman: A Social History of a Labour Force in Metropolitan London, 1829–1914* (2002) is a path-breaking attempt to get at who ordinary Victorian policemen were, the nature of their work experience, and the management aims and techniques of their superiors. Finally, Weinberger's *The Best Police in the World: An Oral History of English Policing* (1995) is a study of the different tasks of policing and the experience of the job from *c.* 1930 to 1960 that draws significantly on interviews with a cross-section of officers of different ranks and from different forces.

References

Ascoli, D. (1979) *The Queen's Peace: The Origins and Development of the Metropolitan Police 1829–1979*. London: Hamish Hamilton.

Beattie, J.M. (2001) *Policing and Punishment in London 1660–1750: Urban Crime and the Limits of Terror*. Oxford: Oxford University Press.

Carrier, J. (1988) *The Campaign for the Employment of Women as Police Officers*. Aldershot: Avebury.

Critchley, T.A. (1978) *A History of Police in England and Wales*. London: Constable.

Desborough (1919 and 1920) *Reports of the Committee on the Police Service of England, Wales and Scotland*, Part 1 (Cmd 253, London: HMSO), Part 2 (Cmd 574, London: HMSO), Evidence (Cmd 874, London: HMSO).

Douglas, R.M. (1999) *Feminist Freikorps: The British Voluntary Women Police, 1914–1940*. Westport, CT, and London: Praeger.

Emsley, C. (1996) *The English Police: A Political and Social History* (2nd edn). London: Longman.

Emsley, C. (1999) 'A typology of nineteenth-century police', *Crime, Histoire et Sociétés/ Crime, History and Societies*, 3: 29–44.

Emsley, C. (2001) 'Sergeant Goddard: the story of a rotten apple, or a diseased orchard?' Paper presented to the IAHCCJ colloquium, European University Institute, Florence.

Klein, J. (2001) 'Blue-collar job, blue collar career: policemen's perplexing struggle for a voice in Birmingham, Liverpool, and Manchester, 1900–1919', *Crime, Histoire et Sociétés/Crime, History and Societies*, 6: 5–29.

Lustgarten, L. (1986) *The Governance of Police*. London: Sweet & Maxwell.

Morgan, J. (1987) *Conflict and Order: Labour Disputes in England and Wales 1900–1939*. Oxford: Clarendon Press.

Oaksey (1949) *Reports of the Committee on Police Conditions of Service*, Part 1 (Cmd 7674, London, HMSO), Part 2 (Cmd 7831, London: HMSO).

Paley, R. (1989) ' "An imperfect, inadequate and wretched system"? Policing in London before Peel', *Criminal Justice History*, 10: 95–130.

Palmer, S.H. (1988) *Police and Protest in England and Ireland 1780–1850*. Cambridge: Cambridge University Press.

Philips, D. and Storch, R.J. (1994) 'Whigs and coppers: the Grey Ministry's National Police Scheme, 1832', *Historical Research*, 67: 75–90.

Philips, D. and Storch, R.J. (1999) *Policing Provincial England 1829–1856: The Politics of Reform*. London: Leicester University Press.

Porter, B. (1987) *The Origins of the Vigilant State: The London Metropolitan Police Special Branch before the First World War*. London: Weidenfeld & Nicholson.

Reith, C. (1938) *The Police Idea*. Oxford: Oxford University Press.

Reith, C. (1943) *British Police and the Democratic Ideal*. Oxford: Oxford University Press.

Reith, C. (1952) *The Blind Eye of History*. London: Faber.

Reynolds, E.A. (1998) *Before the Bobbies: The Night Watch and Police Reform in Metropolitan London 1720–1830*. London: Macmillan.

Shpayer-Makov, H. (2002) *The Making of a Policeman: A Social History of a Labour Force in Metropolitan London 1829–1914*. Aldershot: Ashgate.

Storch, R.D. (1975) ' "The plague of blue locusts": police reform and popular resistance in northern England 1840–1857', *International Review of Social History*, 20: 61–90.

Storch, R.D. (1976) 'The policeman as domestic missionary: urban discipline and popular culture in northern England 1850–1880', *Journal of Social History*, 9: 481–509.

Troup, Sir E. (1928) 'Police administration, local and national', *Police Journal*, 1: 5–18.

Wall, D.S. (1998) *The Chief Constables of England and Wales: The Socio-legal History of a Criminal Justice Elite*. Aldershot: Ashgate.

Weinberger, B. (1991) *Keeping the Peace? Policing Strikes in Britain 1906–1929*. Oxford: Berg.

Weinberger, B. (1995) *The Best Police in the World: An Oral History of English Policing*. Aldershot: Scholar Press.

Chapter 5

Policing since 1945

Tim Newburn

Introduction

According to Bottoms and Stevenson (1992: 10), 'all things considered . . . the omens for the criminal justice policy-maker in 1945 looked good'. However, as they document, and is noted by many commentators, 'the years which followed the war were jaundiced by disappointed hopes' (Critchley 1967: 237). The reasons for this are complex, but certainly include the continual growth of recorded crime and the practical and political consequences it set in train, the emergence of research questioning the efficacy of elements of the criminal justice system and a series of 'scandals', or at least incidents, that served to illustrate some of the problems with policing and to challenge previously held public views about its character and purpose.

It is worth remembering that professional policing in Britain at this time was little more than a century old. The nineteenth and early twentieth centuries had seen the gradual establishment and refinement of the system of policing and, by the 1930s, what had originally been a somewhat amateurish and chaotic system had been replaced by one in which officers earned wages almost one third above the national average (Royal Commission on the Police 1960). Inflation gradually but systematically eroded this pay differential, and increasing postwar prosperity and full employment served to ensure that other advantages once enjoyed by police officers were progressively shared by other occupations, though the disadvantages of police work, of course, were not (Martin and Wilson 1969).

In the period since the Second World War, British policing has, in many respects, undergone remarkable change (though that is not to say that there are not also some very significant continuities). In organising this chapter, four broad themes in policing since 1945 are considered: the role and the image of the police; the relationship between the police and local communities; particularly minority communities; the relationship between government and the police; and the relationship between the police and other policing agencies. The last six decades have seen three royal commissions consider aspects of policing – though only one directly on the police – and numerous other inquiries that have sought to explore and, in some respect, reform policing.

Legislation affecting policing has been so extensive as to be almost impossible to summarise. At the heart of much of the deliberation in this period has been the fundamental issue of the role of the police.

The role and image of the police

Policing in the postwar years was still largely organised on a beat system, the basis of which had been established during the nineteenth century. A number of beat systems existed but, crudely speaking, there were two major types. In rural areas, by and large, constables were responsible for the entire (geographic and temporal) policing of a particular area. In urban areas, where full 24-hour cover was often required, officers worked in shifts, but still walked either a fixed or a variable beat (with support from other officers where necessary). In the late 1940s the idea of motorised patrols was rejected for a number of reasons including that it would diminish 'that contact with the public which is so useful to the police and to the public itself' (cited in Bottoms and Stevenson 1992: 29). The drawbacks of moving to motorised patrol were also noted by the Royal Commission in its interim report and it is undoubtedly the case that attachment to beat policing remained strong, including within the police service, well into the 1960s.

Influenced by recent research, in 1967 the Home Office issued a circular that encouraged police forces to adopt a new system of policing which reduced the number of officers on foot patrol and put them into cars. This system, called 'unit beat policing' (UBP), was felt to have the advantage of allowing much wider geographical areas to be covered on a 24-hour basis and, together with the personal radios that were to be issued, of enabling officers to respond much more quickly to calls from the public. The hope that it would both improve policing and police–community relations is now widely presented as being the polar opposite of what happened in practice partly, it is suggested, because it was undermined by a police culture which played down the 'service' element of the system and exploited the opportunities it provided for 'action' (Holdaway 1983). Reiner (1992b: 76) suggests that with the transformation of patrol into a 'fire brigade' service, the emphasis was placed on 'technology, specialisation and managerial professionalism as the keys to winning the fight against crime'. The main charge laid at the door of UBP is that, albeit unintentionally, it was partly responsible for a sea change in the style and image of British policing, a new style that not everyone was entirely comfortable with. As Chibnall (1977) described it: 'The "British bobby" was recast as the tough, dashing, formidable (but still brave and honest) "Crime-Buster"' (cited in Reiner 1992b: 76). However, just around the corner were a series of well publicised cases that would challenge the reputation for honesty.

In the space of less than ten years at least four separate corruption scandals involving Metropolitan Police officers were uncovered. It all began with journalists from *The Times* tape recording conversations between detectives and criminals in which the covering up of serious crimes was being discussed. Equally as shocking as these revelations was the subsequent apparent inability of those tasked with investigating these abuses to secure co-operation within the force and to discipline those officers involved. This pattern continued with other allegations against officers from the Drug Squad and the Obscene Publications Squad (Cox *et al.* 1977). There were even allegations towards the end of the decade that detectives had been involved in major armed robberies. If the general public had ever accepted the image of PC George Dixon at something approximating face value (see Chapter 11), they were unlikely to do so after this (Sparks 1993).

Corruption of a different sort, sometimes rather misleadingly referred to as 'noble cause corruption', formed part of the impetus behind the establishment of a further Royal Commission in 1981. In these cases the issue was the behaviour of the police during the detention and interrogation of suspects – in particular of people suspected of being involved in Irish Republican terrorism. The police had been under enormous pressure to get results. Throughout the 1970s there was concern about the convictions secured in the aftermath of the bombings in Birmingham, Guildford and elsewhere, with allegations of intimidation, violence and the fabrication of evidence being widely made. The release of the Guildford Four, the Birmingham Six, the Maguires, the acquittal on appeal of the Tottenham Three, and widespread concern about the activities of the West Midlands Serious Crimes Squad were part of the reason that public confidence in the police fell dramatically – though there was evidence of changing public attitudes more generally towards public services (Glennerster 2000).

The Home Secretary responded by appointing a Royal Commission on Criminal Procedure (RCCP). Arguably the commission's greatest impact was in forming the basis for much of what later became the Police and Criminal Evidence Act 1984 (PACE). The RCCP focused on the rights of suspects, an issue that had been debated vociferously for some time, but which had been brought to a head by the 'Confait case' in which, it was eventually found, three boys had been convicted of murder on the basis of false confessions. The Judge's Rules, which at that time formed the basis for suspect's rights, were identified by many commentators, and by the Royal Commission, as being inadequate. PACE not only extended police powers in a number of important ways but also introduced far-reaching procedural safeguards (some of which were revised in 1991) to guard against abuses of these powers. There can be little doubt that the Act has had an impact on the behaviour of police officers, and on the culture of policing, and the worst fears of its critics should certainly have been allayed (though see Chapter 10).

The early 1980s also saw both significant urban disorders and a bitter miners' strike. The very visible public order policing these involved also affected the image of British policing. Though using a degree of hyperbole in describing the policing of the miners' strike, Jefferson (1990: 1–2) suggests that the new image of public order policing was:

> not one of a line of bobbies defensively 'pushing and shoving', but of 'snatch squads': menacing teams of officers, unrecognizable in visored, 'NATO-style' crash helmets and fireproof overalls, advancing behind transparent shields being banged by drawn truncheons, making 'search' sorties into crowds of fleeing demonstrators for the purpose of arrest, or a spot of retributive 'destruction'.

Similarly, the 'television pictures of a police officer apparently hitting a prostrate picket repeatedly with his truncheon at the Orgreave coke works during the miners' strike did immense damage to the police reputation for restraint' (Waddington 1991).

Against this background, public consensus about, and satisfaction with, the style and nature of policing appeared precipitately to decline. The response from within the police was to endeavour to institute a programme which would begin to alter the image and, wherever possible, the reality of policing. The Metropolitan Police instituted a programme of reform – the Plus Programme – and the Association of Chief Police Officers (ACPO) built on this with the release of its *Strategic Policy Document* (ACPO 1990), within which was its 'Statement of Common Purpose and Values'. At the heart of much of this endeavour was the intention to present policing as a *service* rather than as a *force* (Stephens and Becker 1994); the reform programme being both 'a reaction to ... declining public satisfaction and also as a consumerist expression of managerialist policy' (Mawby 2002: 45). Both the Strategic Policy Document and the Operational Policing Review which preceded it identified considerable public dissatisfaction with much of the current style of policing. It was around this time that there emerged ideas associated with 'community policing' and, as one of the more radical chief constables of the period put it, 'police should be much more than law enforcers; to use an older term they should be "peace officers" ' (Alderson 1984: 11). There was a significant shift in emphasis in policing at this time and this could be seen, in part, in the slowly changing role accorded to crime prevention.

Although since the inception of the new police crime prevention has been thought of as a key function, there has generally been a lack of clarity about what this is to mean in practice. It was not until after the publication of the report of the Cornish Committee on the Prevention and Detection of Crime (Home Office 1965) that specialist crime prevention departments began to come into being in any number. Despite the apparent rise in the stock of crime prevention with central government, responsibility *within* police forces for crime prevention work for a long time remained the domain of specialist crime prevention units and crime prevention officers and was initially treated as a peripheral specialism of low status and interest when placed alongside crime-fighting (Graef 1989; Chapter 12). However, as crime continued to rise, despite the increase in resources devoted to policing in the early 1980s, one of the key messages emanating from the police was they could not be expected to carry responsibility for the prevention of crime unaided. Beginning with the Ditchley Circular (211/78), increasing emphasis came to placed upon the 'community' in relation to policing and, later, upon what has since become known as 'inter' or 'multi-agency co-operation'.

This has broadened further more recently, and during the course of the 1990s the stock of what is now generally referred to as 'community safety' rose (Crawford 1998; Hughes *et al.* 2002). In 1990, the Morgan Committee – an inquiry established by the Standing Conference on Crime Prevention – had recommended the imposition of a statutory requirement on local authorities to stimulate crime prevention and community safety programmes at a local level. There was no reform until after the 1997 General Election, however, when the

Labour Party's manifesto commitment to implement the Morgan Committee recommendations was acted upon. In fact what was included in the Crime and Disorder Bill was a variant on the Morgan proposals, the compromise being a provision to give local authorities *and* the police new duties to develop statutory partnerships to help prevent and reduce crime.

The Crime and Disorder Act 1998 placed a statutory duty on chief police officers and local authorities, in co-operation with police authorities, probation committees and health authorities, to formulate and implement a 'strategy for the reduction of crime and disorder in the area', including undertaking and publishing an 'audit' of levels and patterns of crime locally. The language of the late 1990s was dominated by talk of 'partnership', of multi-agency working and of joint responsibilities, and it was in the area of community safety that this was perhaps most visibly seen. The largely 'service-based, consumerist' view of policing espoused by many police managers by the early 1990s (Reiner 1991) certainly held sway within the police service by the end of the century with, for example, the Commissioner of the Metropolitan Police recommending a return to 'Dixon of Dock Green-style bobbies on the beat' (*Guardian* 28 February 2003). Policing, of course, is not like other public services and the nature of the relationship between it and the communities it 'serves' can never be as entirely straightforward as notions of 'service delivery' can make it sound. Nowhere is this clearer than in the relationship between the police and Britain's minority ethnic communities. Responses to the perceived problems of police–community relations have led to calls for significant reform of the police service – by and large from a liberal-idealist position. An exception, this time from the right, has come recently from Hitchens (2003) who, in a critique of contemporary criminal justice, identifies what he feels has been a profound cultural shift in policing as part of a broader trend in which the moral certainties of the immediate postwar period have been replaced by a system in which authority has been undermined and moral relativism rules. The result, in his view, has been that the 'best police force in the world has been reduced to bureaucratic uselessness' (2003: 17). Though not alone in identifying problems in contemporary policing, Hitchens' diagnosis is unusual, indeed a throw-back to previous times, arguing that what is required is a moral counter-revolution reversing the tide of what he perceives to be the broad sweep of liberal progressive reformism in the past 40 years. Many are blamed by Hitchens for the current failings of policing; key, however, among those he holds responsible are Lord Scarman and Sir William Macpherson.

From Scarman to Stephen Lawrence

In the aftermath of the 1981 riots Lord Scarman was appointed to inquire into the causes of the unrest in Brixton and to make recommendations (Scarman 1982). Scarman was critical of the policing of Brixton and especially the heavy-handed 'Swamp 81' 'street saturation' operation. Almost 950 'stops' had been made in the course of this operation, resulting in 118 arrests. More than half the people stopped were black. A total of 75 charges were brought, though only one was for robbery, one for attempted burglary and 20 for theft or attempted theft. As a result of his inquiry, Scarman concluded that the lack of consultation with community representatives prior to 'Swamp 81' was 'an error of judgement' (Scarman 1982: 4.73), that the whole operation 'was a serious mistake, given the tension which existed between the police and local community' (1982: 4.76) and that 'had policing attitudes and methods been adjusted to deal fully with the problems of a multi-racial society, there would have been a review in depth of the public order implications of the operation, which would have included local consultation'.

Scarman's recommendations as a result of the inquiry were wide ranging and took in such diverse areas as recruitment of ethnic minorities to the police, increasing consultation through the introduction of statutory liaison committees, the introduction of lay visiting to police stations, the independent review of complaints against the police and the tightening of regulations regarding racially prejudiced behaviour by officers. In relation to the nature of the policing service being delivered to minority communities, Scarman explicitly rejected 'institutional racism' as an explanation for the problems that had precipitated the inquiry. However, in the careful language of an eminent lawyer, he went on to note that if 'the suggestion being made is that practices may be adopted by public bodies as well as private individuals which are *unwittingly discriminatory* against black people, then this is an allegation which deserves serious consideration, and, where proved, swift remedy' (Scarman 1982, emphasis added). As Stuart Hall noted at the time (1982: 68), 'the idea that oppressive policing is not a set of fortuitous events but a process, a structural condition, is beyond [Scarman's] grasp. The concept of "institutional racism" is not merely repugnant to his sympathies. It is unthinkable within his discourse. This is one limit-point to his reformism'. Nevertheless, the report emphasised the need for change and, despite its limitations, 'was the trigger for a reorientation of policing on a wide front. Indeed by the late 1980s, [Scarman's] ideas had become the predominant conception of policing philosophy amongst Chief Constables' (Reiner 1991).

A little over a decade after the Scarman Inquiry – on 22 April 1993 – 18-year-old Stephen Lawrence was stabbed to death in Eltham, South London, giving rise, albeit over four years later, to another significant inquiry into policing. There are many differences between the Scarman and Stephen Lawrence Inquiries – in terms of the incidents that gave rise to them, the speed with which they were called and their recommendations (Bowling 1999) – but both left a lasting impression on the British policing landscape.

On that evening in April 1993, Stephen Lawrence had been standing at a bus stop with a friend, Duwayne Brooks, when they were approached by a small group of clearly hostile and abusive white youths. Though Brooks was able to escape and call for help, Stephen Lawrence was stabbed twice and died within a short period of time. As the Stephen Lawrence Inquiry, established by Jack Straw in the aftermath of the 1997 General Election, put it (Macpherson 1999: para. 2.1): 'those violent seconds in 1993 have been followed by extraordinary activity, without satisfactory result'. The police investigation found no witnesses to the attack other than Duwayne Brooks and 'other sound evidence against the prime suspects [was] conspicuous by its absence' (1999: para. 2.2). A private prosecution was launched against five suspects in 1996 but failed because of lack of evidence (two suspects were discharged at the committal stage and the other three, who went to trial, were acquitted). Ominously the verdict of the inquest jury was that 'Stephen Lawrence was unlawfully killed in a completely unprovoked racist attack by five white youths'. The Stephen Lawrence Inquiry concluded memorably, and in contrast with Scarman, that: 'There is no doubt but that there were fundamental errors. The investigation was marred by a combination of professional incompetence, *institutional racism* and a failure of leadership by senior officers' (1999: para. 46.1, emphasis added).

The 'professional incompetence' included a lack of direction and organisation in the hours after the murder, little or no pursuit of the suspects, insensitive treatment of both the Lawrence family and Duwayne Brooks (Brooks and Hattenstone 2003), inadequate processing of intelligence, ill-thought-out surveillance and inadequate searches. However, the inquiry concluded that incompetence alone could not account for police failures and it suggested that the very fact that the victim was black led directly to less competent behaviour on the part of officers, in particular with regard to their actions at the scene of the crime, in connection with family liaison, the treatment of Duwayne Brooks and in the use of inappropriate and offensive language. The service, the inquiry suggested, was 'institutionally racist'. This it defined (Macpherson 1999: para. 6.34) as:

> The collective failure of an organisation to provide an appropriate and professional service to people because of their colour, culture or ethnic origin. It can be seen or detected in processes, attitudes and behaviour which amount to discrimination through unwitting prejudice, ignorance, thoughtlessness, and racist stereotyping which disadvantage minority ethnic people.

The inquiry made 70 recommendations which covered the monitoring and assessment of police performance; the reporting and recording of racist incidents and crimes; the investigation and prosecution of racist crime; family liaison; the treatment of victims and witnesses; first aid; training; employment, discipline and complaints; stop and search; and recruitment and retention. These recommendations amounted 'to the most extensive programme of reform in the history of the relationship between the police and ethnic minority communities' (Bowling and Phillips 2002: 16). At the centre of the recommendations was a proposed ministerial priority for the police to seek to 'increase trust and confidence in policing among minority ethnic communities'.

As Reiner (2000: 211) suggests, 'the Macpherson Report . . . has transformed the terms of the political debate about black people and criminal justice . . . what had not [previously] featured in public awareness and political debate was the disproportionate rate at which black people suffered as victims of crime'. In this, the Macpherson Inquiry achieved something that Scarman hadn't. Moreover, as Bowling and Phillips (2002: 18) note:

> Where Scarman was hesitant on the question of accountability, Macpherson was strident. Since the Lawrence Inquiry had concluded that the

failings of the police were systemic and the result of insufficient accountability, it recommended the introduction of lay oversight into all areas of police work, and the creation of a fully independent complaints system. Crucially, the Inquiry recommended bringing the police into the ambit of race relations law, a proposal that had been roundly rejected two decades earlier.

The nature of police relationships with, and the policing of, minority ethnic communities has been the subject of considerable attention, and no little controversy, in the period since the publication of the Stephen Lawrence Inquiry (see Chapter 21). One of the key issues raised by both Scarman and the Stephen Lawrence Inquiry concerns the nature of the relationship between the police, government and local communities and, more particularly, how the police service is effectively to be made accountable.

Centralisation and control

In some respects the most obvious and consistent trend in the history of policing since 1829 is the gradual centralisation of control as government, largely through the Home Office, established greater control over chief officers and their constabularies (see Chapter 4).

There are at least four major ways in which this process of centralisation may be seen in the postwar years:

1. The progressive reduction in the number of police forces in England and Wales (and increased government powers of amalgamation).

2. The increased ability of police forces to co-ordinate their activities across force boundaries together with the formation of new, powerful national policing organisations such as the National Crime Intelligence Service (NCIS) and the National Crime Squad (NCS).

3. The formalisation of the activities of police representative bodies such as the Police Federation and, in particular, ACPO. And perhaps most significantly

4. The increase in government oversight of, and influence over, policing via legislative change and new managerial reforms.

Since 1945 increasing centralisation has seen the amalgamation of forces in England and Wales, and their reduction from almost 200 in 1945 to their current level of 43 (see Chapter 8). These changes were initially brought about by the Police Act 1946 which gave the Home Secretary power compulsorily to amalgamate police forces with populations below 100,000. As a result of the 1946 Act the number of forces was reduced to 125 by 1949, and then was further reduced by 1964 to 117. In its consideration of police governance, the Royal Commission gave serious thought to the possibility of 'nationalisation'. As we know, nationalisation didn't occur, though Bottoms and Stevenson (1989: 10–11) conclude that 'Overall, one is left with the clear impression of a

Commission impressed with some of the logic of the nationalisers' case, but regarding it as simply too radical in the context of the times'. Despite rejection, as its secretary put it, 'the Commission came near to the brink' (Critchley 1967: 282). The trend was unmistakably towards fewer and bigger forces. In the aftermath of the Police Act 1964 there was a very substantial period of consolidation, and the number of forces was reduced to its current level in 1974. Further amalgamations appeared likely in the early 1990s, particularly during the period of Michael Howard's tenure as Home Secretary. New provisions were included in the Police and Magistrates' Courts Act 1994, giving the Home Secretary powers to order force amalgamations without having any form of local inquiry as would have been the case under the Police Act 1964. The provisions contained no requirement on him to justify his plans before an independent inspector, or even to do more than give reasons to those that have objections to his proposals. This represented a remarkable concentration of power centrally over decisions about the structure of local forces, and though no further amalgamations have occurred the pressures are certainly in that direction.

The second aspect of centralisation concerns the increased ability of forces to work across boundaries in support of each other, together with the creation or reinforcement of national policing bodies. The Police Act 1964 provided the basis for the establishment of regional crime squads (RCSs) and within a year nine RCSs had been established. The squads grew in size significantly during the 1970s and 1980s, though their number was reduced from nine to six in the early 1990s. Plans for an NCIS got underway in 1990, the intention being to integrate the work of the existing National Football Intelligence Unit, the Art and Antiques Squad, the National Drugs Intelligence Unit, the regional criminal intelligence offices and a variety of other bodies. NCIS was established in 1992. Growing awareness of crime problems that crossed national borders, and the need to liaise effectively with international policing organisations such as Europol and Interpol, were a significant pressure towards the development of formal national policing bodies. At the 1995 Conservative Party conference the Home Secretary announced that he intended creating an operational NCS to deal with serious crimes, a proposition implicitly endorsed by the Home Affairs Committee in its 1995 report on organised crime. This was put into effect by the Police Act 1997 and the NCS came into operation on 1 April 1998. The Director General of the NCS effectively took control of the RCSs which were absorbed into the structure of the NCS. There have been occasional proposals either for the establishment of a 'British FBI' or for the formation of a national police force. Neither look especially likely currently. Nevertheless, the formation of national squads is indicative of creeping centralisation and although some commentators see this as presaging the eventual nationalisation of policing (see Uglow and Trelford 1997), NCS, NCIS and related agencies with national and international responsibilities still act collaboratively or in support of local constabularies and, to date at least, have not obviously usurped power or status from them. The policing of the miner's strike in 1984 focused attention on the increasingly 'national' nature of policing in Britain. In 1972, the National Reporting Centre (NRC) was established as a system for co-ordinating and managing mutual aid between forces in times of emergency. It had been used on a relatively small number of occasions prior to the miners' dispute, but during the strike was utilised on a hitherto unprecedented scale – the 'high point in the national co-ordination of policing public order' (Reiner 1991: 191). The perception that this vast policing operation was too obviously acting on behalf of government – perhaps the primary fear about the consequence of nationalising policing – left many chief constables feeling uncomfortable, though it appears many also believed that 'it had averted rather than precipitated the formation of a national police force' (Reiner 1991: 188).

In terms of national co-ordination of policing, one of the most significant developments in the postwar period has been the remarkable transformation police representative organisations and, most especially, ACPO. Prior to the establishment of ACPO in 1948, chief officers had been represented by the County Chief Constables' Club and the Chief Constables' Association of England and Wales (for the city and borough forces). Most commentators describe the activities of these organisations as being more like clubs than policy-making or pressure groups (ACPO 1998). Indeed, there is little evidence that ACPO was much different in the first two decades or so of its existence (Savage *et al.* 2000). For the bulk of this period, the impression that the police service was somehow outside politics was successfully maintained. The politicisation of 'law and order' from the late 1960s onwards is by now well documented (see Downes and Morgan 2002). The growing visibility of the police in 'political' debates can be seen both in the changing role of ACPO and in the activities of the Police Federation, beginning in the 1960s with campaigns for better pay. From that point onward, the Police Federation became a relatively vocal and influential pressure group, even going so far as to place an advertisement in the national newspapers in the run-up to the 1979 General Election, linking rising crime with the failure of the Labour adminis- tration's policies (McLaughlin and Murji 1998). The crucial development which saw the police thrust into the centre of political controversy was the election of the radical Thatcher government and, most obviously, the role undertaken by the police in support – as it appeared to some at least – of government attempts to undermine the miners' strike.

In the period since then, and encouraged in many respects by the Home Office, ACPO has become a highly organised and effective national co- ordinating body. It has, less happily for the Home Office, also become a supremely effective lobbying organisation. As comfortable working in the public eye as behind the scenes in the Home Office and Parliament, it is now one of the most important influences on contemporary policing in Britain. The formidable power of ACPO was successfully exercised in the early 1990s when, beginning with Kenneth Clarke and continuing under Michael Howard, the Conservative government attempted to engineer radical reforms in policing and, in particular, to increase central control dramatically and to begin a process of partial privatisation, 'hiving off' or 'contracting out'. A series of inquiries, including the Sheehy Inquiry into Police Responsibilities and Rewards, and the Core and Ancillary Tasks Review (the Posen Inquiry), together with the first drafts of the Police and Magistrates' Courts (PMC) Bill, appeared to herald the possibility of a new era in policing; one in which policing was redefined largely as 'crime fighting', with other functions contracted out, and where government had significantly enhanced powers to hire and fire officers and to manage local policing delivery. That the Posen Inquiry resulted in almost no change at all, that the Sheehy Inquiry had much less impact than had been anticipated in some quarters and that elements of the PMC Bill were successfully resisted is in no small measure due to the influence of ACPO. The erstwhile head of the Audit Commission, Howard Davies, once noted that the police was the least affected of all public services by 'the Thatcher revolution' (McLaughlin and Murji, 1993: 95). This has not been because of a perception that the police were somehow less in need of reform but rather that successive home secretaries up to and including the present incumbent have eventually fought shy of taking on ACPO; for the Thatcher administration partly because of the 'debt' owed in aftermath of the miners' strike; for later administrations more because of the increasing influence and leverage exercised by ACPO. Radical reform of the police service remains a very dim prospect in the absence of a Home Secretary truly willing to confront the association.

Despite the now very powerful position occupied by ACPO, the clearest element of the long-term centralisation of British policing has been the gradual accretion of power over policing by government. This can be seen in two key respects: successive reforms to the tripartite structure for police governance which have progressively enhanced central powers; and the growth of a form of centralised managerialism which seeks to regulate policing primarily by means of performance assessment but which, under New Labour, shows every sign of becoming a form of fairly direct government micro-management. In the postwar period, police governance and accountability were defined and shaped by the Royal Commission on the Police and the subsequent Police Act. The Police Act sought to define, effectively for the first time, the respective roles of the Home Secretary, chief constables and police authorities. It replaced the old system of watch committees and joint standing committees with a single system of police authorities. These authorities were placed under a duty to secure the maintenance of an 'adequate and efficient' force for their area, though these terms were undefined. In terms of governance, the Royal Commission's recommendations, and the Act that followed, were based on the principle that 'there should be stronger central control' (Critchley 1967: 286) and the 1964 Act reinforced the powers of the Home Office and chief constables at the expense of local authorities (Marshall 1978). One of the major changes made by the Act was the enshrining in statute of the fact that supreme responsibility for local policing lay with chief constables, each force thenceforward being 'under the direction and control' of its chief officer. In order to do this the chief officer was empowered by the Act to appoint, promote and discipline all officers up to the rank of chief superintendent. The Home Secretary was given the power to call for reports from chief constables, to approve the appointment of senior officers and to compel the retirement of an inefficient chief constable. Such a description, however, does scant justice to the degree of influence that was exercised even then by the Home Office over policing. As Lustgarten (1986: 100) puts it, 'practice in this area embodies to an extreme degree a notable feature of British politics: its informality and preference for behind the scenes influence, quiet words in ears, and careful selection of key people who can be trusted to share fundamental norms'. The basic structure established by the 1964 Act – and which concentrated greatest powers in the hands of the Home Office and chief constables at the expense of local police authorities – remained the basis of police governance for 30 years until the Police and Magistrates' Courts Act 1994 (for a more extended discussion, see Chapter 24).

The initial proposals in the PMC Bill to establish police authorities independent of local councils, yet subject to significant oversight by the Home Office, prompted Vernon Bogdanor to claim that 'the Bill establishes a national police force under the control of the Home Secretary' (*The Times* 19 January 1994) and the then President of ACPO, Sir John Smith, to comment, 'I am inclined to the view that we are witnessing a move, perhaps unintended, for national control of the police by central government' (cited in Jones and Newburn 1995: 448). As has already been suggested, the original proposals were considerably amended during their passage through Parliament, partly as a result of ACPO's lobbying efforts. In the event, depoliticisation was one of the most visible consequences of the Act. The influence of party politics generally, and the political complexion of authorities in particular, clearly diminished significantly as a result of the reforms (Jones and Newburn 1997). If anything, it was the power of chief constables that was reinforced by the reforms, though there was the potential to reinvigorate police authorities, certainly with regard to financial oversight of local policing.

As far as central control was concerned, though not especially dramatic at that stage, it was the introduction of national objectives for policing that was the clearest illustration of the future direction of change. The growing emphasis on the key elements of 'new public management' (see Chapter 25), and the increasing influence of the Audit Commission were, among other developments, indicators of a shift towards what Reiner called 'calculative and contractual' accountability (1993: 19–20) in which performance is 'judged according to the achievement of a limited range of performance indicators'. Central control through such means was most clearly and most recently articulated in the establishment of the Police Standards Unit.

Its focus is on the management of 'performance' and spreading 'best practice' via the quantitative measurement of police activities and the publication and comparison of results, not just between individual forces but between basic command units. In addition, the Police Reform Act 2002 introduced an Annual Policing Plan, provided powers to promote consistency across police forces through the introduction of statutory codes of practice and introduced new powers to require police forces to take remedial action where they are judged to be inefficient or ineffective by Her Majesty's Inspectorate of Constabulary (HMIC).

The most vivid illustration of what I have called the current trend towards government 'micro-management' of policing is what became known as the 'street crimes initiative'. As a result of growing concern in government about levels of recorded street crime in 2000–1 and 2001–2, and the perceived failure of the police service to respond adequately, there was direct intervention in local policing strategies. A Downing Street 'summit' on street crime resulted in the identification of ten forces in which the greatest street crime problems were believed to exist. For the following six months these ten forces provided weekly crime figures to a designated government minister. At the end of this period of close scrutiny, and after the injection of considerable extra resources to support enhanced police operations within the ten forces, success was claimed for the Prime Minister's promise to have street crime 'under control by September [2002]' (*Police Review* 26 July 2002). The success or otherwise of the initiative is not the issue here. Its importance for policing lies in the extraordinary level of control, and the unusually hands-on manner, exercised by central government, and by the Prime Minister in particular. That government should have deemed this to be necessary, and now be defining it as a success, is likely to mean more of the same in the future. The long-term trend towards greater central control of policing is, on current evidence, unlikely to be reversed.

Policing and the police

The other most significant changes affecting policing in the postwar period are in some ways difficult to characterise. Put crudely they concern a set of processes that have had the consequence of 'pluralising' the provision of policing. At the beginning of the twenty-first century we find ourselves confronted by what often appears to be a bewildering array of organisations that might broadly be thought of as policing bodies (for a discussion see, for example, Chapters 6 and 7). Indeed, so significant do the changes appear to have been that two influential criminologists have argued that 'future generations will look back on our era as a time when one system of policing ended and another took its place' (Bayley and Shearing 1996: 585). A central strand of Bayley and Shearing's argument concerns what they term the 'end of a monopoly' by the public police; something they allege has occurred since the mid-1960s. Though the accuracy of this claim has been contested (see Jones and Newburn 2002), what seems undeniably the case is that the 'policing division of labour' has become more highly differentiated and more complex in recent times.

Thinking more directly about public policing – the primary focus of this chapter – there are a number of distinct processes that can be identified. These include the imposition of tighter financial controls over the police; the related questioning of the appropriateness and effectiveness of the public sector in delivering particular policing functions; and the stimulation of alternative forms of provision through increasing emphasis on partnerships and related forms of citizen 'responsibilisation'. The Metropolitan Police Act 1829 recognised that the commissioner could employ civilian clerks, and indeed this happened from the early days of the force. Furthermore, there was a 'civilian' influence in senior positions prior to the 1950s with a number of commissioners being appointed from outside the service (Loveday 1993). By and large, however, most civilian appointments were confined to clerical or ancillary posts, and it was not until after 1945 that the main expansion in civilian employment took place (Jones *et al.* 1994). There was a very rapid expansion in civilian employment between 1945 and 1975, some slowing during the remainder of the 1970s and then increasing interest in a policy of civilianisation from the Conservative government in the 1980s, supported by bodies like the Audit Commission. The pressures stimulating increasing employment of civilians changed during the postwar period, from a concern initially with ensuring that officers were available for mainstream police duties to a more fiscally driven concern from the 1970s onwards focusing on 'economy' (police expenditure), 'efficiency and effectiveness' (specialist civilian staff in specialist support posts). Whatever the impetus, the policy of civilianisation has had a marked impact on British policing since 1945.

The era of tighter financial control in policing followed hot on the heels of one of the most significant increases in expenditure on policing. In 1979, part of the Conservative Party's 'law and order' election promises concerned a pay deal for the police, and an increase in police numbers. In the five years to 1984 public expenditure on the police doubled from £1,644 million to £3,358 million. A rather naïve belief that this would yield positive results was quickly dashed and recorded crime predictably continued to rise despite the vastly increased financial commitment. Government ministers were deeply unhappy at what they perceived to be a lack of return on their expenditure and from approximately 1982–3 onwards the government began vigorously to pursue its 'Financial Management Initiative' (FMI). This was designed to encourage efficiency and cost savings by applying private sector management methods to the public sector, and imposing market disciplines on them. Home Office Circular 114/1983 (and later the even tougher 106/1988), produced largely without consultation with police representative bodies, signalled that the financial climate had changed. The circular outlined potential new management strategies for the police – now generally referred to as 'policing by objectives' (PBO). Though Kenneth Newman had introduced very similar initiatives into the Metropolitan Police before the circular was published, both ACPO and the Police Federation were often very hostile to the new emphasis on 'value for money', largely because of the potential consequences for the terms and conditions of employment.

In addition to the problem of rising crime, the other major reason that the Conservative government felt able to adopt a stringent financial policy, particularly in its second term of office, was that recorded levels of public satisfaction with the police had been declining for some years (Skogan 1990). The Thatcher administrations of the 1980s were deeply sceptical about both the effectiveness and the efficiency of public services, and placed much greater faith in the efficacy of markets and in the ability of the private sector to deliver services economically. As a consequence, this period saw increased emphasis placed on market pressures and the beginnings of a flirtation with the idea of privatisation in the policing arena. The size and significance of the private security sector were anyway on the increase (Jones and Newburn 1998), there was as we have seen increasing civilianisation (and use of 'specials') within the police (Jones et al. 1994), and plans were floated to privatise the Police National Computer and to formalise a customer–contractor relationship between police forces and the Forensic Science Service, each of which give rise to police fears that more widespread privatisation was possible.

The impact of both financial constraint and the spectre of privatisation was to open up a debate about the future shape of policing in Britain. This debate continued into the 1990s and was given further impetus by the establishment of the Sheehy and Posen Inquiries. From the very outset the Sheehy Inquiry was controversial. It was announced to general surprise at the Police Federation conference in May 1992, and was chaired by Sir Patrick Sheehy, the chairman of BAT industries; neither he nor any of its four other members had any experience of policing. The inquiry reported in July 1993 (Home Office 1993) just two days after the publication of the white paper on police reform. Its 272 recommendations were designed to 'reward good performance and penalise bad' and included fixed-term contracts for new recruits, the introduction of a severance programme for middle-ranking and senior officers, and performance-related pay for chief constables and their assistants.

The Posen Inquiry, established at roughly the same time as Sheehy, had a very specific 'contracting out' focus. Its terms of reference were 'To examine the services provided by the police, to make recommendations about the most cost-effective way of delivering core police services and to assess the scope for relinquishing ancillary tasks' (Posen 1994). The review team suggested that 'some of the resources needed to improve performance in core areas of work supporting key and national objectives will have to be found by releasing resources currently absorbed by peripheral non-essential tasks or by finding more cost-effective ways of delivering core tasks'. The inquiry was, in essence, a further step along the road towards potential privatisation of certain police functions. Though the final report was a damp squib, it reinforced the view that the government was increasingly concerned to ensure value for money from the police and also that it was actively considering how the private sector could play a greater role in policing.

There have been a number of more recent developments that either have had, or are likely to have, an effect on the policing division of labour. New Labour's Crime and Disorder Act 1998 raises a host of issues for policing and how it is to be delivered (for a review, see Newburn 2002). Perhaps the most important – even though it is not a simple, direct or even intended consequence of the Act – concerns the implications for the 'role' of the police in the delivery of 'policing'. Crucially, it appears that the logic of the Crime and Disorder Act is likely to lead, at least in the long term, to further pluralisation of policing. There are a number of reasons for this. First, the Act places a significantly increased emphasis on the identification of local problems and local responses to them. Secondly, it encourages local choice and is likely therefore to stimulate competition. Thirdly, it explicitly encourages partnerships between public, private and municipal providers. And, finally, Best Value requirements are likely further to reinforce this 'marketisation' of criminal justice. Perhaps crucially in this regard, Best Value requires reviews of service provision to be undertaken according to what are known as the 'four Cs': *challenge* why and how a service is being provided; invite *comparison* with others' performance across a range of relevant indicators, taking into account the views of both service users and potential suppliers; *consult* with local taxpayers, service users and the wider business community in the setting of new performance targets; and embrace fair *competition* as a means of securing efficient and effective services (see Chapter 25). Together, the Crime and Disorder Act and Best Value make explicit the impossibility of a 'police solution' to policing and are likely to stimulate increased competition and further change.

Of all the recent inquiries into policing, the most explicit recognition of the increasingly 'plural' nature of policing and security provision was contained in the proposals advanced by the Independent Commission on Policing in Northern Ireland (the Patten Inquiry) (1999) which was set up as part of the Good Friday Agreement (10 April 1998). The Patten Commission's role was to examine policing in Northern Ireland and to make proposals for future policing structures and arrangements, including means of encouraging widespread community support. It recommended a radical overhaul of accountability structures, including the introduction of a Police Ombudsman and a new Policing Board (not *Police* Board) to replace the largely discredited Police Authority. Beneath the Policing Board it recommended the establishment of District Policing Partnership Boards (DPPB) as a committee of the district council with a majority elected membership. In particular, it was envisaged that these boards would have responsibility for promoting partnership of community and police in the collective delivery of community safety. Perhaps most radically in this regard the inquiry recommended that district councils should have the power to contribute an amount initially up to the equivalent of a rate of three pence in the pound towards the improved policing of the district. This could enable DPPBs to purchase additional services from the police or other statutory agencies, or indeed from the private sector. Critics suggested that this would be exploited in such a way as to enable services involving, or even controlled by, paramilitaries to be purchased by DPPBs. Though by no means enacted in full in Northern Ireland (McEvoy *et al.* 2002), and unlikely to be enacted on the mainland in the near future given the police reform programme that is underway, none the less the Patten Inquiry outlined an approach to policing and to police accountability that has the potential to transform policing in England and Wales in important ways, and may yet be seen as a model for reform in the future.

Finally in this regard there are the developments associated with what now appears to be referred to as the 'extended police family' and, more particularly, the increasing visibility of alternative forms of 'police patrol' (see Chapter 7). Of all the elements of the Police Reform Act 2002, it was the proposals for the introduction of community support officers that were most radical, though the idea was by no means a new one. Almost a decade earlier, a committee established by the Police Foundation and the Policy Studies Institute had recommended experimentation with alternative forms of police patrol (Police Foundation/PSI 1994; see also Morgan and Newburn 1997), only to be roundly criticised by ACPO and by New Labour in opposition for recommending 'policing on the cheap'. By 2002, however, the fiscal realities were such that it was difficult for any politician to avoid the conclusion that the level of policing seemingly demanded by the public could not easily be provided from within the public purse. A form of public–private partnership was proposed – not that such language was used. Using the more mellifluous idea of 'an extended police family', and underpinned by the 'broken windows' philosophy (Wilson and Kelling 1982), the white paper proposed, and the Police Reform Act incorporated, proposals that agents and agencies such as neighbourhood and street wardens, security guards in shopping centres, park keepers and 'other authority figures' (Home Office 2001: para. 2.31) could be accredited by, and work alongside, the police in a formal capacity. More controversially, the government proposed a power to enable chief constables to appoint support staff to provide a visible presence (i.e. to patrol) in the community. These 'community support officers' are to be under the control of the chief constable and have limited powers to detain suspects, to stop vehicles and to issue fixed-penalty notices. The Home Office was primarily responding to the problem of limited resources in making such a proposal. While much of the police service appeared sceptical at best, and somewhat hostile in many cases, the Metropolitan Police – also subject to considerable resource pressures – was at the forefront of taking the idea of community support officers forward – the first of the new officers patrolling the capital from late 2002.

Directly and indirectly, through a number of its measures, New Labour has stimulated further moves in the direction of a more complex and fragmented policing division of labour. The Police Reform Act, via the creation of community support officers and the accreditation of extended police family members, is the most visible of the measures. Arguably, however, the Crime and Disorder Act, in conjunction with Best Value and the increasing emphasis placed upon consumer demand, will prove to be just as important in the process of formalising the mixed economy of policing. In outlining Bayley and Shearing's (1996) argument about profound systemic change in the nature of policing systems, I drew attention to the fact that they argued that central to this transformation has been the ending of the public police's monopoly on policing. Of course, in reality, no such monopoly ever existed (Jones and Newburn 2002). Nevertheless, in the not-too-distant past it was at least plausible to talk about the police as if they were synonymous with policing. Perhaps the best measure of the change that has taken place since the Second World War is the impossibility of making such an assumption now.

Conclusion

In attempting to bring some order to half a century of police history, and a period of rapid social change, I have suggested that four sets of issues or trends can be seen to have been dominant in this period. First, I suggested that in some respects the role of the police has expanded – or at least become more complex as the world being policed becomes more complex. At least as importantly the image of the police has fundamentally altered and, in particular, we are now some distance from the high point of police legitimacy in the early years after the Second World War. As a consequence, the very idea of 'policing by consent' is now significantly more problematic than was the case 50 years ago. The result has been an almost continuous debate over the past decade over the 'proper' role and function of the police. Most recently the symbolic image of Dixon of Dock Green has once again reappeared, serving to define a sense of what has been lost and, in the eyes of commentators such as the Commissioner and Deputy Commissioner of the Metropolitan Police and the journalist Peter Hitchens, what now needs to be regained. For the senior management of the Metropolitan Police (*Guardian*, 28 February 2003), the era of Dixon has been invoked in the hope that government and the public can be persuaded that significant increases in police officer numbers are necessary. For Hitchens (2003), Dixon represents a period of policing prior to the damaging changes brought about by 'social liberalism'. In an argument resonant of the critics of 'permissiveness' in the 1960s (Newburn 1992), Hitchens suggests as a result of a cultural campaign by the liberal elite, the police are now hamstrung by rules that have transformed them from an 'effective police force into [an] ineffectual police service' (2003: 291).

The second, and related, set of issues concern the nature of the relationships between the police and the communities its serves, which has been a focus of increasing attention and, frequently, criticism. This has been clearest in relation to police–minority ethnic community relations. Late twentieth-century Britain witnessed a remarkable growth of cultural pluralism. Whereas for much of the postwar period the key sources of social and political identity were based around economic class divisions, we now live in a society in which these are less important. Though concerns about the policing of a diverse society are not new, the apparent gulf between the police and minority ethnic communities has been increasingly visible since at least the time of Lord Scarman's inquiry in the early 1980s, culminating in the Stephen Lawrence Inquiry's description of the Metropolitan Police as 'institutionally racist'. Policing diversity is set to remain a key theme in the coming decades.

The third theme concerns police governance and has been characterised by the progressive neutering of local authorities, the emergence of a form of managerialism that involves ever-closer scrutiny of police performance, the growing authority and influence of police representative bodies and, arguably most important of all, the ever-increasing power and influence of central government in policing. Notwithstanding the creation of new national policing bodies, the increasing visibility of a national senior police officer elite and the increasingly powerful and vocal role taken by ACPO, the differences between individual forces in relation to the most basic aspects of policing such as crime recording (HMIC 1996) and levels of patrol service (Audit Commission 1996) should make one sceptical of the claims made for the creation of a national force by default. Indeed, alongside the centralising tendencies in contemporary policing, there have been simultaneous pressures towards localisation and fragmentation. Indeed, policing appears to be becoming increasingly pluralised. The private sector continues to expand, public–private partnership working is no longer unusual and an array of other policing bodies – ranging from parks police and neighbourhood wardens to community support officers – are now part of the security patchwork. The police service's broad mandate as an emergency service largely remains, but it is undertaken within a context in which they have to compete with providers who are functionally, geographically and legally limited and, therefore, potentially economically advantaged in the policing marketplace.

I noted earlier that the period covered by this chapter has been one of rapid social change. As Rod Morgan and I noted a few years ago, 'were we to resuscitate PC George Dixon he would find his surroundings somewhat strange' (Morgan and Newburn 1997: 11). Yet in surveying the changing nature of British policing here I have made little reference to any of the specific areas of social and cultural change. Space precluded any particular mention, for example, of the changing distribution of income and wealth, the changing nature of employment and of education and training. Nor did I discuss in any detail the very significant changes to the ethnic composition of the British population or to the changing nature of the family, though no doubt each, and all, of these has had an important impact on policing. I can do little more here than make note of this, with perhaps one exception. Numerous commentators (though see in particular Reiner 1992a) have noted the parallels between the changing nature of the social order being policed and the changing nature of policing itself. In this view, social order is in essence 'postmodern' and by implication so is policing (Reiner 1991; Johnston 2000). The impact of these changes can be seen in a number of ways: the fact that the police as a body with an omnibus mandate, symbolising order, seems increasingly anachronistic (Reiner 2000); that the provision of security is increasingly commodified (Johnston and Shearing 2003); and that policing bodies are simultaneously stretched globally and locally. There is one further aspect of 'late modernity', however, that is noteworthy in this regard. We live in increasingly reflexive times and this basic social fact has a potentially profound impact on all our social institutions, including the police. And it is this reflexivity which underpins and influences so much that has happened in the field of policing in the last half century. We are now more critical of policing and the police. We ask for more yet, given the greater visibility of the belly of the beast, feel we receive less. We are more demanding and less trusting, and this makes the role of the police under late modernity particularly difficult to define and to manage. It remains, however, a crucial task at the beginning of the twenty-first century. Though using different language, Sir Robert Mark recognised this over a quarter of a century ago, and perceptively noted the changes and consequences that it meant for the service he led:

> For over a century we have been an artisan service trained to uphold a social system but not to think too much about it whilst doing so . . . The very nature of our role in a society which is better equipped to think for itself, to question custom and precedent, to demand greater equality of opportunity and above all to ask those who govern it the question 'Why?' requires that we ourselves should exercise the same curiosity about our role and the motives and justification for what we do (1977: 117–18).

Selected further reading

Robert Reiner's *The Politics of the Police* (2000 – now in its third edition) remains the most comprehensive and finest book on British policing in the postwar period. Sociologically informed and historically detailed, it should be the starting point for anyone interested in this period in the history of policing. Clive Emsley's *The English Police: A Political and Social History* (1996) provides a longer historical introduction. This reading is then best supported with the detailed work in Bottoms and Stevenson's (1992) chapter in *Unravelling Criminal Justice*, and 'insider accounts' of various types, including Critchley's *A History of the Police in England and Wales, 900–1966* (1967), Robert Mark's *Policing a Perplexed Society* (1977), and John Alderson's *Law and Disorder* (1984). More recent developments are well charted in Ben Bowling and Coretta Phillips' *Racism, Crime and Justice* (2002) and Jones and Newburn's *Private Security and Public Policing* (1998). The two most recent official reports on policing that, in their very different ways, have important things to say, and which should be read in detail, are the Macpherson Report (1999) and the Patten Report (Independent Commission on Policing in Northern Ireland 1999).

Acknowledgements

I am grateful to Janet Foster, Tevor Jones, Rob C. Mawby, Peter Neyroud and Robert Reiner for comments on an initial draft of this chapter.

References

Alderson, J. (1984) *Law and Disorder*. London: Hamish Hamilton.

Association of Chief Police Officers (1990) *Strategic Policy Document*. London: ACPO.

Association of Chief Police Officers (1998) *Fifty Years of Leadership in Policing*. West Mercia: ACPO.

Audit Commission (1996) *Streetwise*. London: Audit Commission.

Bayley, D. and Shearing, C. (1996) 'The future of policing', *Law and Society Review*, 30(3): 585–606.

Bottoms, A.E. and Stevenson, S. (1992) 'What went wrong? Criminal justice policy in England and Wales 1945–70', in D. Downes (ed.) *Unravelling Criminal Justice*. Basingstoke: Macmillan.

Bowling, B. (1999) 'Facing the ugly facts', *Guardian*, 17 February.

Bowling, B. and Phillips, C. (2002) *Racism, Crime and Justice*. Harlow: Longman.

Brooks, D. and Hattenstone, S. (2003) *Steve and Me: Stephen Lawrence and the Search for Justice*. London: Abacus.

Chibnall, S. (1977) *Law and Order News*. London: Tavistock.

Cox, B., Shirley, J. and Short, M. (1977) *The Fall of Scotland Yard*. Harmondsworth: Penguin Books.

Crawford, A. (1998) *Crime Prevention and Community Safety*. Harlow: Longman.

Critchley, T.A. (1967) *A History of Police in England and Wales 900–1966*. London: Constable.

Downes, D. and Morgan, R. (1994) 'Hostages to fortune? The politics of law and order in post-war Britain', in M. Maguire *et al.* (eds) *The Oxford Handbook of Criminology*. Oxford: Oxford University Press.

Downes, D. and Morgan, R. (2002) 'The skeletons in the cupboard: the politics of law and order at the turn of the millennium', in M. Maguire *et al.* (eds) *The Oxford Handbook of Criminology* (3rd edn). Oxford: Oxford University Press, 286–321.

Emsley, C. (1996) *The English Police: A Political and Social History* (2nd edn). London: Longman.

Glennerster, H. (2000) *British Social Policy Since 1945*. Oxford: Blackwell.

Graef, R. (1989) *Talking Blues*. London: Collins.

Hall, S. (1982) 'The lessons of Lord Scarman', *Critical Social Policy*, 2(2): 66–72.

Hitchens, P. (2003) *A Brief History of Crime: The Decline of Order, Justice and Liberty in England*. London: Atlantic Books.

HMIC (1996) *A Review of Crime Recording Procedures*. London: Home Office.

Holdaway, S. (1983) *Inside the British Police*. Oxford: Blackwell.

Home Office (1965) *Report of the Committee on the Prevention and Detection of Crime*. London: HMSO.

Home Office (1993) *Inquiry into Police Responsibilities and Rewards*. London: Home Office.

Home Office (2001) *Policing a New Century: A Blueprint for Reform* (Cm 5326). London: Home Office.

Hughes, G., McLaughlin, E. and Muncie, J. (eds) (2002) *Crime Prevention and Community Safety: New Directions*. London: Sage.

Independent Commission on Policing in Northern Ireland (1999) *A New Beginning: Policing in Northern Ireland – the Report of the Independent Commission on Policing in Northern Ireland* (Patten Report). Belfast: Independent Commission on Policing in Northern Ireland.

Jefferson, T. (1990) *The Case against Paramilitary Policing*. Milton Keynes: Open University Press.

Johnston, L. (2000) *Policing Britain: Risk, Security and Governance*. Harlow: Longman.

Johnston, L. and Shearing, C. (2003) *Governing Security*. London: Routledge.

Jones, T. and Newburn, T. (1995) 'Local government and policing: arresting the decline of local influence', *Local Government Studies*, 21(3): 448–60.

Jones, T. and Newburn, T. (1997) *Policing after the Act: Police Governance after the Police and Magistrates' Courts Act 1994*. London: PSI.

Jones, T. and Newburn, T. (1998) *Private Security and Public Policing*. Oxford: Clarendon Press.

Jones, T. and Newburn, T. (2002) 'The transformation of policing: understanding current trends in policing systems', *British Journal of Criminology*, 42: 129–46.

Jones, T., Newburn, T. and Smith, D.J. (1994) *Democracy and Policing*. London: PSI.

Loveday, B. (1993) 'Civilian staff in the police service', *Policing*, summer.

Lustgarten, L. (1986) *The Governance of Police*. London: Sweet & Maxwell.

Macpherson, Sir William (1999) *The Stephen Lawrence Inquiry – Report* (Cm 4262-I). London: HMSO.

Mark, Sir R. (1977) *Policing a Perplexed Society*. London: George Allen & Unwin.

Marshall, G. (1978) 'Police accountability revisited', in D. Butler and A. Halsey (eds) *Policy and Politics*. London: Macmillan.

Martin, J.P. and Wilson, G. (1969) *The Police: A Study in Manpower*. London: Heinemann Education.

Mawby, R.C. (2002) *Policing Images: Policing, Communication and Legitimacy*. Cullompton: Willan.

McEvoy, K., Gormally, B. and Mika, H. (2002) 'Conflict, crime control and the "re"-construction of state–community relations in Northern Ireland', in G. Hughes *et al.* (eds) *Crime Prevention and Community Safety: New Directions*. London: Sage, 182–212.

McLaughlin, E. and Murji, K. (1993) 'Controlling the Bill: restructuring the police in the 1990s', *Critical Social Policy*, 13: 95–103.

McLaughlin, E. and Murji, K. (1998) 'Resistance through representation: "Story lines", advertising and police federation campaigns', *Policing and Society*, 8: 4.

Morgan, R. and Newburn, T. (1997) *The Future of Policing*. Oxford: Oxford University Press.

Newburn, T. (1992) *Permission and Regulation: Law and Morals in Postwar Britain*. London: Routledge.

Newburn, T. (2002) 'Community safety and policing: some implications of the Crime and Disorder Act 1998', in G. Hughes *et al.* (eds) *Crime Prevention and Community Safety: New Directions.* London: Sage.

Police Foundation/Policy Studies Institute (1994) *Final Report of the Independent Inquiry into the Role and Responsibilities of the Police.* London: Police Foundation/PSI.

Posen, I. (1994) *Review of Police Core and Ancillary Tasks.* London: Home Office.

Reiner, R. (1991) *Chief Constables.* Oxford: Oxford University Press.

Reiner, R. (1992a) 'Policing a postmodern society', *Modern Law Review*, 55(6) 761–81.

Reiner, R. (1992b) *The Politics of the Police* (2nd edn). Brighton: Harvester.

Reiner, R. (1993) 'Police accountability: principles, patterns and practices', in R. Reiner and S. Spencer (eds) *Accountable Policing: Effectiveness, Empowerment and Equity.* London: Institute for Public Policy Research, 1–23.

Reiner, R. (2000) *The Politics of the Police* (3rd edn). Oxford: Oxford University Press.

Royal Commission on the Police (1960) *Interim Report* (Cmnd 1222). London: HMSO.

Royal Commission on the Police (1962) *Final Report* (Cmnd 1728). London: HMSO.

Sanders, A. and Young, R. (1994) *Criminal Justice.* London: Butterworths.

Savage, S., Charman, S. and Cope, S. (2000) *Policing and the Power of Persuasion: The Changing Role of the Association of Chief Police Officers.* London: Blackstone Press.

Scarman, Lord (1982) *The Scarman Report.* Harmondsworth: Penguin Books.

Skogan, W.G. (1990) *The Police and Public in England and Wales: A British Crime Survey Report. Home Office Research Study* 117. London: HMSO.

Sparks, R. (1993) 'Inspector Morse: the last enemy', in G.W. Brandt (ed.) *British Television Drama in the 1980s.* Cambridge: Cambridge University Press.

Stephens, M. and Becker, S. (1994) 'The matrix of care and control', in M. Stephens and S. Becker (eds) *Police Force, Police Service: Care and Control in Britain.* Basingstoke: Macmillan.

Uglow, S. and Trelford, V. (1997) *The Police Act 1997.* London: Jordans.

Waddington, P.A.J. (1991) *The Strong Arm of the Law.* Oxford: Oxford University Press.

Wilson, J.Q. and Kelling, G. (1982) 'Broken windows', *Atlantic Monthly*, March: 29–38.

Part II

The Context of Policing

Tim Newburn

Part II of the handbook can in some respects be viewed in two sections. Whereas the first three chapters deal with the structural and organisational context of policing, the last three chapters deal with police culture, practice and representation. Together, they provide the context within which contemporary policing should be understood. Policing is increasingly international. Bodies, structures and forms of co-operation proliferate in the international arena, and Neil Walker's opening chapter (Chapter 6) describes and explores the nature of the major arrangements in this area. His focus is very explicitly upon '*trans*national' rather than the '*inter*national' dimension of policing. This, as he explains, is because the key developments are by no means confined to policing that is authorised and practised within the territorial and institutional confines of the state. Rather, his focus is at least as much upon policing which is not reducible to co-operation between actors whose main reference point is their state of origin, but instead involves relatively autonomous networks or where authority and allegiance are primarily to other non-state 'polities' or political communities such as the EU. Indeed, Walker's primary focus is on developments within Europe, though he notes the seeming re-emergence of a classic internationalist logic in the increasing visibility and influence of the USA in the aftermath of 11 September.

The context of policing has been changing domestically as well as internationally, and Adam Crawford's focus (Chapter 7) is upon the pattern of policing in the UK. Recent decades have seen a massive expansion in private and quasi-public forms of policing provision and this chapter explores, and provides an overview of, the emerging new policing division of labour. Its primary focus therefore is on 'policing beyond the police': on private security and other non-constabulary forms of provision. Partly, because of the absence of formal regulation until recently, understanding the nature, shape and size of the private security/policing sector has been limited. This chapter demythologises private policing and draws out the similarities and differences between public, private and other forms of policing provision. Considerable attention is paid to the emergence of the new, and increasingly visible, forms of patrol service that are now to be found in many major towns and cities, as well as to what this means for how we understand policing criminologically and sociologically.

The third chapter in this section focuses more directly on the nature of the police service itself. Much of what is written about the police assumes a knowledge of how the service is organised. In my view this is a mistake. Students in particular often have only a passing familiarity with the nature and structure of the police and tend to find that there is no obvious source they can turn to for such information. The chapter by Rob C. Mawby and Alan Wright (Chapter 8) fills this gap. It describes the structure of the British police service and, more particularly, how forces are structured internally. It includes an overview of the rank structure in police organisations, of the different way in which uniformed officers' work is structured (beat, response, etc.), and the division between general and specialist departments and roles. It looks at the location and size of police forces, provides a brief history of police representative bodies such as the Association of Chief Police Officers and the Police Federation, and examines the roles of the growing proliferation of bodies that scrutinise police performance.

Understanding the behaviour and practice of police officers is at the core of the following two chapters. Police 'culture' (Chapter 9) is often considered to be both a cause of police deviance and an obstacle to police reform. Understanding the culture of the police is therefore central to understanding the delivery of policing services. However, as Janet Foster points out, following other recent authors in this field, there is of course not one but several police cultures. Her chapter examines what is currently known about the nature of police cultures, how they are produced and reproduced and, in the light of this, what lessons can be drawn for successful reform of police conduct.

The following chapter (Chapter 10) takes a close look at the use and abuse of police powers, focusing in particular on key areas of activity such as detention and arrest and, in particular, the operation of the Police and Criminal Evidence Act and its impact on the treatment of suspects by the police, including such issues as the right of silence and the right of access to legal advice. It is the very fact of the existence of extensive powers that facilitates the exercise of generalised police authority. Consequently, in order to understand this very particular authority that the police bring to the situations they confront, it is important to understand how particular powers are organised. As the authors, Andrew Sanders and Richard Young, argue 'the importance of legal powers is not that they are *actually* invoked particularly frequently, but that they *could* be'. In reviewing this area, Sanders and Young take a particularly critical look at police practices and are relatively pessimistic about the likelihood of enlightened change in this area pointing, for example, to the Criminal Justice Bill 2003 as a further example of the state's willingness to over-ride civil libertarian concerns about the extent of police powers.

The style and tone of this chapter illustrate one of the important attributes of this volume. In addition to seeking to attract the leading authors in particular fields, we have deliberately sought to include differing viewpoints within the volume. These range from critical criminologists to senior police officers. The inclusion of this variety means that particular chapters have useful counterpoints and can helpfully be read in conjunction with each other. Thus, for example, the Sanders and Young chapter in this part can usefully be read in conjunction with Peter Neyroud's chapter on ethics in Part IV (Chapter 23). Both concern the issue of police conduct and its governance, though they differ in part in both their diagnosis and prognosis. Such differences of approach and opinion, it seems to me, are illustrative of the existence of a serious and healthy debate about both the nature and the future of policing.

Whether criminologists or criminal justice professionals, all the authors in this volume have an intimate knowledge of at least some of the realities of policing. In this they differ from the majority of the public who, if they have any contact with the police, will generally do so relatively fleetingly and occasionally. As such, their impression of the police, of police function and culture, will most likely be largely derived from the media. As Robert Reiner wrote 17 years ago, 'mass media images of the police are of central importance in understanding the political significance and role of policing'. On television (from *Dixon* to *Morse*, and *Ironside* to *NYPD Blue*), in film (from the *Blue Lamp* onwards) and via the press, our mass-mediated images play a vital role in framing how policing is understood and legitimated. Robert Reiner (Chapter 11), in the chapter which closes Part II, examines the changing media representation of policing and how this is linked with changing perceptions of the threat of crime and changing perceptions of police legitimacy. While mass-mediated images of policing have changed markedly, he argues that they continue to display an entrenched police fetishism – an assumption that the police are a functional prerequisite of social order; something without which there would be chaos and uncontrolled disorder. That this should still be so in the face of several decades of fairly intense public scrutiny and no little criticism is testament to this 'Teflon service's' stature as a continuing symbol of order and security.

Chapter 6

The pattern of transnational policing

Neil Walker

Introduction

The purpose of this chapter is to map some of the most salient developments in transnational policing, to locate and explain their causes and to identify current trends and future prospects. Before we proceed to these various stages of discussion, three preliminary issues of orientation should be addressed. The first concerns the title of the chapter. The term *trans*national is preferred to *inter*national for an important reason. If we are concerned with policing other than policing that is authorised and practised within the territorial and institutional confines of the state, then only some such policing can be properly labelled 'international'. That is to say, policing beyond the state may take the form of international policing – police co-operation and common action between officials and bureaucracies who owe their authority and allegiance first and foremost to the discrete states in question – yet it may also take a different form. For some forms of policing beyond the state are not reducible to co-operation between actors whose main reference point is their state of origin, but may instead involve networks which are relatively autonomous of these states of origin or which owe authority and allegiance to other non-state 'polities' or political communities – of which the EU is, in the policing field as in so many others, the primary example.

This leads directly to the second introductory remark. While the general horizon of this chapter is global, constraints of space demand a more selective approach. Accordingly, much of the focus is on European developments, not just because the European domain may be of most immediate interest to the primary readership of this book but also because, due to the emergence of the EU as a post-state polity (Walker 2002b), the EU is presently the limiting case of transnational police co-operation. But of course there are other important themes and developments in transnational policing, many of which take place within a more traditional international paradigm, and with the USA as a particularly important point of influence. Indeed, it is arguable that since 11 September we have seen a resurgence of this classical internationalist logic, and this resurgence and its structural antecedents also deserve – and receive – due attention.

Our third and final introductory remark concerns the formulation of a general framework to bring together our discussion of origins, current trends and future prospects within a coherent framework. Such a framework is supplied by an exploration of the very conditions of possibility of transnational policing, and is to that exploration that we now turn.

The conditions for the possibility of transnational policing

For many, the very idea of transnational policing may strike an incongruous note – may even be viewed as counter-intuitive. One need go no further than the table of contents of this volume to gain the impression that policing is typically and principally treated as an affair of states and their internal security concerns. What arguments, then, underscore the state/policing coupling, and how compelling and how comprehensive in import are these arguments (Walker 2000: Ch. 8; Loader and Walker 2001)?

To begin with, most theories of the modern state place the maintenance of internal (and external) security at or close to the centre of their conceptual scheme. Policing and internal security are often seen as definitive functions of the state – as *necessary* characteristics of statehood. This conceptual centrality is typically elaborated in functional terms. To the extent that the modern state differs from its dynastic and imperial predecessors, it is in its claim to comprehensive and legitimate authority over a definite territory and a definite population. In turn, this seems to require a strong commitment by the state to monopolisation or control of the means of force, both as a 'stick' with which to maintain its own position and as the 'carrot' of the establishment and maintenance of general order that provides the population with a legitimate reason for accepting the authority of the state.

Yet if we bracket off the function of the self-interested, self-preservation of the state, which though it points to the undoubted sociological significance of the self-perpetuation of powerful bureaucracies and the interests with which they are associated (Marenin 1982) tends to view the might of the state in crude, monolithic terms, and if we concentrate instead on the second and more general function – the maintenance of general order – even here we see that the 'stick' and the 'carrot' are closely connected within a unified logic of political action – one which highlights the crucial place of state coercion as both root and vehicle of a socially coherent project of collective security. So for Thomas Hobbes and the social contract theorists, the unitary force at the root of the state was a necessary means of overcoming the problems of collective action that stood in the way of collective security. If each values the peace and the minimisation of everyday threat which all require to pursue their lives effectively, but if no individual or section of the population has the power to guarantee its own security still less the security of all others without the consent of all others, and if there is insufficient mutual trust to bring about or perpetuate such mutual consent – with some concerned that others will abuse whatever coercive power they hold or, alternatively, that even if they do not hold or seek coercive power, they will nevertheless 'free ride' on the costly efforts of more willing parties to provide collective security – then there is a case for the prior establishment of the overweening force of the state as the binding framework of the political community. That is to say, if mutual consent does not naturally occur then the political community as a whole must be persuaded or contracted to the belief that the state and its monopoly of force be secured. Yet – in an inescapable paradox of 'legitimate' coercive authority – effective persuasion is only possible if the state is *already* endowed with the power to prevail against abusers or free-riders, using its coercive threat as an ultimate or 'second order' power to secure the requisite general compliance to guarantee the stable 'first order' resources of coercive capacity necessary for the system of effective policing which the community desires but cannot provide for itself.

If this provides a close linkage between the early modern 'nightwatchman state' (Nozick 1974) and the policing or internal security function, as the state has developed and expanded other equally important ties between the state and policing have been forged. The etymology of the term 'police' indicates its origins in the idea of the general government of a polity or political community, and this link has again become palpable as the modern state has expanded its functions. Familiar contemporary labels and themes such as community policing, multi-agency policing and problem-oriented policing testify to the fact that the tasks of modern policing are woven closely into the fabric of the welfare state. As the modern state has assumed responsibility and claimed credit for the broader well-being of its citizens, the functions of the police have come to interlock closely with those of various other services – health, social security, environmental protection, utility supply, etc. – involved in that broader welfare project. With their 24-hour availability and powers of legal coercion the police have both the presence and authority to reinforce these other services not just as reactive 'stand-ins' (Cohen 1985: 28) at the point of delivery but also as proactive players in the planning and co-ordination of both local and central administration. In this sense, policing has shaped and been shaped by the broader framework of multi-functional, co-ordinated regulatory activity we call government and the general container of government power we call the state.

Finally, the link between policing and state is also symbolic. The deep implication of policing in the consolidation of the coercive power of the state and in its sponsorship of an increasingly broad conception of governance, both of which tasks have also been vital to the social legitimacy of the state, has not been without cultural consequences. The close and venerable instrumental links been policing and the state project have provided copious materials through which the two may also be joined at the level of popular consciousness (Walden 1982; Loader 1997; Emsley 2000; Loader and Mulcahy 2003). If national identity is the main medium through which the state is experienced by its citizens as a community of attachment – as common membership of the polity – then policing is of no little significance as a resource through which this 'we feeling' (Deutsch *et al.* 1957: 36) is developed and sustained or, indeed, dissipated or lost. The presence, practice, reputation and iconography of policing have been important in many nation-building exercises and in forms of collective self-understanding which sustain national feeling, just as they have in the divisions and fractures which rupture national identity (Ellison and Smyth 2000). Crucially, as with coercive power and the development of broad governance capacity, the symbolic relationship between policing and the state is a symbiotic one. The state depends on policing's familiar signifiers as one source of common identification and on its reputation before various populations as a mark of their willing and confident belonging to the political community, but reciprocally, and in a mutually reinforcing logic, policing also depends for its legitimacy and efficacy upon levels of trust in and common feeling with anonymous others associated with common citizenship of a state. For without this social and political bond the public resources for policing conceived of as a public good will not be forthcoming and the levels of consent necessary for an effectively informed and acquiesced policing strategy will be absent (Loader and Walker 2001; Walker 2002a).

For all these close ties to the state project, that policing beyond the state exists and is a growing phenomenon is undeniable. In examining the conditions of possibility of this phenomenon, we can distinguish between those tendencies which complement the close link between policing and the state or at least do not directly challenge it, and those tendencies that invite a more radical reappraisal of the state–police coupling.

As to the first set of factors, we can make a further distinction between political factors and professional factors conducive to policing beyond the state (Walker 2000: ch. 8). The political factors concern the need for states to encourage and allow some measure of liaison and co-operation between their police forces and related criminal justice agencies in order to respond to the dangers posed to their capacity to secure order within their own territory by the planning and perpetration of crime on an international scale. In other words, co-operation between states is encouraged on pragmatic grounds to match and to address the forms of co-operation between deviant groups that cause crime to ramify across borders. This pragmatic justification is most straightforward in the area of 'normal' crime, where the security of the state as such is not at issue and where co-operation is facilitated by the fact that the general framework of criminal law shows a striking similarity across states. Yet even with regard to crime such as terrorism which may present a direct challenge to the 'specific order' (Marenin 1982) of the state and where the state is likely to be most jealous of its policing prerogatives and least trustful of the motives of other states, the international context within which such crimes take place and the urgency of the threat they pose may overcome objections to co-operation. Finally, political pragmatism may also have a more strategic edge. The opening up of an international agenda in police co-operation may displace pressure upwards from national governments uncomfortable with insistent domestic pressures for a successful criminal justice policy and may provide a new and less democratically scrutinised arena within which to argue for more resources and increased powers.

At the professional level, there are also strong pragmatic reasons for co-operation, and these track the motivating factors already alluded to at the political level. Yet the thrust towards professional co-operation is perhaps even more dynamic. Police officers typically have a more immediate sense of the urgency of particular avenues of co-operation than do their political masters.

In addition, notwithstanding the national particularity of police institutions, police officers can find a solidarity, trust and empathy with foreign colleagues born of similar working conditions and priories and even of a similar sense of professional isolation within their national milieus. Furthermore, police officers, partly because they work 'in regions of low visibility' (Van Maanen 1974), and partly because their definition of success is not so closely tied to public approbation, do not necessarily share the broader sensitivities of their political colleagues about the ideological fit and public acceptability of transnational initiatives within a state-dominated paradigm of policing. Indeed, taken together, these factors suggest a conclusion that will be borne out in our subsequent historical overview: although there is often eventual convergence of agendas, the initiative in international police co-operation has frequently been a professional one rather than a political one. More forcefully, their greater predisposition towards co-operation at certain points means that police professionals have often ventured into domains of co-operation where their political masters would not, or at least not so boldly, dare to tread. One recent analysis, indeed, takes the argument about the possible gap between the professional and political worldview a stage further. It ties the emergence of systematic forms of international police co-operation in the nineteenth and early twentieth centuries precisely to the growing institutional autonomy of national police organisations from the political centre of the state, and to the development of a common transnational organisational interest in the fight against international crime which escapes the more cautious prism of general state interests (Deflem 2002: 21–22).

What of these tendencies in transnational policing which involve a more radical reappraisal of the state–policing coupling? Here we are primarily concerned with the way in which in a world of increasing globalisation of economic activity, communications media, cultural influences and forms of political organisation (Held *et al.* 1999), we may observe the emergence of post-state polities which begin to claim authority of a type traditionally associated with state sovereignty (Walker 2002b). As noted in the introduction, the shift has been most profound, and with most significant consequences for policing, in the context of the EU. Here, as we shall see, the political logic of police co-operation is increasingly that of a distinct political community with autonomous capacity, authority and allegiance, even though this logic continues to compete in highly complex ways with a more traditional statist conception of co-operation both within the EU itself and in its relations with other polities. Before we discuss this novel complexity, however, we need to attend to the earlier history of police co-operation.

The growth of transnational policing

Origins and consolidation

The earliest attempts to institutionalise transnational policing involved a series of initiatives among European states in the second half of the nineteenth century to combat what were seen as political threats to the established state autocracies or oligarchies (Deflem 2002: ch. 1). The so-called 'year of revolution' of 1848 provided the impetus for a number of measures aimed at securing the existing political order against a wide range of destabilising political influences, influences which tended to be framed under the conveniently pathologising label 'anarchist' but which in fact covered a wide range of liberal, socialist and nationalist movements. Some of these policing initiatives were bilateral and others multilateral; some were more or less openly institutionalised and others clandestine; some were properly international and others, notably the Police Union of German States of 1851–66, tracked close patterns of political interconnection in a manner which anticipated Europe's much more intense integration project a century later.

The emergence of a similar framework of police organisation in many European states facilitated the co-ordination of these initiatives. Yet that same common bureaucratic development, together with the growth of a sense of a common foundation of professional police knowledge in matters such as criminology and investigation techniques and an increasing appreciation of the contribution of communications and transportation systems to a nascent 'world society' (Deflem 2002: 78) in which transnational criminal opportunities were expanded, also provided the context within which police-led initiatives in operational co-operation concerning ordinary crime became possible. As Fijnaut has argued, slowly but surely there developed a professional 'fraternity which felt it had a moral purpose, a mission to perform for the good of society' (1997: 111). This was no smooth progression, but an untidy accumulation of tentative beginnings and false starts against a backdrop of fragile and fluid international political allegiances and the threat of war and its massive disruption of the general framework of transnational co-operation. Indeed, it was not until after the First World War that the first permanent international agency – the International Criminal Police Commission (ICPC) – provided a general template for international police co-operation. Established in Vienna in 1923, while the ICPC would have been impossible without the prior and complementary establishment of the League of Nations as a more general institutional framework for the international political community, it was nevertheless a professional rather than a political initiative. Both the ICPC and its post-Second World War institutional successor, the French-based International Criminal Police Office (ICPO) – or Interpol as it soon became known – supplied a communications exchange for the participating national police forces as well as providing a 'policeman's club' (Anderson 1989: 43) in which senior officers could nurture professional and social contacts with international colleagues. These organisations were conspicuous in their lack of formal foundations in international law, and with the striking exception of the Nazi takeover of the ICPC in 1938, governmental involvement remained marginal and low key.

The contemporary scenario of transnational policing has seen Interpol expand its activities significantly. Its membership, originally 19, has grown tenfold. In recent years it has begun to regularise its position in international law, it has exploited developments in information technology to increase the flow and quality of its information exchanges through its system of national central bureaus, and it has rationalised its organisational structure to provide a separate European unit. Yet in many ways it remains the paradigm case of a *inter*national police organisation and is limited by the constraints inherent in internationalism. It has never challenged the statist prerogative in police operations and lacks the legal, symbolic and material resources to be anything other than parasitic on national police authorities. Partly because of these restrictions, but also because of a more general expansion in the network of transnational policing relations, it is no longer the dominant actor on the scene.

Two developments over the last 30 years have had a particular impact in this regard. To begin with, there has been a marked internationalisation of US law enforcement activity (Nadelman 1993). Although the USA has always been a player on the international policing stage, often it was a reluctant or peripheral presence. Its geographical distance from the main European stage, the more general legacy of isolationism from its revolutionary beginnings and the fragmented nature of its internal law enforcement design and the attendant difficulties of identifying the most appropriate and legitimate representatives of federal policing interests, all contributed to this. However, particularly since the eruption of international traffic in narcotics in the 1960s and 1970s and President Nixon's declaration of a 'war on drugs', there has been a sharp increase in activity, much of it outside the framework of Interpol. Instead, internationalisation has tended to take the form of the increased concentration of resources on international activities dealing with drugs, internal revenue, organised crime, immigration, etc., including the widespread placement of liaison officers, training units and other support agencies in embassies and law enforcement institutions abroad. In turn, as we shall see below, the end of the Cold War has led to a more pronounced internationalisation of the internal security agenda and, indeed, a blurring of the boundaries between internal and external security. September 11th may have led to a marked consolidation and further intensification of much of this activity, but it is important to appreciate the significance of the structures and attitudes in place even before that seismic event.

The other major development of the past 30 years has been in the policing capacity of the EU, and it is to this that we now turn.

The European Union

The EU may today be hosting the most audacious and potentially far-reaching experiment in transnational policing, but the beginnings of its law enforcement capacity, too, were, inauspicious (Anderson *et al.* 1995: chs 1–2; Denza 2002: ch. 3). While the Pompidou Group had earlier inaugurated policy-level collaboration in the area of drug-trafficking, the Trevi organisation did not provide the first major initiative in the policing field until 1975, a full 18 years after the Treaty of Rome established the supranational initiative which was eventually to become the EU. From its earliest years, aided and abetted by a precociously self-assertive approach by its main judicial organ, the European Court of Justice, the European Communities (as they then were) had carved out an original constitutional niche at an intermediate point between the two traditional Westphalian poles of statehood and international organisation (Weiler 1999: ch. 2). The new supranational entity did not itself aspire to statehood, and in particular its *political* organs remained either weakly democratically legitimated (in particular the Assembly, later to become the Parliament, was originally only indirectly elected, maintained a very low public profile and had few powers of policy-making or policy intervention, while the more powerful Commission, as permanent executive, was merely an appointed body) or, as in the case of the Council, which comprised national executives with veto powers, continued to be dominated by the member states themselves. At the same time, however, through the development of constitutional doctrines of supremacy and direct effect and through an expansive interpretation of their own jurisdiction, the new European Communities – with the European Court of Justice in the vanguard – began to make *legal* claims which in many ways were reminiscent of the state.

Yet policing and criminal justice policy were for a long time not powered by the main engine of legal integration. Certainly, there was an expansion of co-operative activity in parallel with the deepening and widening of the core areas of the community law. Trevi grew from its beginnings in the area of counter-terrorism to cover drugs, organised crime, police training and technology and a range of other matters, and its activities were given a further significant boost with the launch of the Commission's '1992' Single Market Programme after 1985 – a programme which in its explicit aspiration to remove internal border controls over persons, goods and services ushered in the possibility of a new 'security deficit'. The supposed security deficit consequent upon the liberalisation of internal controls was also the catalyst for the other major European criminal justice initiative of that time, namely the Schengen system. The original Schengen Agreement of 1985 covered a core of five member states who committed themselves to a pre-emptive initiative in abolishing border controls. Aided by a later Implementation Agreement of 1990 the Schengen idea gradually expanded to cover all the EU member states with the exception of the island-members, Britain and Ireland, who refused to dismantle their sea and air border controls, and even came to embrace two non-EU members of the Nordic Passport Union – Norway and Iceland. When after various false dawns it eventually became operational in 1995, the Strasbourg-based Schengen organisation incorporated a number of compensatory law enforcement measures, including the computerised Schengen Information System and police co-operation both in the exchange of information and intelligence and through a raft of more concrete operational measures – including 'hot pursuit' across borders, cross-border observation and controlled delivery of illegal substances (Den Boer 2000). But in the final analysis, both Trevi and Schengen remained strictly outside the community structure. For all the political salience of its areas of interest, Trevi was no more than a forum for policy discussion and information exchange, one that operated in the shadow of the supranational legal structure. Schengen had a more elaborate and more entrenched institutional system and, unlike Trevi, could boast a formal legal basis, but again it was quite distinctive from the legal organisation of the European Communities.

Only with the passing of the Maastricht Treaty of 1992 establishing the EU was police co-operation formally integrated into the supranational structure, but even then the legacy of political ambivalence and policy lag continued to show its trace. Police co-operation was located in a new 'Third Pillar' of Justice and Home Affairs alongside criminal justice co-operation, civil jurisdictional matters and immigration, asylum and visa policy (Peers 2000: ch. 2). In this way, it was kept quite distinct from the traditional 'First Pillar' of common market measures (which itself increasingly embraced flanking social measures such as environmental policy, cultural policy and employment policy) as indeed it also was from the new 'Second Pillar' of Common Foreign and Security Policy. Each of the pillars retained its own distinctive institutional methodology, and the single most important differentiating factor between the First Pillar on the one hand and the Second and Third on the other remained the extent to which real policy and implementation power passed from national to supranational authorities. So within the Third Pillar, the member states retained important powers of initiative and control over policy-making; the measures themselves tended to be 'soft' rather than 'hard' – facilitative rather than compulsory – and did not penetrate the national legal systems sufficiently to confer direct rights and obligations on individuals; implementation was controlled by national actors operating through the Council rather than the more supranational Commission; the European Court of Justice was largely excluded from supervising the legality of policy activity and implementation; and other European institutions, such as the Parliament and the new European Ombudsman, were also largely excluded from a supervisory role vis-à-vis the new operational agencies (Walker 2003a).

Nevertheless, the Maastricht Third Pillar was much more than a token initiative. Beneath the Council of Justice and Home Affairs Ministers an elaborate policy-making and policy-implementing structure of steering groups and working parties was established, including a number relating to policing. The most important initiative, however, was the creation of the legal basis for the establishment of Europol as a central organisation in a network of relationships with national units in each member state – which in the case of the UK was the recently established National Criminal Intelligence Service (see Chapter 18). The working premise of Europol was that the central organisation would supply the national units with criminal intelligence and analysis and would receive from them information on themes and issues connected with certain forms of transnational crime. This, together with the integrated policy structure and a novel facility to develop supporting legislative measures in criminal justice co-operation gave a pronounced new impetus to police co-operation.

Yet when the next wave of treaty reform beckoned at Amsterdam in 1997 one of the few matters on which there appeared a broad European consensus was that the Third Pillar initiatives, including the policing measures, had disappointed expectations (Peers 2000: ch. 3; Denza 2002: ch. 5). They were criticised, on the one hand, for their slow and inefficient progress and, on the other, for their opaqueness and lack of accountability. In what has been a recurring theme in the justice and home affairs sphere, the national jealousies which prevented the forging of a fully fledged supranational capacity tended to lead both to a cumbersome and frustrating progression of policy initiatives – with the requirement of unanimity often blocking progress at the behest of the most reluctant member state – and to impede the kinds and degrees of empowerment of European political organs (such as the Parliament and the Court of Justice) in a monitoring capacity that was required to match the scale and scope of the new Europe-wide legislative and executive security function.

Most pertinently, notwithstanding its high-profile conception at Maastricht, Europol itself had a difficult and protracted birth. The German government argued for its early negotiation, but in fact initial progress was tentative, leading only to the creation of a precursor organisation – the Europol Drugs Unit – in 1993. The legal Convention for Europol itself, the draft of which remained within the control of the member states in the Council with the European Parliament not consulted, was not signed until 1995, and the organisation did not become fully operational at its in The Hague head-quarters until 1999. Many factors contributed to its delay but, tellingly, they included arguments over the range of crimes covered by its mandate – going to the question of its efficiency and viable capacity – and unease as to the adequacy of its data protection system and the extent of jurisdiction of the European Court of Justice – going to the question of the sufficiency of its political and legal accountability.

Indeed, by the time Europol was fully operational, with a broad remit to cover all crimes with an 'organised criminal structure', its underlying constitutional basis had already been much revised by the Amsterdam Treaty. This treaty, which remains the main constitutional fundamental of the present EU policing capacity, gave voice to the dissatisfaction of its sponsors and introduced radical changes to the Maastricht framework. Visa, asylum, immigration and other policies related to the free movement of persons were transferred from the Third to the First Pillar, while even in the residual Third Pillar dealing with police and judicial co-operation there has been a move towards a more supranational institutional methodology. The right of initiative is now shared by the Commission and member states, the measures to be used are more formal and better suited to the articulation of stable and authoritative legislative norms as opposed to ad hoc agreements, there is a modest increase in the consultative powers of the European Parliament, and there is clearer recognition of the adjudicatory powers of the European Court of Justice – although this is still limited and uneven and the court is specifically prohibited from ruling on the validity and proportionality of the operations of domestic police forces and other law enforcement agencies, or on the exercise by member states of their responsibilities with regard to the preservation of law and order and internal security.

More specifically, policing competence is extended to embrace operational co-operation between the competent authorities, including the police, customs and other specialised law enforcement services of the member states. Consistent with this new general constitutional permission, Europol is provided with the legal basis to acquire a range of new functions, including the authority to establish joint operational teams to support national investigations, the power to ask the competent authorities of the member states to conduct and co-ordinate investigations in specific cases, the capacity to develop specific expertise which may be put at the disposal of member states to assist them in investigating organised crime, and the facility to promote liaison arrangements between prosecuting or investigating officials specialising in the fight against

organised crime. And alongside these marked increases in policing competence, the Amsterdam Treaty significantly strengthens the capacity to develop
common measures for harmonisation of both substantive and procedural
criminal law and to facilitate co-operation between criminal justice agencies,
as well as incorporating the Schengen arrangements into the new Area of
Freedom, Security and Justice (see below), and distributing them across the
First and Third Pillars.

The significance of Amsterdam, however, cannot be seen merely in
aggregation of new increments in competence and institutional capacity.
Amsterdam also marked a shift in the macro-political climate. Internal security,
it seemed, was no longer to be treated as the poor cousin of European
integration, never able to keep up with its rich relatives, but rather as its
precocious child, one who had made remarkable progress in a very short
period of time and who was ready to treated as a mature member of the
European family. Indeed, to extend the metaphor, in some regards at least,
internal security could be seen to be vying for the mantle of head of the family.
While the Amsterdam Treaty split the old Justice and Home Affairs sector
between two pillars, it also reunited them under one single policy label, namely
'the establishment of an Area of Freedom, Security and Justice'. This label, for
some at least, was seen as a key mobilising project for the union as it entered
the twenty-first century. By the late 1990s, Freedom, Security and Justice was
already the busiest area of policy according to indices such as Council meetings
held and measures proposed (Den Boer and Wallace 2000: 503). At Tampere,
Finland, in October 1999, the European Council – the thrice-yearly meeting of
the Heads of State of the European Union – took the unprecedented step of
focusing their meeting on one single theme, and the development of the Area of
Freedom, Security and Justice provided that theme. The meeting itself sought
to kick start the post-Amsterdam agenda, and in the area of police co-operation
it signalled various other initiatives which were to come to fruition in due
course, including a European Police Chiefs Operational Task Force, a new
European Police College and the launching of Eurojust (composed of prosecutor and magistrates from each member state) as a body which would
complement at the level of judicial investigation the co-ordination and
information-sharing activities of Europol at the operational level.

Again, as with North American law enforcement, the events of 11 September
2001 have given yet additional impetus to the new Area of Freedom, Security
and Justice, but before we examine the effects of this new ingredient in the
mix, let us look more closely at the factors which accounted for the remarkable
growth of European police co-operation until that point.

Explaining recent patterns

In examining the conditions of possibility of transnational policing above we
have already sketched the main explanatory contours of present developments. Beyond the EU domain, the early mix of political and professional
initiatives, the growth and consolidation of ICPC and Interpol and the
late-century surge in North American international activities can all be

explained within the classic parameters of the statist model. We see both the incentives and the limitations to bilateral and multilateral co-operation at the political level, particularly in those areas of 'high' or political policing where the very national interest that makes co-operation crucial also sets limits to that co-operation. We see the importance of professional, practically motivated initiatives, and they have often been in the vanguard of developments where there is an absence of political initiative or even endorsement. We see the development of a strong US capacity in international policing shadowing their more interventionist foreign policy generally in both Cold War and post-Cold War eras. In a globalising world, the USA increasingly responded to the interconnectedness of its economic and political stability with external forces in a proactive manner, and policing was necessarily part of that policy thrust.

But what of the EU? As was said above, it is not plausible to explain the nature and extent of common police activity in its regional setting purely in terms of a statist logic. Certainly, statist thinking played it parts in Trevi and in the original Maastricht settlement, and even after Amsterdam a significant part of the support for police co-operation, especially among the more Euro-sceptic states such as the UK, can be explained in these terms. Nor should we underestimate the importance of professional interests and ideologies. The fact that there is now a permanent Third Pillar bureaucracy under the aegis of the Council, as well as permanent agencies such as Europol and Eurojust, provides an institutional context that amplifies the common interests and sympathies which are at the root of professional co-operation and also creates a new set of vested interests in the consolidation and extension of the very structures and agencies created (Bigo 2000a). However, if only statist political and professional interests were in play, it would be difficult to imagine that a more powerful brake would not have been put on the expansion of policing capacity. Other factors are at work that concern the logic of the political development of the EU itself, and its acquisition of state-like tendencies.

What are these factors? In general terms, we may identify three sets of forces – and three sets of arguments underpinning or rationalising these forces – which contribute to a more distinctive EU dynamic in this area, each of which draws upon one of the rationales linking policing to the state – security, governance and symbolic association (Walker 2000: ch. 8). In addition, these three sets of forces and attendant discourses are in some respects mutually reinforcing.

In the first place, there is the prevalence of a new internal security discourse, one that bears a family resemblance to the traditional security rationale linking policing to the state. The new Area of Freedom, Security and Justice is a telling indication of the maturing of a project which conceives of the EU as a self-standing 'security community' (Adler and Barnett 1998) – even if the relative underdevelopment of the Common Foreign and Security Policy and its high-profile shortcomings in crises such as Kosovo and the Iraq War demonstrate that the external dimension of this project remains seriously underdeveloped in comparison to the state archetype. But to concentrate on the internal dimension, this is premised upon the identification of a range of interests among the peoples and polities of western and central Europe which are increasingly presented as interests held in common rather than merely concurring or overlapping, and also upon the perception of a series of threats to these common interests and of the appropriate security responses to these threats.

There are significant economic and political factors underpinning this matrix of rhetoric, belief and action. The healthy economic prosperity of the EU in the post-Cold War era stands in stark contrast to the insecurity and poverty of the polities to its south and east. The present wave of central European and Mediterranean enlargement which promises to increase the EU from 15 to 27 or 28 by 2007 might seem to have addressed some of these problems, but extending the borders does not resolve the question of the relationship to the 'outside' and, indeed, the strict conditions and delayed rewards of new membership (including, tellingly, in the area of internal security, where trust appears to be in particularly short supply – Walker 2002c) threaten to create a two-tier structure inside the union.

The use of a rhetoric of security with its connotations of urgent threat has provided western European political elites with a conveniently reductionist way of viewing the complex of problems associated with these questions of economic advantage and political pedigree. The security metaphor allows core anxieties associated with the prospect of sharing the privileged European space with outsiders to connect with more specific concerns about the development of criminal organisational links across internal and external borders. In this vein, Bigo has argued that the emergence of an 'internal security ideology' around the institutional edifice of the Area of Freedom, Security and Justice has allowed a number of issues ranging from immigration and asylum and terrorism, organised crime and public order to be located along a single 'security continuum' (Bigo 1994: 164) and treated to a one-dimensional securitised response. When what is projected to be at stake is the security of the western European 'way of life' itself, the argument for the development of a coercive apparatus becomes highly persuasive. Recalling the discussion of the logic of security earlier, we may note that the EU seems to be in the process of severing the Hobbesian connection between the ultimate coercive power of the polity and the capacity of the polity to bind its citizens to a system of compulsory policing. The EU may lack the 'second order' power of the ultimate means of violence, instead still relying on the member states themselves to provide this, but is nevertheless developing a 'first order' policing power which, though historically derived from the states, increasingly possesses an independent momentum and a self-referential authority. The internal security discourse is both a reflection and a reinforcing cause of this growing autonomous power.

A second discourse which contributes to the deepening of the EU internal security capacity, albeit in a much lower key, is that of functional spillover (Lindberg 1963). Since its inception, a key argument associated with the extension of the European project into new domains has been that the development of a programme of intervention in one sector prompts adjustments in related policy sectors, either to secure optimisation in the original sector or to prevent perverse effects in the other sectors. The development of a competence in internal security matters is no exception to this trend. Just as the development of common anti-discrimination and environmental measures are justified, at least in some measure, by the need to ensure that the common market is not distorted by unequal socially responsive side-constraints in different national sectors, so too the development of a competence in Justice and Home Affairs was justified, at least in some measure, by the need to ensure that the opening of borders did not have inordinate consequences in terms of the increase in security risks.

As we have seen, this reasoning provided a significant impetus for the growth of an internal security capacity during the '1992' programme of the pre-Maastricht phase. More generally, functionalist thinking can be seen to resonate very closely with the governance logic associated with state policing. Not only does the prevalence of functionalist thinking help to explain how the EU came to develop a security competence but it also aids our understanding of how policing and related security matters are becoming more deeply embedded within the structure of a multisectoral post-state polity just as they embedded themselves within the structure of the multisectoral state. For wherever a polity develops a broad competence to govern, there is a continuous spillover into the police sector from the range of other 'governed' social activities. To take but two examples from the very recent history of the EU, the introduction of the euro currency in 2002 brought in its wake problems associated with its counterfeiting, and so the argument was successfully made that the combating of this freshly minted economic crime should be added to the functions of Europol. Similarly, the development of EU thrice-yearly councils as high-profile political occasions and, as such, attracting high-profile demonstrations by civil society groups opposed to their political and economic programmes – a trend which reached an early peak in 2001 in Copenhagen and which was part of a broader momentum of anti-globalisation protests at major political occasions, most notoriously at the G7 meeting in Genoa in the same year – provided the impetus for the new European Police Chiefs Operational Task Force initiative in developing a co-ordinated public-order policing capacity at major summits (Bunyan 2003).

Inasmuch as they suggest a compelling relationship between cause and effect, action and reaction, functional arguments for the growth and consolidation of a polity are clearly flawed. Yet precisely because they present matters of political choice as natural or predetermined, functionalist arguments are popular and persuasive within the EU, appealing to a bureaucratic conception of policy and a technocratic conception of policing as tasks insulated from and sustained and nurtured regardless of the broader vicissitudes of political life.

A final discourse affecting the development of a EU policing capacity, one which resonates with the general symbolic dimension linking police and state, is the macro-political discourse of European integration itself. With its citizenship provisions introduced at Maastricht, its new Charter of Fundamental Rights proclaimed in 2000, its grand Constitutional Convention chaired by Valery Giscard D'Estaing in 2002–3, and with its flags, anthems and annual 'Europe day', Europe has become an explicit project in polity-building in recent years (Walker 2003b). Of course this project is challenged by Euro-sceptic voices. Yet we should not underestimate the extent of self-conscious polity-building, not only through these direct symbolic acts but also in the development of particular policy sectors, even in areas, such as policing, where one would expect the forces of statist resistance to supranational ambition to be most resilient. For instance, it is noteworthy that the crucial foundational Third Pillar measures were planned and perpetrated at the high point of institutional self-confidence in the early 1990s, following the success of the Commission in bringing the 1992 project to fruition. In particular, German Chancellor Kohl's initial proposal for Europol in 1991 was well attuned to the political mood, an audacious statement of intent by the increasingly dominant and most explicitly integrationist member state. It was meant, and partly succeeded, as a sign of political virility, chosen and highlighted precisely *because* it challenged one of the traditional areas of state hegemony. Similarly, the priority given to the Area of Freedom, Security and Justice is not just about the pursuit of a vigorous securitisation approach within a particular policy sector, but again a massive statement of symbolic intent. If the idea of the state is about the coincidence of territory, population and authority, then the prioritisation of an explicitly territorialised conception of security conveys a powerful message about the ambitions of the EU as a 'state-*like*' entity, even if not a full-blown state.

More generally, the emphasis on the internal security area speaks eloquently not only to the authority claims of the new polity but also to its identity claims. Recall that policing in the state tradition connects to the formation of political community through the prism of national identity. In order to secure its broader legitimacy the project of polity-building at the European level must also be concerned with issues of identity, and must address the oft-voiced concern that the EU lacks the symbols and vehicles of identity formation – common language, shared sense of historical origins, etc. – which are so central to the 'imagined community' (Anderson 1983) of the state. In the absence of these features, and given the fears of political and economic instability noted earlier, the idea of a security community may acquire a particularly vital cultural dimension. A strong security element within the politics of the EU dramatises what Europeans have in common, even if it is an identity which tends to emphasise what Europe is *not* – the 'other' beyond the borders – rather than its positive features.

Current trends and future prospects

In this final section, we examine three trends in the configuration of transnational policing and then seek to draw a few modest conclusions as to future prospects. Two of these trends, the rise of the EU as an autonomous force and the development of the USA, draw upon on the arguments and analysis set out in the course of the chapter. The other trend, and the first we consider, introduces a new theme, but links it to some of the broader trends in globalisation we have discussed above.

Transnational private policing

Over the last ten years policing studies has at last caught up with the fact that private forms of policing are outstripping public forms in terms of numbers and resources, if not yet perhaps significance and, indeed, have done so for some time. The reasons for this are too familiar to repeat at length; suffice to say that they are related to the fiscal crisis of the social democratic state and its general decentring as the dominant societal steering mechanism, the increased acceptance of cultural and interest pluralism which cuts across territorially defined populations, the rise of 'mass private property' (Shearing and Stenning 1983) which shares many of the same priorities – and problems – as public space, the post-Fordist move away from the large-scale top-down bureaucracy as the paradigm form of social organisation, and a consequent and reinforcing cultural normalisation of private or 'club' (Hope 2000) solutions to questions of security (Jones and Newburn 1998). It would be surprising if this shift did not also impact upon transnational policing, especially since many of the factors which underpin privatisation also underpin transnationalisation (see Chapter 7).

In particular, and running through all the discrete factors named above, the gradual decoupling of territory and population in the structure of our contemporary political forms finds its specific manifestation in policing in the growing distinction between the policing of territory and the policing of 'suspect populations' (Ericson 1994; Sheptycki 2002). Where once the paradigmatic policing sponsor was the state and the paradigmatic object of policing was the territorial citizenry in general, increasingly we see a shift either in the sponsor or object of policing – and often in both – from the territorially general to the non-territorial particular. Much of transnational policing, then, makes sense in terms of the relocation of the particular (sponsor or object, or both) beyond the confines of the state boundary. Where the state or the post-state polity is still the sponsor, this often still takes a public form, as we have seen in the concentration upon particular territorially indistinct populations (drug-traffickers, terrorists, anti-globalisation protesters, irregular migrants, etc.) in EU policing, or indeed in contemporary US policing. Yet, this new particularism often manifests itself in the extension of private forms of security beyond the state, with particular interests or particular forms of expertise that are not commonly found in general police organisations engaged in specific forms of security surveillance or enforcement against limited populations. This trend can be seen, for example, in the corporate security guards of transnational companies, in the involvement of private agents in matters of state security abroad where the interests of 'high politics' and private finance intersect (as in industrial espionage and counter-espionage), and in the employment of specialised private security guards to contain irregular immigrants in secure zones while they await the processing of their cases (Johnston, 2000; Sheptycki 2002: 329–34). It is, of course, difficult to quantify such a diverse, fragmented and sometimes clandestine range of security activities, but such evidence as exists dovetails with our understanding of the nature of the underlying forces at work to suggest that this is very much a growing sector of transnational policing.

The European Union

Earlier we explained how Amsterdam in 1997 and Tampere in 1999 had given a significant boost to police and criminal justice co-operation in the EU, and how a diverse array of powerful professional and political motivations underpinned these developments. Present trends suggest that these dynamics have gained in strength. The new treaty capacities of Europol to take initiatives that will be implemented by national units and to establish joint investigation teams are now successfully enshrined in legislative instruments. The events of 11 September have added to the momentum of the internal security dynamic, and have spawned a number of new initiatives (Bunyan 2003; Gilmore 2003). A task force has been created within Europol for the fight against terrorism and, independently of Europol, multinational ad hoc teams for gathering and exchanging information on terrorists have been set up, while co-ordination meetings and multinational teams to combat and destabilise suspected terrorist groups have also been formed under the aegis of a new framework of EU security and intelligence chiefs. Measures have been passed allowing both for a common list of terrorist organisations and for the approximation of laws against terrorism in the member states; unlike many European First Pillar measures which aim at minimum or 'lowest common denominator' har- monisation, the logic of the approximation instrument seems to be one of maximum harmonisation, with both of the staple components of the definition of terrorism – the 'violence' used and the 'political ends' sought – defined in a very inclusive manner to include theft and property destruction under the first head and a wide range of forms of destabilisation, intimidation and compulsion or frustration of the acts of governments and international organisations under the second head. The classic internationalist instrument of extradition has been all but extinguished within the EU due to the creation of a common arrest warrant which will dispense with most of the national judicial protections associated with the former instrument, most strikingly the principle of double criminality, and so will greatly facilitate the transnational transfer of the accused person (Gilmore 2003). And Europol's younger sibling – Eurojust – has now achieved formal legal status following the Treaty of Nice in 2001 and a series of implementing instruments. Many other developments that expand the network of EU security agencies have also been established or are in the pipeline. The Police Chiefs Operational Task Force, which has an important role in the co-ordination of anti-terrorist and public order policing beyond the confines of Europol, has already been mentioned, and other initiatives which are under serious and sustained consideration include a common European Border Guard and a European Public Prosecutor (Den Boer 2003).

It is difficult to discern an overall pattern in this renewed acceleration of activity, but three trends may be identified which allow us to observe a qualitative shift in the kaleidoscope of new measures and agencies of European police co-operation. In the first place, the anti-terrorist theme has taken centre-stage since 11 September, justifying not only various specific initiatives in the anti-terrorist field but also providing a pretext for the intensification of various other measures, as with the European arrest warrant which covers 32 offences – most of them unconnected with terrorism. Historically, anti-terrorism has been perhaps the most ambivalent theme in transnational police co-operation, the site at which the respective logics of a traditional international approach and a more pervasive transnational ap- proach most directly clash. Because of the gravity of the threat posed, terrorism has often been the catalyst for co-operation, as in some of the early forms of international co-operation in the late nineteenth century and in the development of the Trevi forum. Yet the close connection of terrorism with the specific order of the state has meant that such co-operation has often remained highly contingent on particular circumstances where national interests over-lap, and conditional on the retention of national prerogatives. For instance, despite its important place in the foundations of European police co-operation, terrorism was not included in the first wave of crimes falling within the settled remit of Europol, even if it was soon added. With 11 September, terrorism now seems to be at the centre of the EU's permanent internal security capacity, the urgency of the threat having largely eclipsed national sovereignties' concerns. This may, of course, be revised again in due course, but unless and until it is, it provides a more powerful engine for integration than many of the more prosaic themes of transnational police co-operation.

The other two recent developments are more subtle, but perhaps of equal long-term significance. Secondly, then, although neither Europol nor any of the other transnational agencies have independent powers of legal execution (arrest, search etc.), increasing involvement post-Amsterdam in operational matters and increasing control over operational information are shifting the power balance significantly between transnational and national operational units. The possession of direct legal powers of coercion over the individual citizen has traditionally been seen as a key preserve of sovereign statehood, a non-negotiable dimension of the state's Hobbesian compact with its popula-tion and a guarantee that any transnational police facility will remain in the service of national needs and capacities. Yet the shift in informational and operational resources upwards to the European level, particularly as advanced information technology is peculiarly suited to the proactive styles of policing developed to combat the dispersed security threats targeted within the supranational environment, suggests that executive powers may have become a somewhat outmoded index of control, and may obscure a real transfer of authority to the supranational level.

Thirdly, the field of European police co-operation is increasingly implicated in a broader system of criminal justice co-operation. Earlier, we talked of the importance of functionalist thinking in European integration, but in the first phase of Third Pillar activity, the major point of reference for functionalist extension remained the First Pillar. Put crudely, the First Pillar acted and the Third Pillar reacted. While elements of this relationship remain, the advent of Eurojust, the intensification of harmonisation of substantive and procedural criminal law, and the proposals for a European Public Prosecutor and a European Border Guard speak to the development of an autonomous systemic logic within the security field. Developments in one piece of the security jigsaw tend to support the case for the preparation of another piece. Police co-operation became a feasible proposition against a background of reasonable approximation of substantive and procedural criminal law, and the degree of common purpose and mutual trust this allowed. In turn, the consolidation of police co-operation has provided a favourable empirical backdrop against which the case for greater integration of capacities of judicial investigation and prosecution may be made and, subsequently, we may expect such greater co-ordination at the prosecutorial level to provide an argument for yet more police co-operation. Like all functionalist thinking, the logic of this approach may well be flawed, may present as natural and inevitable that which is often highly contestable, but there is no denying its influence none the less.

Amid the rapid expansion of Third Pillar capacities and agencies and the qualitative shift in the intensity of co-operation this heralds, the current Constitutional Convention might have been expected to provide an opportunity for more considered political reflection on the direction of the Area of Freedom, Security and Justice. In this regard, however, it has demonstrated a somewhat paradoxical character. On the one hand (Convention on the Future of Europe 2002; Walker 2003a), there has been some concern expressed about the proliferation of agencies, powers and activities, and about the lack of adequate mechanisms for accountability for this burgeoning domain. On the other hand, the Constitutional Convention has itself provided another opportunity for the pursuit of the various underlying rationales which have driven the Area of Freedom, Security and Justice so far so quickly. Much of the debate over security matters in the convention has been concerned with the inadequacy of existing instruments to achieve security objectives after 11 September, and this has dovetailed with the strong supranationalist concern to assimilate the various instruments and law-making procedures of the Third Pillar to those of the First Pillar on the one hand, and to ensure that operational co-ordination is firmly co-ordinated within an autonomous European bureaucracy on the other. The outcome will remain unclear until the present process of constitutional reform runs its course with the conclusions of the Intergovernmental Conference in the latter part of 2004, but there is a strong possibility that policing and security will emerge significantly strengthened in terms of capacity and jurisdiction, the ease with which measures may be passed and the extent to which their oper-ationalisation may be co-ordinated independently of the states. This may be accompanied by some improvement of accountability to European institutions, including the European Court of Justice and the European Parliament, but the danger remains that a combination of residual statist ambivalence about strengthening these central institutions, the greater urgency in a climate of increased security fears of the need to ensure 'effectiveness' over the demands of accountability, and the genuine constitutional difficulties of supervising an unparalleled concentration of executive and operational authority in the transnational domain (alongside a similar, but constitutionally more familiar increase in legislative authority) will lead to a highly unbalanced solution.

The USA

One dimension of the EU internal security capacity not yet discussed has been its fast-developing external dimension, its extension to cover co-operative relations with other global regions. Until recently, the major focus of this effort was eastwards, both in preparing the enlargement countries for accession, and in managing relations with those countries situated on or beyond what one former EU ambassador to Moscow termed the 'arc of instability' (*The Economist*, 7 November 1998) from Russia, through the Ukraine, the Balkans and Turkey into the south and eastern Mediterranean – embracing those countries which will provide the new external border post-enlargement and other countries further east and south, which, as suppliers of illegal drugs and immigrants, are perceived to be important sources of Europe's security problem. By comparison, relations with the USA were slow to develop, but received a significant stimulus after 11 September. The tone was set by an early joint statement against terrorism just nine days after the Twin Towers attack, an extraordinary European Council meeting the following day to develop a fuller response and George Bush's open letter to the EU of 16 October containing 47 separate requests for co-operation against terrorism. Many of these initiatives bore fruit in an extensive co-operation agreement signed at Copenhagen in December 2002 (Bunyan 2003). Among other matters, this provides for more intensive co-operation at the level of the exchange of personal data (despite American data protection standards being much lower than EU standards), development of the role of European liaison officers in Washington to include direct co-operation with specific US agencies such as the FBI and the Drug Enforcement Administration (DEA) on intelligence matters and investigative methods, US representation on EU Third Pillar working parties and committees, and greater controls by US officials over the entry of EU persons and goods.

There has been considerable criticism of some of these developments as representing a one-sided US agenda in which EU concerns and priorities are given short shrift (Bunyan 2003). Yet this new form of collaboration is only one component of a new approach to internal security in the USA, which, as noted earlier, was already well developed before 11 September. There has been much talk by security scholars in recent years of the merging of internal and external security agendas (Anderson *et al.* 1995: ch. 6; Bigo 2000b). While in the European domain, it is perhaps more accurate to talk about the transnational extension of the internal security agenda to the boundaries of the EU, with external security matters still primarily controlled by the state, in the USA, by contrast, where jurisdictions over internal and external security are both still coterminous with the sovereign state, the metaphor of merger is more apt (Andreas and Price 2001). In the post-Cold War era we have seen a significant reconfiguration of US security strategy in response to the end of bipolarity. Security threats, and security resources, can no longer be easily compartmentalised into the domestic and the global, with police and military the dominant players in their respective domains. Instead, these threats are perceived as more fluid and more variegated, requiring new security rationales and operational methodologies, but still drawing upon old institutions and rhetorics. So, in a pervasive militarisation of security rhetoric, organised crime has been variously named the 'new Evil Empire' (Raine and Cilluffo 1994) and 'the new communism' (Naylor 1995) and security policy in many domains, particularly Latin America and the Caribbean, is now mainly driven by drugs control, illegal immigration and other issues of law enforcement. Alongside this shift in rhetoric and in priorities we see significant technological change in the conversion of military hardware for police missions, and organisational change in increased linkages and overlaps between police and intelligence communities. This is particularly evident in the creation by the Department of Justice of the Executive Office for National Security and the development of the Special Task Force on Law Enforcement/Intelligence Overseas, and in the increasing deployment of the military in 'military operations other than war' (MOOTW) which owe as much to policing as to traditional soldiering in their methods and objectives (Andreas and Price 2001).

To some extent, 11 September may be seen as a reversion to the tradition of the 'warfare state' (Andreas and Price 2001: 36) with the explicit remilitarisation involved in the 'war against terrorism'. But this, like the slogan itself, would be a gross simplification. Alongside the aggressive military dimension, in many other domains the merging of internal and external security logics can be seen to have accelerated. The very nature of the attack on the Twin Towers served as eloquent testimony to the redundancy of any clear distinction between the internal and the external, and much US security activity since has been aimed precisely at developing a more holistic approach. This can be seen in the new arrangements with the EU mentioned above, which are part of a broader reconsideration of all dimensions of security under the New Transatlantic Agenda. To name but one other prominent initiative, it can also be seen in the launch of the new domestic Department of Homeland Security in November 2002, which brings most of the functions of domestic security – including Immigration and Naturalisation, the Coast Guard, Customs and Federal Emergency management – under one roof, and which will also have close links to police and intelligence service in providing a central clearing house for the assessment of the domestic vulnerability of the USA (Wheeler 2002). Needless to say, much of the preventative and assessment work of the various elements of this new integrated capacity faces outwards to the international environment in its efforts to 'secure' the domestic environment.

Future prospects

Many of the trends set out above in the areas of privatisation of transnational policing, the intensification of EU capacity and the internationalisation of US policing appear deeply embedded, and set to continue into the foreseeable future. Yet as the events of 11 September reminded us, a key characteristic of post-Cold War, post-Westphalian security politics is precisely the shrinking horizons of the foreseeable, and so we should not be surprised if future events significantly disrupt current tendencies. That having been said, two general conclusions as to future prospects may be drawn from current trends.

In the first place, what is striking about the emerging configuration of transnational policing is precisely its lack of any single defining pattern or template. Unlike the earlier phases of internationalism – the Westphalian system with its state monopoly over the means of violence – there is no stable background geopolitical structure to lend coherence to the new tendencies. Supranational absorption of many of the traditional capacities of the state in the EU, the powerful and to some degree unilateral reassertion of national sovereignty in a style which increasingly over-rides the division between internal and external security in the case of the USA, and a more general transcendence of traditional forms of polity-based 'security sovereignty' – state or supranational – in the case of the privatisation of transnational policing, exist simultaneously in a complex matrix of competition and co-operation.

In the second place, in this new age of diversifying and fluidly evolving forms of policing and internal security, one common concern is the resistance to adequate individual and democratic accountability of the new transnational arrangements. Many factors conspire to support this diagnosis. As we have seen in the European domain, an obdurate faith in and reliance on primarily national forms of control for increasingly supranational arrangements is one difficulty. In the US context, there is a parallel problem of mismatch between the democratic 'principal' on the one hand and the policing 'agent' on the other. That is to say, the category of those affected by US policing agencies, given their burgeoning transnational dimension, manifestly and increasingly fail to correspond to the sovereign US citizenry who, at least formally, possess the constitutional capacity to hold US policing to democratic account. And in the context of transnational private policing, the key concern is even more stark, namely that there is *no* available forum of public accountability whatsoever. Furthermore, the problems of tracking fugitive power in each of these three domains are compounded if we consider the active relations which exist between them, and the exponential increase in complexity and opaqueness such networked relations produce. If we add to this the general tendency for questions of democratic accountability and civil liberties to be marginalised in conditions where the security imperative prevails, as in the post 11 September climate, the problems become greater still. Indeed, even where a window of opportunity exists for constitutional reflection on the problem of accountability, as in the EU Constitutional Convention, and even where the urgent security agenda does not obscure the long-term issues at stake, the sheer novelty of the problems of designing adequate accountability arrangements on a scale where the population as a whole only has a weak general attachment to the polity in question (Cederman 2001) and limited specific sympathy with many of those who are subject to transnational policing arrangements may frustrate the discovery of adequate solutions (Den Boer 2002; Hayes 2002; Loader, 2002). Quid custodiet ipsos custodes has always been one of the most profound and pressing questions of statecraft. Where both the custodians and those who provide the object of their concerns come systematically to escape the confines of the state, the problems of finding adequate and legitimate governance arrangements run even deeper and demand yet more urgent consideration.

Selected further reading

On the general history of transnational policing, Deflem's *Policing World Society* (2002) is an excellent general source, and Anderson's *Policing the World* (1989) provides a clear and interesting account of the development of the role of Interpol. Anderson *et al. Policing the European Union* (1995) and Den Boer and Wallace's 'Justice and home affairs' (2000) are good general sources on the origins of policing in the EU, while Nadelman's *Cops across Borders* (1993) remains the best history of the internationalisation of US policing. For more recent European developments, Den Boer's 'Police and judicial co-operation in criminal matters' (2003) is helpful, while the regular *Statewatch* bulletins provide an unrivalled source of critical contemporary commentary. For more recent US development, Andreas and Price's 'From war fighting to crime fighting' (2001) is particularly useful.

Other useful sources for some of the more specific themes covered in this chapter include Sheptycki's 'Accountability across the policing field' (2002) on the operational sociology of transnational policing, Loader's 'Governing European policing' (2002) and Den Boer's 'The incorporation of Schengen into the TEU' (2002) on the accountability of transnational policing, Loader and Walker's 'Policing as a public good' (2001) on the broader normative implications of moving beyond the state as the main source of policing, Johnston's 'Transnational private policing' (2000) on the privatisation of transnational policing, Bigo's 'The European internal security field' (1994) and 'When two become one' (2000) on the politics of transnational policing, Peers' *EU Justice and Home Affairs Law* (2000) and Denza's *The Intergovernmental Pillars of the European Union* (2002) on the legal dimension of transnational policing in the European domain, and Gilmore's *The Twin Towers and the Three Pillars* (2003) and Bunyan's 'The birth of the EU's Interior Ministry?' (2003) on European policing and security responses to 11 September.

References

Adler, B. and Barnett, M. (1998) *Security Communities*. Cambridge: Cambridge University Press.

Anderson, B. (1983) *Imagined Communities: Reflections on the Origins and Spread of Nationalism*. London: New Left Books.

Anderson, M. (1989) *Policing the World: Interpol and the Politics of International Police Co-operation*. Oxford: Clarendon Press.

Anderson, M., Den Boer, M., Cullen, P., Gilmore, W., Raab, C. and Walker, N. (1995) *Policing the European Union: Theory, Law and Practice*. Oxford: Clarendon Press.

Andreas, P. and Price, R. (2001) 'From war fighting to crime fighting: transforming the American national security state', *International Studies*, 4: 31–52.

Bigo, D. (1994) 'The European internal security field: stakes and rivalries in the newly developing area of police intervention' in M. Anderson and M. Den Boer (eds) *Policing across National Boundaries*. London: Pinter, 161–73.

Bigo, D. (2000a) 'Liaison officers in Europe: new officers in the European security field', in J. Sheptycki (ed.) *Issues in Transnational Policing*. London: Routledge, 67–100.

Bigo, D. (2000b) 'When two become one: internal and external securitisations in Europe', in M. Kelstrup and M. Williams (eds) *International Relations Theory and the Politics of European Integration: Power, Security and Community*. London: Routledge, 171–204.

Bunyan, T. (2003) 'The birth of the EU's Interior Ministry?' *Statewatch*, 13(1): 21–3.

Cederman, L.E. (2001) 'Nationalism and bounded integration: what it would take to construct a European Demos', *European Journal of International Relations*, 7: 139–74.

Cohen, H. (1985) 'Authority: the limits of discretion', in F.A. Elliston and M. Feldberg (eds) *Moral Issues in Policework*. Totowa, NJ: Rowan & Allanheld, 27–42.

Convention on the Future of Europe (2002) *Report of Working Group X on 'The Area of Freedom, Security and Justice'. Final Report* (CONV 426/02), Brussels.

Deflem, M. (2002) *Policing World Society: Historical Foundations of International Police Cooperation*. Oxford: Clarendon Press.

Den Boer, M. (2000) 'The incorporation of Schengen into the TEU: a bridge too far?', in J. Monar and W. Wessels (eds) *The Treaty of Amsterdam: Challenges and Opportunities for the European Union*. London: Cessels, 296–318.

Den Boer, M. (2002) 'Towards an accountability regime for an emerging European police governance', *Policing and Society*, 12: 275–90.

Den Boer, M. (2003) 'Police and judicial co-operation in criminal matters: a dynamic policy area', in P. Van Der Hoek (ed.) *Public Administration and Public Policy in the European Union*. New York, NY: Dekker (forthcoming).

Den Boer, M. and Wallace, W. (2000) 'Justice and home affairs', in H. Wallace and W. Wallace (eds) *Policy-making in the European Union*. Oxford: Oxford University Press, 493–530.

Denza, E. (2002) *The Intergovernmental Pillars of the European Union*. Oxford: Oxford University Press.

Deutsch, K., Burrell, S., Kann, R., Lee, M., Lichtermann, M., Loewenheim, F. and Van Wagenen, R. (1957) *Political Community and the North Atlantic Area*. Princeton, NJ: Princeton University Press.

Ellison, G. and Smyth, J. (2000) *The Crowned Harp: Policing Northern Ireland*. London: Pluto.

Emsley, C. (2000) *Gendarmes and the State in Nineteenth Century Europe*. Oxford: Oxford University Press.

Ericson, R. (1994) 'The division of expert knowledge in policing and security', *British Journal of Sociology*, 45: 149–76.

Fijnaut, C. (1997) 'The International Police Commission and the fight against communism, 1923–1945', in M. Mazower (ed.) *The Policing of Politics in the Twentieth Century*. Providence, RI: Berghalin, 107–28.

Gilmore, W. (2003) *The Twin Towers and the Three Pillars*. Florence: European University Institute, Law Department.

Hayes, B. (2002) *The Activities and Development of Europol – towards an Unaccountable 'FBI' in Europe*. London: Statewatch.

Held, D., McGrew, A., Goldblatt, D. and Perraton, J. (1999) *Global Transformations*. Cambridge: Polity Press.

Hope, T. (2000) 'Inequality and the clubbing of private security', in T. Hope and R. Sparks (eds) *Crime, Risk and Insecurity: Law and Order in Everyday Life and Political Discourse*. London: Routledge, 83–106.

Johnston, L. (2000) 'Transnational private policing: the impact of global commercial security', in J. Sheptycki (ed.) *Issues in Transnational Policing*. London: Routledge, 21–42.

Jones, T. and Newburn, T. (1998) *Private Security and Public Policing*. Oxford: Clarendon Press.

Lindberg, L.N. (1963) *The Political Dynamics of European Integration*. Stanford, CA: Stanford University Press.

Loader, I. (1997) 'Policing and the social: questions of symbolic power', *British Journal of Sociology*, 48: 1.

Loader, I. (2002) 'Governing European policing: some problems and prospects', *Policing and Society*, 12: 291–306.

Loader, I. and Mulcahy, A. (2003) *Policing and the Condition of England: Memory, Politics and Culture*. London: Routledge.

Loader, I. and Walker, N. (2001) 'Policing as a public good: reconstituting the connections between policing and the state', *Theoretical Criminology*, 5: 9–35.

Marenin, O. (1982) 'Parking tickets and class repression: the concept of policing in critical theories of criminal justice', *Contemporary Crises*, 6: 241–66.

Nadelman, E. (1993) *Cops across Borders: The Internationalization of US Criminal Law Enforcement*. Philadelphia, PA: Pennsylvania State University Press.

Naylor, R.T. (1995) 'From cold war to crime war: the search for a new "national security" threat', *Transnational Organised Crime*, 1: 37.

Nozick, R. (1974) *Anarchy, State and Utopia*. New York, NY: Basic Books.

Peers, S. (2000) *EU Justice and Home Affairs Law*. Harlow: Longman.

Raine, L.P. and Cilluffo, F.J. (eds) (1994) *Global Organized Crime: The New Evil Empire.* Washington, DC: Center for Strategic and International Studies.

Shearing, C. and Stenning, P. (1983) 'Private security implications for social control', *Social Problems*, 30: 493.

Sheptycki, J. (2002) 'Accountability across the policing field: towards a general cartography of accountability for post-modern policing', *Policing and Society*, 12: 323–38.

Van Maanen, J. (1974) 'Working the street', in H. Jacob (ed.) *The Potential for Reform of Criminal Justice.* Beverly Hills, CA: Sage, 83–130.

Walden, K. (1982) *Visions of Order: The Canadian Mounties in Symbol and Myth.* Toronto: Butterworths.

Walker, N. (2000) *Policing in a Changing Constitutional Order.* London: Sweet & Maxwell.

Walker, N. (2002a) 'The problem of trust in an enlarged area of freedom, security and justice: a conceptual analysis', in M. Anderson and J. Apap (eds) *Police and Justice Co-operation and the New European Borders.* The Hague: Kluwer, 19–34.

Walker, N. (2002b) 'Policing and the supranational', *Policing and Society*, 12: 307–22.

Walker, N (2002c) 'The idea of constitutional pluralism', *Modern Law Review*, 65: 319–59.

Walker, N. (2003a) 'Freedom, security and justice', in B. De Witte (ed.) *Ten Reflections on the Constitutional Treaty for Europe.* Florence: Robert Schuman Centre, 159–82.

Walker, N. (2003b) 'The idea of a European constitution and the *Finalite* of integration', in B. de Witte (ed.) *The Emergence of a European Constitution.* Oxford: Oxford University Press (forthcoming).

Weiler, J.H.H. (1999) *The Constitution of Europe.* Cambridge: Cambridge University Press.

Wheeler, T. (2002) 'Bush's new Department of Homeland Security: the scaffolding of a police state', *World Socialist Web Site* (www.wsws.org) 8 June.

Chapter 7

The pattern of policing in the UK: policing beyond the police

Adam Crawford

Introduction

Until recently policing had become synonymous with the activities of the modern professional police. It was not always so. 'Policing' until the eighteenth and early nineteenth century in Europe referred to a much more general schema of regulation that encompassed diverse institutions engaged in the maintenance of orderly environments, the promotion of public tranquillity and ensuring efficient trade and commerce. Crime was only a marginal element in this body of police regulation. It also included the policing of weights and measures, health and safety, roads and buildings, trade protection, liquor licensing and the general governance of populations. With the birth of the modern professional police in 1829, the responsibility for policing, over time, became firmly located within the state (see Chapter 4). Its paid agents alone ultimately were to be responsible for the nature and form of policing and crime control. In many senses, the development of the professional police was coupled to the formation of the modern state. As a consequence, policing came to be seen as a product of what the police actually do. This is not to say that the private or non-state provision of policing and security services disappeared, but rather they came to assume, or be perceived to occupy, a less significant and more subordinate role (South 1988).

In recent years, however, we have seen a restructuring and proliferation of 'policing beyond the police', as a result of which a more complex division of labour in the fields of policing and security has emerged. A pluralised, fragmented and differentiated patchwork has replaced the idea of the police as the monopolistic guardians of public order. The police are now part of a varied assortment of organisations with policing functions and a diffuse array of policing processes. With this, the study of policing has shifted to encompass a broader assortment of actors and agents. This chapter explores both *a new way of looking at things* – namely, a reconceptualisation of policing – and *a new set of things to look at* – namely, the growth of policing beyond the police. In order to outline the pattern of policing, this chapter considers the activities of a variety of public and municipal, as well as commercial and voluntary, actors with policing functions beyond, and sometimes in conjunction with, the police. The intention of this chapter is not to give a comprehensive overview of all forms of policing but rather to illustrate some of the divergent forms and processes as well as to explore some of the issues raised by the diverse providers of policing and their inter-relationships. The chapter begins by providing a framework within which to situate and understand policing. It then goes on to consider the broader sociopolitical context in which modern policing and its study are located. It provides an overview of policing beyond the police under four headings: specialist policing; municipal policing; civilian policing; and commercial policing. It then goes on to explore some of the economic and technological dynamics stimulating developments in commercial policing and some of the themes provoked by the marketisation of policing and security. The chapter concludes with an assessment of the unfolding relationship between the professional police and other forms of plural policing.

What is policing?

Policing as a set of activities and processes is something that may be performed by a variety of professional and ordinary people. This may be a group of professionals employed by the state in a dedicated organisation called 'the police' with a broad mandate of crime control and order maintenance. In addition, policing may be a task of professionals employed either by (local or central) state agencies with specialist policing functions, such as the regulation of particular types of crimes or offences committed in defined places, or by state departments with other primary functions. Furthermore, policing may be conducted by municipal agents, private security personnel or by the public in their local networks of informal social control. Increasingly, policing may also be the product of new technologies, such as bugging devices and surveillance cameras,[1] or even embedded into the design of the built environment.

Despite the fact that the police constitute but one part of a more varied and complex totality of policing, we tend to operate with an 'intuitive notion of what the police are' (Reiner 2000: 1). Both symbolically and literally the police dominate our conceptions of policing. However, the police in England and Wales are not an undifferentiated body of people. As well as being divided into 43 separate forces, the police are internally ordered into specialist functions and dedicated units as well as a number of national services. Furthermore, within the police organisation policing may be conducted by fully trained professionals or by civilians who cannot draw upon the same extensive powers, status, training or equipment as their professional counterparts. As well as civilian support staff, the police utilise the capacity of volunteers in the form of the Special Constabulary.

For the purpose of this chapter, 'policing' will be taken to mean something that lies between the fuzzy and rather nebulous concept of 'social control' and the narrower definition of police work. Here, Jones and Newburn's (1998: 18–19) definition is a useful starting point. They include:

> those organised forms of order-maintenance, peacekeeping, rule or law enforcement, crime investigation and prevention and other forms of investigation and associated information-brokering – which may involve a conscious exercise of coercive power – undertaken by individuals or organisations, where such activities are viewed by them and/or others as a central or key defining part of their purpose.

Building upon this, we can identify four key elements of policing: first, it entails intentional action or a purposeful condition; secondly, it involves the conscious exercise of power or authority by an individual or organisation; thirdly, it is directed towards rule or norm enforcement, the promotion of order or assurances of safety; and, fourthly, it seeks to govern in the present and/or the future.

Building upon earlier work, Jones and Newburn (1998: 202–3) advance a multidimensional understanding of policing in which they highlight five principal axes around which different forms of policing may be delineated. These are as follows:

- *Functional*: the different tasks that policing agents perform. Traditionally, policing has been divided between order maintenance, law enforcement and a variety of service functions, but also may be allied to much broader, non-policing, functions.

- *Legal*: the nature of powers enjoyed by various agents, be they derived from statute, common law or local bye-laws. Traditionally, this has juxtaposed professional police with specific legal powers against those universal rights of ordinary citizens. However, security staff operating within private property or policing employees can draw upon legal powers derived from property rights and employment contracts. Furthermore, as Stenning (2000) notes, this emphasis upon formal legal powers provides only a partial picture of the 'practical coercive and intrusive powers' used by diverse policing agents, as it tends to ignore the 'tool box' of physical, personal and symbolic resources.

- *Sectoral*: the relationship between particular policing organisations and the state or market. However, Johnston (1993) has drawn our attention to the growing sectoral complexity of policing, which does not fit neatly in either the 'public' or 'private' sectors. The source of funding and the status of employees are often more complex and not easily delineated in such a manner. Johnston prefers to call these 'hybrid' policing bodies.

- *Geographical*: the point along the local–national–international continuum at which policing bodies are organised. This dimension has become increasingly complex in recent years with overlapping and contradictory processes of centralisation and decentralisation, as well as the Europeanisation and even globalisation of elements of policing (Sheptycki 2000; Walker 2000; Chapter 6).

- *Spatial*: the forms of space in which policing bodies operate. This dimension differentiates between residential, commercial, industrial spaces, for example, with regard to their relative accessibility and openness to different people. Even here we have seen the emergence of new social spaces, such as the Internet, that confuse and confound the geographic and type of space differentiation. These spaces are not territorially bounded in any sense but take on a virtual form, constituting a type of 'cyberspace' (see Chapter 20).

In an important recent contribution, Johnston and Shearing (2003) advance a much broader, nodal conception of 'security governance'. They prefer this term to the narrower concept of 'policing', in part to escape what they see as its analytical, state-centred straitjacket and its conventional association with the public police: 'Within this conception of governance no set of nodes is given conceptual priority. Instead, the exact nature of governance, and the precise contribution of the various nodes to it, are matters for empirical enquiry' (Johnston and Shearing 2003: 147). The relationship between different nodes, it is assumed, will vary across time and space. The articulation between agents involved will range from different states of co-operation, from benign neglect to outright conflict. Furthermore, resources may flow across nodes in a variety of different ways. This is a highly pluralistic model of policing that refuses to give conceptual priority to the state in order to highlight the range of governmental nodes that exist and the relationship between them. In so doing, this approach 'by emphasising that the state is no longer a stable locus of government ... defines governance as the property of networks rather than as the product of any single centre of action' (Johnston and Shearing 2003: 148). This model encourages the analysis of governance beyond the state. Yet despite their preference to decentre the state, for conceptual reasons, it often returns within their framework as occupying a dominant position largely because of its empirical position. As I hope to show, the role of the state remains pivotal in its inaction as well as its action. Furthermore, the professional police remain qualitatively different from other forms of policing, in its symbolic power (Loader 1997), generalist mission and regulatory position with regard to other forms of policing.

Throughout this chapter implicit reference will be made to the multidimensional concept of policing advanced above. First, let us consider the broad context within which contemporary policing has emerged and remains located.

The context of contemporary policing

The aim of modern criminal justice, from the nineteenth century onwards, has been primarily one of state-centred control through specialist professional institutions, whose principal concern was the prosecution and punishment of offenders. During the last 30 years or so the foundations upon which this approach was premised have been eroded. This erosion has been stimulated by a number of broad inter-related developments that warrant brief comment.

First, since the late 1970s crime and the fear of crime have come to occupy a new salience within everyday life. The public demand for security has become a dominant feature of contemporary life. This has been reflected in the politicisation of crime, policing and security. Attitude surveys suggest that, for many people, crime and the fear of it constitute the most pressing social issues. Objective risks and subjective anxieties are often out of kilter. And yet quests for security operate at both symbolic and material levels. Latest British Crime Survey (BCS) data suggest that despite reductions in the overall level of crime since the mid-1990s the public continues to believe that crime is rising (Povey *et al.* 2003).

Second, there has been a growing recognition of the limited capacity of the formal criminal justice system, notably police, prosecution, punishment and prisons. The American commentator Marcus Felson (2002: 3) calls this the 'cop-and-courts fallacy' at the heart of modern crime control and criminology, which exaggerates the importance of police, courts and prisons as the key actors in crime prevention. As victimisation surveys remind us, most crimes are never reported to the police. Low clear-up rates (about one in five recorded crimes) and case attrition through the court process only serve further to undermine the deterrent value of the police. The public has increasingly lost confidence in the capacity of the professional police to solve crime problems (Mirrlees-Black 2001).

Third, the sovereign state's monopoly over matters of crime control and security has been increasingly exposed (Garland 1996). The idea that 'sovereign' states alone could guarantee crime control to their subjects in a monopolistic fashion always was merely a 'myth', rather than a reality, albeit a powerful myth. Stan Cohen noted that in privileging the formal state apparatus of social control we had 'bullied ourselves (and others) into thinking that social control is synonymous with state control' (1989: 353). Consequently, there has been an associated acknowledgement of the importance of informal social control. Rather than supplanting informal sources of authority in society, it has increasingly become recognised that the role of public agencies should be to act to support and enhance existing private, communal or parochial forms of control. Yet, there has been a simultaneous structural transformation in the public sphere (Habermas 1989), in ways that have undermined many informal control mechanisms and encouraged sectional or self-interests. This has been reflected in an associated decline in shared public activity, social bonds and communal ties (Etzioni 1993) and a rise in what Lasch refers to as 'privatism' (1980: 25): an introspective preoccupation with the care and development of the self on behalf of individuals, resulting in forms of social and spatial withdrawal. The aspect of personal safety has been an important element in this preoccupation.

Fourth, the financial burden to the public purse of the police specifically – and the criminal justice system more generally – has meant that governments have become more cautious about the use of scarce resources, particularly in the light of the pressure on public expenditure since the fiscal crises of the 1970s. In this context, the appropriateness of the breadth of the services traditionally performed by the professional police became the subject of extensive public scrutiny.

Fifth, the most significant adaptation to the crisis of confidence and competence in the traditional state-centred approach to policing and criminal justice has been the rebirth of *crime prevention* with its emphasis upon instrumental reasoning through risk and security management. Despite the original Peelian vision of crime prevention as a central element of police work, the history of the professional police has been one in which, until recently, crime prevention became defined in increasingly narrow and specialist terms and was pushed to the margins of the police organisation (Harvey et al. 1989). Crime prevention as a residual category became associated with the 'deterrent effect' of institutions of criminal justice – notably the 'scarecrow' function of policing through patrol. More recently, greater emphasis has been placed on the delivery of crime prevention through partnerships – linking an array of organisations and agencies beyond the police.

This connects with a sixth trend, the dispersal of responsibilities for crime control within and beyond the state (Crawford 1997). The last 20 years have seen various governmental 'strategies of responsibilisation' (Garland 2001). A major driver in the pluralisation of policing and the dispersal of responsibilities for crime prevention has been the impact of neoliberal-inspired reforms that have sought to rearticulate the relationship between state, market and civil society. In redrawing the appropriate functions of government, Osborne and Gaebler's thesis suggests that governments become stronger not weaker in that they 'steer' more, but 'do' less (1992: 32).

One consequence of this managerialist agenda has been the quest to hive off traditional state functions. To this end, the 1990s saw considerable governmental effort to try to distinguish 'core' policing tasks from 'ancillary' ones, the implication being that the latter should be devolved to private or voluntary initiative (Home Office 1993, 1995). A broader consequence has been a rearticulation of relations between the state and civil society in matters of crime. Where once citizens were told to 'leave it to the professionals' they are now enlisted as 'partners in crime prevention' in a new corporate approach, notably in the Crime and Disorder Act 1998 (CDA). The logic of the Act has been to encourage and entrench a diversification of policing functions at a local level. In addition, there has been an explicit emphasis upon transferring responsibility on to the business sector both at the stage of design (in term of new products) and service delivery.[2]

Seventh, the extended nature of public fears and associated demands for security have seen a broadening of the focus of policy concern beyond crime, narrowly defined, to include fear of crime, disorder and anti-social behaviour, as well as 'quality of life' issues. In this, the 'discovery' of fear of crime as a social problem – largely through victimisation survey research (Hough and Mayhew 1983) – has been instrumental in policy debates. Hence, 'community safety' – rather than the narrower concept of crime prevention – has become the catch-all term that has emerged in policy discourse (Crawford 1998). Here, Wilson and Kelling's (1982) 'broken windows' thesis has been hugely influential in promoting the policing of disorder, minor nuisances and anti-social behaviour as crucial linchpins in crime prevention and urban regeneration.

This has a number of implications. To begin with, the concern for incivilities, anti-social behaviour, disorder and subcriminal activities constitutes a lowering of the threshold of tolerance and, consequently, an increase in the demand for policing. In this context, the presentation of places as secure and safe locations in which to live, work, do business or enjoy leisure has become crucial to entice insecure people (whether for the purposes of consumption or labour) and nomadic capital. In addition, this emphasis upon fear of crime combined with the public demand for a visible presence has placed considerable pressure on the patrol function of policing and its symbolic import. However, the demand for policing as reassurance is not something that the police alone are able to meet within current resources. Although visible patrol would appear to remain a key element in securing public confidence and addressing perceptions of safety, its place on the agenda of the 'crime-fighting' police has slipped. This has left a mismatch between available resources and public demand.

Finally, in broad parallel to the recent growth of commercial security provision there has been a decline in the number of what Jones and Newburn (2002) have termed 'secondary social control occupations' and of parochial social control institutions. Traditional (often informal) modes of governing, public spaces in particular, through intermediaries such as park keepers, train guards and bus conductors, have all but disappeared. This withdrawal of intermediaries was often justified in terms of neoliberal cost-efficiency arguments. This saw 'capable guardians' replaced by new technologies, if at all. In Britain, there has been 'a marked decrease in employment in a range of occupations providing "natural surveillance" and other low level controls as a corollary to their primary functions' (Jones and Newburn 2002: 140). The point here is that current developments may represent a 'formalisation of social control' or a transformation in its presentation, rather than a fundamental rupture in the history of policing.

In sum, the forces driving change in the nature and form of policing and community safety lie both within, and far beyond, the state. Box 7.1 outlines some of the different forms of plural policing, both within and beyond the public police. Let us consider each of these in more detail.

Specialist policing bodies

Just as the professional police model of specialist state-based regulation developed in relation to crime throughout the nineteenth and twentieth centuries, so specialist regulatory agencies emerged in other fields and in relation to specific crime-related spheres and activities. Today, there are public agencies engaged in tasks related to state security, such as MI5 and MI6, as well as the Ministry of Defence Police and the Atomic Energy Authority constabulary. Secondly, there is also a cluster of non-Home Office police forces with geographically or spatially defined parameters, such as the British Transport Police and the docks and parks forces. The former represents a good example of where the cost of public policing is met by commercial organisations, in this instance the 'privatised' railway companies. Some dock forces, such as the Port of London Authority constabulary, are good examples of private companies performing 'public' functions. Thirdly, there are other specialist bodies performing designated policing functions. For example, a number government departments employ officials to undertake investigative

Box 7.1 Different forms of plural policing

Home Office police forces
- 43 police forces in England and Wales.
- Central services – National Crime Squad, National Crime Intelligence Service.

Specialist policing bodies
- State security services.
- Custom and Excise.
- British Transport Police.
- State departments – DSS, Inland Revenue.
- Regulatory authorities – Health & Safety Executive.

Municipal policing
- Environmental health officers.
- Public auxiliaries – city guards, neighbourhood wardens, local patrols.
- Traffic wardens.
- Community safety partnerships.
- Anti-social behaviour teams.
- Policing through housing and education.

Civilian policing
- Special Constabulary.
- Neighbourhood watch.
- Citizens' patrols.
- Vigilantism.

Commercial policing
- Staffed services – security guards, door supervisors.
- Private investigation services.
- Installation and monitoring of security equipment.

---

and law enforcement functions, such as the Inland Revenue Investigation Unit and HM Customs and Excise.

In addition, large areas of 'regulatory law' are entrusted to central or local government agencies or inspectorates of diverse kinds. These include the Health and Safety Executive (a quasi-autonomous body established by the Health and Safety at Work Act 1974) with regard to the enforcement of industrial safety regulations and the Regional Water Authorities concerned with anti-pollution enforcement. In some instances, regulatory bodies are located within investigative departments of other public authorities, such as the Post Office Investigation Department and the Benefits Agency. In other instances, they constitute 'quangos' outside of government departments. The complex sectoral status of some of these bodies is further illustrated by the role of the National Society for the Prevention of Cruelty to Children (NSPCC) and the Royal Society for the Prevention of Cruelty to Animals (RSPCA), both charitable organisations with statutory powers and a certain 'private status' (see Button 2002).

The role and number of regulatory bodies have expanded over the last century, particularly in the field of business and consumer regulation as the power of corporations has grown (Braithwate 2002; Chapter 18). Recent managerialist reforms and privatisation have served to create novel regulatory agencies with policing functions. One particular growth industry has been the regulation of public bodies by other parts of government: what Hood *et al.* (1999) refer to as 'regulation inside government'. In the 'new regulatory state' the state is both the object and the subject of regulation (Braithwaite 2000). Moreover, public authorities may even be the subject of 'private regulation'.[3]

The historical lesson drawn from the diverse body of regulatory agencies is the manner in which they have prioritised non-punitive modes of enforcement, preferring strategies rooted in persuasion through market-based disciplines and mentalities. As Braithwaite (2003) reminds us, there is a very different history of policing to be derived from the business regulatory field as distinct from the 'police-prisons' arena.

Municipal policing

Local authorities employ a number of specialist policing services. For example, most environmental health officers (EHOs) are employed by local authorities, along with trading standards officers, to carry out a wide range of enforcement work. EHOs are involved with enforcement of legislation on housing, environmental protection, and food safety and standards, and possess a significant range of statutory powers to enter premises and conduct investigations (see Jones and Newburn 1998).

Local authority patrols

Some local authorities have revived an earlier tradition of parks police enforcing local bye-laws and enjoying significant legal powers.[4] A good example is the Wandsworth Parks Constabulary established in 1985 and directly employed by the borough council (Jones and Newburn 1998: 132). Recently a number of local authorities have set up their own policing patrols. Unlike parks police they do not enjoy any formal police powers. One of the earliest and most notable examples has been in Sedgefield, County Durham, where the district council set up its own uniformed 'Community Force', in early 1994, to patrol the local vicinity on a 24-hour basis. Although similar to private security patrols, the Community Force was established as a department of the council, not a commercial company. Officers have no police powers of arrest and work upon the assumption of not using their citizen's powers of arrest. It has a non-confrontational policy of 'observe and report only' acting as a junior partner of the local police who are contacted and called upon in the event of an incident (Wiles 1996). Other local authorities have followed this lead, often focusing upon crime and disorder problems on council-run housing estates. However, pressures on councils to open up their services to competitive tendering (and the emphasis on 'Best Value') have meant that many councils have contracted out this patrolling work to commercial companies rather than retaining it in-house.

Community safety units and anti-social behaviour

The community safety units spawned by the statutory requirements of the CDA have added an additional dimension to policing activities within local authorities (in some metropolitan areas community safety units predated the Act). By and large, these units are not service providers but catalyse and co-ordinate the activities of others. Importantly, s. 17 requires local authorities to anticipate the potential crime and disorder consequences of their policies. This in theory, if less in practice, places 'crime and disorder considerations at the very heart of decision making, where they have always belonged' (Home Office 1997: para. 33). Despite considerable resistance (notably from housing and education departments) in mainstreaming the possible implications of s. 17, some commentators suggest that like 'a wolf in sheep's clothing' this section could come to have far-reaching ramifications (Moss and Pease 1999).

The combined emphasis upon partnership working and the criminalisation of anti-social behaviour has tied local authorities and other public sector agencies much more closely into policing functions, either in their own capacity or jointly with the police. For example, the introduction of 'anti-social behaviour orders' (ASBOs) and 'youth curfews' involves local authorities working alongside or in consultation with police. Under the Police Reform Act 2002 registered social landlords and British Transport Police have been given powers to apply for ASBOs. Furthermore, many councils now have anti-social behaviour teams that bring together police officers and council officials to work side by side. In a similar vein there has been an increasing emphasis upon schools and education authorities working in partnership with the police in relation to the policing of truancy.[5]

Policing through social housing tenancies

One particular area in which municipal authorities have increased their policing activities has been with regard to their own tenants. While the control of tenants' conduct has been an ever-present feature of social landlordism since the late Victorian era, since the 1990s there has been a greater preoccupation in housing management with the policing of anti-social behaviour (Burney 1999). This has seen greater recourse to the use of civil and administrative powers as a means of preventing crime and disorder. The law has been significantly strengthened through changes to tenancy agreements stimulated by the Housing Act 1996. One effect of this is that if the local authority wish to evict, there is no requirement to prove any ground for possession.[6]

The 1996 Act also extends grounds for possession, specifically relating to nuisance and illegal behaviour, introduces new forms of injunctions (so that landlords can order tenants to desist from particular behaviour) and gives authorities the power, for the first time, to exclude certain groups from their waiting lists. The Department of the Environment advice following the Act acknowledged that such exclusions might include those 'with a history of anti-social behaviour' (DoE/DoH 1997: para. 4.27). This enables prevention through exclusion, rather than enforcement. In addition, social landlords have been increasingly resorting to the use of – non-criminal – legal remedies in the policing of tenant behaviour.[7] However, this form of policing anti-social behaviour through housing is tenure specific, relating only to social housing. Private tenants are less likely to be subject to anti-social behaviour clauses in their tenancy agreements. Latest government initiatives as spelt out in the white paper *Respect and Responsibility* (Home Office 2003) and the Anti-Social Behaviour Bill are likely to extend the policing activities of registered social landlords, as well as local education authorities and schools in relation to anti-social behaviour.[8] Social landlords are to be provided with more powers to enable them to take action against anti-social tenants including faster evictions and removing their right to buy their council home.

Public auxiliaries

The growing role of public auxiliaries has drawn much inspiration from the lessons of the earlier Dutch experiences of *Stadswacht* schemes of civic wardens. The first scheme started in 1989 in Dordrecht and thereafter was extended across the Netherlands. The Dutch model employed the young and long-term unemployed as city wardens to help visitors in the city centres feel safer, and provide information, as well as intervene if people litter the streets or engage in disorderly behaviour (Hauber *et al.* 1996). The guards aim to provide a reassuring presence and act as 'ambassadors of the city'. Following the Dutch experience and its positive impact (Hofstra and Shapland 1997), a number of similar initiatives developed in the 1990s in the UK.

Recently, the British government has stimulated the provision of auxiliaries in public places through a series of programmes launching various types of 'wardens'. The explicit government intention has been the creation and rebuilding of layers of intermediary actors within civil society, capable of commanding sufficient authority to act as agents of social control. In this, warden schemes have been closely tied to a governmental agenda of neighbourhood renewal advanced by the Social Exclusion Unit (1998, 2001), proposing a national strategy for improving the conditions of Britain's poorest neighbourhoods. They have also been linked to the government's more recent commitment to revive public spaces outlined in the report *Living Places: Cleaner, Safer, Greener* (ODPM 2002).

This resulted in the launch of the *neighbourhood warden* programme in 2000. Wardens provide concierge duties, patrol or act as 'super caretakers' (Jacobson and Saville 1999), offering a semi-official presence in residential areas with the aim of improving quality of life. This initiative was followed a year later by a *street warden* programme, with a similar remit to neighbourhood wardens, but extending their role beyond residential areas. In addition, street wardens focus more on tackling environmental problems and caring for the physical appearance of areas. While neighbourhood wardens are employed by local authorities and housing associations, street wardens may be employed by other organisations, sometimes private. A third wave of *street crime wardens* was announced in September 2002, concentrating on the reduction of street crime in ten police force areas with the highest street crime, as part of the government's Street Crime Initiative.

In response to the expansion of wardens the Association of Chief Police Officers (ACPO 2000) published their own 'fundamental principles' to govern the establishment and operation of schemes. Of central concern is that there should be no diminution of police powers, wardens should have no enhanced powers beyond that of the ordinary citizen and the appearance of non-police wardens should be distinct from that of the police in terms of uniform and corporate image.

Civilian policing

As some British researchers have shown, there is a rich vein of 'policing by the public' (Shapland and Vagg 1988), albeit often ignored in policy debates. Public participation in policing, and crime control more generally, not only constitutes a fundamental basis for the legitimacy of modern policing through consent but also appeals to our highest civic values. Social ties and informal social control constitute the bedrock of local order (Foster 1995). At one level, informal policing by the public acts as a form of 'social capital' (Putnam 2000) reflecting the ability of groups to realise common values and to regulate their members according to desired principles. Here 'collective efficacy' operates through 'the linkage of mutual trust and the willingness to intervene for the common good' (Sampson *et al.* 1997: 919). This represents the policing *by* communities rather than the policing *of* communities. At another level, civilian participation may also foster synergies between formal and informal mechanisms of control such as to facilitate crime prevention and detection, notably through the flow of information. However, forms of civilian policing may also be at odds with professional police activities, with the result that the provision of information may be considered to constitute 'grassing' (Evans *et al.* 1996).

Government strategies of responsibilisation have sought to encourage 'active citizenry' and 'voluntary collective action' to assist in the provision of local goods and services as the role of the state is withdrawn and redrawn. Civilian policing may take the form of individual or collective action. Individual acts may involve anything from installing personal security measures to contacting the police, giving information to the Crimestoppers phone line or joining the police as volunteers in the Special Constabulary. Collective action may constitute low-level local surveillance through neighbourhood watch as the 'eyes and ears' of the police, street patrols, self-help groups such as the Guardian Angels, organised (and disorganised) vigilantes and gang-related activities or community self-policing as in the case of paramilitaries in Northern Ireland. As this suggests, there is a thin line separating legitimate citizen action and vigilantism (Johnston 1996a). Who defines the normative order to be policed? What form does policing take? Whose interests are served by such policing activities? And what popular support is there for those doing the policing?

The contentious and ambiguous nature of civilian policing was apparent when the then Home Secretary announced in 1994 that neighbourhood watch schemes should get out and 'walk with a purpose' (Howard 1994). Given the hostile reception that this proposal received, particularly from the police themselves, it was hastily revisited and any reference to the idea of 'patrols' was removed in order to avoid the notion that this merely represented 'policing on the cheap'. Furthermore, the proposal also raised concerns about the spectre of vigilantism. This episode exposes crucial ambiguities in the idea of devolving responsibility for crime control to the public and the limitations on civilian policing. A more recent example was the media debate in the light of the conviction for murder of the Norfolk farmer, Tony Martin after he shot dead a burglar in his own home in August 1999.[9] The case highlights the uncertain legal boundaries to legitimate action, particularly with regard to self-defence.

Johnston (2000: 146) draws a distinction between 'responsible' and 'autonomous' forms of citizenship. The former consists of those acts that are directed, supported and sanctioned by the state, while autonomous forms of citizenship are independent of the state. And yet, the levels of support, sanction and legitimisation may be hesitant, begrudging or ambivalent. The attitude of a group towards the police is not a necessary determinant of the police's reciprocal attitude towards the group (Marx 1989). Hence, we need to examine both the extent to which a group sees itself as either 'adversarial' or 'supplemental' to the role of the police, as well as how the police and other relevant organisations (such as local authorities) interpret that relationship. In Britain most of the recent developments in civilian policing have been of a supplemental variety, welcomed or at least tolerated by the police.

Despite some commentators' assertions that organised civilian policing is now to be found 'everywhere' (Bayley and Shearing 1996: 587), the empirical evidence to support such a claim is thin. Aside from occasional media fascination with events such as the outbreaks of vigilantism against alleged paedophiles over the summer of 2000 stimulated by the 'naming and shaming' campaign of the *News of the World* newspaper, most civilian policing is low level and erratic. Community crime prevention research, on the contrary, highlights the difficulty of sustaining citizen involvement in relation to crime issues alone, and suggests the life expectancy of citizen patrols to be rather limited (Rosenbaum 1988). Reactions to crime rarely constitute sufficient grounds for maintaining community interest and enthusiasm over time, even in places where initial levels of awareness and participation are high (Palumbo *et al.* 1997). We should not confuse sporadic bouts of collective responses to given incidents or individual quests for personal safety with organised community-level policing activities.

Commercial policing

Calculating the size of the commercial security industry is notoriously problematic due to the lack of official data (Jones and Newburn 1995). Estimations in Britain suggest that the number of personnel in the private security industry has surpassed the number of public police officers. De Waard (1999: 155) puts the total number of private security personnel at 160,000, which equates to 275 security services personnel per 100,000 inhabitants. Jones and Newburn (2002: 141) have used Census figures to show that the number of private security guards rose from 66,950 in 1951 to 159,704 in 1991. However, the number of police officers also rose during this period (albeit not at the same rate) from 84,585 to 149,964. Table 7.1 presents figures pertaining to the relative number of certain forms of policing in England and Wales in

Table 7.1 Plural policing numbers in England and Wales in 2001–2*

Body	No.
Professional police	131,548
Civilian staff	58,909
Special Constables	11,598
Community support officers	1,281
Traffic wardens	2,233
Neighbourhood wardens	1,454
British Transport Police	2,073
Private security guards	125,000

Note:
*Police figures valid on 30 September 2002. They include 2,054 officers seconded to the National Crime Squad, National Crime Intelligence Service and central services (Hosking and Smith 2003). Civilian staff, special constables and traffic wardens valid on 31 March 2002 (Smith *et al.* 2002). Private security estimates taken from the British Security Industry Association (BSIA 2001). Neighbourhood warden figures taken from Neighbourhood Warden Team – valid as of December 2002 (Office of the Deputy Prime Minister) – and CSOs from the Home Office.

2001–2. What is apparent from these figures is that there is not only a diversity of policing personnel and that commercial security guards are no longer peripheral providers of policing, but also that new forms of policing appear to be expanding the total number of policing agents.

According to the British Security Industry Association (BSIA) (2001):

- the commercial security sector employs some 350,000 individuals;

- there are an estimated 8,000 security companies in the UK market;

- there are an estimated 2,000 staffed security companies;

- the in-house staffed security sector has halved since 1993, due to the rise of contract firms;

- the number of BSIA members' employees in staffed security services had grown from 30,400 in 1988 to 75,500 by 2001, while the number of BSIA members' employees across the sector has on average doubled during this period; and

- the industry turnover in the field of staffed security services (excluding in-house security) was estimated to be £1,678 million in the year 2001.

A significant number of commercial security companies are small in size (some of which are not BSIA members). Jones and Newburn (1998) found that more than half of the companies they sampled employed five or fewer people and 88 per cent fewer than 50 people. Yet, as a result of recent mergers and acquisitions, the commercial security industry has also seen the emergence of a small number of very large-scale companies, operating within national and international arenas. For example, Securitas AB employ 210,000 and Group4 Falck A/S 115,000 people worldwide. Together they have approximately 9 per cent of the total world market (van Dijk and de Waard 2001: 20).

The size of the commercial security industry in Britain is smaller than in the USA, Canada, Australia and South Africa (where the number of security personnel is more than three times greater than Britain). However, Britain leads the rest of Europe when comparing the ratio of security personnel per inhabitant, closely followed by Germany (de Waard 1999: 155). Unlike most other European countries Britain has adopted a very clearly non-intervention-ist stance towards the regulation of the industry, allowing it to grow largely unchecked. Some European countries have imposed more strict forms of regulation. Nevertheless, by early 1997 there were almost 600,000 employees working in the commercial security industry across the 15 EU countries, with an average of 160 per 100,000 inhabitants (de Waard 1999: 168).

Like the police, commercial security firms provide a variety of functions. Johnston (1992) suggests that they offer everything that the professional police do and much more besides. The activities of the commercial sector can be divided into three broad classifications: staffed services; security equipment; and investigation. Staffed services are often the most visible element of commercial policing and include uniformed guarding of both people and property. According to Jones and Newburn (1998), the guarding sector represents only a quarter of the total industry. However, in addition to contract security guards there is a number of in-house security guards or staff with quasi-security functions (whether uniformed or not). The security equipment sector, which Jones and Newburn suggest is the fastest-growing area within commercial security, includes the manufacture and installation of electronic and physical technology, such as CCTV, alarm systems, locks, bolts and bars.

The investigation sector includes private detectives, debt collectors and bailiffs. The literature available shows the private investigation market to be a particularly shadowy element of the commercial security industry. In the UK it is estimated that there are approximately 15,000 private detectives (Button 1998). This compares with 70,000 private detectives and 26,000 store detectives in the USA (Sklansky 1999). Research suggests that most private detectives in Britain are former police officers and they tend to be organised in small companies (Gill and Hart 1997). The differentiated nature of demand is thus reflected in the loose structure of the trade. While private detectives may be commissioned to work for either the defence or prosecution in the preparation of a case, they are more likely to become involved in investigations where prosecution is not the preferred outcome.

This is true of most forms of private policing, which are less likely than their public counterparts to produce 'cases' that end up in courts. The commercial objectives of private security are not necessarily compatible with prosecution. Any adjudication that may occur is more likely to be in the context of private or 'shadow' justice systems. This lack of legal oversight implies a potential deficit in accountability and raises concerns over malpractice. Accountability, here, is more likely to be commercial and exercised through contractual arrangements.

Regulating commercial security

While not holding the full extent of formal legal powers of the professional police, commercial security officers are able to deploy considerable resources that enable them to generate compliance with their demands. In particular, these derive from property laws governing the private property they police, enabling them to deny access to desired goods and services if compliance is not forthcoming. Powers may also stem from employment laws where the people policed are themselves employed by the property owner (such as workplace security). In addition, commercial police (like the public police) possess and deploy an array of personal, physical and symbolic powers. Just as public police power is regulated and checked, so there have been demands for the regulation of commercial security. Most interest has focused upon state regulation; however, as Stenning (2000) notes, this is neither the only, nor the most effective, mode of rendering private police powers accountable.[10]

The private security industry in Britain, unlike many other countries, has – until recently – remained largely unregulated by the state. The Private Security Industry Act 2001 seeks to shift the industry into the mainstream of UK policing services by encouraging a higher degree of professionalism. The Act introduces a compulsory licensing scheme for security officers and their managers, as well as directors and partners of contract security companies. It will also introduce a voluntary approved companies scheme. The Act establishes the Security Industry Authority (SIA), whose role is to license and regulate all 'contract' private security providers. In-house security officers will not be included in the licensing regime, meaning that security staff, employed directly by a business rather than from a security company, are exempt from the licensing requirement.[11] The licence will be granted only after a full criminal record check has been issued from the Criminal Records Bureau. Other factors such as suitable training will also be considered a precondition of licensing. The SIA will oversee the licensing regime and maintain a register of licensees and 'approved companies'. The authority will employ a number of inspectors who will have the right to enter security premises to ensure that personnel carry valid licences.

The Act represents a relatively limited form of regulation, which fails to address some of the concerns for tighter regulation. The failure of the legislation to extend to in-house security officers and the voluntary nature of the 'approved companies scheme' are particular weaknesses. In part, this reflects the fact that the legislation's primary function appears to concern improving the industry's image against a background of public concern over unscrupulous and criminal operators as well as poor standards of training and low-quality service. Nevertheless, the new licensing regime is likely to have significant implications for the future role of private security guards. While the absence of regulation has clearly facilitated the unchecked expansion of the commercial security industry, let us examine some other trends that have stimulated the security market in certain defined social spaces.

Issues raised by the growing market for policing

The growth of commercial policing and the marketisation of security more generally raise broader normative issues about their implications. They also raise questions about the forces stimulating their expansion and the possible limits or boundaries to their development.

Mass private property

As Shearing and Stenning (1981) have argued, the expansion of the private security industry has been fostered and encouraged by changes in land use and property relations, notably the 'privatisation of public space' through the growth of 'mass private property'. By this they refer to facilities that are owned privately but to which the public has access and use, such as shopping malls, entertainment stadia, leisure centres and recreational grounds. The growth of 'mass private property' has seen greater amounts of 'public places' located on private property and policed by private security companies. This important societal development has provided private corporations with the legal space and economic incentive to do their own policing. According to Shearing and Stenning (1983), the advent of 'mass private property' has not only brought about a change in the 'hands of policing' but also in its style and nature: 'Policing changed as its location changed' (Shearing 1992: 423). One of their most important research findings is that the strategies of commercial security tend to differ significantly from those of the traditional police in that they are more instrumental than moral, offering a more proactive rather than reactive approach to problem-solving. They tend to be concerned with loss prevention and risk reduction rather than with law enforcement or the detection and conviction of criminals. In mass private property the regulatory force of 'membership' and 'access' is a powerful mode of control. If the law is invoked it is often likely to be contract law, rather than the criminal law. The powers of removal, dismissal and exclusion – whether from a night-club, shopping mall or municipal park – are potent administrative tools of policing.

The security guard and the shop owner have private, largely commercial, interests to secure that diverge from those of public prosecution. Security guards are more likely to prioritise the plugging of security breaches in the future, the exclusion of likely offenders and ensuring that the appearance of security is not compromised. Symbolic and ritualistic punishments are not a moral imperative. Commercial security tends to inscribe incentives for conformity and orderly conduct: a 'rewards infrastructure' (Kempa et al. 1999: 206). It prefers to operate through consensual forms of control rather than coercive ones as traditionally associated with state regulation. Shearing (2001) thus juxtaposes a past-regarding, reactive, morally toned and punitive mentality of 'justice' against a risk-based, instrumental and future-oriented mentality of 'security'. The former is associated with traditional aspects of police crime detection work (and the activities of state criminal justice agencies more generally). The latter is associated with commercial operatives and is exercised under plural auspices. This juxtaposition is a useful analytic device; however, it is the osmotic relationships between state and commercial developments and the cross-fertilisation of techniques, practices and mentalities which dominate the field. Furthermore, the specific nature of property relations in different countries means that the 'mass private property' thesis developed originally in relation to North America may be less applicable to the UK and other parts of Europe (Jones and Newburn 1999).

Nevertheless, Britain is witnessing the uneven growth of 'propriety communities', where security constitutes a 'club good', exclusive to those who are members. Forms of such 'collective consumption clubs' (Webster 2002) may be *commercial* in the form of shopping malls, *industrial* through science parks and trading estates or *residential*. Let us consider the latter in further detail.

Private residential estates

The growth of private residential estates and 'gated communities' has been relatively slow in Britain where they remain something of a novelty. By comparison, developments in America and South Africa have dramatically refigured the structure of community organisations, local government, land-use control and neighbour relations. The spread of gated communities has sparked considerable debate in the USA (Alexander 1997; Blakely and Snyder 1997), particularly as they often incorporate private forms of policing and security governance. It is estimated that over 40 million Americans (one sixth of the nation's population) live within 231,000 community associations (as against 500 in 1965), and about a fifth of these are gated and walled (CIA 2002). Half of all new homes in major metropolitan areas belong to common interest housing developments or community associations. Not all these are gated or commercially policed. None the less, they constitute 'contractual communities' in which residents sign up to forms of regulation over their private and public activities and behaviour. Here, the state is all but absent. They represent forms of 'private government' in which the public interest has been reconfigured at a parochial level.

In Britain, progress has been far less dramatic. The legal framework for such developments rests in the leasehold covenant, which sets out property rights, obligations and restrictions. Nevertheless, many urban planning commentators suggest that we are likely to see the growth of gated communities in future years. A report published by the Royal Institute of Chartered Surveyors concluded that the popularity of gated enclaves is on the increase in the UK, often fuelled by concerns over education and crime. Their likely expansion, it suggests, will be facilitated by current weaknesses in planning policy with regard to social mixing and the protection of green-belt sites (Minton 2002). As many housing planners recognise, the best way to attract residents back to city centres lies in a 'sticks and carrots' approach, offering incentives to live in brownfield and inner-city sites and limiting the supply of green-belt land for development. Innovative planners look to 'magnet policies' in this regard. Crime prevention features and a visible policing presence may well come to constitute important 'security magnets' for urban regeneration.

Urban fortunes

As a response to the emergence of out-of-town retail and leisure outlets and in part in competition with each other for new positions of influence and wealth in the reorganised national (and international) economy, city centres have become a focus of concern. The repositioning of city centres has been an important element in the competition for inward investment, the generation of local employment and the regeneration of urban spaces. The pressure to reorganise has been particularly acutely felt in old industrial cities especially where there are nearby large regional shopping centres. It has been estimated, for example, that Sheffield city centre lost between 15 and 20 per cent of its trade after the Meadowhall shopping centre opened (cited in Jones and Newburn 1999: 234). For city centres like this, regeneration and rebranding has been fundamental to their urban fortunes. In this, 'local growth coalitions' (Logan and Molotch 1987), often combining municipal authorities and commercial interests, have played an important role. A central element of this re-imagining has been the capacity to present a city as a 'safe place' to shop and do business. Security as a commodity has been important in establishing a competitive advantage over rival cities within local, national or global economies. Here, the commercial sector has, to some degree, set the agenda from which the public provision of security in urban areas has borrowed. For example, local authority town centre managers are increasingly aping modes of regulation and policing deployed in privately owned out-of-town shopping centres. The deployment of 'city guards', 'street wardens' and 'ambassadors' in city centre areas has been an instrumental part of recent strategy to make the city a more attractive and safe place.

Another manner in which city authorities have learnt from commercial developments has been through the embedding of policing technologies into both design features and occupational responsibilities (Shearing and Stenning 1987). Stimulated by 'defensible space' theory (Newman 1972), an array of design practices clustered under the heading of 'crime prevention through environmental design', have seen greater emphasis on 'designing out' crime and disorder features of the urban environment and capitalising upon civilian or 'natural' surveillance. Thus citizens and employees without designated 'security' tasks can be enlisted in policing activities. Urban planners and designers, it is argued, increasingly have regard to the security implications of new developments.[12] Advances in technology have significantly facilitated this 'embedding the governance of security' (Johnston and Shearing 2003: 26), particularly through forms of surveillance.

The expansion of the night-time economy

In line with these broader urban changes many British cities have seen significant expansion in the night-time economy, fuelled notably by alcohol-based, leisure industries. Pubs, clubs and other night-time outlets have become important elements of post-industrial urban prosperity by attracting inward flows of capital investment and new consumers. And yet they have brought with them safety dilemmas, particularly given the alcohol-related crime and disorder problems that have been generated. For example, between 1998 and 2001 there was a 240 per cent increase in the capacity of Manchester city centre's licensed premises. During almost the same period there was a 225 per cent increase in the number of city centre assaults (Home Office 2001a). Hence, this new expansion of the night-time economy has generated new security demands.

In part, these have been met by the private security industry through 'door supervisors' or 'bouncers', whether internally employed or contracted to security firms. For the large numbers of young people that frequent these new leisure economies bouncers are the dominant form of policing. However, given their lingering association with intimidation, violence, drugs and other forms of criminality, bouncers themselves have come to be seen as a safety issue in need of regulation (see Home Affairs Select Committee 1995). Ironically, it is the demands of the potentially violent environment bouncers are employed to police that encourage the physical nature of the job and the violent and intimidatory subculture it sustains (Hobbs *et al.* 2002). Yet it is these aspects of the policing by bouncers that are the cause of much concern. In response, municipal authorities have sought a number of initiatives aimed at regulating and policing both 'troublesome' night-time consumers *and* commercial staff.

In the absence of state regulation of private security staff, local alliances of municipal and private bodies sought to develop their own regulatory licensing schemes (Lister *et al.* 2001). As a result 'door supervisor regulation schemes' emerged, concerned with promoting the safety of the night-time leisure environment. As with the regulation of private security, the intention was to remove the criminal element, improve standards and legitimise the industry by enhancing its image. Another strategy has been to encourage licensed premises operators to club together to purchase additional levels of public police provision. This has been facilitated by recent changes in legislation that have enabled the police to generate income by selling aspects of their services, including the patrolling function.[13] As a strategy, this addresses concerns that police resources are being pulled into policing the crime and disorder consequences of commercial operations by the alcohol-based leisure industries. Such 'polluter pays' schemes have met with government approval as they encourage business to take 'responsibility themselves for the public order implications of their activities' (Home Office 2001b: 97). However, as Lister (2003) notes, they also present potential conflicts of interests particularly as the police retain a statutory role within the court processes of granting, renewing and revoking operational liquor licences. The concern is that the exercise of discretion in this role may be compromised by whether a potential licensee is willing to contribute to such schemes which directly benefit the local police as a source of income generation.

While it is clear that much of the policing of the night-time economy rests in private hands, it would be wrong to suggest that it has occurred regardless of or despite the state's (in)activity. In many senses, the expansion of the night-time economy has been made possible by the existence of a 'free' form of public policing both willing and able to respond to its crimogenic and disorderly consequences.[14] This 'progression of a commercial frontier' has also been actively facilitated by the local state's deregulatory stance and its encouragement of 'municipal entrepreneurship' (Hobbs *et al.* 2003). A related example is to be found in the diverse ways in which professional police activity has encouraged markets for commercial provision of policing. The Police Act 1964 enables police forces to charge for services where providing security at concerts and football stadia. This has been a significant stimulus to the market in stewards and security guards at such events. This is one reason why most of the policing in football stadia is conducted by stewards employed by the clubs themselves and why popular concerts and festivals are policed by a variety of commercial firms. These examples remind us of the interconnected relations between commercial developments and state (in)activity.

The policing of the Internet

A further arena of social change with considerable policing implications has been the development of the Internet. As an example of a shift in the nature of social organisation and communications, the challenge of the Internet powerfully suggests the need to cut definitions of policing free from their traditional territorial bindings. It also illustrates the manner in which techno-logical change connects with, and provides an engine for, the expansion of commercial policing and security services. The policing of cyberspace funda-mentally alters established notions of time and space, while also reconfiguring property relations away from a physical place-based form to the policing of the more fluid form of intellectual property. In cyberspace ideas are more important than objects; image, copyright, trademarks and patentable materials take on a new salience (Wall 2001).

Far from being an unregulated 'free for all', the Internet is actually the site of multi-level governance involving divergent actors with different regulatory purchase over the Internet environment. As well as the professional police, a diversity of quasi-public, private and commercial policing organisations has emerged to regulate this new frontier. This responsibility has sometimes been assumed reluctantly. For example, Internet service providers (ISPs) – often acting in a transnational manner – have increasingly sought to control some of the activities that take place on their servers (see Chapter 20). Against the background of concerns about the circulation of illegal materials, ISPs in the UK established the Internet Watch Foundation, as a quasi-public face of Internet regulation. It has often been the fear of civil sanctions combined with adverse publicity that has encouraged ISPs to assume a policing role (also demanded of them by the states in which they operate).[15] Corporate security organisations have also become increasingly involved in Internet policing primarily serving to protect the interests of large commercial telecommunications and other related organisations. The policing of the Internet also illustrates the manner in which ordinary citizens, as individual users and user groups, perform important (self-)policing functions, some of which resonate with forms of terrestrial 'community self-regulation' (Wall 2002). The wide array of forms of security governance that coalesce around the policing of cyberspace highlights different degrees of complementarity, as divergent definitions of order and security vie with each other as differing models of justice are deployed.

The relationship between the police and other policing organisations

It is clear that the osmotic relationship between state, non-state and commer-cial developments in policing has seen the cross-fertilisation of techniques, practices and mentalities. In many senses, the public police have borrowed strategies and technologies first deployed and developed in arenas of 'private government'. By contrast, the commercial and municipal sectors have borrowed from the professional police elements of image, symbolic power and authority. The interactive nature of developments across the public–private divide is particularly acute with regard to flows of information. There has been a blurring of functional, legal, sectoral, spatial and even geographical dimensions. As the Patten Report (1999) on the future of policing in Northern Ireland noted, a central question for the future is: 'How can professional police officers best adapt to a world in which their own efforts are only a part of the overall policing of a modern society?' In answer to this question we can identify four different, and potentially conflicting, approaches:

1. An *integrationist* model whereby forms of policing are integrated within the 'immediate police family' of the professional state police.

2. A *steering* model whereby the police seek to 'govern at a distance' the policing activities of others.

3. A *networked* model whereby plural policing providers link together in horizontal partnerships (as equals) in local security provision.

4. A *market* model whereby competition structures the relations between the divergent providers.

All these models are to be found coexisting within recent policy and practice developments.

An integrationist model

Johnston and Shearing note that 'the common police response is a defensive and reactionary one: "How can we re-impose state police control over policing?"' (2003: 11). The integrationist model of 'professional police hegemony' (Johnston and Shearing 2003) sees the police directly employ a larger proportion of the security workforce. The expansion of the police force has occurred in a number of ways. First, the number of professional police officers in England and Wales stands at a record number at over 130,000 officers. Secondly, recent managerialist reforms have encouraged the growing civilianisation of policing whereby police tasks have been devolved to civilian staff. There are now nearly 60,000 full-time equivalent civilian staff in England and Wales (see Table 7.1).

More specifically, the Police Reform Act 2002 introduces a new breed of 'second tier' police officers. As proposed in *Policing a New Century: A Blueprint for Reform* (Home Office 2001b), the Act allows for specified police support staff to be given particular powers in various circumstances in order to perform certain defined functions: civilian detention officers, escort officers and investigating officers. In addition, the Act (s. 38) introduces a new form of patrolling officer known as 'community support officers' (CSOs).[16] CSOs will be appointed by the chief police officer to provide a visible presence, combat low-level anti-social behaviour and provide reassurance. They are intended to support police officers and release fully trained officers from tasks that do not require their level of skills. The powers of CSOs are restricted to hand out fixed-penalty tickets for minor disorders, to request the name and address of a person acting in an anti-social manner, to stop vehicles, direct traffic and remove vehicles.[17] It would appear that the trend towards 'creating "quasi-crimes" for minor public acts of public disorder' has produced a new twist as these are now to be 'policed by "quasi-police officers"' (Ormerod and Roberts 2003: 157).

More controversially, CSOs will be able to detain a person for up to 30 minutes pending the arrival of a constable or to accompany that person to a police station with the person's agreement. Significantly, CSOs will also have the power to use reasonable force to enforce that detention. The first wave of 1,206 CSOs were being introduced in more than half (27) of the police forces across England and Wales in late 2002/early 2003. However, in only six of these areas will CSOs have detention powers.[18] The government intends to deploy 4,000 CSOs by the end of 2005 and has earmarked funding to support further recruitment.

According to some police commentators 'the advent of these new patrolling officers is a revolution in British policing' (Blair 2002: 23). Consequently, there has been some significant opposition to their introduction from within the police, notably from the Police Federation (Mulraney 2002; Gilbertson 2003). Paradoxically, one concern relates to the potentially negative impact of CSO recruitment on the Special Constabulary, against a background of declining numbers.[19] The same may be said for traffic wardens, another member of the 'immediate police family', where numbers are also declining.[20] However, the continuing fall in the number of traffic wardens, in part, reflects the increasing role of local authorities in traffic control and the transferral of responsibilities within and between different public auxiliaries and forms of municipal policing.

A steering model

The steering model constitutes an attempt to link plural providers under the co-ordination of the professional police, with the latter at the apex of a pyramid structure. In this model the police are both ideologically and legally dominant. A key element in this strategy is the accreditation and licensing by the police of the policing activities of others. This approach is also apparent in the 2002 Act. It seeks to harness the commitment of those already involved in crime reduction activities, such as traffic wardens, neighbourhood and street wardens and commercial security staff, through the co-ordination and steering of the 'extended police family'. The Act (ss. 40 and 41) makes provision for community safety accreditation schemes and, in certain circumstances, the granting of limited powers to accredited members of those schemes. Before establishing an accreditation scheme the chief officer must consult with the police authority of that force and all the local authorities that lie within the police area. Accredited 'community safety officers' will be employed by local authorities, housing associations or the private sector (such as shopping centre security staff). Accredited persons may be empowered to issue fixed-penalty notices for only trivial offences. Their powers are not as extensive as those of CSOs. The legislation requires that arrangements are in place for employers of the persons accredited to supervise the carrying out by their employees of the community safety functions.

Accredited community safety officers will only partly be under police direction. Accreditation represents a form of 'arm's length' governance through which the police aim to govern 'at a distance'. While accredited officers will not be under the same form of control as CSOs by virtue of not being directly employed by the police, this has its advantages for the police. It potentially allows a response to public demand for high-visibility reassurance policing without the cost. In fact, the police can charge for accreditation. Moreover, it means that the police are not liable for any unlawful conduct in the performance of policing work by accredited officers. This will fall upon their employers. Finally, accreditation facilitates the responsibilisation of private organisations by encouraging them to take greater account of, and responsibility for, their own policing and security matters. At the same time it will allow for greater police control over certain elements of the private security industry. The nature of the relationship between the regulatory system to be established by the SIA and the accreditation schemes as they develop locally will constitute an interesting dynamic in the unfolding regulation of private security.

Accreditation will allow local police to determine which organisations and agencies they wish to work with in the construction of the extended police family. As a consequence, they will be at the centre of local security network formation, not merely because of their formal legal powers, their legitimate use of force, their relationship with the criminal justice system or access to considerable information and data, but also as a result of their new regulatory role over those providing policing beyond the police. However, given the burden and cost associated with applying for accreditation, let alone the transfer of responsibilities that it entails, the extent to which security providers (from within local authorities and private firms) will be keen to apply for this new position is yet to be determined. It is unclear how keen local police forces will be to grant accreditation. Furthermore, the new-found position of the police as accreditor and licensor of other plural policing providers places them in the ambiguous position of service provider and regulator.

Accreditation will give a certain 'public' status to commercial security guards and their employers. Not only will accredited officers be granted certain powers over and above those exercisable by ordinary citizens but also the manner in which they exercise these will be subject to public interest requirements. Despite the Act not specifying that accredited people are caught by the Human Rights Act 1998, never the less it seems clear that private employers and their accredited employees will be treated as 'public authorities' for the purpose of human rights legislation. Nonetheless, this model assumes a relationship in which policing beyond the police serves as the professional police's 'junior partner' (Cunningham and Taylor 1985).

A networked model

A network model is one in which divergent forms of policing are loosely connected through networks and alliances (Johnston and Shearing 2003). No particular node within the network is given priority. What differentiates a networked model from a market model is that the former presupposes an element of co-ordination, whereas the latter presupposes competition. In theory, if not in practice, the CDA, with its emphasis upon local community safety partnerships, sought to advance the local infrastructure for a networked model (Crawford 2001). Despite the rhetoric, the local community safety partnerships to which it gave rise have largely failed to engage in any significant way with the private sector (HMIC 2000). They almost exclusively incorporate public sector agencies and to a lesser degree the voluntary sector.

Ericson and Haggerty (1997), drawing upon Canadian research, have argued that more and more of the public police's time and resources are being deployed to service networks that have security rather than law enforcement as their principal concern. In this view, increasingly the police have become 'knowledge brokers, expert advisors and security managers to the public and other institutions' (Ericson 1994: 164; see Chapter 26). However, the extent to which this is the case in Britain is much less clear. While, communications policing lies at the heart of many partnership arrangements, information often constitutes a central battleground in interagency conflicts. In reality, information flows between security providers may often be hesitant, non-reciprocal and easily disrupted. Given the plurality of security providers, the central question for a networked model concerns the effective co-ordination of the diverse actors and agencies. The reality of partnership working is often one of conflicting ideologies, aims and purposes (Crawford 1997). Local governance through partnerships, by its very nature, embodies structural conflicts over cultural traditions and working practices between the actors. As such, the idea of networks as a descriptive term tends to imply an overly organised understanding of highly fragmented local security arrangements.

A market model

A market model suggests the need for an independent regulatory agency above and outside the competing parties to ensure fair competition, appropriate standards and the safeguarding of the public interest. While the professional police are in competition with other providers, sometimes directly, they stand outside the regulatory frameworks established for other providers. Regulation is segmented. The commercial security industry has a new regulatory body, the SIA, but other forms of policing are regulated differently. Should the police regulate and license the policing activities of others while simultaneously competing with those other providers (see Chapter 24)? The present position may encourage counterproductive competition between public and private providers, in which the police relationship with private providers is coloured by the nature of their competitive market relation rather than the quality of the policing provided or its capacity to serve the public good. To this end, Loader has argued for the creation of national, regional and local policing commissions whose purpose would be 'to formulate policies and co-ordinate service delivery across the policing network, and to bring to democratic account the public, municipal, commercial and voluntary agencies that comprise it' (2000: 337). Such commissions might act to move a market model closer to a networked model, and in so doing regulate the market deficiencies.

For example, market provision may also produce increasingly monopolistic or large-scale providers that undermine free competition. Perversely, this may facilitate the steering and regulation of plural policing by the state or regulatory authority. It may even be in the interests of such authorities to encourage and foster monopolistic tendencies among private providers. Regardless, this may occur as a by-product of regulatory regimes that disadvantage (and hence remove) small-scale providers due to the costs associated with regulation or accreditation.

Of significant concern regarding the growing commodification of security is the inequitable distribution of policing. One of the central paradoxes of crime prevention and security provision is that there is often an inverse relationship between activity and need. Those who can afford it may opt to purchase additional cover, in the form of security equipment and private police, or retreat behind exclusive and gated walls. As policing becomes a 'club good' serving particular parochial interests, there will be implications for the independence and impartiality of the service delivered. Policing may become increasingly segmented into different tiers depending upon the capacity to pay rather than need. This may leave a residual public sphere policed by a residual public police.

Conclusions

The current policing terrain is complex and ambiguous. Contemporary policing is simultaneously 'joined-up but fragmented'. It is also the object of governmental initiatives which are both 'arm's length but hands on' (Crawford 2001). At one moment, the British state appears to have ceded the governance of security and policing in certain spheres to commercial and voluntary interests (CDA for example). The next moment, it seeks to reassert control – sometimes in a tentative fashion – through centrally funded police controlled programmes (such as the various wardens), regimes of regulation (under the Private Security Industries Act 2001) and accreditation schemes (under the Police Reform Act 2002). Diversification has been stimulated by governmental strategies of responsibilisation and marketisation, as well as fundamental changes in the urban political economy and the nature of property relations. In this, technological and commercial innovation has also played a key role, presenting both new opportunities for security and new threats to it. The inexorable, and potentially insatiable, demand for security is, at times, supply driven and an inescapable facet of contemporary sensibilities. Hence, this quest for security through policing may be self-escalating, such that the more we have the more insecure we are and the more we want (Spitzer 1987: 50). Simultaneously, restraining and adequately responding to this demand will be a major challenge for governments and police.

The developments outlined in this chapter demonstrate the 'indivisibility' of policing that requires us to understand the role of the police within the context of the 'diverse totality' of policing, and which demands an analysis of their interconnectedness (Johnston 1996b: 54). In today's context we need to move beyond a simple public/private or state/non-state dichotomy to conceptualise both the publicness of commercial and voluntary forms of policing and the privateness of professional policing. In so doing, we need to hold on to, rather than discard, the distinctiveness of state action. It is the interface between state regulation (or its absence) and activity, including that of the police, on the one hand, and commercial and voluntary activity on the other hand, that helps to explain the complex nature of plural policing developments.

None the less, the future shape of policing will depend upon the way in which the professional police adapt to a context in which they are no longer perceived as a monopolistic provider. Despite innovations, such as CSOs, the police are unlikely to be able to retain policing 'within the police tent' (Blair 2002). Inappropriately, this suggests a 'police solution' to the problem of policing. To attempt to do so is to try to put the genie back in the bottle (if there ever was one in the first instance). What marks the professional police as distinct in the new division of labour is the generalist nature of their work and their symbolic role. As such, they are often a resource of last resort, to be drawn upon where necessary by other policing agencies or required to 'underwrite the actions of these more specialist bodies' (Jones and Newburn 1998: 246). The role of state policing may be being reduced, encircled and transformed, but it continues to constitute more than one node among many. The state's capacity to be the police of last resort remains a fundamental rationale of government. The pressing questions for the future concern the effective co-ordination of diverse policing efforts and the manner in which plural policing arrangements and networks are harnessed to the 'public good'. This requires the establishment of institutional means for connecting diverse policing activities such that they are rendered accountable and guarantee equitable and equal provision.

Notes

1 It is now estimated that there are 2.5 million CCTV cameras in Britain, some 10 per cent of the worldwide total (Meek 2002).
2 A recent Home Office report called for the transfer of responsibility for prosecuting certain shoplifting offences to shops and for commercial organisations to take on a greater share of the costs associated with policing events and premises (PA Consulting 2001: 18). The Policing Bureaucracy Taskforce is currently exploring how to implement this as well as passing responsibility for the delivery of a package of ancillary tasks from the police to local authorities (O'Dowd 2002).
3 In this respect, Scott (2002: 63) cites the illustrative case in which the RSPCA, in its role of monitoring the welfare of police dogs, first suspended the supply of dogs to police forces (pending an investigation), and then successfully prosecuted a police dog officer for cruelty (*Guardian* 11 June 1998).
4 Local Government (Miscellaneous Provisions) Act 1982, s. 40 grants municipal personnel, where sworn in as a constable by a magistrate, powers of arrest in designated parks and public spaces.
5 See s. 16 of the CDA 1998.
6 An introductory tenancy lasts for 12 months, after which time it converts automatically to a secure tenancy.

7 During the period 1996-8 the number of possession actions taken on grounds of anti-social behaviour increased by 127 per cent (Hunter *et al.* 2000: 60).

8 The proposals will give local education authorities and schools powers to ask parents whose children do not attend school regularly or who have been excluded from school to sign parenting contracts to regulate their behaviour.

9 Martin's conviction was reduced to manslaughter on appeal in 2001 and he received a reduced prison sentence of five years. At the appeal Lord Woolf, the Lord Chief Justice, said that the court understood Martin's frustration at the perceived failure of the police, but that 'any shortcomings could not justify Mr Martin taking the law into his own hands'.

10 Stenning notes the role of industry self-regulation, criminal and civil liability, employment law, contractual liability and mechanisms of accountability through the market, all of which 'may be no less effective in influencing and preventing or reducing abuses' (2000: 345).

11 It is expected that the licensing of security officers will commence at the end of 2004. In addition, the SIA will also license door supervisors, wheel-clampers, security consultants, private investigators and keyholders; some of these sectors will be licensed from the end of 2003. Licenses will need to be renewed after three years.

12 To a certain degree s. 17 of the CDA makes this responsibility explicit.

13 Section 9 of the Police and Magistrates' Courts Act 1994.

14 For the moment, the government appears to have backed down from initial proposals to be introduced in its Anti-social Behaviour Bill to pass the cost of policing public disorder around pubs to the licensed trade (*Guardian* 1 March 2003).

15 Despite widespread fears over the lack of policing of the Internet, to date there have been no prosecutions brought against ISPs in the UK.

16 Interestingly they are being referred to as *police* community support officers (PCSOs) by the police themselves in an attempt to reinforce their status as part of the 'immediate police family'.

17 Their enforcement powers are set out in Part 1 of Schedule 4 of the Act.

18 These powers are being piloted for two years (from December 2002 when the powers came into force) and will be the subject of an HMIC evaluation.

19 The number of specials in March 2002 (see Table 7.1) – 11,598 – was 9 per cent less than a year earlier (Smith *et al.* 2002: 8) and represents a 40 per cent drop on the figure six years ago (19,451).

20 Over the year to March 2002 there was an 11 per cent reduction in the number of traffic wardens.

Selected further reading

The subject of policing as defined in this chapter is reasonably wide ranging and this is reflected in the burgeoning literature that informs current developments and debates. The historical shifts in forms of public and private policing in the UK are well covered by South in *Policing for Profit* (1988) and Johnston in *The Rebirth of Private Policing* (1992). The leading empirically informed research study is Jones and Newburn's *Private Security and Public Policing* (1998). Shearing and Stenning's collection of essays entitled *Private Policing* (1987) remains an excellent reference point. The best general discussions are to be found in *Policing Britain* by Johnston (2000), *The Future of Policing* by Morgan and Newburn (1997), *Policing in a Changing Constitutional Order* by Walker (2000) and *Governing Security* by Johnston and Shearing (2003). The wider community safety implications of policing are covered in Crawford's *Crime Prevention and Community Safety* (1998). Button provides a detailed overview of the different forms of policing in his book *Private Policing* (2002). Hobbs and colleagues' recent study of *Bouncers* (2003) is an informative analysis of an under-researched but important aspect of policing. Some of the highlights from the more extensive North American literature include: Bayley and Shearing's essay 'The future of policing' in the *Law and Society Review* (1996), Forst and Manning's *The Privatization of Policing* (1999) and Ericson and Haggerty's *Policing the Risk Society* (1997). Finally, Rigakos's *The New Parapolice* (2002) provides and interesting and detailed ethnographic account of an innovative private security company in Canada.

References

ACPO (2000) *Working the Beat – Fundamental Principles for the Neighbourhood Warden Programme*. London: ACPO.

Alexander, G.S. (1997) 'Civic property', *Social and Legal Studies*, 6(2): 217–34.

Bayley, D. and Shearing, C. (1996) 'The future of policing', *Law and Society Review*, 30(3): 585–606.

Blair, I. (2002) 'The policing revolution: back to the beat', *New Statesman*, 23 September: 21–3.

Blakely, E.J. and Snyder, M.G. (1997) *Fortress America: Gated Communities in the United States*. Washington, DC: Brookings Institution Press.

Braithwaite, J. (2000) 'The new regulatory state and the transformation of criminology', *British Journal of Criminology*, 40: 222–38.

Braithwaite, J. (2002) *Restorative Justice and Responsive Regulation*. Oxford: Oxford University Press.

Braithwaite, J. (2003) 'What's wrong with the sociology of punishment?', *Theoretical Criminology*, 7(1): 5–28.

BSIA (2001) 'Interesting facts and figures in the UK security industry' at http://www.bsia.co.uk/industry.html.

Burney, E. (1999) *Crime and Banishment: Nuisance and Exclusion in Social Housing*. Winchester: Waterside Press.

Button, M. (1998) 'Beyond the public gaze: the exclusion of private investigators from the British debate over regulating private security', *International Journal of the Sociology of Law*, 26: 1–16.

Button, M. (2002) *Private Policing*. Cullompton: Willan.

CAI (2002) 'Facts about community associations', available at http://www.caion-line.org/about/facts.cfm.

Cohen, S. (1989) 'The critical discourse on "social control": notes on the concept as a hammer', *International Journal of the Sociology of Law*, 17: 347–57.

Crawford, A. (1997) *The Local Governance of Crime*. Oxford: Clarendon Press.

Crawford, A. (1998) *Crime Prevention and Community Safety*. Harlow: Longman.

Crawford, A. (2001) 'Joined-up but fragmented', in R. Matthews and J. Pitts (eds) *Crime, Disorder and Community Safety*. London: Routledge, 54–80.

Cunningham, W.C. and Taylor, T. (1985) *Private Security and Police in America*. Boston, MA: Heinemann.

Department of the Environment/Department of Health (1997) *Code of Guidance on the Housing Act 1996, Parts VI and VII*. London: DoE.

De Waard, J. (1999) 'The private security industry in international perspective', *European Journal on Criminal Policy and Research*, 7(2): 143–74.

Ericson, R. (1994) 'The division of expert knowledge in policing and security', *British Journal of Sociology*, 45(2): 149–75.

Ericson, R. and Haggerty, K. (1997) *Policing the Risk Society*. Oxford: Clarendon Press.

Etzioni, A. (1993) *The Spirit of Community*. New York, NY: Simon & Schuster.

Evans, K., Fraser, P. and Walklate, S. (1996) 'Whom can you trust? The politics of "grassing" on an inner city housing estate', *The Sociological Review*, 44(3): 361–80.

Felson, M. (2002) *Crime and Everyday Life*. (3rd edn). London: Sage.

Forst, B. and Manning, P. (1999) *The Privatization of Policing*. Washington, DC: Georgetown University Press.

Foster, J. (1995) 'Informal social control and community crime prevention', *British Journal of Criminology*, 35(4): 563–83.

Garland, D. (1996) 'The limits of the sovereign state: strategies of crime control in contemporary society', *British Journal of Criminology*, 36(4): 445–71.

Garland, D. (2001) *The Culture of Control*. Oxford: Oxford University Press.

Gilbertson, D. (2003) 'Plastic policemen', *Police Review*, 21 February: 28–9.

Gill, M. and Hart, J. (1997) 'Exploring investigative policing', *British Journal of Criminology*, 37: 549–67.

Habermas, J. (1989) *The Structural Transformation of the Public Sphere*. Cambridge: Polity Press.

Harvey, L., Grimshaw, P. and Pease, K. (1989) 'Crime prevention delivery: the work of crime prevention officers', in R. Morgan and D. Smith (eds) *Coming to Terms with Policing*. London: Routledge, 82–96.

Hauber, A., Hofstra, B., Toornvliet, L. and Zandbergen, A. (1996) 'Some new forms of functional social control in the Netherlands and their effects,' *British Journal of Criminology*, 36: 199–219.

Her Majesty's Inspector of Constabulary (2000) *Calling Time on Crime: A Thematic Inspection on Crime and Disorder*. London: Home Office.

Hobbs, D., Hadfield, P., Lister, S. and Winlow, S. (2002) 'Door lore: the art and economics of intimidation,' *British Journal of Criminology*, 42: 352–70.

Hobbs, D., Hadfield, P., Lister, S. and Winlow, S. (2003) *Bouncers: Violence and Governance in the Night-time Economy*. Oxford: Oxford University Press.

Hofstra, B. and Shapland, J. (1997) 'Who is in control?', *Policing and Society*, 6: 265–81.

Home Affairs Select Committee (1995) *The Private Security Industry*, Vols. 1 and 2. London: HMSO.

Home Office (1993) *Inquiry into Police Responsibilities and Rewards*. London: HMSO.

Home Office (1995) *Review of the Police Core and Ancillary Tasks: Final Report*. London: HMSO.

Home Office (1997) *Getting to Grips with Crime: A New Framework for Local Intervention*. London: Home Office.

Home Office (2001a) *Fighting Violent Crime Together: An Action Plan*. London: Home Office.

Home Office (2001b) *Policing a New Century: A Blueprint for Reform*. London: Home Office.

Home Office (2003) *Respect and Responsibility – Taking a Stand Against Anti-social Behaviour*. London: Home Office.

Hood, C., Scott, C., James, O., Jones, G. and Travers, T. (1999) *Regulation inside Government: Waste-watchers, Quality Police and Sleaze-busters*. Oxford: Oxford University Press.

Hosking, R. and Smith, C. (2003) *Police Service Strength England and Wales: 30th September 2002*. Home Office Online Report 23/03 available at http://www.homeoffice.gov.uk/rds/pdfs2/rdsolr2303.pdf.

Hough, M. and Mayhew, P. (1983) *The British Crime Survey: First Report*. London: HMSO.

Howard, M. (1994) 'A volunteer army awaiting the call', *The Times*, 28 February.

Hunter, C., Nixon, J. and Shayer, S. (2000) *Neighbour Nuisance, Social Landlords and the Law*. London: Chartered Institute of Housing.

Jacobson, J. and Saville, E. (1999) *Neighbourhood Warden Schemes: An Overview*. London: Home Office.

Johnston, L. (1992) *The Rebirth of Private Policing*. London: Routledge.

Johnston, L. (1993) 'Privatisation and protection: spatial and sectoral ideologies in British policing and crime prevention', *Modern Law Review*, 56(6): 771–92.

Johnston, L. (1996a) 'What is vigilantism?', *British Journal of Criminology*, 36(2): 220–36.

Johnston, L. (1996b) 'Policing diversity', in F. Leishman *et al.* (eds) *Core Issues in Policing*. Longman: Harlow, 54–70.

Johnston, L. (2000) *Policing Britain*. Longman: Harlow.

Johnston, L. and Shearing, C. (2003) *Governing Security*. London: Routledge.

Jones, T. and Newburn, T. (1995) 'How big is the private security sector?', *Policing and Society*, 5: 221–32.

Jones, T. and Newburn, T. (1998) *Private Security and Public Policing*. Oxford: Clarendon Press.

Jones, T. and Newburn, T. (1999) 'Urban change and policing', *European Journal on Criminal Policy and Research*, 7(2): 225–44.

Jones, T. and Newburn, T. (2002) 'The transformation of policing', *British Journal of Criminology*, 42: 129–46.

Kempa, M., Carrier, R., Wood, J. and Shearing, C. (1999) 'Reflections on the evolving concept of "private policing"', *European Journal on Criminal Policy and Research*, 7(2): 197–223.

Lasch, C. (1980) *The Culture of Narcissism*. London: Sphere Books.

Lister, S. (2003) 'Policing and regulation developments in the night-time economy: corporate hospitality at the disturbed edge of a commercial frontier', in *Criminal Justice Review 2001–2*. Leeds: Centre for Criminal Justice Studies, 19–21.

Lister, S., Hadfield, P., Hobbs, D. and Winlow, S. (2001) 'Accounting for bouncers: occupational licensing as a mechanism for regulation', *Criminal Justice*, 1(4): 363–84.

Loader, I. (1997) 'Policing and the social: questions of symbolic power', *British Journal of Sociology*, 48(1): 1–18.

Loader, I. (2000) 'Plural policing and democratic governance', *Social and Legal Studies*, 9: 323–45.

Logan, J.R. and Molotch, H. (1987) *Urban Fortunes: The Political Economy of Place*. Berkeley, CA: University of California Press.

Marx, G. (1989) 'Some trends and issues in citizen involvement in the law enforcement process', *Crime and Delinquency*, 35(3): 500–19.

Meek, J. (2002) 'Robo Cop', *Guardian*, G2, 13 June: 4.

Minton, A. (2002) *Building Balanced Communities: The US and UK Compared*. London: RICS.

Mirrlees-Black, C. (2001) *Confidence in the Criminal Justice System: Findings from the 2000 British Crime Survey*. London: Home Office.

Morgan, R. and Newburn, T. (1997) *The Future of Policing*. Oxford: Oxford University Press.

Moss, K. and Pease, K. (1999) 'Crime and Disorder Act 1998: Section 17 a wolf in sheep's clothing?', *Crime Prevention and Community Safety*, 1(4): 15–19.

Mulraney, S. (2002) 'Thumbs down', *Police Review*, 26 April: 26–7.

Newman, O. (1972) *Defensible Space: People and Design in the Violent City*. London: Architectural Press.

O'Dowd, D. (2002) *Policing Bureaucracy Taskforce*. (income generation guide available at http://www.policereform.gov.uk/bureaucracy/change_proposal_reports/Management_Support/Income_Generation_Guide/).

Office of the Deputy Prime Minister (2002) *Living Places: Cleaner, Safer, Greener*. London: ODPM.

Ormerod, D. and Roberts, A. (2003) 'The Police Reform Act 2002', *Criminal Law Review*: 141–64.

Osborne, D. and Gaebler, T. (1992) *Reinventing Government*. Reading, MA: Addison-Wesley.

PA Consulting Group (2001) *Diary of a Police Officer*. London: Home Office.

Palumbo, D., Ferguson, J.L. and Stein, J. (1997) 'The conditions needed for successful community crime prevention', in S.P. Lab (ed.) *Crime Prevention at a Crossroads*. Cincinnati, OH: Anderson Publishing, 79–98.

Patten, C. (1999) *A New Beginning: Policing in Northern Ireland. Report of the Independent Commission on Policing for Northern Ireland*. London: HMSO.

Povey, D., Ellis, C. and Nichols, S. (2003) *Crime in England and Wales. Home Office Statistical Bulletin* 02/03. London: Home Office.

Putnam, R. (2000) *Bowling Alone*. New York, NY: Touchstone.

Reiner, R. (2000) *The Politics of the Police* (3rd edn). Oxford: Oxford University Press.

Rigakos, G. (2002) *The New Parapolice*. Toronto: Toronto University Press.

Rosenbaum, D.P. (1988) 'Community crime prevention: a review and synthesis of the literature', *Justice Quarterly*, 5(3): 323–93.

Sampson, R.J., Raudenbush, S.W. and Earls, F. (1997) 'Neighborhoods and violent crime: a multi-level study of collective efficacy', *Science*, 277: 918–23.

Scott, C. (2002) 'Private regulation of the public sector: a neglected facet of contemporary governance', *Journal of Law and Society*, 29(1): 56–76.

Shapland, J. and Vagg, J. (1988) *Policing by the Public*. London: Routledge.

Shearing, C. (1992) 'The relation between public and private policing', *Crime and Justice*, 15: 399–434.

Shearing, C. (2001) 'Punishment and the changing face of governance', *Punishment and Society*, 3(2): 203–20.

Shearing, C. and Stenning, P. (1981) 'Modern private security: its growth and implications', *Crime and Justice*, 3: 193–245.

Shearing, C. and Stenning, P. (1983) 'Private security: implications for social control', *Social Problems*, 30: 493–506.

Shearing, C. and Stenning, P. (1987) 'Say "cheese"!: The Disney order that is not so Mickey Mouse', in C. Shearing and P. Stenning (eds) *Private Policing*. London: Sage, 317–23.

Sheptycki, J. (ed.) (2000) *Issues in Transnational Policing*. London: Routledge.

Sklansky, D.A. (1999) 'The private police', *UCLA Law Review*, 46(4): 1165–287.

Smith, C., Rundle, S. and Hosking, R. (2002) *Police Service Strength: England and Wales, 31 March 2002* 10/02. London: Home Office.

Social Exclusion Unit (1998) *Bringing Britain Together: A National Strategy for Neighbourhood Renewal*. London: Cabinet Office.

Social Exclusion Unit (2001) *National Strategy for Neighbourhood Renewal*. London: Cabinet Office.

South, N. (1988) *Policing for Profit*. London: Sage.

Spitzer, S. (1987) 'Security and control in capitalist societies: the fetishism of security and the secret thereof', in J. Lowman *et al*. (eds) *Transcarceration: Essays in the Sociology of Social Control*, Aldershot: Gower, 43–58.

Stenning, P. (2000) 'Powers and accountability of private police', *European Journal on Criminal Policy and Research*, 8(3): 325–52.

Van Dijk, F. and de Waard, J. (2001) *Public and Private Crime Control: Dutch and International Trends*. The Hague: Ministry of Justice.

Walker, N. (2000) *Policing in a Changing Constitutional Order*. London: Sweet & Maxwell.

Wall, D. (ed.) (2001) *Crime and the Internet*. London: Routledge.

Wall, D. (2002) 'Insecurity and the policing of cyberspace', in A. Crawford (ed.) *Crime and Insecurity: The Governance of Safety in Europe*. Cullompton: Willan, 186–209.

Webster, C. (2002) 'Property rights and the public realm', *Environment and Planning B: Planning and Design*, 29: 397–412.

Wiles, P. (1996) *The Quality of Service of the Sedgefield Community Force*. Sheffield: University of Sheffield.

Wilson, J.Q. and Kelling, G. (1982) 'Broken windows: the police and neighbourhood safety', *The Atlantic Monthly*, March: 29–37.

Chapter 8

The police organisation

Rob C. Mawby and Alan Wright

Introduction

This scene-setting chapter provides the introductory context to the more detailed arguments elsewhere in this volume. It is deliberately descriptive rather than critical. It sets out a factual profile of the public police to enable newcomers to the subject and non-specialists to locate the important substantive debates of the other chapters in their organisational context. The chapter is set out as follows.

First, we set out a basic description of the 43 so-called 'Home Office' forces in England and Wales. Second, we consider the structure of forces, examining the building blocks of the police organisation. This includes headquarters, basic command units and local policing arrangements. Third, we consider the hierarchical rank system and also recruitment, training and promotion. Fourth, we comment on police civilianisation. Fifth, we examine the role and responsibilities of the police and the tasks they routinely perform. Sixth, we describe the management, control and oversight of the public police and highlight the role of influential stakeholders. Seventh, we outline the development of policing agencies at the national level in the fields of both operations and support. To conclude, although this chapter only seeks to provide the introductory context to more detailed arguments elsewhere in the volume, we highlight a number of emerging issues that the police organisation faces.

The police of England and Wales

For readers new to this subject, there is a danger of talking about 'the police' of England and Wales as if they were one organisational entity. From the outset, it is necessary to be clear about what it is to which we are referring. The police in England and Wales are not a unitary body similar to the national police forces that exist in many parts of Europe, such as Finland, France or Hungary. So far, policing in England and Wales has not developed into a single, national police of this kind. Although on some occasions we might refer to 'the police service' as if it were a single entity, it continues to consist of a number of police 'forces', each of which has its own organisational structure.

Indeed the term police 'force' itself may be now somewhat less appropriate than it was hitherto. Readers should be aware of the apparent dichotomy between care and control in policing debated in this volume (see also Stephens and Becker 1994). Many individual police organisations present themselves as providing a 'service' to the public, rather than exercising force. The Metropolitan Police, for example, renamed itself the *Metropolitan Police Service* in 1988, following a study by corporate identity consultants (Wolff Olins 1988). Here, however, we will adopt the convention of referring to individual police organisations that have responsibility for the policing of a specific geographical area as 'police forces'. We will use the term the 'police service' to refer to the police forces of England and Wales as a whole.

With the exception of the City of London Police, all the police forces currently existing in England and Wales (the so-called 'Home Office' forces) have been subject to amalgamations and boundary change. Several amalgamations took place during the 1939–45 war and more followed the Police Acts of 1946 and 1964. The Local Government Act 1972 did away with the remaining county borough police forces. In April 1974, the Home Office consolidated the then existing forces into 41 county or area forces. These, with the addition of the City of London Police and the Metropolitan Police, make up the 43 forces that now carry out the territorial policing of England and Wales (see Figure 8.1).

In addition to the police forces of England and Wales, there are eight regional police forces in Scotland. These comprise Central Scotland Police, Dumfries and Galloway Constabulary, Fife Constabulary, Grampian Police, Lothian and Borders Police, Northern Constabulary, Strathclyde Police and Tayside Police. As was the case in England and Wales, police forces in Scotland were also subject to amalgamations after the passing of the Local Government (Scotland) Act 1973. We will not discuss these forces in detail because Scottish policing works under a different legal tradition and accountability structure from that in England and Wales. Lack of space here precludes the extended discussion of Scottish policing that it deserves (but see Walker 1999).

Similarly, we do not discuss the policing of Northern Ireland. The Police Service of Northern Ireland came into being in November 2001 following the recommendations of the Patten Commission on policing in the province (1999). It replaced the Royal Ulster Constabulary, which itself had been in operation since the disbandment of the Royal Irish Constabulary in 1922. Again, this subject deserves a more extensive discussion than we have space for here (but see Ellison and Smyth 2000; Mulcahy 2000; Chapter 19).

In this chapter, we confine our discussion to the 43 'Home Office' forces in England and Wales. Readers should also be aware of role of the 'non-Home Office' police forces that have a specialised remit and exercise their jurisdiction throughout the UK (Oliver 1997: 96; Button 2002; see Chapter 7). These include the British Transport police (BTP); the Ministry of Defence Police (MDP); and the United Kingdom Atomic Energy Authority Constabulary (UKAEAC). The Jersey, Guernsey and Isle of Man Police are separate organisations that carry out policing in those islands.

Figure 8.1 Police forces in England and Wales and Scotland

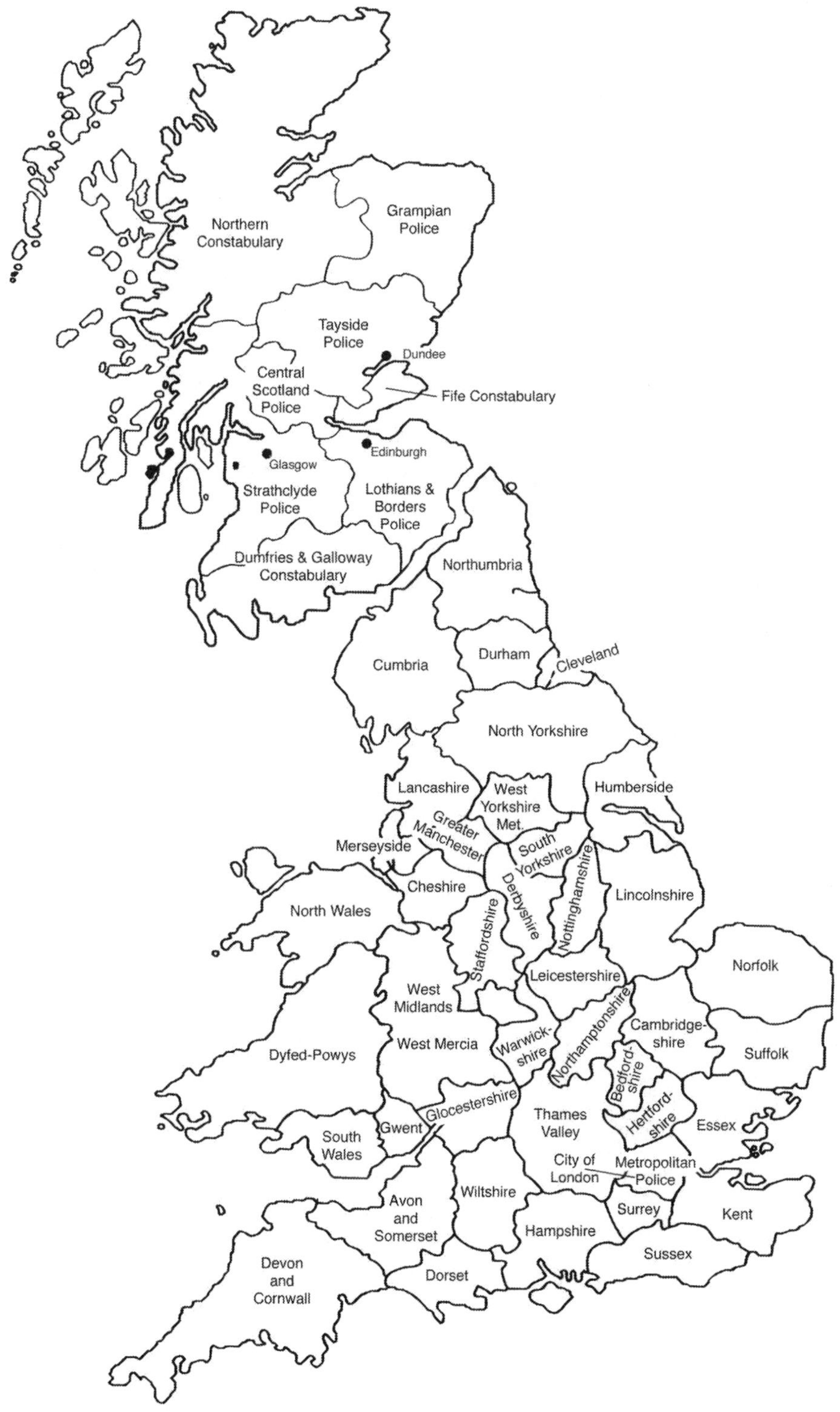

Table 8.1 Police forces in England and Wales (police strengths and other data to 2002)

Force	Location by English government office regions and Wales	Net annual revenue expenditure (£)	Expenditure per 1,000 population (£)	Total police ranks	Total male ranks	Total female ranks	Total minority ethnic officers	Total civilian staff	Total special constables	Total officers per 100,000 population
Avon and Somerset	South West	194,595,000	128,734.5	3,096	2,601	495	41	1,611	364	204.8
Bedfordshire	Eastern	71,807,500	129,011.0	1,069	860	209	49	524	118	188.9
Cambridgeshire	Eastern	84,131,000	115,216.4	1,362	1,140	222	36	733	207	186.5
Cheshire	North West	120,533,000	122,692.4	2,059	1,675	383	12	884	191	209.2
City of London	London	50,941,000	N/A*	764	651	113	24	247	36	*
Cleveland	North East	92,394,000	166,176.3	1,461	1,207	254	19	626	85	262.5
Cumbria	North West	70,487,135	143,320.7	1,100	895	205	4	631	102	224.0
Derbyshire	East Midlands	121,690,000	124,452.9	1,848	1,541	306	53	953	260	189.0
Devon and Cornwall	South West	203,604,000	128,319.2	3,053	2,502	550	15	1,639	689	192.4
Dorset	South West	85,272,276	123,064.0	1,381	1,141	240	10	741	253	197.8
Durham	North East	87,589,000	144,369.5	1,614	1,299	315	17	660	134	266.0
Dyfed–Powys	Wales	62,558,898	129,575.2	1,132	945	187	6	459	157	234.5
Essex	Eastern	190,298,000	116,826.1	2,946	2,433	512	48	1,571	381	180.8
Gloucestershire	South West	71,138,000	125,943.4	1,183	948	234	16	545	154	209.4
Greater Manchester	North West	432,769,000	167,350.7	7,217	5,858	1,358	213	3,135	338	279.1
Gwent	Wales	79,491,000	142,610.3	1,333	1,099	235	16	570	142	239.2
Hampshire	South East	216,200,000	120,331.7	3,480	2,813	667	40	1,597	444	194.8
Hertfordshire	Eastern	130,005,000	123,717.7	1,825	1,448	377	31	1,121	206	173.7
Humberside	Yorkshire/Humber	128,205,904	145,539.7	2,058	1,687	372	17	816	207	233.6
Kent	South East	212,092,000	132,720.7	3,355	2,685	670	51	1,958	327	209.9
Lancashire	North West	197,083,000	137,083.3	3,304	2,698	605	59	1,442	363	231.1
Leicestershire	East Midlands	113,124,000	120,511.2	2,100	1,743	357	97	816	143	223.7
Lincolnshire	East Midlands	76,054,000	119,902.3	1,198	1,009	190	11	600	155	188.9
Merseyside	North West	272,500,000	193,348.5	4,125	3,431	695	81	1,532	468	293.9
Metropolitan Police	London	2,128,386,000	288,841.7	26,223	21,988	4,235	1,286	10,459	680	365.9

Norfolk	Eastern	98,400,000	122,388.1	1,468	1,223	245	15	819	244	182.6
Northamptonshire	East Midlands	77,060,000	123,119.7	1,214	980	234	33	742	177	194.0
Northumbria	North East	221,697,000	156,787.1	3,929	3,264	664	35	1,403	256	277.8
North Wales	Wales	89,451,000	135,985.1	1,506	1,251	255	7	645	125	228.1
North Yorkshire	Yorkshire/Humber	95,000,000	126,011.4	1,417	1,181	236	7	743	185	188.0
Nottinghamshire	East Midlands	140,825,000	136,431.9	2,330	1,977	352	72	1,087	341	225.9
South Wales	Wales	190,643,000	153,833.8	3,222	2,689	534	42	1,435	277	258.7
South Yorkshire	Yorkshire/Humber	189,480,266	145,582.5	3,199	2,577	622	83	1,352	206	245.8
Staffordshire	West Midlands	132,268,329	124,708.5	2,133	1,714	419	31	1,030	384	201.3
Suffolk	Eastern	76,934,000	113,154.9	1,203	984	218	21	692	308	176.9
Surrey	South East	122,050,641	112,942.5	1,992	1,594	398	33	1,043	187	184.3
Sussex	South East	183,875,000	120,773.3	2,893	2,355	538	30	1,507	306	190.0
Thames Valley	South East	251,799,000	118,337.7	3,762	3,087	675	106	2,061	356	176.8
Warwickshire	West Midlands	60,474,000	118,585.8	969	809	160	29	459	209	189.9
West Mercia	West Midlands	135,164,000	117,875.2	2,018	1,670	349	28	1,116	339	176.0
West Midlands	West Midlands	413,600,000	157,922.9	7,681	5,933	1,748	369	3,007	598	293.3
West Yorkshire	Yorkshire/Humber	328,699,800	155,534.0	4,889	3,964	926	152	2364	349	230.5
Wiltshire	South West	75,540,000	123,132.2	1,157	932	226	17	649	147	188.7
England and Wales		8,385,909,749	158,438.3	127,267	104,483	22,784	3,362	58,022	11,598	240.4

Sources: Smith *et al.* (2002); Home Office Research and Statistics Directorate; HM Chief Inspector of Constabulary, Annual Report 2002.
Note *Officers per 100,000 of population for the City of London and Metropolitan Police are combined.

There can be little doubt that policing has been a major policy issue in recent years. As part of the government's drive against crime, and in an attempt to satisfy public concerns, police officer numbers in England and Wales have reached record levels (129,603 officers in total by 2002). Forty forces increased their total officer strengths in the 12 months up to March 2002. In 19 forces, the latest increases have taken officer strengths to record levels. The number of female ranks was up by 4.5 per cent on 2001 totals. Officers from the minority ethnic groups also increased by 14 per cent on the previous year, though from a low base. In 1999, the government introduced race equality targets for the public services. Each police force must achieve a proportion of its police staff that reflects the ethnic mix of its policing area by 2009 (Home Office 2002, 2003).

In Table 8.1 we set out some basic information on the 43 'Home Office' police forces that currently exist in England and Wales. As will be evident in examining this comparative table, police forces differ considerably in size. They also differ in some aspects of their organisation. The fact that the eight 'metropolitan' forces (Greater Manchester, City of London, Merseyside, the Metropolitan Police, Northumbria, South Yorkshire, West Midlands and West Yorkshire) account for 46 per cent of the total police strength in England and Wales has an inevitable effect on their organisation. Larger forces necessarily have larger administrations and central investigation functions, although the structure of local policing through Basic Command Units (BCUs) is similar (see below). The question of the optimum size for a police force runs through the recurring debate over whether there should be further force amalgamations. Citing economies of scale, enhanced performance, improved leadership and adjusting to the challenges of twenty-first century criminality, commentators have argued cases for variously, one national police force with regional commanders; amalgamating the current 43 forces into six forces; and creating between 10 and 25 'super' forces (Hancock 2003).

Recent Home Office publications have included the location of police forces within the geographical areas covered by government offices for the regions or Wales (Smith *et al.* 2002). A growing amount of regionalisation, co-ordinated through the office of the Deputy Prime Minister, seems unlikely to by-pass policing in the medium to longer term. Although we cannot be certain that the clustering of forces under these headings is a precursor to amalgamation into a number of regional police forces, there can be little doubt that the concentration of political and administrative power in the regions will affect policing. If regional assemblies become a reality, it seems likely that they would play an important role in regional police accountability.

The structure of police organisations

International comparison shows that states structure their police forces in varying ways, but patterns of centralised and decentralised policing, and indeed mixed models, do emerge (see R.I. Mawby 1990; Benke *et al.* 1997; Loveday and Reid 2003; Chapter 2). In England and Wales, as described in the section above, policing has retained a decentralised, local character, although there are instances of regional collaboration – for example, the Central

Motorway Patrol Group in the West Midlands. In addition, standardisation is apparent in the development of a national operational communications system (Airwave). Significantly, the Police Reform Act 2002 contained provisions that would facilitate regionalisation or nationalisation.[1]

Forces have developed in ways that depend upon historical and geographical differences. However, the development of the structures of individual forces suggests that there are cyclical patterns of restructuring. These have often involved the reorganisation of forces into smaller or larger subunits, which become hubs of operational policing. Despite the differences between forces, a recognisable structural model exists for the police organisation. Typically, a force comprises a headquarters, which houses the strategic managers and support departments, and a number of BCUs, which deliver policing services within a geographical area. The number of BCUs that forces are organised into ranges from two to 32, but the median is six (Audit Commission 2001).

The Audit Commission (2001) has described the activities of the force headquarters as:

- setting and co-ordinating force-wide strategy, policy and standards;

- scrutinising and monitoring the performance of BCUs and HQ departments;

- allocating resources, in line with the overall budget set by the police authority;

- providing business support, e.g. finance and human resources (HR); and

- direct provision of some specialist operational functions and/or support to BCUs in these areas, e.g. major crime investigation and armed response.

The headquarters purpose is, therefore, both to support and to monitor the force's BCUs, whose core role is to provide basic policing services within a fixed geographical area. These policing services include 'patrol, 24-hour response and investigation of "volume" crime such as burglary, robbery and theft – and to work with local partners to reduce crime and disorder' (Audit Commission 2001).

If we take one shire force (we use Staffordshire as an example), then this has a headquarters and four operational 'territorial' divisions – the BCUs. The headquarters comprises two types of departments – 'Operational Support' and 'Organisational Support and Development'. The former departments include Crime Support, Criminal Justice Administration, the Communications Centre, the Operations Division, the Professional Standards and the Legal Departments. The latter serve the internal requirements of the force – Human Resources, Support Services, Technology Services, Performance Development, Financial Support and Employee Health and Care. The senior command team direct and manage the force from headquarters.

Each territorial Division or BCU has its own headquarters. This is the base for the divisional command team and the divisional support and operations units – for example, the Criminal Investigation Department (CID). It is from here that the divisional commander (a chief superintendent) oversees the delivery of policing in the local policing units (LPUs) or 'sectors' as some forces call them. These are smaller geographical areas in which teams deliver policing at the local level, under the direction of an inspector. At the 'lowest' level of geographical policing, within the LPU uniformed officers may each have personal responsibility for maintaining links with the local community and problem-solving in a small area known as a 'beat'. These are typically aligned to ward boundaries and, in some forces, are subdivided to create 'micro-beats'.

Although there are some variations in the names of units and departments and their precise roles and locations, this model is typical of many provincial and metropolitan forces (see Figure 8.2). However, although there is a degree of structural isomorphism between police forces, size matters. We have already alluded to the larger central investigative, specialist and administrative structures of the metropolitan forces. The Metropolitan Police Service, for example, has large investigative units, based at New Scotland Yard, dealing with forensic services, intelligence, serious crime and terrorism.

Although forces call their territorial policing units by various names, including *areas, districts, divisions, operational command units* and *boroughs,* generically they are all BCUs. BCUs have grown in significance at least since the 1991 Audit Commission Report, *Reviewing the Organisation of Provincial*

Figure 8.2 The structure of a typical provincial force

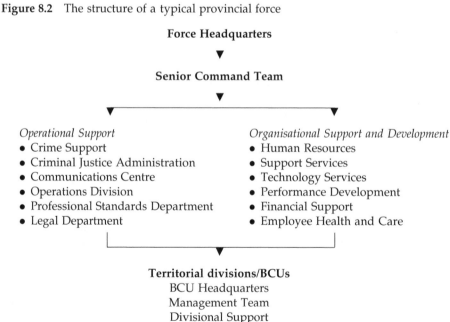

Force Headquarters
▼
Senior Command Team
▼

Operational Support
- Crime Support
- Criminal Justice Administration
- Communications Centre
- Operations Division
- Professional Standards Department
- Legal Department

Organisational Support and Development
- Human Resources
- Support Services
- Technology Services
- Performance Development
- Financial Support
- Employee Health and Care

▼
Territorial divisions/BCUs
BCU Headquarters
Management Team
Divisional Support
Divisional Operations
▼
Local policing units/sectors
Inspector
Community beat officers
Response officers

Police Forces, which argued the case for devolving power to allow local discretion and flexibility in the use of resources. Government efforts to measure performance and improve standards of policing have focused on BCUs as the unit of analysis. The 2001 white paper, *Policing a New Century* (Home Office 2001), put the BCU at the heart of its vision to modernise the service by devolving more power down to the 318 BCUs across England and Wales. The Police Standards Unit (PSU) has a specific mandate to focus on BCUs and since April 2001 they are subject to inspection by Her Majesty's Inspectorate of Constabulary (HMIC). HMIC (2002a) provides a summary of emerging findings from the inspections.

The purpose of this critical gaze is to compare and improve performance across the service nationally, taking into account that BCUs differ in size (from less than 100 to more than 1,000 police officers), population policed (from 4,000 to 300,000 residents) and physical area (from one square mile to several hundred) (Audit Commission 2001). Some cover heavily populated ethnically diverse cities and towns. Others cover large, but sparsely populated, rural areas. The Home Office has undertaken to make public the performance of BCUs using a suite of performance indicators and 'performance radar' diagrams (Home Office 2002: 37–9, paras 11.1–11.2).

In relation to the structuring of BCUs and local policing, it is pertinent to mention that partnership working has become a statutory requirement of police work since the Crime and Disorder Act 1998 that established formal 'Crime and Disorder Reduction Partnerships' (CDRPs) (Newburn 2002). Although partnership working under the Act is primarily at BCU level, in practice BCUs often delegate the implementation of localised schemes within partnerships to local policing units. Taking Staffordshire again as an example, there are nine formal CDRP partnerships operating across the four BCUs. Clearly, for administrative and operational reasons, partnerships can develop, make decisions and operate more easily when their borders are coterminous but, due to historical circumstances, this is not always the case. Most forces in England and Wales have attempted to make BCUs coterminous with borough/district/unitary-level local authorities. However, in the case of some large local authorities (for example Birmingham) there may be several BCUs in one local authority and in the case of smaller local authorities (for example Rutland) the BCU may encompass several local authorities.

Ranks, recruitment and career development

The traditions and symbolism of British policing make considerable play on the claim that police officers are simply 'civilians in uniform' (emphasised by the 1929 Royal Commission on the Police). This has not always sat easily with an organisation that possesses the state mandate for the delivery of coercive force and which appears to be organised on a quasi-military basis.

This mixture of the civilian and the military has its origins in the establishment of the modern police. In the 1820s, opposition existed to the creation of a police force akin to the continental model of policing, which cast the police as overt and covert agents of the state (Chapman 1970). The English were also suspicious of large standing armies and any new police force would need to disassociate itself from both the continental model and the military. The architect of the new police, Peel, and the first Metropolitan Police Commissioners, Rowan (a military colonel) and Mayne (a lawyer), took these factors into account. The police were uniformed, to communicate that they were not spies and the uniform was deliberately a different colour (blue) from military uniforms (black) (Reith 1943: 36; Ascoli 1979: 90). Secondly, the police were unarmed, again to distinguish them from the military, and the truncheons they carried were discretely positioned out of view in the tunic (Reith 1952: 152; Waddington 2000: 170). Thirdly, the low pay discouraged 'gentlemen and commissioned officers' from joining, thus avoiding again the 'taint of militarism' (Emsley 1992: 116).

In 1829, the Metropolitan Police were established with, beneath the two commissioners, a hierarchical rank structure of superintendents, inspectors, sergeants and constables. Only the title of sergeant was taken from the military. The superintendent and inspector titles came from the old parochial and public office systems (Ascoli 1979: 85), while the office of constable was long established (see Emsley 1996: 8–14; Chapter 3). This model has essentially remained intact across police forces, though with the addition of intermediate ranks, such that, at the time of writing, the hierarchy in forces is as shown in Table 8.2.

This organisational structure faced increasing criticism during the 1990s. In April 1992, the House of Commons committee on police co-operation in the European Community reported that the British policing system was suffering

Table 8.2 The police service rank structure

	Provincial and Metropolitan forces	The Metropolitan Police Service	City of London Police
The federated ranks			
Practitioners	Constable	Constable	Constable
Supervisors	Sergeant	Sergeant	Sergeant
Managers	Inspector	Inspector	Inspector
	Chief inspector	Chief inspector	Chief inspector
The superintending ranks			
Middle managers	Superintendent	Superintendent	Superintendent
	Chief superintendent	Chief superintendent	Chief superintendent
The ACPO ranks			
Strategic managers	Assistant chief constable	Commander	Commander
	Deputy chief constable	Deputy assistant commissioner	Assistant commissioner
	Chief constable	Assistant commissioner	Commissioner
		Deputy commissioner	
		Commissioner	

from 'blind incompetence' in its management and called for the end of its 'Heath Robinson structures' (cited in *Institute of Race Relations Police Media Bulletin* 63). In this climate in May 1993 the then Home Secretary, Kenneth Clarke, announced an inquiry to examine the rank structure, remuneration framework and the terms and conditions of service of police officers. Sir Patrick Sheehy's *Inquiry into Police Responsibilities and Rewards* tackled perceived internal management deficiencies, and recommended a flatter rank structure, fixed-term appointments, performance-related pay and the abolition of allowances and perks (Sheehy 1993).

Sheehy recommended flattening the rank structure by dispensing with the ranks of chief inspector, chief superintendent and deputy chief constable. There followed a period when the ranks of chief superintendent and deputy chief constable were no longer used, but both have since been resurrected. In recent years, criticisms of the quality of police supervision and leadership have remained persistent (see Chapter 25). These have run hand in hand with the development of a performance culture that has become an increasingly prominent aspect of policing (McLaughlin and Murji 1997, 2001). This has implications for the recruitment, training and promotion of police officers.

All officers enter the police service at the lowest rank of constable. While forces previously had variable selection criteria, for example concerning height and eyesight, national recruitment standards were introduced in April 2003. No minimum or maximum height requirements exist and the minimum age is 18, but there is no upper limit. An applicant must be a British citizen, an EU/EEA national or Commonwealth citizen or a foreign national with no restrictions applicable on their length of stay in the UK. Regarding educational attainments, there are no formal requirements, but applicants must pass written literacy and numeracy tests. They must also pass a national 'job-related fitness test'. Suitable applicants can apply to any force that has vacancies and is recruiting.

Successful applicants spend two years as probationary officers, completing their foundation training. This comprises residential and on-the-job training in law and policing skills. The current regime (excluding the Metropolitan Police Service, which differs slightly), consists of six stages, as detailed in Table 8.3.

At the time of writing, this training is under review and it is likely that in the future the training will still be completed over two years but in a more flexible way, with the residential period being broken up through Internet-based

Table 8.3 Probationer foundation training

Stage	Probationer training component
1	Two weeks' local induction and familiarisation
2	Fifteen weeks' residential course at a regional centre
3	Two weeks' in-service learning local procedures
4	Ten weeks on patrol with a tutor constable
5	Two weeks' review of additional needs
6	In-service development work for the remaining period

and distance learning. It is also likely that, during the second year, probationers will begin to focus on their possible specialisms. After the satisfactory completion of this period, officers have the opportunity to develop their careers pursuing specialist roles, which include detective work, traffic duties, firearms deployment, etc. Training courses are available to equip them for specialist duties.

While all police officers begin as constables, there has been a recurring debate concerning direct entry to the higher ranks and, to a lesser extent, accelerated promotion schemes (for example, the current Police High Potential Development Scheme) which aim to recruit fast-tracking high-achievers. On the one hand it is argued that it is necessary for prospective chief constables to walk the beat for two years and to have practised policing in order that they can understand and lead a police force. On the other hand, it is argued that the multi-tiered rank system discourages ambitious, able graduates and that a chief constable post is more suited to an experienced professional person with a knowledge of business and finance, strategy and management than a practising police officer.

In order for officers to progress through the ranks, they must pass the sergeants' and inspectors' examinations (OSPRE or, in full, the Objective Structured Performance Related Police Promotion Exam) and then be successful in interview. Promotion to senior posts above the rank of inspector depends on successful assessment. To achieve the ACPO ranks (assistant chief constable and above), an officer must have served as a superintendent for at least two years and must successfully complete the Strategic Command Course (SCC), designed by Centrex (the working name of the Central Police Training and Development Authority). This course has undergone transformations in recent years and has yet to establish its credibility as being the most effective vehicle for producing the strategic leaders required by police forces. Once officers have passed the SCC, they are able to apply for assistant chief constable posts advertised by local police authorities, which devise their own interview and assessment policies. The Police Reform Act 2002 has delegated ministerial approval of candidates to Her Majesty's Chief Inspector of Constabulary (HMCIC), who chairs a panel to consider candidates' suitability (HMCIC 2002: 30–1). It has become commonplace at ACPO level for police authorities to offer fixed-term contracts of between four and seven years.

Civilians in the police organisation

We have focused in the above section on the recruitment, training and promotion of police officers but, as we noted earlier, there has always been references to officers being 'civilians in uniform'. However, while the service's senior officer, the Metropolitan Police Commissioner, is in fact a civilian, in the historical development of the police organisation, civilian support staff have often been treated as second-class citizens with little status and lacking career development structures and prospects (Highmore 1993; Loveday 1993; Berry *et al.* 1998). In recent years, however, there have been increased opportunities for non-police officers to develop careers at different levels and in specialist roles. Since the 1980s, the Home Office has encouraged the police service to recruit civilian staff in specialist functions and it is now possible for professional people to join forces as corporate communications managers, crime analysts, forensic analysts and financial and performance specialists. At a strategic level, since the mid-1990s forces have recruited civilian staff to join the ACPO-level team to provide specialist financial or other strategic input. At yet another level, the skills gaps in certain areas, for example, crime investigation, has opened the doors for forces to recruit retired detectives to assist with investigative work. This is, of course, in addition to the pattern of civilianised policing which is emerging through the employment of community support officers (CSOs) and investigation officers, empowered by the Police Reform Act 2002.

This expansion of civilianised forms of policing is significant to the development of the police organisation. The Police Reform Act 2002, the National Policing Plan for England and Wales 2003–6 and the Policing Bureaucracy Taskforce Report published in September 2002 (www.policereform.gov.uk/bureaucracy) all included provisions relating to greater involvement of civilians in policing, both in the front line and also in support roles. This runs from the recently appointed CSOs to volunteers, including the long-established Special Constabulary. The government introduced uniformed CSOs in September 2002 as a 'second tier' of policing, with the intention of having 4,000 of them in place by 2005. CSOs complement the work of police officers and work under the direction of the local police commander. Under the Police Reform Act 2002, chief constables can give CSOs limited powers to deal with anti-social behaviour and disorder.

It was feared in some quarters that the introduction of paid CSOs might have an impact on the volunteer membership of the Special Constabulary. Consequently there have been a number of high-profile recruitment campaigns and events, including the first 'National Specials Weekend' that was held in February 2003. The Police Act 1964 established the Special Constabulary in its modern form. Each police force has its own Special Constabulary (see Table 8.1 for details of numbers in 2002). These comprise volunteers who commit at least four hours per week to working with and supporting regular police officers. They wear similar uniforms to, and have the same powers as, regular officers. The eligibility criteria for recruitment are also similar to those for regular officers and training is provided by the local force and through a national training package. Specials are subject to the same rules of conduct and disciplinary procedures as regular officers. While specials have been lampooned as 'hobby Bobbies' and in the past have experienced problems of integration and communication with regulars (Berry et al. 1998: 241), they are representatives of their local community and as such remain an important component in local policing.

In addition to special constables, there are other types of civilian volunteers. Ten forces operate voluntary police cadet schemes for 14–18-year-olds.[2] The cadets assist their local force in such activities as crime prevention initiatives and the stewarding of events. Another form of volunteer is that of voluntary support staff. These roles are specific to the needs of individual forces, but generally involve assisting regular support staff with administrative work.

While the civilianisation of policing has consistently encountered opposition, principally from policing stakeholders, but also from other sources, on the grounds of 'policing on the cheap', effectiveness, competency and accountability, it is, nevertheless, an integral part of the future of the police organisation. (See Chapter 7 for a detailed assessment of the civilianisation of policing, and Wright (2002) for the implications of a wider interpretation of the term 'policing' to include civilian and non public-police agencies.)

Mapping policing tasks

So, how does the organisational structure relate to the tasks of policing? To pursue this, we must consider the role of the public police and what they actually do. This is not quite the simple task that it ostensibly sounds; policing is a multifaceted activity in an increasingly complex and fragmented world.

In September 1829, the first commissioners of the new police issued their *General Instructions* to the new recruits. These established the prevention of crime as the principal responsibility of the police, together with the protection of life and property, and the preservation of public tranquillity (Reith 1956: 135–6; Ascoli 1979: 87). The *Police Service Statement of Common Purpose and Values*, introduced in 1990, in part echoed these original instructions, namely, it stated that the purpose of the police service was:

> to uphold the law fairly and firmly; to prevent crime; to pursue and bring to justice those who break the law; to keep the Queen's Peace; to protect, help and reassure the community; and to be seen to do this with integrity, common sense and sound judgement (ACPO 1990: 1).

More concretely, the tasks of the police are shaped locally by policing plans developed by local police authorities (a requirement of the Police and Magistrates' Courts Act (PMCA) 1994 and the Police Act 1996) and ministerial priorities. In addition, since November 2002, the National Policing Plan for England and Wales 2003–6 sets out (for the first time, and as a requirement of the Police Reform Act 2002) the government's strategic priorities for the police service over a three-year period. Paragraph 1.4 of the plan states:

> The primary objective for the police service for the Plan's three-year duration is to deliver improved police performance and greater public reassurance with particular regard to the following priorities:
>
> • Tackling anti-social behaviour and disorder;
>
> • Reducing volume, street, drug-related and violent and gun crime in line with local and national targets;
>
> • Combating serious and organised crime operating across force boundaries;
>
> • Increasing the number of offences brought to justice (Home Office 2002: 3).

Despite this apparent clarity of purpose, in contemporary Britain the public police operate as a multi-functional 24-hour emergency service performing a myriad of tasks. Research suggests that traffic and foot patrol and CID consume approximately 75 per cent of police resources (Audit Commission 1996; Bowling and Foster 2002): a pattern found in police forces around the world (Bayley 1994: 16–30; 1996). Uniformed patrol and response officers deal with a multiplicity of incidents during the course of their shifts, including attending reported crimes, investigating reports of nuisance and disorder, and attending the scenes of accidents and incidents (Manning 1988; Waddington 1993). CID officers pursue the investigation of crime and the targeting of criminals. Specialist police officers are engaged in police work that runs the gamut of firearms, traffic, mounted and dogs sections, child protection, domestic violence, public order, schools liaison, drugs liaison, partnership co-ordination, *ad infinitum*. The chapters in this volume illustrate that variety is the spice of police work and, as R.I. Mawby (2000: 107) has noted, there exists 'a widespread feeling that British policing does – and should – have a broad mandate'.

The police service, therefore, performs a broad range of tasks and Bowling and Foster (2002: 987) have usefully summarised these as including public reassurance, crime reduction, crime investigation, emergency service, peace-keeping, order maintenance and state security (see also Johnston 2000: 36–43). Policing has moved away from the original Peelian ideal of providing crime prevention and public tranquillity to a more fragmented model of a range of tasks, which has proved problematical to define in terms of 'core functions' (Wright 2002: 26–31). This difficulty was evidenced by the *Home Office Review of Police Core and Ancillary Tasks* (Posen 1995) which intended to identify and prioritise core policing tasks and also ancillary tasks that could be dropped or hived off. It concluded that 'there was little scope for the police service, broadly defined, to withdraw completely from large areas of current police work' (Posen 1995: 5).

These issues are reflected in debates over whether the police are primarily a police 'force' or a police 'service' delivering care or control (Punch 1979; Stephens and Becker 1994; Waddington 1999: 4–20; Reiner 2000: 108–15). During the early years of the modern police, the service role was emphasised for the purposes of securing policing by consent (Reiner 2000: ch. 2). The service or force dilemma faced Peel as it faced later policing policy-makers and Reiner (1994: 153) notes that Peel, Mayne and latterly Lord Scarman (when reporting on the Brixton riots of 1981) reinforced the 'preservation of public tranquillity' as the fundamental goal, above law enforcement. Equally Skolnick (1966), Bittner (1980, 1990) and Ericson (1982) have shown that the police play a key role in order maintenance, preserving the status quo, and the key element of this is their power to use legal force. The debate recurs, but is simplistic in that providing service to one sector of the community often involves executing force against another sector of the community. Some police functions, for example, public order policing, include force as part of the service. The police combine both roles and it is the balance between the two that at times comes into conflict.

The controversy over the role of the public police has moved beyond the force/service dichotomy in recent years. Factors influencing the role of the police include the private policing debate (Button 2002; see Chapter 7); transnational pressures (Sheptycki 2000; see Chapter 6); developments in media and information technologies (R.C. Mawby 2002; see Chapter 26); and theorising around the risk society (Ericson and Haggerty 1997; Johnston 2000). What is clear, however, is that the role of the police and the range of public policing remain complex and dynamic. Different and evolving approaches to core tasks, such as patrol work and crime investigation, involve new approaches to policing styles. For example, the focus on intelligence-led policing since the mid-1990s (Audit Commission 1993; see Chapter 13) and the implementation of the National Intelligence Model (NIM) across all forces by April 2004 have wide-ranging implications for the practice and administration of policing. For, as Maguire observes (Chapter 15), the NIM is not only a 'whole new "business model" for the organisation of police responses to crime' but also for the organisation of 'many other areas of police responsibility'. It has also been designed to operate at three interlinking levels of business, namely: local, cross-border and 'serious and organised crime', which is national and international (NCIS 2000: 8; see Chapter 13).

Management, control and oversight

Understanding the police organisation is not just a matter of unravelling the complexities of the local organisation of policing structures, the nature of the hierarchy and surveying the broad range of tasks that the police perform. It also requires consideration of the management, control and oversight of the police organisation and of some of the stakeholders who influence the direction of policing both at the local and national levels.

The current system of holding the 43 forces of England and Wales accountable has been characterised as 'the tripartite structure of police accountability'. Established under the Police Act 1964, following the deliberations of the 1962 Royal Commission on the Police, this remains the basis of police governance. The tripartite system distributes responsibilities between the Home Office, the local police authority and the chief constable of the force. Legislation since the Police Act 1964, including the Police and Magistrates' Courts Act 1994, the Police Act 1996 and the Police Reform Act 2002, has endorsed the tripartite arrangements, though not always uncontroversially.

One intention of the Police and Magistrates' Courts Act 1994 was to strengthen the role of local police authorities by giving them additional powers, including involvement in developing local policing plans. However, the Police Reform Act 2002 moved greater power towards the centre – for example, through the introduction of the National Policing Plan 2003–6 and other measures. Table 8.4 shows the current balance of powers and the respective responsibilities of the tripartite structure (see Chapter 24 for a detailed exposition of the governance and accountability of British policing).

Within each force there are structures for internal decision-making. Typically a force will have a senior management or 'command' team or, in the case of the Metropolitan Police Service, a 'management board'. These teams comprise the senior members of staff, namely, the chief constable, the deputy

Table 8.4 The tripartite system under the Police and Magistrates' Courts Act 1994 and the Police Reform Act 2002

Home Secretary/Home Office	Local police authority	Chief constable
Determines key national policing objectives. Produces annual National Policing Plan and presents it to Parliament.	Responsible for maintaining an effective and efficient force.	Responsible for direction and control of the force.
	Determines local policing priorities. Produces a three-year strategy consistent with National Policing Plan.	Responsible for operational control.
Directs police authorities to establish performance targets. Can require a police force to take remedial action if HMIC judges them inefficient or ineffective.		Drafts local policing plan in conjunction with local police authority.
	Determines arrangements for public consultation.	Responsible for achieving local and national policing objectives.
Determines cash grant to police authorities.	Established as precepting body responsible for budgeting and resource allocation.	Responsible for resource allocation.
Approves appointment of chief constables.	Responsible for appointment and dismissal of the chief constable (subject to ratification by the Secretary of State). Can require suspension or early dismissal on public interest grounds.	Chief constables and deputy/assistant chief constables on fixed-term contracts.
Issues statutory codes of practice and directions to police authorities.		
Issues statutory codes of practice to chief officers.		
Has authority to order amalgamations.	Membership of 17 (usually): 9 from local government, 5 local 'independents', 3 magistrates.	

and assistant chief constables and, in some cases, senior civilian members of staff responsible for finance and administration. The command team provides the strategic direction for the organisation. Below this top-level structure, sometimes, but by no means in all forces, a policy forum brings together the superintendents and senior support staff. This group will, ideally, both provide advice upwards and take policy away for implementation.

At BCU level this model is replicated, with the BCU commander having his or her own command team. Below them, there is a level of local police commanders who both feed information to the command team and who are responsible for policing at the local station level. HMIC (2002a: 4, para. 12) identified the effective leadership of BCUs as *the* critical success factor that differentiates 'BCUs operating in similar contexts but with varying results' (see Chapter 25). The inspectorate emphasised also the importance of preparing police officers for BCU management, through training, and of building a BCU management team with complementary skills. This emphasis on leadership and management echoed the view of the Audit Commission (2001).

While the vertical, hierarchical model of management dominates the police service, at the same time there are horizontal elements that contribute to organisational development – e.g. 'user groups'. These became more common-place during the 1990s as successive governments placed pressure on police forces, and other public sector organisations, to apply business methods and theory to their structures and practices (McLaughlin and Murji 1997, 2001). The business-like approach (exemplified by the Sheehy Inquiry) has seen a tendency towards delayering, the thinning out of officers in the middle management ranks and the encouragement of greater team working. Police forces have found these developments somewhat challenging, having operated so long as extended hierarchies.

Policing stakeholders

One notable feature of contemporary policing is the prominence of a number of police 'voices' and stakeholders that seek to influence the direction and character of policing. These include representatives of street cops and management cops (Reuss-Ianni 1983) such as ACPO, the Police Superintendents' Association (PSA) and the Police Federation, and the more recently formed Gay Police Association (GPA, formerly known as the Lesbian and Gay Police Association or LAGPA), the British Association for Women in Policing (BAWP) and the National Black Police Association (NBPA). Stakeholders outside the organisation include the Association of Police Authorities (APA), the Audit Commission and HMIC. Space precludes an in-depth examination of all these groupings.

The three most prominent police voices are ACPO, the PSA and the Police Federation. Each lobbies publicly and behind the scenes, seeking to influence policing policy. They have formed, at times, strategic alliances to defend and promote policing and, at other times, they have competed for pre-eminence. We will briefly consider five main stakeholders.

The Association of Chief Police Officers

Officers of the rank of assistant chief constable and above are known as the ACPO ranks. The collective influence of these officers has grown (Savage *et al.* 2000; Loader and Mulcahy 2001) and the policy-making and lobbying role of ACPO was recognised by the decision in April 1996 to divide into two bodies. There now exists 'ACPO' which promotes the professional interests of the service and the Chief Police Officers' Staff Association (CPOSA), which is purely a staff association (Barton 1996). Membership of ACPO is now open to senior support staff, in addition to sworn officers.

This collection of senior officers and support staff increasingly projects 'a single police voice' (Wall 1998: 316), and the increased cohesiveness and unity of ACPO as a body exerts a greater influence on police policy-making. Research by Savage and colleagues attributes this trajectory to the political context of the 1980s and 1990s that both encouraged a common view from the police leadership and galvanised the previously fragmented chief officers to unite in the face of threatening police reform. It also reflects the increasingly complex policing environment that heightened the need for specialist ACPO committees to provide advice (Savage *et al.* 2000: 69–80). ACPO, through its structure of thematic 'business areas', is able to provide this advice and pursue proactively its own agenda. This was further strengthened in 2003 with the appointment of its first full-time president, the former Chief Constable of Northamptonshire.

The Police Superintendents' Association

The Police Act 1964 established the Police Superintendents' Association as a staff association, but it now goes beyond that role, providing another police voice and acting as a policing pressure group, representing forces' middle managers. Some years ago Brogden (1982: 162) suggested that the association was powerless as the superintendent was neither the master nor servant in the police hierarchy. However, during the mid-1990s, led by a dynamic chairperson, chief superintendent (subsequently, Lord) Brian Mackenzie, the PSA made something of a breakthrough, reinventing itself to become an influential authority that successfully lobbied politicians and regularly gave evidence to parliamentary home affairs committees. The PSA actively works with the Home Office and other policing stakeholders to achieve its aim of influencing policing policy and practice. Like ACPO, in order to focus its work, the PSA has developed a number of business areas, chaired by members of its National Executive Committee.

The Police Federation

The Police Act 1919 established the Police Federation to represent the views of the federated ranks, namely, officers up to the rank of chief inspector. It came to particular prominence as a police 'voice' during the 1970s when it campaigned to 'to influence politicians to support the "rule of law" and to reverse the liberalising trend in penal and social policy' (Reiner 2000: 72). However, this was not a sudden incursion. McLaughlin and Murji (1998: 376) have traced the Federation's efforts to articulate the police voice, including its first press release and television appearances by its chairman in 1959, through to its 1970s transition from 'humble professional association' to 'media opinion leader' (Reiner 2000: 71). The prominence of the Federation voice has not always met the approval of senior officers. Nevertheless, the Federation is an influential pressure group and an organised lobbyist. Although the emergence of the National Black Police Association and the Gay Police Association has brought into question the capacity of the Federation to speak for *all* rank-and-file police officers, it nevertheless retains a significant presence, presenting a police worldview on law and order issues.

Her Majesty's Inspectorate of Constabulary and the Audit Commission

The first inspectors of constabulary were appointed under the provisions of the County and Borough Police Act 1856. More recently, s. 38 of the Police Act 1964 specified the inspectors' role and gave them the power to inspect and report to the Home Secretary on the efficiency and effectiveness of police forces. The role of HMIC has since been laid out in the Police Acts (1994 and 1996) and, relating to Best Value, the Local Government Act 1999. The inspectorate's role, according to its *statement of purpose*, is:

To promote the efficiency and effectiveness of policing in England, Wales and Northern Ireland through inspection of police organisations and functions to ensure:

- Agreed standards are achieved and maintained;
- Good practice is spread; and
- Performance is improved.

Also to provide advice and support to the tripartite partners (Home Secretary, police authorities and forces) and play an important role in the development of future leaders (HMCIC 2002).

There are six inspectors (four are former chief constables, two are from non-police backgrounds) and three assistant inspectors (two seconded deputy chief constables and one lay inspector who provides a specialist independent perspective on race and diversity issues) (HMCIC 2002: 37). The inspectors are based in regions and conduct their work assisted by staff officers and support staff. The Chief Inspector of Constabulary (HMCIC) co-ordinates their work and advises the Home Secretary on policing matters. Seconded police officers and Home Office civil servants provide support to the Chief Inspector.

In terms of the inspections themselves, HMIC conducts force inspections and specific BCU inspections. It also conducts thematic inspections that focus on a specific area of policing, such as corruption (HMIC 1999), visibility and reassurance (HMIC 2001a) and diversity (HMIC 2003). With the Audit Commission, it also conducts Best Value inspections.

The constitutional position of HMIC is interesting in that inspectors have independent status. They are servants of the Crown and not Home Office employees. This has not reduced criticism that in practice HMIC has sometimes operated within limits defined by the Home Secretary or Home Office officials. This criticism needs to be balanced by the observation that until the appointment of lay inspectors in 1993, inspectors were recruited from the ranks of senior ACPO officers and continue to wear a uniform that is virtually indistinguishable from the uniform of a chief constable.

The work of HMIC involves scrutiny by (mostly) ex-senior police officers but, since 1988 the police have also been scrutinised by 'professional outsiders' in the form of the Audit Commission (Weatheritt 1993: 33). This independent body was established in 1982 by the Local Government Finance Act to monitor and promote economy, efficiency and effectiveness in the management of local government. The Audit Commission first focused on the police in 1988 and early reports scrutinised the financing of police funding and budget allocation (for example, Audit Commission 1988). However, later reports focused on operational matters, including crime management and the promotion of intelligence-led policing (see Audit Commission 1993; Chapter 13) and patrol work (Audit Commission 1996). The Audit Commission has increased in status since its first police report and although its recommendations are not prescriptive, they are commonly implemented. This is no small task. As one (since retired) chief constable noted, between 1997 and 1999 there were 'no less than 27 Audit Commission and Police Inspectorate thematic reports published, incorporating over 300 different recommendations' (Pollard 1999: 28).

The Police Standards Unit and Best Value
In addition to the established framework of oversight by HMIC and the Audit Commission, policing has also become subject to scrutiny through the Best Value regime and the work of the Police Standards Unit (PSU). The Best Value programme placed (from April 2000) a statutory duty on local authorities to deliver services to clear standards by the most effective, economic and efficient means Department of the Environment, Transport and the Regions (DETR) 1998). Local police authorities are included as 'Best Value authorities' and as such police forces are required to demonstrate 'Best Value' (Leigh *et al.* 1999). Accordingly, police forces must report against a series of Best Value performance indicators (Home Office 2002: Annex D).

The PSU was established by the Police Reform Act 2002, but had actually been at work within the Home Office from July 2001. Its role is to identify good policing practice and the means of spreading it. It also has an intervention role. If a force is identified as requiring 'remedial actions', it will intervene to improve performance (Loveday and Reid 2003: 13–14). In this role, the PSU will work closely with HMIC to complete a formidable oversight regime.

The development of national policing structures

As we have described, British policing remains rooted in territorial police forces that the tripartite system holds accountable. How long the current number of forces will remain is an issue of debate. Successive legislation and government policies have increased central control. The potential for force amalgamations is real. Policy-makers have also increasingly recognised that local policing is ill-suited to policing some aspects of modern Britain, both in terms of operations against crime and the co-ordination of support functions that are relevant to all police forces.

Crime does not take account of local, national or international borders. The growth of organised crime, drug trafficking and terrorism has placed a high demand on the police to develop agencies that can operate across geographical borders. Such agencies must be able to co-operate with other law enforcement bodies, both nationally and internationally. In recognition of such factors, the government and the police service have developed the National Crime Squad (NCS) and the National Criminal Intelligence Service (NCIS).

We have already alluded to the need for an approach to operational policing that can combat aspects of cross-border crime. In 1964, regional crime squads (RCS) were set up to provide this capability. The squads were organised in nine regions covering England and Wales. These were supplemented in 1986 by the development of RCS 'drugs wings', which were given the task (in conjunction with HM Customs and Excise) of tackling the expanding market in illicit drugs. In 1993, the RCSs were reorganised into six regions. However, due to their nature, their priorities tended primarily to be regional.

Accordingly, in 1998, the amalgamation of these six regional squads established the NCS. The enabling legislation for the formation of this national unit was the Police Act 1997. Headed by the Director General from its London headquarters, the NCS comprises Eastern, Northern and Western operational units. Police forces in England and Wales second officers to the squad. In 2002, it had 1,176 police officers seconded from territorial policing and 405 civilian staff (Smith *et al.* 2002). For the year 2001–2, the budget of the NCS was £114 million, supplemented by a further £14.2 million for the National High-Tech Crime Unit. The overall remit of NCS is to target criminal organisations committing serious and organised crime. This includes drug trafficking, immigration crime, illegal arms trafficking, money laundering, counterfeit currency, kidnap and extortion. Some 75 per cent of its work involves drug trafficking.

NCS is currently accountable by means of a tripartite structure, mirroring the arrangements in territorial police forces. Under the Police Act 1997, its accountability is to the Home Secretary and to the National Crime Squad Authority. The authority has eleven members (five independent members nominated by the Home Secretary, two elected members from local police authorities, two chief constables, and representatives of HM Customs and Excise and the Home Office). Objectives and performance targets are set by the authority and by the Home Secretary and published in an annual service plan. The constitution of the service authority is changing due to the Criminal Justice and Police Act 2001, although the most recent HMIC inspection of NCS points out that precise working arrangements are yet to be finalised (HMIC 2001b).

During the 1980s, the National Drugs Intelligence Unit (NDIU), which then had its base in the Metropolitan Police area, assisted the work of RCS units and supported local police forces. However, in 1992 following criticism of the existing approach, the Home Office formed the NCIS. This was organised more on a multi-agency basis than had previously been the case. The new service included staff from the Home Office, HM Customs and Excise, the police service and local authorities. The 1997 inspection of NCIS by HMIC highlighted the progress that NCIS had made and set out a number of recommendations (HMIC 1997). The Police Act 1997 provided a firm statutory basis for the service and put into place measures for accountability through a service authority similar to those of the NCS.

By 2002, 287 police officers seconded from territorial policing were working at NCIS. In addition, 482 civilians, many of whom NCIS employed as analysts, were working there. The work of NCIS covers four 'business' areas, namely:

1. Strategic overviews of organised crime.

2. Operational intelligence on the 'top few' criminals.

3. Specialist services and intelligence co-ordination.

4. Knowledge products, including the National Intelligence Model (NIM).

NCIS headquarters are in London and it has offices in Birmingham, Bristol, Glasgow, London, Manchester, Wakefield and Belfast. These provide an interface with other operational and intelligence agencies. The National Central Bureau of Interpol and the UK National Unit of Europol are also sited at NCIS headquarters.

In addition to these operational investigation and intelligence units, many police support functions require a high degree of national co-ordination. This is particularly true of training and information technology. As a consequence in recent years, national organisations have been set up to provide a range of services in these fields in support of the delivery of 'front line' operational policing. These include the Central Police Training and Development Authority (Centrex); the National Centre for Policing Excellence (NCPE); the Police Skills and Standards Organisation (PSSO); and the Police Information Technology Organisation (PITO). In the remainder of this section, we consider briefly the roles and responsibilities of these organisations.

National Police Training (NPT) had been in existence for some years, with its headquarters at Bramshill House in Hampshire. Bramshill was the host to higher police training, to international training and to a number of specialist training and development functions. Regional training centres, which were part of NPT, carried out training for probationer constables, some supervisors and specialist officers. Following an extensive review of police training, including inspection by the HMIC and parliamentary scrutiny through the Select Committee for Home Affairs, the government decided that training needed to be organised under the auspices of a new non-departmental public body. In April 2002, the Central Police Training and Development Authority (Centrex) took over the functions of NPT and introduced a new (and it is intended, more cohesive) approach to the national co-ordination of training.

The Criminal Justice and Police Act 2001 established the mandate and the accountability system for Centrex. Changes introduced by Centrex include the merging of the National Crime Faculty and National Operational Faculty and developments in probationers' foundation training. Among other developments, Centrex took over responsibility for the National Centre for Scientific Support to Crime Investigation. Centrex also hosts the National Centre for Policing Excellence (NCPE), with a remit to enhance the base of knowledge on best practice in police work.

In parallel with the developments in Centrex which affect the delivery of training at all levels, the government and the police service have made concerted efforts to consolidate the framework of competencies which police officers are expected to reach, whatever their rank or role. In June 2001, the PSSO took over as the recognised standards-setting body for the police service. PSSO has developed National Occupational Standards (NOS), and has defined an assessment strategy and a National Competency Framework (NCF). This work informs all aspects of police human resource management, including recruitment, training, performance review, promotion and development. Other current work includes an important project in conjunction with ACPO to professionalise the work of crime investigators.

Like most modern organisations, police forces and national policing bodies have made increasing use of information technology. However, it is important to ensure that information and communications technology is co-ordinated on a national basis to support policing in all of its aspects. To do this, the PITO was set up under the Police Act 1997. The National Policing Plan and the tripartite structure of ACPO, the APA and the Home Office strategically guide the work of PITO. Its work includes projects on communications, identification of suspects, the Police National Computer, 'joined up' criminal justice, intelligence, investigation and police support services. PITO also has a commercial role in trying to secure Best Value for the police service and providing advice on procurement and contract management.

There can be little doubt of the need for national co-ordination in the fields of crime and criminal intelligence, especially where transnational organised crime is involved. Indeed, in July 2003, the Prime Minister established a Cabinet committee to consider the viability of a national policing agency dedicated to combating serious and organised crime. This would have implications for bringing together NCIS and the NCS, agencies that, in general, the police service has received positively. The reception by the service of centralised systems for training and information technology in the past decade has been less sanguine. Some aspects of police training have met with criticism (HMIC 2002b). Projects such as the National Strategy for Police Information Systems (NSPIS) have disappointed (HMCIC 2002). Although the work of organisations such as Centrex, PSSO and NCPE at first sight appears to be highly centralised, their products are the result of extensive consultation inside and outside the police service. Their development is very recent. Only time will tell whether these new departures in training and its management will bring the desired results.

Conclusion

This chapter only seeks to provide the introductory context to the more detailed arguments elsewhere in the volume. We have provided the organisational background to the policing themes and controversies that other chapters investigate and critically appraise. At the same time, however, we have highlighted a number of issues, perennial and emerging, that challenge the police organisation. These include the trends towards centralisation and civilianisation; the shaping of policing by legislation; the debate over core policing tasks as the public police increasingly work among other forms of policing; the questioning of police effectiveness and leadership in a performance-driven context; and the challenge of establishing necessary and appropriate forms of oversight and control. We have suggested that public policing is not simply a matter of performing a number of core legislated tasks. Rather it is complex and dynamic, and this requires the police organisation to evolve constantly. Therein lies the challenge.

Selected further reading

No one text comprehensively discusses the development and structure of the modern police organisation. Waddington's *Policing Citizens* (1999), Reiner's *The Politics of the Police* (2000) and Bowling and Foster's 'Policing and the police' (2002) provide incisive analyses of the police in late modern society. Leishman *et al.*'s *Core Issues in Policing* (2000) comments widely on the themes of policing and the reactions of the police organisation to the changing environment. Johnston's *Policing Britain* (2000) provides an excellent account of the relationship between policing, risk and security. Wright's *Policing* (2002) sets out a critical analysis of policing in an age of social and political fragmentation.

This is a fast-moving area in which texts can quickly date. It is recommended, therefore, that readers make use of electronic resources to remain updated. In particular, we would suggest visiting the Home Office's 'Police Reform' website (http://www.policereform.gov.uk). This contains recent reports and legislation, together with links to other useful sites – for example, to a variety of policing associations and agencies.

Notes

1 The Police Reform Act 2002 introduced a National Policing Plan and s. 7 of the Act empowered the Home Secretary to make provisions requiring all police forces to adopt particular procedures or practices.
2 The ten forces are Bedfordshire, Derbyshire, Gloucestershire, Greater Manchester Police, Hertfordshire, Lincolnshire, the Metropolitan Police Service, South Yorkshire, Sussex and West Mercia.

References

ACPO (1990) *Strategic Policy Document: Setting the Standards for Policing: Meeting Community Expectation*. London: New Scotland Yard.

Ascoli, D. (1979) *The Queen's Peace*. London: Hamish Hamilton.

Audit Commission (1988) *Administrative Support for Operational Police Officers*. London: Audit Commission.

Audit Commission (1991) *Reviewing the Organisation of Provincial Police Forces. Police Paper 9*. London: HMSO.

Audit Commission (1993) *Helping with Enquiries*. London: Audit Commission.

Audit Commission (1996) *Streetwise: Effective Foot Patrol*. London: Audit Commission.

Audit Commission (2001) *Best Foot Forward: Headquarters' Support for Police Basic Command Units*. London: HMSO.

Barton, M. (1996) 'Double vision', *Policing Today*, 2(1): 8–9.

Bayley, D. (1994) *Police for the Future*. Oxford: Oxford University Press.

Bayley, D. (1996) 'What do the police do?', in W. Saulsbury *et al.* (eds) *Themes in Contemporary Policing*. London: Police Foundation/Policy Studies Institute, 29–41.

Benke, M., Buzas, P., Finszter, G., Szkinger, I., Mawby, R.C. and Wright, A. (1997) *Developing Civilian Oversight of the Hungarian Police*. Brussels: European Commission.

Berry, G., Izat, J., Mawby, R.C., Walley, L. and Wright, A. (1998) *Practical Police Management* (2nd edn). London: Police Review Publishing.

Bittner, E. (1980) *The Functions of the Police in Modern Society*. Cambridge, MA: Oelgeschlager, Gunn & Hain.

Bittner, E. (1990) *Aspects of Police Work*. Boston, MA: Northeastern University Press.

Bowling, B. and Foster, J. (2002) 'Policing and the police', in M. Maguire *et al.* (eds) *The Oxford Handbook of Criminology* (3rd edn). Oxford: Oxford University Press, 980–1033.

Brogden, M. (1982) *Autonomy and Consent*. London: Academic Press.

Button, M. (2002) *Private Policing*. Cullompton: Willan.

Chapman, B. (1970) *Police State*. London: Macmillan.

DETR (1998) *Modern Local Government: In Touch with the People* (Cm 4013). London: Home Office.

Ellison, G. and Smyth, J. (2000) *The Crowned Harp: Policing Northern Ireland*. London: Pluto.

Emsley, C. (1992) 'The English Bobby: an indulgent tradition', in R. Porter (ed.) *Myths of the English*. Cambridge: Polity Press, 114–35.

Emsley, C. (1996) *The English Police: A Political and Social History* (2nd edn). London: Longman.

Ericson, R. (1982) *Reproducing Order: A Study of Police Patrol Work*. Toronto: University of Toronto Press.

Ericson, R.V. and Haggerty P. (1997) *Policing the Risk Society*. Oxford: Clarendon Press.

Hancock, P. (2003) 'Size matters', *Police Review*, 16 May: 38.

Highmore, S. (1993) *The Integration of Police Officers and Civilian Staff*. London: Home Office.

HM Chief Inspector of Constabulary (HMCIC) (2002) *Annual Report 2001–2002*. London: HMSO.

HMIC (1997) *The National Criminal Intelligence Service: 1997 Inspection Report*. London: HMIC.

HMIC (1999) *Police Integrity: Securing and Maintaining Public Confidence*. London: Home Office.

HMIC (2001a) *Open All Hours*. London: HMIC.

HMIC (2001b) *The National Crime Squad: 2001–2002 Inspection Report*. London: HMIC.

HMIC (2002a) *Getting Down to Basics: Emerging Findings from BCU Inspections in 2001*. London: HMSO.

HMIC (2002b) *Training Matters*. London: HMIC.

HMIC (2003) *Diversity Matters*. London: HMIC.

Home Office (2001) *Policing a New Century: A Blueprint for Reform* (Cm 5326). London HMSO.

Home Office (2002) *The National Policing Plan 2003–2006*. London: Home Office.

Home Office (2003) *Race Equality: The Home Secretary's Employment Targets: Milestone Report, January 2003*. London: Home Office Communication Directorate.

Johnston, L. (2000) *Policing Britain: Risk, Security and Governance*. London: Longman.

Leigh, A., Mundy, G. and Tuffin, R. (1999) *Best Value Policing: Making Preparations. Policing and Reducing Crime Unit Police Research Series Paper* 116. London: Home Office.

Leishman, F., Loveday, B. and Savage, S.P. (eds) (2000) *Core Issues in Policing* (2nd edn). London: Longman.

Loader, I. and Mulcahy, A. (2001) 'The power of legitimate naming. Part I. Chief constables as social commentators in post-war England', *British Journal of Criminology*, 41(1): 41–55.

Loveday, B. (1993) *Civilian Staff in the Police Force: Competences and Conflict in the Police Force. Studies in Crime, Order and Policing Research Paper* 2. Leicester: CSPO.

Loveday, B. and Reid, A. (2003) *Going Local: Who Should Run Britain's Police?* London: Policy Exchange.

Manning, P.K. (1988) *Symbolic Communication*. Cambridge, MA: MIT Press.

Mawby, R.C. (2002) *Policing Images: Policing, Communication and Legitimacy*. Cullompton: Willan.

Mawby, R.I. (1990) *Comparative Policing Issues*. London: Unwin Hyman.

Mawby, R.I. (2000) 'Core policing: the seductive myth', in F. Leishman *et al.* (eds) *Core Issues in Policing* (2nd edn). London: Longman, 107–23.

McLaughlin, E. and Murji, K. (1997) 'The future lasts a long time: public policework and the managerialist paradox', in P. Francis *et al.* (eds) *Policing Futures: The Police, Law Enforcement and the Twenty-First Century*. London: Macmillan, 80–103.

McLaughlin, E. and Murji, K. (1998) 'Resistance through representation: "storylines", advertising and Police Federation campaigns', *Policing and Society*, 8: 367–99.

McLaughlin, E. and Murji, K. (2001) 'Lost connections and new directions: neo-liberalism, new public managerialism, and the "modernization" of the British police', in K. Stenson and R.R. Sullivan (eds) *Crime, Risk and Justice: The Politics of Crime Control in Liberal Democracies.* Cullompton: Willan, 104–21.

Mulcahy, A. (2000) 'Policing history: the official discourse and organisational memory of the Royal Ulster Constabulary', *British Journal of Criminology,* 40(1): 68–87.

National Criminal Intelligence Service (NCIS) (2000) *The National Intelligence Model.* London: NCIS.

Newburn, T. (2002) 'Community safety and policing: some implications of the Crime and Disorder Act 1998', in G. Hughes *et al.* (eds) *Crime Prevention and Community Safety: New Directions.* London: Sage, 102–22.

Oliver, I. (1997) *Police, Government and Accountability* (2nd edn). London: Macmillan.

Patten, C. (1999) *A New Beginning: Policing in Northern Ireland: The Report of the Independent Commission on Policing for Northern Ireland.* London: HMSO.

Pollard, C. (1999) 'Unnecessary intervention', *Policing Today,* 5(4): 26–8.

Posen, I. (Chair) (1995) *Home Office Review of Police Core and Ancillary Tasks.* London: HMSO.

Punch, M. (1979) 'The secret social service', in S. Holdaway (ed.) *The British Police.* London: Edward Arnold, 102–17.

Reiner, R. (1994) 'What should the police be doing?', *Policing,* 10(3): 151–7.

Reiner, R. (2000) *The Politics of the Police* (3rd edn). Oxford: Oxford University Press.

Reith, C. (1943) *British Police and the Democratic Ideal.* London: Oxford University Press.

Reith, C. (1952) *The Blind Eye of History.* London: Faber & Faber.

Reith, C. (1956) *A New Study of Police History.* Edinburgh: Oliver & Boyd.

Reuss-Ianni, E. (1983) *Two Cultures of Policing: Street Cops and Management Cops.* New Brunswick, NJ: Transaction Books.

Savage, S., Charman, S. and Cope, S. (2000) *Policing and the Power of Persuasion: The Changing Role of the Association of Chief Police Officers.* London: Blackstone Press.

Sheehy, Sir P. (1993) *Inquiry into Police Responsibilities and Rewards* (Cm 2280.1). London: HMSO.

Sheptycki, J. (ed.) (2000) *Issues in Transnational Policing.* London: Routledge.

Skolnick, J. (1966) *Justice Without Trial.* New York, NY: Wiley.

Smith, C., Rundle, S. and Hosking, R. (2002) *Police Service Strength: England and Wales 31 March 2002. Home Office Statistical Bulletin* 10/02. London: Home Office Research and Statistics Directorate.

Stephens, M. and Becker, S. (eds) (1994) *Police Force Police Service.* London: Macmillan.

Waddington, P.A.J. (1993) *Calling the Police.* Aldershot: Avebury.

Waddington, P.A.J. (1999) *Policing Citizens: Authority and Rights.* London: UCL Press.

Waddington, P.A.J. (2000) 'Public order policing: citizenship and moral ambiguity', in F. Leishman *et al.* (eds) *Core Issues in Policing* (2nd edn). London: Longman, 156–75.

Walker, N. (1999) 'Situating Scottish policing', in P. Duff and N. Hutton (eds) *Criminal Justice in Scotland.* Aldershot: Dartmouth.

Wall, D. (1998) *The Chief Constables of England and Wales: The Socio-legal History of a Criminal Justice Elite.* Aldershot: Dartmouth.

Weatheritt, M. (1993) 'Measuring police performance: accounting or accountability?', in R. Reiner and S. Spencer (eds) *Accountable Policing.* London: IPPR, 24–54.

Wolff Olins (1988) *A Force for Change: A Report on the Corporate Identity of the Metropolitan Police.* London: Wolff Olins Corporate Identity.

Wright, A. (2002) *Policing: An Introduction to Concepts and Practice.* Cullompton: Willan.

Chapter 9

Police cultures[1]

Janet Foster

Introduction

Police culture has been used 'to explain and condemn a broad spectrum of policing practice' (Waddington 1999: 287), and is often presented as if it is singular, monolithic and unchanging. Although many unifying and identifiable cultural characteristics exist in police organisations across the world, and their very existence might seem indicative of a singular culture, research suggests that there are important differences within and between a variety of policing subcultures – for example, 'street cops and management cops', detectives and uniform officers and response and community police officers. Police forces and departments also differ because of their history, policing context, traditions, and the leadership or interests of those who head them. It is important therefore not to be too deterministic about police culture, and my choice of the word 'cultures' in the title of this chapter is deliberately intended to convey the nuances and differences *within* and *between* different elements of the police organisation and the people who work in it rather than presenting it as homogeneous and one-dimensional.

This chapter focuses on the cultures of the public police. I describe their key characteristics and how researchers have explained them; the gendered and racialised aspects of police cultures; and the ways in which cultural factors shape 'what *really* matters' (Johnson and Scholes 1999) in policing and, by so doing, fundamentally influence policing priorities and practice. I also discuss how organisational cultures act as inhibitors to change and why some of the most problematic elements of street cop culture, in particular, seem to have been so persistent in police research spanning some 40 years. Given these continuities across time and space I also consider the possibilities for achieving cultural change.

Before embarking on these issues, however, I want briefly to discuss what is meant by organisational culture and the similarities and differences between police and other organisational cultures to provide a context for the subsequent discussion.

What is organisational culture?

Schein (1985: 6) defined organisational culture as the 'deeper level of basic *assumptions and beliefs* that are shared by members of an organisation, that operate unconsciously and define in a basic taken-for-granted fashion an organisation's view of itself and its environment'. All organisations have cultures, and the term is not a pejorative one, despite the fact that many researchers see police culture as malign, because of its more negative characteristics. Organisational cultures do however have a fundamental impact on what their members 'notice and how they interpret it' where a filtering process 'screens out some parts of "reality" while magnifying others' (Kier 1999: 26). This is particularly important for policing where perceptions of danger, a sense of mission and feelings that the police represent a 'thin blue line' between order and chaos fundamentally shape police officer's perceptions of their work and of the social world (Reiner 2000).

Predictability is a vital element in all organisational cultures (Kier 1999: 26), and in occupations where 'reassurance and certainty' are highly valued cultures are often at their strongest (Hampden-Turner 1990: 13, cited in Brown, A. 1998: 73). No matter how desirable, predictability and certainty are of course never fully achievable, especially for police officers who are often exposed to people and situations where behaviour is unpredictable, and sometimes dangerous, and where outcomes can be difficult to anticipate in advance.

Perhaps because of the taken-for-granted qualities of organisational cultures, and the often unacknowledged needs they fulfil, it is sometimes difficult for participants to *perceive* their influence, challenge their core values or to appreciate the structural inequalities that may be embodied within everyday working practices. Indeed, as Kier (1999: 30) argues, 'We can often learn more about a culture from those who reject its assumptions than from those who accept' them.

One of the most powerful, but frequently taken-for-granted features of organisational cultures is their gendered quality (see Morgan 1992). Tradition-ally male-dominated occupations, like the military, fire brigade and police have been close-knit organisations characterised by male-bonding (Gregory and Lees 1999: 50). At one level, such bonding provides a vital foundation for trust relationships in difficult and dangerous situations (Gregory and Less 1999: 50). However, it also means that 'Members of a group identify *with* as well as *against* others' (Kier 1999: 27) which can result in hostile and exclusionary behaviour. North American marines, for example, overtly dem-onstrate the outsider status of women by chanting: 'three-zero-five-six/We don't need no stinkin' chicks!' (Ricks 1995, cited in Kier 1999: 37). This chant is also illustrative of the structured inequalities that emanate from some cultures and that themselves reflect, reinforce and sometimes amplify broader structural inequalities in society. This is the case not only for women but, as I describe later, for any group (or individual) perceived to be 'different' from the dominant culture.

Structured inequalities, or the insider/outsider characteristics inherent in many organisational cultures, rarely feature in the *formal* policies and statements of organisations. Yet, as Johnson and Scholes (1999: 236–7) argue, there are vital differences between the ways in which organisations present themselves publicly and in their everyday practice:

> As organisations increasingly make visible their carefully considered public statements of their values, beliefs and purposes there is a danger that these are seen as useful and accurate descriptions of the organisational paradigm. But they are at best only partially accurate, and at worst misleading, descriptions of the *real* organisational culture. This is not to suggest that there is any organised deception. It is simply that the statements of values and beliefs are often statements of aspiration or strategic intent ... rather than accurate descriptions of the culture as it exists in the minds and hearts of people within and around the organisation. This 'real' culture is evidenced in the way the organisation actually operates: it is the taken-for-granted assumptions about 'how you run an organisation like this' and 'what really matters around here'.

As I describe later these differences between formal policies and informal practice present real challenges to any organisation – especially where the negative elements have the potential, as with policing, to undermine public confidence, damage credibility and invite negative media attention. However, the existence of these parallel organisational imperatives helps to explain why, despite a rapidly changing social and political environment and considerable changes in *formal* policies, procedures and legislation over the four decades covered in this review, *informal* cultural practices have proved highly resilient. Furthermore, as I describe later, the challenge for any police manager is not policy formulation but turning policies into practice.

Do the police have a unique occupational culture?

The uniqueness of the pressures and dangers on the police has frequently been exaggerated by officers and police researchers alike who 'become mesmerized by the police world and ... attribute behaviour uniquely to its culture' instead of acknowledging the many similarities with other occupations (Punch 1985: 187). There are, for example, clear parallels in research on military culture in terms of solidarity and the impact of hierarchy (Winslow 1998; Kier 1999), and with a range of other public and private sector environments too – for example, in relation to risk and performance management (see, for example, Ericson and Haggerty 1997).

However, there are also some interesting differences. In the business world, for example, organisational culture has focused largely on managers and is viewed positively (Brown, A. 1998: 89, 85). In policing research we find the exact opposite. Cop culture has been intrinsically linked with the most junior of officers in front-line policing, with little attention given to middle and senior managers (see Reiner 1991 as an exception). Furthermore, the impact of the culture is seen to be overwhelmingly negative, something many police officers find frustrating. An HMIC (1999: 9) report, for example, suggested that the term 'canteen culture' is 'as misleading as it is mischievous', as it negatively labels officers and fails to acknowledge that those who conduct their work professionally emanate from the exact same culture as those who exhibit its worst characteristics. Elias' (1994: xix) insights from community studies on the *established* and the *outsiders* help us to understand these frustrations and how they might be played out within the police organisation. Elias suggests that established groups judge outsiders by their worst characteristics and behaviour. For the police this contributes to their feelings of being the 'thin blue line' between order and chaos as these emotions are shaped by situations and contacts with the most difficult and problematic people (for which officers feel they deserve support and praise, not condemnation). By contrast, the established group possess a 'self-image' based on the *best* of the group. This enables them continuously to invest in positive elements and evade acknowledgement of the less creditable or negative ones (Elias 1994: xix).

Recently, research has begun to acknowledge more fully the heterogeneous nature of police culture, and the importance of police officers being active agents in the formation, acceptance or rejection of particular aspects of it (Chan 1996; Dixon 1997). However, as Young, a former police superintendent turned anthropologist argues, one of the reasons why police research is so threatening to police officers is that it 'reveals modes of thought and practice which are well known and constituted, but which are necessarily taken for granted. For who inside the system needs to be told that which is well understood?' (1991: 48). Of course, some of what is well understood are, or have, negative aspects. These negative aspects have also been the predominant focus of academic research which leaves the police view of their own culture, and the academic research on it, in rather polarised positions.

It is perhaps important therefore to remind ourselves why understanding and reforming the most negative elements of police cultures are so important – largely because key and persistent negative elements of the culture directly conflict with the police organisation's need to provide a fair and equitable service particularly to the poor, vulnerable and needy with whom they disproportionately come into contact; have a fundamental impact on who joins the police service and who stays in it; and impede the development of more responsive and advanced approaches to crime management and reduction (see, for example, Chan *et al.* 2001).

In the preceding discussion I briefly outlined the issues relating to organisational cultures in general. I now want to turn to a more detailed discussion about the characteristics of police cultures and how these shape policing priorities.

The characteristics of 'cop culture'

[C]op culture has developed as a patterned set of understandings that help officers to cope with and adjust to the pressures and tensions confronting the police (Reiner 2000: 87).

Reiner (2000: 90) suggests that cop culture is a 'subtle and complex intermingling' of police officers' sense of mission, action-oriented behaviour and cynicism where the emphases on danger, suspicion, isolation, solidarity, pragmatism and authority are all core elements of 'cop culture'. I am using the singular 'culture' here as these *general* characteristics appear with remarkable consistency in police research and most are also integral to subcultural groupings *within* the police, although the emphasis given to different aspects may vary, as will the degree to which these characteristics are exhibited by some individuals.

Machismo, intolerance, prejudice and conservatism are also regarded as characteristic features of police culture which has led researchers to ask whether these characteristics reflect those who choose a career in policing or whether these behaviours are learnt and linked with the nature of police work itself. Research suggests that at the point of joining, police recruits have a strong commitment to public service (see, for example, Van Maanen 1973; Fielding 1988; Reiner 2000) and do not exhibit any distinct police personality (see Banton 1964; Skolnick 1966; Bittner 1967; Coleman and Gorman 1982). Indeed, Waddington (1999: 292–3) goes so far as to suggest that police officers' attitudes differ little from those present in broader society:

> it is far from the case that the police are a repository for authoritarianism, racism and conservativism within a liberal population brimming over with the milk of human kindness. Their culture might be less 'sub' than is often supposed and instead be the expression of *common* values, beliefs and attitudes within a police context.

This does not of course justify racism or other kinds of prejudice and disadvantage in the police because we rightly expect our public servants to have higher standards than those of the general population (Mastrofski 1999). Furthermore, even if police officers are no 'more authoritarian than the general population, the "normal" degree of authoritarianism' demonstrated in the culture 'is disturbing in an occupation which wields considerable power over minorities' (Reiner 2000: 100) or indeed any other group where intolerant attitudes abound.

Although fledging officers may begin with ideals about serving the public, research suggests it does not take long before they find themselves 'reassessing their values' and 'their sense of identity' moving away in many cases from an outward-looking public service orientation into a more inwardly focused 'crime control' approach (Fielding 1988: 205). One of the interesting features of this process, as I describe below, is that what police officers come to value as 'real policing' even though this represents a very small proportion of their actual work.

The pursuit of 'real police work'

Despite the image of fast cars and catching criminals, policing is frequently a more mundane and routine activity than it is often portrayed in the media, popular fiction and by police officers themselves. Michael Banton (1964: 127), who conducted the first study of the police in Britain, suggested that patrol officers are in fact peace-makers more than law enforcers, and many aspects of their work are routine. Indeed 'waiting, boredom and paperwork' were an ever present reality (Banton 1964: 85). Almost 40 years later these remain resonant, and persistent themes and 'the working practices of the lower ranks' have changed very little despite our rapidly changing social environment (Holdaway 1995: 111).

Like other police researchers who followed in his footsteps, Banton found that the contrast between police officers' perceptions of their work and his experience of it were very different. 'It is remarkable', he wrote:

> how frequently I have been assured by officers I have been accompanying on patrol . . . that it has been an unusually quiet night; either the laws of chance do not apply to patrol work or the busy shifts impress themselves on the patrolmen's [sic] mind so strongly that all other ones seem to fall below standard (1964: 156).

The proverbial quiet nights also persist in observations of contemporary police work, so it is important to ask why officers define their work in terms of the *extra*ordinary rather than the mundane.

Van Maanen (1973), in an early and classic study of the police in America, argued that the answer in part lies with the kinds of images that recruits had of the police prior to entry. Instead of reorienting their perception of the work, given that danger and excitement are relatively infrequent, officers continue to invest in the atypical 'real policing' activities as these provide 'self-esteem and stimulation' for police officers and a means to reinforce their own 'self-image of performing a worthwhile, exciting and dangerous task' (Van Maanen 2003: 74–5; see also Waddington 1999).

The consequence of this orientation is that the social service tasks police officers are asked to perform are frequently 'viewed as a waste of time and effort' (Pogrebin and Poole 2003: 86). Officers often see these requests as 'trivial, mundane or unfounded' and as being initiated by people perceived as 'too weak or ineffectual to handle their own problems' (Pogrebin and Poole 2003: 86). These perceptions also extend to the treatment of victims, even of serious crimes, whose 'demands' on detectives may be perceived as 'burden-some' and distract them from their 'real' work (i.e. pitching their wits against the criminal) (Stenross and Kleinman 2003: 108; also see Jordan 2001). A Canadian study highlights how absurd at one level this attachment to 'real' policework is:

> During our field observations, police officers who sat doing paperwork complained about not being free to pursue crime. At the same time they recognized that most crimes were not something they could do anything about except create a record for risk management purposes. In some instances officers who complained about the paper burden also stated that there was very little crime in their area, but maintained nevertheless that real police work is crime work (Ericson and Haggerty 1997: 299).

There are many ironies in this quotation but one that is less frequently observed is that paperwork, though often derided by officers and politicians, is of course a crucial component of *all* policing. It provides part of the foundation for transparency and legitimacy of police practices and, without paperwork, good case preparation and successful prosecutions are impossible. Hunt (1984: 287) suggests that one of the reasons for the derision of paperwork in police cultures is that it is perceived as feminised work. This was exemplified in the comments street cops used to describe their office colleagues who were characterised as 'pencil-pushing bureaucrats' and 'inside tit men'.

Van Maanen (2003: 75) suggests that as 'the vast majority of time is spent in tasks other than real police work, there is little incentive for performance' and that officers learn very early on to 'keep their heads down', finding:

> that the most satisfying solution to the labyrinth of hierarchy, the red tape and paperwork, the plethora of rules and regulations, and the 'dirty work' which characterises the occupation is to adopt the group norm stressing staying out of trouble. And the best way ... [to] stay out of trouble is to minimize the set of activities he [*sic*] pursues.

In short, for Van Maanen, street officers' culture is one of 'learning complacency' (2003: 75).

Given its high status 'real policing' also dominates the war stories told by police officers. These provide a very powerful, but 'partial organisational history' (Van Maanen 2003: 70) as well as important 'cues' for police officers' behaviour. As Shearing and Ericson (1991: 491–2) explain:

> In their street talk officers use stories to represent to each other the way things are, not as statements of fact, but as cognitive devices used to gain practical insight into how to do the job of policing ... Such stories ... capture the sedimented residue of generations of police experience and convey it in a form that police officers can capture and use to construct their actions on an on-going basis.

Police culture is not only conveyed through stories. In fact as I describe in the next section 'becoming' a police officer (Van Maanen 1973) requires learning and internalising a vast array of formal and informal knowledge about policing and the way it is conducted.

Learning the 'rules' of policing

Despite the mundane and routine quality of most police work, new recruits learn very quickly that policing can be difficult and stressful involving unpredictable, emotionally challenging and traumatic tasks (for example, dealing with sudden deaths and fatal accidents, pub fights and public disorder). These incidents have a powerful, though often unacknowledged, impact in shaping officers' approaches to their work and may in part explain both the power of the culture and the emphasis on the dangers of the job. Recruits soon learn that to survive their work practically and emotionally requires them to be one of a team. They also become acutely aware that their peers and colleagues have the power to grant or reject their membership of that team (and that with acceptance comes confidence that other members will help them if their safety is threatened). Training school therefore provides 'a rehearsal of how occupational culture can nurture and protect its members' where cultural values 'emanate from the couching of ideas, the examples given and the style of filling-in talk, back chat and corridor conversation' as much as from the formal teaching and curriculum (Fielding 1988: 54).

The training also injects a dose of police 'reality', laying the foundations for cynicism and a perception that the job is impossible (without bending the rules); that officers are not valued or cared for (either externally or internally); and that the only people they can rely on are one another. Through this process recruits also come to value current operational officer's accounts (these are the only people who know what 'real policing' is all about) above those of outsiders (who have no legitimacy or experience) or trainers (they've been away from the sharp end for too long).

One of the most important transitions for new recruits is their journey from 'autonomy' to 'solidarity' (moving from the individual to the group) (Fielding 1988: 189). In the military, individuality is overtly challenged from the outset of training (Ricks 1995: 4) where, as one marine described, there 'is a ban on using the first person' and 'the group is supreme'. When a new recruit dared use 'I' he was strongly admonished: 'I?, I? . . . "I" is gone!' he was told, while 'a staff sergeant explained to the recruits that "before we leave my island, we will be thinking and breathing exactly alike. Nobody's an individual, understand?" ' (Ricks 1995: 4 cited in Kier 1999: 28–9).

Although the police environment is less extreme than the military, police recruits learn quickly that being accepted by the group has primacy over their individual needs. While this is an understandable response, bonding is sometimes achieved at considerable individual and emotional cost, as this officer describes:

> The police reader will be aware, and other readers need to be aware, of the immense pressures involved in being a police officer . . . Having been a part of this environment, I understand why policemen and women need to 'belong' – to identify with, and seek the support of, their own police companions . . . But I have also seen how this highly charged atmosphere . . . can lead to a peculiar bottling-up of emotions; a creation of the tendency to deny one's true feelings and beliefs on a number of issues in order to maintain the acceptance and affirmation given by the group which is so vital in fighting off the pressures both from the outside, and unfortunately, sometimes from the higher, managerial ranks inside the police (police sergeant cited in Burke 1993: 9).

For the military, group cohesion is an integral element of being able to fight, and personnel are encouraged to bond and see the military as 'their family' (Winslow 1998: 352). However, rather like real policing, wars are relatively rare occurrences, and most military activity involves peace-keeping (Winslow 1998: 352) where this strong degree of bonding can generate problems:

We're so connected physically and mentally, that if there's one person that we admire, who does good work, who gains the respect of others, of his superiors and colleagues, the others will group around him. If he incites his group to racist behaviour, they'll follow, even if they don't agree, because they won't distinguish themselves from the group. Because the group's all you've got. If you're in battle, no one else is looking out for you. You can't count on your family, they're in another world (Canadian soldier cited in Winslow 1998: 353).

Although there are some clear differences between the military and policing very similar processes occur, as this officer explains:

I soon realized that no matter how keen or well intentioned a new probationer is, it is difficult to go against the grain of the existing 'old sweats'. So when people talk of 'spades' and 'queens' and 'lefty bastards', it would take a very brave individual indeed who voiced any kind of protest. Most people just keep their mouth shut (cited Burke 1993: 16).

'There are some aspects of it that aren't very savoury', a minority ethnic recruit, who eventually resigned from the police service, described:

but ... it tends to indoctrinate you, well brainwash. Because the police culture it applied even to me ... I found myself doing it. I mean, specifically, I started picking people, putting them into little compartments. I found myself thinking 'Well, that's not quite right, perhaps coming from an ethnic minority myself and having experiences at first hand, I should know better' but I found myself doing it (officer cited in Holdaway and Barron 1997: 126–7).

I will return to these issues later but here I want to focus on the training environment and the powerful informal messages that appear to pervade it. These serve to reinforce rather than challenge received police wisdom 'regardless of the content of the academy instruction' (Van Maanen 2003: 71). Perhaps this is why, as a recent American study (Prokos and Padavic 2002) highlighted, some of the deepest structural disadvantages remain so embedded in police cultures. The researchers found that although:

the explicit curriculum ... at the police academy ... was gender neutral; the hidden curriculum was riddled with gendered lessons [and male recruits] ... by watching and learning from instructors and each other ... developed a form of masculinity that 1) excluded women students and exaggerated differences between them and the men; and 2) denigrated women in general (Prokos and Padavic 2002: 439, 446).

The authors describe how a fictional programme on policing shown during training included a domestic incident where the man arrested said: 'There oughtta be a law against bitches.' This phrase came to symbolise the position of women recruits in the training school and was continuously used after the

Table 9.1 The hidden curriculum in law enforcement training

	Lessons for men	*Lessons for women*
Treating women as outsiders	Social and physical boundaries can be created through language that excludes women, through the assumption that cops are men, through bonding with other recruits around activities that exclude women.	Instructors and other students assume cops are men. Women are virtually ignored in the curriculum and are excluded from social groups.
Exaggerating gender differences	Women and men are very different and this matters more than other differences between people. If women are strong, they are like men, which is inappropriate. 'Feminine' women are incapable of the physical demands of police work.	Women and men are very different and this matters more than other differences between people. Women are the ones who are different, men are the norm, so women will be treated differently.
Denigrating and objectifying women	Women are sexual objects. Women and women's issues (such as victimisation) are not as valuable, good or important as men or men's issues.	The place of women in the criminal justice system is as victims and as objects of men's fantasies and ridicule.
Resisting powerful women	Women in positions of power do not need to be taken seriously.	Women asserting authority will not be taken seriously by male police officers.

Source: Prokos and Padavic (2002: 447).

programme's viewing as a means to 'joke about something that a woman trainee had done or about women in general' (2002: 439). In Table 9.1 Prokos and Padavic (2002: 447) outline the lessons male and female recruits learnt during their time in training school.

These early organisational experiences have a profound impact on police officers' attitudes and behaviour and, as Schein (1971) suggests, a 'psychological contract' is created that joins 'the individual to the constraints and purposes of the organization' (Van Maanen 2003: 67). This process is powerfully demonstrated by Hunt and Manning's (2003: 142) study of police lying and how the nature of police work, and officers' responses to it, opens up a moral and practical minefield and, in so doing, creates the backdrop for a range of illegitimate behaviour and abuse of the rule of law.

In some cases lying is perceived as 'good police work' and motivated by good intent – for example, reducing the distress to victims' families and intervening in times of crisis; in others it is rewarded, as in specialist investigations or roles like undercover work (see Manning 1980; Hunt and Manning 2003). 'Bad' lying, by contrast, would involve actions like giving false testimony in court (Hunt and Manning 2003: 143). Despite the seeming distinctiveness of good and bad lying, even in the training environment recruits begin to understand that the law is enforced differentially and inconsistently. Once on the streets probationers see how blurred these issues really are in practice and their contact with more experienced officers (who tell them to forget everything they learnt at training school – this is the 'real' world now and this is how it *really* is) leads to the development of a belief that the difficulties posed for policing are so considerable that the job cannot be done without corner-cutting, via an informal 'ways and means act' rather than adhering to 'the rule of law' (see PSI 1983; Dixon 1997). '[L]earning to lie' therefore 'is a key to membership' (Hunt and Manning 2003: 143). Even those officers whose behaviour is known to be poor (and therefore questionable) are 'expected to lie', and fellow colleagues may have to collude in their lies (Hunt and Manning 2003: 147). To sustain this morally questionable world, officers:

> develop sophisticated and culturally sanctioned mechanisms for neutralizing the guilt and responsibility that troublesome and even morally ambiguous lying may often entail. In time, accounts which retrospectively justify and excuse a lie may become techniques of neutralisation which prospectively facilitate the construction of new lies with ready-made justifications. When grounds for lying are well-known in advance, it takes a self-reflective act to tell the truth, rather than to passively accept and use lies when they are taken-for-granted and expected (Hunt and Manning 2003: 151).

Seasoned police officers also assume the public lie. This is in part shaped by their experience that things are not always what they seem and that suspicion is a healthy element of a police officer's tool-kit, but Manning and Hunt's study highlights that there might be another element too – that lying is so intrinsically embedded in their way of working that officers simply assume that this is the way the world works.

Does this mean officers lie to police researchers too? In Britain, the bulk of empirical policing research has either been entirely qualitative or has a large qualitative component (see, for example, PSI 1983). Where researchers observe policing *in practice*, they are often present at the time accounts are constructed and are, therefore, in a position to differentiate between officers' accounts of events and their own observation of those events. Furthermore, where interviews and observations are combined researchers can link what officers *say* with what they *do*.

Policing the 'mean streets'

> ... police routinely come into conflict with the most marginal groups in society, and like antagonists generally, they demean their opponents ... If the police can persuade themselves that those against whom coercive authority is exercised are contemptible, no moral dilemmas are experienced – the policed section of the population 'deserve it' (Waddington 1999: 301).

The poor and socially excluded have formed the bulk of the police's business both as victims and offenders ever since the creation of the Metropolitan Police in 1829. Research in the past four decades based on direct observations of police officers' behaviour suggests that those groups with whom the police most frequently come into closest contact are frequently dismissed as 'police property', 'dross' and 'slags' who are seen to be undeserving of better treatment (see PSI 1983; Choongh 1997; Reiner 2000). Officers, particularly in inner-city areas, tend to believe they are 'the thin blue line' engaged in a battle to save the streets from lawless elements, and react strongly against those perceived to be challenging their authority or who fail to show officers the respect and demeanour they believe they deserve (see Werthman and Piliavin 1967; Reiss 1971; PSI 1983). This readily lends itself to negative labelling of people and places, to repeatedly targeting a known, and relatively small, 'suspect population' either through their repeat offending or, as is frequently the case with young black (and increasingly young Asian) men, unquestioned racist stereotyping. The latter appears to be so powerful that even minority ethnic officers can find themselves enacting them. As this officer explained: 'I've done it. It's hard to understand the pressure you're under. If you're in a particular situation and things are slow, then you almost subconsciously find yourself targeting blacks' (cited in Cashmore 2001: 652). Not surprisingly repeated targeting often makes groups feel they are victims of police harassment (which recent research suggests is likely to reduce compliance) and forms a vital backdrop to relationships between minority ethnic communities and the police. Even 'deserving victims', as I noted earlier, are prey to elements of the culture that value crime-fighting over support and victim care.

There has been considerable debate about whether values expressed in 'the canteen culture' (see Fielding 1994), and the opportunities it provides for officers to 'let off steam' (Waddington 1999: 287), shape police behaviour in practice. Although, as Hall *et al.* (1998: 6) argue, 'our basic attitudes do influence how we behave' it is also clear that police officers' behaviour can be highly situated (i.e. differs according to time, place and context). This was aptly demonstrated by the PSI study (1983) where officers openly expressed racist attitudes and 'prejudice' in their talk – but these were less apparent in their practice.

It is also evident that despite the seemingly overwhelming weight of negative cultural values 'the occupational culture has to make its pitch for support' (Fielding 1988: 135) and that while some officers 'embrace it without question' others 'will box and cox against and with it' (Holdaway and Barron 1997: 11). This helps to explain the diversity in practice documented by police researchers. Recent work on stop and searches, for example, reveals differences in officers' understanding of the grounds for stop/search and their execution of these powers (Quinton *et al.* 2000; see also FitzGerald 1999). Such variations highlight that police practice cannot be 'articulated in simple or straightforward ways in all localities' (Walklate 2000: 235), at *all* times and by *all* officers.

The gendered quality of some street encounters illustrates this well. In an Australian study (Braithwaite and Brewer 1998: 286) researchers found that male officers were 'more competitive' in their encounters and used 'tactics which emphasized power over citizens, such as control, threat and physical actions' (see Chapter 22). These often had negative results including verbal abuse and sometimes 'physical resistance'. Women officers, by contrast, even if they adopted the tactics of their male counterparts did not experience similar responses. As the authors noted:

> the tactical choices of male officers more often placed them at risk of physical confrontation ... Females were generally more supportive of citizens, preferring tactics which emphasised mutual power in the interaction ... [They] used coercive tactics less frequently and in different contexts than males and, as a result, experienced less verbal abuse during their discussions with members of the public, and avoided physical resistance (Braithwaite and Brewer 1998: 286).

Mastrofski (1999) argues that there are some fundamental expectations that should shape our treatment at the hands of the police, either as victims or offenders. These include 'attentiveness, reliability, responsiveness, competence, manners and fairness'. As the preceding discussion has shown these principles tend not to be among the most valued aspects of street policing culture. However, as I describe in the next section, some of these elements are apparent in some subcultures of policing, particularly those related to community policing where officers can develop very different orientations to their work and in so doing highlight 'essential divisions' within the seeming hegemonic street cop culture' (Fielding 1995: 11).

In search of variation

Despite the dangers of *generalising* about police culture (as a singular and homogeneous entity), police researchers (myself included) often find it difficult to move away from the general (and seemingly all powerful) characteristics of *the* dominant police culture in part because these elements appear to be common for most, if not all, officers. This has frequently led researchers to assume that the dominant (street cop) culture is representative of policing per se (and that therefore any discussion of difference is unimportant). However, research suggests there are important differences between and within different roles, ranks and specialisms.

Little research has examined either *how* dominant the dominant culture really is, or charted in detail the relationship between different subcultural groupings and 'dominant' cultural characteristics. As I describe later, research has tended to focus either on subcultural grouping or to discuss the impact of the 'culture' at a more general level. We do not even know whether small percentages of dominant and influential officers create an artificial appearance of hegemony, just as the occasional incidents of real policing powerfully shape police officers' perceptions of their work.

These issues are important because, as Reiner's (1978) 'typology of police orientations' (see Table 9.2), drawn from his own and other police research, demonstrates, there is a diverse range of orientations among officers in terms of their reasons for joining the police, the 'attachment' they have towards it,

Table 9.2 A typology of police orientations

	Bobby	Uniform carrier	New centurion	Social worker	Professional	Federationist
Initial attraction	Mixed or instrumental	Could be either	Non-instrumental	Non-instrumental	Non-instrumental	Instrumental
Current attachment	Interest and security	Pay	Interest	Public service	Public service or interest	Interest
Job satisfaction	Moderate to satisfied	Completely unsatisfied	Satisfied	Satisfied to moderate	Satisfied	Satisfied
Promotion system	Mixed reasons	Completely unjust	Unjust: based on irrelevant criteria	Just	Just	Just or mixed
Relations between the ranks	Mainly consensus	Conflict	Conflict	Mainly consensus	Consensus	Contained, limited conflict
Role of police	Includes some social aspects, but mainly crime prevention	No valid function at all	Narrow, should concentrate on crime	Wide, largely a social service	Includes many functions	Includes many functions but must limit

Source: adapted from Reiner (1978).

their job satisfaction, attitudes to promotion, relationship with other ranks and perceptions of the police role, all of which may be influential in shaping their encounters and approaches to their work. Yet their initial training, socialisation and environmental exposure, as I described in the previous section, are very similar.

Almost a quarter of a century after Reiner's research, a study focusing on the implementation of community policing in a US police department (Mastrofski *et al.* 2002) outlined four distinct officer styles:

> *Professionals* who demonstrated ownership, knowledge and awareness, care and attentiveness, communication skills and good order maintenance.
> *Reactors* who were enforcement oriented, 'reactive' rather than proactive and selective about whom they helped.
> *Tough cops* who were cynical, authoritarian and had few conflict resolution skills but saw themselves as 'crime fighters'.
> *Avoiders* who were 'reluctant to engage in any type of encounter'.
> (Mastrofski *et al.* 2002: 88–102).

Depressingly, only the 'professionals', who formed just a fifth of the officers observed, 'exhibited behaviour consistent with the leadership's ideal of how officers should deal with the public', while 'two in five officers showed styles distinctly at odds with the department's ideal' (Mastrofski *et al.* 2002: 106). At a time when increasing emphasis is being placed on the police, by the public and politicians alike, to adopt more sensitive and responsive approaches to communities, this research raises some important questions about whether there are sufficient officers with the appropriate skills to undertake such work. There is no British research that enables us to estimate what proportion of officers would fall into the professional category here (or if the same kinds of typologies are appropriate), but it is at least arguable that because of rather different, more liberal policing traditions, and political pressures on the police in Britain, the proportion of professionals and reactors may be higher than US forces based on paramilitary principles. Nevertheless, recent research in London, for example, still suggests 'a better balance' is required 'between the "crime fighting" objectives and the equally important ones of "peace keeping" and "order maintenance"' (FitzGerald and Hough 2002: 1).

The typologies outlined above offer some insight into the *variations* in officer orientations (and highlight the fact that police officers are not all the same). Below I examine two areas (community policing and research on 'street cops and management cops') to illustrate the subcultural differences in different roles and ranks in the police organisation. Both highlight how the nature of particular kinds of police work and the environment in which it occurs are vital factors in shaping officers' responses.

Community policing

Emergency 24-hour response policing (where all constables begin) is often difficult, frustrating and transient work (likened by one officer to being on a production line – see Fielding 1995: 19). Despite these negative associations response policing is also valued as real policing because it involves driving at high speeds from call to call and has the potential, at least, for dangerous crime-fighting work. As I have already argued the nature of response policing can also have a powerful impact on attitudes and behaviour. As these community officers said of their 24-hour response colleagues: '[they] feel it's too much trouble to say "hello" to somebody. They walk around [people], or turn their eyes away or worse. It's as if they're afraid of the people out there.' Another suggested 24-hour response was ' "thank you very much, somebody will be in touch" and away you go' (cited in Fielding 1995: 19).

Given the difficulties associated with response policing one might expect those who seek other uniform roles – where their work is more involved with problem-solving, where there is both greater and more positive interfaces between the police and public, and where 'you've got time for a bedside manner' (community police officer cited in Fielding 1995: 19) – would find these immensely appealing. Yet rather perversely officers who adopt community roles can often find themselves disparaged by their response colleagues precisely because they are no longer engaged in what is perceived to be real policing (see McConville and Shepherd 1992). Many officers who assume community roles, however, despite much that is 'shared' in terms of 'assumptions about the [police] organization, its environment and sanctioned practices', come to understand their role and interactions with people as less fleeting, more meaningful and satisfactory (both for the officer and the public) (Fielding 1995: 11; see also Bennett 1994; Trojanowicz and Bucqueroux 1998).

Miller (1999) suggests, on the basis of research on a neighbourhood policing programme in a US city, that this kind of approach can transform police officers' attitudes and skills. Neighbourhood officers developed a broader conceptual framework for the problems they encountered; came to see 'crime as part of a larger constellation of social issues, often related to poverty, poor schooling, and blocked opportunities'; acquired a broader range of skills and approaches to their work (which enhanced job satisfaction) and were retained when officers returned to response policing roles; and were 'less cynical about people, more willing to look beyond the immediate crisis to the larger picture and better able to comprehend situations by using a problem-solving approach' (Miller 1999: 211).

What is equally important in cultural terms is that this kind of work detaches officers from well established 'occupational perspectives' and creates possibilities for them to 'become critics as well as insiders' (Fielding 1995: 11). This suggests that attempts to encourage greater community interaction, problem-solving and multi-agency liaison (through the Crime and Disorder Act, for example) are important developments and may in time impact on policing practice. Furthermore, although the American research cited earlier (Mastrofski et al. 2002) suggested a minority of officers conformed to their leaders' ideals, there was evidence that those in the most negative groups were in a minority too. If, as the authors note, there had been a decline of the worst types of officers and a movement towards the middle into the reactor category (who demonstrated a 'willingness to improve their rapport with the public, but only on a reactive and selective basis'), this was at least 'progress toward the department ideal' (Mastrofski et al. 2002: 107).

Street cops and management cops

For a variety of reasons, most research on police culture has focused on street-level officers. Part of this bias is explained by the nature and quality of front-line police work and its potential impact on public attitudes. Accessing street officers, though, is not only easier than observing crime analysts at work or shadowing middle managers, for example, but has also proved far more alluring to researchers who may be as seduced by images of real policing as the officers they observe. What we see therefore is a lot of research on a small proportion of policing (perhaps exacerbating the potential for distortion and oversimplification). Civilian staff, for example, who in many British forces now form a significant proportion of personnel, are rarely researched. We know very little about how they perceive the world of policing, how much dominant cultures influence their attitudes, values and approach to their work, or whether they form a significant subcultural grouping in their own right. These, and other absences in the research, prevent a holistic knowledge and understanding about the police organisation, something that is crucially important for reform and change.

I want to focus my attention here on another area of relative absence: the street cop/management cop divide. Van Maanen (1984) argues that promotion within the police *depends* in large part on jettisoning well developed ways of thinking that are embedded in street cop culture. This in itself suggests that management cultures may be differently characterised. This was certainly reflected in a study of street cops and management cops in New York City where two very contrasting views of policing were identified (Reuss-Ianni and Ianni 1983: 253). Street cops were nostalgic and attached to images of harmony and order both in their relationships with the public and within different levels of the police hierarchy. Whether these perceptions ever approximated to actuality is unclear (but unlikely, because as Pearson (1983) reminds us, we all have a tendency to see the past through rose-tinted spectacles). Street cops perceived their internal working environment as divided and bureaucratic where 'the real loyalties of the bosses' did not reside with the officers (Reuss-Ianni and Ianni 1983: 254).

Management cops, defined not unproblematically in this study as those in headquarters posts, believed in 'efficient organisation, rational decision making, cost-effective procedures, and objective accountability at all levels of policing' (Reuss-Ianni and Ianni 1983: 257). They were also 'politically expedient' and more forward thinking, having accepted that changing social and economic circumstances required a different approach (1983: 270). Given that this study is now 20 years old these themes sound highly familiar!

However, instead of transforming the street cop culture to fit better the needs of contemporary policing the management cop culture secreted in headquarters 'coexist[ed] with rather than contain[ed] the local precinct street culture', characterised at the time of the research as rife with institutionalised corruption (Reuss-Ianni and Ianni 1983: 255–6).

The nature of street police work requires even the newest and most junior of officers to be assertive and exert control over others. This, combined with the levels of discretion exercised by street-level officers and the degree of autonomy and control they impose upon their work (which still pertains even in these performance-driven days), is a powerful mix and one that is potentially very difficult to manage. Indeed, in the New York study, the relationship between the two cultures was described as one of 'gaming' where the 'precinct level response' was 'to test in what way they can maneuver around, outwit, or nullify the moves of headquarters decision makers' by 'foot dragging, absenteeism' and a plethora of other 'coping . . . and self defending techniques' (Reuss-Ianni and Ianni 1983: 259, 270). As an indication of how powerful this resistance was, managers seemed to be unable to get street officers to accept their reforms 'seriously or honestly' (1983: 272).

The dominance of bureaucratic management cops has been equally observable in British policing over the last 20 years. Reiner (1991), for example, in his study of Britain's chief constables highlights the demise of the 'barons, bobbies and bosses' who dominated postwar policing and the rise of the 'bureaucrats' who saw 'policing by consent' and a 'finely tuned balance' between 'enforcement' and . . . 'participation' as the key objective in police work (Reiner 1991: 340; see Chapter 25). By the time of Wall's (1998) research almost a decade later these bureaucrats were firmly entrenched. But the game play persists.

Although it is easy to see how performance culture and managerialism may have reinforced *differences* between street and management cops, it is equally important for us to understand more about the continuities *between* street cops and management cops. Indeed, as Steytler (1990: 107) argued, although research on cultures continues to focus on 'the relatively powerless officers', understanding senior officers' cultures, or what he terms 'high policing', is essential because 'For cop culture to be an adequate analytic tool, it must account for the norms created by, mediated through, and protected by . . . senior officers' (cited in Marks 2000: 571). As I describe below there are some interesting glimpses into the importance of these issues in research examining the gendered and racialised elements of police culture.

The dangers of being 'different'

Without a conscious effort to put the shoe on the other foot it is easy to underestimate how organisational and wider societal factors shape the treatment and experience of particular groups, especially where the processes are subtle or embedded in routinised ways of working that are taken for granted rather than questioned. But 'there is of course a direct and vital link between internal culture in the way people are treated, and external performance' (HMIC 1997: 9).

Despite changes in policy, and recruitment, the police service remains a largely male, white and heterosexual organisation, where those who are perceived to be 'different' by virtue of their race, gender or sexuality have reported significant problems in gaining acceptance, and in some cases recognition or legitimacy for their experiences. Martin (1996: 523), for example, found deeply embedded differences between male and female officers' experiences in a force she studied. Male officers 'denied that a macho or sexist style was evident in their division' and some even suggested 'that people outside the service had an unrealistically negative and exaggerated view of the subculture' (1996: 523). However, the women officers Martin interviewed perceived sexism to be one of the key problems in their workplace. Indeed the majority 'had experienced sexual harassment . . . of a physical nature' and two of these cases happened in the very place male officers believed it did not occur (1996: 519).

In the three sections that follow I examine three areas of *difference*, those based on gender, race and sexuality. It is too simplistic of course to regard these as discrete entities. In practice some officers may experience *difference* as female and black officers, or also be gay. As there is currently little research on the interactions between gender, race and sexuality in policing we can only speculate on what the relationship between these might be but it is likely that there is a complex 'melding of multiple factors' rather than one dominant element (i.e. race, gender or sexuality) (Miller 1999: 155). However, existing research suggests some interesting, and not always predictable, alignments. For example, male minority ethnic officers often ally themselves with the dominant white male culture (as this is where the power is vested in the organisation) and by so doing may end up reinforcing the prejudice experienced by female officers, including those of minority ethnic origin (Martin 1994).

Women in a man's world

The taken for granted ethos of masculinity in police cultures is reflected in the fact that early studies on policing only referred to police*men* (see Banton 1964) as if women were invisible in the organisation (Heidensohn 1992), and even today it is not uncommon to hear journalists, members of the public and some police officers speaking of policemen rather than the gender-neutral, police officers. Given the importance of masculinity as a key cultural attribute in *real* policing it is perhaps unsurprising that despite over a quarter of a century of sex discrimination legislation, and growing numbers of women officers, research continues to demonstrate that policing is still largely viewed, and run, on masculine precepts (Taylor and Mackenzie 1994; Brown and Heidensohn 2000). Indeed 'the widespread and persistent nature of . . . [police culture] suggests it has deep roots and powerful protectors' (Heidensohn 1998: 223). This, combined with the fact that 'Sex roles and gender stereotypes are amongst the most potent and enduring social categorisations' (Brown 1998a: 266–7) means patriarchal attitudes and assumptions about women's domestic roles (Dick and Jankowicz 2001: 81) still present major impediments for women officers who find themselves favoured for some roles (which reinforce gender stereotypes and the 'emotional labour' – Stenross and Kleinman 2003 – that their male colleagues dislike) and are similarly 'kept from others', for example more specialist posts (see Holdaway and Parker 1998).

Waddington (1999: 298) suggests that women officers directly challenge the fundamental task of policing as one that is undertaken by 'real' men (see also Messerschmidt 1993) who must use 'coercive authority' and their physical strength to maintain control of the streets (no matter how unrepresentative this is of policing activity – Jermier *et al.* 1989; Martin 1989 – or problematic as a policing technique – PSI 1983; Braithwaite and Brewer 1998).

The differing styles of conflict resolution and sensitivity that some women officers bring to their work are often dismissed as 'soft' (see Young 1991) and unimportant by their male counterparts. Women officers therefore often struggle to find acceptance (and are constantly reminded they are in a man's world). In this highly gendered and pressured environment they are forced to choose between 'embracing this male culture as their own or fulfilling the more traditional expectations associated with their role' (Walklate 2000: 238), a choice that has been expressed as one where there are *police*women who take the first path and police*women* who take the latter (Martin 1990).

Whichever path they choose women officers often feel isolated and there is little evidence of them working collectively or developing a 'shared conscious-ness' indeed one woman officer described her experience as 'like being in the sisterhood with no sisters'! Silvestri (1999: 8, 18) suggests that those women who seek and succeed in gaining promotion develop 'strategies to minimise their increased visibility, suppressing their consciousness as women wherever possible' – a road that is not without its emotional, practical and personal costs (see Martin 1996; Brown and Heidensohn 2000).

Although it was assumed that as women formed larger percentages of the police organisation that harassment would decline, Brown's (1998b) survey of women officers in more than 30 countries suggests otherwise. Eighty per cent of women officers in the sample from Britain, the USA and Australia reported being sexually harassed. This is a potent and disturbing reminder that women who work in male-dominated worlds are vulnerable, a position that stands in stark contrast to female-dominated professions like nursing and teaching that are not characterised by similar kinds of harassment (see Brown 1998a; Miller 1999). Sexual discrimination therefore seems to be firmly institutionalised in policing but in recent years, as race issues have gained prominence, gender issues have received less coverage and attention.

Racism: inside and outside

As with the gender issues described above, structural disadvantage and discrimination are vital factors in the treatment of minority ethnic communi-ties in British society and in the experiences of police officers and civilian staff who come from those communities (see Hall *et al.* 1978; Gilroy 1987; Bowling 1999). Racial prejudice and stereotyping have formed integral elements of the taken-for-granted assumptions in dominant white cop culture (Holdaway 1995) and, like gender, it is unsurprising that minority ethnic officers often find themselves isolated and in some cases subjected to racialised language, behaviour and stereotypes. However, there are some suggestions, as I describe later, that overt racism has actually become less visible and more subtle over time.

In a classic study of the Metropolitan Police (PSI 1983), commissioned after the Brixton riots in 1981, the 'pervasive' nature of 'racial prejudice and racialist talk' was all too evident. A white police officer cited in the report outlines his views on race relations in Britain at that time (early 1980s):

Blacks today are repaying whites for their bad treatment in colonial days. They aren't just against police but against all white people. The police are an obvious target because they represent white supremacy. Really, until blacks have taken over and evened up the score, the problem won't be solved. I don't blame them really, when they get stuck in places like Brixton. I know that PCs call them spooks, niggers and sooties, but deep down the majority of PCs aren't really against them, although there are some who really hate them and will go out of their way to get them. I call them niggers myself now, but I don't really mean it. I think a relief takes on a personality of its own. Although you still have your own personality, you lose a lot of it to the relief group personality (see Policy Studies Institute 1983: Vol. 4, 115).

In the last 20 years two major reports have focused on the problems associated with policing and race relations: the Scarman Inquiry (1981) and the Lawrence Inquiry (Macpherson 1999). Both were described as 'defining moments' or 'watersheds' in policing history and highlighted very similar themes, advocating that the police service should reflect the diverse communities they serve and the need for more sensitivity and awareness of the problems encountered by minority ethnic communities who have found themselves 'simultaneously over-policed' and 'under-serviced' (Walklate 2000: 235; see Chapters 21 and 28). There was, however, one very significant difference between them. Whereas Lord Scarman adopted the 'bad apple' thesis of police racism (i.e. that individuals rather than the organisation were to blame), the Lawrence Inquiry (Macpherson 1999) emphasised institutional racism. This was defined as:

the collective failure of an organisation to provide an appropriate and professional service to people because of their colour, culture or ethnic origin. It can be seen or detected in processes, attitudes and behaviour which amount to discrimination through unwitting prejudice, ignorance, thoughtlessness, and racist stereotyping which disadvantage minority ethnic people (Macpherson 1999: para. 6.34).

The then Home Secretary, Jack Straw, suggested that:

any long-established, white-dominated organisation is liable to have procedures, practices and a culture that tend to exclude or to disadvantage non-white people. The police service, in that respect, is little different from other parts of the criminal justice system – or from Government Departments, including the Home Office – and many other institutions (*Hansard* 24 February 1999 column 391, cited in Bowling and Phillips 2002: 18).

The fact that almost 20 years after Scarman's recommendations progress with minority ethnic recruitment was lamentable (still only at two per cent by 2000 – Bowling and Phillips 2002) and the service provided to minority ethnic communities remained very problematic (Clancy *et al.* 2001) indicates perhaps how little the grievances of minority ethnic communities were prioritised or understood by the police who perhaps underestimated just how widespread and deep rooted the lack of trust and confidence was in them. Attempts to heal the rift in relationships post-Scarman focused on community policing initiatives and awareness training. These sat, rather uneasily, alongside measures to ensure officers were properly trained and equipped to deal with riot situations in the future. Perhaps highlighting a key weakness in the police organisation more generally, there was little or no evaluation of whether the reforms prompted by Scarman had an impact on routine operational policing practice.

Training is of course not sufficient, in itself, to tackle the negative elements of the dominant culture especially given subtle and informal messages that may serve to reinforce, rather than challenge, deeply held stereotypes. Furthermore, although the 'bad apple' theory was widely believed there was no vigorous campaign to challenge offensive behaviour (or to sack racist officers which would have demonstrated both internally and externally that racist police officers would not be tolerated). Indeed in the late 1990s almost 20 years after Scarman an inquiry by the police inspectorate reported 'overt and covert racism' and although 'longer serving officers had noticed beneficial change from the stories of the 1980s and earlier, . . . there were still too many accounts of distressing behaviour or, at best, managerial indifference towards ethnic minority staff' (HMIC 1999: 29–30). There were also 'a small number of officers whose behaviour' was deemed 'not only unprofessional but morally wrong' (1999: 29–32).

This situation is itself a reflection of a conservative organisation that refutes the need for radical change. The tendency to individualise problems conveniently leaves the organisation intact when in fact 'bad apple' problems can often be reflective of broader organisational failings (see Klockars 1985). This is particularly important for policing and race issues because while it may be the case that a minority of individual officers 'hold consistently extreme attitudes of racial prejudice there is no clear evidence that an explanation of personality traits is sufficient' (Holdaway 1996: 79–80), particularly when officers seem to develop 'increasingly illiberal/intolerant attitudes' towards minority ethnic groups during their service (Colman and Gorman 1982). This pattern also extends to minority ethnic officers. As this constable explained:

At that time I was particularly conscious that I had to try harder to be accepted. I was getting conscious of my colour, my ethnicity, that it was difficult for me, more difficult for me than a white officer to be part of the team. So I tried to guard and stop more black people. If I met an Asian person I would be harder on him, just to prove to my colleagues that I was one of them, that I was a police officer, not an Asian person or a black person (Holdaway and Barron 1997: 144).

Minority officers who challenged racist remarks or behaviour by their colleagues often find themselves ignored or ostracised:

I would say, 'I don't think you should be saying that' and those people that said 'Sorry, I didn't know you were there' would say, 'Well you know what it's like, you get used to it'. 'Well get un-used to it then', I would say, 'you wouldn't like it if I said, "You so-and so"', I mean how would you feel if I said that to you?' . . . They should just give it a bit of thought before they open their mouth and that's what I told them . . . [but] Nobody takes any notice (cited in Holdaway 1997: 395).

Although minority officers often struggle to gain legitimacy within the organisation, and frequently find their colleagues indifferent and sometimes hostile, in incidents where minority officers are abused by the public the situation is rather different:

I remember being sent to a job, domestic dispute . . . and of course the door opened and this guy says, 'What do you want nigger?' And I said 'Domestic dispute, come to sort it out for you, what's your problem?' He said, 'I don't want a nigger policeman dealing with my family, send me a real policeman.' So I said 'Ok' turned on my heels, just radioed through to the control room, said, 'Here sarge, got a guy here doesn't want to see a black policeman. I'm clearing, over'. He said, 'yes fine, log off, not requesting police attention' – nobody went. He rang back and nobody went (Holdaway and Barron 1997: 136–7).

Although this example shows solidarity on one level, it also represents neglect of duty on another. It was not the victim but the perpetrator of domestic violence who abused the officer. By refusing to deal with the incident the victim's needs were not met at all, nor was the racist abuse of the officer. Holdaway and Barron (1997: 136–7) suggest in public encounters where black and Asian officers receive support from their white colleagues 'the identity of "police officer", with all the connotations and denotations of power, authority and occupational values it musters takes precedence over the sustaining of racialised divisions within the police workforce'.

The key question is *why* does the environment permit such racism? In short, because as Sutherland (1949) so aptly put it in the context of white-collar crime, there is an 'excess of definitions favourable to the violation of laws'. Like any other crime, motivated offenders operate within 'awareness spaces' where they feel comfortable and familiar (Brantingham and Brantingham 1984), and where they perceive the likelihood of intervention or apprehension to be low. Without challenging racist, sexist or homophobic behaviour (with a firm and consistent lead at all levels of the organisation) perpetrators are 'left with the impression that their behaviour [is] supported' (Holdaway and Barron 1997: 134).

While recruitment of minority ethnic and women officers has often been viewed as a potential solution to some of the problems faced by the police service, this may do little to change the organisation unless the internal environment is addressed. As this Asian officer explained:

All you'll do is fill the force with more black faces. Good for PR, but it won't make a scrap of difference to how police work gets done. [Another officer said:] it's just an assumption that, if we get more black officers, it will be OK. But, why? It won't achieve a thing . . . We can have an all-black police force and it wouldn't change a thing: you'd still have racism in the police (Cashmore 2002: 333).

The most invisible difference

The experiences of gay and lesbian police officers are the most invisible 'of the three dimensions to equal opportunities ... and consequently the least debated' (Walklate 2000: 242). Again the processes are complex as this gay officer explained: 'I don't actually think recruits join the police more homophobic than the rest of society. It's just that once they've been in the police for a while, they make more of a show of what prejudices they have, because the canteen culture encourages them to do so' (cited in Burke 1993: 32). Based on the limited research available it seems that the dominant culture is as staunchly heterosexual as it is racist and sexist where gay male officers report being ostracised unless they can establish qualities attributed to *real* (heterosexual) men, by proving their masculinity in difficult or violent situations for example. Lesbian officers potentially face double disadvantage, although their gay male counterparts have argued that their sexuality is less threatening and more accepted (see Burke 1993). There is simply insufficient work at this stage to establish whether this evaluation is right. It may be the case, though, that as they have already been marginalised as women their sexual orientation, which is invisible, is less of an issue (although the treatment of Alison Halford, former Assistant Chief Constable in Merseyside Police, suggests that, in some circumstances women's sexuality can be used against them as much as their gender – see Fielding 1994).

Can police cultures be changed?

In an early study of American policing in the 1960s, James Q. Wilson (1968: 4) concluded that 'the constraints' placed on police officers because of 'the nature of [their] function' put 'real limits on the degree to which [their] behaviour can be modified by organizational directives'. Like Banton (1964) before him, Wilson (1968: 7) highlighted the discretion street-level officers possessed, working beyond the visible scrutiny of either supervisors or senior officers most of the time, thus making their work inherently difficult to control. Wilson's scepticism about the possibilities for changing police officers' behaviour was shared by a number of his successors, and the apparent unchanging nature of police culture has, until recently, become part of policing mythology (see Dixon 1997: 18–19). However, as Chan (1997: 92–3) argues, police cultures are not immune to pressures from the external environment, and 'just as most houses on fire offer several escape routes, most environmental constraints allow for numerous adaptive responses' and different cultural forms (Kier 1999: 35–6).

The question is, therefore: what levers are required to transform the negative elements of police cultures into more positive ones and to create the impetus for change? Johnson (1990) cites two important ingredients: the *climate* for change needs to exist; and the *need* for change must either be widely acknowledged or prompted by a significant catalyst (as occurred in South Africa, countries in eastern Europe and Northern Ireland, for example).

In an important study that moved the debate about the possibilities for changing police cultures forward, Chan (1996, 1997) describes how the climate for corruption, which was once endemic and accepted in the New South Wales police department, rapidly changed as managers were forced to acknowledge the impact of corruption scandals and to enforce a focused (and effectively 'zero tolerance') anti-corruption strategy. Officers were left in no doubt that the department would not tolerate this behaviour. By contrast their handling of equally public and damaging scandals connected with the treatment of aboriginal and Island people was very different. Instead of targeted strategies for tackling the problems of 'racism and abuse' among officers head on, generalised crime prevention and community policing programmes were introduced by management and ignored by rank-and-file officers who remained unconvinced about the need to change their approach (Chan 1996: 123–6). In other words neither the external climate nor the management response was sufficiently strong to lever changes in racism and discriminatory practice (Chan 1996: 130).

Leadership and culture: 'two sides of the same coin'

Transformational leadership is a vital component in changing police cultures (see Chapter 25). If challenging racist, sexist and homophobic behaviour were as central to police culture as the myth of crime fighting, the police service would look very different indeed. Leadership and culture, as Schein (1992: 15) argues, are 'two sides of the same coin' where the absence of intervention in 'dysfunctional' cultures results in those cultures 'managing' the leaders (as the study of New York City, described earlier, illustrated – Reuss-Ianni and Ianni 1983). However, in order to tackle the negative elements, sufficient critical distance is required to 'overcome [leaders' own] constraining cultural assumptions' (Schein 1996: 379). This is very difficult in an organisation where all officers begin at the same place (the bottom!), are exposed to the same initial training and socialisation (though its impact is differential) and find themselves confronted with the same kinds of accommodations and moral ambiguities that all street officers encounter. These factors may help to explain why, as Reiner (1991) argues, the links between street and senior cops are perhaps more similar than their differences even though for street cops the divide seems very wide.

Holdaway's (1991) study of minority ethnic recruitment pre-Lawrence provides a useful example of how, despite well intentioned policies and some committed chief officers, change is difficult to achieve without very focused strategies. He argues that although chiefs did not set out to 'to allow the rank-and-file to continue practising policing as they desired' they did not ensure that policy was translated into practice (Holdaway 1995: 118). Indeed 'race relations' was peripheral rather than 'a central feature' of their strategy (Holdaway 1991). The climate post-Lawrence is very different. The Metropolitan Police Service were named and shamed and, along with all police forces in England and Wales, found themselves under intense public and political gaze with externally enforced legislative changes, increased scrutiny (and accountability) of policing practices like stop and search and the introduction of recruitment targets for minority ethnic officers to ensure greater representation. This is a far more directive approach and has enhanced accountability and scrutiny at a number of different levels in the organisation.

For some commentators changes in legislation are pivotal to reducing officer discretion, hindering the 'permissive' elements of the culture and increasing accountability (see Grimshaw and Jefferson 1987: 283; Brogden *et al.* 1988: 170). Perhaps the best illustration of the power of legislation in this regard is the Police and Criminal Evidence Act 1984 (PACE) (though see Chapter 10 dissenting view). As one officer explained: 'I actually saw that [PACE] as a god-send to me, who wanted to be an honest detective and [was] very uncomfortable about the practices ... People had to comply otherwise they wouldn't survive' (Foster forthcoming). Marks (1999: 157–8) suggested similar factors were at play in the public order training unit in South Africa, where white officers, accustomed to working in a repressive and racist regime, recognised that there was no option but to change their tactics in the new South Africa as the nature of their role was transformed and their jobs were on the line.

Miller's (1999) study of a police department in the USA highlights the possibilities for creating a more enlightened internal police environment through the right kind of leadership and reform strategies, even where the external impetus for change is not pressing, and demonstrates that tackling the internal environment can impact favourably on service delivery and improve police/community relationships too. The department she observed developed an enlightened reputation for recruiting women, minority and gay/lesbian officers and became a place where as this officer explained: 'We get quality people ... not the traditional cookie cutter model of a police officer.'

When a community policing programme was introduced (an idea that came in the first instance from a street-level officer), the 'old guard' resisted its introduction cynically seeing it as yet another example of the chiefs' 'wild plans'. This paved the way for a new wave of officers, a large proportion of whom were female and/or from minority ethnic backgrounds who were supportive of neighbourhood policing and whose 'difference' (in terms of gender, race/ethnicity and sexuality) proved advantageous in developing confidence and trust with diverse communities (Miller 1999: 15). Neighbourhood policing was so successful that it moved from the margins to the mainstream and all officers seeking promotion felt working on a neighbourhood policing team was vital (1999: 121). As the impact of working in these teams developed officers' skills and perceptions of their role, neighbourhood policing had a transformative and lasting impact on cultural attitudes too.

Continuity and change

Michael Banton's (1964: vii) pioneering study of policing in Britain sprang from a desire to examine an organisation that was 'working well' and where what, in contemporary terms, we would call best practice might be found. Banton did not use the term 'culture', although some of the characteristics we now associate with police culture, for example solidarity, perceptions of danger and lying for ones colleagues, are very evident in his analysis. It is these and other characteristics described in this chapter that have given discussions of police cultures their timeless quality (Dixon 1997). However, unlike Banton, most studies of policing that followed focused on what has gone badly and 'police culture' has been firmly in the frame.

I began this chapter highlighting the importance of acknowledging the complexity and multifaceted nature of police cultures. Yet, as I conclude I am conscious that I too could be guilty of oversimplifying a rather complex world and of focusing on the negative and powerful elements of a dominant culture rather than the diversity of cultures (which eschew neat generalisations), or more positive cultural aspects that police officers themselves might choose to emphasise (for example, the sense of mission, the desire to rid the streets of 'the bad guys', the dedication and long hours, the willingness, on one level, to do society's dirty work). This imbalance is to some extent a reflection of the kind of research that has been done on police cultures and it is difficult to write a review without *feeling* negative about some of the worst aspects. Researchers, however, as a senior police officer explained to me, see the worlds they observe in relation to how that world *ought* to be, or what they would ideally like it to be. Police officers, by contrast, more rooted in the imperfections and messiness of worlds as they find them, are perhaps both less aspirational or optimistic about the possibilities for change and become rather fragmented in their thinking, and often embattled, where the broader organisational aspirations and goals (which often seem unrealisable) can get lost along the way.

If we want the police organisation to move forward then perhaps it is time for a new approach that seeks to explore more fully police officers' own perceptions of what they value in the organisation, and how they believe they need to move forward. Pioneering work with prison officers (Liebling *et al.* 2001: 162), for example, has used a method called appreciative inquiry (Elliott 1999). Rather like restorative justice, this method focuses on the positive elements of an organisation or group and aims to generate transformational change through supporting and developing rather than criticising and condemning staff (Liebling *et al.* 2001: 163).

Appreciative inquiry might offer new insight and possibilities both for understanding the complexities of police cultures and how they can be changed (since in the final reckoning it does not matter what researchers say about these cultures, but rather how police officers seek to shape them and how they influence their actions). As the preceding discussion illustrates it is possible for officers who might have been steeped in the negativity of 24-hour response policing to adapt to different, and ultimately far more satisfying, ways of policing in neighbourhood or community roles so there is nothing inherent about police officers or their cultures that prevents change (although, as Mastrofski *et al.*'s study revealed, there may be issues about whether the organisation has sufficient numbers of individuals who want, or are able, to police professionally). However, the persistence of some of the most negative cultural characteristics, like sexism and racism, does highlight the vested interests that some (we do not know how large or small this number might be) have in resisting change at all levels of the organisation.

Even where the drive and commitment for change exist 'structural reform' is not a speedy process and requires us to 'temper short term scepticism with long term patience' (Mastrofski 1998: 182–3), something that in the 'can do' action-oriented world of policing is difficult. Nevertheless, as the discussion in this chapter has highlighted, police cultures are not singular and monolithic; they do vary across time and space, and the political, social and economic climate in which policing occurs does offer significant possibilities for transformational change. However, this can only happen if police leaders, and those at all levels of the police organisation, support the positive and tackle the negative in a radical, sustained and focused manner. If not, another review of the literature on police culture in 40 years will be reporting a very similar story.

Selected further reading

There are some very useful texts that review the literature on police cultures. The best is Reiner's *Politics of the Police* (2000: ch. 3). Janet Chan's study of the New South Wales Police, *Changing Police Culture* (1996 and 1997), is an excellent and informative read that highlights both the possibility of change and the central role that political and environmental factors play in this process. Dixon's book, *Law in Policing* (1997), contains a very useful overview of the literature on police culture and the different theoretical approaches to the area. Waddington's (1999) article in the *British Journal of Criminology* is also well worth a read. Miller's (1999) study on *Gender and Community Policing* is the best American monograph on policing I have read for some time. This would be particularly helpful for police officers, especially the last chapter that looks at policy implications.

There are also books and articles that focus on particular aspects of police cultures. On gender, Heidensohn's *Women in Control?* (1992) and Jennifer Brown's (1998a, 1998b) articles on harassment and discrimination are useful starting points. On race, Holdaway's *The Racialisation of British Policing* (1996) is very helpful, as is his co-authored book (with Barron) on *Resigners* (1997). There are very few studies of detectives and most of these are now very dated: Sanders' *Detectives* (1977), Hobbs' *Doing the Business* (1988), Ericson's *Making Crime* (1993) and Innes' recent study on homicide investigation: *Investigating Murder* (2003). There is more research on community policing and culture – see Fielding's *Community Policing* (1995), Trojanowicz and Bucqueroux's *Community Policing* (1998) and Mastrofski *et al.*'s 'Styles of partol in a community policing context' (2002). A good place to begin with the management literature on culture is Andrew Brown's *Organisational Culture* (1998), while Johnson and Scholes' *Exploring Corporate Strategy* (1999) has some very useful case studies on culture from a variety of public and private sector settings. For the vital links between leadership and culture, see Schein's *Organizational Culture and Leadership* (1985).

Note

1 This chapter draws on a literature review of police cultures undertaken for the Home Office in 2001.

References

Banton, M. (1964) *The Policeman in the Community*. London: Tavistock.
Bennett, T. (1994) 'Community policing on the ground: developments in Britain', in D.P. Rosenbaum (ed.) *The Challenge of Community Policing: Testing the Premises*. Thousand Oaks, CA: Sage, 224–46.

Bittner, E. (1967) 'The police on Skid Row: a study of peacekeeping', *American Sociological Review*, 32: 699–715.

Bowling, B. (1999) *Violent Racism: Victimisation, Policing and Social Context*. Oxford: Clarendon Press.

Bowling, B. and Phillips, C. (2002) *Racism, Crime and Justice*. Harlow: Longman.

Braithwaite, H. and Brewer, N. (1998) 'Differences in the conflict resolution tactics of male and female patrol officers', *International Journal of Police Science and Management*, 1(3): 276–87.

Brantingham, P.J. and Brantingham, P.L. (1984) *Patterns in Crime*. New York, NY: Macmillan.

Brogden, M., Jefferson, T. and Walklate, S. (1988) *Introducing Policework*. London: Unwin Hyman.

Brown, A. (1998) *Organisational Culture* (2nd edn). Harlow: Financial Times/Prentice Hall, Pearson Education.

Brown, J. (1998a) 'Aspects of discriminatory treatment of women police officers serving in forces in England and Wales', *British Journal of Criminology*, 38(2): 265–82.

Brown, J. (1998b) 'Comparing charges: the experience of discrimination and harassment among women police officers serving in Australia, the British Isles and the United States of America', *International Journal of Police Science and Management*, 1(3): 227–40.

Brown, J. and Heidensohn, F. (2000) *Gender and Policing: Comparative Perspectives*. Basingstoke: Macmillan.

Burke, M.E. (1993) *Coming out of the Blue*. London: Cassell.

Cashmore, E. (2001) 'The experiences of ethnic minority police officers in Britain: under-recruitment and racial profiling in a performance culture', *Ethnic and Racial Studies*, 24(4): 642–59.

Cashmore, E. (2002) 'Behind the window dressing: ethnic minority police perspectives on cultural diversity', *Journal of Ethnic and Migration Studies*, 28(2): 327–41.

Chan, J. (1996) 'Changing police culture', *British Journal of Criminology*, 36(1): 109–34.

Chan, J. (1997) *Changing Police Culture: Policing in a Multicultural Society*. Cambridge: Cambridge University Press.

Chan, J., Brereton, D., Legosz, M. and Doran, S. (2001) *E-policing: The Impact of Information Technology on Police Practices*. Queensland: Criminal Justice Commission.

Choongh, S. (1997) *Policing as Social Discipline*. Oxford: Oxford University Press.

Clancy, M., Hough, M., Aust, R. and Kershaw, C. (2001) *Crime Policing and Justice: The Experience of Ethnic Minorities: Findings from the 2000 British Crime Survey. Home Office Research Study* 223. London: HMSO.

Colman, A. and Gorman, L. (1982) 'Conservatism, dogmatism, and authoritarianism in British police officers', *Sociology*, 16(1): 1–11.

Dick, P. and Jankowicz, D. (2001) 'A social constructionist account of police culture and its influence on the representation and progression of female officers: a repertory grid analysis in a UK police force', *Policing: An International Journal of Police Strategies and Management*, 24(2): 181–99.

Dixon, D. (1997) *Law in Policing: Legal Regulation and Police Practices*. Oxford: Clarendon Press.

Elias, N. (1994) 'Introduction: a theoretical essay on established and outsider relations.' Originally published 1976 in Elias, N. and Scotson, J. *The Established and the Outsiders* (2nd edn). London: Sage.

Elliott, C.M. (1999) *Locating the Energy for Change: A Practitioner's Guide to Appreciative Inquiry*. Winnipeg: IISD.

Ericson, R. (1993) *Making Crime: A Study of Detective Work* (2nd edn). Toronto: Toronto University Press.

Ericson, R. and Haggerty, K. (1997) *Policing the Risk Society*. Oxford: Clarendon Press.

Fielding, N. (1988) *Joining Forces: Police Training, Socialization and Occupational Competence*. London: Routledge.

Fielding, N. (1994) 'Cop canteen culture', in T. Newburn and E. Stanko (eds) *Just Boys Doing Business: Men, Masculinity*. London: Routledge, 46–63.

Fielding, N. (1995) *Community Policing*. Oxford: Clarendon Press.

FitzGerald, M. (1999) *Searches in London under Section 1 of the Police and Criminal Evidence Act*. London: Metropolitan Police.

FitzGerald, M. and Hough, M. (2002) *Policing for London: Key Findings*. London: Southbank/LSE.

Gilroy, P. (1987) *There Ain't No Black in the Union Jack*. London: Hutchinson.

Gregory, G. and Lees, S. (1999) *Policing Sexual Assault*. London: Routledge.

Grimshaw, R. and Jefferson, T. (1987) *Interpreting Policework: Policy and Practice in Forms of Beat Policing*. London: Allen & Unwin.

Hall, S., Critcher, C., Jefferson, T., Clarke, J. and Roberts, B. (1978) *Policing the Crisis: Mugging, the State and Law and Order*. London: Macmillan.

Hall, S., Lewis, G. and McLaughlin, E. (1998) *The Report on Racial Stereotyping* (prepared for Deighton Guedalla, solicitors for Duwayne Brooks, June 1998). Milton Keynes: Open University Press.

Hampden-Turner, C. (1990) *Corporate Culture: From Vicious to Virtuous Circles*. London: Economist Books.

Heidensohn, F. (1992) *Women in Control?* Oxford: Clarendon Press.

Heidensohn, F. (1998) 'Comparative models of policing and the role of women officers', *International Journal of Police Science and Management*, 1(3): 215–26.

Her Majesty's Inspectorate of Constabulary. (1997) *Winning the Race: Policing Plural Communities*. London: HMSO.

Her Majesty's Inspectorate of Constabulary. (1999) *Winning the Race Revisited*. London: HMSO.

Hobbs, R. (1988) *Doing the Business: Entrepreneurship, the Working Class and Detectives in East London*. Oxford: Oxford University Press.

Holdaway, S. (1991) *Recruiting a Multi-ethnic Police Force*. London: Home Office.

Holdaway, S. (1995) 'Culture, race and policy: some themes of the sociology of the police', *Policing and Society*, 5: 109–20.

Holdaway, S. (1996) *The Racialisation of British Policing*. London: Macmillan.

Holdaway, S. (1997) 'Some recent approaches to the study of race in criminological research: race as social process', *British Journal of Criminology*, 37(3): 383–400.

Holdaway, S. and Barron, A. (1997) *Resigners? The Experience of Black and Asian Police Officers*. Basingstoke: Macmillan.

Holdaway, S. and Parker, S.K. (1998) 'Policing women police: uniform patrol, promotion and representation in the CID', *British Journal of Criminology*, 38(1): 40–60.

Hunt, J. (1984) 'The development of rapport through the negotiation of gender in field work among police', *Human Organization*, 43: 283–96.

Hunt, J. and Manning, P. (1991) 'The social context of police lying', *Symbolic Interaction*, 14(1): 1–20. Reproduced in Pogrebin, M. (ed.) (2003) *Qualitative Approaches to Criminal Justice: Perspectives from the Field*. Thousand Oaks, CA: Sage.

Innes, M. (2003) *Investigating Murder: Detective Work and the Police Response to Criminal Homicide*. Oxford: Oxford University Press.

Jermier, J., Gaines, J. and McIntosh, N. (1989) 'Reactions to physically dangerous work: a conceptual and empirical analysis', *Journal of Organizational Behaviour*, 10: 15–53.

Johnson, G. (1990) 'Managing Strategic Change: the role of symbolic action', *British Journal of Management*, Vol. 1, no. 4: 183–200.

Johnson, G. and Scholes, K. (1999) *Exploring Corporate Strategy* (5th edn). London: Prentice Hall.

Jordan, J. (2001) 'Worlds apart? Women, rape and the police reporting process', *British Journal of Criminology*, 41: 679–706.

Kier, E. (1999) 'Discrimination and military cohesion: an organizational perspective', in M. Fansod Katzenstein and J. Reppy (eds) *Beyond Zero Tolerance: Discrimination in Military Culture*. Lanham, MD: Rowman & Littlefield, 25–52.

Klockars, C. (1985) *The Idea of Police*. Beverly Hills, CA: Sage.

Liebling, A., Elliott, C. and Arnold, H. (2001) 'Transforming the prison: romantic optimism or appreciative realism?', *Criminal Justice*, 1(2): 161–80.

Macpherson, Sir W. (1999) *The Stephen Lawrence Inquiry: Report of an Inquiry by Sir William Macpherson of Cluny* (Cm 4262-1). London: HMSO.

Manning, P. (1980) *Narc's Game*, Cambridge, MA: MIT Press.

Marks, M. (2000) 'Transforming police organizations from within: police dissident groupings in South Africa', *British Journal of Criminology*, 40: 557–73.

Martin, C. (1996) 'The impact of equal opportunities policies on the day-to-day experiences of women police constables', *British Journal of Criminology*, 36(4): 510–28.

Martin, S. (1989) 'Women in policing: the eighties and beyond', in D. Kenney (ed.) *Police and Policing: Contemporary Issues*. New York, NY: Praeger, 3–16.

Martin, S. (1990) *On the Move: The Status of Women in Policing*. Washington, DC: Washington Police Foundation.

Martin, S. (1994) ' "Outsider within" the station house: the impact of race and gender on black women police', *Social Problems*, 41: 383–400.

Marks, M. (1999) 'Changing dilemmas and the dilemmas of change: transforming the public order policing unit in Durban', *Policing and Society*, 9(2): 157–79.

Mastrofski, S. (1998) 'Community policing and police organisational structure', in J.-P. Broduer (ed.) *How to Recognise Good Policing: Problems and Issues*. London: Sage. 161–89

Mastrofski, S. (1999) *Policing for People*. Washington, DC: Police Foundation.

Mastrofski, S., Willis, J. and Snipes, J. (2002) 'Styles of patrol in a community policing context', in M. Morash and J. Ford (eds) *The Move to Community Policing*. Thousand Oaks, CA: Sage, 81–111.

McConville, M. and Shepherd, D. (1992) *Watching Police, Watching Communities*. London: Routledge.

Messerschmidt, J. (1993) *Masculinities and Crime: Critique and Reconceptualization of Theory*. Lanham, MD: Rowman & Littlefield.

Miller, S.L. (1999) *Gender and Community Policing: Walking the Talk*. Boston, MA: North Eastern University Press.

Morgan, D. (1992) *Discovering Men*. London: Routledge.

Pearson, G. (1983) *Hooligan: A History of Respectable Fears*. London: Macmillan.

Pogrebin, M.R. and Poole, E.D. (1988) 'Humor in the briefing room', *Journal of Contemporary Ethnography*, 17(2): 183–210. Reproduced in M. Pogrebin (ed.) (2003) *Qualitative Approaches to Criminal Justice: Perspectives from the Field*. Thousand Oaks, CA: Sage, 80–93.

Policy Studies Institute. (1983) *Police and People in London* Vols 1–4 (Smith, D. *A Survey of Londoners* Vol. 1; Small, S. *A Group of Young Black People* Vol. 2; Smith, D. *A Survey of Officers* Vol. 3; Smith, D. and Gray, J. *The Police in Action* Vol. 4). London: Policy Studies Institute.

Prokos, A. and Padavic, I. (2002) 'There oughtta be a law against bitches: masculinity lessons in police academy training', *Gender, Work and Organization*, 9(4): 439–59.

Punch, M. (1985) *Conduct Unbecoming: The Social Construction of Police Deviance and Control*. London: Tavistock.

Quinton, P., Bland, N. and Miller, J. (2000) *Police Stops, Decision-Making and Practice*. Police Research Series Paper 130. London: Home Office.

Reiner, R. (1978) *The Blue Coated Worker*. Cambridge: Cambridge University Press.

Reiner, R. (1991) *Chief Constables*. Oxford: Oxford University Press.

Reiner, R. (2000) *The Politics of the Police* (3rd edn). Oxford: Oxford University Press.

Reiss, A.J. Jnr. (1971) *The Police and the Public*. New Haven, CT: Yale University Press.

Reuss-Ianni, E. and Ianni, F. (1983) 'Street cops and management cops: the cultures of policing', in M. Punch (ed.) *Control in the Police Organization*. Cambridge, MA: MIT Press, 251–74.

Ricks, T.E. (1995) 'Separation Anxiety: "New" Marines Illustrate Growing Gap Between Military and Society'. *Wall Street Journal*, 27 July: 1.

Sanders, W.B. (1977) *Detectives: A Study of Criminal Investigations*. New York, NY: Free Press.

Scarman, Lord (1981) *The Scarman Report: The Brixton Disorders* (Cmnd 8427). London: HMSO.

Schien, E. (1971) 'Organizational socialization and the profession of management', *Industrial Management Review*, 2: 37–45.

Schein, E. (1985) *Organizational Culture and Leadership*. San Francisco, CA: Jossey-Bass.

Schein, E. (1992) *Organizational Culture and Leadership* (2nd edn). San Francisco, CA: Jossey-Bass.

Schein, E. (1996) *Organizational Culture and Leadership* (3nd edn). San Francisco, CA: Jossey-Bass.

Shearing, C. and Ericson, R. (1991) 'Culture as figurative action', *British Journal of Sociology*, 42(4): 481–506.

Silvestri, M. (1999) 'Being in the sisterhood with no sisters'. Paper presented to the American Society of Criminology conference, Toronto, 17–20 November.

Skolnick, J. (1966) *Justice without Trial*. New York, NY: Wiley.

Stenross, B. and Kleinman, S. (1989) 'The highs and lows of emotional labor: detectives' encounters with criminals and victims', *Journal of Contemporary Ethnography*, 17(4): 435–52. Reproduced in M. Pogrebin (ed.) (2003) *Qualitative Approaches to Criminal Justice: Perspectives from the Field*. Thousand Oaks, CA: Sage, 107–15.

Steytler, N. (1990) 'Policing political opponents: death squads and cop culture', in D. Hannson and D. van Zyl Smit (eds) *Towards Justice? Crime and State Control in South Africa*. Cape Town: Oxford University Press, 106–33.

Sutherland, E. (1949) *White-collar Crime*. New York, NY: Holt, Rinehart & Winston.

Taylor, C. and Mackenzie, I. (1994) 'The glass ceiling at the top of the greasy pole', *Policing*, 10(4): 260–7.

Trojanowicz, R. and Bucqueroux, B. (1998) *Community Policing*. Cincinnati, OH: Anderson.

Van Maanen, J. (1973) 'Observations on the making of policemen', *Human Organization*, 32: 407–18. Reproduced in M. Pogrebin (ed.) (2003) *Qualitative Approaches to Criminal Justice: Perspectives from the Field*. Thousand Oaks, CA: Sage, 66–79.

Van Maanen, J. (1984) 'Making rank: becoming an American police sergeant', *Urban Life*, 13: 155–76.

Waddington, P.A.J. (1999) 'Police (canteen) sub-culture: an appreciation', *British Journal of Criminology*, 39(2): 286–309.

Walklate, S. (2000) 'Equal opportunities and the future of policing', in F. Leishman *et al.* (eds) *Core Issues in Policing* (2nd edn). Harlow: Longman Pearson Education, 232–48.

Wall, D. (1998) *The Chief Constables of England and Wales*. Aldershot: Dartmouth.

Werthman, C. and Piliavin, I. (1967) 'Gang members and the police', in D. Bordua (ed.) *The Police*. New York, NY: Wiley, 56–98.

Wilson, J.Q. (1968) *Varieties of Police Behaviour: The Management of Law and Order in Eight Communities*. Cambridge, MA: Harvard University Press.

Winslow, D. (1998) 'Misplaced loyalties: the role of military culture in the breakdown of discipline in peace operations', *Canadian Review of Sociology and Anthropology*, 35(3): 345–67.

Young, M. (1991) *An Inside Job: Policing and Police Culture in Britain*. Oxford: Oxford University Press.

Chapter 10

Police powers

Andrew Sanders and Richard Young

Introduction

The title of this chapter needs little introduction or explanation. We are all familiar with the idea of the police arresting people, carrying out street searches and detaining suspects so they can be questioned. This chapter will look at these powers, and many more besides. However, it would be easy to create the false impression that policing is primarily a matter of the exercise of powers – of the exercise of coercion. In reality, much policing is by consent, much policing is done with the community, or sections of it, and much criminal activity is condoned, ignored or dealt with in non-coercive ways. Many of the chapters in this book, especially in Part III, look at aspects of policing (such as crime prevention and community policing) where powers are rarely exercised.

Just because a specific power is not invoked it does not follow that power in a more general sense is not brought into play. Power is exercised in many different places in society and has many different sources. But the power of law enforcement agencies (most obviously the police, but also including bodies such as factory inspectors) is special. Much of it derives from specific powers given in legislation, and extended by judicial decisions, to those agencies. For example, many people consent to be searched by police officers not because they are happy about it but because they believe (usually correctly) that if they do not consent the police will be able to invoke a power that allows them to insist anyway. In other words, the existence of extensive police powers facilitates the exercise of generalised police power, and so to understand the latter we need to understand the former. The importance of legal powers is not that they are *actually* invoked particularly frequently, but that they *could* be. And so it has often been said that bargaining, for example, takes place in the shadow of the law.

Another way of saying that the police need not exercise their powers in any particular situation is to say that they exercise discretion. Whether potentially suspect communities are actually subjected to policing (coercive or otherwise) is thus largely a matter for the police. While it is true that the police are open to external influences (such as the Home Office, local police authorities and local communities), police discretionary choices at the level of both force policy and street-level decision-making are usually the key determinant of the use of police power. For example, Miller *et al.* (2000) found that Cleveland, a force noted for its adoption of 'zero tolerance' policies, carried out 101 searches per 1,000 of the population aged ten or over, compared with just six per 1,000 in Humberside, the force most similar according to a range of socioeconomic variables. Further, while police powers are always limited by the legislation or judicial decisions that created them, we shall see that a power that is limited in law is not necessarily limited in action. Crucial issues therefore are the controls on those powers and the redress available when they are breached. This will be the subject of the penultimate section of the chapter.

This chapter focuses on problems created by police power in England and Wales. No doubt much of the time police power is used within the limits of the law and in ways that a majority of people considers uncontroversial. But those in that majority rarely encounter the police in an adversarial setting. This chapter looks at the issues from the perspective of the minority who suffer abuses, and questionable uses, of police power. Although we rely on research evidence in support of our arguments, it must be acknowledged at the outset that the empirical record on some issues is thin. Although the police compare well with many other institutions in their willingness to engage with researchers, the problem is that much discretionary police work is of low visibility and this makes rigorous evidence difficult to obtain. Some of our arguments must accordingly be expressed tentatively.

Before discussing the most important police powers we will examine the applicability of 'models' of criminal justice to the police. This is so that we can rise above the detail of each particular power in order to identify patterns of development, whether they be towards greater protection of victims or of civil liberties, or whether they are geared towards more convictions or greater efficiency. Through this means we aim, in the conclusion, to explore the question of what police powers are for.

'Modelling' police powers

Over 35 years ago Packer (1968) famously characterised criminal justice systems as comprising two ideal types: due process and crime control. 'Due process' values prioritise civil liberties in order to secure the maximal acquittal of the innocent, risking acquittal of many guilty people. 'Crime control' values prioritise the conviction of the guilty, risking the conviction of some (fewer) innocents and infringement of the liberties of some citizens to achieve the system's goals. Due process-based systems tightly control the actions and effects of crime control agencies such as the police. Crime control-based systems do not. No system can correspond exactly with either model. They are best understood as situated at either end of a spectrum, with existing systems located somewhere in between.

If the police wish to interview people they suspect of committing a crime, due process protections, such as the caution against self-incrimination, are triggered. On arrest the suspect is generally taken to a police station. This triggers further due process protections, such as a right of access to lawyers, as civil liberties are further eroded by lengthy detention, interrogation, search of the suspect's home, fingerprinting and so forth. In order to charge, further evidence is required and further protections are provided: the Crown Prosecution Service (CPS) to vet the case and Legal Aid to prepare a defence. In order to convict there must be yet more evidence. So, due process requirements become more stringent at each stage, in parallel with the increased coerciveness of suspicion, accusation and trial. Suspects may be believed to be guilty by the police, and may indeed be guilty 'in truth'. But in the absence of sufficient evidence, due process requires that they be released.

This does not mean that police powers in England and Wales are necessarily located at the due process end of the spectrum. We shall see that little evidence is needed to stop and search someone, and no caution need be given when questioning these suspects; every year hundreds of thousands of people, against whom it is likely that there was little or no evidence of crime, are arrested, detained and released without formal action being taken; and the protection given to suspects who face questioning in the police station pales into insignificance when compared to the experience of that intimidating environment. Doubts about police efficiency and propriety on the part of advocates of due process lead them to argue for more stringent limitations on police powers, while advocates of crime control argue that even the legal protections that we do have obstruct discovery of the truth.

Despite the clarification provided by Packer's models, their value is limited. For example, they do not provide us fully with an answer to the question: what are police powers for? Under the crime control model, this is clear: they are to identify as many criminals as possible with a view to their conviction. But what about the due process model? The aim of police powers can hardly be to protect suspects, for if that were the goal the solution would be simple – we would simply not give the police any powers at all. It seems then that it is hard to get away from the idea that crime control is the goal under both models, and that the only difference between the two is how far pursuit of that goal is tempered by a concern to protect the liberties of suspects. This being the case, there are few, if any, due process protections for suspects that cannot be eroded if a sufficiently strong utilitarian (crime control) argument can be made for doing so. In Packer's models, in other words, protections are always being 'balanced' against police powers. Where that balance is struck determines where in the spectrum a system is located.

Ashworth attempts to provide a structure for this balancing act by developing a framework of ethical principles derived from the European Convention on Human Rights (ECHR) (Ashworth 1998a). This is valuable, particularly now that the Human Rights Act 1998 makes the ECHR applicable to all areas of UK law, but it leaves many conflicts unresolved, as Ashworth's principles are reformulations of key due process principles. Moreover, many of them are vague, such as 'to be treated fairly and without discrimination' and 'reasonable grounds for arrest and detention'. Those that are precise, such as the 'right of innocent persons not to be convicted', are not absolute but may be undercut by the kinds of considerations one finds in the crime control model. None the less, this approach does at least provide a safety net in those areas where rights *are* 'absolute', an example being the ECHR's prohibition of torture.

An alternative approach is our 'freedom model' (Sanders and Young 2000). It starts from the recognition that police powers (and the limits to which they are subject) are intended to further conflicting values, aims and interests in the criminal process, such as convicting the guilty; protecting the innocent from wrongful conviction; protecting human rights by guarding against arbitrary or oppressive treatment; protecting victims; maintaining order; securing public confidence in, and co-operation with, policing and prosecution; and achieving these goals without disproportionate cost and consequent harm to other public services. Politicians like to pretend that these goals are all equally achievable but, in reality, choices have to be made over which are to have priority. The choices that are made give expression to particular philosophical standpoints. The standpoint we prefer establishes the promotion of freedom as the over-riding purpose of the criminal justice system in general, and police powers in particular. All the various interests and goals identified earlier are connected to this underlying goal. For example, arrest is not a valuable activity in itself. Arrests are made in the hope that, where the arrestees are offenders, what follows will reduce their (and everyone else's) propensity to commit crime. This should enhance the freedom of past and potential future victims. Similarly we expect the police to respect the rights of suspects on the street not because limiting police power is in itself a good idea but rather because no more freedom should be taken away from members of the public by state officials than has been constitutionally allowed by Parliament and the courts.

This model allows that different interests come into conflict and prompts us to search for compromises that are likely to maximise overall freedom. This is not a crude form of utilitarianism for it does not oppose a 'human rights' approach to criminal justice. Instead, it suggests that human rights could be better secured if we adopted the language of freedom rather than, or at least as a supplement to, that of rights. We might, for example, more effectively convince the police to respect defendants' rights if we highlight how those rights do not constrain but rather facilitate the achievement of the ultimate criminal justice goal of promoting freedom. This model has obvious links with Faulkner's (1996) account of an inclusionary form of criminal justice in which, because the end of law is to enlarge freedom, authority has to be accountable, solutions to crime must be sought by working with, and within, the community, and young people must be given opportunities rather than be treated as an enemy to be humbled through discipline and social exclusion. This model requires considerable elaboration as to the precise meaning of 'freedom' and a start on this is made elsewhere (Sanders and Young 2000). Here we use the model simply as a sensitising device, as a way of signalling that the use of police power in the pursuit of crime control may be counterproductive.

Just as the freedom approach uses the insights of Ashworth's human rights approach when considering what the law ought to be, so it also uses Packer's insights when assessing the values that currently characterise police powers. But rather than simply classifying the rules regulating police powers in crime

Table 10.1 Types of legal rule and their effect on police behaviour

	Rule expresses crime control values	*Rule expresses due process values*
Influence police	Enabling effect	Inhibitory effect
Do not influence police	Legitimising effect	Presentational effect

control and due process (or human rights) terms, we can also classify them according to how far they influence police behaviour. Table 10.1 identifies four types of rule. First there are rules that express crime control values – which, in other words, give powers to the police. These may be 'enabling rules' that allow the police to do things that they could not do before, such as the rules on stop and search; or they may be 'legitimising rules' that allow the police to do things that they used to do anyway, such as the rules authorising precharge detention (largely doing away with the concept of suspects 'helping the police with their inquiries'). Then there are rules that express due process values. 'Inhibitory' rules, such as those that stop the police from assaulting suspects during a formal interrogation, actually constrain the police, while 'presentational' rules have little or no effect except at the level of appearances. This classification alerts us to the need to go beyond simple comparisons of the 'law in books' with the 'law in action' by analysing the relationship between rules and police behaviour.

Police decisions 'on the street'

In the first decades after the establishment of the police in their present form, sufficient evidence to prosecute was needed before street powers could be exercised. Arrested persons were taken directly before the magistrates, who decided whether to prosecute. In theory, then, police investigation had to take place before arrest (a due process approach), although in reality many people were forced to 'help the police with their inquiries' in custody. Arrests are now often made to facilitate investigation, bringing the formal rules into line with a crime control reality. The current legal position is somewhere between the crime control and due process models. Both stop and search and arrest without judicial warrant are allowed for most 'normal' crimes (including theft, burglary, serious assaults, sexual offences, drugs offences, public order offences and possession of offensive weapons), and the police are periodically given more powers for more offences – for example, in relation to terrorism in the wake of the terrorist attacks on New York and Washington on 11 September 2001. A further extension (to allow the police to stop and search for items carried with a view to causing criminal damage) is provided for by clause 1 of the Criminal Justice Bill, which had reached second reading stage at the time of writing. Clause 9 of the same bill provides a new power to arrest for possession of a Class C drug.

'Reasonable suspicion' and discretion

The police need 'reasonable suspicion' in order to exercise most arrest and stop and search powers. The code of practice on stop and search issued by the Home Office under the authority of the Police and Criminal Evidence Act 1984 (PACE) states that 'there must be some objective basis' for suspicion (para. 1.6), which 'can never be supported on the basis of personal factors alone' (para. 1.7). The 'objective' factors envisaged (which apply equally to arrest) include 'information received', someone 'acting covertly or warily' and someone 'carrying a certain type of article at an unusual time or in a place' where there have been relevant crimes recently (para. 1.6). Other important recent stop and search powers do not require reasonable suspicion, such as the power to stop and search for weapons created under s. 60 of the Criminal Justice and Public Order Act 1994 and extended by subsequent legislation (see, generally, Sanders and Young 2000: chs 2 and 3).

Clearly, police officers have to exercise discretion in deciding whether to stop and search and arrest, for there is little objectivity in perceiving someone to be acting 'warily'. Some people look less 'suspicious' than others, and multitudes of actual or likely offences have to be prioritised. Minor offenders (prostitutes, unlicensed street traders and so forth) are often simply ignored (Smith and Gray 1983). Arrest is used less frequently than informal action even for relatively serious violence (Clarkson *et al.* 1994; Hoyle 1998). Similarly, when officers are able to be proactive (as opposed to their usual reactive mode) they have to use discretion about the offences or offenders in which to invest their time. Discretion is also created as a consequence of the way offences are defined. How carelessly does someone have to drive before an officer is likely to pull him or her over, for example? So, stop and search and arrest decisions are constrained only loosely by law: the powers themselves, based on reasonable suspicion, are ill-defined and subjective; many of the offences for which the powers are exercised are similarly ill-defined; and the police largely set their own priorities. Equally important influences on the exercise of discretion are general policing goals, specific police force policies (e.g. Miller *et al.* 2000) and 'cop culture' (see Chan 1996; Dixon 1997; Reiner 2000).

Patterns of bias and police working rules

Research has found that the weak constraints imposed on discretion by law allow considerable scope for bias in policing. Prior to the implementation of PACE in the mid-1980s, study after study produced similar findings (e.g. Stevens and Willis 1979; Tuck and Southgate 1981; Field and Southgate 1982; Smith and Gray 1983; Willis 1983). Stops were often based on classic stereotypes leading to patterns of bias on lines of age, class, gender and race. PACE was intended to make some difference for, although it gave more, not less, power to the police, it also incorporated more controls than there were before. These include requirements to tell suspects why they are being arrested or stop-searched and to make records of the incident.

Stop and search and arrest decisions are of intrinsically low visibility (Goldstein 1960). Thus written records can be constructed after the event (McConville *et al.* 1991: ch. 5). Accounts of incidents can correspond as much with legal expectations as with the reality of the incidents (Scott and Lyman 1968; Ericson 1981). Thus officers are aware that the precise way in which forms are completed may either help or hinder a member of the public subsequently making a formal complaint about their actions (Bland *et al.* 2000: 73). It is hardly realistic to expect an officer to record on their stop and search form that their reason for exercising a power was that they had come across a 'Rastafarian out at night', yet we know that such reasoning does take place (see below). On the other hand, at least the requirement to record has the potential to focus officers' minds on the limits of their legal powers, and some officers do claim this has an influence on them (Bland *et al.* 2000: 71–2). However, when scrutiny of forms reveals the reasons for searches to be sometimes recorded in such vague terms as 'drugs search', 'info received' and 'acting furtively' (Bland *et al.* 2000: 44), the extent to which there has been a genuine shift in police reasoning is open to question. Moreover, many stops are not recorded at all. This is only a breach of the law if PACE powers are actually exercised (that is, if the stop is not consensual) and if the suspect is searched or arrested (Sanders and Young 2000: ch. 2).

Research has not found the control and accountability mechanisms in PACE to have achieved their intended effects. In one London borough, for example, Norris *et al.* (1992) observed 272 stops, of which 28 per cent were of black people despite only 10 per cent of the local population being black. This over-representation of black people is continued at the arrest stage (Hillyard and Gordon 1999). The problem with most such research is that it compares stop and search or arrest statistics for a particular area with the composition of the resident population for that same area. But MVA and Miller *et al.* (2000) found that over half the available pedestrian population resided outside the five police areas in which they were studying stop and search practices. They argued that when statistics on recorded stops and searches are compared with the population 'available' to be stopped and searched (i.e. those who use public places when and where stops take place) no general pattern of bias against those from ethnic minorities was evident. The most consistently over-represented group in the stop and search statistics, relative to the proportion in the available population, was young males.

Although the method used in this study represents an advance on those which make simplistic comparisons between stop and search patterns and resident populations, one should put in its proper context the finding of no general pattern of bias against ethnic minorities. This study was conducted shortly after the publication of the report of the Stephen Lawrence Inquiry (Macpherson 1999), which highlighted the damaging effect of stop and search practices on ethnic minority confidence in the police (see Chapter 21). Moreover, the five study sites were all involved in piloting a recommendation of that report (which was that all stops and all searches should be recorded, whether consensual or not). This may have made the police more circumspect about carrying out stops and searches of blacks and Asians, or at least in making records of such searches when they were carried out.

Indeed, a separate study by Bland *et al.* (2000) of the same five police areas examined by MVA and Miller *et al.* (2000) found evidence of substantial under-recording of both stops and searches during the pilot period. As the

MVA and Miller *et al.* (2000) study was based on recorded stop-searches the possibility that it underestimated the actual rates of ethnic minority stops and searches is obvious. In addition, the study did not examine whether ethnic minorities were subjected to stops and searches that were not legally justified more often than whites (i.e. when there was no reasonable suspicion), whether the use of stop and search powers resulted in an arrest (i.e. whites may have been drawn further into the system less frequently), and whether the use of stop and search powers was accompanied by differing degrees of respectful treatment according to the colour of the suspect's skin. Finally, and as the authors rightly acknowledge, the study does not controvert the fundamental point that black and Asian people are over-represented in the stop and search figures relative to their presence in the overall population and that this remains 'an important indicator of the actual experience of different ethnic groups within police force areas' (MVA and Miller *et al.* 2000: 88). Black people, Brown concluded in a review of PACE research, are more likely to be stopped than white people or Asians, more likely to be repeatedly stopped, more likely (if stopped) to be searched and more likely to be arrested (1997: chs 2 and 4; see also Chapter 21). Indeed, Bowling has found that s. 60 stops – those that do not require 'reasonable suspicion' – are even more problematic than PACE stops. Section 60 stops are 27 times more likely to be used against blacks, and 18 times more likely to be used against Asians, than they are against whites: 'Wherever officers have the broadest discretion is where you find the greatest disproportionality and discrimination' (cited in Dodd, *Guardian* 21 April 2003).

The research by Bland *et al.* (2000) also confirmed that the manner in which the police exercise their powers is a crucial determinant of whether their actions were regarded as legitimate: 'It's not what they say, it's how they say it' (2000: 87). Offensive and racist language was particularly resented. One Pakistani young adult described his interaction as follows: 'their exact words were, yeah (and I've got witnesses because I was with two other people, yeah) was: "Don't fuck me about right, and I won't fuck you about, where have you got your drugs?" ' (2000: 83). Black people were found to be far less likely than Asian or white people to report any positive experiences of respectful treatment by the police.

McConville *et al.* (1991) identified several 'working rules' which structure police decision-making, such as the general suspiciousness of the suspect and the threat to police authority or public order. Ten years later, Quinton *et al.* (2000) found similar patterns. Given these working rules, it is not surprising to find that stop and search is a very crude instrument of crime control. Although more stops lead to more arrests, the proportion of stops that lead to arrest decreases as the number of stops rises. This consequence of the crime control approach can be observed in most years since PACE was implemented; the number of recorded stops has increased tenfold since 1986 yet the proportion leading to arrest declined from 17 per cent in 1984 to 10 per cent in 1997–8 (Sanders and Young 2000: ch. 2). Not surprisingly, then, as the number of recorded stop-searches declined in the wake of the Macpherson Inquiry (down from a little over a million in 1998–9 to just under 750,000 in 2001–2) the number resulting in arrest rose back up to 13 per cent (Ayres *et al.*

2002). The detail of such trends should not blind us to the most salient points about the use of stop and search powers, however, which is that it is rare for police suspicions to be borne out by evidence on which to base an arrest, and that use of the stop and search power results, at best, in only a marginal impact on crime. Overall, it has been estimated that the various types of searches conducted by the police in 1997 reduced the number of crimes susceptible to this tactic by just 0.2 per cent (Miller *et al.* 2000: 28).

This is not to say that, under certain conditions, changes in formal rules are completely ineffective. Hoyle's (1998) study of domestic violence assessed the impact of a Home Office circular which encouraged arrest wherever there was evidence of an offence. Arrests rose significantly as a result, although not to the extent that full adherence to the circular would have produced. It seems that the police perception of domestic assaults as 'not worth their time' can be overcome, albeit not entirely. As Chan (1996) argues, police culture is not independent of societal pressures and legal rules. Whether, and how, practices and rules correspond are always empirical matters. So, Hoyle found that, in the enthusiasm of police officers to implement this new policy, many arrests took place on inadequate evidence: an example of legal rules being over-ridden by non-legal concerns. It will be harder, however, to change police practice in the direction of less frequent use of their power, or more frequent compliance with safeguards, as can be seen from the earlier discussion about the limited impact of the high-profile Macpherson Report (1999). The pilot project mentioned earlier did not require the police to record the 'frequent informal' stops where 'known criminals' or 'informants' were stopped by the police for the purpose of gathering 'criminal intelligence' because officers had objected that such recording might 'impact on their working practices' (Bland *et al.* 2000: 14–15). Thus members of the public in the pilot sites who reported being stopped and searched repeatedly, sometimes in the course of just one day, were almost never given records of these encounters. Lustgarten (2002) argues that many stop-searches are illegal under a new European Community Race Directive that became operational in July 2003, but it remains to be seen whether this will make any difference to police practice.

Police powers on the street: inclusionary or exclusionary?

Arrests usually follow information from, and complaints by, victims or witnesses (Reiss 1971; Steer 1980; Shapland and Vagg, 1988), although the late 1990s saw a revival of proactive policing (see Chapters 13 and 15). If relatively few arrests are proactive, does discretion, with the patterns of bias that are reflected when it is exercised, really play a major part in determining the shape of the official suspect population? McConville *et al.* (1991) argue that most of the studies cited above are based on indictable offences, missing out the summary offences (such as public order, prostitution, drunkenness, etc.) in which police initiative is more pronounced. Even when the police do not have a proactive role, the initiator of police action may be influenced by similar forms of stereotyping. Store detectives stereotype (Cameron 1964; Murphy 1986), and doubtless 'ordinary' members of the public do too. Citizen initiation usually involves the transmission of rather sketchy and sometimes downright unreliable information to the police (see, for example, Quinton *et al.* 2000: 31–3). Moreover, that information still has to be sifted, evaluated and acted upon (or not) by the police and stereotyping plays an important part in these processes (e.g. Grady 2002). The police are not simply the agents of the public. Thus, the British Crime Survey has repeatedly shown that the police record only about half of all the crime reported to them (Simmons *et al.* 2002).

In other words, police discretion and the exercise of judgement are still operative even when arrests are citizen initiated. The same is true when information is obtained from informants, on whom the police increasingly depend (Maguire and Norris 1992; Field and Pelser 1998). Information from the public is one resource among many upon which the police draw in exercising discretion on the street according to their own priorities. It is only when a community is well organised and vociferous in its demands for changes in policing practices that the police are likely to modify their working rules in favour of working with that community in a genuinely inclusionary way (Miller 2001).

The increased formal powers of stop and search and arrest given to the police since the mid-1980s, combined with the ability of the police to stop and search and arrest largely on the basis of broad intangible suspicion, led to the increased use of this activity throughout the late 1980s and 1990s (Sanders and Young 2000: chs 2 and 3). Other new laws, such as s. 5 of the Public Order Act 1986, provide arrest powers for trivial offences which are used extensively by the police to enforce their authority (Brown and Ellis 1994). Young males, especially from poor and minority sections of the community, bear the brunt of this power (Meehan 1993; Loader 1996; Brown 1997: chs 2 and 4). They feel – with some justification – discriminated against, and the consequent social unrest creates a vicious spiral of yet more policing and more unrest (Scarman 1981; Keith 1993; Macpherson 1999). The police sometimes use arrest powers to stamp their authority on challengers, often without any intention of prosecuting (Choongh 1997; Hillyard and Gordon 1999). The poor and underprivileged, it is claimed, are often treated dismissively as part of, and in order to emphasise, their exclusion from normal standards of protection (Young 1991).

From a freedom model perspective, police powers on the street are clearly drawn too wide and used too indiscriminately. While we have concentrated in considering how police power impacts on suspects and their communities, the situation is similarly problematic when viewed from the perspective of victims or, indeed, of the police themselves. For every arrest which fails to prevent or solve a crime creates a twofold loss of freedom: the arrestee loses some liberty and privacy; and the time, money and resources wasted in the arrest will not have been used to protect potential victims (e.g. through street patrols of high-crime areas) or to provide non-law enforcement public services.

Detention and questioning

On arrest, all suspects, except in exceptional cases, should be taken directly to a police station. It is then for the custody officer (the old station sergeant) to decide whether or not the suspect should be detained. There are only two grounds for detention: in order to charge the suspect; or, where there is insufficient evidence to charge, in order to secure that extra evidence. But this is allowed only where detention is necessary for that purpose, and only for as long as it is necessary. Senior officers are obliged periodically to review detention to ascertain this. Detention is normally limited to 24 hours but, for serious arrestable offences, the police can authorise detention for up to 36 hours and detention in such cases can extend to 96 hours with the leave of the magistrates' courts. Clause 5 of the Criminal Justice Bill makes provision for the police to have the power to detain for up to 36 hours in the case of all arrestable offences, not just those which are serious in nature.

Immediate transit to a police station where a custody officer then becomes responsible for the suspect is designed to ensure that suspects do not remain in the hands of officers who might mistreat them. Time limits are intended to ensure that suspects are not intimidated by the prospect of indefinite detention. However, suspects are often intimidated by the prospect of 24 hours in the cells. Decisions concerning the necessity of detention are consequently of great importance. In recognition of this, the custody officers have to complete custody sheets that record everything that happens to, and is decided about, detained suspects. However, this evidence is written by the members of the agency against whom it is supposed to be a protection – rather like records of stop and search. Thus, despite the outward appearance of everything being done 'by the book', detention is hardly ever refused, reviews of detention can be perfunctory and the suspect might remain in custody for as long as investigating officers wish, subject to the time limits stated in PACE (Dixon *et al.* 1990; McKenzie *et al.* 1990; McConville *et al.* 1991; Phillips and Brown 1998).

When the police do decide to release the suspect, they have to decide what else to do, if anything. Suspects released without charge may be given bail by the police while further inquiries are carried out. When custody officers decide to charge suspects with offences they have to decide whether to release on bail or to hold the suspect in custody pending the next magistrates' court hearing (usually the next morning). Detention is allowed only if the suspect's real name and address cannot be verified, if they are unlikely to appear in court to answer the charge, if they are likely to interfere with witnesses or police investigations or if they are likely to commit a significant crime. According to the case law of the European Court of Human Rights these decisions must be based on evidence, not speculation. However, like much human rights-speak this is both unrealistic and inconsistent with the crime control elements of English law and practice. Most of these provisions require custody officers to predict what might happen if the suspects were released – in other words, to speculate. Around 80 per cent of charged suspects are granted bail by the police, this percentage having risen in recent years after the police were granted powers to set conditions, such as not making contact with the victim (see, generally, Bucke and Brown 1997; Raine and Willson 1997). Just because most suspects are granted bail does not mean that the police have refrained from exercising power over this group. The bail decision gives the police a bargaining tool in interrogation, which can be used to extract information about current and previous offending, other offenders and so on (for an example, see McConville 1992). The fact that the police can make this decision on a largely discretionary basis gives them generalised power that goes far beyond the specific bail powers written into the law. These powers will be further extended by clause 3 of the Criminal Justice Bill (allowing bail to be granted on the street by an arresting officer).

Access to legal advice

PACE requires free legal advice to be provided to all suspects who request it. Information about this unambiguous right has to be provided by the custody officer to the suspect. Advice may be delayed in exceptional cases but not denied outright. Custody records state whether or not suspects were informed of their rights, whether or not suspects requested advice and what (if anything) happened then. Request rates have now risen to around 40 per cent and actual advice rates to around 34 per cent (Bucke and Brown 1997). This is a massive increase over the pre-PACE situation, when less than one in ten suspects requested advice (Sanders and Young 2000: 215) but, even today, two out of every three people do not make use of an entirely free service that is designed to help them. This requires explanation.

Some suspects have negative attitudes towards solicitors, which is not surprising. Advice is frequently provided by telephone, rather than in person, and, in many cases, solicitors do not attend interrogations, and when they do they are often passive. Legal Aid lawyers have a generally non-adversarial stance and take their lead from the police. The behaviour of the police themselves is often an additional factor in suspects' decision-making. The research (summarised by Brown 1997: ch. 6; Sanders and Young 2000: 214–40) shows, first, some suspects do not request advice because they are not informed (wholly or partly) of their rights; some suspects' requests are denied, ignored, or simply not acted upon (custody records recording only some of these instances); and the police often attempt to dissuade suspects from seeking advice and to persuade them to cancel their requests. Such events were used in 331 cases (40 per cent of all cases observed) in the study conducted by Sanders *et al.* (1989) and included such things as disquieting information: 'You'll have to wait in the cells until the solicitor gets here'.

The net result is that the potential for, and likely effect of, getting help from a solicitor are among many factors that suspects must weigh up when detained. Police station legal advice and assistance are now regulated more rigorously (Cape 2002: 111), but the effect of this is undermined by changes to the right of silence (discussed below). Once again, the specific legal power of the police to detain gives them a more generalised power that goes beyond the written law.

Police interrogation

Interrogation has assumed ever greater importance in police investigation over the years. Around three fifths of detained suspects are interrogated (Bucke and Brown 1997: 31). The PACE *Code of Practice for the Detention, Treatment and Questioning of Persons by Police Officers* (Code C) (Home Office 1995) sets out basic standards for interrogation (the provision of proper heating, ventilation, breaks, access to solicitors and others, and so forth), but also states that a police officer is 'entitled to question any person from whom he thinks useful information can be obtained ... A person's declaration that he is unwilling to reply does not alter this entitlement' (Note 1B). So, police officers may attempt to persuade suspects to change their minds about not speaking, and to hold them, subject to the time limits, for as long as that takes.

Many suspects against whom there is plenty of evidence anyway will talk to the police under almost any conditions. Others have to be persuaded. Some are susceptible to 'deals': confessions in exchange for favours such as bail or reduced charges. Then there are those who are intimidated by being held against their will in 'police territory' where the environment is deliberately denuded of psychological supports, by being in fear of spending the night in the cells or by the employment of any number of 'tactics' against them. Examples of such tactics are offering inducements, claiming that there is overwhelming evidence against the suspect and using custodial conditions such as return to the cells. The latter can be particularly effective, given the importance attached by most suspects to the shortest detention possible. To understand the coercive nature of detention, it is necessary to appreciate how it is experienced by suspects: in these conditions, 'time passed exceedingly slowly' (Newburn and Hayman 2002: 97). If a tactic does not work in the initial interrogation, 24 hours (or more) thus allows ample time for the suspect to be psychologically 'softened up' for further interrogation. Evans (1992: 49) found a strong statistical association between the use of tactics and confessions.

Extreme tactics are now unacceptable in formal interrogations since such interactions must be tape recorded. That this is required gives rise to another way of securing confessions: through informal interrogation. This may occur on the way to the police station, before and after formal interrogations, or in the cells under the guise of a 'welfare visit'. Custody officers are supposed to record the precise times at which interviews begin and end, but this does not prevent officers having an 'informal chat before I switch on the tape' (Evans and Ferguson 1991; see also Evans 1992: 36; McConville 1992). Many appeals turn on confessions allegedly made 'informally' but not repeated 'formally'. As one officer told Maguire and Norris (1992: 46–7), there would be nothing to prevent him from distorting the contents of informal conversations 'if I was dishonest'. While it appears that 'tactics' are now used less frequently in formal interrogations than they were before PACE, it is possible that they are now simply being used more under 'low visibility' conditions. The scope for this is reduced in police stations with CCTV cameras (Newburn and Hayman 2002), but at present few have installed them, and the problem of what goes on outside the station will remain.

Coercion occurs in both informal and formal interrogations. This is inevitable under English law, for the job of the police interrogator is to elicit answers even from suspects who have declared a refusal to provide answers: in other words, to persuade them to change their minds. Tactics are designed to do this, and not all tactics are of the 'carrot' variety: 'Sometimes it's necessary to shout at people ... you have to keep up the pressure' (detective cited by McConville *et al.* 1991: 4). Even interrogation practices which would be innocuous to most people are coercive to vulnerable people (Gudjonsson and MacKeith 1982; Littlechild 1995). Procedures for identifying, and making allowances for, vulnerable people in police custody have proved to be inadequate (Bucke and Brown 1997; Phillips and Brown 1998; Young 2002). Thus suspects might be trapped into saying or accepting things that they did not necessarily mean. Doing so can lead to false confessions. 'Falsity' can be a matter of interpretation and degree. McConville *et al.* (1991) argue that interrogation is a process of construction whereby facts are made and not discovered. An example is given by Maguire and Norris (1992: 4), who report a CID sergeant saying that he had been taught to induce people found carrying knives to say that they were for their own protection. This, unknown to the suspect, constitutes admission of the crime of carrying an 'offensive weapon'. This type of confession, with elements of falsity arising from the process of case construction, is probably more common than what is commonly thought of as constituting a 'false confession', and yet is equally likely to lead to wrongful convictions.

McConville *et al.* (1991) argue that false confessions are an inevitable result of crime control values dominating the criminal justice system. This view contrasts with that of Moston (1992), who argues that police failure to verify confessions and avoid leading questions is simply a matter of technical competence and a failure of training. Less confrontational 'investigative interviewing' or 'ethical interviewing' is advocated by him and others instead. A massive programme to train police officers in investigative interviewing was instituted in the 1990s and, by the end of that decade, over two thirds of police officers had received this training. Clarke and Milne (2001) conducted a major evaluation of the effectiveness of this training after a number of smaller-scale studies had indicated that investigative interviewing was not having the impact in the workplace that some had anticipated. Their evaluation involved skilled police officers reviewing and rating the tape recordings of interviews with suspects without knowing whether the interviewing officer had been trained in investigative interviewing or not. The authors claim that, compared to earlier studies, the research indicates a decline in the use of leading questions and the more frequent provision of information required by law, such as the right to legal advice. It is doubtful whether these changes can be attributed to the training, however, since trained and untrained officers were found to interview in much the same way as each other. Moreover, standards of interviewing indicated that the training had failed to bring about a radical change in police behaviour. For example, listening skills were rated as poor, interviews were found to be dominated by the use of closed questions and 10 per cent of the interviews were considered to involve possible breaches of PACE. Interviews with victims and witnesses raised even more concern, and 'damning' evidence was found of interviewers apparently looking to inter-viewees to confirm police suspicions rather than provide their own accounts (Clarke and Milne 2001: 110). The research also found that there was little effective supervision of interviewing and that scant interest had been shown by police leaders in ensuring that their officers actually used the skills taught in training. Maguire (2002: 91) notes that 'changing what is still a strongly ingrained element of police culture – the view that the overriding aim of an interview is to obtain a confession – is an ambitious task, and there is little doubt that poor interviewing practices still persist to a considerable extent'. In our view, miscarriages of justice arising from coercion and false confessions would be more effectively reduced by preventing confession evidence forming the sole basis of convictions, and by providing the defence with the same resources as are provided to the prosecution, than by trying to change interrogation practices.

Over half of all suspects who are interrogated either confess or make incriminating statements to the police (see, for the most recent research, Bucke *et al.* 2000). Only two to four per cent of suspects exercise absolute silence although a further five per cent or so simply make flat denials, while 8–15 per cent answer some questions and not others, and some suspects are silent at the start but then answer questions later (or vice versa) (Leng 1992). Despite this low rate of silence, and the few 'ambush defences' that take advantage of it (Leng 1992), in 1994 the law was changed so that when suspects rely in court on a fact which they could have been reasonably expected to mention when questioned by the police, the court can draw an adverse inference from this silence. Similarly, courts can draw adverse inferences from failures to answer questions in court. Exactly what inferences a court should draw from silence is a matter of debate. The law is still being developed by the English and European courts and is likely to remain a matter of great difficulty for lawyers, police officers and judges for some time to come. Consequently these changes have been castigated on pragmatic (for example, Birch 1999) as well as principled grounds (for example, Sanders and Young 2000: 233–40). Despite Article 6 of the European Court of Human Rights (ECHR) proclaiming that 'Everyone ... shall be presumed innocent until proved guilty by law', the ECHR has accepted the lawfulness of these provisions, although it has sought to reduce their potential impact by declaring that silence cannot be the sole or main basis for a conviction (see, generally, Cape 1997; Birch 1999). As might be expected, the effect of the new provisions is to lower the use of the right of silence, probably because lawyers, who were becoming more adversarial in the early-mid 1990s, became more circumspect again about advising silence. Thus Bucke *et al.* (2000) estimated silence and confessions in the late 1990s to be back down to the rates found in the 1980s.

How well regulated are police powers of detention and questioning?

We have seen that the legal regulation of detention does not prevent it from being lengthy and intimidating, that access to lawyers can be obstructed and is often of little value (particularly now that the right of silence has been further restricted) and that the police apply different forms of pressure. Thus McConville *et al.* (1991) argue that while police powers have changed in an apparently due process direction, generalised police power remains un-diminished. This is controversial (for debate about McConville *et al.* (1991), see McConville *et al.* 1997; Smith, 1997a, 1997b; Duff, 1998; and various chapters in the edited collection by Noaks *et al.* 1995). Dixon (1992) observes that 'sea change theorists' (mostly practitioners) argue that the protections for suspects we have discussed here significantly obstruct crime control aspirations.

Although few academic commentators accept this view, it is attractive to those politicians who seek electoral advantage through the dismantling of protections for suspects. Indeed, it is the underlying message of the discussion of the 'justice gap' in the white paper *Justice for All* (Home Office 2002), leading to yet further proposals for additional crime control-based police powers (most of which are taken forward by the Criminal Justice Bill).

It seems to us that crime control-oriented police practices have shifted rather than been eradicated or even reduced. Thus there is little violence now, but there is more use of other tactics and pressures. As Leo puts it, in the US context: 'The law has also empowered the police to create more specialised and seemingly more effective interrogation strategies ... they can lie, they can cajole, and they can manipulate' (1994: 116). The new rules and constraints to which 'sea change' theorists point are access to lawyers, tape recording of interrogation, custody records and the general supervisory role of the custody officer. As we have seen, these developments hardly represent a 'sea change'. There appears to be a 'balance' between due process and crime control only because we now unquestioningly accept the right of the police to use coercive powers. But why do suspects not want to wait for a lawyer, for instance, to come to the station? Why do suspects 'voluntarily' answer police questions? Only because they are in the police station against their will in the first place. So, for example, most suspects do want lawyers, but the desire to get out of the station quickly is stronger (Brown *et al.* 1992). And why is police station legal work often of poor quality? Perhaps, largely because the police have the power to create the forces that so shape it. Solicitors send unqualified staff, give telephone advice or miss interrogations in part because of all the time they would otherwise spend at relatively low rates of pay (Cape 2002: 110). But it is the police who control the time-frame (Sanders 1996a). The legal 'trading' which undermines adversarialism is forced on to lawyers – who, it has to be admitted, usually need little persuading. And in providing the right to detain in such broad circumstances, the law cedes most practical power to the police.

Why have politicians, lawyers and others allowed this to occur? Is it because they do not bear the brunt of these powers? Research has shown that most people who are stopped, searched, arrested, detained and interrogated are young working-class men, with an over-representation from ethnic minorities. The treatment they are given is frequently humiliating – and often deliberately so (Young 1991; Choongh 1997). Opinion-formers, lawyers and legislators, on the other hand (older, middle-class, white people in the main), are very rarely subjected to such exclusionary processes. In the one sphere of criminality where large numbers of middle-class people come into adversarial contact with the police (motoring offences), extensive use is made of informal warnings, 'tickets' and postal guilty pleas in preference to the more stigmatising processes of arrest, detention, prosecution and formal court appearances. There is evidence that pre-trial processes, including the way in which police power is exercised, are as important to a citizen's sense of the legitimacy of state action as the formal outcome (Tyler 1990). Of course, some middle-class people are roughly treated and some poor people are not, but the contrast between the integrated and the excluded is as striking in the field of criminal justice as in other fields of social policy.

How might a freedom model perspective help us in considering reform in this area? First, it again alerts us to the argument that the frequency and lack of discrimination with which the police resort to detention are counterproductive: all detentions infringe freedom and the majority do not result in any significant net gain in liberty. Secondly, it makes the case for treating detained suspects fairly, and in accordance with legal standards, seem much more compelling. If the freedom of suspects is respected to this extent, it is much more likely that they will co-operate with the police in future (whether as a victim, a witness or a suspect). In our ideal world, the police would internalise the values of human rights and the freedom model, and the need for oversight and other regulatory mechanisms would diminish. Under present conditions, however, it is naïve to expect the police to safeguard suspects' rights when so many of them believe that those rights hinder effective policing. It follows that the rights of suspects should not be dependent on the integrity of custody officers and investigating officers but should be either automatic or guaranteed by a genuine third party. Independent lawyers working in the police station might be a solution, although they would need to attend all interrogations and possess an adversarial ethos. Their position could be buttressed by changes in the rule of evidence to render confessions inadmissible unless made in their presence or, where this is impracticable, unless tape recorded.

Other evidence-gathering powers

This chapter gives a lot of emphasis to the securing of evidence through questioning, but the police have many other evidence-gathering powers. All we can do here is to give an indication of their nature and extent. One of the oldest is the power to enter premises. This can be to search for and arrest a suspect, or to search the premises for evidence or proceeds of crime upon or after an arrest. If such evidence is found, it can be seized and may form the basis for an arrest that could not have been otherwise made. Like arrest, these powers were once exercisable only rarely without a judicial warrant. Warrants would, in principle, have been issued only if the police provided evidence of reasonable suspicion to justify the action. Search warrants, like arrest warrants, are now seldom sought (Brown 1997: 31). Over the last 20 years or so the police have been given increasingly extensive powers of entry, search and seizure, consistent with the growing crime control orientation of the system. PACE, in particular, has led to more police-authorised searches being carried out (Brown 1997: 34). And if evidence of a crime is found, it can be seized even if it has nothing to do with the crime for which the police began the search in the first place (PACE *Code of Practice* B: 6.1; and see, generally, Sharpe 2000).

Under s. 32 of PACE, arresting officers may, without warrant, enter and search premises in which the arrested person had been around the time of the arrest or, under s. 17 of PACE, in order to make an arrest (on warrant or on reasonable grounds). Under common law powers preserved by s. 17(6) of PACE, they may also enter without warrant to deal with, or prevent, a breach of the peace, or to protect someone from serious injury, which can be important in domestic violence incidents. The bulk of recorded searches of premises, however, take place under s. 18 of PACE (Brown 1997: 34), which allows searches without warrant of premises occupied or controlled by a person under arrest for an arrestable offence. The police need a magistrates' warrant in most other circumstances, such as if they believe that a search will reveal evidence relating to a serious crime (see s. 8 of PACE). Magistrates should only issue a warrant when there is a reasonable basis for the claims of the police, but they usually have no way of assessing these claims, as 'suspicion' is often based on unverifiable intelligence, such as information from informers (see Brown 1997: 32–33). Sharpe (2000: ch. 3) observes that magistrates seldom look far below the surface of police claims, and empirical evidence supports the view that magistrates tend to 'rubber stamp' requests for warrants (Brown 1997: 33).

Arrested persons, whether or not originally stop-searched, may be searched for limited purposes by the arresting officer on arrest (s. 32 of PACE). Once in the police station, a thorough search under s. 54 of PACE (including a strip-search and saliva sample if the custody officer so decides) is usual. The Criminal Justice Bill extends the power to take a sample to test for the presence of Class A drugs by lowering the age at which suspects become subject to this power from 18 to 14. An 'intimate' body search for Class A drugs or weapons, governed by s. 55 of PACE, may only be carried out if a senior officer authorises this, and it has to be performed by a nurse or doctor unless a superintendent or more senior officer considers this is not practicable (in which case the search is carried out by a constable). There are generally fewer than 200 intimate searches a year, of which less than 20 per cent find drugs or weapons (Ayres *et al.* 2002).

As with stop and search, there is a PACE code of practice governing searches of people and premises (Code B), stipulating that they should be carried out at a reasonable time, using only reasonable force, with due consideration for the privacy and property of the occupier and so forth. There is little research to indicate how these provisions are generally interpreted and how far they are complied with. However, research by Hillyard (1993) and Choongh (1997) suggests, albeit on the basis of limited data, that these powers are sometimes used in order to discipline suspect populations rather than primarily to gather evidence for prosecution purposes. This may explain Newburn and Hayman's finding that Afro-Caribbean detainees were twice as likely as any other ethnic group to be strip-searched on arrival at Kilburn police station in north London (2002: 50–2).

Similarly to other powers, search and seizure may be carried out with the consent of the person concerned, thereby evading many of the PACE safeguards such as the requirement of reasonable grounds for believing that relevant material will be found. We do not know precisely how often this occurs, but research has shown it to be frequent (Brown 1997: 36–7). Many people think (often correctly – see Brown 1997: 37–8) that if they refuse, the police have the power to go ahead anyway, and that to refuse would be regarded as suspicious in itself. In other instances, the police seek consent because no power to search exists, although suspects might not be told this. Instead, the police play on suspects' ignorance, as when 'consent' is obtained from persons in custody (Brown 1997: 37). Again, we can see that specific police powers (of arrest, detention and search) give the police far more generalised power than is evident simply from the letter of the law in the statute book and judicial decisions.

Reasonable suspicion on which to base an arrest or search sometimes emerges from undercover policing, informers and surveillance methods such as telephone taps, mail interception, 'bugging' of buildings and CCTV. Often these methods are combined. There are some 50,000 informers officially registered with the police, and no one knows how many 'unofficial' or occasional informers there are (*Guardian* 12 October 1998). 'Information received' might lead the police to place undercover officers in the middle of developing criminal conspiracies where they must tread a fine line between observing and participating in crime (Maguire and John 1996). These powers, which might best be regarded as legitimising rules, have increased in the last 20 years. For example, the ECtHR decided in 1984 (*Malone* v. *UK*) that the police did not have the right to tap suspects' telephones, even when authorised by the Home Secretary, because there was no statutory power to do so. This was a breach of Article 8 of the European Convention on Human Rights. However, Parliament passed a statute giving the police these powers, and these and many other powers are now consolidated and expanded by the Police Act 1997 and the Regulation of Investigatory Powers Act 2000, which some have seen as a welcome shift towards the legal regulation of police power in this sphere (e.g. Neyroud and Beckley 2000). Most of the powers legitimised by this legislation can, however, be exercised on the authority of senior police officers. Although the fact that some require judicial authorisation (discussed by Akdeniz *et al.* 2001) makes it appear that due process norms are upheld, authorisation is only applicable because these new powers were created in the first place – a distinctly 'crime control' development. It appears that human rights and other legal norms currently provide scant regulation of what might be described as 'sneaky' forms of policing (Colvin 1998; Field and Pelser 1998; Uglow 1999).

'Proactive' policing, in which specific crimes and specific suspects are targeted by the police, is gradually increasing in importance at the expense of 'reactive' policing. Thus the problem of inadequate legal regulation, along with the problem that stereotyping and working rules underlie the targeting process (Gill 2000), are likely to increase (see Chapter 15).

Police powers in relation to the collection of identification evidence also merit attention. Such evidence might come from victims or other witnesses (including police officers), or might be from DNA or fingerprint samples. The police have the power to take saliva, fingerprints and hairs of detained suspects (see ss. 61 and 63 of PACE). They may also hold identification parades under PACE code of practice D, revised in 2002 to take account of the growing practice of making use of video identification instead. There is not the space here to discuss the problems of identification evidence in detail. While it might be imagined by its nature to be objective, it is susceptible to 'construction' in the same way as confession evidence (Sanders and Young 2000: 337). This, together with the notoriously inflated opinion that witnesses have of their own accuracy (Tinsley 2001), renders it unsurprising that a survey in the USA revealed that mistaken identification evidence was the most common cause of miscarriages of justice (Jackson 2001).

Prosecution

Soon after the police were first established they gradually began to take over responsibility for prosecution, despite the lack of any specific or exclusive prosecution powers. As arrest turned into a tool for (rather than the culmination of) investigation, pre-charge detention arose and the police developed various non-prosecutorial dispositions. Although the police are no longer responsible for continuing prosecutions, they remain in control of the initial decision to charge. There are now well over a million prosecutions initiated by the police per year but, even so, around one in four suspects are released from pre-charge detention with no further action (NFA), and many more suspects are given a formal or informal warning. Police officers decide both whether to arrest and whether to charge, and they are responsible for making the decision to release using their own criteria and on the basis of evidence collected and evaluated by themselves. Thus, arrest does not necessarily lead to prosecution, prosecution need not be the normal response to suspected crime and the specific charge prosecuted is an entirely discretionary matter (see, generally, Sanders 1996b).

We do not generally think of prosecution as a 'police power'. But prosecution powers are closely connected with the powers we have examined so far. Although police powers are provided to enable the police to gather evidence to support a prosecution, it has been claimed they enable the police to wield more generalised power in order to subjugate marginal communities, a point which might be evidenced by the high NFA rates (Choongh 1997; Hillyard and Gordon 1999). The police power over prosecution can also be used to justify earlier action that might be in breach of legal rules (McConville *et al.* 1991). Even warnings can be used as policing tools, for example as part of a 'deal' to secure information. The low visibility of these decisions allows the discretion operating here (as in relation to stops and arrests) to be structured more by working rules than legal rules. Thus it has been found that the police often prosecute cases that are weak and, indeed, these cases often fail (McConville *et al.* 1991; Sanders *et al.* 1997).

This makes no sense in terms of Home Office guidelines, but is perfectly rational in terms of police working rules. Charges are a matter for the arresting officer and custody officer. Very rarely do custody officers caution or NFA when the arresting officer wants a prosecution, or vice versa, for custody officers are in a weak position in inquiring into evidential strength. If they try to evaluate arresting officers' evidence they have only one source of information on which to draw (apart from the suspect): that same arresting officer. In the mid-1980s the CPS was created to operate as a check on these decisions and in an attempt to reduce the number of weak prosecutions. But the police role in constructing the evidence that forms prosecutions, and the charging power that follows, prevent the CPS from exercising much influence, except in more obvious cases, such as those where there is clear racial bias (Mhlanga

2000). The problems created by the concentration of power in the hands of police appears to have been belatedly recognised in policy-making circles, for there are plans to transfer some charging powers from the police to the CPS (Home Office 2002). Only time will tell whether this reform will prove to be inhibitory or merely presentational.

Low visibility sometimes leads traditional police cautioning to be used in a far from 'welfarist' way. Lee (1995) describes many cautioning processes as 'degradation ceremonies', her accounts of which sound similar to the accounts of the humiliation of 'toe rags' in the custody room provided by Choongh (1997) and the non-prosecution processes of the DSS (Cook 1989). We do not know how typical are Lee's findings or those of Choongh because there has been little research on the treatment of suspects and defendants. The early findings on 'restorative cautioning' indicate significant and welcome shifts in police practice but also raise concerns that a traditional police agenda may dominate restorative encounters, leaving offenders and victims in some cases almost as marginalised as before (Young and Goold 1999; Young 2001; see Chapter 27). Thus prosecution processes and many diversionary processes remain exclusionary. It is not the case that prosecutorial discretion must necessarily result in exclusionary practices. Whereas the police charge more often than they NFA or divert from prosecution, most non-police agencies behave in the opposite way and seek to work *with* suspects and offenders in order to promote voluntary compliance with the law. From the point of view of crime prevention and recidivism there seems to be no justification for these different patterns (Braithwaite 2001).

From the freedom perspective, there is a justification for changing these patterns. In particular, it can be argued that the freedom of those with economic, social or political power (high-status suspects often committing high-value or very serious crimes) should not be afforded greater respect than the freedom of the poor, the vulnerable and the marginal (usually committing low-value property offences). As a first step, it might be helpful if prosecution policy and power were concentrated in one body with unified channels of accountability to Parliament, the courts and the democratic representatives of local communities. In that way the great disparities of practice between the various forms of prosecuting agencies might become a matter of public debate, and the advantages of diversion from prosecution more widely accepted.

The misuse of police powers

The extent of police misuse of their powers is not known as it is impossible to research such a vast issue adequately, but the research reviewed above shows that there is considerable misuse. Sometimes misuse stems from corruption (Newburn 1999) but more often the police act in excess of their powers in pursuit of evidence of guilt or to control or intimidate suspect populations.

The fact that trials are conducted in relatively independent unbiased courts, and that defendants are represented by relatively independent lawyers regardless of their financial means, undoubtedly deters much potential abuse of power, provides a way of bringing instances of misuses of power to light and protects against some wrongful convictions. The deterrent and protective effects of prosecutions, however, are bound to be partial. First, as we have seen, many suspects are stopped and/or arrested with no prosecution in mind, and many are released with no charge. When police power is used as a disciplinary mechanism, the letter of the law regulating powers is largely irrelevant. Secondly, the overwhelming majority of defendants plead guilty without a trial. In these cases there is no opportunity to bring misuses of power to light. Thirdly, even if evidence was obtained, for example, following an unlawful search or illegal questioning, it would not necessarily be excluded from the trial. While *oppressively* obtained confessions cannot be used, unfairly obtained confessions (or other evidence obtained in breach of the powers we have discussed) can be (Sharpe 1998). Fourthly, suspects or defendants will not raise the question of misuse of power if they are unaware that it has occurred.

Few people know precisely what the police are, and are not, allowed to do. Apart from the inevitably complicated nature of much of the law, many police practices rely on deception. These practices include 'stings' (such as posing as a drugs buyer or dealer, or setting up a second-hand shop in order to trap sellers of stolen goods), and implying to suspects that they have stronger cases than they really have (Ashworth 1998b). Even if a practice is unlawful, and even if the person at the receiving end knows this (or is told this afterwards by a lawyer), there is the difficulty of proving this. And, quite naturally, the police tend to close ranks when they come under investigation (Sanders and Young 2000: 691–2).

The main way of bringing misuse of powers to light is through the complaints and discipline procedure. Despite the introduction in 1985 of an independent oversight body, the Police Complaints Authority (PCA), very few complaints are substantiated. In 2000–1 only 903 complaints were substantiated – which represents nine per cent of the complaints which were investigated, but only three per cent of the 31,034 complaints initially made (Povey and Cotton 2001). The other 97 per cent of complaints were either dealt with informally (34 per cent), adjudged by the PCA to be not practicable to investigate and so 'dispensed with' (22 per cent), investigated but not substantiated (29 per cent) or withdrawn (12 per cent) – something that often happens because of police pressure (Maguire and Corbett 1991). There are three main possible explanations for the low level of substantiation: that most complaints are unjustified; that most police complaint investigations (and PCA scrutiny) are biased; and that evidence of malpractice cannot be obtained in most cases. All three explanations are doubtless partially true. Regarding bias, the discrediting process discussed by Box and Russell (1975) in relation to the pre-PCA system is unlikely to have been affected by changes in the structure of supervision, for all complaints are still investigated by the police themselves. The PCA is in the same position as is the CPS vis-à-vis investigating police officers. Rather than reinvestigate, the PCA peruses a carefully constructed document. Most complainants interviewed by Maguire and Corbett thought 'that the PCA was on the side of the police' (1991: 176) and this is reiterated in more recent general opinion surveys (Harrison and Cuneen 2000).

The complaints system, therefore, fails all due process tests (openness, not allowing officials to be judges in their own cause, giving all parties a fair hearing and so forth) and to fail to deter the police from crime control practices in general and law-breaking in particular. This should be surprising only if we see incidents that give rise to complaints as the products of pathological 'bad apples'. If they are on the contrary regarded as normal reflections of policing practice (Goldsmith 1991), both the behaviour complained of and the closing of ranks preventing a high proportion of substantiation are to be expected (Irving and Dunnighan 1993). Maguire (1992) notes that police investigators probably do not consciously try to exonerate officers who 'overstep the mark', but 'the mark' is not a clear or unchanging line. It depends on the circumstances at the time, the police working rules being pursued and the characteristics of the complainant. Eventually, most of this has become accepted by the government and the police themselves, especially in the wake of the Stephen Lawrence Inquiry of the late 1990s in which it was finally generally accepted both that the police are 'institutionally racist' and that, as a result, ethnic minorities are unjustly treated. Some changes were made to the system in 1999, most notable among which was the lowering of the standard of proof needed to substantiate a complaint from 'beyond reasonable doubt' to 'on the balance of probabilities' (Police (Conduct) Regulations 1999). A larger overhaul of the system is provided for by the Police Reform Act 2002, which provides for the replacement of the PCA by a new Independent Police Complaints Commission. While the enhancement of the civilian element of the system, to include control of investigations in serious cases, is welcome, the experience of other countries shows that this is no panacea (Goldsmith and Lewis 2000). Of greater significance in the long run may be a shift towards a more inclusionary, restorative, way of handling police complaints that some police leaders are now openly advocating (Hill *et al.* 2003; see Chapter 27).

It is not surprising to find that many people are deterred from complaining, and instead prosecute or sue the police. Prosecutions are rare for obvious reasons (not least because few types of police malpractice are actually criminal) although they were brought (unsuccessfully) against some of the officers in the Birmingham Six case. Prosecutions are occasionally initiated by the DPP following invocation of the complaints procedure, but this happened in only 31 cases in 2000–1 (Povey and Cotton 2001). Increasingly, aggrieved complainants or relatives of people who die in police custody are challenging DPP decisions to not prosecute police and prison officers, or to prosecute only on relatively trivial charges. The fact that some of these challenges have succeeded suggests that the DPP is over-cautious in deciding not to prosecute, in contrast to cases where the police are the complainants and the socially marginalised are the accused (Burton 2001).

All other things being equal, a civil action is more likely to succeed than a prosecution because it involves a lower standard of proof. Punitive damages can be awarded in civil actions, and juries are becoming increasingly alarmed at police behaviour. In a notable case in 1996 (some four years after being punched, kicked, racially abused and illegally detained for 90 minutes), Kenneth Hsu was awarded £220,000 in punitive damages. The officers remain unpunished and undisciplined, and in 1997 the Court of Appeal stated that the maximum sum that could be awarded for abuse of police power was £50,000. Hsu's damages were reduced to £35,000 (Dixon and Smith 1998).

Civil actions are expensive, lengthy and difficult to win, but they have none the less increased in number throughout the 1980s and 1990s, indicating the inadequacy of the other available remedies. The civil law has not kept pace with the growth in police powers, however. While wrongful arrest and false imprisonment are traditional actions in tort, PACE itself created no new torts or crimes. Thus the 'right' to a lawyer is not a real right, for there is no court action available to enforce it or to seek compensation for its denial. The same is true of most unlawful interrogation (Sanders 1988). It seems that it is more important to protect property, reputation and tranquillity than it is to protect the civil liberties of 'police property'. Unlike the complaints system, court-based remedies are open and complainant driven, as distinct from being police driven, but their disadvantages render them almost equally ineffective. If freedom is to be maintained, there must be a sense in society that those infringing the rights of others will be held to account in an effective manner. That, after all, is the essential justification for police powers. The current inadequacy of the remedies for abuse of these powers, however, leaves some sections of society with the distinct impression that the police are a law unto themselves.

Conclusion

The law appears to exert less moral force on the police than is often believed, for there is a gap between many legal rules and the working rules of the police. This means that much of the law is presentational in nature, providing a misleading appearance of a system subject to numerous inhibitory due process safeguards. In reality, law-breaking by the police and lesser failures of due process are tolerated within a system which generally fails to punish and deter the police or to compensate most victims of those practices. It is argued by some that changes to legal rules can change police practices radically rather than marginally (e.g. Brown 1997; Dixon 1997). These commentators point to the apparent effects of PACE on interrogations: 'ethical interviewing', less informal interviewing, fewer confessions and a drop in convictions. Early indications following the introduction of PACE suggested that some such changes had taken place. However, these have been offset by the government's emasculation of the right to silence, thus returning to the police their eroded interrogation power, and by the displacement of crime control activity to other parts of the system. In particular, proactive policing – including the use of informants, surveillance and bugging – is an increasingly important, and less controllable, part of the police armoury (for a European perspective, see Field and Pelser 1998; for an American perspective, see Marx 1988). The government has been quick to provide the necessary enabling and legitimising laws to support this shift and has largely dismissed or ignored civil libertarian concerns about ever-increasing police power in this realm. The Criminal Justice Bill is but the most recent example of this legislative drift away from due process values.

Suspects are not a subset of the wider criminal population; rather, criminals are a subset of the wider (official) suspect population. How closely this relates to the 'actually guilty' population must remain a matter of speculation, but any close relationship could well be coincidental. For we would argue that the criminal justice system is not geared solely to detecting and punishing criminal activity. It – and its modern arm, the police – has always been at least as concerned with high-level politics and low-level disorder: that is, with the control of the less powerful. Police powers are used to discipline and exclude marginal populations and these actions are encouraged by politicians and legislators anxious to establish their 'pro-victim, tough on crime' credentials (Sanders 2002).

Prospects for change depend in part on one's view of the reasons why police powers are used in the way that they are. Bureaucratic explanations, which focus on the values of particular institutions, produce more optimistic scenarios than do societal ones. Our view is that, for so long as the state remains obsessed with 'crime reduction' or 'law and order' as the ultimate goal of the criminal justice system, the freedoms of the marginal, the unpopular and the vulnerable will continue to be eroded. It might be different if more was known about the impact of changes to criminal justice processes. There has been an explosion of criminal justice research in the last 20 years, but most of it is 'top down', trying to solve the system's problems; very little has been 'bottom up', asking what it feels like for suspects and defendants. Research should pay more attention to the experiences of suspects, to the lessons to be drawn from Northern Ireland and to the linking of theoretical, policy and empirical questions (Hudson 1993) for when it has done (notable examples are those of Hillyard 1993; Carlen 1996; Loader 1996; Choongh 1997) the results are illuminating.

The police need power to do their job. But the question of how much power they need depends on how their job is conceptualised. A short-term emphasis on crime control should be replaced with a long-term focus on maintaining and enlarging the sense of a free society. As we have seen, there is a case for a much more discriminating use of police powers on the street. In their overview of the mounting research evidence, Bowling and Foster (2002: 997) conclude that 'the proper management and targeting of police resources is better than unfocused patrol and "fire fighting"' when it comes to tackling crime. Thus, saturation stop and search practices such as witnessed in Cleveland should be discarded in favour of police officers and police services asking themselves what is to be gained, and what lost, by resorting to power in a policing context where it is usual for suspicion to be slight, and the crime suspected to be relatively minor. From a freedom perspective, the case for much greater restraint in the use of stop and search, arrest and detention for questioning is clear. For the police ultimately rely on the community for information and support and, in the long run, cannot afford to alienate large sections of the public.

Only rarely is the fundamental question 'why prosecute?' asked in relation to the kinds of case handled by the police. Prosecution often does both too much (stigmatising offenders and driving a wedge between them and their victims) and too little (failing to protect victims from reoffending). For victims and defendants alike a reintegrative approach would be more effective and less alienating than the punitive dichotomous approach embodied in prosecution. Since victims are generally less punitive than the tabloid media would have us believe, this might be widely welcomed. So there is scope for the development of cautioning schemes and similarly more extensive restorative initiatives under which offenders, victims and their respective 'supporters' come together to discuss the harm caused by an offence and how this might be repaired (see Chapter 27). The introduction of conditional cautions (under which any conditions imposed must be oriented towards rehabilitation or reparation) heralded by the Criminal Justice Bill offers some potential here, although the risks of net-widening and mesh-thinning (Cohen 1985) will need to be guarded against.

The question 'why prosecute?' could only be asked from an inclusionary, freedom-oriented perspective. It is at least implicitly asked in one sphere of criminal justice: 'white-collar' law enforcement. Here, inclusionary policies are adopted by non-police agencies. They avoid prosecution and the other trappings of crime control such as arrest, detention, oppressive interrogation and so forth. Instead they use techniques of 'compliance'. It is hardly credible that these differences are the product of bureaucratic pressures or accident. Present practice reflects processes of inclusion for 'white-collar criminals' and processes of exclusion for the poor, deprived and powerless. This is a society in which some of the most damaging criminals are treated in the most humane ways while those who are arguably society's victims are treated as society's enemies so that, in time, they live up to their labels. It remains to be seen whether the recent enthusiasm for restorative justice will result in more inclusionary, freedom-enhancing ways of responding to street-level crime or simply create new sites for unaccountable extensions of state power wielded to exclusionary ends. If the latter proves to be the case, the blame will not rest solely, and perhaps not even mainly, with the police themselves. Ultimately, it lies in the power of political elites to make clear that police powers should be used to preserve and enlarge the freedom of all citizens and social groups alike.

It is easy when highlighting the many deficiencies in the regulation of police powers in England and Wales to overlook the point that the police are afforded much greater latitude in many other jurisdictions. Indeed, the PACE regime may seem attractive when compared with the lack of regulation or codification of police powers found elsewhere. But it does not follow from the fact that torture is not a common policing tactic in this country that our aspirations for greater control of police power should be reined in. This is still one of the wealthiest countries in the world and one that claims to adhere to liberal democratic values, including human rights norms. We can afford to be aspirational in our thinking. And if the price of freedom is eternal vigilance, then it is appropriate to focus on the gap between the ideals of justice and the reality of police power.

Selected further reading

Several texts on criminal justice examine police powers, among other things. Most take either a 'legal' or a 'social policy' approach. Three books which integrate legal and sociological material are Dixon's *Law in Policing* (1997), Ashworth's *The Criminal Process*

(1998) and Sanders and Young's *Criminal Justice* (2000). These books utilise contrasting theoretical frameworks: Ashworth has a human rights approach, Sanders and Young use Packer's crime control and due-process models for descriptive purposes and the freedom perspective as a prescriptive guide, while Dixon makes use of a comparative approach. For a detailed legal treatment, see Lidstone and Palmer's *The Investigation of Crime – A Guide to Police Powers* (1996). Walker and Starmer's *Miscarriages of Justice: A Review of Justice in Error* (1999) takes miscarriages of justice as its theme. All the chapters, including several on police powers, were written specially for the volume. Recent high-quality monographs which blend theory with strong empirical analysis include Bowling's *Violent Racism* (1998), Hoyle's *Negotiating Domestic Violence* (1998) and Choongh's *Policing as Social Discipline* (1997). The implications of growing police powers of surveillance and data collection, and the concomitant increasing co-operation between the police and other institutions, are explored in Ericson and Haggerty's *Policing the Risk Society* (1997).

Acknowledgements

Warm thanks are due to Tim Newburn, Peter Neyroud, Hannah Young and two anonymous reviewers for their helpful comments on a draft of this chapter. Responsibility for its defects is ours alone.

References

Akdeniz, Y., Taylor, N. and Walker, C. (2001) 'RIPA 2000: BigBrother.gov.uk: state surveillance in the age of information and rights', *Criminal Law Review*: 73.

Ashworth, A. (1998a) *The Criminal Process* (2nd edn). Oxford: Oxford University Press.

Ashworth, A. (1998b) 'Should the police be allowed to use deception?', 114 LQR 108.

Ayres, M. *et al.* (2002) *Arrests for Notifiable Offences and the Operation of Certain Police Powers under PACE. Home Office Statistical Bulletin* 12/02. London: Home Office.

Birch, D. (1999) 'Suffering in silence?', *Criminal Law Review*: 769–88.

Bland, N., Miller, J. and Quinton, P. (2000) *Upping the PACE? An Evaluation of the Recommendations of the Stephen Lawrence Inquiry on Stops and Searches. Police Research Series Paper* 128. London: Home Office.

Bowling, B. (1998) *Violent Racism*. Oxford: Clarendon Press.

Bowling, B. and Foster, J. (2002) 'Policing and the police', in M. Maguire *et al.* (eds) *The Oxford Handbook of Criminology* (3rd edn). Oxford: Oxford University Press, 980–1033.

Box, S. and Russell, K. (1975) 'The politics of discreditability: disarming complaints against the police', *Sociological Review*, 23: 315–46.

Braithwaite, J. (2001) *Restorative Justice and Responsive Regulation*. Oxford: Oxford University Press.

Brown, C. and Ellis, T. (1994) *Policing Low Level Disorder. Home Office Research Study* 135. London: HMSO.

Brown, D. (1997) *PACE Ten Years on: A Review of the Research. Home Office Research Study* 155. London: HMSO.

Brown, D., Ellis, T. and Larcombe, K. (1992) *Changing the Code: Police Detention under the Revised PACE Codes of Practice. Home Office Research Study* 129. London: HMSO.

Bucke, T. and Brown, D. (1997) *In Police Custody: Police Powers and Suspects' Rights under the Revised PACE Codes of Practice. Home Office Research Study* 174. London: HMSO.

Bucke, T., Street, R. and Brown, D. (2000) *The Right of Silence: The Impact of the CJPO 1994. Home Office Research Study* 199. London: HMSO.

Burton, M. (2001) 'Reviewing CPS decisions not to prosecute', *Criminal Law Review*: 374.

Cameron, M. (1964) *The Booster and the Snitch*. New York, NY: Free Press.

Cape, E. (1997) 'Sidelining defence lawyers: police station advice after *Condron*', *International Journal of Evidence and Proof*, 1: 386.

Cape, E. (2002) 'Assisting and advising defendants before trial', in M. McConville and G. Wilson (eds) *The Handbook of the Criminal Justice Process*. Oxford: Oxford University Press.

Carlen, P. (1996) *Jigsaw: A Political Criminology of Youth Homelessness*. Buckingham: Open University Press.

Chan, J. (1996) 'Changing police culture', *British Journal of Criminology*, 36: 109–34.

Choongh, S. (1997) *Policing as Social Discipline*. Oxford: Clarendon Press.

Clarke, C. and Milne, R. (2001) *National Evaluation of the PEACE Investigative Interviewing Scheme. Police Research Award Scheme Report* PRAS/149. London: Home Office.

Clarkson, C., Cretney, A., Davies, G. and Shepherd, J. (1994) 'Criminalising assault', *British Journal of Criminology*, 34: 15–29.

Cohen, S. (1985) *Visions of Social Control*. Cambridge: Polity Press.

Colvin, M. (1998) *Under Surveillance – Covert Policing and Human Rights Standards*. London: JUSTICE.

Cook, D. (1989) *Rich Law, Poor Law*. Milton Keynes: Open University Press.

Dixon, B. and Smith, G. (1998) 'Laying down the law: the police, the courts and legal accountability', *International Journal of the Sociology of Law*, 26: 419–35.

Dixon, D. (1992) 'Legal regulation and policing practice', *Social and Legal Studies*, 1: 515.

Dixon, D. (1997) *Law in Policing*. Oxford: Clarendon Press.

Dixon, D., Bottomley, A., Coleman, C., Gill, M. and Wall, D. (1990) 'Safeguarding the rights of suspects in police custody', *Policing and Society*, 1: 115–40.

Duff, P. (1998) 'Crime control, due process and "the case for the prosecution" ', *British Journal of Criminology*, 38: 611–15.

Ericson, R. (1981) *Making Crime*. London: Butterworths.

Ericson, R. and Haggerty, K. (1997) *Policing the Risk Society*. Oxford: Clarendon Press.

Evans, R. (1992) *The Conduct of Police Interviews with Juveniles. Royal Commission on Criminal Justice Research Study* 8. London: HMSO.

Evans, R. and Ferguson, T. (1991) *Comparing Different Juvenile Cautioning Systems in One Police Force*. London: Home Office (unpublished report).

Faulkner, D. (1996) *Darkness and Light*. London: Howard League.

Field, S. and Pelser, C. (1998) *Invading the Private: State Accountability and New Investigative Methods in Europe*. Aldershot: Dartmouth.

Field, S. and Southgate, P. (1982) *Public Disorder. Home Office Research Study* 72. London: HMSO.

Gill, P. (2000) *Rounding up the Usual Suspects*. Aldershot: Dartmouth.

Goldsmith, A. (ed.) (1991) *Complaints against the Police: A Comparative Study*. Oxford: Oxford University Press.

Goldsmith, A. and Lewis, C. (eds) (2000) *Civilian Oversight of Policing: Governance, Democracy and Human Rights*. Oxford: Hart.

Goldstein, J. (1960) 'Police discretion not to invoke the criminal process: low visibility decisions in the administration of justice', *Yale Law Journal*, 69: 543.

Grady, A. (2002) 'Female-on-male domestic violence: uncommon or ignored?', in C. Hoyle and R. Young (eds) *New Visions of Crime Victims*. Oxford: Hart.

Gudjonsson, G. and MacKeith, J. (1982) 'False confessions', in A. Trankell (ed.) *Reconstructing the Past*. Deventer: Kluwer.

Harrison, J. and Cuneen, M. (2000) *An Independent Police Complaints Commission*. London: Liberty.

Hill, R., Cooper, K., Hoyle, C. and Young, R. (2003) *Introducing Restorative Justice to the Police Complaints System: Close Encounters of the Rare Kind*. Oxford: Centre for Criminological Research, University of Oxford.

Hillyard, P. (1993) *Suspect Community*. London: Pluto.

Hillyard, P. and Gordon, D. (1999) 'Arresting statistics: the drift to informal justice in England and Wales', *Journal of Law and Society*, 26: 502–22.

Home Office (2000) *Complaints against the Police – a Consultation Paper*. London: Home Office.

Home Office (and Attorney General and Lord Chancellor's Department) (2002) *Justice for All* (Cm 5563). London: HMSO.

Hoyle, C. (1998) *Negotiating Domestic Violence*. Oxford: Clarendon Press.

Hudson, B. (1993) *Racism and Criminology*. London: Sage.

Irving, B. and Dunnighan C. (1993) *Human Factors in the Quality Control of CID Investigations. Royal Commission on Criminal Justice Research Study* 21. London: HMSO.

Jackson, J. (2001) 'Review of *Miscarriages of Justice* by Nobles and Schiff', *Journal of Law and Society*, 28: 324.

Keith, M. (1993) *Race, Riots and Policing*. London: UCL Press.

Lee, M. (1995) 'Pre-court diversion and youth justice', in L. Noaks (ed.) *Contemporary Issues in Criminology*. Cardiff: University of Wales Press.

Leng, R. (1992) *The Right to Silence in Police Interrogation. Royal Commission on Criminal Justice Research Study* 10. London: HMSO.

Leo, R. (1994) 'Police interrogation and social control', *Social and Legal Studies*, 3: 93.

Lidstone, K. and Palmer, C. (1996) *The Investigation of Crime – a Guide to Police Powers* (2nd edn). London: Butterworth.

Littlechild, B. (1995) 'Re-assessing the role of the appropriate adult', *Criminal Law Review*: 540.

Loader, I. (1996) *Youth, Policing and Democracy*. Basingstoke: Macmillan.

Lustgarten, L. (2002) 'The future of stop and search', *Criminal Law Review*: 603.

Macpherson, Sir William (1999) *The Stephen Lawrence Inquiry* (Cm 4262-I). London: HMSO.

Maguire, M. (1992) 'Complaints against the police: where now?' Unpublished paper.

Maguire, M. (2002) 'Regulating the police station: the case of the Police and Criminal Evidence Act 1984', in M. McConville and G. Wilson (eds) *The Handbook of the Criminal Justice Process*. Oxford: Oxford University Press.

Maguire, M. and Corbett, C. (1991) *A Study of the Police Complaints System*. London: HMSO.

Maguire, M. and John, T. (1996) 'Covert and deceptive policing in England and Wales', *European Journal of Crime, Criminal Law, and Criminal Justice*, 4: 316–34.

Maguire, M. and Norris, C. (1992) *The Conduct and Supervision of Criminal Investigations. Royal Commission on Criminal Justice Research Study* 5. London: HMSO.

Marx, G. (1988) *Undercover: Police Surveillance in America*. Berkeley, CA: University of California Press.

McConville, M. (1992) 'Videotaping interrogations: police behaviour on and off camera', *Criminal Law Review*: 522–48.

McConville, M., Sanders, A. and Leng, R. (1991) *The Case for the Prosecution*. London: Routledge.

McConville, M., Sanders, A. and Leng, R. (1997) 'Descriptive or critical sociology: the choice is yours', *British Journal of Criminology*, 37: 347–58.

McKenzie, I., Morgan, R. and Reiner, R. (1990) 'Helping the police with their enquiries', *Criminal Law Review*: 22–33.

Meehan, A. (1993) 'Internal police records and the control of juveniles', *British Journal of Criminology*, 33: 504–24.

Mhlanga, B. (2000) *Race and the CPS*. London: HMSO.

Miller, J., Bland, N. and Quinton, P. (2000) *The Impact of Stops and Searches on Crime and the Community. Police Research Series Paper* 127. London: Home Office.

Miller, L. (2001) 'Looking for postmodernism in all the wrong places: implementing a new penology', *British Journal of Criminology*, 41: 168.

Moston, S. (1992) 'Police questioning techniques in tape recorded interviews with criminal suspects', *Policing and Society*, 3.

Murphy, D. (1986) *Customers and Thieves*. Farnborough: Gower.

MVA and Miller, J. (2000) *Profiling Populations Available for Stops and Searches. Police Research Series Paper* 131. London: Home Office.

Newburn, T. (1999) *Understanding and Preventing Police Corruption: Lessons from the Literature. Home Office Police Research Series* 110. London: Home Office.

Newburn, T. and Hayman, S. (2002) *Policing, Surveillance and Social Control*. Cullompton: Willan.

Neyroud, P. and Beckley, A. (2000) 'Regulating informers: RIPA, covert policing and human rights', in R. Billingsley *et al.* (eds) *Informers: Policing, Policy, Practice*. Cullompton: Willan.

Neyroud, P. and Beckley, A. (2001) *Policing, Ethics and Human Rights*. Cullompton: Willan.

Noaks, L., Levi, M. and Maguire, M. (eds) (1995) *Contemporary Issues in Criminology*. Cardiff: University of Wales Press.

Norris, C., Fielding, N., Kemp, C. and Fielding, J. (1992) 'Black and blue: an analysis of the influence of race on being stopped by the police', *British Journal of Sociology*, 43: 207–23.

Packer, H. (1968) *The Limits of the Criminal Sanction*. Stanford, CA: Stanford University Press.

Phillips, C. and Brown, D. (1998) *Entry into the Criminal Justice System. Home Office Research Study* 185. London: Home Office.

Povey, D. and Cotton, J. (2001) *Police Complaints and Discipline: England and Wales, 12 Months to March 2001. Home Office Statistical Bulletin* 21/01. London: Home Office.

Quinton, P., Bland, N. and Miller, J. (2000) *Police Stops, Decision-making and Practice. Police Research Series Paper* 130. London: Home Office.

Raine, J. and Willson, M. (1997) 'Police bail with conditions', *British Journal of Criminology*, 37: 593–607.

Reiner, R. (2000) *The Politics of the Police* (3rd edn). Brighton: Wheatsheaf.

Reiss, A. (1971) *The Police and the Public*. New Haven, CT: Yale University Press.

Sanders, A. (1988) 'Rights, remedies and the PACE Act', *Criminal Law Review*: 802–12.

Sanders, A. (1996a) 'Access to justice in the police station', in R. Young, and D. Wall (eds) *Access to Criminal Justice*. London: Blackstone.

Sanders, A. (ed.) (1996b) *Prosecutions in Common Law Jurisdictions*. Aldershot: Dartmouth.

Sanders, A. (2002) 'Victim participation in an exclusionary criminal justice system', in C. Hoyle and R. Young (eds) *New Visions of Crime Victims*. Oxford: Hart.

Sanders, A., Bridges, L., Mulvaney, A. and Crozier, G. (1989) *Advice and Assistance at Police Stations and the 24 Hour Duty Solicitor Scheme*. London: Lord Chancellor's Department.

Sanders, A., Creaton, J., Bird, S. and Weber, L. (1997) *Victims with Learning Disabilities: Negotiating the Criminal Justice System. Occasional Paper* 17. Oxford: Centre for Criminological Research.

Sanders, A. and Young, R. (2000) *Criminal Justice* (2nd edn). London: Butterworths.

Scarman, Lord (1981) *The Scarman Report: The Brixton Disorders*. London: HMSO.

Scott, M. and Lyman, S. (1968) 'Accounts', *American Sociological Review*, 33: 46–62.

Shapland, J. and Vagg, J. (1988) *Policing by the Public*. London: Routledge.

Sharpe, S. (1998) *Judicial Discretion and Criminal Investigation*. London: Sweet & Maxwell.

Sharpe, S. (2000) *Search and Surveillance: The Movement from Evidence to Information*. Aldershot: Dartmouth.

Simmons, J. *et al.* (2002) *Crime in England and Wales 2001/2002. Home Office Statistical Bulletin* 07/02. London: Home Office.

Smith, D. (1997a) 'Case construction and the goals of the criminal process', *British Journal of Criminology*, 37: 319–46.

Smith, D. (1997b) 'Reform or moral outrage – the choice is yours', *British Journal of Criminology*, 38: 616–22.

Smith, D. and Gray, J. (1983) *Police and People in London*. Aldershot: Gower.

Steer, J. (1980) *Uncovering Crime: The Police Role*. London: HMSO.

Stevens, P. and Willis, C. (1979) *Race, Crime, and Arrests. Home Office Research Study* 58. London: HMSO.

Tinsley, Y. (2001) 'Even better than the real thing? The case for reform of identification procedures', *International Journal of Evidence and Proof*, 5: 235.

Tuck, M. and Southgate, P. (1981) *Ethnic Minorities, Crime and Policing. Home Office Research Study* 70. London: HMSO.

Tyler, R.T. (1990) *Why People Obey the Law*. New Haven, CT, and London: Yale University Press.

Uglow, S. (1999) 'Covert surveillance and the ECHR', *Criminal Law Review*: 287.

Walker, C. and Starmer, K. (eds) (1999) *Miscarriages of Justice: A Review of Justice in Error*. London: Blackstone.

Willis, C. (1983) *The Use, Effectiveness, and Impact of Police Stop and Search Powers. Research and Planning Unit Paper* 15. London: Home Office.

Young, H (2002) 'Securing fair treatment: an examination of the diversion of mentally disordered offenders from police custody'. Unpublished PhD, University of Birmingham.

Young, M. (1991) *An Inside Job*. Oxford: Oxford University Press.

Young, J. (1999) *The Exclusive Society*. London: Sage.

Young, R. (2001) 'Just cops doing "shameful" business?: police-led restorative justice and the lessons of research', in A. Morris and G. Maxwell (eds) *Restorative Justice for Juveniles*. Oxford: Hart.

Young, R. and Goold, B. (1999) 'Restorative police cautioning in Aylesbury: from degrading to reintegrative shaming ceremonies?', *Criminal Law Review*: 126–38.

Chapter 11

Policing and the media

Robert Reiner

Introduction: the Odd Couple – the media and policing

The relationship between policing and the mass media has always been vexed and complex. Sir Robert Mark, Commissioner of the Metropolitan Police in the early 1970s, once referred to it as 'an enduring, if not ecstatically happy, marriage'. In many ways this is an apt metaphor. It captures the mutual dependence and reciprocal reinforcement that underlies a relationship frequently characterised by bickering and tension.

Stories of crime, deviance and how they are policed have always been a prominent part of the content of the mass media. Since the Second World War the police have become increasingly central in news and entertainment stories, as will be shown later. This necessarily makes the media depend on the police as prime sources of their product. Indeed, according to the recent evidence given to the Home Affairs Committee by the editor of *The News of the World*, journalists occasionally pay police officers for information.

In turn the mass media are an important concern to the police. Policing, especially in Britain, has always been a matter of symbolism as much as substance (Walker 1996; Loader 1997; Reiner 2000a, 2000b; Leishman and Mason 2003). Most sophisticated police leaders have realised this. From the architects of modern British policing in the early nineteenth century, such as Sir Robert Peel, up to today's chief officers, there has been a continuing concern with constructing and maintaining a favourable image of policing as a benign, honourable and helpful service (Mawby 1999, 2001, 2002a, 2002b).

Police elites, in Britain and elsewhere, have struggled, largely successfully, to represent policing as the monopolistic source of security, the primary protection for the public against threats and fears about crime and disorder (McLaughlin and Murji 1998; Wilson 2000; Loader and Mulcahy 2001a, 2001b, 2003). This has involved continuous reconstruction and reinterpretation of the nature of policing as patterns of social order, conflict and authority change. But beneath the shifting modes of representation of policing there has remained in place a bedrock theme that I have called 'police fetishism' (Reiner 2000a: 1). By this I mean the assumption that the police are a functional prerequisite of social order, so that without a police force there would be chaos and uncontrolled war of all against all. This is a theme that most people already encounter in contemporary society in children's nursery stories and is deeply embedded in modern culture (Reiner 2000a: 163). What police fetishism blots out is the variety of other forms of policing that have and do and could exist (Jones and Newburn 1998; Johnston and Shearing 2003). Even more importantly, it obscures the fundamental significance of other aspects of social structure and culture for the maintenance and reproduction of order and security (Reiner 2000a: ix–12).

While concern from different points of view about media representations of policing has a long history, in the last quarter of the twentieth century this anxiety took a new turn in the context of the profound social and cultural shifts that have been variously interpreted as post- or late-modernity. It is impossible here to go into the multifaceted arguments about how to characterise contemporary patterns of change. But certain deep-seated aspects of social transformation have had considerable implications for media and policing. Changes in technology and routines of social life have interacted to produce a saturation of social and cultural life by ever more pervasive mass media (Thompson 1995). The media in a proliferating variety of forms (new like the Internet, or developments of the old such as radio, television or CDs) have become omni-present, continuously consumed and almost inescapable. This has been an important feature of such key social changes as the erosion of 'space-time distanciation' (Giddens 1990) through the growing speed of communications across the globe. The proliferation of opportunities to access the media is related to important shifts in social interaction and authority, notably cultural diversification, the questioning of moral absolutes, declining deference, heightened sensitivity to risk and insecurity of diverse kinds and other processes with profound implications for policing.

These changes transform the old debate about the significance of media representations of crime and policing: 'The media are no longer, if they ever were, observers of the scene, they are players in the game' (Simon Lee cited in Peay 1998: 8). Representations of policing are not just after-the-event narratives with more or less worrying implications for the legitimacy of the social order. Increasingly the commission of crimes, public disorder and policing operations are depicted as they happen, a trend most vividly illustrated by the destruction of the World Trade Centre on 11 September 2001, when mass murders were broadcast around the world on live television. This was just the most dramatic example of this trend, and the more general growth of 'reality' television (Fishman and Cavender 1998; Hill 2000). Policing and crime now are shaped – in part at least – by their media representation, in a semiotic loop (Lawrence 2000).

This chapter will examine the long-running debates about media and policing. The first section considers different perspectives on the significance of media representations and constructions of policing. There is then a discussion of media representations before the Second World War and an analysis of their implications for the struggle to establish police legitimacy. The many changes since the Second World War are then examined. In the conclusions the implications of contemporary patterns of representation are considered further.

The debate about the media and social order

The main arena in modern societies where public images of policing are constructed and contested is the mass media. Two polar opposite anxieties about the effects of media representations of crime and policing have flourished. Conservatives frequently claim that the media subvert authority and exacerbate deviance, while liberals and radicals have suggested that the media undermine the rule of law and legitimate authoritarian policing by exaggerating the threat posed by crime (Reiner 2002; Greer 2003). Conservative concerns about the potential impact of mass media of communication on order and policing have existed throughout the history of the media. In the late eighteenth century, Patrick Colquhoun, one of the most prominent champions of the creation of the new police, drew attention to a supposed new wave of 'bawdy ballad singers' and their deleterious effects on 'the morals and habits of the lower ranks in society'. He advocated government support for rival groups of ballad singers who would tour the pubs singing wholesome, uplifting lyrics and remedy the damage done by their subversive counterparts (Reiner 2002: 376).

During the twentieth century successive waves of new technological forms of mass media – cinema, radio, television, video, satellite, the Internet – sparked a series of moral panics spreading alarm about their alleged detrimental effect on morality, crime and violence (Barker and Petley 2001; Carter and Weaver 2003). Police voices have often been in the vanguard of these anxieties. In 1916 John Percival, Chief Constable of Wigan, declared in evidence to an inquiry by the 'National Council for Morals' that 'the cinema is responsible for the increase in juvenile crime' (Mathews 1994: 27). That same year a report representing all chief constables concluded that 'The establishment of a central Government censor of cinematograph films is essential and will conduce to the reduction of juvenile crime in the country' (Mathews 1994: 25). These comments typify a long history of 'respectable fears' (Pearson 1983) held by older, well established people about threats to morality posed by the young and outsiders, supposedly egged on by noxious cultural influences.

Radical and liberal analyses have often had the opposite worry. They have regarded the media as fomenting unrealistic public fears, vastly exaggerating the extent, seriousness and violence of crime. This has the effect of undermining popular support for the rule of law, thus legitimating undemocratic and authoritarian forms of policing and criminal justice, including vigilantism. The systematic tendency of the media to encourage tough policing and law and order solutions to crime is attributed by radical analyses to the interests that the elites who dominate media industries have in maintaining the socioeconomic and political status quo. Media demonisation of offenders diverts public anxiety away from other sources of insecurity, and solutions to the crime problem are portrayed in terms of strengthening the forces of order rather than reform of the social system.

One result of both these anxieties has been a veritable industry of research attempting to assess the content, effects and sources of media representations (recent reviews include Livingstone 1996; Howitt 1998; Reiner 2002). Much of this detailed research has tended to support a 'third way' position. The pattern of media representation, even if it confirms some of the anxieties of critics, emerges from a web of interactions and influences in a complex process of production, and cannot be attributed to a straightforward political ideology or vested interest (Reiner 2002; Greer 2003).

Much of the research on media effects has been conducted within a positivist psychological frame of reference, seeking to establish whether exposure to particular images has clearly identifiable consequences either for 'anti-social' attitudes or actions, or for fear of crime. Perhaps unsurprisingly the prodigious efforts to isolate a 'pure' media effect tend to result in such masterpieces of inconsequentiality as the conclusion of one major study that 'for some children, under some conditions, some television is harmful. For some children under the same conditions, or for the same children under [different] conditions, it may be beneficial. For most children, under most conditions, most television is probably neither particularly harmful nor particularly beneficial' (Schramm *et al.* 1961: 11).

The majority of studies, whether conducted in laboratory or 'natural' conditions *do* find some effects in the expected direction but usually very small ones. For example, one study of 34 matched sets of US cities between 1951 and 1955 found that larceny increased by about five per cent in the cities that gained access to television for the first time, compared to cities without TV or which had been receiving it for some time (Hennigan *et al.* 1982). The weight of evidence does also suggest some effects on fear of crime, although these are equivocal (Reiner 2002: 399–402).

It is not surprising that the vast research enterprise on media effects has been rather inconclusive. Most of it has been focused on testing the allegations which have flourished for centuries in political debate, and indeed have been circulated by the media themselves, about direct causal relationships between exposure to images and subsequent behaviour. The implicit model behind such anxieties is implausibly simplistic: the media as an autonomous and powerful ideological hypodermic syringe, injecting ideas and values into a passive public of cultural dopes.

It is far more plausible to suggest that media images do indeed have profound consequences (Philo 1999), but not in a pure and directly determin-istic manner. Audiences may interpret media images in differing ways, according to their particular social experiences and interests. The media themselves do not change autonomously but reflect developments in social perceptions and practices that have other origins. The media–society relation-ship is dialectical: each develops in interaction with the other, in a complex loop of interdependence. Media representations have significant consequences, although the hunt for pure effects that can be experimentally isolated is chimerical. The question is not 'how the media make us act or think, but rather how the media contribute to making us who we are' (Livingstone 1996: 31–2).

Constructing police fetishism: images of policing and the media before the Second World War

The media representation of the police has always been one key aspect of the general debate about media and crime. The media have also been an important arena within which the legitimacy of the police has been contested and constructed. The creators of the modern British police in the early nineteenth century faced an enormously resistant market for their product. Throughout the eighteenth century a succession of proposals had been put forward calling for reform of the policing arrangements that had been inherited from the Middle Ages, which were a patchwork quilt of entrepreneurial and citizen bodies, backed up ultimately by the army (Emsley 1996: ch. 1, 2002: 211–13; Reiner 2000a: ch. 1; Rawlings 1999: chs 2, 5, 2002: chs 2–5; see Chapters 3 and 4).

Literary advocates of a new, modern police, such as Defoe and the Fielding brothers, wrote lurid accounts of rising crime and disorder in London and other cities, although these are not borne out by the fragmentary statistical evidence, at any rate until the later eighteenth century (Rawlings 1999: 35–8, 70–2; 2002: 106–7). In the reformers' accounts the old forms of policing were either corrupt or bumblingly incompetent, and there was a clear need for a rational, professional, modern organisation.

During the second half of the eighteenth century the reform arguments gathered force, in a context of increasing questioning of the whole criminal justice process by Enlightenment and utilitarian thinkers such as Beccaria and Bentham. In much of Europe this found expression in a flourishing 'science of police' which sought to analyse the techniques for effectively regulating and disciplining the populations of modern societies (Pasquino 1978). The leading British exponent of this new branch of political economy was the Middlesex magistrate Patrick Colquhoun, whose *A Treatise on the Police of the Metropolis* (Colquhoun 1795) was an important influence on Bentham and other champions of the police idea (Reiner 1988; McMullan 1998; Garland 1997: 177; 2002: 19–25).

In eighteenth and early nineteenth-century Britain there was clearly widespread and deep hostility to the police, evidenced by the protracted struggle around the creation of the new police. The campaign to establish a modern police only succeeded after 1829 and Peel's Metropolitan Police Act which created a model that eventually spread through the whole country following the County and Borough Police Act 1856.

The sources of opposition to the new police lay at the top and bottom of the social hierarchy – the middle class were the strongest bastion of support for the police idea. The rhetoric which justified opposition to the police was much the same at both ends of the social scale. The police were represented as oppressive threats to the cherished liberties of the British people. They were said to be an alien import from France, Russia, Prussia or some other European police states, who would necessarily be brutal and corrupt agents of political tyranny.

Ultimately during the first half of the nineteenth century this widespread rejection of the police was gradually overcome. Peel and other police leaders packaged and marketed the police in a way that succeeded in selling them to an increasing part of the public. This was made possible by changes in the political economy and social structure that reduced the sources of opposition. The legitimation of the police involved the careful construction of an image that subtly combined the representation of the police as both paragons of virtue and panaceas for crime and disorder. Between the middle of the nineteenth and the middle of the twentieth centuries this succeeded in displacing the opposing image of the police as oppressive pariahs, in the eyes of most British people (Reiner 2000a: ch. 2).

The elements of the successful marketing of the police by Peel (and Rowan and Mayne, the first two Commissioners of the Metropolitan Police) were directed at defusing the various strands of the opposition. They developed the image of the British bobby as a citizen in uniform, subject to the rule of law not party politics, and operating with minimal force, backed by the consent of the community rather than coercive powers. This paragon of virtue would protect the public from crime and disorder more effectively than a force that relied upon the state's monopoly of the means of violence, its unique advantage being the cultivation of public support. The marketing of this image succeeded only in part because of its own virtues. A precondition for policing by consent was the slow, faltering and never complete incorporation of the mass of the British population into a common citizenship (Marshall 1950). A more harmonious, if still highly unequal, society was much more receptive to accepting the police as a symbol of its integration.

The nineteenth-century conflicts about the establishment and acceptability of the police were played out in the media of the day, the press, the novel and the music hall (Miller, D. A. 1988; Miller, W. 1999: ch. 5). Popular literature and journalism began to feature the exploits of police 'detective officers' from the mid-1840s, and Dickens 'virtually appointed himself patron and publicist to the Detective Department' (Ousby 1976: 65–6). The genre of police memoirs (pioneered by the celebrated 1828 *Memoires* of Vidocq, head of the Sûreté in Paris from 1812 to 1827), was imported to Britain in 1849 when a long-running series *Recollections of a Detective Police-officer* first appeared in *Chambers' Edinburgh Journal* (Ousby 1976: 66).

The advent of the cinema as the primary medium of mass entertainment early in the twentieth century stimulated the kind of respectable anxiety that has accompanied each successive form of technological innovation, from television to the Internet (Black 1994: ch. 1). Cinema history has been continuously punctuated by conflicts about the supposedly anti-social aspects of its representation of crime (Rafter 2000; Leitch 2002). As illustrated earlier, the police have been prominent in campaigns to censor cinema because of fears about its criminogenic consequences. There was also continuing concern about the cinema's representation of the police, which was alleged to undermine their authority. As early as 1910 the International Association of Chiefs of Police adopted a resolution condemning the cinema's treatment of the police (Reiner 1981: 197). Its president complained that 'in moving pictures the police are sometimes made to appear ridiculous, and in view of the large number of young people, children, who attend these moving picture shows, it gives them an improper idea of the policeman' (Reiner 1981: 197). The police were alarmed by being lampooned as the Keystone Cops, and by appearing dull and ineffectual in comparison with heroic private investigators or glamourised gangsters.

These fears reached a height in the early 1930s with the cycle of classic gangster movies such as *Little Caesar*, *Public Enemy* and *Scarface*. Concern about these was a major factor in the enforcement from 1934 of the Hays Code, which laid down strict rules about how Hollywood could depict crime and law enforcement, as well as more general moral issues (Black 1994: ch. 5). In the early 1930s the Director of the FBI, J. Edgar Hoover, the first of many media-conscious police chiefs, initiated a policy of co-operating with Hollywood in return for control over how his agency was represented (Powers 1983: ch. 4; Potter 1998). The result of the Hays Code and Hoover's moral entrepreneurship was the birth of the first cycle of films featuring law enforcement heroes, beginning in 1935 with *G-men*, a paean to the bureau replete with documentary-style footage on FBI training and forensic methods (Reiner 1981: 200–3).

The G-men films were unusual in popular entertainment before the Second World War in featuring professional law enforcers as the protagonists. Police heroes were rare in the cinema and in popular literature until the late 1940s. Television, which began to be the dominant form of popular entertainment after the early 1950s, is the only medium that has always represented the police as central characters in fiction. Before the Second World War the main heroes in crime fiction in all media were amateur sleuths, private detectives or bystanders inadvertently drawn into crime as victims, suspects and/or investigators (Reiner 1981, 2000a: ch. 5; Rafter 2000: ch. 3; Leitch 2002). In the predominant subgenres of crime fiction before the Second World War (notably the classical whodunnit à la Conan Doyle or Agatha Christie, and the private eye stories of Hammett, Chandler *et al.*), the police appear as minor characters, often portrayed negatively as either comic or corrupt.

A darker shade of blue: police and the media since the Second World War

In the immediate aftermath of the Second World War the police achieved a zenith of public popularity. This was crystallised in the image epitomised by the fictional hero PC George Dixon, the quintessential representation of the British bobby ideal, introduced in the 1949 Ealing film *The Blue Lamp*. Murdered after only 45 minutes of *The Blue Lamp*, the Dixon character made such a popular impact that he was resurrected in 1955 for a BBC television series that lasted until 1976.[1] Dixon remains a potent symbol of all that was supposedly best in British policing, and politicians or police chiefs under pressure regularly call for the return of Dixon. On 28 February 2003, for example, the *Guardian* reported that the Commissioner and Deputy Commissioner of the Metropolitan Police believed 'it's time to bring back Dixon' (Hopkins 2003).

In the late 1960s the long-term process of increasing the popular legitimacy of policing went into reverse (Reiner 2000a: chs 2, 7). The ultimate source of this lay in deep cultural and social changes that undermined the structural basis of police legitimation (Reiner 1992). Culturally the whole postwar period saw a slow decline in deference, increasing desubordination (Miliband 1978) and a widespread challenging of authority. In the early 1970s there began a sustained economic recession with permanently high levels of unemployment. It became increasingly clear that this was not cyclical but a fundamental change in the nature of the economy. Developing technology and globalisation had generated a structurally excluded 'underclass' that 'the majority class does not need to maintain or even increase its standard of living' (Dahrendorf 1985: 101). This excluded minority of about one third of the population has become increasingly criminalised due to the pressures of hopelessness and the erosion of the most potent socialising agencies, work and family (Currie 1998; Davies 1998; Taylor 1999; Young 1999).

As crime and disorder increased and the police tried to stem this, the unintended consequence was the reversal of the ingredients of the Peelian police image. The media began to spotlight scandals concerning police corruption and malpractice, miscarriages of justice, racism, sexism and a militarisation of public order tactics. They also focused increasingly on apparent police ineffectiveness in crime control as indicated by soaring crime and plummeting clear-up rates. The result was declining public confidence, as indicated by many surveys and other evidence (Sims 2003: 108). Successive governments and police chiefs have tried various strategies to reverse this. For most of the 1980s and the early 1990s the relegitimation strategy was 'back to the future'. Its blueprint was the 1981 report by Lord Scarman on the Brixton disorders (Scarman 1981), with its prioritisation of 'peace-keeping'. By the early 1990s the police elite had began to restructure policing around a consumerist, 'quality of service' ethos, at least rhetorically (Waters 2000). This attempt at relegitimation appeared to succeed during the 1990s in arresting the decline of public confidence measured by surveys (Bucke 1996; Sims 2003: 108).

In 1993–4 a major shift in official definitions of the police mission was implemented by Home Secretary, Kenneth Clarke, and by his successor, Michael Howard. As defined in the 1993 white paper on *Police Reform* the overriding police objective became simply 'catching criminals', as if life was a gangster movie. The supposed means of achieving this was reorganisation on 'businesslike' lines (as detailed in the Sheehy Report published in the same week as the white paper). This proposed market disciplines – short-term contracts, performance-related pay and so on – to restructure policing around a performance culture. Although much modified during its legislative passage, the Police and Magistrates' Courts Act 1994 heralded a significant tilt towards the 'businesslike' crime control ethos (Morgan and Newburn 1997). Tony Blair's 'New Labour' government in 1997 continued the fundamentals of this approach. The police mission was defined primarily as crime reduction, and a quasi-market model, involving continuous setting and monitoring of performance targets from the centre, was seen as the vehicle for effective delivery (Leishman *et al.* 2000; Reiner 2000a; Bowling and Foster 2002).

The police image encouraged by government seems to have considerably narrowed from the traditional broad peace-keeping, consensus-building model. Since 1993 the aim has been to sell the police as crime fighters, downplaying the service function and problems of legality. Despite periodic calls in moments of challenge to police legitimacy for a return to the Dixon of Dock Green police culture (see, for example, Hopkins 2003), these amount to little more than blips in the drive towards a crime control performance culture.

The media representation of policing has become an increasingly central aspect of the struggles over police legitimacy in the period since 1945.

Reflecting this, the police became more prominent in all media during the second half of the twentieth century, whether in fiction, news stories and 'factions' – as Leishman and Mason call the increasingly prevalent genre of entertainment/documentary hybrids (Doyle 1998; Hill 2000; Leishman and Mason 2003).

The same two broad perspectives found in the general debate about crime and the media are echoed in current controversies about the representation of the police. On one hand, there has been a continuation of the long-running conservative anxiety about media images undermining order, with fears about how they portray the police, who are of course the front-line embodiments of the state's authority. On the other hand, there has been concern among liberal and radical commentators that the media presentation of crime and policing is detrimental to popular support for principles of legality and fosters authoritarianism.

There has been considerable research in Britain and North America in the last 30 years studying the content of media representations of policing (usually as an aspect of a more general concern with images of crime and criminal justice). There has also been some research on the processes of production, and the perception of media images by the public, and by police officers themselves (Perlmutter 2000). The police themselves are generally very sensitive about their image in the media. Sir Robert Mark advocated a more open approach to the media while he was Metropolitan Commissioner in the early 1970s. None the less in 1974 he declared to the London Press Club that the police were 'without doubt the most abused, the most unfairly criticised and the most silent minority in this country' (Chibnall 1979). Police reactions to their media representation suggest a kind of *Catch-22* paranoia. Stories about police deviance are understandably regarded with concern, even though they are usually framed within a perspective that legitimates the police institution itself (Chibnall 1977; Schlesinger and Tumber 1994). Somewhat less predictably, officers are also worried about positive representations of policing, which could lead the public to expect too much of the police, in terms of crime-fighting wizardry or superhuman patience, tact and integrity (Perlmutter 2000). They fear that TV cop shows breed an assumption that crimes can be cleared up routinely in half an hour minus commercial breaks: 'You can't take fingerprints off water', as one officer put it in a survey (Arcuri 1977).

Anxiety about the media representation of policing has stimulated police leaders and professional associations to try to cultivate positive relations. The most common strategy in the postwar period has been to pre-empt problems by co-operation with media producers, and by training police spokespersons for media appearances (Chibnall 1977; Schlesinger and Tumber 1994; Crandon and Dunne 1997; Boyle 1999; Mawby 1999, 2002a, 2000b; Innes 1999, 2003; Leishman and Mason 2003: ch. 3). Unfortunately, there is also a pattern of negative reactions to particular programmes stimulating cyclical periods of police–media conflict (Reiner 2000a: 143–7).

The numerous content analyses of news and fiction stories about crime suggest that the predominant representation of policing is an extremely favourable one, contrary to the perennial police anxiety about this. Interestingly, similar patterns of representation have been found in studies of both fiction and news/documentary stories about crime and law enforcement. Although there are some variations in the representation of crime and policing between different media, operating with varying technologies and in different markets, and between different genres, the following broad patterns have been found by studies conducted at different times and places:[2]

1. Stories about crime and law enforcement are perennially prominent in all media. Their precise proportion varies in different studies, according to the definitions that they adopt. More substantively, the extent and prominence of crime stories vary between different media and the markets they operate in, whatever the research methods used by researchers. The general prominence of crime stories flows in part from the very nature of news and story-telling. As one study of news-making put it, 'deviance is *the* defining characteristic of what journalists regard as newsworthy' (Ericson *et al.* 1987: 4). This is clearly almost tautologous: news implies some element of novelty and extraordinariness, and the same applies to fictional story-telling. In this sense crime, deviance and control, 'some disruption of the social order', are intrinsic to all narrative (Leitch 2002: 11–13), so the empirical finding of perpetual media fascination with crime and police stories is hardly astonishing.

2. The media concentrate on stories of serious crimes against the person, particularly homicide and sexual offences. These offences, which constitute only a small proportion of crime recorded in official statistics or victim surveys, are the focus of the overwhelming majority of media accounts.

3. The media concentrate on crimes that are already or are likely to become solved. Offences which are reported in the news when they occur are typically the most serious cases of interpersonal violence, which have the highest clear-up rates. Most other offences are reported only at the stage of an arrest or trial, and the reports are usually filtered through the perspective of the police, prosecutor or judge. Fictional crimes are almost invariably cleared up, as a result of the exercise of remarkable skill and daring by police or other law enforcement heroes. This contrasts with the picture given in official statistics, which shows that only two per cent of offences reported in victim surveys result in a conviction. Studies of detection indicate that few of these clear-ups are the product of skilful detection; the majority are either virtually self-clearing cases or solved due to effective interrogation tactics and bureaucratic processes (Innes 2003).

4. Offenders and victims reported in news stories are disproportionately older, white, middle or upper class. The same demographic pattern of offenders and victims features in most fiction. The media picture contrasts sharply with the characteristics of convicted offenders or victims portrayed in official statistics (Barclay and Tavares 1999). These are mostly young, from the most marginal socioeconomic groups, and disproportionately black. This portrait of the demography of crime skews it to the more serious, rational end of the spectrum, making the usual triumph of law enforcement all the more impressive.

The overall picture of crime and control presented in the media, whether fiction or news, is thus highly favourable to the police image. Crime is represented as a serious threat to vulnerable individual victims, but one that the police routinely tackle successfully because of their prowess and heroism. The police accordingly appear as the seldom-failing guardians of the public in general, essential bulwarks of the social order – the essence of 'police fetishism'.

The police are sensitive about the regular appearance of stories that focus on police deviance. Corrupt police officers have high news value, as do all stories of authority figures caught in wrongdoing. The news media will hunt these scandals out with great gusto. None the less, the overall framework for presenting particular stories about police corruption or malpractice tends to legitimate institutions of law enforcement in general. In the past such stories have typically portrayed deviant police as 'one bad apple' in an otherwise sound barrel (Chibnall 1977). As stories about police malpractice have multiplied in the last three decades this narrative has become less credible. Nevertheless the overall framework of police deviance stories continues to legitimate the organisation per se. This is accomplished by constructing a narrative of progressive reform. Cases of deviance are presented within an overarching account of how organisational procedures are being changed to prevent the recurrence of malpractice in the future (Schlesinger and Tumber 1994). The fundamental theme is that the police may have erred but now they are getting their house in order and, indeed, they tend to use classic police techniques in the process.

Police corruption features less often in fiction, but where it does the protagonists are often the cops who fight corruption (as in *The Untouchables* or *Between the Lines*). When the deviance takes the form of rule-breaking to catch criminals, what Metropolitan Police Commissioner Paul Condon notoriously referred to as 'noble cause corruption', this vigilante style policing is often celebrated (as in *Dirty Harry* or *The Sweeney*). Thus the presentation of police deviance by both news and fiction helps reproduce police fetishism, the overwhelmingly favourable police image in the media as successful and heroic guardians of the public without whom social order is impossible.

The sources of this overwhelmingly favourable police image lie more in the practical exigencies of production processes than any direct consequences of the ideology of those responsible for creating the content of media output. It is true that the British press has been predominantly conservative and overtly champions 'law and order', and even liberal newspapers support the police role although they are concerned about civil liberties. Traditional crime reporters working for popular tabloid newspapers have felt themselves under an obligation to present the police in a favourable light whenever possible, representing them as the 'goodies' (Chibnall 1977: 145).

However as 'law and order' has become increasingly controversial as a political issue (Downes and Morgan 2002), the broadsheet press at the 'quality' end of the market have also appointed specialist editors in this area. They are more commonly referred to as 'home affairs' or 'legal' correspondents than 'crime' reporters (Schlesinger and Tumber 1994), and do not share the police-centred perspective of their tabloid counterparts. The producers of broadcast news, as well as the creators of crime fiction in any medium, do not intentionally act as police cheerleaders either. Their primary self-conception is as purveyors of objective information or non-ideological entertainment. Both values would lead to assiduous pursuit of police failure or malpractice, in exactly the way that the police themselves fear. Moreover, according to one empirical study of the contemporary 'Hollywood elite', responsible for producing the most popular entertainment for large and small screens around the world, they are quintessential children of the 1960s, with liberal, permissive and anti-authoritarian values (Powers *et al.* 1996). If the outcome none the less is the overall legitimation of the police role that is found by content analyses, then the source of this cannot be the direct ideological intention of the creative personnel working in the media.

The origins of the fundamentally favourable representation of the police in the media lie in a combination of professional conceptions of what counts as a 'good story' for news or fiction, and practical exigencies in the production process. The concentration of news on the most serious interpersonal crimes of violence, especially murder or sexual offences, is due to what reporters perceive as the essence of newsworthiness: individualisation, immediacy, drama, titillation, novelty (Chibnall 1977: 22–45; Hall *et al.* 1978; Ericson *et al.* 1987, 1989, 1991). These crimes are portrayed primarily as specific cases rather than in terms of broader social causes because the basic format of news schedules involves an event orientation – what's happened since the last news (Rock 1973: 76–9). Perceptions of 'good stories' by writers and producers of popular fiction share a similar sense of what interests audiences (and audience interviews confirm this – Livingstone *et al.* 2001).

Another ingredient of the conception of a 'good story' held by creators and audiences is a structure which resolves tension with a clear, satisfying outcome, as encapsulated in Miss Prism's celebrated definition of fiction in Wilde's *Lady Windermere's Fan*: 'The good ended happily, and the bad unhappily'. This inclines towards stories with crimes that are cleared up, since the majority of audience members are positioned with the victim or the law enforcers by most conventional crime stories (Sparks 1992; Rafter 2000; Livingstone *et al.* 2001; Leitch 2002).

In addition to the professional sense of what kinds of narratives interest and satisfy audiences, practical exigencies exert pressures and incline producers towards a police-filtered perspective. The most overt of these have been formal and informal censorship pressures, deriving from a variety of moral entrepreneurs concerned about the criminogenic or destabilising consequences of media representations of crime and law enforcement. A clear example discussed earlier was the Hays Code which in 1934 forced Hollywood to switch from producing films with gangster protagonists to ones featuring the FBI as heroes. More generally it meant that until the Hays Code became ineffective in the mid-1950s all Hollywood films had to conform to a 'crime doesn't pay' message (Black 1994: ch. 5; Rafter 2000: ch. 1; Leitch 2002: ch. 2).

More consistently important than negative censorship pressures has been the need of producers of news and fiction to achieve and maintain practical co-operation with the police. The exigencies of news production in particular have several unintended pro-police ideological consequences. The focus on cleared-up cases, which creates a misleading image of police effectiveness, is primarily a result of the economics of allocating reporting resources, leading to the deployment of personnel to institutional settings such as courts where newsworthy events can be expected to recur regularly. Considerations of convenience and personal safety lead camera crews and reporters typically to cover incidents such as riots from behind police positions, creating an image of the police as 'us', and the people they are dealing with as 'them' (Murdock 1982: 108–9).

Above all, the police control much of the information on which crime news reporters depend, which gives them an inevitable degree of power as essential and accredited sources (Chibnall 1977; Ericson *et al.* 1987, 1989, 1991). This allows the police often to be the 'primary definers' of crime news, which is often framed by their perspective (Hall *et al.* 1978: 58). There is considerable variation between news production processes and procedures according to the medium and market in which they work, and contingency and cock-up play a central role in determining day-to-day content (Ericson *et al.* 1991: 93–4). None the less, the most comprehensive study of the creation of crime news concluded that 'the news media are as much an agency of *policing* as the law-enforcement agencies whose activities and classifications are reported on' (Ericson *et al.* 1991: 74). They reproduce order while representing it. Although there are no systematic studies of the production of crime fiction in any medium, the hallmark of police stories above all has been a realist style and the appearance of verisimilitude. It is likely that this too sets up pressures to obtain police co-operation which are analogous to those for news production, albeit not as pervasive or tight.

While crime stories in both news and fiction have generally legitimated the police, as shown by studies of content and production, there have been considerable changes over time in the extent and the way that this has been accomplished (Reiner *et al.* 2000a, 2000b, 2003). There are also important differences between different media, and within any medium at different market levels, for example between the popular and 'quality' newspapers (Ericson *et al.* 1991).

In fiction the police seldom figured as central characters before the Second World War, as was noted earlier. The police emerged as heroic protagonists during the late 1940s in the subgenre of crime fiction usually referred to as the 'police procedural' (Dove 1982; Dove and Bargainnier 1986; Winston and Mellerski 1992; Reiner 1978, 1981, 2000a: ch. 5; Wilson 2000: ch. 2; Leishman and Mason 2003: ch. 4). This form of narrative, in which police 'organisation men' successfully solve crimes through the bureaucratic use of routine police procedures, developed simultaneously in several media in the immediate postwar years, on both sides of the Atlantic. British examples include *The Blue Lamp/Dixon of Dock Green*, *PC 49*, *Fabian of the Yard*, *Shadow Squad/Murder Bag* and John Creasey's Inspector West and Gideon of Scotland Yard novels (the latter subsequently became a TV series and a John Ford film). The leading US examples are the 1947 movie *The Naked City* (subsequently a TV series), the novels of Lawrence Treat, Hillary Waugh and Ed McBain (Dove 1982: ch. 2), and above all *Dragnet*, originally a radio series and subsequently a pattern-setting TV series and movie. *Dragnet* inspired many imitations such as *Highway Patrol*, *Racket Squad*, *Gangbusters* and *The Untouchables*.

The emergence after the Second World War of the police procedural subgenre was the first time that police featured regularly as central characters in either print, radio or cinema fiction. However, it coincided with the advent of television as the primary entertainment medium, and police heroes have been prominent in television fiction throughout its history. There have been many studies of the television representation of the police.[3] In an earlier article I attempted to periodise the British television representation of policing as a dialectic development (Reiner 1994). Starting from the cosily consensual world of *Dixon of Dock Green* in the 1950s, the thesis, it moved through a transitional phase with a gradually hardening image in *Z-Cars* in the 1960s, to the antithesis of *The Sweeney* and its tough vigilantism in the 1970s. The synthesis of this dialectic was *The Bill*, which projected an array of contrasting images of the police from cosy community constables in the Dixon mould to tough, rule-bending Sweeney-style thief-takers. *The Bill* was also a demographic synthesis, representing the spectrum of contemporary policing in terms of gender, race, organisational specialism and rank. More broadly in the 1980s and 1990s television police series became diversified into an array of contrasting styles encapsulating the whole previous development of the genre. The range extended from the nostalgic worlds of *Heartbeat* and classic sleuth stories like *Morse*, and the Dixon-in-drag community policing of *Juliet Bravo* and *The Gentle Touch*, to Sweeney-esque crime-busters such as *Dempsey and Makepeace*.

Recently Leishman and Mason have suggested that the synthesis embodied in *The Bill* in the 1980s can be seen as the thesis of a new dialectic (2003: ch. 6). *The Bill* foreshadowed recognition of the diverse demographic make-up of contemporary police organisation and its conflict-ridden bureaucratic dimensions. This developed into a transitional stage of series featuring a diversity of police types and more politicised aspects of policing, of which *Prime Suspect* was emblematic. These explore the more problematic aspects of traditional police culture, such as gender and race discrimination. The antithesis is represented by the culmination of these trends, *Between the Lines*, which focused on a unit responsible for the investigation of police corruption and malpractice (Brunsdon 2000 is a stimulating analysis of these series). In the mid-1990s a new set of transitional series began to emerge. These echo the tensions of 'third way' crime control policy, 'tough on crime, tough on the causes of crime'. They feature protagonists who are psychologically or morally flawed or at least ambiguous, the antithesis of the overgrown boy-scout image of Dixon or Dragnet, but none the less function as effective community or crime-fighting police. Examples include *The Cops, Thief-takers* and *The Vice* or (in the USA) *NYPD Blue, Homicide* or *The Shield*. This pattern was heralded by 1970s vigilante films such as *Dirty Harry*, but the deviance of the central characters of contemporary movies often makes them seem like model citizens (King 1999 is a useful study of American cop movies since 1980). The contemporary anti-heroes are none the less courageous, resourceful, even if rule-breaking protectors of the weak and vulnerable from extremely violent crime and terrorism. Often the protagonists are forensic scientists of some kind (like *Cracker* or *CSI*), allowing a distinction between the fallibly human context of their own lives and the unsullied virtue of their security function (Brunsdon 2000: 216–17; Leishman and Mason 2003: 102–3). In Leishman and Mason's analysis, *The Bill* remains the synthesis of the dialectic. Over the course of the 1990s *The Bill*'s leading characters became increasingly flawed or even corrupt, encapsulating the gamut of deviance represented in other contemporary series (Leishman and Mason 2003: 103–4).

A more systematic analysis of the changing images of police in the media is provided by a historical content analysis of changing representations of crime and criminal justice that I conducted with Sonia Livingstone and Jessica Allen (Allen *et al.* 1998; Reiner *et al.* 2000a, 2000b, 2003). This analysed a sample of the crime films that were top box-office successes in Britain between 1945 and 1991, a random sample of crime-related stories from *The Times* and *The Mirror* in that period and the crime series that were most popular on British TV between 1955 and 1991.

The different media varied in the extent to which the police figured prominently in the stories analysed. The police typically played a minor role in cinema films until the mid-1960s. Hardly any films in our random sample between 1945 and 1965 featured police heroes, but after the late 1960s police protagonists become the most frequent type. The police have, however, always been the most common protagonists of television crime series. In the period up to 1979, 64 per cent of the top-rated TV crime series had police heroes. Although in the 1980s this fell to 43 per cent, the police remain the most frequent hero figures in TV series. In newspapers the proportion of stories which focused on policing and the criminal justice system (as distinct from specific crimes) rose in the period studied, but was always greater in *The Times* than *The Mirror*. Criminal justice stories rose from two per cent of all stories on average between 1945 and 1951 to six per cent between 1985 and 1991 in *The Mirror*, and from three to nine per cent in *The Times*. Overall the police are more frequently the central protagonists in stories in all the media now than in the immediate postwar period. The change is most marked in the cinema, and least on television, where stories have always been dominated by police heroes.

In all media the representation of the police became somewhat *less* supportive over the postwar period as a whole, although still remaining predominantly positive. However, this declining trend overall in favourable images of policing masks some important complexities. In the cinema representation of the integrity and the effectiveness of the police we found a clear curvilinear pattern. The police are presented most positively in the first part of our period, from 1945 to 1963, and most negatively in the middle, from 1964 to 1979. In the last years of our period, 1980–91, there is some slight overall improvement in the representation of police ethics and efficiency. However, this recovery is ambiguous: the total figures mask a bifurcation of images in recent years between extremely negative ones and attempts to resuscitate the earlier positive representations. In newspaper stories there is a more straightforward linear trend towards an increasingly negative portrayal of police effectiveness and integrity.

The extent to which crime is cleared up in media stories illustrates this. In cinema films the offender was brought to justice in 39 per cent of cases in 1945–64, and killed in another nine per cent. After 1965 they were brought to justice in less than 15 per cent of films, but killed in 35 per cent (Reiner *et al.* 2000a, 2000b). In press stories, the proportion of the principal crimes reported that was cleared up was 73 per cent between 1945 and 1964, 63 per cent between 1965 and 1979 and 51 per cent between 1980 and 1991 (Reiner *et al.* 2003). Thus although the broad conclusions of previous content analyses are confirmed by our study – the police are typically represented as effective in bringing offenders to justice – this is to a diminishing extent in all media.

A similar trend can be seen in representations of police malpractice. Excessive use of force by police was shown in only three per cent of films in 1945–63, but 44 per cent in 1964–79, and 25 per cent in 1980–91. Illicit investigation methods were shown in 11 per cent of films in the first period, 80 per cent in the second and 67 per cent in the third. Corruption featured in no films in our sample before 1963, 13 per cent from 1964 to 1979 and 15 per cent from 1980 to 1991. In newspaper stories there is a steady trend upwards in the representation of police deviance. Between 1945 and 1964 only 10 per cent of all crime news stories primarily concerned police deviance, but this rose to 12 per cent 1965–79 and to 19 per cent in 1981–91. The largest single category of police deviance stories reported abuse of powers (42 per cent 1945–64; 59 per cent 1965–79; 45 per cent 1981–91). Stories about race or gender discrimination by police had become the next most common by the end of the period, taking over from reports of personal corruption. Of police deviance stories, 21 per cent in 1945–64 were about personal corruption but only 14 per cent in 1981–91. The proportion of stories about discrimination in these respective periods was almost the reverse: 14 and 24 per cent (Reiner *et al.* 2003).

The personal characteristics of the police in films show the same pattern. Until 1963 no films had police protagonists whose lifestyle was deviant in any way. Between 1964 and 1979 this appeared in 33 per cent of films, but only 17 per cent from 1980 to 1991. Between 1945 and 1963, 50 per cent of police protagonists were caring and pleasant in manner; only 19 per cent from 1964 to 1979; and 39 per cent after 1980. In the earliest period only 26 per cent of police protagonists were reacted to as sexually attractive within the narrative; but this was 63 per cent in the middle period and 59 per cent after 1980. News stories about police engaged in deviant conduct short of illegality actually declined during the period studied (from 21 per cent of police deviance stories to 14 per cent), possibly because the disappearance of fictional police with boy-scout lifestyles and the generally greater social liberalism made minor police peccadilloes less newsworthy.

The overall pattern of representation of police since 1945 thus seems curvilinear. Positive images are increasingly challenged after the mid-1960s, but with some bifurcation after the early 1980s between attempts to restore the past and even more negative representations of policing as ineffective or unjust. In news stories the trend is more straightforwardly negative, with increasing proportions of stories featuring police malpractice and declining success in clearing up crime. Overall, however, the prevailing representation remains positive in all media. The characteristic portrayal of the police is as ethical and effective guardians of the public.

Conclusion: the Teflon service and the reproduction of police fetishism

Policing is at best a palliative and not a panacea for the social harms of crime, disorder and insecurity. The point was made most pithily by Raymond

Chandler in the classic 1953 crime novel, *The Long Goodbye*: 'Crime isn't a disease, it's a symptom', claims Chandler's hero, private eye Philip Marlowe. 'Cops are like a doctor that gives you an aspirin for a brain tumour' (Chandler 1977: 599). This is confirmed by most social scientific analyses of the police and policing (I have tried to summarise the arguments and evidence in Reiner 2000a). Yet there is a deeply entrenched cultural denial of this, the myth of police indispensability that I referred to earlier as 'police fetishism'. It became ingrained during the nineteenth century through an intertwined process of socioeconomic and political changes that disciplined modern societies, and the gradual legitimation of the police as the symbols of this.

As conflict in modern societies became increasingly institutionalised, and crime and disorder declined, so the police became the totems of this broader civilising process for which they tacitly gained the credit. News stories about crime testified to this. For the first two thirds of the twentieth century, crime was not seen as a major threat or policy problem. Crime stories were mainly confined to the popular press and concentrated on spectacular cases that the police were usually successful in solving. Police heroes were almost entirely absent from crime fiction, but paradoxically this implicitly assumed police success in regulating routine crime. Detective stories created a fantasy world of genteel crime in country houses. Idiosyncratic victims, perpetrators and red-herring bystanders became embroiled in puzzles that were solved by eccentric amateur or private investigators massively well endowed with what Agatha Christie's Poirot called 'little grey cells'. The tacit assumption was of a society so well ordered that the most minute deviations from routine constituted clues to crime.

After the Second World War, and particularly from the mid-1950s, crime became perceived as a growing problem, and recorded crime rates began a seemingly inexorable rise. At first this continued to be interpreted as a marginal issue that social amelioration and reformist criminal justice interventions would contain successfully. The rise of the fictional police hero suggests, however, that crime was coming to be perceived as a problem requiring the attentions of a professional bureaucracy, not enthusiastic amateurs.

After the late 1960s the conception of crime and criminal justice in political discourse and popular culture begins to change profoundly. Crime and disorder come to be seen as profound threats, to individuals and to the social fabric. The control of crime, under the new rubric of 'law and order', becomes a prominent political issue that parties contest with growing ferocity (Garland 2001; Downes and Morgan 2002). Media representations reflect and reinforce this process, as indicated above. In fiction the police are increasingly celebrated as vigilantes who must break the rules of legality to crack crime. News stories more often report police failure and police deviance. At first this was associated with considerable debate and evidence of a loss of police legitimacy in public opinion surveys.

However, in the mid-1990s there was a consolidation of policy around the conception of policing as crime control, with 'businesslike' organisation seen as the means of achieving this. Media representations reflect this in portraying the police as what Leishman and Mason graphically call 'the thin blurred line' (2003: 83). Police officers are no longer portrayed as paragons of virtue but as effective if often venal protectors of the mainstream public – 'us' – against risks posed by a variety of demonised others – 'them', including serial killers, paedophiles, international organised criminals and terrorists. If the police fail the media usually blame the thinning of the blue line: the answer is more and tougher policing. Banished from serious political and media discussion is anything beyond police fetishism, such as a consideration of what aspects of social structure and culture may contribute towards the development of the evils that threaten. The police seem to be a 'Teflon service' that has survived a long period of increasing revelations of failure and malpractice to remain a powerful political and cultural force (Reiner 2000a: 47). Although the media have increasingly highlighted scandals and controversy about policing, they have also perpetuated the myth of police fetishism. Crime and disorder are identified as the key elements of social threat, and policing solutions as the only conceivable ones. The police remain the most potent symbols of security in popular consciousness (Wilson 2000; Loader and Mulcahy 2003). Media stories of morally flawed but courageous and determined cops as shields against victimisation continue to reproduce police fetishism.

Selected further reading

As the long reference section implies, there is now an extensive literature on policing and the media. Without doubt the most useful and important single reading is the excellent new text by Leishman and Mason: *Policing the Media: Facts, Fictions and Factions* (2003), which provides a comprehensive and stimulating overview of the area. There are many articles that offer analytic accounts of the media presentation of policing, including: Clarke's ' "You're nicked!" Television police series and the fictional representation of law and order' (1992), Reiner's 'Mystifying the police: the media presentation of policing' (2000) and Brunsdon's 'The structure of anxiety: recent British crime drama' (2000). Mawby's *Policing Images: Policing, Communication and Legitimacy* (2002) is a comprehensive analysis of police use of the media to promote their image. General reviews of the research on media representation of crime and criminal justice generally are Surette's *Media, Crime and Criminal Justice* (1998), Howitt's *Crime, the Media and the Law* (1998) and Reiner's 'Media made criminality' (2002). The website for the latter (www.oup.co.uk/best.textbooks/law/maguire) contains links to a number of useful British and American websites on media, crime and policing.

Notes

1 Willis (1950) is a novelisation of *The Blue Lamp*. Several stories drawn from scripts for the television series were published as Edwards (1974). For discussions of the significance of Dixon, see Clarke (1983), Reiner (1994), Barr (1998: 80–105), Leishman and Mason (2003: 49–54).
2 These conclusions are drawn mainly from Roshier (1973), Chibnall (1977), Dominick (1978), Pandiani (1978), Garofalo (1981), Ditton and Duffy (1983), Ericson *et al.* (1987, 1989, 1991), Marsh (1991), Williams and Dickinson (1993), Lichter *et al.* (1994), Sacco (1995), Bailey and Hale (1998), Howitt (1998), Surette (1998), Reiner (2000a: ch. 5; 2002).

3 See, for example, Hurd (1979), Inciardi and Dee (1987), Buxton (1990), Laing (1991), Clarke (1982, 1983, 1986, 1992), Sparks (1992, 1993), Leishman (1995), Eaton (1996), Stead (1999), Brunsdon (2000), Reiner (1994, 2000a: ch. 5, 2000b), Leishman and Mason (2003).

References

Allen, J., Livingstone, S. and Reiner, R. (1998) 'True lies: changing images of crime in British postwar cinema', *European Journal of Communication*, 47(4): 1–13.

Arcuri, A. (1977) 'You can't take fingerprints off water: police officers' views towards "cop" television shows', *Human Relations*, 30(2): 237–47.

Bailey, F. and Hale, D. (eds) (1998) *Popular Culture, Crime and Justice*. Belmont, CA: Wadsworth.

Barclay, G. and Tavares, C. (1999) *Information on the Criminal Justice System in England and Wales. Digest* 4. London: Home Office.

Barker, M. and Petley, J. (eds) (2001) *Ill Effects: The Media/Violence Debate* (2nd edn). London: Routledge.

Barr, C. (1998) *Ealing Studios*. Moffat: Cameron & Hollis.

Black, G.D. (1994) *Hollywood Censored*. Cambridge: Cambridge University Press.

Bowling, B. and Foster, J. (2002) 'Policing and the police' in M. Maguire *et al.* (eds) *The Oxford Handbook of Criminology* (3rd edn). Oxford: Oxford University Press, 980–1033.

Boyle, R. (1999) 'Spotlighting the police: changing UK police–media relations in the 1990s', *International Journal of the Sociology of Law*, 27(2): 229–50.

Brunsdon, C. (2000) 'The structure of anxiety: recent British television crime fiction', in E. Buscombe (ed.) *British Television*. Oxford: Oxford University Press, 195–217.

Bucke, T. (1996) *Policing and the Police: Findings from the 1994 British Crime Survey*. London: Home Office.

Buxton, D. (1990) *From The Avengers to Miami Vice: Form and Ideology in Television Series*. Manchester: Manchester University Press.

Carter, C. and Weaver, C.K. (2003) *Violence and the Media*. Buckingham: Open University Press.

Chandler, R. (1977) *The Long Goodbye*. London: Heinemann (originally published 1953).

Chibnall, S. (1977) *Law-and-order News*. London: Tavistock.

Chibnall, S. (1979) 'The Metropolitan Police and the news media', in S. Holdaway (ed.) *The British Police*. London: Arnold, 135–49.

Clarke, A. (1982) *Television Police Series and Law and Order* (Popular Culture Course Unit 22). Milton Keynes: Open University.

Clarke, A. (1983) 'Holding the blue lamp: television and the police in Britain', *Crime and Social Justice*, 19: 44–51.

Clarke, A. (1986) 'This is not the Boy Scouts: television police series and definitions of law and order', in T. Bennett *et al.* (eds) *Popular Culture and Social Relations*. Milton Keynes: Open University Press, 219–32.

Clarke, A. (1992) ' "You're nicked!" Television police series and the fictional representation of law and order', in D. Strinati and S. Wagg (eds) *Come on Down? Popular Media Culture in Post-War Britain*. London: Routledge, 232–53.

Colquhoun, P. (1795) *A Treatise on the Police of the Metropolis*. London: J. Mowman.

Crandon, G. and Dunne, S. (1997) 'Symbiosis or vassalage? The media and law enforcers', *Policing and Society*, 8(1): 77–91.

Currie, E. (1998) 'Crime and market society: lessons from the United States', in P. Walton and J. Young (eds) *The New Criminology Revisited*. London: Macmillan, 130–42.

Dahrendorf, R. (1985) *Law and Order*. London: Sweet & Maxwell.

Davies, N. (1998) *Dark Heart*. London: Verso.

Ditton, J. and Duffy, J. (1983) 'Bias in the newspaper reporting of crime news', *British Journal of Criminology*, 23(2): 159–65.

Dominick, J. (1978) 'Crime and law enforcement in the mass media', in C. Winick (ed.) *Deviance and Mass Media*. Beverly Hills, CA: Sage, 105–28.

Dove, G. (1982) *The Police Procedural*. Bowling Green, KY: Popular Press.

Dove, G. and Bargainnier, E. (eds) (1986) *Cops and Constables: American and British Fictional Policemen*. Bowling Green, KY: Popular Press.

Downes, D. and Morgan, R. (2002) 'The skeletons in the cupboard: the politics of law and order at the turn of the millennium', in M. Maguire *et al.* (eds) *The Oxford Handbook of Criminology* (3rd edn). Oxford: Oxford University Press, 286–321.

Doyle, A. (1998) ' "Cops": television policing as policing reality', in M. Fishman and G. Cavender (eds) *Entertaining Crime*. New York, NY: Aldine de Gruyter, 95–116.

Eaton, M. (1996) 'A fair cop? Viewing the effects of the canteen culture in *Prime Suspect* and *Between the Lines*', in D. Kidd-Hewitt and R. Osborne (eds) *Crime and the Media: The Post-Modern Spectacle*. London: Pluto, 164–84.

Edwards, R. (1974) *Dixon of Dock Green*. London: Pan.

Emsley, C. (1996) *The English Police: A Political and Social History* (2nd edn). London: Longman.

Emsley, C. (2002) 'The history of crime and crime control institutions', in M. Maguire *et al.* (eds) *The Oxford Handbook of Criminology* (3rd edn). Oxford: Oxford University Press, 203–30.

Ericson, R., Baranek, P. and Chan, J. (1987) *Visualising Deviance*. Milton Keynes: Open University Press.

Ericson, R., Baranek, P. and Chan, J. (1989) *Negotiating Control*. Milton Keynes: Open University Press.

Ericson, R., Baranek, P. and Chan, J. (1991) *Representing Order*. Milton Keynes: Open University Press.

Fishman, M. and Cavender, G. (1998) *Entertaining Crime: Television Reality Programmes*. New York, NY: Aldine de Gruyter.

Garland, D. (1997) ' "Governmentality" and the problem of crime', *Theoretical Criminology*, 1(2): 173–214.

Garland, D. (2001) *The Culture of Control*. Oxford: Oxford University Press.

Garland, D. (2002) 'Of crime and criminals: the development of criminology in Britain', in M. Maguire *et al.* (eds) *The Oxford Handbook of Criminology* (3rd edn). Oxford: Oxford University Press, 7–50.

Garofalo, J. (1981) 'Crime and the mass media: a selective review of research,' *Journal of Research in Crime and Delinquency*, 18(2): 319–50.

Giddens, A. (1990) *The Consequences of Modernity*. Cambridge: Polity Press.

Greer, C. (2003) *Sex Crime and the Media: Sex Offending and the Press in a Divided Society*. Cullompton: Willan.

Hall, S., Critchley, C., Jefferson, T., Clarke, J. and Roberts, B. (1978) *Policing the Crisis*. London: Macmillan.

Hennigan, K.M., Delrosario, M.L., Heath, L., Cook, J.D. and Calder, B.J. (1982) 'Impact of the introduction of television crime in the United States: empirical findings and theoretical implications', *Journal of Personality and Social Psychology*, 42(3): 461–77.

Hill, A. (2000) 'Crime and crisis: British reality television in action', in E. Buscombe (ed.) *British Television*. Oxford: Oxford University Press, 218–34.

Hopkins, N. (2003) 'It's time to bring back Dixon, says Met', *Guardian*, 28 February: 15.

Howitt, S. (1998) *Crime, the Media and the Law*. London: Wiley.

Hurd, G. (1979) 'The television presentation of the police', in S. Holdaway (ed.) *The British Police*. London: Arnold, 118–34.

Inciardi, J. and Dee, J.L. (1987) 'From the Keystone Cops to Miami Vice: images of policing in American popular culture', *Journal of Popular Culture*, 21(2): 84–102.

Innes, M. (1999) 'The media as an investigative resource in murder enquiries', *British Journal of Criminology*, 39(2): 268–85.

Innes, M. (2003) *Investigating Murder*. Oxford: Oxford University Press.

Johnston, L. and Shearing, C. (2003) *Governing Security*. London: Routledge.

Jones, T. and Newburn, T. (1998) *Private Security and Public Policing*. Oxford: Oxford University Press.

King, N. (1999) *Heroes in Hard Times: Cop Action Movies in the US*. Philadelphia, PA: Temple University Press.

Laing, S. (1991) 'Banging in some reality: the original "Z-Cars"', in J. Corner (ed.) *Popular Television in Britain*. London: British Film Institute, 125–43.

Lawrence, R.G. (2000) *The Politics of Force: Media and the Construction of Police Brutality*. Berkeley, CA: University of California Press.

Leishman, F. (1995) 'On screen – police on TV', *Policing*, 11(2): 143–52.

Leishman, F., Loveday, B. and Savage, S. (eds) (2000) *Core Issues in Policing* (2nd edn). London: Longman.

Leishman, F. and Mason, P. (2003) *Policing and the Media: Facts, Fictions and Factions*. Cullompton: Willan.

Leitch, T. (2002) *Crime Films*. Cambridge: Cambridge University Press.

Lichter, R.S., Lichter, L.S. and Rothman, S. (1994) *Prime Time: How TV Portrays American Culture*. Washington, DC: Regnery.

Livingstone, S. (1996) 'On the continuing problem of media effects', in J. Curran and M. Gurevitch (eds) *Mass Media and Society*. London: Arnold, 305–24.

Livingstone, S., Allen, J. and Reiner, R. (2001) 'Audiences for crime media 1946–91: A historical approach to reception studies', *Communication Review*, 4(2): 165–92.

Loader, I. (1997) 'Policing and the social: questions of symbolic power', *British Journal of Sociology*, 48(1): 1–18.

Loader, I. and Mulcahy, A. (2001a) 'The power of legitimate naming: chief constables as social commentators in post-war England', *British Journal of Criminology*, 41(1): 41–55.

Loader, I. and Mulcahy, A. (2001b) 'The power of legitimate naming: making sense of the elite police voice', *British Journal of Criminology*, 41(2): 252–65.

Loader, I. and Mulcahy, A. (2003) *Policing and the Condition of England*. Oxford: Oxford University Press.

Marsh, H.L. (1991) 'A comparative analysis of crime coverage in newspapers in the United States and other countries from 1960–1989: a review of the literature', *Journal of Criminal Justice*, 19(1): 67–80.

Marshall, T.H. (1950) *Citizenship and Social Class*. Cambridge: Cambridge University Press.

Mathews, T.D. (1994) *Censored*. London: Chatto & Windus.

Mawby, R.C. (1999) 'Visibility, transparency, and police–media relations', *Policing and Society*, 9(3): 263–86.

Mawby, R.C. (2001) 'Promoting the police? The rise of police image work', *Criminal Justice Matters*, 43: 44–5.

Mawby, R.C. (2002a) *Policing Images: Policing, Communication and Legitimacy*. Cullompton: Willan.

Mawby, R.C. (2002b) 'Continuity and change, convergence and divergence: the policy and practice of police–media relations', *Criminal Justice*, 2(3): 303–24.

McLaughlin, E. and Murji, K. (1998) 'Resistance through representation: "storylines", advertising and Police Federation campaigns', *Policing and Society*, 8(4): 367–99.

McMullan, J. (1998) 'Social surveillance and the rise of the "police machine"', *Theoretical Criminology*, 2(1): 93–117.

Miliband, R. (1978) 'A state of desubordination', *British Journal of Sociology*, 29(4): 399–409.

Miller, D.A. (1988) *The Novel and the Police*. Berkeley, CA: University of California Press.

Miller, W. (1999) *Cops and Bobbies* (2nd edn). Columbus, OH: Ohio State University Press.

Morgan, R. and Newburn, T. (1997) *The Future of Policing*. Oxford: Oxford University Press.

Murdock, G. (1982) 'Disorderly images', in C. Sumner (ed.) *Crime, Justice and the Mass Media*. Cropwood Papers 14. Cambridge: Institute of Criminology, 104–23.

Ousby, I. (1976) *Bloodhounds of Heaven: The Detective in English Fiction from Godwin to Doyle*. Cambridge, MA: Harvard University Press.

Pandiani, J. (1978) 'Crime time TV: if all we knew is what we saw . . .', *Contemporary Crises*, 2(4): 437–58.

Pasquino, P. (1978) 'Theatrum politicum: the genealogy of capital – police and the state of prosperity', *Ideology and Consciousness*, 4(1): 41–54.

Pearson, G. (1983) *Hooligan*. London: Macmillan.

Peay, J. (1998) 'The power of the popular', in T. Newburn and J. Vagg (eds) *Emerging Themes in Criminology*. Loughborough: British Society of Criminology.

Perlmutter, D. (2000) *Policing the Media*. Thousand Oaks, CA: Sage.

Philo, G. (ed.) (1999) *Message Received*. London: Longman.

Potter, C.B. (1998) *War on Crime: Bandits, G-Men, and the Politics of Mass Culture*. Brunswick, NJ: Rutgers University Press.

Powers, R.G. (1983) *G-Men: Hoover's FBI in American Popular Culture*. Carbondale, IL: Southern Illinois University Press.

Powers, S.P., Rothman, D.J. and Rothman, S. (1996) *Hollywood's America: Social and Political Themes in Motion Pictures*. Boulder, CO: Westview Press.

Rafter, N. (2000) *Shots in the Mirror: Crime Films and Society*. New York, NY: Oxford University Press.

Rawlings, P. (1999) *Crime and Power: A History of Criminal Justice 1688–1998*. London: Longman.

Rawlings, P. (2002) *Policing: A Short History*. Cullompton: Willan.

Reiner, R. (1978) 'The new blue films', *New Society*, 43(808): 706–8.

Reiner, R. (1981) 'Keystone to Kojak: the Hollywood cop', in P. Davies and B. Neve (eds) *Politics, Society and Cinema in America*. Manchester: Manchester University Press, 195–220.

Reiner, R. (1988) 'British criminology and the state', *British Journal of Criminology*, 29(1): 138–58.

Reiner, R. (1992) 'Policing a postmodern society', *Modern Law Review*, 55(6): 761–81.

Reiner, R. (1994) 'The dialectics of Dixon: the changing image of the TV cop', in M. Stephens and S. Becker (eds) *Police Force, Police Service*. London: Macmillan, 11–32.

Reiner, R. (2000a) *The Politics of the Police* (3rd edn). Oxford: Oxford University Press.

Reiner, R. (2000b) 'Romantic realism: policing and the media', in F. Leishman *et al.* (eds) *Core Issues in Policing* (2nd edn). London: Longman, 52–66.

Reiner, R. (2001) 'The rise of virtual vigilantism: crime reporting since World War II', *Criminal Justice Matters*, 43: 4–5.

Reiner, R. (2002) 'Media made criminality', in M. Maguire *et al.* (eds) *The Oxford Handbook of Criminology* (3rd edn). Oxford: Oxford University Press, 376–416.

Reiner, R., Livingstone, S. and Allen, J. (2000a) 'Casino culture: media and crime in a winner–loser society', in K. Stenson and R. Sullivan (eds) *Crime, Risk and Justice*. Cullompton: Willan, 175–93.

Reiner, R., Livingstone, S. and Allen, J. (2000b) 'No more happy endings? The media and popular concern about crime since the Second World War', in T. Hope and R. Sparks (eds) *Crime, Risk and Insecurity*. London: Routledge, 107–25.

Reiner, R., Livingstone, S. and Allen, J. (2003) 'From law and order to lynch mobs: crime news since the Second World War', in P. Mason (ed.) *Criminal Visions: Media Representations of Crime and Justice*. Cullompton: Willan.

Rock, P. (1973) 'News as eternal recurrence', in S. Cohen and J. Young (eds) *The Manufacture of News*. London: Constable, 64–70.

Roshier, B. (1973) 'The selection of crime news by the press', in S. Cohen and J. Young (eds) *The Manufacture of News*. London: Constable, 40–51.

Sacco, V.F. (1995) 'Media constructions of crime', *The Annals of the American Academy of Political and Social Sciences*, 539(1): 141–54.

Scarman, Lord (1981) *The Scarman Report: The Brixton Disorders*. London: HMSO.

Schlesinger, P. and Tumber, H. (1994) *Reporting Crime*. Oxford: Oxford University Press.

Schramm, W., Lyle, J. and Parker, E.B. (1961) *Television in the Lives of our Children*. Stanford, CA: Stanford University Press.

Sims, L. (2003) 'Policing and the public', in C. Flood-Page and J. Taylor (eds) *Crime in England and Wales 2001/2: Supplementary Volume. Home Office Statistical Bulletin* 01/03. London: Home Office, 105–18.

Sparks, R. (1992) *Television and the Drama of Crime*. Buckingham: Open University Press.

Sparks, R. (1993) 'Inspector Morse', in G. Brandt (ed.) *British Television Drama in the 1980s*. Cambridge: Cambridge University Press.

Stead, P. (1999) ' "It's not all about nicking folks": dramatizing the police', in D.W. Howell and K.O. Morgan (eds) *Crime, Protest and Police in Modern British Society*. Cardiff: University of Wales Press, 207–37.

Surette, R. (1998) *Media, Crime and Criminal Justice* (2nd edn). Belmont, CA: Wadsworth.

Taylor, I. (1999) *Crime in Context: A Critical Criminology of Market Societies*. Cambridge: Polity Press.

Thompson, J.B. (1995) *The Media and Modernity*. Cambridge: Polity Press.

Walker, N. (1996) 'Defining core police tasks: the neglect of the symbolic dimension', *Policing and Society*, 6(1): 53–71.

Waters, I. (2000) 'Quality and performance monitoring', in F. Leishman *et al.* (eds) *Core Issues in Policing* (2nd edn). London: Longman, 264–87.

Williams, P. and Dickinson, J. (1993) 'Fear of crime: read all about it? The relationship between newspaper crime reporting and fear of crime', *British Journal of Criminology*, 33(1): 33–56.

Willis, T. (1950) *The Blue Lamp*. London: Convoy Publications.

Wilson, C.P. (2000) *Cop Knowledge: Police Power and Cultural Narrative in Twentieth Century America*. Chicago, IL: University of Chicago Press.

Winston, C.P. and Mellerski, N. (1992) *The Police Eye: Ideology and the Police Procedural*. London: Macmillan.

Young, J. (1999) *The Exclusive Society*. London: Sage.

Part III

Doing Policing

Tim Newburn

What do the police do and how has what they do changed? Part III of the handbook looks at how the police operate, ranging from crime prevention and investigation to major issues such as drugs, terrorism and organised crime. Simon Byrne and Ken Pease (Chapter 12) open this part of the book by examining the history and reality of police crime prevention activities and by considering the increasingly central role that community safety has become in local responses to crime. The police, of course, now increasingly work in 'partnership' with other bodies, particularly local authorities, in the creation of community safety audits and subsequent plans. This chapter explores the emergence of these new working structures, how they operate in practice and how best they should be understood within current theoretical frameworks. In doing so a number of important assertions are made by the authors. First, they argue that though crime reduction (their preferred term) is often assigned considerable importance within the police organisation, it generally remains of low status. Secondly, the increasing emphasis on partnership has largely been instituted as an act of faith rather than being evidence based. Thirdly, that the most appropriate role for the police in this regard should be to act as champions of evidence-based crime reduction, and to draw other organisations in to this activity where appropriate. And, finally, they quite rightly suggest that this separately and collectively represents a very significant challenge to the police and their leaders.

The gap between the rhetoric and reality of evidence-led policing is further explored by Nick Tilley (Chapter 13). Though less discussed now that at its height in the 1980s and 1990s, community policing and its variants still underpins much of what contemporary British policing aims to be: responsive to local concerns, based on consultation and problem-solving in approach. Tilley's chapter explores both the theory and the reality of community policing, and subsequent approaches such as intelligence-led and problem-oriented policing. These 'reform movements' seek to shift policing away from its traditionally reactive stance towards a mindset and a variety of practices that are more proactive and analytical. Though the emergence of the National Intelligence Model in recent years has given added impetus to the idea of intelligence-led policing, Tilley notes that attempts to implement all three models have faced very significant difficulties. Despite such barriers, all such approaches have much to commend them. In comparing and assessing the three, Tilley favours problem-oriented policing. However, he suggests that a significant move in that direction would require not only a conducive external political environment but also a revolution in terms of police culture, organisation and capacity for analysis.

Picking up this theme, Nina Cope (Chapter 14) explores the nature and use of crime analysis within the police service. She explores the major methods of crime analysis, including GIS and offender profiling, and examines the work of crime analysts within the police, and assesses their role in investigation and detection. The central assumption, and argument, of the chapter is that analysis is a potentially vital tool in modern policing but, currently, is underdeveloped and underused. There are a number of very serious barriers to greater usage of crime analysis; put basically, they concern the number of shortcomings in the data used by the police service (inconsistency, lack of timeliness and unreliability), together with the generally limited understanding of analysis by officers, and of policing by analysts.

The idea that in the early twenty-first century the police service remains some distance from being 'intelligence-led' may come as a surprise to some readers. Mike Maguire (Chapter 15) puts this into context in his chapter on criminal investigation. He opens with a historical overview of the development of criminal investigation in the late nineteenth and twentieth centuries and then moves on to examine the key features of the working practices of the three main types of detective unit through which criminal investigation was organised in the twentieth century: 'generalist' CID offices, specialist squads and ad hoc major inquiry teams. In part because of a rather inglorious recent past, peppered with allegations of corruption and malpractice, there have been significant reform attempts, both within the police service and outside, designed to restore public confidence and improve investigative practice. Though significant in themselves, Maguire argues that these changes may prefigure much more radical reform of the nature and practice of criminal investigation in years to come.

One of the other areas of police practice that has come under considerable public scrutiny in recent decades has been public order policing or, as Tank Waddington (Chapter 16) calls it, the policing of contention. Though such activities are often separated from other aspects of policing, Waddington argues that the differences are less obvious in practice. Thus, though the public image may be one of riot-gear-clad officers ducking petrol bombs, the bulk of public protests are policed by officers in normal uniforms and are accompanied by few arrests and little violence. Moreover, the term 'public order' gives a superficial coherence to a potentially very broad range of circumstances and situations. Indeed, the policing of contention, he argues, poses very real dangers to the police. In particular, they very easily become the 'meat in the sandwich' between protesters with legitimate grievances, on the one hand, and the state with its own interests on the other. A fine balancing act, he suggests, is the staple task in the policing of contention.

In a similar vein, Nigel South and Maggy Lee (Chapter 17) open their chapter by arguing that the 'policing of drugs reflects wider politics, social change and perceptions of threats to social order and everyday life'. They examine the range of policing practices from low-level drugs enforcement to the increasingly important arena of transnational policing. The history of the policing of drugs is a complex and fascinating one, and South and Lee trace this from the early twentieth century – where concerns both about servicemen and about refugees in the First World War put the issue of drug control more firmly on the official agenda – all the way through to present-day issues of 'zero tolerance', harm reduction and the links between drugs, terrorism and organised crime. The bulk of criminological literature has focused on 'good ordinary crime' and this is as true of the policing literature as any other. Far less attention has generally been paid to crimes of the suites than the crimes of the streets. The policing of organised or white-collar crime is the subject taken up by Mike Levi (Chapter 18). He outlines the institutional response to organised and financial crime, including within this the development of the National Crime Squad and the National Criminal Intelligence Service, the work of the Serious Fraud Squad as well as the increasing number of regulatory – as opposed to police – bodies that are operating in this arena.

With the increasing number and size of the scandals involving financial crime, the policing of such activities is treated with greater seriousness and accorded greater resources. Despite this, Levi argues, the relative absence of fear of white-collar crime holds back activity in this area. One area that currently stimulates considerable trepidation, and consequently much police activity, is terrorism. Intriguingly, however, as Mario Matassa and Tim Newburn note (Chapter 19), criminologists have paid relatively little attention to this area of policing and those scholars who have specialist expertise in the area of terrorism tend to pay little regard to the role of the police. In part this is because of the important role that has generally been played by the security services in response to terrorist threats. Nevertheless, as the chapter illustrates, the police have themselves had an important and relatively long-standing role in counter-terrorism, one that has provided them with vastly increased powers utilisable in everyday policing activity and not just in the terrorist arena. The future of policing in this arena – especially post 11 September – is uncertain. What seems indisputable, however, is that the subject is likely to rise further up the academic and criminological agenda.

The final subject in this part of the book (Chapter 20) concerns a relatively new area of policing activity – that connected with the policing of cybercrimes. Yvonne Jewkes, one of a small but growing band of criminologists with expertise in this area, examines the nature of cybercrimes and the nature of the police response in this area. Perhaps not surprisingly given the relative immaturity of this as a subject for police investigation and detection she concludes that we are somewhat poorly geared to deal with the apparent threats posed by Internet-based crime. In response, she suggests three potentially important responses. First, some amendment to the criminal law is required both better to define the nature of problem and to facilitate its investigation. Secondly, and echoing other chapters, she suggests that greater emphasis needs to be placed on prevention and, finally, that attention must be paid to equipping police officers with the necessary skills for work in this area. Without this, the police and other agencies are likely to be quickly outstripped by the pace of technological and social change.

Chapter 12

Crime reduction and community safety

Simon Byrne and Ken Pease

Introduction

This chapter makes four assertions about crime reduction within policing:

1. Crime reduction has hitherto not been accorded a status commensurate with the importance organisationally assigned to it. This is changing.

2. Recent legislation and guidance have led to an emphasis on partnership working as a good in itself, with too little attention being given to what has been demonstrated to be effective in crime reduction.

3. That the appropriate goal for the police is to champion evidence-led crime reduction, drawing on the resources and skills of other organisations in realising it, and where appropriate assigning responsibility to those organisations to give effect to it.

4. That this goal presents a huge challenge to police leadership.

To understand current tensions and practices within police crime reduction, we must first seek to map out the terrain, the paradoxes attending the terms used and the uncharted waters of partnership upon which policing now sails. That done, a very brief account will be given of how organisational arrangements for crime reduction have changed over time. We go on to note the current demonstrated effectiveness of some types of crime reduction, and the criminological facts with which they have to come to terms. Finally, we make suggestions about how the police service, and especially its leadership, might best respond.

Crime reduction and community safety: Tweedledum and Tweedledee?[1]

Ford Motor Company (Europe) makes and sells motor vehicles. To do this, it is organised into a variety of divisions, such as marketing, personnel and research. Each of these has a separate and clear function in ensuring that motor vehicles are produced and sold, and that successive model generations prove ever more appealing to purchasers. Eyebrows might be raised if the Ford organisation were to include a division labelled 'manufacturing and selling motor vehicles'. One would suppose that the function of such a department should permeate the entire organisation, and hence the existence of the department would be unnecessary and likely to cause confusion. Ford might just get away with a division labelled 'manufacturing and selling motor vehicles' if it reported directly to the Chief Executive Officer (or board) and dealt with company strategy.

A Ford division labelled 'manufacturing and selling motor vehicles' is no odder than a function within the police service labelled 'crime reduction'. Almost 200 years since the birth of modern policing in London, it is timely to remember that crime prevention was at the heart of what latter-day organisational gurus would describe as the mission statement of the Metropolitan Police. The enactment of the Crime and Disorder Act in 1998, and the contemporary emphasis on partnerships as the resolution of many societal problems, develops the motifs of 1829. With the inception of the Metropolitan Police and the Crime and Disorder Act 1998 bracketing nearly two centuries of professional policing, we reluctantly conclude that crime prevention has never fully permeated police thinking and practice. Neither has it enjoyed the compensating virtue of prestige and privileged access to chief officers.

Before outlining the role of crime reduction within the police service, some terms must be defined. In the UK, some police officers have carried the title 'crime prevention officers'. In recent years, the term 'crime reduction' has been favoured in government publications and on the Home Office website.[2] Individual acts of crime *prevention* result, in the aggregate, in crime *reduction*. The arrangements put in place by police and crime reduction partnerships to achieve the prevention or reduction of crime have at their heart the community safety officer within the local authority. Stopping crime is thus interchangeably referred to as preventing or reducing crime, or achieving community safety. In this chapter the terms 'crime prevention' and 'crime reduction' are preferred. The relationship between crime reduction and community safety is not straightforward. The introduction of the term 'community safety' originally provided a way of wresting ownership of discourse about crime from the police by politicians of the left (see Hughes 2002), but was much more than a political ploy. It has long been recognised that crime is a product of physical and social arrangements over which the police have little control (with a few exceptions such as making recommendations about the granting of liquor licences). Seeking to locate responsibility for crime reduction with those whose actions facilitate crime represents progress. The difficulty which we have is not with the wider permeation of responsibility for crime reduction but with the underpinning and usage of the term community safety. As one of us has argued elsewhere (Wiles and Pease 2000; Pease 2001a) the term is a misnomer, since the function as circumscribed within the Crime and Disorder Act 1998 deals only with those sources of danger which are occasioned by human agents acting criminally or in a disorderly way. This matters, in so far as it distorts recognition and prioritisation of all threats to safety which a community may encounter, and neglects the distributive justice which is appropriately achieved by the equitable sharing of unavoidable risks. Community safety is currently a function legislated *within* a Crime and Disorder Act. This is the wrong way round. Crime is only one of the things which threaten community safety. In real life, crime and disorder reduction should fit within a Community Safety Act, since the slings and arrows of outrageous misfortune include accidents, poisonings and infectious and contagious diseases as well as crime. The point is made here primarily to justify our preference for the term crime reduction in what follows, but also to highlight the dangers of using the term community safety exclusively in relation to risks occasioned by crime. There is little sign of the paradox having been recognised. People need urgent help for a variety of reasons. Rather than start with crime per se we believe it would be more useful to start with the broader issue of hazard and hazard management, of which crime and disorder are then subsets. When people dial 999, they are asked which of the emergency services they need. Urgent help is needed of various kinds. Public demand has to be quickly subdivided to make the assistance appropriate. With this limited exception, we require the public to decide who can help them before they contact a hoped-for helper. They need to decide that the police service is the best body to advise about noisy neighbours rather than environmental health or housing, that the fire service rather than the police is relevant to a wheelybin on fire and so on. This segmentation of help based upon citizen perception of the problem has many obvious disadvantages, not least that co-ordinated response to complex problems is thereby made difficult. Furthermore, while strictly outside the scope of this chapter an ill-informed public will often make the wrong choices about which service to contact, increasing demand unnecessarily, while at the same time adding to their own frustration and diminishing confidence in public services to do anything to help them as they become more confused about who does what in a segmented world. In short, characterising crime reduction as community safety unnecessarily muddies the waters of service provision. As will be argued later, it also confuses the comparison of tactics of crime reduction which are crime limited and those tactics which are likely to have other benefits.

Crime reduction within policing thus finds itself in a strange land, where a core organisational purpose has begun to escape from its peripheral position, only to be subsumed in a partnership with agencies outside the organisation, which share neither the police service's informing ideologies nor its emphasis on immediate action. We now briefly outline the history of crime prevention within the police service to clarify some current issues.

Crime reduction within the police service: aspirations and achievements

We can address the status and development of crime reduction within the police service by considering the infrastructure of and perceived responsibility for crime reduction. These two aspects are obviously linked. The infrastructure is a product of the perceived responsibility, lagging somewhat as the latter changes.

For the purposes of this chapter, the starting line is taken to be the point at which crime prevention took upon an independent existence within police forces, in the mid-1960s. In 1965, the Cornish Committee on the Prevention and Detection of Crime reported (Home Office 1965; and see Weatheritt 1986). By 1965, a few forces had already established crime prevention sections, typically within CID. The Cornish Committee contended that expertise in security hardware and crime prevention publicity was now such as to demand specialist officers keep abreast of developments. The committee recommended that an officer of at least inspector rank should be designated force crime prevention officer, with sergeants on each division assigned to carry out security surveys and liaise with patrol officers. The year 1967 saw the establishment of the Home Office Standing Committee on Crime Prevention, as recommended by Cornish, who also recommended the setting up of crime prevention panels in all towns with a population of more than 150,000. The extent to which these local bodies were formed and became active varied hugely by police force area.

Until the mid-1990s, the status of crime prevention relative to general policing was mirrored by their respective training bases. Senior officers and those on high-prestige specialist courses would find themselves at Bramshill, a stunningly beautiful Tudor mansion in rural Hampshire, once offered to the Duke of Wellington for services to the nation. Trainee crime prevention officers, by contrast, would find themselves in a Portakabin behind Staffordshire Police Headquarters, being lectured to predominantly by business people who stood to gain commercial advantage as providers of products to the police service. In 1986, Mollie Weatheritt suggested that the role of the crime prevention officer was seen as a fairly undemanding pre-retirement placement for CID officers:

> Until recently, when the figure has fallen to about fifteen years, the average length of service of constables and sergeants attending the basic training course for newly appointed crime prevention officers at the Crime Prevention Centre was twenty years, just five years short of the period at which police officers become eligible for pensionable retirement on half pay (pp. 49–50).

Research some years later reinforced Weatheritt's picture, although it showed a migration from CID to community liaison as the headquarters line of responsibility for such work (Grimshaw et al. 1989). This suggests that within the police service at that time, the emphasis was moving from 'locks, bolts and bars' to engagement with the community. This is noteworthy since this was the period at which from the Home Office perspective, at least, the stress on target-hardening was in its pomp. It is more comprehensible given the emphasis on crime control through community engagement by the most influential chief constable of his generation, John Alderson (see Alderson 1979).

The somewhat modest reality described by Weatheritt and later by Grimshaw and her colleagues diverged grotesquely from the aspirations for the crime prevention officer. A working party of the Association of Chief Police

Officers (ACPO) in 1979, unpublished but extensively reported in Weatheritt (1986: 13–14), summarised the tasks which should fall to the crime prevention officer as follows:

a. the cultivation of a working two-way relationship between beat patrol officers and the crime prevention officer, and the encouragement of all officers to report matters of crime prevention interest;

b. the acquisition of a thorough knowledge of technical aids to security, by study of appropriate journals and visits to manufacturers of locks, safes etc.;

c. the inspection of property where there are special or difficult security features: and the keeping of records of such visits to enable follow-up visits to be made at appropriate times;

d. maintaining a firm relationship with local authorities and all their bodies to whom advice can be given on crime prevention;

e. the giving of talks to local bodies on crime prevention and personal protection, and the giving of advice to householders on request or whenever the opportunity arises;

f. ensuring that crime prevention literature is used to its best effect and displayed or distributed on all appropriate occasions: the crime prevention officer should always have available a collection of physical protection devices for selective display;

g. the regular giving of lectures at probationer and refresher courses and the issue of a crime prevention booklet for the guidance of all members of the force;

h. to support and liaise with other departments of the force in the task of community relations and preventive policing and to co-operate with social agencies concerned with the welfare of children and young persons;

i. to co-operate and liaise with the security industry, and with fire prevention officers, to ensure that security standards do not conflict with fire safety requirements;

j. to give advice on security to builders and architects in the planning stages of buildings, and if necessary survey premises from plans; to maintain liaison with architects and local authority planning departments;

k. to encourage the activities of crime prevention panels;

l. to prepare articles for inclusion in local publications and newspapers in collaboration with the force public relations officer.

Despite all the changes since 1979, the flavour of crime prevention officer (CPO) work remains recognisable from the list. Subsequent changes have had less effect on the routines implied by the list than might have been supposed, apart from providing the crime reduction officer with a new raft of colleagues within local authorities and elsewhere. More recently the Audit Commission (1999) found on average only one per cent of officers working full time on crime prevention activities, which seems extraordinarily modest in relation to the tasks enumerated above. As late as 1998, commentators could refer to crime prevention in the delivery of modern policing as a 'Cinderella of police work' (see Hough and Tilley 1998). Yet the kudos attending crime reduction has increased. Contemporary crime reduction officers belie the stereotype of the 'one-eyed, tired pre-retirement bobby', although to this day a background in crime reduction is not what the most able and/or ambitious officer would choose to facilitate progress up the greasy pole to chief officer rank, compared to (for example) experience as a detective.

But things are changing. In the late 1990s West Yorkshire Police began setting questions about community safety as part of its process of selection for promotion (see Audit Commission 1999), thus reinforcing its importance in the corporate mindset of aspiring leaders. An increasing number of forces now second middle-ranking officers to local authority and other strategic posts to help lead and co-ordinate the policing and crime reduction agenda. As a third marker of the somewhat enhanced status of crime reduction, in 1995 training moved to the Crime Prevention College in Easingwold, North Yorkshire, where it is better resourced and correspondingly more professional. At the time of writing, the training of crime reduction officers seems likely to be moved again, this time to Bramshill. While this can rightly be heralded as a tardy recognition of the importance of crime reduction, it is perhaps ironic that the Easingwold facility will now concentrate on the training in crime reduction of local authority community safety officers and other, non-police personnel. Thus, while the rhetoric emphasises partnership, the separation of training is about as geographically great as is possible within England and Wales.

If there remains a circumscribed and low-status role for crime reduction in the police hierarchy, albeit one which is being remedied slowly and in piecemeal fashion, to what should we ascribe this state of affairs? It is too easy to describe anything as a consequence of police 'culture', but it is unarguable that the wish for thrill and attention seeking is one element of the attractiveness of police work, fuelled by media representations of the service (see Chapter 11). Front-line officers often derive more satisfaction from arresting offenders and detecting crimes, which inevitably have victims and consequences, rather than preventing the commission of crime and disorder in the first place. This predilection for prevention and reduction *through detection* is paradoxical, since a preventable crime has taken place, before detection becomes relevant.

Published in 1996, *Towards 2000*, the ACPO strategy for crime prevention in the twenty-first century, saw prevention as the responsibility of all officers (see Leishman *et al.* 2000). New styles of policing are only now starting to emerge based upon leadership, ownership and accountability for enhanced levels of performance at a 'neighbourhood' level. This evolution of what has previously been described as 'community policing' is more consistent with modern government doctrine for public service delivery where the responsibility for action and decision-making is pushed to the lowest possible level (see Office of Public Services Reform 2002). In this new model of policing, constables, sergeants and inspectors are wrestling with the thorny issues of crime reduction and are slowly changing the craft of street policing from a focus almost exclusively on enforcement and detection to that of sustainable reductions in crime and disorder through prevention and problem-solving (see Chapter 13). This of course brings opportunities for attendant improvements to the quality of life of residents in local neighbourhoods. These same people, victims, witnesses and informants, may come to know the name of their neighbourhood officer and believe that they care and indeed act in relation to their neighbourhood problems. This sea change in policing style is doubtless complemented by a focus on problem-solving as a way of doing business rather than concentrating on responding to incidents. There is also as an emerging recognition that it lends itself neatly to the tactical delivery of crime and disorder reduction partnership strategies in particular and neighbourhood renewal in general.

Are there any other reasons, beyond officers' lust for excitement, why crime reduction's moment is arriving so tardily within the police organisation? One contributory reason is surely the historic emphasis on offenders rather than presenting opportunities. If crime is simply the natural work of evil or damaged people, then convicting and incapacitating evil and damaged people lies at the heart of police work. For those of the left politically, the emphasis is on damage, occasioned through deprivation of one kind or another. Marcus Felson (1994) refers to this as the 'pestilence fallacy', which asserts that bad things come from other bad things. He writes:

> Why then do the most prosperous nations of the world ... have high property crime rates? Why do the poor nations of the world have generally low property crime rates? ... Why was the major period of crime rate increase in the United States 1963 to 1975, also a period of healthy economic growth and relatively low unemployment? Why did Sweden's crime rates increase greatly as its Social Democratic government brought more and more programmes to enhance equality and protect the poor? (pp. 11–12).

Felson concludes 'crime seems to march to its own drummer', and that the richness of crime opportunities is the crucial factor determining the beat. This is a conclusion of fundamental importance for crime reduction, suggesting that the regulation of the supply of crime opportunities is central to the reduction enterprise. Over the past 25 years or so there has been a gradually increasing recognition of the possibilities offered by focusing on criminal events rather than on offenders (Gilling 1997; Crawford 1998). In parallel with this, and in our view relatively unmindful of the developments within criminology, the responsibility for crime reduction has been diffused from the police into local crime and disorder reduction partnerships.

The coming of partnership?

The point at which the primary responsibility for crime reduction began to move from the police service will be dated by most observers to the publication of the Morgan Report (Standing Conference on Crime Prevention 1991), although the rhetoric of crime prevention had been settled along the same lines much earlier, for instance in the unnumbered Home Office circular *Crime Prevention*, issued on 17 May 1968. It is very evident in the identically titled Home Office Circular 8/84. Its emergence as an idea whose time has come is well documented in Koch (1998) and Newburn (2003). The starting point, fully formed in the Morgan Report, was that it was inappropriate for the police to 'own' the crime problem, and with it information about crime and disorder. Local authorities have many relevant powers, in relation to planning, tenancies, leisure and education, all of which impact on the development of criminal inclinations and their realisation in action. Morgan proposed that local authorities assume statutory responsibility for 'community safety'. This was from the beginning of the process, marked by the publication of the Morgan Report, conceived narrowly as meaning safety from *criminal* predation. While seven years elapsed between the publication of the Morgan Report and legislative action, during that period the Labour Party made clear its intention of give effect to its central recommendation once in power, and many local authorities acted in anticipation of that.

A variant of the central Morgan proposal was realised by the Crime and Disorder Act 1998. It gave statutory responsibility to local crime and disorder reduction *partnerships*, comprising police and local authority acting jointly. Partnerships are required by the legislation to prepare crime audits every three years, to consult with citizens and to devise local strategies reflecting audits and consultation.[3] This approach sidestepped the issue of a 'lead' agency in crime prevention. The government was not persuaded by the Morgan view that giving local authorities lead responsibility would be workable in practice. Its views, rather, were that the 'principles of partnership' required collective responsibility. Consequently, the responsibility now lies jointly with the relevant senior police officer and the relevant local authority. Perhaps the most important element of the Act is s. 17, which imposes a statutory duty on local authorities to consider the crime consequences of all their decisions, and has potentially profound implications (Moss and Pease 1999).

Garland (2000) speculates on the origins of notions of preventive partnership, and emphasises the profundity of changes which must yet occur for their intended level of joint responsibility to be fully realised. In brief, his analysis contends that we find ourselves in societies where high rates of crime are perceived to be normal, and that one part of the response of central government to this perception has been to divert from itself and diffuse throughout society the responsibility for reducing crime. Garland is persuasive about the degree of change which such diversion implies:

> ... the key question relates to [the preventive partnership's] ability to mobilize a new rationality of crime control – a new way of thinking and acting that differs quite radically from previous modes of crime control.

Preventive partnerships involve a whole new infrastructure of arrangements whereby state and non-state agencies co-ordinate their practices in
order to enhance community safety through the reduction of criminal
opportunities and the extension of crime-consciousness ... This strategy
also entails a set of criminological assumptions ... a style of governance
... and a repertoire of techniques and knowledges, all of which are quite
novel and at variance from the previously established ways of thinking
and acting (2000: 349).

Central government shaping of the crime reduction landscape

Alongside the diffusion of responsibility for crime reduction comes what
Garland (2000) terms a 'sovereign state strategy' stressing enhanced control.
Certainly an important strand in the emerging crime reduction infrastructure
has been the efforts of central government to steer the enterprise in directions
of which it approves. A number of phases in this effort will illustrate the trend.
The first is experience of the Home Office's crime reduction initiative around
the turn of the century. The second is the regionalisation of Home Office
influence on the practice of crime reduction.

In the Home Office's £400 million crime reduction initiative launched in
1999, the distribution of the available funding reflects Home Office priorities
by offence type and tactics to be deployed. Most dramatic was the £150 million
earmarked for CCTV systems. To oversimplify, whatever the presenting crime
problem, 40 per cent of the answer was deemed to be CCTV. Gossip held that
this resulted from a particular enthusiasm (not evidence based) of the
Financial Secretary for the Treasury at the time. Apocryphal though it
probably is, the currency of this story illustrates a willingness to believe that
crime reduction priorities danced to the Treasury tune, and begat cynicism
(among the successful bidders) and bitterness (among those who failed). The
second author has been called upon from time to time to act as referee for
community safety organisers applying for jobs in other areas or of other kinds.
Without exception, the successes to which their CVs call attention lie in the
amount of money attracted from central government, seldom if ever the
success which such money yielded under their stewardship in reducing crime.
In the beauty contest in which they saw themselves as competing, victory
consisted in garnering money, not spending it to good effect. The form which
the process of granting money under the crime reduction programme took
illustrates perfectly the balance between central direction and devolved
responsibility. Area-based bids for funding were invited, which were judged
by central government (on criteria which included a local partnership
element). Central government also funded the evaluation of outcomes. Thus
the raft of initiatives which sprang up was shaped by central government, but
failure could be assigned to local implementation.

The second recent development worth mentioning here is the regionalisation
of community safety funding. The appointment of regional crime directors and
their fast-increasing influence serve to allow central government fuller control
of the crime reduction enterprise. The location of such directors within an
organisational context which is primarily economic has also served to favour

the perception of economic development as a crime control strategy, despite the tenuousness (and complex nature) of the link between crime and areal economic indicators (Field 1998). Regional directors as conduits for central government funds allow a degree of central oversight of local partnerships which was not hitherto possible, and favour community development re- sponses to crime problems at the expense of more focused situational or design factors. One such director is located in each of the ten regional government offices. They are either civil servants or former police officers (typically assistant chief constables). Because of their role in allocating funds, their frequent meetings with Home Office ministers and their increased control of evaluative functions, the role has clearly increased in influence and importance.[4]

The developments listed above are illustrations of Garland's point that central control of the crime reduction agenda is maintained despite the diffusion of responsibility. The sacking in 2001 of the Chief Constable of Sussex, Paul Whitehouse, under pressure from a new Home Secretary seemed like a statement of intent about the limits of police operational independence. The *Police Reform* white paper of 2001, and the debate which followed it, also reflects intensified concern with the balance of local and central power (see Chapters 5 and 24). While crime reduction forms only a minor part of the more general debate about policing, the trends illustrated suggest that it is the bell-wether of central government shaping of force policy – a point not lost in the direction and impetus given to contemporary efforts to reduce street crime in a number of the larger forces.

The final strand of central government prescription and direction is evident in the recently published and first-ever National Policing Plan for England and Wales (see Home Office 2002). It is a bold attempt at co-ordination and clarity and has already prompted much debate among senior police professionals about the extent to which this plan strikes a balance between government intervention and direction with devolution of authority and resources and the unique nature of the local context of policing. Of greater relevance to this chapter is the absence of any explicit reference to crime reduction in the plan. What are the implications of the National Policing Plan for the issues outlined here? First, there will be a record number of police officers on our streets by 2004. Secondly, guardianship of public space will be enhanced by the presence of community support officers and ultimately in some areas, police-accredited staff employed in local warden schemes, etc. (see Chapter 7). The proliferation of quasi-police officers bespeaks the progressive incorporation of the policing function within a wider local partnership setting, albeit within a framework chosen by the Home Office.

Love and loathing in the age of partnerships

It seems almost heretical to aver that partnership working is not always appropriate and brings its own disadvantages. In practice it seems extremely patchy in its implementation, with health authorities being particularly disinclined to become fully involved (see Phillips *et al.* 2002), and data exchange between partners proving very contentious (Moss and Brookes 2003). Michael Scott (2000), writing as a former US police chief and an experienced criminological researcher, notes more problems. Reviewing 20 years of problem-oriented policing, he describes instances in the USA where non-police agencies have so absorbed a police agenda as to act oppressively, including the deployment of physical force against putative offenders. He prefers to advocate not partnership but agencies acting in ways in which they are mandated to, guided by a shared crime reduction agenda. He sees collaboration in the choice of ways in which contributing agencies perform those actions which they traditionally saw as their responsibility. Like Garland, but with the added weight of the practitioner behind his words, he sees even the limited collaboration which he prefers as representing such a change of focus that it has proven much easier to implement for limited periods in small areas than as an ongoing mode of working more generally.

Frustrations with the experience of partnership working are not adequately reflected in the literature on the topic. Most Home Office publications on the topic are remarkably anodyne in tone, and are focused upon how to get partnerships to work, almost irrespective of the partners involved, or their possible contributions to crime reduction (see, for example, Bullock *et al.* 2000; Hester 2000; Hedderman and Williams 2001). The balance of the published output of the Home Office's Research and Statistics Directorate is moving towards notions of good practice whose quality is not evidenced by demonstrated crime reductions. There now exists a separate publication series reporting this kind of work. There is certainly a place for such reports, but the genre is threatening to become co-terminous with the official literature on the topic. More central questions about our criminological preconceptions and what has been shown to work in crime reduction need to be asked.

In our experience, common police frustrations with the partnership experience include the following:

- A high ratio of talk to action.

- Lengthy delays between decisions to act and action.

- Varying enthusiasm for partnership working among local authority departments, with 'people-processing' departments generally more keen than those who make physical changes.

The third issue may be of particular importance. In so far as (for example) probation and social service departments play a full role in crime reduction, and housing, health and direct works (for example) do not, the profile of crime reduction work in an area will take on a particular shape, irrespective of evidence about effectiveness. This is the fate which we envisage for partnership working in crime reduction, alias community safety.

How does one think about crime reduction?

As trailed at the end of the preceding section, there is a danger of the crime reduction enterprise being shaped by the preferences and prejudices of those most eager to be engaged in partnership working. For that reason, we need to be explicit about what we know. To rehearse a point made earlier, crime reduction is taken to be aggregated crime prevention. Installing an immobiliser on one's car is crime prevention. The cumulative effect of people installing immobilisers is crime reduction. Prevention (in the aggregate reduction) involves securing the non-occurrence of something that may otherwise have happened. While some would argue that this makes the measurement of prevention impossible, the difficulties are no greater than in medicine, where preventive medicine requires disease not to develop after an intervention which occurs in its absence.

One lesson from preventive medicine is the crucial importance of seeking to understand the mechanism by which a disease (or crime) manifests itself. The physician John Snow showed that the link between cholera sufferers in a London epidemic was the well from which they drew their drinking water (see Gilbert 1958; Tufte 1983). This identifies the disease agent as water-borne, and was the first step in understanding the mechanism of cholera transmission. Sometimes the mechanism is context specific, so that (for example) hydrangeas bloom in different colours depending upon soil acidity. Crime is a product of interacting social conditions, context, time, genetic factors predisposing to criminality and opportunities to commit crime. There are thus multiple means whereby the path leading to the crime event may be blocked.

This is reflected in Paul Ekblom's model representing the conjunction of criminal opportunity (Ekblom 2000).[5] He sees his framework as the 'universal story' of the criminal event, a development of the routine activities approach of Marcus Felson (1994). An *offender* who is prepared and able to commit a crime seeks out or engineers a crime *situation*. This combines a vulnerable and attractive *target* of crime, in a favourable *environment* and in the absence of capable *preventers*. Ekblom's framework distinguishes remote causes and immediate precursors, with 11 generic kinds of cause. These may be primarily concerned with the situation which an offender encounters, characteristics of the offender or some combination of the two. Each element may be thought of both as a remote cause and an immediate precursor. In a pub argument, the immediate precursor is a glass which can be broken to make a weapon. The remote causes entail the resistance of breweries to introduce glasses which fragment rather than leaving sharp edges, or licensing magistrates to control pubs whose poor management is reflected in frequent disorder. Likewise, an offender's lack of skills may be immediate or remote. Remote causes include the lack of educational or technical skills conferring employability. Immediate precursors may reflect an inability to talk one's way out of a conflict. The Ekblom framework helps crime reduction practitioners envisage, communicate and implement specific interventions, and to integrate approaches.

What works?

At the stage of evaluation, the characterisation of crime reduction as community safety comes back to haunt one. This is because the more remote the cause addressed (in Ekblom's terms) – i.e. the more distant from the denial of crime opportunities – the more likely an initiative is to have other benefits.

Community safety, in its restricted, crime reductive usage, invites evaluation exclusively in crime reductive terms. This is not reasonable. It is not fair to judge (for example) education enrichment programmes on the basis of crime reduction benefits alone. Let us take as an example the most famous such programme, the Perry Preschool programme (Schweinhart *et al.* 1993). The assertion tested was that a good preschool programme can help children in poverty make a better start in life. Children aged 3–4 were assigned randomly to a group which received the programme and a group which did not. At age 27, the group receiving the preschool intervention had half the arrests of the control group. However, they also had almost three times the level of home ownership, a higher level of education and fewer had received welfare benefits during their adult lives. Thus the apparent effects of preschool education on adult criminality were only one element in a much wider range of benefits.

Put briefly, programmes which impact on a wide range of human behaviour should be assessed using criteria which reflect that width. The caveat is that, just because a programme addresses a remote 'cause' of crime, it cannot be assumed that it would prove successful *in any terms*. This is both because remote causes of crime are based more on assertion than evidence (see, for example, Rich Harris 1998), and because stating a rationale is far easier than making a difference. Merely invoking preschool disadvantage as a programme's rationale will not guarantee its success.

Scott (2000) notes the continued seductive appeal of the police-led drug education programme DARE, in the face of repeated negative outcome evaluations. Scott argues that this is because of its benign effects on police image. Some evidence from the Sure Start programme in the UK throws up disturbing evidence about programme implementation problems and lack of clarity in conception (see Smithson 2002). This is perhaps reflected in the general paucity of demonstrations of the efficacy of correctional programmes (see Farrington 2000), and in the annual publications of statistics which tabulate the almost complete predictability of rates of reconviction on the basis of age and previous convictions.

To summarise our position:

- Early intervention programmes can impact upon a range of measures of quality of life, and to consider them alongside situational measures of crime reduction is unfair on both: on early intervention because it narrows its evaluated impact to crime reduction, and on situational measures because, by setting them alongside an enterprise which is palpably worthy in terms of the realisation of human potential, makes situational prevention seem overly narrow and amoral.

- Some programmes will flourish less because of their impact than their image, and the reflected glory on those who seek to implement it. In such a case, implementation failure is almost certain, since what drives the development of such programmes is not outcome linked.

So what is the well intentioned police officer to do? As citizen, he or she has good reason to argue for well designed early intervention programmes. Such intervention in the early childhood of offenders in due course may reduce levels of crime (Farrington and Welsh 1999), but more importantly will enrich the quality of life of those undergoing it. It does not need to be justified in terms of crime reduction. There has been a process in recent decades often referred to as the criminalisation of social policy, whereby measures of crime are taken to be central in judging the efficacy of social policy. In our view, re-badging crime reduction as community safety is one means whereby this pernicious process is advanced.

Interventions in the lives of those already embarked upon a criminal career seem to be less profitable than good early intervention in reducing levels of crime (Goldblatt and Lewis 1998; Sherman *et al.* 1998), so the police officer as citizen should not feel impelled to advocate such programmes. As police officer, he or she should demand evidence for the likely success of correctional elements in community safety programmes. To overstate the case, one often feels in meetings to decide a local strategy that a balance is sought between situational change elements (which have a good chance of being successful) and offender change elements (which on the evidence have much less chance). The balance achieved locally may therefore be between the effective and the ineffective.

The question which remains for day-to-day policing is whether opportunity reduction measures and short-run community initiatives really can be effective in preventing crime. The bulk of *policing* decisions in crime reduction will centre on such techniques.

Ekblom's distinction between remote and immediate precursors of crime is accepted, with most policing decisions concerning immediate precursors. However, the oft-made distinction between social and situational crime prevention is explicitly rejected. Even the crudest target-hardening techniques operate through social mediators. An impregnable door lock makes no difference if the intending burglar is confident that no one will intervene when hearing him break a window to gain entry. A robber will not proceed if an intended victim is seen as too powerful (or too poor). As will be seen later, even some interventions which look as though they work in simple opportunity reduction ways, in fact operate otherwise.

There are enough successful case studies of situational prevention to inspire confidence that such an approach will confer worthwhile levels of crime reduction, even before early interventions along the lines of the Perry Preschool Project are implemented and come to have their effect. Since we have already been waiting nearly 40 years for an adequate UK replication of the Perry project, this is just as well for our hopes of success in prevention. The upcoming evaluation of the Home Office's reducing-burglary initiative is likely to conclude that the target-hardening of the homes of the vulnerable was the tactic which yielded the most obvious successes, and work in preparation by Guerette and Clarke will demonstrate that increased attention to the security of automated teller machines (ATMs) in New York and Los Angeles was associated with reductions in crime associated with them.

Intelligently conceived and implemented situational prevention is typically successful in reducing crime. Such a claim is invariably followed by the sceptic's assertion that crime prevented by situational means simply goes

Table 12.1 The 16 techniques of primary prevention

Increasing the effort	Increasing the risks	Reducing the reward	Removing excuses
Target hardening Steering locks Anti-robber screens	*Entry/exit screening* Baggage screening Merchandise tags	*Target removal* Keep car in garage Removable car radio fascia	*Rule-setting* Customs declaration Hotel registration
Access control Entryphones Computer passwords	*Formal surveillance* CCTV Automatic number plate recognition	*Identify property* Product serial numbers Vehicle licence plate	*Stimulating conscience* Roadside speed displays Drink-drive campaigns
Deflecting offenders Cul-de-sacs Routing away fans at soccer matches	*Employee surveillance* Park wardens Club door staff	*Removing inducements* Rapid repair of damaged property Removing graffiti	*Controlling disinhibitors* Drinking age laws Parental controls on Internet
Controlling means Weapons availability Photographs on credit cards	*Natural surveillance* Street lighting Windows	*Rule setting* Tenancy agreements Software copyright agreement before installation	*Facilitating compliance* Fine deduction from salary Ample litter bins

Source: Clarke (1997).

somewhere else to happen (displacement). The research simply does not show this to be the case to such an extent as to offset preventive effects (see, for example, Hesseling 1994). Indeed in some cases the opposite of displacement (known as diffusion of benefits) occurs instead (an account of these matters and references to other work can be found in Pease 2002).

A classification of situational prevention approaches was developed by Ron Clarke and Ross Homel (Clarke 1992; Clarke and Homel 1997) and is reproduced as Table 12.1 in summarised form. It is included here because it is influential and because it provides real-life examples. Two common misconceptions are dispelled by it. That primary prevention equates to:

1. target-hardening; and

2. physical intervention.

Only one of the 16 alternatives distinguished in Table 12.1 involves target-hardening. Many alternatives clearly operate through a change in perception. Natural surveillance works in so far as the offender's calculation of risks and rewards is modified. Access control by badge only works when someone responds to someone else's lack of a badge.[6] Table 12.1 makes it clear that primary crime prevention is concerned with *all* the circumstances surrounding the crime event, and their manipulation to remove crime opportunities.

Situational prevention is particularly desirable in that it is less intrusive than programmes directed at offenders or those deemed to be on the threshold of offending. One of the most universal facts about crime is its age and gender profile. In virtually all countries studied, those officially processed for offending are disproportionately male and disproportionately young. Moffitt (2003) distinguishes life-course persistent offenders from adolescent-limited offenders. The latter are distinguishable in that they will desist from crime in their late teens and early twenties. For them, the task is to so order society that they reach the age of 24 having done least harm and having suffered least damage, both self-inflicted and through criminal justice. Designing out the immediate precursors of crime is perhaps the most obvious means of achieving this end. For life-course persistent offenders, this is less relevant. So, if situational prevention is the most desirable strategy, how should it be focused?

Where to concentrate crime reduction effort: hotspots and repeat victimisation

Crime is heavily concentrated on particular areas, and within them on particular locations and people. Some US communities have homicide rates 20 times higher than the average (Sherman *et al.* 1995). In England and Wales, 32 (of 376) crime reduction partnerships account for half the robberies committed nationally. Within an area, crime clusters at 'hotspots' (see Sherman *et al.* 1989; Sherman 1995). Some locations are long-standing hotspots (Spelman 1995). Intervention there makes sense in that crime will be high in the future, as it was in the past. Some hotspots are time limited, however, bringing the danger that resources are wasted (Townsley and Pease 2002). The danger is that overuse of hotspot analysis will yield many transient hotspots for each stable hotspot. We are aware of the practice of requiring the nomination of a given number of hotspots for tasking and co-ordination purposes. We are also aware that, since police presence is a desideratum for local politicians, each councillor will become exercised by the absence of a local hotspot. Politically, every ward should have one so that the councillor can point to increased police presence on local streets. This is linked to the problem about whether it is reasonable to focus exclusively on stable hotspots (at least until they cool down) or to some extent on areas which are unusually hot relative to their own (generally cool) climate. This we call the 'winter in Florida, summer in Alaska' problem. If you go purely on temperature, you always attend to Florida rather than Alaska. However, if you are influenced by whether the temperature is unusual, you give attention to Alaska during its summer, even if it remains colder than Florida throughout the year. Nor can we rely on police officers' awareness of hotspots, since this is surprisingly poor (Ratcliffe and McCullagh 2001).

Despite the problems in practice, crime mapping is perhaps *the* growth industry in criminology (see, for example, Weisburd and McEwen 1998; Harries 1999; Hirschfield and Bowers 2001; Murray *et al.* 2001; see Chapter 14). Like all fashions, it should be looked at with circumspection (Pease 2001b).

There will be a step change in the utility of mapping when it becomes prospective – that is, when it plots tomorrow's crimes rather than yesterday's. Lest this sound fanciful, Groff and La Vigne (2002) review attempts to move in that direction, and in the UK, Kate Bowers and Shane Johnson are approaching the problem from a distinctive perspective, based upon their analyses of crime spates within small areas.

Concentration at the personal or household level is known as repeat victimisation (see Farrell and Pease 2001). For some offences (pre-eminently domestic violence), preventing repeat crimes against the same target prevents most crime of the type. This is less obvious but also true for crime types like commercial burglary (see Mirrlees-Black and Ross 1995). Two per cent of manufacturers suffer a quarter of the burglaries. Domestic burglary (Shaw and Pease 2000), bank robberies (Matthews *et al.* 2001) and racial attacks (Sampson and Phillips 1992) also conform to the pattern. Many repeats happen within days or weeks of the preceding crime, suggesting that precautions to prevent repeats should be put in place quickly. The prevention of repeat victimisation may prove a cost-efficient strategy of crime prevention generally, the more so since it seems to be predominantly prolific offenders who return to the same household or victim (Everson 2000; Everson and Pease 2001).

What to do

The literature on hotspots and repeat victimisation suggests where and when to prioritise crime reductive effort, but what works? The debate in situational prevention has moved from 'does it work?' to 'how can we make it work quickly and cheaply?' The police officer does not lack sources of advice, the largest source in the UK being the Home Office crime reduction website. This comprises a 'knowledge base', 'toolkits' (evaluated best practice), a discussion forum, strategy statement and so on.[7] There are other websites of both British and North American origin also offering crime reduction advice.[8] Of these, the COPS guides deserve special mention as clearly written by those whose experience includes that as a police officer. Two volumes (Clarke 1992, 1997) detail successful situational initiatives. These show the range of approaches that work, the common factor being the meshing of mechanism and context. Helpful as these are, a further frustration is often getting crime preventers to use such libraries of good practice. This raises further questions about (1) how we share knowledge in the first place; and (2) how we ensure adherence to what works at a strategic and tactical level. This is an issue for police leaders and is expanded upon later.

It was contended above that, while making opportunity-limiting changes to situations will reduce crime, the mechanism can be more subtle than might appear at first sight. One such illustration of the point concerns lighting. The obvious mechanism by which lighting enhancement works concerns an area's surveillability in the dark. Accordingly, lighting's effectiveness was for a long time judged in terms of changes in night/day ratios in crime. Lights make a difference only in the dark, so their crime reductive effects should be limited to the hours of darkness. It turns out that lighting effects in crime reduction are evident in the day as well, so one has to think in terms of changes in resident confidence, or use of the street throughout the day and night, or some similar mechanism. The lighting example is instructive in that even the most obvious mechanism might not be the correct one (Pease 1999).

Over the last two years, evidence has begun to be reported to suggest that very many situational measures, as for lighting, do not work in the way we would like to think they do. In some 40 per cent of published case studies reporting crime prevention success, the success occurred too soon to have been a product of the obvious situational change (Smith *et al.* 2002). This is a staggering proportion and should be enough to give pause to those who regard situational crime prevention as simple (not to say simple minded). The most obvious reason for these 'anticipatory benefits' involves pre-launch publicity. Sallybanks (2000) shows that during a period of deployment of decoy vehicles[9] in Stockton-on-Tees there was a small reduction in vehicle theft. When the vehicles were withdrawn but the initiative was publicised, the reduction of vehicle theft, relative to surrounding areas, was much greater. Thus publicity seemed to work better than actually deploying decoy vehicles. Information exchange by word of mouth is a major feature of offending groups. Manipulating these through viral marketing is a legitimate crime reduction tactic, so far woefully neglected. Anticipatory effects seem to be particularly characteristic of CCTV schemes, as (from observation of two schemes) seems to be a subsequent decline in their effects upon crime (see Smith *et al.* 2002). If changed perception is the most active ingredient in CCTV schemes, there are obvious implications for how CCTV should be implemented (and regularly changed thereafter). The importance of anticipatory benefits in crime reduction has been highlighted recently by the observation that in around one third of the sites where the reducing burglary initiative was implemented saw burglary reductions which predated implementation. A substantial proportion of the burglary reduction could be ascribed to such anticipatory benefits.

Understanding anticipatory changes in crime levels should be a major research focus. Identifying 'active ingredients' in crime reduction is crucial. If we can deploy them better, more cheaply and hence more generally, major success will follow. Indeed, greater use of the media and other forms of communication and marketing presents a huge opportunity to the budding crime preventer based on this interesting phenomenon. This is particularly potent given that the police are a regular and available source of information to news gatherers (see Mawby 2002), and that the period 1989–99 saw an 800 per cent increase in the supply of television news alone! The question surely must be what use is being made of this somewhat untapped resource? We are not advocating 'spin doctoring' as a crime prevention tactic, but seeking to begin a debate about how better and more thoughtful links between the police and the public – defining and meeting public expectations – can not only help reduce crime but also increase police visibility in the eyes of a public that draws so much of its information from the media.

Making a difference: police colleagues

Ask an officer responding to a 999 call about his or her priority and it is likely to be to attend on time and deal with the incident. Ask an officer serving in a

303

specialist squad what he or she is there to do and it is likely to be to serve the aims of that squad – usually arresting offenders (see Hough and Tilley 1998). In the context of performance indicators, which do not always chime with crime reductive purposes, what can be done to direct police attention to the latter? There are a number of steps which should be taken:

1. To train all officers in what we know about effective crime reduction. There are enough evaluated successes to allow officers to become more sensitive to what can be done to prevent crime at the individual and areal level, and thus to become truly expert in their dealings outside the police service.

2. To avoid premature closure of incidents. As to victims, we know that a crime event is a good predictor of imminent crime in the same place or nearby. The original crime report must be seen as the start of a process whereby repetition is prevented and the mechanisms underpinning a crime are understood, rather than a book-keeping exercise whose completion reflects termination of interest in a case. This will involve more focused use of the skills of police analysts (see Chapter 14).

3. To avoid premature closure of dealings with putative offenders. We know that certain behaviours are markers or triggers of other kinds of criminal involvement. For example, as yet unpublished research by Schneider shows the enormous rates at which shop theft and burglary constitute complementary crimes by the same offenders. Treating the shop thief as a burglar on his of her day off, and acting accordingly, is likely to serve as an effective enforcement action in the cause of prevention. Other 'trigger' events include driving while disqualified (Rose 2000) and parking in bays for the disabled (Chenery et al. 1999). It should not be forgotten that the Yorkshire Ripper was apprehended because a boot was searched when a number plate was 'wrong'. Ted Bundy was apprehended because his vehicle had no lights. David Berkowitz (son of Sam) was apprehended through a parking ticket. In each case, these events triggered police officer suspicions, which in turn resulted in these serial killers being brought to justice.

4. Service-level agreements should be reached so as to give concrete effect to collaborative action between community safety 'partners'.

Taken together, these four steps should make it more likely that the crime reduction enterprise be moved to a more evidence-based position. Fundamental to a way ahead along the lines set out here is effective and forceful leadership (see Chapter 25). Leadership can be exercised at any rank, and there are numerous examples of individual officers who have achieved real change by collaboration with other agencies. Many of these are represented among the candidates for the Tilley Award, and described on the Home Office's crime reduction website. Writing about the lowly status of crime prevention, Hough and Tilley (1998) suggested that the preconditions for successful crime prevention were as follows:

• Commitment to crime prevention from senior officers , including ACPO ranks.

- Adequate resources to service dedicated crime prevention efforts.

- An explicit emphasis on crime prevention by basic command unit (BCU) commanders.

- Systems that hold officers of all ranks accountable for crime prevention.

- Incentives to encourage effective preventive work.

- An officer with specific responsibility for developing and implementing crime prevention strategy.

- Crime prevention accorded the status of an expert profession for some specialists.

- Education and training.

- Integration of detective and preventive functions in local crime management.

Not everyone will agree with the whole list, and what is missing, being implicit rather than explicit, is making crime reduction a key part of every police officer's role. What is self-evident is this is not reality at present and part of the blame must lie with leadership, both central and local.

An important weapon in the police armoury is s. 17 of the Crime and Disorder Act 1998, which imposes a statutory responsibility on local authorities to consider the crime consequences of their decisions. Moss (2003) argues that this places the police in a powerful position in so far as they can plausibly present themselves as local experts in the crime consequences of planning, maintenance and other decisions. The writers have seen at first hand the anxieties which are evoked when local authority officials are advised of such consequences, and the effect of s. 17 to date should not be underestimated. There is a risk of doing so, in the light of the absence of court process testing the relevance of s. 17 (see Moss 2003).

The suggestion above that collaboration needs to be shaped, perhaps by service-level agreements between the police and local authority departments, will also place local commanders in a more routinely politicised environment than they have hitherto been wont to inhabit.

Policing style

In the literature on attitude and behaviour change, a number of factors have been identified as relevant:

- The degree of change required. For example, the assimilation-contrast theory suggests that small changes can be induced, but when the change required goes beyond a particular extent, the change attempt will lead to a reaction against the hoped-for change (see Insko 1967).

- The congruity of the changed position with other attitudes and beliefs (as in Heider's (1946) balance theory and Festinger's (1957) cognitive dissonance theory).

- Awareness of the implications of the changed position (as in Kelly's (1950) personal construct theory).

If the agenda for change set out in the foregoing were to be adopted, what are the implications for police leadership? Perhaps the central leadership task is climate-setting, which stresses the purposes of policing and the relationship of crime reduction tasks to them. The advantage is that most police work can be conceived as crime reductive in the right climate. One of the major tragedies of policing is that somehow actions have become divorced from their underlying purpose, to remain justified only by minimum standards of performance bureaucratically expressed. Arresting and imprisoning an offender is 'a good result' only in so far as it precludes the commission of further crime by the same person. Dispersing 'disorderly youths' is a success in so far as it provides respite, but a real success only in so far as the problem is reduced in the longer term. Taking a crime report is a prelude to the prevention of repeats, not a book-keeping exercise. The climate-setting task, in reasserting purposes over processes of practice, provides the means whereby any given level of change is perceptually minimised, in pursuit of the attempt to bring change within the range where it will be assimilated by officers. Thus the first aim of climate-setting leadership in the service of crime reduction is to reassert the purposes behind the processes.

The second aim of climate-setting is to ensure the purposes behind the processes are couched in ways which are most consistent with the values and self-perception of police officers. Let us assume that most police officers, like most other people, want to do a good job. They will characterise what a good job means in terms familiar from their life outside the police service: in terms of helpfulness, loyalty to people and principles, and honesty. All professional lives compromise or mitigate the expression of these standards, so that the professional persona deviates from the private one. The teacher cannot hug the distressed child for fear of accusations of paedophilia; the solicitor does not invite social contact with clients. It is interesting that in the literature on police corruption, 'noble cause corruption' looms large. Here personal principles and beliefs swamp professional standards to generate corrupt behaviour, albeit justified by appeal to noble principles. Climate-setting in the spirit discussed here appeals explicitly to principles and standards which will be shared by the officer. Thus, for example, attempts to prevent repeat victimisation can invoke notions of fairness in the distribution of harms. The wish to protect children and the elderly means that (for example) invocation of this purpose in the prevention of repeated burglary by distraction will seldom meet objections from police officers. Subtle climate-setting would involve stressing that most delinquency is adolescent limited, so that situational prevention is a way of keeping those with brief criminal careers away from serious delinquency until maturity takes over. If coupled with a strong emphasis on enforcement for chronic offenders, such a climate could be sustained on the basis of congruence with standards applying outside the police service.

The final role of leadership is to elaborate what is possible and what has been successful in crime reduction. Just as personal change does not occur until one realises the implications of the position to which one changes, so until he or she is familiar with the literature on what has worked, the officer will not change. This involves a huge training and motivational effort. It will have the incidental effect of injecting real expertise into partnership processes, which expertise is now lacking. One can muse on how a patient would react to the information that their brain surgery was being undertaken by a partnership. In skills-based procedures, a designated leader with relevant qualifications and experience seems desirable, and that role will typically be assumed in partnerships by a police officer, who now typically knows little about evidenced crime reduction. For such an officer to be prepared to occupy a role based on expertise rather than formal position, a substantial training effort must be made before the changes mooted earlier in this chapter become realistically achievable.

Selected further reading

There are two distinct literatures in crime reduction. One concerns its politics and position among social policy purposes. Books in this tradition have been written by Gilling (*Crime Prevention*, 1997), Crawford (*The Local Governance of Crime*, 1997; *Crime Prevention and Community Safety*, 1998) and Hughes (*Understanding Crime Prevention*, 2002). The second literature concerns the question of which kinds of intervention have, on the basis of experience and evaluation, proven worth while. For work of this kind, see Clarke's *Situational Crime Prevention* (1992, second edition 1997) and the US website www.usdoj.gov/cops/cp_resources/pubs_ppse/default.htm.

Work in any Home Office publication series under the authorship of Clarke, Ekblom, Webb, Tilley or Laycock will be relevant. This and other work can be identified and downloaded from the relevant Home Office website (www.crimereduction.gov.uk). The reader should be aware that much unevaluated work also features on the website, and should be read in an agnostic spirit.

Notes

1 With apologies to Paul Wiles for use of Lewis Carroll's simile first applied by him with the second author (Wiles and Pease 2000).
2 www.crimereduction.gov.uk.
3 http://www.audit-commission.gov.uk/comsafe/
4 Details of crime directors and their staffs are available on the Home Office's crime reduction website (www.crimereduction.gov.uk).
5 See also www.crimereduction.gov.uk/cco.htm.
6 Is actually thought by intending offenders likely to act on the absence of a badge.
7 http://www.crimereduction.gov.uk.
8 http://www.usdoj.gov/cops/cp_resources/pubs_ppse/default.htm#Guide_series; http://crimeprevention.rutgers.edu; www.usdoj.gov/cops/cp_resources/pubs_ppse/default.htm; http://www.preventingcrime.net/; http://www.be-safe.org/.
9 Vehicles rigged to facilitate detection of those entering it illegally. Methods of achieving this can include tracking or camera systems, or physical restraint systems, whereby an intruder is unable to leave the vehicle.

References

Alderson, J. (1979) *Policing Freedom*. Plymouth: McDonald & Evans.

Audit Commission (1999) *Safety in Numbers – Promoting Community Safety*. London: Audit Commission.

Bullock, K., Moss, K. and Smith, J. (2000) *Anticipating the Impact of Section 17 of the Crime and Disorder Act 1998. Briefing Note* 11/00. London: Home Office.

Chenery, S., Henshaw, C. and Pease, K. (1999) *Illegal Parking in Disabled Bays: A Means of Offender Targeting. Briefing Note* 1/99. London: Home Office.

Clarke, R.V. (1992) *Situational Crime Prevention: Successful Case Studies*. New York, NY: Harrow & Heston.

Clarke, R.V. (1997) *Situational Crime Prevention: Successful Case Studies*. (2nd edn). New York, NY: Harrow & Heston.

Clarke, R.V.G. and Homel, R. (1997) 'A revised classification of situational crime prevention techniques', in S. Lab (ed.) *Crime Prevention at a Crossroads*. Nashville, KY: Anderson, 17–27.

Crawford, A. (1997) *The Local Governance of Crime: Appeals to Community and Partnerships*. Oxford: Clarendon Press.

Crawford, A. (1998) *Crime Prevention and Community Safety: Politics, Policies and Practices*. Harlow: Longman.

Ekblom, P. (2000) 'The conjunction of criminal opportunity – a tool for clear, joined-up thinking about community safety and crime reduction', in S. Ballantyne *et al.* (eds) *Secure Foundations: Issues in Crime Prevention, Crime Reduction and Community Safety*. London: IPPR.

Everson, S. (2000) 'Repeat victims and repeat offenders'. Unpublished PhD thesis, University of Huddersfield.

Everson, S. and Pease, K. (2001) 'Crime against the same person and place: detection opportunity and offender targeting', in G. Farrell and K. Pease (eds) *Repeat Victimisation*. Monsey, NY: Criminal Justice Press, 199–220.

Farrell, G. and Pease, K. (eds) (2001) *Repeat Victimisation*. Monsey, NY: Criminal Justice Press.

Farrington, D.P. (2000) 'Monetary costs and benefits of crime prevention programmes', *Crime and Justice*, 27: 305–61.

Farrington, D.P. and Welsh, B.C. (1999) 'Delinquency prevention using family-based interventions', *Children and Society*, 13: 287–303.

Felson, M. (1994) *Crime and Everyday Life*. Thousand Oaks, CA: Pine Forge Press.

Festinger, L. (1957) *A Theory of Cognitive Dissonance*. Stanford, CA: Stanford Universsity Press.

Field, S. (1998) *Trends in Crime Revisited*. London: Home Office.

Garland, D. (2000) 'The culture of high crime societies: some preconditions of recent law and order policies', *British Journal of Criminology*, 40: 347–75.

Gilbert, E.W. (1958) 'Pioneer maps of health and disease in England', *Geographical Journal*, 124: 172–83.

Gilling, D. (1997) *Crime Prevention*. London: Routledge.

Goldblatt, P. and Lewis, C. (eds) (1998) *Reducing Offending: An Assessment of Research Evidence on Ways of Dealing with Offending Behaviour. Home Office Research Study* 187. London: HMSO.

Grimshaw, P., Harvey, L. and Pease, K. (1989) 'Crime prevention delivery: the work of police crime prevention officers', in R. Morgan and D. Smith (eds) *Coming to Terms with Policing*. London: Routledge.

Harries, K. (1999) *Mapping Crime: Principle and Practice*. Washington, DC: National Institute of Justice.

Hedderman, C. and Williams, C. (2001) *Making Partnerships Work: Emerging Findings from the Reducing Burglary Initiative. Briefing Note 1/01.* London: Home Office.

Heider, F. (1946) 'Attitudes and cognitive organisation', *Journal of Psychology*, 21: 107–12.

Hesseling, R.B.P. (1994) 'Displacement: a review of the empirical literature', in R.V. Clarke (ed.) *Crime Prevention Studies 3.* Monsey, NY: Willow Tree Press, 197–230.

Hester, R. (2000) *Crime and Disorder Partnerships: Voluntary and Community Sector Partnerships. Briefing Note 10/00.* London: Home Office.

Hirschfield, A. and Bowers, K. (2001) *Mapping and Analysing Crime Data.* London: Taylor & Francis.

Home Office (1965) *Report of the Committee on the Prevention and Detection of Crime* (Cornish Committee). London: Home Office.

Home Office (1968) *Crime Prevention.* Unnumbered circular, 17 May.

Home Office (1984) *Crime Prevention. Circular 8/84.* London: Home Office.

Home Office (2002) *The National Policing Plan 2003–2006.* London: Home Office Communication Directorate.

Hough, M. and Tilley, N. (1998) *Getting the Grease to the Squeak, Research Lessons for Crime Prevention. Crime Detection and Prevention Series Paper 85.* London: Home Office.

Hughes, G. (2002) *Understanding Crime Prevention.* Buckingham: Open University Press.

Insko, C.A. (1967) *Theories of Attitude Change.* New York, NY: Appleton-Century-Crofts.

Kelly, G. (1950) *The Psychology of Personal Constructs.* New York, NY: McGraw-Hill.

Koch, B.C.M. (1998) *The Politics of Crime Prevention.* Aldershot: Ashgate.

Leishman, F., Loveday, B. and Savage, S. (2000) *Core Issues in Policing* (2nd edn). Harlow: Pearson Education.

Matthews, R., Pease, C. and Pease, K. (2001) 'Repeated bank robbery: theme and variations', in G. Farrell and K. Pease (eds) *Repeat Victimisation.* Monsey, NY: Criminal Justice Press, 154–64.

Mawby, R.C. (2002) *Policing Images: Policing, Communication and Legitimacy.* Cullompton: Willan.

Mirrlees-Black, C. and Ross, A. (1995) *Crime against Retail and Manufacturing Premises: Findings from the 1994 Commercial Victimisation Survey. Home Office Research Study 146.* London: HMSO.

Moffitt, T.E. (2003) 'Life-course persistent vs adolescent-limited anti-social behaviour', in D. Cicchetti and D. Cohen (eds) *Developmental Psychopathology* (2nd edn). New York, NY: Wiley.

Moss, K. (2003) 'Crime prevention v planning: is Section 17 a material consideration?', *Crime Prevention and Community Safety: An International Journal*, in press.

Moss, K. and Brookes, S. (2003) *Data Exchange in Crime and Disorder Partnerships: The Long and Winding Road*, submitted for publication.

Moss, K. and Pease, K. (1999) 'Section 17 Crime and Disorder Act 1998: a wolf in sheep's clothing?', *International Journal of Crime Prevention and Community Safety*, 1: 15–19.

Murray, A.T., McGuffog, I., Western, J.S. and Mullins, P. (2001) 'Exploratory spatial data analysis techniques for examining urban crime', *British Journal of Criminology*, 41: 309–29.

Newburn, T. (2003) *Crime and Criminal Justice Policy* (2nd edn). Harlow: Addison, Wesley, Longman.

Office of Public Services Reform (2002) *Reforming our Public Services, Principles into Practice.* London: Cabinet Office.

Pease, K. (1999) 'The effects of street lighting on crime', in K. Painter and N. Tilley (eds) *Surveillance and Crime Control.* Guilderland, NY: Harrow & Heston, 47–76.

Pease, K. (2001a) 'Distributive justice', in R. Matthews and J. Pitts (eds) *Crime, Disorder and Community Safety: A New Agenda?* London: Routledge.

Pease K. (2001b) 'What's to do about it? Let's turn off our minds and GIS', in A. Hirschfield and K. Bowers (eds) *Mapping and Analysing Crime Data*. London: Taylor & Francis, 225–36.

Pease, K. (2002) 'Crime reduction', in M. Maguire *et al.* (eds) *Oxford Handbook of Criminology* (3rd edn). Oxford: Oxford University Press, 947–79.

Phillips, C., Jacobson, J., Prime, R., Carter, M. and Considine, M. (2002) *Crime and Disorder Reduction Partnerships: Round One Progress. Police Research Paper* 151. London: Home Office.

Ratcliffe, J.H. and McCullagh, M.J. (2001) 'Chasing ghosts? Police perceptions of high crime areas', *British Journal of Criminology*, 41: 330–41.

Rich Harris, J. (1998) *The Nurture Assumption*. London: Bloomsbury.

Rose, G.N.G. (2000) *The Criminal Histories of Serious Traffic Offenders. Home Office Research Study* 206. London: Home Office.

Sallybanks, J. (2000) *Assessing the Police Use of Decoy Vehicles. Police Research Series* 137. London: Home Office.

Sampson, A. and Phillips, C. (1992) *Multiple Victimisation: Racial Attacks on an East London Estate. Crime Prevention Unit Paper* 36. London: Home Office.

Schweinhart, L.J., Barnes, H.V. and Weikart, D.P. (1993) *Young Children Grow up: The Effects of the Perry Preschool Program Study through Age 27*. Ypsilanti, MI: High/Scope Press.

Scott, M. (2000) *Problem-Oriented Policing: Reflections on the First 20 Years*. Washington, DC: US Department of Justice.

Shaw, M. and Pease, K. (2000) *Research on Repeat Victimisation in Scotland*. Edinburgh: Scottish Executive.

Sherman, L.W. (1995) 'Hot spots of crime and criminal careers of place', in J.E. Eck and D. Weisburd (eds) *Crime and Place*. Monsey, NY: Willow Tree Press, 35–52.

Sherman, L.W., Gartin, P. and Buerger, M.E. (1989) 'Hot spots of predatory crime: routine activities and the criminology of place', *Criminology*, 27: 27–55.

Sherman, L.W, Gottfredson, D., Mackenzie, D., Eck, J., Reuter, P. and Bushway, S. (1998) *Preventing Crime: What Works, What Doesn't, What's Promising*. Washington, DC: National Institute of Justice.

Sherman, L.W., Shaw, J.W. and Rogan, D.P. (1995) *The Kansas City Gun Experiment: Research in Brief*. Washington, DC: National Institute of Justice.

Smith, M., Clarke, R.V. and Pease, K. (2002) 'Anticipatory benefits in crime prevention', in N. Tilley (ed.) *Analysis for Crime Prevention*. Monsey, NY: Criminal Justice Press, 71–88.

Smithson, H. (2002) 'Reducing the risk of offending through early intervention'. Unpublished PhD thesis, University of Manchester.

Spelman, W. (1995) 'Criminal careers of public places', in J.E. Eck and D. Weisburd (eds) *Crime and Place*. Monsey, NY: Willow Tree Press, 115–44.

Standing Conference on Crime Prevention (1991) *Safer Communities: The Local Delivery of Crime Prevention through the Partnership Approach* (Morgan Report). London: Home Office.

Townsley, M. and Pease, K. (2002) 'Winter in Bermuda and Summer in Alaska: hot spots, crime and climate', in N. Tilley (ed.) *Analysis for Crime Prevention*. Monsey, NY: Criminal Justice Press, 59–70.

Tufte, E.R. (1983) *The Visual Display of Quantitative Information*. Cheshire, CT: Graphics Press.

Weatheritt, M. (1986) *Innovations in Policing*. London: Croom Helm.

Weisburd, D. and McEwen, T. (1998) *Crime Mapping and Crime Prevention*. Monsey, NY: Criminal Justice Press.

Wiles, P. and Pease, K. (2000) 'Crime prevention and community safety: Tweedledum and Tweedledee?', in S. Ballintyne *et al.* (eds) *Secure Foundations: Key Issues in Crime Prevention, Crime Reduction and Community Safety*. London: IPPR, 21–9.

Chapter 13

Community policing, problem-oriented policing and intelligence-led policing

Nick Tilley

Introduction: old and new models for policing

Community policing, problem-oriented policing and intelligence-led policing all comprise reform movements for the police. Built into each there is, thus, a critique of policing as deemed normally done as well as a vision of some preferable alternative. All call on the police to be less reactive and more proactive. All thus call on the police not simply to respond to calls for service as they come in. All are premised on the assumption that policing can be and needs to be improved. Community policing and problem-oriented policing are global movements, though the latter has distinctly American origins. Intelligence-led policing is home grown in the UK, though is exciting interest in other countries also.

The main impetus for community policing derives from a sense that police–community relations are unsatisfactory. In Britain, John Alderson argued in the 1970s that traditional 'authoritarian' policing was proving inadequate and inappropriate in a plural, 'libertarian society' with increasing levels of crime. A different, community model of policing was needed (Alderson 1977, 1979). The Scarman Report on riots in Brixton in 1981 went on to highlight the need for the police to engage more closely with the communities served (Scarman 1982). Likewise, in the USA, the movement for community-oriented policing was stimulated by the perceived need for the police to lessen their distance from the community (Weisel and Eck 1994: 63). Policing calls for co-operation with members of the community. Mistrust among substantial sections of the community makes policing difficult. Policing by consent implies community confidence that the police are acting with and for citizens. Mawby compares policing in England and Wales with policing in continental Europe and Northern Ireland. He concludes that 'in many respects there does appear to be a much more explicit tradition of community involvement in England and Wales' (Mawby 1992: 125). Recent arguments in favour of community policing thus comprise in part a case for a return to the true, distinctive roots of policing, where there has been a move away from them. As Alderson points out, however, the means of crime control envisaged by Peel at the dawn of professional policing did not much engage the community. Community policing aspires to greater involvement of and with the community than envisaged by Peel (Alderson 1979). The problems addressed by the movement for community policing have arisen most acutely where the police have most lost the confidence of particular subsections of the community, often members of minority ethnic groups, as in the case of Brixton.

The main impetus for problem-oriented policing springs from a sense that the demand on police has become overwhelming. Moreover, underlying problems producing calls for service are not being addressed. The police are called on to deal with a very wide range of emergency problems, which include crimes but much else besides that also rightly falls to a police agency. With a diminishing resource per call the police are often able to do little more than log individual incidents. They are thereby failing to address the issues producing the calls. This is both inefficient and ineffective. Problem-oriented policing involves adopting an analytic approach that takes community concerns seriously. It develops strategic responses that aim to deal effectively with issues underlying police-relevant community problems. The origins of problem-oriented policing lie in the work of Herman Goldstein (1979, 1990), who had been an adviser to the Chicago Police Department before becoming an academic. Goldstein highlighted shortcomings in the so-called 'professional model' of policing, which had developed in the USA to deal with police inefficiency, corruption and abuse of discretion. Research had shown that the prescribed professional policing was not in practice what was delivered and also that many standard police responses were in any case ineffective. Fresh ways of working were needed, making more use of analysis, officer imagination, local discretion and also community resources where it was relevant to do so.

Goldstein was critical of police services that had lost sight of their purposes and had instead become obsessed with procedure. Ironically, though an American writing at the time principally about American policing, Goldstein began the 1979 paper which first laid out his vision for problem-oriented policing with a British tale:

> Complaints from passengers wishing to use the Bagnall to Greenfields bus service that 'the drivers were speeding past queues of at least 30 people with a smile and a wave of a hand' have been met by a statement pointing out that 'it is impossible for the drivers to keep to their timetable if they have to stop for passengers' (1979: 236).

This quotation captures the aspiration of problem-oriented policing to return to purpose and substance from a preoccupation with form and its performance management corollaries. British police services have flirted with problem-oriented policing since Goldstein first floated the idea, with the Metropolitan

Police Service under Sir Kenneth Newman the first to experiment with it in the early 1980s. The ideas have taken a more substantial hold in the early years of the new century.

The main impetus for intelligence-led policing comprises the supposed failure of the police to address the systemic sources of crime and crime patterns. Crime detection was predominantly responsive and opportunistic. Police clear-up rates were poor. Offenders are located in networks. A small number of prolific offenders is responsible for the majority of crimes. In a paper stimulating the development of intelligence-led policing, the Audit Commission (1993) prescribed a proactive approach, targeting the criminal not the crime, making much more and much better use of intelligence. This was picked up by several forces that ran demonstration projects (Maguire and John 1995; Amey et al. 1996a, 1996b), the most extensive and influential of which was the work in Kent, under Sir David Phillips. Intelligence-led policing draws on the notion that the police can and do know a great deal about offending patterns. Intelligence-led policing involves effectively sourcing, assembling and analysing 'intelligence' about criminals and their activities better to disrupt their offending, by targeting enforcement and patrol where it can be expected to yield highest dividends. Dealing with individual offences reactive-ly and trying to solve them one at a time as evidence happens to be available is not an efficient or effective way of allocating police efforts. Instead, the police can and should actively pursue information about criminals and their organisation. This is expected simultaneously to lead to improvements in both the detection and prevention of crime. The Kent model in particular has been enormously influential, and the National Intelligence Model (see Chapter 14), the vehicle for delivering intelligence-led policing, has been formally endorsed by the Association of Chief Police Officers (ACPO), by Her Majesty's Inspectorate of Constabulary (HMIC) and by Home Office ministers.

All three models are critical of and aim to replace 'reactive' policing. 'Reactive policing' describes a model where the police respond case by case to issues as they arise. Reactive policing is also sometimes referred to a 'fire brigade' policing, involving responses to emergencies as they arise but little else. The fire is put out, the case is dealt with and then the police withdraw to await the next incident that requires attention. There is nothing strategic about response policing. There are no long-term objectives. There is no purpose beyond coping with the here and now. Community policing, problem-oriented policing and intelligence-led policing are all concerned with reforming policing in ways that will give it greater direction. The next section lays out the ends and means specified in or assumed by each of the three models.

The three models outlined

The following discussion lays out the key elements of each of the three models. It will become obvious that the models vary in the degree to which they have been articulated. In some cases it will be necessary to impute implicit though critical elements.

Community policing

Community policing in the USA has been variously described as the 'new orthodoxy' (Eck and Rosenbaum 1994: 3) and as the 'national mantra of the American police' (Greene 2000: 301). It has also been supported in Britain, though less avidly as an overarching basis for a new model of policing to which police services as a whole need to be committed.[1] In 1994 Bennett noted that over the previous decade there had been a programme of reform drawn up by police and government aimed at 'improving the quality of the police service and customer satisfaction'. Bennett added that 'Although the publications and official declarations relating to this process use the term [community policing] fairly infrequently, they contain many references to the concept of a greater working partnership between the police and the public'. (1994: 224).

Bennett's comments hold true also for the following decade. There has been a continuing programme of reform, involving both police and government, which aims to improve police service and customer satisfaction, and the emphasis has again been on partnership, though with relatively infrequent explicit references to community policing as such.

So, what exactly is community policing and what is it for? In the UK in an influential account, John Alderson laid out objectives for 'a police system for the future in a free, permissive and participatory society', as follows:

1. To contribute to liberty, equality and fraternity.

2. To help reconcile freedom with security and to uphold the law.

3. To uphold and protect human rights and thus help achieve human dignity.

4. To dispel criminogenic social conditions, through co-operative social action.

5. To help create trust in communities.

6. To strengthen security and feelings of security.

7. To investigate, detect and activate the prosecution of crimes.

8. To facilitate free movement along public thoroughfares.

9. To curb public disorder.

10. To deal with crises and help those in distress involving other agencies where needed (1979: 199).

In the USA, Trojanowicz and Bucqueroux (1990: xiii–xv) listed some key principles of community policing, the first of which was that 'Community policing is both a philosophy and organisational strategy to allow community residents and police to work together in new ways to solve problems of crime, fear of crime, physical and social disorder and neighbourhood decay'. Trojanowicz and Bucqueroux went on to indicate that this means involving all members of the police organisation, employing community policing officers, adopting a proactive approach, engaging in problem-solving with community members and other agencies and adopting decentralised ways of working.

Though their emphases differ, both Alderson in the UK and Trojanowicz and Bucqueroux in the USA clearly call for closer working relationships with communities. Community policing stresses policing *with* and *for* the community rather than policing *of* the community. It aspires to improve the quality of life in communities. In improving the quality of life it aims to solve community problems alongside the community and as defined by the community.

Beyond this it has, however, proven difficult to pin down what specifically is involved in implementing community policing. On that there is broad agreement among scholars and many police officers.

Reiner quotes one chief constable as saying '[community policing] doesn't mean a damn thing. It's just one of those terms you use which are a recent invention by some of our, dare I say it, mock academics' (1991: 112). Many real academics on both sides of the Atlantic go along with this, repeatedly stressing community policing's ambiguities (Weatheritt 1988; Eck and Rosenbaum 1994; Kelling and Coles 1996; Skogan and Hartnett 1997). Bayley (1994: 104) reports that he has heard the police describe community policing as being 'foot patrol, aggressive enforcement of minor ordinances, electronic surveillance of shopping malls, enhanced traffic enforcement, and any police action that instills public confidence', adding that 'The phrase has been so often used imprecisely, it has been cheapened'.

The term 'community' itself is notoriously slippery. It often seems to imply shared norms, values and ways of life. Groups with these attributes need not be geographically defined, of course. In practice the community of community policing most often does amount to 'neighbourhood'. Neighbourhoods, though, can often be divided. Indeed the most problematic ones characteristically are quite seriously fractured, with conflicts over use of space, legitimate lifestyles and appropriate forms of policing. For the practical purposes of community policing, members of the community normally comprise self-selected citizens or representatives of other private sector, public sector or volunteer agencies. It rarely, if ever, comprises all residents, or a representative sample of them. Indeed it is scarcely conceivable that it could do so. The 'community' of 'community policing' is elusive and may in many cases be illusory. Ironically, those least likely to take part in it are just those whose disaffection with the police lay behind many calls for community policing.

So far I have suggested that 'community policing' is widely endorsed, though at the same time widely seen to be close to meaningless. I have also highlighted difficulties that arise in relation to the term 'community' itself and its interpretation in the context of community policing. Several scholars, while acknowledging these difficulties, have still attempted to distil a coherent account of what is involved in conducting community policing.

While agreeing that '[In] a definitional sense, community policing is not something one can easily characterise', Skogan and Hartnett try to draw out what is involved in principle and what is done in practice in community policing. As they put it, 'it involves reforming decision-making and creating new cultures within police departments; it is not a packet of specific tactical plans' (1997: 5). They go on to state that community policing requires organisational decentralisation, patrol designed to facilitate two-way communication between the police and public, a commitment to broadly focused problem-oriented policing, responsiveness to citizens' demands, problems and priorities, and help for neighbourhoods to solve crime problems on their own.

Skogan and Hartnett also give examples of what is done in practice in community policing. These include:

> opening small neighborhood substations, conducting surveys to measure community satisfaction, organizing meetings and crime-prevention seminars, publishing newsletters, forming neighborhood watch programs, establishing advisory panels, organizing youth activities, conducting drug-education projects and media campaigns, patrolling on horses and bicycles, and working with municipal agencies to enforce health and safety regulations (1997: 5–6).

Bayley (1994: 102–15) also tries to distil the core elements of community policing. These include consultation, adaptation, mobilisation and problem-solving (CAMPS). Communities are consulted. Police services adapt by becoming decentralised and locally responsive. The public and other agencies are mobilised in efforts to address crime problems since the police cannot deal with them effectively on their own. Patterns of crime and disorder problems are identified and dealt with proactively in the aggregate rather than simply as a series of discrete incidents calling for a response.

Kelling and Coles (1996) echo others' comments about the diverse ways in which community policing has been understood. They say that it has 'come to mean all things to all people', and that some 'believe [it] is no more than an undefinable set of concepts and public relations con intended to restore public confidence in a seriously tarnished and disgraced occupation' (Kelling and Coles 1996: 158). Yet Kelling and Coles do believe that community policing can be defined. Community policing, they say, assigns the police broad functions extending beyond enforcement and responses to crimes. These functions include 'keeping the peace and public order, protecting constitutional liberties, ensuring security, resolving conflicts, assisting persons in danger who cannot help themselves, managing problems that endanger citizens and/or communities, and responding to emergencies' (1996: 158). Police dependence on citizens for authority, information about problems and collaboration in problem-solving is recognised. Officers do not function as automata responding to standard events but have to learn to apply knowledge and skills to specific situations. Officers avoid general tactics and instead use their discretion in relation to the particular issues facing them, working alongside citizens and other agencies. Because of the need to respond locally to local problems, authority is devolved downwards, and away from the centre. Moreover, because communities differ in characteristics and policing needs, what specifically is delivered by way of community policing will vary from one place to another. That what is implemented is not always the same is, thus, no surprise. Indeed, were this to be the case that would comprise a perversion of community policing properly understood.

These accounts of community policing highlight key points at which community plays a part in policing, marking community policing off from response policing. The community is involved in:

- defining what constitute problems or policing needs;

- shaping forms of local policing by the police service;

- examining identified local problems alongside the police service;

- determining responses to identified issues;

- implementing responses to issues as participants in community policing;

- joint work with the police to address community-defined problems; and

- informing or supplementing the operational work of police officers.

A corollary of this for police organisation is that decentralisation is needed, providing for discretion in adapting priorities and tactics to local circumstances and needs. This in turn suggests that what is done in practice is likely to vary quite widely from place to place. The diversity in what is implemented on the ground is, thus, fully to be expected and not an indication that the notion of community policing is inherently incoherent.

Box 13.1 summarises one of Skogan and Hartnett's examples from their Chicago study, illustrating what goes on in community policing in practice. The example shows broad community involvement with the police in identifying a local problem, in deciding what to do about the problem, in playing a major part in implementing the planned solution and in learning lessons from the efforts made.

Box 13.1 The case of the street-corner drug dealers: an example of community policing in action

> In Englewood, in response to citizen concerns raised at beat meetings, a local minister and the police organised a series of anti-drug marches, and 'positive loitering' at street corners where troublemakers were known to congregate. The plan was to drive dealers from the area by hitting all sites till the dealers left. Over 60 residents took part in the first march. The minister preached through a megaphone about the evils of drugs and led marchers' chants. Gang members watched and laughed at them. Fewer, mostly older residents took part in the second march. Their optimism about effectiveness waned. There were fears about retaliation and displacement of dealing locations. Lessons were learnt by the police and community: a wider range of clergy needed to be involved; a wider geographical area for citizen mobilisation was needed; and youth needed to participate as well as older community members.

Source: Skogan and Hartnett (1997: 174–5).

Problem-oriented policing

Problem-oriented policing is often bracketed with community policing, especially in the USA where both are enthusiastically embraced. In Britain, in varying ways and to differing degrees almost all police services purport to engage in problem-oriented policing (Read and Tilley 2000).

As with community policing, problem-oriented policing incorporates an explicit conception of the nature and role of modern policing. Goldstein laid out the purposes of policing, as he saw them, in a book that preceded his writings focusing specifically on problem-oriented policing. These purposes were to:

1. prevent and control conduct threatening life and property;

2. aid crime victims and protect people in danger of physical harm;

3. protect constitutional guarantees;

4. facilitate the movement of people and vehicles;

5. assist those who cannot care for themselves;

6. resolve conflict between individuals, between groups or between citizens and their government;

7. identify problems that may become more serious for individuals, the police or the government; and

8. create and maintain a feeling of security in the community (Goldstein 1977, as described in Scott 2000).

Problem-oriented policing is concerned with achieving these purposes of policing by systematically addressing relevant problems in the community. Identified problems should be thoroughly researched and understood. Relevant responses should be identified and targeted on the basis of this analysis. Enforcement is but one means among many. A police force that concentrates on enforcement is confusing means with ends. Moreover traditional police methods – for example, response, stakeouts, sting operations, patrol, crackdown, investigation, detection, arrest, etc. – have been found to be largely ineffective in providing sustainable solutions to police-relevant community problems (Clarke and Goldstein 2002).

Problems comprise patterned issues of community concern that fit within the police remit. Goldstein stressed their broad range. His examples in 1979 included 'street robberies, residential burglaries, battered wives, vandalism, speeding cars, runaway children, accidents, acts of terrorism, even fear' (p. 242).

The nature of the patterns shown by problems can vary widely (see Tilley and Laycock 2002). Frequently found examples include the following:

• *Repeat victimisation*: the increased risk to those who have suffered crime and the time course of heightened risk.

• *Hotspots*: the concentration of incidents in particular places or categories of place.

• *Prolific offenders*: the concentration of offending on particular persons.

• *Hot products*: the attractiveness of particular products as targets for theft.

• *Hot classes of victim*: the heightened vulnerability of types of person to specific types of crime.

- *Seasonality*: the times of the day, week or year when incidents tend to be more frequent.

Problem-oriented policing calls for the close specification of problems. Rather than addressing, say, 'burglary' as a problem with a solution, problem-oriented policing requires a more detailed account of a common class of burglaries. The common class of burglaries relates to some means by which they are patterned. The means by which their patterning is defined needs to be relevant to ways in which the problem might effectively be dealt with. The example shown in Box 13.2 illustrates the point.

Box 13.2 The case of the stolen appliances: an example of problem-oriented policing in practice

---

Clarke and Goldstein (2002) describe a problem-oriented policing initiative in Charlotte-Mecklenburg. The initial presenting problem, which had resisted reduction using traditional police responses, was 'theft at construction sites'. This, though, was too broad for problem-oriented policing. A more sharply defined issue was needed. Eventually, the problem targeted became that of 'theft of household appliances at newly completed houses'. Other forms of theft at construction sites, for example, theft of tools and machinery and of building materials, would require a different form of attention.

The extent of the problem was assessed – 109 of 485 commercial burglaries in 1998 in the target area of Charlotte-Mecklenburg were in houses under construction and involved loss of domestic appliances. The problem was understood as a function of readily available valuable goods in poorly guarded, easily accessible premises while the houses awaited occupation and a good market for the stolen goods. Cookers, microwaves and dishwashers were most often taken, with hard-wired appliances less likely to be taken than those just plugged in. Costs of the thefts to the builders experiencing the losses were calculated.

The response lit on was that of postponing installation of plug-in appliances until the houses became occupied. The attractive targets for theft would thereby no longer be available. In practice getting this response implemented proved difficult. Builders had to be persuaded to alter their existing practices. A pitch to the larger builders was made proposing a six-month trial, including police monitoring of compliance to the agreed new practices, prior to longer-term adoption of the policy if it proved effective. Ten builders agreed at once to take part, though two more did so in practice from the start of the trial period. These 12 comprised 35 per cent of the construction in the relevant area of Charlotte-Mecklenburg. Compliance was monitored by the police. Builders failing to comply were reminded of what they needed to do to do so. All builders' appliance installation practices were tracked.

The outcome of the trial was then evaluated. For the targeted appliances rate of loss in burglaries was 0.9 per 100 houses for builders rarely (<17 per cent) installing plug-in appliances prior to resident occupancy, but was 3.9 per 100 houses for builders which often (>70 per cent) installed them. The 12 participating builders were also convinced the measures had been effective and continued with them. Efforts were made to extend their practices to other builders.

Several key features of problem-oriented policing emerge from the example given in Box 13.2:

- The problem eventually addressed was more specific than the initially presenting one.

- Analysis focused on understanding the conditions generating the problem.

- The response targeted a pinch point in producing the problem.

- Part of the response involved applying leverage to those in a position to act (the builders).

- The planned responses were monitored.

- Outcome evaluation was undertaken.

- The problem and potential response may well be significant beyond the specific part of Charlotte-Mecklenburg where the initiative was run.

It is also worth drawing attention to several features of this initiative that mark it out from other ways of policing and dealing with crime problems:

- The problem was not defined in terms of neighbourhood.

- The response did not address a 'root cause' of the criminality of those involved in the offending; indeed, it didn't focus on offenders at all.

- The problem was not addressed 'bottom up'.

- The problem did not involve engagement with the community, as community is ordinarily understood.

- The response did not involve enforcement or the criminal justice system.

This is not to say that problem-oriented policing can never focus on neighbourhood-related problems, address 'root causes' (whatever they may be), work in a bottom-up way, engage the community or involve enforcement or the criminal justice system in addressing a problem. The point in problem-oriented policing is that the problem and its analysis come first. What is done is a function of the problem as revealed through analysis and the most efficient and effective, ethical way of addressing it. The emphasis is on the end not the means, and the end is addressing police-relevant community problems.

Problem-oriented policing has come conventionally to involve the use of certain tools. These include most notably the problem analysis triangle (PAT), which is sometimes referred to as the 'crime triangle', and the SARA process, which describes 'scanning, analysis, response and assessment' as four broadly sequenced stages in dealing with problems.

The problem analysis triangle invites those looking at problems to consider three features that all problems have: an offender or source of complaint, a victim or class of victims and a location or characteristic of locations. The problem analysis triangle has affinities with routine activities theory according to which crimes and crime patterns can be understood in terms of the co-presence of likely offenders and suitable targets in the absence of effective intercedants, be they guardians of the potential target/victim or handlers of the potential offender (see Cohen and Felson 1979; Felson 1998). Problems can be removed or ameliorated by altering one or more of the three crucial problem features. Looking at them carefully may help identify common factors and plausible pinch points. The SARA process is intended to capture what has to be done to engage in problem-oriented policing. Problems have to be identified through scanning. They then have to be interrogated in detail during analysis. On the basis of analysis a plausible response is devised. Then the effectiveness of the response in dealing with the problem is gauged through assessment. In practice there is a good deal of feedback and overlap between stages, making the process messier than this tidy reconstruction might suggest.

Intelligence-led policing

Intelligence-led policing describes a way of doing police business. It is primarily a practical notion of how better to deliver police work. No explicit philosophy of policing lies behind its development. The aims and functions of policing remain largely tacit and taken for granted. Intelligence-led policing is essentially about doing the practical business of policing more smartly, incorporating modern information technology and modern methods. It is not about taking a critical line on what that business is. It is no surprise that it has been stimulated by the Audit Commission, with its interest in effectiveness and efficiency.

The National Intelligence Model (NIM) has become the major vehicle for conducting intelligence-led policing. NIM was developed by the National Criminal Intelligence Service (NCIS) on behalf of the Crime Committee of the Association of Chief Police Officers. It is being rolled out to all 43 police services in England and Wales, and has Home Office and HMIC support. It is also being implemented in Scotland. The account given here of intelligence-led policing relies heavily on the NCIS publication describing the NIM (NCIS 2000). The NIM claims to 'represent the collected wisdom and best practice in intelligence-led policing and law enforcement' (NCIS 2000: 7).

Intelligence-led policing takes the police essentially to be an enforcement agency, albeit one among many. It accepts that this enforcement role needs to be oriented among other things to partnership and community safety. The focus on enforcement implies a preoccupation with law-breaking and law-breakers, with crime and criminals. Thus, we are told:

> The law enforcement business is about the successful management and reduction of law enforcement problems. It involves identifying and limiting the activities of volume criminals and dangerous offenders, controlling disorder and tackling the many problems that adversely affect community safety and the quality of life. The specific outcomes required are improved community safety, reduced crime rates and the control of criminality and disorder (NCIS 2000: 11).

Intelligence-led policing involves developing and maintaining a detailed and up-to-date picture of patterns of crime and criminality in order to intervene in it most effectively to disrupt networks and remove prolific offenders. Doing so requires staffing, procedures and structures to elicit information, interpret it and act on it promptly and systematically.

The emphasis placed by intelligence-led policing on informed and coherent enforcement responses to crime problems is seen in the following opening remarks about the NIM:

> The model provides important opportunities for law enforcement managers whether from the Police Service or another enforcement agency ... Acceptance of the basic precepts of the model will greatly aid the effort to 'join up' law enforcement activity.

> It is the outcome of a desire to professionalise the intelligence discipline within law enforcement (NCIS 2000: 7).

In practice the NIM works at various interconnecting levels, drawing together and interpreting information about crime and criminals. It distinguishes among:

- Level 1, covering local issues, including the whole range of categories and levels of crime, notably volume crime.

- Level 2, covering cross-border issues, where crime issues cross jurisdictional borders and where intelligence therefore needs to be shared, and

- Level 3, covering serious and organised crime operating on a national or international scale.

The 'Tasking and Co-ordination Group' (TCG) is central. Regular 'tactical' meetings set the agenda for intelligence gathering, receiving intelligence, making tactical assessments, allocating law enforcement efforts and reviewing progress. 'Strategic' TCG meetings occur much less frequently and set priorities on the basis of nationally and locally set objectives.

The tactical TCG uses a menu, comprising four elements:

1. Targeting offenders.

2. Management of hotspots.

3. Investigation of offences forming series.

4. Application of 'preventative measures such as CCTV, lighting or community action initiatives' (NCIS 2000: 14).

While the first three points refer to traditional policing methods of investigation, enforcement and patrol, the last shows the intelligence-led model not to be exclusively oriented to these (though even here CCTV and lighting upgrades would be construed by many as aids to more effective enforcement).

Intelligence-led policing is fed by 'intelligence products' There are four types. *Strategic assessments* provide a longer-term picture of trends possibly with forecasts for the future, and are used to inform priorities and resource allocation. *Tactical assessments* are short term and are aligned to the tactical menu. *Target profiles* describe offenders and their associates to inform operations against them. *Problem profiles* identify emerging series of offences or hotspots for crime. Series can then be used in investigations to identify offenders. Hotspots are used to work out crime reduction initiatives and as a basis for looking for offenders operating in them.

What comprises the intelligence to feed into these products is not discussed in detail, but can evidently be wide ranging and is often obtained by covert means. There is a strong emphasis on being up to date. As NCIS puts it: 'The law enforcement environment is a fast moving one in which matters requiring urgent attention are frequently likely to come to notice' (2000: 22). Information on what is happening may not just be received; it may also be actively sought. This may involve tasking informants, deploying undercover officers and making use of covert technical means (NCIS 2000: 22). The information obtained thereby is not, of course, in the public domain. It refers to intelligence secretly constructed about current activities of particular offenders and groups of offenders – their plans, ways of life and organisation – in order that their criminality may more effectively be disrupted. It can all seem rather cloak and dagger. As NCIS says:

> The need to know principle is widely recognised as the backbone of the intelligence doctrine. 'Need to know' is a security principle that the dissemination of information should be no wider than is required for the efficient conduct of the business in hand and restricted to those who have authorised access (2000: 28).

Cultivation of intelligence of this covert kind is a long-standing part of the stock-in-trade of policing. Intelligence-led policing in general, and the NIM in particular, formalises this and makes available a wider sweep of information. It also takes intelligence beyond the local and personal information and sources normally used previously. This more systematic approach to intelligence is needed now because, 'as criminality becomes more sophisticated and mobile, the identification of patterns is beyond the capability of localised, informal methods of identification' (NCIS 2000: 27).

Box 13.3 shows a case study of intelligence-led policing provided by NCIS. The example brings out the core emphases of the intelligence-led model:

- The focus is on crime.

- The means used in addressing the problem are enforcement and disruption.

- The enforcement and disruption measures are aimed at reducing the problem by undermining the ability of criminals to do their business.

- The enforcement and disruption activities are informed by intelligence work aimed at understanding the business and those involved in it.

- The tactics are co-ordinated at a relevant level, in this instance level 3 since the problem is of international dimensions and involves organised crime.

- The organisations involved are all enforcement agencies.

Box 13.3 The case of international vehicle crime: an example of intelligence-led policing

> The problem concerns the international traffic in stolen vehicles. Those involved need to have technical skills. They also need to understand and have access to overseas markets. The market is growing because of increased profitability and a 'relatively unco-ordinated law enforcement response, which reduces the chance of detection'. Investigators across jurisdictions have pooled knowledge and looked for better joint working. A tasking and co-ordination group was set up to establish intelligence requirements, to find out who the main players are and how the markets and criminal business works. A multinational control strategy group will support the tactical options in overseeing the effort to 'join up' the targeting of individuals and organisations involved in trafficking stolen vehicles wherever they may be based, and it will oversee efforts to link patterns of vehicle criminality. It will take the lead in the development of disruption strategies.

Source: NCIS (2000: 41).

The relationships between the models

Table 13.1 sets out core features of intelligence-led, community and problem-oriented policing. Though a simplification it attempts to capture the distinctive emphases of each model compared to the others by highlighting its particular focus. The contrasts are thereby made more stark than they would be in practice.

The first set of contrasts concerns the background and *raison d'être* of each model. The main problems addressed are quite different. Intelligence-led policing is concerned with traditional police priorities: the detection of crime and the apprehension of serious and prolific offenders. Crime is deemed better controllable by better targeting of offenders. The public will thereby be better served. The presenting problem addressed by community policing is quite different. It relates to perceived police legitimacy, in particular among members of minority communities. A sine qua non of much policing is good community relations and where they are unsatisfactory the police cannot satisfactorily serve the citizenry. For problem-oriented policing, the difficulty is the way in which growth in demand for police services is outpacing growth in resources. The police are deemed to have been less attentive to and effective than they might be in relation to patterns of police-related problems that come to their attention. Dealing with them effectively would both better serve the public and comprise a means of containing demand.

For intelligence-led policing law enforcement is assumed to be the key function of the police. The law shapes what the police are concerned with and what they can do. Public protection is protection primarily from law-breakers. Others may have a useful part to play in helping the police enforce the law and the police may assist those in other agencies enforcing the law. Enforcement can be made smarter by assiduously assembling, analysing and acting on information relating to the activities and organisation of major and prolific offenders. Enforcement efforts can in this way be better targeted and

Table 13.1 Dimensions of intelligence-led, community and problem-oriented policing

Dimension	Intelligence-led policing	Community policing	Problem-oriented policing
Background and raison d'être			
1. Problem addressed	Poor detection rates	Lack of legitimacy	Demand exceeding capacity
2. Critique of traditional policing	Ineffective at clearing crime, inadequate at providing protection	Detached from community which funds policing and on whom policing depends; issue of consent	Ineffective in dealing with spiralling demand, not oriented to core problems
3. Inspiration	David Phillips	John Alderson, Robert Trojanowicz	Herman Goldstein
Conception of policing and police officers			
4. Police mission	Law enforcement	Community governance	Deal with police-relevant problems
5. Who defines policing needs	Police	Community	Constitution/law/rights
6. Scope of policing	Narrowed to law enforcement	Broadened to all community concerns/demands	Mid-range, police function defined
7. Dominant discourse	Law	Politics/ideology	Science
8. Core personnel	Intelligence units/Tasking and Co-ordinating groups	Community beat officers	Analysts
9. Openness to others	Enforcement contingent	Value in itself	Problem contingent
10. Source of legitimacy	Government/authority	Local community	Core police functions
11. Appeal	To the police	To the community	To government
Characteristic forms of thinking and action			
12. Problem diagnosis	Bad people	Communities in need	Unintentional crime opportunities
13. Intervention focus	Person	Place	Event pattern
14. Analytic inputs	Evidence/intelligence	Community concerns	Data

Table 13.1 *Continued*

Dimension	*Intelligence-led policing*	*Community policing*	*Problem-oriented policing*
15. Technology	Computerised intelligence	Not important/mobile phone!	Computers
16. Preferred tactic	Arrest	Community mobilisation	Any – problem contingent
17. Preferred control mechanism	Incapacitation	Informal social control	Blocked opportunity
18. Key police quality	Action/brawn	Empathy/heart	Reason/brain
Success criteria			
19. Main indicator	Serious/prolific villains caught	Satisfied community	Police functions performed effectively
20. Expected benefit	Reduced crime	Reduced crime	Reduced crime

the community thereby better served. Community policing puts less emphasis on law enforcement. The police mandate comes from the community served. The police do have authority, of course. But they are there to exercise it on behalf of, and with, the community to achieve community-defined ends. Laws are not enforced for their own sake. Moreover community interests can often be achieved more effectively by means other than enforcement. Indeed, enforcement will often be irrelevant to troubles communities bring to their local police. An important value in itself for community policing is involvement with the community. This is not simply some means to another police-defined end. Problem-oriented policing embraces concerns that extend beyond law enforcement, but are not all-encompassing. The police may adopt a variety of means to deal with police-related problems. These may or may not involve work with the community. Both enforcement and community involvement are contingent on the nature of the police-relevant problem being addressed. And the problem has to be analysed coolly and scientifically to work through what the most effective, equitable and efficient solution will be.

The focus that intelligence-led policing has on law-breaking leads naturally to attention to law-breakers as dangerous folk from whom protection is required. It is these criminals who need to be dealt with by either treatment or punishment. The trick is to identify them and obtain a legal mandate to intervene with them to try to effect incapacitation or personal changes so that they no longer pose a threat. The computer enables better management of the flow of information that the police receive about criminals, their behaviour, organisation and lifestyle. Smarter action can then be taken to control them through deterrence, disruption, arrest or incarceration. Up-to-date intelligence allows for speedy, well targeted interventions in an ever-changing world of criminals and criminal organisation. Community policing, in contrast, tends to situate problems in community contexts. The relationship between community dynamics, offending, conflict, disorderly behaviour and informal social control needs to be grasped better to know what forms of intervention are needed and for what purposes. The police need to work closely with the community in determining what needs to be done and by whom. Enforcement may occur but it is undertaken with and for the community served and takes place alongside other efforts to deal with underlying issues. Problem-oriented policing has an affinity with situational crime prevention (Tilley 1999; Braga 2002). Both propose a systematic approach to defining problems with data and to developing and using informed responses to them. Situational crime prevention proposes that crime problems are normally the unintended consequences of social arrangements that have simply evolved or have benign purposes. Better management of everyday life can reduce opportunities, typically by increasing risk to potential offenders, reducing rewards otherwise available from crime or making offending more difficult. This entails neither a social nor an individual pathology. Of course, problem-oriented policing does not require a situational response. Particular problems may call for enforcement or community engagement or a combination of both with or without situational measures. It all depends on the particular police-relevant problem at hand. Working through what the problem is and what might work out well as a way of dealing with it is often time-consuming and intellectually challenging.

Success in intelligence-led policing comes with 'good arrests' and 'good sentences', by which is meant conviction of serious and prolific offenders and their severe punishment, keeping them from those they would otherwise harm. Success in community policing is associated with smooth and contented community functioning achieved through community members and community institutions. Success in problem-oriented policing occurs with the successful amelioration, removal or management of specific police-related community problems. All models expect crime levels to be better controlled than through traditional reactive policing.

The three models of policing outlined and discussed here clearly differ from one another substantially and across a range of dimensions. They have different means, ends, key players and priorities. Can they, nevertheless, coexist in the same police service? Is each so all-encompassing that it could not tolerate the others? If more than one model operates in a police service, must one take priority as the prevailing way of doing police work?

If the models are taken to describe overall ways of conceiving of and doing policing, then it is difficult to see how they could work together. They simply suggest different functions, priorities and ways of working. But policing may be construed to be a complex social institution with many functions, none of which can or should be abandoned. Emergencies have to be responded to. Crimes have to be investigated and known offenders brought to book, especially those committing serious crime or large numbers of crimes. Order has to be maintained. In a democratic society communities should shape policing priorities. For the sake of longer-term public protection as well as in the interests of efficiency, police-related problems should be addressed by the police even where enforcement is not the most effective or efficient means of doing so.

Moreover, there are clearly some points of convergence when it comes to the practice implied in the models, marking their operations off from those in traditional policing. The following comprise some examples:

- Problem-oriented policing implies attention to problems exploiting pinch-points in the conditions generating problems (Tilley 2002). This may include targeting prolific offenders criminal organisations, those recruiting new criminals, or stolen goods markets, any or all of which are likely to be focused on also in well executed intelligence-led policing. Likewise problem-oriented policing calls for attention to police-relevant community problems and for use of non-traditional enforcement responses, which would also comprise part of the proper mission of community policing.

- All three models would naturally steer attention to repeat victims. For problem-oriented policing repeat victimisation comprises one major pattern of events that calls for systematic attention, and there have been successes in achieving crime reduction by focusing on it (see, for example, Farrell 1995; Pease 1998; Farrell and Pease 1993, 2001). Moreover, non-crime events of interest to the police also display repeat patterns that are open to interventions (Read *et al.* 1999). There is an association between repeat victimisation and prolific offending. Repeat offenders appear to be largely responsible for repeat offences (Everson and Pease 2001), and concentrating on already-victimised targets proactively is an efficient way of finding prolific offenders. It thus again forms a natural element of high-quality intelligence-led policing. With regard to reducing repeat incidents, community mobilisation has been found to be one important means – for example, in relation to domestic burglary and domestic violence (Forrester *et al.* 1988; Anderson *et al.* 1994; Hanmer *et al.* 1998). This would certainly form part of the agenda of purposive community policing.

- Crackdown and consolidation strategies are plausible candidates for many problems addressed in problem-oriented policing (see Wright 1994; Farrell *et al.* 1998). The crackdown side sits well with intelligence-led policing. It involves efforts to target intensive, well publicised enforcement to incapacitate and/or deter offenders generating problems, an approach found often to have beneficial side-effects beyond the temporal operation of the crackdown itself (Sherman 1990). The consolidation side may sit well with community policing. It involves using the window of opportunity created by the crime lull effected by the crackdown to build longer-term measures to sustain the impact, many of which will sit well with community policing and may involve interventions by community members and non-police agencies.

- Procedurally, both problem-oriented policing and intelligence-led policing call for far more specialist analysis than is conducted in conventional, response policing. They make use of data held by the police and may require special data-collecting exercises. They suggest targeting in the light of the analyses. Intelligence-led policing leaves space for non-enforcement problem-oriented work though it pays it relatively little attention. Similarly, problem-oriented policing leaves space for enforcement when it is appropriate to the problem being addressed and its analysis.

- Problem-solving is widely deemed to comprise one key element of community policing (see, for example, Skogan *et al.* 1999). In its widest sense problem-oriented policing also endorses problem-solving, though the steer specifically towards *problem orientation* implies a strictly analytic, data-using, pattern-finding approach that is not entailed by or indeed practised in much *problem-solving* in community policing.

In most police services it is likely that different specialist units concentrate on different activities conforming more or less to policing according to the different models. So, community policing is conducted mainly by community beat officers and schools liaison officers. Intelligence-led policing is done mainly by intelligence officers and CID. Problem-oriented policing is done mainly by crime prevention officers and crime pattern analysts. Patrol officers and senior officers respectively are deployed and oversee the activities involved in each model as and when required, making sure that where there are potential tensions at the point of practice they do not occur and where there are potential complementarities they are exploited.

The models in practice

Let us turn now to the operation of these models in practice. There is a significant literature on community policing, especially in the USA, and on problem-oriented policing, more of which is British. There is so far rather less on intelligence-led policing which emerged more recently than the other two models.

Problem-oriented policing

The implementation of problem-oriented policing has been found to face substantial challenges both in the UK and the USA (Leigh *et al.* 1996, 1998; Read and Tilley 2000; Scott 2000). Difficulties have included the following.

Cultural resistance
Police officers believe that real policing involves crime fighting, crime fighting entails dealing with miscreants and dealing with miscreants effectively involves catching and punishing them. Real policing is thus deemed primarily to be oriented to enforcement.

Lack of data for analysing problems
Traditional, enforcement-oriented policing uses information to catch and disrupt offending. A premium is put on recency. If several cases are linked it

tends to be because the same offender or group of offenders is thought to be responsible. Longer-term trends and wider-scale patterns not connected because of offender-related links are hard to discern in data which are not collected with this purpose in mind and hence do not reliably and accurately record incidents using standard precoded categories. Most police data are poorly configured for aggregate problem-analytic purposes.

Problems in analysis
Weaknesses in data collection practices clearly inhibit analysis. Also, data analysis to identify patterns is technically and intellectually difficult. Police services have found it very hard to attract and retain analysts with the appropriate skills (see Chapter 14). It is not clear that these analytic capacities are ever likely to be adequate for analysing enduring problems resistant to standard responses (Bullock and Tilley 2003a).

External imperatives
Police services are under pressure to satisfy external imperatives of various sorts, which limit the extent to which problem-oriented policing can be put in place in accordance with the ideal model. For example, the imposition of specific performance indicators steers attention to particular problems. They may also steer police services to particular forms of social control where specified responses, for example, clear-up rates, are measured. These measurements are anathema to problem-oriented policing. Yet new public management methods make them increasingly common.

Demands for response
As an emergency service the police face an inescapable responsibility to respond when called upon to do so. There is certainly a sense among many police officers that they are so busy that they are unable to find the time or resources for standing back and engaging in longer-term problem-oriented work. Ironically, the very stimulus to problem orientation – the growth in demand relative to resources – is taken to comprise a key block to its implementation.

Organisational obstacles
The introduction of problem-oriented policing requires a substantial change in ways of police working. Implementation cannot take place overnight. Sustained and committed leadership backed up by training programmes, appointment of new forms of staff, changed promotion criteria, altered commendation practices, etc., are all needed. In the absence of a sustained and committed change programme problem orientation is likely to remain an occasional fad or the preserve of a few exceptional officers. This is largely the current situation. Senior officers have shorter-term time horizons and wide responsibilities. Driving problem orientation for long enough and across a wide-enough front for it to become a new routine way of doing business has yet to happen in any major force. Mid-range managers (sergeants and shift inspectors in particular) are often caught between the requirement to respond to immediate public demands and calls to work out sustainable solutions to

long-term problems. It is not surprising that the imperatives of the here and now characteristically take precedence.

Where problem-oriented policing has been put in place, the analyses have tended to be weak and the evaluations of the effectiveness of measures introduced unsystematic. Much of the work has comprised relatively low-level problem-solving – useful in itself but not what was intended in Goldstein's model. There has been rather little problem-oriented policing taking substantial and long-term problems, analysing them and putting in place strategies informed by local analysis and established research (Read and Tilley 2000).

As a response to some of these difficulties in implementing problem-oriented policing a series of problem-specific guides is being produced under the auspices of the Office for Community Oriented Policing at the National Institute of Justice in Washington, DC. These provide advice to those attempting to address problems as to the sorts of analysis needed and the kinds of response that might be appropriate in the local conditions in which local problems manifest themselves. At the time of writing some 20 of these have appeared, covering issues such as street prostitution (Scott 2001), theft of and from cars at parking facilities (Clarke 2002), acquaintance rape of college students (Sampson 2002) and burglary of single-family houses (Weisel 2002). More general guides have also appeared covering analysis for and evaluation of initiatives (respectively, Bynum 2001 and Eck 2002). The use and impact of these general and specific guides are not yet known.

Community policing

The fluid ways in which community policing has been characterised mean that what is done in its name varies very widely. Implementing it comprehensively has proved to be very difficult. Those communities most in need of community policing seem to have taken to it least enthusiastically. The marginalised and disaffected and those living in fractured communities, among whom relationships with the police have been least trusting, have not been quick to embrace a redefinition of policing (Sadd and Grinc 1994: 44). Moreover, those who would like to work more closely with the police can be deterred because of intimidation from other residents (Sadd and Grinc 1994: 44; Hancock 2001). Likewise, police officers have also been reluctant fundamentally to alter the ways in which they work. Well organised, well ordered community groups who already trust the police (and who are already trusted by the police) have more readily co-operated in community policing than those in highly disorganised areas (Laycock and Tilley 1995). They also more readily create new organisations in which to work with the police (Sadd and Grinc 1994: 42–3). Even in middle-class communities, however, many instruments of community policing such as Neighbourhood Watch have tended not to remain active for long.

Community police officers in particular are frequently put down (Sadd and Grinc 1994). Officers are referred to by their colleagues, for example, as 'hobby bobbies', 'empty holsters' or 'officer friendlies'. They are not deemed to be doing real policing at the sharp end. Instead, they are deemed, disparagingly, to be engaged in social work (Sadd and Grinc 1994: 37; Skogan and Hartnett 1997: 71). Moreover, some of those allocated to community policing duties fail to present themselves within neighbourhoods in ways that elicit trust (Hancock 2001). They may do what can be measured by monitoring their activities, but fail to follow this up with problem-solving and action (Skogan and Hartnett 1997: 72). The monitoring and supervision of officers who have to learn the intelligent and sensitive use of discretion called for in community policing are tricky (Greene 2000). Community policing processes are hard to manage, and this creates problems in a disciplined organisation focused on adherence to rules (see Skogan and Hartnett 1997: 73).

Community policing has sat uneasily with some of the work the police are otherwise expected to do. If the police are expected one day to enforce order, it is difficult the next to redefine the relationship in terms of community engagement. If arrests to meet community concerns are agreed with a community officer their credibility is jeopardised if colleagues fail to play their part, perhaps because of wider concerns about organised crime (Hancock 2001: 144).

Performance management requirements can be important inhibitors to the changes called for in community policing (Skogan and Hartnett 1997; Greene 2000). As Greene, reflecting on American experience, puts it:

> American policing is in a catch-22 situation where it at once announces to the community and to the police that they should expect something different from the police and yet measures those things that are most associated with traditional policing, such as crime reporting and arrests. In systems where there is a disjuncture between preaching and practice, it should be expected that employees would follow the path of what is measured, rewarded and punished (2000: 359).

In practice much of what passes for community policing merely comprises an adjunct to traditional policing aligned to traditional achievement measurements. Moreover this adjunct involves those who are already supportive of the police as they currently operate: those who are law abiding and living conventional lifestyles. The community, construed in this way, can furnish 'eyes and ears' for the police. They can alert police officers to suspicious behaviour. They may even help out in operations by providing premises from which covert observations can be made. The community in this account is ancillary to the police service. Neighbourhood Watch can often operate in this way. Special constables work directly within the police as a formal volunteer support service. Those attracted to working with the police on these terms are rarely the disaffected whose relatively poor relations with the police prompted recommendations for community policing. Indeed, there is a risk that it might reinforce notions among the disaffected that there is too cosy a relationship between some sections of the community, with their own interests and the police service. Community beat officers weave into (or infiltrate) local neighbourhood life to elicit intelligence and to mobilise support for the police service and its agenda. The community, be they local citizens or members of other agencies, becomes a valuable medium through which police services can operate more efficiently and effectively, with more trust and less resistance (see

Brake and Hale 1992: 77–8). In Bayley's terms, the accent here is on police *mobilisation* of the community for its own ends, but without the consultation, adaptation or problem-solving (see Bayley 1994).

Intelligence-led policing

The research community has been less involved in the development, implementation, observation and evaluation of intelligence-led policing than they have in problem-oriented and community policing. As a formalised way of policing it is also much more recent. Though there have been studies of its early implementation (Maguire and John 1995; Amey *et al.* 1996a, 1996b) time will yet tell what happens in the longer term with the NIM as a vehicle for delivering it. Maguire and John and Amey *et al.* found various problems in efforts to implement intelligence-led policing prior to the NIM. These included the following:

- Continued officer involvement in response-led policing creating problems in setting aside time for proactive work.

- Difficulties in creating and maintaining a steady flow of intelligence, analysis, preparation of target packages and conduct of operations.

- Lack of training, senior officer commitment and poor communication between specialist units.

- Usympathetic attitudes, cultural resistance and low morale among officers performing less attractive roles.

In the one area Maguire and John looked at where radical changes had been introduced to produce 'an integrated, intelligence-driven approach to crime investigation', implementation was least problematic. Partial, ad hoc implementation had been less successful. The NIM as a vehicle for delivering intelligence-led policing aspires to inform that integrated approach which Maguire and John find to be most promising in implementation terms.

Will the NIM be taken up enthusiastically? Will it be subject to development and enhancement? Will it wither? So far the NIM has enjoyed wide support from chief police officers, HMIC and the Home Office. It is formally being rolled out nationally. Tasking and co-ordination meetings are being held widely. Patrol is being informed by analyst-defined hotspots. Individuals and groups are being targeted for special police attention on the basis of intelligence about who is actively involved in crime and who is networked with whom. Moreover, new techniques are being devised to establish 'harder' links between offenders and crime scenes and between one offender and another. FLINTS (the Forensic Led Intelligence System) is an important example. This carries a database of links established through physical evidence, notably fingerprints and DNA profiles, between known and unknown individuals and scenes. It enables networks and linkages among and between individuals and crimes scenes to be established and represented. It can thereby inform police targeting of enforcement efforts, where it can be expected to have maximum impact.

Despite some resistance to the immediate changes effected, intelligence-led policing may come to play better with traditional grass-roots police officers than community or problem-oriented policing. The primary activity embraced for police officers is enforcement. The main means of control comprise deterrence and containment through incarceration. The distinction between the offender and the non-offender is maintained and problems are firmly laid at the doors of the offender. All this fits well with prevailing assumptions. None of it challenges current ways of thinking. The image added to the police is a flattering one. Who would not want to be seen to be 'intelligence led'? The form of policing suggested is also likely to receive support from the public and politicians. It continues to be hard on the criminal, but targets that hardness on the worst offenders.

None of this means that intelligence-led policing will necessarily be effective in controlling crime or dealing with police-related community problems. Goldstein, commenting almost a quarter of a century ago, expresses scepticism about the then forerunners to intelligence-led policing, where he says:

> Some police departments have, through the use of computers, developed sophisticated programs to analyse reported crimes. Unfortunately, these analyses are almost always put to very limited use – to apprehend a professional car thief or deter a well-known cat burglar – rather than serving as a basis for rethinking the overall police response to the problem of car theft or cat burglaries (1979: 244).

And it remains the case that we lack systematic independent evaluations of intelligence-led policing to see whether it can reach out beyond enforcement to other effective means of dealing with problems. Potential ethical and operational problems in the covert means mobilised by intelligence-led policing have also been noted by some commentators, including the risk that privacy will be invaded disproportionately to the potential benefits from its breach, that crime itself might be overlooked, that crime might be inadvertently encouraged and that there may be tensions between short-term prevention and longer-term detection, etc. (see, for example, Maguire and John 1995; Maguire 2000; Norris and Dunninghan 2000).

Conclusion: prospects for the three models

While community policing, problem-oriented policing and intelligence-led policing differ substantially in their origins and rationales and in the purposes they assign to policing, at the point of service delivery there are substantial areas of overlap where different models will agree on needed new practices.

Efforts to implement significant change in policing, of whatever kind, have been found to encounter severe difficulties. Front-line police services are notoriously resistant to change (see Skogan and Hartnett 1997: 74ff). Police officers cannot for the most part be seen as they perform their duties. In practice, they have to exercise discretion whatever model of policing is purportedly in place. They are also accustomed to changing fads, fancies and directives from their bosses (see Sadd and Grinc 1994: 39–40), or their bosses' bosses. They are often understandably cynical about what is being asked from the 'dream factory', as headquarters are sometimes called. Unsympathetic officers can often get away with minimal compliance. They can weather new-fangled ideas and continue to deliver the policing they feel is appropriate. There is ample scope for subversion of new thinking from within (Rogers 2002). Moreover, high rates of senior staff turnover, external political pressures and traditional performance measurements are all apt to inhibit efforts to implement sustained change programmes.

Despite these difficulties there have been some successes in putting in place new models. Skogan and Hartnett report significant change in officer attitudes along intended lines in prototype areas where community policing was being implemented in the Chicago Alternative Policing Strategy. Wycoff and Skogan (1994: 88–9) likewise found in Madison that it had been possible to 'bend granite' and effect changes in police organisation, leading to higher levels of community involvement. One British superintendent in Lancashire, committed to problem-oriented policing and apparently effective in doing so in his patch, likened effecting change in his force to dealing with a large liner. The ship moves steadily in one direction through inertia. Stopping and changing direction quickly are not possible. But change had been made over time with a consistent steer.

Also, and notwithstanding the difficulties encountered in changing police organisations as a whole, many individual officers are committed to one or other new model of policing and act accordingly. Many try to police in ways they believe appropriate, drawing on the new models. And some outstanding work can be seen as a result – for example, in entries to the American Goldstein Award for problem-oriented policing and its British counterpart, the Tilley Award.

Is there a 'best buy' among the models discussed here? The following comprise reasons for thinking that intelligence-led policing, under the auspices of the NIM, may be more likely to take hold and if so to take hold more quickly that problem-oriented or community policing:

1. Its assumptions, priorities and ways of working accord well with traditional policing.

2. It tasks police officers with specific jobs and does not expect them to exercise substantial discretion.

3. It is endorsed by senior police officers, ACPO, HMIC and the Home Office.

4. It is attuned to delivering outcomes that fit with traditional measurements of police effectiveness.

5. The changes required do not threaten significant police subgroup interests, processes or cultural beliefs.

6. It is framed to be able to accommodate some problem-oriented policing.

7. It leaves a residual role for community engagement in the interests of feeding information into the model.

We have, though, yet to see how well and how extensively the intelligence-led model is implemented and what outcome benefits, if any, it produces. We have also yet to see whether or not it is able to deliver ethical policing (see Chapter 23).

If it could be put in place successfully, however, most benefits would accrue from problem-oriented policing. It is evidence based. It has an explicit account of the distinctive role and purpose of policing. It provides space for community policing and intelligence-led enforcement as required by the problems being addressed. It stresses substance and effectiveness over process and style. Since it is attentive to emerging problems it is adaptable to changed conditions. Yet at its most ambitious it would require a revolution in terms of police culture, organisation and capacity for analysis. It would also require a conducive external political environment. In having these requirements it may at worst be utopian and at best a very long-term project.

Selected further reading

An influential early rationale for intelligence-led policing can be found in the Audit Commission's *Helping with Enquiries: Tackling Crime Effectively* (1993). A statement of what is deemed to be involved in doing intelligence-led policing through the NIM is to be found in the NCIS's *The National Intelligence Model* (2000). An account of some experience of intelligence-led methods of policing in practice is to be found in Maguire and John's *Intelligence, Surveillance and Informants* (1995). A short, accessible account of the principles and practice of problem-oriented policing is to be found in Braga's *Problem-oriented Policing and Crime Prevention* (2002). Goldstein's classic *Problem-oriented Policing* (1990) repays reading and rereading. An account of the British experience of delivering problem-oriented policing can be found in Read and Tilley's *Not Rocket Science: Problem-solving and Crime Reduction* (2000).

For an account of thinking behind community policing in the UK, see Alderson's *Policing Freedom* (1979). The most extensive and systematic account of community policing in practice is Skogan and Hartnett's *Community Policing Chicago Style* (1997). A useful collection on the nature and experience of community policing is Rosenbaum's *The Challenge of Community Policing* (1994). Two collections with discussions covering problem-oriented policing, intelligence-led policing and community policing are Skogan's *Community Policing: Can it Work?* (2003) and Bullock and Tilley's *Crime Reduction and Problem-oriented Policing* (2003).

Note

1 This may be because there is a longer-term and stronger tradition of police working with communities in Britain than in the USA (see Mawby 1992; Greene 2000).

References

Alderson, J. (1977) *Communal Policing*. Exeter: Devon and Cornwall Constabulary.
Alderson, J. (1979) *Policing Freedom*. Plymouth: Macdonald & Evans.

Amey, P., Hale, C. and Uglow, S. (1996a) *Development and Evaluation of a Crime Management Model. Police Research Series Paper* 18. London: Home Office.

Amey, P., Hale, C. and Uglow, S. (1996b) *Proactive Policing*. Edinburgh: Scottish Central Research Unit.

Anderson, D., Chenery, S. and Pease, K. (1994) *Biting Back: Tackling Repeat Burglary and Car Crime. Crime Detection and Prevention Series* Paper 58. London: Home Office.

Audit Commission (1993) *Helping with Enquiries: Tackling Crime Effectively. Police Paper* 12. London: HMSO.

Bayley, D. (1994) *Police for the Future*. New York, NY: Oxford University Press.

Bennett, T. (1994) 'Community policing on the ground: developments in Britain', in D. Rosenbaum (ed.) *The Challenge of Community Policing*. Thousand Oaks, CA: Sage, 224–46.

Braga, A. (2002) *Problem-oriented Policing and Crime Prevention*. Monsey, NY: Criminal Justice Press.

Brake, M. and Hale, C. (1992) *Public Order and Private Lives*. London: Routledge.

Bullock, K. and Tilley, N. (2003a) 'The role of research and analysis: lessons from the crime reduction programme', in J. Knutsson (ed.) *Problem-oriented Policing: From Innovation to Mainstream. Crime Prevention Studies Series* 15. Cullompton: Willan, 147–81.

Bullock, K. and Tilley, N. (2003b) *Crime Reduction and Problem-oriented Policing*. Cullompton: Willan.

Bynum, T. (2001) *Using Analysis for Problem-solving*. Washington, DC: US Department of Justice Office of Community-oriented Policing Services.

Clarke, R. (2002) *Thefts of and from Cars in Parking Facilities. Problem-oriented Guides for Police Series* 10. Washington, DC: US Department of Justice Office of Community-oriented Policing Services.

Clarke, R. and Goldstein, H. (2002) 'Reducing thefts at construction sites: lessons from a problem-oriented project', in N. Tilley (ed.) *Analysis for Crime Prevention. Crime Prevention Studies Series* 13. Monsey, NY: Criminal Justice Press, 89–130.

Cohen, L. and Felson, M. (1979) 'Social change and crime rate trends: a routine activity approach', *American Sociological Review*, 44: 588–605.

Eck, J. (2002) *Assessing Responses to Problems: An Introductory Guide for Police Problem-solvers. Problem-oriented Guides for Police Series*. Washington, DC: US Department of Justice Office of Community-oriented Policing Services.

Eck, J. and Rosenbaum, D. (1994) 'The new police order: effectiveness, equity, and efficiency in community policing', in D. Rosenbaum (ed.) *The Challenge of Community Policing*. Thousand Oaks, CA: Sage, 3–23.

Everson, S. and Pease, K. (2001) 'Crime against the same person and place: detection opportunity and offender targeting', in G. Farrell and K. Pease (eds) *Repeat Victimization. Crime Prevention Studies Series* 12. Monsey, NY: Criminal Justice Press, 199–220.

Farrell, G. (1995) 'Preventing repeat victimisation', in M. Tonry and D. Farrington (eds) *Building a Safer Society: Strategic Approaches to Crime Prevention. Crime and Justice. Vol. 19*. Chicago, IL: University of Chicago Press, 469–534.

Farrell, G., Chenery, S. and Pease, K. (1998) *Consolidating Police Crackdowns: Findings from an Anti-burglary Project. Police Research Series Paper* 113. London: Home Office.

Farrell, G. and Pease, K. (1993) *Once Bitten, Twice Bitten: Repeat Victimisation and its Implications for Crime Prevention. Crime Prevention Unit Paper* 46. London: Home Office.

Farrell, G. and Pease, K. (2001) *Repeat Victimization. Crime Prevention Studies Series* 12. Monsey, NY: Criminal Justice Press.

Felson, M. (1998) *Crime and Everyday Life*. Thousand Oaks, CA: Pine Forge Press.

Forrester, D., Chatterton, M. and Pease, K. (1988) *The Kirkholt Burglary Prevention Project. Crime Prevention Unit Paper* 13. London: Home Office.

Goldstein, H. (1977) *Policing in a Free Society*. Cambridge, MA: Ballinger.

Goldstein, H. (1979) 'Improving policing: a problem-oriented approach', *Crime and Delinquency*, 25: 236–58.

Goldstein, H. (1990) *Problem-oriented Policing*. New York, NY: McGraw-Hill.

Greene, J. (2000) 'Community policing in America: changing the nature, structure, and function of the police', in J. Horney (ed.) *Policies, Processes and Decisions of the Criminal Justice System. Criminal Justice 2000*. Washington, DC: US Department of Justice Office of Justice Programs, 299–370.

Hancock, L. (2001) *Community, Crime and Disorder: Safety and Regeneration in Urban Neighbourhoods*. Basingstoke: Palgrave.

Hanmer, J., Griffiths, S. and Jerwood, D. (1998) *Arresting Evidence: Domestic Violence and Repeat Victimisation. Crime Detection and Prevention Series Paper* 104. London: Home Office.

Kelling, G. and Coles, C. (1996) *Fixing Broken Windows*. New York, NY: Free Press.

Laycock, G. and Tilley, N. (1995) *Policing and Neighbourhood Watch: Strategic Issues. Crime Detection and Prevention Series Paper* 60. London: Home Office.

Leigh, A., Read, T. and Tilley, N. (1996) *Problem-oriented Policing: Brit Pop. Crime Prevention and Detection Series Paper* 75. London: Home Office.

Leigh, A., Read, T. and Tilley, N. (1998) *Brit Pop II: Problem-oriented Policing in Practice. Police Research Series Paper* 93. London: Home Office.

Maguire, M. (2000) 'Policing by risks and targets: some dimensions and implications of intelligence-led crime control,' *Policing and Society*, 9: 315–36.

Maguire, M. and John, T. (1995) *Intelligence, Surveillance and Informants: Integrated Approaches. Crime Prevention and Detection Series Paper* 64. London: Home Office.

Mawby, R. (1992) 'Comparative police systems: searching for a continental model', in K. Bottomley *et al.* (eds) *Criminal Justice Theory and Practice*. London: British Society of Criminology, 108–32.

Metcalfe, B. (2001) 'The strategic integration of POP and performance management: a viable partnership?', *Policing and Society*, 11: 209–34.

National Criminal Intelligence Service (NCIS) (2000) *The National Intelligence Model*. London: NCIS.

Norris, C. and Dunninghan, C. (2000) 'Subterranean blues: conflict as an unintended consequence of the police use of informers', *Policing and Society*, 9: 385–412.

Pease, K. (1998) *Repeat Victimisation: Taking Stock. Crime Detection and Prevention Series Paper* 90. London: Home Office.

Read, T. and Tilley, N. (2000) *Not Rocket Science: Problem-solving and Crime Reduction. Crime Reduction Research Series Paper* 6. London: Home Office.

Read, T., Tilley, N., White, J., Wilson, M. and Leigh, A. (1999) 'Repeat calls for service and problem-oriented policing', *Studies on Crime and Crime Prevention*, 8: 265–79.

Reiner, R. (1991) *Chief Constables*. Oxford: Oxford University Press.

Rogers, C. (2002) 'Community safety and zero tolerance: a study in partnership policing.' Unpublished PhD thesis, University of Glamorgan.

Rosenbaum, D. (1994) *The Challenge of Community Policing*. Thousand Oaks, CA: Sage.

Sadd, S. and Grinc, R. (1994) 'Innovative neighborhood oriented policing: an evaluation of community policing plans in eight cities', in D. Rosenbaum (ed.) *The Challenge of Community Policing*. Thousand Oaks, CA: Sage, 27–52.

Sampson, R. (2002) *Acquaintance Rape of College Students. Problem-oriented Guides for Police Series* 17. Washington, DC: US Department of Justice Office of Community-oriented Policing Services.

Scarman, Lord (1982) *The Scarman Report: The Brixton Disorders, 10–12 April 1981*. Harmondsworth: Penguin Books.

Scott, M. (2000) *Problem-oriented Policing: Reflections on the First 20 Years*. Washington, DC: Department of Justice, Office of Community-oriented Policing Services.

Scott, M. (2001) *Street Prostitution. Problem-oriented Guides for Police Series* 2. Washington, DC: US Department of Justice Office of Community-oriented Policing Services.

Sherman, L. (1990) 'Police crackdowns: initial and residual deterrence', in M. Tonry and N. Morris (eds) *Crime and Justice: A Review of Research. Vol. 12.* Chicago, IL: University of Chicago Press, 1–47.

Skogan, W. (2003) *Community Policing: Can it Work?.* Belmont, CA: Wadsworth.

Skogan, W. and Hartnett, S. (1997) *Community Policing Chicago Style.* New York, NY: Oxford University Press.

Skogan, W., Hartnett, S., DuBois, J., Comey, J., Kaiser, M. and Lovig, J. (1999) *On the Beat: Police and Community Problem Solving.* Boulder, CO: Westview Press.

Tilley, N. (1999) 'The relationship between crime prevention and problem-oriented policing', in C. Sole Brito and T. Allan (eds) *Problem-oriented Policing: Crime-specific Problems, Critical Issues and Making POP Work. Vol. 2.* Washington, DC: Police Executive Research Forum, 253–80.

Tilley, N. (2002) 'Introduction: analysis for crime prevention', in N. Tilley (ed.) *Analysis for Crime Prevention. Crime Prevention Studies Series* 13. Monsey, NY: Criminal Justice Press, 1–13.

Tilley, N. and Laycock, G. (2002) *Working out what to Do: Evidence-based Crime Reduction. Crime Reduction Research Paper* 11. London: Home Office.

Trojanowicz, R. and Bucqueroux, B. (1990) *Community Policing: A Contemporary Perspective.* Cincinnati, OH: Anderson.

Weatheritt, M. (1988) 'Community policing: rhetoric or reality?', in J. Greene and S. Mastrofski (eds) *Community Policing: Rhetoric or Reality.* New York, NY: Praeger, 153–76.

Weisel, D. (2002) *Burglary of Single-family Houses. Problem-oriented Guides for Police Series* 18. Washington, DC: US Department of Justice Office of Community-oriented Policing Services.

Weisel, D. and Eck, J. (1994) 'Towards a practical approach to organizational change: community policing initiatives in six cities', in D. Rosenbaum (ed.) *The Challenge of Community Policing.* Thousand Oaks, CA: Sage, 53–72.

Wright, A. (1994) 'Short-term crackdowns and long-term objectives', *Policing*, 10(4): 253–9.

Wycoff, M. and Skogan, W. (1994) 'Community policing in Madison: an analysis of implementation and impact', in D. Rosenbaum (ed.) *The Challenge of Community Policing.* Thousand Oaks, CA: Sage, 75–91.

Chapter 14

Crime analysis: principles and practice

Nina Cope[1]

Introduction

Crime analysis involves the synthesis of police and other relevant data to identify and interpret patterns and trends in crime to inform police and judicial practice (Gill 2000). Engaging in the process of analysis suggests patterns of crime can be identified among offenders, offences, victims, spaces and places. Crime analysis supports the prevention, reduction and investigation of crime by providing the police with information that enables them to prioritise interventions. Local crime analysis identifies the location of crime problems, criminal targets and vulnerable victims to prevent and reduce crime, while investigative analysis assists with solving crimes and the prosecution of offenders by providing information for presentation at court.

The expansion of crime analysis is closely associated with recent developments in policing, including the emphasis on problem-oriented interventions, the use of intelligence to target police activity (see Chapter 13) and advancing information technology that has dramatically increased the capacity of the police to store and retrieve information (see Chapter 26). However, the position, status and quality of crime analysis can vary considerably between police forces. Currently, analysis within UK police forces is influenced by the National Intelligence Model (NIM), which identifies three levels of crime: level 1, covering local crime; level 2, cross border crime; and level 3, including national, transnational, serious and organised crime (NCIS 2000; see Chapters 13 and 15). Crime analysts are frequently located in intelligence units, at level 1 and 2 within police forces (analysis at level 3 is the responsibility of the National Criminal Intelligence Service – NCIS), although some forces may also have analysts attached to special inquiry units, such as murder investigation teams. The number of crime analysts working within forces varies. The Metropolitan Police, for example, have 150 analyst positions across 32 local intelligence units at level 1, with another 100 analytical positions at level 2. Cope *et al.* (2001) in their study of intelligence-led policing found a county force had only two crime analysts working in each of the three local

340

intelligence units, compared to a metropolitan force that had up to six analysts working in the local intelligence units included in the research.

This chapter is divided into four sections. The first section considers why analysis is desirable within policing and outlines a five-stage analytical process. The chapter goes on to consider a number of analytical techniques, including offender profiling, which are used in the analysis of crime. The third section of the chapter addresses the frequently atheoretical approach of analytical techniques by introducing useful theory for developing explanation in volume crime analysis. Finally, the chapter considers the context of analysis and some of the principal limitations to the use of crime analysis in operational policing.

The purpose and process of crime analysis in policing

As crime analysis supports the police by providing detailed information about crime problems to target appropriate interventions, it has become integral to problem-oriented and intelligence-led approaches. Problem-oriented approaches suggest the police, by shifting their emphasis away from responding to the symptoms of problems, have a significant role in crime prevention and reduction (Goldstein 1990). Intelligence-led policing also aims to shift the emphasis of the police away from demand-driven interventions towards proactive methods of crime control. The importance of using intelligence, understood as information developed for action, to focus police activity on offenders who were responsible for the majority of the police workload, was outlined in the Audit Commission report, *Helping with Enquiries: Tackling Crime Effectively* (1993). Intelligence-led policing has developed within the broader context of the 'risk society' that has influenced the proliferation of risk management strategies throughout criminal justice agencies (Ericson and Haggerty 1997; Maguire 2000). Currently, the NIM (NCIS 2000) offers a framework for the implementation of intelligence-led approaches in UK police forces.

New modes of public management (Bottoms and Wiles 1996; see Chapter 25) and ongoing debates around capturing police performance and accountability (Johnston 2000; see Chapter 24) have also influenced the development of crime analysis. Perhaps the starkest example of monitoring performance and accountability is COMPSTAT, a process that relies on the delivery of accurate and timely computerised statistics to assess crime problems and police response. Crime analysis supports the COMPSTAT process by providing crime maps that 'visualise crime problems' (McGuire 2000) so that, in an era of rationalised police resources, analysis is crucial for identifying priority areas where the impact of interventions will be greatest (Manning 2001).

Crime analysis supports problem-oriented and intelligence-led approaches by reviewing large volumes of information to identify problems, thereby enabling 'tailor-made' interventions to be developed (Tilley 2002a), and police activity to be targeted towards identified risks (Maguire 2000). Analysis facilitates the dissemination of critical intelligence and the development of preventative strategies (Ekblom 1988; Martens 1990). A systematic, five-stage analytical process is outlined in Figure 14.1.

Figure 14.1 The analytical process

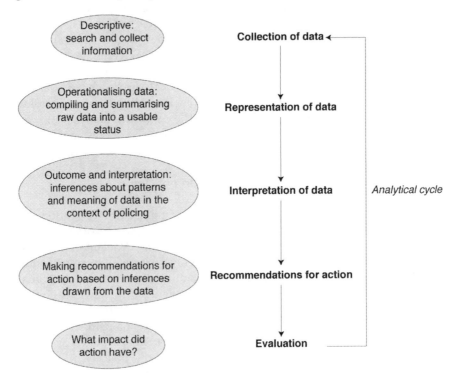

The first stage of crime analysis concerns the *collection* of data. This is the initial research phase, which will involve the analysts pulling together a range of data sources. In the main, analysts focus on police data and information held by other criminal justice agencies, although arguably this should extend to include relevant quantitative and qualitative research that would provide a broader insight into crime and criminality. Collecting information for analysis can take time, especially when the technology has not been designed with analysis in mind and therefore simply stores a range of data in no particular order or coding system to facilitate interrogation. The growth of computer and information technology has supported the increasing demand for information and intelligence, reinforcing the role of the police as key providers of risk-related information (Ratcliffe 2002a). This usually means a lot of information is stored 'just in case' although little may be useful for analysis because the guidance from police forces around what to store is vague, probably due to the difficulty of assessing the relevance of data (Maguire and John 1995; Ericson and Haggerty 1997; Ratcliffe 2002a). Further issues concerning data standards, the format and accuracy of data recording, and protocols of information sharing with other criminal justice agencies also complicates the collection of data.

The second stage of analysis focuses on the *representation of data*. Technology has dramatically affected the capacity of crime analysis to chart key variables associated with crime data, such as the peak days and time of offending,

Table 14.1 Key information to consider in the process of crime analysis

Variable	Explanation
Nature of offence	Legal category and grounds of offence
Location of offence	Space and place of offending
Time of offence	Includes day and time of day
Method of offence	How the offence was committed
Target of offence	The objective of the offence
Victim characteristics	Includes the age, gender and activity at the time of offence
Physical and social circumstances of the offence	Environmental and situational factors and how they contributed to the offence

offenders' association networks and the spatial characteristics of crime (Weisburd and McEwen 1998). Indeed, the reliance of crime analysis on technology has led research to suggest that some key stages, such as the collection and representation of data, could be automated (Read and Oldfield 1995). For example, FLINTS (the Forensic Linked Intelligence System), a computer system developed by the West Midlands Police in the UK, facilitates the search and presentation of data for further analysis. Developing an analytical picture of crime involves analysts seeking basic information to explore the 'who, what, where, when, how and why' of offending. Ekblom (1988: 12; see Table 14.1) identified seven key variables for crime analysis to consider when sorting and developing data.

While the representation of data is an extremely powerful tool, which supports the visualisation of crime, the data presented are, in the main, descriptive. Maps, for example, are retrospective. They describe where crime *has* occurred and where offences *were* concentrated, but do not necessarily explain *why* this pattern emerged, *what* might occur in the future and *how* it should influence decisions around police deployment (Groff and La Vigne 2002). Descriptive data have a basic informative value in that they present information in a flexible, simple format (Eck *et al.* 2000) and, in a performance-driven culture, having some knowledge about the size and location of current crime problems is crucial (McGuire 2000). Furthermore, the ability to present volumes of data in an easily recogniseable and understandable form has led to analytical techniques being used to prepare investigative data for court proceedings. However, it is crucial that crime analysis interprets information to support proactive policing.

Interpretation is arguably where *analysis* really begins as it moves from the descriptive presentation of data to explanation so that the patterns and distribution of crime can be explained and understood. To demonstrate the process I want to consider an increase in burglaries in a locality. The first task for the analyst is to collect all the relevant information pertaining to the area and the crimes. To sort these data the analyst is likely to use analytical techniques to represent the problem. This may include mapping the location of offences, tracking the property taken, the time, method and victims of the offences. The interpretation of data will consider what the emerging patterns mean. For example, can a linked series of offences be inferred from the method or forensic information? The location of offences may lead an analyst to suggest potential suspects based on their residence. The review of offending method may offer an insight into potential crime generators or patterns of repeat victimisation. Finally, tracking the property taken may lead an analyst to deduce the nature of the stolen-goods market in the locality. The example highlights that while maps of offences are revealing, they will also conceal a large amount of information as they 'cry out for interpretation because they are crude and must be seen from some social perspective' (Manning 2001: 96).

The ability to map or present volumes of data in a visual form is an achievement for policing, but it cannot be understood as crime analysis, which is a far more *cognitive* than technical and computer-driven process (Buslik and Maltz 1998). As the data for analysis can be fragmented, incomplete and inexact inferences need to be drawn to ensure the implications of the patterns, profile and crime distribution are interpreted to support police decision-making (Kelly 1990; Eck 1998). The process of interpretation in crime analysis is both deductive and inductive. A *deductive* method involves the development of a theory, which is then tested through empirical research. In analysis this may be the hypothesis that young men commit more violent crime than young women, which is then validated through the analysis of crime trends. *Induction* is the reverse of deduction and involves developing explanations and theories based on observation and research. For example, the representation of data reveals that theft is concentrated in a socially deprived area that has recently experienced gentrification, culminating in the development of a large entertainment and residential complex. An analyst might consider the impact of the development on the population and opportunities for crime in order to explain the crime trend.

Maintaining the distinction between description and explanation in analysis is important, not least because analytical representations of crime can be misleading (see later discussion). However, interpretation in crime analysis can be difficult to achieve in practice, especially when analysts' computer skills mean they are frequently called upon to fulfil a range of administrative functions (Gill 2000) and provide descriptive statistical information for management that summarises rather than initiates police action (Cope *et al.* 2001). Furthermore, the training and knowledge of analysts and police officers may not support the development of interpretation. As Eck (1998: 381) notes: 'our ability to use maps effectively depends as much on how we incorporate theories in the maps of data'. This sentiment can be extended to other techniques of analysis where data patterns are represented but not explained.

The fourth stage of the analytical process involves *recommendations for action*. By reviewing the data, crime analysts can identify and prioritise crime problems so that police activity can be focused where an intervention is most likely to impact on crime reduction. Crime analysis can also guide investigations towards likely suspects. To return to the above example of analysing burglaries, by reviewing potential offenders, linked series offences, repeat victims and the stolen-goods market, analysis can *support* the investigation of key offenders, direct crime prevention to vulnerable victims and assist with developing market reduction strategies. Analytical recommendations can include police tactics, the collection of further information to increase research and the development of problem-oriented interventions and crime prevention.

The final stage of the analytical process is *evaluation*. Generally the police do not capture the impact of their activity because they are continually responding to new or different problems, or they do not have the time, resources, people, skills or motivation to evaluate practice. Increasingly 'what works' research has aimed to provide an evidence base for policing and crime reduction interventions (Goldblatt and Lewis 1998; Sherman *et al.* 1998), although there is some way to go before the knowledge developed from research is fully integrated into police practice (Ekblom 2002). Evaluation, understood as research that aims to assess the impact of activity to inform policy, is crucial for developing evidence-based decision-making (Ratcliffe 2002a; Tilley 2002b). In the complex environment of policing and crime it is especially important for evaluation to capture the context of interventions and the mechanisms than make them successful or otherwise (Pawson and Tilley 1997). The role of analysis in continually monitoring crime places it in a good position to evaluate police practice.

Perfect pictures: the techniques of crime analysis

The possibility of crime analysis in policing has increased alongside the proliferation of a range of technology and specialised software packages, which support the stages of the analytical process. The frequently computerised techniques aim to provide a detailed picture of offending to facilitate the interpretation of trends, patterns and incidents. Analytical techniques focus on the analysis of *trends*, *spaces*, *times* and particular crime types, criminal associations and offenders through the development of *profiles*. Crime analysis can be both tactical and strategic. *Tactical analysis* aims to maximise the impact of enforcement by reviewing current crime problems and prolific offenders to inform investigations and operations. *Strategic analysis* identifies longer-term crime problems and future trends to provide management with an understanding of the scope and dimension of criminal activity in order to assist with local policy development and planning. The appropriate analytical technique should be selected according to the problem being investigated, the data available for analysis, the tactical or strategic focus of the analysis and the analytical report being produced. This chapter provides a general introduction to the techniques of analysis and analytical products, their rationale and some of the associated strengths and weaknesses (see Table 14.2 for a summary). The more specialised technical aspects of analytical software and data can be found in practitioner and expert guides (for example, see Harries 1999).

The strengths and weaknesses of analytical techniques

Computer-based techniques aid analysis by presenting data in a format that can be easily understood. However, 'any analytical technique, no matter how

Table 14.2 Summary of analytical techniques and outputs/products

	Explanation
Analytical techniques	
Statistical analysis	The monitoring of all statistical data pertaining to crime and police activity. Provides an overview to identify areas for more detailed analysis.
Crime pattern analysis	A widely used term that generally refers to the analysis of spatial patterns of crime and the identification of crime hotspots to target police deployment. Crime pattern analysis is usually associated with geographic information systems (GIS) that support the mapping of crime and other social data.
Temporal	Monitors the temporal patterns of offending around days and hours. Identifies any trends to assist with targeting police deployment.
Seasonal	A strategic form of analysis that monitors seasonal trends in crime, to enable potential crime problems to be anticipated.
Network analysis	Usually associated with tactical analysis, it assesses the associations and linkages between offenders to identify areas for intervention. Frequently supported by analysts software such as I2.
Telephone record analysis	A form of tactical network analysis that assesses the trends and patterns of phone records. Often used in investigative analysis to support the prosecution of offenders.
Time series analysis	A form of network analysis that reviews the pattern and frequency of criminal activity within a given period of time. Useful for assessing prolific offending patterns and the escalation of offending.
Analytical outputs/products	
Criminal market analysis	Assesses the operation of criminal markets and networks. Can facilitate a market-focused crime reduction strategy.
Demographic and social trend analysis	A product in the NIM that assesses the context of broader demographic and social issues and their impact on crime. Will involve the analysis of data from other criminal justice agencies. Useful for strategic analysis as it considers issues associated with population, employment, education and their potential impact on offending patterns.
Results analysis	A product in the NIM that assesses the impact of activity (or no activity) on crime problems. Facilitates an understanding of 'what works' and an evidence base for future decision-making and deployment.
Risk analysis	A product in the NIM that assesses the extent to which crime problems are persistent or irregular and the imperative for police intervention. Considers the impact of intervention or non-intervention.
Target profile	A tactical form of analysis that assesses the criminal activity and methods of a prolific offender.

Source: Peterson (1994); NCIS (2000).

elaborate or elegant, will not replace good data or make up for poor or inadequate information' (Ianni and Reuss-Ianni 1990). Therefore, it is important to consider the quality of the information that is presented by analytical techniques, such as crime maps or offender network association charts.

Considering the prolific role of crime maps in policing (Weisburd and McEwen 1998) and their strength at representing volumes of spatial information (Ratcliffe and McCullagh 2001), the extent to which maps represent an accurate picture of crime needs to be discussed. Maps rely on accurate data, which can be undermined by the lack of knowledge about the exact location of offences and the recording of incomplete addresses, or incorrectly spelt street names. To map data within a geographic information system (GIS), geographical references are applied to addresses, known as geo-coding. However, some police computer systems do not support geo-coding (Ratcliffe 2000). Furthermore, the methodology of mapping is important as different approaches to spatial analysis may result in the identification of different 'hotspots' (Ratcliffe 2002b). Some maps count crime in localities producing the computer equivalent of manual 'drawing-pin' maps that adorned office walls prior to the introduction of mapping technologies. Another type of hotspot map draws ellipses to delineate a general area where crime is concentrated. The latter can identify broad areas for intervention but may not be as accurate as the more information-laden dot-map version (Harries 1999).

A further limitation of maps is that they count data but do not offer an insight into the relative risk of crime (Craglia *et al.* 2000). For example, a burglary hotspot map does not indicate how likely a resident in the area is to be burgled. To assess the relative risk of burglary an analyst would need to take account of the number of households in the area and to what extent they represent the target population. However, the degree of random error in mapping affects the extent to which the relative risk of offending can be assessed. While maps are exceptionally good at drawing attention to areas where crime is high and low, they provide little insight into the causes of crime because, unless they are properly constructed and interpreted, they tend to ignore the geography of an area and other factors that may affect levels of crime.

Offender profiling

Some techniques of crime analysis are more specialised, focusing on particular offences or aspects of crime. Offender profiling refers broadly to the process of inferring the characteristics of an offender based on a detailed analysis of his or her crimes (Alison and Canter 1999). Offender profiling is founded on the assertion that while an offenders' behaviour may change and develop over time, an offence will have key 'psychological signatures' that will be consistent and can be interpreted to provide further insight into offenders' motivations, social and occupational status, criminality and personality (Grubin 1995). For example, Britton's (1997) accurate profile of John Bostock, who admitted to two counts of murder in 1986, highlighted the age range of the offender, his sexual immaturity, lack of social skills, physical strength and area of employment.

The nature of offender profiling makes it best suited to exploring serious crimes, such as linked sexual assaults or murders.

While the contribution of offender profiling to criminal investigations is relatively recent, the principle of studying the association between the characteristics of offences and the offenders is long established and has often been mythologised in literary portrayals of detectives, such as Sherlock Holmes. Despite the competent representation of profiling within fictional accounts, in practice there is considerable debate around the different approaches to examining crimes and the professionalisation of profilers. To illustrate this it is useful to consider the development of profiling, including two critical approaches, the typologies of the Federal Bureau of Investigations (FBI) and the work of David Canter, a pioneer of profiling in the UK. The section goes on to explore the limitations of offender profiling.

Approaches to offender profiling

The case of the 'Mad Bomber' in 1956, where James A. Brussel, a psychiatrist, assisted the police by providing a remarkably accurate profile based on a psychoanalytical interpretation of the crime scene, initiated public interest in profiling. However, a process to support systematic offender profiling was not developed by the Behaviour Science Unit (currently the Investigative Support Unit) of the FBI until the early 1970s (Ainsworth 2001). The FBI developed a typology of sexual assault and murders, based on officers' experiences of investigating serious crimes and interviews with offenders convicted of rape and murder. The early framework developed by Ressler facilitated the investigative distinction between organised and disorganised styles of attack in murder cases, where the former would be carried out with restraint, compared to the erratic, impulsive actions involved in the latter (Canter 1994). The FBI asserted that the classification of crimes reflected the personality of the offender. The protagonist of an organised crime would be more intelligent, socially skilled and sexually competent, while a disorganised offender would be more likely to live alone, near the crime scene and have limited social skills and sexual experience (Ainsworth 2001). The FBI typology of rape cases categorised offenders as either selfish or unselfish. The first type would engage in the act to satisfy himself, while the unselfish rapist would engage in a pretence of intimacy with the victim. An extended rape classification system that includes power reassurance type, power assertive type, anger retaliatory type and anger excitement type highlights the complex motivations for serious sexual assault.

There is some debate around the usefulness of such typologies and classification systems in offender profiling. Coleman and Norris (2000) question the possibility of classifying offences as either organised or disorganised and the extent to which a consistent motivation, implicit in a classification system, can be assumed in multiple offences. Canter (1994) also highlighted the difficulty of maintaining boundaries between the categories and argues they are inherently ambiguous. The methodology of developing the classification system has been widely criticised as unsystematic and as relying too heavily on the experience and intuition of investigators, rather than a theoretically grounded study of crime (Alison and Canter 1999; Rossmo

2000). A demand for profilers throughout the 1980s and 1990s reinforced the atheoretical approach, as the proliferation of profiling procedures was largely unguided by an evidence base (Grubin 1995).

Canter's approach to profiling was a departure from the FBI processes in so far as it explicitly aimed to include psychological theory in the study of crimes. The case of John Duffy, the Railway Rapist, was Canter's introduction to the practice of profiling and the possibility of applying psychology to criminal investigations. John Duffy exhibited 13 of the 17 attributes identified in Canter's profile, matching the predicted employment, marital status, home address and offending history (Ormerod 1999). Canter went on to research profiling hypotheses, developing the scientific discipline of investigative psychology and ensuring later forays into profiling were more theoretically driven than the initial experience on the Duffy investigation. An example is the circle of crime theory. The profile of John Duffy included his residential location, based on the analysis of the location and proximity of offences. Canter developed the concept of mental maps as a method of interpreting the geographic distribution of offending. The theory is supported by evidence that highlights the close proximity of rapes to offenders' home address (also see Davies and Dale 1995) and the volume of offenders who live within a circle drawn around the location of their offences (Godwin and Canter 1997).

Canter's research has led him to outline five important characteristics to help criminal investigations (Ainsworth 2001):

1. Residential location.

2. Criminal biography.

3. Domestic and social characteristics.

4. Personal characteristics.

5. Occupational/educational history.

From the above it appears Canter did not entirely depart from the categorisation of crime developed by the FBI. However, the investigative psychology approach aims to base the development of such categories on the systematic analysis of data (Canter, D. 2000). For example, Canter and Heritage (1990), based on a detailed study of over 60 sexual assault cases, developed a list of 33 common offence features of sexual crimes. By further exploring the association between the factors, Canter was able to develop an insight into the most critical characteristics of rape. More recently, Canter and colleagues have developed 'facet theory', the study of associations between variables, to explore the complexity of criminal situations and identify common crime scene characteristics that can be distinguished from unusual features in the process of criminal investigations (Ainsworth 2001).

Critiques of offender profiling

Despite the considerable advances in the field, offender profiling has been subject to debate and criticism. As with all analytical techniques, profiling relies on accurate information about crimes being reported to the police, something that cannot be relied upon in serious crime investigations (Ainsworth 2001). Offender profiling continues to be plagued by broader questions about its aim, definition and impact. Copson (1995) noted some confusion among police officers about how to use profiling advice in the course of police investigations. Indeed, Copson's study of offender profiling in UK police forces found that assessing the impact of profiles on investigations was complicated by a range of different perceptions of usefulness. Thus, over four fifths of respondents agreed that the profile advanced their understanding of the offender, but less than three per cent agreed it had led to the identification of the offender. This also reflects the often-confused and vague objective of profiling – whether it is intended to add advice, direct an investigation or be used in court to support prosecution (Wilson and Soothill 1995).

While this chapter has outlined two approaches to offender profiling, in practice there continues to be little commonality in methods between profilers. Approaches can be idiosyncratic, based on accepted wisdom and the skills and personality of the profiler (Copson and Marshall 1999). This potentially means that good profilers may get it right, without fully understanding why (Grubin 1995), pointing to a broader question about the role of expertise in developing profiles. Not all profilers subscribe to the Canter approach but actively draw on a wealth of clinical, professional and intuitive experience when developing profiles. The key issue with such experiential approaches is assessing their reliability and validity (Ormerod 1999) in a context where getting it wrong can potentially have considerable consequences (Ainsworth 2001). Crime profiler Paul Britton's now infamous connection with the Rachel Nickel murder on Wimbledon Common and the subsequent arrest, prosecution and acquittal of Colin Stagg exemplifies a number of potential problems associated with using profiles. The Stagg case was dismissed and the judge rejected the use of profiles as evidence stating that the court 'would not wish to give encouragement either to investigating or prosecuting authorities . . . to supplement their cases on this basis' (Ormerod 1999: 209). While the court did not totally dismiss the assistance of psychology in cases, it indicated that consideration needed to be given about the boundaries of its influence in investigations. Recent developments in forensic technology may provide the opportunity to test profiles using other investigative techniques. Certainly, if the terms of reference are clear, and the basis on which the profile is developed is understood, the potential for profiling to contribute positively to the investigation of serious crime seems more likely.

Theory for practice: developing explanation in volume crime analysis

The discussion above highlights the possibility that analytical techniques may be used atheoretically in policing, limiting their capacity to interpret and explain crime reliably. It is important therefore to consider the value of criminological theory in supporting interpretation in crime analysis. In illustrating this I want to focus on the review of volume crime conducted at a local level in policing, where criminological theory can develop a detailed understanding of crime to support crime prevention and investigations.

Crime analysis goes back to environmental criminology (Bottoms and Wiles 2002). For example, the Chicago School scholars, as early pioneers of environmental criminology, drew on the disciplines of urban sociology and human ecology to illustrate the association between crime, social disorganisation and poverty in urban settings (Weisburd and McEwen 1998). While the influence of ecological theories has diminished within criminology, exploring the spatial distribution of crime continues to be important and has found new energy, especially among practitioners, with the development of technology that supports the computerised mapping of geographic information.

As with all research processes, an integral relationship exists between theory and analysis (see Bottoms 2000). Criminological theory can support analysis through its capacity to reveal and explain consistent empirical *facts* about crime, concerning its distribution or the risk factors associated with offending and victimisation (see, for example, Braithwaite 1989; Farrington 2002). Indeed, the mere fact that an analyst asks particular sorts of questions or anticipates certain patterns of crime reflects the importance of theory for the interpretation of data in analytical inquiry (Eck 1998).

Figure 14.2 introduces some of the factors we know about crime that influence and support analysis. The figure draws on Ekblom's (1996) conceptual model that makes a distinction between *distal* (background) and *proximal* (immediate) factors that influence crime. I want to focus on the proximal circumstances of offending to consider how theory could enhance explanation

Figure 14.2   Some factors about crime that support analysis

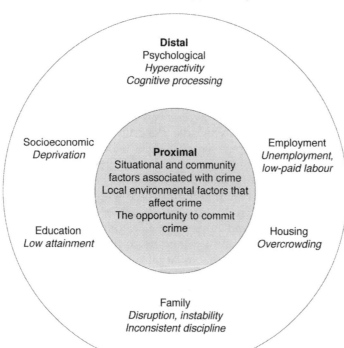

in volume crime analysis. This is not to overlook the importance of understanding the distal causes of crime, which will in turn influence the proximal circumstances of offending. As Ekblom (1996: 61) notes: 'it is to the meso-levels and micro-levels . . . that we might look to try and understand why a particular offender frequents a particular situation and how the components of the situation itself have come together to produce a criminal event'. It is the complex interplay between macro (societal), meso (local) and micro (individual) factors in the commission of crime that needs to be incorporated into crime analysis so that analytical recommendations can consider a range of tactical and strategic interventions. As an example I want to return to burglary. Research suggests that residents in deprived areas are more likely to be victims of burglary (Ratcliffe and McCullagh 1999). However, people are not simply victims of burglary because they are poor. They are more likely to be victims because they live near burglars, who are unlikely to travel long distances to offend (Craglia *et al.* 2000). Policing alone cannot tackle poverty, a distal cause of crime. However, by analysing the pattern and opportunities to commit crime, the police are able to develop a range of interventions to address the proximal circumstances of offending. Space precludes a lengthy discussion of all the relevant theories and their critiques. Therefore, I want to focus on key theoretical concepts that relate to local crime analysis and crime prevention to demonstrate how the application of criminology can support the interpretation of analytical data.

Reason, rationality and routine: theory for crime analysis

Opportunity-based theories of crime consider the situational and environmental characteristics of offending. A long tradition of research has indicated that the distribution of crime in space is not random. Despite the contribution of early studies on the spatial attributes of offending, for example, Shaw and McKay's (1942) work on social disorganisation, the broad focus of spatial analysis has limited ability to address the more detailed causal analysis of crime in a particular place (Sherman *et al.* 1989). Therefore, more detailed research of the micro-context is necessary because, as Felson (1998: 52) has observed: '[Offenders] typically behave like criminals only in certain settings, that is, slices of time and space within which relevant people and things are assembled'. Drawing on control theory (Hirschi 1969), which emphasised the importance of understanding why people do not commit crime, Felson (1998: 23) noted that crime was committed by people who were 'tempted more but controlled less', and aimed to explore the relationship between the daily routines of everyday life and opportunities to offend. *Routine activity theory* asserted that for crime to occur a minimum of three factors needed to come together in time and space: a suitable target, a likely offender and the absence of a capable guardian (Felson 1998). Crime rates are not only affected by the prevalence of the three factors but also the frequency at which they converge together in time and space creating a hotspot of crime (Sherman *et al.* 1989). Therefore, an explanation for the high levels of crime around a train station might refer to the volume of suitable targets and likely offenders, but also the absence of capable guardians and low levels of informal social control exercised in such a transient and impersonal space.

Routine activity theory stresses the importance of assessing the suitability of the target through the eyes of the offender using the acronym VIVA: the *value* of the target, the *inertia* of the target, the *visibility* of the target and *access* for an offender (Felson 1998). Routine activity approaches provide a theory for crime analysis through which to deconstruct criminal events and understand situations where crime is more likely to occur. Felson and Clarke (1998) suggested the theory provides a robust explanation for burglary increases in western Europe and the USA throughout the 1960s and 1970s as the ownership of portable and desirable technology proliferated.

A further crucial component of analysis is to explore the decision-making process of the offender. The *rational choice perspective* starts with the premise that offenders seek to advantage themselves through their offending. This involves making decisions to commit crime, which are rational within the constraints of their time and ability (Cornish and Clarke 1986; Clarke 1997). Of course, there are inherent problems with assessing what is and is not rational (Tilley 1997). Nevertheless, the perspective has directed attention to the structure of choice and decision-making associated with offending. Rational choice theory is supported by a range of interview-based research that has indicated a decision-making process is involved in the commission of crime (Cromwell *et al.* 1991). As with routine activity, rational choice theory focuses on the circumstances of the offence, facilitating the analysis of offenders' motivations and modus operandi to understand how they might influence the pattern and frequency of offending.

Rational choice and routine activity theories suggest the distribution of crime is not random but varies in time and space (Sherman *et al.* 1989). Burglary, for example, is more concentrated in areas of low socioeconomic status (Bottoms and Wiles 2002). Crime pattern theory draws together a range of disciplines to explain this distribution of offending. For example, descriptive crime analysis might indicate the close proximity of an offender's home address to his or her offences; however, theory enables us to interpret this pattern of crime further. Brantingham and Brantingham (1981, 1991) explored the extent to which offenders' daily life patterns influenced the location of their offences. They suggested that we all carry 'cognitive maps' of the places we live. The maps will include 'awareness spaces' – that is, the areas we know very well because we socialise, go to work or college or carry out daily chores in the locality. Understanding offenders' 'awareness spaces' through the process of detailed crime analysis is important because, in the main, criminal opportunities would intersect with *cognitively known areas* (Bottoms and Wiles 2002). This has been supported by research that indicates offenders tend not to travel long distances to commit offences (Wiles and Costello 2000). This work is also crucial for supporting the investigation of serious offences through 'geographic profiling', a strategic management information system that links psychological profiling with spatial analytical techniques (Rossmo 2000). While forming only part of a criminal investigation, geographic profiling aims to explore the location of crime, offender type, hunting style, targets, travel pathways, land use and demographics to provide further insight into the offender and the crime. The critical relationship between offending pattern and the residential location of the offender highlights the importance of mapping burglary and serious sexual assaults, and interpreting the emerging patterns in light of the theory to narrow the focus of police activity towards particular suspects.

Aside from focusing on the activity of the offender and the spatial distribution of offences, crime analysis can enhance the interpretation of crime by exploring patterns of victimisation. Repeat victimisation focuses on the repetitious nature of offending, which means a small number of victims, encompassing both people and property, experience a large proportion of crime (Farrell and Pease 2001). Explanations for repeat victimisation focus on the enduring vulnerability of the target to crime, or an initial offence increasing the likelihood of subsequent offences (Pease 1998). Research also highlights the temporal trends associated with repeat victimisation, which suggests when it does occur, it happens quickly (Robinson 1998).

Crime analysis, by exploring the spatial distribution and time series of repeat victimisation, may offer an insight into crime that cannot be gained from focusing on the offence or the offender. For example, exploring repeat victimisation may provide further understanding of geographical concentrations of crime, or hotspots (Farrell and Sousa 2001). Hotspots may reflect high levels of crime incidents per victim, rather than indicating multiple opportunities for offending (Farrell *et al.* 1996).

'Opportunity blocked': analysis, action and results

By understanding the proximal circumstances of offences, crime analysis can suggest 'tailor-made' interventions to prevent and reduce crime (Tilley 2002a). Situational crime prevention focuses on developing interventions to disrupt the immediate circumstances of the offence. Clarke (1997) outlines four classifications for crime prevention. First, crime prevention aims to make committing crime more difficult through target-hardening, based on the rational choice perspective that offenders would be more likely to be attracted to an easy target. Secondly, crime prevention aims to increase the risks associated with crime. This may, for example, involve surveillance or controlling exits in shopping centres. Thirdly, crime prevention aims to reduce the rewards of offending through marking property or by making stolen items unusable after theft. Finally, crime prevention aims to remove the excuses for offending, acknowledging that a moral paradigm may be involved in offenders' rational decision-making. Such an approach provides the rationale for signs and posters that warn of prosecution and harsh sentences for crimes.

It is assumed that targeting the situation of offences may displace offending. Simply put, this involves offenders moving crime to another space, time, target, or causing them to adopt a different tactic to commit offences (Repetto 1976). Displacement must not become a 'catch-all' for unexplained increases and decreases in crime, not least because the theories discussed above would suggest that the displacement of crime is not inevitable (Clarke 1997). Indeed if displacement did occur, it would be difficult to detect through crime analysis as 'some displaced crime will probably fall outside the areas and types of crime being studied or be so dispersed as to be masked by background variation' (Barr and Pease 1990: 293).

The theories discussed above suggest crime analysis needs to take account of four critical generators of crime: the offender, the victim, the community and the situation of offences (Tilley *et al.* 1999). Table 14.3 summarises the theories and their potential contribution to developing interpretation in volume crime analysis.

The context of analysis: the problems of integrating crime analysis into policing

This chapter has focused on the foundation and the technical and theoretical aspects of crime analysis. However, understanding how analysis operates in the context of policing is important for appreciating its limitations and the extent to which it influences police activity. Notwithstanding the emphasis on crime analysis within intelligence-led policing, its status in practice is far more equivocal. Research has identified that despite a belief among officers that analysis supports an intelligence-led approach to police work, a lack of understanding of analysis among police officers, and policing among analysts, severely limits its contribution and development (Cope forthcoming). Indeed, to achieve crime analysis in practice requires two problems to be overcome: the problem of data and the problem of culture.

The problem of data

To support analysis the police must gather and store a range of data relating to crime and criminal activity. This not only requires appropriate technology but it also demands an exchange of information within policing. However, research has recognised a range of *experiential* knowledge is not systematically recorded by the police but is held in officers' heads (Manning 1992). Indeed, a limitation of intelligence-led crime control is its reliance on formal methods of communicating and storing data, when many police officers continue to share information informally (Gill 1998).

Crime analysis is also limited by the quality of the information that is available to be analysed (Cope *et al.* 2001). Canter (2000: 4) notes that data for analysis should be relevant, reliable, accurate and timely. However, attaining data standards to facilitate analysis is complicated. The relevance of information is temporal, influenced by current priorities, agendas and criminal activity. For example, a small red car spotted late at night in a bingo-hall car park is arguably irrelevant until a small red car is identified as being involved in a robbery of the same bingo hall. Then the analyst will need to explore more about the original sighting. Was the robbery planned? Did the suspect use the bingo hall? Essentially the data become relevant when the offence has been committed, highlighting how challenging it can be routinely to link information to develop proactive interventions.

In addition to the difficulty of assessing the relevance of data is the difficulty that information is frequently unreliable and inaccurate, which affects the quality of analytical reports. As collecting and recording information can be highly bureaucratic it can undermine the timeliness of information, which also

Table 14.3 A summary integrating theory into volume crime analysis

Theory	Definition	Analysis
Routine activities theory	Opportunities for crime are associated with the routine activities of everyday life. Three conditions are needed for crime to occur: a likely offender, a suitable target and the absence of a capable guardian. The acronym VIVA is used to assess the suitability of targets.	Focuses on the offender, offence and situation of crime. Provides an insight into opportunities for crime and how they might relate to offenders' lifestyles and daily activities. This may further explain crime patterns, increase the understanding of hotspots (where the three factors for crime regularly coincide) and enable the identification of potential 'hot products' that are desirable to steal.
Rational choice theory	Offenders seek advantages through crime and make decisions about offending that are rational within the constraints of time and ability.	Focuses on the offender and offence. Supports the analysis of approaches to crime and modus operandi. Interpreting decision-making processes from crime patterns and targets in detailed profiles of offenders may offer an insight into potential crimes that have been committed by the same person, or enable predictive crime patterns to be hypothesised.
Crime pattern approaches	A general term applied to the study of the interaction between the offender and his or her environment.	Focuses on the spatial and situational aspects of crime. Facilitates the interpretation of crime patterns by exploring the relationship between opportunity for crimes and offenders' awareness spaces. Also supports criminal investigations.
Repeat victimisation	When the same location, person, business, organisation, household or vehicle experiences more than one crime within a specified time frame.	Offers an insight into patterns of victimisation. Understanding the temporal and spatial distribution of repeat victimisation may provide the means to 'predict' patterns of victimisation.
Situational crime prevention	A process that aims to reduce crime by intervening in the proximal causes of offences.	Focuses on the situation of crime. A useful analytical recommendation that follows from understanding the opportunities and circumstances of offences.
Displacement	The process by which offenders seek alternative methods of offending when opportunities to commit crime are blocked. Displacement can be temporal, spatial, involve different tactics or be directed towards different targets.	Helpful for evaluation (results analysis). Important to consider the intended and 'unintended', positive and negative consequences of police interventions.

helps to explain officers' scepticism towards formal methods of exchanging information. Indeed, in the 'reactive' environment of policing, where the speed of the response is prioritised, the time needed to record all information on computers is perceived to limit the effectiveness of data analysis (Chapter 26).

The problem of culture

More reliable sources of information will not automatically lead to the greater use of data in policing as there are broader cultural barriers to the integration of analysis. A number of features of police culture (Chapter 9) – the value attached to action-oriented police work, along with experience, *grounded* knowledge and the use of discretion by the police – directly impact on the integration of crime analysis into police work. As crime analysis is frequently office based and computer driven, it represents the antithesis of action-oriented police work. As Kelly (1990: 151) notes: 'analysts and investigators . . . inhabit positions . . . which breed friction . . . the intelligence analyst is situated in an information processing . . . unit, while the street investigator [is] working with . . . others [that] may not able to see the forest for the trees'.

Considerable misunderstanding often exists between police officers and analysts of one another's roles. The background and experience of analysts are highly variable across UK police forces. Within the Metropolitan Police, for example, while police officers do occupy analytical positions, the majority of analysts are civilian graduates or have prior experience working within the police, in control rooms or crime desks, for example. All civilian analysts are ranked (often equivalent to an inspector) and while forces may have a senior or principal analyst who is often responsible for the development of strategy and training, day-to-day management analysis is often undertaken by a police officer, who may not fully understand the role and potential of analysis. This can frequently lead to the misuse and exclusion of analysis from operational practice (Cope forthcoming).

The process of analysis often involves decontextualising data to provide overviews of crime (Peterson 1990). This differs from police practice, which validates knowledge gathered and understood through the experience of policing (Manning and Hawkins 1989), not knowledge interpreted from computer systems through the experience of analysis. Nevertheless, it is the different approach to assessing data that makes analysis valuable for the police. An overview of crime is important, especially as changes in officers' deployment means they may not have an opportunity to 'get to know their beat'. Furthermore, crime problems, such as vehicle crime, can be so voluminous as to make it impossible for an individual, through his or her experiences of dealing with a small number of offences, to grasp the breadth of the problem (Ratcliffe and McCullagh 2001).

A significant factor in the use of analysis to direct activity is the extent to which it further inhibits police officers' already diminishing discretion to act (Chan 2001). Traditionally a valued aspect of police work, it is argued that the ability for police officers to exercise discretion has gradually been eroded as the need to rationalise resources, target interventions and maintain accountability has increased (Manning 2001). As analysis draws together different sources of data to establish trends and patterns, the information provided to police officers may not always be specific. If officers do not trust the process of analysis, they are unlikely to respond to analysts' information. This may be further exacerbated by some police officers high expectations that intelligence will always deliver specific information that leads to an arrest (Chan 2001; Cope *et al*. 2001). It also suggests that the current offerings from analysis are not always valued, as some police officers continue to think 'they should be doing what the intelligence analysts are doing, and also believe they can do this more effectively and less expensively than analysts' (Moore 1977 cited in Kelly 1990: 151). This suggests the strength of crime analysis can only be realised if both police officers and analysts, who often work in separate habitats, learn to understand, co-operate and support one another.

Conclusion

Crime analysis includes a range of techniques that explore trends and patterns in crime data to influence police activity. The expansion of analysis in policing has been encouraged by the emphasis on problem-oriented and intelligence-led approaches in UK forces, and is supported by the proliferation of technology that has increased the capacity of the police to store, retrieve and search data. Indeed, it is the accessibility of analytical software that has ensured visual representations of crime now support crime reduction, prevention, investigation and monitor performance. However, crime analysis is more than simply providing maps, graphs and network charts. Analysis can interpret and explain data, providing the police with an understanding of crime problems and trends. Without interpretation, analysis tends to provide the police with descriptive, retrospective information about crime. This does not undermine the value of analytical representations of crime but stresses the importance of supporting both the *cognitive* and the *technical* aspects of crime analysis within policing. The integration of theory and exploring the social context of crime data are crucial for advancing explanation in crime analysis.

While recent developments have reinforced the importance to police forces of having an analytical capability, there remains insufficient understanding within the police service of why analysis is desirable and possible. The quality of crime analysis is integrally linked to the quality of data stored by police forces. Furthermore, the potential of analysis is only realised when it is systematically integrated into practice and informs the deployment of resources. However for this to happen, the relevance and reliability of analysis need to be developed. While analysts and police officers work in the same world, they frequently occupy different habitats. By sharing the benefits of each other's experiences, further insight and understanding of crime can be developed.

Selected further reading

Ekblom's (1988) early Home Office study, *Getting the Best out of Crime Analysis*, provides a sound introduction. Recent volumes by edited by Tilley (2002), *Analysis for Crime*

Prevention and *Evaluation for Crime Prevention*, provide practical examples and useful theoretical discussions on the relationship between analysis, theory and research. Ainsworth's *Offender Profiling and Crime Analysis* (2001) provides a good introductory discussion of offender profiling. Goldsmith *et al.*'s *Analyzing Crime Patterns* (2000) and Weisburd and McEwen's *Crime Mapping and Crime Prevention* (1998) offer useful discussions of crime analysis in practice. Felson's *Crime and Everyday Life* (1998) and Bottoms and Wiles's chapter 'Environmental criminology' in the *Oxford Handbook of Criminology* (2002) provide an excellent introduction to the theory for analysis. Practitioners should consult the National Intelligence Model (NCIS 2000) to review the techniques of analysis. As the technology advances quickly it may be helpful to consult websites, for example, the Crime Mapping Research Center (www.ojp.usdoj.gov/nij/maps) or the International Association of Crime Analysts (www.IACA.net) to review current developments.

Note

1 The views expressed by the author are not necessarily those of the Metropolitan Police Service.

References

Ainsworth, P. (2001) *Offender Profiling and Crime Analysis*. Cullompton: Willan.

Alison, L. and Canter, D. (1999) 'Profiling in policy and practice', in L. Alison and D. Canter (eds) *Profiling in Policy and Practice*. Aldershot: Ashgate, 3–22.

Audit Commission (1993) *Helping with Enquiries: Tackling Crime Effectively*. London: HMSO.

Barr, R. and Pease, K. (1990) 'Crime placement, displacement and deflection', in M. Tonry and N. Morris (eds) *Crime and Justice: A Review of Research*. Vol. 12. Chicago, IL: University of Chicago Press, 196–216.

Bottoms, A. (2000) 'The relationship between theory and research in criminology,' in R.D. King and E. Wincup (eds) *Doing Research on Crime and Justice*. Oxford: Clarendon Press, 15–60.

Bottoms, A. and Wiles, P. (1996) 'Understanding crime prevention in late modern societies', in T. Bennett (ed.) *Preventing Crime and Disorder: Targeting Strategies and Responsibilities. Cropwood Conference Series*. Cambridge: University of Cambridge, 620–56.

Bottoms, A. and Wiles, P. (2002) 'Environmental criminology', in M. Maguire *et al.* (eds) *The Oxford Handbook of Criminology* (3rd edn). Oxford: Oxford University Press, 620–56.

Braithwaite, J. (1989) *Crime, Shame and Reintegration*. Cambridge: Cambridge University Press.

Brantingham, P.L. and Brantingham, P.J. (1981) 'Notes on the geography of crime', in P.J. Brantingham and P.l. Brantingham (eds) *Environmental Criminology*. Beverly Hills, CA: Sage.

Brantingham, P.L. and Brantingham, P.J. (1991) *Environmental Criminology* (2nd edn). Prospect Heights, IL: Waveland Press.

Britton, P. (1997) *The Jigsaw Man*. London: Bantam Press.

Buslik, M. and Maltz, M. (1998) 'Power to the people: mapping and information sharing in the Chicago Police Department', in D. Weisburd and T. McEwen (eds) *Crime Mapping and Crime Prevention*. Monsey, NY: Criminal Justice Press, 113–30.

Canter, D. (1994) *Criminal Shadows: Inside the Mind of a Serial Killer*. London: HarperCollins.

Canter, D. (2000) 'Offender profiling and criminal differentiation', *Legal and Criminological Psychology*, 5: 23–46.

Canter, D. and Heritage, R. (1990) 'A multi-variate model of sexual offence behaviour', *Journal of Forensic Psychiatry*, 1: 185–210.

Canter, P. (2000) 'Using a geographic information system for tactical crime analysis', in V. Goldsmith *et al.* (eds) *Analyzing Crime Patterns, Frontiers of Practice*. Thousand Oaks, CA: Sage, 3–10.

Chan, J. (2001) 'The technology game: how information technology is transforming police practice', *Criminal Justice*, 1: 139–59.

Clarke, R.V. (ed.) (1997) *Situational Crime Prevention, Successful Case Studies* (2nd edn). Albany, NY: Harrow & Heston.

Coleman, C. and Norris, C. (2000) *Introducing Criminology*. Cullompton: Willan.

Cope, N. (forthcoming) 'Intelligence led policing or policing led intelligence: integrating volume crime analysis into policing', *British Journal of Criminology*.

Cope, N., Innes, M. and Fielding, N. (2001) *Smart Policing? The Theory and Practice of Intelligence-led Policing*. London: Home Office.

Copson, G. (1995) *Coals to Newcastle? A Study of Offender Profiling*. Police Research Group Special Interest Paper 7. London: Home Office.

Copson, G. and Marshall, N. (1999) 'Mind over matter', *Police Review*, 11 June: 16–17.

Cornish, D.B. and Clarke, R.V. (1986) *The Reasoning Criminal: Rational Choice Perspectives on Offending*. New York, NY: Springer-Verlag.

Craglia, M., Haining, R. and Wiles, P. (2000) 'A comparative evaluation of approaches to urban crime pattern analysis', *Urban Studies*, 37: 711–29.

Cromwell, P., Olson, J. and Wester Avary, D. (1991) *Breaking and Entering: An Ethnographic Analysis of Burglary*. Studies in Crime, Law and Justice 8. Thousand Oaks, CA: Sage.

Davies, A. and Dale, A. (1995) *Locating the Stranger Rapist*. Police Research Group Special Interest Paper 3. London: Home Office.

Eck, J. (1998) 'What do those dots mean? Mapping theories with data', in D. Weisburd and T. McEwen (eds) *Crime Mapping and Crime Prevention*. Monsey, NY: Criminal Justice Press, 379–406.

Eck, J., Gersh, J. and Taylor, C. (2000) 'Finding crime hot spots through repeats address mapping', in V. Goldsmith *et al.* (eds) *Analyzing Crime Patterns, Frontiers of Practice*. Thousand Oaks, CA: Sage, 49–63.

Ekblom, P. (1988) *Getting the Best out of Crime Analysis*. Crime Prevention Unit Paper 10. London: Home Office.

Ekblom, P. (1996) 'Towards a discipline of crime prevention: a systematic approach to its nature, range and concepts,' in T. Bennett (ed.) *Preventing Crime and Disorder. Cropwood Conference Series*. Cambridge: University of Cambridge, 43–97.

Ekblom, P. (2002) 'From the source to the mainstream is uphill: the challenge of transferring knowledge of crime prevention through replication, innovation and anticipation', in N. Tilley (ed.) *Analysis for Crime Prevention*. Monsey, NY: Criminal Justice Press, 131–94.

Ericson, R.V. and Haggerty, K. (1997) *Policing the Risk Society*. Oxford: Clarendon Press.

Farrell, G., Ellingworth, D. and Pease, K. (1996) 'High crime rates, repeat victimisation and routine activities', in T. Bennett (ed.) *Preventing Crime and Disorder. Cropwood Conferences Series*. Cambridge: University of Cambridge, 276–96.

Farrell, G. and Pease, K. (2001) 'Why repeat victimization matters', in G. Farrell and K. Pease (eds) *Repeat Victimization*. Monsey, NY: Criminal Justice Press, 1–4.

Farrell, G. and Sousa, W. (2001) 'Repeat victimization and hot spots: the overlap and its implications for crime control and problem-oriented policing', in G. Farrell and K. Pease (eds) *Repeat Victimization*. Monsey, NY: Criminal Justice Press, 221–40.

Farrington, D. (2002) 'Developmental criminology and risk focused prevention', in M. Maguire *et al.* (eds) *The Oxford Handbook of Criminology* (3rd edn). Oxford: Oxford University Press, 657–701.

Felson, M. (1998) *Crime and Everyday Life*. Thousand Oaks, CA: Pine Forge Press.

Felson, M. and Clarke, R.V. (1998) *Opportunity Makes the Thief. Practical Theory for Crime Prevention. Police Research Series Paper* 98. London: Home Office.

Gill, P. (1998) 'Police intelligence process: a study of criminal intelligence units in Canada', *Policing and Society*, 8: 339–65.

Gill, P. (2000) *Rounding up the Usual Suspects? Developments in Contemporary Law Enforcement Intelligence*. Aldershot: Ashgate.

Godwin, M. and Canter, D. (1997) 'Encounter and death: the spatial behaviour of US serial killers', *Policing*, 20: 24–38.

Goldblatt, P. and Lewis, C. (eds) (1998) *Reducing Offending: An Assessment of Research Evidence on Ways of Dealing with Offending Behaviour. Research Study* 187. London: Home Office.

Goldsmith, V., McGuire, P., Mollenkopf, J.H. and Ross, T. (eds) (2000) *Analyzing Crime Patterns, Frontiers of Practice*. Thousand Oaks, CA: Sage.

Goldstein, H. (1990) *Problem-oriented Policing*. New York, NY: McGraw-Hill.

Groff, E. and La Vigne, N. (2002) 'Forecasting the future of predictive mapping', in N. Tilley (ed.) *Analysis for Crime Prevention*. Monsey, NY: Criminal Justice Press, 28–57.

Grubin, D. (1995) 'Offender profiling', *Journal of Forensic Psychiatry*, 6: 259–62.

Harries, K. (1999) *Mapping Crime Principle and Practice*. Washington, DC: National Institute of Justice.

Hirschi, T. (1969) *Causes of Delinquency*. Berkeley, CA: University of California Press.

Ianni, F.A.J. and Reuss-Ianni, E. (1990) 'Network analysis,' in P. Andrews and M. Peterson (eds) *Criminal Intelligence Analysis*. Loomis, CA: Palmer Enterprises, 67–84.

Johnston, L. (2000) *Policing Britain*. Harlow: Longman.

Kelly, R. (1990) 'The development of inferences in the assessment of intelligence data', in P. Andrews and M. Peterson (eds) *Criminal Intelligence Analysis*. Loomis, CA: Palmer Enterprises, 149–80.

Maguire, M. (2000) 'Policing by risks and targets: some implications of intelligence-led crime control', *Policing and Society*, 9: 315–36.

Maguire, M. and John, T. (1995) *Intelligence, Surveillance and Informants: Integrated Approaches. Crime Detection and Prevention Series Paper* 64. London: Home Office.

Manning, P. (1992) 'Information technologies and the police', in M. Tonry and N. Morris (eds) *Modern Policing. Crime and Justice*. Vol. 15. Chicago, IL: University of Chicago Press, 349–99.

Manning, P. (2001) 'Technology's ways: information technology, crime analysis and the rationalizing of policing', *Criminal Justice*, 1: 83–104.

Manning, P. and Hawkins, K. (1989) 'Police decision making', in M. Weatheritt (ed.) *Police Research: Some Future Prospects*. Aldershot: Avebury, 139–56.

Martens, F. (1990) 'The intelligence function', in P. Andrews and M. Peterson (eds) *Criminal Intelligence Analysis*. Loomis, CA: Palmer Enterprises, 1–20.

McGuire, P. (2000) 'The New York Police Department COMPSTAT process: mapping for analysis, evaluation and accountability', in V. Goldsmith *et al.* (eds) *Analyzing Crime Patterns, Frontiers of Practice*. Thousand Oaks, CA: Sage, 11–22.

NCIS (2000) *The National Intelligence Model*. London: NCIS.

Ormerod, D. (1999) 'Criminal profiling: trial by judge and jury, not criminal psychologist', in L. Alison and D. Canter (eds) *Profiling in Policy and Practice*. Aldershot: Ashgate, 209–61.

Pawson, R. and Tilley, N. (1997) *Realistic Evaluation*. London: Sage.

Pease, K. (1998) *Repeat Victimisation: Taking Stock. Crime Detection and Prevention Series Paper* 90. London: Home Office.

Peterson, M. (1990) 'The context of analysis', in P. Andrews and M. Peterson (eds) *Criminal Intelligence Analysis*. Loomis, CA: Palmer Enterprises, 21–65.

Peterson, M. (1994) *Applications in Criminal Analysis: A Sourcebook*. Westport, CT: Greenwood Press.

Ratcliffe, J. (2000) 'Implementing and integrating crime mapping into a police intelligence environment', *International Journal of Police Science and Management*, 2: 313–23.

Ratcliffe, J. (2002a) 'Intelligence-led policing and the problems of turning rhetoric into practice', *Policing and Society*, 12: 53–66.

Ratcliffe, J. (2002b) 'Damned if you don't, damned if you do: crime mapping and its implications in the real world', *Policing and Society*, 12: 211–25.

Ratcliffe, J. and McCullagh, M. (1999) 'Burglary, victimisation and social deprivation', *Crime Prevention and Community Safety*, 1: 37–46.

Ratcliffe, J.H. and McCullagh, M.J. (2001) 'Chasing ghosts? Police perceptions of high crime areas', *British Journal of Criminology*, 41: 330–41.

Read, T. and Oldfield D. (1995) *Local Crime Analysis. Crime Detection and Prevention Series Paper* 65. London: Home Office.

Repetto, T.A. (1976) 'Crime prevention and the displacement phenomenon', *Crime and Delinquency*, 22: 166–77.

Robinson, M. (1998) 'Burglary revictimisation: the time period of heightened risk', *British Journal of Criminology*, 38: 78–87.

Rossmo, K. (2000) *Geographic Profiling*. Boca Raton, FL: CRC Press.

Shaw, C. and McKay, H. (1942) *Juvenile Delinquency and Urban Areas*. Chicago, IL: University of Chicago Press.

Sherman, L., Gartin, P. and Buerger, M. (1989) 'Hot spots of predatory crime: routine activities and the criminology of place', *Criminology*, 37: 27–55.

Sherman, L., Gottfredson, D., MacKenzie, D., Eck, J., Reuter, P. and Bushway, S. (1998) *Preventing Crime: What Works, what Doesn't and what's Promising*. Washington, DC: National Institute of Justice.

Tilley, N. (1997) 'Realism, situational rationality and crime prevention', in G. Newman *et al.* (eds) *Rational Choices and Situational Crime Prevention*. Aldershot: Ashgate, 95–114.

Tilley, N. (ed.) (2002a) *Analysis for Crime Prevention*. Monsey, NY: Criminal Justice Press.

Tilley, N. (ed.) (2002b) *Evaluation for Crime Prevention*. Monsey, NY: Criminal Justice Press.

Tilley, N., Pease, K., Hough, M. and Brown, R. (1999) *Burglary Prevention: Early Lesson from the Crime Reduction Programme. Crime Reduction Series Paper* 1. London: Home Office.

Weisburd, D. and McEwen, T. (eds) (1998) *Crime Mapping and Crime Prevention*. Monsey, NY: Criminal Justice Press.

Wiles, P. and Costello, A. (2000) *The 'Road to Nowhere': The Evidence for Travelling Criminals. Home Office Research Study* 207. London: Home Office.

Wilson, P. and Soothill, K. (1995) 'Psychological profiling: red, green or amber?', *Police Journal*, 69: 12–20.

Chapter 15

Criminal investigation and crime control

Mike Maguire

Introduction

This chapter in divided into three main sections. The first provides a brief historical perspective on the development of criminal investigation in the late nineteenth and twentieth centuries as a set of routine practices (both formal and formal), locating it as a core component of the 'modern' approaches to crime control that emerged with the growth of centralised bureaucracies and the nation-state. It also identifies common 'myths' about the nature of criminal investigation and considers some theoretical approaches that present an alternative perspective.

The second section examines key features of the working practices of the three main types of detective unit through which criminal investigation was organised in the twentieth century: generalist criminal investigation department (CID) offices, specialist squads and ad hoc major inquiry teams. In doing so, it identifies the major risks and weaknesses associated with each, noting that the history of the CID has been littered with, on the one hand, criticisms of ineffectiveness and, on the other, scandals involving corruption, malpractice and/or miscarriages of justice. Such criticism, it will be shown, was particularly strong and sustained during the 1970s and 1980s when something of a 'crisis in legitimacy' became apparent.

The third section describes the initiation since this period of a variety of substantial reforms, internal and external, designed to restore public confidence and improve the efficiency, integrity and accountability of investigative practice. These have included attempts at more systematic prioritisation of cases likely to yield 'results', encouragement of greater use of so-called 'proactive' methods of investigation and mechanisms to improve the integrity of the production of evidence, especially in relation to police interviewing. It will be argued, however, that such reforms may be only the precursors of much more fundamental change. Strong challenges are looming to some of the core assumptions behind twentieth-century approaches to crime control: in particular, that crime can be effectively controlled through the routine investigation and processing of individual cases by the police and criminal justice system. In response, some potentially far-reaching developments have begun to take shape – notably the imminent implementation of the National Intelligence Model, and the growth of formal partnership, data sharing and joint operational planning with other agencies. These may prefigure a major shift towards genuinely new strategic and 'risk oriented' approaches, driven by threat assessments, prioritisation, forward planning and 'problem-solving' objectives, and incorporating serious efforts to widen responsibility for tackling crime. In this context, the meaning of the term 'crime investigation', and its boundaries within the broader concept of 'crime control', are already becoming much less clear than in the past.

As with other contributions, although some reference will be made to practice elsewhere, the main focus of the chapter will be on England and Wales. Inquisitorial systems are not covered here, but it is important to be aware that in most other European jurisdictions, police investigations are conducted under the direction of judges or lawyers, which has significant implications for their regulation (see, for example, Field and Pelser 1998). There is also no space here for another topic of major importance – that of the emergence of transnational forms of crime investigation, especially in relation to cross-border and organised crime (Sheptychi 1998, 2000).

Historical and theoretical perspectives

The CID and the birth of 'modern' investigative practice

Examples of what might loosely be described as 'criminal investigation' (obvious cases being the tracking down and capture of thieves, bandits or highwaymen) can be found in many societies throughout history. Equally, some of the methods familiar in current investigative practice (such as the use of informers and the interrogation of suspects) were employed in, for example, Elizabethan England and Napoleonic France for the somewhat different purpose of identifying and eliminating political enemies. However, 'modern' forms of criminal investigation – the routine application by the (public) police of an established body of practices and techniques to detect offenders and gather evidence – date only from the middle to late nineteenth century. In the eighteenth and early nineteenth centuries, although a variety of (often part-time) local watchmen and constables provided some rudimentary 'official' responses to local crime, the extent to which thieves or robbers were pursued and prosecuted depended largely on whether victims, or other wealthy people in the neighbourhood, were prepared to make 'citizen's arrests' and pay to bring private prosecutions under the common law. Some victims also hired the services of 'thief-takers' (in some ways forerunners of private detectives) who had contacts among criminal groups and would negotiate the return of stolen property or deliver offenders to justice for reward money – although the thief-takers were often suspected of organising the thefts themselves. In broad terms, then, crime was perceived as an agglomeration of private wrongs against individuals rather than as a social problem, and responses to it remained highly localised and variable (for further discussion of these issues, see Radzinowicz 1956; Gatrell *et al.* 1980; Emsley 1996a, 2002; see also Chapter 4 in this volume).

Even after the establishment of the 'New Police' in 1829, which marked a key point in the general growth in bureaucratic regulation of the population associated with the emergence of the modern state, it was many years before criminal investigation became a significant and firmly established component of the new apparatus of social control.[1] As Emsley (1996b; see Chapter 4) makes clear, the 'New Police' were oriented primarily towards order mainten-ance, street patrol and the prevention, rather than investigation and detection, of crime. Indeed, 'detective work' was widely regarded with suspicion, and unobtrusive investigation in plain clothes was officially frowned upon, owing to its perceived association with autocratic governments and 'continental' methods such as the use of agents provocateurs and informers (see also Critchley 1978; Ascoli 1979). It was not until 1842 that the first small detective department was formed within the Metropolitan Police, and there was little further growth until the 1870s, when public concerns about rising street crime in London began to put serious pressure on politicians for more effective policing of the problem. It was eventually agreed in 1877 to set up a substantial and autonomous Criminal Investigation Department in the capital, initially with 250 officers.

From then on, 'crime control' rapidly became established as a major plank of the policing agenda, and the CID established itself as the body that 'owned' it. The principal means by which it was to be achieved was the detection, arrest and prosecution of offenders – in a nutshell, criminal investigation.[2] Senior CID officers took every opportunity to portray detectives as possessing a monopoly on expertise in this area, and to free themselves from any 'interference' or control by the uniform branch. Although never entirely successful in these respects (uniformed officers have always played a much greater role than tends to be acknowledged), they were greatly helped in the early years by events such as the Fenian bombing campaign in London in the mid-1880s, in which the investigative tactics of the CID's 'Special Irish Squad' came to be seen as more effective than the uniform branch's preventive strategy of guarding buildings.[3] In 1901, too, the establishment of an effective fingerprinting system and the Criminal Records Office both demonstrably enhanced detectives' arsenal of weapons against repeat offenders, allowing the CID to consolidate its independent position and expand its numbers. Indeed, it is fair to say that the subsequent history of criminal investigation, including the development of its standard methodologies and the informal practices (and frequent scandals) that grew up around them, has been inextricably tied up with the history and 'culture' of the CID. This will be explored in more detail presently.

Key roles of criminal investigation

Throughout this period, too, criminal investigation has been a subject of enduring interest to the general public, and a considerable mythology has grown up around it. This can be understood not just in terms of the 'glamour' of the subject of 'catching criminals', which has consistently ensured a good living for thousands of authors, film-makers, television directors and so on, but also in terms of both the real and the symbolic importance of successful criminal investigation in delivering one of the key 'promises' of the modern centralised state, on which a significant portion of its legitimacy has rested: the promise of providing effective security to its citizens (Garland 1996, 2001).

Security from crime, of course, has always depended heavily on a myriad of informal and community-based mechanisms of social regulation and control. However, the core contribution of the 'modern' state was the construction of the huge institutional edifice intended to underpin and back up all other forms of crime control: the criminal justice and penal system. In crude terms, the basic message about crime given by western democratic governments during the twentieth century was that it could be controlled by 'catching' criminals and processing them through the system. This would in many cases 'change' the individual offender;[4] at the same time, the threat of being caught and sentenced would act as a general deterrent to others tempted to commit crime. Criminal investigation has always played three critical roles in this edifice. First, it provides the 'gateway' into the system: criminal courts, prisons and probation services can only deal with those who have been arrested and charged with specific offences. Secondly, it is central to the deterrence function: if effective, it should convince anyone tempted to offend that there is high risk of 'getting caught'. And, thirdly, it plays a major part in the 'reassurance' agenda – that is, in efforts to convince the public that the police are 'beating crime' and protecting them from the worst offenders. In last two roles, it should be noted, the impression created is arguably as important as the 'real' level of investigative performance.

For the above reasons, the most prominent aim of criminal investigation has generally been that of 'bringing offenders to justice', and much of the following discussion of long-established investigative practice will be centred around this notion. However, it is important to recognise that a considerable proportion of investigative activity has always been aimed at other objectives, such as the collection of 'intelligence'. Moreover, as will be discussed in the final part of the chapter, recent doubts about the effectiveness of crime control in general may eventually alter basic assumptions about the purposes of investigation and its part in the wider picture.

Myths and misunderstandings: the ghost of Sherlock Holmes

Given its importance to the modern state's claim of delivering effective security, the police (especially the CID) clearly have a strong interest in portraying a positive picture of the effectiveness of criminal investigation in 'solving crimes' and 'catching criminals'. This partly explains why so much police effort is put into the detection of certain crimes, such as particular kinds of murder, which capture the public (and media) imagination and arouse fear: the symbolic importance of success in such cases is considerable (Morgan 1990). It also underlines the huge value to a police force of encouraging general belief in a slogan such as 'Mounties always get their man', or of creating legends about the prowess of particular detectives who 'cracked' celebrated cases, such as 'Nipper of the Yard'. Myths about investigative work are further perpetuated through literary fiction and films, the popular appeal of which is partly due to a combination of the arousal of deep-seated fears (about danger from the criminal 'other') and the reassurance that comes from the usual 'happy ending' of the criminal being caught by the police and removed to prison (see also Chapter 11 in this volume).

The stereotypical image which tends to be promoted through most media and fictional representations (and is frequently reflected also in detectives' memoirs and police training manuals) is of a 'case' in which detectives perform a 'Sherlock Holmes' type of role,[5] usually involving the following sequence of events:

1. A member of the public reports a crime to the police.

2. Detectives examine the scene for 'clues', interview victims and witnesses, and make other inquiries.

3. A suspect is identified and confronted with incontrovertible evidence of his or her 'guilt', resulting in a confession and criminal charges.

This picture contains within it a number of assumptions about the nature of investigative work, namely:

- that it is 'reactive' (i.e. that the police respond to a crime complaint from the public rather than generate the investigation themselves);

- that it is focused on an offence which has already taken place;

- that the offence which is being investigated is clear from the outset;

- that the inquiries are geared to uncovering the 'truth' about what happened;

- that it is carried out by detective (CID) officers; and

- that the main investigative skills lie in discovering and interpreting 'clues' to find out 'who did it'.

While it is not difficult to find real cases which follow the above sequence and appear to support these assumptions – in particular, what are sometimes referred to by the police as 'hard-to-solve major inquiries' (to be discussed later) – such an account gives a highly misleading impression of the day-to-day reality of most investigative work, past or present. In the following analysis, indeed, it will be shown that all the above assumptions are contradicted on many occasions.

Challenging the myths: 'suspect centred' investigation and 'case construction'

A radically different picture that has emerged from academic research is that, far from focusing on the scenes of individual offences, the bulk of investigative work has always been what might be dubbed 'suspect centred'. McConville *et al.* (1991), indeed, portray it as essentially a process of 'case construction' against members of 'suspect populations' – principally, those people who have built up a set of previous convictions and have become well known to the local police. In its crudest form, this involves the practice encapsulated in the line from the film *Casablanca*, 'round up the usual suspects': that is (without any evidence to link them to specific offences) frequently detaining and questioning 'known criminals' in the hope that they will admit to, or reveal information about, their own or their associates' recent criminal activities. Blatant 'fishing expeditions' of this kind have been explicitly forbidden in England and Wales since 1985 by the Police and Criminal Evidence Act (PACE) 1984, but the authors argue that they continue in more hidden guises.

More broadly, the notion of case construction against suspects calls into question the claim that crime investigation involves a 'search for the truth'. This claim has been questioned at two levels. McConville *et al.* (1991) and Sanders and Young (2002; see Chapter 10) focus mainly on the influence of the organisational aims and culture of the police. Adapting a distinction made long before by Herbert Packer (1968), they argue that police officers are driven mainly by a 'crime control' as opposed to 'due process' orientation towards their work: in short, their main priority is to bring to justice those they 'know' to be guilty of crime, rather than to ensure that suspects' rights are fully guarded and that designated procedures are meticulously followed (the main priority of many lawyers). This being so, once a person becomes a suspect, he or she is placed into an adversarial relationship with the police rather than one in which the latter seek 'the truth' in a neutral and 'objective' fashion. Thereafter, detectives, starting from a premise of guilt, selectively weave together available pieces of information, or statements by suspects and witnesses, to produce a simplified and coherent story of 'what happened' which they hope will eventually be used as the basis of the prosecution case in court.

The other way in which the claim has been questioned is at an epistemological level through the social constructionist argument that, even if they wanted to, investigators would not be able to discover 'the truth'. In this view, 'crimes' are social or legal constructs, not objective realities, and criminal investigation is inevitably and inherently a creative and interpretative activity. Ultimately, it is about translating 'social reality' into a 'legal reality' that can be dealt with by prosecutors and the courts. In this sense, 'offences' are 'created' retrospectively, in many cases through the medium of astute questioning of suspects in which they are persuaded to admit to actions or intentions that are necessary to the legal proof that a particular offence has occurred and that they have committed it. In addition to 'case construction', this process has been described as 'making crime' (Ericson 1993) or the construction of 'event narratives' (Innes 2003).

Taking account of variation

Such an account provides a valuable broad lens through which to view the process of criminal investigation and an important corrective to the stereotypical images referred to earlier. In particular, it offers a framework for understanding one of the core features of the investigative practices which developed during the twentieth century: the central role played by police interviews in the production of evidence, and hence the extent to which the successful prosecution of offenders (and thereby, arguably, the effectiveness of the whole criminal justice process) came to depend on *confessions*. This point will be picked up again later when discussing reasons for changes that have occurred in recent years.

At the same time, however, general arguments about 'case construction' tend to take little account of the fact that, in practice, investigative activity takes a number of considerably different forms. On the whole, constructionist arguments tend to focus on the evidence-building process that occurs – especially through interviewing – once the police have identified a strong suspect. They have relatively little to say, by contrast, about *how the police initially come to believe that particular people have committed particular crimes*, and hence how they decide how to structure their questioning. This is unproblematic if, for example, a well-known previous offender is arrested at the scene of a burglary, but in other situations it is by no means so straightforward. Clearly (unless the police were to resort to blatant threats, violence or fabrication), simply 'rounding up' and questioning the 'usual suspects' would be unlikely to be a very productive strategy unless the interviewer had at least a minimal idea of what they had been doing. Without this, he or she would have limited levers with which to persuade them to 'talk'.

In other words, if we wish to develop explanations of investigative activity which take account of its full variety and the different situations in which it is set in motion, it is necessary to do so within a wider descriptive framework. Ideally, one would like to create a typology to divide it into neat, mutually exclusive categories, but unfortunately there appears to be no entirely satisfactory way of doing this.

The 'reactive-proactive' distinction

Probably the most common distinctions made have been those based on the opposing terms *reactive* and *proactive* (see, for example, Maguire and Norris 1992; Irving *et al.* 1996; Wright 2002: ch. 4). However, these terms are used in a variety of senses and can often produce more ambiguity and confusion than clarity. They are probably most helpful as a means of distinguishing between two broadly different approaches to the use of investigative resources: reactive approaches giving priority to responding to day-to-day demands (in particular, dealing with crimes reported by the public) and proactive approaches giving more weight to longer-term planning and to agendas set by the police. On the other hand, the terms also tend to be used to distinguish between investigations with different kinds of aims or focus (e.g. reactive investigations to identify the perpetrators of a given offence, in contrast to proactive operations to discover the future plans of known criminal groups), between investigations 'triggered' in different ways (e.g. by a reported crime, as opposed to an intelligence report), and even between different kinds of investigative methods (e.g. forensic examination of crime scenes may be described as a reactive method, covert surveillance as a proactive method). Confusion can be caused when, for example, so-called 'proactive methods' (tasking of informants, surveillance, etc.) are prominent in an apparently 'reactive investigation' (say, a robbery investigation triggered by a 999 call).

Overall, while distinctions based on these terms are by no means valueless, it is essential to clarify in each case the sense in which they are employed.

'Knowledge ' and 'evidence'

A distinction which is arguably more helpful to understanding the variety of forms that investigative practice takes is that between two basic objectives (or tasks): the generation of (police) 'knowledge' and the production of 'evidence'. This has the advantage, first of all, that it draws attention to the centrality of the gathering and manipulation of *information* to detective work – a point stressed in much of the literature (and discussed further below).[6] It also adds a new dimension to the notion of investigation as essentially a process of 'construction'.

Knowledge here refers primarily to the conclusions and understandings reached by the police[7] as to what crimes have been (or are likely to be) committed, by whom, how and why. Numerous factors can play a part in shaping this knowledge (the 'truth' of which is often contested), including a host of information sources and the perceptual lenses and prejudices of those receiving them, but one important aspect which will receive particular attention later is the production and use of 'intelligence'.

Evidence, of course, refers to material that may be presented in court to help establish whether an alleged criminal offence has been committed, and whether an accused person committed it. The main forms it takes are physical traces linking a person to a particular offence ('forensic' evidence), statements by victims or witnesses and responses by suspects to questioning in interviews. Its production requires skill and care and is surrounded by rules designed to ensure that it has been obtained fairly and is presented to the courts in a 'valid' form.

Depending upon the type of inquiry concerned, the production of knowledge and of evidence has normally entailed a number of the following basic tasks:

Production of 'knowledge'

- Determining that one or more criminal offences have been committed.

- Producing a 'narrative' of the circumstances surrounding offences.

- Determining the most promising 'lines of inquiry'.

- Identifying and/or eliminating 'suspects'.

- Exploring the backgrounds, motivations, lifestyles and activities of suspects or 'known offenders' and their associates.

- Gathering intelligence about planned offences.

Production of 'evidence'

- Producing evidence that specific offences were committed (or were planned).

- Producing evidence to link suspected persons with particular offences.

These tasks can be undertaken in different orders or different combinations. Investigators will sometimes start with a specific offence and seek to find out (and/or find evidence to 'prove') who committed it. At other times, they will start by identifying 'suspect' individuals or groups and seek to find out (and/or find evidence to 'prove') what offences they have committed (or are likely to commit in the near future). Often, too, the various tasks will become blurred within the same inquiry.

Individual cases can also vary greatly in the difficulty, complexity and contentiousness of the various tasks involved. For example, most alleged incidents of 'date rape' involve only one suspect who is known to the complainant, so identification is not an issue. However, if the suspect claims that the woman gave consent, the production of sufficient evidence to convince a jury that an offence has taken place may be an extremely difficult task. Moreover – especially in the days before guidance was given that people claiming to be victims of sexual crime should be believed in the first instance (Home Office Circular 69/1986; see also Harris and Grace 1999) – the amount of effort put into this task may be greatly influenced by police 'knowledge', in the shape of the judgements of investigating officers as to who is telling the truth.[8] By contrast, in a 'hit and run' incident it is normally clear that an offence has occurred, and once a suspect is found it may be quite easy to prove guilt (for example, from damage to the car), but identifying the driver and the vehicle in the first place may be extremely difficult.

Twentieth-century investigative practice: key features, risks and crises

Many of the general points made in the previous section can now be illustrated through a closer examination of the formal and informal working practices that were developed and carried out by CID officers during most of the twentieth century. The following discussion will be structured simply around the three main organisational units within which such work was (and to a considerable extent, still is) undertaken. It is recognised that uniformed officers also played an important role in investigation over this period (a role which has since grown in importance – see final section), but the focus at this stage is on detective practice only.

The three main organisational structures

Despite a certain amount of individual variation, the basic pattern – at least until the 1980s – was for forces to maintain a generalist CID office in each division, and a number of dedicated specialist squads (serious crime squads, drugs squads and so on) at headquarters. In addition, if an exceptionally serious crime was reported, an ad hoc major inquiry team might be set up to investigate it. The first and third of these organisational units have generally been associated with 'reactive' approaches to investigation, with squads being considered more 'proactive'. However, these associations are not as clear cut as is often assumed.

'Generalist' CID offices
The work of local CID offices – which employ the greatest numbers of officers – is the hardest to describe or categorise. Perhaps its clearest feature is that it

has always been structured to some extent by the expectation that detectives will respond promptly to any significant crimes that are reported in their area. Most obviously, if a murder, 'stranger rape' or other major crime is reported, substantial numbers of CID officers (as well as uniformed officers) may be abstracted immediately from other duties to take part in the investigation: in some cases, this might tie them up for several months. To this extent, the work of such units has always been 'driven by events' and can be fairly described as 'reactive'. However, once one begins to look at offences below this level, the picture becomes more complicated.

On the one hand, a common feature of local CID work in the twentieth century (which, again, has by no means disappeared) was the daily reception of the latest crime reports (emanating mainly from members of the public) and their allocation by supervisors as 'cases' to be dealt with by individual detectives. The latter were then expected to undertake some form of investigation into each case – usually, at a minimum, visiting the scene of the crime – and to file a report on progress by a certain date. This appears to reflect an assumption that the basic approach of investigators at all levels should be a 'reactive' one, the aim being to 'solve' each individual 'case' as it appears. Such a view, it should be noted, is further supported by the choice of the 'clear-up rate' – i.e. the percentage of recorded crimes which have been 'detected'[9] – as the key national measure to assess the effectiveness of the police in controlling crime (Burrows and Tarling 1982; Burrows 1986; Maguire *et al.* 1992; Maguire 1994).

On the other hand, it is clear from previous research that CID officers working under this system did not follow through all their individual cases rigorously: if after visiting the scene and talking to victims and witnesses there was no clear indication of the offender's identity, they would commonly 'spike' the case and take no further action unless any other relevant information happened to come to their attention (see, for example, Maguire and Norris 1992). The general difficulty in making any further progress in such cases is evident from findings such as those of Greenwood *et al.* (1977) in California, that unless there was a strong lead on the offender's identity within the first 24 hours, the percentage of burglaries detected was almost negligible; or Steer's (1980) finding in Oxford that matching fingerprints contributed to under one per cent of detections. Maguire *et al.* (1992), too, found very small detection rates among cases allocated to CID officers in which there was no immediate suspect. Moreover, where there *was* a clear early identification of a suspect, this was in the great majority of cases provided by the victim or a direct eye-witness, rather than by any complex form of 'sleuthing' by detectives.

In summary, then, in 'reactive' investigations of offences reported by the public and allocated to individual detectives, the overall picture found by research comprised two main types of cases: those which involved the alleged offender's identity being handed to the police as it were 'on a plate' by the victim or an eye-witness; and those where the identity of the offender was unknown at the outset and (despite the best efforts of detectives) was likely to remain unknown thereafter.

However, two important qualifications need to be made to this picture. First, while the identity of a suspect may be handed to detectives on a plate, this does not necessarily mean that the case against that suspect can be easily proved in court. On the contrary, as in the 'date rape' example given above, the production of evidence in such cases may be very difficult (another example might be an allegation of theft in which the 'suspect' claims that the 'stolen' property belongs to him or her, not the self-styled 'victim'). This is a good illustration of the more general point that, while the skills of Sherlock Holmes in interpreting 'clues' would be a very helpful bonus, among the most important skills required by detectives in their day-to-day work are a combination of legal knowledge (e.g. about what evidence is necessary to prove intent), understanding of technical procedures such as the preservation of physical evidence and competence in conducting formal interviews (Morgan 1990; Maguire *et al.* 1992).

The second qualification is that, in cases where the identity of the offender is not immediately apparent and the scene reveals no obvious 'clues', this is not necessarily the end of the story. If the offence is serious enough, or if it becomes clear from the modus operandi (MO) that it is part of a 'series' committed by the same (unknown) offender, much more effort may be put into the task of identification, including the use of methods such as instructing paid informants to make inquiries among their criminal associates. Equally, the offence may come into view again much later as a by-product of another inquiry – as when, for example, an arrested offender is persuaded to 'come clean' about all his or her criminal activity over recent months and (perhaps unexpectedly) admits to this particular offence.

This last point brings us to the other main feature of twentieth-century CID practice at the local level: what was earlier called 'suspect centred' investigative work, in the sense of placing the main focus on monitoring and gathering evidence about the activities of 'known offenders' rather than on 'solving' individual crimes. Although this kind of work is more strongly associated with specialist squads at force level (see below), it has always played a significant part also in divisional CID work. For one thing, many local CID offices set up small squads, usually on a temporary basis, to tackle people known to be frequently involved in particular kinds of offence (drugs squads and burglary squads probably being the most common) – though, as Maguire and Norris (1992) point out, their members were often pulled away from this task to help out with other demands on the office. Secondly, a similar 'monitoring' role, albeit less systematic, was also a key aspect of routine CID activity. Many detectives ran their own informants, who would give them information about what local criminal groups were doing. This would allow them, occasionally, to mount successful raids to recover stolen property or even (if the information was good enough) surveillance operations to 'catch them in the act' of committing planned offences. They also made use of routinely stored information (intelligence logs reporting 'sightings', records of offenders' MOs and so on) in order to, as it were, come at the problem from the other direction: in other words, to try to link up information about reported offences with information about known offenders.

Matza (1969), indeed, saw this process – which he termed the 'bureaucratic' approach, or 'policing by suspicion' – as lying at the heart of the policing of crime in the twentieth century. In short, he argued, it entailed (1) the routine collection and storage of information about a pool of local people with criminal records; (2) searches for recent reported offences which in some way 'fitted' this information; and (3) attempts to establish the link through detaining, questioning and trying to 'construct a case' against the most likely 'candidates' for these offences. Seeing criminal investigation – or, rather, day-to-day investigative work in local CID offices in the late twentieth century – as a dynamic, two-way process of this kind is more illuminating than focusing only on the final 'case construction' element, and offers a partial answer to the question posed earlier as to how the police decided which suspects to ask about which specific offences (as opposed to questioning people and constructing cases, as it were, in a vacuum). Put another way, it illustrates how the generation of police 'knowledge' interacts with the production of 'evidence'.

Specialist squads

The main argument for the formation of specialist squads has always been that certain forms of crime, and certain kinds of offenders, cannot be effectively dealt with by routine responses of the kinds described above and hence require special measures. This applies especially to less 'visible' and more 'organised' kinds of crime, including the supply of illegal goods and services through activities like drug dealing and prostitution: such behaviour is only infrequently reported to the police as 'crime' by members of the public, so if the police are to take action they have to generate it proactively. Even so, more conventional crimes such as robbery and vehicle theft have also frequently been tackled through specialist squads. Generally speaking, the aim of squads has been to identify and 'target' key groups or individuals involved in the relevant activities, gathering 'intelligence' and evidence about their activities and eventually effecting planned arrests. This kind of work often appears glamorous to outsiders, and certain squads acquired highly exaggerated reputations for daring exploits through fictional representations of their work. A classic example from the early 1930s (though its successes were exaggerated by the media) was the Prohibition Bureau, the team of agents led by Elliot Ness which pursued Al Capone and others involved in the supply of illegal alcohol during the prohibition period in Chicago (Hoffman 1993). The 'Flying Squad' also achieved a prominent and mainly positive public profile in London in the 1960s when concerns about organised crime were exceptionally high. At the same time, however (as discussed below), others have been at heart of some of the biggest corruption scandals that have afflicted the police.

In Britain, centrally located squads were particularly common in the 1970s and 1980s. As noted earlier, many divisions set up small local squads, but the focus here is on the larger units operating at force or regional level. These tended to work independently, set their own agendas and, in some cases, retained the same members for long periods. They usually claimed to work 'proactively' in the sense of focusing on particular categories of offender ('organised', 'serious', 'travelling' and so on) and setting up longer-term operations against 'targets', rather than responding ad hoc to individual reported offences. Such offenders often go to some lengths to conceal their activities, or at least to avoid leaving evidence which will convict them easily in court. To meet this challenge, squad detectives often used unconventional methods of obtaining both knowledge and evidence, including close social interaction with active criminals, either openly (it being common practice for detectives to drink in the same pubs and clubs as 'villains') or covertly (for example, through surveillance, recruiting group members as participant informants or working undercover). Hobbs (1988) further argues that in this (under)world, information was a valuable commodity and (as suggested by the title of his book, *Doing the Business*) such interactions could be understood as trading in a 'market' in it: for example, 'deals' would be negotiated in which key information would be given to detectives in return for money, the dropping of charges or even confidential police information. As will be discussed shortly, associations of these kinds clearly contain some serious risks.

Even so, as Maguire and Norris (1992) found, the extent and sophistication of strategic planning and intelligence gathering and analysis that squads employed were often exaggerated, and they quite often acted in a sense in a 'reactive' manner: for example, it was quite common to respond to, say, a 'tip off' from an informant that a house contained stolen property by simply arranging an immediate raid and gaining the 'quick win' of an arrest, rather than exploring the possibilities of setting up a wider-ranging operation to explore the ramifications of the information and possibly to capture a bigger network of offenders.

Major inquiry teams

The third main mode of criminal investigation developed during the twentieth century is the 'major inquiry'. Clearly a 'reactive' form of investigation, this refers to the formation of an ad hoc team of detectives (often assisted by uniformed officers) and the setting up of an incident room, under the direction of a senior investigating officer (SIO), in response to an apparent murder or other very serious offence or series of offences.

Although, as will be discussed later, the way in which such investigations are managed has changed considerably over time, the core elements of the situation have always remained basically the same. The decision to set up a major inquiry is determined by a number of factors, including the seriousness of the offence, whether a 'series' is involved (as where a 'serial rapist' appears to be active), the likelihood of major media attention and the likely difficulty of identifying the offender. In his study of murder investigations, Innes (2003) distinguishes between 'whodunits' and 'self-solvers': the latter, where the identity of the offenders appears certain from the outset, may be dealt with by a much smaller-scale response. One of the main differences between major inquiries and investigations of less serious crimes is that, whereas the difficulty of identifying a clear suspect for, say, a burglary often leads to an early reduction in investigative effort, large numbers of detectives may continue to work on a 'hard-to-solve' murder with few 'leads' for many months or even years.

Risk and failures

The above three kinds of unit, then – generalist local CID offices, specialist squads and ad hoc major inquiry teams – together formed what might be called the 'tripartite' structure on which police investigative responses to crime, particularly in the mid to late twentieth century, were largely built. However, both the CID in general, and the different approaches that each unit employed, came in for serious criticism at intervals over many years, culminating in a growing crisis in legitimacy between the late 1970s and 1990 which led to some significant changes in regulation and practice. This crisis, it will be argued, arose out of risks that were inherently attached to the standard ways of operating that had developed in the CID over many years: practices, it should be emphasised, that had originated to some extent as attempts to solve some of the fundamental problems of responding effectively to crime.

A history of scandal and failure?

The principal concerns about crime control practice that have arisen repeatedly over the years can be summarised crudely as follows:

1. Ineffectiveness in 'catching criminals' (both in general and in individual high-profile cases).

2. Miscarriages of justice (especially arresting and charging the 'wrong person').

3. Abuses of power, corruption and perversion of criminal justice.

4. Erosions of civil liberties (especially through the use of intrusive methods of investigation).

5. Lack of transparency and accountability.

These concerns have been reflected in numerous ways, ranging from ongoing criticisms of day-to-day CID practice and performance (by academics, lawyers and, in some cases, senior police officers, politicians or the media) to major scandals in individual cases resulting in headline news coverage, high-level inquiries and/or significant policy or legislative changes. For example, one recurring theme throughout the twentieth century was the isolation of the CID from mainstream policing, and hence from many of the disciplinary controls exercised by uniform supervisors. Concerns about this became so great in the early part of the twentieth century that a leading police historian (admittedly, a strong supporter of the uniform branch) felt able to write that 'by 1922 the CID had become a thoroughly venal private army' (Ascoli 1979: 210). Similar accusations abounded in the 1970s, when the CID was frequently described as a 'firm within a firm'. This period was also blighted by a series of corruption scandals which eventually prompted the Commissioner of the Metropolitan Police, Robert Mark, to demand the resignation of many CID officers and to introduce institutional reforms to realign the 'balance of power' towards the uniform branch (Cox *et al.* 1977; Mark 1978; Hobbs 1988).

Concerns about CID ineffectiveness (either in failing to bring *anyone* to justice or in bringing the *wrong people* to justice) have also emerged periodically. These have generally grown at times of rising crime rates and were prominent in the late 1970s and early 1980s, fuelled by research studies which suggested that detectives were wasting too much time in simply 'processing' minor cases or on routine visits to scenes of crimes with little hope of a detection (Greenwood *et al.* 1977; Steer 1980; Eck 1983; Clarke and Hough 1984; Burrows 1986; Hough 1987). Probably most damaging, however, have been spectacular failures in major cases, from the inability of investigators to catch 'Jack the Ripper' in the late nineteenth century to the blunders evident in the 'Yorkshire Ripper' case in the 1980s (Byford Report 1981) and the Stephen Lawrence case in the 1990s (Macpherson 1999). Such failures, it should be said, have sometimes had the beneficial result of stimulating improvements following official inquiries. This applies to all the above cases, as well as to a highly critical general report on CID weaknesses by the Detective Committee in 1938, which led to a major rationalisation of detective resources, more systematic training, improved forensic and laboratory facilities, and a revamping of systems of communication (Emsley 2002: 218).

Specific risk factors

To gain a better understanding why the above kinds of problem have been so recurrent, and especially to throw light on the sustained 'crisis' surrounding the CID that began in the mid-1970s, it is helpful to identify key risk factors associated with specific aspects of, or approaches to, criminal investigation. While these were present to some degree in all three kinds of detective unit described (and, it could be argued, will always exist in criminal investigation however it is organised), the patterns and degrees of risk varied with their different environments and working practices. In order to illustrate this, let us begin by briefly reiterating the most salient features of the work of each unit. Although (as has already been made clear) the picture has never been so neat in practice, these may be characterised as in Table 15.1.

At least four major 'risk factors' can be identified which are linked directly to the various working practices and sources of evidence outlined. These relate to 'pressure to perform'; to the tendency for over-reliance on interview evidence; to the need for close dealings with 'known criminals' outside the police station; and to the increasing use of covert and deceptive methods of investigation.

Pressure to perform: Pressure to 'perform' has virtually always been an integral element of CID work and its influence has been strong in all three kinds of detective unit described. Where local CID offices were concerned, Maguire and Norris (1992) found in interviews with detectives that it was generally understood that those who failed to generate sufficient numbers of arrests or other overt evidence of productivity were at risk of being 'put back in uniform' – seen by many as a sign of failure and almost a form of demotion. This was symbolised in a note pinned up on an office wall: 'A sus a day keeps the helmet away'.

In addition to pressure from senior officers, many officers generated pressure on themselves. The culture in some offices encouraged 'workaholic' tendencies and driving ambitions among individuals to increase their numbers of arrests or to put certain offenders 'behind bars'. While desirable in some respects, this ran the risk of tipping over into a situation in which terms like

Table 15.1 Investigative units: key features

	Working environment	Standard procedures	Common working practices	Main sources of evidence	Main skills employed
Local CID offices	Dominated by unpredictable daily demands.	Allocation to officers of individual 'cases' (usually crimes reported by the public) requiring preliminary investigation and report.	1. Visits to scenes of crimes and some local inquiries, but most investigative time spent 'processing' those cases with a clear suspect from the outset. 2. Monitoring of 'known offenders' in the hope of linking them to specific crimes (either already reported or coming to light through the monitoring process).	Statements by victims and witnesses. Admissions in interviews.	1. Use of legal knowledge, production of valid evidence, competence in formal interviewing. 2. Ability to communicate with regular offenders, find out what they are doing, and 'get them to talk'.
Specialist squads	Closed, relatively autonomous, less pressure of immediate events.	Targeting of individuals and groups; collection and analysis of intelligence; planning and execution of 'operations'.	1. Use of covert methods (informants, surveillance, etc.). 2. Willingness to consider methods of crime control beyond arrest and conviction, and to 'use a sprat to catch a mackerel'.	Surveillance; documentary material (e.g. bank transactions); statements by offenders persuaded to give evidence against associates; planned 'raids'.	Individual initiative, handling of informants, 'negotiation'.
Major inquiry teams	Hierarchical to consultative, depending on style of SIO. Often strong background pressure for an 'early result'.	Systematic collection of evidence, determination of lines of inquiry, identification and elimination of suspects.	Officers divided into groups and allocated specific tasks. All information pooled and collated.	Forensic, witness statements, interviews with suspects.	SIOs: personnel and resource management, dealing with external pressure, handling of large amounts of evidence, clear thought about lines of inquiry.

'bending the rules', 'cutting corners', 'using the Ways and Means Act' or 'gilding the lily' became part of the language of day-to-day work, and individual officers went further and further towards routine by-passing of suspects' rights or even fabrication of evidence.

However, pressures to perform (and their consequences) could be much more highly magnified in both central squads and major inquiry teams. In the case of squads, the criminal groups targeted tended to be more sophisticated and resourceful than most offenders pursued at local level, making successful arrests more difficult and putting more pressure for 'results' on the whole team. In the close-knit squads that were revealed as having breached rules and broken the law on a major scale in the 1970s, it was clear that the 'rot' had often permeated the whole team, rather than being restricted to individual 'bad apples'. In some cases, the malpractice took the form of financial corruption and was clearly driven by greed, but in others pressure to perform was a strong factor: the term 'noble cause corruption' was sometimes used to identify instances in which an almost obsessive desire to 'convict criminals' drove officers to widespread rule-breaking and fabrication of evidence (for discussion of the seminal case of Lundy, see Short 1992).

Where major inquiries are concerned, the 'pressure for a result' has tended to come from both external and internal sources. Certain kinds of murder – especially what appear to be sexually motivated murders of women or children by unknown strangers – often stimulate massive media coverage and create an atmosphere of fear in the surrounding area, so the SIO, in particular, faces daily pressure to demonstrate progress with the investigation and to make an early arrest. At the same time, such inquiries can be extremely expensive and can tie up police officers for long periods, so the SIO also tends to face increasing pressure from senior officers to expedite the inquiry. Traditionally, SIOs tended to be given complete responsibility for and control over major inquiries, with little external assistance. The obvious risks were, first, poor decisions on which 'lines of inquiry' to follow, potentially resulting in a major waste of resources and the investigation being led up a blind alley; and, secondly, miscarriages of justice arising from a blinkered notion that a particular person is guilty, combined with the above pressures to 'wrap up' the case as quickly as possible (Maguire and Norris 1992; Rozenberg 1992; Walker 2002; Walker and Starmer 1999).

Reliance on interview evidence: One of the most prominent features of 'generalist' investigative work as described above was its heavy reliance (and often over-reliance) on interview evidence. Major inquiries, too, quite often produced insufficient evidence to convict without some form of admission from the main suspects. In both cases, the need for this kind of evidence in itself created a temptation for investigators to treat interviewing as nothing more than a vehicle for obtaining a 'confession', closing their minds to anything said that contradicted their 'knowledge' of the situation. This attitude was further encouraged by the prevailing police culture, the 'crime control' (as opposed to 'due process') orientation of most police officers and the institutional pressures on investigators referred to above. At the same time, the fact that people could be detained in police stations for considerable (and unspecified) lengths of time, without contact with relatives or a solicitor, produced an essentially coercive situation, which detained persons often experienced as frightening and psychologically disorienting (Irving and Hilgendorf 1980; Irving and McKenzie 1989; Gudjonsson 1992).

In the light of all the above circumstances, there were clearly in-built risks that (1) police officers might become oppressive in their questioning; (2) people might be unfairly persuaded to make or sign self-incriminating statements (for example, in response to hints that 'co-operation' would bring quicker release); (3) some suspects (especially those with mental disabilities) might become so disoriented and vulnerable to suggestion that they would make entirely false confessions to crimes mentioned by interviewers; or (4) some police officers would, in their records of interviews, distort or embellish what had been said or even invent it entirely.

These kinds of risks were seen to be all too real and came to public and political attention in England and Wales in spectacular fashion in the late 1970s through a high-profile inquiry into the clearly wrongful conviction of three adolescents for the murder of Henry Confait, based on false confessions made under oppressive questioning (Fisher 1977). Several other major miscarriages of justice dating from this period and arising partly or wholly from unsafe confession evidence did not come to light until the late 1980s, when they caused further serious questioning of the integrity of police investigations (Rozenberg 1992).

Close dealings with criminals: If (as was the case with most 'squads') a core objective of investigators is to find out as much as possible about the lifestyles, activities and plans of selected 'targets', it is necessary in some way to 'get close to them'. In some of the major squads operating in the 1970s and 1980s, close proximity to criminal groups with considerable power and resources, combined with the closed and autonomous nature of the squads and poorly regulated operating methods, clearly carried major risks and almost inevitably led to some serious and deeply embedded forms of malpractice. These included the plain corruption of officers who were tempted by offers of shares in the proceeds of crime, or who in some cases fell victim to blackmail or other pressures put on them by resourceful criminals. They also included malpractice which was encouraged by risks inherent in the cultivation of informants. A common problem here was of 'the tail wagging the dog': informants used their relationship with detectives to further their own criminal interests and were sometimes given almost 'carte blanche' to continue their activities in return for information about others. They also 'set up' rival criminals by giving false information or acting as agents provocateurs.[10]

Among the most notorious examples of endemic and enduring malpractice were the activities of several detective units in London in the 1970s (Cox *et al.* 1977; Mark 1978) and the West Midlands Serious Crimes Squad (Kaye 1991). A later example from continental Europe involved a Dutch police team, ostensibly under the direction of lawyers but in reality out of control, which became involved in a series of large deliveries of drugs into the country. This eventually led to a major scandal, a parliamentary inquiry and several high-level resignations (Fijnaut and Huberts 2002).

Covert, intrusive and deceptive methods: The final risk factor concerns the use of covert, intrusive or deceptive methods of investigation, in particular the interception of communications, 'bugging', the use of undercover officers or participating informants and 'sting' operations. These pose a potential threat to basic civil liberties, especially privacy, as well as a risk of unfair prosecutions and convictions. The employment of such methods was for many years associated with high-level specialist squads, although it has become increasingly common at all levels of policing. Apart from telephone tapping, for which rules were established under the Interception of Communications Act 1985, there was no statutory regulation of intrusive surveillance methods in England and Wales until the late 1990s. In its absence, determining the acceptability of various means of obtaining evidence was largely left to internal police rules and the discretion of senior officers, together with the occasional judgement in the British courts or the European Court of Human Rights, but neither provided consistent principles or guidance to investigators, nor effective controls on an increasing disregard of civil liberties (see, for example, Maguire and John 1996; Colvin and Noorlander 1998). Marx (1988) drew attention to a phenomenon of 'surveillance creep', whereby the police gradually push at the boundaries of what methods are considered acceptable by the courts and the public, with the effect that is hardly noticed that individual rights taken for granted ten years ago are breached routinely today almost without anyone noticing.

As well as police disregard for rights to privacy, an issue of growing concern was the lack of clear limits on the use of deceptive methods such as 'sting' operations, whereby people are tricked or tempted by undercover officers or police informants into taking part in some form of criminal activity and subsequently arrested. These range from fairly 'passive' operations such as leaving a lorry full of goods unattended to see if anyone will steal from it, to those in which a 'known offender' may be actively persuaded to take part in a crime – an example being an attempt to persuade a known drug trafficker to buy and smuggle a large consignment of heroin. The latter is clearly a case of 'entrapment' by an agent provocateur, and the case would almost certainly be dismissed if the facts came to light in court. However, concerns were expressed about cases in which the involvement of an informant was hidden from the courts (and the defendant). Moreover, the limits of entrapment-like behaviour were defined only through case law, which left them unclear. An important illustrative case was that of Colin Stagg, a suspect in a high-profile murder case, who was befriended by a female police officer who repeatedly tried to trap him into admissions by pretending that she found it stimulating to listen to talk about violence against women (*R* v. *Stagg* (1994) *The Times* 15 September). In this case, the evidence was excluded and the police officers involved were strongly criticised, although it was pointed out in their defence that there had been no clear law or legal precedent preventing the use of this kind of tactic (for further discussion of regulatory issues around covert and deceptive methods, see Maguire and John 1996; Field and Pelser 1998; Sharpe 2002).

Responses to the crisis: glimpses of a radically different future?

The various scandals, recurrent criticisms and growing awareness of the risk factors outlined above led eventually to a number of legislative and policy initiatives, organisational reforms and shifts in thinking, particularly over the 1980s and 1990s, which between them have already contributed to some substantial changes in the ways that police investigations are regulated, managed and carried out. In this final section, the most important of these changes will be summarised, and the question will be posed whether they represent merely a number of superficial reforms aimed at taking the steam out of the persistent criticisms of CID practice, or whether they signal a much more radical shift in approaches to crime control.

Responses to concerns about integrity

The concerns about police interviewing raised by the Confait case (Fisher 1977) led to the setting up of the Royal Commission on Criminal Procedure (1981) and, eventually, following its recommendations, to a key piece of legislation to monitor the integrity of evidence production, the Police and Criminal Evidence Act (PACE) 1984: in particular the codes of practice for the detention and questioning of suspects in police stations. The main safeguards introduced were the appointment of a 'custody officer', who decides whether detention is justified, maintains a written record of what happens (the 'custody record') and is responsible for suspects' welfare while in custody; limits on the length of time for which suspects can be detained; a right of access to legal advice during questioning; and the obligation to make a contemporaneous (normally tape recorded) record of what is said in interviews (Zander 1985; Home Office 1995). The impact of this system has been the subject of a great deal of empirical research and vigorous academic debate, opinions ranging from those who conclude that it has had little effect on police attitudes and that they have found it relatively easy to circumvent the rules, to those who argue that it has transformed attitudes and virtually eliminated the risk of mistreatment or oppressive interviewing in police custody (for a flavour of these debates, see McConville *et al.* 1991; Dixon 1995; Morgan 1995; for a recent overview, see Maguire 2002).

However, concerns about integrity continued to emerge, and matters again came to a head in 1991 after another series of major miscarriages of justice (most dating back to pre-PACE days), with the setting up of the Royal Commission on Criminal Justice in 1991, supported by several specially commissioned pieces of research. While the new commission's report (1993) was disappointing to those who sought greater statutory controls over police investigations, the inquiry certainly focused the minds of senior police managers and sparked off some important internal reforms. These included significant reductions in the numbers of specialist squads (particularly at police-force level) and limitations on the length of time for which officers could be members of particular teams or how long they could remain in the CID without a temporary return to uniform; in some forces, indeed, the CID was virtually disbanded for a period and, in most, new arrangements were made to facilitate closer joint working with uniform staff. There was also an increase in the emphasis put upon integrity in training courses, including the introduction of concepts such as 'ethical interviewing' (sometimes also called 'investigative interviewing') aimed at teaching officers to keep a more open mind and also to behave less aggressively when questioning suspects (Williamson 1996).

Where the problem of 'getting too close to criminals' is concerned, the practice of detectives routinely drinking in pubs and clubs with 'villains' (Hobbs 1988) was generally forbidden. By the mid-1990s, too, many forces also claimed to have greatly reduced the risks of corruption or the perversion of justice by improving their systems of informant handling. However, serious doubts were cast on this claim in a highly critical study by Dunnighan and Norris (1996), which found many instances of informants not being registered, unrecorded payments being made and the prior involvement of informants being concealed from court cases. Strong national guidelines have since been produced by the Association of Chief Police Officers (ACPO). These underline the principle that informants (now officially referred to as 'covert human intelligence sources', or CHISs) are 'owned' by the police force, not by the individual officer, and stipulate that that they should always be officially registered, that two 'handlers' should be appointed (under the supervision of a 'controller' who is responsible for all informant management in the area) and that a record should be kept of all meetings. The extent to which practice now matches the aspirations is a question that requires research (for more general research on preventing corruption, see Newburn 1999).

More recent legislation has tended to reflect concerns about the protection of civil liberties (and possible breaches of the European Convention of Human Rights, which was incorporated into English law via the Human Rights Act 1998), and hence to focus on the regulation of covert forms of evidence or intelligence gathering. In particular, the Police Act 1997 required the formulation of clear rules to govern the authorisation of 'bugging' (Home Office 1998), and the Regulation of Investigatory Powers Act 2000 introduced for the first time statutory guidelines on the use and handling of CHISs. Critics have argued that these Acts do little more than legitimise pre-existing police rules and practices, as well as protecting the police from challenges under the Human Rights Act, but the creation of statutory rules in these areas is surely preferable to the uncertain position that existed previously (for discussion, see John and Maguire 1998; Neville 2000; Sharpe 2002).

Efforts to improve effectiveness

As well as responding to concerns about integrity, from the mid-1980s onwards police managers were increasingly faced with the challenge of how to improve their effectiveness in terms of crime control. Already on the defensive over rising crime rates and falling detection rates, they began also to come under the general spotlight that was shone on the performance of the public services by the Thatcher government through its Financial Management Initiative and its focus on the 'three Es' (economy, efficiency, effectiveness). Ironically, it appeared to many, the more effective they became in ensuring integrity, the bigger this second challenge became. In particular, the new regulation of post-arrest procedures under PACE – even though not as restrictive as many first feared – made it increasingly clear to the more far-sighted that the ingrained habit of reliance on confession evidence to secure the bulk of convictions had to be confronted, and it was time to grasp the nettle of implementing new investigative strategies across the whole police service. Indeed, the whole 'reactive', case-based approach (whereby CID officers were expected to make some effort at investigating each individual crime as it was reported) began to come under serious questioning.

Two complementary concepts were particularly prominent in discussions of the 'way forward': 'crime management' and 'proactive' approaches.

The idea that the flow of crime should be 'managed', rather than allowing officers' working days to be dominated by the need to respond to increasingly large numbers of individual crime reports, became widely accepted during the 1980s. It was manifested in a number of organisational changes that took place in many police forces. One was the setting up of 'crime management units' (or units with similar names) at divisional level, acting as a 'one-stop shop' and co-ordinating centre of investigative activities. Many operated a system of 'crime screening' (Eck 1983), whereby reports of crimes were sifted on the basis of what had been found by the uniformed officers who conducted the initial visit to the scene: for example, if the offence appeared to be fairly minor, and there was no clear evidence of who had been responsible, the case might be immediately 'screened out' and not allocated to a CID officer for further investigation. Such systems were sometimes based on discretion, though in other cases they used a formal scoring system whereby points were awarded on the basis of indicators of 'detectability', such as whether there were fingerprints, eye witnesses and so on.

A further aspect of crime management was an increasing trend towards specialisation of tasks within CID offices. Rather than expect individual detectives to follow through their own cases 'from the cradle to the grave', it became much more common for small groups of officers to take on specific tasks such as interviewing arrested persons or preparing court papers for all cases flowing through the office.

At the same time, the notion of using more 'proactive' approaches or methods became increasingly widely supported. It was given a major boost by the Audit Commission's (1993) report, *Helping with Enquiries: Tackling Crime Effectively*, which criticised traditional case-based methods of working and urged police forces to 'target the criminal, not just the crime': in other words, to focus on groups and individuals known to be actively involved in crime and to collect intelligence and evidence about their movements and activities. This might include attempts to link them (e.g. through forensic evidence or their modus operandi) to previously recorded offences or series of offences, but might also be aimed at discovering their future intentions and ideally at catching and arresting them 'in the act'. The report also advocated much greater use of informants, which it deemed to be the most 'cost-effective' source of intelligence (though this was strongly disputed later by Dunnighan and Norris 1999). Such approaches were hardly new – as already discussed, they were common in specialist squads, and local CID units used them spasmodically – but the intention was to apply them in a much more systematic manner than in the past, with greater organisational resources and support and, importantly, drawing in the uniform branch as well as the CID.

One of the pioneering police forces in this respect was Kent, where the Chief Constable, David Phillips, experimented by introducing a holistic 'intelligence led' system of policing into two police stations (see Maguire and John 1995; Amey *et al.* 1996). This entailed a major reorganisation of existing roles and functions, the idea being that everyone on the staff would contribute in some way to the achievement of a clear set of goals. The main units set up were an intelligence cell, a tactical arrest team and a case preparation team. Most existing CID staff were reallocated to one of these specialised units, only a small number remaining as a 'reactive' investigative team to deal with day-to-day offences reported by the public (though the majority of these offences were 'screened out' so that the team could focus on the most serious). The intelligence cell played a key role in collecting and analysing information and identifying 'targets', its director meeting regularly with senior operational officers as part of the 'Tasking and Control Group' that made all the main decisions about how resources would be deployed. All activity was highly focused, the objective being to identify the most prolific offenders (at one point, a 'top 40' list was constructed) and then to collect information and evidence about them in a systematic way, including giving patrol officers specific tasks relating to them, paying informants to find out more about them and setting up surveillance operations. Arrests were usually planned in advance and carried out by the tactical team. While the system experienced some significant practical problems – especially 'blockages' in the flow of intelligence, delays in processing cases after arrest, failures in communication and losses of morale among officers not selected for their preferred roles – it was seen by most officers as a successful experiment in terms of tackling the main crime problems in the area. Moreover, few victims complained once it was explained to them why a crime they had reported would not be directly investigated (Maguire and John 1995).

Although many other police forces also paid lip-service to an intention of practising 'intelligence-led policing' (ILP), and although some set up one or more of the necessary tools for doing so (such as improving intelligence systems or introducing dedicated surveillance teams), the number of 'proactive' operations implemented was generally small and there were few signs of major changes to the traditional reactive patterns of working, Kent remaining more the exception than the rule. As Maguire and John (1995) showed, if a local police division was really to be 'intelligence led', it had both to undertake significant reorganisation in order to establish a genuinely integrated system and to address deep-seated cultural resistance (see also Barton and Evans 1999; HMIC 1999; Heaton 2000). It will be argued below that a more fundamental change of this kind may finally be imminent. However, it is first necessary to complete the picture of police managers' responses to the 'crisis' by charting recent reforms in the crucial area of major inquiries.

Improvements to major inquiries

In terms of the attention of the media, politicians and the public, concerns about other aspects of crime control tend to grow cumulatively, but mistakes in one high-profile major inquiry can take on a sudden huge significance that remains in the public mind for many years. Two inquiries in particular have received more media and public attention and have had a greater influence on police reforms in this area than any other: the 'Yorkshire Ripper' case in the early 1980s and the Stephen Lawrence case in the mid-1990s.

The 'Ripper' case was notable not just for the public fear it caused while the murders continued but also for the highly publicised misjudgements made by the inquiry team, in particular in putting 'all their eggs in one basket' in pursuing a fruitless line of inquiry and in failing to spot several strong indications of the identity of the murderer within the huge volume of material generated by the inquiry. The concerns raised by the case led eventually to some important reforms in the organisation of major inquiries, notably the introduction of a computer system, the Home Office Large Major Inquiry System (HOLMES, later updated to HOLMES 2), to facilitate the systematic storage and analysis of investigative material, and various mechanisms to reduce the burden and pressure on SIOs. The latter included devolving some responsibilities to other members of teams and the introduction of a system of formal external reviews in cases which still remained undetected after a set period of time – the objective being for the case to be examined through a 'fresh pair of eyes' (Maguire and Norris 1992; Berry *et al.* 1995; Innes 2003).

Despite these reforms, the investigation of the murder of Stephen Lawrence in 1993 demonstrated that by no means all the lessons of previous mistakes had been learnt, as well as drawing attention to the influence of racial prejudice on the conduct and outcome of a major inquiry, including on the important early stages when evidence should be preserved by the first officers on the scene (Macpherson 1999). The ramifications of the case went far beyond the mechanics of investigative practice (see, for example, Stanley 1999; see also Chapter 21 in this volume), but in relation to procedures in major inquiries, subsequent developments have included the production of a comprehensive 'Murder Manual' (Innes 2003; Brookman forthcoming) and more honest recognition of major skills deficits among SIOs, leading to a search for new ways of assessing and improving their quality (Smith and Flanagan 2000).

Signs of more fundamental change

Returning finally to the 'bigger picture', it is interesting to speculate in this final section whether what was earlier referred to as the 'modern' approach to crime control – embodied, as far as the police contribution is concerned, in the investigative practices of the three kinds of units through which CID work was organised for most of the twentieth century (generalist offices, squads and major inquiry teams) – may be in the early stages of a radical transformation. Writers such as Garland (1996, 2001) and Rose (2000) have identified a growing belief that, in the more complex, individualised and deracinated communities that are coming to characterise 'late modern' societies, crime can no longer be effectively controlled by what have now become the traditional responses of the central state and the criminal justice institutions. This, they argue, has set in motion major shifts in thinking and practice across all the core state agencies. Perhaps more significantly for the longer term, it has also fuelled the beginnings of what may become a general dispersal of responsibility for the control or 'governance' of crime away from the major government and criminal justice institutions towards voluntary and private organisations, local communities and, ultimately, the 'responsibilised' individual (Johnston 2000; Rose 2000; for a more sceptical view, see Jones and Newburn 2002).

One major feature of this shift in 'penality' (Garland 2001) has been a growing focus on the *identification and management of risk* as an organising principle of the work of all the main criminal justice agencies.[11] Another has been an increasing recognition that their 'effectiveness' in this task depends on sharing data and working more closely together, illustrated in the rapid and widespread development of *partnerships* aimed at reducing crime (Hughes 1998; Pease 2002). As these trends become more manifest in the shape of new formal structures and practices underpinned by legislation, such as 'community safety partnerships', 'crime audits', 'crime reduction plans' and the like, the role of 'criminal investigation' (and even the descriptive usefulness of the term) becomes increasingly unclear.

In more concrete terms, probably the most significant sign of a truly radical change in police approaches to crime control is the development and imminent implementation of the National Intelligence Model (NIM). This instrument, developed initially under the auspices of the National Criminal Intelligence Service (NCIS), is essentially a blueprint for a whole new 'business model' for the organisation of police responses to crime (and, indeed, of many other areas of police responsibility). It is based primarily on the notion that the core business of policing is to collect relevant information to allow clear and accurate identification and analysis of current and likely future 'problems'; to prioritise the most important of these problems and plan responses to them; to implement the plans; and, finally, to evaluate what has been done and to feed back the experience and knowledge. At its heart are the preparation of a comprehensive 'strategic assessment' of current and predicted crime threats in the relevant area and of 'tactical assessments' to identify particular targets – which may be people, places or activities – on which the police should most profitably focus their plans for managing these problems (for more details, see NCIS 2000; John and Maguire 2003). If applied correctly, the NIM allows for 'solutions' to be sought outside the criminal justice system. For example, it could lend support to approaches such as gathering information about the nature of particular criminal markets in order to find ways of 'disrupting' them and the criminal networks that control them (Kock *et al.* 1995; Clarke 1999; Sutton *et al.* 2001).

As such, the NIM represents a step change from the traditional individualistic, case-based approach to criminal investigation described in the first part of this chapter. It also represents a major advance from early attempts to rationalise the use of investigative resources, such as the introduction of crime management units and crime screening in the 1980s, and indeed from the under-resourced and often token efforts to practise 'proactive' or 'intelligence led' policing at local level in the 1990s. Like the specialist squads of the 1980s, few of those ostensibly involved in ILP researched their problems or planned their strategies with any analytical depth and, as Gill (2000) argues, such approaches often amounted in practice to little more than a more focused 'rounding up of the usual suspects': put another way, it could be argued that, despite their aspirations, most investigative units remained (in the broadest sense of the word) 'reactive' in character. Of course, the big 'if' surrounding the NIM is whether those driving its implementation will be able to overcome familiar obstacles to translating intentions into reality: not least, passive resistance among police middle managers and officers arising from the challenge which the rigorous analytical approach, and even the 'alien' tone and language, of the model represents to traditional police cultures and ways of working (John and Maguire 2003).

Selected further reading

The Audit Commission's *Helping with Enquiries: Tackling Crime Effectively* (1993) is probably the report with biggest influence on crime investigation over the last decade. It strongly advocates a shift from 'reactive' to 'proactive' approaches and greater use of informants. Innes' *Investigating Murder: Detective Work and the Police Response to Criminal Homicide* (2003) is a detailed and up-to-date study of murder investigations, based on analysis of case files and interviews with detectives. It provides a useful typology of investigations and applies theories of 'narrative' to the construction of cases. It also covers wider theories about detective work. Maguire's 'Policing by risks and targets: some dimensions and implications of intelligence-led crime control' (2000) is a brief overview of contemporary developments in crime control and criminal investigation, summarising recent literature on risk and policing, and considering some of the implications of what appears to be a broad shift away from the traditional focus on individual cases and reliance on the criminal justice system towards more strategic, 'problem-solving' and risk-focused approaches.

Maguire and Norris's *The Conduct and Supervision of Criminal Investigations* (1992) is one of the main research reports commissioned by the Royal Commission on Criminal Justice in the area of the regulation of detective practice. It examines in some detail problems and risks inherent in routine CID work, the activities of proactive squads and major inquiries. McConville *et al.*'s *The Case for the Prosecution* (1991) is a controversial and highly influential book which revived Packer's concepts of 'crime control' and 'due process', questioned the impact of PACE and framed 1990s academic debate on the regulation of police behaviour. Wright's *Policing: An Introduction to Concepts and Practice* (2002) is a highly recommended overview of recent issues in policing, combining sociological theory with practical knowledge and experience, and including an excellent chapter on crime investigation.

Notes

1 For broader discussions of the concept of 'modernity' and its expression in the growth of bureaucratic, 'scientific' and classificatory systems of social control, see, for example, Foucault (1977) and Garland (1990, 2001).
2 In England and Wales, prosecution decisions remained a police function until the establishment of the independent Crown Prosecution System in 1985 (see Sanders 2002; Sanders and Young 2002).
3 This squad remained operational afterwards, and formed the nucleus of Special Branch, which has continued ever since to deal with offences against state security: see Chapter 4.

4 To what extent such change was to be achieved through punishment and individual deterrence (e.g. by fines, flogging or long prison sentences) or by 'rehabilitation' (e.g. through probation 'treatment' or 'therapy') varied over time with changing circumstances, theories or politics (Garland 1990, 2001).

5 Though note, of course, that Sherlock Holmes was an 'amateur' who regularly made a fool of the slower-witted and incompetent professional detectives who appear in the stories (especially Inspector Lestrade). This theme reflects the scepticism about the effectiveness of the police as investigators which remained strong throughout the nineteenth century. Twentieth-century detective fiction (including films and television series) is much more likely to portray police officers as experts in 'solving' crime (Morgan 1990; for broader discussions of the police in fiction, see Sparks 1992; Reiner *et al.* 2001).

6 Indeed, many writers have characterised information as the 'lifeblood', the 'essential raw material' or the 'currency' of investigative work, and the trade of the detective as revolving around its acquisition, analysis and interpretation (see, for example, Hobbs 1988; Ericson 1993; Innes 2003).

7 Although this chapter focuses on the (public) police, they are not the only agency which investigates crime, and the same would apply to, for example, Customs officers investigating drugs importation or Inland Revenue officers investigating tax fraud.

8 These, in turn, may be influenced not just by their impressions of the individuals concerned but also by their own previous experience of such cases, personal prejudices, the police 'culture' and so on.

9 More precisely, the clear-up rate shows the percentage of officially recorded crimes for which one or more people have been charged, summonsed, cautioned or otherwise dealt with on the basis of an admission or reasonable evidence that they were the perpetrator(s). This includes admissions to additional offences which convicted offenders agree to have 'taken into consideration' by the court without extra charges being laid and later admissions in prison ('prison write-offs') – both of which are usually referred to as 'secondary detections'. It also includes offences in which, for example, the offender was too young, elderly or ill for charges to be laid. A 'not guilty' verdict does not negate a 'detection'.

10 For further discussion of the risks relating to informants, see Reuter (1983), Marx (1985), Hobbs (1988), Maguire and Norris (1992), Maguire and John (1996), Stelfox (1998), Dunnighan and Norris (1996, 1999), Billingsley *et al.* (2001), Sharpe (2002).

11 For general discussions of this issue, see Ericson and Haggerty (1997), Kemshall (1998), Maguire (2000), Kemshall and Maguire (2001), Hudson (2002), Loader and Sparks (2002).

References

Amey, P., Hale, C. and Uglow, S. (1996) *Development and Evaluation of a Crime Management Model. Police Research Series Paper* 18. London: Home Office.

Ascoli, D. (1979) *The Queen's Peace: The Origins and Development of the Metropolitan Police 1829–1979.* London: Hamish Hamilton.

Audit Commission (1993) *Helping with Enquiries: Tackling Crime Effectively.* London: Audit Commission.

Barton, A. and Evans, R. (1999) *Proactive Policing on Merseyside. Police Research Series Paper* 105. London: Home Office.

Berry, G., Mawby, R.C. and Walley, L. (1995) *The Management and Organisation of Serious Crime Investigations.* Satfford: Staffordshire University.

Billingsley, R., Nemitz, T. and Bean, P. (2001) *Informers: Policing, Policy, Practice.* Cullompton: Willan.

Brookman, F. (forthcoming) *Homicide in the UK.* London: Sage.

Burrows, J. (1986) *Investigating Burglary: The Measurement of Police Performance. Home Office Research Study* 88. London: HMSO.

Burrows, J. and Tarling, R. (1982) *Clearing up Crime.* London: Home Office.

Byford, L. (1981) 'The Yorkshire Ripper case: review of the police investigation of the case'. HM Inspectorate of Constabulary (unpublished).

Clarke, R. (1999) *Hot Products: Understanding, Anticipating and Reducing Demand for Stolen Goods. Police Research Series Paper* 112. London: Home Office.

Clarke, R. and Hough, J.M. (1984) *Crime and Police Effectiveness. Home Office Research Study* 79. London: HMSO.

Colvin, M. and Noorlander, P. (1998) *Under Surveillance: Covert Policing and Human Rights Standards. Report.* London: JUSTICE.

Cox, B., Shirley, J. and Short, M. (1977) *The Fall of Scotland Yard.* Harmondsworth: Penguin Books.

Critchley, T. (1978) *A History of Police in England and Wales.* London: Constable.

Dixon, D. (1995) 'New left pessimism', in L. Noaks *et al.* (eds) *Contemporary Issues in Criminology.* Cardiff: University of Wales Press, 216–23.

Dunnighan, C. and Norris, C. (1996) 'A risky business: the recruitment and running of informers by English police officers', *Police Studies*, 19(2): 1–25.

Dunnighan, C. and Norris, C. (1999) 'The detective, the snout and the Audit Commission: the real costs of using informants', *Howard Journal*, 38: 67–86.

Eck, J. (1983) *Solving Crimes: The Investigation of Burglary and Robbery.* Washington, DC: Police Executive Research Forum.

Emsley, C. (1996a) *Crime and Society in England 1750–1900.* London: Longman.

Emsley, C. (1996b) *The English Police: A Political and Social History.* London: Longman.

Emsley, C. (2002) 'The history of crime and crime control institutions', in M. Maguire *et al.* (eds) *The Oxford Handbook of Criminology* (3rd edn). Oxford: Oxford University Press, 203–30.

Ericson, R. (1993) *Making Crime: A Study of Detective Work* (2nd edn). Toronto: Toronto University Press.

Ericson, R. and Haggerty, K. (1997) *Policing the Risk Society.* Oxford: Clarendon Press.

Field, S. and Pelser, C. (eds) (1998) *Invading the Private: State Accountability and New Investigative Methods in Europe.* Aldershot: Dartmouth.

Fijnaut, C. and Huberts, L. (eds) (2002) *Corruption, Integrity and Law Enforcement.* The Hague: Kluwer.

Fisher, Sir H. (1977) *The Confait Case: Report.* London: HMSO.

Foucault, M. (1977) *Discipline and Punish: The Birth of the Prison.* London: Allen Lane.

Garland, D. (1990) *Punishment and Modern Society: A Study in Social Theory.* Oxford: Clarendon Press.

Garland, D. (1996) 'The limits of the sovereign state: strategies of crime control in contemporary society', *British Journal of Criminology*, 36(4): 445–71.

Garland, D. (2001) *The Culture of Control.* Oxford: Oxford University Press.

Gatrell, V., Lenman, B. and Parker, G. (eds) (1980) *Crime and the Law: The Social History of Crime in Western Europe Since 1500.* London: Europa.

Gill, P. (2000) *Rounding up the Usual Suspects? Developments in Contemporary Law Enforcement Intelligence.* Aldershot: Ashgate.

Greenwood, P., Chaiken, P. and Petersilia, J. (1977) *The Criminal Investigation Process.* Lexington, MA: Heath.

Gudjonsson, G. (1992) *The Psychology of Interrogations, Confessions and Testimony.* Chichester: Wiley.

Harris, J. and Grace, S. (1999) *A Question of Evidence? Investigating and Prosecuting Rape in the 1990s. Research Study* 196. London: Home Office.

Heaton, R. (2000) 'The prospects for intelligence-led policing: some historical and quantitative considerations', *Policing and Society*, 9: 337–56.

HMIC (1999) *Policing with Intelligence*. London: Her Majesty's Inspectorate of Constabulary.

Hobbs, D. (1988) *Doing the Business*. Oxford: Oxford University Press.

Hoffman, D. (1993) *Scarface Al and the Crime Crusaders*. Carbondale, IL: Southern Illinois University Press.

Home Office (1995) *Revised Code of Practice for the Detention, Treatment and Questioning of Persons by Police Officers*. London: Home Office.

Home Office (1998) *Intrusive Surveillance: Code of Practice*. London: Home Office.

Hough, J.M. (1987) 'Thinking about effectiveness', *British Journal of Criminology*, 27(1): 70–9.

Hudson, B. (2002) 'Punishment and control', in M. Maguire *et al.* (eds) *The Oxford Handbook of Criminology* (3rd edn). Oxford: Oxford University Press, 233–63.

Hughes, G. (1998) *Understanding Crime Prevention: Social Control Risk and Late Modernity*. Milton Keynes: Open University Press.

Innes, M. (2003) *Investigating Murder: Detective Work and the Police Response to Criminal Homicide*. Oxford: Clarendon Press.

Irving, B., Faulkner, D., Frosdick, S. and Topping, P. (1996) *Reacting to Crime: The Management of Police Resources*. London: Home Office.

Irving, B. and Hilgendorf, L. (1980) *Police Interrogation: A Case Study of Current Practice. Royal Commission on Criminal Procedure Research Study* 2. London: HMSO.

Irving, B. and McKenzie, I. (1989) *Police Interrogation*. London: Police Foundation.

John, T. and Maguire, M. (1998) 'Police surveillance and its regulation in England and Wales', in S. Field and C. Pelser (eds) *Invading the Private: State Accountability and New Investigative Methods in Europe*. Aldershot: Dartmouth.

John, T. and Maguire, M. (2003) 'Rolling out the national intelligence model: key challenges', in K. Bullock and N. Tilley (eds) *Essays in Problem-oriented Policing*. Cullompton: Willan, 38–68.

Johnston, L. (2000) *Policing Britain: Risk, Security and Governance*. Harlow: Longman.

Jones, T. and Newburn, T. (2002) 'The transformation of policing? Understanding current trends in policing systems', *British Journal of Criminology*, 42: 129–46.

Kaye, T. (1991) *Unsafe and Unsatisfactory? Report of the Independent Inquiry into Working Practices of the West Midlands Crime Squad*. London: Civil Liberties Trust.

Kemshall, H. (1998) *Risk in Probation Practice*. Aldershot: Ashgate.

Kemshall, H. and Maguire, M. (2001) 'Public protection, partnership and risk penality: the multi-agency risk management of sexual and violent offenders', *Punishment and Society*, 3(2): 237–64.

Kock, E., Kemp, T. and Rix, B. (1995) *Disrupting the Distribution of Stolen Electrical Goods. Crime Prevention and Detection Series* 69. London: Home Office.

Loader, I. and Sparks, R. (2002) 'Contemporary landscapes of crime, order and control: governance, risk and globalization', in M. Maguire *et al.* (eds) *The Oxford Handbook of Criminology* (3rd edn). Oxford: Oxford University Press, 83–111.

Macpherson, Sir W. (1999) *The Stephen Lawrence Inquiry: Report of an Inquiry by Sir William Macpherson of Cluny* (Cm 4262). London: HMSO.

Maguire, M. (1994) 'Assessing investigative performance: the clear up rate and beyond', *Focus*, 1(4): 22.

Maguire, M. (2000) 'Policing by risks and targets: some dimensions and implications of intelligence-led crime control', *Policing and Society*, 9: 315–36.

Maguire, M. (2002) 'Regulating the police station: the case of the Police and Criminal Evidence Act 1984', in M. McConville and G. Wilson (eds) *The Handbook of the Criminal Justice Process*. Oxford: Oxford University Press, 75–98.

Maguire, M., Hobbs, D., Noaks, L. and Brearley, N. (1992) *Assessing Investigative Performance. Report to Home Office*. Cardiff: Cardiff University Social Research Unit.

Maguire, M. and John, T. (1995) *Intelligence, Surveillance and Informants: Integrated Approaches. Crime Detection and Prevention Series Paper* 64. London: Home Office.

Maguire, M. and John, T. (1996) 'Covert and deceptive policing in England and Wales: issues in regulation and practice', *European Journal of Crime, Criminal Law and Criminal Justice*, 4: 316–34.

Maguire, M. and Norris, C. (1992) *The Conduct and Supervision of Criminal Investigations. Royal Commission on Criminal Justice Research Report* 5. London: HMSO.

Mark, R. (1978) *In the Office of Constable*. London: Collins.

Marx, G. (1985) 'Who really gets stung? Some issues raised by the new police undercover work', in F. Elliston and M. Feldberg (eds) *Moral Issues in Police Work*. Totowa, NJ: Rowan & Allanheld.

Marx, G. (1988) *Police Surveillance in America*. Berkeley, CA: University of California Press.

Matza, D. (1969) *Becoming Deviant*. Englewood Cliffs, NJ: Prentice Hall.

McConville, M., Sanders, A. and Leng, R. (1991) *The Case for the Prosecution*. London: Routledge.

Morgan, J.B. (1990) *The Police Function and the Investigation of Crime*. Aldershot: Avebury.

Morgan, R. (1995) 'Authors meet critics: the case for the prosecution', in L. Noaks *et al.* (eds) *Contemporary Issues in Criminology*. Cardiff: University of Wales Press, 224–30.

NCIS (2000) *The National Intelligence Model*. London: National Criminal Intelligence Service.

Neville, E. (2000) 'The public's right to know: the individual's right to privacy', *Policing and Society*, 9: 413–28.

Newburn, T. (1999) *Understanding and Preventing Police Corruption: Lessons from the Literature. Police Research Series Paper* 112. London: Home Office.

Packer, H. (1968) *The Limits of the Criminal Sanction*. Stanford, CA: Stanford University Press.

Pease, K. (2002) 'Crime reduction', in M. Maguire *et al.* (eds) *The Oxford Handbook of Criminology* (3rd edn). Oxford: Oxford University Press, 947–79.

Radzinowicz, L. (1956) *A History of the Criminal Law and its Administration from 1750. Vol. 2. The Clash Between Private Initiative and Public Interest in the Enforcement of Law*. London: Stevens.

Reiner, R., Livingstone, S. and Allen, J. (2001) 'Casino culture: media and crime in a winner-loser society', in K. Stenson and R. Sullivan (eds) *Crime, Risk and Justice: The Politics of Crime Control in Liberal Democracies*. Cullompton: Willan, 175–93.

Reuter, P. (1983) 'Licensing criminals: police and informants', in G. Caplan (ed.) *Abscam Ethics*. Washington, DC: The Police Foundation.

Rose, N. (2000) 'Government and control', *British Journal of Criminology*, 40: 321–39.

Royal Commission on Criminal Justice (1993) *Report* (Cm 2263). London: HMSO.

Royal Commission on Criminal Procedure (1981) *The Investigation and Prosecution of Criminal Offences in England and Wales: The Law and Procedure* (Cmnd 8092-1). London: HMSO.

Rozenberg, J. (1992) 'Miscarriages of justice', in E. Stockdale and S. Casale (eds) *Criminal Justice under Stress*. London: Blackstone Press, 91–117.

Sanders, A. (2002) 'Prosecution systems', in M. McConville and G. Wilson (eds) *The Handbook of the Criminal Justice Process*. Oxford: Oxford University Press, 149–66.

Sanders, A. and Young, R. (2002) 'From suspect to trial', in M. Maguire *et al.* (eds) *The Oxford Handbook of Criminology* (3rd edn). Oxford: Oxford University Press, 1034–75.

Sharpe, S. (2002) 'Covert surveillance and the use of informants', in M. McConville and G. Wilson (eds) *The Handbook of the Criminal Justice Process*. Oxford: Oxford University Press, 59–74.

Sheptychi, J. (1998) 'The global cops cometh', *British Journal of Sociology*, 49(1): 57–74.

Sheptychi, J. (2000) *Issues in Transnational Policing*. London: Routledge.

Short, M. (1992) *Lundy: The Destruction of Scotland Yard's Finest Detective*. London: Grafton.

Smith, N. and Flanagan, C. (2000) *The Effective Detective: Identifying the Skills of an Effective SIO. Police Research Series Paper* 122. London: Home Office.

Sparks, R. (1992) *Television and the Drama of Crime*. Buckingham: Open University Press.

Stanley, L. (ed.) (1999) 'The Stephen Lawrence murder and the Macpherson Inquiry report' (special issue), *Sociological Research Online*, 4(1).

Steer, D. (1980) *Uncovering Crime: The Police Role. Royal Commission on Criminal Procedure Research Study* 7. London: HMSO.

Stelfox, P. (1998) 'Policing lower levels of organised crime in England and Wales', *Howard Journal*, 37: 393–406.

Sutton, M., Schneider, J. and Hetherington. S. (2001) *Tackling Theft with the Market Reduction Approach*. London: Home Office.

Walker, C. and Starmer, K. (1999) *Miscarriages of Justice*. London: Blackstone.

Walker, C. (2002) 'Miscarriages of justice and the correction of error', in M. McConville and G. Wilson (eds) *The Handbook of the Criminal Justice Process*. Oxford: Oxford University Press, 505–24.

Williamson, T. (1996) 'Police investigation: the changing criminal justice context', in F. Leishman *et al.* (eds) *Core Issues in Policing*. London: Longman.

Wright, A. (2002) *Policing: An Introduction to Concepts and Practice*. Cullompton: Willan.

Zander, M. (1985) *The Police and Criminal Evidence Act 1984*. London: Sweet & Maxwell.

Chapter 16

Policing public order and political contention

P.A.J. Waddington

Introduction

The policing of public disorder and civil strife is quite straightforward: police fight with their opponents. Police in most jurisdictions are trained in techniques and tactics, but everywhere the outcome is much the same: since no plan survives contact with the enemy (to quote a military aphorism), quelling disorder is as chaotic as any battle. Police are often hurt and occasionally killed in such fracas, but it is their opponents who usually suffer more, particularly in jurisdictions where police are armed.

In my experience, what police officers want from academic analysis is not a manual of how to fight battles on the streets – they know that well enough. Instead, they want and need a wider understanding of why disorder erupts at all and with what consequences. Fortunately, this is something about which academic research has much to contribute.

Public order: a distinct policing task?

Public order policing is often implicitly distinguished from other policing tasks such as law enforcement, but upon close inspection that distinctiveness is far from clear. The phrase 'public order policing' evokes an image of riot-clad officers engaged in forceful confrontation with political dissidents, pickets and those engaged in 'community disorders'. However, this is misleading for several reasons: first, protests and picketing are overwhelmingly policed in most jurisdictions by officers in normal uniforms and are accompanied by few arrests and little or no violence (della Porta and Reiter 1998). Secondly, eruptions of violence and its forceful suppression arise in a much broader spectrum of contexts: leisure activities, most notably soccer hooliganism, and street carnivals like that in Notting Hill, London; and occasions associated with youth culture such as the confrontations of 'mods and rockers' in the 1960s to the difficulties in accommodating 'peace convoys' and 'raves' in the

1990s (for a general review of public disorder in Britain, see Waddington, D. 1992; King and Brearley 1996). Viewed historically, the notion of public order policing embraces inter-faith conflicts – for example, the Murphy riots of the mid-nineteenth century. Cross-culturally, deadly ethnic riots have claimed vast numbers of lives, such as the wholesale slaughter of Sikhs that followed the assassination of Mrs Ghandi (Brass 1996; Horowitz 2001).

Nor is 'public order policing' distinguished from other forms of policing by officers being deployed en masse under superior control, for police act collectively in very different types of circumstances, such as at civil disaster (Hills 1997). Indeed, as the Hillsborough disaster reminds us, the line between a public order operation and a disaster may be very blurred, at least so far as the police are initially concerned (Taylor 1989). Such a line may become even more blurred in the future by the prospect of police enforcing the quarantine of whole communities afflicted by biological attack by terrorists.

Policing contention

Given the ambiguities that inevitably surround the concept of 'public order', I propose to concentrate here upon one aspect that does present a range of particular issues. That is, the policing of what Charles Tilly usefully describes as 'contentious politics' (1995), for while it is true that not all contentious politics falls into the ambit of policing, much of it is pursued through protest and related activity. On the other hand, 'contention' is not synonymous with 'protest': 'contention' is more inclusive and does not imply that events are explicitly politically motivated.

Why is contention worth attention? Because, as I have argued elsewhere (Waddington 1995), it creates a policing context in which police legitimacy is intrinsically problematic. The legitimacy of law enforcement may at any time become problematic, but it is not intrinsically so. Criminals are ipso facto beyond the moral community and police can readily don the mantle of moral superiority. This is quite different when those whom the police seek to restrain or suppress are motivated by ideals (and even self-interest can be presented as the pursuit of 'justice'). In these circumstances, *any* police action (even their mere presence) may be interpreted as illegitimate. If 'challengers' have right on their side, then police action (that is other than conspicuously benign) must be in the wrong. Even 'neutral' policing would unacceptably equate those in the right and those in the wrong. In other words, policing contention is unavoidably 'political'.

Policing contention: the historical experience in Britain

The introduction of the police in 1829 was partly justified by its role in controlling 'the mob' (Palmer 1988). In the aftermath of the so-called 'Peterloo massacre', in which troops had charged into a forbidden protest gathering near Manchester, leaving 11 dead and 100 injured, the demand for a less lethal alternative to the military became irresistible (Waddington 1999). Yet, from their inception it was a task surrounded by controversy. In 1833 Constable

Culley was murdered during the so-called 'Battle of Cold Bath Fields'; worse still, the inquest jury returned a verdict of 'justifiably homicide' that was subsequently overturned on appeal. This illustrates the distrust with which the infant Metropolitan Police was viewed. The remainder of the nineteenth century was punctuated by confrontations between police and contentious gatherings, often surrounded by controversy. However, the police gradually replaced the military as solely responsible for the control of public order and while public order policing could be still be bloody, the number of fatalities decreased enormously.

The left

During the twentieth century the greatest challenges to public order came from the opposite poles of the political spectrum – the Labour movement and fascism. Confrontations between increasingly powerful trade unions and the state culminated in the General Strike of 1927. Then, as the Great Depression seized the economy, confrontations occurred during 'hunger marches' organised by the left-wing National Unemployed Workers Movement. The 1950s and 1960s were largely quiescent with police–picket confrontations becoming ritualised 'pushing and shoving' (Geary 1985). Towards the end of the 1960s Britain's poor economic performance was blamed increasingly on trade union militancy and during the 1970s there were repeated confrontations on picket lines. These confrontations increased markedly during the 1980s as Mrs Thatcher's government embraced the market and traditional 'coal-stack' industries crumbled. Steel workers, miners and printers were at the forefront of these confrontations. The year-long miners' strike epitomised the climate of the times, with thousands of police drafted into the coalfields to protect working miners and break the strike. For the first time, officers policing industrial disputes were attired in riot gear and used tactics that were aggressive. The result was that the unions were subdued.

The final flicker of resistance from the left was in the early 1990s when protesters opposed the introduction of the poll tax, the climax of which was the poll tax riot in Trafalgar Square and the surrounding area. Since then 'the left' has embraced not only socialists but also environmentalists and others without a clear ideological position. As the millennium came to an end, there were confrontations associated with the construction of roads and airports, as well as opposition to 'globalisation'.

The politics of race

The opposite end of the spectrum finds fascist parties. In the 1930s fascism was explicitly the ideology of Moseley's 'black shirts'. Their marches and gatherings provoked anti-fascist resistance and police were often caught separating the two sides and allegedly defending the fascists against their opponents (Thurlow 1993). Much the same pattern was repeated during the post-Second World War era, reaching a crescendo in the 1970s when the National Front and British National Party staged provocative marches through areas of high ethnic minority settlement. With each successive wave of concern about immigration, asylum-seekers and so forth, the far right has been on hand to exploit it, but not on the scale of earlier confrontations.

The politics of race was not exclusively orchestrated by the far right; during the 1980s there was widespread rioting by ethnic minorities living in Britain's 'inner cities' and 'dump estates'. St Paul's, Bristol, Southall (1980), Brixton, Liverpool 8, and Moss Side, Manchester (1981), Handsworth, Birmingham, Brixton and, infamously, Broadwater Farm, Tottenham (1985), all came to epitomise these confrontations. The Scarman Report (1981) into the Brixton riot laid the blame on social and economic disadvantage, combined with oppressive policing. As the millennium dawned, similar outbreaks of 'community disorder' erupted in several of Britain's northern towns and cities, notably Oldham, Burnley and Bradford. However, this time they were more closely associated with Asian youth rather than Afro-Caribbeans and appeared to have been sparked by opposition to far-right political activity in conditions of increased racial tension (Ritchie 2001; Clark 2002).

It seems safe to conclude that the control of contentious politics is a persistent feature of policing. Certainly, it has been so throughout the western world. The USA witnessed serious ghetto riots during the 1960s and campus rebellions against the Vietnam War. In 1968 student rebellion also erupted in Germany, Italy and, most explosively, in Paris. More recently, opposition to global capitalism has been a worldwide phenomenon. So, how have the police responded?

The police response

In Britain the police were originally conceived as an alternative to heavy-handed militarism. While the military were available as a lethal longstop for much of the nineteenth century, political contention became progressively less violent reaching a low point in the 1950s. Since then, the police have significantly increased their coercive capacity: in the early 1970s a national mechanism was installed for the mobilisation of 'mutual aid' between forces and police were organised in squads for public order purposes (police support units); in the 1980s police acquired riot equipment (helmets, body armour, shields and the yet-to-be-used plastic baton rounds); and gradually tactics evolved in favour of a more aggressive response to disorder. All this has proven immensely controversial.

Challengers

Policing contention, like most other aspects of policing, entails a *relationship*, in this case with 'challengers'. Who are the 'challengers' whom police encounter in this context? What are their motives? What strategies and tactics do they use? Indeed, much of the literature on the *policing* of political contention is actually dominated not by policing as such but by analyses of 'challengers'. Analysts are correct to do so, because how 'challengers' conduct themselves has obvious implications for how they are policed.

Debating with Le Bon's ghost

For much of the twentieth century, sociology was accused of being preoccupied with a debate with the ghost of Karl Marx. While Marx's ghost clanks around the terrain of contentious politics, a far more prominent apparition is that of the ghost of Gustav Le Bon. He too was a nineteenth-century social and political thinker, whose book *The Crowd* (1895) succeeded in defining the terms of the debate about contentious gatherings for a century (McPhail 1991). His influence continues to be felt in manuals on riot control.

Central the Le Bon's thesis was the fear that in the type of society created by industrialisation and urbanisation, people could gather in very large numbers and be swayed by irrational feelings that they would resist in other contexts. He envisaged a process of 'emotional contagion' that swept through a gathering and created a single 'crowd mind' that overpowered the cognitive processes of its members. During the twentieth century, psychologists were to add flesh to the outline that Le Bon had proposed, most notably Miller and Dollard (1941), whose theory of 'frustration-aggression' posits that if experimental subjects are sufficiently frustrated in some endeavour, they will indiscriminately act with aggression once given the opportunity. Combined with the notion of relative deprivation (Gurr 1968) this creates a plausible scenario in which those who feel deprived become progressively frustrated by their plight and then engage in indiscriminate aggression under the guise of some form of protest.

If this is accurate then it has profound implications for policing, since it gives legitimacy to, if not encouraging, outright suppression. McPhail (1991) has correctly insisted that there is little or no credible evidence that participants in gatherings are *necessarily* or *frequently* afflicted by emotional contagion – what he calls the 'myth of the madding crowd'. Even in the most extreme situations, such as the immediate aftermath of disasters, people are not cognitively impaired; on the contrary, they are perfectly able to assess their circumstances and act appropriately to achieve their goals. Even collective violence can have a rational basis: if those who have a purpose are obstructed they will tend to overcome the obstruction. This is one reason why the policing of contention is more than simply 'crowd control': challengers are distinguished by their clarity of, and commitment to, a purpose. When police obstruct that purpose confrontation can be expected. Yet it is not mindless rage: violence tends to be purposive – damage tends to be targeted against property that rioters find offensive (Reicher 1984) and looting tends to be as selective as any shopping expedition (Berk and Aldrich 1972)! Equally, challengers might seek violence – for instance, believing that change can only be achieved by such means, or that it is essential for some form of social cleansing (Horowitz 2001). As McPhail (1994) makes plain, being *rational* is not synonymous with being *reasonable* – this is the 'dark side of purpose'.

On the other hand, it should not be assumed that everyone in every situation is rational. A sound criterion for judging the rationality of action is whether it advances or harms the realisation of one's goals. This appears straightforward at first but conceals difficulties. Horowitz (2001) emphasises how those engaged in 'deadly ethnic riots' carefully select their targets and appraise the risks and rewards of attacking particular groups. Yet, many such riots result in outcomes that are in no way to the advantage of the rioters – not even in their own terms. Moreover, we should not ignore the influence of intoxicants: drunken groups have been responsible for violent disorder in Britain (where they were once dubbed 'lager louts') and North America (where 'beer riots' are commonplace).

As Rule (1989) points out, actors are not condemned only to being either 'rational' or 'irrational'; in many cases their behaviour can better be described *non-rational*, a prominent example of which is religious conflict – for instance, the conflict between Hindus and Muslims regarding the mosque at Ayodhya (see Chaturvedi and Chaturvedi 1996), or the conflict that has long surrounded the Temple Mount in Jerusalem (Friedland and Hecht 1996). In these and many other circumstances, the conflict is *symbolic*.

In symbolic conflict means and ends tend to be fused, rather than activity serving some extrinsic purpose. Marching becomes not simply a means by which a gathering proceeds collectively from one location to another but also a display and possibly a provocation. Marches by far-right activists in Skokie, Illinois (Sherr 1989), and areas of high ethnic settlement in Britain and elsewhere (Clutterbuck 1980); republicans and loyalists in Northern Ireland (Jarman and Bryan 1996); and Hindus, Sikhs and Muslims in India (van der Veer 1996) are just some of the many occasions upon which marching acquires enormous symbolic significance and leads to contention, if not also violence and disorder.

Thus, while a great deal of contentious activism is devoted to the purposive pursuit of rational goals that allows negotiation, persuasion and compromise, there are some activities that do not. More to the point, *within* any social movement, campaign or protest action there may be some adherents for whom the issues and the means of achieving them are rational and purposive, whereas for others they are non-negotiable and symbolic. It is these latter conflicts that are most productive of coercive encounters with the police, or where the failure of the police to intervene forcefully itself becomes a cause of contention.

'Riff-raff' v. the 'ballot-box of the poor'

A related, but separate, issue surrounds those who engage in contention and their motives for doing so: what is often depicted as the 'riff-raff' theory, on the one hand, and the 'ballot-box of the poor' on the other. 'Riff-raff' theory proposes that disorder arises from wanton hooliganism by members of the criminal classes, whereas the 'ballot-box' view regards violent contention as genuine attempts to remedy justified grievances. If the former is correct, then robust policing is amply justified, but if it is the latter then repression merely heaps injustice upon grievance and aggravates conflict. As this implies, this is predominantly a normative argument about the alleged causes of disorder and their remedies (Grimshaw and Bowen 1968; Taylor 1984; Waddington 1991), neither of which is convincing.

Consistent with its normative orientation, the 'ballot-box' explanation is very selectively applied: ethnic minorities, striking workers, disadvantaged youth and other favoured downtrodden groups are seen as expressing grievances; but not neofascists, Ulster loyalists and the like (Waddington 1991). In other words, 'grievance theory' is an application of 'underdog' sociology (Jefferson 1993) and suffers the generic weaknesses of that approach (Hammersley 2000).

What sustains this view is the sentimental assumption that 'underdogs' prey upon 'fat cats'. Sometimes they do, but equally they can inflict suffering upon their neighbours – participants in deadly ethnic riots believe they too suffer grievances that justify slaughter (Horowitz 2001).

Grievance and 'riff-raff' theories share a common assumption that riot, disorder and protest are the province of the poor, but this is hard to sustain. Participants in violent disorder and protest tend *not* to be the most deprived: arrest data and post-incident surveys indicate that they are more likely than non-participants to be employed and no more likely that non-participants to have criminal records (for a review of this literature see Field and Southgate 1982). At the aggregate level, Spilerman (1970, 1971, 1976) could find no indicators of deprivation that reliably distinguished between American cities that suffered violence during the ghetto riots of the 1960s and those that did not – a conclusion confirmed in a much smaller-scale study in Britain following the inner-city riots of the early 1980s (Parry *et al.* 1987). Analysis of individuals similarly failed to find evidence of deprivation (McPhail 1971). Protest is the pastime of the middle classes and 'unattached intellectuals' (not least university students), not the downtrodden masses (Klandermans 1997; della Porta and Diani 1999). Finally, it needs to be appreciated that the concept of *relative* deprivation was invoked in order to explain the *lack of fit* between objective deprivation and protest or resistance. Indeed, resource mobilisation theory insists that protest activity depends upon the economic affluence that allows adherents and sympathisers to use their disposable income and other resources, such as spare time, in pursuit of favoured causes (McCarthy and Zald 1977; Jenkins 1983).

Theoretically too there are problems with the notion that grievances provoke protest and disorder. As Tilly (1978) has observed, grievances are simply so ubiquitous that they cannot explain the variance in protest activity or violence. There is little evidence that the grievances of ethnic minorities in America and Britain were alleviated in the wake of the disorders that afflicted their cities in the 1960s and 1980s respectively, so why then did they cease? In an attempt to fill the explanatory gap, theorists have relied upon the idea that while grievances provide a background condition conducive to contentious politics and disorder, it must be supplemented by some event(s) that focus discontent. These events have been described as 'precipitating conditions' (Smelser 1962) or 'flashpoints' (Waddington *et al.* 1989; Waddington 1992, 1998). However, as I have argued elsewhere (Waddington 1991, 2000), the identification of such events is inevitably retrospective and open to considerable bias (since one theorist's 'flashpoint' is another's 'innocuous act'). Moreover, 'grievance' theories tend to make the Le Bonian assumption that collective action is unitary, whereas available evidence suggests that those who participate do so for a plurality of motives (for example, see Keith 1993).

An alternative theoretical paradigm

If the conventional debate has proven sterile, an alternative has emerged from 30 years of social movements research based on three basic components:

(1) the structure of political opportunities and constraints confronting the movement; (2) the forms of organisation (informal as well as formal), available to insurgents; and (3) the collective processes of interpretation, attribution, and social construction that mediate between opportunity and action. Or perhaps it will be easier to refer to these three factors by the conventional shorthand designations of political opportunities, mobilising structures, and framing processes (McAdam *et al.* 1996: 2).

What implications does this consensus hold for the policing of contention? Obviously, there is much more that could be said about these three components (for a review, see della Porta and Diani 1999), but here the perspective will be narrowed to the implications for policing.

Political opportunities

The key observation of the current consensus is that grievances do not explain why contention erupts when and where it does. African-Americans had long harboured grievances about their treatment, especially in the southern states. So, why was their challenge to segregation delayed until the mid-1950s? The answer given by McAdam's authoritative analysis of the American Civil Rights Movement (1982) is that three 'political opportunities' presented themselves at this crucial time: first, the collapse of 'King Cotton' as the staple commodity of the South caused displaced labour to migrate to the cities and the northern states. Consequently, African-Americans became concentrated in urban centres away from small rural communities where they had previously been vulnerable to harassment and intimidation. Secondly, the earlier creation of segregated black colleges and churches unwittingly produced an African-American intelligentsia and a network through which it could mobilise. Thirdly, the National Association for the Advancement of Colored Peoples provided a continent-wide organisational infrastructure for promoting the campaign for desegregation. It was these conditions that *allowed* the movement to prosper.

Protest cycles

Protest rarely occurs in isolation but, rather, there are periods during which protest revolves around a broad, but related, range of issues reaching a peak and then subsiding – the 'protest cycle' (Tarrow 1994). The existence of such a cycle has direct implications for the police, for it is the 'early risers' (Tarrow 1989) who dominate the initial stages of a protest cycle. They are distinguished by the innovative tactics they employ to wrong-foot opponents, including the police, and attract public attention, giving campaigners valuable momentum. Examples include tactics like the 'lunch-counter sit-ins' of the Civil Rights Movement, 'teach-ins' of 1970s student radicals and contemporary 'stunts' by gay rights activists. Always, these tactics are disorderly even when non-violent, because they breach established patterns; sometimes, they are overtly violent, such as the tactic of 'suicide bombing' used by militant Palestinians during the Intifada. Almost invariably, it provokes a coercive response from the security forces as they struggle to gain control of the new expression of dissent.

'Early risers' gain the initiative and others tend to flock to the cause (McAdam 1983). However, this is a mixed blessing, for as the cycle gathers momentum it sacrifices radicalism. Mainstream social moments seek to regain the authority and leadership lost to militants. This involves them in taking up many of the issues pioneered by the 'early risers' and transforming them into negotiable positions capable of compromise. As compromises are reached, so 'soft' support for radical and militant action tends to ebb away. Simultaneously, the police evolve means of countering the threats posed by radical innovations. As the security forces gradually obtain the upper hand and the costs of protest thereby increase (as protesters are arrested and penalised by the courts), support ebbs away.

As the protest cycle tends to decline, a new dynamic is initiated, with potentially very violent consequences: the pool of available adherents to the campaign shrinks and radical factions compete for adherents by increasing militancy. At its most extreme, this can lead small factions into terrorism (della Porta 1995). This produces a counter-response from the security forces, such as the special unit of the *carabinieri* that hunted down and eliminated all but the remnants of the Italian Red Brigades (Collin 1985). The severity of state response is facilitated by the illegitimacy that militant/terrorist groups have acquired.

Mobilising structures

Organisation

It will now be apparent that this alternative paradigm harbours no sentimentality in its analysis of social movements. This 'realist' perspective is maintained in its analysis of what makes movements successful or not. The answer is 'organisation' – the effective use of resources. An ad hoc gathering that expresses its grievances presents no threat; if it is violent, it can be suppressed with little likelihood of repercussions. 'Grass roots' get trampled!

So how are successful challenges organised? The answer is that it is 'whom you know' that matters. Challengers who are isolated fail: those who are connected to networks have more success (for a general review, see Klandermans 1997). The Black Civil Rights Movement did not just spring spontaneously from the fertile soil of generations of racial oppression, it relied on a dense network of black churches and colleges to communicate not only grievances and aspirations, but – more importantly – tactics also (McAdam 1982, 1983).

Networks may include purely personal contacts, but often (as in the case of the Civil Rights Movement) they are facilitated by formal organisations. Indeed, social movements research has discovered that the normal mode of recruitment is that it occurs in 'blocks', as activists in related areas of contention ally themselves en masse with others. However, the cost of relatively easy recruitment is factionalism. Campaigns and individual protests are very rarely homogeneous in their composition; instead they consist of a dense patchwork of different groups.

One way in which heterogeneity can be gauged is in terms of the relative militancy of different component groups. These differences often build tensions into the internal dynamics of social movements, for moderates have an ambivalent relationship with the militant fringe (Henriques 1991). On the one hand, militants are very useful to a movement, for they tend to capture headlines through their militant actions (see, for example, Lange 1990; Short 1991). Militants can also be wielded by moderates as a threat in negotiations, indicating a constituency within the movement that moderates need to placate with valuable concessions. At the same time, moderates must maintain some distance from militants to avoid moral contamination. Thus when militants go 'too far' they tend to be disowned by moderates.

The *heterogeneity* of social movements, campaigns and discrete protests is of enormous importance to how contentious politics is policed for, as Stott and Reicher (1998) argue, when police respond to the actions of *some* sections of a gathering (and, by extension, a campaign or wider movement) as if it was the consensual act of all, they thereby weld together the entire gathering, campaign or movement. Militants know this and a well worn tactic is to provoke the police into this reaction.

Beyond the core of activists and adherents lie 'conscience constituencies' (McCarthy and Zald 1977) predisposed to support a range of causes. It is these constituencies that activists need to mobilise to bring pressure to bear upon those with power. This is crucial to policing for, if the police act in ways that can be depicted as brutal and oppressive, then consequent moral outrage among sympathetic 'conscience constituencies' becomes a source of leverage. For example, during the early stages of the American Civil Rights Movement a more (Barkan 1980) or less (Morris 1993) conscious decision was made to provoke the authorities into making mass arrests that would clog the gaols and courts. 'Bull' Connor's cops in Birmingham, Alabama, took the bait and in a desperate attempt to suppress the protests resorted to fire-hoses, police dogs and birdshot against non-violent schoolchildren. All this was broadcast on network television news and helped to prompt federal intervention. The police in Albany, Georgia, however, resisted the bait, adopted a strategy of arresting protesters without overt force and releasing them on bail, thus defeating the purpose of the protest.

Violence and rampage

This brings us to the part that violence plays in protest. Many 'underdog' accounts of political contention depict violence as a symptom of collective wrath – people who have reached the end of their tether because of the grievances they suffer. The alternative paradigm has no such illusions: violence is one of the few resources available to the powerless and dispossessed (Eisinger 1973; Wilson 1976): 'Encoded in a group's actions and tactics are a good many messages, but none more significant than the degree of threat embodied in the movement' (McAdam 1996: 341). And violence works! Gamson reviewed a large array of American social movements and found that those who made recourse to violence succeeded more often than those that did not (Gamson 1975; Frey *et al.* 1992).

However it is important not to get violence out of proportion, for it is far from prevalent. In contentious gatherings violence (or even confrontation) is typically engaged in episodically by relatively few individuals at any one moment. Very often 'violence' extends to little more than bystanders cheering and gesticulating in support of, or opposition to, the actions of a few militants. Even in those settings most associated with violence, outbreaks are episodic and often ritualistic. Marsh *et al.* (1977) illustrate this in connection with confrontations among soccer 'hooligans' who taunt each other, 'square up' as if to fight and withdraw after others intervene. Armstrong's portrayal of 'football hooliganism' confirms that many of the 'confrontations' that he witnessed amounted to little more than inconsequential dashing back and forth (Armstrong 1998).

Elite sponsorship

Violence works, but is not nearly so important as having 'friends' in the corridors of power. States vary in the extent to which the political elite is divided, but divisions are commonplace and equally commonly exploited by campaigners. Movements try to align themselves with the agendas of elite interests, such as political parties seeking to appeal to a 'conscience constituency' attracted to the plight of some group or to a cause (Jenkins and Perrow 1977). Sometimes distinct agencies or sections of government have their own reform agenda which they pursue vicariously through campaigners whom they supply with 'leaked' information and other resources. At its most extreme, elite sponsorship might extend to a whole tier of government, as when the Kennedy–Johnson Federal administrations came to support the Civil Rights Movement in the South because it saw the opportunity of securing precious black votes in the cities of the North and feared the international consequences of scenes of racial oppression broadcast on television (McAdam 1982).

Of course, this means that the campaigns are less divorced from elite institutions than they would often like to pretend. This is a two-edged sword for, while elite sponsorship can provide much needed resources, the campaign is constrained to act within limits acceptable to their sponsors. The militancy of the 'Black Power' movement and the eruption of violence in the streets of American cities during the 'long, hot summers' of the 1960s did much to undermine the Civil Rights Movement, especially among white opinion (McAdam 1982). So, elite sponsorship is a component of the process of institutionalising politics, so that it conforms to what is acceptable to dominant interests and values (Piven and Cloward 1977, 1992). At its most extreme, it takes the form of state licensing, through the acceptance of tax breaks that are predicated upon the charitable status of campaigning organisations (McCarthy *et al.* 1991).

Legitimacy and the courts

In this context, a state institution that has escaped much attention is that of the law and the courts. This is particularly surprising given the significance that legality has for legitimacy. The famous decision of the US Supreme Court in *Brown* v. *Board of Education* that effectively ended segregated schooling in the South is a conspicuous example. This established not only that segregation was wrong in schooling but also powerfully endorsed the view that African-Americans were widely denied their constitutional rights. This emboldened and energised the nascent Civil Rights Movement (Scheingold 1974). Post-incident judicial inquiries also often serve as both forums within which campaigners can pursue political goals and as endorsers of their claims of injustice. Recent examples include the Scarman Report into the Brixton riot (1981) and the Taylor report on the Hillsborough disaster (1989).

Dramatic incidents offer fortuitous opportunities for campaigners to gain access to the policy agenda (McCarthy *et al.* 1996). However, those opportunities need to be exploited and the events that open the window of opportunity must be depicted in a manner that gives them lasting significance. Court cases and public inquiries offer campaigners that opportunity. Whether or not disorder erupted because of repressed grievances is less important than that it is *thought* than grievances and injustices were the motive. For instance, there seems to be little objective difference between the disorders that occurred in Britain's northern towns and cities in 2001 and those that occurred throughout the inner cities almost exactly 20 years previously. Yet there was a marked difference in how those events were interpreted. In stark contrast to the sympathetic analysis of Lord Scarman's report, reports on the 2001 disturbances were quite dismissive of claims that the predominantly Asian rioters were victims of injustice (Ritchie 2001; Clark 2002).

Framing processes

This brings us to the third leg of the current consensus on social movements, how campaigners 'frame' their cause. Since grievances are too ubiquitous to explain the variance in challenges (Tilly 1978), those grievances must be 'framed' to have any mobilising force. That is, social movements need to persuade potential adherents that something is wrong; that someone is to blame; and that it is capable of remedy by a programme of challenging action, thereby creating a 'collective action frame' (for a review of this literature, see Klandermans 1997). How events are 'framed' as the movement progresses is crucial to its continued survival and achieving any measure of success (Gamson and Meyer 1996). Hence, activists expend considerable resources in attempting to portray their relationships with police, authorities and opponents in ways most flattering to themselves. Increasingly activists are becoming media savvy in conveying their vision to a wider audience (Klandermans and Goslinga 1996; McCarthy *et al.* 1996). Hence, for the police, only half the 'battle' is fought on the streets; equally important is the 'battle' that is fought in the media following a confrontation. The police too must 'frame' events and thus, wittingly or otherwise, create a 'symbolic contest' (Gamson 1992).

Just as important is the collective will of the authorities to resist insurgency. The police are custodians of the state's monopoly of legitimate force over its own citizens. If the state itself lacks legitimacy, the police may lack the will to coerce fellow citizens. According to Oberschall (1996) this is what happened in eastern Europe during the revolutions of 1989, when international, as well as internal, events had eroded the legitimacy of the regimes to the point where their own security apparatus lacked the motivation to resist.

The police

How, then, do police attempt to cope with the complex patchwork of challenging groups for whom disorder and violence are resources to be used?

Authoritarianism, paramilitarism and 'tooling up'

Overwhelmingly, the problem of policing contention is one that confronts the police of liberal democracies. Social movements are products of democratic politics in which political opportunities exist for the pursuit of causes and interests. Of course, even authoritarian states may face resistance. However, the security forces in such states are much less constrained in crushing it, as was most vividly illustrated by the bloodshed and subsequent repression of pro-democracy activism in Tiananmen Square, China in 1989 (Calhoun 1989). It is perhaps surprising that the police of authoritarian (states that are so reliant on overt repression for their survival) are also least adept at dealing with resistance. Inquiries into major episodes of disorder during the apartheid regime's state of emergency in the late 1980s repeatedly disclosed muddle and incompetence (Kannenmeyer 1985; Goldstone 1990; Waddington, P.A.J. 1992).

However, even authoritarian regimes find it difficult to rely wholly upon repression. Oberschall (1996) argues that it is legitimacy – the moral authority of the state – that ultimately secures its existence. Once that legitimacy begins to be undermined, as it did in eastern Europe in 1989, then the repressive capacity itself begins to crumble. It was divisions among the elite, but particularly an international context that increasingly exposed the communist regimes of eastern Europe to delegitimation. Emboldened by international support, challengers increased the pressure on the regime while, internally, delegitimation sapped the will of the security forces to defend the state. This is an important observation for, if true, it places the policing of contention at the heart of politics, for how regimes react to challenges is an integral feature of their legitimacy.

Given the importance of legitimacy to the survival of the state, it is to be expected that liberal democracies are sensitive to criticisms that they are becoming authoritarian. Of course, challenging groups will be eager to present almost any police action in the most negative light. On the one hand, it is likely to fit into their existing 'collective action frame' to do so (Klandermans 1997) and they will genuinely believe the complaints they make. On the other hand, they have a vested interest in doing so, because the more enfeebled the state's security apparatus, the greater the challengers' room for manoeuvre. Frequently, therefore, the policing of protest itself becomes a political issue (Waddington 1991). Thus, the heavy-handed repression of the protests against the Democratic Party Convention in Chicago in 1968 (Walker 1968) and the confrontational policing of the 1984–5 British miners' strike became weapons in the ideological struggle between challengers and their respective state adversaries (Fine and Millar 1985; McCabe et al. 1988).

These are relatively short-term issues. Of longer-term significance is the claim that the state is drifting towards greater authoritarianism (Hall 1979). While this too may be the expression of a 'collective action frame' or a tactical ideological ploy, there can be little doubt that the police extended their repressive capability during the last quarter of the twentieth century (Waddington 1991; King and Brearley 1996). Riot squads now conform to an international stereotyped appearance of visored helmets, body armour, flame-retardant overalls, carrying shields and batons. They also tend to deploy in squad formations under superior command and control, instead of acting as individual officers exercising discretion. Successive legislation over a 20-year period has also added to the legal armoury of the British police. These developments have been stimulated by incidents and temporary fashions that have prompted 'moral panics'. Paradoxically, they have also been prompted by society-wide changes that are intolerant of risk and promote equality (HMIC 1999). Following both the poll tax riot in 1990 and community disorders in Britain's northern towns and cities in 2001, police unions protested strongly about the scale of injuries to officers. The extension of health and safety regulations to police has added authority to demands that officers be properly protected while engaged in work that is intrinsically risky.

Changes in public order policing have also occurred within a wider policing context that reinforces the suspicion that the emphasis has changed towards greater coercion. The growth in the use of firearms by police (Kraska and Kappeler 1997) and the widespread availability of low-lethality weapons such as CS sprays (Rappert 2003) both contribute to an impression that the police are becoming increasingly *paramilitary*. Why is this such a potent criticism?

One of the most compelling arguments in favour of the establishment of a professional civil police in 1829 was that it would be able to suppress 'the mob' without recourse to military force (Palmer 1988). While the military continued to act as a lethal longstop to the police until the early years of the twentieth century (see Chapter 4), the police acquired the monopoly over public order (Vogler 1991). I have argued elsewhere (Waddington 1999) that this reflected the growing acceptance that the British population enjoyed political citizenship and, therefore, could not be 'hacked down like an enemy' as they had been at 'Peterloo' (Critchley 1970). Paradoxically, the military disengaged from the control of civil disorder just as its repressive capacity increased markedly. This represented no universal trend, however, for the policing of the British Empire continued to be militaristic and often brutal (Anderson and Killingray 1991, 1992). The infamous Amritsar massacre is instructive: volleys of military gunfire were aimed directly into a non-violent and unresisting crowd that had defied a ban on protest gatherings. It left 379 dead and 1,200 wounded (the unofficial, but widely accepted, estimate is closer to 2,000 deaths). Its purpose was, in the words of General Dyer (the officer commanding), to 'produce the necessary moral and widespread effect' (Furneaux 1963: 13). When Dyer was disciplined for this outrage, he received the backing of the House of Lords, a substantial number of Conservative MPs, the courts, the press and also the public who in large numbers subscribed financially to an appeal on behalf of the general.

What was acceptable riot control when used against colonial peoples became unacceptable when used in a domestic British context. This was but one expression of the distinction between policing Britain and policing the Empire and reflected the importance of the citizenship with which the British civil population was endowed (Waddington 1999). This continues to make itself felt for, while plastic baton rounds have been used as a riot control weapons in Northern Ireland for many years, its possible use on the mainland of Britain remains highly controversial. However, citizenship *is* divisible and 'second-class citizens' have received more coercive policing than their more respectable peers. Notably, soccer supporters have become familiar with policing tactics that present a forceful appearance long before there has been an indication that violence was likely. The initial police response to the Hillsborough Stadium disaster was to assume that fans trying to escape the crush were hooligans to be beaten back (Taylor 1989).

Citizenship, while qualified, has imposed a restraining hand on the control of protest and other forms of contention. This is illustrated by the intensification of the search for effective 'non-lethal weapons'. Rappert (2003) persuasively argues that these are not merely devices capable of only technological appraisal; they are weapons that are interpreted socially. Indeed, their development and adoption are part of the process through which states seek to legitimate themselves and which challengers attempt to undermine – the state professes restraint while challengers complain of repression. This political process is neatly illustrated by the controversy that has surrounded the use of baton rounds in Northern Ireland. It is now widely accepted that the lethality rate of plastic baton rounds is less that one per 5,000 firings (Patten 1999). This is an enviable record for such a weapon, yet it remains highly controversial because it is seen as a weapon of oppression.

Similarly complex is the issue of intelligence gathering. Traditionally, liberals have worried that intelligence gathering by the police is likely to 'chill' political debate. Indeed, reflecting on the anti-Vietnam War and other campus protests of the 1960s, Marx (1974) suggests that police acted as agents provocateurs in order to discredit dissidents. Alternatively, if police have too little or inadequate intelligence then they may be criticised for over-reacting to minor threats (Stark 1972). Indeed, what is striking is that, in Britain, the police have extended their intelligence gathering of politics with a wariness that has not been evident elsewhere. Royal ceremonials are the object of intensive intelligence gathering, including the identification of so-called 'royal watchers' – people with what is deemed to be an 'unhealthy' fascination for the Royal Family – who, if found in the vicinity of a ceremonial, are liable to be detained on some pretext until it is over (Waddington 1994). At the other end of the spectrum, those deemed to be 'soccer hooligans' can expect to be the object of similarly intensive surveillance and intelligence gathering. Yet police intelligence relating to campaigning groups and protest activity is notable for its paucity. What intelligence there is, is often gained from the protest organisers themselves. Here police rely on the factionalism that is a common characteristic of social movements. Protest organisers tend to be recruited from the mainstream of the movements and are anxious lest more militant factions engage in actions sufficiently extreme as to discredit the cause. Police seek to ally themselves with organisers to protect the protest from 'infiltration' by such extreme groups. The police recognise the sensitivity that surrounds intelligence gathering in the context of contentious politics and are cautious in its use.

From 'escalated force' to 'negotiated management'

In contrast to the pessimism of the 'tooling-up' vision of contemporary public order police, a more optimistic view is the theme of a recent body of literature (see, for example, the essays contained in della Porta and Reiter 1998). Research in various jurisdictions has found that police typically seek to negotiate agreed arrangements with protest organisers. For example, my own observations of nearly a hundred major public order operations in London (Waddington 1994) found that control over protesters was achieved overwhelmingly by guile rather than force. Police commanders sought to convince protesters to 'police themselves' by offering advice, guidance and favours in the hope that this would be reciprocated with compliance. In so far as control was exercised during marches and the like, it usually fell to the traffic patrol officers to do it by enclosing the demonstration in a traffic-free 'bubble' surrounded by a 'moving wall of steel'. The result was that most demonstrations were not only peaceful but also *minimally disruptive*: protesters assembled at an agreed location, proceeded along a 'standard route' that created minimum traffic disruption, concluding with a rally at a prearranged venue. Strikingly, this pattern is replicated even among police units as notorious as the French riot police – the CRS (Fillieule and Jobard 1998).

Nor is this style of policing restricted to organised political protest for, despite the additional powers that police have acquired to deal with public disorder, there is still a preference for seeking negotiated settlements. For instance, legislation that made trespass a criminal offence under certain circumstances that were designed to counter 'New Age travellers', 'raves', hunt sabotage and environmental protests against new roads, airport runways and the like, have been significantly under-enforced (Bucke and James 1998). To a considerable extent this reflects purely practical constraints on the ability to enforce the law, such as the unavailability of sufficient officers. However, there are also democratic constraints, such as the presence of civil liberties lawyers and activists in anti-roads and other environmental protests. While the 'law in books' might appear draconian, police shy away from testing it in court for fear that precedent will constrain their future actions.

The emergence of this style of policing can be traced to the very origins of professional policing in the late eighteenth and early nineteenth centuries. As Tilly (1995) has documented, there was a significant decline in violence during this period. On the one hand, social movements as we now understand them, became established. They were organised attempts to introduce change and their leaders recognised the benefits that accrued from retaining legitimacy and negotiating settlements of grievances. While the threat of violence and disorder was a valuable resource, it was normally held in reserve, while the demonstration, meeting and petition became the means of expressing dissent. On the other hand, 'citizenship' was spluttering into existence and states found it increasingly difficult to repress the civil population too vigorously (even those who were disenfranchised).

The mutual conspiracy to 'cool it' is aptly illustrated in the cauldron of industrial strife. Geary (1985) explains how, during the first half of the twentieth century, 'stoning and shooting' was replaced by relatively benign 'pushing and shoving'. The growth of the Labour Movement created a common interest shared among trade unions, the state and, to a lesser extent, employers to reduce overt conflict: the nascent Labour Movement did not wish to undermine its electoral appeal by its industrial arm being associated with violence and disorder; the state did not want to encourage sympathy for the Labour Movement by appearing to act in a heavy-handed manner. The outcome was a massive decline in violence and disorder connected with industrial disputes throughout much of the twentieth century (Dunning et al. 1987). Moreover, this pattern was replicated in the USA, albeit somewhat later in the century. Until the 1930s industrial conflict was marked by exceptional violence, with considerable loss of life. The reforms of the Roosevelt era and the Taft–Hartley Act in the post-Second World War period transformed the picture (Taft and Ross 1979).

In the political realm, McPhail et al. (1998) have charted the transition in the USA from what they call the 'escalated force' model of public order policing to the adoption of 'negotiated management'. In the 1960s the USA was prominent among those states in which people had been killed in the course of civil unrest (Gurr 1979). This reflected the prevailing belief that the police should confront and trump any display or use of force by protesters; that is, it was deliberately escalatory. However, the political climate began to change, mainly as a result of a succession of Supreme Court judgements that reinforced First Amendment rights to freedom of speech and assembly. As protesters' rights were recognised, so the emphasis changed not only in favour of respecting these rights but also the practical necessity to negotiate mutually acceptable arrangements wherever possible. These negotiations have revolved around the issuing of permits and the ability of the police to constrain the 'time, manner and place' of the protest.

However, this is not untrammelled good news for democratic freedoms for, as McPhail et al. (1998) remark, the danger is that protest will be stripped of its political potential and institutionalised as a neutered ritual. On the other hand, this kind of negotiated settlement is exactly the kind of model that the Parades Commission in Northern Ireland is seeking to implement in order to reduce civil strife and the threat to the peace process (North 1997).

Ebbs and flows in tolerance

This account might suggest a 'Whig history' of inevitable progress towards civilised conduct by both the state (and its agents, the police) and challengers. Unfortunately, reality is neither so cosy nor so simple. There are cross-cutting pressures that lead to contradictions.

The first pressure encouraging more forceful action on the part of the police are political demands to take action. 'Moral panics' may or may not be exploited by the police, right-wing politicians and the media (Cohen 1972; Goode and Ben-Yehuda 1994), but either way they impact upon the police as a political force. Social movements beget counter-movements and the latter often demand stern action by the police. However, the capacity to apply such pressure is not equally distributed. Thus Bucke and James (1998) found that the police were much more susceptible to political pressure from the government's Highways Agency than they were to the fox-hunting squirearchy whom they tended to view with little more than contempt.

Secondly, apart from 'political muscle' what seems to influence policing is the perceived legitimacy of the protest and protesters (which is quite different from whether or not police officers agree with it). Both della Porta (1998) and I (Waddington 1994) in the Italian and British context respectively have noted how police distinguish between 'good' and 'bad' protesters. 'Good' protesters are 'ordinary decent people' who feel genuinely aggrieved but have no desire to cause disorder. 'Bad' protesters are militants and extremists who will jump on any bandwagon simply in order to 'come out and fight us'. It is interesting to note how this parallels the distinction drawn by social movement theorists between mainstream and militant factions within movements and how 'early risers' catch the authorities off guard.

Finally, of course, the easiest method of vitiating legitimacy is for protest to become violent and disorderly. This then licenses the police to take robust action to prevent any repetition.

Digging ditches

Senior public order commanders in London showed no enthusiasm for confrontation. They regarded this as the last resort, or what they referred to as being obliged to 'die in a ditch', for they believed that once disorder broke out the police were in a 'no win' position. They were vulnerable to complaints that they had failed to prevent disorder or quell it quickly enough to prevent damage and injury, as well as allegations that they had over-reacted and responded with more force than was necessary. However, there were certain occasions, locations and personalities for which and whom they were prepared to 'die in a ditch'. Typically, these were state occasions often associated with royalty (Waddington 1993, 1994).

Proverbial 'ditches' are not 'dug' by the police (except possibly inadvertently through unfamiliarity with public order; see Critcher 1996). They are 'dug' by others with the power to do so: the state that the police serve. Usually, the 'ditches' are well marked on the political terrain and long established, but occasionally they are hastily created by powerful interests. Such was the situation in the early 1980s when the Thatcher government pursued a vigorous policy of economic restructuring that involved dismantling many of the traditional 'coal-stack' industries. Resistance to these policies by labour unions, particularly steel workers, coalminers and print workers was regarded as a threat to constitutional government rather than a conflict between employers and employees. Particularly during the year-long miners' strike, government rhetoric emphasised the illegality and illegitimacy of the union's actions, and the mass mobilisation of police on a national basis had all the hallmarks of a state of emergency, even though there was no declaration of such (Sunday Times Insight Team 1985). The confrontational style of policing that stretched the letter of the law (McCabe *et al.* 1988) was consistent with police feeling obliged by the circumstances to 'die in a ditch'.

'Divided societies'

As the previous section implies, politics is never far from policing, especially the policing of public order. I have argued elsewhere (Waddington 1999) that routine policing reflects prevailing notions of respectability. However, this is only half the story, if that, for it omits what Steven Lukes (1973) has called the 'third dimension' of power. Power relationships are built into the very fabric of society. For instance, institutions of private property obviously favour those who possess such property, while civil wrongs such as trespass and criminal offences such as burglary tend to impact upon the property-less. Police need act with no bias in capturing the burglar or assisting with the eviction of squatters also to be shoring up the power relationships inherent in the society they serve.

As in routine policing, the reality of these power relationships is often obscured during public order situations. A strike can be represented as merely conflict between two parties, between whom the police occupy a position of ostentatious neutrality. Even disorder erupting in the course of a political protest against the state can be framed by the police in terms of the need to enforce neutral laws that protect the wider interest. However, when the state itself is the object of contention then the police role as ultimate servants of the state (as opposed to any particular government) becomes visible. Neutrality is not an option when the state itself is or is thought to be under threat and in these circumstances the proverbial 'velvet gloves' are often removed. An example of this was seen in the immediate aftermath of the First World War when the fear of Bolshevism gripped the ruling elite of the time. In Britain, this produced a secret system of civil contingency planning that remained in place despite changes in governing political parties, and became increasingly established with the passage of time (Jeffery and Hennessy 1983). Despite the appearance of a localised police structure, these arrangements covertly organised policing on a national basis subordinated to central government so that, by the outbreak of the Second World War, a national police force existed in all but name (Morgan 1987). Yet here is the irony: for while these arrangements remained in place throughout the post-Second World War era, the 1950s were quiescent for policing, especially the policing of public order. The explanation is simple: in the 1950s the threat of a Bolshevist revolution had all but disappeared. However, when it was believed that trade union militancy once again threatened the British state in the 1970s and 1980s, the police abandoned their neutrality in favour of more confrontational tactics (Geary 1985).

Social movements in liberal democracies are overwhelmingly reformist rather than revolutionary, and those that are the latter are usually so enfeebled that they pose no credible threat. However, state power is so perilously secured in some societies that there is a credible prospect that mobilisation around any political issue could topple it. Among those states are 'divided societies' (Weitzer 1985, 1990; Brewer 1991), the 'usual suspects' being Northern Ireland, Israel and apartheid South Africa, but the issues arising in these cases pale into insignificance alongside Sri Lanka and many sub-Sahara African countries. I have argued elsewhere (Waddington 1999) that division is not the essence of the problem in these societies, for most states embrace divisions, some of which erupt into hotly contested political issues. Thus, in the USA since the Supreme Court decision in *Roe* v. *Wade*, 'pro-life' and 'pro-choice' militants have occasionally clashed, sometime with bloody results. However, this dispute hardly challenges the foundation of the American Constitution; on the contrary, both sides treasure the Constitution, clashing instead over how it should be interpreted. Correspondingly, the police can adopt a position of more or less relaxed neutrality and 'negotiated management'.

Neutrality is not a stance that the police can adopt in states like Northern Ireland, Israel and apartheid South Africa where the state itself is or was challenged from within or outside its borders, or both. Sinn Fein, the Palestine Liberation Organisation and the African National Congress seek or sought not only to change specific policies but also to eliminate or transform fundamentally the state. As South Africa demonstrated, this is not an idle threat and it is not one about which the state's monopolists of legitimate force can be neutral. The same was true of colonial possessions, where the first duty of the police was not the maintenance of law and order but the preservation of the colonial territory. Brute political facts encourage or dictate that in these circumstances policing is militaristic and coercive, even though during the era of 'end of Empire' the British strove consciously to export to their colonies a more consensual style of policing modelled on the domestic bobby (Anderson and Killingray 1992; Sinclair 2002).

Into the future

Globalisation and new social movements

In contrast to the optimism of McPhail *et al.* (1998), recent events have led to fears that even liberal democratic states are reverting to more confrontational methods of public order policing. This achieved prominence during the so-called 'Battle of Seattle' in November 1999, since when there have been repeated violent confrontations between police and anti-globalisation/anti-capitalist protesters in cities worldwide that have played host to international gatherings of heads of state and economic organisations like the International Monetary Fund and World Trade Organisation. In Gothenberg, Sweden, and Genoa, Italy, these confrontations resulted in police opening fire, causing injury and death. In London and other cities around the globe May Day celebrations have become associated with violent confrontations between police and mainly youthful protesters opposing globalisation and capitalism, and advocating environmentalism. Is this new? Is the police response different from what it has been in the past?

There is a body of literature that does assert that the movements represented at many of these events are a new phenomenon (della Porta and Diani 1999). In nutshell what this literature suggests is that changes in the economy have undermined traditional class-based social movements founded on socialist ideology; instead, opportunities have opened for alternative movements to prosper. The increase in female employment; the growth of the state, especially in connection with welfare that intrudes into the lives of citizens; the globalisation of finance; and the growth of knowledge-based work have together produced new sources of conflict and grievance, and new social formations. The 'new class' is neither proletariat nor bourgeois in outlook. Its members embrace individualism but eschew competitiveness and value social welfare. New social movements are less concerned with advancing sectional interests (such as those of employees), but focus instead on issues of identity (for instance, respecting gender differences and sexuality), post-material values (for example, the environment) and moral concerns affecting human-kind generally (the exemplar of which is 'peace'). Such movements also draw upon a very wide 'conscience constituency' among an increasing swathe of the workforce that is people oriented (Pinard and Hamilton 1989) rather than technocratic (Kriesi 1989).

To what extent are 'new social movements' genuinely 'new'? Plotke (1990) suggests that this is a Eurocentric view, for in Europe class conflict and socialism have been the predominant axis around which contentious politics revolved. But even in Europe there have been social movements that, while they may have sheltered under the umbrella of the left, were quite distinct from it. A clear example of this has been the peace movement. While the Campaign for Nuclear Disarmament was closely affiliated to the Labour Movement, its composition was distinctly middle class and the orientation of its adherents was highly moralistic (Parkin 1968).

There is, however, one respect in which certain movements diverge from the past. For their independence from class politics and socialist ideology means that adherents need be less restrained by the interests of the wider movement than sections of the Labour Movement have been in the past. Whereas labour conflict was restrained by trade unions for fear that it might discredit the Labour Party and harm its electoral interests (Geary 1985), those who now protest against global capitalism and promote the interests of the environment have no such restraining hand. Yet, in many respects, the types of militancy displayed by anti-capitalist, anti-globalisation protesters and environmental-ists reflect earlier campaigns. 'Early risers' have extended the repertoire of protest activities and caught the authorities and their opponents off guard. Militant environmentalist groups like 'Earth First!' (Lange 1990; Short 1991; Purkis 1996) illustrate this well by the series of 'stunts' that they have pulled and their tactic of 'monkey wrenching' (for example, 'spiking' trees vulnerable to being felled by loggers, causing chainsaws to break and impeding the logging operation and endangering loggers). However, while novel, this is the continuation of the established pattern of the early stages of a protest cycle, rather than a wholly new departure. Correspondingly, the heavy-handed response by police to protests aimed at international meetings (Ericson and Doyle 1999) is the other side of this established pattern: caught off guard and with a yawning 'ditch' in which to 'die', security forces resort to their ultimate resource – the use of force.

However, in this context it is worth reminding ourselves of Tarrow's comment made long before '9/11', namely that the most prominent, genuinely global social movement is that of militant Islam (Tarrow 1994).

Privatisation

A development that has paralleled the emergence of new social movements has been the involvement of private security in their control. There is nothing new in this either: private security was often involved in the more bloody confrontations that occurred in the USA in the first half of the twentieth century (Weiss 1986, 1987). However, the institutionalisation of labour conflict during that century in most liberal democracies saw not only an accommodation between the two sides of industry but also the involvement of the public police as more or less neutral arbiters. However, movements associated with environmentalism have shifted the site of action back to the private sphere. Protests against the building of roads and airport runways have often taken place on private land. In Britain, the legal remedy for the removal of those obstructing such constructions is civil, rather than criminal, and the appropriate authority is that of the under-sheriff assisted by bailiffs and private security personnel (Button and John 2002; Button *et al*. 2002). Police attend these locations ostensibly to 'preserve the peace', but are drawn into the conflict as protesters challenge the authority of the under-sheriff. Sometimes, police find themselves unwillingly enmeshed in the conflict because of what they regard as the ineptness of the bailiffs and, often hastily recruited, security guards.

Conclusions

Policing the politics of contention is rarely dangerous, but it is threatening to police institutions. Unlike criminals and disorderly individuals that are the staple of routine police work, protesters and campaigners are motivated by principle – believing that they have right on their side – and the capacity to articulate not only their political demands but also complaints and grievances about how they are policed. Since protest is the preserve of the powerless, those who engage in it have little to lose. Beyond activists there often lies a broad swathe of opinion – the 'conscience constituency' – sympathetic to the aims, if not always the means, of the campaign. It is in the interests of campaigners to arouse moral indignation among this spectrum of opinion by alleging that police have behaved oppressively and brutally.

Behind the police are powerful forces – government, other state institutions, powerful economic and social institutions – all of which have a vested interest in 'digging' proverbial 'ditches' in which they would have the police 'die'. The order that the police are duty bound to uphold inevitably favours these powerful interests and so the room to manoeuvre is limited. No wonder, then, that police often liken their public order role to being the 'meat in the sandwich'!

Yet the freedom to express contentious opinions is the life-blood of a democratic society, so it is essential that the police are able effectively to balance these competing pressures. The second half of the twentieth century witnessed considerable success in achieving this balance in jurisdictions throughout the western world, and even beyond. In the wake of '9/11', the twenty-first century has opened with perhaps the gravest threat to the maintenance of this balance. Militant Islamic fundamentalism threatens to open a yawning fissure in the domestic context as much as it does internationally. Faced with unprecedented terrorist menace, the danger is that the police (and other representatives of the state) will face almost irresistible pressure to abandon balance and embrace repression.

Selected further reading

Understanding political contention and its policing requires both historical and cross-cultural perspectives. Critchley's *The Conquest of Violence* (1970) is a much criticised, but none the less valuable and accurate account of the historical development of the policing of political contention in Britain. Palmer's monumental work, *Police and Protest in England and Ireland, 1780–1850* (1988), provides a fascinating historical comparative analysis of the divergent paths trod by policing either side of the Irish Sea. Collections of essays edited by Brass – *Riots and Pogroms* (1996) – and Panayi – *Racial Violence in Britain, 1840–1950* (1993) – usefully combine historical and wide-ranging comparative perspectives. A comparative perspective on contemporary public order policing can be found in the collection edited by della Porta and Reiter, *Policing Protest: The Control of Mass Demonstrations in Western Democracies* (1998).

Social movements have generated an enormous literature in recent years, but fortunately this has been accompanied by a number of very good general texts. Foremost among these are della Porta and Diani's *Social Movements: An Introduction* (1999), Klandermans' *The Social Psychology of Protest* (1997) and Marx and McAdam's *Collective Behaviour and Social Movements: Process and Structure* (1994). An excellent critical review of the literature on gatherings is to be found in McPhail's *The Myth of the Madding Crowd* (1991).

References

Anderson, D.M. and Killingray, D. (1991) *Policing the Empire: Government, Authority and Control, 1830–1940*. Manchester: Manchester University Press.

Anderson, D.M. and Killingray, D. (1992) *Policing and Decolonisation: Politics, Nationalism and the Police, 1917–65*. Manchester: Manchester University Press.

Armstrong, G. (1998) *Football Hooligans: Knowing the Score*. Oxford: Berg.

Barkan, S.E. (1980) 'Criminal prosecutions in the southern civil rights and anti-Vietnam war movements: repression and dissent in political trials', in S. Spitzer (ed.) *Research in Law and Sociology*. New York, NY: JAI Press, 279–99.

Berk, R. and Aldrich, H. (1972) 'Patterns of vandalism during civil disorder as an indicator of selection of targets', *American Sociological Review*, 37: 533–47.

Brass, P.R. (1996) *Riots and Pogroms*. Basingstoke: Macmillan.

Brewer, J.D. (1991) 'Policing in divided societies: theorising a type of policing', *Policing and Society*, 1: 179–91.

Bucke, T. and James, Z. (1998) *Trespass and Protest: Policing under the Criminal Justice and Public Order Act 1994*. London: Research, Development and Statistics Directorate, Home Office.

Button, M. and John, T. (2002) ' "Plural policing" in action: a review of the policing of environmental protests in England and Wales', *Policing and Society*, 12(2): 111–21.

Button, M., John, T. and Brearley, N. (2002). 'New challenges in public order policing: the professionalisation of environmental protest and the emergence of the militant environmental activist', *International Journal of the Sociology of Law*, 30(1): 17–32.

Calhoun, C. (1989) 'Revolution and repression in Tiananmen Square', *Society*, 26(6): 21–38.

Chaturvedi, J. and Chaturvedi, G. (1996) 'Dharma Yudh: communal violence, riots and public space in Ayodhya and Agra City: 1990 and 1992', in P.R. Brass (ed.) *Riots and Progroms*. Basingstoke: Macmillan, 177–200.

Clark, L.T. (2002) *Report of the Burnley Task Force*. Burnley: Burnley Task Force.

Clutterbuck, R. (1980) *Britain in Agony*. Harmondsworth: Penguin Books.

Cohen, S. (1972) *Folk Devils and Moral Panics*. Oxford: Martin Robertson.

Collin, R.O. (1985) 'The blunt instruments: Italy and the police', in J. Roach and J. Thomaneck (eds) *Police and Public Order in Europe*. London: Croom Helm, 185–214.

Critcher, C. (1996) 'On the waterfront: applying the flashpoints model to protest against live animal exports', in C. Critcher and D. Waddington (eds) *Policing Public Order: Theoretical and Practical Issues*. Aldershot: Avebury, 53–70.

Critchley, T. (1970) *The Conquest of Violence*. London: Constable.

della Porta, D. (1995) *Social Movements, Political Violence, and the State*. Cambridge: Cambridge University Press.

della Porta, D. (1998) 'Police knowledge and protest policing: some reflections on the Italian case', in D. della Porta and H. Reiter (eds) *Policing Protest: The Control of Mass Demonstrations in Western Democracies*. Minneapolis, MN: University of Minnesota Press, 228–52.

della Porta, D. and Diani, M. (1999) *Social Movements: An Introduction*. Oxford: Blackwell.

della Porta, D. and Reiter, H. (eds) (1998) *Policing Protest: The Control of Mass Demonstrations in Western Democracies*. Minneapolis, MN: University of Minnesota Press.

Dunning, E., Murphy, P., Newburn, T. and Waddington, I. (1987) 'Violent disorders in twentieth century Britain', in G. Gaskell and R. Benewick (eds) *The Crowd in Contemporary Britain*. London: Sage, 19–75.

Eisinger, P. (1973) 'The conditions of protest behaviour in American cities', *American Political Science Review*, 67: 11–28.

Ericson, R. and Doyle, A. (1999) 'Globalization and the policing of protest', *British Journal of Sociology*, 50: 589–608.

Field, S. and Southgate, P. (1982) *Public Disorder: A Review of Research and a Study in One Inner City Area*. London: HMSO.

Fillieule, O. and Jobard, F. (1998) 'The policing of protest in France: toward a model of protest policing', in D. della Porta and H. Reiter (eds) *Policing Protest: The Control of Mass Demonstrations in Western Democracies*. Minneapolis, MN: University of Minnesota Press, 70–90.

Fine, B. and Millar, R. (1985) *Policing the Miners' Strike*. London: Lawrence & Wishart.

Frey, R.S., Dietz, T. and Kalof, L. (1992) 'Characteristics of successful American protest groups – another look at Gamson's strategy of social protest', *American Journal of Sociology*, 98(2): 368–87.

Friedland, R. and Hecht, R.D. (1996) 'Divisions at the center: the organisation of political violence at Jerusalem's Temple Mount/Al-Haram Al-Sharif – 1929 and 1990', in P. R. Brass (ed.) *Riots and Progroms*. Basingstoke: Macmillan, 114–53.

Furneaux, R. (1963) *Massacre at Amritsar*. London: George Allen & Unwin.

Gamson, W.A. (1975) *The Strategy of Social Protest*. Homewood, IL: Dorsey.

Gamson, W.A. (1992) *Talking Politics*. Cambridge: Cambridge University Press.

Gamson, W.A. and Meyer, D.S. (1996) 'Framing political opportunity', in D. McAdam *et al.* (eds) *Comparative Perspectives on Social Movements*. Cambridge: Cambridge University Press, 275–90.

Geary, R. (1985) *Policing Industrial Disputes: 1893 to 1985*. Cambridge: Cambridge University Press.

Goldstone, H.H.R.J. (1990) *Report of the Commission of Enquiry into the Incidents at Sebokeng, Boipatong, Lekoa, Sharpeville and Evaton on 26 March 1990*. Johannesburg: South African Government.

Goode, E. and Ben-Yehuda, N. (1994) *Moral Panics: The Social Construction of Deviance*. Oxford: Blackwell.

Grimshaw, A.D. and Bowen, D.R. (1968) 'Three views of urban violence: civil disturbance, racial revolt, class assault', in L. H. Masotti and D. R. Bowen (eds) *Civil Violence in the Urban Community.* Beverly Hills, CA: Sage, 103–19.

Gurr, T.R. (1968) *Why Men Rebel.* Princeton, NJ: Princeton University Press.

Gurr, T.R. (1979) 'Political protest and rebellion in the 1960s', in H. D. Graham and T. R. Gurr (eds) *Violence in America.* Beverly Hills, CA: Sage, 49–76.

Hall, S. (1979) *Drifting into a Law and Order Society.* London: Cobden Trust.

Hammersley, M. (2000) *Taking Sides in Social Research.* London: Routledge.

Henriques, K.A. (1991) 'A case study and analysis of a nonviolent direct action campaign and coalition building', in M. Spencer (ed.) *Research in Social Movements, Conflict and Change.* Greenwich, CT: JAI Press, 77–89.

Her Majesty's Inspectorate of Constabulary (HMIC) (1999) *Keeping the Peace: Policing Disorder.* London: HMSO.

Hills, A. (1997) 'Care and control: the role of the UK police in extreme circumstances', *Policing and Society,* 7(3): 177–90.

Horowitz, D.L. (2001) *The Deadly Ethnic Riot.* Berkeley, CA: University of California Press.

Jarman, N. and Bryan, D. (1996) *Parade and Protest: A Discussion of Parading Disputes in Northern Ireland.* Coleraine: Centre for the Study of Conflict, University of Ulster.

Jefferson, T. (1993) 'Pondering paramilitarism', *British Journal of Criminology,* 33(3): 374–81.

Jeffery, K. and Hennessy, P. (1983) *States of Emergency.* London: Routledge & Kegan Paul.

Jenkins, J.C. (1983) 'Resource mobilization theory and the study of social movements', *Annual Review of Sociology,* 9: 527–53.

Jenkins, J.C. and Perrow, C. (1977) 'Insurgency of the powerless: farm worker movements (1946–1972)', *American Sociological Review,* 42: 249–68.

Kannenmeyer, D.D.V. (1985) *Report of the Commission Appointed to Inquire into the Incident which Occurred on 21 March 1985 at Uitenhage.* Republic of South Africa, Pretoria.

Keith, M. (1993) *Race, Riots and Policing: Lore and Disorder in a Multi-racist Society.* London: UCL Press.

King, M. and Brearley, N. (1996) *Public Order Policing.* Leicester: Perpetuity.

Klandermans, B. (1997) *The Social Psychology of Protest.* Oxford: Blackwell.

Klandermans, B. and Goslinga, S. (1996) 'Media discourse, movement publicity, and the generation of collective action frames: theoretical and empirical exercises in meaning construction', in D. McAdam *et al.* (eds) *Comparative Perspectives on Social Movements.* Cambridge: Cambridge University Press, 312–37.

Kraska, P.B. and Kappeler, V.E. (1997) 'Militarizing American police: the rise and normalization of paramilitary units', *Social Problems,* 44(1): 1–18.

Kriesi, H. (1989) 'New social movements and the new class in the Netherlands', *American Journal of Sociology,* 94(5): 1078–116.

Lange, J.I. (1990) 'Refusal to compromise: the case of Earth First!', *Journal of Speech Communication,* 54: 473–94.

Le Bon, G. (1895) *The Crowd.* New Brunswick, NJ: Viking.

Lukes, S. (1974) *Power: a Radical View.* Oxford: Macmillan.

Marsh, P., Rosser, E. and Harre, R. (1977) *Rules of Disorder.* London: Routledge & Kegan Paul.

Marx, G.T. (1974) 'Thoughts on a neglected category of social movement participant: the agent provocateur and the informant', *American Journal of Sociology,* 80(2): 402–42.

Marx, G.T. and McAdam, D. (1994) *Collective Behaviour and Social Movements: Process and Structure.* Englewood Cliffs, NJ: Prentice-Hall.

McAdam, D. (1982) *Political Process and the Development of Black Insurgency*. Chicago, IL: University of Chicago Press.

McAdam, D. (1983) 'Tactical innovation and the pace of insurgency', *American Sociological Review*, 48: 735–54.

McAdam, D. (1996) 'The framing function of movement tactics: strategic dramaturgy in the American civil rights movement', in D. McAdam *et al.* (eds) *Comparative Perspectives on Social Movements*. Cambridge: Cambridge University Press, 338–56.

McAdam, D., McCarthy, J.D. and Zald, M.N. (1996) 'Introduction: opportunities, mobilizing structures, and framing processes – toward a synthetic, comparative perspective on social movements', in D. McAdam *et al.* (eds) *Comparative Perspectives on Social Movements*. Cambridge: Cambridge University Press, 1–20.

McCabe, S., Wallington, P. with Alderson, J., Gostin, L. and Mason, C. (1988) *The Police, Public Order and Civil Liberties: Legacies of the Miners' Strike*. London: Routledge.

McCarthy, J.D., Britt, D.W. and Wolfson, M. (1991) 'The institutional channelling of social movements by the state in the United States', in M. Spencer (ed.) *Research in Social Movements, Conflict and Change*. Greenwich, CT: JAI Press, 45–76.

McCarthy, J.D., Smith, J. and Zald, M.N. (1996) 'Accessing public, media, electoral, and governmental agendas', in D. McAdam *et al.* (eds) *Comparative Perspectives on Social Movements*. Cambridge: Cambridge University Press, 291–311.

McCarthy, J.D. and Zald, M.N. (1977) 'Resource mobilization and social movements: a partial theory', *American Journal of Sociology*, 82: 1212–41.

McPhail, C. (1971) 'Civil disorder participation', *American Sociological Review*, 36: 1058–72.

McPhail, C. (1991) *The Myth of the Madding Crowd*. Hawthorne, NY: Aldine de Gruyter.

McPhail, C. (1994) 'The dark side of purpose: individual and collective violence in temporary gatherings', *Sociological Quarterly*, 35(1): 1–32.

McPhail, C., Schweingruber, D. and McCarthy, J. (1998) 'Policing protest in the United States: 1960–1995', in D. della Porta and H. Reiter (eds) *Policing Protest: The Control of Mass Demonstrations in Western Democracies*. Minneapolis, MN: University of Minnesota Press, 49–69.

Miller, N. and Dollard, J. (1941) *Social Learning and Imitation*. New Haven, CT: Yale University Press.

Morgan, J. (1987) *Conflict and Order: The Police and Labour Disputes in England and Wales 1900–1939*. Oxford: Clarendon Press.

Morris, A. (1993) 'Birmingham confrontation reconsidered: an analysis of the dynamics and tactics of mobilization', *American Sociological Review*, 58(5): 621–36.

North, D. P. (1997) *Report of the Independent Review of Parades and Marches*. Belfast: HMSO.

Oberschall, A. (1996) 'Opportunities and framing in the Eastern European revolts of 1989', in D. McAdam *et al.* (eds) *Comparative Perspectives on Social Movements*. Cambridge: Cambridge University Press, 93–121.

Palmer, S.H. (1988) *Police and Protest in England and Ireland, 1780–1850*. Cambridge: Cambridge University Press.

Panayi, P. (ed.) (1993) *Racial Violence in Britain, 1840–1950*. Leicester: Leicester University Press.

Parkin, F. (1968) *Middle Class Radicalism*. Manchester: Manchester University Press.

Parry, G., Moyser, G. and Wagstaffe, M. (1987) 'The crowd and the community: context, content and aftermath', in G. Gaskell and R. Benewick (eds) *The Crowd in Contemporary Britain*. London: Sage, 212–55.

Patten, C., Rt Hon. (1999) *A New Beginning – Policing in Northern Ireland*. Belfast: The Independent Commission on the Policing for Northern Ireland.

Pinard, M. and Hamilton, R. (1989) 'Intellectuals and the leadership of social movements', in L. Kriesberg (ed.) *Conflict and Change*. Greenwich, CT: JAI Press, 73–107.

Piven, F.F. and Cloward, R.A. (1977) *Poor People's Movements: Why they Succeed, How they Fail*. New York: Random House.

Piven, F.F. and Cloward, R.A. (1992) 'Normalizing collective protest', in A.D. Morris and C.M. Mueller (eds) *Frontiers in Social Movement Theory*. New Haven, CT: Yale University Press, 301–25.

Plotke, D. (1990) 'What's so new about new social movements?', *Socialist Review*, 20(1): 81–102.

Purkis, J. (1996) 'Daring to dream: idealism in the philosophy, organization and campaigning strategies of Earth First!', in C. Barker and P. Kennedy (eds) *To Make another World: Studies in Protest and Collective Action*. Aldershot: Avebury, 197–218.

Rappert, B. (2003) *Non-lethal Weapons as Legitimating Forces? Technology, Politics and the Management of Conflict*. London: Frank Cass.

Reicher, S.D. (1984) 'The St Paul's riot: an explanation of the limits of crowd action in terms of a social identity model', *European Journal of Social Psychology*, 14: 1–21.

Ritchie, D. (2001) *Oldham Independent Review: One Oldham, One Future*. Oldham: Oldham Independent Review.

Rule, J.B. (1989) 'Rationality and non-rationality in militant collective action', *Sociological Theory*, 7: 145–60.

Scarman, L., Rt Hon. the Lord (1981) *The Brixton Disorders 10–12 April 1981: Report of an Inquiry by the Rt. Hon. The Lord Scarman, O.B.E.* London: HMSO.

Scheingold, S. A. (1974) *The Politics of Rights: Lawyers, Public Policy, and Political Change*. New Haven, CT: Yale University Press.

Sherr, A. (1989) *Freedom of Protest, Public Order and the Law*. Oxford: Blackwell.

Short, B. (1991) 'Earth First! and the rhetoric of moral confrontation', *Communication Studies*, 42(2): 172–88.

Sinclair, G.S. (2002) ' "Settlers' men" or policemen? The ambiguities of "Colonial" policing, 1945–1980'. Unpublished Phd thesis. Reading: The University of Reading.

Smelser, N.J. (1962) *Theory of Collective Behaviour*. London: Routledge & Kegan Paul.

Spilerman, S. (1970) 'The causes of racial disturbances: a comparison of alternative explanations', *American Sociological Review*, 35: 627–49.

Spilerman, S. (1971) 'The causes of racial disturbances: tests of an explanation', *American Sociological Review*, 36: 427–42.

Spilerman, S. (1976) 'Structural characteristics of cities and the severity of racial disorders', *American Sociological Review*, 41: 771–93.

Stark, R. (1972) *Police Riots: Collective Violence and Law Enforcement*. Belmont, CA: Wadsworth.

Stott, C. and Reicher, S. (1998) 'How conflict escalates: the inter-group dynamics of collective football crowd "violence" ', *Sociology*, 32(2): 353–77.

Sunday Times Insight Team (1985) *Strike*. London: Coronet.

Taft, P. and Ross, P. (1979) 'American labor violence: its causes, character, and outcome', in H.D. Graham and T.R. Gurr (eds) *Violence in America*. Beverly Hills, CA: Sage, 187–241.

Tarrow, S. (1989) *Democracy and Disorder: Protest Politics in Italy, 1965– 1975*. Oxford: Oxford University Press.

Tarrow, S. (1994) *Power in Movement: Social Movements, Collective Action and Politics*. New York, NY: Cambridge University Press.

Taylor, P., Lord Justice (1989) *The Hillsborough Stadium Disaster, 15 April 1989*. London: HMSO.

Taylor, S. (1984) 'The Scarman Report and explanations of riots', in J. Benyon (ed.) *Scarman and After*. London: Pergamon, 20–35.

Thurlow, R. (1993) 'Blaming the Blackshirts: the authorities and the anti-Jewish disturbances in the 1930s', in P. Panayi (ed.). *Racial Violence in Britain, 1840–1950*. Leicester: Leicester University Press, 112–29.

Tilly, C. (1978) *From Mobilization to Revolution*. Reading, MA: Addison-Wesley.

Tilly, C. (1995) *Popular Contention in Great Britain, 1758–1834*. Cambridge, MA: Harvard University Press.

van der Veer, P. (1996) 'Riots and rituals: the construction of violence and public space in Hindu nationalism', in P.R. Brass (ed.) *Riots and Progroms*. Basingstoke: Macmillan, 154–76.

Vogler, R. (1991) *Reading the Riot Act: The Magistracy, the Police and the Army in Civil Disorder*. Milton Keynes: Open University Press.

Waddington, D. (1992) *Contemporary Issues in Public Disorder*. London: Routledge.

Waddington, D. (1998) 'Waddington versus Waddington: public order theory on trial', *Theoretical Criminology*, 2(3): 373–94.

Waddington, D., Jones, K. and Critcher, C. (1989) *Flashpoints: Studies in Public Disorder*. London: Routledge.

Waddington, P.A.J. (1991) *The Strong Arm of the Law*. Oxford: Clarendon.

Waddington, P.A.J. (1992) *An Inquiry into the Police Response to, and Investigation of, Events in Boipatong on 17 June 1992*. Submitted to the Commission of Inquiry Regarding the Prevention of Public Violence and Intimidation. The Honourable Mr R.J. Goldstone, chariman. Pretoria 20 July.

Waddington, P.A.J. (1993) 'Dying in a ditch: the use of police powers in public order', *International Journal of the Sociology of Law*, 21(4): 335–53.

Waddington, P.A.J. (1994) *Liberty and Order: Policing Public Order in a Capital City*. London: UCL Press.

Waddington, P.A.J. (1995) 'Public order policing: citizenship and moral ambiguity', in F. Leishman *et al.* (eds) *Core Issues in Policing*. London: Longman, 114–30.

Waddington, P.A.J. (1999) *Policing Citizens*. London: UCL Press.

Waddington, P.A.J. 2000. 'Orthodoxy and advocacy in criminology', *Theoretical Criminology*, 4(1): 93–111.

Walker, D. (1968) *Rights in Conflict: The Violent Confrontation of Demonstrators and Police, during the Week of the Democratic National Convention*. New York, NY: Banton.

Weiss, R.P. (1986) 'Private detective agencies and labour discipline in the United States, 1855–1946', *Historical Journal*, 29(1): 87–107.

Weiss, R.P. (1987) 'From "slugging detective" to "labor relations": policing labour at Ford, 1930–1947', in C.D. Shearing and P.C. Stenning (eds) *Private Policing*. Newbury Park, CA: Sage, 110–30.

Weitzer, R. (1985) 'Policing a divided society: obstacles to normalization in Northern Ireland', *Social Problems*, 33(1): 41–55.

Weitzer, R. (1990) *Transforming Settler States: Communal Conflict and Internal Security in Northern Ireland and Zimbabwe*. Berkeley, CA: University of California Press.

Wilson, J. (1976) 'Social protest and social control', *Social Problems*, 24: 469–81.

Chapter 17

Drugs policing

Maggy Lee and Nigel South

Introduction

Just as drugs policy is 'never purely about drugs' (Dorn 1998: 11) so too the policing of drugs reflects wider politics, social change and perceptions of threats to social order and everyday life. Illegal drugs are a source of fear for many and demonised by authorities and the media: often representing a 'plague' or source of 'corruption' identified with external 'others' that requires the mobilisation of defences and resources to fight a 'war' (Christie 1986; Home Affairs Committee 1986; South 1999). Throughout the twentieth century, police were key contributors to the development of this discourse although, importantly, this was not to the exclusion of innovations such as the accommodation in the 1980s of harm reduction principles (Dorn and South 1994), the creation of arrest referral schemes (Dorn *et al.* 1990) or reservations from some 'thinking coppers' about the implications of the 'drugs war mentality' for British policing (Grieve 1993; Blanchard 2003). In the closing decades of the twentieth century, drugs policing was a particularly high-profile field and it remains so despite the anti-terrorism agenda of the new century. Indeed the links between terrorism and drug trafficking as a source of funding are of particular interest to intelligence analysts and investigators (see Chapter 19).

As an area of priority and specialisation, drugs law enforcement has often led the way in precedents and developments for both policing and Customs and Excise. Examples include changes in organisation and techniques (specialist squads, undercover work, informant use, intelligence gathering and so on) and in relation to partnerships with communities and the business sector and multi-agency strategies.

Thus, though potentially very broad in scope, this chapter focuses primarily on the early history and foundations of the development of drugs policing; forms of organisation and specialisation, including financial policing; as well as transnational/global, national and local drugs policing (including corruption).

Early history

Drugs policing is not new. By definition, from the beginnings of the process of their criminalisation, possession of and dealing in certain drugs became both a target for the police and a spur to the development of various styles and techniques of policing.

Prior to the First World War, an international drug conference in the Hague in 1912 agreed the principle that the use of opium, morphine and cocaine should be limited to 'legitimate medical purposes'. However commercial considerations such as German and British interests in, respectively, cocaine and morphine production meant little of the agreement was pursued at the time. In the domestic legislative context, only some tightening of regulations relating to prescribing and over-the-counter sales followed (Kohn 1992: 42). The First World War sharpened national interest in the legal status of drugs in several ways.

First, in 1915 and 1916 several stories emerged linking servicemen with the use of drugs. Most famously, Canadian soldiers based in Folkestone were found to be using cocaine supplied by a petty criminal, Horace Kingsley, and a London prostitute, Rose Edwards. This triangle of 'crime–prostitution–corruption' was linked to the further threat of 'outsiders' – Canadians – bringing the 'habit' of cocaine use to Britain and was a powerful image in news reporting. However, rather more telling about the availability of drugs in Britain was that the supplier to the Folkestone troops, Kingsley, was not part of some elaborate illegal chain of traffickers but merely exploited a lax regulatory system in which some pharmacists were happy to supply cocaine without a prescription or proper record of the transaction (Kohn 1992).

Secondly, the war meant London police became increasingly interested in the refugees who had fled Europe and the contributions that some made to the West End underworld. Prostitutes, petty criminals and others among the undesirable 'foreigners' now mixed in the milieu of local criminals rumoured to be associated with cocaine supply, and all became the subject of police attention employing informants and surveillance. For example, information received by an inspector at Paddington in early 1916 named one Willy Johnson as part of a supply gang and led to observation being carried out by Police Sergeants Hedges and Venner which led to Johnson's arrest and, as Kohn (1992: 37) puts it, 'London's first drugs bust'. In response to the Folkestone case and other concerns, the Army Council recognised the ill-defined nature of drugs offences and banned any unauthorised supply to soldiers of a variety of drugs that might be abused. In civilian life, however, swift remedy of what now appeared an unsatisfactory situation was not so easy. The Poisons and Pharmacy Act 1868 was designed to regulate sales by pharmacists, not the criminal trade. Furthermore, in the Johnson case, Hedges and Venner had not actually witnessed a completed drug deal, merely Johnson's attempts to hustle and offer cocaine for sale. Johnson was acquitted (Kohn 1992: 38), leading to support from all ranks of the police service for change. Sergeant Hedges noted in a report that 'unless the existing regulations are supplemented, it is useless for Police to devote further time' to drug dealers (a police lament repeated down the years) (1992: 39). Johnson's prosecution failed on the basis of the law as it stood but provided the opportunity for the police to air their case for reform, with the counsel for the police suggesting the idea of a prohibitive addition to the Defence of the Realm Act (DORA).

Subsequent arrests of dealers, concerns about drug use in the Bohemia of clubland and café society, sensational journalism linking drugs with the influence of 'foreigners' and threats to mental and moral health all raised drugs control to a far higher level of policy concern than had been the case in the prewar deliberations before and after the 1912 Hague meeting. The idea of employing DORA and adding a new regulation struck a chord. Within the Home Office the leading figure supporting new legislation was Sir Malcolm Delevingne, an under-secretary and diplomat who contributed not only to domestic policy but also to the drafting of subsequent international treaties (South 1998; McAllister 2000). Delevingne candidly acknowledged that amendment of DORA as a means of introducing drug control was perhaps stretching the point, saying in terms of 'its bearing on the "Defence of the Realm"' the nature of the drug problem 'is neither very direct nor important' (Kohn 1992: 43). None the less this was a way of avoiding the need for legislation that might face greater opposition if taken through Parliament. From 28 July 1916, DORA Regulation 40B required that possession of cocaine or opium be a criminal offence except where possession was by authorised persons (Berridge 1978). The Commissioner of the Metropolitan Police, Sir Edward Henry, was particularly convinced of the baleful consequences of cocaine use and was therefore a strong supporter of any such regulatory measures, arguing for the criminalisation of drugs and imprisonment for dealing and possession, and linking drugs with other social and moral scourges of society. Given the laws and powers, urged Sir Edward, the police might then find it possible 'to deal severely with the unauthorised persons who, using as their tools burglars, thieves, prostitutes, sodomites, men living upon the earnings of women and other nefarious persons, are at present with impunity doing such infinite harm' (Kohn 1992: 43). The drug cultures and markets of the streets had been born but so too had 'get tough' drugs law enforcement.

In these same years, the criminalisation agenda was pursued with even more vigour and success in the USA where prohibitionist sentiment was ascendant, and the Harrison Act 1914 laid foundations for an enforcement-led public policy that endures today. In Britain however, criminalisation was tempered by the compromise that became known as 'the British System' (Strang and Gossop 1994). The different trajectories of policy and hence policing had political and moral roots, but policy also reflected the particularity of circumstances in the two countries. In the USA, the rapid growth of the new urban centres and their social problems, the growth of a criminal underworld and development of an addiction problem considerably more serious than Britain experienced all meant a law enforcement approach received easy acceptance. Opponents, including doctors who wished to prescribe drugs, and their addict patients, were vilified and faced sanctions. In Britain, on the other hand, the success of a medical-oriented approach to a system of maintenance prescribing for the addicted was achievable not least because as Parssinen (1983: 220) put it, 'the addict population was small, elderly and dying off'. The acceptance of the Rolleston Committee Report to the Ministry of Health in 1926 led to establishment of a system that was undoubtedly humane but not altogether professionally selfless (many addicts were themselves medical practitioners who had abused their access to drugs). It was significant in two other ways: it laid the foundations for the harm reduction principles that emerged in the 1980s; and it was also an example of British compromise in so far as a medical and treatment approach was permitted within and subordinate to a wider context of criminal justice prohibitions and powers for the police.

Police powers were exercised in the break-up of the small subcultures of drugs use as still existed in the late 1920s, and the absence of conflict between the medical and law enforcement models over the next three decades was not so much the triumph of the British System that is often portrayed as a reflection of the absence of a drugs problem to respond to (Downes 1977). Only during the late 1950s did police and the Home Office begin to detect evidence of new patterns of drug availability – principally cannabis and heroin – and once again the clubland of London's West End was identified as the site and source of the 'drug problem' (on reasons for the emergence of the problem and responses at this time, see Spear 2002). This identification of the London drug scene re-emphasised that it was the Metropolitan Police that held a special position as the force with most responsibility for, and experience with, drug users and dealers, though ironically it was also this aura of elitism and autonomy that led in the 1970s to the Metropolitan Drugs Squad lying (in both senses) at the centre of scandals revolving around endemic corruption in police specialised units (Cox *et al.* 1977).

From the 1960s, the social and cultural contexts of drug use and drugs-related crime underwent significant changes and so too did drugs policy and policing. New patterns of drug availability were emerging. The abuse of the prescribing system by both addicts and doctors led to the growth of a street market in heroin and cocaine causing alarm in policy circles, while media and public were simultaneously fascinated and appalled by new youth cultures and associated drug use (amphetamine, LSD). In succession, the Drugs (Prevention of Misuse) Act 1964, and then the Dangerous Drugs Acts of 1965 and 1967 extended controls, ratified the 1961 United Nations Single Convention on Narcotic Drugs in British legislation, and created the framework for the new system of clinics or drug dependency units. These would now regulate the prescribing of heroin and cocaine in regimes generally aimed at maintenance with the ultimate goal of abstinence and with a treatment orientation dominated by psychiatry, representing a shift from a welfare to control model. As Shapiro (1999: 29) remarks, it is interesting that in a decade that in other respects saw 'unprecedented liberalising legislation' and relaxation of controls 'on gambling, censorship, abortion, homosexuality ... the laws against drug use were tightened'. Specialist drugs policing – squads, intelligence units and innovative techniques – were to follow. Developments in drugs policing on the street, and the shadow history of cases of corruption, will be discussed below. First we describe organisational changes and trends.

Organisation and specialisation

At least since the 1970s, an increasing amount of what has been categorised as 'serious crime' has been directly or indirectly drug related. Direct relationships may involve drug distribution, related violence including homicide and the laundering of proceeds from drug crime (Dorn *et al.* 1992; South 1992; Bean 2002). Less directly, illegal enterprises may be involved in illicit markets for a variety of commodities including drugs (Reuter 1983; Ruggiero and South 1997; South 2000) or in serious 'project crimes' that may be funded from the proceeds of drug trafficking. Indeed, reflecting analysis of drugs as simply one business commodity among others for entrepreneurial criminals (Hobbs 1995), the National Crime Squad (NCS) sees their criminal targets as 'entrepreneurs who will traffic in whatever commodity they think presents the least risk and the greatest profit at any one point in time' (NCS website January 2003; see Chapter 18).

In 1964, regional crime squads (RCSs) covering nine regions were established as a response to concern about the increasing mobility of the postwar criminal committing crimes of an organised nature across force boundaries. Local police were seen as ill-placed to react to such crime not only because of their geographical limits but also because new degrees of seriousness and sophistication were becoming evident. The RCSs were followed by the establishment of criminal intelligence branches in each of the regions (ACPO 1975: 2; Dorn *et al.* 1992: 154) and specialist operational 'drugs wings' in the mid-1980s following the recommendations of the Broome Committee Report (ACPO 1985). In a move to improve effectiveness, the RCSs were amalgamated into six regions in 1993. However, just two years later, growing unease about the threat of organised crime led the Parliamentary Home Affairs Select Committee to conclude that the RCS structure was out of date and a nationally co-ordinated structure was now required.

Increasing specialisation of skills and functions reflected not only the perceived need to match the sophistication of serious criminals but also a general shift away from reactive investigation and detection of individual crimes to a strategic approach to crime control. The growth of what came to be described as 'intelligence-led' policing (see Chapter 13) and a proactive 'targeted' approach (e.g. monitoring sales of the precursor chemicals used to manufacture synthetic drugs) was a characteristic key feature of drugs-related policing from the mid-1980s, initially in relation to high to middle-level drugs crime enterprises and markets. As we shall see, the approach also became a part of strategies for low-level drug enforcement.

The development and direction of capacity for intelligence analysis relating to drugs and other serious crimes followed the establishment of the RCSs, and the value of intelligence-led/targeted policing is now fully embraced and promoted in generic policing (cf. the Audit Commission's (1993) recommendation to the police to 'target the criminal, not just the crime'). The importance of intelligence and informant use in specialist policing throughout the UK has grown enormously, whether in metropolitan or small-town locations (Maguire and Norris 1992: 78–96; Collison 1995; South 2001). However, London and its police have remained central to organisational and capacity developments. In

1973 a Central Drugs and Illegal Immigration Unit (CDIIU) was established at Scotland Yard, linking two issues seen to represent increasingly important threats from external sources.

Thirty years later the work of the National Criminal Intelligence Service and NCS (below) feature these issues prominently in their work. The former traces its roots back to the CDIIU, its specialisation a year later as the Central Drugs Intelligence Unit serving nationally but still based with the Metropolitan Police, and then the National Drugs Intelligence Unit, formed in 1985 as a joint police and customs service intelligence-gathering and clearing house. As Dorn *et al.* (1992: 154) note:

> historically, the organisation of drugs intelligence in Britain has been influenced . . . by the Metropolitan Police's assumption of a quasi-national role . . . As a succession of reports shows, ACPO's expert and considered assessment has tended to be that the relationship between trafficking and other crimes is close enough to merit integration of intelligence functions. Thus the 'Baumber report' (ACPO 1975) saw integration of intelligence functions as the way forward at national level and suggested the setting up of an integrated national criminal intelligence office. This recommendation was repeated more firmly a decade later by the 'Ratcliffe report' (ACPO 1986) which also foresaw 'the integration of the National Drugs Intelligence Unit'. . .

into a new national criminal intelligence office or service.

This emerged in 1992 as the broader National Criminal Intelligence Service and drew together various specialist police database operations. However, as with the work of the NCS, a large proportion of NCIS work is drug related.

The NCS was launched on 1 April 1998, with Eastern, Western and Northern geographical divisions and a London headquarters. Although the squad describes the range of criminal activity 'targeted' as including drugs and arms trafficking, immigration crime, money laundering and counterfeiting, kidnap and extortion, it notes that 'currently approximately 75 per cent of operations involve drug trafficking in whole or in part' (NCS 2002). In reporting its progress after four years, the NCS listed achievements that included the disruption of 1,062 criminal organisations of which 821 were involved in drug trafficking, and almost 1,300 operations of which over 70 per cent were drug related (NCS 2002). The NCS works with NCIS and HM Customs and Excise and is mirrored in Scotland by the Scottish Drug Enforcement Agency (SDEA), established on 1 June 2000. The SDEA incorporates the former Scottish Crime Squad and clearly signals via its title that although investigation of other serious and organised crime falls within its remit, drug-related crime is its main *raison d'être*.

Financial detection

Targeted policing and 'problem'-oriented approaches to crime control have developed hand in hand with new financial tracking capabilities, involving police access to financial data held by banks and others. The Proceeds of Crime

Act came into force on 30 December 2002, accompanied by a government pledge to double the amount of money seized from criminals. The Act applies across the UK and is administered by a new Assets Recovery Agency. It enhances powers first introduced under the Drug Trafficking Offences Act (DTOA) 1986 and allows for the freezing of assets at the start of an investigation to avoid their sudden disappearance from sight or jurisdiction and the granting of monitoring orders to the police and other investigators to trace transactions taking place on a given bank account. The DTOA is worth further brief discussion because of the precedent it set for action by the courts (reversing the burden of proof from the prosecution to the defendant, who now had to show that his or her assets were legally acquired) and because it is an example of the great influence that American legislation (such as the Racketeer Influenced and Corrupt Organizations Law – see, for example, Goldsmith 1988) and law enforcement developments have had on UK drugs law and policing.

In the early to mid-1980s, the unprecedented rise in heroin and other drug problems, alongside associated crime, led to a cross-party parliamentary consensus that was not averse to the use of images of 'invasion' and 'war' (Social Services Committee 1985; Home Affairs Committee 1986: iv–v). The Conservative government certainly had backing for tough action against traffickers but needed an innovative instrument. The grounds for financial policing to be applied to drugs cases were strong: as the result of an earlier appeal it had been established that the Misuse of Drugs Act 1971 could not be used to enable seizure of assets held to be of criminal provenance. The 1985 Home Affairs Committee urged emulation of American practice, to 'give the courts draconian powers in both civil and criminal law to strip drug dealers of all the assets acquired from their dealings in drugs' (Home Affairs Committee 1986: iv–v) and the DTOA was the result. In practice, the confiscation of criminal assets was neither widely nor always successfully pursued, and the new 2002 legislation and administrative agency reflect this.

Such laws have been criticised for eroding civil liberties and, in 2000, the Scottish Criminal Court of Appeal held that the Proceeds of Crime (Scotland) Act 1995 was unlawful because the presumption that assets are derived from crime unless otherwise proven is a violation of the European Convention on Human Rights. Furthermore, provision for the exchange of financial data relating to individuals may raise similar concerns to those debated in relation to cases involving the exchange of personal data between the police and other bodies (e.g. probation, social services, housing and health departments). A set of general data protection principles established at European level and in the Data Protection Act 1998 applies to this kind of data although Maguire (2000) has argued that, in reality, multi-agency protocols are essentially 'facilitative' rather than 'restrictive', containing many broad data protection exemptions and 'few meaningful barriers' to the sharing of a wide range and volume of personal information, with little regard to privacy issues. Increasingly then, law enforcement measures and some legislation aim to push serious criminals outside the protection of rights-based law, yet at the same time rights-based laws can be used to challenge such attempts! As in many areas of drugs law enforcement, tensions and contradictions abound.

Transnationalisation of drugs policing

Between the First and Second World Wars, the USA promoted drugs prohibition at home and internationally. As head of the foreign control section of the USA's prohibition unit in the 1920s, Harry Anslinger met like-minded drugs officials such as Sir Malcolm Delevingne at international meetings and, despite occasional disagreements (McAllister 2000; Sheptycki 2000: 21), such policy entrepreneurs set in motion a strong movement towards transnational control and law enforcement. In 1930, Anslinger became the first US Narcotics Commissioner at the age of 38, a position from which he systematically set out to help build up the contemporary demonology of drugs that was highly influential in global law enforcement circles for decades. Following the war the USA embraced a new internationalism and, as Sheptycki (2000: 211) notes: 'in steering the international drug control agenda the USA had created a vehicle for sending policing personnel abroad in numbers never before seen . . . from the 1960's onwards, the number of authorised US overseas "law enforcement" personnel greatly surpassed the number of conventional overseas "secret service" posts.' In the UK, although overseas postings and liaison had a long history based on Commonwealth ties and Anglo-American links, as well as the operation from the 1920s of Interpol, it was really in the mid-1980s that the drug strategy of the Conservative government promised greater commitment of police and customs to international and bilateral anti-drugs efforts.

Dorn (1998; Dorn et al. 1996) has described the variety of internal differences in controls and judicial attitudes towards drugs, as well as some less than fraternal disputes, occurring between member states of the EU. However what is also noteworthy is that at the 'high end' of policing and in relation to the external presentation of policy and policing by the EU, there has been 'a marked convergence of efforts, techniques and aims' between member states, such that by the late 1990s 'action against drug trafficking had become *the* site for the convergence of policing systems in Europe as anti-terrorist police co-operation had been in the 1970s' (Sheptycki 2000: 214). Despite this and strong encouragement of law enforcement co-operation, as Gregory (2000: 128) notes, 'generally speaking states have not sought to create any form of supranational policing' and neither the long-standing Interpol nor the newer EU Police Office – Europol – have either operational or executive powers but exist principally as hubs for networks of co-operation and exchange of information. Europol was created by the Maastricht Treaty and the Europol Convention of the 1990s as the criminal intelligence agency for the EU, acting as a clearing house and analyst of information concerning serious crimes specified by the EU Justice and Home Affairs Council (see Chapter 6). Unsurprisingly drugs trafficking, illegal immigration and trafficking in human beings are high priorities and, in 1999, Jurgen Storbeck, Director General of Europol, argued for the diversion of resources away from low-level policing towards the high-level threats to European security associated with the growth of cross-border organised crime and in particular the growth of drug markets (Bigo 2000: 69–71; Sheptycki 2000: 214).

Since September 2001, anti-terrorism has obviously returned to a central place in high-level and transnational police co-operation and convergence, and the agenda now links drugs law enforcement, anti-money laundering initiatives, immigration control and anti-terrorism (see Chapter 19).

From the global back to the local

By January 2003 government and police intelligence were aware that stockpiles of opium in Afghanistan and Pakistan were much larger than had been estimated. Despite initial optimism, the war on the Taliban and terrorism is unlikely to have generated a welcome dividend for drug control. Efforts to encourage crop substitution for opium farming and trading seem to have failed (*Druglink* 2002: 3) and it is assumed that heroin smuggling will increase, although NCIS also assumes that 'traffickers will do all they can to prevent a flooding of the market, so maintaining prices and their profits' (*Druglink* 2002: 4). None the less, a year later, Hopkins (*Guardian* 6 January 2003) reported that 'members of the inter-agency drugs action group, made up of the security services, the national crime squad, customs and excise and the police' were of the view that 'unless the Afghan production of heroin is curbed "traditional law enforcement cannot hope to win" the war against the traffickers'.

While no specific source for this statement is given, the message can be read in at least two inter-related ways relevant to drugs interdiction and law enforcement. First, it re-emphasis that policing drugs is a global issue and requires transnational efforts to undermine production, stockpiling and manipulation of the market at this level. Secondly, the police 'back home' cannot be blamed for ineffectiveness against drugs on the street when overall supply is so plentiful and evidently beyond their control. In the 1980s and 1990s local drugs squads (Dorn *et al.* 1992; Collison 1995) had recognised the displacement or 'balloon effect' ('press down here and it pops up over there') that follows targeting of dealing sites, acknowledging that such operations could disrupt local markets but not cut the steady flow of supply. Since then the volume of drugs produced for the international market has expanded even further. As Makarenko (2001: 20) notes:

> production of opium in Afghanistan increased 100% between 1988 and 1991. Between 1991 and 1999 production expanded from an estimated 2,000 tons to a record 4,600 tons. By the end of 1999 Afghanistan was said to produce 75% of the global supply of opium, from which 80% of global heroin is produced.

Production, distribution and availability have also increased in relation to cocaine and cannabis. In the 1990s NCIS acknowledged that record seizures had made no discernible impact on street price and that seizures of drugs are a fraction of estimated smuggled imports (South 2002: 930). Hence the ability to 'shut down' a local market has become correspondingly more difficult and, in such a context, modest success at local level will make little difference to overall availability.

For some this suggests it may be more appropriate to pursue a strategy focused on the external and upper levels of the chain (i.e. sources of production and organisers of distribution). This idea is not new; in fact a combination of local policing and international co-operation goes back to the mid-twentieth century. In the late 1960s and the 1970s both British and Dutch police were targeting the growing heroin markets of London and Amsterdam which were seeing seizures of 'Chinese' heroin but also working with police in Hong Kong and elsewhere in southeast Asia. In the 1980s and 1990s, the focus shifted to the posting of liaison officers in Pakistan with an interest in opium production in the 'Golden Crescent' region, including Afghanistan. Bigo (2000: 74 and *passim*) notes the increasing importance of such police officers as 'new transnational agents' occupying specialist liaison posts 'responsible for the prevention of terrorism, drugs and organised crime' (2000: 73) and draws the important distinction between 'bilateral liaison officers (posted abroad in foreign police agencies) and so-called European liaison officers (posted at Europol Headquarters in the Hague)' (2000: 74). Clearly the transnational terrain is increasingly important but also increasingly complex. UK police and customs follow production and distribution of crop-based drugs from overseas origins to local streets, and money trails from UK banks to states regarded as having lax banking regulations. At the same time, however, UK crime entrepreneurs manufacture synthetic drugs for both domestic *and* overseas markets, and Jersey and the Isle of Man are listed by US and Canadian police agencies as offshore banking havens for money laundering.

Against a background of critical evaluations of 'high level' approaches to drug enforcement and continuing questions about the impact of police efforts to curtail distribution and availability, the local dimension has become much more prominent in policy and practice debates. Perhaps more significantly, police enthusiasm about low-level drug enforcement has to be understood as part of the response to the pressure to deliver 'results' and to focus on 'what works' measures.

National and local drugs policing

'Counting' drug enforcement

According to Home Office figures, there were 124,350 reported seizures involving controlled drugs within the UK in 2000 (with the vast majority involving Class B drugs) (Corkery 2002). In general, NCS and customs seized most of the cocaine, heroin, ecstasy-type drugs, herbal cannabis and anabolic steroids recovered within the UK while local police forces seized most of the cannabis plants and crack. At one end of the scale, the report from NCS (2002) on their first four years of operation to March 2002 indicated seizure of drugs with a potential street value of £695 million and identification of illegally obtained assets worth £104 million notified to the courts. At the other end of the scale, drug seizures by the local police are of small quantities more typical of the user or petty-dealer end of the market rather than that of major dealers or traffickers.

Some commentators have argued that the mundane reality of drug law enforcement involves the police making 'shit-bum arrests' (Wilson 1978: 80) against street-level hustlers or user-dealers who are often drug users as well; in Collison's (1995: 12) words, these are the 'little league players in the drug game'. Indeed, May et al. (2002) found in their study of the policing of cannabis a significant degree of police action against 'simple possession' with no concurrent offences. Some officers reported using possession arrests as a 'door opener' to other offences, though in practice the offences which actually came to light were almost all relatively minor. Others suggested that cannabis possession arrests were easy to 'notch up' for probationers, as there was a ready supply of suspects who were likely to be carrying cannabis. By contrast, Newburn and Elliott (1998) found in their national survey and research study in six police forces that police enforcement activities have been reoriented away from possession offences and towards higher-level trafficking. Such contradictory findings probably reflect not only the lack of consistent and specific guidance on anti-drugs policing but also the high degree of local autonomy available to police generally and their drugs specialists, the discretion exercised by front-line police officers and the inherent difficulty in regulating drugs work 'on the ground'.

In the context of proactive policing and target selection in drug enforcement, questions may be asked about the cost of processing large numbers of minor drug offenders. Godfrey et al. (2002: 28) have calculated that, for the year 2000, the estimated cost of Class A drug possession arrests for *young recreational* users was £3,766,108. Writing about the estimated cost of policing cannabis, May et al. (2002) suggest that this could be as high as £350 million in 1999 (i.e. five per cent of the annual police budget) or as low as £38 million (i.e. half a per cent of the annual police budget or £500 for processing each cannabis offence).

As Collison (1995: 3) reminded us, it is also important to consider 'the various organizational and reputational costs borne by the police as the result of the strategies and practices developed and deployed in the everyday world of the drug game, strategies which ... impact most heavily on those local communities already disenchanted with the possibility of consensual policing' (see also Akhtar and South 2000). The use of stop and search powers by the police is particularly relevant to our discussion here, as Phillips and Brown (1998) found in their study that nearly one half of police arrests for drugs offences are a result of stop and searches. May et al. (2002) suggest that the over-policing of cannabis (i.e. a tenfold increase in numbers found guilty or cautioned for cannabis possession in the UK since 1974) was most likely a result of an upward trend in consumption combined with the growth in the use of stop and search by the police until the late 1990s. Following the publication of the Macpherson Report in February 1999, there was an overall fall in the number of stop and searches and a corresponding fall in drug arrests and the number of cautions given by police although this trend was short lived. While some police officers were openly critical of any further limitations of police search and arrest powers that might follow the reclassification of cannabis as a Class C drug, seeing this as an impediment to street-level drug policing and likely to 'frustrate both our ability to clear up other crimes and the intelligence gathering process' (Monaghan 2002: 9), others have pointed to serious problems long associated with police use of stop and search powers (Lea 2000). May et al. (2002) found that police officers reported using stop and search where suspicions about more serious offences proved unfounded. The over-policing of particular sections of society has serious implications, especially against a background of conflicts between the police and black communities (see Chapter 21).

Low-level drug enforcement

Targeted policing which combines a problem-solving approach with what is often referred to as low-level drug enforcement (Dorn and Murji 1992; Lee 1996; Murji 1998; Jacobson 1999) has sometimes followed dissatisfaction with the expense and seemingly poor results of attempts to disrupt wholesale trafficking and the middle markets. 'Low level' is taken to mean the suppliers and users at the retail level of the drug market, with police reorganisation and intelligence development broadly mirroring the perceived hierarchy of the market. In the context of drug enforcement, locally based police initiatives can involve any combination of a number of elements which inhibit drug transactions or 'manage' the drug market, 'trying to keep it from growing or causing too much disruption locally' (Lupton *et al.* 2002: 42–3) – for example, by increasing the risks of arrest and general inconvenience faced by buyers and sellers, disrupting the criminal business or removing key individuals from the area. Enforcement activities most commonly take the form of surveillance, use of intelligence, test-purchase operations, highly visible patrols and police crackdowns. Police initiatives may also include more treatment-oriented interventions to 'break the cycle of drug-related offending', such as referral to drug advice agencies or support for the court's use of Drugs Treatment and Testing Orders, and the proposed supervision of heroin injecting in specialist units in police stations (ACPO 2002).

Low-level drug enforcement has also been closely associated with a 'community damage limitation' approach to drugs control. The aims of this approach are multifaceted, including reducing fears of drug-related crime, reducing levels of visible drug dealing, protecting communities from drug-related nuisance and anti-social behaviour, promoting drug education in schools and minimising threats to public health. Such thinking is apparent in the Advisory Council on the Misuse of Drugs Report, *Police, Drug Misusers and the Community* (ACMD 1994), in *Tackling Drugs Together* (HM Government 1994), in the Labour government's strategy on drugs, *Tackling Drugs to Build a Better Britain* (HM Government 1998) and its (post-Drug Czar) *Updated Drug Strategy* (Home Office Drugs Strategy Directorate 2002). A particularly neat reinterpretation of what counts as success (an example of the glass being seen as half full, not half empty) can be found in the 1994 ACMD report: thus, if a police:

> crackdown on dealing in a public place leads to dealers switching their business operations to a private house and drug availability and consumption remain undiminished, this may be regarded as a failure in enforcement terms. But the other outcome may be to restore a public amenity for the benefit of the wider community, in which case the police should be given the credit (1994: 27).

This broadening of policing objectives fits with the police's own argument that – as in other areas of police activity – performance cannot be measured solely in the quantifiable terms of detection rates and drug seizures. In the process, the police mission has been redefined in terms of being responsive to the expressed needs of local communities, creating a 'consistent' and 'co-ordinated' response to the drugs problem, and measuring their performance based on a 'realistic' assessment of the scale of the problem. The public is asked to accept that the elimination of the drugs trade is impossible, and containment or minimisation of the various harms associated with drug misuse is the best that can be achieved. In the last decade what constitutes success in drugs law enforcement has been constantly redefined and the dismal record of the government in achieving the targets set in its 1998 strategy will simply confirm for the future the wisdom of modest targets and flexible interpretation. 'Good' results no longer need to be measured in the conventional sense of drug seizures or court-based punishments. Indeed, Chatterton *et al.* (1998) were able to come up with a 'robust suite of performance indicators (PIs) for evaluating police anti-drugs strategies' comprising 48 main and 142 complementary performance indicators from which police forces could pick and mix to suit their local needs.

Problem-solving approaches to drug enforcement have been developed in partnership with local agencies that bring together various responsibilities and areas of concern. In the mid-1990s, Drug Action Teams and drug action groups were formed to 'tackle drugs together' in the light of local needs and priorities, generally involving representatives of education, health and local authorities, drug agencies, the police and other criminal justice partners. The orientation towards problem-solving has led to a redefining of the ownership of the drugs problem. This involves the police seeking to impact on crime not only in a direct way (e.g. through detective investigation) but also by activating statutory and non-statutory agencies and/or using civil procedures or administrative powers possessed by other agencies to deal with drugs and drugs-related problems outside the criminal justice and penal systems. The emphasis on the police fighting crime in a strategic and targeted manner, in partnership with other social agencies, has been given further statutory impetus by the Crime and Disorder Act 1998. Under the Act, all local authorities have a statutory duty, in collaboration with the police and other agencies, to produce and implement a formal 'crime and disorder strategy' and where necessary to seek court orders to restrict the movements or behaviour of individuals seen as posing a threat to community safety. In this context, highly visible though relatively minor forms of street dealing are a prime target of crime and disorder strategies. The community is also given a crime prevention role through emphasis on physical measures to 'design out' crime and situational strategies to reduce opportunities for drugs selling and buying. For example, 'place managers' in fast-food restaurants and betting shops can be trained to be aware of drug dealing in such popular meeting places and transaction sites and take remedial measures (e.g. by discouraging long-stay customers, installing blue lighting in toilets to make injection of drugs more difficult) (Edmunds *et al.* 1996). The public as 'active citizens' have also been mobilised to co-operate with the police in the fight against drug-related nuisance, for instance by calling drug hotlines.

'Community' is, of course, not an unproblematic concept in relation to policing (Crawford 1997; Hughes *et al.* 2002). As Cohen (1979: 609) has argued, a 'new mode of deviancy control' premised on the presence of community is advocated 'just at the historical moment when every commonplace critique of "technological", "postindustrial" or "mass" society mourns the irreplaceable loss of community'. The idea that drug buyers and sellers come from 'outside' the boundaries of community is a popular one, supported by some studies though challenged by other evidence on local drug markets in white working-class communities (Forsyth *et al.* 1992; Parker *et al.* 1998b; Lupton *et al.* 2002).

In the context of intelligence-led anti-drugs policing, police 'partnership' with social agencies has involved a normalisation of exchanges of personal information with limited critical scrutiny (on 'grey information' provided by the private security sector, see Lee 1995). Critics have argued that enforcement measures using civil standards of proof can be seen as 'an unjustifiable "back door" method of using the power of the criminal law to control [anti-social] behaviour . . . about which there may not be reliable evidence' (Maguire 2000: 324). For example, local authorities can evict 'suspected' drug dealers by enforcing tenancy conditions and local councils and the police can apply for an anti-social behaviour order to exclude 'troublesome' individuals (e.g. drug sellers) from particular areas. These civil sanctions can in turn give rise to strong criminal sanctions when breached, though in practice civil sanctions are seldom invoked because of the time, financial costs and other obstacles involved (e.g. reluctance of local authorities to evict tenants whom they may ultimately have to rehouse elsewhere – Lupton *et al.* 2002: 61).

Police partnership with the community can also be regarded as problematic if we consider the complex and contradictory nature of social reaction to drug policing in inner cities. In the USA, for example, there is some evidence to suggest that 'public support for aggressive enforcement is the strongest among persons *most likely* to be the target of that enforcement, namely African Americans, Hispanics, low income residents, renters, and persons of limited education' (Rosenbaum 1993: 76, emphasis added). Proponents of intensive police operations are able to point to survey results which suggest that, while ethnic minorities are strongly opposed to police use of excessive force (more so than whites), the same groups of the most disadvantaged residents may call upon the police 'to do whatever it takes' to remove the local drug problem (Rosenbaum 1993). In practice, police crackdowns and the 'war on drugs' have filled up many juvenile institutions, jails and prisons with drug convicts, impacting disproportionately on young black men and minority communities (Mauer 2000).

Similarly in Britain, the invocation of a police alliance with black communities has been evident in special police operations such as the Metropolitan Police's 'Operation Trident'. Trident was presented as 'a police response to "community" pressure', especially 'from the black community over concerns about gun crime' (Murji 2002: 33). But the question of 'who speaks for or represents "the community"' remains (2002: 33). Furthermore, police racialisation of the drug problem and the chequered history of police crackdowns on drugs in some areas (e.g. Brixton and Notting Hill in London) suggest that anti-drugs policing does not occur in a vacuum. In the past high-profile anti-drugs police operations were sometimes scaled down or closed because of allegations of racism. Indeed, social reaction to drugs is highly complex and sometimes contradictory in nature. As Murji (1998: 151–2) has argued:

> it is possible to see the police as both promoting the idea of yardies as a black mafia and seeking to play it down. Black politicians have simultaneously complained about stereotypes and called for a war on drugs in the name of the black community. Drugs researchers and agencies have both criticised the pre-occupation with crack (or any other drug on its own) while some have discovered crack and perhaps used that as the basis for their continued funding (cf. *Druglink* January/February 1993).

There are other important questions associated with locally based police initiatives in drug enforcement. Questions may be asked about their effectiveness. Targeted police operations appear to have limited long-term impact on drug-dealing activities and drug availability (Lupton *et al.* 2002; May *et al.* 2002). In Manchester, for example, high-profile police presence was found to have 'little, if [any] at all, impact' on drug hotspots and local 'drugs economies continue to flourish and grow' (Chatterton *et al.* 1998: 7–8). Drug dealers, runners and buyers are known to have adapted their modus operandi in response to police tactics (e.g. greater use of mobile phones, requirement for new buyers to consume drugs on site). Some research studies have also highlighted the problem of displacement of the drugs problem, though the precise nature and impact on a variety of constituencies (e.g. businesses, commuters, drug workers, police and residents in various neighbourhoods) are still open to debate (Edmunds *et al.* 1996; Lee 1996; Jacobson 1999).

Evaluations of different types of local drug referral schemes at the point of arrest have raised a different set of issues. Surveys suggest that by the end of the 1990s just over half the country was covered by some type of arrest referral scheme (Newburn and Elliott 1998). Some studies have highlighted the 'modest gains' of referral schemes in facilitating some drug users' access to help and information (Dorn and South 1994; Murji 1998: 83, 113–16) while Edmunds *et al.* (1998: vi) reported 'very substantial reductions in both drug use and crime' (though potential 'response bias' was acknowledged). However, efforts by the police and drug workers to deliver referrals and to intervene at a critical point in the careers of active offenders have sometimes raised uncomfortable questions about client confidentiality, costs and benefits, and the role of compulsion in drug treatment. This last point has become even more relevant given the police powers to drug test detainees for 'trigger offences' (mainly property offences) under the Criminal Justice and Court Services Act 2000 and the proposal to strengthen the links between 'a positive test result' for Class A drugs and 'treatment targeting'. As Mallender *et al.* (2002: 4) have pointed out, 'some stakeholders have suggested that testing by the police should be allowed to have an impact on police bail . . . [as] this will increase the deterrence effect of drug testing'. All this, coupled with the scepticism of many front-line officers towards the police role in harm reduction, illustrates the perennial tensions of combining welfare and crime control elements in police work.

Rule-bending and other forms of police misconduct

There is one further aspect of intelligence-led drug policing that has raised concerns among some critics – i.e. the widespread use of criminal informants (Reuter 1983; Norris and Dunninghan 2000; South 2001). As Maguire (2000: 325) argues, 'any policing system which places informants at the heart of its operational strategy runs a constant risk of "the wheel coming off" through rule bending and worse'. In drug enforcement, participating or non-participating informers and undercover police may be used by drug squads to infiltrate the drug trade – for example, through drug busts or controlled deliveries. Such actions arguably stretch 'the limits of policing in a democratic society' and foster 'an entrepreneurial approach to detection which, once perfected in the drug game ... can all too easily slip over into more mainstream police work' (Collison 1995: 196). People may be 'set up' by informants acting as agents provocateurs; and police may end up facilitating rather than repressing crime (e.g. officers turning a blind eye to informants' criminal activities in return for information). There are also risks of officers dishonestly concealing the involvement of informants from the authorities, the courts, and defendants and their lawyers, thereby undermining rather than promoting justice.

The collapse of prosecutions in several high-profile drug-smuggling cases and a series of damning reports into the practices of Customs and Excise (for example, the Hosker Report in 1999; the Butler Report in 2000; the Gower–Hammond Report in 2001) provide vivid examples of 'the wheel coming off' when individuals or whole teams were systematically involved in rule-bending with the aim of achieving 'good' results. Customs and Excise, especially its elite enforcement arm, the National Investigation Service, has been criticised for its 'culture ... of carelessness and recklessness – a catalogue of flawed procedures, misleading requests, illegalities and incompetence' (*Guardian* 2 November 2002). In particular, in a collapsed prosecution case relating to the importation of cocaine valued at over £30 million in Bristol in 1999, the Customs and Excise investigation methods were criticised by the presiding judge as 'socially corrosive and destructive' (*The Daily Telegraph* 9 June 2000). A police investigation, Operation Brandfield, has also been launched into at least 11 major drug-smuggling operations. Most of these operations involved 'controlled deliveries' believed to involve the importation of up to 200 kg of heroin into the UK by customs, some of which 'went missing' and ended up on the streets (*Guardian* 2 November 2002).

Such insights into rule-bending are particularly important to understanding police corruption in Britain and elsewhere (Sherman 1974; Mollen Commission 1994; Punch 1985, 2000: 312–13). Indeed, research and official inquiries have found evidence of a range of corrupt activities in drugs-related police work, including opportunistic theft (e.g. stealing from drug arrestees); acceptance of bribes to lie on oath and to provide confidential records; the planting of drugs; illegal searches; the protection of informants; involvement in violence; participation by police officers in drug dealing; and protection of major drug operations. In 1998, the Commissioner of the Metropolitan Police acknowledged that there could be up to 250 corrupt police officers serving in his force, believed to be implicated in offences that include large-scale drug dealing. More recently, in April 2001, five police officers from the Derbyshire and Nottinghamshire police forces, including two serving with the elite NCS, were arrested for allegedly dealing in cannabis and cocaine (*The Independent on Sunday* 29 April 2001).

In a review of the literature, Newburn (1999: 25–7) suggests that drug enforcement has a number of characteristics, some shared with other forms of policing, that make it particularly prone to corrupt practice. These include the difficulty in regulating legally suppressed markets where there is an absence of a 'victim'; the secretive and quasi-legal nature of drug enforcement; the widespread use of informants; pressure for results generated by the 'war on drugs' rhetoric; the difficulty in securing sufficient evidence to convict (hence the temptation to engage in process corruption); the need to buy or occasionally use drugs in the course of anti-drugs policing; and the large sums of money available in the drugs trade. As Newburn (1999: 27) sums up, corrupt practices tend to be especially entrenched in drug-related policing precisely because:

> those areas of police work that have the strongest link with, or are closest to, the 'invitational edge' [of corruption] are also those which are generally subject to the least managerial scrutiny and . . . are increasingly associated with extraordinarily large sums of money and therefore very high levels of [financial] temptation.

Conclusion

Drugs policing has been shaped by many of the same influences and changes as mainstream policing but is also characterised by a 'special' status, both figurative and actual. It is a site of policy and strategic significance; of innovations in law, methods and technology; of much that is valued by the police culture (action, risk and crime targeting); and of a particular and favourable image held by society and media (doing 'dirty work' to protect our communities and young people). However, if drugs policing were *ever* straightforward, this is certainly not the case today.

In the contemporary context, drugs have become a feature of everyday life not experienced since the nineteenth century (South 1999). The argument that drugs have become in some sense 'normalised' in society, whether via increased consumption of drugs such as cannabis and ecstasy, or simply through enormously increased familiarity with drugs as part of the cultural wallpaper, has been supported by some (Parker *et al.* 1998a; Hammersley *et al.* 2003) and contested by others (Shiner and Newburn 1999). However none would dispute that the late modern landscape of drug use, related crime and policing that began to emerge from the late 1970s is profoundly different from that of preceding decades.

At several points in this chapter we have noted tensions in drugs policing and wider policy. Of course such tensions are not restricted to this field but reflect the wider co-existence of liberal versus punitive responses to crime in late modernity, occasionally perceived as complementary but frequently appearing diametrically opposed. In this respect drugs policing reflects the tension or contradiction between Garland's (2001: 137) 'two criminologies': between concerns with normal, rational offenders (drug users' shoplifting, burgling and small-scale dealing) and, on the other hand, 'threatening outcasts' (the corrupting 'drug dealers at the school gates' image) and 'fearsome strangers' (the alien traffickers image). Drugs policing is constituted by both a 'criminology of the self' (the normalisation of the rational, choosing actor in crime) and a 'criminology of the "other"' (the subversive interloper from 'outside'). As Garland (2001: 137) amplifies, the first 'is invoked to routinize crime, to allay disproportionate fears and to promote preventative action. The other functions to demonize the criminal, to act out popular fears and resentment and to promote support for state punishment'. We have referred to some of the different strands in the story(ies) of drugs policing that find reflection in Garland's two criminologies, from the early history of drugs policing through to recent tensions between the treatment and punishment aims of community-based initiatives. However further investigation of these various tensions and contradictions would be valuable.

As Berridge and Edwards (1987: 244) have remarked, 'the roots of action on any drug issue appear to be mixed, with influences which interact and mutually amplify'. Actors from within and without the state (e.g. 'non-state actors' and 'sub-state agents' – Sheptycki 2000: 217) play significant roles in the formation of drugs policy and hence directions for policing. The construction of consensus and incorporation or rejection of opposition produces a complex picture of enforcement and treatment, both punitive and liberalising. As a future research agenda, the investigation of policy networks (Duke 2000) and application of actor network theory (Manning 2002) may help reveal how contradictions are constantly (re)produced and then negotiated in drugs policy and policing.

Selected further reading

Collison's *Police, Drugs and Community* (1995) is an important ethnographic study of a force-level drug squad at work. It examines the strategic, cultural and political effects of contemporary drug policing against a background of the limits and possibilities of policing in a democratic society. Jacobson's *Policing Drug Hot-spots* (1999) is a useful overview of research studies on the application of situational crime prevention methods to the policing of local drug markets in the USA and Britain. It also highlights the problems as well as the conditions of successful multi-agency, preventive initiatives against local drug markets. Murji's *Policing Drugs* (1998) is about the policing of drugs and the social reaction to particular types of drug and drug offender in Britain. It provides a critical analysis of low-level drug enforcement and drug referral schemes, drug legalisation and decriminalisation, and official and media reactions to various drug scares. South's 'Drugs, alcohol and crime' (2002) is a comprehensive overview of key studies of the use, distribution and control of illegal drugs and alcohol in the UK, with reference to international developments.

References

Advisory Council on the Misuse of Drugs (ACMD) (1994) *Drug Misusers and the Criminal Justice System. Part II. Police, Drug Misusers and the Community.* London: HMSO.

Akhtar, S. and South, N. (2000) 'Hidden from heroin's history: heroin and dealing within an English Asian community – a case study', in M. Hough and M. Natarajan (eds) *International Drug Markets: From Research to Policy.* New York, NY: Criminal Justice Press, 153–77.

Association of Chief Police Officers (ACPO) (1975) *Report of the Sub-committee on Criminal Intelligence* (Baumber Report). Unpublished.

ACPO (1985) *Final Report of the Working Party on Drugs Related Crime* (Broome Report). Unpublished; extracts in the Appendix to Dorn *et al.* (1992).

ACPO (1986) *Second Report of the Working Party on Operational Intelligence* (Ratcliffe Report). Unpublished.

ACPO (2002) *Review of Drug Policy and Proposals for the Future.* London: ACPO Drugs Committee.

Audit Commission (1993) *Helping with Enquiries: Tackling Crime Effectively.* London: HMSO.

Bean, P. (2002) *Drugs and Crime.* Cullompton: Willan.

Berridge, V. (1978) 'War conditions and narcotics control: the passing of the Defence of the Realm Act Regulation 40B', *Journal of Social Policy,* 7(3): 285–304.

Berridge, V. and Edwards, G. (1987) *Opium and the People: Opiate Use in Nineteenth Century England.* London: Yale University Press.

Bigo, D. (2000) 'Liaison officers in Europe: new officers in the European security field', in J. Sheptycki (ed.) *Issues in Transnational Policing.* London: Routledge, 67–99.

Blanchard, S. (2003) 'Licensing drugs: a thinkable solution' (http://www.idmu.co.uk/police.htm). Originally published in *Police Review,* 3 June 1994.

Carrabine, E., Cox, P., Lee, M. and South, N. (2002) *Crime in Modern Britain.* Oxford: Oxford University Press.

Carrabine, E., Lee, M. and South, N. (2000) 'Social wrongs and human rights in late modern Britain', *Social Justice,* 27(2): 193–211.

Chatterton, M., Varley, M. and Langmead-Jones, P. (1998) *Testing Performance Indicators for Local Anti-drugs Strategies. Home Office Police Research Series* 97. London: Home Office.

Christie, N. (1986) 'Suitable enemies', in H. Bianchi and R. van Swaaningen (eds) *Abolitionism: Towards a Non-repressive Approach to Crime.* Amsterdam: Free University Press, 42–54.

Cohen, S. (1979) 'Community control in a new utopia', *New Society,* 15: 609–11.

Collison, M. (1995) *Police, Drugs and Community.* London: Free Association Books.

Corkery, J. (2002) *Drug Seizure and Offender Statistics. Home Office Statistical Bulletin* 4/02. London: Home Office.

Cox, B., Shirley, J. and Short, M. (1977) *The Fall of Scotland Yard.* Harmondsworth: Penguin Books.

Crawford, A. (1997) *The Local Governance of Crime.* Oxford: Clarendon Press.

Currie, E. (1998) *Crime and Punishment in America.* New York, NY: Metropolitan Books.

Dorn, N. (1998) 'Editorial: drug policies and the European Union', *Drugs: Education, Prevention and Policy,* 5(1): 5–13.

Dorn, N., Jepson, J. and Savona, E. (eds) (1996) *European Drug Policy and Enforcement.* Basingstoke: Macmillan.

Dorn, N. and Murji, K. (1992) 'Low level drug enforcement', *International Journal of the Sociology of Law,* 20: 159–71.

Dorn, N., Murji, K. and South, N. (1990) 'Drug referral schemes', *Policing*, 6: 482–92.

Dorn, N., Murji, K. and South, N. (1992) *Traffickers: Drug Markets and Law Enforcement.* London: Routledge.

Dorn, N. and South, N. (1994) 'The power behind practice: drug control and harm minimisation in inter-agency and criminal law-contexts', in J. Strang and M. Gossop (eds) *Heroin Addiction and Drug Policy: The British System.* Oxford: Oxford University Medical Press, 292–303.

Downes, D. (1977) 'The drug addict as a folk-devil', in P. Rock (ed.) *Drugs and Politics.* New Brunswick, NJ: Transaction, 89–98.

Duke, K. (2000) 'Prison drugs policy since 1980: shifting agendas and policy networks', *Drugs: Education, Prevention and Policy*, 7(4): 393–408.

Edmunds, M., Hough, M. and Urquia, M. (1996) *Tackling Local Drug Markets. Crime Detection and Prevention Series Paper* 80. London: Home Office.

Edmunds, M., May, T., Hearnden, I. and Hough, M. (1998) *Arrest Referral: Emerging Lessons from Research. Drugs Prevention Initiative Paper* 23. London: Home Office.

Forsyth, A., Hammersley, R., Lavelle, T. and Murray, K. (1992) 'Geographical aspects of scoring illegal drugs', *British Journal of Criminology*, 32(3): 292–309.

Garland, D. (2001) *The Culture of Control.* Oxford: Oxford University Press.

Godfrey, C., Eaton, G., McDougall, C. and Culyer, A. (2002) *The Economic and Social Costs of Class A Drug Use in England and Wales 2000.* Home Office Research Study 249. London: Home Office.

Goldsmith, M. (1988) 'RICO and enterprise criminality: a response to Gerard E. Lynch', *Columbia Law Review*, 88(4): 774–801.

Gower, J. and Hammond, Sir A. (2001) *Review of Prosecutions Conducted by the Solicitor's Office of HM Customs and Excise.* London: The Legal Secretariat to the Law Officers (www.lslo.gov.uk).

Gregory, F. (2000) 'Private criminality as a matter of international concern', in J. Sheptycki (ed.) *Issues in Transnational Policing.* London: Routledge, 100–34.

Grieve, J. (1993) 'Thinking the "unthinkable" ', *Criminal Justice Matters*, 12: 8.

Hammersley, R., Marsland, L. and Reid, M. (2003) *Substance Use by Young Offenders.* Home Office Research Findings 192. London: Home Office.

HM Government (1994) *Tackling Drugs Together: A Consultation Document Strategy for England, 1995–1998.* London: HMSO.

HM Government (1998) *Tackling Drugs to Build a Better Britain: The Government's Ten-year Strategy for Tackling Drugs Misuse* (Cm 3945). London: HMSO.

Hobbs, D. (1995) *Bad Business: Professional Crime in Modern Britain.* Oxford: Oxford University Press.

Home Affairs Committee (1986) *Misuse of Hard Drugs.* Session 1985/6. London: House of Commons.

Home Office Drugs Strategy Directorate (2002) *Updated Drug Strategy.* London: Home Office.

Hughes, G., McLaughlin, E. and Muncie, J. (eds) (2002) *Crime Prevention and Community Safety: New Directions.* London: Sage.

Jacobson, J. (1999) *Policing Drug Hot-spots. Home Office Police Research Series* 109. London: Home Office.

Kohn, M. (1992) *Dope Girls: The Birth of the British Drug Underground.* London: Lawrence & Wishart.

Lea, J. (2000) 'The Macpherson Report and the question of institutional racism', *Howard Journal of Criminal Justice*, 39(2): 219–37.

Lee, M. (1995) 'Across the public–private divide? Private policing, grey intelligence and civil actions in local drugs control', *European Journal of Crime, Criminal Law and Criminal Justice*, 3(4): 381–94.

Lee, M. (1996) 'London: "community damage limitation" through policing?', in N. Dorn *et al.* (eds) *European Drug Policy and Enforcement*. Basingstoke: Macmillan, 33–54.

Lupton, R., Wilson, A., May, T., Warburton, H. and Turnbull, P. (2002) *A Rock and a Hard Place: Drug Markets in Deprived Neighbourhoods*. Home Office Research Study 240. London: Home Office.

Macpherson Commission (1999) *The Stephen Lawrence Inquiry: Report of an Inquiry by Sir William Macpherson of Cluny*. London: Home Office.

Maguire, M. (2000) 'Policing by risks and targets: some dimensions and implications of intelligence-led crime control', *Policing and Society*, 9: 315–36.

Maguire, M. and Norris, C. (1992) *The Conduct and Supervision of Criminal Investigations. Royal Commission on Criminal Justice Research Study 5*. London: HMSO.

Makarenko, T. (2001) 'Getting to market', *Druglink*, 16(5): 19–22.

Mallender, J., Roberts, E. and Seddon, T. (2002) *Evaluation of Drug Testing in the Criminal Justice System in Three Pilot Areas. Research, Development and Statistics Directorate Findings* 176. London: Home Office.

Manning, N. (2002) 'Actor networks, policy networks and personality disorder', *Sociology of Health and Illness*, 24(5): 644–66.

Mauer, M. (2000) *Race to Incarcerate*. New York, NY: New Press.

May, T., Warburton, H., Turnbull, P. and Hough, M. (2002) *Times They Are A-changing: Policing of Cannabis*. York: YPS for the Joseph Rowntree Foundation.

McAllister, W. (2000) *Drug Diplomacy in the Twentieth Century*. London: Routledge.

Mollen Commission (1994) *Report of the Commission to Investigate Allegations of Police Corruption and the Anti-corruption Procedures of the Police Department*. New York, NY: Mollen Commission.

Monaghan, G. (2002) 'Policing cannabis reclassification – easy as ABC', *Druglink*, 17(1): 7–9.

Murji, K. (1998) *Policing Drugs*. Aldershot: Ashgate.

Murji, K. (2002) 'It's not a black thing', *Criminal Justice Matters*, 47: 32–3.

National Crime Squad (2002) *National Crime Squad Performance – the First Four Years*. NCS Web Site.

Newburn, T. (1999) *Understanding and Preventing Police Corruption: Lessons from the Literature. Home Office Police Research Studies* 110. London: Home Office.

Newburn, T. and Elliott, J. (1998) *Policing Anti-drug Strategies: Tackling Drugs Together Three Years on. Crime Detection and Prevention Series Paper* 89. London: Home Office Police Research Group.

Norris, C. and Dunnighan, C. (2000) 'Subterranean blues: conflict as an unintended consequence of the police use of informers', *Policing and Society*, 9: 385–412.

Parker, H., Aldridge, J. and Measham, F. (1998a) *Illegal Leisure: The Normalization of Adolescent Recreational Drug Use*. London: Routledge.

Parker, H., Bury, C. and Egginton, R. (1998b) *New Heroin Outbreaks among Young People in England and Wales. Crime Prevention and Detection Paper* 92. London: Home Office.

Parssinen, T. (1983) *Secret Passions, Secret Remedies: Narcotic Drugs in British Society, 1820–1930*. Manchester: Manchester University Press.

Phillips, C. and Brown, D. (1998) *Entry into the Criminal Justice System: A Survey of Police Arrests and their Outcomes. Home Office Research Study* 185. London: Home Office.

Punch, M. (1985) *Conduct Unbecoming*. London: Tavistock.

Punch, M. (2000) 'Police corruption and its prevention', *European Journal on Criminal Policy and Research*, 8: 301–24.

Reuter, P. (1983) 'Licensing criminals: police and informants', in G. Caplan (ed.) *Abscam Ethics*. Washington, DC: The Police Foundation.

Rosenbaum, D. (1993) 'Civil liberties and aggressive enforcement: balancing the rights of individuals and society in the drug war', in R. Davis *et al.* (eds) *Drugs and the Community*. Springfield, IL: Charles Thomas.

Ruggiero, V. and South, N. (1997) 'The late-modern city as a bazaar: drug markets, illegal enterprise and the barricades', *British Journal of Sociology*, 48(1): 55–71.

Shapiro, H. (1999) 'Dances with drugs: pop music, drugs and youth culture', in N. South (ed.) *Drugs: Cultures, Controls and Everyday Life*. London: Sage, 17–35.

Sheptycki, J. (ed.) (2000) *Issues in Transnational Policing*. London: Routledge.

Sherman, L. (1974) *Police Corruption*. New York, NY: Anchor.

Shiner, M. and Newburn, T. (1999) 'Taking tea with Noel: the place and meaning of drug use in everyday life', in N. South (ed.) *Drugs: Cultures, Controls and Everyday Life*. London: Sage, 139–59.

Social Services Committee (1985) *Misuse of Hard Drugs*. London: HMSO.

South, N. (1992) 'Moving murky money: drug trafficking, law enforcement and the pursuit of criminal profits', in D. Farrington and S. Walklate (eds) *Offenders and Victims: Theory and Policy*. London: British Society of Criminology/ISTD, 167–93.

South, N. (1998) 'Tackling drug control in Britain: from Sir Malcolm Delevingne to the new drug strategies', in R. Coomber (ed.) *The Control of Drugs and Drug Users: Reason or Reaction*. Amsterdam: Harwood, 87–106.

South, N. (1999) 'Debating drugs and everyday life: normalisation, prohibition and "otherness"', in N. South (ed.) *Drugs: Cultures, Controls and Everyday Life*. London: Sage, 1–15.

South, N. (2000) 'Illicit markets', in C. Bryant *et al.* (eds) *The International Encyclopaedia of Criminology and Deviant Behaviour*. Washington, DC: Brunner, 207–9.

South, N. (2001) 'Police, security and information: the use of informants and agents in a liberal democracy', in M. Amir and S. Einstein (eds) *Policing, Security and Democracy. Vol. 2. Special Aspects of Democratic Policing*. Huntsville, TX: Office of International Criminal Justice Press, 87–103.

South, N. (2002) 'Drugs, alcohol and crime', in M. Maguire *et al.* (eds) *The Oxford Handbook of Criminology*. Oxford: Oxford University Press, 914–44.

Spear, B. (2002) *Heroin Addiction, Care and Control: The 'British System' 1916–1984*. London: Drugscope.

Storbeck, J. (1999) *Organised Crime in the European Union – the Role of Europol. 1999 Police Foundation Lecture*. London: Police Foundation.

Strang, J. and Gossop, M. (eds) (1994) *Heroin Addiction and Drug Policy: The British System*. Oxford: Oxford University Medical Press.

Wilson, J.Q. (1978) *The Investigators*. New York, NY: Basic Books.

Chapter 18

Organised and financial crime

Michael Levi

Introduction

This chapter deals with the policing of two overlapping categories of crime that present even greater conceptual boundary problems than do others discussed in this book: organised crime and white-collar crime. Before we discuss policing, let us briefly review the behavioural context in which it takes place. Influenced as we are by profound cultural images of the Sicilian Mafia and the Italian-American Mafia that have brought *The Godfather* and *The Sopranos* to our screens, it is difficult not to be seduced by the assumption that this hierarchical, deeply embedded cultural and family mode of organisation is the natural evolution of serious crime: the general public, criminals and the police are all subjected to (and sometimes entranced by) these images of power and 'threat to society'. However, before his assassination, Italian investigating judge Falcone appreciated that this threat was much more complex than a subculture or alien conspiracy model, and that the organised crime phenomenon could not be controlled without tackling political and business alliances, as well as police, prosecutorial and judicial corruption. This is equally true of contemporary countries in the Balkans and elsewhere (see Gambetta 1994; Stille 1996; Arlacchi 1986, 1998; Jamieson 2000; Paoli 2002 for different accounts of Italian organised crime). However, where it is harder to develop corrupt alliances between criminal justice officials, politicians and suppliers of illicit commodities or predatory criminals, organised crime is unlikely to flourish. This is important because to the extent that organised criminals represent a set of people who are 'really dangerous' to the essential integrity of the state, and who trigger (especially in continental European legal systems) special investigative powers because of this threat, it would be helpful to know how special are their threats and what they constitute.

Some academics (e.g. Hobbs 1998) consider that all crime is essentially local in character (though connected somehow to the global economy); others (van Duyne 1996) – though understanding that value-added tax and European Community frauds require transnational networks (or, with the aid of

corruption or counterfeiters, paperwork that *simulates* the transnational movement of goods) – regard the issue of transnational organised crime as
overblown and under-analysed by the 'threat assessment industry'. Others still
regard the sceptics as naïve theorists who fail to appreciate the creeping threat
posed by cross-border criminal co-operation (for a collection that reviews some
of these issues, see Berdal and Serrano 2002; see also Levi 2002a). The nature
of what Hobbs (1997) termed 'criminal collaboration' varies in different
countries, but affects the kind of control strategies (policing and administrative) that it makes sense to adopt.

'Organised crime' used to be a phenomenon that was central only to
American and Italian crime discourses about 'the Mafia', but – stimulated by
the growth of the international drugs and people migration trades[1] and by the
freeing up of borders since the collapse of the USSR – the debate about it and
specific national and transnational powers to deal with 'it' has extended to
Britain and other parts of Europe and beyond in the course of the 1990s.
However unclear it may be about how 'we' can assess whether crime is
'organised' or not, the term is a unifying framework around which international police and judicial co-operation can be structured. Definitional ambiguities do not seem to inhibit confident statements about the 'scale of the
problem' of transnational organised crime, which is always asserted to be
'growing' and often said to be using hi-tech methods, as if crossing borders by
plane, motor vehicle, digital phone or computer were not also done by
business people, professionals and the general population, probably in greater
proportions than criminals at work do. Some crimes such as 'identity theft'
associated with fraud, organised crime and terrorism are also plausibly said
to be growing.[2]

By contrast , 'white-collar crime' is a term used more by criminologists
(Croall 2001; Nelken 2002; Levi and Pithouse forthcoming) than by police and
politicians, especially in Britain where it has only rarely been a major crime
issue (and then only in relation to identity fraud and deposit and investment
'widows and orphans' frauds). In keeping with the more general moral
entrepreneurship of US 'law and order' politics, the media, politicians and law
enforcement officials there are paradoxically *more* likely to discuss it, both (1)
for crimes *against* business (like credit card fraud); and (2) for crimes against
investors *by* prestigious and by racketeer-run business alike. Though 'corporate crime' is more common nowadays, some academics also use 'white-collar
crime' to refer to the regulation of employers' legal duties to ensure the
workplace health and safety of their employees.[3] For reasons of space and
coherence, I will deal primarily here with the policing of one subset of
white-collar crime – fraud – which itself encompasses a range of victim–
offender activities and social statuses. 'The problem of fraud' and official
responses to it lack the 'Evil Empire' rhetoric of the construction of the
'organised crime problem', even though *some* large aggregate frauds against
the Treasury – evasion of excise duty on alcohol and tobacco – are included in
the category of the most serious organised crime threats facing the UK in the
assessment of the National Criminal Intelligence Service (NCIS 2002) and,
peculiarly, tend to be seen as 'organised crime' rather than 'fraud'. Nevertheless, if we look at frauds not so much by the number of each type reported but

by the amount of money lost, we can better appreciate why (largely reactive) institutions such as the Serious Fraud Office (SFO) were created in 1987 and still exist. They exist because the 'new classes' of victim – for example, shareholders in privatised utilities and collectors of early retirement and redundancy pay – are a *political risk* which calls for a response. The SFO exists also because Britain was concerned about its reputation in the global marketplace and, given that (despite large redundancies in 2002 and 2003) as many as one in five Londoners in employment works in financial services, they are strategically important in an economy of seriously declining manufacturing and agricultural industries (see Levi and Pithouse forthcoming). At the volume fraud end of the fraud spectrum (such as credit card fraud – see Levi 1998) and even at the level of infiltration into financial institutions and corruption of those already there, there is an overlap between 'organised' and 'white-collar' criminals, since many such frauds are committed by diversified offender networks. One consequence of this is that the policing of fraud may overlap more with the policing of organised crime than it would have done in the past.

At the risk of confirming the view of policing as 'things that the police do', I will largely exclude here the policing of corporate crimes such as health and safety at work offences. However, though usually less dramatic than drive-by shootings in our major cities, it should not be forgotten that in 2000–1 in the UK, employees suffered 215 workplace deaths (up 53 from the previous year), while the self-employed suffered 80 deaths (up 22 from the previous year) (HSC 2002). We should also note the differences in discourse embodied in non-police policing of serious risks to life (e.g. the mission statement of the Health and Safety Commission is 'to ensure that risks to people's health and safety from work activities are properly controlled'). In seeking to achieve this 'proper control' in 2001–2, 192,693 regular contacts were made with industry; over 40,000 incidents and complaints were investigated; 10,641 improvement and prohibition notices were issued; and information laid for 1,618 prosecutions, mostly under the 'strict liability' provisions of the Health and Safety at Work Act 1974.[4]

The standard method of dealing with the wide range of *non*-police cases is advice and prodding of the unco-operative, with slowly escalating sanctions for persistent violation. If one wished to characterise crudely the difference in the mode of treatment of organised and white-collar crimes, one might do so by suggesting that organised criminals are people who – whatever they do, including purchasing apparently legitimate businesses with proceeds of crime – are deemed to be socially dangerous, whereas white-collar criminals are people who – with some highly stigmatised exceptions such as some pension fund fraudsters[5] – are viewed as being essentially amenable to restorative justice methods. These differences may be justifiable on a risk-based model of policing, but we tend to take for granted the assumptions on which they are based. As one long-term (bankruptcy) fraudster told me, 'I only wanted to make enough money to afford to be honest' (see, further, Levi 1981, 1999). This may be equally true of *some* drugs traffickers and other National Criminal Intelligence Service (NCIS) and National Crime Squad (NCS)/Customs and Excise targets, but a policy decision has been taken not to allow them to integrate into the legitimate enterprise world, both on moral grounds and on the assumption of future dangerousness. This chapter will explore the similarities and differences in styles of policing for different forms of serious crime and the groups and networks who commit them.

The organisation of organised crime policing

At the international level, policy responses have been to pressurise states into passing legislation and to set up mutual legal assistance mechanisms to facilitate international exchanges of intelligence and to progress cases. However at an *operational* national level, in response to these threats, a common British police response has been to set up specialist force squads, initially focused around types of crime (e.g. drugs squads, fraud squads, vice squads) (see Morgan *et al.* 1996 who pointed out that there was very little serious problem definition or supervision of what these squads were for). These were then broadened out into more generalist serious crime squads at a force level, with a centralisation in the 1990s into the NCIS and the National Crime Squad, funded by 'top slicing' from the (often protesting) police forces. In addition, HM Customs and Excise Investigations Division focuses on Class A drugs importation (see Chapter 17) and on various types of fraud, especially excise fraud (alcohol and tobacco), value-added tax fraud and oil fraud. The NCS *can* take on fraud cases, but in practice they do so only when these are related to counterfeiting and forgery and/or are committed by people identified as serious international offenders at level 3.[6] This could be characterised as dealing with frauds only when committed by 'the usual suspects' or persons connected with them. Fraud is examined later.

The NCS was formed in April 1998 through the amalgamation of the six former regional crime squads and is tasked with combating serious and organised crime within, or affecting, England and Wales. The organisation is under the day-to-day direction and control of the Director General who is accountable to the National Crime Squad Service Authority, some of whose members overlap with the NCIS Authority. The 2002–3 staff total of 1,944 includes the core strength of 1,333 seconded police officers and 432 support staff plus the staff who make up the National Hi-Tech Crime Unit, Project Reflex (on organised immigration crime) and other areas of activity that receive direct funding. The NCS has three Operational Command Units (OCUs), Northern, Eastern and Western, covering the whole of England and Wales. Each OCU comprises of several branch offices where operational teams are based.

On 1 April 2002, following the Criminal Justice and Police Act 2001, the National Crime Squad became a non-departmental public body (NDPB), defined as 'a body which has a role in the process of national government, but is not a Government department or part of one, and which accordingly operates to a greater or lesser extent at arm's length from Ministers' (NCS 2002). The crime-related objectives of the National Crime Squad[7] are to dismantle or disrupt criminal enterprises engaged in Class A drug trafficking, organised immigration crime and other activities 'according to agreed priorities'. It also aims 'to proactively seek to identify and implement opportunities for improved interagency working including providing an appropriate level of specialist support to forces and other agencies'. In common with organised crime 'task force' concepts internationally, the principal policing style of the NCS is (1) the development of informants (for regulated financial benefits or, in a formalised way and in collaboration with the Crown Prosecution Service, for reduced criminal charges or promises of positive mentions of their contribution to sentencing judges or parole authorities); (2) undercover infiltration, including 'sting' operations in which officers pose as buyers or sellers of illegal products and services (such as drugs, vice and money laundering); and (3) a range of covert electronic and physical surveillance methods.

Apart from its own officers and analysts who develop tactical packages, one of the key sources of intelligence on organised crime is the NCIS (see Chapters 13 and 14) whose annual budget doubled to £90 million in the four years to 2001–2. NCIS has two objectives set by the Home Secretary, namely, to provide high-quality assessments and actionable intelligence (1) on Class A drugs supply reduction and on combating organised immigration crime; and (2) to increase disruption of criminal enterprises engaged in other forms of serious and organised crime; plus two fairly amorphous co-operation objectives set by the service. The Security Services (MI5) and the Secret Intelligence Service (MI6) also play an increasingly important role in intelligence gathering and disruption of major crime networks.

The control of organised crime internationally

As Justice and Home Affairs has become a key component of EU 'Third Pillar' activities (involving the Council of the EU as well as the European Commission because national governments do not wish to allow EU bodies to gain control over law and order issues), and organised crime has ascended in importance as a political issue for the EU and the G-8 most powerful industrialised countries, it is no longer possible to see 'serious crime' policy in purely national terms. Part of the 1998 Joint Action (an agreement to step up action against organised crime) was a commitment to criminalise membership of criminal organisations – influenced by the Italian experience of Mafia and Mafia-type hierarchical organisations but harder to apply in less regimented settings – and tough action against criminal offshore finance centres.

There are two sorts of shift in approach to the control of organised crime. The first shift relates to traditional criminal justice approaches, and the second – which is not incompatible – relates to prevention. Criminal justice approaches include the following:

1. Substantive legislation, relating especially to money-laundering and proceeds of crime legislation (see, for the UK, Levi and Osofsky 1995; PIU 2000; Proceeds of Crime Act 2002; and, for a critical account, Alldridge 2003).

2. Procedural laws involving mutual legal assistance (including the establishment of Europol and Eurojust, whose detached national prosecutors and investigative judges are expected to facilitate urgent cases, and the European arrest warrant and asset-freezing orders).

3. Investigative resources, including the formation of specialist organisations and police units. In the UK, this includes the National Hi-Tech Crime Unit and even some mixed private–public funded ones such as the Dedicated Cheque and Plastic Crime Unit (established April 2002 for an initial two-year experiment).

There has been ongoing reform of anti-laundering and crime proceeds legislation around the world (Gilmore 1999; Stessens 2000), 'responsibilising' (under threat of imprisonment and being banned from doing business) bankers and lawyers by requiring them to keep records, actively to look for 'suspicious' transactions and to report their suspicions to financial intelligence units (NCIS in the UK). There has been greater policing (including Customs and Excise) involvement in financial investigation, still mainly in the drugs field but increasingly in excise tax fraud and, post-11 September 2001, terrorism (Levi and Gilmore 2003). Laundering is the cleansing of funds so that they can be used in a way indistinguishable from legitimate money and in essence, bankers and lawyers have been forced to keep tight records and report their suspicions of their clients to central bodies (NCIS in the UK). If and when those official surveillance capabilities increase – as they did steadily during the 1990s, accelerating after the millennium and especially after 11 September – funds that were just hidden become vulnerable to enforcement intervention and perhaps confiscation (Levi 2002b).

There has developed an Egmont Group of Financial Investigation Units (FIUs) worldwide, whose aim (not always realised in practice) is to facilitate inter-FIU inquiries across borders, transforming the *potential* for intelligence-led policing (and disruption) of organised crime activity across borders. Criminal finance monitoring has been supplemented by attempts to cut down on 'people trafficking' and, despite human rights appeals to the European Court which have led to relaxation of the policy, lorry drivers have been fined heavily for carrying illegal migrants across the English Channel, even when there was no evidence that the drivers knew they had climbed on board through soft-sided canvas: this led large firms to introduce new technology for checking (by carbon dioxide levels) whether their trucks were stowaway-free. There has also been a focus on 'taking out' drugs manufacturers and distributors in countries of origin, rather than waiting till they were close to the shores of the UK or other European countries. Problematic issues related to informers (or, in the language of the Regulation of Investigatory Powers Act 2000, 'covert human intelligence sources') have also become more prominent, and failure to disclose participating informants has led to the collapse of several drugs trafficking and excise fraud cases, particularly (but not exclusively) those prosecuted by HM Customs and Excise.

The concept of 'cross-border' tends to mean different things in different contexts. Thus, those that have national police forces and/or that are concerned with crimes across national boundaries will see it in one way. In the UK it has tended to be seen within the traditional constabulary divisions and the typical orientation of sector policing towards the local rather than the national or international. The Phillips Report (1996) – set up by ACPO to look at police responses to cross-border crime – noted that 43 per cent of central squad work (drugs, fraud, vehicle, etc.) was cross-(force) border: of that figure, over a third of fraud work was undertaken internationally and under a third nationwide. Militating against such work, however, was management reluctance to commit resources to out-of-force investigations; knowledge about whom to contact in another force; incompatible equipment; and a lack of the necessary relevant intelligence. Since then, there has been a growing bifurcation between (1) the growing decentralisation of efforts at a neighbourhood level; and (2) the growing internationalisation of links with other countries by the NCIS and NCS, as well as in the policing and prosecution of fraud, to which we now turn.

Responses to fraud

Police policy and fraud in the UK

In 1946, the joint Metropolitan and City Police Company Fraud Department was set up to deal with deception risks for newly demobilised military personnel. Outside London, however, the establishment and maintenance of fraud squads has been episodic, depending largely on the interest of chief constables who get little external pressure to expand them compared with neighbourhood policing. Since the late 1990s, there has been an Economic Crime section of the Association of Chief Police Officers' Crime Committee. Despite this, senior police indifference extends to all crimes with corporate victims, and even to some crimes against investors (Levi 1987; Doig and Levi 2001; Levi and Pithouse forthcoming). In this respect, little has changed since the mid-1980s, though periodic booms in complex inquiries into mortgage frauds and local authority corruption have sometimes generated larger fraud squads. The explanation for this neglect is far from clear, but it appears to relate in part to some Victorian conception of prudence whereby everyone who does not take sufficient care of his or her own property deserves little sympathy. There are also a number of pragmatic factors, three of which are of key importance:

1. There has been little central or local political pressure on forces to do more about fraud (e.g. via key performance indicators or local indicators in policing plans).

2. The apparent low productivity of fraud squad staff in relation to standard police performance indicators, fraud being more labour intensive to investigate.

3. Chief officers' own relatively unsophisticated appreciation of the business world and the possible impact of fraud losses on the local and national economy.

By 1998, only one UK force was without a fraud squad (though some have subsequently merged their fraud investigators into a generic serious crimes squad). There are a number of fraud squads in specialist police forces (including the Ministry of Defence Police and British Transport Police) and in the UK Crown Dependencies (Guernsey, the Isle of Man and Jersey). Most fraud squads have very flat structures, headed by detective inspectors, and in 1998 there were only eight at the rank of superintendent or above (almost all of whom were also heads of other squads, such as major crime units, which included murder, major robbery, drugs, kidnapping and fraud work). Most squads have shrunk, though over a quarter increased in size in 1993–8, and their case acceptance criteria vary in different parts of the country and according to how busy they are, despite which over a third had no service-level agreements with divisions (Doig and Levi 2001).

Half the forces stated that fraud investigation was not specifically mentioned at all in force written policy. Only one mainland force – the City of London Police, whose area is largely financially and internationally focused – includes fraud within the published local policing plan which describes briefly the place of the Specialist Crime Department, responsible for fraud investigation, within the structure of the force and profiles the make-up of the 'City', linking fraud investigation to the business orientation of the area. The plan identifies preventing and detecting fraud as main priorities.

Observation over the past three decades indicates little evidence in the UK to support the notion advanced by Ericson and Haggerty (1997) that the police act as handmaidens and risk managers for the commercial sector. The main pressure for fraud policing comes from (1) the impact of globalisation on the demand for investigation in key financial services countries (e.g. to investigate bribes paid to foreign leaders); and (2) broadened share ownership, both direct and via stock market investments by pension funds, creates demand for regulation of abuses and investigations of 'failed' entrepreneurs (Levi and Pithouse forthcoming).

New public management and fraud policing

A number of changes – broadly summarised under the rubric of 'new public management' – have affected public services, including frauds and police responses to them, in the past 25 years. Under the Conservative government of 1979–97, 'Next Steps' agencies were expected to create the organisational context for cultural change towards private sector high-energy service values. These included the Benefits Agency (now JobCentre Plus), which deals with social security fraud investigation as well as service delivery, and the Revenue departments, which deal with tax fraud.

Out-sourcing of public sector contracts generated more corruption and public sector fraud inquiries for the police, but the stripping-out of middle ranks, the devolution of most policing responsibilities to divisions, the downsizing of headquarters staff and pressure on staffing complements of central squads were commonplace. Within this context of organisational change, several relevant reports and developments had implications for the policing of fraud. The Audit Commission (1993) suggested that 12 months was the minimum period before a detective was 'fully productive' in a fraud squad and that four years was the minimum tenure period (three months and one year was proposed for cheque fraud). These were to be allied to intelligence-led, proactive policing, though the relationship between this and low-rate, high-value sophisticated fraudsters (or, for that matter, organised crime investigations) was never properly considered at the time or subsequently. Secondly, Morgan *et al.* (1996) suggested that, while all forces had case review systems, they lacked any substantive evidence of performance measurement or management review by senior force management. They concluded that fraud squads should become regional, with smaller cases being handled directly by basic command units; and that the police should stop investigating frauds which do not directly harm the general public: larger frauds should be dealt with by businesses, where the latter were victims.

Developing fraud investigations

Except where offenders are linked to organised crime networks and groups, fraud investigations remain overwhelmingly reactive in character (see Chapter 15), though some are triggered by suspicious transaction reports from financial institutions in advance of any report from the public. The latter include investigations of Nigerian 'advance fee' frauds in which targets are offered (by mail or, increasingly, email) the 'opportunity' of helping the fraudster get (imaginary) billions of dollars out of the country that have been obtained by corruption. The ability to be proactive or to develop crime pattern analysis is hampered by the lack of resources and the length and complexity of referred work. Over a third of forces admitted that they performed reactive policing only, although one force stated that it would begin to undertake proactive functions following a pending review. Over a half of forces replied that they also undertook proactive investigations, although a significant minority of these indicated that this was only occasionally. Most forces had access to technical support, surveillance and computer staff but, for most, developing proactive police work was constrained by the same issues currently inhibiting more effective reactive policing. The greater the amount of interagency, inter-force and (especially) international work needed, the more resources are actually consumed.

While the larger forces are relatively well provided with specialist equipment, the majority are not, and the variety of, and variations in, software and hardware clearly militate against inter-force communication and co-operation (see Chapters 14 and 26). Indeed, when asked what would expedite fraud investigations, it was the issues of ease of inter-fraud squad communication, access to a national database, intelligence-led proactive policing and liaison between forces that figured most strongly.

Fraud policing may be usefully bifurcated into (1) high policing, represented by the work of the Serious Fraud Office (SFO) – discussed later – and (2) (relatively) low policing, represented by the regulation of plastic fraud with only a modest input from the police (Levi *et al.* 1991; Levi 2000; Levi and Handley 1998, 2002). At the 'low policing' end of the fraud spectrum, the pressure on diminishing fraud squad resources was increased by the rise in high-volume, low-cost fraud in the private sector during the 1980s in those industries who had traditionally seen fraud squads as responsible for dealing with the threats from 'white-collar' criminals, leading to a further loss of interest in the high-volume credit card crimes (and reduction of service to businesses relocating from London). This was understandable because reactive investigation was inhibited by poor forensics – customers could take away the signed receipt with their fingerprints on, or bank handling of cheques made data recovery difficult – while plastic fraudsters were not 'dangerous enough' either in terms of how crucial they were to organised crime groups/networks or in terms of committing high enough priority offences to interest force or national squads dealing with 'serious crime'. The rapid rise in plastic card fraud in the late 1980s and early 1990s encouraged an industry strategy which, under the auspices of the Association for Payment Clearing Services (APACS), led to a number of committees and initiatives to foster co-operation among financial services institutions that comprise their membership, producing a major drop in fraud levels (Levi and Handley 1998), even though plastic fraud subsequently more than doubled to £424.6 million in 2002 (Levi and Pithouse forthcoming). The Association of Chief Police Officers' (ACPO) response to the report of Levi et al. (1991) (and the heavy political interest that accompanied it) and to enhanced industry fraud prevention efforts was the introduction of a number of their own proposals: a consistent and co-ordinated approach to cheque and credit card fraud, central reference points in each force and the possibility of establishing dedicated squads. However in practice, the police response was patchy (Levi and Handley 2002), and business dissatisfaction with this led in April 2002 to their three quarters funding of a new Dedicated Cheque and Plastic Crime Unit (the Home Office paying one quarter) for an initial two-year period.[8]

Not only the private sector but also, internal corruption excepted, the public sector has largely taken its fraud inquiries out of police hands. There are some 9,000 non-police fraud investigators in the public sector, from the Department of Work and Pensions Fraud Investigation Service and Jobcentre Plus (with some 7–7,500), Inland Revenue, HM Customs and Excise, to the Charity Commissioners and local authorities (where up to 1,000 investigators deal primarily with Housing Benefit fraud). Further, a number of these agencies have both discrete legislation and their own prosecution capability which substantially mitigates the need to rely on the police, the Crown Prosecution Service or more generic legislation.

Mutual co-operation between police fraud squads

Of the 41 squads responding to the question on current cases involving work outside the force area (OFA), 15 replied that all their cases involved OFA work and only six reported that half their work or less was OFA (Doig and Levi 2001).[9] Only two forces replied that none of their *current* cases involved outside the UK, and a third had at least five current international cases. Although most forces allocate OFA cases among each other on an informal basis, forces can use (and 15 have used) agreed evaluation criteria for referral of cases from one force to another: these are based on points allocated according to the location of the crime, the suspects and the witnesses, and the force to which the crime was first reported. However, as with many forms of conflict, informal settlement is preferred.

There is also much 'partnership fraud policing': the agencies with whom police forces most commonly work are (in no particular order) the Department of Work and Pensions (DWP), HM Customs and Excise, the Department of Trade and Industry (DTI), Inland Revenue, the Serious Fraud Office and Trading Standards. Again, however, there is enormous variation in quality of joint work, and differences in objectives – especially in civil recovery or taking people off benefit versus criminal prosecution – bedevil such interagency work. The principal aims of the tax authorities and, in a different way because they are an expenditure body, the DWP are to maximise revenue: fraud investigation (and, a fortiori, prosecution) are very much subsidiary to this core purpose, by contrast with the police which is primarily a court-oriented, non-revenue-raising body. Additionally, there are issues of investigative timing, since the Inland Revenue and even Customs and Excise have longer time-frames than the police and DWP.

Prosecution and relationship to policing fraud

All the components of the criminal justice system are 'loose coupled' in the sense that they have an interactive relationship in which one part's expectations of what the others will do inform their own behaviour (though this can sometimes lead to deviance to achieve crime control goals). However the organisation of policing in fraud is especially difficult to separate out from the organisation of prosecution, since following the Fraud Trials Committee Report (Roskill 1986), the government took a conscious decision to violate the newly established principle of separating investigation and prosecution by setting up the Serious Fraud Office (SFO). It is crucial to understand the cultural differences that underlie the prosecution and regulation of different kinds of frauds. If and when reported to the police and accepted by them as crimes, credit frauds and most deceptions committed against individuals and businesses are dealt with by police and, where the evidence is sufficient, are prosecuted by the Crown Prosecution Service (CPS) in most cases or by the SFO where specialist accountancy and other skills are required, special powers may be needed, the sum at risk is estimated to be at least £1 million (normally) and the case is likely to give rise to national publicity and widespread public concern. These include cases involving government departments, public bodies, the governments of other countries and commercial cases of public interest.[10] It is important to keep this development in perspective: the SFO deals only with the top slice of non-revenue frauds, totalling about 100 cases annually (including those that may take several years to dispose of), and there are seldom more than ten SFO trials annually. So the vast proportion of fraud policing is prosecuted (if at all) by the CPS following police investigations that have minimal accounting or legal advice from outside the police.

As noted earlier, the SFO was set up by the Criminal Justice Act 1987 to pursue more effectively and quickly 'serious or complex fraud' in the aftermath of the Fraud Trials Committee (1986) chaired by Lord Roskill. The size of the SFO was determined by the Treasury, and Lord Roskill's intention (personal interviews 1986 and 1992) to include Customs, DTI and Inland Revenue investigations and prosecutions within it failed due to bureaucratic out-manoeuvring. The SFO is a government department, responsible to the Attorney General, staffed by lawyers, financial investigators, forensic account-ants and administrative support personnel. It is not part of the police service but police officers are provided 'on loan' to the SFO at the discretion of their chief constables or commissioners, in theory according to a memorandum of understanding agreed between the SFO Director and ACPO. Police officers are needed to execute search warrants in order to enter premises to seize evidence; to make arrests and to charge suspects; and to monitor compliance with bail conditions. The police also conduct interviews (other than those under s. 2 of the Criminal Justice Act 1987 in which there is no right to silence). Policing priorities may mean that the SFO is not always able to count on as many policing resources as it would like to have, and resource conflicts sometimes mean that officers (for example, from the Metropolitan Police) prefer to work from their own offices rather than from those of the SFO. In 2003, the SFO planned move to new offices where they would be co-located with part of the City of London police fraud squad, who retained a strong, dedicated fraud resource.

In 2001–2, the SFO worked with over 30 police forces in the UK, including one case in April 2002 when a combined team of over 200 police officers (mainly from the NCS, Metropolitan and Strathclyde Police) and SFO staff was put together to mount a series of evidential searches during the course of one day at 27 premises throughout mainland UK (SFO 2002) (see Table 18.1).

Notwithstanding bodies such as the SFO, an unintended effect of policing policy and the practice of requiring firm proof of fraud before accepting cases was to shift the economic burden of crime investigation on to victims, in particular corporate victims, thus transferring public law back into the sphere of private law. At the high end of the fraud-policing spectrum, there has been some tension between some fraud squads and the SFO over what some police see as the 'cost (in)effective' deployment of resources and whether the SFO in-house lawyers who act as case controllers are the best judges of how to manage cases (Levi 1993), while police 'Authorised Investigator' schemes in

Table 18.1 The origins of Serious Fraud Office cases

	1999–2000	2000–1	2001–2
Police	41	40	40
Department of Trade and Industry	14	9	11
Arising from existing SFO cases	3	2	6
Crown Prosecution Service	2	4	2
Financial Services Authority (or predecessor bodies)	1	2	4
Occupational Pensions Regulatory Authority	—	2	2
Office of the Supervision of Solicitors	—	1	1
Foreign authorities	—	2	0
Other	20	8	9
Total	81	70	75

the late 1990s to license private investigators (at victims' own expense) and to conduct fraud inquiries 'in collaboration' with the police had very limited success (Levi and Pithouse forthcoming). One of the advantages of reporting a case to the SFO is that better access to specialist accountancy and forensic investigation is available than from cash-strapped forces or from the CPS. A memorandum of understanding in principle describes what gets reported to the SFO; the relative roles and responsibilities in each case (and a clear recording system and an arbitration procedure in case of dispute); case review; and line management responsibility for staff. At present the police pay for the time of their own staff, the costs of gathering evidence and looking after exhibits. The SFO pay for their staff, ICT costs and the costs associated with a case once it is in court.

By contrast with the police and the CPS/SFO, the non-police agencies – principally the DWP, Customs and Excise, DTI, Inland Revenue and local-authority trading standards officers – that deal with frauds appropriate to their function prosecute only as a last resort or for strategic reasons such as the desire to generate greater publicity or to generate revenue or enhance deterrence. The closest to routine prosecution-mindedness is the DWP (though even they prosecute in only a minority of cases identified), but income tax and value-added tax frauds typically are dealt with by financial penalties rather than prosecution, while trading standards officers (who deal with counterfeit goods and other consumer issues) prefer advice and warning to traders, and also are constrained by their lack of resources, which means that every time they prosecute, they tie up resources that could be used in investigation.

The DTI, the Financial Services Authority (created under the Financial Services and Markets Act 2000, which has responsibility for deciding whether or not those who conduct investment business are 'fit and proper' and for disciplining rule-breakers), the SFO, HM Customs and Excise and the Inland Revenue are involved in the exercise of substantial state power. (The fact that such powers seldom lead to prosecution does not mean that they are not employed or are not important to those against whom they are exercised.) Under s. 2 of the Criminal Justice Act 1987, when authorised by the Director of the SFO, and without the need to go to court, legal and accountancy and *non*-police investigative staff at the SFO are given power to require anyone believed to be connected with a serious fraud case to attend – instantly if the SFO wishes – to produce documents and/or to answer questions. There is no right to silence even for potential defendants, though admissions by the accused under compulsory questioning are not admissible in evidence against them. The use of these powers of compulsory disclosure has increased considerably, partly reflecting the heavy involvement in major corporate manipulations of professional people with obligations of confidentiality who seek the protection of compulsion under law to allow them to talk – what the SFO refers to as 'willing recipients' – and partly reflecting increased flexing of regulatory muscles. In the period 1988–2002, the number of s. 2 notices issued by the SFO rose from 233 to 1,055 for UK institutions and people, plus another 262 on behalf of overseas authorities, which international co-operation was largely unknown in the late 1980s.

The future of fraud investigation

A number of fraud squads consider that the first stage to improve the efficiency and effectiveness of fraud investigations is access to information and intelligence on a regional or inter-force basis. Neither NCIS – which is concerned solely with those people identified as a serious threat, the criteria for which exclude specialist fraudsters other than those involved in major smuggling excise evasion – nor the NCS displays any significant interest in most fraudsters, and the SFO does not have a brief to deal with most of the fraud cases that come to fraud squads, let alone those that come (or would come if they were willing to take them) to divisional CID. A substantial gap is left in the service offered to fraud victims, which is hardly unique in contemporary policing but is seldom the result of explicit policy analysis or reviews of either harms or clear-up possibilities. There are many things victims with resources can and will do through the civil sphere, including asset-freezing injunctions and search orders to freeze assets and require entry (though usually accompanied by a police officer), but though there may be some regional consolidation, there seems little chance of any substantial rise in police resources outside the City of London area. The experimental Dedicated Cheque and Plastic Crime Unit is an intriguing example of public–private partnership policing, but there is limited private sector willingness to pay for public policing in addition to their taxes.

Regulatory, disruption and non-criminal justice approaches to serious crime control

Regulation and the control of fraud

Finally, we have the different mode of controlling financial abuses, namely, the regulation of financial services and, less rigorously, though the DTI can apply to the court to have a company wound up 'in the public interest', other companies. Within the financial sector and in professional organisations, regulators such as the Financial Services Authority (FSA), the Law Society and the varied accountancy bodies have extensive powers to vet the moral suitability and competence of potential employees ('fit and proper person' tests) – which criteria may vary depending on the level of employment, say, at bank-director level – and to discipline both individuals and firms, including financial penalties. The FSA can also prosecute in the criminal courts for market abuse offences under the Financial Services and Markets Act 2000 (see, further, Croall 2003; Levi and Pithouse forthcoming). On the other hand, in the volume fraud arena, the preventative work is done by the industry themselves, with only very modest input from the police and none from the FSA, while industrial firms have to rely on business credit checks, private security vetting, more limited industrial security networks and their own judgement for preventative purposes. Some of these commercial security networks are transnational, as are payment card schemes such as American Express, MasterCard and Visa. Regulators, too, link up in membership of the International Organization of Securities Commissions and Bank for International Settlements.

Thus, an overall picture of the different public sector groups involved in consumer advice or protection, regulation or investigation of fraud would include those groups shown in Box 18.1.

Box 18.1 UK professional and public sector groups involved in fraud advice, prosecution and regulation

---

Civil Aviation Authority (CAA)
The Civil Aviation Authority operates the Air Travel Organisers' Licensing (ATOL) scheme. Most firms selling air travel and holidays are required by law to hold an ATOL, which protects consumers from losing money or being stranded abroad, should the firm go bust. The CAA also deals with inquiries from the public about air travel firms that do not hold ATOLs in order to ensure consumers are protected (for more information, see www.caa.co.uk).

Crown Prosecution Service (CPS)
The CPS is the government department which prosecutes people in England and Wales who have been charged by the police with a criminal offence (for more information, see www.cps.gov.uk).

Financial Services Authority (FSA)
The FSA has powers to investigate in the financial sector and to prosecute, under the Financial Services and Markets Act 2000 (for more information, see www.FSA.gov.uk).

Insolvency Practitioners Association
This body aims to promote a better understanding of insolvency administration. The association regulates and monitors its members' practices and works to maintain and improve the conduct and standards of performance of insolvency practitioners and their staff (for more information, see www.ipa.uk.com).

Insolvency Service
The Insolvency Service administers and investigates the affairs of bankrupts and companies in compulsory liquidation and has a duty to establish the reasons for the insolvency and to report misconduct (for more information, see www.insolvency.gov.uk).

LACOTS
LACOTS – the Local Authorities Co-ordinating Body on Food and Trading Standards – was set up in 1978 by the local authority associations in England, Scotland and Northern Ireland to improve the quality of local authority regulation by promoting consistency and the co-ordination of enforcement. In addition to developing operational guidance, advice and information for local regulatory authorities, LACOTS provides technical input to legislative proposals. Partnership arrangements operate within central government, trade and consumer organisations as well as enforcement agencies throughout the European Community (for more information, see www.lacots.org.uk).

The Law Society
The Law Society is the professional body for solicitors in England and Wales. Complaints about solicitors are dealt with by the Office for the Supervision of Solicitors (for more information, see www.lawsociety.org.uk). Scotland and Northern Ireland have their own governing bodies.

Box 18.1   *Continued*

LIFFE

LIFFE is a recognised investment exchange under the terms of the UK Financial Services Act 1986 and as such it is required to operate its markets with due regard to the protection of investors and to ensure that trading is conducted in an orderly and fair manner. The exchange monitors and enforces compliance with its rules and co-operates with other regulatory bodies and seeks to promote and maintain high standards of integrity (for more information, see www.liffe.com).

Local authorities

Local authorities employ trading standards officers who are responsible for the enforcement of consumer protection legislation and the investigation of complaints about goods and services. They will prosecute where necessary (for more information, see www.tradingstandards.gov.uk).

London Team Against Fraud (LTAF)

LTAF is a non-profit organisation which does not investigate fraud but collates information and assists in sharing information via a multi-agency network (for more information, see www.ltaf.org.uk).

Ministry of Defence Police (MDP)

This force is a fully constituted police force acting under the Ministry of Defence Police Act 1987. It provides civil policing across the MoD and operates independently of political or departmental influence in the maintenance and operation of the law. Its jurisdiction includes all those organisations and individuals with whom the MoD does business (for more information, see www.mod.uk/mdp/fraud.htm#fraud).

Office of Fair Trading

While not an investigatory body, the Office of Fair Trading is interested in receiving information regarding the conduct of companies and individuals holding consumer credit licences (for more information, see www.oft.gov.uk). The Enterprise Act 2002 substantially changed the legal powers and environment for competition enforcement.

OPRA

OPRA was set up by Parliament in the aftermath of the Maxwell pension fund frauds to help make sure that occupational pension schemes are safe and well run. Under the Pensions Act 1995, OPRA investigates and takes action where there is carelessness or negligence that could put occupational pension schemes at risk (for more information, see www.opra.gov.uk).

OTE (Organisation for Timeshare in Europe)

Formerly known as the Timeshare Council, OTE is the official trade association for the timeshare industry in Europe, representing companies and organisations with legitimate interests in the industry. All OTE members abide by OTE's code of ethics, ensuring that consumers' rights are protected. It also offers a free conciliation service for members' related queries and general advice about timeshare (for more information, see www.ote-info.com).

Police forces

Individual police fraud departments investigate fraud, theft and other apparent offences committed in their areas.

Box 18.1 *Continued*

The Serious Fraud Office
The SFO has powers (under the Criminal Justice Act 1987) to investigate and prosecute any case of suspected serious and complex fraud (for more information, see www.sfo.gov.uk).

The Society of Lloyd's
The FSA oversees Lloyd's regulation to ensure consistency with general standards in financial services. In practical terms, however, in order to avoid unnecessary duplication, the FSA delegates a substantial part of its regulatory activity to the Council of Lloyd's and focuses on a supervisory role. The Council of Lloyd's is the governing body of the society, under the Lloyd's Act 1982. Day-to-day supervision of the market is undertaken by the Risk Management Division of the Corporation of Lloyd's (for further information, see www.lloyds.com).

Regulation and the prevention of organised crime

Prevention has long been the primary focus in financial services frauds but, in recent years, there has been a shift in interest towards it in organised crime. One important aspect of this is the use of powers in the financial and tax areas, where in essence the focus of the attack is upon the financial assets of organised criminals rather than on criminal prosecution as such. Banks, building societies and the professions have been required to report clients and customers whom they subjectively suspect and, increasingly, have reasonable cause to suspect of serious crime (both frauds and trafficking in drugs and people). The use of tax prosecutions against 'organised criminals' and, for that matter, against wealthy individuals and corporations suspected of dishonestly evading large sums from the proceeds of otherwise legal activities, varies in Europe. For financial prevention, most countries rely on post-conviction confiscation, often with a provision that after conviction, defendants must justify the legitimate origin of their assets if they are to avoid their confiscation (Levi 2001). Thus, in the Irish Republic (Criminal Assets Bureau Act 1996) and the UK (Proceeds of Crime Act 2002), as well as in the USA, South Africa and Australia, *civil* law means and standards of proof are used to 'recover' for the state the assets deemed to be derived from crime, *irrespective of whether or not anyone is ever convicted or even prosecuted for those crimes*. The aim here is to undermine both the motivation of criminals to become 'top organisers' and their resources to be able to do so. This can be reinforced by extended powers to confiscate large cash sums inland that do not have a legitimate explanation, as contained in the Proceeds of Crime Act 2002.

A second, rather different, aspect is the use of the regulatory powers of local authorities, environmental and licensing agencies and the like, to disrupt the 'businesses' of organised criminals by making it more difficult for them to obtain necessary licences, find suitable premises and so on. This can be seen in experiments in the Wallen 'red light' district of Amsterdam, where tight controls are exercised over property ownership, with intensive reviews of intending and existing owners and their associates to 'keep organised crime out' (Levi and Maguire forthcoming). Since 1970, civil injunctions have been used under US Federal and State Racketeer-Influenced and Corrupt Organizations (RICO) laws to place corrupt unions and businesses under court-approved management, and quite apart from high-profile arrests that may accompany the civil measures, this appears to have had an impact on this highly visible form of structured organised crime, measured for example by garbage disposal and fish-market prices (Jacobs 1999; Levi and Smith 2002), though there is less evidence of impact on other crime phenomena. Where otherwise legitimate businesses that would be profitable without crime engage in systematic patterns of crime facilitation, there seems no reason in principle why they should not be placed under public interest management or even forfeited as instrumentalities of crime, providing that proportionality under the European Convention is satisfied.

The prevention of organised and financial crime

Where data are good, as they are in payment card fraud, some impact of preventative measures can be discerned (Levi and Handley 1998, 2002), though it remains difficult to attribute any measurable effects to police activity per se. However the impact of anti-organised crime measures on *outcomes* remains insufficiently analysed, since there are few reliable data on the 'before' or 'after' levels or organisation of drugs and people trafficking, EU fraud, etc. (Reuter and Kleiman 1986; Black *et al.* 2000; Naylor 2002; Levi and Maguire forthcoming). For example, the law enforcement agencies in EU and Council of Europe member countries are required to return annual counts of the number of organised crime groups but, quite apart from quality-monitoring issues, it is not obvious whether a reduction in the number is a good thing (less harm has been caused or there is a lesser threat to society) or is a bad thing (it is an indicator of monopoly or oligopoly rather than of looser networking, and therefore a *greater* threat to society).

Some approximations for illicit use can be made from self-report studies or from sophisticated techniques for estimating prevalence, but these do not explain or enable inferences to be made about how offending is *organised*. Very few financial institutions, even in offshore finance centres, will now accept strangers or even established clients bringing in briefcases full of cash. However, there is no evidence that fewer drugs or trafficked women and children have become available as a result of the sorts of measures discussed above (which is not to say there has been no effect). In the private sector sphere, industry and public sector fraud data suggest some impact from data matching and from the co-ordination of data at an industry-wide level (Levi and Handley, 1998; Levi and Pithouse forthcoming), but other forms of fraud data are too poor to permit easy inferences.

Irrespective of whether or not 'organised crime' will truly threaten the state – and it is important to think about how one would recognise that condition if one came to it – one can and should try to anticipate shifts in serious crime activities (Williams and Godson 2002). One may also try to develop strategies to reduce market opportunities for 'hot products' (Clarke 1999) and disruption mechanisms for criminal markets by breaking up the prerequisites of serious crime for gain into their constituent parts (Ekblom 2000; and see Hicks 1998 for an attempt to examine links between local communities, police and organised crime prevention). Sutton *et al.* (2001) suggest that in both commercial fence supplies and commercial sales markets, investigative and preventive efforts should focus on thieves and purchasers of stolen goods – because here there are no 'innocent' consumers. Attention should be paid to business people who buy stolen goods so that the 'crime facilitators' and the thieves who supply them will need to invest more effort and face greater risks if they want to convert stolen property into cash. This might involve identifying through systematic analysis which shops and businesses thieves visit in order to sell stolen goods; requiring traders to obtain proof of identity from and to keep records of anyone who sells them second-hand goods (and checking covertly whether or not they do so); and using administrative measures as well as criminal prosecutions to control misconduct. The police might use mobile CCTV cameras and surveillance teams to gather evidence by observing the homes of known or suspected residential fences; and might seek to close down bars and other places used for trading in stolen goods as well as drugs.

Despite exhortations to shift practices towards crime reduction in the UK, it is not always obvious how much policing has changed (see Chapter 12): there has been little general police or investigative judge support for radical shifts in staff to financial investigation from equally prized and media-supported areas of crime and disorder. But to supplement traditional law enforcement, alternative problem-solving approaches to complex social issues are being explored. For example, the strong recent focus on trafficking in women (Kelly and Regan 2000; Richard 2000; Vocks and Nijboer 2000; Aronowitz 2001) may cause us to think about better co-ordination between immigration and policing to encourage exploited sex workers to complain and give evidence rather than simply deporting them and, by 2003, this had begun to happen. The measurement of changes in organised crime and the assessment of whether these are beneficial or not are in their infancy, but it seems worth while to think of different strategies such as building in fraud and other technological prevention measures at the point of production and distribution, rather than waiting for crime to grow and then trying to police it. Whether the policing panopticon will ever extend to encompass all types of fraud, however, is extremely unlikely, for despite the growth in public concern about their direct and indirect (via pension funds, etc.) investments in the stock markets and about identity theft and other crime risks associated with the cyberworld, the iconography of fear of crime is more difficult to develop and sustain for 'white-collar' than for 'organised' crime.

Selected further reading

There is no text that adequately captures the policing of both fraud and organised crime. For a general discussion of the nature of organised crime and reactions to it, see Levi's 'The organisation of serious crimes' (2002). For wider approaches to research and transnational policing, see also Edwards and Gill's *Transnational Organised Crime* (2003) and Sheptycki's *Issues in Transnational Policing* (2000). For a deeply sceptical critique of the role that law enforcement *could* play in dealing with 'market offences' such as drugs, see Naylor's *Wages of Crime* (2002). For a good overall review of the control of white-collar crime, see Croall's *Understanding White-collar Crime* (2001). Changes in the regulation and trial of commercial fraud are discussed in the special issue of the *Journal of Financial Crime* (July 2003) (especially articles by Croall, Huber (on Germany) and Levi). Otherwise, there is Fooks' 'In the Kingdom of the Blind the one-eyed man is king: corporate crime and the myopia of financial regulation' (2003).

Notes

1 Analytically, both these trades are artefacts of criminalisation in the sense that if no artificial constraints were placed on demand, there would be no need for illegal businesses (Naylor 2002; for a more general discussion of organised crime, see Levi 2002a). However, though true, a similar argument could be made about property rights generally so it is not as profound a point as is often claimed.

2 Though there is a statistical inflation from treating all deceptions as to 'who we are' as 'identity theft' (see www.cifas.org.uk for some data on increased identity fraud).

3 I make this distinction because employees' risks of assault on the way to and from work is not their employer's legal responsibility. The extent of the duty of care is not always obvious where – as in the case of the police – the occupation is inherently dangerous and is known by employees to be so at the point of employment contracts. However there is always an obligation on the employer to take reasonable care.

4 Contrast with normal American approaches to violent crime the fact that of some 200,000 workplace deaths since the creation of the US Federal Occupational Safety and Health Administration in 1972, the administration has referred just 151 cases to the Justice Department. Federal prosecutors declined to act on more than half of those referrals; 11 people have been sentenced to prison (*The New York Times* 10 January 2003). For more extended discussion of workplace violence in the context of ordinary violent crime, see Levi with Maguire (2002). The separate report on enforcement and prosecutions (http://www.hse.gov.uk/action/content/off01-02.pdf) states: '4.10 It is HSE policy to investigate all work-related deaths which are reported to us unless there are good reasons for not doing so, in which case those reasons will be recorded. In the last three years the average fine in cases following a death has been between about £20,000 and £30,000. Last year's average was £32,700, about two thirds higher than the averages for the previous couple of years'.

Later, discussing relations to the mainstream prosecution system, the report notes: '5.16 During 2001/2002, the police referred 43 cases of work-related death to the CPS, in sectors where HSE is the health and safety enforcing authority, to consider possible manslaughter charges. The CPS have so far started prosecutions for manslaughter in 5 of these cases. Since April 1992, a total of 224 possible manslaughter cases have been referred to the CPS. The CPS have brought prosecutions for manslaughter in 55 cases, 11 of which have resulted in convictions. Only 8 directors have been disqualified for conduct in relation to health and safety offences since the Company Directors Disqualification Act 1986.' All individual and corporate offenders prosecuted are logged on a publicly available database' (http://www.hse-databases.co.uk/prosecutions/case).

5 The point at which financial services firms accused of 'mis-selling' by what is now the Financial Services Authority become defined as 'fraudsters' is intriguing, but it

may be that this is the most sensible way of getting them to compensate clients so long as they have the capacity to do so (see Levi and Pithouse forthcoming).

6   Level 1 covers local issues, including the whole range of categories and levels of crime, notably volume crime; level 2 covers cross-border issues, where crime issues cross jurisdictional borders and where intelligence needs to be shared across borders to address them; and level 3 covers serious and organised crime operating on a national or international scale.

7   In a small island economy, an entrepreneur can exercise almost total domination, through charisma, corruption or prospective economic damage should he or she withdraw. Where leading politicians personally have a large (declared or unde-clared) stake in the interests affected, the difficulties of engineering change are most acute. In such cases, there may have to be incapacitation at the international level, as in the economic sanctions imposed by the USA in their kingpins and other legislation which makes it an offence to transact business for particular individuals or even nation-states such as Iraq or Libya.

8   An NCS press release in June 2002 stated that over the past four years 'the Squad has fine-tuned its ability to tackle the top tier of criminality. Success in dismantling organised crime networks – whether trading in Class A drugs, human trafficking or hi-tech criminality – result from a highly focused, professional approach and joint working with partner agencies to fight serious and organised crime.

The underlying theme has been that of continuing to target a higher and more sophisticated level of criminality than had been possible under the previous Regional Crime Squad system. In its first public report on the work of the Squad, HM Inspectorate of Constabulary found the organisation to be efficient and effective with clear development plans. During the first four years (1 April 1998 to 31 March 2002) of operations the National Crime Squad has achieved results including; Arrests – 3,697 suspects arrested. Of those, 163 were the alleged kingpins of organised crime believed to be at the heart of major criminal conspiracies. Disruption of criminal organisations – 1,062 criminal organisations, including 821 drug trafficking gangs, have been disrupted or dismantled. Drugs – Drugs with a total potential street value of £695 million (including £443 million of cocaine, heroin and ecstasy), weighing over 85,000 kilos, were seized. Assets confiscation – Over £104 million of illegally gained assets, in respect of convicted criminals, have been traced and identified to the courts for confiscation. Operations – Almost 1,300 operations, over 70% drug related, have been undertaken solely by the Squad and an increasing number have been carried out jointly with HM Customs & Excise, police forces and other agencies. Support to forces – More than 242,000 hours of officers' time has been given to police forces on 700 other operations'.

9   Interviews with participants: the author is leading a Morgan Harris Burrows evaluation team for this experimental public–private policing project.

10 There is a distinction between 'the public interest' and 'what interests the public'.

References

Alldridge, P. (2003) *Proceeds of Crime*. Oxford: Hart.

Arlacchi, P. (1986) *Mafia Business: The Mafia Ethic and the Spirit of Capitalism*. London: Verso.

Arlacchi, P. (1998) 'Some observations on illegal markets', in V. Ruggiero *et al.* (eds) *The New European Criminology*. London: Routledge.

Aronowitz, A. (2001) 'Smuggling and trafficking in human beings: the phenomenon, the markets that drive it and the organisations that promote it', *European Journal on Criminal Policy and Research*, 9(2): 163–95.

Audit Commission (1993) *Helping with Enquiries: Tackling Crime Effectively*. London: HMSO.

Berdal, M. and Serrano, M. (eds) (2002) *Transnational Organized Crime: New Challenges to International Security.* Boulder, CO: Lynne Rienner.

Black, C., van der Beken, T. and de Ruyver, B. (2000) *Measuring Organised Crime in Belgium.* Antwerp: Maklu.

Clarke, R. (1999) *Hot Products.* London: Home Office.

Croall, H. (2001) *Understanding White-collar Crime* (2nd edn). Milton Keynes: Open University Press.

Croall, H. (2003) 'Combating financial crime: regulatory versus crime control approaches', *Journal of Financial Crime*, 11(1): 45–55.

Doig, A. and Levi, M. (2001) 'New public management, old populism and the policing of fraud', *Public Policy and Administration*, 16(1): 91–113.

Edwards, A. and Gill, P. (eds) *Transnational Organised Crime: The Policy and Politics of the Global Crime Problem.* London: Routledge.

Ekblom, P. (2000) 'Preventing organised crime: a conceptual framework'. Paper presented at the Europol workshop on organised crime, The Hague, May (available from the author).

Ericson, R. and Haggerty, K. (1997) *Policing the Risk Society.* Oxford: Clarendon Press, 450.

Fooks, G. (2003) 'In the Kingdom of the Blind the one-eyed man is king: corporate crime and the myopia of financial regulation', in S. Tombs and D. Whyte (eds) *Researching the Powerful: Scrutinizing States and Corporations.* New York, NY: Peter Lang.

Gambetta, D. (1994) *The Sicilian Mafia.* Cambridge, MA: Harvard University Press.

Gilmore, W. (1999) *Dirty Money: The Evolution of Money Laundering Counter-measures* (2nd edn). Strasbourg: Council of Europe Publishing.

Hicks, D.C. (1998) 'Thinking about organized crime prevention', *Journal of Contemporary Criminal Justice*, 14(4): 325–51.

Hobbs, D. (1997) 'Criminal collaboration' in M. Maguire *et al.* (eds) *The Oxford Handbook of Criminology* (2nd edn). Oxford: Oxford University Press.

Hobbs, D. (1998) 'Going down the glocal: the local context of organised crime', *The Howard Journal of Criminal Justice*, (37)4: 407–22.

HSC (2002) Annual Report 2001–2002, Health and Safety Commission, London: 446.

Jacobs, J. (1999) *Gotham Unbound.* New York, NY: New York University Press.

Jamieson, A. (2000) *The AntiMafia: Italy's Fight against Organized Crime.* London: Macmillan.

Kelly, L. and Regan, L. (2000) *Stopping Traffic: Exploring the Extent of, and Responses to, Trafficking in Women for Sexual Exploitation in the UK. Police Research Series Paper* 125. London: Home Office.

Killick, M. (1998) *Fraudbusters.* London: Gollancz.

Levi, M. (1981) *The Phantom Capitalists: The Organisation and Control of Long-term Fraud.* Aldershot: Gower.

Levi, M. (1993) *The Investigation, Prosecution, and Trial of Serious Fraud. Royal Commission on Criminal Justice Research Study* 14. London: HMSO.

Levi, M. (1995) 'Covert policing and the investigation of "organized fraud": the English experience in international context', in C. Fijnaut and G. Marx (eds) *Police Surveillance in Comparative Perspective.* The Hague: Kluwer, 195–212.

Levi, M. (1998) 'Organising plastic fraud: enterprise criminals and the side-stepping of fraud prevention', *The Howard Journal of Criminal Justice*, 37(4): 423–38.

Levi, M. (1999) 'Regulating fraud revisited', in P. Davies *et al.* (Eds) *Invisible Crimes.* Basingstoke: Macmillan.

Levi, M. (2000) *Reversal of the Burden of Proof in Confiscation of the Proceeds of Crime: A Council of Europe Best Practice Survey.* Strasbourg: Council of Europe.

Levi, M. (2002a) 'The organisation of serious crimes', in M. Maguire *et al.* (eds) *The Oxford Handbook of Criminology* (3rd edn). Oxford: Oxford University Press, 878–913.

Levi, M. (2002b) 'Money laundering and its regulation', *Annals of the American Academy of Social and Political Science*, 582: 181–94.

Levi, M., Bissell, P. and Richardson, T. (1991) *The Prevention of Cheque and Credit Card Fraud. Crime Prevention Unit Paper* 26. London: Home Office.

Levi, M. and Gilmore, W. (2003) 'Terrorist finance, money laundering and the rise and rise of mutual evaluation: a new paradigm for crime control?', *European Journal of Law Reform*, 4(2): 337–64.

Levi, M. and Handley, J. (1998) *The Prevention of Plastic and Cheque Fraud Revisited. Home Office Research Study* 184. London: Home Office.

Levi, M. and Handley, J. (2002) *Criminal Justice and the Future of Payment Card Fraud.* London: Institute for Public Policy Research.

Levi, M. with Maguire, M. (2002) 'Violent crime', in M. Maguire et al. (eds) *The Oxford Handbook of Criminology* (3rd edn). Oxford: Oxford University Press, 795–843.

Levi, M. and Maguire, M. (forthcoming) 'Organised crime prevention: conceptual difficulties and practical potential', *Crime, Law and Social Change* (special issue).

Levi, M. and Osofsky, L. (1995) *Investigating, Seizing and Confiscating the Proceeds of Crime. Police Research Group Paper* 61. London: Home Office.

Levi, M. (1987) *Regulated Fraud*, London: Routledge, 450.

Levi, M. and Pithouse, A. (forthcoming) *White-collar Crime and its Victims.* Oxford: Clarendon Press.

Levi, M. and Smith, A. (2002) *A Comparative Analysis of Organised Crime Conspiracy Legislation and Practice and their Relevance to England and Wales. Online Report* 17/02, London: Home Office.

Morgan, J., McCulloch, L. and Burrows, J. (1996) *Central Specialist Squads: A Framework for Monitoring and Evaluation. Police Research Series Paper* 17. London: Home Office.

Naylor, R. (2002) *Wages of Crime: Black Markets, Illegal Finance, and the Underworld Economy.* Ithaca, NY: Cornell University Press.

NCIS (2002) *UK Threat Assessment, 2002.* London: National Criminal Intelligence Service.

Nelken, D. (2002) 'White-collar crime', in M. Maguire *et al.* (eds) *The Oxford Handbook of Criminology* (3rd edn). Oxford: Oxford University Press, 844–77.

Paoli, L. (2002) 'The paradoxes of organized crime', *Crime, Law and Social Change*, 37: 51–97.

PIU (2000) *Recovering the Proceeds of Crime.* London: Cabinet Office Performance and Innovation Unit.

Reuter, P. and Kleiman, M. (1986) 'Risks and prices: an economic analysis of drug enforcement', in M. Tonry and N. Morris (eds) *Crime and Justice: A Review of Research.* Vol. 7. Chicago, IL: Chicago University Press.

Richard, A. (2000) *International Trafficking in Women to the United States: A Contemporary Manifestation of Slavery and Organized Crime.* Washington, DC: US Central Intelligence Agency.

Roskill, Lord (1986) *Report of the Fraud Trials Committee.* London: HMSO.

SFO (2002) Annual Report 2001–2, Serious Fraud Office, London: 461.

Sheptycki, J. (2000) (ed.) *Issues in Transnational Policing.* London: Routledge.

Stessens, G. (2000) *Money Laundering: An International Enforcement Model.* Cambridge: Cambridge University Press.

Stille, A. (1996) *Excellent Cadavers.* London: Vintage.

Sutton, M., Schneider, J. and Hetherington, S. (2001) *Tackling Theft with the Market Reduction Approach.* London: Home Office.

van Duyne, P. (1996), 'The phantom and threat of organised crime', *Crime, Law and Social Change*, 24: 341–77.

Vocks, J. and Nijboer, J. (2000) 'The promised land: a study of trafficking in women from central and eastern Europe to the Netherlands', *European Journal on Criminal Policy and Research*, 8(3): 379–88.

Williams, P. and Godson, R. (2002) 'Anticipating organized and transnational crime', *Crime, Law and Social Change*, 37(4): 311–55.

Chapter 19

Policing and terrorism

Mario Matassa and Tim Newburn

Introduction

In popular fiction and the public imagination the 'policing' of terrorism is often seen as being 'synonymous with espionage and skullduggery, with the sexual blackmail of a Mata Hari and the cloak-and-dagger exploits of a James Bond' (Shulsky and Schmitt 2002: 1). Views of the unusual nature of such activities are reinforced by images of specialist military units, such as the camouflaged SAS storming the Iranian embassy to rescue hostages held captive by hooded terrorists. Political rhetoric about the 'war on terrorism' further cements such views in the public mind. In reality, however, much terrorist activity is regarded by the state as a form of criminal behaviour and consequently a matter for the state's agencies of law and order – the police and the criminal justice system. Moreover, as we shall argue, much of this policing activity employs traditional policing tactics and powers – though abuse of such powers has been a continuing concern. These policing responses, the context in which they are to be understood and how they should be regulated, form the primary focus here.

What is terrorism?

Terrorism is not unique to the modern era. Though the terms 'terrorism' and 'terrorist' are relatively new, dating back two centuries to 1798 (Laqueur 1987), and there is a tendency to think of terrorism as a 'new mode of conflict' (Jenkins 1974), the use of 'terror' to achieve political ends has a far longer history. Modern-day terrorism, which dates back to the 1960s (Shafritz *et al.* 1991: xi), is a product both of historical and wider technological, social and political changes.

Prior to the 1960s most terrorist activity was localised, either confined within specific geographic jurisdictions or limited to certain regions as a consequence of cross-border intrusions. Rapid advances in transportation and communication technology brought about a shift in the nature and scale of the terrorist threat. Some commentators have suggested that such advances heralded a new form of terrorism – non-territorial terrorism (Sloan 1978), particularly in the wake of the 1967 Arab–Israeli conflict and reprisal attacks perpetrated against Israeli targets in foreign states – though, arguably, the fundamental logic of terrorism remained unaltered. The seizure of 53 American hostages at the US Embassy in Tehran in November 1979 opened a further chapter in the history of terrorism with the use of 'armed diplomacy' by so-called rogue states as an instrument of foreign policy (Sloan 1982: 23), and forms of 'state-sponsored' terrorism which continue today (see Cabinet Office 2002).

It has become customary to begin any analysis of the concept of terrorism with an attempt to define the nature of the subject matter. Doing so is problematic: 'any definition of political terrorism venturing beyond noting the systematic use of murder, injury, and destruction or the threats of such acts towards achieving political ends [being] bound to lead to endless controversies' (Laquer 1987: 72).

Most definitions of terrorism make reference to political intent and means and, for the purposes of this chapter, the definition from s. 1 of the Terrorism Act 2000 suffices. Stated crudely, it includes actual or threatened acts of violence against people and/or property designed to influence the government, to intimidate the public or a section of the public, or to advance a political, religious or ideological cause.

Terrorism in the UK

The Troubles

Until recently, for the police and security services in the UK, the major anti-terrorist activity has been as a result of the Troubles in Northern Ireland since 1969. Indeed, taking a longer perspective, it is possible to suggest that terrorism in Northern Ireland has been a strategic driver for developments in policing on the mainland since at least the introduction of the new police in the early nineteenth century. Since 1969 over 3,000 people have died because of political violence in Northern Ireland, and the conflict has affected people far beyond the borders of the region, leading to the deaths of approximately 200 people in Great Britain, the Republic of Ireland and elsewhere in Europe (O'Leary and McGarry 1993; McKittrick et al. 1999). Put crudely, the terrorist campaigns emanate from two primary sources: Republican groups (the Provisional IRA, the Irish National Liberation Army, and the 'dissident groups', the 'real' IRA and the Continuity IRA) and Loyalist paramilitary organisations (primarily the Ulster Volunteer Force, the Ulster Defence Association and the Loyalist Volunteer Force). The terrorist activity has included attacks on members of the police and the army; political assassinations and attempted assassinations (such as the bombing of the Conservative Party Conference in Brighton in 1984); bombings of shops, pubs, hotels and other targets in city centres in Northern Ireland and in England; and sectarian-inspired violence and murder. We return to the policing of the Troubles in greater detail below.

Political extremism

The two other major foci of attention in the field of domestic political violence have been so-called 'animal rights extremists' and the activities of far-right political groups such as Combat 18, which together with related forms of hate crime and violent xenophobia form what is often thought of as 'domestic terrorism'. Established in the early 1990s, Combat 18 was 'a by-product of the rising militancy within the British National Party' which by that time had replaced the National Front as the main far-right party in the UK (Lowles 2001). In addition to its involvement in numerous violent attacks, Combat 18 was also believed to be linked to Loyalist paramilitaries in Northern Ireland, in particular the Ulster Defence Association (and also the Ulster Volunteer Force), having been monitored by the Metropolitan Police Special Branch throughout the 1990s (Lowles 2001).

At the most contentious end of animal rights action lie various forms of civil disobedience which, at their most extreme, are held to constitute a form of terrorism. These include industrial sabotage, destruction of property, raids on premises associated with animal exploitation (to gather evidence, to sabotage, to free animals), together with the intimidation of, and attacks upon, individuals held to be in breach of 'animal rights'. One example of the latter is Professor Colin Blakemore, Director of Oxford University's Centre for Cognitive Neuroscience, who has been sent letter bombs, attacked, received kidnap threats against his family and is accompanied by a police escort when travelling. In addition to the specific anti-terrorist legislation, there are a number of other provisions that can be used in this regard, including the Protection from Harassment Act 1997 and the Malicious Communications Act 1998. Activity in this area has been taking place in the UK for over a decade now. In the early 1990s the Animal Liberation Front began a fire-bomb campaign in Scotland and one of its offshoots, the Justice Department, sent a series of parcel bombs to high-profile members of the meat trade. Available evidence suggest that the full range of intelligence activities has been used against animal rights extremists. The main database, the Animal Rights National Index, was incorporated into the National Public Order Intelligence Unit in March 1999 (HMIC 1999).

International terrorism and the UK

The bulk of terrorist activity in the UK since the Second World War has been connected with the Troubles in Northern Ireland. Examples, to date, of international terrorists targeting the UK or UK assets and citizens abroad have been relatively few. A number of major incidents have, however, occurred. The explosion of a bomb on Pan Am Flight 103, flying over the Scottish borders close to the small town of Lockerbie, killed 270 people – all 259 on board the plane and a further 11 on the ground.

Much of the international terrorism in the UK has been connected to the Middle East, though with links far beyond, particularly to Africa. In 1970, the Black September group assassinated the Jordanian Ambassador in London and, in June 1982, the Abu Nidal group killed the Israeli Ambassador in London. The Israeli Embassy in London, and other Jewish targets, were bombed in 1994, and there were a number of incidents in the mid-1990s involving Sikh terrorists (Taylor 2002). Overseas, terrorism-related activities include the kidnappings of Terry Waite, John McCarthy and others in Beirut in 1986–7, as well as other incidents in Yemen, Chechnya, and the murder of the British military attaché in Athens in June 2000. Finally, of course, the 11 September attacks have drawn particular attention to the threat posed by militant Islamic groups. British citizens were among those tourists killed in Luxor in 1997 by Egyptian terrorists and at least 65 Britons died on 11 September.

Responding to terrorism: national and international structures

The Metropolitan Police and other forces

One of the earliest incidents in the postwar period was a hit-and-run machine-gun attack on the US Embassy in August 1967. Early in 1968 there followed attacks on the Spanish Embassy, the American Officers' Club and six further bomb attacks occurred in London between then and mid-1970 (all but one directed at Spanish targets). Later in 1970 the targets changed to senior British officials and, in Ascoli's (1979: 325) words, it appeared 'the international anarchists had given way to urban guerillas': the 'Angry Brigade' had been formed. Further attacks on a BBC van and on the Department of Employment still seemingly caused relatively little concern at Scotland Yard. A small investigation unit was established with the Metropolitan Police (henceforward 'the Met') in 1970 in response to an apparent rise in politically motivated crime in London, but it was only with an attack on the home of the then Employment Minister, Robert Carr, involving two bombs, that more co-ordinated action began slowly to unfold.

The realisation that 'a dangerous and well organised body' was at work led directly to the formation of the Met Bomb Squad in 1971 (initially as an ad hoc squad of four, and then expanded quickly to 20, drawn from Special Branch, the Flying Squad and ex-army explosives experts – Huntley, 1977). Successful prosecutions in the following year led to the demise of the Angry Brigade but this proved to be 'only a prologue; the main drama was yet to come' (Ascoli 1979: 328). Indeed, during the course of the trial a letter bomb exploded, killing a cultural counsellor at the Israeli Embassy – the first strike of the Black September movement. In the four months to the end of January 1973, 43 letter bombs were posted to Israeli individuals or organisations. A car bomb outside army barracks in Aldershot in February 1972 was the first sign that the IRA were also operating in England. The first attack appears to have been the work of the 'Official' IRA. Thereafter, beginning with a series of car bombs and continuing with incendiary attacks in major department stores (Huntley 1977), the Provisional IRA constituted the main urban terrorist threat in London.

In the aftermath of 'the new and bloody battle' (Huntley 1977: 192), the Bomb Squad was renamed the Anti-terrorist Branch in 1976. There are a number of other agencies that can provide support to anti-terrorist officers (Wilkinson 2001):

- Special Branch.

- Technical Support Branch (expertise in surveillance devices and communications technology).

- Specialist Firearms Squad.

- Diplomatic Protection Group.

- Royalty Protection Group.

- Crime Operations Group (mounts special operations against organised crime).

- Metropolitan Police Forensic Science Laboratory and Chemists' Inspection Unit.

All these specialist units are located in a section known as Specialist Operations, under the command of an assistant commissioner. The Anti-terrorist Branch (SO13) is one of a number of specialist units and has responsibility not only for the investigation of terrorist activities within the capital but also across the country (at the invitation of the relevant chief constable); being the largest force by far, the Met is the only constabulary in the UK to have a dedicated anti-terrorist squad, though there are satellite exhibit liaison officers and POLSA (police search advisers) teams that provide specialist skills outside London, together with Special Branch units in all 52 constabularies in the UK (HMIC 2003). The Commander of SO13 is appointed by the Association of Chief Police Officers (ACPO) as the national co-ordinator for the investigation of acts of terrorism and cases involving animal rights extremism and eco-terrorism. The branch also takes responsibility for counter-terrorism. The Met not only has lead responsibility in the police service for such work but also has the 'lion's share' of the expertise. In addition, however, the police in the West Midlands and Greater Manchester have also built up resources and expertise in this area as, of course, have the Royal Ulster Constabulary (RUC) (now the Police Service for Northern Ireland – PSNI).

As Wilkinson (2001: 111) says: 'the fact that . . . M15 has taken over the lead intelligence-gathering role on the Irish Republican threat may have misled members of the public into thinking that the Metropolitan Police role . . . has been discontinued. Nothing could be further from the truth'. Both the Metropolitan Police Special Branch and SO13 are closely involved, work closely together and with the Security Services. Wilkinson gives as his main example of such joint activity the operation that led to the conviction of seven men for plots to bomb the main feeder electricity substations in London and the south east of England.[1] During this operation, tens of thousands of surveillance hours were undertaken, and over 5,000 pages of false documents, 8,500 exhibits and 20,000 hours of CCTV film were provided by the police to the prosecution – giving some sense of the scale of such anti-terrorist activity. SO13 works bilaterally with police services in other countries against terrorism. Thus, for example, a Met team worked in Athens permanently after the assassination of the British Military attaché there in June 2000, investigating the 17 November group believed to be responsible for the murder.

According to the Home Office (1994), 'Special Branches exist primarily to acquire intelligence, to assess its potential operational value, and to contribute more generally to its interpretation'. Countering the threat of terrorism is Special Branch's most important single function. As noted above, each police force has its own special branch, though the size of these varies significantly, depending on the nature and extent of their responsibilities. It is the Metropolitan Police Special Branch that has a national role in relation to extremist political and terrorist activity, and which is responsible for liaising with local and international organisations. Special branches are involved in risk assessment in relation to terrorist threats and provide armed personal protection for people judged to be at risk. Because of their anti-terrorist role, Special Branch officers are permanently stationed at ports and airports to gather intelligence, identify suspects and to provide support to other anti-terrorist activity. In addition, government advice (Home Office 1994) on the role of Special Branch suggests it has three other main functions in support of the Security Service: counter-espionage, counter-proliferation and counter-subversion.

The primary responsibility for gathering information on animal rights extremists, and seeking to prevent attacks on persons and property by such groups, has generally rested with special branches in most forces, and Special Branch was the main channel for intelligence between forces and the main database, the Animal Rights National Index, throughout the 1990s. The ACPO Terrorism and Allied Matters business area has primary responsibility for the formulation of policy at a national level, with the Security Service having co-opted status at senior level in recognition of the close relationship between the organisations. The two major policing organisations outside the constabularies are the National Crime Squad (NCS) and the National Criminal Intelligence Service (NCIS), both of which play important functions in relation to organised crime (see Chapter 18). Currently, Special Branch has limited dealings with NCIS, confined primarily to interception matters and information stored on covert human intelligence sources. It has even fewer dealings with NCS. There now exists, therefore, an extensive and relatively complex Special Branch network, something which has seen substantial increases in resources in recent times. Nevertheless, a recent Her Majesty's Inspectorate of Constabulary (HMIC) thematic review (2003: 30) concluded that there remain 'significant weaknesses in the current structure ... to the detriment of the Branch's ability to respond consistently to the current level of terrorist threat facing this country'. One option for reform considered by HMIC was the possibility of establishing a National Special Branch. This it rejected, arguing that it would put at risk 'the golden thread' of local coverage made possible by the current structure. In doing so it underlined the idea that the community-based responses to crime apply just as much to terrorism as to other areas.

The Security Services

The Security Service – more usually known as MI5 – is the UK's security intelligence agency. Its role is to protect national security and to support law enforcement agencies in preventing and detecting serious crime. MI5 is responsible for security intelligence work against covertly organised threats to the UK and advises government of protective security measures. The Secret Service Bureau had been established in 1909 to combat German espionage. The expansion of the work of the bureau led to the splitting of responsibilities into counter-espionage within the British Isles (MI5) and the gathering of intelligence from overseas (MI6).

Prior to the Great War the bureau had about 10 staff; by the end of the war MI5 alone had 850. The Russian Revolution led to the Security Service taking responsibility for countering the threat of communist subversion and, from the 1930s onwards, fascist subversion was added to the list. In 1952 the Prime Minister, Churchill, passed personal responsibility for the Security Service to the Home Secretary (Bunyan 1977). The directive issued at that time, which set out the responsibilities of the service, formed the basis for its work until 1989 and the passage of the Security Service Act. From the 1970s onward, resources were progressively diverted from counter-subversion work into international (particulary because of the perceived threat from Palestinian terrorists) and Irish counter-terrorism.

As we have noted, MI5 is also responsible for monitoring the threat from other terrorist groups in the UK. Responsibility for intelligence activity against Irish republican terrorism on the British mainland was transferred to MI5 from the Metropolitan Police in 1992 against police wishes, and those of the Special Branch in particular. In 1996, new legislation extended MI5's statutory remit to include supporting law enforcement agencies in the work against serious crime (see Chapter 18).

Interpol

In the growing, and increasingly complex, world of international police co-operation, it is Interpol which is the longest-standing arrangement. Primarily a clearing house for intelligence, 'Interpol's battle with terrorism has always been an uphill battle' (Bresler 1992: 257). For many years, involvement had been resisted because of the 'political' nature of such activity. Interpol's involvement in anti-terrorist activity was established as a result of a resolution at the 54th General Assesmbly in 1985 which called for the creation of a specialised group within the then Police Division to 'co-ordinate and enhance co-operation in combating international terrorism'. Even then, according to Bresler, it was not until 1987 that the group became operational. The then Secretary General is quoted as saying 'it took 15 years from [Interpol's] lowest point at the Munich Olympic Games in 1972 to do something that could have been done in two years' (cited in Bresler 1992: 257). The Public Safety and Terrorism sub-directorate of Interpol deals with terrorism; firearms and explosives; attacks and threats against civil aviation; maritime piracy; and weapons of mass destruction.

Two major and continuing problems with Interpol have generally been identified. First, because it was perceived not to be tackling terrorist crime adequately in the 1970s, European states made other anti-terrorist arrangements, notably in the establishment of the Trevi group and the European Police Working Group. Secondly, there have been persistent doubts about the security of Interpol's communications network (House of Commons 1990: 43;

George and Watson 1992). Nevertheless, despite these problems, there remain a number of reasons why Interpol is important in international policing of terrorist activity:

- When national police want to make an arrest outside their jurisdiction they have to go through Interpol.
- Interpol is used when an investigation into terrorism in Europe extends beyond European borders.
- Interpol provides specialist advice on explosives, and firearms in particular.
- Interpol has developed a reputation for providing warnings of potential terrorist activity, especially involving hi-jacks or air bombings.

Trevi

When established in 1976, anti-terrorism was its founding mandate. Subsequently, one of the responses to the perceived ineffectiveness or inadequacy of Interpol was a decision by European ministers of justice to establish a regular meeting to deal with matters of policy. A programme of action was published in the name of EC interior ministers in 1990 which attempted 'a synthesis of the arrangements considered between police and security services with a view to more effective prevention and repression . . . of terrorism, drug trafficking or any forms of crime including organised illegal immigration' (cited in Hebenton and Thomas 1995). The programme also revealed that by that stage the Trevi group was already relatively far advanced in the development of a rapid and protected communications system for collecting and disseminating information about terrorism and terrorists. Trevi meetings were largely superseded by the more formalised arrangements made for the EU under the Maastricht Treaty.

Maastricht Treaty

Signed in February 1992, the treaty seeks to 'facilitate the development of the European Community into a political and an economic and monetary union' (European Commission 1992). With pressure resulting from the lowering of internal frontiers and from the need to provide a collective response to ethnic and territorial instability resulting from the significant changes taking place in former communist states, the Third Pillar of the treaty covers co-operation in matters of justice and home affairs (though subsequent to the Treaty of Amsterdam in 1997 much of justice and home affairs was moved into the First Pillar). It also formalised much of the work that had previously been undertaken by bodies such as Trevi. Chalk (1994) suggests that there are five main ways in which the Maastricht Treaty could have a positive impact on anti-terrorist activity:

1. By establishing a union-wide system it may help produce more integrated policies and tactics.

2. It establishes the beginnings of an effective EU crisis management structure, incorporating police, customs and judicial authorities.

3. (As amended at Amsterdam) it establishes a general justice and security framework, with Europol at the centre, with a number of supporting capacities of working groups, etc.

4. The strengthening of the outer frontier through integrated immigration and asylum policies.

5. Through exploiting its potential to develop a coherent intelligence initiative for serious international crime.

Europol

Europol is the EU law enforcement organisation that handles criminal intelligence. Its mission is to assist the law enforcement authorities of member states in their fight against serious forms of organised crime (see Chapter 6). It was established in the Maastricht Treaty in 1992. Based in The Hague, Europol started limited operations in early 1994, specifically in relation to drugs. A counter-terrorism preparatory group was established in 1998. The group identified a number of functions that Europol should perform in this regard and in December 1998 the EU confirmed the intention to extend Europol's mandate to include counter-terrorism (Rauchs and Koenig 2001). From 2002 Europol's mandate was formally extended to deal with all serious forms of international crime, including terrorism. Europol supports member states by:

- facilitating the exchange of information, in accordance with national law, between Europol liaison officers (ELOs). ELOs are seconded to Europol by the member states as representatives of their national law enforcement agencies;

- providing operational analysis in support of member states' operations;

- generating strategic reports (e.g. threat assessments) and crime analysis on the basis of information and intelligence supplied by member states, generated by Europol or gathered from other sources; and

- providing expertise and technical support for investigations and operations carried out within the EU, under the supervision and the legal responsibility of the member states concerned.

Europol is also active in promoting crime analysis and harmonisation of investigative techniques within the member states. A preparatory group was established in the late 1990s comprising 11 counter-terrorism experts who have been seconded by the member states, with the remit of advising how Europol can support its members in the field (Marotta 1999).

The EU has passed new anti-terrorist legislation since 11 September, part of which involves a recommendation on establishing multinational police investigation teams: 'Since this measure takes the form of a Recommendation, it was not subject to democratic scrutiny and will not be subject to judicial scrutiny, although it will likely have important practical consequences' (Peers 2003: 239–40). Peers suggests that the original aim of the proposal was to provide an operational capability in relation to activities that potentially threaten national security but which are non-criminal. The investigations will be subject to national law, and accountability will be provided for in the same way. These teams will be separate from Europol, the latter's convention expressly preventing joint participation (and particularly participation in non-criminal investigations), though Europol's operational capacities in this field are expanding fast.

Responding to terrorism: the use of legislation

As Walker (2000b) notes, special laws against terrorism were a constant feature of British political and legal life throughout the twentieth century, and are set to remain. The emergency powers that were introduced in the 50 years after 1922 were largely incorporated into the Emergency Powers Act 1973 after the discontinuation of the Stormont Parliament (Donohue 2001), and a Prevention of Terrorism Act has been in continuous use since 1974. Whether the introduction of such legislation had a significant impact on the nature of the prevention and control of terrorism is much debated (see Walker 1992; Hillyard 1993). Moreover, the Prevention of Terrorism Acts have been much criticised, in part because of their perceived effects, but equally because of what is perceived to be the rather ill-considered and rushed way they have come about. By and large, such legislation has 'been hastily drafted in circumstances of crisis, and has remained fragmented' (Walker 2000b: 1). A summary of the principal legislative measures in the UK for countering terrorism is contained in Box 19.1.

In terms of police powers, according to Walker (2000b) the differences between the policing of terrorism and 'ordinary' policing are narrowing. In part, this is because the Police and Criminal Evidence Act 1984 (PACE) and its related codes of practice are having an impact on inquiries relating to terrorism – by streamlining investigative interviewing, for example – and also, conversely, that broader interviewing techniques aimed at developing intelligence and informers, often associated with terrorism-related inquiries, are more and more a feature of policing generally. Similarly, Donohue (2001) describes a long-term process of 'normalisation' whereby the exceptional powers granted, temporarily, under the Emergency Powers Acts from 1973 to 1996 were, via the prevention of terrorism legislation, implemented throughout the UK. According to Hillyard (1993) normalisation has three major features. First, legislation introduced as a temporary measure over time is transformed into a permanent piece of law. Secondly, a symbiotic relationship develops between ordinary criminal law and emergency legislation whereby elements of one progressively become incorporated into the other. The result is 'general tightening up throughout the statutory law' (Hillyard 1993: 263). In explaining such 'normalisation', Walker suggests that the primary reason for this was that policing by consent was becoming less feasible during the 1970s

Box 19.1 Anti-terrorist legislation

The Northern Ireland (Emergency Provisions) Act 1973
It made it possible to exclude from Great Britain, from Northern Ireland or from the UK as a whole, persons involved in terrorism associated with Northern Ireland; and provided the police with powers to arrest suspected terrorists and detain them for 48 hours on their own authority, with the possibility of an extension of detention for a further period of up to five days authorised by the Secretary of State.

The Prevention of Terrorism (Temporary Provisions) Act 1974
- Provides powers to proscribe organisations concerned with terrorism relating to Northern Irish affairs.
- Provides the power to exclude UK citizens either from living in Great Britain or Northern Ireland.
- Gives the police powers of arrest, search and detention without a warrant of people where there is a reasonable suspicion that they belong to a proscribed organisation, are subject to an exclusion order or are concerned in the commission, preparation or instigation of terrorism.
- Makes it an offence to withhold information from the police about future acts of terrorism, or people involved in terrorism.

The Prevention of Terrorism (Temporary Provisions) Act 1984
It re-enacted the provisions of the 1976 Act with some modifications, particularly to exclusion orders, to incorporate the changes recommended by Lord Jellicoe in his review of the operation of the 1976 Act.

The Prevention of Terrorism (Temporary Provisions) Act 1989
- Provides for the proscription of terrorist organisations.
- Makes it an offence to solicit support, or display support, for a proscribed organisation.
- Provides powers of exclusion from Great Britain, Northern Ireland or the UK.
- Provides powers to stop, search and detain persons suspected of terrorism.
- Provides the police with increased powers to search financial records, and to enter property.

Intelligence Services Act 1994
It provides for a system under which MI6 and the Government Communications Headquarters (GCHQ) may lawfully interfere with the civil liberties of the UK public. Some provisions also apply to the Security Service (MI5).

The Prevention of Terrorism (Additional Powers) Act 1996
Extended police powers available in Northern Ireland to the police in Great Britain, including powers to:
- stop and search pedestrians within designated areas for terrorist items;
- cordon off areas and impose temporary parking restrictions in response to perceived threats; and
- search non-residential premises (e.g. lorry parks, lock-up garages).
Provided powers to police in the UK to search unaccompanied freight at ports.

Police Act 1997
Established the Office of Surveillance Commissioners, a non-departmental public body responsible for the oversight of covert surveillance.

Box 19.1   *Continued*

The Northern Ireland (Emergency Provisions) Act 1998

- Amended the range of cases dealt with by the Diplock courts (the trial of certain offences by judges alone).
- Repealed the powers to detain without trial persons suspected of being terrorists.

The Criminal Justice (Terrorism and Conspiracy) Act 1998

- Opinion of a police officer admissible in court as evidence of membership of a terrorist organisation.
- Courts allowed to draw inferences from refusal to answer questions during an investigation into membership of a terrorist organisation.
- On conviction, assets used in furtherance of a proscribed organisation would be forfeited.
- Created the offence of conspiring in the UK to commit a terrorist act abroad.

The Terrorism Act 2000

- Significantly broadens the definition of 'terrorism'.
- Gives the Home Secretary powers to proscribe organisations involved in, or supportive of, terrorism.
- Extends police powers of arrest without a warrant (linked with the new definition of terrorism).
- Introduces new safeguards governing extended detention and audiotaping of interviews.

The Regulation of Investigatory Powers Act 2000

Provides for, and regulates the use of, a range of investigative powers by a variety of public bodies. The powers covered include:

- interception of communications and acquisition and disclosure of communications data;
- cover surveillance, agents, informants and undercover officers; and
- investigation of electronic data protected by encryption.

Provides for independent judicial oversight of the powers in the Act.

The Anti-terrorism, Crime and Security Act 2001

- Increased powers of detention of immigrants suspected of terrorism (but otherwise protected by Article 3 of the European Convention on Human Rights because they would face torture in the country to which they would be returned).
- Extends the circumstances under which the police can undertake 'examinations to ascertain a suspect's identity' (fingerprinting, photographing, removal of clothing).
- Extends the powers of the Ministry of Defence Police and British Transport Police.
- (Re)creation of an offence of failing to disclose information about terrorism.
- Extension of the Crime and Disorder Act 1998 provisions so that a criminal offence can now be 'religiously aggravated'.

---

and 1980s, 'especially as some ethnic minorities in Britain to some degree mirror the alienation experienced by Nationalists in Northern Ireland' (1992: 257).

The third feature of normalisation concerns the use of emergency powers to deal with 'ordinary crime' (Hillyard 1993). It was alleged, for example, in the mid-1980s that hunt saboteurs were arrested under the Prevention of Terrorism Act (PTA), and Hillyard's study shows numerous examples of people originally arrested under the PTA eventually being charged with criminal offences such as motoring and theft offences. One of the dangers in this area is that of 'spillover' from anti-terrorist concerns to other areas of policing, particularly public order policing (i.e. the bracketing of rowdy and occasionally violent street protests with terrorism in the minds of the police and politicians, and the use of anti-terrorist measures (both legal and policing) to deal with them).

As Walker (1992: 25) noted in the early 1990s, 'despite the wider contexts in which terrorism now takes place, British legislation opposing it has been traditionally preoccupied with the Irish variety'. The majority of special powers available to the police have been provided by the Emergency Provisions Acts (in Northern Ireland) and the Prevention of Terrorism (Temporary Provisions) Acts (applicable throughout the UK). A number of factors – the Human Rights Act 1998, the peace process in Northern Ireland and the fact that the existing legislation in Northern Ireland was set to expire in August 2000 – provided the potential for some of this fragmentation to be cleared up (Walker 2000b). The Terrorism Act 2000 replaced the previous PTAs and related legislation, though the bulk of their provisions were unaltered. The 2000 Act extended the financial offences relating to terrorism. In particular it does so in order to incorporate the threat of foreign terrorism (though the offence must either be committed in the UK or, if committed abroad, constitute an offence in the UK). The greatest changes brought about by the Act in this area were the powers of seizure of cash at national borders.

In Walker's (2000b: 29) view, having overhauled the legislation in 2000, with broad parliamentary support, it would 'be a fine development if . . . the UK government and its security forces could have the confidence and ability to rely increasingly on "normal" policing powers'. Writing prior to 11 September, Walker was not optimistic of this, and was right not to be. The Anti-terrorism, Crime and Security Bill was published on 12 November 2001 and became an Act of Parliament by 13 December. The Anti-terrorism, Crime and Security Act 2001 includes provisions which will allow the indefinite detention without trial of non-British citizens suspected of terrorism creating, in the words of one commentator, 'the possibility of internment' (Fenwick 2002: 737). According to Liberty,[2] by 19th December eight people had been detained under its 'internment' provisions. In a statement by the Home Secretary in September 2002, a total of 12 suspects had been detained under the new legislation by that time, two of whom had voluntarily left the country.[3]

According to Wilkinson (2001), one of the difficulties in assessing the efficacy of anti-terrorist legislation arises from the wide range of aims for which it can be employed. He identifies at least six aims of such legislation, of which it is only the last two in the list that are most usually assumed to be the main objectives:

1. Prophylaxis – dealing with underlying grievances and problems.

2. Deterrence – severe penalties for particular offences.

3. Increasing powers – over international co-operation, extradition, search, seizure, etc.

4. Symbolic or expressive aims – to express perceived public revulsion.

5. Enhancing public security.

6. Suppressing terrorist organisations.

Perhaps more fundamentally, as with all potentially preventative measures, the difficulty of assessment lies in establishing some evidence about the non-commission of particular acts. Walker (1992), in his survey of anti-terrorist legislation, suggests that special powers have occasionally been helpful but, equally, have had negative unintended consequences including encouraging secrecy (as a result of proscribing organisations) and by removing suspects from known haunts (using powers of exclusion). He concludes that: 'the criminal justice system has taken its toll. Yet most of the successes were attributable to chance, routine police work and terrorist incompetence. The special powers and port controls have been a contributory element in some cases but have rarely been the decisive factor' (1992: 249).

Elements of this analysis may be somewhat overstated. In particular, it might be argued that it is precisely competent, professional routine police work that makes it possible to identify and to take advantage of chance, or terrorist incompetence. Nevertheless, Walker's central argument – that there is little evidence that special powers have been the decisive factor in anti-terrorist policing – has much support. Even some of the staunchest defenders of the attempts by liberal states to fight terrorism point to the limited impact of legislative efforts: 'By definition terrorist groups are making war on legality' (Wilkinson 2001: 114). One doesn't have to accept Wilkinson's implicit understanding of the relationship between the nation-state and terrorism to accept his underlying point which is that organisations that perceive themselves to be in conflict with particular governments or nations are unlikely to be especially concerned about the legislation passed by such governments – though they can, and do, seek to use democratic and legal safeguards in their own defence. As even Wilkinson acknowledges, the special powers that most liberal states introduce at some point in response to terrorism often carry risks, sometimes grave risks, for the democratic system itself. The use of internment in Northern Ireland would be an example of one such measure. Indeed, the policing of 'the Troubles' provides a useful insight into the nature, the achievements and some of the pitfalls of anti-terrorist policing.

Responding to terrorism: policing 'the Troubles'

Wilkinson notes that the 'political culture and traditions in Northern Ireland . . . are so steeped in violence that the province became a virtual laboratory for deploying protracted terrorism as a weapon within a liberal democratic state' (2001: 30). Equally, since 1969 Northern Ireland has acted as an 'ideal training ground' for testing and developing new styles, methods and strategies of policing (Hillyard 1985).

Ni Aolain (2000), in her detailed review of the use of force by the state during the troubles, identifies three phases in the cycle of 'policing' – the *militarisation* phase between 1969 and 1974, the *normalisation* phase between 1975 and 1980 and the *counter-insurgency* phase between 1981 and 1994. Other commentators note similar trends, namely militarisation, Ulsterisation – a shift which became known as the 'primacy of the police' – and professionalisation (cf. Boyle *et al.* 1975; Hillyard 1994; Weitzer 1990). Hillyard (1997: 170) also notes a fourth trend, 'covertisation', which denotes the increased use of undercover and clandestine surveillance tactics, in addition to the overwhelming reliance on informers in gathering intelligence to combat the terrorist threat.

The first phase – militarisation – represents the immediate reaction by the state to the outbreak of civil disturbance. During these early years the army assumed 'primacy' for the maintenance of order. Though there were proposals for significant reform of the RUC at the time – effectively to civilianise and disarm it – these were dropped and the RUC assumed a dual role of 'normal' and security policing, being subordinate to the army in respect to the latter. Faced with increasing violence from both Protestant and Nationalist paramilitaries, the army adopted a policy of direct confrontation. Blanket measures, such as the introduction of internment in 1971, house-to-house searches and the Falls Road curfew were introduced, many against the advice of senior army officers, who considered such measures indiscriminate and counterproductive. Considerable criticism was also made of army interrogation techniques – techniques which led eventually to the Irish government taking the British government to the European Court of Human Rights, which found it guilty of inhuman and degrading treatment (Taylor 2001) and led Lord Gardiner in the report of an official inquiry to note that:

> The blame . . . must lie with those who, many years ago, decided that in emergency conditions in Colonial-type situations we should abandon our legal, well-tried and highly successful wartime interrogation methods and replace them by procedures that were secret, illegal, not morally justifiable and alien to [democratic] traditions (cited in Taylor 2001: 73).

The central message – that anti-terrorist policing methods should be governed by the same principles and ethics as all policing methods – is one that will be repeated throughout this chapter. There can be little doubt that the nature of terrorism brings forth a sometimes understandably strong response. However, the key lesson from policing experience in this field appears that the long-term disbenefits of overly repressive tactics far outweigh any short-term advantages. As Taylor (2001: 75) notes of the 'policing' tactics in Northern Ireland in this period: 'However many lives the "Brits" say internment and "in-depth" interrogation may have saved, there is no denying that after its introduction the death toll soared'.

This situation lasted until 1976 at which point the British government, recognising that military operations and tactics appeared if anything to be contributing to a worsening of the situation, reversed the position so that the army became the 'junior partner' in the security field – a shift known as the 'primacy of the police' and 'Ulsterisation' policies. The shift was not achieved without considerable resistance from the military hierarchy. This was in part fuelled by suspicion about the competence of the RUC to assume responsibility for intelligence gathering.

The policy of normalisation was born out of the failed attempt to apply a military solution to what was ostensibly a political problem. The political objective and rationale underpinning the shift was the restoration of civil institutions of order, thereby divesting paramilitaries of any vestige of political legitimacy. Vital to this policy was the fundamental reorganisation of the police and restructuring of the criminal justice system to meet the demands of the situation. The changes to the latter were rooted in the recommendations of the Scarman (1972) and Diplock Report (1972). Changes were initiated on two levels: first, the removal of 'special category status' for those convicted of politically motivated offences after 1976; and, secondly, the modification of the court system through the enactment of the Emergency Provisions Act (EPA) 1973. The EPA removed the right of trial by jury for defined scheduled offences. Upon arrest for a scheduled offence, the arrestee was subject to emergency arrest, detention and trial procedures (in what were known as the 'Diplock courts').

The enactment of the EPA illustrated the paradox of policing in Northern Ireland. On the one hand there was the official desire to 'normalise' political violence while, on the other, introducing special powers implicitly recognising the apparent 'abnormality' of the situation. Emergency legislation provided the RUC with the mechanism for developing and pursuing a proactive strategy to combat terrorist violence.

The Ulsterisation process required a fundamental reorganisation of the RUC which at the time was ill-equipped to assume the primary role in intelligence gathering. When the Provisional IRA formed in late 1970 the intelligence held by the RUC was inadequate and outdated (Bishop and Mallie 1987). The need to gain better intelligence, and to develop effective structures for doing so, were vital to the RUC's strategy to respond to escalating levels of terrorist violence. Responsibility for riot control, counter-insurgency operations and intelligence gathering was therefore gradually transferred to the RUC. This was another key period in which developments in policing in Northern Ireland acted as a driver for contemporaneous or subsequent developments on the mainland (though the process was in some ways an iterative one). Sir Kenneth Newman, then Chief Constable of the RUC, being familiar with developments in surveillance and technology for volume crime being used by the Metropolitan Police, immediately instituted four major changes aimed at streamlining intelligence collection and sharing. First, intelligence collection was centralised with the establishment of the Criminal Intelligence Unit (CIU) established at the RUC headquarters (though area intelligence units were also established). The CIU had access to the army's computer at Lisburn and to the Met's Special Branch records.

The second major change was the reorganisation of CID. In addition to the existing divisional CID, Newman introduced four regional crime squads based on a combination of similar squads formed on the mainland to tackle serious crime and the 'A' squad, set up by his predecessor, James Flanagan, to tackle sectarian murders. The four regional crime squads were to take primary responsibility for the gathering of intelligence and became, in effect, the cornerstone of the RUC's strategy to combat terrorism. While investigations were geographically determined, the majority of interrogations were carried out at Castlereagh.

Thirdly, the surveillance techniques and systems used by the RUC were radically overhauled at this time. The fourth, and final, reform made by Newman, although it was never publicly hailed as such, was the establishment of a full-time centralised, Specialist Interrogation Centre in Castlereagh. The CIU collated the information and disseminated it to the regional crime squads who, in turn, interrogated terrorist suspects detained at Castlereagh, incommunicado under the provisions of emergency legislation. The aim was to gather intelligence and elicit signed confessions. This was the only evidence that was offered by the prosecution in the majority of cases that came before the new Diplock courts.

In the aftermath of the assassination of Christopher Ewart-Biggs, recently appointed British Ambassador to Dublin, the Chief Constable issued a new directive on terrorist suspects which distinguished between 'an "interview" – the result of which criminal charges were to be preferred – and an "interrogation" conducted for the purpose of obtaining intelligence' (Taylor 1980: 68). The directive stipulated that the Judges Rules, at that stage a suspect's main safeguard against abuse in custody, applied to an 'interview' and not an 'interrogation'. While officers were directed to stipulate if a suspect was to be interviewed or interrogated when brought into custody, the fact that the Judges Rules did not seem to apply to 'interrogations' gave officers 'unaccustomed freedom' (Taylor 1980: 69).

The policy of police primacy was officially introduced in January 1977 with the signing of a joint directive between the RUC and the army relegating the army to the position of 'military aid to the civil power' (MACP) and firmly establishing the front-line role of the RUC in the 'war' against Irish terrorism. The traditional hostility between the police and the army over intelligence sources was temporarily abated with the creation of integrated intelligence centres called Tasking and Co-ordination Groups.

The operational vacuum left by the shift to 'primacy of the police' simultaneously resulted in moves towards further militarisation of the RUC while modernising the force and integrating it within mainland police structures and practices. Militarisation was symbolised, in reality and perception, by sophisticated weaponry and the establishment of specialist units to facilitate the counter-insurgency role. In 1980 divisional mobile support units (DMSUs) were established, trained in riot and crowd control. These were intended to provide emergency support where 'ordinary' policing proved to be inadequate.

While the moves towards paramilitarism might seem at odds with the dual objectives of criminalisation and normalisation, they were, for Newman, an integral component of his 'total strategy' and fully compatible with the policy of 'Ulsterisation' (Newman 1978a, 1978b). Increasing the resources devoted to intelligence gathering and surveillance was a major development sponsored by Newman, who was concerned about the gap in the RUC's capabilities in this regard (Ryder 1989).

This 'gap', it might be said, was made manifest by the shift in the nature of the IRA from one of relative disorganisation to its gradual emergence as a highly sophisticated urban/semi-rural guerrilla army. By the mid-1980s Weitzer (1985: 53) concluded that:

> policing has not come full circle to the pre-1970s state of affairs, but instead consists of an uneasy blend of positive and retrogressive developments. While trends can be discerned in the direction of both normalization and militarization, official policy has tended to accent the former at the expense of the latter.

The friction between the army and the police came to a head in August 1979 following the killing of 18 British soldiers in an IRA ambush in Co. Down. Senior military staff sought political support for the reassertion of operational supremacy. In the event, Newman convinced the Prime Minister to allow the recruitment of an additional 1,000 police officers. In order to appease the military – and to resolve the continuing rivalry between the army and the RUC over intelligence – Maurice Oldfield, previously a director of MI6, was appointed as security co-ordinator (Ellison and Smyth 2000: 109). With the remit of taking over control of all intelligence gathering and collation, Oldfield established a directorate known as 'The Department' – a committee including representatives from a range of security agencies including the SAS, military intelligence, RUC Special Branch, the SPG, MI5 and MI6. The aim was to co-ordinate intelligence collection between the RUC Special Branch and the army. Although Oldfield's stay in Northern Ireland was short lived the closer working relationship between the police and the army was to continue throughout the 1980s and into the 1990s.

In the wake of restructuring and retraining in the late 1970s, the specialist surveillance and operational units assumed a more active operational counter-insurgency role in the early 1980s. In late 1982 a number of fatal shooting incidents by officers from the mobile support units provoked strong international and local condemnation. A number of inquiries were set up to investigate allegations that a shoot-to-kill policy was in operation. The most notable of these was the Stalker Inquiry, headed by the then Deputy Chief Constable of Greater Manchester Police in 1984. Stalker alleged that he was obstructed from carrying out his investigation and before it was completed he was removed from duty under controversial circumstances. The inquiry, which was completed by Colin Sampson in 1987, was never published. Stalker described the activities of RUC Special Branch in great detail in his autobiography, and concluded that he had 'never experienced, nor had any of my team, such an influence over the entire police force by one small section' (1988: 56–7) – a point also made by witnesses to the Patten Inquiry in the late 1990s (see Independent Commission 1999: 72).

The apparent failure of the RUC to take on the operational counter-insurgency role successfully, coupled with the collapse of the supergrass system (see below) at that time, is held by some to have resulted in the shift of responsibility for counter-insurgency operations back to the army, primarily the SAS. The RUC was relegated to the function of supporting the army in covert operations and providing the informer intelligence that allowed preplanning of 'set-piece' operations – specialist operations resulting in the use of deadly force, such as the shooting of three unarmed IRA members in Gibraltar in 1988 (Ni Aolain 2000; Taylor 2001).

The 'emergency' situation in Northern Ireland blurred the line between 'normal' and 'counter-insurgency' policing. Counter-insurgency policing became 'institutionalised', overshadowing efforts to employ traditional methods. Indeed, emphasis on the former tended to undermine the latter, being a 'hollow PR effort and a thinly disguised mode of repression, in the form of intelligence gathering' (Weitzer 1995: 287). In addition to the 'normal' array of policing tactics, and in response to the very grave threats, and the enormous loss of life since 1969 (see McKittrick *et al.* 1999), the British security forces in Northern Ireland employed a myriad of counter-insurgency tactics, including: internment without trial; the abolition of trial by jury; the progressive elimination of common law safeguards; the use of brutal methods of interrogation; alleged abuse of army and police powers of arrest, stop and search; the use of supergrasses to obtain convictions; and, at its most extreme, the adoption of an alleged 'shoot-to-kill policy'. For some critical commentators, such tactics debased normal police practice and further exacerbated the existing divisions of a divided society (for example, Hillyard 1988).

Whatever one's position on this, what seems clear is that the panoply of special policing measures to combat terrorism failed to suppress paramilitary violence in Northern Ireland and, if anything, increased the perception of policing as an instrument of state repression. This was the legacy that the Patten Commission confronted and which meant that fundamental changes to policing were all but inevitable. One emerging lesson of anti-terrorist activity appears to be that whatever the short-term gains of the more extreme policing methods – and these may appear very significant indeed – the longer-term costs may be greater. In particular, one risk is that the integrity of a police service is itself undermined and becomes part of the problem rather than the 'solution'. As was well illustrated in the peace process in Northern Ireland, as in many 'transitional societies', the move towards 'peace' tends under such circumstances not only to involve the reform of the political process and the political system but reform of the police service too (on the South African experience, see Brogden and Shearing 1993). That solutions are inevitably political and centre on questions of legitimacy is neatly captured in the process that saw the RUC transformed into the Police Service for Northern Ireland (PSNI).

Police powers and anti-terrorist tactics

Understanding the area of police powers and tactics in anti-terrorism, as in the area of anti-terrorist legislation, means focusing at least in part on the nature of the relationship between 'special' and 'normal' powers. Put crudely, there is an argument which holds that the most successful policing strategies in relation to terrorism are precisely those that utilise normal policing methods. On the other hand, there are those that argue that the very nature of terrorism requires special tactics and approaches. In thinking briefly about policing in this area we rely primarily, but not exclusively, on the example of policing terrorist activity during the Troubles.

As outlined above, the PTA legislation includes special powers of arrest, though Walker (1992) argues that the majority of terrorist arrests in England, Wales and Northern Ireland could be made under PACE provisions. Hillyard (1993: 148) and others argue that there is considerable evidence to suggest that the primary object of a large proportion of arrests that are made under PTA legislation is 'either to gather intelligence or to screen the Irish community'. In parallel with observations about the use of arrest under the PTA, it is suggested by some commentators that the primary objective of interrogation is either to gather intelligence or to recruit informants (Hillyard 1993), though this is by no means necessarily problematic. Policing terrorism in Northern Ireland has for the past 30 years centred upon developing more effective practices for gathering intelligence. Two distinct trends can be discerned, the first focusing upon the use of technology and the second employing human intelligence sources (now known as CHIS – 'covert human intelligence source') (Taylor 1993). The trend, which Hillyard (1997) labels 'covertisation', signals increased use of surveillance and clandestine undercover techniques, in addition to the use of CHIS to supply information on those involved in political violence (now subject to supervision by civil commissioners under the Regulation of Ivestigatory Powers Act 2000).

Northern Ireland was a favoured site for testing and developing an array of new technology, including helicopter monitoring equipment fitted with surveillance and night-vision cameras, telephone taps, advanced communications and automatic vehicle tracking systems and computerised data intelligence banks with remote access to terminals in police vehicles and at border check points (Hillyard 1997: 173). Responsibility for conducting covert surveillance operations has rested jointly between the RUC and the specialist army units.

On the British mainland there has been increasing emphasis on the use of technology in the attempt to prevent terrorism. According to Walker and McGuinness (2002), after the first major bombing in 1992 in the City of London, the ideas of private responsibility for security and the creation of 'defensible space' were heavily promoted both by the local police and by the City of London Corporation and the Home Office. In part, this was facilitated by both the geography of the City – a dense, relatively easily 'surveilled' space – and by the financial power of its occupants. By contrast, the private security response to the Manchester bombing was much less visible. In practice, though, it would anyway be difficult to establish, and there is little evidence as to the efficacy of such surveillance as a means of prevention. So far as CCTV is concerned, it appears more likely to be used as a source of evidence in investigations and later prosecutions (though such work is hugely resource intensive), such as that of David Copeland, the man responsible for the 'hate crime' bombings in London in 1999.

In parallel with the use of technical intelligence-gathering systems has been a concomitant reliance upon human intelligence from a number of different sources, including agents, CHIS and, for a period, the use of 'supergrasses' acquired during interrogations at the Specialist Interrogation Centre in Castlereagh (Morton 1995; Greer 2001). Following the end of the use of detention without trial in Northern Ireland, the pressure on the security forces and the police to secure convictions increased. However, after a highly critical report into allegations of mistreatment at the Castlereagh Holding Centre, 'the policy of securing convictions on confession alone consequently lost the viability it once had' (Walsh 1983: 63) and new opportunities for gathering intelligence and securing convictions were needed. In late 1981 a new and 'distinct counterinsurgency initiative: the supergrass system' was born (Greer 1988: 73). After two days in detention, Christopher Black, who had been arrested at a road block, began to give statements implicating himself and others in a range of terrorist offences. He was granted immunity from prosecution and in a subsequent trial gave evidence against 38 accused, of whom 35 were later convicted. This case is generally taken as the beginning of the 'supergrass system'.

Conviction rates in the early stages were high. The first three trials resulted in the conviction of 56 of 64 defendants, with 31 of those convictions resting solely on the uncorroborated testimony of the supergrass (Greer 1988). In total, between 1981 and 1984 the supergrass system yielded approximately 25 informants (7 Loyalist and 18 Republican) resulting in almost 600 people being arrested and charged with terrorist offences in Northern Ireland (Greer 1988: 73). Ultimately, however, most of the convictions were overturned on appeal. The credibility of witnesses who had received inducements to testify, together with controversy surrounding the viability of uncorroborated evidence, effectively ended the tactic. Greer argues (1988: 94) that 'these factors seem to have prompted the judiciary to reassess its original choice between uncritical loyalty to counterinsurgency policy as conceived by the executive and loyalty to the ideology of the rule of law'.

Finally, it is worth noting that despite the lack of long-term success, the supergrass system proved indirectly beneficial to the security effort in a number of ways. First, the use of the technique was disruptive to terrorist organisations, evidenced by the reaction by paramilitary organisations to the threat posed to their internal security within their own communities. Secondly, it provided the RUC with current intelligence on terrorist suspects and activities. And, finally, although most convictions were later quashed, many suspects spent considerable periods in remand awaiting trial, giving credence to the view that it amounted to a form of 'internment by remand' (Greer 1984).

The infiltration of political groups, or the encouragement of informants within them, has become another standard tactic in anti-terrorist activity (Stevens 2003). Lowles' (2001) history of Combat 18 (C18), for example, suggests that at least one, if not more than one, leading member of the organisation was a paid informant of the Security Service/Special Branch in the late 1990s. Indeed he goes further. Initially, he argues, it appeared that C18 was not significantly hampered by the police and security services, arousing suspicion in some circles – including the far right – that it was being used to destabilise and disrupt the far right, which had been having some political success. From around 1995, however, 'there seemed to be a more determined effort on the part of the police to curtail the excesses of C18 . . . [and the police] . . . increased their intelligence on the group' (Lowles 2001: 261). Evidence came from a number of sources, including investigative journalists and, it appeared, an intelligence source within C18 (see issues of *Searchlight* during the period). For Lowles (2001), though the extent of the attention paid to such groups at the time indicates the seriousness with which they were taken, it was also an illustration of the success of the operation.

Finally in relation to police powers and tactics, recent years have seen increasing emphasis placed on forfeiture and asset seizure as a means of hampering the work of terrorist organisations. Considerable powers are included in the PTA, covering the seizure of assets, whether direct or indirect fruits of terrorism, so long as the assets are money or other property. As Levi and Gilmore (2002) note, however, 'it is difficult, even with hindsight, to work out when and how the view developed that attacking the money trail was a key element in the fight against organised crime'. Some place it in the mid-1980s when the FBI and others began using the Racketeer Influenced Corrupt Organizations (RICO) legislation passed in 1970 (Wechsler 2001), and the original focus of the bulk of such activity, especially internationally, was on drugs trafficking (Nadelmann 1993). Prior to 11 September the link between crimes for economic gain with terrorism was not high on the agenda of the USA and of many of the major international investigative bodies, including the G-7 established Financial Action Task Force (FATF) (Levi and Gilmore 2002) – though the links between NORAID and Irish terrorism, for example, had long been known and targeted in the UK. Domestically, the UK PTA gave greater powers than were available elsewhere and, consequently, greater prominence to such a strategy than in many jurisdictions (Levi and Osofsky 1995). Internationally, though al Qa'eda assets had been targeted since at least the East Africa Embassy bombings in 1998, there had been little apparent urgency.

Since 11 September the change has been swift. At a rhetorical level, the 'war on crime' that was extended to terrorism was described in part as a 'financial war'. Within the UK the National Terrorist Financial Investigation Unit, based within the Met's Special Branch, has trebled its staff resources and according to the Cabinet Office (2002) assets worth over $100 million have been frozen since 11 September. Internationally, the basis for financial investigative activity has remained the FATF, though it quickly sought to extend its work beyond money laundering to terrorist financing. In this connection there are a number of suggested differences between the funding of terrorism and other forms of 'organised' criminal activity. First, some forms of terrorism may be state sponsored. Secondly, and linked to this, some terrorist organisations can rely wholly, or in part, on donations and contributions from supporters for their funding. Thirdly, many terrorist organisations engage in legitimate business activities as a means of supporting themselves (Navias 2002), though the latter is certainly true of much organised crime too.

Levi and Gilmore (2002) suggest that the closest analogues of terrorist funds laundering are (1) the corporate and political 'slush funds' used for transnational corruption and political finance; and (2) tax evasion on non-criminal activities. To this might be added (3) the appropriation of finance intended as aid; and (4) the profits from arms dealing (Gilmore 1999).

Anti-terrorist policing activity in the UK has seen the progressive extension of policing powers, the development of new technologies and techniques and, from time to time, the deployment of tactics well beyond the limits of the law (Goldstein 1975). The temptation to stray beyond the law is, of course, present in all policing; a temptation perhaps exacerbated in this area because of the nature and threats posed. It is all the more important, therefore, that anti-terrorist policing is carefully and systematically governed.

Anti-terrorism: accountability and control

> Successful anti-terrorist co-operation cannot be measured purely in terms of operational effectiveness ... it has to be regarded as socially legitimate (Chalk 1994: 120).

Another way of expressing Chalk's observation is to follow Lustgarten's (2003) suggestion that the term 'national security' be assumed to have inherent within it the notion of effective democracy. Without this, the activities of any regime seeking to protect and maintain itself could be legitimised in the name of 'national security'. If 'effective democracy' is assumed, the logical consequence is that limits are immediately placed upon what national security institutions, including the police, may do and how they may do it. More particularly, this means ruling illegitimate any activities that are themselves in violation of democratic principles. In relation to policing that means resisting the temptation to accrue increasingly intrusive and repressive powers, and accepting the need to work directly with communities, and within ethical guidelines, against terrorist activity. Of course, while sensible in principle this is, as Lustgarten among others recognises, far from straightforward in practice, for the tactics and approaches of terrorists are not governed by the same standards or principles. The trick, he says, 'is to prevent any advantage the opponent may thereby obtain from leading to serious damage, without employing unacceptable means to do so. This should be recognised as a fairly serious dilemma' (2003: 321).

Adherence to the principles of democratic practice means a number of things. According to Lustgarten (2003) it means, at the very least, compliance with the rule of law. In addition, it should encompass, he argues, some form of effective public decision-making in the choice of the aims and operative framework of the agencies and also the creation of oversight machinery capable of ensuring that they respect democratic values. Though frequently invoked, 'democratic values' are rarely spelt out. In one of the few attempts to specify such values, Jones et al. (1994) argue that at least seven principles can be identified: *equity, delivery of service, responsiveness, distribution of power, information, redress* and *participation*. It is these democratic values, they argue, that should inform and direct the governance of policing. Following Lustgarten and others, we would argue that the policing of terrorist activities should be subject to at least as much democratic oversight as other areas of policing. Chalk outlines a number of guiding principles for governance in this arena:

1. *Limitation*: that strategies adopted do not go beyond what is needed and are directed only against terrorists. There is currently concern among some critics that the old external threat of communism has been replaced by the perceived new threat of mass immigration. The equation of immigration with crime, and terrorism, has given rise, some argue, to an increasingly militarised response to border protection – a response that involves the police who have replaced 'the army as the central instrument of coercion' (Bigo cited in Chalk 1994: 123).

2. *Credibility*: that citizens should be convinced that actions are appropriate and effective. Arguably, knowledge of EU-wide agencies and policies is far from good as 'the lines of communication between the general population and those involved with the Maastricht third pillar are extremely limited' (Chalk 1994: 125).

3. *Accountability*: that there should be parliamentary supervision and judicial oversight.

The space available here only allows for a brief description of the current arrangements for the governance of anti-terrorist activity in the UK and in other arenas in which the UK is involved. To begin with, there are perhaps two general observations that we might make. First, there have been a number of developments in recent years that have sought to increase the degree of oversight and accountability of the agencies involved in anti-terrorism. Secondly, it is arguably the case that there remain a number of democratic deficits in this regard.

In relation to the first observation, there are a number of developments we might point to. In the UK, as Lustgarten and Leigh (1994) argue, there has been particular concern about the accountability of the Security Service. Thus, whereas in Australia and Canada, following police corruption scandals, the trend has been towards the empowerment of security agencies, in the UK the view among policy-makers has been that the arrangements for the governance of the police are more robust than those for the Security Service. The consequences of this have been to ensure a continuing leading role for the police service in anti-terrorist activity, and a number of attempts better to regulate the Security Service. The Security Service Act 1989 (as amended in 1996) places the organisation under the authority of the Home Secretary and sets out its functions and the responsibilities of its Director General. The Intelligence Services Act 1994 established the Intelligence and Security Committee – a parliamentary committee – with responsibility for overseeing the expenditure, administration and policy of the security and intelligence services (MI5, MI6 and GCHQ). The Police Act 1997 and the Regulation of Investigatory Powers Act 2000 have significantly enhanced the structures and systems for oversight of policing by establishing the Office of Surveillance Commissioners, a Commissioner for the Intelligence Services and a tribunal to examine complaints and hear proceedings under s. 7 of the Human Rights Act 1998. As a result of these and other developments, there is undeniably now a far greater degree of openness about the activities of the Security Service and of covert policing activities generally.

In Northern Ireland an Ombudsman's Office has been established, providing significantly enhanced oversight of policing in all areas of activity, including anti-terrorist activity. The office, though relatively recently established, has already published a number of hard-hitting reports focusing on, for example, the Omagh bombing (Police Ombudsman 2001); the use of batons (Police Ombudsman 2002, 2003a); and the treatment of solicitors and barristers by the police (Police Ombudsman 2003b). Finally, on the mainland, after following consultation and reports from both KPMG and Liberty, the decision was taken to reform the police complaints system and to establish an Independent Police Complaints Commission, which will be operational from April 2004. In the context of the focus of this chapter, its independence, and its ability to investigate the activities of Special Branch, make it a potentially important development. The recent Stevens Inquiry (2003) makes numerous recommendations designed further to regulate covert police activity including the introduction of integrity testing and quality assurance checks and the formation of an overarching group of all relevant agencies (Gold group) to ensure effective intelligence sharing and to respond to community concerns.

Nevertheless, it remains the case that much work in this area remains shrouded in secrecy. A number of major democratic deficits remain – in relation to both police and security agencies. This is perhaps particularly vivid in the international arena. The growing number of international policing bodies working in this area remains poorly regulated and largely unaccountable (see Chapter 6). In many respects, Benyon et al.'s (1993: 210) conclusion that 'informal arrangements for co-operation have evolved which may or may not be backed up by more official policies and structures' remains accurate. Each of the major policing systems – Interpol, Trevi, Schengen and Europol – has different relationships to the institutions of the EU and, more importantly in this regard, each has rather inadequate legislative foundations. Indeed, 'popular accountability controls over the relevant institutions are equally meagre' (Anderson et al. 1995: 253) and due process safeguards remain underdeveloped. If anything, the situation has probably deteriorated since 11 September. A number of new measures have increased police powers and co-operation. Europol has increased its powers of information gathering from national forces and to co-ordinate arrests made by them. Europol now has a specialist anti-terrorist team, and the EU has given it a mandate to work with its US counterparts (Grant 2002). As yet, the increased powers have not been paralleled by increased oversight.

In the last few years anti-terrorist activity in the UK has been co-ordinated by three ministerial committees (two of which were established after 11 September): the War Cabinet, chaired by the Prime Minister, which oversees all the work; a further committee chaired by the Home Secretary which co-ordinates policy on protective and preventative security; and the Civil Contingencies Committee (CCC), also chaired by the Home Secretary, which has responsibility for supplies and essential services during emergencies (Cabinet Office 2002). Within London, considered to be at greatest threat, a London Resilience Cabinet, chaired by the Minister for London, has been established, as has an interagency London Resilience Team. A new strategic emergency planning regime for London, headed by the minister and the

Mayor, has been introduced and revised command, control and communication arrangements developed. Following 11 September the Security Service and the police have been working in the National Counter Terrorism and Security Office (NaCTSO) to deal with new terrorist tactics, and on the operational side the Police International Counter Terrorist Unit (PICTU) was established, staffed by Special Branch, Anti-terrorist Branch and Security Service officers to co-ordinate operations against international terrorism. The Security Service continues to lead on countering the threat from international terrorism (working closely with SIS, GCHQ, government departments and law enforcement agencies). Domestically, then, arrangements for governmental oversight are now reasonably well established. Democratic oversight – through the introduction of the Police Ombudsman for Northern Ireland and the Independent Police Complaints Commission – has recently been enhanced, but may still require further empowerment.

(Super)terrorism and the emergence of market societies

Just as the advent of globalised communications is held to have brought significant changes to the nature of the late modern world so, some would argue, it has heralded a shift in the nature of the terrorist threat. Political developments and further technological advances are said to have resulted in the emergence of new threats (such as those posed by weapons of mass destruction (WMD) and cyber-terrorism). Taylor and Horgan (1999: 84) predict three fundamentally different sources of future terrorism:

1. *International sources*, which will relate to the absorption of terrorism within conventional warfare.

2. *Focused issue-based terrorism*, which might be local in character like the Oaklahoma bombing or narrow but international in character, such as anti-abortion terrorism.

3. *Organised crime-related terrorism*, where the techniques of terrorism may be used for political ends to achieve financial gain.

Recent events, such as the sarin attack on the Tokyo subway, the Oaklahoma bombing and the separate attacks by al Qa'eda terrorists in New York and Washington, DC, would suggest that traditional constraints that inhibited high-impact/high-casualty methods might no longer apply. As Weinberg and Eubank observe: 'At one time terrorists wanted a lot of people watching, not a lot of people dead. Now they evidently want both, or so it is widely believed' (1999: 94). This does not necessarily mean that the principles of terrorism have changed, merely its scale. None the less, according to some influential commentators, terrorism is now both a more complex phenomena and, arguably, a greater danger than has been the case hitherto in modern times. And, as Gearson (2002: 22) puts it, 'modern states are actually not particularly well equipped to fight, or even capable of fighting, transnational and stateless terrorism'. Some would go further even than this. Bobbitt's influential thesis (2002) argues that the environment of unprecedented uncertainty associated with WMD and the new technologies requires, indeed, will bring, a fundamental reworking of the state itself. His argument is that the enormous power of the new technologies can be utilised by small numbers of people – operating independently of any state – and can deal a fatal blow to a nation-state. Moreover, the origin of such an attack can be partially, if not fully, disguised. 'Such attacks', he says, 'will not arrive with labels that tell us whether they are the result of a terrorist's attack, or a strategic assault by another state, or just the afternoon diversions of a teenager in California' (2002: 812). Under the circumstances of such a disguised attack, he argues, three deadly risks arise:

1. A state, unwilling or unable to suppress those believed to be responsible, will forfeit its sovereignty, be subject to attack and even occupation.

2. A state that is attacked will turn on its own people – or a minority – with violence and despotic police methods.

3. A state, despite denial of responsibility, will be deemed responsible and will itself become a target.

We face a future, he suggests, in which we will inevitably see much greater involvement of private interests in national security, and one in which 'national security' will cease to be defined by the borders of nation-states. The new emerging structures he calls 'market states'. Where the nation-state justified itself as a means of maximising the welfare of its citizens, including their safety, the market state is focused on maximising the opportunities enjoyed by its members. It is, therefore, a system less concerned with matters such as the rule of law, of concerns about justice and ethics, except in so far as they work to stimulate opportunity. The future, he asserts, is one in which what have hitherto been considered to be the three certainties of national security – 'that it is national (not international), that it is public (not private), and that it seeks victory (not stalemate) . . . are all about to be turned upside down' (2002: 816). The future, he argues, is very unlikely to be like the past. The policing arrangements are also likely to be radically reworked. It is, of course, impossible to judge whether Bobbitt is correct in his diagnosis. What seems undeniable, however, is that the USA – with the passage of the Homeland Security Act – the UK – with considerable increases in resources in anti-terrorist activity – and the EU – in response to pressure from the USA – are now organising their anti-terrorist activities in ways that in many cases would have been considered out of proportion to the threats posed – and perhaps even unpalatable – prior to 11 September.

Conclusion

Although this chapter concludes with a lengthy list of references to academic work, it is interesting to note, compared with other areas of police work, just how little has actually been written about the policing of terrorist activities. In part, no doubt, this is explained by the relative secrecy that surrounds such work. Nevertheless, even those scholars with a particular interest in the area of counter-terrorism appear to have relatively little to say about the role of the police. Wilkinson, for example, who notes that 'the main burden of containing and defeating terrorism in liberal democratic states is carried by the police services' (2001: 110) provides almost no detail of how they do this, outside a basic description of the structure of anti-terrorist work within the Met. Equally, policing scholars have tended to pay relatively little attention to anti-terrorist activity though, for understandable reasons, this is less true of those located in Northern Ireland than elsewhere in the UK. As the focus of concern shifts from domestic to international terrorism it will be interesting to see whether the focus of academic concern also moves (see Walker 2003).

This is not the place for a lengthy summary of the material presented earlier. Rather, we wish to make a small number of general observations about the policing of terrorism. The first is that much of the activity undertaken by the police in relation to terrorism is often merely a more intensive version of routine police work, of a problem-oriented variety (in particular through the collection of intelligence, often via the use of informants and surveillance). Though tempting to believe that something more sophisticated than 'normal' policing – and perhaps not so constrained by law – is required, there are good reasons to resist this. Secondly, because of the nature of the threats posed, and sometimes the sophistication of the terrorists themselves, there is an inherent pressure towards ever-increasing powers. Terrorist activities tend to elicit a strong reaction on the part of the state and, all too often, this has involved the passage of new, emergency legislation, generally providing for the extension of the powers available to the police and/or the Security Services. This leads to the third observation which is that, even though such measures are often presented as being 'temporary', the reality is that over time there is a long-term process of 'normalisation' in which the gap between special and normal policing powers narrows or even disappears. This is an area, therefore, in which oversight and accountability of police activities are especially important. The limitations of existing mechanisms for governing policing in the UK are well rehearsed (see Chapter 24). In the area of anti-terrorist activity, where there is an increasing role for transnational police organisations, the problems are arguably even greater and in more urgent need of reform (see Chapter 6).

Notwithstanding the general point made above, the policing of terrorist activity can be distinguished, to a degree, from other policing activities by the greater attention that is paid to *prevention* in the former compared with the latter. As Lustgarten (2003: 328) notes, the police task in this regard 'is to protect fundamental values and institutions from harm, not punish those who perpetrate it after the damage is done'. To act in this manner is to be proactive, to use information and intelligence to gauge threats. It is, in short, an area of policing that is governed by the notion of 'risk'. One question which arises here, therefore, is whether there should be, indeed are, any differences of institutional focus in this regard. More particularly, should security services be primarily concerned with 'protection' and the police with 'punishment'? Current arrangements and the lessons of recent practice suggest that maintaining such an institutional division of labour is neither healthy nor realistic. The tasks associated with 'protection' – intelligence gathering, surveillance, etc. – are just as much the stuff of routine policing as they are of the work national security agencies. Moreover, the greater transparency of constabularies, when compared with security services, rather reinforces the desirability of at least some police involvement in such activity in a democracy.

Walker and McGuinness (2002) argue that the police response to political crime exhibits some of the features of Ericson and Haggerty's (1997) 'policing the risk society' model, including the management of criminal risk through surveillance; information gathering; and communication and brokering both by the police themselves and by powerful non-police bodies including, for example, financial institutions. The most recent example of this idea may be seen in the adoption of 'community risk assessment' in anti-terrorist activity – derived from the Stephen Lawrence Inquiry. It is important, however, not to exaggerate the extent to which such policing is risk focused and, in particular, to overstate the abilities of the police and security services in this regard. Though there have been very significant successes (and these are often not very visible), there have also been some pretty spectacular failures including, most notably, in relation to the terrorist attacks on the World Trade Center and the Pentagon which, according to Ball (2002: 60):

> involved the worst intelligence failure by the US intelligence community since Pearl Harbor in 1941 ... a failure at all phases of the intelligence cycle, from the setting of priorities and tasks, through the gamut of collection activities, to the analytical, assessment and dissemination processes which should have provided some warning of the event.

In his report in the aftermath of the Brixton riots, Lord Scarman observed that policing must aim to strike a balance between the prevention of crime, the protection of life and property and the preservation of order. In doing so, Scarman argued, the duty of the police to maintain order must override all other concerns. It may also reasonably be argued that 'this principle applies equally to terrorism' (Crawshaw 1987: 19). Two points may be made here. First, the nature of anti-terrorist policing is, at heart, little different from other areas of policing and, more particularly, with regard to the rules and procedures governing it, should be no different at all. Secondly, that a failure to recognise and abide by this is likely simply to serve to reinforce the inequities and problems that are the major source of the threats being policed.

How are we to conclude? We began the chapter by asking 'what is terrorism?' Crudely, terrorism may be viewed as 'political violence' or violence for political ends. In responding to such violence, or the threat of such violence, it is clear that security services, and the police in particular, have an important role to play in the maintenance of order and security. However, it is equally important that this role should not be confused or conflated with the idea that policing represents some form of 'solution' to the problem of terrorism. Indeed, as most commentators agree, to talk of solutions is anyway rather naïve. Rather, and using Wilkinson's (2001) terminology, we might better think of pathways out or away from terrorism. The lesson closest to home, in Northern Ireland, suggests that just as terrorism is political, so are the pathways away from it. Democratic states are unlikely to find that law enforcement and judicial control are a sufficient response. Moreover, to the extent that law enforcement is a central part of the response to terrorist threats, the model in this area should be 'community-based', 'democratic' and 'ethical' policing, as it should in all others.

Selected further reading

There is nothing that could be described as a comprehensive text in this area. Wilkinson's *Terrorism versus Democracy* (2001) provides a useful overview from a particular vantage point, but should generally be read in conjunction with more critical accounts. The policing of the Troubles is well covered from a number of vantage points: by journalists such as Taylor (*States of Terror* 1993; *Brits: The War against the IRA* 2001), historians of the police (Weitzer's *Policing Under Fire* – 1995), as well as criminologists of various hues (e.g. Brewer's 'Policing in divided societies' (1991) and Hillyard's *Suspect Community* (1993)). Walker's *The Prevention of Terrorism in British Law* (1992), though now out of date, is a good guide to anti-terrorist legislation in the UK. For developments beyond the UK, Hebenton and Thomas's *Policing Europe* (1995) and Nadelmann's *Cops across Borders* (1993) are good sources, as is Walker's *Policing in a Changing Constitutional Order* (2000). Lustgarten and Leigh's *In from the Cold* (1994) provides the most thoroughgoing review of the work of security services, and Bobbitt's *The Shield of Achilles* (2002) is one of the most influential, if somewhat dystopian, theses on the emerging new world order. There are numerous websites full of pertinent information. On policing, legislative developments and civil liberties, the best is probably Statewatch (www.statewatch.org).

Notes

1   As an example that there is relatively little that can be found that is truly new about 'modern' terrorist activities, a similar plan had been hatched by the IRA and was revealed in the *News of the World* on 5 February 1939.
2   www.liberty-human-rights.org.uk/resources/articles/pdfs/the-anti-terrorism-crime-and-security-act-2001.pdf.
3   www.cabinet-office.gov.uk/sept11/coi-0809.doc.

Acknowledgements

Warm thanks are due to Lawrence Lustgarten, Peter Neyroud and Neil Walker for helpful comments on an early version of this chapter.

References

Anderson, M., den Boer, M., Cullen, P., Gilmore, P., Raab, C.D. and Walker, N. (1995) *Policing the European Union: Theory, Law and Practice*. Oxford: Clarendon Press.
Ascoli, D. (1979) *The Queen's Peace: The Origins and Development of the Metropolitan Police 1829–1979*. London: Hamish Hamilton.

Ball, D. (2002) 'Desperately seeking Bin Laden: the intelligence dimension of the war against terrorism', in K. Booth and T. Dunne (eds) *Worlds in Collision: Terror and the Future of Global Order*. Basingstoke: Palgrave, 60–73.

Benyon, J., Turnbull, A., Willis, R., Woodward, R. and Beck, A. (1993) *Police Co-operation in Europe: An Investigation*. Leicester: Centre for the Study of Public Order.

Bishop, P. and Mallie, E. (1987) *The Provisional IRA*. London: Heinemann.

Bobbitt, P. (2002) *The Shield of Achilles: War, Peace and the Course of History*. London: Penguin Books.

Boyle, K., Hadden, T. and Hillyard, P. (1975) *Law and the State: The Case of Northern Ireland*. London: Martin Robinson.

Bresler, F. (1992) *Interpol*. London: Sinclair Stevenson.

Brogden, M. and Shearing, C. (1993) *Policing for a New South Africa*. London: Routledge.

Bunyan, T. (1977) *The History and Practice of the Political Police in Britain*. London: Quartet.

Cabinet Office (2002) *The United Kingdom and the Campaign against International Terrorism*. London: Cabinet Office (http://www.cabinet-office.gov.uk/reports/sept11/coi-0809.pdf).

Chalk, P. (1994) 'EU counter-terrorism, the Maastricht Third Pillar and liberal democratic acceptability', *Terrorism and Political Violence*, 6(2): 103–45.

Crawshaw, S. (1987) 'Countering terrorism: the British model', in R.H. Ward and H.E. Smith (eds) *International Terrorism: The Domestic Response*. Chicago, IL: Office of International Criminal Justice, 11–22.

Diplock Report (1972) *Report of the Commission to Consider Legal Procedures to Deal with Terrorist Activity in Northern Ireland* (Cmnd 5185). London: HMSO.

Donohue, L. (2001) *Counter-terrorist Law and Emergency Powers in the United Kingdom, 1922–2000*. Dublin: Irish Academic Press.

Ellison, G. and Smyth, J. (2000) *The Crowned Harp: Policing Northern Ireland*. London: Pluto Press.

Ericson, R. and Haggerty, K. (1997) *Policing the Risk Society*. Oxford: Clarendon Press.

European Commission (1992) *Commission of the EC European Union*. Luxembourg: Office for Official Publications of the EC.

Fenwick, H. (2002) 'The Anti-terrorism, Crime and Security Act 2001: a proportionate response to 11 September?', 65(5): 724–62.

Gearson, J. (2002) 'The nature of modern terrorism', in L. Freedman (ed.) *Superterrorism: Policy Responses*. Oxford: Blackwell, 7–24.

George, B. and Watson, T. (1992) 'Combating international terrorism after 1992', in Y. Alexander and D.A. Pluchinsky (eds) *European Terrorism Today and Tomorrow*. Washington, DC: Brassey's Terrorism Library.

Gilmore, W. (1999) *Dirty Money: The Evolution of Money-laundering Counter-measures*. Strasbourg: Council of Europe.

Goldstein, H. (1975) *Police Corruption: A Perspective on its Nature and Control*. Washington, DC: Police Foundation.

Grant, C. (2002) 'The eleventh of September and beyond: the impact on the European Union', in L. Freedman (ed.) *Superterrorism: Policy Responses*. London: Blackwell, 135–53.

Greer, S. (1984) 'Internment with a judge's stamp', *Fortnight*, April.

Greer, S. (1988) 'The supergrass system', in A. Jennings (ed.) *Justice Under Fire*. London: Pluto Press, 73–103.

Greer, S. (2001) 'Where the grass is greener: supergrasses in comparative perspective', in R. Billingsley *et al.* (eds) *Informers: Policing, Policy and Practice*. Cullompton: Willan.

Hebenton, B. and Thomas, T. (1995) *Policing Europe: Co-operation, Conflict and Control*. Basingstoke: Macmillan.

Her Majesty's Inspectorate of Constabulary (1999) *Keeping the Peace: Policing Disorder*. London: HMIC.

Her Majesty's Inspectorate of Constabulary (2003) *A Need to Know: HMIC Thematic Inspection of Special Branch and Ports Policing*. London: HMIC.

Hillyard, P. (1985) 'Lessons from Ireland', in B. Fine and R. Millar (eds) *Policing the Miners' Strike*. London: Lawrence & Wishart.

Hillyard, P. (1988) 'Political and social dimensions of emergency law in Northern Ireland', in A. Jennings (ed.) *Justice under Fire*. London: Pluto, 191–212.

Hillyard, P. (1993) *Suspect Community: People's Experience of the Prevention of Terrorism Acts in Britain*. London: Pluto.

Hillyard, P. (1994) 'The normalization of special powers', in N. Lacey (ed.) *A Reader on Criminal Justice*. Oxford: Oxford University Press.

Hillyard, P. (1997) 'Policing divided societies: trends and prospects in Northern Ireland and Britain', in P. Francis *et al.* (eds) *Policing Futures: The Police, Law Enforcement and the Twenty-first Century*. Basingstoke: Macmillan, 163–85.

Home Office (1994) *Guidelines on Special Branch Work in Great Britain*. London: Home Office and Scottish Office Home and Health Department.

House of Commons (1990) *Practical Police Co-operation in the European Community. Home Affairs Committee (7th Report) Session 1989–90*. London: HMSO.

Huntley, B. (1977) *Bomb Squad*. London: W.H. Allen.

Independent Commission on Policing in Northern Ireland (1999) *A New Beginning: Policing in Northern Ireland* (the Patten Report). Belfast: ICPNI.

Jenkins, B. (1974) *International Terrorism: A New Mode of Conflict*. Los Angeles, CA: Crescent.

Jones, T., Newburn, T. and Smith, D.J. (1994) *Democracy and Policing*. London: Policy Studies Institute.

Laquer, W. (1987) *The Age of Terrorism*. Boston, MA: Little Brown & Co.

Levi, M. and Gilmore, B. (2002) 'Terrorist finance, money laundering and the rise and rise of mutual evaluation: a new paradigm for crime control?', *European Journal of Law Reform*, 4(2): 337–64.

Levi, M. and Osofsky, L. (1995) *Investigating, Seizing and Confiscating the Proceeds of Crime. Police Research Group Paper* 61. London: Home Office.

Lowles, N. (2001) *White Riot: The Violent Story of Combat 18*. Bury: Milo Books.

Lustgarten, L. (2003) 'National security and political policing: some thoughts on values, ends and the law', in J.P. Brodeur *et al.* (eds) *Democracy, Law and Security: Internal Security Services in Europe*. Aldershot: Ashgate.

Lustgarten, L. and Leigh, I. (1994) *In from the Cold: National Security and Parliamentary Democracy*. Oxford: Oxford University Press.

Marotta, E. (1999) 'Europol's role in anti-terrorism policing', in M. Taylor and J. Horgan (eds) *The Future of Terrorism*. London: Frank Cass, 15–18.

McKittrick, D., Kelters, S., Feeney, B. and Thornton, S. (1999) *Lost Lives: The Stories of the Men, Women and Children who Died as a Result of the Northern Ireland Troubles*. London: Mainstream Publishing.

Morton, J. (1995) *Supergrasses and Informers: An Informal History of Undercover Police Work*. London: Little Brown.

Nadelmann, E. (1993) *Cops across Borders*. State Park, PA: Pennsylvania State University Press.

Navias, M.S. (2002) 'Finance warfare as a response to international terrorism', in L. Freedman (ed.) *Superterrorism: Policy Responses*. Oxford: Blackwell, 57–79.

Newman, K. (1978a) 'Violence in Northern Ireland', *Constabulary Gazette*, March: 7–10.

Newman, K. (1978b) *Prevention in Extremis: The Preventative Role of the Police in Northern Ireland. The Cranfield Papers*. London: Peel Press.

Ni Aolain, F. (2000) *The Politics of Force: Conflict Management and State Violence in Northern Ireland*. Belfast: Blackstaff.

O'Leary, B. and McGarry, J. (1993) *The Politics of Antagonism: Understanding Northern Ireland*. London: Athlone Press.

Peers, S. (2003) 'EU responses to terrorism', *International and Comparative Law Quarterly*, 52: 227–43.

Police Ombudsman for Northern Ireland (2001) *A Statement by the Police Ombudsman for Northern Ireland on her Investigation of Matters Relating to the Omagh Bombing on August 15 1998*, Belfast: Office of the Police Ombudsman.

Police Ombudsman for Northern Ireland (2002) *A Summary of Reports by the Police Ombudsman for Northern Ireland on the Discharge of Baton Rounds by Police Officers during 2001 and 2002*. Belfast: Office of the Police Ombudsman.

Police Ombudsman for Northern Ireland (2003a) *A Study of Complaints Involving the Use of Batons by the Police in Northern Ireland*. Belfast: Office of the Police Ombudsman.

Police Ombudsman for Northern Ireland (2003b) *A Study of the Treatment of Solicitors and Barristers by the Police in Northern Ireland*. Belfast: Office of the Police Ombudsman.

Rauchs, G. and Koenig, D.J. (2001) 'Europol', in D.J. Koenig and D.K. Das (eds) *International Police Cooperation: A World Perspective*. Lanham, MA: Lexington Books.

Ryder, C. (1989) *The Royal Ulster Constabulary: A Force Under Fire*. London: Methuen.

Scarman, Lord (1972) *Violence and Civil Disturbances in Northern Ireland in 1969. Report of a Tribunal of Inquiry* (Cmnd 566). London: HMSO.

Shafritz, E.F. Jr, Gibbons, J.R. and Scott G.E. (1991) *Almanac of Modern Terrorism*. New York, NY: Facts on File.

Shulsky, A.N. and Schmitt, G.J. (2002) *Silent Warfare: Understanding the World of Intelligence* (3rd edn). Washington, DC: Brassey's.

Sloan, S. (1978) *The Anatomy of Non-territorial Terrorism: An Analytical Essay. Clandestine Tactics and Technology Series*. Gaithersburg: The International Association of Chiefs of Police.

Sloan, S. (1982) 'International terrorism, conceptual problems and implications', *Journal of Thought: An Interdisciplinary Quarterly*, 17(2).

Stalker, J. (1988) *Stalker*. London: Harrap.

Stevens, Sir J. (2003) *Stevens Inquiry: Summary and Recommendations*. London: Metropolitan Police.

Taylor, M, and Horgan, J. (1999) 'Future developments of political terrorism in Europe', *Terrorism and Political Violence*, 11(4): 83–93.

Taylor, P. (1980) *Beating the Terrorists?* Harmondsworth: Penguin Books.

Taylor, P. (1993) *States of Terror: Democracy and Political Violence*. London: BBC Books.

Taylor, P. (2001) *Brits: The War against the IRA*. London: Bloomsbury.

Taylor, T. (2002) 'United Kingdom', in Y. Alexander (ed.) *Combating Terrorism: Strategies of Ten Countries*. Ann Arbor, MI: University of Michigan Press, 187–226.

Walker, C. (1992) *The Prevention of Terrorism in British Law*. Manchester: Manchester University Press.

Walker, C. (2000b) 'Briefing on the Terrorism Act 2000', *Terrorism and Political Violence*, 12(2): 1–36.

Walker, C. and McGuinness, M. (2002) 'Commercial risk, political violence and policing the city of London', in A. Crawford (ed.) *Crime and Insecurity: The Governance of Safety in Europe*. Cullompton: Willan, 234–59.

Walker, N. (2000a) *Policing in a Changing Constitutional Order*. London: Sweet & Maxwell.

Walker, C. (2003) 'Policy options and priorities: British perspectives', in M. Van Leeuwen (ed.) *Confronting Terrorism: European Experiences, Threat Perceptions and Policies*, The Hague: Kluwer Law International.

Walsh, D.P.J. (1983) *The Use and Abuse of Emergency Legislation in Northern Ireland*. London: Cobden Trust.

Weinberg, L. and Eubank, W. (1999) 'Terrorism and the shape of things to come', *Terrorism and Political Violence*, 11(4): 94–105.

Weitzer, R. (1985) 'Policing a divided society: obstacles to normalization in Northern Ireland', *Social Problems*, 33(2): 41–55.

Weitzer, R. (1995) *Policing Under Fire: Ethnic Conflict and Police–Community Relations in Northern Ireland*. Albany, NY: State University of New York Press.

Wilkinson, P. (2001) *Terrorism versus Democracy: The Liberal State Response*. London: Frank Cass.

Chapter 20

Policing cybercrime

Yvonne Jewkes

Introduction

In April 2001, the National Hi-Tech Crime Unit (NHTCU) was established amid a fanfare of publicity and optimistic predictions concerning its future impact on cybercrime. Part of a wider £25 million strategy funded by the government, the NHTCU is a multi-agency organisation comprising representatives from the National Crime Squad, the National Criminal Intelligence Service, HM Customs and Excise, the Ministry of Defence and seconded police officers. Its aims are to work in conjunction with local police forces, offering advice and technical assistance, and co-ordinating operations carried out at a local or regional level. In addition, the unit conducts its own investigations and develops intelligence about computer-related crime – including hacking, virus writing, drugs trafficking on the Internet and computer-mediated child abuse – nationally and internationally. In its first year of operation, the NHTCU declared its achievements (10 proactive operations, 30 arrests and recovery of over three-and-a-half terabytes of information) proof of its status as 'the lynchpin in the UK's co-ordinated response to cybercrime' (www.ncis.co.uk/press/2002). In July 2002 the National Criminal Intelligence Service (NCIS) augmented these accomplishments with the release of a statement heralding the success of an operation code-named Twins, co-ordinated between the NCIS, NHTCU and Europol. Following raids carried out simultaneously across seven countries, several arrests were made and substantial quantities of computer and video equipment containing abusive images of children were seized. This success prompted Detective Chief Superintendent, Len Hynds, head of the NHTCU, to declare that Operation Twins demonstrated how 'international law enforcement works in partnership, across multi-geographical jurisdictions, to identify and bring to justice those responsible for and engaged in serious sexual abuse of children' (www.ncis.co.uk/press/2002). However, just a few months later the NHTCU was reportedly 'creaking at the seams' (*Guardian*, 12 November 2002) and 'unable to cope' (BBC News, 13 January 2003) with the volume of intelligence it was receiving about users of child pornography on the Internet. In the words of a spokesman from the NHTCU, Operation Ore – a police investigation of over 7,000 UK subscribers to an American child pornography portal – had 'hammered' the unit and 'crippled' their capabilities to investigate other high-priority cybercrimes (telephone conversation, 8 April 2003).

The establishment of the NHTCU may have seemed attractive to those who have been alarmed by recent moral panics concerning the apparent expansion and increased visibility of cybercrimes and may, superficially at least, have appeared to fulfil prophesies of an international law enforcement agency patrolling the electronic beat and hunting down paedophiles, pornographers and criminal masterminds. But the first two years of NHTCU's operation – while notable for successes such as Operation Twins – have also demonstrated that some expectations of the organisation were wildly ambitious and unrealistic, at least within the context of the finite resources within which it has to operate. The sheer size and scope of the Internet, the volume of electronic traffic it facilitates, the varying legal responses to cybercrime in different countries and other inter-jurisdictional difficulties combine to ensure that the police feel they remain in a perpetual game of 'catch-up' with the vast numbers of criminally minded individuals who lurk in the shadowy corners of cyberspace.

This chapter examines some of the unique challenges facing the police in their attempts to tackle cybercrime. At the present time the Home Office does not compile statistics on cybercrime and, in any case, figures on the precise scale and breakdown of computer-mediated crime are notoriously unreliable as they are invariably out of date by the time they are published. The chapter therefore steers clear of quantitative measurements and discusses some of the offences that – within a generally low-visibility category of crime that has no specific reference point in law – are (in the broadest sense) 'policed'. It then explores the factors which impede effective policing of cybercrime (in the more narrow sense of proactive law enforcement and intelligence gathering by the state-funded public police) and considers the particular case of child pornography and Operation Ore which, it argues, has paradoxically both accelerated and hampered the police's commitment to combating cybercrime. Finally, the chapter reflects on emerging trends and priorities in policing cybercrime and considers the challenges for the future.

Policing cybercrime

Before discussing the characteristics of cybercrime, and the specific role of the police in combating the problem, it should briefly be noted that much of the monitoring, regulation, protection and enforcement related to cybercrimes is not the responsibility of state-controlled public police forces. Governments, the police, Internet service providers (ISPs) and Internet users all broadly agree that the latter two groups – ISPs and users – must bear the primary responsibility for cleaning up cyberspace. For example, individual Internet users can monitor their own use and that of others, evict offensive participants from chat rooms or report harmful or illegal material on websites. Parents and teachers of young Internet users can utilise software which denies access to material containing sexually explicit words, or restrict children's use of the Net on the basis of rating systems provided by independent regulatory bodies such as the Internet Watch Foundation (IWF). ISPs can draw up codes of conduct which their members and subscribers must follow, monitor the content of their sites and remove offending content or take other appropriate action. In addition there are a growing number of interest groups – such as Women Halting Online Abuse (WHOA), Internet Hotline Providers in Europe (IN-HOPE) and Cyberangels – who support a particular cause or aspect of regulation. There also exist numerous organisations that support specific business interests, such as the Business Software Alliance (BSA) which represents many of the big software companies and works closely with law enforcement agencies to enforce copyright laws and investigate cases of software theft. Finally, in recent years there has been a proliferation of private security firms set up to protect corporate data for commercial businesses who place a premium on discretion and privacy when it comes to their computerised records and data systems.

Even the police themselves are becoming part of a more diverse assortment of bodies with policing functions, and the array of activities we term 'policing' is becoming increasingly diffuse within and between nation-states (Reiner 2000; see Chapter 7). Just as the policing of terrestrial space has demanded a 'joined-up approach' between individual citizens, private sector agencies and the police, so too has the policing of cyberspace become a pluralistic endeavour, as the establishment of the NHTCU illustrates. When commentators talk of 'cybercops' they may be referring to a wide range of different bodies or strategies encompassing those whose primary aim is to 'protect', for example, authorities who use encryption and digital 'fingerprinting' techniques to protect copyrighted material, to those whose primary aim is to 'enforce', for example, the National Crime Squad and the NCIS. The international police co-ordination body, Interpol, and its European equivalent, Europol, also support cross-border investigation and act as conduits for the pooling of intelligence and expert knowledge (see Chapter 6). However, although Interpol and Europol have put themselves forward as the most effective organisations to establish a global cyberpolice force, in reality such a move is some way off (Glick 2001). Co-operation between member states is undoubtedly desirable, but in reality it is hard to achieve and investigations can be held up for months while law enforcement agents from different countries struggle to find compatible modus operandi (Glick 2001).

While a review of the literature on policing cyberspace reveals that much of it is not concerned with 'the police' at all, but is about non-police regulatory bodies, a great deal of discussion that *is* explicitly concerned with the police service's role in combating cybercrime (even from within the police's own ranks) is scathing about their commitment to the task (Goodman 1997; Hyde 1999). Yet, great strides have been made in recent years and it is certainly not the case that all police officers are Luddites seeking to thwart progress within the force. Since the first police operation targeting paedophiles using the Internet for networking purposes – code named Starburst – took place in 1998, there have been a number of successful investigations including Cathedral (an international operation targeting the notorious 'W0nderland Club' in 2001); Artus (in which an international paedophile network known as the 'Round

Table' was uncovered in March 2002); Magenta (in which 27 people were arrested in the UK in April 2002); Amethyst (a nationwide swoop by Ireland's Sexual Assault and Domestic Violence Unit in May 2002); as well as Twins and Ore. Furthermore, alongside the establishment of the NHTCU, the government has provided funding for a minimum complement of two officers in every force to carry out proactive investigations of online criminality and forensic examinations of seized computer hardware.

In addition, government targets requiring all public agencies to provide their services online by 2005 are accelerating the progress of e-policing strategies across all forces (albeit that some are responding with greater speed and enthusiasm than others). A national website (www.online.police.uk) permits minor, non-emergency crimes to be reported online, and an e-policing management group has been established to develop strategy in this area. Of course, e-policing is different from policing cybercrime: the former pertains to the police's own use of technology to improve their efficiency and deliver a better service to the public, while the latter concerns the investigation of crimes committed by means of computer technologies. However, as will be discussed in greater detail later, many police officers believe that the two issues are intrinsically related, and that the police service cannot be expected to respond with eagerness to the problems of cybercrime when individual police officers are not encouraged to employ technology to improve their service or even routinely given an email address.

What is cybercrime?

Throughout this chapter the term 'cybercrime' is used to describe what, elsewhere, might encompass 'computer crime', 'Internet crime' and 'high-tech' or 'hi-tech' crime; terms that tend to be used interchangeably despite their differences.[1] So what are 'cybercrimes' and what kinds of challenges do they pose for the police and other law enforcement agencies? Broadly speaking, cybercrimes can be classified in two categories: crimes that cannot be committed in any other way or against any other type of victim (in other words, where the computer is the target of the offence; for example, unauthorised access to systems, tampering with programs and data, planting of viruses and so on); and familiar or conventional crimes that are facilitated by computer and information technologies ('cyber' versions of fraud, identity theft, stalking and so on). In some cases, criminal activities may encompass both categories. For example, acts of terrorism can involve qualitatively new offences enabled by computer technologies or, alternatively, may integrate cyberspace into more traditional activities such as planning, intelligence, logistics, finance and so on (Goodman and Brenner 2002). Finally, there are a number of activities that are not illegal but may constitute what most people would consider harmful to some users (such as some forms of pornography, gambling, unsolicited email, unregulated sales of medicines and prescription drugs and so on). The following section provides an outline of some of the crimes unique to, or significantly enhanced by, computer technologies, together with a brief consideration of policing strategies relating to these offences.

Pornography

The most high-profile form of 'policing' aimed at the Internet to date has been targeted at pornography, especially material which exploits children. The specific case of Operation Ore, a police investigation targeting UK subscribers to child pornography sites, will be examined in detail later in the chapter. However, while the trade in abusive images of children has dominated debates about the potentially subversive role of the Internet, the issue of pornography generally (i.e. the kind of 'adult' pornography that in pre-Internet times was to be found on the top shelves of newsagents) is rather more ambiguous. It is a subject that provokes fear and fascination in equal measure and, while online pornography was the force that propelled the rapid growth of the Internet and demonstrated its commercial potential, equally it was pornography that precipitated the establishment of some of the most high-profile organisations which police the Net. 'Adult' cyberporn has democratised sexual gratification and provided greater freedom of access to women, as well as its traditional customers, men (Jewkes and Sharp 2003), yet at the same time it has reignited debates about the exploitation of women and the relationship between pornography and rape (Aitkenhead 2003). But perhaps most surprisingly, the Internet has normalised 'adult' pornography to the extent that when rock star Pete Townshend faced allegations of downloading abusive images of children and said he was not a paedophile but had used adult porn all his life, the latter was barely commented on in the British media. The distinction between sexually explicit images of adults and sexually explicit images of children is interesting in the current context. The former, even at its most hard core and illegal, is not considered to be a policing priority, while the latter is (as will be argued later) the moral panic of our age, with all the attendant implications that moral panics tend to have on government and policing priorities.

Hate crime

The promotion of racial hatred is widespread and the Internet is a relatively cheap and accessible means of connecting similarly minded people across the world and coalescing their belief systems. The Net is a sophisticated tool for recruitment and unification, providing links between hate movements that were previously diverse and fractured, and facilitating the creation of a collective identity and empowering sense of community (Perry 2001: 177). Various groups on the political far right – neo-Nazis, skinheads and groups with ties to the Ku Klux Klan – are using the Net to target a youthful and impressionable audience with racist, anti-semitic and homophobic propaganda with little fear of the kind of legal sanction that might accompany the circulation of such material in more 'traditional' forms (Whine 1997; Zickmund 2000). Although Germany and many other European countries have criminalised the publication and distribution of hate propaganda, the Internet remains largely unregulated and there is little the police can do unless a specific crime is reported. It is estimated that there are thousands of websites propagating violence and intolerance and many contain practical guides (such as bomb-making instructions) to assist proponents of hate in their criminal endeavours in the physical world. But more insidious than sites that attract those who are already involved in, or predisposed towards, acts of crime and violence, are those which purport to be 'mainstream' and are used to target the 'unconverted'. For example, in an effort to change the demographics of hate movements by recruiting young students and professionals, many sites feature audio excerpts of CDs, downloadable album covers and online lyrics – a blatant appeal to the 'MTV generation' (Perry 2001: 178).

The use of the Internet to promote hatred is not confined to racially motivated attacks. In July 2001 the ISP, Demon, won a change to the injunction protecting the killers of two-year-old James Bulger when they were released from custody and given new identities. The original form of the injunction, designed to prevent the mass media from publishing or broadcasting details of the offenders or their whereabouts, was deemed 'inappropriate' for the Internet because of the risks of a service provider inadvertently providing access to material about the pair and consequently being found in contempt of court. ISPs are now compelled to take all reasonable measures to prevent this from happening, although stories about the pair – posted on sites in other parts of the world – still abound on the Net.

Electronic theft and intellectual property rights

One of the most obvious consequences of the new information and communications revolution is its creation and distribution of unimaginably more information-based products which force us to re-evaluate traditionally held ideas about crime and criminality. For example, theft has commonly involved one person taking something belonging to another person without his or her permission – the result being that the first party no longer has possession of the property taken. Investigation of this type of offence is usually relatively straightforward in so far as it involves property that is tangible, visible and atom based (Goodman 1997). But in a virtual context, it is quite possible for one person to take something that belongs to another person without permission and make a perfect copy of the item, the result being that the original owner still has the property even though the thief now has a version as well (Goodman 1997). Such acts challenge conventional and legal definitions of offences and render traditional copyright laws irrelevant.

Electronic reproduction of data can take many forms. One of the most common is 'peer-to-peer' file-sharing, which has arguably returned to the Internet a sense of the liberal, collective ethos and benign anarchy that characterised its early days in the 1960s and 1970s. But for the film and music industries who are losing millions of dollars in lost sales, this form of 'digital piracy' taking place in teenagers' bedrooms the world over is every bit as unlawful as the knowing and criminal use of the Internet to market or distribute copyrighted software. The industry has been slow to respond to the problem of file-sharing, and broadband technology has made it even quicker and easier to download music and movies illegally. However, some CDs are now being manufactured in such a way as to make it impossible to play them (and copy them) on a PC. Meanwhile, the Record Industry Association of America (RIAA) is taking legal action against individuals it alleges offer file-swapping services on university campuses, and the Movie Picture Association of America is attempting to close down sites that distribute films online. But many believe that big corporations are being forced into playing cat-and-mouse games they can't possibly hope to win because – as the RIAA's infamous closure of Napster demonstrated – when the illegal business of one outfit is terminated, numerous others will appear in its wake.

Invasion of privacy and theft of identity

The entitlement to security of person is regarded as a fundamental human right, yet the scope and pervasiveness of digital technologies open up new areas of social vulnerability. Invasion of privacy takes many forms from 'spamming' to online defamation, stalking and violence. Spamming has thus far been considered little more than an extension of conventional junk mail, although it is increasingly being recognised as an insidious and frequently illegal activity. It can encompass electronic chain letters, links to pornographic sites, scams claiming that there are extensive funds – for example, from over-invoiced business contracts or a deceased relative's will – available for immediate transfer into the target's bank account, fraudulent pyramid investment schemes, phoney cancer cures and bogus test kits for anthrax. The sheer volume of spam – which, according to a European Commission study, will soon average 60 unwanted messages per day for every user (Schofield 2002) – obviously poses difficulties for those trying to stem the tide of unsolicited mail, and pressure is mounting on ISPs to do more to stop spam at source.

The law offers greater protection to individuals whose reputation is slurred by defamatory Internet content. Teachers and lecturers seem particularly vulnerable to such attacks. In 2000, Demon paid over £230,000 to a British university lecturer who claimed that the ISP had failed to remove two anonymous Internet postings defaming him, while in America a 'teacher review' site set up by students at the City College of San Fransisco resulted in one teacher filing a lawsuit against the site, denouncing it as a 'disgusting, lie-filled, destructive force' (Curzon-Brown 2000: 91). The phenomenally successful 'Friends Reunited' site (www.friendsreunited.co.uk) allows participants to share memories of former teachers, but urges users to report abusive messages to the site support team who instantly remove them. However, individual users of the site can still be prosecuted as a former pupil of Jim Murray found out when he was taken to court for posting defamatory remarks about the teacher in May 2002. In this case the court ordered the defendant, Jonathan Spencer (who, ironically is himself now a teacher), to pay Murray damages of £1,400.

Another cybercrime related to privacy is the theft of personal identity, a practice that has dramatically increased in the last few years. The American Federal Trade Commission report that of the 204,000 complaints it received in 2001, 42 per cent involved stolen identities. It further estimated that up to 750,000 US citizens had their identities stolen in 2002 for the purposes of accessing credit card accounts, securing loans and cashing cheques. Identity theft encompasses a full range of offences from the appropriation and use of credit card numbers (see Chapter 18) to the wholesale adoption of someone else's persona (Finch 2003). It can be mundane and opportunistic; for example, many identity thieves rummage through dustbins for discarded credit card statements or pick up receipts left at bank ATMs. However, more high-tech versions include hacking into an individual's personal computer in order to steal his or her bank and credit card details, using software programs designed to work out or randomly generate PIN numbers, and 'skimming' credit cards in shops and restaurants to produce a near perfect copy of the original card.

Information security, personal security and cyber-trespass

Collectively known as 'hackers', individuals who seek to infiltrate computerised information systems can be driven by a wide range of motives including a relatively benign belief in freedom of access to information for all or, even, simply, a desire for mastery for its own sake (Taylor 2003). But it is those who perpetrate acts of vandalism, incapacitation, espionage or terrorism (who more accurately should be termed 'crackers') that receive most attention.

Three acts of trespass commonly occur in cyberspace. First is the deliberate planting of viruses which either act immediately to disable systems ('denial-of-service' attacks) or are 'sleeping viruses' to be activated or neutralised at a later date when ransom negotiations have taken place or when the virus originator has long since disappeared from the organisation targeted. An example of the former was the denial-of-service attack targeting eBay, Yahoo, Amazon and CNN, among others, which effectively shut down their websites for hours at an estimated cost of $1.2 billion. The culprit was found to be a 15-year-old hacker from Montreal, dubbed Mafiaboy, who eventually served an eight-month sentence in a Canadian detention centre. An example of a sleeping virus concerned the case of Timothy Lloyd, a senior programmer for defence contractor Omega Engineering, manufacturers of sophisticated measurement and control systems for, among others, NASA and the US Navy. Anticipating his imminent dismissal, Lloyd exacted his revenge by planting a software time bomb that was detonated 20 days after he left the company, deleting critical computer programs at a cost of over $10 million to the company and 80 job losses.

The second form of cyber-trespass concerns the deliberate manipulation or defacement of presentational data such as home pages, a practice which increased fivefold in 2001 to 22,337 cases, according to hacker tracker Alldas.de (Heikkila 2001). One case involved the identification by Italian police of six members of a hacker group (aged 15–23) who attacked over 600 websites in 62 countries, replacing official home pages with anti-globalisation slogans. The case was notable for the number and significance of the targets, which included the Pentagon, NASA, the Chinese government, US law courts, universities, media organisations, ISP, political parties and celebrities.

Thirdly, trespass can involve acts of extortion, spying or terrorism whereby computer systems are infiltrated and access gained to companies' classified information, or systems of the armed forces, police, defence or intelligence agencies. The scope and anonymity afforded by the Internet – together with the fact that increasingly money only exists in electronic form – are attracting organised gangsters to turn to computer fraud. In an article entitled 'Hacker hit men for hire', *Business Week Online* reports that Internet mercenaries are now offering their services in destroying 'your Web enemy' (Blank 2001). In countries where wages are low and opportunities are limited but computer literacy is advanced, the Internet has spawned an enterprise culture involving the sale of various services. For the right price, Internet outlaws will steal information from a rival company, obtain credit card details of thousands of customers at a time in order to hold a business to ransom or bombard the chosen target with tens of thousands of emails in a single day thus jamming computer networks and disrupting normal business. One company held to ransom over its electronic data was the American music retailer, CD Universe. In 2001 a 19-year-old Russian student calling himself 'Maxim' stole 300,000 credit card numbers from the company's database and threatened to reveal the data unless he received $100,000 cash. When CD Universe failed to respond quickly enough, he carried out his threat, publishing online the credit card and personal details of 25,000 CD Universe customers (Goodman and Brenner 2002).

The penetration of any security system may be damaging enough, but the risk of harm increases exponentially with the size of organisation targeted. Among the potential consequences of deliberate acts of sabotage are the capacity to disrupt or damage water, gas and electricity supplies, close all international communications, manipulate air traffic control or military systems, hack into a hospital's computer system and alter details of medical conditions and treatments, tamper with National Insurance numbers or tax codes and paralyse financial systems. Although 'cyberhomicide' has not yet been reported many of these activities suggest that it may only be a matter of time (Goodman and Brenner 2002). Nevertheless, most commentators believe that, while these kinds of possibilities are terrifying to contemplate, the likelihood of such calamitous events occurring through human or software error is far greater than the chance of malicious hackers, mercenaries or terrorists bringing down a country's infrastructure (Hamelink 2000) and, for the time being at least, they remain hypothetical possibilities rather than perpetrated acts of aggression.

Industrial espionage and workplace sabotage

A great deal more prevalent than the incidents described above are the acts of sabotage perpetrated by employees on their employers; indeed four out of five of all known Internet-related crimes are committed from within an organisation (McGibbon 2001). Although some of these infiltrators might define themselves as hackers, and many will be disgruntled employees who have a grudge against the company, many more are 'ordinary' office workers – usually women – who disrupt the rhythm and routine of work by sabotaging their computers. Often, the sabotage will be unwitting, the result of carelessness or ignorance of security procedures (as when viruses are spread by people opening corrupted email attachments). But, as I argue elsewhere (Jewkes 2003b), damage to company computer systems may be the result of more knowing acts of resistance as office workers assert their agency in the face of depersonalised and routinised systems by disrupting the flow of organisational communications and work. Management are usually fully cognisant of the damage caused by their workforce, which accounts for infinitely more computer downtime and information loss every year than is caused by the demonised figure of the hacker. But corporations who are dependent on digital systems of communication and information storage are understandably reticent to admit the extent to which they are vulnerable to such attacks and many cases are not reported to the police (Ross 1991). Most companies do not wish to publicise that sensitive information has been accessed from within, but privately admit that access to passwords, confidential data and knowledge of an organisation's information systems can make it relatively easy for employees to exploit their security loopholes (McGibbon 2001).

Specialist units for policing cybercrime

The crimes outlined above pose significant challenges for the police service. Although many are familiar offences, their context and scope, and the technical expertise required to investigate them, have compelled the police to examine their capacity to respond. In addition to the two specialist officers in every force provided by government funding as part of its national high-tech crime initiative, several forces have gone much further and now have specialist units concentrating expertise in computer-related crime. However, it is not the case that each force has its own distinct and easily identifiable 'cybercrime unit' dedicated to investigating only computer-mediated crimes. Some forces have established departments that deal solely or predominantly with cybercrimes; others employ one or two specialist personnel with 'high-tech' expertise within the much broader context of, for example, a serious crime unit.

The names and precise operational remits of specialist units dealing with cybercrime vary, then, from force to force (and in some forces will differ from the examples given below). In the main, however, they fall into four categories. First, there are scientific support units or forensic investigation units which carry out forensic examinations of seized computer equipment and data recovery, as well as investigating cases involving DNA, fingerprints and so on. Secondly, there are departments which gather intelligence on major crimes, usually in support of a force CID or fraud squad. Variously called (among other names) the 'Force Intelligence Bureau', 'Crime Squad', 'Specialist Investigations Department', or 'Intelligence and Specialist Operations', personnel in these units tend to work on major, cross-boundary investigations such as terrorism and fraud, and they gather intelligence on persistent, known, 'career' offenders. The third group of specialist units are those with a broader remit to investigate offences committed against computer systems as well as to investigate traditional crimes that have a 'high-tech' element. These include force hi-tech crime units, computer crime units or telecoms and computer crime units. Finally, there are units that deal with obscene images of children and/or investigate paedophile networks. These include child protection units or child protection and investigation units, paedophile units, abusive images units, obscene publications units and vice squads. The names of these departments indicate some of their differing functions but, while all may have a duty to investigate sexual images of children on the Net, not all of them will include within their remits the safeguarding of children in chat rooms or the more general welfare of children in the community. One of the most high-profile units dealing with children's welfare is the Metropolitan Police's Paedophile Unit based at New Scotland Yard. It is charged with carrying out proactive and reactive operations against those who manufacture and distribute paedophile material, including via the Internet. But it also carries out operations against high-risk predatory paedophiles operating within the 'real' (as opposed to virtual) community and is part of a wider group – the Child Protection Operational Command Unit (SO5) – which itself comes under the auspices of the Met's Serious Crime Group. SO5 has a far wider range of responsibilities in relation to child welfare than only computer-related offences and, in addition to the Paedophile Unit, incorporates 27 child protection teams and 4 major investigation teams who work in partnership with professional agencies such as social services, and health and education authorities (www.met.police.uk/so/so5.htm).

Most forces have at least one specialist unit which falls into one of the four categories outlined above, although in some forces one department will be responsible for all the offences mentioned, albeit in conjunction with officers from other, more 'traditional' departments such as CID or special branch. The picture is further complicated by the fact that some police forces have complex structures, with departments containing numerous specialist units with overlapping responsibilities. An example is Hampshire Constabulary whose CID contains the Specialist Investigations Department, which includes a Financial Investigation Unit, Fraud Squad, Computer Crime Unit, Child Protection Unit and Paedophile Unit. Kent Constabulary, on the other hand, has a Central Operations Unit that incorporates Intelligence and Specialist Operations, Major, Serious and Organised Crime, Forensic Investigation, Tactical Operations and Special Branch, any or all of which might be called upon to investigate cybercrime. Although the lack of consistency in structure across police forces reflects the 'local' nature of the history of policing and justice, it is still somewhat surprising that such a 'micro' approach prevails in the boundless and borderless sphere of cyberspace. It is arguable that a more consistent and compatible structure could improve co-operation between forces dealing with crimes that cross boundaries (local and national, as well as global). This suggestion brings our discussion to the problems associated with policing cybercrime. The section that follows explores the particular challenges facing the police with regard to investigating cybercrime, and the internal and external factors that are preventing them from carrying out their work in this area as effectively as they might.

Problems with policing cyberspace

The volume and scope of cybercrime and the problem of jurisdiction

The main obstacles to the effective policing of cybercrime are the sheer volume of material generated, the global scope of the problem and the difficulty in applying laws to criminal activities across geographical boundaries. All three aspects are illustrated by the 'Love Bug' virus which took two hours to spread around the world destroying computer files and data. Assessments of the financial cost of the Love Bug virus vary, but are thought to be at least $2 billion (and potentially as high as $10 billion), while an estimated 45 million users in 20 countries were victims (Goodman and Brenner 2002). Virus experts from the FBI traced the Love Bug to a computer science student in the Philippines, but their investigation was thwarted when it became apparent that the Philippines had no cybercrime laws, which meant that Love Bug's creator had not committed a criminal offence in that jurisdiction. The suspect was charged with theft and credit card fraud on the basis that the virus was designed to steal passwords which, in turn, could be fraudulently used to obtain Internet services and goods, but the charges were dismissed as inapplicable and unfounded. He could not be extradited to the USA which does have laws governing cybercrime because extradition treaties require 'double criminality'; in other words, they require that the act for which the person is being extradited is a crime in both the extraditing nation and the nation seeking extradition (Goodmand and Brenner 2002). Although the Philippines has since adopted new legislation which would result in heavy fines and/or a custodial sentence for the creator of a computer virus, the legislation came too late for the investigators of the Love Bug, and no one was ever brought to trial.

The Love Bug case illustrates why efforts to police cyberspace have, to date, been considered largely futile. Two points are germane here. First, as Lenk (1997: 129) points out, the mindset related to jurisdiction has always been somewhat parochial: 'letting foreign police tread a square metre of their soil in hard pursuit of criminals is still anathema to ... national governments'. Lack of co-operation or compatibility between forces *within* a country can also be an obstacle to investigation, as mentioned in the previous section. In Canada, Operation Snowball, the country's largest child pornography inquiry, has resulted in the arrest of less than five per cent of suspects in over two years, and one of its leading investigators, Detective Sergeant Paul Gillespie, underlined the problems inherent in investigations that rely on collaboration between federal, provincial and municipal forces saying: 'International co-operation is a dream – national co-operation is a nightmare' (cited in Akdeniz 2003: 3). Secondly, the difficulties facing Internet regulators are compounded by different moral codes and divergent legal responses in different countries. In many countries it is a criminal offence to publish 'hate speech' or otherwise incite racial hatred, including via the Internet. Yet in the USA, for example, such activity may be protected by the First Amendment. Similarly, material that is considered mildly pornographic in the UK and Ireland may not be censured at all in Sweden or the Netherlands but may be subject to much stricter regulation in the Middle East. Diversity of definition is brought most sharply into focus in relation to communications between countries with a tradition of freedom of speech and those that are more repressive. For example, in China all ISPs have to register with the police and all Internet users must sign a declaration that they will not visit forbidden sites (among those routinely blocked are news, health and education sites, yet pornography sites are virtually unregulated), while in Saudi Arabia the government has approached the problem of harmful content by allowing only one state-controlled provider of Internet access (Hamelink 2000). But perhaps most punitive of all countries is Burma where the authorities are so hostile towards the Internet (because of its potential for political dissidence) that even owning a computer with a network connection constitutes a criminal act (Hamelink 2000).

The Internet's capacity to allow individuals and organisations to evade authorities 'by slipping into anonymity and by retreating beyond the bounds of their jurisdictions' (Slevin 2000: 214) has made it attractive to organised criminals, who have been quick to exploit legal loopholes exposed within countries that have relatively relaxed attitudes to cybercrime. For example, the Safer Internet Campaign reports that Russia has become a major source of child pornography because it has no specific laws governing the production or circulation of such material. Thus, while numerous criminal groups from other countries use Russian Internet sites to broadcast child pornography around the world, it is estimated that less than one per cent of the content is actually produced in Russia (www.saferinternet.org/news/safer21.htm). Illegal trading also originates from former eastern bloc countries and predominantly involves the sale of counterfeit goods (perfumes and other toiletries, alcohol, cigarettes and designer-label goods) and the illegal distribution of 'genuine' cut-price drugs, tobacco and alcohol. Online casinos are also proliferating on the Internet; unsurprisingly since gambling is illegal in many jurisdictions.

Under-reporting of cybercrime

Global statistics, though unreliable, indicate that cybercrime is dramatically increasing in number and severity. Despite evidence that people are becoming more willing to report offences to the police and other authorities, it is estimated that still only 10 per cent of computer-related crime is reported and fewer than two per cent of cases result in a successful prosecution (www.intergov.org). The reasons for the under-reporting of cybercrime are complex, but there are three predominant reasons for its low visibility. First, there may be a failure on the part of some victims of cybercrime to recognise that a crime has taken place, or alternatively that an act to which they have been subjected is illegal. Offences such as cyberstalking and identity theft may be carried out over a relatively long period of time before the victim realises that something is amiss and, in some cases, crimes and their perpetrators remain unknown and their effects are not felt (Finch 2003; Joseph 2003). Thus, although the notion of any crimes being 'victimless' has been vigorously challenged, especially in the criminological literature on white-collar crime, locating cyber-victimisation can be problematic because victims can remain as anonymous as offenders. This was sensationally illustrated in a case of stolen identity in 2003 when Derek Bond, a 72-year-old British tourist on a wine-tasting holiday in South Africa, was arrested and held in custody for three weeks after being mistaken for a fraudster wanted by the FBI. It transpired that the conman had been using a duplicate passport for 14 years without Mr Bond's knowledge. Locating victimisation is further problematised in cases of virus propagation because the numbers of victims affected may be simply too large and dispersed to identify, and because viruses can continue to create new victims long after the virus was created and – hypothetically speaking, given the rarity of successful investigations and prosecutions – long after the offender has been caught and punished (Goodman and Brenner 2002).

The second factor in the under-reporting of cybercrime is the reluctance on the part of some victims to involve the police or make public their misfortune. As noted earlier, businesses and corporations may be especially unwilling to admit the extent to which they are vulnerable to attacks on their systems, either by their own workforce or by outsiders, for fear of damaging their credibility or embarrassing their shareholders. Anxiety about negative publicity and future loss of revenue as customer confidence is damaged makes many in the business community turn, not to the state-funded police service, but rather to privately operated security services; an arrangement that has multiple benefits for the victimised company (see Chapter 7). For example, not only can an investigation into cybercrime against a business or corporation be conducted in secret in order to avoid damaging relations with consumers and shareholders but there may also be a perception that dedicated security services will have a better understanding of the problems caused by cybercrime and the most effective ways of combating it than the police who deal with an infinitely more diverse range of criminal activities. It has even been suggested that private security companies have an advantage over the police in so far as they are uninterested in bringing the culprits to justice – merely in thwarting their criminal activities in relation to a specific company. The hacker can not only be stopped in his or her tracks but also he or she can be thrown 'back into the marketplace, hopefully to attack their competition down the street' (Goodman 1997: 16).

Finally, the whole subject of cybercrime (with the notable exception of child pornography) tends to be met with public apathy. Like the more general category of white-collar crime, cybercrime seems remote and intangible, especially when compared to offences such as interpersonal violence, street crime, domestic burglary, car theft and sexual assault. To paraphrase Box (1983: 31) the public understands much more easily what it means for an old lady to have £5 snatched from her purse than to grasp the financial significance of cybercrime. Public indifference to such crime is mirrored in the attitude of many senior police personnel who rarely view crime involving corporate victims or even corporate offenders (as much cybercrime is) as 'real' police work; a viewpoint that may be understandable given the reluctance of many corporations to involve the police in investigations of internal wrong-doings.

Police culture

The need for the police to 'raise their game' is not simply an issue about inter-force co-operation, public priorities or even resources (see below), but one that highlights the need for a change of attitude on the part of the police. The police have been variously characterised as professional crime-fighters (Manning 1997); action heroes with a strong sense of mission (Holdaway 1983; Reiner 2000); pragmatic conservatives suspicious of technological experimentation (Crank 1998; Reiner 2000); or a thin blue line safeguarding social order and protecting the public they serve (Goodman 1997). Many officers develop expectations about the police well before joining up, possibly influenced by media representations (Goodman 1997; Leishman and Mason 2003; see Chapter 11) which tend to stress action and adventure as opposed to any desk-based activity. Their tardiness in responding to computer-mediated crime is therefore unsurprising. The culture of the police is one in which machismo and heroism co-exist with an aversion to innovation, particularly if it makes officers more office bound than they are already (see Chapter 9). Goodman (1997: 11), though referring to American law enforcement agents, outlines an argument that relates equally to the police in the UK and elsewhere:

> Uniformed patrol officers and personnel assigned to high-risk duties such as the Special Weapons and Tactics ('SWAT') team . . . are perceived to be the *real* cops . . . Since the internal culture of police departments places a lower value on catching non-violent offenders, it should come as no surprise that officers are not clamouring to investigate computer crimes.

However, the problem may be wider than simply a reluctance to investigate cybercrime. While technophobia may be no more prevalent within the police than it is in the public at large (itself a point of debate for many commentators), a lack of computer savvy *is* a serious problem for the police and is compounded by insufficient training on either computer usage or computer crime (Goodman 1997; Hyde 1999; Woods 2002). Although the police are routinely trained in the use of criminal database systems, the skills required are rudimentary and they do not prepare officers for tackling cybercrimes. Quite simply, for some critics, the under-utilisation of computer resources within local and regional police stations illustrates how far the police have to go before they can adequately tackle sophisticated computer crime. The potential impact of new technology on the criminal justice system – including training, funding, co-ordination and consistency – is currently under review and was one of the tasks granted to the Foresight Panel, a Department of Trade and Industry initiative (Pease 2001). Their report, *Turning the Corner* (Foresight 2000) calls for the establishment of a national e-crime strategy including the formulation of a specialist hi-tech crime reduction training academy for both law enforcement and business.

It is conceivable, then, that the initiative likely to have greatest impact on the culture of policing cybercrime will be the drive towards a national e-policing strategy which, although in its infancy, is already changing perceptions of information technology within local police forces. Several forces are currently developing e-policing projects which, in part, derive from recommendations made in a report commissioned by the Home Secretary who was concerned at the amount of time officers spend in police stations completing paperwork (Home Office 2001). It emerged that 250 different types of form are in regular use by police officers who spend approximately half their working hours filling them in. But as an alternative it has been suggested that officers could be issued with palmtop computers (PDAs or personal digital assistants) which would enable them to complete electronic forms at a crime scene, check information 'remotely' and write up reports without the need to return to the station. Electronic forms could also be simplified to eliminate errors and could be 'intelligent' in order to cut out irrelevant questions or unnecessary information (e.g. asking a male his 'maiden' name). Furthermore, it has been calculated that reducing its paper burden by just one per cent would save the police £200,000 and 16,000 hours of officers' time (http://news.bbc.co.uk 12 March 2002). One of the forces at the cutting edge of e-policing initiatives is Wiltshire Police, which is working in partnership with Hewlett-Packard and Microsoft to reduce the administrative burden faced by the police. The officer leading the project compares the benefits of e-forms with conventional ones:

> the [paper] form was costing around £10k to produce each year, of which over half of the forms were rejected because of the poor quality of completion. When the paper form was turned into an electronic process, rejection rates were reduced to zero, production costs were eliminated and it became possible to re-deploy three data clerks to other duties (Ogden, www.publicservice.co.uk/pdf/home_office/summer2002).

For some within the police service, e-policing cannot happen too soon, although it is conceded that one of the barriers to an effective e-policing strategy may be the culture of an organisation resistant to change. A report compiled by HMIC admits that not only might forces experience difficulty in recruiting and retaining staff with the skills needed for e-policing but also that in the wider culture of police forces, the very existence of an e-policing vision and strategy may 'unsettle staff' (2001: 158).

Limited resources

The lack of consensus regarding definitions of cybercrime and the difficulties associated with compiling accurate statistics on such a rapidly evolving area of crime make it difficult for the police to formulate a coherent response to the commission of such offences and deploy their resources accordingly. The 'fuzziness' surrounding the concept of cybercrime is, according to Goodman (1997), exacerbated by the fact that many of today's police managers have risen up through the ranks of a force they first joined in a pre-computer age and continue to think they can 'get by' without having to devote additional resources to cybercrime because that is what has been done in the past. In addition, the fact that the physical distance between offender and victim might cross countries or even continents means that the co-ordination required between different police authorities (which may necessitate individual officers making trips around the world to liase with their overseas counterparts) can be an expensive undertaking. In these times of fiscal constraint and public demands for more localised community policing programmes, chief constables are arguably unlikely to direct precious resources into a type of crime that is costly, difficult to investigate and low down on most people's priorities for their police service. Yet one crime – and one specific police operation – has precipitated widespread media interest in the allocation of police resources and presented a unique challenge to investigators.

The challenge of Operation Ore

Given the obstacles to investigation and prosecution highlighted in this chapter, it is hardly surprising that, in general, the police aim for what Goodman (1997: 14) calls the 'low-hanging fruit': those criminals who commit 'ordinary' and serious crimes but may require fewer resources and less complicated investigations in order to secure an arrest and conviction. Of course, police priorities are inevitably linked to government-set performance targets which are themselves frequently a reaction to public anxiety following high-profile criminal cases. Yet while cybercrime has, on the whole, failed to cause public consternation, the figure of the paedophile preying on victims in chat rooms and on dedicated porn sites *does* haunt the public imagination, and it is arguable that Operation Ore has done more to propel the British police towards computer literacy and technological expertise than any other factor. Paedophilia – in the broad sense in which it is increasingly used, encompassing those whom the police informally term 'lookers' as well as 'doers' (Silverman and Wilson 2002) – is undoubtedly the moral panic of our age and dominates debates about the Internet.[2].

Ore was launched in the UK in May 2002 after the FBI passed to the NCIS details of 7,272 British subscribers who had accessed a Texas-based subscription website called Landslide, a gateway to pornography sites whose names (e.g. Cyber Lolita and Child Rape) indicate their content. The seizure of Landslide's database by police and the US Postal Inspection Service yielded the names and credit card details of some 390,000 subscribers in 60 countries, including around 35,000 subscribers in the USA. Of the 7,272 British subscribers, only a fraction have been investigated, with police prioritising individuals in positions of authority and those who have access to children. As of January 2003, approximately 1,300 search warrants have been issued, 1,200 arrests made and only a handful of cases have been brought to court.

As mentioned in the introduction, this return is viewed as woefully inadequate by many, although the majority of criticism has been directed at the government for failing to provide sufficient funding, rather than at the NHTCU who are making some headway despite operating within financial constraints. It goes without saying that the volume and scope of child pornography are vast, and growing exponentially as the Internet itself expands its global reach. Yet arguably, more debilitating than any of the factors highlighted above is the problem of limited resources. Despite the fact that child protection is listed as a national policing priority, the government's attitude to the ongoing funding shortfall experienced by the NHTCU raises questions about the seriousness with which it views such work and of the capacity of the Home Office to respond to change. John Carr, an adviser on Internet safety for children's charities, notes that the prospect of over 7,200 names arriving in one hit to any intelligence-based environment presents a significant challenge and that such an unprecedented task requires an unprecedented level of response from the police (Carr 2002). Yet when the police requested extra resources to enable them to carry out preliminary routine work (estimated at £2 million) the Home Office turned them down, saying that it was a matter for the police to manage within existing budgets. Of course, the government's frugality on this issue might be justifiable in the sense that cybercrime is potentially as limitless as cyberspace itself, and any funding strategy must rapidly start to resemble a bottomless money pit which can never be satisfactorily filled. But reticence at government level adequately to resource the policing of cybercrime inevitably has a bearing on the decisions made by managers at a local policing level. Every single police force in the country received names from the list passed on by the FBI, but Carr believes that some chief constables have done little or nothing with those names and consequently that the ability of local police officers to deal effectively with cybercrime depends largely on which force they are in. And although the government has set down as a minimum criterion that every force should employ two specialist staff to deal with computer-mediated crime (one network investigator and one forensic examiner) some forces report that they are struggling to recruit suitable applicants (see Chapter 14). The problem is not restricted to the failure of the police to offer salaries to computer graduates that are commensurate with other sectors. As a spokesperson (who wished to remain anonymous) at the NHTCU told me, it is relatively easy to take good police officers and give them adequate training in computer technologies, but it is much more difficult to take computer 'whizzkids' and turn them into good police officers; it requires a 'different mindset that can be difficult to reach' (telephone conversation 8 April 2003).

It might be argued, then, that the problem of under-funding is inherently related to police culture – 'cop culture' even. But, perversely, Operation Ore has none the less benefited cybercrime investigation. Prior to Ore, the national policing units struggled to persuade some divisional commanders that their beat now extends beyond traditional boundaries to a 'cyberbeat which can encompass anywhere in the world' (telephone conversation 8 April 2003) and that this makes the problem of Internet paedophilia a local, as well as global, concern. No force has been left untouched by Operation Ore, and every police probationer now receives training in high-tech crime (as do detectives, child protection officers and others). But it is still early days. Silverman and Wilson (2002: 86) note with some incredulity that the Paedophile Unit within the 'largest and best-resourced police force in the country', the Metropolitan Police, was set up as recently as 1994, and that the first conviction for downloading child pornography via the Internet was in 1996 (2002: 88).

Specialist units such as the Met's are among those that have been criticised for their concentration on low-hanging fruit which yields results; in this case, individuals who download and pass on abusive images of children, or who use Internet chat rooms to prey on young victims. Meanwhile, the more difficult task of policing the producers and distributors of child pornography is largely ignored (Jenkins 2001). Comparisons with the drugs trade are obvious here, but for Silverman and Wilson the analogy is misguided as it implies that 'users' should be treated with compassion rather than punishment. As they point out, 'photographs of child sexual abuse are photographs of a crime in progress' (2002: 90) and, by definition, no child can give consent to his or her involvement in this trade. In any case, the notion that any investigation in this area is straightforward is a fallacy. It might be assumed that the only problem facing the officers involved in Operation Ore is following up the names and credit card details of the Landslide subscribers; few paedophile investigations have benefited from such a visible electronic trail from supplier to user (members of the clandestine W0nderland Club, by contrast, used sophisticated encryption to mask their activities). But, of course, the sheer numbers involved make it a daunting task for investigators, and some subscribers will have used stolen credit cards to make their transactions. Furthermore, the growing capacity of computer hard drives to store increasing amounts of data means that police investigators are facing an ever-ascending uphill struggle. The spokesperson at the NHTCU said that it could take one officer the whole of his working career to investigate thoroughly the contents of a 10 Gb hard drive. Computers are now being produced with 160 Gb storage capacity (telephone conversation 8 April 2003).

Policing cybercrime: emerging trends and challenges for the future

There are clearly no easy solutions to the problems of policing and prosecuting cybercrimes but, as an initial step forward, progress could arguably be made in three areas. The first is legislation.

An area of legislation that requires attention in the UK and elsewhere is the modernisation of substantive *and* procedural laws so that not only is there international agreement on what constitutes criminal activity in cyberspace but there is also an adequate legal framework in place for its investigation. Currently, the police may be hampered by antiquated procedural law which, for example, only authorises the issue of warrants to search for and seize tangible evidence, a requirement which can be counterproductive to the investigation and prosecution of cybercrimes where evidence may be regarded as intangible (Goodman and Brenner 2002). Under existing UK legislation, someone who steals a PC can be investigated and prosecuted, but someone who steals a database cannot. A report by US consultancy McConnell International notes that, although many countries still rely on archaic laws that predate the birth of cyberspace, ironically, of the 52 countries analysed, only one – the Philippines – had updated its statute book to deal with cybercrime; a direct consequence, as mentioned earlier, of their failure to prosecute the creator of the Love Bug (Glick 2001).

Governments need to review existing laws but avoid drafting hasty and ill-thought-out legislation on the back of media campaigns and public anxiety. One such newly proposed law, announced by the Home Secretary in November 2002, is the charge of 'grooming' which is causing concern among civil liberties groups because it is designed to target adults who meet a child after contact has been made on the Internet but *before* any offence has taken place. This raises the question of whether *thinking* about sexual acts is the same as committing them and – even if a case reaches court – proving intent is notoriously difficult for the police and prosecutors. Secondly, in addition to reviewing and updating their legal statutes which will help the police build a case for prosecution when cybercrimes are committed, governments must also do more to prevent such offences occurring in the first place. Their collective failure to do so is part of a wider neglect of the potential scope and costs of cybercrime and the harm that it can cause. Somewhat belatedly in March 2003 the UK the Department of Trade and Industry announced a new 'Foresight' project on Cyber Trust and Crime Prevention. In a statement, John Denham, then Minister for Crime Reduction and Policing, claimed that the initiative would 'help ensure that technology is used to benefit society and ... police officers have the latest tools and technology to protect and police our communities and to minimise criminal misuse' (www.foresight.gov.uk). Many critics will be wary of a government initiative designed, as its press release states, to ensure that 'long term financial information is held in a consistent and compatible format that allows its retrieval in 20 years or more'. And while few would question the need for the police or Customs and Excise to 'protect and detect in the virtual world as in the real' (news release, www.foresight.gov.uk), especially in their efforts to counter terrorist and cyber-terrorist threats, more may be troubled by the use of technology to hold sensitive or confidential information about individual citizens.

Thirdly, greater attention needs to be paid to the information and computer literacy skills of police officers at all levels of command and in national, regional *and* local contexts. The raising of competence levels may seem a completely different issue from that of policing cybercrime but, for many critics, the problems are inter-related. If the police are to be considered competent in tackling cybercrime, they must present an image of a technologically savvy force of cybercops, rather than a disunited band of 'technoplods' struggling to play catch-up with organised criminals and computer-literate deviants. The imperative on the 43 forces of England and Wales to get up to speed in their approach to cybercrime has been brought dramatically into focus by media reports detailing how the NHTCU has failed to cope with the information passed to it by the FBI concerning Internet users of child pornography. This case illustrates that police forces which assume that cybercrime is not part of their remit and that they can call upon the national police agencies if necessary, may be making a serious error. Goodman (1997) calls for police managers to think strategically about computer crime in terms of recruitment, education, training and allocation of resources, and advises that officers should be encouraged to think about how technology might help them improve operations. He also suggests that computer science graduates should be targeted in police recruitment campaigns and further implies that the appointment of officers with qualifications in computing and related areas will help to change the culture of an institution in urgent need of modernisation (Goodman 1997). Unfortunately, at the present time, the police cannot easily offer attractive salaries to recruit skilled staff in what is a very competitive market, and the costs of ongoing training in a fast-moving, constantly evolving environment may be beyond the budgets of most chief constables.

The need for a national e-policing strategy is highlighted in numerous in-house police documents. The HMIC (2001) report *Open All Hours* notes that forces are currently at different stages of developing their electronic services, but that with a target date of 2005 for e-services to be up and running it is a matter of concern that a national strategic framework has not yet been fully developed and that the police service is still operating 43 variations of the same product.

Each of the forces in England and Wales has its own individual site (linked via the national police website) which are almost exclusively 'first generation' sites; that is, sites primarily designed as a public relations tool to promote that force and to disseminate public information, as opposed to 'second generation' interactive or transactional sites, or 'third generation' sites which adjust dynamically to individual user requirements. The lack of interaction between the public and police is, according to Superintendent Woods, a missed opportunity: '[I]t is not just information that 21st century citizens want from the police via the Internet. They also want to use everyday police services, just as they could if they called a police officer to their home address or visited a police station ... there is a significant demand for interactive online police services that the police service are not yet satisfying' (www.e-policingregre-port.com). While there is a danger that the police could become the victims of information overload (Woods also suggests, for example, that the public should be able to text the police on their mobile phones to report minor crimes, a move which would surely stretch the current infrastructure well beyond its limits), there is no doubt that computer technologies could improve both the accessibility of police services and communication with the public. This is a major issue in relation to child abuse. As with many other areas of criminal activity, the perpetrators of such crimes using the Internet are often protected by the fear and shame felt by many of their victims. It may take years for allegations to come to light, if they ever do, and – given the numbers of Internet child porn sites alone, estimated by US Customs at over 100,000 sites worldwide (Cullen 2003) – the assurance of a spokesperson for the NCIS Serious Sex Offenders Unit that 'the public can rest assured that the law will eventually hunt these people down' (www.ncis.co.uk/press) seems woefully optimistic. But the facility to report sexual abuse online might alleviate some of the fear and stigma experienced by some victims and offer them a familiar and non-confrontational means of reporting an offence – certainly one which, in the initial stages at least, gives them a feeling of control. In support, it can be noted that the arrest and conviction of Jonathan King in 2001 for sexual assaults on children going back to the 1970s was precipitated by an email sent to the NCIS by one of King's victims.

The problem of child abuse generally, and Operation Ore specifically, has proved to be a double-edged sword for the specialist police officers and other investigators who are charged with tackling cybercrime. It has undoubtedly brought cybercrime to public attention, raised awareness among police managers of the scale and depth of the problem and enhanced the profile of the regional and national squads that have been set up to deal with it. But at the same time Ore has highlighted the inadequacy of the current funding strategy, caused other serious cybercrimes to slip down the investigation priority list and resulted in the diversion of resources from, for example, child protection units with the result, some maintain, of actually putting children at risk (Cullen 2003). And Operation Ore will by no means be the last nationwide investigation of its type that the police service in England and Wales have to face. It is estimated that up to 250,000 British subscribers are currently using sites like those linked to Landslide (Cullen 2003). Even if this figure is overestimated, the challenges for the police and criminal justice system look set to multiply in future years.

Selected further reading

There is still comparatively little written about policing cybercrime. As the references indicate, much of the most useful material is to be found on the Internet, and it is worth visiting the police force websites (linked via www.police.uk) to monitor the progress of individual forces' e-policing strategies and their approaches to crimes involving computers. Among books on cybercrime, there are several edited collections, the most relevant of which are Jewkes' *Dot.cons: Crime, Deviance and Identity on the Internet* (2003), Loader's *The Governance of Cyberspace: Politics, Technology and Global Restructuring* (1997) and Wall's *Crime and the Internet* (2001). David Wall has also written several chapters on the regulation of cyberspace – e.g. 'Policing the virtual community: the Internet, cyberspace and cybercrime' (1997) and 'Insecurity and the policing of cyberspace' (2002). In relation to specific cybercrimes, the most extensive list of resources is probably devoted to hackers and hacking. Two of the best of are Taylor's *Hackers: Crime in the Digital Sublime* (1999) and Himanen's *The Hacker Ethic and the Spirit of the Information Age* (2001). On child pornography and the Internet, two recent texts are worth reading, not least for the oppositional views they take on those who download and trade in abusive images of children. They are Jenkins' *Beyond Tolerance: Child Pornography on the Internet* (2001) and Silverman and Wilson's *Innocence Betrayed: Paedophilia, the Media and Society* (2002). More general critiques of the role of the Internet, its regulation and its creation of social problems can be found in Hamelink's *The Ethics of Cyberspace* (2000) and Slevin's *The Internet and Society* (2000).

Notes

1   Goodman and Brenner (2002) note that computer crimes differ in type and scale from cybercrimes and date back to the origins of computer systems in the 1960s when the first cases of computer manipulation, sabotage, espionage and illegal uses of computers were reported. They state that the size of early computers and their restricted access meant that virtually all computer crimes were committed by 'insiders': legitimate computer users with authorised access to the hardware and software. Strictly speaking, then, computer crimes are offences that target computers, while cybercrimes are offences committed with the assistance of or by means of computers, computer networks and related information and communications technologies. 'High-tech' crime had traditionally related to the theft of computer parts, although the Home Office Research and Statistics Directorate refer to 'hi-tech' crime in a broader and more nebulous way (www.homeoffice.gov.uk/rds). 'Internet crimes' are offences that take place via the network that supports email, the World Wide Web and Internet Relay Chat.

2   I have used the term 'paedophilia' in a deliberately broad and uncritical sense. This chapter is not the place to discuss definitions of paedophilia or to enter into the debate about whether pornography use and child molestation are intimately related. For an insight into this subject, see Silverman and Wilson (2002), Bell (2003) and Jenkins (2001, 2003).

References

Aitkenhead, D. (2003) 'Net porn', *Observer Review*, 30 March: 1.

Akdeniz, Y. (2003) 'Regulation of child pornography on the Internet' (www.cyber-rights.org/reports/child.htm).

Bell, J. (2003) 'I cannot admit what I am to myself', *Guardian*, 23 January (www.guardian.co.uk).

Blank, D. (2001) 'Hacker hit men for hire' (www.businessweek.com).

Box, S. (1983) *Power, Crime and Mystification*. London: Tavistock.

Carr, J. (2002) 'A force to be reckoned with', *Guardian*, 12 November (www.guardian.co.uk).

Crank, J.P. (1998) *Understanding Police Culture*. Cincinnati, OH: Anderson.

Cullen, D. (2003) 'Child porn list leaked to Sunday Times' (www.theregister.co.uk).

Curzon-Brown, D. (2000) 'The teacher review debate part II: the dark side of the Internet', in D. Gauntlett (ed.) *Web.studies: Rewiring Media Studies for the Digital Age*. London: Arnold, 91–4.

Finch, E. (2003) 'What a tangled web we weave: identity theft and the Internet', in Y. Jewkes (ed.) *Dot.cons: Crime, Deviance and Identity on the Internet*. Cullompton: Willan, 86–104.

Foresight (2000) *Turning the Corner. Report of the Crime Prevention Panel*. London: Department of Trade and Industry (www.foresight.gov.uk).

Glick, B. (2001) 'Cyber criminals mock arcane legal boundaries' (www.vnunet.com).

Goodman, M. (1997) 'Why the police don't care about cybercrime', *Harvard Journal of Law and Technology*, 10: 465–94.

Goodman, M. and Brenner, S. (2002) 'The emerging consensus on criminal conduct in cyberspace', *International Journal of Law and Information Technology*, 10(2), 139–223.

Hamelink, C.J. (2000) *The Ethics of Cyberspace*. London: Sage.

Heikkila, P. (2001) 'Defacements increase five-fold in 2001' (www.silicon.com).

Himanen, P. (2001) *The Hacker Ethics and the Spirit of the Information Age*. London: Vintage.

HMIC (2001) *Open All Hours: A Thematic Inspection Report on the Role of Police Visibility and Accessibility in Public Reassurance*. London: Home Office.

Holdaway, S. (1983) *Inside the British Police*. Oxford: Blackwell.

Home Office (2001) *Diary of a Police Officer*. Police Research Paper 149 (available at www.homeoffice.gov.uk/rds).

Hyde, S. (1999) 'A few coppers change', *Journal of Information, Law and Technology* (available at http://elj.warwick.ac.uk/jilt/99-2/hyde.html).

Jenkins, P. (2001) *Beyond Tolerance: Child Pornography on the Internet*. New York, NY: New York University Press.

Jenkins, P. (2003) 'Cut child porn link to abusers', *Guardian*, 23 January (www.guardian.co.uk).

Jewkes, Y. (ed.) (2003a) *Dot.cons: Crime, Deviance and Identity on the Internet*. Cullompton: Willan.

Jewkes, Y. (2003b) 'Policing the net: crime, regulation and surveillance in cyberspace', in Y. Jewkes (ed.) *Dot.cons: Crime, Deviance and Identity on the Internet*. Cullompton: Willan, 15–35.

Jewkes, Y. and Sharp, K. (2003) 'Crime, deviance and the disembodied self: transcending the dangers of corporeality', in Y. Jewkes (ed.) *Dot.cons: Crime, Deviance and Identity on the Internet*. Cullompton: Willan, 36–52.

Joseph, J. (2003) 'Cyberstalking: an international perspective', in Y. Jewkes (ed.) *Dot.cons: Crime, Deviance and Identity on the Internet*. Cullompton: Willan, 105–25.

Leishman, F. and Mason, P. (2003) *Policing and the Media: Facts, Fictions and Factions*. Cullompton: Willan.

Lenk, K. (1997) 'The challenge of cyberspatial forms of human interaction to territorial governance and policing', in B. Loader (ed.) *The Governance of Cyberspace: Politics, Technology and Global Restructuring*. London: Routledge, 126–35.

Loader, B. (ed.) (1997) *The Governance of Cyberspace: Politics, Technology and Global Restructuring*. London: Routledge.

Manning, P. (1997) *Police Work* (2nd edn). Prospect Heights, IL: Waveland Press.

McGibbon, A. (2001) 'Beware the security enemy within', *Network News*, 13 June (www.vnu.com).

Pease, K. (2001) 'Crime futures and foresight: challenging criminal behaviour in the information age', in D. Wall (ed.) *Crime and the Internet*. London: Routledge, 18–28.

Perry, B. (2001) *In the Name of Hate: Understanding Hate Crimes*. New York, NY: Routledge.

Reiner, R. (2000) *The Politics of the Police* (3rd edn). Oxford: Oxford University Press.

Ross, A. (1991) *Strange Weather: Culture, Science and Technology in the Age of Limits*. London: Verso.

Schofield, J. (2002) 'Can the spam', *Guardian*, 25 April (www.guardian.co.uk/archive).

Silverman, J. and Wilson, D. (2002) *Innocence Betrayed: Paedophilia, the Media and Society*. Cambridge: Polity Press.

Slevin, J. (2000) *The Internet and Society*. London: Routledge.

Tang, P. (1997) 'Multimedia information products and services: a need for "cyber-cops"?' in B. Loader (ed.) *The Governance of Cyberspace: Politics, Technology and Global Restructuring*. London: Routledge, 190–208.

Taylor, P. (1999) *Crime in the Digital Sublime*. London: Routledge.

Taylor, P.A. (2003) 'Maestros or misogynists? Gender and the social construction of hacking', in Y. Jewkes (ed.) *Dot.cons: Crime, Deviance and Identity on the Internet*. Cullompton: Willan, 126–46.

Wall, D. (1997) 'Policing the virtual community: the Internet, cyberspace and cyber-crime', in P. Francis *et al.* (eds) *Policing Futures: The Police, Law Enforcement and the Twenty-first Century*. London: Macmillan, 208–36.

Wall, D. (ed.) (2001) *Crime and the Internet*. London: Routledge.

Wall, D. (2002) 'Insecurity and the policing of cyberspace', in A. Crawford (ed.) *Crime and Insecurity*. Cullompton: Willan, 186–209.

Whine, M. (1997) 'The far right on the Internet', in B. Loader (ed.) *The Governance of Cyberspace: Politics, Technology and Global Restructuring*. London: Routledge, 209–27.

Woods, P. (2002) *E-Policing* (www.e-policingreport.com).

Zickmund, S. (2000) 'Approaches to the radical other: the discursive culture of cyberhate', in D. Bell and B.M. Kennedy (eds) *The Cybercultures Reader*. London: Routledge, 237–53.

Part IV

Themes and Debates in Policing

Tim Newburn

By its very nature much of policing is controversial and conflictual. This part of the handbook examines some of the major themes and debates in contemporary British policing. Thus, for example, from the Scarman Report in the early 1980s to the Macpherson Report in the late 1990s, race and racism have been a major issue both for the police service as an organisation and in understanding and framing how particular communities are policed. The opening chapter by Ben Bowling and Coretta Phillips (Chapter 21) explores the key theoretical, professional and policy issues in this area. As they argue, there is considerable evidence that the 'service' provided by the police is experienced as being much less satisfactory by minority ethnic communities than others. The authors explore the nature of this, and potential explanations for it, together with possible methods of reform. They are particularly critical of what they take to be the trend towards a more 'military' crime-fighting orientation in British policing, something at odds with the democratic forms of policing they identify as holding out the greatest hope for positive change in the area of racism, crime and justice.

Staying with diversity issues, Frances Heidensohn's chapter (Chapter 22) considers women's experiences of law enforcement, both on the inside and the outside. How are we to understand the role and experiences of policewomen? What are the implications of this for the police organisation and for the delivery of policing as a service? How is domestic violence and other forms of violence against women policed and how is this changing? Is there a female cop culture and to what extent does it differ from the dominant masculine ethos in policing? Policing, as she concludes, remains highly gendered, though women are now far more visible in policing – and increasingly so at the most senior levels. The traditional model of policing was organised around a highly masculine, macho cop culture. Not only is this being challenged by a gendered agenda but, Heidensohn, suggests also looks and feels increasingly out of step with the priorities of policing in a modern (or postmodern) world 'where new priorities, new styles and new technologies are employed'.

In thinking about policing practices for a complicated, diverse and challenging world, in my view the most useful recent addition has been the increased attention that is now being paid to questions of ethics and the possibility of something akin to 'ethical policing'. The challenge of exploring the nature of the relationship between policing and ethical considerations is taken up by Peter Neyroud (Chapter 23), currently Chief Constable of Thames Valley Police. He sketches a brief history of police ethics and offers a guide to the principles of policing. In this context he examines the nature of police professionalism, covert policing and the use of force, the nature of performance ethics and the possibility – indeed, he argues, the necessity – of greater public participation in policing. Without this, he suggests, even the most ethical, professional police service will lack the legitimacy it requires to police communities successfully.

The area in which there has historically been the most prolonged, and occasionally heated, debate about participation has been in connection with issues of police governance and accountability. For as long as there has been a police service there have been concerns about who guards the guardians. Trevor Jones' chapter (Chapter 24) explores issues of police governance, how it is best to be understood and how it works in practice. As he notes, this is an area that has, in recent years, lost some of its political bite. We live in managerialist and technocratic times, with many policing debates being dominated by fiscal and administrative concerns. Like Neyroud, Jones explores the fundamental values in policing and considers how these might most appropriately inform a system of governance and accountability – particularly in the context of the increasingly complex environment of the multifaceted policing division of labour that now exists.

Delivering policing effectively and ethically poses considerable challenges for police leaders. Matt Long (Chapter 25) examines questions of leadership and performance management in the police service. He charts the shift towards the current emphasis on managerial forms of performance assessment and outlines the current regimes, including Best Value and the related systems of auditing and inspection. Recent years have seen the beginnings of a major overhaul of senior police officer training and Long outlines the restructuring of rank-based leadership courses in the National Police Leadership Centre and he argues that we are witnessing a shift in emphasis towards 'transformational' rather than 'transactional' leadership – albeit that this change is not yet especially well developed.

One of the other very significant changes impacting upon policing is the extraordinary rate at which technologies are now developing. How have the police responded to the information technology age? Janet Chan's chapter (Chapter 26) explores how developments in ICT and other technologies have had an impact on the nature and organisation of policing, what the barriers to changed practices have been and what future prospects appear to be. As authors of previous chapters on both crime analysis and on the Internet noted, police familiarity with, and utilisation of, new technologies sometimes leaves something to be desired. Similarly, Janet Chan concludes that while ICT offers opportunities for the institutionalisation of a more effective, more evidence-based and more accountable model of policing, the technology alone does and will not turn police forces into 'thinking' or 'learning' organisations. Nevertheless, policing practices and 'technologies' are being challenged in many ways. One of these concerns the interest in restorative justice (RJ) which has been burgeoning in recent years. Carolyn Hoyle and Richard Young (Chapter 27) explore the police role in RJ developments. In particular they explore the development of restorative cautioning in Thames Valley, together with other initiatives which aim to improve the relationship between the police and victims of crime. The chapter examines not only the current realities of such RJ practice but also considers what 'restorative policing' might look like. As is true of many of the challenges facing the police, the authors conclude that 'real cultural change' is necessary if RJ is to fulfil its potential, particularly with regard to acknowledging and respecting the interests of victims in the criminal justice process, and organising policing in ways that are more inclusionary and reintegrative.

The book concludes with a look at the future of policing. Predicting the future is notoriously problematic, yet Tim Newburn (Chapter 28) suggests that there are a number of trends, already identifiable, that look set to exert considerable influence over the likely shape and style of policing in the near future. These are the continuing commodification of security and pluralisation of policing; the growth of responsibilisation and citizen involvement; the pressures towards both centralisation and regionalisation; the growing visibility of transnational policing bodies and activities and the consequent problem of transnational democratic governance; and the demand for local responsiveness in a climate of managerialism. In such a context, it is hard to deny that policing in the near future faces some fairly dramatic challenges.

Chapter 21

Policing ethnic minority communities

*Ben Bowling and Coretta Phillips,
with the assistance of Ankur Shah*

Introduction

The delivery of policing – whether in the form of 'force' or 'service' – should not be greatly inferior for some social groups than others. And yet, the research evidence shows that, in general, people who are seen as are 'white' tend to have a more satisfactory experience of the police than people whose ancestry lies in Asia, Africa and the 'islands of the sea'.[1] The so-called 'colour-line' that the pioneering sociologist W.E.B. Du Bois (1901/1989: 13) predicted would be the 'problem of the twentieth century' can be discerned clearly a hundred years later in the relationship between police and ethnic minority communities in numerous countries around the world.[2]

In this chapter, we examine policing practices, making comparisons between the policing of 'white', 'black' and 'Asian' communities in Britain.[3] We begin with a discussion of the history of policing ethnic minority communities and how they have been targeted for particular forms of policing. We look at both 'public-initiated' encounters with the police – such as reporting crime – and 'police-initiated' encounters such as stop and search and the decisions to arrest and charge. Having looked at the problems in policing, and attempted to explain them, we go on to look at some of the solutions, including the recruitment of a more diverse police service and renewed accountability mechanisms. We consider the changes that have occurred over the past two decades – between the Scarman Inquiry of 1981 and the Lawrence Inquiry of 1999 – and point to new directions in the development of research in this field.

Discrimination in policing: police culture and its context

The experience of black and Asian communities in British society has undergone a fundamental transformation in recent years. Until well into the

1960s while there were a few people from ethnic minority communities represented in sport, business, politics and the civil service, there were no black and Asian police officers whatsoever. Now, while they are much under-represented, they make a significant contribution to the social, economic and political life of British society and are slowly forming a more representative part of the criminal justice system.

None the less, racist beliefs, xenophobic attitudes and racial prejudices remain widespread in British society. While the most overt forms of racism – activism within an extreme right political party (such as the British National Party) and participation in the 'white power' movement – is rare, racist attitudes, anti-immigrant feelings and xenophobic values have a deep and powerful well-spring on which to draw. If police officers are a cross-section of society, then it can be expected that some will be racially prejudiced. Research on policing conducted in the 1970s, 1980s and early 1990s indicated that racism and racial prejudice in police culture were more widespread and more extreme than in wider society. Studies found that 'racial prejudice and racialist talk ... [were] pervasive ... expected, accepted and even fashionable' (Smith and Gray 1985: 388–9) while negative views of people from ethnic minorities and support for extreme right political parties were widespread (Smith and Gray 1985; Holdaway 1983, 1997: 78; Reiner 2000: 98–100, 115–21).

Research evidence over the past three decades has found that specific stereotypes are commonly used by police officers to classify people on the basis of their ethnic origin. Studies found that Asians tended to be regarded as devious, liars and potential illegal immigrants (Cain 1973; Graef 1989: 131). Black people, by contrast, are thought prone to violent crime and drug abuse, to be incomprehensible, suspicious, hard to handle, naturally excitable, aggressive, lacking brainpower, troublesome and 'tooled up' (Graef 1989; Reiner 1991). These findings have not been restricted to constables but have been found throughout the ranks (see Reiner 1991: 44). A 1997 inspection of community and race relations policies and practices within the police service conducted by Her Majesty's Chief Inspector of Constabulary concluded that 'racial discrimination, both direct and indirect, and harassment are endemic within our society and the police service is no exception ...' and that there was 'a direct and vital link between internal culture in the way people are treated and external performance' (HMIC 1997: 18). On the basis of the inspection and accounts of racist behaviour by police officers from members of the public, HMIC concluded that even 'if the majority of the accounts are dismissed as either the products of third party articulation or even exaggeration, a picture still emerges of pockets of wholly unacceptable racist policing' (1997: 18). Improvements have been noted in subsequent inspection reports, but there is a concern that these are occurring in isolated pockets rather than across police force areas, with some front-line supervisors still not intervening in challenging inappropriate behaviour and language, and with key issues such as the prudent use of discretion in stop and search marginalised in police training, or actively resisted (HMIC 1999, 2000, 2003).

We have reached the view that although the links are complex, racially prejudiced attitudes do affect the way in which people behave (Bowling and Phillips 2002: 161–2). Hall et al. (1998) argue that 'while there is no automatic or straightforward link between racially prejudiced attitudes and language and discriminatory or differential behaviour ... there is a consistency in the pervasive nature and expression of racial stereotypes and their influence on police expectations and behaviours'. Discrimination is most likely where there are no clear guidelines or criteria for decision-making, where decisions depend on subjective judgements rather than (or in addition to) objective criteria, where decision-making criteria are not strictly relevant to decisions and have a disproportionately adverse impact on certain groups; where there is considerable scope for exercise of individual discretion; where there is no requirement to record or monitor decisions or decision-making process; and where local and organisational cultural norms (rather than the requirements of service delivery) strongly influence decision-making (FitzGerald 1993).

Police targeting: the criminalisation of ethnic minority communities

Research documenting the experience among minority communities of being subjected to oppressive policing in Britain can be traced back to the 1960s when a report to the West Indian Standing Council alleged that the police engaged in practices that they referred to as 'nigger hunting' (Hunte 1966). Stuart Hall *et al.*'s (1978) seminal work, *Policing the Crisis*, shows clearly how, on the basis of pre-existing beliefs about their supposed criminality, black people were subject to extraordinary policing, and portrayed by the media, politicians and criminal justice agents as a 'social problem'. Hall *et al.* describe the demonisation of the British black population and the creation of a new and powerful 'folk devil'. This demonic status created a rationale for policing minority communities in a way which white populations (certainly those in the middle and 'respectable' working classes) had not experienced since the nineteenth century (Howe 1988: 13–16). For some commentators, policing British ethnic minority communities was merely an extension of colonial policing which had existed for decades in the Caribbean, India and Africa, and which had now been turned inward to police the 'domestic colonies' (Sivanandan 1982; Fryer 1984; Howe 1988).

One of the most controversial areas of police targeting relates to the policing of immigration and the people who are defined as 'immigrants'. During the 1960s and 1970s 'coloured immigration' was not only a potent political issue but also one that framed black and Asian people's experiences of policing. Many research studies uncovered evidence that ordinary policing often involved checking immigration status (asking, for instance, for passports) when people from ethnic minorities reported crimes of which they had been the victim. The Immigration Act 1971 gave the police and immigration authorities considerable powers to detain and question those people who were suspected of being in breach of immigration law, such as entering illegally or overstaying terms of entry (see Gordon 1984). Gordon (1984) suggests that the Immigration Act 1971 began to shift the control of immigration from external border controls to internal controls, or 'pass laws' for people of African, Caribbean and Asian descent resident in Britain (Sivanandan, 1982: 135). In the months following the implementation of the Act, numerous high-profile passport raids were conducted, amounting to a 'witch hunt' of African, Caribbean and Asian communities, according to Gordon (1984).

A study in Birmingham found that more than one third recounted personal experiences of police harassment or brutality and half mentioned an incident relating to a close friend (All Faiths for One Race 1978). Many specifically accused the police of racial abuse. An Institute of Race Relations report (1979: 2) concluded that police officers demonstrated little regard for the civil liberties of black and Asian people. It described persistent foot and vehicle stops, racially abusive questioning, arbitrary arrest, violence on arrest, the arrest of witnesses and bystanders, punitive and indiscriminate attacks, victimisation on reporting crime, forced entry and violence, provocative and unnecessary armed raids, repeated harassment and trawling for suspects, and the use of riot-squad paramilitary equipment. They also identified continuous intelligence gathering and surveillance of 'symbolic locations' – coded language for the centres of Britain's black and Asian communities (see also Newham Monitoring Project 1985, 1988; Keith 1993).

'Race', riots and the police: public order policing in ethnic minority communities

The increasingly strained relationship between black communities and the police collapsed vividly in the public disorder of Bristol in 1980 and then in the London neighbourhood of Brixton in April 1981, followed by Manchester, Liverpool, Birmingham and other towns and cities in July (Solomos 1993: 154). The Brixton riots were triggered by 'Operation Swamp '81'. For a week, 120 plain-clothes and uniformed police officers patrolled Brixton with specific instructions to stop and question anyone who looked 'suspicious'. In all, 943 people were stopped over the course of four days. Of these 118 were arrested, more than half of whom were black. Among the 75 who were charged, only one was for robbery, one for attempted burglary and 18 for theft or attempted theft. People familiar with the experiences of black Britain had predicted disorder for some years (see Pryce 1979). The images of riot, burning, looting and the threat of a 'collapse of social order' were brought home as scenes of pitched battles between police and people were beamed on to television screens across the country. In Brixton more than 300 people were injured, while many vehicles and 28 buildings were destroyed, some of those by fire.

For Lord Scarman (1981: 45), appointed to chair the public inquiry into the riots, these were 'essentially an outburst of anger and resentment by young black people against the police'. Although he noted that not all the people involved in the disturbance were black, Scarman identified a problem of policing 'a multi-racial community in a deprived inner city area where unemployment, especially among young black people, is high and hopes are low' (1981: 15). Scarman recommended identifying racial prejudice among police recruits, efforts to recruit more ethnic minority police officers, improving community relations and handling public disorder, closer supervision of front-line police constables, improvements in the management training of inspectors and sergeants (especially in conducting stop and search operations), and making the display of racially prejudiced behaviour a dismissal offence. To increase public confidence in the police a greater degree of consultation with the public was recommended, introducing lay visitors to make random checks on police stations, and an independent element in the system for considering complaints against the police.

The Scarman Report was welcomed by the political mainstream, but the right-wing *Daily Mail* thought it was 'telling the police to turn a blind eye to black crime' and dismissed what it considered a 'call for positive discrimination' (Kettle and Hodges 1982). Critics on the left thought Scarman's analysis fundamentally flawed, echoing racist pathologies of black people (Gilroy 1987) and failing to explain properly why people were so angry with the police and its roots in their experiences of oppressive policing. Most fundamentally, Scarman failed to 'grasp the nettle' in relation to the key issues of stop and search, the investigation of complaints against the police and police accountability (Bridges 1982; Howe 1988). For these commentators, unless the police could be brought under democratic control, continued frustration and anger were inevitable and further disorder a clear possibility.

As predicted, disorder flared again in 1985. The riots in September in the Lozells Road area of Handsworth in Birmingham resulted in the deaths of two Asian men and the injury of more than one hundred people. The value of the damaged property was put at £7.5 million. A month later riots on the Broadwater Farm were triggered by the death of Cynthia Jarret in Tottenham, north London. During the disorders, a community policeman, PC Keith Blakelock, was stabbed to death. More than 250 people were injured and there was widespread damage to property. The media portrayal of the 1985 riots served to confirm media images of black communities as inherently and pathologically deviant and disorderly (Gilroy 1987). However, many of the conditions which had commanded attention five years earlier – such as unemployment, housing and welfare provision – had steadily worsened (Scarman 1981; Solomos 1993: 160). In the inner cities in 1985, levels of unemployment were up to two or three times higher than in the 1980–1 disorders (Cross and Smith 1987). Moreover, nothing had been done to tackle the problems of racial discrimination and inequality (Scarman 1981: XVII; Solomos 1993: 160).

After the mid-1980s, disorders involving black people were less frequently reported in the media and were either rarer or considered less newsworthy. Anxiety about 'race' and crime was displaced to a large extent by a concern with 'youth' in general. The 'Poll Tax riot' in Trafalgar Square on 31 March 1991 – arguably *the* most serious peacetime disorder in London in the twentieth century – symbolised both the end of the Thatcher era and the myth that riot was a 'black thing'. Keith (1993) argues that after the mid-1980s, disorder in England had become 'naturalised'. When white youth rioted in the 1990s – most spectacularly in Oxford and the north east of England – there was relatively little surprise, compared with the shocked and outraged response a decade before. He also suggests that the changing demography of the rioters should not be taken as evidence of a resolution of the conflict between black youth and the police; certainly, the media were still obsessed with questions of 'black criminality' and disorderliness. The material conditions that gave rise to the riots of the 1980s had only worsened.

Among the few outbreaks of public disorder to merit official attention in the mid-1990s were the riots in the Manningham area of Bradford on 9–11 June 1995 (Bradford Commission 1996). These disorders erupted when two police officers intervened in a group of young Asian men playing football in the road. After a struggle, three young men were arrested, a crowd gathered, accusations and counter-accusations ensued, leading to the intervention of a large number of police officers. Although the official report of the inquiry argued that 'the direct cause of the disorder ... was the unacceptable behaviour of those relatively few people who behaved so anti-socially', Foundation 2000, a community organisation based in Manningham, concluded the riots occurred in the context of a 'severe loss of confidence in the police' because of police action that was 'highly questionable, extremely provocative and unreasonable' (Foundation 2000: 11; 1995).

The summer months of May, June and July 2001 saw a spate of disturbances in Burnley, Bradford and Oldham, former mill towns in the north of England. The riots – dubbed by numerous media reports as the 'worst on mainland Britain for 20 years' – started on 26 May after a series of attacks by white youths on Asian homes in Glodwick, an area of Oldham with a significant Asian population. By the end of the riot two days later, 15 officers had been injured, pubs and offices and been damaged and 17 people were arrested (Ritchie 2001). The small Lancashire town of Burnley saw rioting on 23 June after reports of attacks by racist groups in the Stoneyholme area (Clarke 2001). The riots were finally calmed down by the police presence on 24 June. The Manningham district of Bradford (scene of the 1995 riots) erupted on the 7 July when the National Front reacted to an Anti-Nazi League rally of around 600 people, resulting in 200 police officers injured, two people stabbed and 36 arrested. Once the initial destruction and uncertainty had passed and calm was restored, the soul-searching began. The initial responses remarked on the presence of white extremists, the increase in attacks by Asians on whites and the view that this was merely an example of 'mindless criminality', or stemmed from a failure to respond to local drug dealing. The wider issues of policing a society divided along the lines of class, faith and culture and the context of segregation, deprivation and social exclusion were examined in the numerous official reports (Burnley Task Force 2001; Cantle 2001; Ousley 2001; Ritchie 2001). The reports called for more ethnic minority police officers and better communication to tackle distrust between police and community (see also Waddington 2001; Webster 2002).

Excessive force: police violence and deaths in custody

It is an axiom of the liberal tradition in policing that the police use of force must be *essential* (used as a tactic of last resort), *minimal* (no more than needed to prevent anticipated harm), *legitimate* and *accountable* (Uglow 1988; McLaughlin 1991; Morgan 1989, 1992). There is a considerable amount of material which questions the extent to which the police have adhered to the principle of the 'minimum use of force' in their dealings with African, Caribbean, Asian and other minority communities. The Institute of Race Relations (1991) paper, *Deadly Silence: Black Deaths in Custody*, documents 16 cases between 1969 and 1991 in which the death of a black person came about either through lack of care or through the use of oppressive control techniques. The Institute of Race Relations (1991) notes that there is a tendency to obscure information on deaths in custody and to create 'official misinformation' that explains the deaths as accidental, or a misadventure or 'even the fault of the victim, because of his or her behaviour, drunkenness, abuse of drugs, or mental or physical condition' (IRR, 1991: 5). This deflects attention 'from police deviance to questions of the victim's deviance' (Kappeler *et al.* 1994: 164). There is convincing evidence that racist assumptions about 'dangerous', 'out-of-control', 'drug addicts' or 'schizophrenics' can lead police officers to overlook signs of physical illness which remain untreated and lead to tragic fatalities (IRR 1991; Kappeler *et al.* 1994; Chigwada-Bailey 1997).

For the UK as a whole, in 2001–2, 70 people died in police custody or 'otherwise in the hands of the police', an increase of 32 per cent on the previous year. In addition, ethnic minorities make up the bulk of those who have died as a result of physical force (other than guns) by the police or the use of restraints (Inquest 1996). The recent figures for 2001–02 indicate a lower proportion of ethnic minority deaths in custody relative to their representation in the arrested population (see Home Office 2003). Whether these figures represent the start of a positive trend in the equitable use of police force remains to be seen.

Proactive policing: the use of stop and search powers

The use of stop and search powers by the police has been the most controversial issue in debates about policing ethnic minority communities. As the late Bernie Grant, formerly MP for Haringey, said:

> nothing has been more damaging to the relationship between the police and the black community than the ill judged use of stop and search powers. For young black men in particular, the humiliating experience of being repeatedly stopped and searched is a fact of life, in some parts of London at least. It is hardly surprising that those on the receiving end of this treatment should develop hostile attitudes towards the police. The right to walk the streets is a fundamental one, and one that is quite rightly jealously guarded (NACRO 1997: 3).

Since the nineteenth century, police forces have had wide-ranging local powers to stop and search individuals whom they suspect of criminal intent (Brown 1997). During the 1970s, the so-called 'sus' laws permitted the police to arrest and prosecute people under the Vagrancy Act 1824 (ss. 4 and 6) for frequenting or loitering in a public place with intent to commit an arrestable offence. As we have discussed earlier, evidence pointed to the extremely heavy use of these powers against people from ethnic minority communities, particularly young black people. Following the work of such organisations as the Scrap Sus Campaign (1979) and the conclusions of the Royal Commission on Criminal Procedure (1981), the Police and Criminal Evidence Act 1984 (widely known as PACE) was introduced to regulate police powers.

According to the PACE Code of Practice A, the primary purpose of the power is 'to enable officers to allay or confirm suspicions about individuals without exercising their power of arrest'. In relation to s. 1 of the Police and Criminal Evidence Act 1984, s. 23 Misuse of Drugs Act 1971 and s. 47 Firearms Act 1968, police officers must have reasonable grounds to suspect that that a person is in possession of stolen or prohibited articles. While 'reasonable grounds' will depend on circumstances, there must be an *objective basis* for suspicion based on accurate and relevant 'facts, information, and/or intelligence'. It adds that:

> reasonable suspicion can never be supported on the basis of personal factors alone without reliable or supporting intelligence or information or some specific behaviour by the person concerned. For example, a person's race, age, appearance, or the fact that the person is known to have a previous conviction, cannot be used alone or in combination with each other as the reason for searching that person. Reasonable suspicion cannot be based on generalisations or stereotypical images of certain groups or categories of people as more likely to be involved in criminal activity (PACE Code of Practice A).

The power to stop and search is primarily an *investigative* power used for the purposes of crime detection or prevention in relation to a specific individual at a specific time (Lustgarten 2002). In practice, however, police officers frequently use stop and search powers for other purposes such as 'gaining intelligence' on people 'known' to the police, to break up groups of young people and for 'social control' more generally (FitzGerald 1999; cf. Waddington *et al.* 2002). The police and government argue that the police need to use stop and search tactics to identify criminals, even though Home Office research concluded that the tactic has an extremely limited impact on crime – including its role in detection, disruption and deterrence (Miller *et al.* 2000; see also Bowling and Foster 2002).

Young (1994) argues that the legal regulation of stop and search powers does not prevent the abuse of discretion. Police officers have to interpret legal rules for which no amount of guidance could cover every eventuality. The concept of 'reasonable suspicion' is vague and police officers differ widely in their understanding of it (Quinton *et al.*, 2000). Moreover, searches 'consented' to by suspects invoke neither PACE powers nor protections and this is very problematic since the concept of 'consent' is slippery because suspects may be ignorant of their rights to refuse to be searched (Dixon *et al.* 1990). Finally, stops and searches, like many aspects of police work, are largely invisible to supervisory officers and, therefore, 'the norms and working practices of the street level police officer take priority over outside regulation' (Young 1994: 14).

Disproportionality in the use of stop and search

One of the most consistent research findings in this field is that people from ethnic minority communities – and black people in particular – are far more likely to be stopped and searched by the police in comparison with white people. Comparing numbers of stop and search with the resident population of an area enables the calculation of the number of stops and searches per capita. In England and Wales in 2001–2, the rate for white people was 13 stops per 1,000 population, while the figure for black people was 106 and for Asian people 35 per 1,000. These data are the source for the widely reported statistic that black people are eight times and Asian people three times more likely to be stopped and searched by the police in comparison with their white counterparts.

Data from the 1999 British Crime Survey (BCS) were consistent with this pattern, although white respondents and those of Indian origin were less likely to have been stopped in a car (12 per cent) during 1999, compared with black, Pakistani and Bangladeshi respondents (15 per cent), with little differences between ethnic groups for foot stops. The BCS found wide variation in the extent of multiple stops. Of those stopped in a car, black people were the group most likely to be stopped on multiple occasions with 14 per cent stopped five or more times compared with four per cent of white respondents, six per cent of Indians and 11 per cent of Pakistanis and Bangladeshis (Clancy *et al.* 2001).

Stops and searches under s. 60 of the Criminal Justice and Public Order Act 1994 can be authorised by a senior police officer (of the rank of inspector or above) based upon 'a reasonable belief that incidents involving serious violence may take place or that people are carrying dangerous instruments or offensive weapons' within any locality. These powers were introduced to prevent violent offences at sporting and other large-scale events, but are now being used extensively in ethnic minority communities. In England and Wales, the police conducted 44,000 stops and searches under s. 60 of the Criminal Justice and Public Order Act over the past four years, nearly tripling between 1998–99 and 2001–2. Figures on the use of s. 60 in England and Wales show that black people are 28 times more likely and Asian people 18 times more likely to be searched than white people.

The BCS found wide ethnic differences in the extent to which a reason was given for vehicle stops and whether the reasons given were thought to be acceptable. Of those stopped in a car, 93 per cent of white respondents stopped were given a reason, compared with 86 per cent of black respondents and 88 per cent of Indian, Pakistani and Bangladeshi respondents. While 80 per cent of white respondents felt that the reason given for the stop was adequate, this was true of 61 per cent of black respondents, 68 per cent of Indian respondents and 67 per cent of Pakistani and Bangladeshi respondents (Clancy *et al.* 2001: 59–60). This evidence is consistent with earlier research that indicated that stops and searches involving black people were more likely to be speculative (Norris *et al.* 1992).

Disproportionate use of stop and search powers has also been found in the use of ss. 13A and 13B of the Prevention of Terrorism Act 1989, designed specifically to combat terrorism from the Provisional Irish Republican Army. Of the 13,760 people stopped under these powers in 1997–8, seven per cent were Black and five per cent Asian (Home Office 1998: 14). No statistics on the ethnic breakdown of stop and searches under s. 44(1) or 44(2) of the Terrorism Act 2000 are available, but it seems likely these powers will have been used extensively against people from ethnic minority communities.

Explaining disproportionality

In attempting to explain ethnic disproportionality in stop and search, some commentators, such as FitzGerald and Sibbitt (1997), have noted the import-ance of taking account of different ethnic groups' 'availability'[4] to be stopped and searched, according to time spent on the streets and other public places. Two recent studies which have explored availability have found that ethnic minorities have a higher presence on the street than suggested by resident populations. This means that per capita measures of the use of stop and search may be overstating the extent of ethnic disproportionality. In the two studies which together covered six police force areas, stop and search patterns based on available street presence indicated that at an aggregate level, white people tended to be stopped at a higher rate than would be expected, while black and Asian people were largely under-represented or proportionately represented among those stopped and searched on foot or in their vehicles (MVA and Miller 2000; Waddington *et al.* 2002).

While this research emphasises the problems with per capita measures of stop and search, it should be remembered that the legal principles which govern the use of police stop and search powers require officers to have reasonable grounds for suspicion that a person is in possession of stolen or prohibited articles. It is of particular concern that research by FitzGerald (1999) and Quinton *et al.* (2000) suggests that many police officers are unclear about the concept of 'reasonable suspicion', and the extent and limitation of their powers. Being a member of a group who are stereotypically assumed to be more likely to be involved in crime cannot be used as grounds for suspicion. Yet there is some evidence of the use of 'racial profiling', described by minority ethnic officers interviewed by Cashmore (2001: 652) who reported being advised to stop 'black kids with baseball caps, wearing all the jewellery', in order to boost their recordable activities and enhance their performance. Other officers were said to 'subscribe to the philosophy that, if you see four black youths in a car, it's worth giving them a pull, as at least one of them is going to be guilty of something or other'.

This type of thinking is consistent with patterns of selective enforcement by police officers, based on stereotyping and their heightened suspicion of ethnic minorities. In 1981, Lord Scarman (1981: 64) noted that 'some officers . . . lapse into an unthinking assumption that all young black people are potential criminals', and the more recent research evidence also indicates such stereotyping among police officers (see, for example, FitzGerald and Sibbitt 1997; Quinton *et al.* 2000). As one Home Office study put it:

> the police contribute to the large ethnic differences in the PACE data by virtue of their heightened suspiciousness of black people. This is pervasive and deeply entrenched; and it may significantly increase the

chances of black people coming to the attention of the police relative to other groups (FitzGerald and Sibbitt 1997: 66).

Asian communities are likewise finding themselves in similarly, if slightly less in number, problematic stop and search situations. Indirect discrimination may also play a part in disproportionality. MVA and Miller (2000: 87) note that, in some of their research areas, 'stops and searches were targeted at some areas where there [were] disproportionate numbers of those from minority ethnic backgrounds, yet where the local crime rates did not appear to justify this attention'.

Arrest and the decision to charge

Arrest marks the first stage of the criminal justice process and the initial decisions about whether an individual enters the formal criminal justice system. Only a small minority of stop and searches – 13 per cent of all minority ethnic groups in 2001–2 – led to an arrest, and only seven per cent of arrests for notifiable offences have followed a stop and search (Home Office 2003). Although both proportions are slightly higher for black and Asian people, it is clear that most arrests result from reactive behaviour by the police following notification of an offence by a member of the public (see Phillips and Brown 1998). This means that stop and search makes a significant but rather modest contribution to the representation of white and ethnic minority people in the arrest population. Official statistics showed that, in 2001–2, the number of black people arrested was on average five times higher than white people relative to their proportion in the general population. The arrest rate for Asians was two times higher than it was for whites (Home Office 2003).

Although comprehensive data on arrest outcomes are not yet available nationally, there is mounting evidence which indicates that the police are 'overcharging' some ethnic minorities following their arrest. Phillips and Brown (1998), for example, reported that the Crown Prosecution Service (CPS) terminated proportionately more cases involving ethnic minorities compared with white defendants, largely because of insufficient evidence. This pattern of results has been similarly found in Mhlanga's (1999) more recent study of CPS and court decision-making at 22 CPS branches in cases involving defendants aged under 22 years in 1996. Case termination rates were higher for black (17 per cent) and Asian defendants (19 per cent) than for white defendants (13 per cent). These differences remained once other legally relevant factors had been taken account of, leading Mhlanga (1999: 26–7) to note that it was possible that the CPS were 'downgrading, or even rejecting outright, cases where the police have shown bias against minorities'. Further evidence to support overcharging practices by the police in some cases involving ethnic minority suspects comes from a recent review by Her Majesty's Crown Prosecution Service Inspectorate (2002). The higher termination rates for ethnic minority defendants suggest that the police may be presuming guilt in the case of some black and Asian suspects as a result of negative stereotyping yet where there is insufficient evidence to proceed against them.

Attitudes towards the police

Survey data provide a 'consumer's perspective' on policing. The overall picture shows that black respondents are somewhat less satisfied with police action and they perceive the police to be unfair to certain groups and, therefore, not surprisingly, are less willing to co-operate with the police than white respondents (see Mayhew *et al.* 1993;, Skogan 1990, 1994; Chigwada-Bailey 1997; Spencer and Hough 2000; Clancy *et al.* 2001). The findings with respect to Asians are more mixed, with less disapproval of the police than black and white respondents reported in some studies, whereas in others Asians tend to hold views that put them between black and white respondents. The general pattern has been confirmed by the 2000 BCS which reported that twice as many black respondents (38 per cent) as white respondents (19 per cent) could recall being 'really annoyed' by the behaviour of a police officer in the last five years; for Asian respondents the figure was 23 per cent. The main reasons cited by those interviewed were that the police had been rude, unfriendly, behaved unreasonably or had failed to do anything (Sims and Myhill 2001). More generally, while 54 per cent of white respondents saw the police as doing a good or excellent job, this was true of only 40 per cent of black respondents and 42 per cent of Asian respondents (Mirrlees-Black 2001).

Public satisfaction with the police at a local level is based on the percentage of respondents saying that the police do a 'very good job' in their area. In 1988, the first year that comparisons among ethnic groups were made in the BCS, 26 per cent of white respondents gave the police the highest rating in comparison with 16 per cent of black and Asian respondents. By 1996, the figure for white respondents had dropped to 22 per cent, that for black respondents had stayed the same and that for Asians had risen to 19 per cent. In the 2000 BCS, only 20 per cent of white respondents found that their local police do a very good job, compared with 19 per cent of black respondents, 16 per cent of Indians and 15 per cent of Bangladeshis. The figures for 2000 suggest a positive trend in the responses of black people to local policing while the Asian figure has dropped by three per cent, and that of the white community by a further two per cent.

Contacting the police

Among all ethnic groups the most common reason for contacting the police is to report a crime, but white respondents are significantly more likely than any other group to call the police in order to give information, to report suspicious circumstances, a disturbance or nuisance (Clancy *et al.* 2001). The generally lower opinion of the police among ethnic minority communities does not at first sight appear to affect the extent to which black and Asian people call on their help when they are victimised. Evidence from the 1988, 1992 and 1996 BCS (Skogan 1990; FitzGerald and Hale 1996, Bucke 1997) found that black, Indian and Pakistani victims were, if anything, *more* likely to report household crimes to the police. For personal offences, only the Indian group was more likely to report than whites, while black people had reporting rates that were somewhat lower than similar white victims once the seriousness of the offence had been taken into account (Skogan 1994; FitzGerald and Hale 1996). Victims from ethnic minority communities who report crimes are generally less satisfied with the police response than white victims (see Clancy *et al.* 2001: Figure 4.7). Clancy *et al.* found that 33 per cent of black, 43 per cent of Indian, 27 per cent of Pakistani and Bangladeshi and 47 per cent of white individuals felt they were satisfied by their experience with the police in the 16–29 age group.

The police response to racist violence

Although ethnic minority communities have been the targets of racist violence throughout their history in Britain it was only in 1981 that the British government and police officially recognised the problem and started recording it (Home Office 1981; Bowling 1999). By the mid-1980s, racist violence was established as an 'urgent priority' for a range of governmental agencies – including the Home Office, police and local authorities – although numerous reports suggested that the police on the ground were still not taking the problem seriously enough (Bowling 1999). The research evidence suggests that, until recently at least, rank-and-file police officers saw 'lower level' racist incidents as 'rubbish' and not worthy of investigation and officers were unwilling to ascribe a racial motive to an attack even if this was the victim's belief (Bowling 1999: 246).

Victims of racial incidents are much less likely to be satisfied with police service than victims of crime in general. In Bowling's (1999) study in east London, for example, the most common complaint among those who were dissatisfied with the police response was that the police did not 'do enough', that they failed to keep the victim informed and that they seemed not to be interested. Only a very small minority felt generally very satisfied with the way in which racist harassment was dealt with in their area and less than one third were at all satisfied.

The racist murder of Stephen Lawrence in 1993 and the subsequent public inquiry set up in July 1997 – to which we return later in this chapter – focused public attention on the issue of racist violence as never before. The report recommended improvements in the recording, investigation and prosecution of racist incidents. In response, the Home Office produced a *Code of Practice on Reporting and Recording Racist Incidents* in April 2000 which applied to all statutory, voluntary and community groups, and the Association of Chief Police Officers (ACPO) drafted its own guidance, *Identifying and Combating Hate Crimes* (2000), which is now used by all police forces. The Metropolitan Police Service (MPS) implemented a number of changes in addition to those recommended by the Lawrence Inquiry, including the creation of a Racial and Violent Crimes Task Force and the establishment of community safety units (CSUs) in all boroughs across London in 1999, with officers specially trained to investigate 'hate crimes', and similar specialist units have also been created in other forces.

These policies have had some impact on police practice. It is clear, for example, that there has been an increase in the willingness and ability of the police to record racist incidents and to file intelligence reports, with some cases referred to the Racial and Violent Crime Unit for more intensive investigation. There remains the risk, however, that if racist violence remains the preserve of specialist departments it will continue to be seen as separate from the 'real business of policing and an isolated caricature of what [the police] should be doing in respect of all crime problems' (Baggott 2000: 15).

A multi-ethnic force? Black and Asian officers in the British police

As people from ethnic minorities struggled to join the police service in the 1970s and 1980s, their treatment by their colleagues was often hostile as well as being hostile towards minority communities in general. Reading today Smith and Gray's (1985) study of 'the police in action', it is staggering to recall the language police officers used in speaking about black and Asian people. The centrality of racism in the subculture of the police served – and still does in some places – to alienate, marginalise and discriminate against ethnic minority officers. Even the most recent evidence shows that some supervisory and senior police officers fail to discourage and discipline racist comments and actions by police officers (HMIC 1998, 1999).

Increasing the recruitment of ethnic minority police officers was on the agenda of the Home Office and senior police officers even before the Scarman Report. There has been an increase in the proportion of serving police officers who are from ethnic minorities from 0.7 per cent in 1986 to three per cent in 2001–2 (Home Office 2003). This means that they remain considerably under-represented given that around seven per cent of the economically active population are from ethnic minorities.

Experiences in the job

The overwhelming majority of black and Asian police officers interviewed by Holdaway (1993) reported that racist comments and jokes were routinely part of officers' conversations (see also Holdaway and Barron 1997). Even in the post-Macpherson policing climate, ethnic minority police officers have referred to abuse by colleagues as a way of testing their commitment to the job (Cashmore 2002). Until relatively recently, senior officers appeared not to be concerned with challenging and changing this aspect of the police culture (HMIC 1997, 1999). As HMIC reported 'there were still too many accounts of distressing behaviour, or at best, managerial indifference towards ethnic minority staff'. Holdaway notes that the choice between tolerating or challenging racist remarks affected working relations because 'stereotypical thinking and team membership go hand in hand' (1996: 158). Thus, it is unsurprising that some black and Asian officers may find themselves marginalised from work and social networks because they fail to collude with negative representations of ethnic minorities, or where in the case of some Asian officers, religious observance prevents socialising that revolves around drinking.

Retention

The retention rate for ethnic minority police officers is predictably lower than for white officers and worsened in the period 1994–8. Holdaway and Barron (1997) studied the reasons for resignation among a sample of 28 former

African-Caribbean and Asian police officers in comparison with a group of 18 white resigners. Holdaway and Barron note that the resignation decision was not something taken lightly; typically, resigners said that they thought about resigning for more than five months. As one of Holdaway and Barron's (1997: 145) interviewees put it: 'Obviously, it doesn't make you feel good at all because you're working with people who you know, who don't really like Asians and blacks'. The most common specific reasons for the resignation of black and Asian officers were poor management within the police service, domestic/personal reasons, the difficulties of integration into the occupational culture and frustration with the way supervisory and senior officers dealt with everyday racist banter, and the aggressive policing of ethnic minorities. Since HMIC (1997) recommended that police forces should have mentoring, informal networking and welfare support as part of their retention policies, various support groups and forums for minority officers have come to the fore. These groups provide support networks, a forum for officers and also serve campaigning and lobbying functions. Foremost among the professional organisations is the National Black Police Association and the Black Police Associates in the Metropolitan Police Service.

Promotion

In 2001–2 only 16 per cent of ethnic minority officers were to be found in the promoted ranks within the police service compared to 22 per cent of white officers. Seven per cent of white officers were in ranks above sergeant, whereas this was true of five per cent of ethnic minority officers (Home Office 2003). Ethnic minority officers (HMIC 1995) have reported that due to constant threats to their status and the subsequent need continually to reassert their position, seeking promotion was sometimes too large an endeavour or something to be delayed (Bland *et al.* 1999). Where promotion is sought, the time to promotion is longer for ethnic minorities. Bland *et al.* (1999) found that ethnic minority police officers take an average of around 12 months longer to be promoted to the sergeant rank (five months longer for Asian officers and 18 months for African-Caribbean officers). It was suggested that this reflected selection bias once officers had passed the sergeant examination that made them eligible for promotion. The time taken by ethnic minorities to reach the rank of inspector was also longer than for their white counterparts (Bland *et al.* 1999). The data for specialist police officers are more encouraging. HMIC data for 1997–8 indicate an adequate representation of ethnic minority officers as detectives (this did however tend to come later in the career of ethnic minority officers). White officers were much more likely to have been posted to a traffic department or planning/performance posts and national secondments than their ethnic minority counterparts (Bland *et al.* 1999).

Meeting recruitment targets

In 1998, the Home Secretary published local and national targets for the increased recruitment, retention, career progression and senior level representation of ethnic minority staff in the Home Office, police, prisons and probation services (Home Office 1999). Positive action aims to achieve equality of representation over a given time and has a symbolic value to demonstrate the commitment to recruiting police officers who reflect the community they serve. Research shows that a higher success rate for complainants, greater under-standing and sympathy for those alleging discrimination, and more effective procedures and remedies will enhance the credibility of the law in the eyes of ethnic minorities both within and outside the force (Rotterdam Charter 1996). Practical efforts to encourage local people from ethnic minority backgrounds to join the police service, such as conducting targeted recruitment campaigns with the assistance of community organisations and contacts, running famil-iarisation and access courses, placement schemes, and providing application forms in minority languages, are all positive ways forward. However, these efforts are hindered by the fact that applicants will carefully consider their likely experiences of racism and discrimination. Indeed, HMIC (1995) reported that ethnic minority officers were sometimes unwilling to recommend the police service to potential recruits because of the difficulties they would face in the job. Clearly, the negative perception that ethnic minorities have of the police has hindered police forces' efforts to recruit ethnic minority police officers (Stone and Tuffin 2000; see also Cashmore 2001).

Linking equal opportunities with equality of service

Even if the numbers of ethnic minority police officers increased very dramatically, it will remain important to consider the working practices of white staff who will inevitably form the overwhelming majority, comprising, as they do, 92 per cent of the working population. The literature on the criminal justice professions highlights the importance of the relationship between equality of opportunity for employees *within* a service and the quality of service that it provides to the public. The Commission for Racial Equality, for example, argues that producing a police service which more closely reflects the population it serves is important not only as a goal but also as a means to the end of improving service provision. That is, it increases the chances that the services provided will be appropriate, relevant and accessible to all members of the community. As Brown (1997) points out, including groups previously excluded can have the effect of transforming the organisation; just by 'being there', women inevitably bring new and different perspectives and become catalysts for change within the organisation. Similarly, the presence of black officers affects some features of the organisational culture. It seems clear, for example, that the increasing presence of black and Asian officers within the organisation has reduced the willingness of all police officers to use racist 'banter' or engage in other more overt forms of racial prejudice and discrimination within the service. Furthermore, the actual positions that minority workers hold is crucial to maximising their contribution to the change process. To have any real effect on service provision, they must be able to contribute to decision-making. It should not be thought, however that, in service delivery terms, representation of ethnic minority groups in the higher ranks of the service will achieve more than the goal of equal employment opportunities. Policing needs to do more than simply accommodate women and ethnic minority officers, but make them a 'visible feature of the policing landscape' (Brown 1997).

Discrimination and police governance

In a democracy, structures of police governance should reflect the demographic characteristics of the community being policed. However, ethnic minority communities are under-represented among chief police officers, middling or senior ranks of the Home Office and in police authorities that make up the three elements of the tripartite structure of police governance (Jones and Newburn 1997). The idea of policing by consent is compromised if systems of accountability fail to reflect the ethnic diversity of the population. This 'democratic deficit' has long been recognised and attempts have been made to increase the responsiveness of the police to minority communities. Specialist 'community relations departments' have existed since African, Caribbean and Asian populations were first perceived to present a 'community relations problem' for the police from the late 1950s onwards (see Pope 1976). Scarman specifically cited a failure to consult and inform communities as a cause of the 1981 riots. However, the police community consultative groups[5] recommended by Scarman are widely viewed by police and public alike to be ineffective (Morgan 1989; see Chapter 24). Recent changes under the Crime and Disorder Act 1998 require community consultation in co-operation between local authorities and the police. This also requires consultation of the 'hard to reach' groups under s. 6 of the Act, which may include some of the ethnic minorities.

Independent monitoring is important because it offers the opportunity to provide transparency, openness and accountability in policing. In practice, however, such processes face great challenges to their effectiveness. In many instances, consultative arrangements have offered few opportunities for local communities to exert any control over the police organisation because consultation does not amount to accountability (Bridges 1982). Reviews of such mechanisms in England have concluded that they are of marginal importance to the principal areas of police activity (Morgan 1989; CRE 1991: 3). Moreover, the deficit in legal and political accountability is not fully redressed by the creation of new systems of consultation. Despite the sometimes disappointing experience of mechanisms to enable police accountability, we are of the view that this is one of the most important spheres for future work. In the UK, the police have historically thought of independent monitoring groups as obstructive and unhelpful. However, in recent years senior police officers have become increasingly conscious of the fact that such organisations provide information about crime and policing that can be gained from no other source. Independent advisory groups, if they can work to overcome some of the problems set out above, can also play a role in creating a greater visibility of policing practices (by using the media and public meetings, for example) and challenge stereotypical, narrow and discriminatory thinking among police officers.

Complaints procedures

The process by which the public can formally complain about instances of error and misconduct is the touchstone of police accountability. It is through this process that the police may be called upon to explain and account for allegations of misconduct and impropriety and, where necessary, make amends for injury and deaths arising from the use of force. The ways in which complaints by black and Asian people against the police have been handled has been the subject of much criticism (IRR 1979: 87). The first study in this area found that ethnic minority groups were much more likely to complain of misconduct than would have been expected from their numbers in the population but complaints made by black and Asian people were also significantly less likely to be substantiated (Stevens and Willis 1981). The report noted that these results might be explained by the fact that complaints of assault, particularly in the police cells after arrest, were more common among black complainants and that these types of allegations generally have a low substantiation rate.

The Police Complaints Authority (PCA) does not provide breakdowns of complaints against the police by ethnic origin but, since 1990, has collected separate figures for complaints of racially discriminatory behaviour by police officers. In the first full year of recording in 1991, there were 49 such complaints, which increased twelve-fold in a decade to 579 in 2000 (PCA 2000: 18). The substantiation rate for all complaints is about two per cent, while that for allegations of racially discriminatory conduct is much lower. The PCA notes that there are difficulties in substantiating these complaints, many of which allege incivility or the misuse of stop and search powers: 'in the former case, officers are unlikely to use offensive or racist language in the presence of independent witnesses. In the latter, it is difficult to prove beyond reasonable doubt that the complainant was picked out specifically because of his or her racial origin' (1997: 52). In 1996–7 a total of four officers were found guilty of racially discriminatory behaviour and were either dismissed or resigned from the service and a fifth officer subsequently resigned before the disciplinary hearing (PCA 1997: 52).

In response to numerous calls from the aggrieved members of the public and politicians alike, in 2000 the Home Office announced the setting up of the Independent Police Complaints Commission (IPCC). The IPCC, it is hoped, will offer 'a much more independent and proactive role to build a system in which all sections of the community, and the police service, can have confidence'. However, exactly how it will achieve this ambitious aim and whether the funding will be sufficient to maintain it remain to be seen. In addition this new system will apply only to members of the regular force, excluding special constables and civilian employees. As Bowling and Foster (2002) argue, the problems of investigating the police, such as the 'blue wall of silence' (internal policing cover-ups) (Kappeler *et al.* 1994), political interference (Manby 2000; Gordon 2001) and insufficient resources (Melville 1999), are unlikely to be solved by the IPCC.

Redress through civil litigation

Perceived and actual ineffectiveness in the police complaints procedure and 'fear of themselves being criminalised or harassed' (IRR 1987: 45) have meant that victims of alleged police misconduct have increasingly forgone the official complaints procedures and have instead taken civil court proceedings for damages against the police (though this has all happened within a general context of increased litigiousness). The use of the civil courts has increased dramatically over the past two decades. In London in 1979, only seven cases against the Metropolitan Police were heard, resulting in damages of £1,991 being paid; in 1986, there were 126 cases heard, resulting in damages to victims of £373,000 (IRR 1987: 86). By 1994–5 in the Metropolitan Police this had leaped to 731 threatened actions, and 1,000 in 1996–7 (Metropolitan Police 1997: 83), while damage payments tripled from £1.3 million in 1994–5 to £3.9 million in 1999–2000 (Metropolitan Police 2001). The primary difficulty with compensatory litigation is that it in some respects it deflects attention from the root of the problem. While damage payments have tripled from 1994–5 to 1999–2000 the quality of service perceived by sections of the black and Asian community has not improved significantly. This leads to the conclusion that while funds are being spent on costly litigation – and which clearly provides some remedy for the victims of police wrongdoing – the necessary changes in structure and attitude are not being made.

The Lawrence Inquiry: towards a new agenda?

The questions of policing, racism, inequality, fairness and justice raised more than two decades earlier in the Scarman Report leaped again to centre-stage at the turn of the twenty-first century. The cause célèbre which acted as 'lightning rod' for these issues was the murder, on 22 April 1993, of Stephen Lawrence, a black teenager stabbed to death in south London in a completely unprovoked racist attack by five white youths (Macpherson 1999). The Macpherson Report concluded that the fundamental flaws in the conduct of his murder investigation resulted from 'professional incompetence, institutional racism and a failure of leadership by senior officers' (1999: 137). More broadly, the report identified an absence of 'confidence and trust' in the police among ethnic minority communities. This was partly the result of a failure to respond properly to racist violence, but also a more widespread concern about the inequitable use of stop and search powers, deaths in police custody, racial discrimination and a lack of openness and accountability. The report concluded that the black community was 'over policed . . . and under protected' (1999: 312).

The report made 70 recommendations, almost all of which were accepted by the government, amounting to the most extensive programme of reform in the history of the relationship between the police and ethnic minority communities. It recommended a 'ministerial priority' to 'increase trust and confidence in policing among ethnic minority communities' by demonstrating fairness in all aspects of policing, more vigorous inspections and the application of freedom of information and anti-discrimination legislation to the police service. It recommended improvements in the handling of racist incidents, first-aid training, family liaison and the handling of victims and witnesses. It also recommended improvements in training, recruitment and retention policies; handling discipline and complaints; and the regulation of stop and search powers.

In the years since the Stephen Lawrence Inquiry, the primary difficulty has been in assessing whether or not real changes have occurred. Bourne (2001: 13) argues that 'the promise the report appeared to hold out is not being met', a view shared by Doreen Lawrence, the murdered teenager's mother, who said that 'nothing has changed' and that 'black people are still on the outside looking in' (*The Observer* 24 February 2002). As critics like Bourne (2001) and Bridges (2001) point out, the government is attempting to eradicate racism with one hand, but entrenching it with the other. They argue that legislation such as the Immigration and Asylum Act 1999 and the Criminal Justice Bill 2002 will disproportionately affect ethnic minorities because of strongly engrained institutional racism (Bourne 2002; Bridges 2001). The Anti-Terrorism Act 2001 likewise is argued to be discriminatory, and is perceived to be eroding many basic rights on the grounds of national security (McLaughlin and Murji 1999: 382).

One area which may be taken as the litmus test of progress 'post-Lawrence' is in the use of stop and search powers. In the immediate aftermath of the publication of the Macpherson Report, levels of recorded stop and search fell from an all-time high in 1998 of around 1 million to around three quarters of a million in 2002. This reduction has many causes, but it was probably at least partly attributable to the criticism that the use of the power was frequently unlawful and unjustified. It was also argued by some police critics that officers were afraid of using the power against black people in case they were accused of racism. However, police statistics show that while the number of stops of white people dropped very sharply, the numbers for black and Asian people fell to a much smaller extent. As a consequence, the racial disproportionality in the use of the power actually increased from a black/white ratio of 5 to 1 in 1999 to 8 to 1 in 2002, suggesting that black people are now more likely to be unfairly targeted than at the time of the Lawrence Inquiry. At the same time, as we discussed earlier, there is growing use of other powers, such as s. 60 of the Criminal Justice and Public Order Act 1994, which are even more extensively used in ethnic minority communities.

The Home Secretary's *Third Annual Progress Report* (2002) makes for more optimistic reading, suggesting new measures from the appointment of two full-time non-police assistant inspectors recruited to specialise in race and diversity issues to the introduction of the new independent police complaints authority. Further grounds for optimism can be found in strenuous efforts on the part of the police service to improve their policies in dealing with racist violence, improving the response to ethnic minority crime victims in general and in recruiting a more diverse police service. There are certainly many police officers who are committed to transforming the police service into a responsive, professional organisation for the twenty-first century.

The Lawrence Inquiry was heralded as a watershed in race relations and it was undoubtedly significant in its recognition of institutional racism and the measures that were subsequently implemented to respond to it. Of these, the most important legislative change was the Race Relations (Amendment) Act 2000 which applies the Race Relations Act 1976 to public authorities including the police, who had hitherto been exempt. In principle this represents a very significant step forward because it makes unlawful both direct and indirect discrimination in the provision of police services and in the use of coercive powers. The question now is whether the courts will be willing to find in favour of plaintiffs alleging discrimination in such spheres as stop and search, arrest, the use of force and so on. We can anticipate test cases in the courts in the coming years.

While the Lawrence Inquiry was welcomed by many people, there were also individuals and groups both inside and outside the police service who objected strongly to its conclusions and recommendations. Some saw its finding of 'institutional racism' as unjustifiably 'tarring all police officers with the same brush' while others saw it as letting individual officers 'off the hook', by drawing attention away from individual responsibility. Those who rejected Macpherson's definition of the problem also rejected the solutions – such as diversity training, regulating police powers and increasing accountability. At the time of the Lawrence inquiry, senior officers described what they saw as a 'push back' by rank-and-file officers against the reform process (see also HMIC 2003). Many were resistant to change and morale declined as a consequence. There is also evidence of a more powerful 'backlash' where ethnic minority officers and those white officers who have taken an overt anti-racist stance have been targets of hate mail and malicious complaints.

Since the publication of the Lawrence Inquiry, the problem of crime within black and Asian communities has been the focus of increased public anxiety and media attention and this has also highlighted the role of the police. In the months following the Lawrence Inquiry, there was a large rise in recorded robbery, particularly involving the theft of mobile phones, and police statistics pointed to an over-representation of black youth among those suspected and arrested. The so-called 'race riots' in the north west of England in 2001 involving young Asian men led to suggestions that 'Asian gangs' and 'Asian criminality' were growing problems. At the same time, some police officers have expressed anxiety about increasing levels of inter-ethnic tension and violence. Most significantly, perhaps, the attacks of September 11 in the USA in the same year and subsequent panic about 'Islamic terrorism', have fundamentally changed the nature of debates about ethnicity, crime and terrorism with some pundits making a direct link between migration and insecurity. Most recently, increases in drug-related shootings across the country (but especially the deaths of Letisha Shakespeare and Charlene Ellis in Birmingham in January 2003) have once again focused public attention on crime within black communities.

There is a view that 'black on black' crime and 'Asian criminality' have been exaggerated by police and media as a means to renew police legitimacy. On the other hand, it can be argued that it is now ethnic minority communities themselves that are demanding police action to restore peace and safety. These developments underscore the central paradox of policing that, in their efforts to protect the public, the tactics most frequently used involve the use of intrusion, coercion and force against the very people crying out for protection. The crucial question is how community safety is to be achieved without repeating the mistakes of the past 25 years.

Conclusion

In common with experiences in many parts of the world, the relationship between the British police and ethnic minority communities has not been a happy one. Today's controversy about the abuse of police power, the failure to investigate crimes against people from ethnic minority communities properly and the view that the police are unresponsive and unaccountable to the communities they serve, echoes this long and troubled history. This is not to say that nothing has changed. On the contrary, the face of the British police service has been changed radically by the recruitment of police officers from ethnic minority communities. Racism is less overt and changes in police culture have occurred as the 'field' of policing and its social and political context have changed (Chan 1997). None the less, discrimination, xenophobia and intolerance persist in the British police. Racism has led to unnecessary deaths, physical and psychological injuries, as well as disaffection and frustration within black and Asian communities. Racism strikes at the very core of the idea of democratic policing. Because the police are guardians of liberty and the gatekeepers of the criminal process, discriminatory policing has the effect of criminalising entire communities and denying them justice.

In recent years, the British police have drifted further towards a 'military model' of policing that emphasises crime fighting, the pursuit of 'enemies within' and adopts practices such as stop and search 'swamps', surveillance and proactive intelligence gathering (Bowling and Foster 2002). It is perhaps understandable that police commanders and hawkish politicians fearing the 'soft on crime label' would opt for this approach in the face of stubbornly high rates of crime and violence. However, this shift to a 'law and order society' is likely to be both counterproductive and undermine fundamental human rights. Paramilitary policing is part of a vicious circle that contributes to the criminalisation of marginalised communities and undermines not only the 'confidence and trust' in the police but also the legitimacy of the state itself. This undermines voluntary compliance with the rule of law and fails to reduce violence in the community.

There have been a number of attempts to reform policing through legal changes and attempts to transform police culture and restructuring systems of police accountability. In our view, reform should begin with a clear commitment to democratic policing based on responsiveness, accountability to the community and adherence to internationally recognised human rights standards (see Chapter 23). These provide us with the basis to ensure the maintenance of peace and the protection of the rights to life, liberty and security of the person. It is crucial that the police service is internally democratic, reflects the demography of the communities served and is accountable to them. The challenge for the future is to envision effective ways of reducing crime and disorder by including young people in the social life of the community. Part of this process must be through defining a new role for the police away from the resort to military-style, intelligence-led coercion and towards positive policing where officers are guardians of public peace and co-producers of community safety.

Selected further reading

This chapter draws on the authors' book *Racism, Crime and Justice* (2002), which sets the research on the policing of minority communities in the broader social context of ethnicity, inequality and racism, in the fields of social policy, criminology and criminal justice. The first major sociological study of racism and British policing is Hall *et al.*'s *Policing the Crisis* (1978), which inspired other theoretically informed studies including Gilroy's *There Ain't No Black in the Union Jack* (1987) and Keith's *Race, Riots and Policing* (1993). Empirical research conducted during the 1980s and 1990s specifically on policing and ethnic minority communities, and on 'race' and racism within the police service is very extensive – most of which is cited in the present article. Among the few other books in this field are Holdaway's *The Racialisation of British Policing* (1996) and Cashmore and McLaughlin's edited collection, *Out of Order? Policing Black People* (1991). More recent books include Britton's *Black Justice? Race, Criminal Justice and Identity* (2000), which explores the meaning of 'race' in the custody process, FitzGerald *et al.*'s (2002) *Policing for London* (2002) and Marlow and Loveday's edited volume, *After MacPherson* (2000), the latter two of which consider policing minority communities in the post-Macpherson period. Statistical data on policing practices such as stops, searches, deaths in police custody, arrests and cautioning are published in the Home Office Section 95 publication, *Statistics on Race and the Criminal Justice System* (1998, 2001, 2003). Readers looking for a broader international perspective are directed towards Chan's *Changing Police Culture* (1997), which analyses 'race' and policing in New South Wales, Australia, and Dulaney's readable and fastidiously researched *Black Police in America* (1996).

Notes

1 Categorisation by 'race' or 'ethnicity' is deeply problematic (see Bowling and Phillips 2002: 23–35). We reject the idea that humanity can be divided into fixed biological or cultural categories and yet there are clear differences in experience among groups defined on the basis of physical appearance. We acknowledge the difficulties inherent in rejecting essentialism while retaining ethnic categories to illuminate racialised patterns of human experience (Bowling and Phillips 2002: xvii; Phillips and Bowling 2003).

2 We have restricted our analysis to the extensive British policing literature. This should not be taken to imply that the relationship between the British police and minorities is uniquely troubled. Elsewhere, we have compared policing in the USA, Australia and South Africa with that in Britain (Bowling *et al.* 2001) and found similar issues and problems in each country.

3 This chapter focuses largely on communities with origins in the Indian subcontinent, Africa and the Caribbean whose experiences of policing are the most extensively documented. There will be both similarities and differences in the experience of other minority groups resident in the UK, such as the Irish, Turkish and Cypriot groups, travellers, Romany, Roma from eastern Europe, Kosovans and Kurds.

4 For a critique of the concept of 'availability', see Bowling and Phillips (2002: 144–5).

5 Police community consultative groups (PCCGs), or 'Scarman committees', were formalised in s. 106 of PACE and consolidated in s. 96 of the Police Act 1996.

References

All Faiths for One Race (1978) *Talking Blues*. London: AFFOR.

Baggott, M. (2000): 'Breaking the power of fear and hate – relationships and renewal: a new "policing style" agenda?', *Policing Today*, Autumn: 14–17.

Bland, N., Mundy, G., Russell, J. and Tuffin, R. (1999) *Career Progression of Ethnic Minority Police Officers. Home Office Police Research Series Paper* 107. London: Home Office.

Bourne, J. (2001) 'The life and times of institutional racism', *Race and Class*, 43(2): 7–22.

Bowling, B. (1999) *Violent Racism: Victimisation, Policing and Social Context* (revised edn). Oxford: Oxford University Press.

Bowling, B. and Foster, J. (2002) 'Policing and the police', in M. Maguire *et al.* (eds) *The Oxford Handbook of Criminology* (3rd edn). Oxford: Oxford University Press, 980–1033.

Bowling, B. and Phillips, C. (2002) *Racism, Crime and Justice*. Harlow: Longman.

Bowling, B., Phillips, C.,Campbell, A and Docking, M. (2001) *Human Rights and Policing: Eliminating Discrimination, Intolerance and the Abuse of Power from Policework*. Geneva: UN Research Institute for Social Development.

Bradford Commission (1996) *The Bradford Commission Report: The Report of an Inquiry into the Wider Implications of Public Disorders in Bradford which Occurred on 9, 10 and 11 June 1995* (Bradford Congress). London: HMSO.

Bridges, L. (1982) 'Racial attacks', *Legal Action Group Bulletin*, January.

Bridges, L. (2001) 'Race, law and the state', *Race and Class*, 43(2): 61–76.

Bright, M. (2002) ' "Nothing has changed," says mother of Stephen Lawrence', *The Observer*, 24 February.

Britton (2000) *Black Justice? Race, Criminal Justice and Identity*. Stoke-on-Trent: Trentham Books.

Brown, D. (1997) *PACE Ten Years on: A Review of the Research. Home Office Research Study* 155. London: Home Office.

Brown, J. (1997) 'Equal opportunities and the police in England and Wales: past, present and future possibilities', in P. Francis *et al.* (eds) *Policing Futures: The Police, Law Enforcement and the 21st Century*. Basingstoke: Macmillan.

Bucke, T. (1997) *Ethnicity and Contacts with the Police: Latest Findings from the British Crime Survey. Home Office Research Findings* 59. London: Home Office.

Burnley Task Force (2001) *Burnley Task Force Report*, 11 December (http://www.burnleytaskforce.org.uk/reports/taskforcereport.pdf).

Cain, M. (1973) *Society and the Policeman's Role*. London: Routledge.

Cantle, T. (2001) *Community Cohesion: A Report of the Independent Review Team*. London: Home Office.

Cashmore, E. (2001) 'The experiences of ethnic minority police officers in Britain: under-recruitment and racial profiling in a performance culture', *Ethnic and Racial Studies*, 24(4): 642–59.

Cashmore, E. (2002) 'Behind the window dressing: ethnic minority police perspectives on cultural diversity', *Journal of Ethnic and Migration Studies*, 28(2): 327–41.

Cashmore, E. and McLaughlin, E. (1991) (eds) *Out of Order? Policing Black People*. London: Routledge.

Chan, J. (1997) *Changing Police Culture: Policing in a Multicultural Society*. Cambridge: Cambridge University Press.

Chigwada-Bailey, R. (1997) *Black Women's Experiences of Criminal Justice: Discourse on Disadvantage*. Winchester: Waterside Press.

Clancy, A., Hough, M., Aust, R. and Kershaw, C. (2001) *Crime, Policing and Justice: The Experience of Ethnic Minorities*. London: Home Office.

Clarke, A. Lord (2001) *Report of the Burnley Task Force*. Burnley: Burnley Borough Council.

Commission for Racial Equality (1991) *The Point of Order: A Study of Consultative Arrangements under Section 106 of the Police and Criminal Evidence Act*. London: Commission for Racial Equality.

Cross, M. and Smith, D.I. (1987) *Black Youth Futures: Ethnic Minorities and the Youth Training Scheme*. Leicester: National Youth Bureau.

Dixon, D., Coleman, C. and Bottomley, K. (1990) 'Consent and the legal regulation of policing', *Journal of Law and Society*, 17(3): 345–59.

Du Bois, W.E.B. (1901, 1989) *The Souls of Black Folk*. Harmondsworth: Penguin Books.

Dulaney (1996) *Black People in America*. Bloomington, IN: Indiana University Press.

Fitzgerald, M. (1993) *Ethnic Minorities in the Criminal Justice System. London: HMSO.*

FitzGerald, M. (1999) Searches in London under Section 1 of the Police and Criminal Evidence Act: London: Metropolitan Police.

FitzGerald, M. and Hale, C. (1996) *Ethnic Minorities: Victimisation and Racial Harassment: Findings from the 1988 and 1992 British Crime Surveys. Home Office Research Study* 154. London: Home Office.

FitzGerald, M., Hough, M., Joseph, I. and Qureshi, T. (2002) *Policing for London*. Cullompton: Willan.

FitzGerald, M. and Sibbitt, R. (1997) *Ethnic Monitoring in Police Forces: A Beginning. Home Office Research Study* 173. London: Home Office.

Foundation 2000 (1995) *Bradford Riots*.

Fryer, P. (1984) *Staying Power: The History of Black People in Britain*. London: Pluto.

Gilroy, P. (1987) *There Ain't No Black in the Union Jack*. London: Hutchinson.

Gordon, D. (2001) 'Democratic consolidation and community policing: conflicting imperatives in South Africa', *Policing and Society*, 11(2): 121–50.

Gordon, P. (1984) *White Law*. London: Pluto.

Graef, R. (1989) *Talking Blues: The Police in their Own Words*. London: Collins Harvill.

Hall, S., Critcher, C., Jefferson, T., Clarke, J. and Roberts, B. (1978) *Policing the Crisis: Mugging, the State and Law and Order*. London: Macmillan.

Hall, S., Lewis, G. and McLaughlin, E. (1998) *The Report on Racial Stereotyping (Prepared for Deighton Guedalla, Solicitors for Duwayne Brooks, June 1998)*. Milton Keynes: Open University.

Her Majesty's Crown Prosecution Service Inspectorate (2002) *Report on the Thematic Review of Casework Having a Minority Ethnic Dimension*. London: HM CPSI.

Her Majesty's Inspectorate of Constabulary (1995) *Developing Diversity in the Police Service*. Equal Opportunities Thematic Inspection Report 1995. London: Home Office.

Her Majesty's Inspectorate of Constabulary (1997) *Winning the Race: Policing Plural Communities. HMIC Thematic Inspection Report on Police Community and Race Relations 1996/7*. London: Home Office.

Her Majesty's Inspectorate of Constabulary (1999) *Winning the Race (Revised): Policing Plural Communities. HMIC Thematic Inspection Report on Police Community and Race Relations 1996/7*. London: Home Office.

Her Majesty's Inspectorate of Constabulary (2000) *Winning the Race: Embracing Diversity. Consolidation Inspection of Police Community and Race Relations 2000*. London: Home Office.

Her Majesty's Inspectorate of Constabulary (2003) *Diversity Matters*. London: Home Office.

Holdaway, S. (1983) *Inside the British Police*. Oxford: Blackwell.

Holdaway, S. (1993) *The Resignation of Black and Asian Officers from the Police Service*. London: Home Office.

Holdaway, S. (1996) *The Racialisation of British Policing*. London: Macmillan.

Holdaway, S. (1997) 'Some recent approaches to the study of race in criminological research: race as social process', *British Journal of Criminology*, 37(3): 383–400.

Holdaway, S. and Barron, A. (1997) *Resigners? The Experience of Black and Asian Police Officers*. London: Macmillan.

Home Office (1981) *Racial Attacks*. London: Home Office.

Home Office (1998) *Statistics on Race and the Criminal Justice System 1998: A Home Office Publication under Section 95 of the Criminal Justice Act 1991*. London: Home Office.

Home Office (1999) *Staff Targets for the Home Office, the Prison, the Police, the Fire and the Probation Services*. London: Home Office.

Home Office (2001) *Statistics on Race and the Criminal Justice System 2001: A Home Office Publication under Section 95 of the Criminal Justice Act 1991*. London: Home Office.

Home Office (2002a) *Stephen Lawrence Inquiry: Home Secretary's Action Plan Third Annual Report on Progress*. London: Home Office.

Home Office (2002b) *Control of Immigration Statistics. Home Office Statistical Bulletin* 11/02. London: Home Office.

Home Office (2003) *Statistics on Race and the Criminal Justice System 2002: A Home Office Publication under Section 95 of the Criminal Justice Act 1991*. London: Home Office.

Howe, D. (1988) *From Bobby to Babylon: Blacks and the British Police*. London: Race Today Publications.

Hunte, J. (1966) *Nigger Hunting in England?* London: West Indian Standing Conference.

Inquest (1996) *Lobbying from Below: INQUEST in Defence of Civil Liberties*. London: UCL Press.

Institute of Race Relations (1979) *Police against Black People: Evidence Submitted to the Royal Commission on Criminal Procedure*. London: IRR.

Institute of Race Relations (1987) *Policing against Black People*. London: IRR.

Institute of Race Relations (1991) *Deadly Silence: Black Deaths in Custody*. London: IRR.

Jones, T. and Newburn, T. (1997) *Policing after the Act*. London: Policy Studies Institute.

Kappeler, V.E., Sluder, R.D. and Alpert, G.P. (1994) *Forces of Deviance: Understanding the Dark Side of Policing*. Prospect Heights, IL: Waveland Press.

Keith, M. (1993) *Race, Riots and Policing: Lore and Disorder in a Multi-racist Society*. London: UCL Press.

Kettle, M. and Hodges, L. (1982) *Uprising!: The Police, the People and the Riots in Britain's Cities*. London: Pluto.

Lustgarten, L. (2002) 'The future of stop and search', *Criminal Law Review*, 603.

Macpherson, W. (1999) *The Stephen Lawrence Inquiry*. Report of an Inquiry by Sir William Macpherson of Cluny. Advised by Tom Cook, The Right Reverend Dr John Sentamu and Dr Richard Stone (Cm 4262-1). London: HMSO.

Manby, B. (2000) 'The South African Independent Complaints Directorate', in A. Goldsmith and C. Lewis (eds) *Civilian Oversight of Policing*. Oxford: Hart.

Marlow, A. and Loveday, B. (eds) (2000) *After Macpherson: Policing after the Stephen Lawrence Inquiry*. Lyme Regis: Russell House Publishing.

Matthews, R. and Pitts, J. (2001) (ed.) *Crime, Disorder and Community Safety*. New York, NY: Routledge.

Mayhew, P., Aye Maung, N. and Mirrlees-Black, C. (1993) *The 1992 British Crime Survey. Home Office Research Study* 132. London: HMSO.

McLaughlin, E. (1991) 'Police accountability and black people: into the 1990s', in E. Cashmore and E. McLaughlin (eds) *Out of Order?: Policing Black People*. London: Routledge.

McLaughlin, E. and Murji, K. (1999) 'After the Stephen Lawrence Report', *Critical Social Policy*, 19(3): 371–85.

Melville, N. (1999) *The Taming of the Blue: Regulating Police Misconduct in South Africa*. Pretoria: Human Sciences Research Council.

Metropolitan Police Service (1997) *Annual Report*. London: MPS.

Metropolitan Police Service (2001) *Annual Report*. London: MPS.

Mhlanga, B. (1997) *The Colour of English Justice: A Multivariate Analysis*. Aldershot: Avebury.

Mhlanga, B. (1999) *Race and Crown Prosecution Service Decisions*. Hull: Centre for Criminology and Criminal Justice.

Miller, J., Bland, N. and Quinton, P. (2000) *The Impact of Stops and Searches on Crime and the Community. Police Research Series Paper* 127. London: Home Office.

Mirrlees-Black, C. (2001) *Confidence in the Criminal Justice System: Findings from the 2000 British Crime Survey. Research Findings* 137. London: Home Office.

Morgan, R. (1989) 'Policing by consent: legitimating the doctrine', in R. Morgan and D.J. Smith (eds) *Coming to Terms with Policing: Perspectives on Policy*. London: Routledge.

Morgan, R. (1992) *Talking about Policing*. London: MacMillan.

MVA and Miller, J. (2000) *Profiling Populations Available for Stops and Searches. Police Research Series Paper* 131. London: Home Office.

NACRO (1997) *Policing Local Communities: The Tottenham Experiment*. London: NACRO.

Newham Monitoring Project (1985, 1988) *Annual Reports*. London: NMP.

Norris, C., Fielding, N., Kemp, C. and Fielding, J. (1992) 'Black and Blue: an analysis of the influence of race on being stopped by the police', *British Journal of Sociology*, 43(2): 207–23.

Ousley, H. (2001) *Community Pride not Prejudice: Making Diversity work in Bradford*. Bradford: Bradford Vision 2001.

Phillips, C. and Bowling, B. (2003) 'Racism, race and ethnicity: developing minority perspectives in criminology', *British Journal of Criminology*, 43(2): 269–90.

Phillips, C. and Brown, D. (1998) *Entry into the Criminal Justice System: A Survey of Police Arrests and their Outcomes. Home Office Research Study* 185. London: Home Office.

Police Complaints Authority (1997) *Report by the Police Complaints Authority on the Investigation of a Complaint against the Metropolitan Police Service by Mr N. and Mrs D. Lawrence*. London: Home Office.

Police Complaints Authority (2000) *Annual Report*. London: PCA.

Pope, D. (1976) *Community Relations – the Police Response*. London: Runnymede Trust.

Pryce, K. (1979) *Endless Pressure*. Harmondsworth: Penguin Books.

Quinton, P., Bland, N. and Miller, J. (2000) *Police Stops, Decision-making and Practice. Police Research Series Paper* 130. London: Home Office.

Reiner, R. (1991) *Chief Constables*. Oxford: Oxford University Press.

Reiner, R. (2000) *The Politics of the Police*. (3rd edn). London: Harvester Wheatsheaf.

Ritchie, D. (2001) *Panel Report, 11 December 2001: One Oldham, One Future*. Manchester: Government Office for the North West.

Rotterdam Charter (1996) *Policing for a Multi-ethnic Society*. Rotterdam: Rotterdam Conference.

Royal Commission (1981) *The Investigation and Prosecution of Criminal Offences in England and Wales: Law and Procedure*. London: Home Office.

Scarman, L. (1981) *The Scarman Report*. London: HMSO.

Scrap Sus Campaign (1979) *A Fair Deal for All: Evidence and Recommendations to the Royal Commission on Criminal Procedure*. London: Scrap Sus Campaign – Steering Committee.

Sims, L. and Myhill, A. (2001) *Policing and the Public: Findings from the 2000 British Crime Survey. Home Office Research Findings* 136. London: Home Office.

Sivanandan, A. (1982) *A Different Hunger: Writings on Black Resistance*. London: Pluto.

Skogan, W.G. (1990) *The Police and the Public in England and Wales: A British Crime Survey Report. Home Office Research Study* 117. London: HMSO.

Skogan, W.G. (1994) *Contacts between Police and Public: Findings from the 1992 British Crime Survey. Home Office Research Study* 134. London: HMSO.

Smith, D.J. and Gray, J. (1985) *Police and People in London*. London: Gower.

Solomos, J. (1993) *Race and Racism in Contemporary Britain*. London: Macmillan.

Spencer, A.J. and Hough, M. (2000) *Policing Diversity: Lessons from Lambeth. Policing Research Series Paper* 121. London: Home Office.

Stevens, P. and Willis, C.F. (1981) *Ethnic Minorities and Complaints against the Police*. London: Home Office.

Stone, V. and Tuffin, R. (2000) *Attitudes of People from Minority Ethnic Communities towards a Career in the Police Service. Police Research Series Paper* 136. London: Home Office.

Uglow, S. (1988) *Policing Liberal Society*. Oxford: Oxford University Press.

Waddington, D. (2001) 'Trouble at mill towns', *The Psychologist*, 14(9): 454–5.

Waddington, D., Stenson, K. and Don, D. (2002) 'Disproportionality in police stop and search in Reading and Slough'. Summary report for Thames Valley Police. Unpublished.

Webster, C. (2002) 'Race, space and fear: imagined geographies of racism, crime, violence and disorder in northern England', *Capital and Class*, December.

Young, J. (1994) *Policing the Streets: Stops and Searches in North London*. Middlesex: Centre for Criminology, Enfield, Middlesex University.

Chapter 22

Gender and policing

Frances Heidensohn

Introduction

Gender became a key feature of the study and concerns of criminal justice systems in the late twentieth century. Criminological theories were challenged, research agendas revised and major policy shifts achieved (Gelsthorpe 2002; Heidensohn 1996, 2002). Debates continue about how effective and widespread these paradigm changes have been, but they are certainly inscribed in the history of criminology (Holdaway and Rock 1998; Heidensohn 2000). The most notable aspect of these developments has been the very belated recognition of the importance of gender in patterns of offending and of victimisation, and also the need for theories to acknowledge this and criminal justice systems to adapt to it.

Police and studies of policing are somewhat distinctive in that the importance of gender had been accepted, albeit in a very different way, almost from the earliest studies of policing. As Robert Reiner put it 'The police world is one of old-fashioned machismo' and he cites in a telling footnote (2000: 107) a researcher's war story about a very macho episode involving police officers he observed in a local drinking club. Reiner is more appreciative than analytical of this key aspect of cop culture. In this he follows in the footsteps of the pioneer US police researchers who acknowledged and described the existence of a highly masculinised core to policing. Danger, authority and the need to achieve results were the three key factors which Skolnick identified as forming the 'working personality' of the urban police officer. Drawing on his own and Westley's empirical studies (originally carried out in the 1940s and 1950s), Skolnick argues that when faced with public hostility officers responded with aggression and violence. This situation then escalated into more threats and tension and led to a secretive and self-protective reaction (1966). In trying to define the distinctive nature of the role of the police, another pioneer scholar insisted on 'their capacity for decisive action. ... The policeman and the policeman alone, is equipped, entitled and required to deal with every exigency in which force may have to be used, to meet it' (Bittner 1974).

In sum, these authors are emphasising aspects of policing which are clearly gendered. Unlike, however, the later feminist – influenced work in criminal justice studies, it is *masculine* gender to which they draw attention and especially to what Connell calls the 'emphasised' masculinity of the use of force, the assertion of authority and the unquestioned loyalty of bands of brothers, bound to each other by the nature of the dangers they confront and their consequent needs for solidarity and protection. Yet, while this is a *recognised* theme in all early projects on the police, it is not one which is subject either to serious discussion or deconstruction. Rather it is a taken-for-granted assumption that policing is a *male* occupation which inevitably means that it must have a *masculine* culture, or even one where, because of threats and powers unique to it, this culture will take an extreme and exaggerated form.

Studies of gender in policing thus began, somewhat unusually, with a focus on men and masculinity. However, as the examples cited above indicate, these themes have not been explored in any great depth in the literature. Despite the urgings of Newburn and Stanko (1994), masculinity has been treated as a single, homogeneous phenomenon which does not have to be explained. There are a few academic insider accounts by men of policing (e.g. Holdaway 1983; Young 1991) which show awareness of difference and complexity in this area. Male officers who are homosexual while they have an active association to which they can belong have only been the subject of very limited research (e.g. Burke 1993). Ironically, one recent article which presents a challenge to academic researchers to provide an appreciative account of police subculture, emphasises that 'the core of the police's oral tradition lies in the glorification of violence over which they hold the legitimate monopoly . . . this celebration is generalised to a "cult of masculinity"' (Waddington 1999: 298). This approach allows for no variation in ideas of masculinity, nor in the varied experiences of male officers. There is still a gap in the literature, although studies of police culture have begun to address this (see Chapter 9).

It is, of course, true that for most of the first 75 years after the founding of the 'new' police in London in 1829, all British recruits were male, as required by the Police Acts, that 'fit men' be appointed, as indeed they were in law enforcement worldwide. However, the period at the turn of the nineteenth and twentieth centuries saw the emergence of a policewomen's movement, whose supporters advocated the employment of female officers and, within a few years, the recruitment of the world's first policewomen. The twentieth century witnessed a series of major shifts, based on this first key development and, in the twenty-first, women officers are widely established in law enforcement albeit still as a minority. Their presence has been the focus of considerable discussion about their role and has opened debates about the gendered nature of policing. These raise questions not only about law enforcement as an *occupation* for women (and men) but also about the experiences of women as the *subjects* of policing activities. Indeed, the aims of the supporters of the policewomen's movement were to improve performance and transform action in those areas. These themes will form the main topics of this chapter. First, though, I want to reflect briefly on the ways in which the initial, unquestioning stance on the inevitability of a macho cop culture has been modified.

In an influential article published in the early 1970s, Egon Bittner developed his 'theory of the police' around the need to use force in some circumstances. He suggests that the police are caught in a time warp and contaminated by their association with 'so-called dangerous classes' and thus 'in the efforts to control violence, depredation and evil, police work took on' some of the features of its targets and became a tainted occupation' (1974a). With what almost sounds like nostalgia, he argues that there has been:

> a profound shift of values, away from virtues associated with masculine prowess and combativeness, and toward virtues associated with assidu-ous enterprise and material progress. There is still some glamour left in being an adventurer or warrior, but true success belongs to the business-man and to the professional (1974a).

Bittner here shows sympathy for those he always refers to as police*men* and claims 'I have written as a spokesman of these officers' (1974a). He sees neither militarisation nor increased educational or recruitment standards as having improved policing and insists that only honest recognition of the proper tasks of policing will do so.

A study of relations between the police and public in London and of the Metropolitan Police as an organisation was completed within a decade of Bittner's work but tackles the issue of the subculture in a very different way. Smith and Gray (1985) carried out extensive fieldwork for their project and illustrate their views with numerous examples, concluding that:

> the dominant values of the Force are still in many ways those of an all-male institution such as a rugby club or boys' school – in the emphasis on remaining dominant in any encounter and not losing face … on masculine solidarity and on backing the other men in the group especially when they are in the wrong … the importance given to physical courage and the glamour attached to violence. This set of attitudes and norms amounts to a 'cult of masculinity' (1985: 372).

Smith and Gray did not find universal acceptance of these values, but they were quite pervasive. However, they suggest that some of the men's talk was fantasy and the result of the officers' own insecurities. They recognised the presence of female officers, clearly sought them out for private interviews and record their own observations of gendered interactions as well as various examples of 'bawdy talk' which they, as male researchers, heard. The Policy Studies Institute (PSI) study (Smith and Gray 1985) has, among its recommen-dations, that more women should be recruited and that they should be more fully integrated into the organisation (they formed about nine per cent of the strength of the Metropolitan Police at the time of the PSI study and an informal – and illegal – quota on recruitment existed).

While this major report has a great deal to say about subcultures within the Metropolitan Police, its main focus is on their racist rather than their sexist aspects. As the authors make clear, their work was carried out during a time of great strain and suspicion between police and people from ethnic minorities in London, with the New Cross fire in Deptford (when 13 young black people died) and the Brixton riots as crisis events. Other studies which analyse the problems caused by the predominance of a gendered and gender-based 'canteen' culture have also been undertaken where racial incidents and alleged police racism have led to highly publicised crises. In March 1991, a video camera recorded on tape the beating by Los Angeles Police Department (LAPD) officers of a black man, Rodney King, who had been arrested after a car chase. An official report (the Christopher Commission) inquired into the incident and into the culture of the LAPD, pointing to its macho character, use of excessive force, marginalising and ridiculing of black and female officers. In a wide-ranging review of police use of excessive force in the USA in cases such as those of Rodney King, Skolnick and Fyfe conclude:

> where police brutality has been a significant issue in recent years, it has generally involved departments . . . led by strong charismatic officials who have adhered to and espoused a style of policing informed, influenced, and reinforced by the kind of blue-collar macho one hears in cops' bars late at night (1993: 240).

A similar, if much less brutal, event led to Janet Chan's (1997) study of police culture in New South Wales. A documentary *Cop It Sweet* showed the New South Wales police as 'racist, sexist, ignorant, insensitive and hypocritical' (1997: 3), despite the fact that they were supposedly on their best behaviour and knew they were being observed and filmed by TV cameras (an echo perhaps of the Roger Graef documentary on the treatment of women victims 20 years previously). Chan, whose purpose is to dissect the nature and sources of police subcultures, rejects the functionalist argument that the ways in which police subcultures develop are a response to the constraints of the job and are inevitable. On the contrary, she maintains, police officers construct their own culture for policing:

> Instead of thinking of police officers being 'socialised' into all encompassing, homogeneous and unchanging police culture . . . a new framework for understanding police culture . . . emphasises the active role played by police actors in developing, reinforcing, resisting or transforming cultural knowledge and institutionalised practice (1997: 225).

Chan insists, as many recent authors have done, on the diversity and choice possible within occupational culture and thus the scope for change. She is in no doubt that change is possible and necessary, given the harmful scandals which affected police forces in Australia which she describes; she also stresses that 'researchers who emphasise the importance of police occupational culture considerably underestimate the power of the field, i.e. the social, economic, legal and political sites in which politics takes place' (1997: 232). Chan contrasts cultural explanations of racism and corruption with institutionalised racism (1997: 38) and sees the former as more compelling. Bowling and Foster (2002: 1012–13) link the two and relate them closely to machismo. They also note the continued influences of these features on police work, the barriers to change and accountability which can be mounted and the sometimes disastrous and costly results, as manifested in the findings of the inquiry into the death of Stephen Lawrence (Macpherson 1999). A contradictory note is struck in a challenging article by Waddington (1999) who argues that 'canteen culture' is just that, a rhetorical device, a 'defensive solidarity of the lower ranks' which they use protectively because of their 'recognition of the precariousness of their position' (1999: 302). They are in danger, he insists, not so much from physical threats or closeness to crime but because they work on the margins of society and can have their key activity ('the exercise of coercive authority') challenged at any time. Waddington seeks to reach an appreciative understanding of police subculture and to reinstate, in revised form, the argument that police subcultures are primarily functional, for the police themselves. He does not address in any way questions as to whether society can afford, or should morally accept, the high costs caused by the impact of these defensive forms. These issues are beyond the scope of this chapter. What is relevant is how all contemporary authors, even those like Waddington who write positively of machismo, have to engage with issues of gender and acknowledge how they form part of the problems to be tackled in law enforcement today. This is a significant shift and is an important background to the central themes to which we now turn.

Women in policing and policing of and for women

Modern policing, as launched in London in the early nineteenth century and developed in its much discussed format in both Britain and the USA as Anglo-American policing (see Chapter 2), did not include women among its recruits. The foundations of the movements which ultimately led to women's entry into policing were nevertheless laid down before the middle of the nineteenth century. They had their origins less in career ambitions for individual women than in campaigns to improve the lot of their unfortunate sisters in prisons, reformatories and 'rescue' missions. Elizabeth Fry advocated wholesale prison reform, insisting that, at all times, women in prison should be segregated from men and, because of the dangers of exploitation and abuse, supervised only by women (Fry 1827). Prison matrons were appointed in 1823, but her other aims were not achieved in Britain for a long time. In 1845 in the USA, the Women's Prison Association and the American Female Moral Reform Society succeeded in having matrons hired to supervise women in gaols. Their aim was to eliminate prostitution and they argued that matrons were needed to protect vulnerable women from abuse by policemen, male prisoners and other hardened women offenders (Feinman 1986). Parallel steps were taken in Britain, with the forming of the Society Promoting the Return of Women as Poor Law Guardians in 1861, which aimed to bring the influence of women of feeling and education to counteract that of men. By the turn of the century, there were groups which advocated the introduction of police-women in the USA, Britain, Europe (especially Holland and Germany) and Australia. The aims of these advocates were the moral reform and rescue of their less fortunate sisters.

Dorothy Schulz (1995) has noted that the policewomen's movement which brought Alice Stebbins Wells to be hired in 1910 by the LAPD as Los Angeles', America's, first female officer, overlapped with the prison matron and police matron movements. Neither of these causes had ever gained the same strength in Britain yet, in 1915, Edith Smith was sworn in and given powers of arrest in Grantham. By this time, particular circumstances existed in this country which gave shape to, and still in the twenty-first century, affect, the pattern of policing by women. These were the effects of the First World War, the aftermath of the struggle for women's suffrage and the aims of the pioneers who led the British movement (Carrier 1988).

Several key figures, including Margaret Damer Dawson, Mary Allen and Nina Boyle, who had all been associated with first wave feminism, pressed for volunteer policewomen to patrol British cities. They argued that the upheavals caused by large-scale movements of troops and of refugees were putting both vulnerable women *and* innocent soldiers at risk. Independently wealthy, very well connected to the heart of the British establishment, they got their way (Lock 1979) and the first Women Police Volunteers went on patrol. Later, after internal conflicts, they became the Women Police Service and mainly worked at policing the women workers in ammunitions factories. Significantly, and unlike their American counterparts, they wore uniforms and, while their work was distinctively specialised, directed at women and juveniles, they aimed at a very early stage at attaining the full status of sworn officers. However, the pioneer days in Britain were marked by sharp rivalries between the various volunteer groups, rivalries vividly illustrated by the evidence given by many of the witnesses to the Baird Committee (1921) who recorded their differing claims to the territory of policing by women. The winners in this turf war were the Voluntary Women Patrols, who provided the leader for the Metropolitan Police Women Patrols.

The cause of women in policing was very much reinforced by the success of the wartime patrols – Baird Committee members as well as independent witnesses refer to this frequently – but there was a lengthy and hard-fought fight to maintain the women in post and to give them police powers. Support was widespread as it had been before 1914 and now included the first women MPs, notably Nancy Astor, as well as bishops, politicians and senior policemen converted to the cause. Their case was aided by the Savidge Inquiry, a report into a scandal in which an interview of a young woman at Scotland Yard was mishandled, and was eventually won in 1931.

Until after the Second World War women's position in policing remained a limited one. The 'victory' of attested status was gained by intense lobbying, but what was achieved was a separate sphere for female police. They had their own distinctive duties and specialised tasks, for which they received additional training. Providing escorts for female prisoners, interviewing and searching women offenders, dealing with female victims, juveniles and at-risk and vulnerable girls and youths were their tasks. They worked in their own departments and had their own hierarchy, including senior officers, but were accountable to all-male upper ranks. Their pay was lower, their uniforms different, they were never armed and their numbers stagnated.

These formative early years cast long shadows even when, with little preparation or training, UK police forces integrated women officers into the mainstream following the passing of the Sex Discrimination Act in 1975. Although that step led to fundamental changes in the role of women in policing, the lasting impact of key aspects of the pioneer days can be summarised thus:

1. The *moral*, especially the save–rescue–control, *basis* of the policewomen's movement, which differentiated it markedly from the origins of the new police and the ways in which their mission had evolved.

2. *Volunteers*: Britain's first women police were volunteers; they modelled themselves on the numerous philanthropic bodies which women had founded and run and through which they achieved some entry into public policy space during the nineteenth century. In this again they were quite different from the male police who joined for the job and typically came, when they had outside experience, from the military.

3. *Class and education*: the first British policewomen were middle or upper class, well educated and with training as nurses or teachers. Male constables were only expected to have the most basic skills when they joined the police.

4. *Specialisation*: pioneer policewomen were specialists, carrying out for themselves a distinct mandate and emphasising unique skills and responsibilities. They worked within the existing police organisations and, by the post Second World War era, were informally expanding their role (Lock 1979), but their numbers were still subject to restrictive quotas and their tasks limited.

5. The *mission* supporting the entry of women into policing and sustaining them in their role was a significant cause in Britain, as it was in several other countries. Most of this support lay *outside* the main law enforcement agencies. In the early part of the twentieth century, alliances linked to the cause were successful, but their influence faded and became something of a liability (Schulz 1995).

6. *Opposition*: one of the main reasons for the growth and maintenance of policewomen's movements was the strength of the opposition they encountered. This was much more marked in Britain than in the USA and came chiefly from within the police themselves, both lower ranks and senior levels. (There were always some keen individual believers and converts.) Lilian Wyles, one of the first women sergeants, later recalled 'To a man, they deprecated this utterly foolish experiment' (1951).

7. *International alliances*: the policewomen's movement was notably international, with its main protagonists using many of the networks which had been built up to promote other feminist and welfare causes.
   The strongest links were between English-speaking nations, where shared allegiance to the movement was promoted, but it also included two 'missions' from Britain to Germany after each world war (Heidensohn 2000).

What the first, long phase after women's entry into policing had achieved was paradoxical. There were female officers with powers of arrest, who wore uniforms and who had their own ranks and establishment. Their numbers had grown considerably, doubling during the Second World War from 282 to 418 and reaching almost 4,000, nearly four per cent of total national strength before integration in 1971 (Jones 1986: 4–5). Yet, despite formal and informal expansion of their roles, they did not carry out the full range of police duties, were paid only about 90 per cent of male pay, were subject to recruitment quotas and were still working in what was a distinct and separate sphere of policing.

Integration and afterwards

British police forces were integrated rapidly in the 1970s when, despite concerted resistance, the Labour government decided that the police should not be exempted from sex discrimination legislation. Similar developments occurred in the USA as a consequence of Title VII of the Civil Rights Act 1964 and in most agencies around the world. In Britain, as in the USA, the pressure came from *outside* the police, from equality legislation imposed on them. Social changes in what Chan (1997) calls 'the field' also meant that public expectations of the police had changed (Jones 1986). The consequences of integration can be seen everywhere, in numbers, deployment, promotion, etc. One of the chief differences is that there is now a substantial body of research and of official reports which demonstrate and analyse these changes. In reporting on this era below, I draw on this material illustratively; it is now too extensive to include it all. My focus is primarily on Britain and I have therefore used British or comparative studies which cover Britain as far as possible. Other studies are used where they have been especially significant and/or influential.

Four themes stand out from the records of the three decades since integration was enforced:

1. Models of equality.

2. Coming to terms with police culture.

3. Career issues.

4. New agendas.

They do not exhaust all the topics and debates which have flourished in this period but a considerable range of issues fit into this framework.

Models of equality

The models of equality for women (and other minorities) when they joined the police were based on the assumption that they should undertake their duties as much like men would as possible. In the 1970s, following the deployment of women officers on patrol for the first time in the USA, a series of evaluative studies were carried out to ascertain: 'can policewomen perform the duties traditionally assigned to men and as effectively as the men?' (Feinman 1986:

95; Bloch and Anderson 1973, 1974). I was able to trace 11 such projects and observed that they generally found only slight differences between male and female officers (Heidensohn 1992: 94–5). In an evaluation of these performance studies, Morash and Greene point out how heavily male stereotyped the items evaluated were and how far they lend 'credence to the idea that the underlying dimension . . . is conformity with the masculine values of dealing with danger, and hostile citizenry, aggressiveness in action and physical powers' (1986: 243–5). Studies undertaken in the decade or so after integration found that despite this body of evidence 'male officers' attitudes to their female colleagues and their *subjective* appraisals of performance were almost universally negative' (Jones 1986: 170 emphasis in original). Striving to achieve equality in performance is a repeated theme in accounts given by women both in the early years of adjustment and more recently. Thus I found (1992) a senior woman who 'described how she had first convinced male colleagues in the CID of her value by "sheer involvement" '; in one post, this meant that she stayed in a chair in the office night and day until her male colleagues agreed to her joining them on a case.

My comparative study of how female officers in Britain and the USA handled public order situations, traditionally regarded as the defining test of sex differences in competence, showed that the women managed in reasonably similar ways to men, but that they were conscious all the time of what they were doing:

> Women interviewed in this study had developed ways to construct 'presences' and demonstrate them in challenging situations. All officers must do this to some extent; females differ in that they know that the 'proper' presence for their role was masculine for a very long time. *They have to adjust to this without losing their potential to be effective in policing* (Heidensohn 1994: 300 emphasis added).

In this same era I also observed a series of what I called 'transformation scenes' in the professional lives of policewomen where 'they described events in which they proved themselves in some way, thereby earning the respect of their colleagues . . . the women themselves felt their confidence strengthened and their male colleagues granted them admission of a kind to the fraternity of real police' (Hediensohn 1992: 142). All these women were only too aware that each such admission was *conditional*, a provisional licence to police which had to be regained with every job move or promotion.

Over the next ten years, numerous reports, reviews and recommendations considerably raised the profile of equal opportunities and questioned many practices (e.g. HMIC 1992, 1996). Nevertheless, in the study which Jennifer Brown and I undertook in the late 1990s, a new generation of younger women were reporting almost identical episodes: 'I chased three and arrested three on foot . . . then the shift were completely different towards me . . . "yeah, you've proved yourself now, . . . one of the boys, you can get involved" ' (Brown and Heidensohn 2000: 140). Marisa Silvestri (2000, 2003) also found that her sample of senior women officers had to emulate male models, some of which, such as the 'smart macho' formula, were themselves innovative adaptations to the new public management.

There are in the twenty-first century some signs of a few modifications to the male-based notion of equality: a respray, perhaps, rather than a brand-new, gender-neutral model. An extensive review of police training (HMIC 1999) and government proposals to reform its content and structure in the UK (Home Office 1999) are notable for their emphasis on gender-neutral curricula and characteristics. Research on the results of the OSPRE℗ Part II exam (this is the Objective Structured Performance Related Examination, designed to select sergeants and inspectors nationally) showed that women consistently outperform men in the assessment centre used to test candidates (Hartley *et al.* 2002; McGuigan *et al.* 2002). McGuigan *et al.* conclude that they can find no bias *against men* in the tests, although they do recommend further research; they suggest their findings indicate 'that women candidates have shown a greater potential to perform as inspectors (managers). Ultimately these differences should translate into comparative levels of on-the-job performance' (2002: 25). Finally, the production of a document entitled *The Gender Agenda* by a coalition of British Association of Women Police (BAWP) and their allies is in itself noteworthy; even more significantly, the authors state as their first long-term aim for the twenty-first century 'For the Police Service to demonstrate consistently that it values women officers' and to put at the top of their list as causes of the failure of the equality of opportunity so far 'the perpetuation of dated stereotypes and myths' (BAWP *et al.* n.d.).

Coming to terms with police culture

While *The Gender Agenda* 'recognises and credits the [police] organisation for the positive progress it has made over the last ten years' (BAWP n.d.: 3), also rates 'failure to recognise the impact and consequences of the predominant and dominating culture on minority groups' (p. 3). It refers, too, to the need for ' "macho" culture' to be acknowledged and itemises some of the 'barriers to progress' caused by the 'dominating male culture' (p. 16); however, there are no examples listed under 'examples of bad practice', a surprising or tactical omission. However, there is a very considerable body of data from numerous sources which attests to the persistence of various forms of traditional cop culture, often manifested in harassment and of a range of strategies and resources employed by female officers to cope with these.

In the USA, legal challenges to police departments, based on allegations of discrimination and harassment, have been fairly common (Heidensohn 1989, 1992). There have been far fewer of these in the UK, although one very high-profile claim of sexual discrimination brought by Assistant Chief Constable Alison Halford, against Merseyside Police, highlighted a very florid version of machismo flourishing at the highest levels (Halford 1993). Apart from such autobiographical accounts and legal cases (where settlement terms sometimes include 'no comment' clauses), evidence for continued harassment and machismo comes from research sources. One of the first and most cited is Martin's (1980) Washington, DC, study in which she sought to understand how women adapt to the male occupational culture when they:

are excluded from the information exchange network and informal social life ... Policewomen's behaviour is circumscribed by the stereotyped roles in which they are cast ... which reminds women that as females they are sex objects, vulnerable to harassment, yet held responsible for the outcomes of the interaction (Martin 1980: 85).

Having carried out a participant observation study on the capital's police department, Martin described the women's responses to police culture as falling along a continuum from 'defeminised' women, super-professionals whose competence masks their femininity, to 'deprofessionalised' women who use feminine wiles to gain protection and concessions. She called the first *police*women and the second police*women* and although only seven of her sample of 28 were at either of the two extremes, her typology is often cited solely in that form. Jones (1986) describes the 'ritual arguments' from male colleagues against their presence with which women officers had to cope. She found a predominance of *police*women in her sample, and it does seem that the 'traditional' response similar to the police*women* disappeared as an option with integration. (Indeed in Britain, women who wished to do so were allowed to leave the force in 1975.) In my first study, *Women in Control?* (1992) I found that female officers in Britain used a range of strategies and techniques for managing their encounters with the occupational culture. Two predominated: first, their profound sense of *mission* – a belief in the values of law and order and their roles as peace officers. Several of these subjects were at a senior level and had joined before 1975, often having had to put formidable efforts into getting in. Secondly, they also stressed *professionalism* and their personal commitment to very high standards (Heidensohn 1992: ch. 4). It was apparent that these strategies could be successful, but that they came at great cost and were essentially loner/challenger solutions to being so constantly treated with scorn and hostility and as out of place in the police.

In our later study, Jenny Brown and I drew on a wide range of sources both to analyse the forms in which scorn and hostility and indeed acceptance were expressed in the dominant culture and to explore the ways in which policewomen were coping with all these at the end of the twentieth century. One fascinating representation of stereotypes of policewomen came from cartoons from police journals which we traced, noting how very much more explicit, sexual and belittling they became as the equality agenda advanced (Brown and Heidensohn 2000: ch. 3). We also carried out surveys and interviews to assess levels of discrimination and harassment in an international sample. About one fifth of all women officers in our sample felt they were not accepted by some or a few of their male colleagues, over half had experienced discrimination in deployment and 74 per cent had been sexually harassed by male officers at some time, though only 7 per cent reported this as 'often' (2000: 110–12). While these data are from a multinational sample, they mirror results from other work done in the British Isles (Brown 2000). We tried to establish various features of the ways in which women coped with these issues. These included:

- the range of such strategies;
- the types of support they used;

- the relationship, if any, between levels of discrimination and numbers of women, type of force and date at which women entered (Brown and Heidensohn 2000: Ch. 5).

Briefly summarising some complex findings, we concluded that 'women officers use a range of support and coping mechanisms and many use a combination' (2000: 113–15). Many relied on their own resources; one pattern seemed counter-intuitive, suggesting that 'greater activation of support and coping strategies is associated with *higher* levels of reported discrimination and harassment' (2000: 113–15), which we take to be an effect of greater awareness and higher standards in forces where women had the earliest dates of entry.

Time proved to be a key comparative dimension in measuring police-women's experiences of dealing with various aspects of discrimination, again in a way which may seem unexpected. Women from the forces we called the 'elders' (i.e. the ones which were the first to admit women) 'were almost twice as likely to report being discriminated against and to experience sexual harassment than those from fledgling forces only recently recruiting women' (Brown and Heidensohn 2000: 123). We tested out a typology of different models of policing as experienced by women, using our subjects' reports of their own contacts with police cultures as the classifying material. This provided us with some interesting distinctions. Our proposed framework, derived partly from other comparative work, included:

- cops;

- gendarmes;

- transitionals;

- colonial history.

We found that policewomen from two English-speaking nations, Australia and Northern Ireland, proved empirically to be respectively more similar to jurisdictions having a shared former colonial history and to European gendarmeries with their militaristic origins. These were significant results, aiding us to see that, while women encounter a common core of police culture globally, their experiences and responses are likely to be affected by historical stages and distinctive police cultures.

Our study also tried to explore the link between the gender ratio and rates of discriminatory behaviour. Kanter has argued that when the percentage of females or of members of another visible minority group rises above 25 per cent or so, discriminatory behaviour will decline. We found no such distinct relationship: 'In general, it did appear that as a gender balance was achieved, this was associated with lower levels, although not elimination, of discrimination' (Brown and Heidensohn 2000: 124). Our overall and somewhat discouraging conclusion was that 'the impacts of the occupational culture are hugely potent and can override an individual's efforts' (2000: 125).

Careers

There is an overall trend for more women to choose policing as a career. In England and Wales the numbers of women police doubled in the 1990s, from under 11,000 to over 20,000, representing 17 per cent of total numbers in 2000. Women are now about a quarter of recruits and, while promotion rates varied after integration, they picked up again by the end of the twentieth century, with three female chief constables and 12 assistant chiefs in post. Westmarland (2001: 21) argues that women may now have relatively better promotion chances than men. She examined the deployment of women in a provincial force, where she found that women were 'working in specialisms linked particularly to child victims' but argues that this is likely to be their choice rather than the effect of gendered coercion, as is the male preference for 'guns, cars and horses' (2001: 21).

Despite the stronger legislative framework in the USA, in which affirmative action and class actions are permissible and they are confident, positive attitudes towards equality, in 2001 women accounted for only 12.7 per cent of sworn law enforcement positions in large agencies, and one report (Lonsway *et al.* 2002) suggests that numbers there have stagnated or even declined, from 14.3 per cent in 1999 to 13.0 per cent in 2000 and 12.7 per cent in 2001. The US authors attribute this fall to internal matters – harassment and discrimination – as well as external factors such as the removal of formal legal pressures. Under so-called 'consent decrees' the city of Pittsburgh reached a high of 27 per cent women in the police department, a share which fell rapidly when the decree was removed – consent decrees 'lapse' after a period of conformity to their requirements (Lonsway *et al.* 2002). In Britain, career issues have included flexible working practices, part-time working, support for networking and better equipment (BAWP n.d.).

Research by Marisa Silvestri (2000, 2003) has highlighted a number of critical aspects of the careers of very senior women officers. She found that many of them felt themselves to be 'inside the sisterhood with no sisters' – i.e. that their promotion out of the ranks had placed them in relatively isolated positions. Her subjects often claimed not to have planned their careers, but she suggests that they had devised their own routes to success, but they could easily be outsmarted by their 'smart macho' male colleagues.

Silvestri (2003) concludes her path-breaking study of senior women officers who have cracked the glass ceiling by warning that her respondents focused on 'representation and retention issues rather than changing the culture'. This 'together with a continued emphasis of success based on merit and competence fosters a continuing myth that if women work hard they will succeed' (2003).

New agendas

Policing has been markedly affected by major changes in the social and political climate, and many of these are closely linked to questions of gender. Thus issues with which police have to deal as priorities have shifted towards a gendered agenda. Domestic violence, rape, sexual assault and the physical and sexual abuse of children all have a very much higher public profile today than they did 15–20 years ago. In most of these cases, too, there are explicit government targets to be met. Paradoxically, perhaps, the 'new' agenda topics which may be used to enhance the position of women police are often presented as being 'gender neutral' rather than, say, 'feminine'. Yet, compared with older styles of policing, with their emphasis on physical strength rather than intellectual ability or athletic prowess not investigative powers, the new subjects and styles are much more 'feminine' and resemble the original mission of the pioneer policewomen.

The next section will briefly cover aspects of these developments as they have affected policing of and for women; here I wish to highlight those that affect the gendering of policing, though there is some overlap. Jones *et al.*, (1994, ch. 3) present a detailed account, based in part on research in four provincial UK police forces on 'new policing responses to crimes against women and children'. They examine the policing of three areas: sexual assault, domestic violence and child abuse. They noted various common features – the setting up of *specialist teams* primarily for cases of child abuse, but also units dealing with rape and sexual assault though 'domestic violence generally came fairly low down on the agenda' (1994: 118), the creation of *new facilities* such as 'rape suites' following the lead of the Metropolitan Police, *improved training* and *written force guidelines*. The most significant changes they observed were in the new interagency procedures set up to deal with child abuse (1994: 127). On balance they found that 'policing (accepting . . . that practice has not always kept pace with policy) has changed in a direction which emphasises sympathetic treatment of victims of rape and sexual assault, of domestic violence and of child abuse' which reflect a wider cultural shift in which the needs and concerns of women and children have, albeit slowly, moved progressively centre-stage (1994: 159). Their analysis identifies several key players in producing these major changes: the Association of Chief Police Officers (ACPO) and senior Home Office officials were very influential, but Jones *et al.*, record that public opinion, affected by scandals such as the Cleveland Inquiry and the plight of rape victims and, in particular, organised feminist opinion, all 'produced pressure for something to be done' (1994: 164).

These changes have still not been fully embedded into police practice. The *Report into the Death of Victoria Climbié* (Laming 2003) gives a harrowing account of the murder of an eight-year-old girl from the Ivory Coast at the hands of her carers. Almost 50 of its pages are devoted to a detailed and devastating critique of the actions and accountabilities of two of the child protection teams of the Metropolitan Police in 1999 (Laming 2003: 295–343). Lord Laming observes the inadequacy of training and experience of the officers involved (2003: 296, 309) and records:

> I was very concerned to hear from a large number of officers who gave evidence before me, that child protection teams [CPTs] within the Metropolitan Police Service [MPS] were considered to be somehow 'different' from other police units. In particular, several officers told me that CPTs were the 'poor cousins' or 'Cinderellas' of the force (2003: 331).

While evidence to the inquiry was 'unclear' on this, Laming found that child protection training had actually been stopped completely by the MPS training department in 1996. Low status for CPTs still appeared to be an issue in 1999 in the MPS. One senior officer told the inquiry:

> there was a significant amount of 'macho nonsense' in the force concerning the work of CPTs, which were sometimes referred to in a derogatory way such as 'cardigan squads'. One of the consequences of this low status was that the best detectives would be put off from applying to join these teams (2003: 334).

This lead to them also having very low priority with regard to numbers of staff, to accommodation, vehicles, equipment and management attention. One MPS commander even stated: 'Anecdotal information would suggest that following the Macpherson Inquiry into the death of Stephen Lawrence, *child protection teams were plundered* in order to increase the numbers of personnel on murder investigation teams' (2003: 333 emphasis added).

The Climbié case is one, tragic episode which involved two CPTs; it may not represent typical practice, although Laming makes all his recommendations applicable to constabularies and their authorities in general and not just to London. His report depicts a situation (in 1999) where a key priority within a 'service' rather than a 'control' agenda (Stephens and Becker 1994) was formally acknowledged but failed to be implemented because it was still not taken as seriously, despite some 30 similar cases since the 1970s, as other 'real' crime issues.

Somewhat remarkably, and contradicting the findings of research in this area, Laming was told that Haringey (the Social Services Department responsible for the child at the time of her death) was dominant in the relationship with the police: 'they are extremely powerful within the protection network and some social workers work hard to actually prevent police involvement'. He concluded: 'there appeared to me to be no sense of equal partnership between the two agencies . . . I heard enough evidence from other witnesses to conclude that the police in Haringey allowed themselves to be "led by the nose" by Haringey Social Services' (2003: 312–13). Clearly, a new gender agenda, in which women officers and suitable male officers (the front-line officers assigned to the Climbié case were women) play a leading role and influence the agenda, can only be achieved through good multi-agency working. Fielding and Conroy (1994: 209) had found, like Jones *et al.* (1994), that this was happening: 'the differences in perspective of those police and social workers directly involved [in child sexual abuse cases] proved to be mild'. They observed genuine culture shifts in both organisations: 'The practice of joint investigation better reconciled social services to control and made the police alert to welfare considerations' (1994: 209). The Climbié Report identifies numerous failings of management at the highest levels in several organisations. The authors of *The Gender Agenda* argue that to improve conditions for women officers and thus to ensure the police service is 'the best deliverer of service to the public, its policies *must be gender proofed*' (BAWP n.d.: 3). The failures identified in the case of Victoria Climbié seem to combine a downgrading of the protection of children, arguably a 'traditional' gender issue, with an inadequate, amateurish approach to criminal investigation, surely a central part of the core mandate of policing. Had both approaches been fully combined, as the BAWP document proposes, a less tragic outcome might have been achieved.

In her study of the deployment of women police in two British forces, Westmarland (2001) found evidence of differential deployment of women in CPTs. In one of them, 14 of the 17 members of the CPT were women; the other was more 'balanced' with 17 females out of 32, although all nine supervisory posts were filled by men (2001: 35, Table 21). She observes that 'as the officially designated experts, women are back in their "policewomen's" departments and, worse, they are now supervised by men so even the autonomy of self rule is lost to them' (2001: 35, Table 21). However, she cautions that this pattern is not necessarily caused by 'paternalistic male structures' (2001: 45) but instead probably by women officers' preferences for 'clean', indoor environments. When considering sexual offences, she found that:

> women are dealing with most of the sexual offences which are reported, and in some cases this is because their male colleagues are leaving this work to them. *As the trained experts*, women are perceived to be the 'safest' officers to cope with the often complicated and distressing aspects of sexual assaults (2001: 85).

When researching departments with very low numbers of women officers serving in them, Westmarland found them 'strongly "anti-women" ' with an exaggerated 'cult of masculinity' (2001: 186–7). Unlike some other studies, she did not find such marked gender differences in patrol work and suggests that 'the traditional image of the high adrenaline, "macho cop" arrest being made only by men now seems unsupportable' (p. 85).

American researchers and activists argue that 'community-oriented policing' is a particularly 'feminine' approach to law enforcement and that 'the structure of community policing capitalises on the skills that have been actually designated as feminine, and therefore undervalued' (Miller 1999: 226). Indeed, in Miller's study of 'Jackson City' she found that when neighbourhood officers were first introduced in the 1980s, only female officers and two black males took these posts. Only later did white males become interested, and Miller documents what she describes as the 'dramatic' move from patrol to neighbourhood policing and how these two had the images of crime fighter and social worker, respectively (1999: 101), images strongly linked to masculinity and femininity. Since in the USA 'community policing represents a new approach to modern law enforcement, emphasising communication and cooperation with citizens as well as informal problem solving' (Lonsway 2000: 4), it is arguably there an item on the gendered agenda. However, the situation is somewhat different in the UK where the promotion of community policing came via a different route. Policing in Britain has, in any case, generally been seen as having remained closer to this model of 'service' (Bayley 1994). Nevertheless, this is an aspect of policing where, as Miller suggests, there is a need for ' "women's work" to-day [to be] reconceptionalised and reframed as a new approach to police work involving gender-neutral job skills' (1999: 225).

One final, and contentious, aspect of US research in this arena should be noted which, so far, has no British parallel. Studies by the National Center for Women and Policing (NCWP) assert that male officers use excessive force much more than their female colleagues and that, as a result:

> the average male officer on a big city police agency costs taxpayers somewhere between two and a half and five and a half times more than the average woman officer in excessive force liability lawsuit payouts. He is over eight and a half times more likely to have an allegation of excessive force sustained against him and . . . more likely to have a citizen name him in a complaint of excessive force (NCWP 2002).

These data are used by the NCWP to promote 'the importance of hiring more women as a strategy', but it can equally support arguments in favour of styles of policing other than the traditional macho and in favour of less confrontational and more subtle ones – more androgynous, even more feminine, perhaps?

Policing women and policing for women

At the beginning of this chapter I outlined the origins of women's entry into policing and showed how they grew from the determination of a number of women (and some men) to chaperone female and juvenile victims and offenders, to control the disreputable activities of their own sex and generally to promote moral reform of society. Indeed, it is possible to argue that the focus of this era for women in policing was on 'vice' and protection. They did succeed in their aims of introducing new areas and new styles of policing into the traditional world which confronted them, but they did not alter the police organisation in very significant ways.

Reports by the pioneers of the twentieth century's 'new' policing, by women, for women, girls and children stress how welcome their activities were to their clients and how grateful they could be (e.g. *Police Woman's Review* 1927–1933), but no systematic reviews of consumers' views were undertaken. What is clear is that several achievements can be credited to this era and to those who promoted the gendering of policing in a new way. First, another career opportunity was opened up in a public service for women. The women who took up this opportunity were generally, and are still today, better educated than their male colleagues and have more professional or vocational qualifications (McGuigan *et al.* 2002). Since the activities of some working-class women were the focus or their surveillance and control, they could be said to have *disadvantaged* them, although others may have gained some support.

It was women and children, not men, whom the first policewomen sought to police, although their focus on 'vice' led them to intervene when 'public indecency' was occurring or when they believed unwary soldiers might be lead astray (Lock 1979). Ironically, one of the main concerns of nineteenth-century crusaders in this area was the rejection or removal of state regulation of women. The key issues here were the campaigns to repeal the Contagious Diseases Acts which forced medical examination and treatment on prostitute women in garrison towns (Bolt 1993). Instead of the public regulation of women's behaviour, feminist campaigners of this era proposed private and welfare-based solutions – rescue homes, girls' clubs, city missions.

There is a marked contrast with the concerns of the modern phase when, as Jones *et al.* point out, there have been successful campaigns to relocate 'certain forms of violence and aggression within the public sphere . . . with consequent increasing pressure on the police to recognise the pervasiveness of male violence and intervene in ways which ensure women's and children's safety' (1994: 154). In short, in the pre-integration era there was a major translation of the *private concerns* of groups of (mainly female) moral reformers into *public causes*. This in turn led to the *policing of private behaviour which had public consequences*: this could be soliciting or enticement, almost any 'waywardness' in children or young women could be targeted.

In the late twentieth century it was gendered violence rather than 'vice' which became the major issue and once again one which impacted on policing from *outside* its organisation. Domestic violence, sexual assault, rape and the physical and sexual abuse of children have all been raised both together and separately as vital, indeed, crisis issues. As we saw above, there has been some considerable, if varied, response to all these, including major shifts in policies and procedures (Home Office 2003: 25–6).

Space does not allow me to cover all these topics in depth, but there are key points to pick out which relate to the central themes of this chapter. The policing of domestic violence has, for instance, been the subject of extensive reviews and major changes in policing procedures. The most discussed issue has been the pro-arrest policy introduced in some US jurisdictions and also advocated in the UK. Even the evaluative research programmes on this topic are contentious. What they do appear to show is there is 'a consistent reduction in the incidents of victimisation due to arrest [thus supporting] the continued use of arrests as a preferred law enforcement response for reducing subsequent victimisation of women by their intimate partners' (Maxwell *et al.* 2002: 69). Nevertheless, 40 per cent of the women in this study continued to be victimised (2002: 71), so this solution does not work for every case. Moreover, there are many other complications. In a British study of the Thames Valley Police Force's policing of domestic violence, Hoyle (1998: 214) found that 'only a third of the victims in the study wanted the officers to arrest the suspect and many of these did not want the police to proceed any further'. She suggests that many women who called the police only wanted 'immediate help to halt a particular incident rather than an attempt to get the perpetrator prosecuted' (1998: 214). Another caution is introduced by Chesney-Lind who argues that an unintended consequence of mandatory arrests in cases of domestic violence is to increase the arrest rates of women and girls, especially those from minority ethnic groups (2002: 82).

Police responses to rape victims have also been the subject both of extensive critiques and major changes. Temkin (1997, 2002) has been a severe critic of the treatment of rape victims. She notes the various formal changes in procedures which had been introduced by the late 1990s but observes that 'old police attitudes and practices, widely assumed to have vanished, are still in evidence and continue to cause victims pain and trauma' (1997: 527). Of her sample of 23 rape cases in Sussex, the majority were positive about their experience, but ten were not (1997: 527).

Gregory and Lees, in their study of victims of sexual assault in London, were more positive:

> Over the past decade the facilities for dealing with victims have improved ... rape examination suites are available in all areas. Most complainants ... were on the whole satisfied with the way they were personally dealt with by the women police ... There was, however, much less satisfaction with the way the case was investigated and followed up. A quarter of the women were still not satisfied with attitudes of the male police officers investigating their case and pointed to the unsympathetic way they had been treated (1999: 165).

A study in New Zealand which aimed to find out if Temkin's conclusions were reflected there concluded that police and victims were 'worlds apart' and that a seismic shift in attitudes was needed. Even so, 64 per cent were satisfied with their treatment at the reporting stage (Jordan 2001: 687) but 32 per cent were dissatisfied. Overall ratings were very polarised – 20 per cent very positive, 20 per cent were very negative. One result of Jordan's project has been a shift to new police procedures in New Zealand.

Police and policing remain gendered in the twenty-first century. The macho culture is still alive in some forces even now, although it is also a source of embarrassment. The majority of officers are male, especially at the most senior levels. Nevertheless, there have been and continue to be changes. Policing as an institution is notable for having changes imposed upon it from the outside, rather than generating them from within. Twice in the twentieth century, law enforcement was affected by the introduction of contentious issues to do with gender. The first time involved a small group of women storming this stern, male bastion and bringing with them new styles and subjects to the police realm. The second, in a still incomplete revolution, sought to change policing priorities and procedures to a more gendered agenda. Although somewhat battered, the institution of the police remains intact and, at the same time, some of the aims of the pioneers and campaigners have been achieved.

Gender perspectives provide powerful lenses for focusing on policing in the twenty-first century and its future development. There are, still, the issues which they highlight of the nature of police culture and how to change it. So much has already changed in modern law enforcement in the mission of policing, its recruitment, training and even its legal framework. If the traditional model of policing was one based on a macho cop culture, this is surely no longer fit for a modern (or postmodern) version where new priorities, new styles and new technologies are employed.

As far as the roles of women in policing are concerned, while these have expanded enormously since the early twentieth century, there are signs still of some of the original issues of the pioneer era persisting. The first policewomen had a protective mission in mind when they sought entry into policing. They wanted to shield their own sex, juveniles and children and to intervene to re-moralise the society of their day. At the same time, they also saw law enforcement as another area of opportunity for the newly emancipated women of the period, although this was originally a secondary aim for the movement. The first half century of policing by women was focused on this specific, specialist task; the next phase was marked much more by an emphasis on opening up opportunities and achieving equality. However, the protective agenda has not disappeared and indeed has gained new importance in the twenty-first century with concerns about domestic violence, child abuse and sexual assaults. How these matters should be policed, who should do it, how offenders be dealt with, are high-profile topics for all law enforcement agencies. For women officers, the tensions between the missions of protection and progress remain to be resolved.

Selected further reading

On the history of women in policing, the classic books are Lock's *The British Policewoman: Her Story.* (1979) and Carrier's *The Campaign for the Employment of Women as Police Officers* (1988). Martin's *Breaking and Entering* (1980) was the first major modern research study. Heidensohn's *Women in Control? The Role of Women in Law Enforcement* (1992) was the first international comparative study and provides comprehensive coverage of the research and issues. Brown and Heidensohn's *Gender and Policing: Comparative Perspectives* (2000) is a multinational study and analyses key themes in the literature. Heidensohn's *Sexual Politics and Social Control* (2000) contains chapters on the international policewomen's movements. The National Center for Women and Policing maintains an excellent US-focused website (www.womenandpolicing.org).

References

Baird Report (1921) *Minutes of Evidence. Committee on the Employment of Women on Police Duties* (Cmd 1133). London: HMSO.

Bayley, D. (1994) *Police for the Future.* New York, NY: Oxford University Press.

Bittner, E. (1974a) 'The functions of the police in modern society', in E. Bittner (1990) *Aspects of Police Work.* Boston, MA: Northeastern University Press.

Bittner, E. (1974b) 'Florence Nightingale in pursuit of Willie Sutton', in E. Bittner (1990) *Aspects of Police Work.* Boston, MA: Northeastern University Press.

Bittner, E. (1990) *Aspects of Police Work.* Boston, MA: Northeastern University Press.

Bloch, P. and Anderson, D. (1974) *Policewomen on Patrol – Final Report: Methodology, Tables and Measurement Instruments.* Washington, DC: Police Foundation.

Bloch, P. and Anderson, D. *et al.* (1973) *Policewomen on Patrol – Major Findings: First Report.* Vol. 1. Washington, DC: Police Foundation.

Bolt, C. (1993) *The Women's Movements in the US and Britain from the 1790s to the 1970s.* Hemel Hempstead: Harvester Wheatsheaf.

Bowling, B. and Foster, J. (2002) 'Policing and the police', in M. Maguire *et al.* (eds) *The Oxford Handbook of Criminology.* Oxford: Oxford University Press, 980–1033.

British Association of Women Police (no date) *The Gender Agenda.*

Brown, J.M. (2000) 'Discriminatory experiences of women police: a comparison', *International Journal of the Sociology of Law*, 29(1): 1–21.

Brown, J. and Heidensohn, F.M. (2000) *Gender and Policing*. Basingstoke: Palgrave/ Macmillan.

Bryant, L. and Penfold, J.W. (1985) 'One of the boys?' *Policing*, 1(4).

Burke, M.E. (1993) *Coming Out of the Blue*. London: Cassell.

Carrier, J. (1988) *The Campaign for the Employment of Women as Police Officers*. Aldershot: Avebury.

Chan, J. (1997) *Changing Police Culture*. Cambridge: Cambridge University Press.

Chesney-Lind, M. (2002) 'Criminalizing victimization: the unintended consequences of pro-arrest policies for girls and women', *Criminology and Public Policy*, 2(1): 81–90.

Doan, L. (1997) ' "Gross indency between women": policing lesbians or policing lesbian police?', *Social and Legal Studies*, 6: 4.

Feinman, C. (1986) *Women in the Criminal Justice System* (2nd edn). New York, NY: Praeger.

Fielding, N. and Conroy, S. (1994) 'Against the grain: co-operation in child sexual abuse investigations', in M. Stephens and S. Becker (eds) *Police Force, Police Service*. Basingstoke: Macmillan.

Fry, E. (1827) *Observations on the Visiting Superintendence and Government of Female Prisoners*. London: Arch.

Gelsthorpe, L. (2002) 'Feminism and criminology', in M. Maguire *et al.* (eds). *The Oxford Handbook of Criminology*. Oxford: Oxford University Press, 112–43.

Gregory, J. and Lees, S. (1999) *Policing Sexual Assault*. London: Routledge.

Halford, A. (1993) *No Way up the Greasy Pole*. London: Constable.

Hartley, S., Stevenson, K. and Rogerson, J. (2002) *Sex Differences in the OSPRE® Part II Assessment Centre*. Harrogate: Centrex.

Heidensohn, F.M. (1989) *Women in Policing in the USA*. London: Police Foundation.

Heidensohn, F.M. (1992) *Women in Control? The Role of Women in Law Enforcement*. Oxford: Clarendon Press.

Heidensohn, F.M. (1994) ' "We can handle it out here": Women officers in Britain and the USA and the policing of public order', *Policing and Society*, 4(4): 293–303.

Heidensohn, F.M. (2000) *Sexual Politics and Social Control*. Buckingham: Open University Press.

Heidensohn, F.M. (2002) 'Gender and crime', in M. Maguire *et al.* (eds) *The Oxford Handbook of Criminology*. Oxford: Oxford University Press, 491–530.

Heidensohn, F.M. with the assistance of Silvestri, M. (1996) *Women and Crime* (2nd edn). Basingstoke: Macmillan.

Her Majesty's Inspectorate of Constabulary (1992) *Equal Opportunities in the Police Service*. London: Home Office.

Her Majesty's Inspectorate of Constabulary (1996) *Developing Diversity in the Police Service*. London: Home Office.

Her Majesty's Inspectorate of Constabulary (1999) *Managing Learning. A Study of Police Training*. London: Home Office.

Holdaway, S. (1983) *Inside the British Police*. Oxford: Blackwell.

Holdaway, S. and Rock, P. (eds) (1998) *Thinking about Criminology*. London: UCL Press.

Home Office (2003) *Safety and Justice: The Government's Proposals on Domestic Violence*. Cm 5847.

Hoyle, C. (1998) *Negotiating Domestic Violence*. Oxford: University Press.

Jones, S. (1986) *Policewomen and Equality*. London: Macmillan.

Jones, T., Newburn, T. and Smith, D. (1994) *Democracy and Policing*. London: PSI.

Jordan, J. (2001) 'Worlds apart? Women, rape and the police reporting process', *British Journal of Criminology*, 41(4): 679–706.

Laming, H. (2003) *The Victoria Climbié Inquiry. Report of an Inquiry by Lord Laming* (Cm 5730). London: HMSO.

Levene, P. (1994) ' "Walking the streets in a way no decent woman should": women police in World War I'. *Journal of Modern History*, March: 3478.

Lock, J. (1979) *The British Policewoman: Her Story*. London: Hale.

Lonsway, K. (2000) *Hiring and Retaining More Women: The Advantages to Law Enforcement Agencies*. Los Angeles, CA: Feminist Minority Foundation.

Lonsway, K., Carrington, S., Aguire, P. and Wood, M. (2002) *Equality Denied. The Status of Women in Policing: 2001*. Los Angeles, CA: National Center for Women and Policing.

Macpherson, W. (1999) *The Stephen Lawrence Inquiry* (Cm 4262). London: HMSO.

Martin, S.E. (1979) 'POLICEwomen and policeWOMEN: occupational role dilemmas and choices of female officers', *Journal of Police Science and Administration*, 2(3): 314–23.

Martin, S.E. (1980) *Breaking and Entering*. Berkeley, CA: University of California Press.

Maxwell, C., Garner, J. and Fagan, J. (2002) 'The preventive effects of arrest on intimate partner violence: research policy and theory', *Criminology and Public Policy*, 2(1): 51–80.

McGuigan, C., Sampson, F. and Rogerson, J. (2002) *A Soft Touch*? Harrogate: Centrex.

Miller, S.L. (1999) *Gender and Community Policing*. Boston, MA: Northeastern University Press.

Morash, M. and Greene, J.R. (1986) 'Evaluating women on patrol: a critique of contemporary wisdom', *Evaluation Review*, 10(2).

NCWP (2002) *Men, Women, and Police Excessive Force: A Tale of Two Genders*. Los Angeles, CA: Feminist Majority Foundation.

Newburn, T. and Stanko, B. (1994) *Just Boys Doing Business*. London: Routledge.

Radford, J. (1989) 'Women and policing: contradictions old and new', in J. Hanmer *et al.* (eds) *Women, Policing and Male Violence*. London: Routledge.

Reiner, R. (2000) *The Politics of the Police*. (3rd edn). Oxford: Oxford University Press.

Schulz, D.M. (1995) *From Social Worker to Crime Fighter: Women in US Municipal Policing*. Westport, CT: Praeger.

Sherman, L. and Berk, R. (1983) *The Minneapolis Domestic Violence Experiment*. Washington, DC: Police Foundation.

Silvestri, M. (2000) 'Visions of the future.' PhD thesis, University of London.

Silvestri, M. (2003) *Women in Charge: Policing, Gender and Leadership*. Cullompton: Willan.

Skolnick, J. (1966) *Justice without Trial*. New York, NY: Wiley.

Skolnick, J. and Fyfe, J. (1993) *Above the Law*. New York, NY: Free Press.

Smith, D.J. and Gray, J. (1985) *Police and People in London. The PSI Report*. Aldershot: Gower.

Southgate, P. (1981) 'Women in the police', *The Police Journal*, 54: 2.

Stephens, M. and Becker, S. (1994) 'The matrix of Care and Control', in M. Stephens and S. Becker (eds) *Police Force, Police Service*. Basingstoke: Macmillan.

Stephens, M. and Becker, S. (eds) (1994) *Police Force, Police Service*. Basingstoke: Macmillan.

Temkin, J. (1997) 'Plus ca change: reporting rape in the 1990s', *British Journal of Criminology*, 37(4): 507–28.

Temkin, J. (2002) *Rape and Legal Process* (2nd edn). Oxford: Oxford University Press.

Waddington, P.J. (1999) 'Police (canteen) sub-culture: an appreciation', *British Journal of Criminology*, 39(2): 286–309.

Westmarland, L. (2001) *Gender and Policing*. Cullompton: Willan.

Wyles, L. (1951) *A Woman at Scotland Yard*. London: Faber.

Young, M. (1991) *An Inside Job*. Oxford: Oxford University Press.

Chapter 23

Policing and ethics

Peter Neyroud

Introduction

In the introduction to the Council of Europe's European Code of Police Ethics published in September 2001, the Committee of Ministers identified a number of factors that highlight the importance of such a code of ethics for policing. First, that criminal justice, within which they include policing, plays an essential role in safeguarding the rule of law. Secondly, the police activities are 'performed in close contact with the public and police efficiency is dependent upon public support'. Finally, public confidence in the police is 'closely related to their attitude and behaviour towards the public and in particular their respect for human dignity and fundamental rights and freedoms of the individual as enshrined in particular in the European Convention on Human Rights'. The Ministers recognised the importance of police ethics, an importance that has been increasingly highlighted in a number of studies through the last ten years (Kleinig 1996a; Neyroud and Beckley 2001).

The creation of such an international code for police ethics highlights not just the importance of the issue politically but also the growing complexity and challenge of ethics for policing in Europe. 'Ethical policing' is no longer a matter for negotiation with reasonably homogeneous local communities defined by geography, but now has to be mediated with national governments and supra-national bodies and take account of communities that are increasingly diverse. With diversity come seemingly irresolvable dilemmas for law enforcement. This chapter will focus on how police forces seek to cope with these dilemmas and on what ethical policing might look like in the twenty-first century, drawing primarily on the UK perspective but also pulling in comparisons from the USA and worldwide experience. It will seek to show why ethics in policing have become so much more important and consequently so much more debated, to set out the changes that the growth of human rights philosophy has made to policing and to show where ethical policing might be heading.

It is important to start by sketching in some of the national and international context of policing which impacts on ethics. Indeed, some form of internationally recognised standard of ethics has become essential as transnational policing has become ever more a reality with the globalisation of trade and politics. With international peace-keeping missions that need not just military personnel but police officers has come a need for global standards and indeed global definitions of policing. This in itself is not easy because, in national terms within the UK and a number of western democracies, the monopoly of the 'public police' or the nineteenth-century model of policing – carried out by local police forces who had a monopoly both of powers and patrol – has, if it ever did exist, now most certainly ceased to (Jones and Newburn 2002). The new 'mixed economy of policing' and patrol which was highlighted in the Labour government's White Paper *Policing a New Century: A Blueprint for Reform* (Home Office 2001) has formalised the broadening of the concept of policing from the uniformed police to a welter of wardens, accredited security personnel, civilian support staff within the police and partly empowered community support officers. This parallels developments elsewhere in both the USA and Europe (Johnston 2000). All these could reasonably, for the purpose of policing ethics, be said to come within the ambit of policing. They pose new challenges for both the professional standards and the accountability of policing: challenges that are recognised in the European code.

Alongside the structural changes, the national and international debate about criminal justice policy has become highly politicised. Policing and the reduction of crime have both in America (Giuliani 2002) and in Europe risen to the top of the political agenda. The 2002 Street Crime Initiative driven by the Labour government was the first crime initiative to be personally headed by a Prime Minister within recent political memory and was paralleled by a similar initiative in a number of European countries such as France. They highlight, as Philip Bobbit (2002) observes, that the modern 'market' state is driven not by the paternalist welfare agenda of its modern predecessor but by a more fragile and turbulent desire to satisfy popular demand and create the conditions for people to enjoy themselves. Equally events such as the terrorist attack on the World Trade Center on the 11 September 2001 and the embedded sense of living in a high crime society (Garland 2001) have created an unsettled society concerned and increasingly demanding about crime and the quality of its policing, safety and security (Neyroud 2002).

The product of these changes within the UK and their impact on 'ethics' can be seen in a number of ways:

• There has been a see-sawing of the definition of the role of policing over the last decade. Kleinig (1996a) suggested that the purposes of policing provide the 'moral foundation' of policing. The see-sawing has certainly disturbed those foundations, shifting quite dramatically between order maintenance and crime fighting as the predominant role. The 1962 Willink Royal Commission (Critchley 1978) defined a broad role for policing, ranging from crime reduction to assisting the public. Twenty years later, the Scarman Report emphasised that order maintenance must take precedence over crime fighting (1982). In stark contrast, the 1993 White Paper issued by the then Conservative government shifted that towards crime fighting. The pendulum swung again and the new Labour government in 1997 produced the 'overarching aims and objectives', recreating the Willink mandate but

579

adjusting to include human rights and a broad definition of the outcomes in terms of 'safer society'. Furthermore, in the Crime and Disorder Act 1998, Labour formally recognised that the police role in reducing crime and disorder was interdependent with other parts of local and central government. The *Blueprint on Policing*, the 2001 White Paper (Home Office 2001) and the subsequent National Policing Plan have re-emphasised the 1993 emphasis on crime fighting into crime reduction and crime detection. There has also been a new stronger emphasis on the prosecution of offenders with targets to increase the number of offenders brought to justice – targets that are dependent on much closer co-operation between the criminal justice agencies. In each case, there have been implications for police officers and police leaders as to what the 'right choices' are in policing and how to make those choices jointly with leaders in local government and fellow managers in the criminal justice agencies. This last point has presented a fundamental challenge to cherished concepts of constabulary independence – a challenge that was recognised by Patten's new formula of 'operational responsibility' (Patten 1999; see Chapter 24).

- Connected with the shifts of role, there has been a gradual change of structure in policing and with it major shifts in the methods of accountability and balance of local and central control. The 1994 legislation brought in national objectives and an increased managerial focus. The 2001–2 police reform programme less than a decade later tightened that central control to include new powers of intervention and a National Policing Plan. The plan itself created a comprehensive framework of plans and targets to be required of every local police force. As with the see-sawing of role definition, the changing balance of stakeholder influence has a profound effect on decision-making, particularly if influence is supported by powers of dismissal. The new interventionist and managerialist approach of government paralleled approaches taken by Giuliani at a municipal level in New York (Giuliani 2002).

- There has been an increasing pressure for 'performance' and this has had an increasingly quantitative focus, despite well recognised concerns about this (Fitzgerald *et al.* 2002). Initially defined as value for money through the 1980s, then seen in terms of a small number of national objectives, in 2002 the managerialist framework for policing was tightened into a Treasury-based linkage between a set of performance targets and the revenue budgets for police forces (Home Office 2002a).

- There has been a pressure for modernisation which is not unique to the police service but a general trend in the public sectors, and that pressure has included not just the performance agenda but also new pay and reward structures, civilianisation and the use of auxiliaries and a demand for increased responsiveness both to central government and to local 'citizen' focus (Home Office 2001, 2002a).

These changes have come at a time when there has also been an increasing focus on evidence-based practice or the 'best' ways (or in ethical terms, the 'right' ways) to police, both in the UK and the USA (Sherman *et al.* 1997; Sherman 1998). One of the first things the Labour Home Secretary did in 1998 was to publish a compendium of evidence-based practice on reducing crime (Home Office 1998). This strong steer towards what works in policing has been re-emphasised in the UK by the introduction of a Police Standards Unit and by the strong emphasis on developing professional practice in the White Paper, including the introduction of a National Centre for Policing Excellence with a mandate to produce codes and the regulation of recommended practice (Home Office 2001, 2002a).

These changes are an important context for ethics, which are about 'how police officers and police leaders make the right judgements and do the right things, for the right reasons' (Neyroud and Beckley 2001: 37). Ethics have also been described by Honderich (1995) as the theoretical basis for the 'principles of moral behaviour' and, as such, they provide both the boundaries for morality and the pathways for proper thinking about real-life choices. As the Ministers agreeing the Council of Europe Code of Ethics set out, ethics are important in policing because of the nature of the powers and the position that police officers have in the citizen's life. Ethical standards are important in policing not only because of the adverse impact of corruption but also because we know that perceptions of fairness and high standards in the way the police do their job are an intrinsic part of reducing crime and affecting criminal behaviour (Tyler and Huo 2002).

What follows in this chapter is not a comprehensive discussion of police ethics, for that would be impossible in the space (see Kleinig 1996a; Neyroud and Beckley 2001), but a focus on some of the key aspects: personal ethics and police professionalism, performance ethics, participation in policing and policing in action – in particular, the use of force. The conclusion will outline where and how ethical policing is being and can be approached.

A brief history of police ethics

Neyroud and Beckley (2001) suggested that policing is in both transition and crisis at the start of the twenty-first century. As I have already indicated, it is certainly in transition. A good indicator of whether it is in crisis would appear to be, from past history, the level of publication of books on police ethics. For, with every apparent crisis of either police professionalism, conduct or corruption, there comes a generation of literature identifying a different angle on police ethics. We can divide the main themes of these debates as follows.

Police professionalism

A twentieth-century drive towards police professionalism can be typified by August Vollmer's, the 'father of modern policing' and his disciple, O.W. Wilson's, vision of the police service as a highly trained core of officers independent of politics and acting with impartiality and integrity (Fogelson 1977). This vision provoked criticism by Westley (1970) and Skolnick (1975) who looked at the differences between the prescribed conduct and what they found in terms of the reality of day-to-day police work, particularly the conflict they saw between the use of coercive force and respect for the law and upholding individual rights.

Police discretion

At a time when a series of high-profile cases in the USA, including *Miranda* v. *Arizona*, were questioning the extent of police discretion and its potential for adversely impacting citizens' rights, Goldstein (1977) and Muir (1977) looked at police discretion in a more optimistic light. For Goldstein, discretion could be properly exercised through proper training and guidelines and for Muir it was an essential component of good street policing. For others, like Skolnick, and, in the UK context, Jefferson and Grimshaw (1984), solutions lay in severely limiting it and reducing the free will of police officers to exercise judgement.

Covert policing

Through the 1980s the increasing use of covert methods of policing raised questions both about police intrusion on privacy and about the police use of deception. Elliston and Feldberg (1985) highlighted how complex were the ethical judgements that needed to be exercised by police officers using covert techniques and how simple 'means and ends' utilitarian approaches simply failed to meet the needs of decision-makers. The complexity of the issues was also highlighted by Gary Marx (1988) who documented the delicate balance between 'ethical deception' authorised by the citizenry and controlled by the law and 'deceptive ethics' or the less appropriate or proportionate use of covert approaches which he felt damaged the privacy, trust and freedom of expression of citizens. The key difference between the two was the right framework of ethics, control systems and accountability.

Police corruption

There have been several waves of concern about police corruption and, in turn, several approaches to dealing with the problem in literature. For Edwin Delattre (1989) the problem and the solution lay in the character of the individual police officer. For Lawrence Sherman (1974, 1978) it was more about the environment of temptation, the systems of control and creating a framework that clearly articulated the boundaries between ethical practice and the slippery slope from small gifts to major graft. In a UK context, Michael Zander (1994) looked at the issue of miscarriages of justice and 'noble cause corruption'. He argued that it was the outcome orientation of police officers that had led to many of the miscarriages and that a reliance on corrupt means could never be justified by the outcome. Crank and Caldero (2000) developed the 'noble cause' theme in a US context following continuing concerns about the intractability of 'noble cause corruption' problems in US police departments. More recently, Fitzgerald *et al.* (2002) have highlighted how an outcome orientation applied in a managerial context carries the danger of administrative corruption.

* * *

The UK debate on police ethics has rarely focused specifically on ethics as a topic but rather on culture (Reiner 1978), on accountability and the democratic deficit in policing (Reiner 1985), on the exercise of discretion and its relationship with community support (Scarman 1982), on corruption (Punch 1985; Newburn 1999), on the treatment and rights of suspects (see Chapter 10) and on policing and human rights (Crawshaw *et al.* 1999).

While each of the works have come at police ethics from a different angle and looked at it through a different lens, both the books and their context are neatly summarised by Waddington (1999) when he commented that policing is always waiting for the next scandal because it 'operates in a netherworld just beyond the limits of respectability'. Waddington, like Skolnick and others before him, appeared to doubt the possibility of police realising any aspiration towards ethical policing, because of the very nature of the work and the 'irresolvable' (Bauman 1993) choices that it presented. It is certainly possible by looking at the literature both in the USA and the UK to see a series of cycles of concern about crime and disorder, followed by pressure on the police to produce short-term results, emerging concerns about corruption – whether it be economic graft (Sherman 1978), noble cause corruption (Crank and Caldero 2000) or administrative corruption (Fitzgerald *et al.* 2002) – followed by a rule-tightening reaction and possibly reorganisation with then new rules and a commitment to new norms. This vicious cycle can be seen in both UK and US contexts (Crank and Caldero 2000; Neyroud and Beckley 2001: 10). Part of the problem with each turn of the cycle is an overemphasis on one aspect of policing. Whether it be a push for crime fighting or a demand for increased detection, these demands have rarely been seen in a context of a wider, more authoritative framework of policing ethics but, then, does such a framework exist?

The principles of policing

Identifying those areas where police officers have clearly acted unethically, over-reaching their discretion, failing to meet the professional standards, acting corruptly or following poor professional practice, is relatively straight-forward. To attempt to describe a scheme of ethics that fits across policing and which copes with the wide variety of policing contexts is far more difficult and far more controversial. There are several major philosophical approaches to ethics that have been applied to policing. They are fundamentally different in their approach to describing ethical behaviour. Mostly obviously in respect of policing, these are the Kantian ethics of duty with their presumption of a universal law of right and wrong, which are often contrasted with the consequentialist ethics of utility with their over-riding concern with positive outcomes. Classically (though not necessarily accurately) these two approaches are seen as juxtaposed and reduced to a debate about 'right means' versus 'right ends'. But then there are also the ethics of virtue, most ably set out by MacIntyre (1981) and adopted by Delattre (1989) in which it is the inner goodness of character that will produce good ends and good actions. Finally, the ethics of care derived from the works of authors such as Gilligan (1982) and Baier (1985) focus on relationships and needs, rather than rights and universal laws. There are important connections between the ethics of care and the restorative justice approaches which have become very significant alternatives to traditional approaches to the criminal justice system (Braithwaite 1989).

Each of these classical theories of ethics provides dilemmas and contradictions which they themselves cannot overcome (Bauman 1993). For instance, policing frequently provides the police officer with choices between an individual's needs and that of a wider community. Each theory would provide a different rationale and, often, outcome for such a choice. The choices provided by classical theory can also be ambiguous and uncertain. In a profession where choices need to be made rapidly and may have potentially far-reaching consequences – including, literally, life or death – officers cannot afford the luxury of ambiguity in decision-making. This suggests a need to search instead for a best fit between the mission of policing, the character of the good police officer and the practice of good policing. For a number of authors (Ross 1930; Gillon 1994; Lawton 1998) this fit can be found better by looking for prima facie principles and applying them in a practical way. Lawton, whose analysis was designed for public service generally not just for policing, saw this as a chain linking value to virtues to principle and practice. Neyroud and Beckley drew from ethical theory, Lawton and Gillon and their professional experience to suggest such a set of principles that might be used as a framework for policing (Box 23.1).

Principles that are very similar to these can be seen running through a number of key publications through the 1990s, which examined standards and integrity in public service, notably in a UK context the Nolan Report on standards in public life (1995), the HMIC integrity inspection of police forces

Box 23.1 Principles of policing

Respect for personal autonomy: this is derived from the ethics of duty and in policing would include respecting the rights of citizens, showing dignity and respect for them and to colleagues and not using either as a means to an end.

Beneficence and non-malificence (Ross 1930) require police officers to help people without harming others.

Justice, including, above all, respect for people's human rights and for morally respectable laws.

Responsibility, which would require police officers to justify their actions and take personal ownership of them (Mulgan 1997).

Care, emphasising the interdependence of police officers and the individuals they deal with and the communities they serve.

Honesty, which is, as McIntyre (1981) identified, a key virtue and one that is central to policing and the authority and legitimacy of individual officers.

Stewardship, which emphasises the idea of trusteeship over the powerless and over police powers.

Source: Neyroud and Beckley (2001).

(HMIC 1999), the Macpherson Report on the death of Steven Lawrence (Macpherson, 1999) and the Patten Report on policing in Northern Ireland (1999), which itself proposed the creation of an ethical code to underpin policing in Northern Ireland.

However, as with the debate about ethical codes, so with principles we still end up with the question as to how principles should be used, how they might be applied and how they might impact upon policing. Here it is important to link the principles with another dimension of police ethics, that of the 'new agenda' in the UK policing – human rights (Neyroud and Beckley 2001). While there has been a UN Declaration of Human Rights since just after the Second World War, human rights had not been a component of police training within the UK until the late 1990s and the application of a human rights approach to law enforcement has been a relatively recent addition into the international protocols (Crawshaw *et al.* 1999). The reasons for this are complex but at least partly related to the globalisation of late twentieth-century trade, politics and crime (Mulgan 1997) and the emerging need for an internationally recognised body of law.

The introduction of the Human Rights Act into UK law in 1998 brought both a new language to policing and a new decision-making calculus that links closely with the ethical principles that have been set out above. Critical to this calculus is the concept of proportionality or, as Starmer puts it, 'the need to find a fair balance between the protection of individual rights and the interests of the community at large' (1999: 169). Proportionality requires a police officer to balance the means proposed against the outcome intended and to ensure that any action is proportionate to the legitimate aim pursued (*Handyside* v. *the UK* 1976). Moreover, proportionality requires a balance of means and ends so that not only does the outcome desired have to be sufficient to justify the means taken but also the means themselves have to be procedurally fair and linked with the concepts of legality, necessity and accountability. This provides a rough-and-ready reckoner between the ethics of duty and utility and has fundamentally shifted the way in which police officers not only make their decisions but also set out their justifications (Neyroud and Beckley 2001).

The British police service has responded to human rights with a significant shift in training, a comprehensive process of auditing of policies and practices against an ethical and human rights framework (Neyroud and Beckley 2001) and codification of decision-making and decision logs. This has turned the theory of human rights into a routine day-to-day practice. The removal of police immunity (*Osman* v. *UK* 2000), the creation of a legal duty to act in a human rights compliant way and the ability for complainants to challenge compliance have all served to reinforce this (Starmer 1999).

It can, however, equally be argued that human rights, like classical ethical theory, provides no firm base for police ethics. Certainly, there are few absolute rights (such as the right to life or freedom from torture), and qualified rights such as privacy and freedom of expression can be seen as complex and subject to considerable flexibility of interpretation. Indeed, the European Court of Human Rights itself recognises a 'margin of appreciation' which allows rights to be interpreted within local, national traditions. The threat of terrorism and organised crime has been seen by some commentators as shifting the legal framework very significantly away from individual liberty (Justice 2002). In each of the areas of policing which will now be examined, the legal, society and professional context will be shown to be extremely important. Policing is, after all, an extremely significant manifestation of government and a very significant touchstone of the nature of the relationship between government and the governed.

The police as professionals

Although long desired by senior police officers and clearly central to the creation of USA-based International Association of Chiefs of Police and the changing role of the Association of Chief Police Officers in the UK (Savage and Charman 1996), the 'gospel of professionalism' (Fogelson 1977: 155) or the desire of the police service to be an independent profession working to high ethical standards deploying a recognised body of professional knowledge is an aspiration that remains to be achieved. On a strict taxonomic approach policing falls short of many of the elements necessary to qualify for full professional status (Friedson 1983). Kleinig's (1996b) assessment of the police service against the traits of a profession confirmed this judgement. On the first point, the provision of a public service, there is no doubt that policing is and should be a public service, but some (Waddington 1999) have argued that the coercive core of policing, the deployment of the use of force, sits uneasily with the concept of service and this has contributed to a long-standing debate about the nature of policing (Stephens and Becker 1994). Secondly, policing is neither a graduate profession nor is there a well established culture of life-long learning and reaccreditation. This situation is changing in the UK with the establishment of a National Training Organisation, the Police Standards and Skills Organisation, in which both accredited learning and mandatory re-qualification will be a critical component to future police training (Home Office 2001). Thirdly, the police service in the UK has no code of ethics. There are a number of ethical statements such as the Oath of Attestation, the Association of Chief Police Officers' (ACPO) 1990 Statement of Common Purpose and Values and the Police Code of Conduct. However, the latter is much more of a discipline code than a statement of ethics. ACPO's draft statement of ethical principles, which dates back to 1992 and was endorsed by the Patten Report (1999), has never been issued as a recommended statement within the British police service. Even the European Code of Ethics was sent to police forces with a gentle ministerial note inviting chief officers to take account of it. ACPO did not formally adopt it.

On the remainder of Kleinig's points, policing is not self-regulating and, while police officers have considerable discretion within the law, there is a substantial legal framework of accountability which restricts the exercise of discretion. Last but not least, the body of knowledge in policing and its codification into standards of professional practice is unfinished business. The White Paper on policing (Home Office 2001) and the creation of the National Centre of Policing Excellence have signalled a strong intention to embark in that direction with codes, regulations and the development of the Police

Standards Unit. Furthermore, there is a push from some professionals and academics to develop 'evidence-based policing' and systemise the evaluation of police strategies (Sherman 1998). However, this is qualitatively different from a self-regulated profession such as the medical or legal profession where the professional organisations themselves have taken responsibility and have been entrusted by the state with the role of developing the body of knowledge.

It is arguable that moves towards greater professionalism are not essential to achieving a more ethical practice. Indeed some would argue that the drive to be professional is more about securing a monopoly and a market than it is about achieving better standards of ethical practice (Parry et al. 1979; Anderson et al. 1981). Others would also argue that professions have had a decidedly mixed reputation in their ability to cope with diversity and to be inclusive in the way in which they encourage both employment of minorities and service provision towards minority communities (Dale and Foster 1986; Edwards 1989; Bowling 1999). From a different angle, Waddington (1999) has argued that the rise of the managerialist culture within not just policing but the wider public service, has compromised professional development by substituting for professional skills and knowledge a new command structure in the form of a performance culture. This we will return to in the next section.

However, none of these are convincing perspectives placed against the prospect of a police service investing in better training, understanding better what works and ensuring that good practice is mandated, developing and re-enforcing standards of professional practice and behaviour and being able to signal those developments to the public they serve. This applies whether the authors are advocating community policing professionalism in the case of Rosenbaum (1994) and Skogan and Hartnett (1997) or a more professional approach to crime investigation.

Where a number of authors have been critical of the police profession has been through analysis of its occupational culture. Authors such as Reiner (1992) and Skolnick (1975) have characterised the police culture as in conflict with the formal values of the police mission. Through work with front-line police officers, they have identified a cynical, suspicious, isolated, conservative, macho, prejudiced and above all pragmatist culture which they have contrasted with the statements such as Wilson's about a new professional mission. A more positive slant – the commitment to a 'noble cause' – still, according to Crank and Caldero, has potentially difficult consequences when harnessed to 'outcome orientation'. However, as Chan (1997) and Foster (see Chapter 9) identify, the culture of the police service is far from being monolithic or immutable. Many of the negative qualities identified by Reiner and others are paralled by positives, as Small and Watson (1999) have demonstrated in a small study of the core-level values of policing. Similarly, Westmarland's (2003) study of front-line officers' integrity suggests high levels of consensus around many types of improper behaviour. This study, above all, illustrates the need for those debates around the boundaries of ethics to be more fully exposed within policing and more openly debated. It is particularly important, as a number of studies, but in particular Chan (1997), have shown, how changes in the external framework such as the legislative changes in the Human Rights Act combined with and underpinned by leadership

587

recruitment, education training and a focus on the decision-making processes in the police service can have a substantial impact on the occupational culture. This suggests that, far from police culture being an impassable barrier, a concerted drive towards a more professional model of policing can potentially edge the service nearer a more professional occupational culture.

A critical component of a more professional culture must be the way in which officers exercise discretion or their professional judgement. Police discretion has had a mixed reception in academic circles, being hugely controversial in the 1970s (Davis 1975) because of it being regarded as usurping judicial functions. Yet from another perspective (Pollock 1998) police discretion is a vital part of balancing the strict enforcement of the law with respect for human beings and care for communities. Indeed, Davis (1996) considered discretion the essence of informed professionalism in policing and has argued strongly against those who would bind the police professional. Discretion, professionalism and human rights policing dovetail together in a clear requirement for individual officers to be personally accountable for decisions that adeptly balance competing rights and to be able to demonstrate clear and justified decision-making. However, replacing rule-bound bureaucracy with flexible professional practice still requires the systematic body of professional knowledge against which the practitioner can be tested.

Key components of any police professional practitioner's decision-making will be their personal and professional integrity. Police officers have both responsibilities and rights. They have as individuals the right to be protected and rights such as privacy and family life and freedom of expression. However, both by human rights law and by the nature of the role, their freedom to be members of groups and associations, to be involved in politics and to accept gifts, gratuities or sponsorship are properly limited. The extent of that limitation has been a subject of considerable debate, notably around the issue of freemasonry, where public concern about the perception of partiality and secrecy has remained problematic and has raised just the questions that Lord Nolan sought to answer in his report on public standards in public life (1995). He suggested that public servants, including police officers, should avoid real and apparent conflicts of interests. Conflicts of interest can be difficult, however, when they are matters of religion, as they are in Northern Ireland, or of sexuality or gender. The extent to which a police officer's personal morality can conflict with his or her professional office has been given starkly contrasting treatments by, on the one hand, the USA-based International Association of Chiefs of Police Code of Ethics which clearly allows intrusion into private life and the censoring of private behaviour, and the European Court of Human Rights whose judgements have clearly underpinned the values of pluralism, tolerance and broad-mindedness. This is just the sort of fundamental difference in values which is increasingly facing police leaders in their choices in policing diverse communities (Guyot 1991).

Perhaps the most hotly debated boundary of virtue and professional integrity has been that of gifts and gratuities. In Westmarland's (2003) survey, accepting free meals and gifts at Christmas was not seen as particularly serious by the majority of officers, although a substantial number recognised that both were contrary to force procedure. However, accepting a free drink for not reporting a landlord for transgressing licensing law was seen as very serious by the vast majority. This is one area where the applications of the principles that we debated above can provide a reasonably clear guide on professional practice. Gifts whose purpose and outcome are the cementing of good relationships in the community (the principles of beneficence and care) and whose net value is trifling may well be appropriate and may not be seen as impacting on the perceived impartiality of the organisation or the officer (stewardship). Furthermore, that rule must be universally applicable and preferably formally sanctioned otherwise, as Sherman (1985) has suggested, gratuities could be the beginning of a psychological process that would gradually lead the officer to self-identify with less ethical practice and could create obligations or credit for future legal or illegal favours, quite apart from delivering an inequitable service. The latter could be a powerful argument in the debate around sponsorship which can, however well handled, create the impression of impartiality even if the substance may be different.

All in all, the striving towards professional status is an important component of modern police professional ideals. In the UK, all three staff associations, ACPO, the Superintendents Association and the Police Federation, have put developing professional practice at the top of their agendas. It is, as the above has identified, not a simple passage. The ideal is an important signal of intent but, as yet, not underpinned by the sort of professional infrastructure – such as ethical codes and established professional standards of practice – which might underpin discretion and develop integrity. Without the professional status, there is little to distinguish the fully empowered police officer from the partly or unempowered patroller and in the world of the mixed economy of policing, such distinctions are increasingly important.

Performance ethics

Ethics has been described above as making the right judgements and doing the right actions for the right reasons. Performance management could be described in a connected way as being the process by which police leaders and stakeholders consider those judgements and the resulting performance. Performance management in the police service is a complex matter. As has been described above, the purpose and expectations of what police services should deliver have see-sawed and remain unclear. Apparently straightforward approaches such as published league tables of detection and crime levels not only fail to exemplify what really concerns the public (Fitzgerald *et al.* 2002) but also, because what gets measured has a very significant effect on what gets done and what is prioritised, create consequences with considerable ethical implications. Collier (2002) has described in detail the relationship between the inputs, outputs and outcomes of policing and the control system of new public management in the UK. He has argued persuasively that the perceived rationality of the existing system does not hold up to detailed analysis, leaving managers bridging the gaps between a ritualistic system of accountability based on targets that bear little relationship to the capacity and capability of the organisation, and the public's expectations of policing.

However, there is a case to be made for the managerialist approach to performance management and one that can probably be linked to ethical practice. A key development in this field has been the Compstat system credited to New York and to the New York Police Department. Its development is set out by Jack Maple (1999), Deputy Commssioner, and by his Commissioner, Bill Bratton (1998), and the principles they enunciate as its core are far removed from the managerialist interpretation placed on it by Giuliani, the Mayor, in his autobiography (2002). Compstat (and its impact on falling crime rates in New York) has been hotly debated. However a strong argument can be sustained that the creation of clear aims linked to clear targets and clear responsibilities for each layer in the organisation creates both a clarity of expectation and of responsibility within the organisation that both advantages public accountability and assists the performance of the organisation. There are however downsides to this approach. First of all, as Fitzgerald et al. (2002) have argued, as soon as the police role is framed through a managerialist lens, there is a danger that crime fighting will sit high on the list of quantifiable indicators. Crime-fighting objectives have the appearance at least of being easily quantifiable. Cracking down on crime is a straightforward populist slogan and the police are strongly linked in the public's minds with the reduction of crime. However, that causal linkage is often complex and the effective tactics that police can deploy (Sherman et al. 1997) need partnership with other wider community strategies to effect long-term change. A simplistic expectation of a close coupled relationship between policing tactics and operations and reductions in crime makes no sense at all, particularly when it appears to hold the police 'directly' accountable for the level of crime (Fitzgerald et al. 2002).

For the managerialist approach to performance management to meet the standards of ethical practices a number of tests would have to be satisfied. First, the data produced by the means of collection would have to be clear and verifiable – a key component of Maple's approach to Compstat (1999). This is far from unproblematic in the case of police-recorded crime statistics (Maguire 2002) or, indeed, incident statistics, which are strongly related to the quality of public–police interaction and organisational practice. Secondly, the outcomes and the targets which measure their achievement would have to be clearly linked to national and local public requirements of the police. Arguably the targets in the first National Policing Plan (Home Office 2002a) have been drawn from priorities identified by the British Crime Survey. However, as *Policing for London* (Fitzgerald et al. 2002) identified, the existing UK targets do not adequately describe the public expectations of the service they want from the police but are, instead, over-focused on a small number of narrow crime reduction targets. Thirdly, the setting of the targets would need to be done in a way that protected properly those areas of policing service (such as child protection, the policing of family violence, dealing with bereavement and the myriad of requirements for assistance from the public) which are not easily measured and where the quality of the service delivered, in professional and emotional support, is often far more important than the narrow performance outcome. Without these types of work being properly ring-fenced and protected in taking into account the requirements to meet a target, managers are left with irresolvable dilemmas in prioritisation.

Finally, the targets would need to engage and be owned by the officers who are endeavouring to achieve them. Without this last requirement, it is debatable whether performance targets and professional practice will ever meet. The impact of Collier's (2002) observations about the unrealistic and ritualistic nature of much target setting and performance management is, as Fitzgerald *et al.* (2002) demonstrate, a high degree of cynicism about the performance framework from front-line officers and an unwillingness to be held responsible for what is not within their capability to achieve. The conclusion of *Policing for London* was that 'performance monitoring is not about the setting of targets for goal achievement, but about monitoring police practice against professional and ethical standards' (2002: 141). Therefore, the Metropolitan Police Service needed to be able to develop ways of managing performance that placed greater emphasis on achieving professional standards and less emphasis on hitting numerical targets. The emphasis placed on quantitative measures distorted performance and reduced the quality of service, which was the gold standard by which the people of London actually measured the police.

Public participation in policing

One potential way of improving the linkage between performance management in policing and professional practice is through public participation in policing (Fitzgerald *et al.* 2002). Participation can be divided in to four different aspects: consultation; lay oversight and inspection; active citizenship; and complementary policing (Neyroud 2001). These four areas share a common theme of taking part or having a share in policing. Each approach can have important benefits for policing. For instance, research evidence suggests a strong association between effective policing and effective crime reduction and local ownership and participation (Puttnam 2000). Secondly, policing in a democratic society is firmly grounded in the concept of policing by consent and the legitimacy and public support for the police being dependent on both a broad consensus and a series of 'rights of renewal' such as local consultation meetings (Neyroud 2001). Thirdly, lay oversight and audit can provide not just critical challenge to professional practice (vital in its development) but can also, as Scarman pointed out, open up controversial areas of policing to community scrutiny (1982). Finally, public participation in an active way in policing such as through Neighbourhood Watch, local patrolling schemes and crime reductions initiatives can provide just the sort of linking or 'interpenetration' of the public and voluntary sector that has been identified as a vital part of the social capital of communities, building trust and communication, which may in the context of crime and fear of crime be a vital part of reassurance (Maloney *et al.* 2000; Puttnam 2000).

Public participation can be seen as a challenge to police independence and, in the eyes of some police leaders, their impartiality. However, while police operations need to be independent of partisan politics they also need to be seen as encompassing the needs of diverse groups. This mediation of contradictions (Larsen 2000) needs opportunities for critique or, in Larsen's words, multiple competing public spaces ensure that different interpretations have the opportunity to be expressed. The police service in the UK has for 20 years relied largely on a formulaic approach of police consultative committees for which there is mixed evidence of success (Jones *et al.* 1994). More recent approaches to consultation about policing plans have had a similarly mixed reception (Jones and Newburn 1997). Through the 1990s and beyond 2000 the direction of initiatives in UK policing has become more and more centralist (see Chapter 24). The Police Reform Act 2002 provided a renewed framework of central control in the form of a National Policing Plan and new powers of intervention for Ministers in failing local forces. As such the right things that the police should be doing have become increasingly nationally defined and nationally prescribed. Just as there are challenges for policing in local participation, so there are disadvantages to being seen to be closely aligned to the political will of central government. The latter and the central framework can limit the opportunity for the police to be locally responsive and also for local needs to influence the priority of those 'right things' and, equally crucially, to be perceived to be doing so. The more that the agenda is set by the National Policing Plan, the less that the consultation locally about local policing plans has any real content. It can become a process of explaining what the police are going to do, not seeking the views of local people about what they should be doing.

Yet there is scope for more open and responsive local approaches as Patten (1999) set out in his report on the policing of Northern Ireland. In seeking to define a solution to the policing of a divided community, Patten proposed not just a police board at force level but also local partnership boards that had a non-executive role in holding local commanders to account and contributing to local policing strategies. Similar approaches to that suggested in the Patten Report have been adopted in West Mercia and Thames Valley. Area partnership boards at local command level have been established. They provide local oversight of the policing strategies in each command area and assist local commanders in planning the delivery of local resources (Neyroud 2001). There is scope for area partnership boards, very local beat meetings with local officers and the wider responsibilities of local police authorities to be developed to ensure that local police forces are more responsive and more engaged with the different communities they police. This sort of multilayered approach seems to offer a reasonable balance between local independence and responsiveness, local accountability and national direction (Neyroud 2001).

Lay or independent oversight of policing has developed in the UK since the Scarman Report in which lay visitors to police custody centres were proposed. Initially a voluntary scheme with no statutory authority, this has now developed into a statutory scheme with a significant track record of performance. Following the Macpherson Report and its criticisms of the police relationship with minority communities (1999), independent advisory groups have been created in order to open up police policy-making and operational decision-making in critical incidents to lay and particularly lay minority scrutiny. Such oversight does not resolve problems of itself. It can still offer conflicting advice and it does not solve the complexities of dealing with restricted resources, plural communities and, therefore, plural priorities. Nor, above all, does it shift the responsibility for taking decisions because these remain with the police officers. As Goldstein (1977) has argued, being responsive to lay advice should never be confused with being accountable. However, for a senior commander managing a complex operation, for a senior investigator dealing with the delicate critical incident or a local community officer policing a complex plural community, lay involvement close in to the decision-maker can enhance the personal responsibility for decisions by providing personal challenge and visibility of both the decisions and the decision-maker (Kleinig 1996a). Furthermore, public and media involvement in processes like Compstat as has been developed in Philadelphia cannot but improve public understanding of the operational challenges for policing and encourage less insular practice by the police themselves. Ethical practice in policing requires both challenge and transparency (Jones *et al.* 1994).

There is a further significant attraction to public participation in the context of ethical policing and that is that participation implies a philosophical shift in the police role from leading or controlling towards 'enabling' (Neyroud and Beckley 2001) or, perhaps, put more simply, an acceptance that good policing is interdependent with the community and many other agencies. This philosophical shift encourages senior managers to give their local officers considerable flexibility and autonomy to work with partners towards local outcomes. It also argues for a greater emphasis on very local priority setting within a broad framework. It has a strong resonance with the UK Labour government's agenda for modernisation (Cabinet Office 1999) which highlighted the need to deliver high-quality public services which are clearly focused on the results which 'matter to people' and within that a strong emphasis on the 'right to choose' services. This approach implies a knowledgeable and informed public, which will be difficult to achieve without significant levels of participation: an element of public choice would be impossible to achieve without participation, and a participative approach has considerable scope to achieve a process for monitoring and reporting progress. Furthermore, without effective transparency through public participation it is particularly difficult to see how police in a democratic society can negotiate the right choices for controversial areas of policing, such as covert policing, the use of force or the policing of diverse communities, in which conflicts of rights – for the suspect, victim, police officer or community – are most clearly exposed. It is to the first two of these that we now turn.

The police in action

A great deal of the literature about ethics in policing has, somewhat naturally, been focused on police operations and particularly on covert policing and the police use of force. Intrinsically, both these present significant ethical problems. In the first, covert policing, the police can be portrayed as using deceptive means in order to detect crime and prosecute offenders and, furthermore, those deceptive means can create significant intrusions on the rights of citizens, notably through electronic or physical surveillance or the deployment of informants. The problem, as Marx (1988) has stated, is not the use of such techniques but the question of how to control the use to which they are put, particularly as 'covert policing' is not in the public view. Covert policing has become significantly more important within the last 20 years. It is vital in detecting invisible or consensual offences such as drugs, drug dealing, corruption and vice. It is important in allowing the investigation of secret, organised and, particularly, terrorist groups and essential in the detection of robbery and volume crime such as burglary (Neyroud and Beckley 2001). There are some categories of crime and criminals which are clearly beyond investigation without the use of covert methods (Vahlenkamp and Hauer 1996). This in itself raises the ethical concern about any law enforcement system which could only investigate simple cases or offenders lacking the sophistication or wealth to cloak their crime in privacy (Clutter-buck 1997). On the other hand, there are clearly significant concerns about the boundaries of deception. Skolnick (1975) drew a distinction between the investigation where deception can be acceptable, and the interview and trial where it cannot. Furthermore, the boundaries between circumstances in which covert policing could have been considered to have inspired the crime rather than prevented it have been proved highly controversial (*Teixeira del Castro* v. *Portugal* 1998).

The complexity and sensitivity of covert policing argue for a model of compliance that deals with both the internal controls and the external oversight. In Table 23.1 such a model is set out. It incorporates three linked layers of compliance: the tactical and operational requirements of day-to-day management; the strategic responsibilities of the chief officers for leadership and control of covert policing; and the legal and societal control systems and the ethical principles that must underpin covert policing. It can been seen that a model of compliance in such a difficult area of policing needs to operate at not just a series of different levels but also through managerial systems, political and citizen oversight and professional standards. Internally, there are six main areas of control: the quality of frontline supervision; internal practice guidelines; authorisation procedure; budgets; performance management of the practice; and the results of operations and review. Externally, these are complemented by legislative framework, democratic control through the role of police authorities and, in the case of the Regulation of Investigatory Powers Act (RIPA) 2000, the Surveillance Commissioner reporting to Parliament. On top of these are inspection and audit by the Police Inspectorate and by the Office of the Surveillance Commission, judicial and commissioner oversight of warrantry and the serious intrusion decisions and the complaints procedure. None of these in itself will produce a ethical approach to covert policing, but if they are underpinned by effective training, a careful appreciation of the risks involved in particular operations and an interventionist and engaged style of management and a performance management framework that does not overemphasise the outcomes of operations against their process, then there is an opportunity for professional covert policing standards to develop into professional covert policing practice.

The position with the use of force is not dissimilar for, like covert policing, it starts with a difficult moral dilemma. The potential for the use of force is at the core of policing (Bittner 1975) but it can be argued to be intrinsically wrong

Table 23.1 Framework for ethical covert policing

	Compliance requirement	*Source of compliance*
Tactical/operational The day-to-day implementation and management of covert policing operations	• Manual of standards on covert policing • Trained staff (such as informant handlers and controllers) • Record-keeping and audit trails • Leadership, supervision and support	• ACPO manuals of guidance on covert policing • National Intelligence Model • ACPO manuals and RIPA codes of practice
Strategic Chief officer management and control of covert policing	• Intelligence/covert policing strategy • Nationally agreed standards • National training standards • Control and audit systems • Leadership	• National Intelligence and Covert Policing Standards
Legal and societal The legal and societal control systems	• Clear and comprehensive legislative provision with supporting guidance • Independent oversight/ audit of applications and operations • An independent complaints system • Public consultation about the nature and extent of covert policing • Democratic oversight of covert policing	• RIPA 2000, the Police Act 1997 and the accompanying codes of practice under both Acts • The commissioner system (RIPA) and Her Majesty's Inspectorate of Constabulary inspections • Tribunal system (RIPA) and police complaints system • PCCGs set up under s. 106 Police and Criminal Evidence Act 1984 • Parliamentary scrutiny of the commissioner (RIPA) and the police authority
Ethical principles The ethical principles which must underpin covert policing	• Respect for personal autonomy • Beneficence and non-maleficence • Justice • Responsibility • Care • Honesty • Stewardship	• As set out in this chapter

Source: Neyroud and Beckley (2001).

in that from a Kantian perspective it conflicts with the duty to accord dignity and personal autonomy to every individual. On the other hand, the police officer also has a duty of beneficence towards any individual threatened with force, quite apart from a human rights duty to preserve life. The use of force and at the extreme the taking of life by a police officer must therefore be ethically justified as being proportionate to the threat and absolutely necessary in the terms of Article 2 of the European Convention on Human Rights.

Added to the complexity of the ethical dilemmas about the use of force is the experience of the linkages between the use of force and police misconduct. In Westmarland's (2003) study of police officer integrity, while officers were clear where the boundaries of dishonesty lay and clear as well that they would be prepared to report colleagues crossing that boundary, there was far less clarity about the boundaries of the use of force and far less willingness to report colleagues who crossed it. For Waddington (1999), the use of force exposes officers to the repeated potential to cross the limits of respectability.

Those boundaries between the acceptable use of force and misconduct become ever more critical as the use of force moves up the continuum towards the lethal options, such as firearms, and the less lethal alternatives to them. If minimisation is the aim of the ethical use of force by police as Kleinig (1996a) has argued, then there is a strong moral imperative on the police to look for alternatives to lethal force albeit one that is not easily accomplished. After significant concern in the UK about a number of police shootings, the ACPO[1] embarked on a programme of research together with the Police Scientific Development Branch at the Home Office (Home Office 2002b) to look for alternatives to firearms and, in the context of public order, to the plastic baton round. The latter was particularly pertinent because of the recommendations of the Patten Report (1999: recommendations 69 and 70). The research started with a careful gap analysis of the operational effectiveness of existing equipment. This was used to identify an operational requirement and to test the existing available equipment within the policing market. The third hurdle was the medical impact of the weapons and a comparison between that and existing equipment and, finally, an acceptability matrix was devised which included the parameters of human rights compliance, community acceptability and consultation with a number of non-governmental organisations. This approach produced a range of options for deployment.

In itself, such a structured approach to police use of force goes only so far. What it does not do, as Rappert (2002) has pointed out, is deal with the operational deployment of the equipment. Rappert's research on the use of CS highlights the problems with the guidelines for deployment of CS and their interpretation by officers operating in uncertain and perhaps volatile condi- tions. Even with the latest comprehensive less lethal research programme, it is unlikely that any of the weaponry or approaches available will be appropriate in all the conditions in which they are utilised. Rappert suggests 'the disparity between the working and presentational rules surrounding the sprays is evidence of what Ericson (1981) has called the organisational hypocrisy of the police' (2002: 702). This seems a rather harsh judgement given that, in the case of both CS and the latest research on less lethal weapons, much of the research and medical evidence has been placed in the public arena. Moreover, the

Table 23.2 Framework for the ethical use of force

	US Supreme Court	Geller and Toch (1996)	ACPO
Tactical and operational	• Kind of weapons available to the officer • Operational tactics on deployment, engagement and warnings • Training and recertification	• Conflict management training • Intervention training of officers to reduce 'bystanderism' • Coaching and mentoring of officers to make them 'highly skilled'	• Training which is accredited and maintained in conflict management and each specific weapon tactic deployed • A manual of operational tactics • Individual record-making
Strategic	• Reporting and review systems for the use of force • A clear framework of policy designed to minimise the use of force	• An 'officer safety' initiative • A departmental style that emphasises 'community policing' and 'peace-keeping' rather than 'crime fighting' • A clear policy emphasising minimal use of force • A national reporting system on the use of force	• An 'officer safety' strategy • Monitoring of use of force locally and nationally • Review of tactics and equipment in the light of monitoring • A clear command and control structure, with a cadre of trained commanders
Societal/legal	A legal framework that emphasises 'reasonableness' in balancing the 'intrusion' of force with the necessity of action	• Public consultation about the use of force, including sharing • Effective complaints system with an independent element	• 'Legality': a clear framework of accessible and available law governing the use of force • 'Remedy' for the citizen, including an independent remedy in serious cases

Source: Neyroud and Beckley (2001).

police service performance in the use of force, including the use of CS, new batons and firearms, has been openly subjected to public scrutiny by the Police Complaints Authority (2000). However, Rappert is right in arguing that safety, in purely medical terms, is not a sufficient yardstick for the adoption of any less lethal technology or use-of-force technique. Acceptability – itself a complex construct – is a much more important assessment. As with covert policing, acceptability has to be seen at a variety of levels.

It can be seen from Table 23.2 that, as with covert policing, at a tactical and operational level, training tactical standards, a range of equipment and proper records are essential to ensuring that officers are confident in the way they use and deploy force and also properly to monitor and to take responsiblity for their deployments. At strategic level, a clear policy framework and standards, together with a proper monitoring and review process, are essential to ensure that the outcomes of the use of force both in terms of civilian and police injuries and complaints and misconduct is properly analysed on a regular basis. And, finally, that there is an effective consultation and complaints system which allows the proper sharing of information about the use of force, a proper debate about its acceptability and an effective independent way of dealing with misconduct.

Towards ethical policing

Several times it has been argued in this chapter that ethics in policing is about police officers doing the right things for the right reasons. What the proceeding sections of this chapter have sought to demonstrate are the ways in which policing can achieve that standard and work towards the principles that were identified earlier. Following on from the initial discussion of the context of policing, the 'history' of police ethics and the potential principles of ethical, human rights compliant policing, four areas were debated:

1. *Policing as a profession*: here the message must be one of unfinished business. The service's clear desire, particularly in a UK context, to achieve a more professional status has yet to be achieved. However, the significance of achieving that aspiration for a more ethical approach to policing was clearly endorsed.

2. In *performance ethics*, some dilemmas in achieving the right balance of holding individuals to account for their performance and doing so in a way that does not so skew that performance as to present potentially unethical choices to officers and their leaders were debated. Here, above all, a greater emphasis on measuring professional practice rather than simply measuring a limited number of quantitative performance targets was suggested as a critical development of performance management frameworks.

3. *Participation in policing* was outlined as a key component of ethical policing – above all in terms of ensuring the police are responsive to their community and in providing challenge to police practice and decision-

making and critical stimulus to the learning cycle about good professional standards.

4. Finally, in *policing in action* the role of the police in covert policing and the police use of force were discussed, and a multilayered framework for creating ethical compliance was set out for both areas but a framework that is equally applicable in other controversial areas of policing. The framework was constructed with elements of professional practice, performance management of professional practice and public participation incorporated to form a credible whole.

It is with participation and a strong sense that, for policing to be ethical, it must be negotiated with the policed that I must conclude. The police could become superbly professional, technically proficient and with sparkling integrity, but they would still lack legitimacy without negotiating their mission, strategies and tactics with local and national communities. Furthermore, there has to be recognition that the commitment to such negotiation is a central part of the mission, a complex and enabling one, not a simple one-line fight against crime. The unsettled and diverse communities of the twenty-first century need a leadership in policing which listens, learns and delivers services that meet their widely differing needs.

Selected further reading

There are a number of good treatments of ethics in policing, of which the most accessible are Delattre's *Character and Cops* (1989), Kleinig's *The Ethics of Policing* (1996) and the companion volume of essays (Kleinig's *Handled with Discretion* – 1996), Neyroud and Beckley's *Policing, Ethics and Human Rights* (2001) and Crank and Caldero's *Police Ethics* (2000). Pollock's *Ethics in Crime and Justice* (1998) and Lawton's *Ethical Management for the Public Services* (1998) put the issues into the wider context of criminal justice and the public services. On more specific issues, Sherman's *Police Corruption* (1974) and *Scandal and Reform* (1978) and Newburn's *Understanding and Preventing Police Corruption* (1999) provide good coverage of corruption, Marx's *Undercover* (1988) and Justice's *Under Surveillance* (1998) provide excellent treatment of covert policing, and Geller and Toch's *Police Violence* (1996) of police use of force.

Note

1   The author was one of those leading this research as the Secretary to the ACPO's Police Use of Firearms Committee from 2000 to 2002.

References

Anderson, D., Lait, J. and Marsland, D. (1981) *Breaking the Spell of the Welfare State.* London: Social Affairs Unit.

Baier, A. (1985) *Postures of the Mind: Essays on Mind and Morals.* Minneapolis, MN: University of Minnesota Press.

Bauman, Z. (1993) *Post-modern Ethics*. Oxford: Blackwell.

Bittner, E. (1975) *The Functions of Police in Modern Society*. Chevy Chase: National Institute of Mental Health.

Bobbit, P. (2002) *The Shield of Achilles: War, Peace and the Course of History*. London: Allen Lane.

Bowling, B. (1999) *Violent Racism*. Oxford: Clarendon Press.

Braithwaite, J. (1989) *Crime, Shame and Reintegration*. Cambridge: Cambridge University Press.

Bratton, W. with Knobler, P. (1998) *Turnaround: How America's Top Cop Reversed the Crime Epidemic*. New York, NY: Random House.

Cabinet Office (1999) *Modernising Government*. London: HMSO.

Chan, J. (1997) *Changing Police Culture: Policing in a Multi-cultural Society*. Cambridge: Cambridge University Press.

Clutterbuck, R. (1997) *Public Safety and Civil Liberties*. Basingstoke: Macmillan.

Collier, P.M. (2002) 'The tortuous triangle: public demand, the performance culture and human rights', *Police Research and Management*, 5–4: 85–101.

Crank, J.P. and Caldero, M. (2000) *Police Ethics: The Corruption of Noble Cause*. Cincinnati, OH: Anderson.

Crawshaw, R., Devlin, B. and Williamson, T. (1999) *Human Rights and Policing: Standards for Good Behaviour and a Strategy for Change*. The Hague: Kluwer International.

Critchley, T.A. (1978) *A History of the Police in England and Wales*. London: Constable.

Dale, J. and Foster, P. (1986) *Feminists and State Welfare*. London: Routledge.

Davis, K.C. (1975) *Police Discretion*. St Paul, MN: West.

Davis, M. (1996) 'Police, discretion and professions', in J. Kleinig (ed.) *Handled with Discretion: Ethical Issues in Police Decision-Making*. Lanham, MD: Rowman & Littlefield.

Delattre, E.J. (1989) *Character and Cops: Ethics in Policing*. Washington, DC: American Enterprise Institute for Public Policy Research.

Edwards, S.M. (1989) *Policing 'Domestic' Violence*. London: Sage.

Elliston, F.A. and Feldberg, M. (eds) (1985) *Moral Issues in Police Work*. Totowa, NJ: Rowman & Allenheld.

Ericson, R. (1981) 'Rules for police deviance', in C. Shearing (ed.) *Organisational Police Deviance*. Toronto: Butterworths.

Fitzgerald, M., Hough, M., Joseph, I. and Qureshi, T. (2002) *Policing for London*. Cullompton: Willan.

Fogelson, R. (1977) *Big City Police*. Cambridge, MA: Harvard University Press.

Friedson, E. (1983) 'The theory of the professions', in J. Dingwall and P. Lewis (eds) *The Sociology of the Professions*. Oxford: Oxford University Press.

Garland, D. (2001) *The Culture of Control: Crime and Social Order in Contemporary Society*. Oxford: Oxford University Press.

Geller, W.A. and Toch, H. (eds) (1996) *Police Violence*. New Haven, CT: Yale University Press.

Gilligan, C. (1982) *In a Different Voice*. Cambridge: Polity Press.

Gillon, R. (1994) 'Medical ethics: four principles plus attention to scope', *British Medical Journal*, 309: 184–8.

Giuliani, R. (2002) *Leadership*. London: Little Brown.

Goldstein, H. (1977) *Policing a Free Society*. Cambridge, MA: Ballinger.

Guyot, D. (1991) *Policing as though People Matter*. Philadelphia, PA: Temple University Press.

HMIC (1999) *Policing Integrity: Securing and Maintaining Public Confidence*. Report of Her Majesty's Inspectorate of Constabulary. London: HMIC.

Home Office (1998) *Reducing Offending: An Assessment of the Research Evidence on Ways of Dealing with Offending Behaviour. Home Office Research Study* 187. London: Home Office.

Home Office (2001) *Policing a New Century: A Blueprint for Reform.* (Cm 5326). London: HMSO.

Home Office (2002a) *The National Policing Plan.* London: HMSO.

Home Office (2002b) *Less Lethal Technologies: Initial Prioritisation and Evaluation.* London: Home Office Police Scientific Development Branch.

Honderich, T. (ed.) (1995) *The Oxford Companion to Philosophy.* Oxford: Oxford University Press.

Jefferson, T. and Grimshaw, R. (1984) *Controlling the Constable: Police Accountability in England and Wales.* London: Frederick Muller.

Johnston, L. (2000) *Policing Britain: Risk, Security and Governance.* Harlow: Pearson Education.

Jones, T. and Newburn, T. (1997) *Policing after the Act: Police Governance after the Police and Magistrates Court Act 1994.* London: PSI.

Jones, T. and Newburn, T. (2002) 'The transformation of policing? Understanding current trends in policing systems', *British Journal of Criminology*, 42(1): 129–47.

Jones, T., Newburn, T. and Smith, D. (1994) *Democracy and Policing.* London: PSI.

Justice (1998) *Under Surveillance.* London: Justice.

Justice (2002) *Annual Conference on Human Rights.* London: Justice.

Kleinig, J. (1996a) *The Ethics of Policing.* Cambridge: Cambridge University Press.

Kleinig, J. (ed.) (1996b) *Handled with Discretion: Ethical Issues in Police Decision-making.* Lanham, MD: Rowman & Littlefield.

Larsen, O. (2000) *Administration, Ethics and Democracy.* Aldershot: Ashgate.

Lawton, A. (1998) *Ethical Management for the Public Services.* Buckingham: Open University Press.

MacIntyre, A. (1981) *After Virtue.* Notre Dame, IN: University of Notre Dame Press.

Macpherson, Sir W. (1999) *Report of the Stephen Lawrence Inquiry.* London: HMSO.

Maguire, M. (2002) 'Crime statistics, patterns and trends: changing perceptions and their implications', in M. Maguire *et al.* (eds) *The Oxford Handbook of Criminology* (3rd edn). Oxford: Oxford University Press, 322–75.

Maloney, W., Smith, G. and Stoker, G. (2000) 'Social capital and urban governance: adding a more contextualised "top-down" perspective', *Political Studies*, 48: 802–20.

Maple, J. with Mitchell, C. (1999) *The Crime Fighter: How You Can Make your Community Crime Free.* New York, NY: Doubleday.

Marx, G. (1988) *Undercover: Police Surveillance in America.* Berkeley, CA: University of California Press.

Muir, W.K. (1977) *Police: Street Corner Politicians.* Chicago, IL: Chicago University Press.

Mulgan, G. (1997) *Connexity: How to Live in a Connected World.* London: Chatto & Windus.

Newburn, T. (1999) *Understanding and Preventing Police Corruption: Lessons from the Literature.* Home Office Police Research Series Paper 110. London: Home Office.

Neyroud, P.W. (2001) *Public Participation in Policing.* London: Institute of Public Policy Research.

Neyroud, P.W. (2002) 'The unsettled society.' Institute of Public Policy Research lecture.

Neyroud, P.W. and Beckley, A. (2001) *Policing, Ethics and Human Rights.* Cullompton: Willan.

Nolan, Lord (1995) *Standards in Public Life. First Report of the Committee on Standards in Public Life.* London: HMSO.

Parry, N., Rustin, M. and Satyamurti, C. (1979) *Social Work, Welfare and the State.* London: Arnold.

Patten, C. (1999) *A New Beginning: Policing in Northern Ireland: The Report of the Independent Commission on Policing for Northern Ireland.* London: HMSO.

Police Complaints Authority (2000) *CS Spray: Increasing Public Safety?* London: Police Complaints Authority.

Pollock, J. (1998) *Ethics in Crime and Justice.* Belmont, CA: Wadsworth.

Punch, M. (1985) *Conduct Unbecoming: The Social Construction of Police Deviance and Control.* London: Tavistock.

Puttnam, R.D. (2000) *Bowling Alone: The Collapse and Revival of American Community.* New York, NY: Simon & Schuster.

Rappert, B. (2002) 'Constructions of legitimate force: the case of CS Sprays', *British Journal of Criminology*, 42(4): 689–709.

Reiner, R. (1978) *The Blue Coated Worker.* Cambridge: Cambridge University Press.

Reiner, R. (1992) *The Politics of the Police.* Hemel Hempstead: Harvester Wheatsheaf.

Rosenbaum, D.P. (ed.) (1994) *The Challenge of Community Policing: Testing the Promises.* Thousand Oaks, CA: Sage.

Ross, W.D. (1930) *The Right and the Good.* Oxford: Clarendon Press.

Savage, S. and Charman, S. (1996) 'Managing change', in F. Leishman *et al.* (eds) *Core Issues in Policing.* London: Longman.

Scarman, Lord (1982) *The Scarman Report.* Harmondsworth: Penguin Books.

Sherman, L. (ed.) (1974) *Police Corruption: A Sociological Perspective.* New York, NY: Anchor.

Sherman, L. (1978) *Scandal and Reform: Controlling Police Corruption.* Berkeley, CA: University of California Press.

Sherman, L. (1998) *Evidence-based Policing.* Washington, DC: Police Foundation.

Sherman, L., Gottfredson, D., Mackenzie, D., Eck, J., Reuter, P. and Bushway, S. (1997) *Preventing Crime: What Works, What Doesn't and What's Promising.* Washington, DC: Office of Justice Programs.

Sherman, L. (1985) Becoming Bent: Moral careers of corrupt policemen, in F.A. Elliston and M. Feldberg (eds) *Moral Issues in Police Work.* Totowa, New Jersey: Rowan and Allanheld.

Skogan, W. and Hartnett, S.M. (1997) *Community Policing: Chicago Style.* New York, NY: Oxford University Press.

Skolnick, J. (1975) *Justice without Trial.* New York, NY: Wiley.

Small, J.J.C. and Watson, R.C. (1999) 'Police values and police misconduct: the Western Australian Police', *The Police Journal*, July: 225–37.

Starmer, K. (1999) *European Human Rights Law: The Human Rights Act 1998 and the European Convention on Human Rights.* London: Legal Action Group.

Stephens, M. and Becker, S. (1994) *Police Force: Police Service: Care and Control in Britain.* Basingstoke: Macmillan.

Tyler, T.R. and Huo, Y.J. (2002) *Trust in the Law: Encouraging Public Cooperation with the Police and Courts.* New York, NY: Russell Sage Foundation.

Vahlenkamp, W. and Hauer, P. (1996) *Organised Crime – Criminal Logistics and Preventive Approaches.* Wiesbaden: Federal Criminal Police Office.

Waddington, P. (1999) *Policing Citizens: Authority and Rights.* London: UCL Press.

Westley, W. (1970) *Violence and the Police.* Cambridge, MA: MIT Press.

Westmarland, L. (2003) 'Policing integrity: Britain's thin blue line', in C.B. Klockars *et al.* (eds) *The Contours of Police Integrity.* Thousand Oaks, CA: Sage.

Zander, M. (1994) 'Ethics and crime investigation', *Policing*, 10(1): 39–48.

Chapter 24

The governance and accountability of policing

Trevor Jones

Introduction

In recent years, debates about police accountability have lost some of the political bite that they once held, particularly compared with the early 1980s. Although controversy still periodically resurfaces, this tends to focus primarily upon police performance and effectiveness. It seems that there is less political and academic interest in arguments surrounding the respective roles of local communities, national and local politicians, and chief constables in the framing of policing *policy*. This partly reflects the decline of overtly 'ideological' politics in general. It may also be related to reforms promoted by successive governments over recent decades. A central theme of these reforms has been a self-conscious aim to 'take the politics out' of policing policy, and locate discussions of policing firmly in the supposedly value-neutral arena of technical competence and managerial expertise. However, beneath the surface, the complexities surrounding police governance and accountability remain profoundly political and of major significance. Indeed, contemporary developments such as the pluralisation of policing and the increasing influence of transnational policing institutions render the issues of police governance and accountability more important than ever.

This chapter is divided into five sections. The first attempts to clarify the meanings of the three key concepts explored within the chapter: 'policing', 'governance' and 'accountability'. The second section considers why issues of governance and accountability are important, and how they might contribute to 'democratic' policing arrangements. The third section provides an overview of the 'tripartite' framework of police governance in England and Wales,[1] and key legislative developments since the 1960s. The fourth section explores four long-term trends in police governance, and the final section assesses the 'democratic' content of the current system in England and Wales.

Definitions

Policing

It has now become standard practice for criminologists to distinguish the activity of 'policing' from the institution of 'the police' (Johnston 1992, 2000; Loader 2000). While criminological studies of policing remain primarily focused upon the specialist state agency tasked with law enforcement and peace-keeping, a growing body of work recognises that 'policing' consists of a variety of activities and processes, carried out by a range of individuals and organisations. This harks back to a much older conception of the term 'police' (Garland 1996; Loader and Walker 2001). In the late eighteenth and early nineteenth centuries, the term was used to denote to the wider system of formal regulation designed to promote the security and well-being of populations, and covered many administrative functions as well as law enforcement ones (see Chapter 3). The renewed focus upon older senses of the term 'policing' has helped to challenge the dominant preoccupation with the public police. However, broader definitions can be problematic when considering specific manifestations of organised social control (Cohen 1985). In particular, it is important to distinguish designated and recognised social control activities from broader governing processes. This chapter will focus upon the more formal and organised manifestations of social control and regulation. In doing so, it will rely upon an earlier 'working definition' developed with Tim Newburn (Jones and Newburn 1998). We took 'policing' to mean a set of functions and processes that form a subset of 'organised forms of social control'. This includes individuals and organisations involved in regulatory, investigation and enforcement activities, part of whose defining purpose is to apply social controls. Although this clearly includes policing activities undertaken by commercial (and other non-state) bodies, space dictates that the primary focus here will be upon the accountability of public policing.[2] However, there will be a discussion of the problems of bringing policing activities undertaken by non-state policing bodies under democratic oversight and direction.

Governance

Within writing on policing, the term 'governance' tends to be used in two distinct ways. Recent usage of the term has emerged from a body of work in political science examining the broader systems of regulation and ordering that have developed in contemporary societies. This maps out the increasing complexity in the ways that western industrial societies govern themselves (Rhodes 1997). It is argued that 'political power is exercised today through a profusion of shifting alliances between diverse authorities in projects to govern a multitude of facets of economic activity, social life and individual contact' (Rose and Miller 1992: 174). Thus, the governmental process is dispersed within a network of agencies throughout the social field, rather than remaining concentrated in the institutions of the state. Such developments have included the emergence of supranational governmental institutions (above the state), market-oriented forms of governing by commercial organisations (beyond the state) and new forms of community governance at the local level (below the state). There have also been important developments within state-provided public services, including the introduction of 'new public management', privatisation and contracting-out, and the creation of semi-autonomous service delivery agencies. 'Governance' is thus used as a general term to denote governmental strategies originating from both inside and outside the state.[3] This notion of governance has resonated clearly in recent writing on policing and security (Johnston and Shearing 2002).

Although these developments are important, for the sake of clarity this chapter will continue in a similar vein to much previous writing about police 'governance', in which the term simply denoted the constitutional and institutional arrangements for framing and directing the policies of the police (Lustgarten 1986; Walker 2000). This approach also implies a belief in the continued relevance and importance of state-organised policing arrangements (Loader and Walker 2001; Jones and Newburn 2002). However, in light of the important developments highlighted by the broader notions of governance, there will be some discussion of the accountability problems posed by plural policing forms (see Chapter 7).

Accountability

Although 'accountability' is a central component of democratic governance of policing, it has been described as a 'chameleon' term with a range of meanings, including 'answerability, responsiveness, openness, efficient estate management, not to mention participation and obedience to external laws' (Day and Klein 1987). For the purposes of this chapter, two key distinctions are important. The first is between the accountability of individual policing agents as they go about their day-to-day activities, and the broader organisational policing policies concerned with overall priorities, resource allocation and policing styles (Reiner 1995). Clearly, the two dimensions are not completely distinct since the behaviour of individual policing agents will clearly be influenced by broader organisational policies and practices, and vice versa. However, although these are clearly important aspects of accountability, space precludes an extensive discussion of the mechanisms used to regulate individual policing agents via complaints systems and legal redress. The second key distinction is between *internal* and *external* mechanisms of accountability. Over-reliance upon external controls may actually be counter-productive if they foster indifference or resistance within policing organisations and weaken internal monitoring systems (Stenning 1995). So although the primary focus here is upon *external* mechanisms of accountability, it is clear that these can only be effective if they complement well developed internal forms of control. The framework of police governance is but one of a range of processes and institutions that may shape 'democratically accountable' policing. The extent to which this framework is effective depends crucially upon its relationship with the variety of other mechanisms, at both individual and organisational level, and within wider society.[4]

Democratic and accountable policing

Why should we be concerned with the arrangements for the governance and accountability of policing? Perhaps the most important reason for our interest in such questions concerns the unique relationship between policing and the institutions of democracy and their legitimacy. The powers that the police possess to protect fundamental liberties simultaneously provide the potential for severe abuse of these freedoms. The paradox of police governance is that the state is both the ultimate source of a solution to the problem of police accountability and the main beneficiary of the reproduction of the specific order (Walker 2000). Thus, the state must promote the best arrangements both to empower and constrain the police, but at the same time impose clear limitations on its ability to influence policing in its own favour. The way in which society regulates and controls the organisation and powers of the police is therefore a crucial indicator of the nature of the political and social order.

A second key strand to democratic accountability concerns the fundamentally *political* nature of policing. Although questions about management and audit are increasingly presented as value-neutral technical matters, policing remains inescapably political. It concerns the expression of fundamental values and, ultimately, the exercise of raw power by intervening authoritatively (and, if necessary, forcefully) in social conflict (see Chapter 16). It also involves choices, given limited resources, between policing priorities and policing styles. Such questions cannot be left to policing agents alone, but should be located within the realm of political debate. Although there needs to be a degree of professional autonomy and insulation from partisan interests, in a democracy such questions are ultimately the responsibility of representative bodies. A third reason why the police should be held accountable, and one that has become of central concern in recent years, involves questions of financial stewardship and audit. As public expenditure on policing spirals ever higher, it is proper that police managers should be held to account for their use of the public resources provided to them and that policing services are delivered as effectively and efficiently as possible. Police accountability also involves broader questions of police effectiveness. Even in our increasingly globalised world, much crime and disorder remains essentially local in character. Police effectiveness in dealing with such problems depends crucially upon information and co-operation provided by the public. In turn, this depends on the police service being viewed as legitimate and worthy of trust and co-operation. Effective mechanisms of accountability and governance are vital in promoting such legitimacy.

While most would agree that the system of police governance should promote 'democratic' policing, the specific meaning of 'democracy' within this context is rarely made explicit. In an earlier piece of work we explored the multiple meanings of 'democracy' in the sphere of policing and highlighted seven 'democratic criteria' that might be used to assess frameworks of police governance (Jones *et al.* 1994). These were as follows:

1. *Equity*: policing services should be distributed fairly between groups and individuals. When the police are enforcing the law, the pattern of

enforcement should be fair and not targeted unjustifiably on particular individuals or groups.

2. *Service delivery*: the police should deliver the appropriate services (determined on other criteria) as effectively and efficiently as possible.

3. *Responsiveness*: the police should be responsive to the views of representative bodies in determining priorities, allocating resources between different objectives and the choice of policing methods.

4. *Distribution of power*: power to influence and review policing policy should not be overly concentrated but should be distributed across a number of institutions and agencies.

5. *Information*: there should be clear and accurate information available to relevant bodies and community groups about funding, expenditure, activities and outputs of policing.

6. *Redress*: representative bodies should have the power to dismiss an incompetent or corrupt police officer. There should be effective means of redress for the unlawful or unreasonable behaviour of individual police officers.

7. *Participation*: as far as possible, citizens from all social groups should have the opportunities to participate in discussions of policing policy and have real influence over policy choices.

All these elements are essential to a democratic framework of police governance. However, various models will clearly place different weights on each of the values. Recent reforms have seen an almost overwhelming concern with the second element, service delivery, at the expense of concerns with factors such as participation and distribution of power.

The framework of police governance in England and Wales

There are now a number of detailed and authoritative accounts of the historical development of the system of police governance since the founding of the 'new police' in 1829 (Lustgarten 1986; Reiner 2000; Walker 2000; see Chapter 4). An awareness of the historical events that lie behind our current system of policing is clearly vital to the understanding of the contemporary arrangements for police governance. However, the focus here is upon the more recent historical period. This section will provide an overview of the key legislative developments over the past 40 years that have shaped the 'tripartite structure' of police governance.

The Police Act 1964

The formal basis of the current system of police governance in England and Wales remains the Police Act 1964, although significant reforms were made during the 1990s. The Act (and the 1962 Royal Commission that preceded it) attempted to address a number of problems that had arisen over previous decades. In particular, it tried to resolve tensions between national and local influences, to unify the fragmented nature of the policing system and to clarify the relative powers of local authorities, national government and chief constables in the framing and implementation of policing policy. The Act contained much studied ambiguity as to the relative influence of the different parties within the police governance system. It was aptly described by Morgan (1986: 86) as a ' "gentlemen's" agreement to gloss over the ambiguities and contradictions concerning the responsibilities for framing, monitoring and financing policing policy'. As Walker (2000) points out, this 'under-specification' of legal powers and responsibilities was quite deliberate and designed to allow enough flexibility for the negotiation of pragmatic compromises between parties with different roles in the system.

Prior to the 1964 Act, there was a dual system of police governance outside London. In urban areas, the chief constable was accountable to 'watch committees' (consisting entirely of local councillors) who in many cases took an active role in the development and monitoring of local police policy-making (Lustgarten 1986). By contrast, in rural areas, the chief was in theory responsible to a committee of local magistrates who tended in practice to allow him a considerable degree of autonomy. The 1964 Act provided for a unified system of local government involvement in policing in both rural and urban provincial forces of England and Wales and established the 'tripartite structure' of police governance. For the 41 provincial police forces, the Act divided responsibility for policing policy between local police authorities (consisting of two thirds elected councillors and one third magistrates), chief constables and the Home Office. However, in London the police authority for the Metropolitan Police was the Home Secretary, a situation that remained until the Greater London Authority Act 1999, which introduced a statutory police authority for London including local government representation. The 1964 Act gave police authorities the duty to secure the maintenance of an 'adequate and efficient' force for their area, and to offer advice and guidance to the chief constable concerning the policing of the area. While the police authority had responsibility for appointing the chief constable (and other senior command posts within the force), this power was crucially subject to the approval of the Home Secretary. Other police authority powers were also subject to Home Office and/or chief constable co-operation. For example, the police authority power to call upon the chief constable for a report on any aspect of policing the local area could be resisted if the chief constable could convince the Home Secretary that such a report was not in the public interest.

The 1964 Act placed each force under the 'direction and control' of its chief constable. The mode of accountability to external bodies established by the Act was, in Marshall's (1978) terms, 'explanatory and co-operative' rather than 'subordinate and obedient'. That is, chief constables were required to *give account* for their decisions to various authorities, but were under no legal requirement actually to *take account* of any critical response (Reiner 1995). The Act also provided the Home Secretary with an array of powers and established in statute the increasing dominance of central government within the framework of police governance. As noted above, the Home Secretary formed the police authority of the largest and most influential police force – the Metropolitan Police. With regard to provincial forces, the Home Secretary had a number of key powers. For example, he could require the chief constable to resign in the interests of efficiency, could call for reports into any aspect of the policing of an area and set up a local inquiry into policing matters. In addition, the Home Secretary was provided with a number of powers of approval over police authority appointments. A vital aspect of central government influence under the 1964 Act concerned the system of funding of the police service. Until 1995, the Home Office provided 51 per cent of police expenditure and directly controlled police staffing levels and capital spending in the provincial forces. In practice, the proportion of centrally provided funding was much higher, since only a relatively small percentage of the revenue provided by local authorities actually came from local taxation.[5]

The Police and Criminal Evidence Act 1984

Following large-scale inner-city disorder in the early 1980s, the Scarman Report into the disturbances in Brixton argued that the police had lost the confidence of local populations, particularly in many inner-city areas with high concentrations of minority ethnic communities (Scarman 1981). A subsequent Home Office circular recommended the establishment of 'local consultative committees' in order to improve discussion and communication between local police commanders and the people in their areas. These became a statutory requirement under the Police and Criminal Evidence Act 1984.[6] Research on these committees suggested that they tended to be rather unrepresentative and lacked any real input into local policing policy (Morgan 1992). However, these arrangements continue under the present system and many forces still see them as a significant vehicle for local consultation.

The Police and Magistrates Courts Act 1994

The 1990s were a crucial period of reform in the system of police governance, with the central piece of legislation during this time being the Police and Magistrates' Courts Act 1994 (later consolidated under the Police Act 1996). The Act introduced a number of major reforms to the tripartite structure within a framework of national planning and performance management. The Act attempted to clarify some of the previous ambiguities and overlapping responsibilities in the powers and duties of all three parties in the tripartite structure.

Police authorities became independent bodies set apart from the local government structure. Their duty under the Act was to provide for an 'efficient and effective' police force. The Act restricted the size of most authorities to 17 members (with a small number of exceptions), consisting of nine councillors, three magistrates and five 'independent' members. These independent members were to be appointed according to complex process but with significant local involvement (rather than appointed by the Home Secretary as was the original intention). The local police authority is now responsible for publishing an annual 'local policing plan' including specific national and local policing objectives, and associated performance targets. The chief constable drafts the plan for his or her area in consultation with the police authority, although the latter body ultimately 'owns' the plan. Under the reformed system chief constables were given responsibility to 'direct and control' their police forces. They took over from the police authority responsibility for detailed management of staffing and budgets and became the responsible employer for civilian police employees. As stated above, the chief constable drafts the local policing plan and sets the annual budget and may now be subject to fixed-term contract. The Act provided the Home Office with a number of new powers. First, it allowed the Home Secretary to set annual national objectives and direct performance targets for forces. The Home Office also has the power to issue codes of practice and give directions to police authorities that are perceived to be failing. In addition, the Home Secretary can set a minimum budget for a police force and require a police authority to meet its commitments within this. The Act gave greater power to the Home Secretary to amalgamate police forces. Finally, under the new system, the Home Office relinquished detailed controls over staffing and capital spending budgets within police forces and henceforth simply provided an annual cash-limited grant to police forces. This provided for greater control of overall spending but less detailed control over the details of what the grant is spent on (Newburn and Jones 1996).

The Crime and Disorder Act 1998

The period following the election of the Labour government in May 1997 was a time of frenetic legislative activity (Newburn 1998). The Crime and Disorder Act 1998 was the key piece of legislation within the sphere of criminal justice and policing. Although this covered a range of issues, the Act had potentially important consequences for the system of police governance. The Act placed a statutory duty upon local authorities for crime and disorder reduction and required the establishment of local multi-agency partnerships (including the police, probation and a range of other public services) (see Chapter 12). These partnerships were required to publish a local crime and disorder reduction plan and to consult widely upon local crime and disorder problems (and the methods via which they should be tackled). Despite problems of implementation, these partnerships provide a potential framework for reinvigorating local influences over community safety and policing policy (Loveday 2000).

The Police Reform Act 2002

Although strongly critical of previous Conservative governments' police reforms at the time, once in office leading Labour politicians enthusiastically embraced managerialism. The appointment of David Blunkett as Home Secretary in 2001 signalled a renewed vigour in approaches to police reform. In his first year as Home Secretary, Blunkett introduced a radical Police Reform Bill including proposals that led to a storm of protest from all levels of the police service. Some of the more radical provisions of the bill (as in previous eras) were subsequently shelved following strong police lobbying. However, when the Act was passed in 2002 it still retained some highly significant provisions in terms of police governance, including the following:

- The introduction of an Annual Policing Plan setting out the government's strategic priorities for policing and requiring police authorities to produce a three-year strategy plan consistent with the National Policing Plan.

- Provision of powers to the Home Secretary to ensure consistent application of good practice across the country through statutory codes of practice, plus a power to make regulations governing policing practices and procedures.

- Provision of powers to the Home Secretary to require a police force to take remedial action where they are judged by Her Majesty's Inspectorate of Constabulary (HMIC) to be inefficient or ineffective.

- Strengthening police authorities' powers to require the early departure of, or to suspend, a chief constable in the public interest.

The Act[7] also has significant implications for the 'pluralisation' of policing (see Chapter 7). It enables chief constables to designate police authority support staff as 'community support officers', investigating officers, detention officers or escort officers in order to support police officers in tackling low-level crime and anti-social behaviour. In addition, it introduced arrangements for the accreditation of neighbourhood and street wardens and embraced the concept of the 'extended police family'.

Long-term trends in police governance

The last 30 years or so has therefore seen a great deal of legislative activity in the arena of police governance. Many of the reforms outlined above have helped to consolidate and in some cases accelerate a raft of trends that have been visible over the longer history of policing in England and Wales. We focus here upon four key long-term developments: professionalisation, nationalisation, marketisation and pluralisation.

Professionalisation

The twentieth century saw a growing emphasis on the professional autonomy of police officers in a sense that sets them apart from other public servants. The most important aspect of professionalisation here relates to the idea that policing *policy* decisions must be insulated from political interference and left to the professional judgement of senior police officers. This doctrine of 'constabulary independence' is 'central to contemporary attempts to understand – and to change – the world of police governance' in England and Wales (Walker 2000: 44).

Up until about 1920 there was no legal tradition preventing politicians from directing chief police officers in general policy matters. In fact, during the late nineteenth and early twentieth centuries, urban police forces outside London and the Metropolitan Police were given detailed policy direction by watch committees and the Home Secretary respectively (Lustgarten 1986). However, the role of politicians in the framing of policing policy was increasingly challenged during the first half of the twentieth century. The case that is widely perceived to have first established the doctrine of 'constabulary independence' is that of *Fisher* v. *Oldham Corporation* ([1930] 2 KB 364). Fisher had been arrested and released following a case of mistaken identity, and sued Oldham Corporation and its watch committee for wrongful imprisonment. The judge found against Fisher on the basis that there could be no 'master–servant relationship' between the arresting police officers and the watch committee (and local authority). The judge's ruling had two main strands. First, following *Stanbury* v. *Exeter Corporation* ([1905] 2KB 838), he argued that because police officers have national as well as local functions, local authorities could not be held vicariously liable for their actions. Secondly, because powers are invested directly in the office of constable (rather than being conferred on individual officers), police officers cannot be subject to the direction of their paymasters.

The Fisher case came to be used as the primary legal justification for limiting the liability of local police authorities for the actions of their officers and for arguing that local police authorities cannot direct law enforcement activities (Walker 2000). Over time, the notion of constabulary independence became extended and entrenched to protect the autonomy of chief constables' policy-making as well as the discretion of constables in individual cases. Lustgarten (1986) provides a comprehensive legal critique of this development, arguing that the threat of partisan control over policing has been used to prevent full democratic scrutiny of policing policy. Nevertheless, despite the dubious legal basis of 'constabulary independence', the notion has become deeply entrenched in the minds of senior police officers, politicians and judges.

Recent legal developments show that the courts remain reluctant to challenge chief constables' professional autonomy. The 1995 case, *R* v. *Chief Constable of Sussex ex parte International Traders Ferry (ITF) Ltd* ([1995] All E.R. 364; [1997] 2 All E.R. 65) involved the applicants applying for judicial review of the chief constable's decision to scale down the police response to demonstrations against the company's role in the export of live animals from Shoreham. ITF asked the divisional court to quash the chief constable's decision on two main grounds. First, they argued that by providing reduced police resources for the demonstrations the chief constable was in breach of his duty to keep the peace and enforce the law. Secondly, they argued that his decision amounted to restraint of trade between European member states. Although the court found that they could not interfere under domestic law (thus confirming the principle of constabulary independence), they did uphold the second point. However, the Court of Appeal reversed this ruling, finding that the chief constable was acting proportionately in the pursuit of the legitimate public policy objective of providing adequate levels of policing across the entire force area. Thus, the famous Blackburn ruling (*R.* v. *Metropolitan Police Commissioner, ex parte Blackburn* ([1968] All E.R. 763)) that in matters of law enforcement the chief constable was responsible 'to the law and to the law alone' remains 'pre-eminent as an authoritative statement of the constitutional status of the police in domestic law' (Dixon and Smith 1998: 422). The courts accepted the basic practical need for policing be rationed, and accepted that these rationing decisions (within reason) were to be the ultimate responsibility of the chief constable.[8] Dixon and Smith (1998) outline how judicial uncertainty about the exact nature of the police function serves to preserve a broad interpretation of 'constabulary independence' and hamper effective legal forms of organisational accountability. The lack of a statutory definition of the general duty of the police in England and Wales means that the courts find it difficult to hold the police to account for alleged breaches of that duty.

Although recent case law has thus supported 'constabulary independence', two significant threats have emerged to its central position within the system of police governance. First, the growing nationalisation of policing and the application of market-based reforms have constrained the autonomy of senior police officers to an extent that radical Labour councillors could only have dreamt about in the 1980s. Senior police officers have become increasingly constrained by a national performance framework. As Walker notes, during the 1990s, the 'immovable object of operational independence was buffeted by a sidewind carrying the irresistible force of the new managerialism' (2000: 296). Secondly, the Patten Commission on policing reform in Northern Ireland critically analysed the doctrine of constabulary independence and proposed replacing this with the notion of 'operational responsibility' (Patten 1999). This would protect the professional autonomy of senior police officers to take operational decisions but open those decisions to rigorous post hoc review by representative bodies. This combines prospective direction by the police with retrospective answerability to external bodies (Walker 2000). Although subsequent legislation did not explicitly recognise the concept of 'operational responsibility' it is highly significant that the recommendations of the Patten Commission were accepted in principle (Northern Ireland Office 2000).[9]

Nationalisation

The decline of local influences within the tripartite structure has been a well documented feature of police governance in England and Wales (Jones et al. 1994; Jones and Newburn 1997; Johnston 2000; Loveday 2000). In fact, it was argued that by the early 1990s the balance had tipped so far towards the centre that England and Wales had a de facto national police force (Reiner 1993).

Perhaps the key aspect of the nationalisation of police governance has been the growing influence of central government, visible in a number of ways. First, there was a significant reduction in the total number of police forces over the twentieth century, and successive reforms have made it progressively easier for the Home Secretary to require forces to amalgamate for reasons of efficiency (see Chapter 28). Secondly, since the early 1980s there has been a marked increase in the number and specificity of policy circulars from the Home Office (Jones et al. 1994). Although these circulars remain officially 'advisory', police forces have come under increasing pressure to regard them as de facto policy directives. The dominance of the centre has also been underlined in case law. Although the 1964 Act gave Police Authorities the primary duty for providing resources and equipment to their chief constables, the central provision of services has increasingly impinged upon this. In the late 1980s, Northumbria police authority sought judicial review of a Home Office circular that offered to supply CS gas or plastic bullets centrally to chief constables whose police authorities refused to provide such equipment. The Court of Appeal judgement in *R* v. *Secretary of State for the Home Department, ex parte Northumbria Police Authority* ([1988] 2 WLR 590) ruled that the Home Secretary had the right to provide plastic bullets to a chief constable in the face of opposition from the police authority. Another key aspect of increased central government influence concerns the fact that the Home Office has been increasingly able to shape the broader outlook of senior police officers through control of the central training institutions (Reiner 1995). These trends were consolidated and extended by reforms during the 1990s and after. The Police and Magistrates' Court Act 1994 allowed the Home Office to establish national policing objectives, and the Police Reform Act 2002 extends these powers with the advent of an annual 'national policing plan' (including a further body of related objectives and measurable targets) published by the Home Secretary (Home Office 2002b). In addition, a national 'Police Standards Unit' has been established with a remit to improve performance of local geographical policing units ('basic command units') across England and Wales.

The flip-side to this growing central control has been increasing limits on the influence of local police authorities. The early 1980s saw radical Labour administrations elected in many of the large urban areas of England covered by the then metropolitan counties. Many of these attempted to challenge their chief constables' autonomy using the powers they had under the 1964 Act, and also by setting up police monitoring groups (Regan 1991; McLaughlin 1994). These conflicts came to a head during the 1984–5 miners' strike, when some police authorities challenged the participation of their forces 'mutual aid' for the national anti-picketing operation and sought to limit their expenditure on such arrangements. In every case, the Home Secretary or the courts ruled in favour of chief constables. These more active attempts to influence policing policy came to an end with the abolition of the metropolitan counties in 1985. The metropolitan police authorities were replaced with 'joint boards', consisting of magistrates and councillors appointed from the constituent district councils within the metropolitan areas. The joint boards proved to be less cohesive and more open to police influence (Loveday 1991). Research carried out by the Policy Studies Institute during the early 1990s found that a number of factors lay behind the apparent lack of influence of local police authorities within the tripartite structure (Jones *et al.* 1994). These included limitations on their statutory powers, as interpreted by the courts and the Home Office. Although many chief constables did seek to consult with their police authorities in local policy-making, this was more a matter of 'wise statecraft' than any real local influence (Reiner 1991). However, the lack of statutory powers was not the only factor behind police authority impotence. Prior to 1995, many police authorities were too large and unwieldy to provide an effective input into policy-making. Police authorities were further hampered by a lack of information and expertise and their dependence upon chief constables for information about policy-making. In addition, police authority members often adopted a rather narrow view of their own role and in many areas offered unconditional support for, rather than an independent review of, the chief constable's decisions. Given this, the reforms introduced by the Police and Magistrates' Courts Act 1994 offered at least the potential for some reinvigoration of local police authority influence (Jones and Newburn 1995), although in practice it seems that the dominance of central influences has continued.

Another key aspect of nationalisation has been the increasing importance of the inspection process coupled with much more vigorous external scrutiny by bodies such as the Audit Commission. The HMIC was a key lever via which the Home Office exercised its duty to promote effectiveness and efficiency throughout police forces in England and Wales. During the 1980s, the role of the HMIC was substantially enhanced (Weatheritt 1986). The inspection process was standardised and strengthened, and younger chief constables were seconded to the inspectorate (along with senior 'lay' inspectors from outside the police service). HMIC reports were published from 1988 onwards and increasingly monitored the extent to which local forces were following national policy guidelines (Reiner 1991). The Audit Commission was established in 1982 with a remit to monitor and promote economy, efficiency and effectiveness in the management of local government. Since the mid-1980s, it has subjected a number of areas of policing to increasing scrutiny and it is widely recognised to have played an important role in promoting standard approaches between police forces.

The enhanced role in national policy-making of the Association of Chief Police Officers (ACPO) has been a key centralising influence. During the late 1980s, ACPO transformed itself into a more effective policy-making and lobbying body, appointing a full-time secretariat and establishing a number of policy committees each chaired by a chief constable. At about the same time, ACPO began to promote a collective 'national' voice on policing issues. Under the 'presumption in favour of compliance' (Savage et al. 1996) it was agreed that once a common policy is ratified by ACPO it is assumed that all chiefs are bound by it, unless they provide specific reasons for doing otherwise. The enhanced policy influence of ACPO was confirmed by research during the 1990s suggesting that the association were effectively 'joint authors' of many Home Office policy circulars (Jones et al. 1994).

A final key aspect of nationalisation has been the emergence of new institutions that potentially compromise the autonomy of local police forces. The National Criminal Intelligence Service (NCIS) was established in April 1992 (although not formally recognised by statute until the Police Act 1997). This incorporated a number of previously existing national units providing criminal intelligence reports to local police forces on matters such as football hooliganism and drug trafficking (Johnston 2000; see Chapters 8 and 18). The system of governance of NCIS mirrors the tripartite structure of control over local police forces. The three parties include the Director (chief constable rank), the Home Secretary and the NCIS 'service authority' (which includes, among others, some elected members from local police authorities). The Home Secretary has a dominant role within this structure since he appoints the chair of the service authority and sets annual objectives and performance targets (Johnston 2000; Walker 2000). The Police Act 1997 also established the National Crime Squad (NCS), whose governance structure is similar to (and overlaps with) that of NCIS, and many of the broad issues remain the same. A number of authors have expressed strong doubts about whether the 'service authorities' constitute an effective third strand in the governance arrangements for these national institutions (Johnston 2000; Walker 2000). It has been argued that the creation of these national policing institutions may be 'another step towards the eventual nationalisation of policing in the UK' (Uglow with Telford 1997: 36). However, others argue that the establishment of such institutions may be an inevitable and even welcome development in practical policing terms, the challenge for the future being to find more effective accountability mechanisms at the national level (Morgan and Newburn 1997; Johnston 2000).[10]

Although 'nationalising' trends have clearly been important, the emerging structure of governance still retains at least the potential for enhanced local influence. For example, there is some evidence that the 1990s reforms provided police authorities with potential opportunities for a more active input into policy-making (Jones and Newburn 1997; Savage et al. 2000). During recent years, police authorities have increasingly organised at the national level via a representative body, the Association of Police Authorities (APA). Savage et al. (2000: 40) have argued that the APA 'has embarked on a programme to make the [local police authorities] full, active and even "equal partners" in the tripartite framework'. Further research is required to explore what influence, if any, this has had upon policing at the local level. In addition, the emergence of Crime and Disorder Reduction Partnerships provides another potentially important local lever of influence over policing within the broader remit of community safety. Three further trends also complicate the picture. First, devolved government in Scotland, Wales and Northern Ireland may come to provide a significant regional tier of influence between provincial forces and the UK government. Secondly, the emergence of transnational policing institutions indicates the growing importance of governance arrangements above the state.[11] Thirdly, increasing national influence should not necessarily be equated with enhanced central government control. Indeed, there are now a number of national sources of influence that may challenge the dominance of central government (Savage et al. 2000). Not least among these is ACPO, which has provided a countervailing influence to the central government reform programmes.

Marketisation

The term 'marketisation' is used here in a general sense to denote the drive to improve cost efficiency and performance effectiveness via the imposition of market disciplines on the police service. This aspect of police reform has been closely linked with the long-term trend towards centralisation of control discussed above: 'In the absence of a conventional market in policing ... the fashioning of a common police product and the supply of methods of assessing its quality and cost effectiveness necessarily presupposed a high degree of central decision-making and standard-setting' (Walker 2000: 102). From the early 1980s on, successive Conservative governments applied market disciplines to a range of public services, although it was some time before these reforms impinged in any significant way on the police service. The process began when the government's 'Financial Management Initiative' (designed to promote the economy, efficiency and effectiveness of public services) was extended to the police service in 1983. This was the first significant attempt to bring about more central budgetary control of policing by linking increases in police staffing levels to evidence that police forces had 'civilianised' posts (Jones *et al.* 1994). From the mid-1980s the Audit Commission was increasingly active in promoting efficient and effective financial management within police forces. By the end of the 1980s, however, senior Conservative politicians were becoming frustrated with the apparent lack of results following major increases in public expenditure on the police (Baker 1993). During the early 1990s, a number of major reports began to map out a programme of radical reform for the police service. Two of these were of central importance – the 1993 Sheehy Inquiry into police responsibilities and rewards, and the white paper on police reform (that subsequently became the Police and Magistrates' Courts Bill).

The Sheehy Inquiry focused upon the internal organisation and structure of policing, and proposed a range of radical reforms. These included fixed-term contracts for all police officers, a performance-related element in pay, the ending of many forms of overtime payment, flatter organisational structures and the abolition of certain ranks (Jones and Newburn 1997). The proposals met with a storm of protest from the police staff associations, who succeeded in neutralising many of its more radical elements. During the same year, the government produced its white paper on police reform (Home Office 1993) containing proposals radically to overhaul the framework for external police governance in England and Wales. The white paper displayed a 'rigorous instrumentalism' with its focus upon providing the most appropriate institutional framework of police governance for promoting efficient and effective service delivery (Walker 2000: 98). When the subsequent Police and Magistrates' Courts Act 1994 was eventually passed into law, its provisions had been substantially modified from those originally proposed in the white paper. Nevertheless, the reforms of the 1990s retained a substantive element of 'marketisation' that was to be subsequently confirmed and expanded under later governments. Of particular importance in this regard were the following:

- The purchaser–provider split between police authority and force.
- National policing objectives and key performance indicators.
- Costed 'business plans' for policing.
- Reduction in size of local police authorities and the appointment of independent members.
- Sponsorship and charging for police services.
- Devolution of budgetary controls.

These themes have accelerated under New Labour. For example from April 2000 the 'Best Value' framework has been applied to police authorities and forces. The legislation requires them to review their service delivery over a five-year cycle and apply what are called the '4Cs': 'challenging' whether a particular service is required in the first place, 'consulting' about service provision, 'comparing' the service with other providers and reviewing 'competitive' alternative providers (Leigh *et al.* 1999). These continued pressures towards marketisation have been supplemented by the significant developments within the Police Reform Act 2002. This applied an even more stringent national planning framework and established the Police Standards Unit to promote performance improvements. All this has been accompanied by an ever more strident rhetoric on the part of government ministers expressing frustration at levels of police performance and the need for more radical reform. In early 2002, Home Secretary David Blunkett fired a shot across the bows of the Metropolitan Police, by publicly stating that if the force continued to fail to deal with spiralling levels of street crime, he would take action to replace the commissioner (Travis 2002). The Street Crime Action Group, established in March 2002, involved more direct intervention in day-to-day policing by senior government ministers than had ever been contemplated under Conservative administrations (Loveday and Reid 2003). In response to the Prime Minister's public undertaking to have street crime 'under control' by September 2002, senior officers in ten selected force areas were required to report on a regular basis to government ministers on progress towards targets (Home Office 2002a).

Direct privatisation – in the sense of hiving off public police functions to commercial providers – has had limited impact in the field of core policing services.[12] However, the expansion of policing providers outside of Home Office police forces has been widely noted. Although we will consider this aspect of marketisation in more detail below, it is worth noting here that the government has introduced a range of provisions relevant to this 'market' for policing services. In particular, it has introduced a system of national regulation for the contract security industry (Button and George 2001) and expressly recognised the existence of an 'extended police family'. As noted above, the Police Reform Act encourages alternative forms of patrol provision such as 'neighbourhood warden' schemes and the possible addition of 'community support officers' within police forces.

Pluralisation

A number of commentators have highlighted a 'pluralisation' of policing visible in many western countries (Johnston 2000; Shearing 2000). This includes the expansion of the commercial security sector (Jones and Newburn 1998; Johnston 2000); new forms of public sector policing provision such as local authority patrol forces and municipal police forces (see Chapter 7); the hiring of commercial security by local authorities (Loader 2000); the increase in reported examples of informal policing such as vigilantism (Johnston 1996); and, finally, the emergence of new transnational policing forms above the state (Sheptycki 2000; see Chapter 6). Criminologists have also drawn attention to the policing roles played by a host of regulatory agencies attached to national and local government such as environmental health officers (Johnston 1992). The pluralised provision of policing services poses significant challenges for those concerned to bring policing (as a whole) under the direction and control of democratic influences. As Loader (2000: 324) has argued, 'the questions . . . that have long vexed discussions of police policy and (mal)practice in liberal democratic societies press themselves with renewed force under the altered conditions of plural policing'. Much of this chapter demonstrates the difficulties encountered in framing effective forms of accountability and control over the public police. These problems are multiplied when considering the problem of devising new institutions of accountability that ensure the range of forms of policing provided by bodies other than state constabularies.

Loader (2000) has proposed the establishment of local, regional and national 'policing commissions' with a statutory responsibility to monitor and direct *policing* policy as exercised by a wide range of 'policing' agencies and institutions. Clifford Shearing (2000) has similarly argued strongly for a 'nodal' conception of police governance. Shearing's involvement on the Patten Commission was probably crucial in its recommendation for the establishment of 'district policing partnership boards' – a committee of the local authority that would have the power to 'buy in' extra local policing resources from providers other than the public police. It also recommended that at force level, a 'Policing Board' (not a 'Police Board') should be established that would have substantially more powers than the existing police authority (Walker 2000). It was suggested that this body might be given responsibility for regulating all policing providers, including commercial firms, and co-ordinating provision across policing networks. The government's legislative response to the Patten Commission ultimately held back from some of these elements. However, although perhaps its time had not yet come, the model laid down by Patten provides a sensible way of approaching the problem of governing local security networks. This requires the effective management of the diversity of policing provision and the maintenance of standards of accountability and equity (Johnston 2000). It seems clear that a more active local input from elected local bodies is required. Such bodies should have both a general responsibility for public safety provision and the possibility of funding activities at the local level.

However, some notes of caution should be sounded here. First, there are significant differences in the nature and degree of 'pluralisation', within and between nation-states (Jones and Newburn 2002). While governance and accountability mechanisms should clearly fit the policing world within which they operate, they will in turn work to shape that world. The introduction of radical reforms – based on the assumption of significant and essentially new plural forms of policing – may effectively institutionalise a quasi-market in policing services and actually further encourage fragmentation and inequity. Secondly, proposals to introduce broader 'policing' accountability mechanisms require more explicit definitions of which functions carried out by which bodies are to be regulated. For example, it seems quite sensible that the operation of contract security guards in public places (or semi-public places such as shopping centres) is an important part of the wider public's experience of policing. But it is less easy to justify political oversight of non-state policing activities that appear to have little impact on the public realm (Jones and Newburn 1998). What is clear is that debates on accountability and governance need to pay more attention to plural forms of policing, both in terms of the co-ordination and effectiveness of policing overall, and in terms of equitable service delivery. There is clearly a variety of policing activities – undertaken by a range of public and private bodies – with potentially significant impacts on the lives of citizens. These activities, as well as those of the public police, should be subject to public regulation and scrutiny. The difficulties of achieving this in practice are, however, complex and daunting.

The democratic framework of police governance

By way of conclusion, this section briefly examines recent developments in the governance of policing in England and Wales in light of the 'democratic criteria' outlined earlier.[13] Despite the gloomy predictions that often accompany major reform, there have been some positive developments since the 1960s. Of course, successive governments' reform programmes have not been without fault, and in particular there is much to criticise in the continued obsession with a narrow performance model. However, at the same time it is hard to deny that there have been some significant improvements in policing, and its framework of governance, over the past 40 years or so.

In terms of *equity*, while trends since the 1960s have been disappointing, this relates primarily to factors outside the immediate framework of policing. Increasing inequality and social polarisation have arisen from wider socioeconomic trends and government policies. Within the context of policing, it has long been noted that services are unequally distributed both in terms of police protection and in the unequal targeting of law enforcement. For example, despite considerable official concern in the arena of race relations, policing still has significantly different impacts on different ethnic groups (see Chapter 21). There is the potential within the reforms outlined above to entrench such inequities. For example, the commitment to a crude 'performance' model based around reduction of particular categories of street crime is likely to enhance rather than reduce inequalities. However, improving the effectiveness of service delivery need not necessarily conflict with equity. New realist criminology highlighted that it is disadvantaged communities whose lives are most blighted by experiences of crime and disorder (Young 1997). These groups have much to gain from efficient and effective policing, so long as such services are concerned with equity. The introduction of performance targets can be used to channel more police attention and resources to disadvantaged victims, for example those of domestic or racial violence (Jones and Newburn 1997). Finally, increased central influence need not necessarily conflict with equity. For example, central government has played an important role in promoting the Macpherson agenda, although clearly much remains to be done in this regard. Nevertheless, there are potential problems with current trends. The continued official adherence to a particularly vigorous form of managerialism threatens further to dilute the impact of local representative bodies at the same time as over-focusing police attention on crude indicators of crime control. Market-based reforms and pluralised policing may increase inequity between local areas (for example, between those local authorities that can afford to pay for extra 'community support officers' or neighbourhood wardens and those who cannot). We still lack accountability institutions at the local level with the necessary power and expertise to ensure that state-run policing is delivered equitably, and that plural policing forms do not simply further polarise provision.

As noted above, questions of efficient and effective *service delivery* have been at the heart of reforms of police governance since the 1980s. It would be difficult to argue that this has had entirely negative effects. Police managers have become significantly more accountable for the efficient and effective use of public resources (Reiner 1993). However, a major problem exists in the managerialist model of 'police performance' that has been uncritically accepted by both Conservative and Labour administrations, and its false implication that policing is a politically neutral exercise. As Walker (2000) points out, performance audit may obscure but cannot circumvent wider questions about policing priorities, styles and methods. Arguably, consumerist pressures have weakened the importance of local democratic deliberations about policing in the arena where they are most important. While central government – as the provider of the overwhelming proportion of police resources – has a legitimate interest in ensuring that these resources are used as effectively as possible, the lack of local democratic deliberation about policing undermines this effectiveness in the longer term. The instrumental achievement of police efficiency and effectiveness may actually be better served by more vigorous local democratic input into policing than by a centrally driven performance model (Walker 2000: 147). There remains much in policing that is not easily captured via routine performance indicators. While they provide a useful aid to democratic accountability, they cannot be a substitute for it.

In a number of ways, policing in England and Wales has become increasingly *responsive* to external bodies. The expansion of central government influence has been well documented, but the police are also increasingly responsive to central bodies other than the Home Office within the national policing policy community (Savage *et al.* 2000). In addition, increasing emphasis on 'consultation' has in some areas led to increased responsiveness to local needs (Jones and Newburn 2001). Nevertheless, the overall picture is arguably one of a declining responsiveness to representative bodies, in particular, locally elected ones. Although local police authorities were provided with significant new powers during the 1990s, these bodies had a substantially reduced elected element. In addition, their influence appears to have been mainly channelled into promoting the same performance model that has been driving central government reforms. Responsiveness to local representative bodies was explicitly downgraded by these reforms and set against what was seen as the more important goal of achieving effective and efficient service delivery. However, it is worth re-emphasising the point that these two should not be seen as mutually exclusive.

A concern with the *distribution of power* has been visible throughout the history of police governance. A key aim of the tripartite structure was to institutionalise a system of countervailing powers over policing. However, this has also been set against the aim of effective service delivery, which has been the primary justification for the growing influence of national institutions. However, as Savage *et al.* (2000) note, this has not resulted in a straightforward concentration in the power of central government. Rather, it has seen the emergence of competing centres of power at the national level, including ACPO and the APA. The pluralisation of policing has also distributed power over service provision, with the emergence of alternative providers that may be more directly accountable to the communities they serve (Johnston and Shearing 2002). However, once again there remains a crucial democratic deficit at the local level. Although there have been opportunities to enhance local influences over policing, these have yet to be grasped in a coherent way. Police authorities are organised at a broad regional level, and their elected component has been substantially reduced. Furthermore, they remain focused primarily upon performance issues concerning the public police and have little influence over forms of policing other than those provided by traditional constabularies. Crime and disorder partnerships may eventually provide an opportunity for improved local democratic co-ordination of policing and community safety activities across the many public and private providers, but at present this remains hope rather than reality (Crawford and Lister 2003).

A central part of the drive for improved service delivery has been the need for better public *information* about the funding, expenditure, activities and outputs of policing. There has also been a continued increase in the productivity of policy and academic research on policing, which has enhanced the amount of information available. The development of the 'marketisation' policies outlined above has required a more rigorous measurement of police performance and a costing of police activities. However, too much information, or information of the wrong sort, is unhelpful to a system of democratic governance. An earlier study of police governance suggested that levels of performance information 'have gone beyond the point where it clarifies matters for the citizen, and is actually in danger of confusing the citizen' (Jones and Newburn 1997: 215). While such information may be a necessary component of democratic accountability, it is certainly not a sufficient one. Information needs of police managers and police authority members clearly overlap to a degree, but they are not identical. It is important to recognise the 'political' uses to which crude performance statistics can be put (see, for example, the recent debate over government claims regarding its Street Crime Initiative). Although the amount of information concerning policing has clearly grown, along with a wider ability to understand and interpret it, recent reforms have done little to address a major problem identified in earlier work. The key mechanism of local police governance, the police authority, still does not have sufficient resources of staff or expertise to provide an effective independent review of, and input into, local policing policies.

As noted in earlier studies, *participation* has often been the key democratic criterion applied in many discussions of police accountability. However, the most appropriate mode of participation in deliberations about policing policy is a difficult and contentious question. Radical analyses still tend to place participation at the centre of reform suggestions – for example, Loader's (2000) proposal for the establishment of policing commissions at the local, regional and national level. This places emphasis on a participatory approach to democracy, actively seeking to incorporate the views of disadvantaged populations in local decisions about policing policy, and obliging senior police officers to respond to such views. Johnston (2000) has also argued for the need to democratise local police governance but accepts that the fragmented state of local civic institutions makes this difficult. The challenge is to develop vibrant local democratic influences over policing styles and priorities in the face of the weakened influence and popularity of local government and local civic society in the UK, and the declining share of police expenditure that comes from local taxation. Nevertheless, especially given the discussions regarding police effectiveness above, it is hard to disagree with Walker's (2000) call for a 'less ambivalent' approach to the virtues of local democracy. Clearly, this cannot be divorced from a discussion of the vibrancy and effectiveness of local democratic service provision in general. As Johnston (2000) has argued, policing policies need to be integrated more firmly within wider debates about social and economic security.

This brief overview of 'democratic criteria' suggests mixed developments in the system of police governance in England and Wales over recent years. In some ways, the police are more accountable than they have ever been – they are certainly under greater scrutiny. Media and public debate about policing has become more informed and critical. The gaze of external bodies such as the Audit Commission (and more recently, the Police Standards Unit) has become ever more intense, coupled with a rigorous measurement of elements of what the police do and how they do it. Police officers are better trained and more politically informed than in previous eras. In particular, most basic command unit commanders are acutely aware of the need for dialogue with the key constituencies on their patch, and many make energetic attempts to consult as widely as possible. These developments have many positive aspects. Nevertheless, the recent history of police governance also throws up some worrying trends. Of particular concern are the continued expansion of national influences at the expense of local democratic institutions; the pressure on the police to chase crude performance targets; persistent inequalities in the policing experiences of different social groups; and the twin threats of inequity and ineffectiveness posed by the pluralisation of policing.

To conclude, perhaps three key points should be made. First, future arrangements for governance and accountability of the police must take account of plural forms of policing. State constabularies will probably remain central within the network of agencies contributing to public safety and security, at least for the foreseeable future. However, we must find more effective and equitable ways of co-ordinating and controlling the plethora of 'policing' activities, many of which are far from new, that contribute to local security networks. Secondly, these arrangements need to address the emerging democratic deficit at the local level. For reasons outlined at the beginning of this chapter, much concern about crime and insecurity is firmly rooted in the characteristics of local areas. For similar reasons, sources of legitimacy and trust of policing bodies are also fundamentally local. The development of vibrant democratic fora that can provide a positive input into local policy decisions regarding policing and security provision must be a key objective of any reform to the current system of police governance. Finally, whatever the precise shape of the institutional infrastructure of police governance, it should embody and promote an explicit set of 'democratic' values. An important example of such an approach to police governance is provided by the Patten Commission (1999) which explicitly adopted a human rights framework as the basis of police reform. It argued for the adoption of an explicit code of policing ethics (Chapter 23) and also for arrangements that would internalise the protection of human rights as the fundamental basis of all policing. The central premise of the Patten Report (1999: 18) – that the basic purpose of democratic policing is 'the protection and vindication of the human rights of all' – has significance not just for policing in Northern Ireland but in England and Wales, and beyond.

Selected further reading

For a more detailed discussion of some of the issues raised in this chapter, the reader is referred to Walker's excellent analysis of police governance: *Policing in a Changing Constitutional Order* (2000). This book addresses an important omission in much British writing on police governance in that it covers the distinctive systems of Scotland and Northern Ireland as well as that of England and Wales. Lustgarten's *The Governance of Police* (1986) remains the central legal critique of the English and Welsh system of police governance up until the early 1980s. The Patten Report (1999) provides important insights into the accountability of policing and many of the issues it raises apply universally. Finally, a significant omission from the chapter concerns the role of complaints systems within the wider framework of police governance. To address this gap, the reader is referred to the comprehensive collection edited by Goldsmith and Lewis – *Civilian Oversight of Policing* (2000).

Notes

1 Space restrictions mean that this chapter will continue the Anglo-centric focus of much criminological writing on police accountability in the UK. For a comprehensive analysis of UK police governance arrangements including the distinctive Scottish and Northern Irish systems, see Walker (2000).

2 This is not intended to downplay the importance of the pluralising trends identified in recent literature. However, there is a tendency to overstate the extent and novelty of the 'transformation' of policing arrangements in many modern industrial societies, and underemphasise the abiding importance of state-provided policing arrangements (Jones and Newburn 2002).

3 Significant though these trends clearly are, it is important to note that the 'new governance' literature is not without its critics, many of whom argue that the fragmentation of the modern nation-state has been overstated. For example, Atkinson and Coleman (1992: 166) have been critical of what they call a 'slavish devotion to pluralist images of the state' and highlight the continued importance of national state institutions in the development of policy.

4 Likewise, we do not have the space to consider the range of other factors that form an important part of the web of mechanisms that might render policing 'accountable' in a broad sense. This includes the 'watchdog' function of the media, and the general openness and visibility of the police organisation.

5 Taking account of central government support grants to local authorities, the actual proportion of central government funding of the police service has risen to over 90 per cent.

6 This Act was arguably of much greater significance in the arena of *individual* police accountability. It introduced a system of regulation of police powers relating to criminal investigation and stop and search (Maguire 2002).

7 The Act also had important implications for the individual dimension of police accountability in that it established new independent arrangements for the investigation of complaints against the police.

8 Although individual forms of accountability are not the focus of this chapter, Dixon and Smith (1998) review several recent cases that demonstrate how the civil law has increasingly been used as a remedy for police misconduct. In particular, civil actions have been seen as an increasingly popular alternative to police complaints systems as a means of redress for police misconduct.

9 The Patten Commission also made a number of other highly significant recommendations regarding police accountability at the local level, and concerning the pluralisation of policing, which will be considered later.

10 Another key development in terms of national policing institutions concerns the role of the security services in 'normal' crime control. The Security Services Act 1996 laid down provisions for the active collaboration of security services in support of the police and other agencies in the prevention and detection of serious crime. Concerns have been raised about the 'hidden' nature of the security services involvement, and the lack of transparency and accountability that this entails (Walker 2000).

11 For a discussion of the problems of transnational police governance, see Walker (2000; see Chapter 6).

12 Although the establishment of the Posen Review of police core and ancillary tasks during the 1990s was accompanied by rumours of radical proposals (such as the privatisation of traffic policing), in the event the final report was rather cautious and restricted itself to rather uncontroversial functions such as escorting heavy loads or the provision of canteen services (Home Office 1995).

13 This discussion does not cover *redress* because the primary focus of this chapter is upon the collective organisational aspects of police accountability.

References

Atkinson, M. and Coleman, W. (1992) 'Policy Networks, Policy Communities and the Problems of Governance', *Governance*, 5(2): 154–80.

Baker, K. (1993) *The Turbulent Years: My Life in Politics*. London: Faber & Faber.

Button, M. and George, B. (2001) 'Government regulation in the United Kingdom security industry: the myth of non-regulation', *Security Journal*, 14: 55–66.

Cohen, S. (1985) *Visions of Social Control*. Cambridge: Polity Press.

Crawford, A. and Lister, S. (2003) 'Plural policing: policing beyond the police in England'. Paper presented at the Canadian Law Commission Conference, 'In search of security', Montreal, 20 February.

Day, P. and Klein, R. (1987) *Accountabilities*. London: Tavistock.

Dixon, W. and Smith, G. (1998) 'Laying down the law: the police, the courts and legal accountability', *International Journal of the Sociology of Law*, 26: 419–35.

Garland, D. (1996) 'The limits of the sovereign state', *British Journal of Criminology*, 36(4) pp. 445–71.

Goldsmith, A. and Lewis, C. (eds) (2000) *Civilian Oversight of Policing: Governance, Democracy and Human Rights*. Portland, Oregon: Hart.

Home Office (1993) *Inquiry into Police Responsibilities and Rewards*. London: HMSO.

Home Office (1995) *Review of Core and Ancillary Tasks: Final Report*. London: HMSO.

Home Office (2002a) *Delivering the Street Crime Initiative: Partnership in Operation*. London: HMSO.

Home Office (2002b) *The National Policing Plan 2003–2006*. London: Home Office.

Johnston, L. (1992) *The Rebirth of Private Policing*. London: Routledge.

Johnston, L. (1996) 'What is vigilantism?', *British Journal of Criminology*, 36(2): 220–36.

Johnston, L. (2000) *Policing Britain: Risk, Security and Governance*. London: Longman.

Johnston, L. and Shearing, C. (2002) *Governing Security: Explorations in Policing and Justice*. London: Routledge.

Jones, T. and Newburn, T. (1995) 'Local government and policing: arresting the decline of local influence', *Local Government Studies*, 21(3): 448–60.

Jones, T. and Newburn, T. (1997) *Policing after the Act: Police Governance after the Police and Magistrates' Courts Act 1994*. London: Policy Studies Institute.

Jones, T. and Newburn, T. (1998) *Private Security and Public Policing*. Oxford: Clarendon Press.

Jones, T. and Newburn, T. (2001) *Widening Access: Improving Relations with 'Hard to Reach Groups'*. London: Home Office.

Jones, T. and Newburn, T. (2002) 'The transformation of policing? Understanding current trends in policing systems', *British Journal of Criminology*, 42(1): 129–46.

Jones, T., Newburn, T. and Smith, D. (1994) *Democracy and Policing*. London: Policy Studies Institute.

Jones, T., Newburn, T. and Smith, D. (1996) 'Policing and the idea of democracy', *British Journal of Criminology*, 36(2): 182–98.

Leigh, A., Mundy, G. and Tuffin, R. (1999) *Best Value Policing: Making Preparations. Police Research Series Paper* 116. London: Home Office.

Loader, I. (2000) 'Plural policing and democratic governance', *Social and Legal Studies*, 9(3): 323–45.

Loader, I. and Walker, N. (2001) 'Policing as a public good: reconstituting the connections between policing and state', *Theoretical Criminology*, 5(1): 9–35.

Loveday, B. (1991) 'The new police authorities in the metropolitan counties', *Policing and Society*, 1(3): 193–212.

Loveday, B. (2000) 'New directions in accountability', in F. Leishman *et al.* (eds) *Core Issues in Policing*. Harlow: Longman, 213–31.

Loveday, B. and Reid, A. (2003) *Going Local: Who Should Run Britain's Police?* London: Policy Exchange.

Lustgarten, L. (1986) *The Governance of Police*. London: Sweet & Maxwell.

Maguire, M. (2002) 'Regulating the police station: the case of the Police and Criminal Evidence Act 1984', in M. McConville and G. Wilson (eds) *The Handbook of the Criminal Justice Process*. Oxford: Oxford University Press, 75–97.

Marshall, G. (1978) 'Police accountability revisited', in D. Butler and A.H. Halsey (eds) *Policy and Politics*. London: Macmillan, 51–65.

McLaughlin, E. (1994) *Community, Policing and Accountability*. Aldershot: Avebury.

Morgan, R. (1986) 'Police consultative groups: the implications for the governance of the police', *Political Quarterly*, 57(1).

Morgan, R. (1992) 'Talking about policing', in D. Downes (ed.) *Unravelling Criminal Justice*. London: Macmillan, 165–83.

Morgan, R. and Newburn, T. (1997) *The Future of Policing*. Oxford: Oxford University Press.

Newburn, T. (1998) 'Tackling youth crime and reforming youth justice: the origins and nature of New Labour policy', *Policy Studies*, 19(3/4): 199–214.

Newburn, T. and Jones, T. (1996) 'Police accountability', in W. Saulsbury *et al.* (eds) *Themes in Contemporary Policing*. London: Policy Studies Institute/Police Foundation, 120–32.

Northern Ireland Office (2000) *Patten Report: Secretary of State's Implementation Plan*. Belfast: HMSO.

Patten, C. (1999) *A New Beginning for Policing in Northern Ireland: The Report of the Independent Commission on Policing for Northern Ireland*. Belfast: HMSO.

Rawlings, P. (2002) *Policing: A Short History*. Cullompton: Willan.

Regan, D. (1991) *Local Government versus the Police: The Rise and Fall of Police Monitoring in Britain*. London: The Hampden Trust.

Reiner, R. (1991) *Chief Constables*. Oxford: Oxford University Press.

Reiner, R. (1993) 'Police accountability: principles, patterns and practices', in R. Reiner and S. Spencer (eds) *Accountable Policing: Effectiveness, Empowerment and Equity*. London: Institute for Public Policy Research, 1–23.

Reiner, R. (1995) 'Counting the coppers', in P. Stenning (ed.) *Accountability for Criminal Justice: Selected Essays*. Toronto: University of Toronto Press, 74–92.

Reiner, R. (2000) *The Politics of the Police*. Oxford: Oxford University Press.

Rhodes, R. (1997) *Understanding Governance: Policy Networks, Governance, Reflexivity and Accountability*. Buckingham: Open University Press.

Rose, N. and Miller, P. (1992) 'Political power beyond the state: problematics of government', *British Journal of Sociology*, 43(2): pp. 173–205.

Savage, S., Charman, S. and Cope, S. (1996) 'Police governance, the Association of Chief Police Officers and constitutional change', *Public Policy and Administration*, 11(2): 92–106.

Savage, S., Charman, S. and Cope, S. (2000) 'The policy-making context: who shapes policing policy?', in F. Leishman *et al.* (eds) *Core Issues in Policing*. Harlow: Longman, 30–51.

Scarman, Lord (1981) *The Brixton Disorders 10–12 April 1981: Report of an Inquiry by Lord Scarman*. London: HMSO.

Shearing, C. (2000) ' "A new beginning" for policing', *Journal of Law and Society*, 27(3): 386–93.

Sheptycki, J. (ed.) (2000) *Issues in Transnational Policing*. London: Routledge.

Stenning, P. (ed.) (1995) *Accountability for Criminal Justice: Selected Essays*. Toronto: University of Toronto Press.

Travis, A. (2002) 'Met police get six month deadline to tackle crime', *Guardian*, 15 February.

Uglow, S. with Telford, V. (1997) *The Police Act 1997*. London: Jordans.

Walker, N. (2000) *Policing in a Changing Constitutional Order*. London: Sweet & Maxwell.

Weatheritt, M. (1986) *Innovations in Policing*. Beckenhem: Croom Helm.

Young, J. (1997) 'Left realist criminology', in M. Maguire *et al.* (eds) *The Oxford Handbook of Criminology*. Oxford: Oxford University Press, 473–98.

Chapter 25

Leadership and performance management

Matt Long

Introduction

'Leadership' is 'one of the most observed and least understood phenomena on earth' (Burns 1978: 2). According to Bryman (1986: 16), 'Of all the confounding areas in social psychology, leadership theory undoubtedly contends for top nomination. And, ironically, probably more has been written and less is known about leadership than about any other topic in the behavioural sciences'. He maintains (1986: 1) that 'The basic problem is that not only is there a range of definitions, but there is also no consensually agreed one'. For the purposes of this chapter we will adopt Rauch and Behling's (1984: 46) definition which sees leadership 'as the process of influencing the activities of an organised group toward achievement'.

The chapter explores current issues in public sector leadership and their impact on the police organisation in the UK. The shift from 'welfare' to 'managerialism' is examined and illustrated by the example of the philosophy and practice of Best Value, and the recent publication of the first-ever National Policing Plan. The chapter then moves on to consider the challenges for police leadership posed by the performance culture engendered by the 'new' managerialism and explores the ways in which higher police training has attempted to respond to these challenges. The perpetual tensions between police 'management' and 'leadership' are then explored with reference to the discourse of 'competency' and the associated framework, which has been more recently developed.

Crisis in public sector leadership?

The debate over how the public services should be led, managed and governed has been raging during New Labour's second term in government. The extent to which the private sector should have a role in the running of public sector organisations such as health, education and policing is particularly contentious. In early 2002, the Prime Minister Tony Blair criticised the fiercest union critics of public service reform as 'conservatives' and 'wreckers' (see Wintour 2002: 2). In response, the general secretary of the TUC, John Monks, suggested the statements were 'bizarre' and 'juvenile'. Just two weeks later, the *Guardian* carried the headline 'Public sector mutiny' (Carvel 2002: 1), in reference to an open letter to the PM, signed by the Metropolitan police commissioner, Sir John Stevens, and a group of senior public sector managers. The letter contained a message warning of an impending collapse of morale among public servants due to media criticism, political interference and added 'red tape' caused by a more intensive inspection culture.

The rise of audit and inspection across the pubic sector (see Clarke *et al.* 2000) is characteristic of a political culture which is less trusting of professional public sector workers and which challenges their autonomy and claims to continued self-regulation. Public sector leaders who are deemed to be 'failing' in their requirements to deliver 'value for money' to citizens, who are now being treated increasingly as 'consumers' of public services, run the risk of being replaced by 'hit teams'. We have, for instance, seen the 'superhead' system introduced into schools to replace headteachers deemed to be 'failing' according to the managerial calculus of audit and inspection. The sense of 'crisis' in public sector leadership is most evident in New Labour's proposals for a far greater role to be given to private business in the running of the public sector. Since New Labour's re-election in 2001, government ministers have expanded the opportunities for private firms to build hospitals and manage NHS surgical units as well as taking over 'failing' schools and the rebuilding of the London Underground. Police leadership has to be viewed in the context of the political elite's perception that there is a problem in public sector leadership more generally.

A crisis in police leadership?

The paramount importance of police leadership is almost impossible to overestimate at the beginning of the twenty-first century. The observations made by Sir William Macpherson in his inquiry into the murder of Stephen Lawrence and the subsequent police investigation (1999: 317) suggesting the police service delivered had been characterised by 'professional incompetence' and a 'lack of direction and organisation' were damning (Alderson 2003). Coupled with this, a look at any of the recent Basic Command Unit (BCU) inspections conducted by Her Majesty's Inspectorate of Constabulary (see, for example, HMIC, 2001a) reveals 'leadership' to be the 'critical success factor' in BCU performance. The requirements of New Labour's Best Value regime, underpinned by the Local Government Act 1999, effectively mean that police leaders have to be more 'visible' than ever before (see, for example, HMIC 2001b). While in narrow, legalistic terms, the Local Government Act 1999 puts the onus of responsibility on police authorities to secure the delivery of 'continuous improvements' in performance (Dobson 2000), in practice the wider culture of the Best Value regime requires police leaders and managers to be far more active and interventionist than they have been in the past. This requires a shift from 'transactional' to 'transformational' leadership (Drodge and Murphy 2002), where leaders have to understand the importance of developing their own 'emotional intelligence' (Goleman 1995). This shift is itself underpinned by the belief that 'intelligent leadership' (Hooper and Potter 2000) should be less about command and control and more about empowering others. Moreover, if leadership is a genuine attempt at culture creation and reformation, then, according to Schein (1992: 374), 'leadership can occur anywhere in the organisation'.

To understand this shift, one must first consider exactly how a society which is characterised by an unwritten 'welfare settlement' came to be replaced by one characterised by more 'managerial' modes of governance (Clarke and Newman 1997).

The shift from welfare to managerialism

The growth of the welfare state and the corresponding social settlement upon which it was founded is located historically in the context of political consensus shared by the parliamentary parties in the 1950s and 1960s. As well as the adoption of Keynesian economic principles, which reaffirmed the belief in the pursuit of full employment, the unwritten 'social contract' was one which implied the belief in a certain level of public provision through state intervention. A classic example was the Beveridge Report's attack on the 'five giants of Want, Disease, Idleness, Ignorance and Squalor' through, among other things, the establishment of a National Health Service (Timmins 1995).

This settlement required a commitment to both bureaucratic administration and professionalism. This period of consensus came under severe challenge in the 1970s due to the OPEC oil crisis and the Winter of Discontent. According to Halsey (1988: 185), 'Mrs. Thatcher had ridden to power in 1979 on a national mood of disenchantment with the welfare state'. The policies of the first Thatcher government in particular were based upon 'a new economic calculus which treated public spending as a drain on the competitive viability of individuals, corporations and nations' (Clarke and Newman 1997: 9). Economically, state intervention was criticised on the grounds that administrative and bureaucratic methods were inferior to markets as a means of allocating resources. Secondly, on more philosophical grounds, the revival of the so-called 'Victorian values' of thrift and self-help meant that the moral basis of the welfare state was also questioned.

The political programme of the New Right was aimed at constructing a new relationship between the state and social welfare. According to Clarke and Newman (1997: 14), 'The special contribution of the New Right in Britain was to tell a particular – and particularly effective – story about these conditions of crisis and to lay the ground for the reconstruction of the relationship between the state and social welfare'. Thatcher and the Conservatives argued that Britain had become the sick man of Europe when the Labour administration under Callaghan was forced to go to the IMF for help in the late 1970s, and it was specifically 'over-manning' in the public sector which was presented as being one of the major reasons why this had occurred. Public sector employees, previously viewed as relatively selfless professionals, were progressively redefined as self-interested and inefficient 'empire builders'.

State intervention in the marketplace was condemned as a 'distortion' and good governance was equated with less government. In this emerging model, politicians increasingly sought to exercise power by setting policy (steering) rather than actually delivering the services (rowing) themselves (Osborne and Gaebler 1992). Thatcher's political programme was underpinned by what Gamble (1994: 35–6) refers to as, 'the doctrine of the free economy and the strong state'. As well as the pursuit of monetarist economic policies, the latter part of the doctrine involved the re-exertion of state authority over the 'new class' of professional public sector employees (e.g. nurses, teachers and police officers) who were seen to have a vested interest in the continuance of bureaucratic public sector practices. The emergent form of governance has been termed the 'new public management' (see Clarke and Newman 1997).

What is the new public management?

According to Wright (2000: 291), 'In policing, modern rational management has been promoted as the method through which an economical, efficient and effective police is to be achieved'. While he credits management gurus such as Drucker (1964) with driving a 'results-oriented approach' (Wright 2000: 291), it was in fact the work of Lubans and Edgar (1979) which first suggested objective-setting in the specific context of policing. The new public management (NPM) began with an attempt to introduce an agenda around 'economy', 'efficiency' and 'effectiveness' into the governance of public sector organisations through Home Office circular 114 of 1983. It meant a shift away from a focus on 'inputs' in favour of measuring what public sector organisations actually produced, or 'outputs'. In order for this to be achieved, 'outputs', were primarily to be assessed through measurement, according to quantifiable, numerical criteria. This was further consolidated legislatively by means of the Police and Magistrates Courts Act 1994 (see Chapter 24). This process was by no means specific to the UK, being particularly associated with the development of Compstat in New York City in the 1990s, whereby local commanders were held to account for the performance of their precincts (Silverman 2001). As a result of such developments, public sector organisations, including the police, could be ranked according to the performance indicators by which their relative 'success' or 'failure' were benchmarked. There was, furthermore, an attempt to get public sector organisations to mirror elements of the practice of private sector organisations by focusing on what were perceived to be their main priorities (Home Office 1995). This was reinforced by attempts to contract out to the private sector (see Chapter 5) so-called 'non-core' activities, under a regime referred to as compulsory competitive tendering.

Waters (2000: 265) points out that 'up until 1987 there was greater managerial emphasis on reducing costs of services and controlling inputs, but that after 1987 the emphasis on quality and consumer demands came to the fore'. Following the Operational Policing Review and the Association of Chief Police Officers' (ACPO) strategic policy document, *Setting the Standards for*

Policing: Meeting Community Expectation, both in 1990, the national Quality of Service programme in the police was launched. A key element of the ACPO initiative in the early to mid-1990s was the application of performance indicators, which attempted to assess customer satisfaction, and six indicators proposed by ACPO were incorporated into the Audit Commission's suite of indicators in 1996–7.

After replacing the Conservatives in government in 1997, New Labour took the view that public sector organisations should be less autonomous and more interdependent, in order that improvements in social outcomes be achieved. Underpinning managerial reform was the belief that 'citizens' should be given a more active role in articulating their needs in terms of service provision. By treating them in ways similar to that which a private business treats, or is believed to treat, its customers, it was felt that they would become more genuine stakeholders. This was reflected in what has been collectively described as the move towards 'Quality of Service' from the early 1990s onwards (Police Federation 1990), underpinned initially by John Major's 'Citizen's Charter'. These, and related changes, were indicative of the broader shift towards what is generally referred to as 'new public management' (NPM). According to McLaughlin *et al.* (2001), NPM has the following nine features:

1. The increased emphasis on achieving results rather than administering processes.

2. The setting of explicit targets and performance indicators to enable the auditing of efficiency and effectiveness.

3. The publication of league tables illustrating comparative performance.

4. The identification of core competencies.

5. The costing and market testing of all activities to ensure value for money.

6. The externalisation of non-essential responsibilities.

7. The establishment of a purchaser–provider split.

8. The encouragement of interagency co-operation.

9. The redesignation of clients as 'customers'.

Under NPM the status, power and, more importantly, the autonomy of the professional were increasingly questioned; professional autonomy and claims to the right of self-regulation were increasingly difficult to sustain. Central among the managerialist reforms introduced in the late 1990s were those generally referred to as 'Best Value' reforms.

The philosophy and practice of Best Value policing

In June 1997, the New Labour government announced the introduction of a new duty for local authorities in order to ensure 'best value' for the public.

The Government's consultation paper, *Modern Local Government: Improving Local Services through Best Value*, was launched in March 1998 and highlighted the need for both local and national standards of performance. It recommended that each year councils should have to review around a quarter of their services with a view to assessing how they could improve performance in line with both short and long-term targets. It was suggested in the paper that, as part of every service review, councils (namely, 'police authorities' in the policing context) should:

- 'challenge' exactly what services they provide and ask why they provide them;
- open up the services which they provide to 'competition';
- benchmark the performance of their forces (and BCUs within forces) in terms of the 'comparison' element of the regime; and
- 'consult' the communities which their forces policed.

In July 1998, the consultation paper was followed by the white paper, *Modern Local Government: In Touch with the People* (DETR 1998). As well as espousing the philosophy of 'continuous improvements' in terms of both the quality and cost of services, the white paper announced the intention to develop a new set of national performance indicators, in consultation primarily with the Audit Commission. Following the Local Government Act 1999, the general duty of Best Value authorities was to make arrangements to secure continuous improvement in the way in which their functions are exercised, having regard to a combination of economy, efficiency and effectiveness. The Act makes police authorities statutorily responsible for delivering Best Value. While the police authority is statutorily responsible under the legislation, in practice, police authorities are having to work very much in partnership with their forces since it is the force which ultimately has to deliver Best Value to the communities which are being policed. This is not so much a new role for police authorities for, under the Police Act 1996, they have a statutory responsibility to maintain an efficient and effective police force for their area. What the Best Value regime seems to require is that police authorities continue to do this but perhaps in a more active and interventionist way than before. Police authorities are required to undertake Best Value reviews and are required to prepare a Best Value performance plan for each financial year. These plans are intended as the primary means by which authorities are held to account for the efficiency and effectiveness of their services and for outlining its plans for the future. The performance plan is meant to be compatible with the requirement that authorities ensure that their proposed aggregate efficiency gains are consistent with the two per cent per annum target which is set for local authority expenditure as a whole. Best Value authorities must publish their plans each financial year and they are subject to audit with the information in the plan being scrutinised to ensure that it is reasonable and robust.

Performance indicators

All local authorities have, since 1992, been statutorily required to collect and publish performance indicators, which were specified annually by the Audit Commission. These indicators were, in part, superseded by a 'new' suite, which was specified by central government, under the Best Value legislation. The Local Government Act 1999 established a set of national Best Value performance indicators (BVPIs), along with the Audit Commission Act 1998 which facilitated the establishment of local authority performance indicators. These two pieces of legislation taken together provide the statutory framework for the 'family of indicators' which underpin the Best Value regime. This 'family of indicators' comprises the following four components.

Local performance indicators
Local authorities are encouraged to develop and use performance measures. There is, however, still a strong pull from 'the centre' in the sense that the Audit Commission has published guides to devising sets of performance indicators and to setting and monitoring local performance targets.

Corporate health and service delivery performance indicators
There are some 18 corporate health indicators which are intended to reflect a small number of council-wide 'general health' indicators that seek to reflect the overall performance of an authority. Along with these, the DETR (1999) outlined 11 proposed police corporate health performance indicators. These performance indicators focus on efficiency gains; estate running costs; Police and Criminal Evidence Act (PACE) 1984 complaints' satisfaction surveys; female and minority ethnic police strength; sickness; staff turnover; management overheads; and medical retirements. The emergency service performance indicators, which have a specific impact on policing, were developed after the 1998 comprehensive spending review. These BVPIs were developed by a centrally co-ordinated group made up of police authority representatives, police force managers, HMIC and the Audit Commission. The indicators fall into the following areas:

- Strategic objectives – including both the level and fear of crime as well as public safety and confidence.

- Cost/efficiency – which looks at the resources committed to a service and the efficiency with which they are turned to outputs.

- Service delivery outcomes – which addresses how well a service has operated in order to achieve strategic objectives. The indicators are concerned with recorded crime, burglary, violent crime, theft of motor vehicles, youth crime, public disorder, files processed and road traffic collisions.

- Quality – which is intended to be a reflection of users' experiences of services. There are indicators around response times; 999 calls; victim and witness satisfaction; charges; summons and cautions; and custody suites with drug arrest referral schemes.

- Fair access – which focuses on ease and equality of access to services. There are indicators, for example, around PACE stops of white and minority ethnic persons and complaints for breach of PACE codes and racial incidents.

Audit Commission indicators

The commission has been involved in specifying and collecting performance indicators for local authorities since 1993–4 and there is now a statutory duty to do so under the Audit Commission Act 1998 to specify local authority performance indicators.[1]

Other indicators

Indicators are published by the government which concern the performance of a wide range of public bodies, such as education, health and social services. There is, for example, an indicator around the total net spending per head of the population as well as cross-cutting performance indicators around racial harassment and domestic violence.

League tables and beacon status

For certain indicators which reflect both efficiency and quality, the government asks authorities to set targets which are consistent with reaching, over five years, the performance level of the top 25 per cent of authorities at the time the targets were set. According to the DETR (1999: 13), 'This approach will put more pressure on those authorities that are performing poorly and will, over time, narrow the range of performance and improve the level of performance overall' and, furthermore, ' . . . those authorities which are already in the top 25 per cent will of course still need to seek continuous improvement'. According to the Audit Commission (1999) the style and content of these 'top quartile' inspections should 'celebrate' the work being done by these councils. Some top-quartile performers can bid to become 'beacons' in certain areas, the idea being that these, 'very best performing councils . . . will set the pace of change and encourage the rest to innovate and to modernise' (DETR 1998: para 2.18). The idea is that by establishing a scheme and awarding beacon status to certain councils, others will be able to learn from these 'centres of excellence'. In making applications for consideration for beacon status, forces must demonstrate results which are capable of being usefully disseminated to other forces and to other BCUs as the basis for spreading best practice.

Beneath the top-quartile performers, the second 25 per cent are referred to as the 'striving' quartile, for whom it is intended that the inspection process should seek to 'encourage' to go the 'extra mile' to get into the top-quartile band. The third quartile is referred to as the 'coasting' quartile who should be 'persuaded' to make improvements through the style and content of the inspection process. The bottom quartile is referred to as the 'failing' quartile and, for this band, the inspection process is intended to be one where these authorities are 'challenged' as to their performance and in some cases referred to the Home Secretary for further consideration.

From a strictly legal perspective, because the statutory responsibility for the delivery of Best Value lies with the police authorities, one would expect to find police authorities being ranked according to these quartile arrangements. In practice, of course, police authorities put the onus of responsibility on their chief officers for the delivery of performance. In fact, as a result of HMIC's rolling five-year programme of BCU inspections, the future is likely to see the onus of responsibility for service delivery being transferred from chief officers to BCU commanders and their respective command teams. This is in line with the government's wider view that effective performance delivery should take place at local level. In due course, the quartile system is likely to be applied to BCUs rather than simply forces or police authorities.

Audit and inspection

Under the auspices of the Audit Commission, the government established a new Best Value Inspectorate, which began work in April 2000. The Local Government Act amends the 1996 Police Act in order to enable HMIC to inspect and to report to the Secretary of State on police authority compliance with the Best Value requirements. The division of responsibility between the Audit Commission and HMIC with regard to audit and inspection is explained by the Home Office in the following way:

> Broadly speaking, the division of responsibility between HMIC and the Audit Commission is that Commission-appointed auditors will check that the Best Value Performance Plan (BVPP) is informed by public consultation, contains comparative performance information, and sets out improvement targets that are realistic and challenging. Auditors will liaise with HMIC before finalising their report on the BVPP and submitting copies to the police authority and the Audit Commission. The auditor's report on the BVPP will be a public document. The auditor may recommend that the authority revise the BVPP to ensure compliance with statutory provision. In exceptional cases, the auditor may have such reservations about the BVPP, and the process underpinning it, that a referral will be made to the Audit Commission or the Secretary of State (Home Office 1999: para. 5).

Between April and June each year, HMIC tests and confirms the main elements of the BVPP by means of 'reality checking'. The two primary questions which the 'reality checks' will ask are: (1) has the force the managerial capacity and commitment to secure improvement; and (2) have resources been deployed in a way that will enable objectives to be achieved? Customer perceptions of service delivery are also evaluated (via surveys and public focus groups) to see whether they match claims made about performance. Following the BVPP audit process, HMIC undertakes a risk assessment of all forces to determine the schedule for subsequent inspections. Risk assessments, which identify 'poor performers', are intended to provide the stimulus for further HMIC inspections at a later date.

If satisfied with the BVPP, the auditors will issue a certificate, which states that the audit has been completed in accordance with the relevant legislation. However, if dissatisfied, the auditors can recommend that the plan should be amended to comply with the statutory requirements – that the Audit Commission should carry out a Best Value inspection of the authority or that the Secretary of State should intervene where the authority is perceived to have failed to put in place adequate systems to measure performance to meet national standards and targets. Unsatisfactory performance means that the Home Secretary can direct a police authority to: (1) prepare or amend a performance plan; (2) follow specific procedures in relation to a performance plan; and (3) carry out a review of its exercise of specified functions. Each results in a specified deadline being set, by which time a statement of action for making improvements had to be produced and published. Where an authority is deemed to be failing, the Home Secretary has the power to transfer particular functions from authorities to a nominee or to make an outsourcing direction, in effect allowing a private sector contractor to take over statutory functions which were previously carried out by a relevant authority.

Following the passage of the Police Reform Act 2002, the Home Secretary produced the first National Policing Plan (Home Office 2003). The plan provides the strategic national overview against which chief officers and police authorities should prepare their own local three-year strategy plans and annual policing plans. While the plan 'aims to strike a balance between key strategic national priorities and the varying needs of local communities' (Home Office 2003: 5), in reality it is a centralising measure. This is precisely because it sets out a clear national framework within which the BVPIs are incorporated and by which both forces and BCUs can be ranked. This is a clear case where the language of devolution of power and resources and the supposed empowerment of BCU command teams meet the practice of increasing centralisation. Once again, the Home Secretary's hand is increasingly strengthened within the tripartite structure as established by the Police Act 1964 (see Chapters 5 and 24).

Leadership and performance management: future challenges

While Best Value reviews are conducted and inspected at force level, the wider culture of continually improving performance, which Best Value seeks to engender, focuses increasingly on the local or BCU level. The term 'performance culture' is used here to denote an emphasis on targets, results and benchmarking to compare standards. This term is narrower than the 'new public management' in that the latter is more all-encompassing and includes such things as contracting out and the introduction of purchaser–provider splits. Increasingly, managerialism and the emergence of the new performance culture have, predictably, had important consequences for police leadership. Indeed, as the requirements expected of police managers have changed so, arguably, has the character of police leaders itself altered. On the basis of his research on chief constables conducted in the early 1990s, Reiner (1991) identified four 'ideal types' of chief officer:

1. The *Baron* typically had 'more military experience than most chief con- stables' (1991: 306) and his leadership style[2] could be described as

'paternalistic', with a strong preference for 'hierarchical structure' and 'norms of deference' to enable him to 'lead from the front' (1991: 6).

2. The *Bobby* – typically working class in pedigree and, coupled with this, has 'a lack of higher education' and is 'in a nutshell ... the bobby on the beat promoted to the top job in the constabulary' (1991: 306).

3. The *Boss* – whose leadership style is typically based on 'authority not power'. As with the Baron, the style is very much 'top-down' and one where 'troops have to toe the line'.

4. The *Bureaucrat* ideally attempts to 'combine a mastery of modern managerial approaches with the charismatic image of a traditional bobby or detective' (1991: 308). The leadership style of the Bureaucrat is far more democratic and empowering than that of the previous three ideal types because it is based on both 'professionalism and diplomacy' (1991: 308).

Though Reiner's research was done some years ago, his typology remains helpful in focusing attention on some of the most significant changes that have occurred in the last decade. There are a number of observations we might make in this regard. First, there has been a very significant shift away from the forms of leadership associated with the first three ideal types. Thus, the style associated with 'the Baron' is discouraged today because of what is perceived to be its now outmoded belief in leadership as a 'top down' process. Similarly, 'the Bobby' has become increasingly rare because of the requirement most forces have for middle-ranking officers and above to possess substantial academic qualifications. Indeed, candidates on the High Potential Development Scheme, for example, are expected to undertake study leading to a policing-related masters degree. The style of leadership associated with 'the Boss' is also not encouraged, being perceived to be a relatively inflexible approach and therefore not in line with the more modern ideology that the organisation should encourage 360 degree feedback, with junior officers giving feedback to more senior officers as well as vice versa. We might also note in this regard that all three of these ideal types are furthermore male centred (all chiefs were male at the time Reiner's research was undertaken) and ignore the massive contribution which women now make at BCU leadership and ACPO levels – a contribution historically denied women in the policing context (Brown and Heidensohn 2000; see Chapter 22).

As Reiner (1991: 348) noted, 'a combination of the changing exigencies of large police organisations and pressure from the centre, especially emanating from the Financial Management Initiative, has pushed all chief constables in the "bureaucratic" direction'. Indeed, we can go further than this and suggest that not only do contemporary police leaders conform much more to the 'bureaucratic' ideal type but also that the location of leadership has changed and been extended downwards. That is, the bureaucrat is now to be found all the way down to BCU commander – and possibly beyond. One of the shortcomings of NPM has been its relatively narrow – and bureaucratic – model of performance measurement and its similarly narrow implicit model of the management of performance. Put crudely, NPM has placed primary emphasis on the 'management' rather than the 'leadership' elements of the police officer's role. Indeed, it is only relatively recently that significant emphasis has been placed on leadership within the service. Hitherto, there had been an assumption, usually unspoken, that leadership within the service was relatively unproblematic. According to Villiers (2003: 26) there is, however, a paradox in policing: 'On the one hand, police officers are usually, at least on the surface, entirely confident in their problem-solving abilities. It is a can-do culture, and any problem can be solved ... On the other hand, [there is] a fundamental lack of inner confidence in many police leaders'. The lack of confidence is manifest, he suggests, in three main ways: 'presenteeism' (an inability to delegate or to distinguish clearly between urgency and importance); unwillingness to consider alternatives; and autocracy. Much of the increased interest in policing circles in management theory stems from a desire to move beyond such models of leadership.

The performance culture of today presents numerous challenges for the police leader of today, three of which are arguably key: the need for continuous improvement, the dual requirements of management and leadership, and partnership working.

Continuous improvement

The police leader of today must be able to meet the demands of a modern performance culture where 'continuous improvements' have to be demonstrated. In 1999, the Home Office commissioned a study by Leeds University to prepare two sets of 'families' – one of crime and disorder reduction partnerships and one of police BCUs. The 'families' were to be formed by grouping together areas with similar socioeconomic and demographic characteristics. The work culminated in early 2000 with the publication for the first time of crime statistics for local policing areas (BCUs). From April 2001, HMIC began to carry out inspections of BCUs as well as force-wide reviews. As middle managers in the police service, senior officers in the basic command team (superintendents and chief inspectors) are expected to play a pivotal role in terms of the delivery of Best Value in policing. The Audit Commission (2001: 5) now refers to performance management in policing as being characterised by 'a culture of devolved responsibility'. According to the former HM Chief Inspector of Constabulary:

> policing is essentially a local service; the vast bulk of patrol work and investigation of volume crime is managed at BCU level, as are crime and disorder partnerships. So it is not surprising that the commitment we all share to enhance police performance leads us to look at how well BCUs are doing (HMIC 2001b).

It is therefore arguably now the case that the focus on performance is now directed at BCU command teams almost as much as it is at the ACPO ranks.

The police middle manager is now expected to take on duties which used to be the responsibility of more senior officers. This is partly as a result of the delayering of the middle ranks which occurred in the 1990s. There was, for example, a 37 per cent decrease in the number of superintendents between

1988 and 1997, with a gradual decline between 1988 and 1992 but a marked decline of 35 per cent between 1992 and 1997 (HMIC 1998). Interestingly, the judgement of 'High Potential Development Scheme' candidates[3] is now done according to superintendent competencies, whereas previously under the old-style 'Special' and 'Accelerated Promotion Courses' they had been judged according to ACPO competencies. This is significant in the sense that it reflects a broader political agenda based on a view that the pivotal leadership positions in policing are to be found at BCU command level rather than ACPO level.

According to HMIC (2001b: 8), 'the hallmark of success for BCU commanders is to achieve the increasingly challenging performance targets set for their areas'. Continuous improvements, for example, have to be achieved, and there is a requirement to sustain a two per cent year-on-year efficiency saving. Demonstrating such continuous improvement means that one of the key future challenges for police leaders lies in ensuring that performance information is recorded ethically and with integrity (Neyroud and Beckley 2001). The potential tension between this and NPM hardly needs spelling out and HMIC (1999), for example, have highlighted the way in which the current 'performance culture' may encourage unhealthy competition between officers in terms of rates of arrest. The challenge for police leaders lies partly then in managing performance constructively, while recognising the danger that the Best Value 'league tables' regime may lead to greater problems of misrepresentation of performance. In the context of crime recording, for example, Loveday (2000) has argued that despite attempts to introduce independent audit mechanisms to encourage ethical recording, corrupt practices continue to flourish. It is not just that with the quartile system police managers will be under pressure to avoid being in the bottom or 'failing' quartile. Top-quartile or 'beacon' performers also receive more attention under the spotlight of audit and inspection, in order that good practice be shared, and this may lead to pressure to manufacture underperformance. This has been referred to as 'institutionalised under-working' (Roy 1954) and more recently by Smith (1995) as the 'convergence' effect. Under Best Value, the inspection regime is likely to increase such pressures at both the bottom and top of league tables and ethical police managers will have to perform while under pressure and in the spotlight (see Chapter 23). It is no longer sufficient to be a 'specialist' police leader who is solely concerned with the performance of one's own organisation. In addition to managing the requirement to demonstrate 'continuous improvements' in service delivery and the bureaucratic burden spawned by the regime, the modern police leader faces the challenge of having to be a 'generalist' who can work together with other public sector leaders.

Partnership working

The police leader of today must have the ability to work in partnership with other agencies so that crime is managed as a social problem and not just a policing problem. Police commanders and their command teams (superintending and inspecting ranks) are now tasked with working together with chief executives of local authorities in order to meet with the statutory requirements of the Crime and Disorder Act 1998. Public sector managers have, in the past, been guilty of what Smith (1995) refers to as both 'suboptimisation' and 'myopia'. The former is where public sector leaders have concentrated almost exclusively on their own narrow objectives at the expense of taking a broader, strategic perspective and the latter is a term used to describe how public sector leaders have to a large extent been guilty of 'short-termism'. As a response to this, the philosophy of 'joined-up working' which underpins the crime and disorder legislation means the police leaders of today must display an ability to develop a more holistic perspective on social problems (Long 2000). It is a challenge to the traditional style of leadership in which officers were generally left to deal with the challenges presented by the daily management of their own functional 'silos'.

As in other areas, there exists a tension between the demands of NPM and the practice of partnership working. There is an uneasy relationship between the government's message that crime is a social problem which requires 'joined-up working' and the NPM-inspired performance culture in which success tends to be measured quite narrowly and where rather than just a policing problem, 'failure' at BCU level may result in the removal and replacement of the particular command team. It is for these reasons that Clarke and Newman (1997: 116) suggest that public sector managers are 'constrained by a variety of often incompatible expectations'.

Management and leadership

The police leader of today must have the ability to manage the organisation while at the same time being able to motivate and inspire individual officers. In policing, as in many other organisations, senior staff – and increasingly staff at other levels – are expected to show both skill and dedication in management and in leadership. This is by no means straightforward, for the skills and attributes associated with rational and careful management are not necessarily, or even usually, those associated with successful leadership. Moreover, management and leadership requirements may conflict with each other: 'The cautious, artful, consensus-seeking manager – who knows the cost of everything, who is determined to please everyone and upset no-one, and whose quota is always fulfilled – may be quite incapable of swift and dynamic leadership when the situation requires it' (Villiers and Adlam 2003: xii).

As I have argued, being an inspirational leader is arguably increasingly difficult to achieve because of the sheer bureaucratic burden placed on the middle manager in the police today as a result of servicing the performance regime driven by HMIC, the Audit Commission and the government. Anticipating future trends, one former chief constable (Butler 2000: 317) suggested that 'The skill will be to manage the process in such a way as to allow the people who can deliver results to get on with the tasks free from overbearing control and scrutiny'. The challenge facing modern police leaders is, in some respects, even more complex than this. Police leaders are now faced with two competing, and in some ways incompatible, sets of expectations. On the one hand, there are the managerialist pressures of fairly narrow goal achievement – as measured by increasing rafts of peformance indicators. On the other hand, there is the increasing emphasis on ethics and human rights –

something which sits uneasily with the constraining of professional autonomy characteristic of NPM. As Neyroud and Beckley (2001) argue, three issues have tended to dominate police performance: crime, police numbers and police expenditure. There are a number of reasons why these individually, and collectively, provide an inadequate basis for assessing the delivery of policing services. Crucially what is absent from this rational-calculative model is any means of stimulating coherent organisational learning. Though current performance models give the appearance of rational management, in practice 'there is an absence of rationality because of the absence of understanding about the relationship between input, behaviour, output and outcome' (Neyroud and Beckley 2001: 121). What is required is a value-systems approach in which managers are enabled not simply to manage resources but to lead the organisation in a direction based on agreed principles and values. This is an approach which is congruent with what I will outline below as 'transformational leadership'.

In order that these challenges be met, as one might expect, there has been a corresponding shift in both the philosophy and practice of higher police training.

The response of higher police training to the challenges of leadership

A number of years ago Richards (1985) noticed that most of the content of 'command courses' at Bramshill was given over to an admixture of police-related social science and 'management' studies – along with a focus of police operational matters. However, 'ethics' and the exploration of other serious spheres of philosophy relevant to policing were 'set aside' (Adlam 2003: 35).

'Higher' police training is located at Centrex (formerly National Police Training), Bramshill. Historically, the National Police Leadership Faculty[4] has trained police leaders from the inspecting ranks and above by means of the rank-based 'Junior', 'Intermediate' and 'Special' and Senior command courses, the latter of which is a mandatory requirement for progression to the ACPO ranks within the service (Adlam 2001). Much has changed in police training in the past 20 years. One of the consequences is that it would no longer be possible to say that consideration of ethics and philosophy is 'set aside'. Indeed, it is increasingly recognised that a full consideration of such issues is central to the development of modern police managers. An exploration of the philosophy and practice of higher police leadership training illuminates the kind of response which is being made to the challenges faced by the modern police leader.

Philosophy

Leadership is more than a position of command
Embodied in the philosophy of higher police training is the belief that leadership is no longer about 'headship'. That is, it is no longer simply about

formal power and authority within an organisational structure. Historically, the study of leadership, which initially focused on military and political leaders, tended to be based on the idea of the 'Great Man' as leader. Hooper and Potter (2000: 54) argue that, 'For many people, up until the latter part of the twentieth century . . . leadership has been thought of as a concept which is primarily male, military and Western'. This line of thinking began to change, however, in the late 1950s and 1960s following Festinger's (1957) work on 'cognitive dissonance'. This psychological condition was said to be exhibited typically by individuals in command leadership positions who had a strong desire for structure and chains of command within hierarchies. Festinger (1957) argued that such leaders tended to make decisions all too quickly, despite the fact that they often had less than adequate data. In addition, such leaders were poor at dealing with new information, particularly when it contradicted their own reasoning. In addition, the idea that 'leadership' should be about much more than 'command' was developed in Dixon's (1976) classic research into 'military incompetence'. This work pointed out that the very traits often much admired by the military in times of crisis could actually lead to poor decision-making. As a result of these related studies of leadership, many organisations, including the police service, have moved well away from the idea that the military-style command leadership is *the* ideal type of leadership for all contexts.

'Leadership' is no longer assumed to be about the formalised division of roles into a leadership collective, residing at the top of an organisation or what Hodgson *et al.* (1965) refer to as 'leadership role constellation'. In recent years there has been a growing acknowledgement that leadership is a social process which is shared between people. De Vries (1999) terms this 'distributed leadership' to imply that it is not restricted to a single person or group of people in an organisation. According to Hooper and Potter (2000: 68–9): 'Being a leader today requires more subtle skills than in the past and a different emphasis, as organisational cultures change. The movement is from a "comfortable" command and control approach to an "uncomfortable" requirement to be an empowerer, a coach, a facilitator and an educator.' An example of this would be the encouragement of more junior officers at both the sergeant and constable ranks to develop their own problem-solving solutions to community policing issues (Skogan and Hartnett 1997). Leadership, in this context, becomes a 'bottom up' rather than a 'top down' exercise. In principle, the more junior ranking officers are increasingly empowered to effect change. Yet, at the same time, of course, the demands of accountability and responsibility on more senior officers are equally as great.

The importance of transformational as well as transactional leadership

The philosophy which underpins modern higher police training acknowledges that there is a distinction between 'leadership' and 'management'. Much of this philosophy has to be credited to the work of Bennis (1989), who pointed out that managers 'administer' whereas leaders 'innovate'. Management was said to be about 'control', whereas leadership was said to be about inspiring 'trust'. Management was furthermore said to be about 'doing things right', whereas leadership was the ability to challenge the status quo, where necessary, in order to 'do the right things'. The distinction between management and leadership may also be related to a further distinction: that between 'transactional' and 'transformational' leadership. 'Transactional' leadership is almost like a contractual agreement or a form of basic management which is based on 'contingency reward' and 'management by exception' (Barling *et al.* 2000). A practical example of this would be file preparation for court cases. 'Transactional' leadership, though important to satisfying the bureaucratic and legal requirements of the criminal justice system, is only part of the solution to the challenge of public sector leadership in the twenty-first century. Tichy and Devanna (1986: 4) note this, arguing that 'The traditional managerial skills, such as financial acumen, manufacturing expertise, and marketing process, are important ingredients in most organisational success stories but not sufficient for organisational transformation'. Similarly, in the context of policing, as Grieve (2003: ix) notes, leadership:

> is no longer a mechanical task, if it ever were. It is not enough, in order to be able to carry out a covert operation with official approval, for the senior detective simply to complete the latest proforma and hope for the best. When the challenges come, as come they will with increasing speed and subtle trajectory, an understanding of the underpinning principles and conflicting values of policing is vital for organisational survival.

By contrast, 'transformational' leadership is characterised by 'idealised influence', 'inspirational motivation', 'intellectual stimulation' and 'individualised consideration'. In the words of Barker (2001: 266), 'Transformational leadership theory encompasses those being led, the employees, subordinates or followers, in the leadership process'. It is said to be a reciprocal process, whereby 'followers' feel admiration, trust, loyalty and respect for the 'leader'. This is precisely why, according to Tichy and Devanna (1986: 4), 'It demands the commitment of the many not the few'. According to Hooper and Potter (2000: 58): 'Leadership has to be a transformational process, or as we call it a transcendent process, unlocking the potential contained in every human being, rather than simply being a contractual or transactional arrangement where people perform simply to gain personal rewards, financial or otherwise'. In emphasising the motivational aspect of transformational leadership, Hooper and Potter (2000: 64) maintain that 'This process is one of alignment. It is similar to stroking iron filings with a magnet: people are magnetised towards the same direction by the prospect of the vision becoming reality'. Likewise, Bass (1990: 21) strongly emphasises the motivational nature of transformational process in issuing a rallying call to leaders who can 'broaden and elevate the interests of their employees' plus the will to 'stir their employees to look beyond their own self-interest for the good of the group'. This type of transformational leadership is much more than the issuing of routine directives and expecting followers mechanically to comply; it is very much about winning 'hearts and minds' (Katz and Kahn 1978) in order to 'change the way people think about what is desirable, possible and necessary' (Zaleznik 1977: 71). Practical examples of where transformational police leadership is exhibited would include where senior officers empower the more junior ranks to develop innovative ideas around anti-burglary and anti-robbery initiatives, and drug arrest referral schemes, as well as community policing initiatives which might involve engaging young people in recreational and sporting activities or, indeed, of course, any other area of work.

There is a need for the police leader of today to be able to exhibit flexibility in leadership styles. Some aspects of policing are non-negotiable and require strictly transactional leadership, as with the example of file preparation for court cases. On the other hand, the skilled police leader has to recognise where transactional leadership would unnecessarily constrain and inhibit more junior officers and prevent them from making a valuable contribution to organisational success. When it comes to encouraging the development of innovative and creative proposals in the field of crime detection and prevention, to tap in to the hidden talents of more junior officers requires transformational leadership. The skilled police leader has to know exactly where the boundaries of transactional and transformational leadership are, and has to be able to move effortlessly between the two styles. It is not only the case that a single model of leadership is likely to be inappropriate to the entire organisation (Panzarella 2003) but also that a single model is unlikely to be sufficient for any individual leader.

Leaders have to develop their emotional intelligence

Not only has police work changed; so have the public and the communities into which it is separated. No longer do people uncritically accept whatever the police are doing in the name of a war on crime. People identify problems and want solutions. They want the police to be effective and accountable. To meet those demands, police leaders have to change themselves, their organisations and their people (Pagon 2003: 167).

According to Goleman (1995), 'emotional intelligence' is a prerequisite for good leadership. This is the ability to understand and manage one's emotions and thus act as a role model and to understand and manage the emotions of others, in order to be able to enhance the trust of others. The individual must be prepared to learn continually and develop and so this philosophy 'embodies the notion that leadership is not static and that leadership behaviours should be an integral part of continuous learning agendas' (Barling et al. 2000: 209). It is notable that in the High Potential Development Scheme for 'fast track' officers identified as the aspiring police chiefs of tomorrow, the module entitled 'Leadership and Self' acts as the gateway module which candidates must pass through before further progression on the course. This core module, which is pivotal for future learning, is very much underpinned by the belief in the necessity of fostering emotional intelligence.

Every officer is a leader

The view of leadership as a role-based rather than a rank-based activity was espoused by Schein (1992: 374), who maintained that 'leadership can occur anywhere in the organisation'. As Barling et al. (2000: 209) put it, and as has been illustrated throughout this chapter, 'Police leadership is no longer simply about the formal leader'. According to the chief executive of the Police Skills and Standards Organisation (PSSO) – the national training organisation for the police service in the UK – 'Constables are often the first officers on the scene . . . the public looks to a constable for leadership. It starts at constable level and needs to be developed from there' (cited in Munro-Orr 2003: 20). Indeed, PSSO recently argued that leadership should no longer be the preserve of the senior ranks precisely because by the time senior officers received their training their attitudes and mental schemas would already be pretty firmly set (Munro-Orr 2003: 20). The idea that every officer should be a leader is compatible with the theory of transformational leadership, and both should be encouraged within the wider political context where power, resources and responsibility are devolved to lower levels in organisations (Anderson 2000).

Practice

During the last five years or so the training at Centrex, Bramshill, has been restructured to accommodate the emergence of a belief that leadership should be a 'role based' rather than a 'rank based' activity. Part of the restructuring took place in 1999, when the Junior Command Course (for inspecting ranks) and Intermediate Command Course (for superintending ranks) were merged to form the Command Team Programme, which has subsequently been renamed the Senior Leadership Development Programme. This was partly due to the recognition that clear distinctions in role, between the ranks, were breaking down and that many chief inspectors needed to be displaying the same leadership qualities as their Superintendent colleagues in BCU commander positions. (see Table 25.1).

It is not surprising that there has been a gradual shift away from the type of behavioural trait theories of leadership. Trait theories not only have little to say about the context in which leadership interactions occur but they also assume that there are relatively fixed and enduring aspects of personality which can be identified. This points in the direction of the argument that leaders are 'born' and not 'made' and potentially calls leadership training into

Table 25.1 The restructuring of rank-based leadership courses in the National Police Leadership Centre

	1990s	*2003*
Name	The Senior Command Course	The Strategic Command Course
Ranks	Superintendents with ACPO potential	Superintendents with ACPO potential
Name	The Intermediate Command Course	
Ranks	Newly promoted superintendents	
Name		The Senior Leadership Development Programme
Ranks		Superintendents and chief inspectors
Name	The Junior Command Course	
Ranks	Newly promoted chief inspectors	

question. This has been accompanied by a move away from didactic 'chalk and talk'-style training towards facilitation at Bramshill (Adlam 2001: 271); a process that has been taking place gradually over the last 30 years or so:

> Beginning in the 1970's a very small number of tutors at Bramshill rejected 'authoritarian' models of education and sought to practice the 'catalytic' style of intervention ... They were aware of the new theories of management that stressed the importance of 'ownership', empowerment and person-centredness. They understood that an authoritarian model of education would only serve to collude with a discredited authoritarian model of management.

The rise of 'facilitative' learning is coupled with the belief that, for learning to be effective, it should be experiential and this has led in practice to the use of case studies and simulations on leadership courses. Rather than long residential courses, increasingly leadership courses are much shorter and are themed into modules, with students being expected to undertake distance learning prior to attendance. This is itself consistent with the idea that 'students' be increasingly treated as 'customers', with their being able to be empowered to shape their own learning and career development more generally (a shift that is itself part of a larger set of changes associated with NPM).

Future tensions: introducing the discourse of competence

In an attempt to ensure that police leaders have the right skills for the twenty-first century, the PSSO was established as a National Training Organisation in March 2001. One of the key responsibilities of the PSSO is in terms of its role as a standard-setting body. A new national framework was introduced in October 2001. This framework was an attempt to introduce a single, consistent approach to all 44 police services in England, Wales and Northern Ireland, it being applicable to 160,000 police officers and 84,000 support staff (Warner 2002). This framework is intended to offer a comprehensive source of behavioural information through the introduction of both rank and role-specific profiles. By meeting the development needs of serving officers as well as assisting in the selection of suitable recruits, the framework is integrated into the performance management process for the police, with the aim of encouraging consistent standards of behaviour in all forces.

On the positive side, the new national competency framework is an attempt at assessing individual police performance – something which has been notoriously absent in the past, partly for practical reasons and partly because of police resistance (Reiner 1998) – as evidenced by the Wembley Rally, attended by tens of thousands of officers, following the publication of the Sheehy Report in 1993. Reiner (1998: 71) argues that 'Assessment of individual police performance is not only desirable as the atomic basis of democratic accountability, but is inevitable', though he points out that 'assessment can never be on a precisely calibrated scale' because 'the most common police activities can be evaluated only in terms of the quality of the process involved'. This view was endorsed by Butler (2000: 307) who stressed that 'It would be unrealistic and of potentially little value to attempt to measure every element of policing by means of individual performance indicators'. While some would point out that 'competencies' are different from actual performance targets, the fact remains that this new national framework is a massive step in the direction of attempting to quantify individual police performance. In this context, the modern police leader has the difficult task of trying to ensure that their officers meet the national competencies for their ranks and roles in the organisation, while simultaneously ensuring that the service delivery to the local victim or crime or 'customer' is of the highest quality.

While the new national competency framework could be considered to be politically progressive in some senses, one has to question whether the discourse of 'competency' is suited to the shift towards 'transformational' leadership. 'Competency' assumes that performance in general, and leadership more particularly, can in some way be accurately measured, though many argue that such activities are not easily quantified. As Drodge and Murphy (2002: 201) put it, 'Competencies may say something about a leader at a given moment in time, but not about leadership, because competencies ebb and flow as they get played out in the complex personal and social worlds every person inhabits'. Adlam (2001: 273) is damning in his critique of the new language of 'competence', arguing that competency frameworks tend to be 'banal but strikingly obvious'. 'No systematic analysis', he argues (2003: 40):

> is offered concerning the ways in which police leadership is a) like all other manifestations of leadership b) like some other types of leadership (e.g. public service) and c) like no other form of leadership (in virtue of its specific tasks and functions).

It certainly does seem to be the case that competency frameworks are better suited to 'transactional' leadership, as they measure tangibles which one associates with management rather than the intangibles of leadership, such as charisma, motivation, ethics and moral responsibility.

It remains to be seen whether the shift towards evidence-based practice and contemporary discourse of 'competence' will be central to ensuring that our police officers of tomorrow are equipped for the challenge of leadership. If used properly, evidence-based practice and the necessity to prove 'competence' on the one hand can be used to great effect to make sure the right leaders are to be allocated suitable roles and promoted to the right positions. On the other hand, there is a real danger that the requirements to demonstrate 'competence' through evidence-based practice could result in both a bureaucratic nightmare for the organisation and police leaders who 'look good on paper' but who are less well suited to the task of motivating and leading others. Should this occur then the competency framework could be considered to be detrimental in that it may contribute very little to improvements in the practical delivery of everyday policing services.

Conclusions

In the first half of this chapter I outlined a number of the most significant changes that have taken place over the past decade in relation to the management of the performance of the police service. As this and other chapters (5, 24 and 25) in this volume indicate, despite the rhetoric of decentralisation and devolution, in practice the governance of policing has become increasingly centralised. It is subject to more and more state control through the managerial calculus of national performance indicators. For at least part of the 1980s and 1990s, one of the consequences of these processes was that as increasing attention was paid to management, questions of leadership fell somewhat off the radar. In the second half of the chapter I examined the changing nature of leadership and leadership training in the police service, and argued that we are witnessing a shift in a direction which places greater emphasis on 'transformational' rather than 'transactional' leadership – albeit that we are probably still in the early stages of this change. Though leadership is now firmly back on the agenda, there remain a significant number of tensions between the processes that are necessary to the inculcation and stimulation of progressive forms of leadership and those that underpin the contemporary culture of performance management. What this chapter has highlighted is that good leadership cannot merely be reduced to good performance management. As Neyroud and Beckley (2001: 220) argue, 'good policing in the twenty first century requires more than "good performance". It needs a renewal of contract between police officer and the citizen'. This, they suggest, in turn requires more openness and scrutiny of policing, continuously improving professional standards and, at heart, a firm commitment to ethics. These elements are mutually reinforcing. Thus, as Alderson (2003: 57) observes:

> Any consideration of [the murder of Stephen Lawrence and the subsequent Inquiry] is likely to come to the conclusion that the principles under which the police should operate in a modern society, with its multi-racial make-up, have not been as clearly defined as is desirable. It is not possible to demand accountability for excellence in police affairs if the road to accountability is not clearly defined.

Our police leaders must be held accountable, but accountability itself cannot merely be reduced to the narrow managerial calculus. In broad agreement with Neyroud and Beckley's argument, Alderson goes on to argue that 'the police need to know what it is that is fundamentally valued by society, what they are supposed to be protecting or defending' (2003: 57) or, as Villiers (2003: 21) puts it, 'the police service of the twenty-first century needs to recognise and declare its doctrine, in the sense of a recognised body of knowledge and an authoritative set of principles'. For the police service of the twenty first century to evolve into a genuinely progressive 'learning organisation', Neyroud and Beckley's illustration of a 'virtuous circle' in which the police service transforms itself along lines consistent with human rights is a helpful starting point (see Figure 25.1).

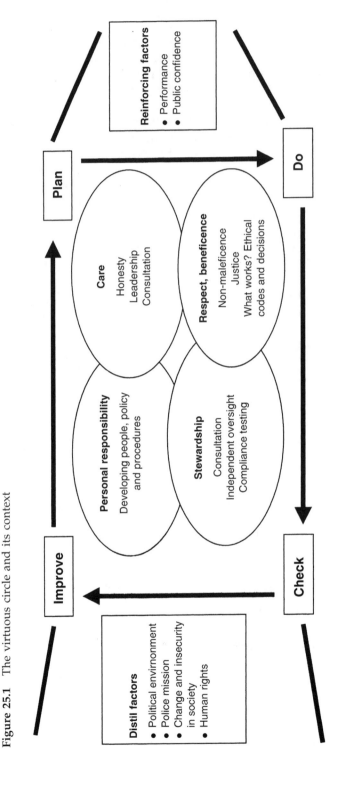

Figure 25.1 The virtuous circle and its context

Source: Neyroud and Beckley (2001): 219.

Selected further reading

Alexander's 'Police and best value: applicability and adaptation' (2000) serves as a useful introduction to the basic tenets of the Best Value legislation and the wider inspection culture in which it is located. The Audit Commission's *Seeing is Believing* (1999) gives the reader a great deal of insight into some of the principles and practices which inform the Audit Commission's approach to the Best Value regime. Ferlie and Fitzgerald's chapter, 'The sustainability of the new public management in the UK' (2002), while not focusing explicitly on policing, is more than useful in that it challenges the reader to consider the likely future existence of the new public sector management as a mode of governance.

The Home Office's *Policing a New Century* (available online: http://www.police reform.gov.uk) gives the reader a great deal of insight into the government's vision for policing in the future in terms of what kind of leadership qualities and management practices are required to drive policy forward. Johnson and Scholes' *Exploring Public Sector Strategy* (2001) enables the reader to be able to understand that policing reform is not specific to the organisation but rather that the type of ideologies, policies and practices which drive the reform agenda are similar across the public sector.

Keenan's 'Just how new is best value?' (2000) enables the reader to appreciate that the present managerial policy of Best Value is not something which is new but, rather, it is the culmination of a variety of social processes and policies which have a long history. McLaughlin *et al.*'s 'The permanent revolution: New Labour, new public management and the modernisation of criminal justice' (2001) sets New Labour's managerial reform agenda of policing in the broader context of other criminal justice agencies, such as the courts and prisons. Finally, McLaughlin *et al.*'s *New Public Management* (2002) is a comprehensive account of the history, context and current challenges posed by the new public sector managerialism.

Notes

1 The Audit Commission has not specified any statutory indicators for local authorities for 2002–3.
2 There were no women chief constables at the time of Reiner's study in the early 1990s.
3 This scheme was introduced on 1 April 2002 to replace both the Accelerated Promotion Scheme and the Accelerated Promotion Scheme for graduates.
4 Renamed the National Police Leadership Centre in 2003.

References

Adlam, R. (2001) 'Provision of police leadership development opportunities, Bramshill: problem, solution and a critical engagement', *International Journal of Police Science and Management*, 3(3): 260–78.

Adlam, R. (2003) 'Nice people, big questions, heritage concepts', in R. Adlam and P. Villiers (eds) *Police Leadership in the Twenty-first Century*. Winchester: Waterside Press: 34–55.

Alderson, J. (2003) 'Police leadership: a search for principles', in R. Adlam and P. Villiers (eds) *Police Leadership in the Twenty-first Century*. Winchester: Waterside Press: 56–67.

Alexander, A. (2000) 'Police and Best Value: applicability and adaptation', *Policing and Society*, 10(3): 263–75.

Anderson, T. (2000) *Every Officer is a Leader: Transforming Leadership in Police, Justice and Public Safety*. London: St Lucie Press.

Audit Commission (1999) *Seeing is Believing. How the Audit Commission will Carry out Best Value Inspections in England*. London: HMSO.

Audit Commission (2001) *Best Foot Forward: Headquarters Support for Police Basic Command Units*. London: Audit Commission for Local Authorities and the National Health Service in England and Wales.

Barker, R.A. (2001) 'The nature of leadership', *Human Relations*, 54: 469–93.

Barling *et al.* (2000) 'Transformational leadership and emotional intelligence: an exploratory study', *Leadership and Organisation Development Journal*, 21(3): 157–61.

Bass, N.M. (1990) 'From transactional to transformational leadership: learning to share the vision', *Organisational Dynamics*, 18(13): 19–36.

Bennis, W. (1989) *On Becoming a Leader*. Reading, MA: Addison-Wesley.

Blair, T. (1998) *The Third Way. New Politics for the New Century*. London: Fabian Society.

Brown, J. and Heidensohn, F. (2000) *Gender and Policing: Comparative Perspectives*. Basingstoke: Macmillan.

Bryman, A. (1986) *Leadership and Organizations*. London: Routledge & Kegan Paul.

Burns, J.M. (1978) *Leadership*. New York, NY: Harper & Row.

Butler, T. (2000) 'Managing the future: a chief constable's view', in F. Leishman *et al.* (eds) *Core Issues in Policing*. (2nd edn). Harlow: Pearson.

Carvel, J. (2002) 'Public sector mutiny', *Guardian*, 21 February.

Clarke, J., Gerwitz, S. and McLaughlin, E. (2000) *New Managerialism: New Welfare?* London: Sage.

Clarke, J. and Newman, J. (1997) *The Managerial State: Power, Politics and Ideology in the Remaking of Social Welfare*. London. Sage.

DETR (1998) *Modern Local Government: In Touch with the People*. Wetherby: DETR Free Literature.

DETR (1999) *Performance Indicators for 2000/2001. A Joint Consultation Document Produced by DETR and the Audit Commission on Best Value and Local Authority Performance Indicators for 2000/2001*. Wetherby: DETR Free Literature.

De Vries, M.F.R. Kets (1999) 'High performance teams: lessons from the pygmies',

Dixon, N. (1976) *On the Psychology of Military Incompetence*. London: Jonathan Cape.

Dobson, N. (2000) *Best Value: Law and Management*. Bristol: Jordans.

Drodge, E.N. and Murphy, S.A. (2002) 'Police leadership as a transformational social process', *International Journal of Police Science and Management*, 4(3): 198–212.

Drucker, P. (1964) *Managing for Results*. London: Heinemann.

Ferlie, E. and Fitzgerald, L. (2002) 'The sustainability of the new public management in the UK', in K. McLaughlin *et al.* (eds) *New Public Management: Current Trends and Future Prospects*. London. Routledge.

Festinger, L. (1957) *A Theory of Cognitive Dissonance*. Row Peterson.

Gamble, A. (1994) *The Free Economy and the Strong State: The Politics of Thatcherism* (2nd edn). London: Macmillan.

Goleman, D. (1995) *Emotional Intelligence*. New York, NY: Bantam.

Grieve, J. (2003) 'Foreword', in R. Adlam and P. Villiers (eds) *Police Leadership in the Twenty-first Century*. Winchester: Waterside Press.

Halsey, A.H. (1988) 'A sociologist's view of Thatcherism', in R. Skidelsky (eds) *Thatcherism*. London: Chatto & Windus, 173–89.

HMIC (1998) *What Price Policing: A Study of Efficiency and Value for Money in the Police Service*. London: HMIC.

HMIC (1999) *Report on Police Integrity*. London: HMIC.

HMIC (2001) *Inspection of Central BCU in Bristol* (online) (http://www.homeoffice.gov.uk/hmic/pubs.htm).

HMIC (2001b) *Going Local: The BCU Inspection Handbook*. London: HMIC.

Hodgson, R.C., Levinson, D.J. and Zaleznic, A. (1965) *The Executive Role Constellation: An analysis of personality and role relations in management*. Boston: Harvard University, Graduate School of Business Administration.

Home Office (1983) *Manpower, Effectiveness and Efficiency in the Police Service*. London: HMSO.

Home Office (1995) *Review of Core and Ancillary Tasks*. London: HMSO.

Home Office (1999) *Best Value: Briefing Notes for the Police Service, Audit and Inspection*. London: Home Office.

Home Office (2001c) *Policing a New Century* (Available online: http://www.policereform.gov.uk).

Home Office (2003) *The National Policing Plan, 2003–2006*. London: HMSO.

Hooper, A. and Potter, J. (2000) *Intelligent Leadership*. London: Random House.

Johnson, G. and Scholes, K. (2001) *Exploring Public Sector Strategy*. Harlow: Financial Times/Prentice Hall.

Katz, D. and Kahn, R.L. (1978) *The Social Psychology of Organizations*. New York, NY: Wiley.

Keenan, J. (2000) 'Just how new is best value?', *Public Money and Management*, 20(3): 45–9.

Long, M. (2000) 'Picking up the bill for our kids? The policing of youth and the Crime and Disorder Act', in J. Pickford (ed.) *Youth Justice: Theory and Practice*. Cavendish.

Loveday, B. (2000) 'Policing performance: the effects of performance targets on police culture', *Criminal Justice Matters*, 40: 23–4.

Lubans, V.A. and Edgar, J.M. (1979) *Policing by Objectives*. Hartford, CT: Social Development Corporation.

Macpherson, Sir W. (1999) *The Stephen Lawrence Inquiry*. London. HMSO.

McLaughlin, E. *et al.* (2001) 'The permanent revolution: New Labour, new public management and the modernization of criminal justice', *Criminal Justice*, 1(3): 301–18.

McLaughlin, K. *et al.* (2002) *New Public Management. Current Trends and Future Prospects*. London: Routledge.

Munro-Orr, T. (2003) 'Leading edge', *Police Review*, 111(5715): 20–1.

Neyroud, P. and Beckley, A. (2001) *Policing, Ethics and Human Rights*. Cullompton: Willan.

Osborne, D. and Gaebler, T. (1992) *Reinventing Government: How the Entrepreneurial Spirit is Transforming the Public Sector*. Reading, MA: Addison-Wesley.

Pagon, M. (2003) 'The need for a paradigm shift in police leadership', in R. Adlam and P. Villiers (eds) *Police Leadership in the Twenty-first Century*. Winchester: Waterside Press.

Panzarella, R. (2003) 'Leadership myths and realities', in R. Adlam and P. Villiers (eds) *Police Leadership in the Twenty-first Century*. Winchester: Waterside Press.

Police Federation (1990) *Operational Policing Review*. Surbiton: Joint Consultative Committee of the Police Staff Associations.

Rauch, C.F. and Behling, O. (1984) 'Functionalism: basis for an alternate approach to the study of leadership', in J.G. Hunt (ed.) *Leaders and Managers: International Perspectives on Managerial Behaviour and Leadership*. New York, NY: Pergamon.

Reiner, R. (1991) *Chief Constables: Bobbies, Bosses or Bureaucrats?* Oxford: Oxford University Press.

Reiner, R. (1998) 'Process or product? Problems of assessing individual police performance', in J.P. Brodeur (ed.) *How to Recognize Good Policing: Problems and Issues*. London: Sage, 55–72.

Richards, N. (1985) 'A plea for applied ethics', in R. Thackrah (ed.) *Contemporary Policing: A Study of Society in the 1980s*. London: Sphere Reference.

Ritzer, G. (2000) *The McDonaldization of Society*. London: Sage.

Roy, D. (1954) 'Efficiency and "The fix": informal intergroup relations in a piecework machine shop', *American Journal of Sociology*, 60(3): 255–66.

Schein, E.H. (1992) *Organizational Culture and Leadership*. New York, NY: Maxwell Macmillan.

Silverman, E. (2001) *NYPD Battles Crime: Innovative Strategies in Policing*. Boston, MA: Northeastern University Press.

Skogan, W.G. and Hartnett, S.M. (1997) *Community Policing, Chicago Style*. New York, NY: Oxford University Press.

Smith, P. (1995) 'Outcome-related performance indicators and organizational control in the public sector', in J. Holloway *et al.* (eds) *Performance Measurement and Evaluation*. London: Sage, 192–216.

Stogdill, R.M. (1950) 'Leadership, membership and organization', *Psychological Bulletin*, 47: 1–14.

Tichy, N. and Devanna, M. (1986) *The Transformational Leader*. New York, NY: Wiley.

Timmins, N. (1995) *The Five Giants: A Biography of the Welfare State*. London: HarperCollins.

Villiers, P. (2003) 'Philosophy, doctrine and leadership: some core beliefs', in R. Adlam and P. Villiers (eds) *Police Leadership in the Twenty-first century*. Winchester: Waterside Press.

Villiers, P. and Adlam, R. (2003) 'Introduction', in R. Adlam and P. Villiers (eds) *Police Leadership in the Twenty-first century*. Winchester: Waterside Press.

Warner, J. (2002) 'Creating a consistent set of standards for Britain's police', *Competency and Emotional Intelligence*, 9(3): 15–18, 24.

Waters, I. (2000) 'Quality and performance monitoring', in F. Leishman *et al.* (eds) *Core Issues in Policing* (2nd edn). Harlow: Pearson, 264–87.

Winchester, R. (2002) 'Ahead of the game', *Community Care*, 14–20 March: 32–3.

Wintour, P. (2002) 'Blair's warning angers unions', *Guardian* 5 February: 2.

Wright, A. (2000) 'Managing the future: an academic's view', in F. Leishman *et al.* (eds) *Core Issues in Policing* (2nd edn). Harlow: Pearson, 288–304.

Zaleznik, A. (1977) 'Managers and leaders: are they different?', *Harvard Business Review*: 67–78.

Chapter 26

Police and new technologies

Janet B.L. Chan

New technologies and policing

Technology has always shaped policing – in both visible and invisible ways. One of the most visible changes in modern policing was in the technology for mobility (Nogala 1995),[1] the use of cars for patrolling the streets and responding to calls for service. Less visibly, advances in communication technologies, such as two-way radios, the widespread availability of tele-phones, together with computer-aided dispatch (CAD) systems, have radically transformed the social organisation of police work (Manning 1992a). There is therefore every reason to expect that dramatic breakthroughs in information technology since the early 1970s (Castells 2000) would have an equally dramatic effect on policing. With recent advances in surveillance, detection and identification technologies, the new technological revolution has virtually taken over social life. Surveillance technologies have become ubiquitous in the UK and other western countries (Graham 1998: 490; Lyon 2001; Marx 2002). In general, the proliferation of 'social control technologies' in the last 50 years has been phenomenal: not only are they increasingly sophisticated (two examples given by Marx are global positioning satellites and night vision scopes) but they are also remarkable in terms of 'scale and relatively greater scientific precision, continual invention and experimentation and rapid global diffusion' (Marx 2001: 15,506; see also Nunn 2001b).

New technologies promise improved effectiveness and efficiency in policing. Technologies extend the physical capacity of police officers to see, hear, recognise, record, remember, match, verify, analyse and communicate (cf. Haggerty and Ericson 1999: 237). Computerised systems offer ready access, ease of use, speed of retrieval, and virtually limitless storage and analytical capacity for information processing. Advances in digitised image and video technologies have expanded the scope of what can be stored as information. These systems have also become increasingly portable, economical and mutually compatible. Computer technologies are considered a 'force multi-plier', meaning that technology can improve a police organisation's efficiency and capability without employing extra staff (Nunn and Quinet 2002: 84).

New technologies can also enhance the professional status of police and the legitimacy of police organisations (Ericson and Shearing 1986; Manning 1992a; Ericson and Haggerty 1997). New technologies build cultural and symbolic capital by improving police officers' computer literacy, technical skills and capacity to deal with sophisticated crimes and criminals (Nogala 1995; Chan *et al.* 2001: 58–60). Information technology, in particular, is especially suited for developing 'smart' policing strategies that are problem oriented, intelligence led and evidence based (see, for example, Sherman 1998; Abt Associates 2000; Maguire 2000). Such technology is also ideal for making police officers and police organisations more self-regulating and more publicly accountable (Chan 1999; Chan *et al.* 2001).

It is easy to be carried away by the hype of new technologies or the apocalyptic vision of their critics, but as Postman reminds us, 'Every technology is both a burden and a blessing' (1992: 4–5), policing technologies being no exception. This chapter is an attempt to answer some of the questions raised by this rapid growth in policing technologies: have new technologies made a difference to policing? What sort of impact have they had? How do we explain the nature of this impact (or lack of impact)? The focus is mainly on the use of information and communication technologies[2] by public police organisations. The first section summarises the research evidence[3] on how new technologies have affected police work and police organisation. The chapter then goes on to analyse the impact of technologies in terms of changes in the structure (*field*) and culture (*habitus*) of policing. Next, these results are interpreted in terms of theories of technological change. The final section of the chapter discusses the opportunities for policing reform occasioned by technological change.

The impact of information technology on policing

The use of information technology has become part of everyday life in the twenty-first century for many individuals and the vast majority of organisations. While the purchase of computers may once have been considered a 'novelty' for police (Dupont 2001: 39), by the late 1980s computers were considered 'necessities, essential parts of police work' by police (Northrop *et al.* 1995). By the mid-1990s, virtually all police forces in the UK, the USA and other western countries had invested heavily in computerised information systems (Mullen 1996; Hoey 1998; Abt Associates 2000). A recent report noted that the annual cost of the PNC (Police National Computer) to the police forces of England and Wales was £17.6 million (HMIC 2000: 78). Similarly, the US Department of Justice's Office has since 1994 'provided upwards of one billion [US] dollars in grants to state and local police agencies for information technology development and enhancement' (Abt Associates 2000: iii). Current technologies support a variety of information systems for operations, command and control, management, geographic analysis and problem-solving (Abt Associates 2000: 15). These are augmented by a variety of identification, detection and surveillance technologies operated by the police, local authorities and private industries (Hoey 1998). To analyse the impact of all this technology on policing, it is important briefly to recap on the role of information in policing.

The role of information in policing

Despite media representations of police work as full of action and danger, the most important aspect of police work is in fact 'information work' (Nogala 1995: 193). Police are 'knowledge workers' (Ericson and Haggerty 1997: 19; Sheptycki 1998), and information is the 'central "input" and basis for action' in policing (Manning 1992a: 352). Research has shown that police officers 'spend most of their time conducting surveillance, interviewing citizens for information relevant to making cases, and writing reports', often spending 'more time writing accounts in official bureaucratic forms than in the actual activity being reported on' (Ericson and Shearing 1986: 138). Conceptually, police work can be regarded as an endless cycle of information collection and processing – penetration, surveillance, information, registration, knowledge, administration – for social control (Ericson and Shearing 1986: 138). The demand for information has historically been driven by crime control and police internal administrative purposes (see Chapter 10), but it is now increasingly also driven by the requirements of external agencies and institutions for their own risk management purposes (Ericson and Haggerty 1997: 21–7).

Impact of information technology on police work

Given the central significance of information in police work, it is natural to assume that advances in information technology would have had a major impact on policing, but such an assumption is not necessarily correct. A major review of the literature published a decade ago suggests that information technologies 'have been constrained by the traditional structure of policing and by the traditional role of the officer' (Manning 1992a: 350). Drawing on evaluation studies published in the 1970s and 1980s (e.g. Chaiken *et al.* 1975; Rheinier *et al.* 1977; Colton 1978; Hough 1980a), Manning described the disappointing results of various technological innovations such as CAD systems, attempts to reduce response time, car locator and tracking systems, crime-mapping techniques and management information systems. He concluded that 'Such research as exists is often inconclusive or suggests that new technologies have less effect on police practices than their proponents predict or prefer' (Manning 1992a: 382).

Manning's conclusion is not really surprising given the technical capacity of these earlier innovations and the social contexts in which they were introduced. Even though the 'information technology revolution' was born in the 1970s, it was not until the mid to late 1990s that the pace of technological change had accelerated sufficiently for these technologies to be widely diffused and culturally accepted (Castells 2000: 31). Early technological innovations in policing would have been cumbersome and expensive by today's standards. However, their most serious problems were not technical. Some of the systems were doomed to failure as they were designed with little understanding of the nature of police work, the expectations of citizens, and the social organisation of policing (Hough 1980b; Manning 1992a: 373–383). For example, attempts to use statistical modelling in the 1970s for assigning police cars to calls assumed that minimising response time would enhance police effectiveness. This assumption did not take into account the fact that there is usually considerable time lapse between crime occurrence and citizens' decision to call the police. It also did not consider the reality that the ability of police to clear crimes depends on numerous factors other than response time – for example, the availability of witnesses, the presence of physical evidence and so on. These innovations were also introduced at a time when computer literacy and acceptance of technological change were not high among police officers. In general it is important to bear in mind that the impact of technological innovations may vary with time and a range of global and organisational factors (see below). Locally, the type of technology, the work focus of police units, individual skills and competencies, their rank and responsibilities can all make a difference (Manning 1992a: 383–6; Nogala 1995: 195).

Collection and management of information
Even before the widespread installation of information technology, police officers often complained about the amount of 'paperwork' they have to do (Ericson 1982; Ericson and Haggerty 1997: 296). Information technology has greatly enhanced the ability of police to collect information and store it for future use (Ericson and Shearing 1986: 141). The seemingly unlimited capacity of modern computer systems to hold and retrieve large volumes of data has meant that police are collecting greater amounts of information, in relation to a wider range of social and personal variables, from a broader variety of government and non-government sources, in statistical, textual and audio-visual formats, over a longer span of time and from a greater physical distance (Haggerty and Ericson 1999: 239–42). Advances in surveillance and detection technologies have also facilitated certain types of undercover 'intelligence' work (Marx 1988: 55). Information captured by these audio-visual means can now be stored in computers for future access and analysis. As Marx observes, 'Computers qualitatively alter the nature of surveillance – routinising, broadening and deepening it' (1988: 208).

The availability of modern computerised information systems does not guarantee, however, that what is entered is complete, accurate and timely. An audit conducted by the HM Inspectorate of Constabulary (HMIC) on crime recording among police forces in England and Wales found:

> widespread and varying interpretation of the [Home Office counting] rules [for recorded crime], offences wrongly classified, . . . the failure to record the correct number of crimes, an error rate of between 15% and 65% of the crime records examined, [and] inappropriate reclassifying of recorded crimes (2000: ix).

There was also substantial under-recording of crime, the average non-recording rate being 24 per cent (HMIC 2000: x). Poor-quality data can have serious operational, investigative, analytical, managerial and legal implications (HMIC 2000; Chan *et al.* 2001: 76–79). It is therefore not surprising that as a result of the HMIC report, the Association of Chief Police Officers established a National Crime Recording Standard in 2001 to promote consistency in crime recording across police forces.

No matter how sophisticated the computer system is, it cannot make officers share information they want to keep to themselves. Manning has observed that sharing of information is not a common practice among police officers, who normally keep information in their own 'case files, private notes, or log books', if not inside their own heads (1992a: 370). There is evidence that the introduction of information technology has not substantially changed this reluctance to share information (see Tan and Al-Hawamdeh 2001; Sheptycki 2003; Chapter 14). In his review of the influence of strategic intelligence on the policing of organised crime, Sheptycki (2003) cites 'intelligence hoarding' and 'information silos' as problems that impeded the flow of police intelligence. Nevertheless, nearly 70 per cent of respondents in Chan et al.'s (2001: 58–9) survey and 83 per cent in a similar survey in Chicago (Chicago Community Policing Evaluation Consortium 2003: 148) agreed that information technology has led to increased information sharing between police officers.

Analysis and use of information
Information retrieval is the most frequently performed task on computers by patrol officers and detectives alike (Northrop et al. 1995). Patrol officers mainly use computers for 'routine lookups', such as checking suspicious persons for outstanding warrants or car licence numbers for stolen vehicles (Northrop et al. 1995). This kind of checking was routine even in the early days of slow main-frame computers (Ericson 1982: 138–42). Certain groups tended to be targeted for this: young men of lower socioeconomic status, especially those who were unco-operative towards the police (Ericson 1982: 141) – i.e. precisely those populations generally subject to policing.

New information technology systems have made checking easier, faster and resulting in more 'hits' (Northrop et al. 1995). Chan et al. (2001) found in their study of an Australian police force that as a result of the introduction of mobile data units in patrol cars, the number of warrants executed more than doubled in two years. This increase in enforcement activity had a flow-on effect on the number of fine defaulters admitted to prison, which also more than doubled in roughly the same period of time (2001: 63–4). Similarly, Meehan's (1998) study of a small suburban American police force found that the installation of mobile data terminals (MDT) in patrol cars had not only led to increased proactive checking and stopping of motorists ('traffic work') but it also created new opportunities for patrol officers to engage in 'investigative work' through 'running plates' in parking lots of restaurants known to be frequented by drug dealers or other criminals, often leading to arrests.

While mobile data units have dramatically facilitated traditional street-level law enforcement activities, they appear to be less useful for officers engaged in problem-oriented policing (POP). Nunn and Quinet's evaluation of the use of cellular digital packet data (CDPD) systems (mobile computers that connect to a mobile phone network) in a US state police agency found that even though the technology made checking of persons and vehicles much easier and faster, it 'did not appear to offer special benefits to officers practicing POP techniques'

(2002: 103). The productivity and performance of POP officers were virtually the same whether or not they had access to the technology. The researchers suggest that the technology did not make a difference partly because 'the activities associated with this new form of policing [POP] may not require any new technologies at all and may actually suggest a retreat from technologies of any kind that reflect traditional policing activities or that distance the police from the community they serve' (Nunn and Quinet 2002: 104).

Detectives also use computers for searches, but they tend to access a variety of sources and systems to build an investigation (Northrop *et al.* 1995). Where different systems are not integrated, these searches can be time-consuming and frustrating. Nevertheless, American detectives reported using computer files significantly more frequently in 1988 than in 1976, and they attributed higher rates of arrests and clearance to computerised information (Northrop *et al.* 1995: 264). Harper's (1991) research on the use of a computerised crime reporting system by detectives in a British police constabulary also found that not only did the computerised information system make it easier and faster to access and retrieve information, it had also transformed the 'spatio-temporal context in which detectives operate': detectives no longer need to travel to different places to locate records and they have virtually 24-hour access to files. The most famous criminal investigation system available to all police forces in the UK is the Home Office Large Major Enquiry System (HOLMES), which was introduced in the mid-1980s. It has recently been replaced by HOLMES 2, which is an integrated investigation management system, combining a variety of functions such as information and document management, information processing and graphical indexing, as well as task management and court preparation.[4] At the time of writing, I have not been able to find any published systematic studies of the impact of HOLMES or its second-generation equivalent on major crime investigations.

Computerised information systems can also be used for more advanced and systematic searching such as matching and profiling (Marx and Reichman 1984). Crime information is now increasingly used for strategic and tactical 'crime analysis' (see Sheptycki 2003; Chapter 14). The explosion of public and private databases and their linkage via computer and communication networks have taken computer matching to a more sophisticated and intrusive level (Haggerty and Ericson 1999: 240–1).

Having access to large volumes of information is not necessarily beneficial. Chan *et al.*'s (2001: 58–9) survey of police officers found that nearly half the respondents felt that information technology had led to information overload among police. This feeling was particularly prevalent among more senior, as well as older and more experienced officers. Electronic mail was also said to be a major cause of information overload. Sheptycki found that 'intelligence overload' occurred among intelligence units as a result of 'noise' (low-grade intelligence or unusable analysis), staff's lack of analytic capacity and administrative support, and the 'compulsive data demand' of intelligence systems (2003: 26–7). In some police forces, it is now increasingly recognised that intelligence officers require specialist training in a variety of software packages and 'To be effective, intelligence analysis has to sit on a solid theoretical framework' (Ratcliffe 2002: 57; see Chapter 14). Ironically, the solution to information overload is to be found in various 'knowledge management', artificial intelligence or expert systems (Haggerty and Ericson 1999: 241).

Ericson and Haggerty (1997) found that some police officers actively resisted some aspects of information technology through refusal to participate, aversion to use or other forms of subtle resistance. Resistance was likely where officers perceived that such technology was used as a surveillance mechanism by supervisors or where the systems were technically difficult or cumbersome. As Manning (1992a) points out, the mere availability and accessibility of information do not necessarily mean that information is used effectively or appropriately by police officers and managers. In general, the use of computer technology may increase productivity without resulting in any gain in efficiency (cf. Henman 1996).

Impact on police organisation

New technologies have been found to 'often destabilise the power balance between organisational segments by altering communication patterns, roles relationships, the division of labor, established formats for organisational communication, and taken-for-granted routines' (Manning 1996: 54). Ericson and Haggerty's (1997) study of Canadian police organisations suggests that information technology has had a profound impact on the way officers think, act and report on their activities. They have concluded that 'Communication technologies . . . radically alter the structure of police organisation by levelling hierarchies, blurring traditional divisions of labor, dispersing supervisory capacities and limiting individual discretion. In the process, traditional rank structures of command and control are replaced by system surveillance mechanisms for regulating police conduct' (1997: 388). Information technology has also created new cultures of policing and rendered police organisations more transparent (1997: 412). Individual police discretion is severely circum-scribed by the rules, formats and technologies of the reporting systems, whereas supervision has been tightened both *prospectively* as details of police activities are embedded in the 'required fields' of information technology systems and *retrospectively* as supervisors take more seriously their scrutiny of filed reports. The capability of information technology is such that it has become an effective tool for the surveillance of police supervisors, the detection of misconduct, and all types of audits, monitoring and risk management (1997: 398–9).

Chan *et al.*'s (2001) study came to some similar conclusions. Survey respondents thought that information technology had led to closer scrutiny of police work by supervisors and made supervisors more aware of the day-to-day activities and workload of officers under their command. This increased awareness of work activities by supervisors was perceived most frequently by detectives, who traditionally enjoyed a great degree of autonomy and freedom in their daily activities. There was general agreement that with the introduction of technology, police were required to report on their activities more frequently. Senior officers with management or supervisory responsibilities reported spending more time on paperwork, planning and checking the work of their staff for 'compliance'. However, the capacity provided by technology for checking has not been fully utilised by supervisors because they 'didn't have time'. The majority of police thought that information technology had led to improved police accountability, which some regarded as an overemphasis on accountability. Officers were concerned that accountability requirements had increased at the expense of 'core' police work, while the organisation had gone 'risk-management crazy'. Some felt that the amount of auditing and checking had gone too far and become counterproductive. Police were suspicious of systems that monitor their decisions and fearful that information technology may be used for punishment. They were concerned that technology-generated performance indicators may be misused by management. They particularly resented demands for accountability from external agencies (Chan 2001: 155).

The organisational impact of information technology is, of course, not deterministic. Manning's (1996) study of the use of cellular (mobile) phones by police suggests that while technology can change work organisation physically, socially, politically and symbolically, meanings of technology are negotiated and often reconstituted as a result. Instead of restricting discretion and tightening supervision, the introduction of cellular phones 'reduces the capacity of the command segment to anticipate, monitor, supervise, and control the actions of field officers', especially in organisations where such phone communications are not recorded (Manning 1996: 59). Officers in some cases used the phones 'to call friends, avoid supervision, reduce work by handling complaints by phone and, more generally, avoid work where possible' (1996: 59). Such 'counter-appropriation' of the technology may be short lived, however, as police departments are increasingly bringing in MDTs into patrol cars which can turn cellular phones into 'another source of potentially controlling surveillance' (1996: 60). Meehan's (1998) study found, however, that MDT technology had in fact increased the autonomy of patrol officers, who no longer had to rely on the dispatcher for information. Supervisors also complained that they could no longer keep track of what was happening out on the street through listening to the radio. Nevertheless, the CAD/MDT interface had the potential to segment job assignments and increase supervisors' control of workload allocation since officers not dispatched to a scene were no longer given detailed information about the nature of the case.

There is evidence that information technology has led to increased civilianisation as well as a larger percentage of technical personnel in police forces. Nunn's analysis of a 1993 survey of 188 municipal police forces[5] in the USA found that 'highly computerised cities reported larger shares of total employees in technical positions', spent more per capita, and seemed to deliver services with fewer officers per capita than municipal agencies reporting lower levels of computerisation' (2001a: 232). One interpretation of the higher level of civilian employees as a result of computerisation is that information technology may have delivered some of the efficiencies promised, at least in terms of 'input' costs (2001a: 231).

With the advent of information technology, police have become suppliers of information for a large number of external agencies: apart from the routine supply of crime and criminal record information to courts and other parts of the criminal justice system, police regularly make available crime occurrence and traffic accident data to insurance companies, law firms, loss assessors and mercantile agents; they also service the requests of external agencies to provide criminal history checks for the vetting of job applicants for certain types of work (Ericson and Haggerty 1997; Chan *et al.* 2001: 31, 102–3). In the UK, police also provide data for crime and disorder partnerships, HMIC and others. Part of the driving force behind this is the 'climate of accountability' leading to new reporting requirements. For example, the victims' rights movement and pressure groups were regarded as 'caus[ing] more forms to be created' (Ericson and Haggerty 1997: 303). Government policies (e.g. freedom of information), new laws and watchdog organisations all demand additional reporting requirements for accountability purposes (Chan *et al.* 2001: 28–30). This created a great deal of resentment among operational officers, who felt that these demands were placing increased burden on officers and detracting from the core business of policing (2001: 102–4). Nevertheless, police organisations have no choice but to comply with legislative requirements and, where possible and appropriate, information is commodified and sold to external institutions either for a fixed fee or a charge per hour of police time (Ericson and Haggerty 1997: 343–4).

Information technology would appear to have had a positive impact on workplace relations: it has led to improved communication and facilitated teamwork (Chan *et al.* 2001). However, in some organisations it can also reinforce old cultural conflicts between central administration and local operations, between police and civilians and between management police and operational police. It can also create new divisions between operational police and information technology personnel. The perception among operational police in the Australian study was that central administration, civilians, management and information technology staff did not understand operational policing needs and were more concerned with their own careers and 'empire building'. Operational police also resented what they saw as inequitable distribution of resources and their perception was that, while they had to live with outdated and inadequate computer equipment, civilians and headquarters staff were provided with more and better computer resources (Chan *et al.* 2001: 99–102).

Technological impact on the *field* and *habitus* of policing

A useful way to analyse technological change is to examine its relationship to the 'field' and 'habitus' of policing (Bourdieu and Wacquant 1992; see Chan 1997; Chan *et al.*). For Bourdieu, a field is like a game; it is a social space of conflict and competition, where participants struggle to establish control over specific power and authority. Central to Bourdieu's concept of field is the notion of 'capital'. Various forms of capital operate in different social fields – these include economic capital, cultural or informational capital, social capital and symbolic capital (Bourdieu 1987: 3–4). Habitus is a 'feel for the game'. It is a system of dispositions which agents acquire either individually, through family and the education system, or as a group, through organisational socialisation. Bourdieu's framework suggests that changes in the game (field) would create new *necessities* which may require the creation of new strategies (habitus) for coping. Technological change, to the extent that it redefines the game of policing, can bring about changes in the field (through various constraints and resources) as well as transform the habitus (e.g. classifications, assumptions and sensibilities).

Impact on the field

Information technology has fundamentally altered the field of policing through the various *resources* ('capital') it provides and *constraints* ('necessities') it imposes on police work.

Technology as a resource

Nogala sees technology as a 'power-amplifier' – new technologies provide 'new possibilities, capabilities and abilities for the police'; these include the power to recognise, to ask, to know, to act and to prevent (1995: 193–4). Technology is a resource that police can draw on 'to get the work done'; as such, it is used much more often than the law (Ericson and Shearing 1986: 134–5). Police officers have generally welcomed the technology and thought that it has made their work easier and more effective (Chan *et al.* 2001; Chicago Community Policing Evaluation Consortium 2003). Information delivered by technology such as MDT can provide useful resources for 'constructing an understanding of "place" . . . or "area knowledge" . . . critical to policing': knowledge of prior police dispatches to an address can be used strategically by officers to effect control and to protect themselves against potential dangers (Meehan 1998: 239–40). Information technology is also a valuable communication resource for police: not only does it facilitate teamwork and information sharing, but it also allows people in different cities and even different countries to work together. Technical (IT) expertise has become a much valued form of cultural capital. As one intelligence officer explained, 'As intel officers we were considered the leaders in IT. We knew nothing, but we knew so much more than the basic [officer] who knew practically nothing. We were gods to them' (Chan *et al.* 2001: 115). The growth in funding and staffing of IT-related functions within the police is often a source of much envy and some bitterness among some officers. The ascendancy of officers with IT expertise may also threaten the traditional power structure of an organisation where previously leaders have predominantly been drawn from the criminal investigation branch (Chan *et al.* 2001).

Technology as constraint

New technology has also created constraints for police work. The computerisation of police reporting systems has not led to any decrease in 'paperwork' (Chicago Community Policing Evaluation Consortium 2003), while greater demands for information both internally and externally have led to the introduction of additional fields and indexes that are mandatory to fill in (Ericson and Haggerty 1997). Chan *et al.*'s case study in Australia found that police reported spending on average about 3 hours and 37 minutes per eight-hour shift using information technology to undertake various administrative tasks (2001: 53). Officers perceived that they were spending more time satisfying accountability requirements and less time 'on the streets'. Higher-ranking police were even more likely to have this perception, as one officer-in-charge explained: 'I could spend six or seven hours a day just doing compliance without even looking at police work. Officers-in-charge of bigger stations probably would need half a dozen staff to do that properly. Nobody does it properly – we're all aware of that. It's very frustrating' (2001: 150). There is no doubt that information technology has given police supervisors a greater capacity to scrutinise the work of their staff, but whether this capacity has been utilised effectively is debatable. An officer-in-charge explained that the new incident management system allows supervisors to check where their cars are, what their officers are doing, how far they have got in their crime report and whether they have done their job properly; however, this officer said that he doesn't really use the system, because he doesn't have time to do it (Chan 2001: 152).

Information technology can also limit police discretion in that they literally cannot do their work without using the technology (Ericson and Haggerty 1997: 394). Avoidance of paperwork becomes more difficult (Meehan 1998: 246) or in some cases no longer possible as reporting fields have been made mandatory (Ericson and Haggerty 1997: 395). As pointed out by some officers: 'there are no shortcuts – the system was designed in such a way that it cannot be circumvented ... In fact, the system is capable of monitoring short-cuts' (Chan 2001: 150–151).

Technological impact on the habitus

To what extent have these changes in the field made a difference to the habitus of policing – that is, the cultural assumptions about the aims of policing, appropriate ways of seeing and behaving, and treasured values and beliefs? One way to clarify the impact of technological change on the habitus is to examine changes and continuities in assumptions about: (1) what police information is for; (2) what is considered relevant information; (3) how information is obtained and used; and (4) how information ought to be obtained and used.

The purpose of information

Different models of policing make different assumptions about what police information is for. Traditional policing models see information primarily in terms of incident-based operational and administrative purposes, while community-oriented and POP models promote the use of information for problem identification, the search for solution and evaluation of responses (Abt Associates 2000: 11–13; see Chapter 13). The available research evidence points to very little change among police in their basic assumption about the purpose of police information. In Chan et al.'s (2001) survey, less than four in ten respondents agreed that information technology has led to a more problem-oriented police service or better proactive policing. In general, officers see information as useful only if it leads to arrests, as one senior information technology manager observed: '. . . even our [intelligence] people, even the high-end users, our power users, generally see information from an offender perspective – in other words, information analysis is all about how we can . . . find an offender . . . how do you nick someone, and so that limits what becomes useful information' (2001: 110). According to this manager, there was not a clear vision of what POP might offer; it was still seen as 'soft' and marginal. Information technology has, in effect, 'made things easier, rather than made things different' (2001: 109).

What is relevant information?

Assumptions about the purpose of police information often determine what is considered relevant information. If the 'good pinch' is the primary aim, then only incident-based data and what can be used as evidence in a particular case would be considered relevant information (cf. Sheptycki 2003; see Chapter 14). But if information were to be used for problem-solving, what counts as relevant information becomes quite broad: crime trends, data on community profiles, economic conditions, community attitudes, etc., are all part of 'environmental scanning' (Abt Associates 2000: 12). As far as the available research evidence shows, police assumptions about what is considered relevant information have remained unchanged in spite of the introduction of information technology. Police in the focus groups conducted by Chan *et al.* (2001) were aware of the potential for using technology for 'smarter' policing strategies, 'intelligence-driven patrols', analysis of 'hotspots' and repeat offenders, and proactive crime investigations, but they said there were not sufficient time or resources to realise this potential. The problem in this police force was also exacerbated by the inappropriate use of intelligence officers to collate statistics for senior police. The assumption that information is relevant only if it leads to arrest and conviction may be partly responsible for police resentment and resistance against having to fill out long and detailed computer reports for external accountability purposes. Ironically, as Ericson and Haggerty point out, 'Most of the crime-related knowledge produced by the police is disseminated to other institutions . . . for their risk management needs, rather than used for criminal prosecution and punishment' (1997: 446).

How information is obtained and used

Traditional policing models typically rely on a narrow range of information sources (e.g. calls for service, crime occurrence), with a heavy emphasis on reactive strategy, retrospective investigation and law enforcement outcomes (Abt Associates 2000: 12–13). As Chan *et al.* (2001) discovered in their case study, the most successful use of information technology for proactive policing was in support of traditional law enforcement: the use of mobile data systems in police cars to check for outstanding traffic offence warrants. This technology was enthusiastically received by police and, as mentioned earlier, had resulted in an exponential increase in the collection of fines as well as the imprisonment of fine defaulters. Meehan (1998) observed a similar enthusiasm among patrol officers in a small American police force in relation to the use of MDT for 'running plates' and conducting stops, both in targeting traffic violations and for potential arrests of offenders with outstanding warrants. In a separate study of a medium-sized suburban police force, Meehan and Ponder (2002) found that MDT technology may also have facilitated 'racial profiling' by police: while African-Americans are generally over-represented in proactive queries compared with white Americans, the rates of queries and stops of African-Americans were about one and a half times higher among a small group of high MDT users, compared with low and medium MDT users.

In police organisations where a more analytical and problem-oriented approach to crime is taken, there appears to be a clash of cultures between police and analysts. Among operational police there is a general mistrust of information retrieved from a computer system, as well as a cultural aversion to depersonalised and decontextualised data generated by crime analysts (see Chapter 14). Among detectives there is a tendency to 'co-opt crime analysis for the purposes of crime investigation', thus reducing 'the intelligence process to evidence gathering and evaluation', instead of a broader analysis of trends and patterns for crime prevention (Sheptycki 2003: ch. 3). The reluctance of police to share information, the non-reporting or non-recording of crime and intelligence information, and the doubtful quality of data entered into computer are all indicative of the assumption that law enforcement ('good pinch') is the main purpose of information (Sheptycki 2003; see Chapter 14).

An emerging trend in some jurisdictions is the use of spatial and temporal trend data for the management of local police commanders' performance, the most famous example being the Compstat process pioneered in New York City (Eck and Maguire 2000; Silverman 2001; Henry 2002; McDonald 2002; Dixon and Maher 2003). Compstat makes use of information and mapping technologies to produce statistical profiles of arrests and crimes in each local area (precinct), and local commanders are held accountable for crime patterns in their precincts through regular briefings and 'grillings' by top executives. In 1996, NYPD's Compstat received an Innovations in American Government award and since then has become the 'Lourdes of policing', with numerous police forces within America and around the world visiting the city, wanting to learn about the process (Silverman 2001: 207). A similar system called Operations and Crime Reviews has been implemented in the New South Wales Police service since 1998. While the process has enormous potential for problem-solving and making police commanders accountable, the NSW process was criticised by some commanders as implementing 'management by fear' and by an independent auditor as being too narrowly focused on crime statistics as performance indicators (HayGroup 2000; Dixon 2001).

One positive change that information technology has brought about is reflected in the way information is used to make police procedures more transparent and police organisations more accountable. For example, case information recorded on computer systems allows victims and complainants to get faster feedback on the progress of their cases and police to provide better service to 'customers' by accessing this information (Chan et al. 2001: 65; see also Ericson and Haggerty 1997: 412). In other instances, transparency can be forced upon police organisations, as when MDT communications following the Rodney King beating was introduced as evidence in court (Meehan 1998: 245).

At a more informal level, Meehan (2000) found that police officers have incorporated audio and video records produced by information and surveillance technologies into the oral tradition of the police occupational culture. In the same way that 'war stories' have served to reinforce solidarity and maintained cultural myths, copies of entertaining or dramatic tapes of police in action are shared, bootlegged and circulated among officers. These records reinforce the traditional values of police culture and 'lend an authenticity and credibility to the police world view' (Meehan 2000: 111).

How information should be obtained and used
Information technology has increased the capacity for police to be more strategic and problem oriented in their methods: they can draw on a wide range of 'environmental' information, share information with other organisations, conduct in-depth analysis of crime and social data, search for workable solutions and evaluate their strategies (Abt Associates 2000: 12–13). This was indeed the ideal of the so-called 'Compstat paradigm' (Henry 2002) and the intention of the architects of the systems in the Australian case study. As a senior information technology manager told the researchers: 'The idea was to move gradually from an ad hoc, operationally oriented system to an integrated, tactically, strategically and eventually policy-oriented system'. However, this was expected to be a longer-term objective, as the organisation has yet to move to the next level of maturity and capability (Chan 2001: 153). Meanwhile, police have become heavily reliant on information technology for information, and some are not comfortable with this situation. To these officers, reliance on technology has meant that police are no longer carrying knowledge in their heads, leading to the loss of 'local knowledge' and the neglect of traditional hands-on intelligence gathering (Chan 2001: 154; see also Meehan 1998: 251 regarding 'deskilling' as a result of increased use of information technology). As pointed out earlier, the prevalent attitude of the police appears still to favour case-by-case investigation rather than crime analysis, evidence gathering rather than intelligence analysis, secrecy rather than openness in information sharing. In some organisations, there is a general mistrust of computerised information and resentment against data collection for internal risk management and external accountability purposes.

The research evidence therefore suggests that technological change has left more continuities than changes in the habitus of policing. But a note of caution is in order: cultural change takes time – the pace of technological change is such that the longer-term effect of information technology is difficult to predict.

Understanding technological change

To understand the mixed impact of information technology on policing – why certain aspects of technological innovations made a difference and others didn't – it is useful to interpret these research findings in relation to various theories of technological change. Researchers who study the impact of technology on social life have long argued that technology should not be seen as consisting of a physical, material dimension only; rather, technology operates in a social context and its meaning is perceived differently by people in different social and organisational positions (Ackroyd *et al.* 1992; Manning 1992a; Ericson and Shearing 1986; Orlikowski and Gash 1994). While techno-logical changes have the capacity to transform social and organisational life, technology is itself shaped by social and organisational conditions. The impact of a specific technology on social life is often determined by factors beyond its technical capacity – psychological, social, political or cultural factors. Hence, technology may be constraining or enabling, but people have the ability to 'adapt, bend, shape, develop, subvert, misuse and otherwise manipulate technological specifications for various purposes' (Ackroyd *et al.* 1992: 11). Orlikowski and Robey explain this as the underlying 'duality' of information technology: 'Information technology is both an antecedent and a consequence of organisational action' (1991: 151).

The impact of technological change on organisational structure, work practices, communication channels and performance cannot be understood in a *deterministic* or rationalist way (Orlikowski 1996: 64). Instead, the conse-quences of information technology should be viewed via an *interpretive* or *emergent* model – i.e. that they result from the 'interplay among computing infrastructures, conflicting objectives and preferences of different social groups, and the operation of chance' and that information technology is open to interpretation during implementation and use (Robey and Sahay 1996: 95). These models stress the active role of organisational members and the importance of social context and processes that produce the meanings of technology. From this perspective, technology is 'an occasion for, not a determinant of, organisational change' (Barley 1986).

As Nogala (1995: 199–206) points out, the impact of technology on police organisations depends on a range of internal and external driving forces as well as counterforces. Broadly speaking, we can distinguish four types of factors that influence the course of technological change and its impact on organisations: (1) *global trends* which refer to larger societal developments that generally affect all organisations; (2) *technical design and implementation* which include the nature of technology itself and how technological change is managed; (3) *political issues* which refer to the interests at stake in technological change and the conflict or bargaining that may result; and (4) *cultural frames* which include the assumptions inherent in the introduced technology and the extent to which these are congruent with those held by users within organisations. These are, of course, analytic categories that are not meant to be mutually exclusive: global trends affect, and are constituted by, organisational issues, while technical design is not politically or culturally neutral.

Global trends

Nogala (1995) has enumerated a number of external driving forces that favour 'further technification of police work'; these include the general development of technology, the increasing desire for more security, the growing security industry, and the general tendency towards the 'industrialisation of social control' (1995: 202–3). There are also a number of driving forces internal to the policing sector that favour such developments. These include the reinforce-ment of international police co-operation, the new emphasis on preventive policing, the expansion of technology-related crimes, the continuing process of police professionalisation and specialisation, the requirements of rationalisation and the promise of technical solutions (1995: 200–1).

The growing importance of knowledge (Burton-Jones 1999), especially the knowledge of risk (Beck 1992), and the increasing dominance of neoliberal rationality (Dean 1999), have been facilitated by the information technology revolution (Castells 2000). Advances in information and communication technology have in turn fuelled the demand for more knowledge of risk and better management of risk.

The rise of neoliberalist rationality (in the form of 'new public management' – NPM) in western democracies in the 1980s saw a new emphasis on the use of private sector managerial techniques and administrative structures, including decentralisation of management, cutting back of the public sector, cost control, efficiency, performance indicators, risk assessment and auditing (Leishman *et al.* 1996; Power 1997; Dean 1999). The need to demonstrate 'value for money' has intensified the search for more effective policing models and investment in an 'armoury' of information and communication technology (Maguire 2000).

Associated with NPM is a new conception of public accountability which involves 'a shift in regulatory style from centralised control towards a combination of self-regulation and external oversight' (Chan 1999: 255; see also Power 1997). In policing, implementing the new accountability involves a range of technologies and accounting devices to measure performance and make decisions auditable. Police are being scrutinised externally by 'watchdog' agencies, public complaints systems and central auditors, and internally by management systems, internal audits and routine surveillance. Information technology provides the means through which police performance and decisions can be monitored, and individual as well as organisational risk factors assessed. Once established, police information systems are obliged to maintain audit trails or implement new data collection fields to meet legislative and accountability requirements (Chan *et al.* 2001: 28–30).

With the production of security being a main concern of both public and private institutions in 'risk society' came a growing demand for information for risk management. Public police organisations have therefore become prime producers and disseminators of crime-related knowledge external institutions such as insurance companies and traffic authorities (Ericson and Haggerty 1997). They are major hubs in the network (Castells 2000: 443) of 'risk communication' (Ericson and Haggerty 1997; Haggerty and Ericson 1999: 238). As such, police actually make wider contributions to the regulation of society through the communication of risk knowledge than through traditional law enforcement and order maintenance (Ericson and Haggerty 1997: 11–12).

Technical design and implementation

Technological change can have a large or small impact on organisations depending on the nature and design of the technology and the way in which technological change is managed. Early American police experience with information technology was negative partly because of poor design: 'Most agencies built their information systems on the advice and counsel of the vendors who were selling them equipment and systems. Internal technical expertise for assessing needs and matching equipment and systems to those needs was essentially non-existent' (Abt Associates 2000: 158). Not surprisingly, Northrop *et al.*'s (1995) survey of police officers found that the two most important factors associated with the frequency of computer usage were user friendliness and technical stability of the system.

Ericson and Haggerty's (1997) research suggests that information technology has had a substantial impact on policing partly because of the design and implementation of a more *coercive* technology which is difficult to avoid or bypass: when the basic routines of police work are built into the system, officers are literally not able to work without using the technology (1997: 394). In fact, where systems are less coercive or less effective, technology can be called upon to correct the problem (1997: 414).

Sparrow has long emphasised the importance of *managing* information systems properly:

> [I]f badly managed, they can frustrate managerial purposes, enshrine old values, focus attention on outdated an inappropriate performance measures, give power to the wrong people, cast in concrete old ways of doing business, create false or misleading public expectations, destroy partnerships and impose crippling restrictions to new styles of operation – quite apart from their propensity to consume millions and millions of tax dollars (1991: 26)

Examples of technical and implementation problems of information technology in policing include flaws in system design, poor system performance, inadequacy of infrastructure, lack of integration of different systems, and various training and support problems (Hough 1980b; Chan *et al.* 2001; Manning 2001; Chicago Community Policing Evaluation Consortium 2003).

Political issues

As Manning (1996: 54) observes, technological changes can often destabilise the power balance within an organisation. Since information itself is a source of power, information technology can lead to power struggles, adaptations or reactions which may subvert the original intentions of the new technology (Orlikowski and Robey 1991: 155).

In policing, the introduction of information technology can restrict the discretion and autonomy of 'street level' police officers, while at the same time enhance the status of information technology specialists (Ericson and Haggerty 1997: 406). Such developments alter the balance of power between workers and supervisors and between police and civilians. When officers feel that their autonomy is threatened by internal surveillance or external interference, they are likely to resort to resistance or sabotage where possible. Ericson and Haggerty gave examples of patrol officers collaborating with dispatchers to avoid being tracked by computer-aided dispatch systems (1997: 414) and of officers refusing or resisting the mandatory reporting of family violence as an 'externally driven surveillance technology based on an outlook of distrust' (1997: 386).

Cultural frames

Technology is not simply an objective, physical given; people have to make sense of it and, in the process, 'develop particular assumptions, expectations and knowledge of the technology, which then serve to shape subsequent actions toward it' (Orlikowski and Gash 1994: 175). Orlikowski and Gash coin the term 'technological frames' to describe a subset of the cognitive schemas shared by members of social groups (Schein 1985; Sackmann 1991). Technological frames can be both helpful and constraining: they can help 'structure' people's experience and reduce organisational uncertainty, but they can also inhibit creativity and reinforce established assumptions (Orlikowski and Gash 1994: 176–7). Technological frames generally vary between social groups, according to the 'purpose, context, power, knowledge base, and the [technological] artifact itself' (1994: 179). In their case study, Orlikowski and Gash distinguished between three domains of technological frames: (1) the nature of technology – people's understanding of *what* technology is capable of; (2) technology strategy – their view of *why* technology was introduced in their organisation; and (3) technology in use – their understanding of *how* technology is to be routinely used and the consequences of such use (1994: 183–4). The impact of information technology on organisations can then be explained in terms of the existence of *congruence* or *incongruence* in technological frames between certain social groups. Where incongruent technological frames exist, the introduction of technology is likely to encounter conflicts and difficulties.

The incongruence between the technological frames of information technology designers and those of the police was evident in the mismatch between the models of policing implicit in the technology introduced in the 1970s and the reality of policing (Hough 1980b: 351–2). Such incongruence can create tension in the workplace as workers seek to adjust their practices to conform to the system's requirements (Ackroyd *et al.* 1992: 119).

Sparrow (1991) shows the difficulty in trying to make a CAD system designed for traditional-style policing serve a community-based, problem-solving style of policing that management in the Houston Police Department wanted to adopt. Problems such as 'call stacking' (holding calls for beat officers to deal with), 'checking by' (allowing patrol cars to do proactive work instead of servicing non-urgent calls), 'call histories' (the amount of time call information should be retained on-line) and 'cherry picking' (officers taking the 'good' calls and leaving the unpleasant ones) revealed the fundamental conflict between traditional-style policing where response time was a major concern and problem-solving policing where police were expected to do proactive work, analyse call histories and make mature, responsible decisions about their work.

A clash in 'technological frames' between the users and the architects of the systems was also evident in the Australian case study (Chan *et al.* 2001). Users of the technology, even the more advanced ones, expected it to make their work easier and more efficient, without their having to change existing policing and management styles. Architects of the systems, on the other hand, have intended the organisation to move towards a more sophisticated mode of information usage – for resource management, tactical policing, strategic planning and policy decisions. Yet the case study has shown that users' technological frames are not immutable. While police resent the additional workload generated by managerial and accountability demands, they have also become willing players in the new technological game. The coercive nature of the technology gave them no other alternatives. Thus, despite constant complaints about various technical problems, police have generally responded positively to the new technology. Ironically, rather than resisting the burden imposed by the technology, they demand more and better technology in the hope of lightening this burden (Chan 2001: 156–7).

Dynamics of technological change

The introduction of new technology is merely the beginning of a 'technological drama' (Manning 1992b, 1996) of normalisation, adjustment, reconstitution and reintegration. The resultant reintegration and normalisation may be manifested in various changes as well as continuities in organisational life. Orlikowski (1996) offers a 'situated change' perspective which sees organisational change as emergent and continuous rather than rapid and discontinuous: 'through a series of ongoing and situated accommodations, adaptations, and alterations ... sufficient modifications may be enacted over time that fundamental changes are achieved' (1996: 66). Her study of the introduction of a call-tracking system found that the organisational structures and practices of the department had changed considerably over the two years following the implementation of the new technology, but the transformation, 'while enabled by the technology, was not caused by it' (1996: 69). Rather, members of the department 'attempted to make sense of and appropriate the new technology and its embedded constraints and enablements' and through their daily actions and interactions in response to the technology, they enacted 'a series of metamorphic changes in their organising practices and structures' (1996: 89).

Conclusion: mobilising technology for better policing

Information technology has certainly enhanced the capacity of police to collect, retrieve and analyse information. It has altered important aspects of the *field* of policing – it has redefined the value of communicative and technical resources, institutionalised accountability through built-in formats and procedures of reporting, and restructured the daily routines of operational policing. The impact of technology on the *habitus* of policing, however, appears to be much less substantial. The advantage brought about by technology – the capacity for a more responsive and problem-oriented approach to policing – has not been fully exploited. This is because operational police's 'technological frame' sees information as relevant only for the purpose of arrest and conviction. While officers are aware of the potential for 'smarter' policing approaches, the preference is still to focus on collecting evidence for law enforcement rather than broader analysis for crime prevention. Technologies that support a traditional law-enforcement style of policing are the most successful ones. Where a more analytical approach is taken in relation to crime and intelligence, there is often a clash of cultures between police and analysts. Supervisors are aware of the capabilities that technology provides for better accountability and supervision, but these capabilities are also underutilised because they do not have time. The cultural suspicion and cynicism against management and external watchdogs remain at a high level.

These findings are consistent with the view that the meaning of technology is constituted by members of organisations. The impact of technology on police work and organisation is often determined by factors beyond its technical capacity. Global trends such as the shift to a knowledge economy, the demand for risk knowledge to provide security, the dominance of neoliberal rationality and the dramatic advances in information technology all favour the increased 'technification' of police work. However, the acceptance or rejection of technological change in any specific setting can depend on its design and implementation, the political issues it raises and its degree of congruence with the technological frames of users. As Manning (1996) points out, the introduction of new technology is the beginning of a series of adjustments and adaptations, symbolic statements and counter-statements, which can result in changes as well as continuities in organisational life. Ericson and Haggerty (1997) are correct in emphasising the fundamental changes to policing brought about by the global forces of risk society and its demand for security through surveillance and risk management – changes which have been accelerated by advances in information and communication technologies. Nevertheless, and somewhat ironically, in spite of their vital role in the communication of risk knowledge, police organisations themselves have not yet become active and willing participants in the risk management enterprise. Officers are most enthusiastic about technologies that advance traditional law enforcement objectives of arrest and conviction. Efforts to change policing from an incident-based, reactive and unreflective approach to a more analytical, proactive and reflective one have not been met with great success.

The lesson from the experience of police with new technologies is the obvious one that 'giving police access to computers, increasing the range and quantity of information that is stored electronically and automating what were previously manual processes will not necessarily increase organisational effectiveness or change how the business of policing is conducted by the agency' (Chan *et al.* 2001: 116). Information technology offers opportunities for the institutionalisation of a more effective, more evidence-based and more accountable model of policing, but technology alone will not turn police forces into 'thinking' or 'learning' organisations (Abt Associates 2000: 154). On the other hand, information technology can create new risks such as illegal or unauthorised use of information (Chan *et al.* 2001: 112), the spreading of inaccurate or misleading information (Ericson and Shearing 1986: 144; HMIC 2000), and the unfair targeting of specific groups based on 'categorical suspicion' (Marx 1988; Meehan and Ponder 2002). Mobilising technology for better policing requires tying the development of technology to a strategy of *planned* organisational change, one that explicitly spells out the types of competencies and work practices that are to be encouraged and supported by organisational resources and reward structures. Technology is not neutral, but, as Postman warns, 'when we admit a new technology to the culture, we must do so with our eyes wide open' (1992: 7).

Selected further readings

Manning's 'Information technologies and the police' (1992) provides a good basic introduction to the key issues. Though not as accessible, Ericson and Haggerty's *Policing the Risk Society* (1997) is the most thorough and theoretically groundbreaking study of changes in policing partly as a result of technology. Abt Associates's *Police Department Information Systems Technology Enhancement Project* (2000) is useful for understanding how information technology can be designed to support community-oriented and problem-oriented policing. It also contains a number of American case studies. Chan *et al.*'s *e-Policing* (2001) and Chicago Community Policing Evaluation Consortium's *Community Policing in Chicago* (2003) provide recent case studies in Queensland, Australia, and Chicago, respectively. Given the pace of technological change, readers should expect more systematic research studies to be published in the near future.

Acknowledgements

I would like to thank Tim Newburn and an anonymous reviewer for their comments on a previous draft of the chapter, Kyungja Jung for her research assistance and David Dixon for insights on Compstat. Some material that first appeared in Chan (2001) has been incorporated here with permission from the editor of *Criminal Justice*. Excerpts from Chan *et al.* (2001) originally written by the author have also been incorporated without quotation marks to avoid the cumbersome use of extended quotations.

Notes

1 Nogala has established a useful scheme for classifying new police technologies. These include surveillance and detection technologies, identification technologies, information-processing technologies, communication technologies, organisation and administration technologies, intervention technologies and technologies for mobility (1995: 199).
2 The majority of new police technologies (the first five of Nogala's 1995 seven categories) can be regarded as *information* technologies as they represent different stages of information management: collection, storage, authentication, matching, analysis and communication.
3 Although the use of information technology is widespread among police forces in the UK, there have not been many systematic studies of the impact of technology on policing. Most of the recent studies cited in this chapter were conducted in the USA, Canada and Australia. As Meehan (1998) points out, to assess the impact of

technology on policing, it is important to study the *in situ* use of technology by police rather than infer from policy documents and user manuals how technology ought to be used.

4   This is based on information provided at www.unisys.com (accessed 24 April 2003).

5   Nunn's analysis was based on the 1993 US Department of Justice Law Enforcement Management and Administrative Statistics survey of all law enforcement agencies with more than 100 officers. The survey resulted in 831 respondents, representing a response rate of 97 per cent. Nunn's sample consisted of 188 agencies in cities with a population of 100,000 or more.

6   There seems to be a contradiction between what the regression results show and the author's final conclusion. The conclusion was consistent with the analysis of means (Table 5) but not with the regression analysis where a number of control variables were included.

References

Abt Associates (2000) *Police Department Information Systems Technology Enhancement Project (ISTEP)*. Washington, DC: Department of Justice, Office of Community Oriented Policing Services.

Ackroyd, S., Harper, R., Hughes, J.A., Shapiro, D. and Soothill K. (1992) *New Technology and Practical Police Work*. Buckingham: Open University Press.

Barley, S. (1986) 'Technology as an occasion for structuring: evidence from observations of CT scanners and the social order of radiology departments', *Administrative Science Quarterly*, 31: 78–108.

Beck, U. (1992) *Risk Society: Towards a New Modernity*. London: Sage.

Bourdieu, P. (1987) 'What makes a social class? On the theoretical and practical existence of groups', *Berkeley Journal of Sociology*, 32: 1–18.

Bourdieu, P. and Wacquant, L.J.D. (1992) *An Invitation to Reflexive Sociology*. Cambridge: Polity Press.

Burton-Jones, A. (1999) *Knowledge Capitalism: Business, Work, and Learning in the New Economy*. Oxford: Oxford University Press.

Castells, M. (2000) *The Information Age: Economy, Society and Culture. Volume I. The Rise of the Network Society* (2nd edn). Oxford: Blackwell.

Chaiken, J., Crabill, T., Holliday, L., Jaquett, D., Lawless, M. and Quade, E. (1975) *Criminal Justice Models: An Overview*. Santa Monica, CA: Rand.

Chan, J. (1997) *Changing Police Culture: Policing in a Multicultural Society*. Melbourne: Cambridge University Press.

Chan, J. (1999) 'Governing police practice: limits of the new accountability', *British Journal of Sociology*, 50(2): 249–68.

Chan, J. (2001) 'The technological game: how information technology is transforming police practice', *Criminal Justice*, 1(2): 139–59.

Chan, J., Brereton, D., Legosz, M. and Doran, S. (2001) *e-Policing: The Impact of Information Technology on Police Practices*. Brisbane: Criminal Justice Commission.

Chan, J. with Devery, C. and Doran, S. (2003) *Fair Cop: Learning the Art of Policing*. Toronto: University of Toronto Press.

Chicago Community Policing Evaluation Consortium (2003) *Community Policing in Chicago, Years Eight and Nine: An Evaluation of Chicago's Alternative Policing Strategy and Information Technology Initiative*. Chicago, IL: Illinois Criminal Justice Information Authority.

Colton, K. (ed.) (1978) *Police Computer Technology*. Lexington, MA: D.C. Heath.

Dean, M. (1999) *Governmentality: Power and Rule in Modern Society*. London: Sage.

Dixon, D. (2001) ' "A transformed organisation"? The NSW Police Service since the royal commission', *Current Issues in Criminal Justice*, 13(2): 203–18.

Dixon, D. and Maher, L. (2003) 'Containment, quality of life, and crime reduction: policy transfers in the policing of a heroin market', in T. Newburn and R. Sparks (eds) *Criminal Justice and Political Cultures*. Cullompton: Willan, forthcoming.

Dupont, B. (2001) 'Policing in the information age: technological errors of the past in perspective', in M. Enders and B. Dupont (eds) *Policing the Lucky Country*. Sydney: Hawkins Press.

Eck, J.E. and Maguire, E.R. (2000) 'Have changes in policing reduced violent crime? An assessment of the evidence,' in A. Blumstein and J. Wallman (eds) *The Crime Drop in America*. Cambridge: Cambridge University Press.

Ericson, R.V. (1982) *Reproducing Order: A Study of Police Patrol Work*. Toronto: University of Toronto Press.

Ericson, R.V. and Haggerty, K.D. (1997) *Policing the Risk Society*. Toronto: University of Toronto Press.

Ericson, R.V. and Shearing, C.D. (1986) 'The scientification of police work', in G. Böhme and N. Stehr (eds) *The Knowledge Society: The Growing Impact of Scientific Knowledge on Social Relations*. Dordrecht: Reidel.

Graham, S. (1998) 'Spaces of surveillant simulation: new technologies, digital representations, and material geographies', *Environment and Planning D: Society and Space*, 16: 483–504.

Haggerty, K.D. and Ericson, R.V. (1999) 'The militarization of policing in the information age', *Journal of Political and Military Sociology*, 27: 233–55.

Harper, R.R. (1991) 'The computer game: detectives, suspects, and technology', *British Journal of Criminology*, 31(3): 292–307.

HayGroup (2000) *Qualitative and Strategic Audit of the Reform Process (QSARP) of the NSW Police Service: Report for Year 1 (March 1999–March 2000)*. Sydney: HayGroup.

Henman, P. (1996) 'Does computerisation save governments money?' *Information Infrastructure and Policy*, 5: 235–51.

Henry, V. (2002) *The Compstat Paradigm*. Flushing, NY: Looseleaf Law.

Her Majesty's Inspectorate of Constabulary (2000) *On the Record: Thematic Inspection Report on Police Crime Recording, the Police National Computer and Phoenix Intelligence System Data Quality*. London: HMIC.

Hoey, A. (1998) 'Techno-cops: information technology and law enforcement', *International Journal of Law and Information Technology*, 6(1): 69–90.

Hough, J.M. (1980a) *Uniformed Police Work and Management Technology*. London: UK Home Office.

Hough, J.M. (1980b) 'Managing with less technology – the impact of information technology on police management', *British Journal of Criminology*, 20(4): 344–57.

Leishman, F., Loveday, B. and Savage, S.P. (eds) (1996) *Core Issues in Policing*. London: Longman.

Lyon, D. (2001) *Surveillance Society: Monitoring Everyday Life*. Buckingham: Open University Press.

Maguire, M. (2000) 'Policing by risks and targets: some dimensions and implications of intelligence-led crime control', *Policing and Society*, 9: 315–36.

Manning, P.K. (1992a) 'Information technologies and the police.' in M. Tonry and N. Morris (eds) *Modern Policing: Crime and Justice, A Review of Research. Vol. 15*. Chicago, IL: University of Chicago Press, 349–98.

Manning, P.K. (1992b) 'Technological dramas and the police: statement and counter-statement in organizational analysis'. *Criminology*, 30(3): 327–46.

Manning, P.K. (1996) 'Information technology in the police context: the "Sailor" phone', *Information Systems Research*, 7(1): 52–62.

Manning, P. (2001) 'Technology's ways: information technology, crime analysis and the rationalizing of policing', *Criminal Justice*, 1(1): 83–104.

Marx, G.T. (1988) *Undercover: Police Surveillance in America*. Berkeley, CA: University of California Press.

Marx, G.T. (2001) 'Technology and social control', in *International Encyclopedia of the Social and Behavioral Sciences*. Amsterdam, NY: Elsevier.

Marx, G.T. (2002) 'What's new about the "new surveillance"? Classifying for change and continuity', *Surveillance and Society*, 1(1): 9–29.

Marx, G.T. and Reichman, N. (1984) 'Routinizing the discovery of secrets: computers as informants', *American Behavioral Scientist*, 27(4): 423–52.

McDonald, P.P. (2002) *Managing Police Operations: Implementing the New York Crime Control Model – CompStat*. Belmont, CA: Wadsworth.

Meehan, A.J. (1998) 'The impact of mobile data terminal (MDT) information technology on communication and recordkeeping in patrol work', *Qualitative Sociology*, 21(3): 225–54.

Meehan, A.J. (2000) 'Transformation of the oral tradition of the police subculture through the introduction of information technology', *Sociology of Crime, Law and Deviance*, 2: 107–32.

Meehan, A.J. and Ponder, M.C. (2002) 'Race and place: the ecology of racial profiling african amercian motorists', *Justice Quarterly*, 19(3): 399–430.

Mullen, K.L. (1996) 'The computerization of law enforcement: a diffusion of innovation study'. PhD thesis, State University of New York.

Nogala, D. (1995) 'The future role of technology in policing', in J.-P. Brodeur (ed.) *Comparisons in Policing: An International Perspective*. Aldershot: Avebury.

Northrop, A., Kraemer, K.L., and King, J.L. (1995) 'Police use of computers', *Journal of Criminal Justice*, 23(3): 259–75.

Nunn, S. (2001a) 'Police information technology: assessing the effects of computerization on urban police functions', *Public Administration Review*, 61(2): 221–34.

Nunn, S. (2001b) 'Police technology in cities: changes and challenges', *Technology in Society*, 23: 11–27.

Nunn, S. and Quinet, K. (2002) 'Evaluating the effects of information technology on problem-oriented-policing: if it doesn't fit, must we quit?', *Evaluation Review*, 26(1): 81–108.

Orlikowski, W.J. (1996) 'Improvising organizational transformation over time – a situated change perspective', *Information Systems Research*, 7(1): 63–92.

Orlikowski, W.J. and Gash, D.C. (1994) 'Technological frames – making sense of information technology in organizations', *ACM Transactions on Information Systems*, 12(2): 174–207.

Orlikowski, W. and Robey, D. (1991) 'Information technology and the structuring of organizations', *Information Systems Research*, 2: 143–69.

Postman, N. (1992) *Technopoly: The Surrender of Culture to Technology*. New York, NY: Vintage Books.

Power, M. (1997) *The Audit Society: Rituals of Verification*. Oxford: Oxford University Press.

Ratcliffe, J. (2002) 'Intelligence-led policing and the problems of turning rhetoric into practice', *Policing and Society*, 12(1): 53–66.

Rheinier, B., Greeless, M.R., Gibbens, M.H. and Marshall, S.P. (1979) *Crime Analysis in Support of Patrol. Law Enforcement Assistance Administration Report*. Washington, DC.: US Government Printing Office.

Robey, D. and Sahay, S. (1996) 'Transforming work through information technology: a comparative case study of geographic information systems in county government', *Information Systems Research*, 7(1): 93–110.

Sackmann, S. (1991) *Cultural Knowledge in Organizations*. Newbury Park, CA: Sage.

Schein, E. (1985) *Organizational Culture and Leadership*. San Francisco, CA: Jossey-Bass.

Sheptycki, J. (1998) 'The global cops cometh: reflections on transnationalization, knowledge work and policing subculture', *British Journal of Sociology*, 49(1): 57–74.

Sheptycki, J. (2003) *Review of the Influence of Strategic Intelligence on Organised Crime Policy and Practice. Final Report*. London: Home Office.

Sherman, L.W. (1998) 'Evidence-based policing', in *Ideas in American Policing*. Washington, DC: Police Foundation.

Silverman, E.B. (2001) *NYPD Battles Crime: Innovative Strategies in Policing*. Boston, MA: Northeastern University Press.

Sparrow, M. (1991) 'Information systems: a help or hindrance in the evolution of policing?', *The Police Chief*, 58(4): 26–44.

Tan, W.L. and Al-Hawamdeh, S. (2001) 'Knowledge management in the public sector: principles and practices in police work', *Journal of Information Science*, 27(5): 311–18.

Chapter 27

Restorative justice, victims and the police

Carolyn Hoyle and Richard Young

Introduction

This chapter explores the various ways in which the police are experimenting with the principles of restorative justice in the UK.[1] In particular, it considers the attempt to transform standard police cautioning practices into 'restorative cautioning', a shift associated with Thames Valley Police but one that is now taking place in other police services. This transformation, along with related initiatives such as the introduction of victim impact statements and youth offending teams, has brought the police into a new set of relations with victims and carries the potential to improve victim satisfaction with the criminal justice system. The chapter will consider the nature and implications of these changed relations and presents original data concerning victims' views of police-led restorative justice. It will conclude by exploring the potential for greater use of restorative principles in policing generally, including the mediation of community disputes and the handling of complaints by the public made against individual police officers. A key conclusion is that police involvement in restorative justice may result in the blurring of some well established ideological distinctions between offenders and victims.[2]

The literature on restorative justice is now almost as enormous as those on victims and on policing, and problems of definition arise in relation to all three terms. We will focus primarily on victims of crime in the conventional sense – that is to say, as people who experience crime directly. It is important to remember, however, that deciding who is the victim and who the offender in any given incident is often difficult, that many people suffer the effects of crime indirectly (e.g. children living in a burgled house, residents of a street where motorists speed – Young 2000) and that there is much overlap between offenders and victims (Sanders and Young 2000: 53–8). If the police are to provide a decent service to victims, and to gain their support and co-operation, it is important that they treat people fairly whatever ascribed role (offender, victim or member of the public) they may currently be occupying.

As far as policing is concerned, our focus in this chapter will be on the public police. Policing in the private sector is undoubtedly a topic of major importance but, while the application of restorative justice to this sphere is beginning to be debated (White 2000; Young 2002), we cannot do justice to the issues involved in the space available here. We are also unable to explore the contrasting approaches to prosecution of the public police and other state-funded regulatory agencies, and the implications this has for restorative justice (but see Sanders 2002).

We need to pause a little longer over the concept of restorative justice. There are almost as many definitions of restorative justice as there are academics interested in it and considerable divergence over what practices and principles it embraces.

In the late 1990s many restorativists concurred that Tony Marshall's definition came closest to their understanding: 'Restorative justice is a process whereby all the parties with a stake in a particular offence come together to resolve collectively how to deal with the aftermath of the offence and its implications for the future' (1996: 37). Most agree that those who have a 'stake' in a particular offence are the offender, the victim and their 'communities', which usually means supporters, such as their families and friends, but could be conceived of as geographical communities. Marshall's definition has, however, been criticised for not making clear what the substantive aim of the process is, and for restricting restorative justice to those cases where the relevant parties are willing to come together to discuss and resolve the matter collectively (Dignan 2002: 171–5). As Walgrave (2002b: 194) puts it: 'the recognition of deliberative processes as crucial tools to enhance the quality of restorative practice must not lead us to consider them to be the key characteristics of restorative justice. Restoration is the key objective'.

This emphasis on the substantive aim of restoration is in line with our own position (Hoyle and Young 2002b) and facilitates an understanding that restorative justice can be of differing degrees of quality (Van Ness 2002). Restorative justice may address a wide range of harms, including material and psychological damage, as well as damage to relationships and the more general social order. The greater the range of harms a justice practice seeks to repair, the more restorative it will tend to be. One useful typology (McCold 2000) is based on the extent to which a restorative practice involves the direct stakeholders in a criminal matter – i.e. victims, offenders and their respective 'communities of care' (such as family or friends). As McCold and Wachtel (2002: 115) argue: 'The emotional exchange necessary for meeting the needs of all those directly affected cannot occur with only one set of stakeholders participating'. Reparative approaches that deal with only one set of stakeholders, such as victim compensation schemes and other reparative services for victims, are according-ly termed 'partly restorative', whereas victim–offender mediation schemes which exclude 'communities of care' are 'mostly restorative'. Only when a reparative process involves all direct stakeholders, as in a restorative justice conference, is it deemed to be 'fully restorative'. We find this typology helpful for present purposes and will adopt it throughout this chapter. As will be seen below, the police have been involved in organising all three types of restorative justice, although fully restorative encounters remain relatively rare events.

The development of a police role in restorative justice in England and Wales

In this section we explore the way in which the police have become increasingly engaged with victims through restorative justice initiatives. This engagement began through initiatives that offered new services to victims without any attempt at involving offenders or 'communities of care'. Subsequently some police services have sought to facilitate reparative communication between victims, offenders and others concerned about an offence. In McCold's terms, the police appear to be developing their role within restorative justice in the direction of fully restorative justice processes.

Partly restorative justice: one-stop shop and victim statement schemes

The one-stop shop (OSS) and victim statement schemes (VSS) were both introduced in 1996 by the second Victim's Charter. The OSS was aimed at keeping victims informed about the progress of their case (with the police taking the responsibility for this), and the VSS provided victims with the opportunity to describe the impact of the crime upon them (including psychological, financial, physical and emotional impacts). Since these victim services included among their aims the lessening of both the sense of injustice and powerlessness following a crime, and the secondary harm that victims have historically suffered in their encounters with the criminal justice system, they were 'partly restorative' in orientation. The VSS could also be seen as furthering a restorative rationale to the extent that it prompted reparative sentencing outcomes such as compensation orders (Edwards 2001: 42). However, these schemes constituted a relatively weak form of partly restorative justice as victim reparation was only one among a number of objectives that they sought to serve. Indeed, the purposes to be served by VSSs were unclear from the outset. For example, it was never decided whether or not this scheme was supposed to affect sentences (Sanders *et al.* 2001: 449).[3] In practice, neither scheme fully succeeded in its most basic aim of improving communication between victims and the criminal justice system.

Part of the problem lay in poor implementation. A substantial minority of victims did not recall being told of basic decisions, about which OSS schemes undertook to inform them. And a third felt that they had received the information too late (either too late to attend court hearings, or after they had received the information from another source, such as through verdicts being published in the local newspaper). Much dissatisfaction of victims lay, however, in the non-dialogic nature of the schemes. Thus, a quarter were unhappy with the manner in which they received the information; they would have preferred the chance to discuss the information provided with the key decision-makers. Not surprisingly, the more victims were told the more they wanted to know, in terms of clarification, explanation for decisions and so forth. Hence, expectations were raised by the promise of information and then dashed by inadequate or insufficient information, with no opportunity for meaningful dialogue with the key decision-makers in their case. The evaluators concluded: 'The general message from our research, and experience in other jurisdictions, is that schemes that provide information to victims without interaction and discussion with them do not in themselves increase satisfaction with the criminal justice process' (Sanders *et al.* 2001: 452).

While the design of the VSS lies at the root of these problems, the police, as the agency responsible for taking the statement from victims, became the focus of victim dissatisfaction. The victims' opinions of the Crown Prosecution Service, magistrates and judges hardly changed, but they lost confidence in the police. They were on the whole much less satisfied with the police when their cases were over than when they started: the proportion of victims who considered the police were doing a 'good' or a 'very good' job declined from 54 to 36 per cent and the proportion who thought they were doing a very poor job increased from 16 to 36 per cent (Hoyle *et al.* 1998). The dangers to the police of taking the lead role in partly restorative justice schemes are evident.

While public confidence in the police is generally high, a substantial minority of victims are less than satisfied with how the police handle their case. The 1998 British Crime Survey found that the police received higher ratings when they had face-to-face contact with the victim (Yeo and Budd 2000). This seems to bear out what Shapland (1986: 214) concluded from her review of several victim studies in the UK and the USA: 'the rule was: the more contact [with criminal justice agents], the greater the level of satisfaction'. However, as the above discussion has shown, victims are not satisfied if this contact is not meaningful; if the police, for example, do not keep them fully informed and if they do not take sufficient notice of their feelings and opinions. As Strang (2002) argues, many victims want more information about both the processing and outcome of their cases, but they also want to participate in their case so that their views on outcomes count. Without such participation, many victims will remain at the periphery of their own case (Hoyle 2002) and the police will continue to bear the brunt of their dissatisfaction. The deliberative processes associated with mostly and fully restorative justice appear to offer victims a greater degree of participation. One might hypothesise, therefore, that victim satisfaction with the police will increase where the latter take the lead in facilitating such processes.

Mostly and fully restorative justice: restorative cautioning and restorative conferencing

Not surprisingly, those involved in the early police-led fully restorative initiatives are unequivocal in their support for a police role. Most notable among these advocates is Terry O'Connell, whose pioneering work in Wagga Wagga, Australia, in the early 1990s greatly influenced subsequent developments in a number of police services around the world. O'Connell argues that in order to become widespread, restorative practices need to be channelled through organs of the modern state (Ritchie and O'Connell 2001: 150). Many academics agree that state agencies, including the police, have a useful role to play in restorative justice. For example, Weitkamp *et al.*, (2003: 319–20) argue that:

> it is absolutely necessary to include the police in a model which is supposed to make community safer, reduce fear of crime levels, create

and implement successful prevention strategies, improve the quality of life in a given community, restore peace within the community through a restorative justice approach, and improve the relationship between police and citizens in order to achieve higher levels of satisfaction with the police work.

They propose a restorative problem-solving police prevention programme structured and implemented by the community, victims, offenders and the police together.

The term 'restorative justice' was not in wide usage in the UK until the mid-1990s and practice on the ground before that time tended to consist of small-scale initiatives which struggled to attract case referrals and resources.[4] However, Thames Valley Police had been developing community and problem-solving approaches since the start of the 1990s, and were therefore well placed to implement the first large-scale attempt to transform cautioning practices. On 1 April 1998, following a period of experimentation, it stipulated that all cautioning activity (for both youth and adult offenders) was henceforth to be restorative in nature. Heavily influenced by the family conferencing approach to juvenile justice developed in Wagga Wagga (Moore *et al.* 1995), the Thames Valley model envisages that a structured dialogue about the offence and its implications, according to a particular sequence of speakers and issues, will have benefits for all concerned. To achieve this structure and sequence, police facilitators are provided with a 'script' which sets out an ordered set of explanatory statements, questions and prompts. The process is aimed at promoting constructive dialogue between all parties to improve the chances of restorative outcomes.

Under the Thames Valley programme, cases destined for a caution, rather than for prosecution, would be processed by 'restorative justice co-ordinators' who would try to arrange 'restorative conferences' involving offenders, victims and their respective 'supporters'. Where there was no victim able and willing to meet with the offender, a 'restorative caution' would take place instead, in which the police officer facilitating the process would 'theme in' any victim's views at the appropriate point. In the first three years of the restorative initiative, 1,915 restorative conferences and 12,065 restorative cautions took place (Hoyle *et al.* 2002).

It can readily be seen that only a small minority (14 per cent) of restorative work taking place in the Thames Valley has been, in McCold's terms, 'fully restorative' with the bulk of work taking the form of 'mostly restorative', victim-absent cautions. Low rates of victim participation are not uncommon in the UK context. For example, a restorative cautioning scheme in Mountpottinger, Northern Ireland (using the Thames Valley model), is reported to have brought offenders together with victims in only seven per cent of cases (O'Mahony *et al.* 2002: 4).

Thames Valley's restorative cautioning programme has received a great deal of publicity. The then Chief Constable, Sir Charles Pollard, did much to publicise the concept nationally and internationally through conference presentations, publications (e.g. Pollard 2000a) and in discussions with key policy-makers. His campaigning zeal and media savvy played a major part in persuading policy-makers and practitioners of the potential value of restorative justice as a mainstream way of responding to crime (Young and Hoyle 2003). Other forces, most notably those serving the counties of Nottinghamshire and Surrey and the Police Service of Northern Ireland, were soon conducting experimental work of their own in this field. The academic scrutiny of the Thames Valley programme (Young and Goold 1999; Hoyle *et al.* 2002) and the other well-known police-led experiment located in Canberra[5] also contributed to the high profile of police-led restorative justice.

Support for the development of a police role in these more intense forms of restorative justice was quickly forthcoming from political elites. The Labour government elected in 1997 strongly endorsed Thames Valley's 'restorative cautioning' programme (Young and Goold 1999) and determined to 'reshape the criminal justice system in England and Wales' to produce more constructive outcomes with young offenders while building on 'three major concepts of restorative justice: responsibility, restoration and reintegration' (Morris and Gelsthorpe 2000: 19). The Crime and Disorder Act 1998 and the Youth Justice and Criminal Evidence Act 1999 put this plan into effect in ways that have major implications for relations between the police and victims (for a more detailed discussion, see Crawford and Newburn 2003: chs 1 and 2).

The 1998 Act replaced police cautions for young offenders with 'reprimands' and 'warnings'. The police are responsible for deciding whether a reprimand or warning should be given, although they are supposed to seek the views of any victim before taking this decision. Work with young offenders is carried out by youth offending teams (YOTs), overseen by a national supervisory body set up under the 1998 Act, the Youth Justice Board of England and Wales. When the government issued advice on how YOTs should deliver reprimands and warnings, it specifically drew attention to restorative justice initiatives set up by Thames Valley Police (Home Office *et al.* 1998), and the Youth Justice Board has since funded many YOT-run restorative justice schemes.

The police remain central players in this part of the youth justice system since s. 65 of the 1988 Act requires that all reprimands and warnings must be administered by a mainstream or a YOT police officer (Home Office/Youth Justice Board 2002). Bearing in mind that the police also remain solely responsible for the cautioning of adult offenders, it is apparent that they bear a significant degree of responsibility for any restorative work now taking place in cases not destined for court.[6]

The Crime and Disorder Act also provides scope for restorative justice and a consultative role for victims by the power given to the courts to impose reparation orders and action plan orders on young offenders. The following year the Youth Justice and Criminal Evidence Act 1999 introduced a new mandatory sentence of referral to a youth offender panel for most young offenders pleading guilty and appearing before a youth or magistrates' court for the first time. Victims should be asked if they wish to attend the panel and thereby contribute to the establishment of a reparative and rehabilitative programme for the offender and the 'contract' for its completion. Thus, the procedures followed at a panel meeting, and any activities specified in the resulting contract, should be informed by principles of restorative justice: taking responsibility for the consequences of offending behaviour, making reparation to the victim and achieving reintegration (or integration) into the community.

The various new youth justice measures create the potential for, and sometimes the duty to engage in, interaction with victims. In almost two thirds of the restorative justice schemes funded by the Youth Justice Board it was the YOT police officer who made at least initial contact with the victims (Wilcox with Hoyle 2002: 22). Guidance issued in November 2002 now makes it clear that, once the police have made the initial contact, YOTs may use specialist liaison officers to work with victims so long as the latter consent to this (Home Office/Youth Justice Board 2002).[7] None the less, the police are, more than ever, bound by legislation into relationships with victims of crime.

Looking beyond legislative duties, the police have remained at the forefront of the drive to spread restorative justice practices throughout the criminal justice process. In 2000 the Youth Justice Board, impressed by the early achievements of Thames Valley Police, provided funds so that its officers could train police and youth justice practitioners across the UK in restorative conferencing techniques (Young and Hoyle 2003). In 2002 Thames Valley Police entered into a formal agreement with Real Justice UK, the leading training organisation in the field of restorative justice (itself run by a former Thames Valley Police officer), to offer joint training to a range of other agencies in conferencing. The police are also involved, as conference facilitators, in the Home Office-funded experiments with scripted restorative justice for adult and relatively serious offenders in Thames Valley, Northumbria and London. It is clear, then, that the police role within restorative justice has developed to the point where many officers now find themselves promoting victim–offender contact. The notion that the police might act as facilitators of a reparative and reintegrative process no longer seems strange although, as we shall see, it remains controversial.

Changing relationships between victims and the police

While it is fair to say that traditionally the police had more to do with victims than did any other criminal justice agency, their obligations typically went no further than acquiring an evidential statement and trying to appear vaguely sympathetic,[8] and indeed there is evidence that they sometimes failed to be respectful or sympathetic, especially in relation to minority groups (Choongh 1997; Clancy et al. 2001). Obligations were owed to the state rather than to victims in person. Victims were conceived of as suppliers of evidence to help the state make its case against the offender, and sympathetic treatment was offered primarily to secure the co-operation of victims in that endeavour.

By contrast many recent criminal justice initiatives conceive of victims as holders of process and substantive rights, including the right to involvement in their own cases, and the right to repair. At the very least victims are now seen as having legitimate expectations vis-à-vis criminal justice agencies, with the latter becoming accountable to them as part of the multiple accountabilities to which they are subject as a public service (Shapland 2000). As we have documented, recent legislation has imposed many victim-centred duties on the police. But even before these, the Home Office Victims' Charters increased their responsibilities to victims and the Macpherson Report (1999) made clear that the police were expected to improve considerably the quality of their liaison with victims and their families.

It is thus no longer enough for the police to appear vaguely sympathetic. They now have a responsibility to victims to ensure that their primary harms are addressed and that secondary harm (i.e. that which may result from engagement with the criminal process) is minimised. Whereas victims once provided a service to the police (the supply of evidence), the police are now supposed to be providing a service to victims. We have seen that this service needs to go beyond simple information transmission if victims expectations are to be met. But do dialogic forms of restorative justice actually satisfy victims? And have police relations with victims changed at the level of day-to-day practice? In addressing these questions we will draw on the data gathered in our evaluation of restorative cautioning.

Police-facilitated restorative cautioning: the victim perspective

Restorative cautioning, as practised by Thames Valley Police, is supposed to provide victims with a satisfying opportunity to learn more about the offence and the offender *and* to participate in the criminal justice response to 'their offender'. In our study, sessions with no victims present (i.e. restorative cautions) generally qualified as mostly restorative because of the presence and participation of the offender's community of care (usually family members). In practice, restorative cautions can themselves be placed on a continuum of restorativeness. At the least restorative end would fall those cautions in which only an adult offender and police officer were present to discuss an offence widely regarded as victimless, such as possession of cannabis, as this would mean that two sets of direct stakeholders (victims and communities of care) were neither present nor invited to play any role. A caution of this type would clearly be no more than a partly restorative process. At the most restorative end of the continuum would be found those cautions involving an offender and several supporters and in which either a surrogate[9] victim was present or in which the actual victim's views were presented in a comprehensive way within the process by a victim representative or by the facilitator, *and* in which efforts were made by the facilitator to enable indirect communication between the offender and the actual victim. Restorative cautions of this nature arguably fall just short of the boundary line between mostly and fully restorative processes.

In this section, however, we concentrate primarily on cases where actual victims met offenders in the presence of their respective supporters (i.e. restorative conferences) as these fully restorative processes provide the strongest contrast with the partly restorative information transmission schemes discussed earlier.

Participation and fairness

Procedural fairness is regarded by the Thames Valley Police as a key component of the restorative cautioning initiative. The prospects of a free exchange of views, of offenders taking responsibility for the harm caused and of victims and others making reintegrative gestures are all much reduced if the participants perceive themselves to be treated unfairly. Furthermore, there is empirical evidence that participants experiencing fair process are more likely to accept the outcomes of that process as legitimate, even if they are burdensome (Tyler 1990). That sense of legitimacy may in turn increase the likelihood that offenders honour reparation agreements to victims and others. Furthermore, regardless of instrumental goals, restorative processes, like court processes, should be fair.

Fairness is not only related to what happens in a restorative conference. The victim's role in a restorative meeting can be influenced by prior perceptions of the opportunity that they will have to participate fully in the process, which are dependent on how adequately the police prepare them. Inadequate preparation impacted greatly on our sample of victims, many of whom had chosen not to attend the meeting because they were told little or nothing about it (Hoyle 2002; see also Miers et al. 2001). The majority had spoken only briefly on the telephone with either the facilitator or an administrator and over half of the victims who attended conferences with offenders reported not having been asked by the police whether they would like someone to accompany them (Hoyle et al. 2002). We found, however, that even where preparation was poor, and support was lacking, good facilitation during the session usually enabled victims to feel comfortable enough to participate fully. Detailed analysis of the 56 cautions in the final phase of our longitudinal research revealed generally good practice in terms of police facilitation of the victims' stories. For example, in three quarters of the cases where victims were present we judged that the facilitator had given them sufficient time to tell their stories.

Almost all (94 per cent) the victims who met with their offender felt the process had been fair[10] because they had been given the opportunity to say what they wanted to say (for example, in 90 per cent of the cases where the victim was present the facilitator asked the victim for his or her views on reparation), and almost three quarters (71 per cent) felt that the meeting had been facilitated well. The bottom line on procedural fairness is therefore that restorative conferences were generally seen by victims as legitimate even in cases where preparation had been poor. By contrast, victims whose involvement extended no further than providing the police with their views for theming in to a restorative caution were noticeably less satisfied (Hoyle 2002; Hill 2003). Thus, notwithstanding poor or mediocre implementation of the model in many cases, it was clear that victims who met with offenders in the presence of other affected parties were much more likely to feel that they had experienced a fair and inclusive process than victims who had been involved in partly or mostly restorative processes such as the victim statement scheme or a restorative caution.

Satisfaction of victims with the conference

Despite concerns expressed by both critics and advocates about the role of victims in restorative justice encounters,[11] a consistent picture of high aggregate victim satisfaction with police-led processes emerges from the research (over 90 per cent in Wagga Wagga (Moore and O'Connell 1994) and

96 per cent in Bethlehem (McCold and Wachtel 1998)).[12] In our own study, 97 per cent of the victims interviewed said that it had been a good idea to meet with the offender in a restorative conference. Almost all felt either a little or a lot better, with only one victim saying that she felt worse for the experience.

Many victims entered restorative meetings with somewhat altruistic aims. Like facilitators, they tended towards optimism about the deterrent and educational impact of the process. In many cases this optimism was well placed; the victims were able to help offenders to recognise the harms they had caused to victims and take responsibility for the offence and for putting things right. As part of the constructive interaction that occurs in well facilitated conferences, recognition of harms done by the offender often results in attempts by the victim to reintegrate the offender. In 70 per cent of cases where the victim was present he or she made reintegrative gestures towards the offender as a result of the dialogue. However, consistent with findings from South Australia (Daly 2002), there were relatively few instances of victims and offenders demonstrating strong empathy for one another's positions and even fewer where they left the conference fully reconciled. As Daly notes, the 'real story' of restorative justice more often involves worthwhile but modest achievements than the dramatic stories of redemption and forgiveness which litter the accounts of many restorativists.

Satisfaction of victims with the police

In summary, most victims are clearly satisfied with the police-led restorative approach. We might hypothesise, therefore, that their satisfaction with the police would increase accordingly. The majority of the victims involved in the restorative conferences were typical of the general public in that they did not enter this process with hostile feelings towards the police. In officers' language, just under a quarter were 'pro-police' and the same proportion were 'anti-police'. The remainder held neutral views, feeling that the police were 'basically OK' or 'fine'. Just over half said that their experience of restorative justice had made no difference to their opinions about the police, but a third indicated a small increase in their respect for the police, and a couple of victims a large increase. One victim had entered the process with feelings of scepticism: 'I was a bit cynical about it, whether it was a good thing or not . . . Looking at it as a do-gooder's sort of thing'. However, he went on to praise restorative cautioning and the police role in the process, concluding, 'I hope it spreads out throughout the country'.

Overall, while few victims experienced a substantial change in their attitudes towards the police, the majority either continued to feel the same way about the police or felt more admiration for them as a result of their experiences with restorative conferencing. This was not true of victims who participated in the VS and OSS schemes. A restorative conference, because it is a genuinely dialogic process, brings on average, higher satisfaction rates and more positive relations between police and victims than other processes involving victim participation. Another way of putting this is that, as one might expect from the work of McCold and Wachtel (2002), victims who experienced a fully restorative process were more satisfied on average than victims who experienced a partly restorative process. However, these positive findings have to be weighed against concerns that restorative cautioning gives the police too much power and fears that the majority of police officers cannot be truly 'restorative'.

Can the police be restorative?

There has been, for some time, unease about whether it is appropriate for conferences to be led by the police, with a reasonable fear that police facilitation places too much power in their hands.[13] The concern is that officers will investigate, arrest, judge and punish someone without legal safeguards. In other words, they will expand their punitive function, and could abuse it, as was starkly illustrated by a number of cases from our 'interim study' (Young 2001). As we have noted elsewhere:

> Police officers are ... responsible for enforcing the law through pro-
> cedures that often stigmatise, and they frequently engage in practices
> which infringe the rights of suspects or inflict social discipline upon them.
> To expect the police against this backdrop to be able to facilitate a
> restorative encounter in a fair, neutral and effective manner is to ask a lot
> (Young and Hoyle 2003: 289–90).

The participant perspective

Braithwaite notes that the Police–Citizens Consultative Committee in Wagga Wagga have argued that the police lend 'gravitas' to proceedings, and that police facilitation, indeed, the presence of the police in uniform, helps victims feel secure. He concludes, however, that 'there is no evidence to support the importance of such alleged advantages. Conversely, there is no evidence to support counterclaims that offenders are intimidated by the presence of a police uniform during the conference or by a police station as a venue' (2002: 161). We do, however, have some evidence on these points.

Only nine per cent of the 178 participants we interviewed expressed disapproval of the police facilitating restorative cautions. The vast majority felt that police officers introduced a welcome degree of authority and formality to the meeting, with a few people (not all of them victims) mentioning that the police presence made them feel safer. A few offenders felt uncomfortable speaking openly in front of the police, but 71 per cent were supportive of this way of running cautions, and better preparation by the police may have done much to alleviate the concerns of the minority.

Cautioning was generally seen by participants as a legitimate option for 'first-time' offenders, but only so long as the matter was treated as serious and responded to authoritatively. Police facilitation was seen as giving the process some gravitas, enhanced by officers being in uniform. In total, over half of participants expressed approval for the police being in uniform and over half of these expressed strong approval. Less than a quarter thought it was a bad idea, with 16 per cent feeling indifferent. There was also clear majority support for conferences being held in police stations, with almost three quarters of participants feeling that this is an appropriate place (and over a third of those expressing strong approval for the police station). Again, the most common reason they gave was that it made the process more official and helped the offenders to take it more seriously.

It is likely that concerns about police facilitation would be greater in communities where the police suffer a pronounced legitimacy deficit.[14] Even in Northern Ireland, however, police-led restorative cautioning appears to be quite popular among participants, although the small-scale nature of the published evaluation means that too much weight should not be placed on this finding (O'Mahony et al. 2002: 39).

The academic perspective

Concerns that restorative justice can extend unaccountable police power are addressed in some detail by Young (2001) and discussed by Braithwaite (2002: 161–3) and Roche (2003) and will not be reiterated here. However, it is helpful to revisit Young's conclusion about the role of the police in leading restorative conferences in the Thames Valley, as this initiative is under scrutiny here. Young showed that 'traditional police culture, and the authoritarian and questionable practices it can generate, present a significant obstacle to the successful implementation of restorative justice' (2001: 220–1). Not all the facilitators we observed subscribed to those less desirable cultural values. Some had clearly taken the lead from their then chief constable and adjusted their norms, practices and commitments to fit more closely with restorative values. However, the anticipated cultural shift was incomplete. Some facilitators seemed to be so deeply entrenched in what academics refer to as cop culture (see Chapter 9) that the process they facilitated was in many ways far from restorative. Our conclusion was that poor police practice was not unalterable but that consistent, accountable and legitimate police facilitation required sound training in, and understanding and acceptance of, restorative justice values, as well as adequate resources, trust in the 'script' and regular monitoring of behaviour.

There remains the question of whether anybody else could do a better job than the police in facilitating restorative cautions. As Daly (2001: 65) has noted, no systematic research has been carried out on this question. Although many commentators favour the idea of community-based facilitation, McCold (1998) found that victims were more supportive of programmes run by professional facilitators than by trained volunteers. While Ashworth's (2002) principled objection to an investigating body such as the police also determining or shaping case outcomes merits attention, there seems little doubt that police-led restorative justice will continue to spread (Young 2001). As a matter of practical politics the most pressing question is whether police involvement will undermine the *perceived* legitimacy of restorative justice. O'Mahony et al. (2002: 16–18) reviewed the literature and data on police-led facilitation and concluded:

> Together, the data would seem to suggest that both victims and offenders trust police to organise a fair and non-authoritarian conference in which

both sides can feel safe in dialogue. Overall, it would seem less important to have in place a neutral facilitator than to have a facilitator in place who is perceived as being fair ... With a lack of empirical data to the contrary, the results of the studies to date would seem to suggest that police-run conferencing is as consistent an idea with restorative justice principles as other mediation programmes.

They warned, however, that the police need to adopt a 'whole agency' approach to restorative justice if the achievements of facilitators in improving police–community relations are not to be undermined by illegitimate or punitive policing strategies and tactics by fellow officers (2002: 47). Culture change is a legitimate aspiration. As Braithwaite (2002: 162–3) acknowledges, an:

> argument for institutional location of conferencing in a police service is about the transformation of police cautioning and police culture more broadly ... Not just in formal cautioning but also in daily interaction on the street, the challenge of transforming police culture from a stigmatising to a restorative style is important.

The question of whether a restorative policing culture can be engendered across an entire police service is explored in the next section.

The police perspective

According to the Halliday Report (2001: 123), only 37 per cent of British police officers support the idea of restorative justice. This is unsurprising. While many police services are running small-scale experiments, and all services have police officers attached to YOTs who will necessarily be involved in restorative activity, the majority of police officers in the UK have scant experience of restorative justice. The evidence suggests that when restorative activity is restricted to relatively few officers, there will be little impact on general policing attitudes.

In a high-profile initiative in Pennsylvania, where the impact of a police-led restorative justice scheme on general policing culture was carefully measured, the results were disappointing (McCold and Wachtel 1998). Those who facilitated conferences were positive about restorative justice (displaying a shift away from a crime control conception of policing) but officers not involved in this somewhat self-contained initiative were generally unmoved. The inference one might draw from this is that restorative justice has to be embraced throughout a police service if culture change is to be achieved.

It is probably fair to say that no police service worldwide has committed itself to restorative justice to such a degree as Thames Valley Police (Braithwaite 2002: 163). It therefore represents a good test for the hypothesis that extensive police involvement in restorative justice will influence general police culture. Terry O'Connell, who provided training in restorative justice for Thames Valley Police officers, has always been adamant that the police ownership of restorative conferencing would ultimately transform police culture and permeate all police–citizen encounters.[15] Indeed, it is under his influence that Thames Valley Police has started recently to experiment with the introducion of restorative procedures into its internal grievances and police complaints processes and in its responses to conflict within schools and the wider community.

We sought information on cultural change from two main sources: interviews with those responsible for the restorative cautioning initiative and questionnaire responses to a force-wide survey.

Interview data

Restorative cautioning represents such a different style of police activity from 'old-style' cautioning that it was acknowledged from the outset by key officers promoting the initiative that there would be an element of cultural resistance to change which would need to be overcome. In 1998 we conducted systematic interviews with restorative justice co-ordinators across Thames Valley Police as well as with key staff at police headquarters (who formed a 'restorative justice consultancy'). One of the issues we explored was cultural resistance to change. Our interviewees acknowledged that, initially, there had been a widespread perception among police officers that the restorative cautioning initiative had ushered in an ineffective watered-down version of the 'old-style' caution. Restorative cautioning was routinely accorded such epithets as 'pink and fluffy' 'namby-pamby' and 'airy-fairy'. But according to our interviewees, many officers had subsequently been 'won round' by the training organised by headquarters (full training to run restorative conferences, less intensive instruction to run a restorative caution or minimal 'awareness training' given to the majority of officers) and by observing restorative sessions. Only some of those who were fully trained took up roles as facilitators or co-ordinators and used their new skills. However, those officers who were able and willing to put theory into practice told us that the shift in their thinking brought about by experiencing the emotional intensity of some restorative sessions was profound, as so colourfully put by this interviewee:

> I was sceptical at first. Oh God, well I told you, I didn't really want the job. Now? Believe you me, I mean you can talk about it forever and a day really but you have got to experience it. Well it's awesome. I mean sometimes you don't get quite such a vibrant one, but Christ yes, when they rock and roll, they do, bloody hell.

Facilitators had noticed a clear difference in the attitudes of police officers; those who had been trained were offering practical support whereas those who had not were carping.

To overcome resistance, some facilitators built up a repertoire of anecdotal evidence and 'good news stories' on which they drew in illustrating the potential of restorative cautioning. Others spoke of the benefits of inviting officers to observe the process:[16]

> These people phone up and they ask me about a file and it's like 'oh we're going to do one of these Andy-Pandy type things' you know, and I say,

'so why don't you come along, have a look and see what you think?' . . .
You don't know how effective it is until you've actually sat in on one. I
think lots of people have been converted just by coming and watching.

It is worth stressing, however, that the interviews revealed a bias towards
thinking of restorative justice as a technique for reducing the risk of
reoffending rather than as a process that showed equal concern for the
interests of offenders, victims and their communities. None of this is to deny
that the introduction of restorative cautioning had made an impact on police
culture, but the main effect appeared to have been a shift from deterrent to
rehabilitative thinking. The possibility of a drift towards an offender-focused
conception of restorative justice is something that will need to be guarded
against given the current political enthusiasm for 'crime reduction', a point to
which we return in concluding.

Some of the police interviewees had been active over a considerable period
of time in introducing restorative justice practices into their areas. They were
thus able to speak about the extent of cultural change achieved in those areas
that were in the vanguard of the restorative cautioning initiative. As one line
manager put it: 'There has been tremendous change in the last two years. We
had a lot of cynical comments about soft options, getting away with things.
Now we have police officers . . . recommending restorative cautioning as a
disposal for their cases'. There were still some operational officers, we were
told, who had no faith in restorative justice, typically those who had not been
trained and, more importantly, not seen a restorative conference for themselves. Many interviewees saw a dichotomy between officers who were
sceptical about the new initiative but who, in time, would be 'on board' and
the 'old die-hards' who could not be converted:

We've actually had a couple of custody officers say to us: 'I'm not going
to put anyone through this RJ rubbish, I'm just going to charge, charge
charge.' They're so traditional. It goes back to police culture, change, our
inability to adapt to change. Because we're moving so fast, Thames Valley
Police, the officers are being left behind.

A small study conducted by Smith in 2002 suggests that there is still at least
a perception of two separate cultures with quite disparate attitudes existing in
two of the English police services which have introduced restorative justice
practices. Interviews with key figures in the Thames Valley Police indicate that
officers who are trained in restorative justice techniques and who are involved
in facilitating conferences remain culturally distinct from those who have no
involvement. Smith (2002: 16) quotes one 'key figure' as saying 'some [officers]
did 180 degree turns in thinking from hardened 20 year coppers to becoming
almost evangelical'. By contrast, many officers with no experience of taking
part in conferences remain very retributive, tending to see restorative justice
as a 'soft option'. He gives examples of officers approaching facilitators who
are planning to offer a restorative conference to 'their offenders' and saying
'Hey! Drop this RJ stuff. I want this offender to get the full sentence'. He also
describes a senior officer with the Metropolitan Police explaining that

non-facilitators who do support the idea are persuaded not by positive outcomes for victims but by the potential for reducing reoffending. More generally, Smith's research suggests that doubts are harboured about the potential of restorative justice to make a difference to front-line policing activities such as street patrols. As someone in charge of implementing the restorative programme in Thames Valley Police put it to Smith:

> Community officers and schools officers have picked it up. But if you're a PC working on a shift in Reading dealing with minute-to-minute shit then it doesn't factor. There are almost two cultures. You need that hard policing too of course. When you have a bar brawl in Carfax [Oxford city centre location] late on a Friday night, you can't use a conference (2002: 17).

The interview data, taken as a whole, suggest that some cultural change has been achieved within Thames Valley Police, and provide useful insights into the causal mechanisms involved. This change appears to have been somewhat patchy and to focus more on promoting offender desistance than victim repair. But in order to assess more accurately the degree of change involved it is necessary to turn to survey data.

Survey data

Surveys of Thames Valley Police staff (both police and civilian) were conducted in 1994 and 1999 in order to learn more about the culture of the service (DOCSA 1994, 1999) and thus provide a measure of cultural change over the period during which restorative cautioning had been introduced into the service.

The general message of the two surveys was that the aggregate level of job satisfaction within this police service was in decline. All other things being equal, had restorative justice changed police culture substantially, we would have expected to see more open and discursive relations between police supervisors and their staff and a recognition of the move towards more community-based policing. In fact, neither shift was apparent in the data. Thus, a substantially larger proportion of the respondents in 1999 than in 1994 believed that changes were typically implemented by management decree, with senior managers considering consultation with employees to be a necessary evil. As the then chief constable noted, many people thought that mistakes were severely punished, that people are only told when they make a mistake, that conflicts are covered up, and that one is left to face the consequences when a mistake is made (Pollard 2000b). This hierarchical and punitive style of management is a long way removed from the kind of restorative culture that Ritchie and O'Connell (2001) argue is desirable within bureaucracies.

The findings were just as discouraging on the issue of external relations. When asked to rank the importance of 23 characteristics of their 'ideal job', the 1999 respondents were less 'community focused' than those from the 1994 survey. For example, 'serving the local community' had dropped from 15 on the list to 20 and having opportunities for helping other people had dropped from 10 to 14.

The obvious difficulty in drawing inferences from these findings is that there are no comparable data for the same period from other police forces. Hence it is difficult to assess whether the introduction of restorative cautioning exacerbated or ameliorated declining job satisfaction and the trend towards an authoritarian management style. However, there were indications from the specific questions concerning restorative justice that amelioration was the more likely effect.[17]

The survey data confirmed that awareness of restorative justice was widespread by 1999, with only four per cent of respondents claiming never to have heard of the concept. However, just over half the respondents felt that restorative justice had made no difference to their work, with just under a quarter feeling that it had. As one might expect, the greater the level of training and experience, the more likely it was that a respondent would acknowledge such a difference. It is almost self-evident that those who have facilitated a conference would tend to say that their work had changed because of restorative justice (83 per cent of the 84 respondents in this subgroup said this). But just over a quarter of those who had received nothing more than awareness training, and just under a fifth of those who had heard of restorative justice but received no training at all, also considered that restorative justice had made a difference to their work. This provides some evidence that the impact of the restorative cautioning initiative on police practices had spread beyond those facilitating restorative processes. Perhaps the most striking result was that three fifths considered that the police service was the right organisation to manage restorative justice, with only 12 per cent believing that the police should not facilitate restorative justice conferences. This is a much higher level of support than found by the Halliday Report among officers nationwide.

Towards restorative policing

In this section we examine a number of other restorative initiatives taking place within Thames Valley in order to assess the prospects of a true shift towards 'restorative policing'. The identity of 'the victim' in these initiatives is less clear than is usually the case with restorative cautioning.

One important policing activity where an attempt is being made to embed restorative justice principles is the handling of public complaints and internal grievances. In 1998 the Police Complaints Authority (PCA), together with Thames Valley Police, considered the use of restorative principles within the formal and highly regulated police complaints process.[18] They believed that it might provide a constructive solution to conflict between police and the public, and between police officers and their employers or colleagues. An experienced restorative justice co-ordinator based at headquarters has been given responsibility for training complaints handlers in restorative techniques. She also encourages the use of restorative methods in the handling of internal disputes between police officers.

In the internal grievance context there is usually no allegation of a crime and, in any case, the labels of 'offender' and 'victim' are seen as largely irrelevant.[19] By contrast, a restorative intervention within the formal police complaints context could work similarly to a restorative caution or conference. Where the parties agree, a meeting takes place between the complainant(s) and the officer(s) complained against in the presence of a facilitator trained in restorative justice principles. The facilitator should encourage the expression of thoughts and feelings about the relevant issues, respectful listening, the taking of responsibility for wrongdoing and a discussion about how any harm caused might be repaired. This would seem to be in line with what many complainants seek from the police. Indeed, complainants are similar to victims of crime in seeking dialogue with 'the other side' as well as active involvement in the processing of their case (Hill *et al.* 2003). Not all complainants have been the target of criminal or even unacceptable behaviour by the police, but they typically feel that one or more officers have flouted rules or social norms and thus feel unjustly treated. None the less they do not necessarily want to see the police officer treated as an 'offender' or seek a formal investigation and punishment. Instead, many seek a less polarised approach in the hope that the officer will come to see their point of view and voluntarily change his or her behaviour in future.

It is clear from an interim evaluation, however, that progress up to the end of 2001 had been slow, with few officers other than the principal co-ordinator managing to bring complainants and police officers together (Hill *et al.* 2003). How do we explain this? Braithwaite (2002: 163) notes that 'cultural change is never rapid and always resisted'. While this is true, there remains the issue of explaining why change in the cautioning sphere was achieved so much more rapidly than is occurring in the complaints sphere. A particular obstacle to change in the complaints setting may be that the police are being asked to contemplate taking on the role of a quasi-offender (rather than, as under the traditional complaints system, the role of an accused) by acknowledging the concerns of a quasi-victim. Indeed, one of the most interesting aspects of the police complaints initiative is the challenge it presents to traditional dichotomised representations of offenders and victims, and the threat it poses to the police belief that they are always on the side of victims. Reiner (2000: 89) has noted that the 'core justification of policing is a victim-centred perspective . . . the protection of the weak against the predatory'. It is difficult for the police to see themselves as predators, or as having victimised the weak. Indeed, research suggests that police officers tend to believe that they are the victims of malicious complainants (Maguire and Corbett 1991: 66). It is perhaps only through dialogue that the police will come to appreciate complainants' positions more fully and move away from this entrenched position (see HMIC 2001: 45).

The Thames Valley initiative in this field has attracted widespread attention (McLaughlin and Johansen 2002) and is likely to be replicated in other police services, not least because the new framework for the police complaints system established by the Police Reform Act 2002 made formal provision for restorative conferences. It is impossible to predict whether restorative justice will come to play a marginal or major part in the reformed system and, as yet, we do not know whether it will lead to greater satisfaction among complainants and police officers.

Thames Valley Police has also changed the way it works with schools. Instead of simply visiting all schools once a term to deliver standard lectures and talks, schools are now treated as 'community beats'. 'At-risk' schools and pupils are prioritised and officers work in partnership with school staff to respond restoratively to truancy, bullying, disruptive behaviour and crime. More strategically, Thames Valley Police has actively encouraged schools (through conference presentations and the dissemination of literature) to adopt a restorative style in dealing with internal conflict. Other police services have undertaken similar initiatives. For example, six schools in Nottinghamshire have adopted restorative practices under the Home Office-sponsored Crime Reduction in Secondary Schools programme. This project grew out of the enthusiasm of Nottinghamshire Police for using restorative conferencing (in preference to school exclusions or a formal criminal justice measure) as a response to school bullying and harassment.[20] The government (Home Office and Department for Education and Skills 2002) has commended the use of restorative justice in this sphere, regarding it as compatible with its professed aim of combating social exclusion. Again, one of the interesting aspects of this development is that it operates, at least in theory, without resort to the formal labels of 'offender' and 'victim'.

Another change evident within Thames Valley Police has been the introduction of restorative conferencing techniques for neighbourhood and community disputes where no criminal offence has yet taken place or where it is not considered expedient to caution or prosecute anyone. In addition, they now use restorative justice techniques in the setting and monitoring of so-called 'acceptable behaviour contracts' (ABCs), as a response to anti-social behaviour (not necessarily criminal) in the community (Bowes 2002: 5).

Restorative justice has the potential to offer a more effective and reintegrative response to community problems (Pollard 2001; Young 2002: 162–3) but, as with many of the initiatives discussed here, there is as yet little by way of proper evaluation evidence. While this remains so, it is legitimate to question whether these developments are all as benign as they are presented to be. Fears that, through restorative justice, the police are extending the nets of formal social control into schools and other civil settings are understandable even if the evidence from other jurisdictions (Braithwaite 2002: 148–50) tends to run counter to this thesis. What matters most are the values that underpin police work in civil settings. Where these values favour dialogue and reintegration over criminalisation and formal punishment the dangers of increased state control are much reduced.

Thames Valley police are explicit in their intention that their own operational restorative initiatives are part of its strategy to '[promote] fundamental cultural change within the police service itself' (Bowes 2002: 4). The service has tried to articulate the common principles to restorative policing: the focus is on changing behaviour through persuasion; the aim is to encourage people to face up to the consequences of their actions; and the practice involves the whole community, victims, offenders and the police who enable the process (Bowes 2002: 8–9). Thames Valley Police come closer, however, to a genuinely strategic approach when they refer to:

a long overdue shift from a militaristic, law enforcement police *force* paradigm, to that of a problem-solving, community safety focused police *service*, concentrating on crime prevention, and where this is not possible, diversion from the criminal justice system … Restorative policing … aims to engender a new way of thinking amongst police officers, such that they think and act restoratively, *all* the time and in *all* their dealings, not just with victims and offenders but with work colleagues, community members, even family and friends (Bowes 2002: 10–11 emphasis in original).

They go on to explain that restorative policing relies on multi-agency working and partnerships with all groups in the community, and the development of ethical codes and ethical decision-making (see Chapter 23). However, more radically, they claim that restorative policing is about pressing for greater use of the civil courts for minor offences, about questioning the inconsistency of 'cracking down' on minor 'street' offending while more serious white-collar offenders (such as tax evaders) receive little sanction, incorporating strategies to avoid net-widening and about fostering greater engagement with faith communities. This is a radical programme which, if fully realised, would amount to a fundamental reorientation of policing, a reduction in formal state control for minor offences and a corresponding increase for some currently neglected major offences, and a radical questioning of stereotypical notions of offenders and victims. In practice, it is probably more realistic to anticipate a less coherent set of achievements. Any police service is bound to be influenced to at least some extent by the prevailing sociopolitical agenda, an agenda on which a shift to restorative policing is unlikely to figure highly.

Conclusion

Our research on restorative cautioning suggests that there is a great deal of support, particularly among victims and the general public, for the police to use restorative practices in responding to criminal behaviour. There is also some evidence that restorative practices improve relations between the police and the public. However, our data also show that police officers within the Thames Valley have yet to be fully convinced that restorative justice is the right path to take or that the police should be on that path at all. Nor have they all fully grasped the meaning of restorative justice and its implications for the way they interact with victims. As we have seen, many police officers tend to see restorative justice in offender-focused terms, and so seek to use victims as a prop to rehabilitative efforts or (less frequently) as a way of increasing the punitive or deterrent bite of 'the intervention'. If victims are unwilling to support these efforts by coming face to face with offenders, the police often seem to lose interest in them (Hoyle 2002; Hill 2003).

Real cultural change is necessary if restorative justice is to fulfil its theoretical potential of showing equal respect for the interests of victims, offenders and communities through inclusionary and reintegrative processes. The experimental use of restorative justice in wider settings, such as the complaints system, schools and communities, carries the potential for dichotomised views of 'victims' and 'offenders' as 'us' and 'them' to be challenged still further. It is true that many of the applications of restorative justice discussed here remain largely aspirational (and under-researched), but such aspirations are a necessary precondition to achieving change. Achieving cultural change is never easy but police culture is neither monolithic nor immutable. When police officers are given the opportunity to be reflexive, and when organisational support is apparent, they are likely to have faith in restorative justice. However, without strong leadership from within the force, the restorative bandwagon is likely often to stall, may occasionally break down and perhaps derail. However, support from the government is also crucial. It seems to us that a restorative policing style does not cohere well with many of the performance measures and ideological messages which are in favour with the present Labour government.

We acknowledge that this government has made genuine commitments to improving the position of victims, through support services[21] and initiatives to provide victims with fuller information about their cases and to give them a (limited) role in the criminal process (see Sanders 2002). However, the difficulties of achieving enduring cultural change within police services will remain enormous while so many government policies remain sharply non-restorative in nature. At the time of writing, some very controversial changes to the criminal justice process, proposed in the Criminal Justice Bill, put before Parliament in November 2002, have been introduced purportedly 'to put the needs of victims and witnesses at the very heart of the criminal justice system' (Home Office 2002). The government is disingenuous in portraying 'reforms' such as introducing the possibility of defendants facing double jeopardy, or changes to the rules on evidence to make it easier to admit evidence of previous convictions, as measures for victims. Various measures introduced under the pretext of helping victims are in fact ploys for securing more convictions and longer or otherwise harsher sentences (Garland 2001; Sanders 2002).

The Labour government of 2003 seems less confident in its home affairs policies than it did in the early days of our research. Punitive populism seems to be creeping back into government policy and crime reduction (almost regardless of the means of achieving this) would appear to be all that matters. None the less, the current Home Secretary has inherited some positive measures in the Crime and Disorder Act and the Youth Justice and Criminal Evidence Act which, unless watered down by future policies, should keep the lifeblood of restorative justice flowing and ensure victims (and others) have a voice in processes that matter to them. It is to be hoped that the police service will be given the political space to experiment further with restorative principles so that we can learn more about the pitfalls and potential of this very different way of thinking about victims, policing and justice.

Selected further reading

Braithwaite's *Restorative Justice and Responsive Regulation* (2002) provides the reader with a comprehensive and international analysis of the history, potential and pitfalls of restorative justice informed by his scholarship on business regulation. Crawford and Goodey's *Integrating a Victim Perspective within Criminal Justice* (2000) brings together some of the leading commentators in the fields of victims and restorative justice to look critically at the role of victims in the criminal justice process. Hoyle and Young's *New Visions of Crime Victims* (2002) is an innovative collection of original theoretical analyses and previously unpublished empirical research on criminal victimisation.

Hoyle *et al.*'s *Proceed with Caution* (2000) documents the findings of a three-year study in the Thames Valley and provides a unique insight into the development and achievements of the first large-scale restorative justice programme in this country. Johnstone's *Restorative Justice* (2002) provides a balanced appraisal of restorative justice, introducing the reader to the key issues and debates in the field. Morris and Maxwell's *Restorative Justice for Juveniles* (2001) is a genuinely international collection of writings on restorative justice, focusing exclusively on work with juveniles. Contributions discuss work in New Zealand, South Africa, Australia, North America and various European countries, including the UK.

Strang and Braithwaite's *Restorative Justice and Civil Society* (2001) provides the reader with a diverse and international collection of chapters by academics and practitioners in the field of restorative justice whose remit was to address the role of restorative justice in various aspects of civil society, including schools, families, churches, the women's movement and indigenous groups. Strang's *Repair or Revenge* (2002) analyses victim satisfaction with restorative justice, drawing on data from the RISE experiments in Canberra, Australia, which compared participants' experiences of restorative justice with court processes and outcomes.

Von Hirsch *et al.*'s *Restorative Justice and Criminal Justice* (2003) situates critiques of restorative justice within criminal justice. Its internationally renowned contributors examine critically its aims, the limits on its application and the extent to which restorative justice can and should replace criminal justice. Walgrave's *Restorative Justice and the Law* (2002) is an edited collection that explores the social and ethical foundations of restorative justice within a discussion of rehabilitation and punishment. It questions the extent to which restorative justice can become part of the mainstream response to crime. Finally, Weitekamp and Kerner's *Restorative Justice* (2002) provides a comprehensive review of international practice and directions in the field of restorative justice, examining its application in less usual areas such as domestic violence, other serious forms of violence and corporate crime.

Notes

1 On the influence of police-led restorative justice worldwide, see Young (2001).
2 We have spent the last six years researching restorative justice (see Young and Hoyle 2000; Hoyle *et al.* 1998, 2002; Wilcox with Hoyle 2002; Hill *et al.* 2003). Data from all these projects inform this chapter.
3 As Edwards (2001) notes, no rationale has subsequently assumed prominence.
4 This is still the case with a number of schemes: see Wilcox with Hoyle (2002).
5 The Canberra (RISE) experiment has been extensively reported on by Sherman, Braithwaite, Strang and others (at www.aic.gov.au/rjustice) and in various publications including, most recently, Strang (2002).
6 The extent to which reprimands and warnings are actually delivered according to restorative principles undoubtedly varies around the country. Evans and Puech (2001) found little evidence of a restorative approach in the YOT they studied.
7 This reflects the pre-existing practice of some YOTs: Burnett and Appleton, (forthcoming).

8 For a discussion of these issues, see various recent edited collections on victims, for example, Hoyle and Young (2002b) (in particular, Sanders) or Crawford and Goodey (2000) (in particular, chapters by Reeves and Mulley and Shapland).

9 For example, some 'retail theft' schemes bring those who have committed theft from shops face to face with a nominated shop manager from the local shopping centre. Shop managers take part in such schemes on a rota basis and will therefore meet offenders who have stolen from their own particular store only by chance (see Young 2002).

10 This finding is almost identical to McCold and Wachtel's (1998) study in which 96 per cent of the victims experienced the restorative process as fair.

11 See, for example, Reeves and Mulley (2000); Ashworth (2002).

12 For the most comprehensive review of the literature on victim satisfaction, see Braithwaite (2002: 45–53).

13 See Polk (1994); Blagg (1997); Cunneen (1997); Ashworth (2002).

14 Mahony et al. (2002: 46) claim that a 'significant number of respondents expressed unease at the conference being held in a police station' although it appears that only three of the people who had actually experienced the police station venue expressed any reservation, with the rest said to be 'happy enough' (2000: 40) with where the meeting took place.

15 The authors have observed over two weeks of O'Connell's training and had many discussions about these matters with him over the past five years. See also Ritchie and O'Connell (2001).

16 The importance of directly exposing police officers to the conference process has been identified elsewhere (see the discussion of the police-led conferencing programme in Rochester, New York in 'Conferencing, Policing and Community', at www.restorativepractices.org (checked 2 February 2003)).

17 There were, of course, no questions on restorative justice in the 1994 survey but we added some questions on this topic to the survey when it was repeated in 1999. We are grateful to Sir Charles Pollard and Superintendent Steve Roberts of Thames Valley Police and to DOCSA Ltd for their co-operation in this matter.

18 The only force that has undertaken a similar level of experimentation with restorative justice in the police complaints context is New South Wales in Australia (Ritchie and O'Connell 2001), although other forces in the UK, including West Mercia and the Metropolitan Police Service, have expressed an interest in the Thames Valley experiment (Johnson 2001).

19 This work is reported to have met with a high degree of success, although no independent evaluation has yet been conducted.

20 See 'Restorative Justice in Schools – Some Practitioners from Nottingham and the Thames Valley Share their Experiences' at www.transformingconflict.org (checked 10 February 2003).

21 For example, they have more than doubled funding for Victim Support, from £11.7 million in 1997 to £28 million in 2002 and have for the first time directly funded other victims' groups, including the Rape Crisis Federation and the self-help group Support after Murder and Manslaughter (Home Office 2002).

Acknowledgements

The authors would like to thank Ros Burnett, Tim Newburn, David Rose, Andrew Sanders and Hannah Young for their helpful comments on previous drafts of this chapter.

References

Ashworth, A. (2002) 'Responsibilities, rights and restorative justice', *British Journal of Criminology*, 42: 578.

Blagg, H. (1997) 'A just measure of shame? Aboriginal youth and conferencing in Australia', *British Journal of Criminology*, 37: 481.

Bowes, D. (2002) *Restorative Policing: Beyond 'Community' to a New Philosophy for Policing* (unpublished).

Braithwaite, J. (2002) *Restorative Justice and Responsive Regulation*. Oxford: Oxford University Press.

Burnett, R. and Appleton, C. (forthcoming) *Joined-up Youth Justice: Tackling Youth Crime in Partnership*. Lyme Regis: Russell House.

Choongh, S. (1997) *Policing as Social Discipline*. Oxford: Oxford University Press.

Clancy, A., Hough, M., Aust, R. and Kershaw, C. (2001) *Crime, Policing and Justice: The Experiences of Ethnic Minorities. Findings from the 2000 British Crime Survey*. London: Home Office.

Crawford, A. and Goodey, J. (eds) (2000) *Integrating a Victim Perspective within Criminal Justice*. Aldershot: Ashgate.

Crawford, A. and Newburn, T. (2003) *Youth Offending and Restorative Justice: Implementing Reform in Youth Justice*. Cullompton: Willan.

Cunneen, C. (1997) 'Community conferencing and the fiction of indigenous control', *Australian and New Zealand Journal of Criminology*, 30: 1.

Daly, K. (2001) 'Conferencing in Australia and New Zealand: variations, research findings, and prospects', in A. Morris and G. Maxwell (eds) *Restorative Justice for Juveniles*. Oxford: Hart.

Daly, K. (2002) 'Restorative justice: the real story', *Punishment and Society*, 4(1): 55.

Dignan, J. (2002) 'Restorative justice and the law: the case for an integrated systemic approach', in L. Walgrave (ed.) *Restorative Justice and the Law*. Cullompton: Willan, 168–90.

DOCSA (1994) *Thames Valley Police Customer Satisfaction and Organisation Culture Survey*. Amersham: DOCSA.

DOCSA (1999) *Thames Valley Police Customer Satisfaction and Organisation Culture Survey*. Amersham: DOCSA.

Edwards, I. (2001) 'Victim participation in sentencing: the problems of incoherence', *Howard Journal*, 40: 39.

Evans, R. and Puech, K. (2001) 'Reprimands and warnings: populist punitiveness or restorative justice?', *Criminal Law Review*: 794.

Garland, D. (2001) *The Culture of Control: Crime and Social Order in Contemporary Society*. Oxford, Oxford University Press.

Halliday Report (2001) *Making Punishments Work: Report of a Review of the Sentencing Framework for England and Wales*. London: Home Office.

Hill, R. (2003) 'Restorative justice and the absent victim: new data from the Thames Valley', *International Review of Victimology*, 9(1): 273.

Hill, R., Cooper, K., Hoyle, C. and Young, R. (2003) *Introducing Restorative Justice to the Police Complaints System: Close Encounters of the Rare Kind. Occasional Paper* 20. Oxford: Centre for Criminological Research.

Her Majesty's Inspectorate of Constabulary (2001) *A Report by Her Majesty's Inspectorate of Constabulary, 2001 Inspection Thames Valley Police*. London: Home Office.

Home Office (2002) *A Better Deal for Victims and Witnesses*. London: Home Office Communications Directorate.

Home Office and Department for Education and Skills (2002) *Tackling it Together: Truancy and Crime*. London: Home Office and Department for Education and Skills.

Home Office, Department of Health, Welsh Office and Department for Education and Employment (1998) *The Crime and Disorder Act Interdepartmental Circular on Establishing Youth Offending Teams*. London: Home Office.

Home Office/Youth Justice Board (2002) *Final Warning Scheme: Guidance for the Police and Youth Offending Teams*. London: Home Office and Youth Justice Board.

Hoyle, C. (2002) 'Restorative justice and the "non-participating victim" ', in C. Hoyle and R. Young (eds) *New Visions of Crime Victims*. Oxford: Hart.

Hoyle, C., Cape, E., Morgan, R. and Sanders, A. (1998) *Evaluation of the 'One Stop Shop' and Victim Statement Pilot Projects*. London, Home Office.

Hoyle, C. and Young, R. (eds) (2002a) *New Visions of Crime Victims*. Oxford: Hart Publishing.

Hoyle, C. and Young, R. (2002b) 'Restorative justice', in M. McConville and G. Wilson (eds) *The Handbook of the Criminal Justice Process*. Oxford: Oxford University Press.

Hoyle, C., Young, R. and Hill, R. (2002) *Proceed with Caution: An Evaluation of the Thames Valley Initiative in Restorative Cautioning*. York: York Publishing Services.

Johnson, A. (2001) *Restorative Justice and Police Complaints. Report to the Professional Standards and Performance Monitoring Committee of the Metropolitan Police Authority*.

Johnstone, G. (2002) *Restorative Justice: Ideas, Values, Debates*. Cullompton: Willan.

Macpherson, Sir W. (1999) *The Stephen Lawrence Inquiry: Report of an Inquiry*. London: HMSO.

Maguire, M. and Corbett, C. (1991) *A Study of the Police Complaints System*. London: HMSO.

Marshall, T. (1996) 'Criminal mediation in Great Britain 1980–1996', *European Journal on Criminal Policy and Research*, 4: 21.

McCold, P. (1998) 'Police-facilitated restorative conferencing: what the data show'. Paper presented to the second annual conference on restorative justice for juveniles, Fort Lauderdale, Florida, November.

McCold, P. (2000) 'Toward a mid-range theory of restorative criminal justice: a reply to the maximalist model', *Contemporary Justice Review*, 3(4): 357–72.

McCold, P. and Wachtel, B. (1998) *Restorative Policing Experiment: The Bethlehem Pennsylvania Police Family Group Conferencing Project*. Pipersville, PA: Community Service Foundation.

McCold, P. and Wachtel, T. (2002) 'Restorative justice theory validation', in E. Weitekamp and H.-J. Kerner (eds) *Restorative Justice: Theoretical Foundations*. Cullompton: Willan.

McLaughlin, E. and Johansen, A. (2002) 'A force for change? The prospects for applying restorative justice to citizen complaints against the police in England and Wales', *British Journal of Criminology*, 42: 635.

Miers, D., Maguire, M., Goldie, S., Sharpe, K., Hale, C., Netten, A., Uglow, S., Doolin, K., Hallam, A., Enterkin, J. and Newburn, T. (2001) *An Exploratory Evaluation of Restorative Justice Schemes. Crime Reduction Research Series Paper 9*. London: Home Office.

Moore, D., Forsythe, L. and O'Connell, T. (1995) *A New Approach to Juvenile Justice: An Evaluation of Family Conferencing in Wagga Wagga*. Wagga Wagga: Charles Stuart University.

Moore, D. and O'Connell, T. (1994) 'Family conferencing in Wagga Wagga: a communitarian model of justice', in C. Alder and J. Wundersitz (eds) *Family Conferencing and Juvenile Justice*. Canberra: Australian Studies in Law, Crime and Justice, Australian Institute of Criminology.

Morris, A. and Gelsthorpe, L. (2000) 'Something old, something borrowed, something blue, but something new? A comment on the prospects for restorative justice under the Crime and Disorder Act 1998', *Criminal Law Review*: 18.

Morris, A. and Maxwell, G. (eds) (2001) *Restorative Justice for Juveniles*. Oxford: Hart Publishing.

O'Mahony, D., Chapman, T. and Doak, J. (2002) *Restorative Cautioning: A Study of Police-based Restorative Cautioning Pilots in Northern Ireland. Northern Ireland and Statistical Series Report* 4. Belfast: Statistics and Research Branch of the Northern Ireland Office.

Polk, K. (1994) 'Family conferencing: theoretical and evaluative concerns', in C. Adler and J. Wundersitz (eds) *Family Conferencing and Juvenile Justice: The Way Forward or Misplaced Optimism?* Canberra: Australian Institute of Criminology.

Pollard, C. (2000a) 'Victims and the criminal justice system: a new vision', Criminal Law Review: 5.

Pollard, C. (2000b) 'Restorative justice and police complaints'. Paper presented at the second international conference on conferencing and circles, 10–12 August, Toronto.

Pollard, C. (2001) 'If your only tool is a hammer, all your problems will look like nails', in H. Strang and J. Braithwaite (eds) *Restorative Justice and Civil Society*. Cambridge: Cambridge University Press.

Reeves, H. and Mulley, K. (2000) 'The New Status of Victims in the UK: Opportunities and Threats', in A. Crawford and J. Goodey (eds) *Integrating a Victim Perspective within Criminal Justice*. Aldershot: Ashgate.

Reiner, R. (2000) *The Politics of the Police*. (3rd edn). Oxford: Oxford University Press.

Ritchie, J. and O'Connell, T. (2001), 'Restorative justice and the need for restorative environments in bureaucracies and corporations', in H. Strang and J. Braithwaite (eds) *Restorative Justice and Civil Society*. Cambridge: Cambridge University Press.

Roche, D. (2003) *Accountability in Restorative Justice*. Oxford: Oxford University Press.

Sanders, A. (2002) 'Victim participation in an exclusionary criminal justice system', in C. Hoyle and R. Young (eds) *New Visions of Crime Victims*. Oxford: Hart.

Sanders, A., Hoyle, C., Morgan, R. and Cape, E. (2001) 'Victim impact statements: don't work, can't work', *Criminal Law Review*: 447.

Sanders, A. and Young, R. (2000) *Criminal Justice* (2nd edn). London: Butterworths.

Shapland, J. (1986) 'Victims and the criminal justice system', in E. Fattah (ed.) *From Crime Policy to Victim Policy: Reorienting the Justice System*. London: Macmillan.

Shapland, J. (2000) 'Victims and criminal justice: creating responsible criminal justice agencies', in A. Crawford and J. Goodey (eds) *Integrating a Victim Perspective within Criminal Justice*. Aldershot: Ashgate.

Smith, P. (2002) *The Rise of 'Law and Order' and its Implications for Restorative Justice*. Oxford: Reuters Foundation and Green College (unpublished David Low Fellowship Paper).

Strang, H. (2002) *Repair or Revenge: Victims and Restorative Justice*. Oxford: Clarendon Press.

Strang, H. and Braithwaite, J. (eds) (2001) *Restorative Justice and Civil Society*. Cambridge: Cambridge University Press.

Tyler, T. (1990) *Why People Obey the Law*. New Haven, CT: Yale University Press.

Van Ness, D. (2002) 'Creating restorative systems', in L. Walgrave (ed.) *Restorative Justice and the Law*. Cullompton: Willan, 130–49.

von Hirsch, A. Roberts, J. Bottoms, A.E., Roach, K. and M. Schiff (eds) (2003) *Restorative Justice and Criminal Justice: Competing or Reconcilable Paradigms?* Oxford: Hart Publishing.

Walgrave, L. (ed.) (2002a) *Restorative Justice and the Law*. Cullompton: Willan.

Walgrave, L. (2002b) 'Restorative justice and the law: socio-ethical and juridical foundations for a systemic approach', in L Walgrave (ed.) *Restorative Justice and the Law*. Cullompton: Willan, 191–218.

Weitekamp, E. and Kerner, H-J. (eds) (2002) *Restorative Justice: Theoretical Foundations*. Cullompton: Willan.

Weitkamp, E., Kerner, H.-J., and Meier, U. (2003) 'Community and problem-oriented policing in the context of restorative justice', in E. Weitkamp and H.-J. Kerner (eds) *Restorative Justice in Context: International Practice and Directions*. Cullompton: Willan.

Wilcox, A. with Hoyle, C. (2002) *Final Report to the Youth Justice Board on the National Evaluation of Restorative Justice Projects*. Draft Report, April 2002.

White, R. (2000) 'Social justice, community building and restorative strategies', *Contemporary Justice Review*, 3: 53.

Yeo, H. and Budd, T. (2000) *Policing and the Public: Findings from the 1998 British Crime Survey. Research Findings* 113. London: Home Office Research Development and Statistics Directorate.

Young, R. (2001) 'Just cops doing "shameful" business? Police-led restorative justice and the lessons of research', in A. Morris and G. Maxwell (eds) *Restorative Justice for Juveniles: Conferencing, Mediation and Circles*. Oxford: Hart.

Young, R. (2002) 'Testing the limits of restorative justice: the case of corporate victims', in C. Hoyle and R. Young (eds) *New Visions of Crime Victims*. Oxford: Hart.

Young, R. and Goold, B. (1999) 'Restorative police cautioning in Aylesbury from degrading to reintegrative shaming ceremonies?', *Criminal Law Review*: 126.

Young, R. and Hoyle, C. (2000) 'Examining the guts of restorative justice', *Criminal Justice Matters*, 40: 32.

Young, R. and Hoyle, C. (2003) 'New, improved police-led restorative justice? Action-research and the Thames Valley Police initiative', in A. von Hirsch *et al.* (eds) *Restorative Justice and Criminal Justice Competing or Reconcilable Paradigms?* Oxford: Hart.

Chapter 28

The future of policing

Tim Newburn

Introduction

This, the final chapter in the volume, looks at the likely future of policing. Of course, we should note to begin with that policing has many possible futures. Moreover, this is not a matter about which criminologists are likely to agree. As many of the previous chapters have indicated, making sense of how we find ourselves in our current position – something about which we at least have some evidence to base our ideas on – is itself a source of contention. Thinking about, and attempting to predict the future, is for obvious reasons more difficult still. Not only is it inherently problematic but, in some respects, it appears our ability to predict the future with any accuracy is getting more difficult all the time. We live, as Walker (see Chapter 6) notes, in times that are characterised by 'shrinking horizons of the foreseeable'. Why is this? First and foremost, the pace of social, economic and technological change is increasing. Secondly, the sources of change are becoming more diverse.

And, yet, in thinking about the future it would be a mistake in this regard to overemphasise change and minimise continuity. Despite the very real changes that have taken place (and continue to take place) in policing, it is hard not to be struck by many of the consistent themes in its history. Despite this, it remains the case, in my view, that many criminologists tend to focus their attention on what they take to be novel or changing in policing and, in this process, deflect attention from the nature and sources of stability and continuity. This is a particular danger when attempting to offer ideas about future directions in policing. The temptation is to identify those areas in which social, legal and/or technological changes are most likely and to read from these likely implications for policing. And, indeed, much of this short chapter focuses on just such changes. However, by adopting such a focus I would not like to convey the idea that I think that we are facing epochal or especially radical change in the immediate or relatively near future. Change in this area as in many others is likely, in my view, to be *incremental*. That said, let us explore what this future might hold.

Changing social context of policing

Before moving on to consider the changes to policing specifically, we should begin by the very briefest overview of those broader social changes that might result in, or even demand, changes to the nature of policing arrangements. At the very least we may assume that trends in some or all of the following will have some appreciable impact on the shape of policing arrangements in the future: income, wealth and inequality; employment and unemployment; sociodemographic change including the ethnic make-up of the population and the nature of family formation; and, of course, levels and patterns of crime and fear of crime. Then there is the related, but also independent, issue of politics. This, by any estimate, is a formidable list of changes to attempt to take account of. In attempting a similar summary a few years ago, Rod Morgan and I (Morgan and Newburn 1997: 42) argued that:

> Our world is changing quickly and, so goes the argument, it is the traditional bases of security which are being destroyed. Jobs for life no longer exist. The welfare state safety net has more and more large holes in it through which the unemployed, the poor, the infirm and the elderly slip in ever-larger numbers. The growth of global markets and consumer individualism has progressively undermined civic society. Local communities and neighbourhoods are increasingly blighted by levels of incivility and crime which leave all but the most hardy fearful for their property and their safety. With increasing prosperity has come increased geographical and social mobility, and a spectacular change in the nature of consumption.

These changes, we suggested, form the backdrop to current developments and preoccupations in policing. Many of those developments in policing have been explored in detail in the other substantive chapters in this volume. Before moving to consider some of them, and what they might have to tell us about likely futures, I want to return to the general question of the nature of the changes we are experiencing. One of the more influential, and radical, readings of our policing present and possible future, is one recently offered by David Bayley and Clifford Shearing (1996).

According to Bayley and Shearing (1996: 585), modern developed economies 'have reached a watershed in the evolution of their systems of crime control and law enforcement'. They go on to argue that 'future generations will look back on our era as a time when one system of policing ended and another took its place'. This is not a position with which I feel entirely comfortable (see Jones and Newburn 2002). However, the reasons that they advance in support of this argument are important for, disagreements about how they should be interpreted notwithstanding, they provide a useful frame of reference for thinking about the future(s) of policing. For Bayley and Shearing, the core of the changes we are witnessing centre on the fact that recent decades are held to have witnessed the breaking of the state's monopoly on policing. In particular, they point to the emergence of a broad range of 'private and community-based agencies that prevent crime, deter criminality, catch law-breakers, investigate offences, and stop conflict' (1996: 586). What we are witnessing, they suggest, is the 'pluralisation of policing' (see Chapter 7).

Bayley and Shearing's description and analysis of the major indicators of this epochal change is detailed. For our purposes here, however, it is possible to identify a number of core components. These are, first, that the state monopoly on policing has been fractured since the mid-1960s. Secondly, that we have seen a spectacular increase in the size and visibility of the private security sector since that time. Thirdly, that citizen involvement in policing has also spread, and become normalised, in a relatively short period to a point where the 'police are no longer the primary crime-deterrent presence in society' (1996: 587). Alongside this growing pluralisation of policing they highlight the increasing questioning of the role of the police – particularly by the service itself. 'This is attributable', Bayley and Shearing (1996: 588) argue, 'to growing doubts about the effectiveness of their traditional strategies in safeguarding the public from crime'. Somewhat in the same vein as David Garland's (1995) thesis about the crisis of penal modernism, they argue that we are witnessing a fracturing of trust in our system of public policing. In thinking about policing futures, what seems undeniable, at the very least therefore, is that we are witnessing some important changes in the policing division of labour.

The further pluralisation of policing?

Perceived changes in policing have seen the sociology of policing shift from a preoccupation with *the police*, to a broader concern with *policing*. More recently still, and as a result of the proliferation of providers it is clear are now involved in such activities, a number of commentators have begun to move away from the focus on 'policing' and to talk of 'security networks' (Shearing 1996; Johnston 2000a; Johnston and Shearing 2003) and, indeed, of the 'commodification' of security and policing. As Loader (1997: 147) summarises it:

> It is becoming more and more difficult to conceive of security provision purely or even principally in terms of what the public police do. Security must now be taken to refer to a whole range of technologies and practices provided, not only by public bodies such as the police or local authorities, but also by commercial concerns competing in the marketplace. We have unfolding in Britain an uneven, patchwork of security hardware and services, provision increasingly determined by people's willingness and ability to pay.

There are multiple changes that might reasonably be located under the heading of 'pluralisation'. These include both the increasing size of the private security sector and its pervasiveness. The proliferation of private security has both involved the spread of new technologies, such as closed-circuit television (CCTV), and the incursion of the private sector into forms of work, or areas of activity, more usually associated with public policing. Recent examples include the enforcement of parking and traffic regulations, the transport and guarding of prisoners and, most important of all at a symbolic level, the patrolling of public streets. In addition, there has been the growing 'com-modification' of policing. Loader (1999) summarises these under three head-ings: 'managerialism' (becoming more 'business-like'); 'consumerism' (the re-presentation of public policing as a 'service' and of the public as 'consumers'); and 'promotionalism' (the increasingly professional promotion of the 'product'). Relatedly, from the 1980s onwards we have seen successive waves of 'civilianisation' and the beginning of discussions about possibilities of privatisation. As Adam Crawford (see Chapter 7) illustrates, these trends continue apace in British policing. They are currently captured – though rather oddly – by the term 'the extended police/policing family', designed to recognise both the existence and the legitimate role of the plurality of providers. There is little sign, or prospect, of a slowdown in the growth of private sources of security provision. Undoubtedly, the future of policing is one that is likely to be characterised by the increasing visibility of a broad, and perhaps broadening, range of providers of policing and security services. One of the key challenges, therefore, will concern the governance of policing services, defined broadly, so as both to maximise effectiveness and minimise inequity in provision.

Increasing responsibilisation and citizen involvement

Another identifiable, and in some senses, linked trend in contemporary criminal justice that is likely to have a continuing impact concerns what we might characterise as the changing relationship between the state and the public in crime control. This changing relationship has, put crudely, seen a growing sense of the limited capability of the state in crime control together with an increasing emphasis on citizen involvement and responsibility. With regard to the former – the increasing visibility of the 'limits of the sovereign state' (Garland 1996) – there has in recent decades been an emerging recognition that the formal justice system, as organised by the state, is unable to guarantee security – or, rather, to maintain the fiction of this possibility. The late modern state, having taken on the role of security guarantor, is now faced with the predicament in which it needs to withdraw from its claim to be the primary provider of crime control, yet recognises the likely significant political and symbolic costs of doing so.

The second element of this set of changes is what Garland (2001) and others (O'Malley 1996) have referred to as a 'responsibilisation strategy': an 'attempt to extend the reach of state agencies by linking them up with the practices of actors in the "private sector" and "the community"' (Garland 2001: 124). The command structure of the nation-state is, so the argument goes, being progressively replaced by a new form of governing in which new responsibil-ities are identified – where ideas such as 'partnership', 'co-operation' and 'citizen involvement' come to the fore. Within criminal justice this increased citizen involvement and participation can be seen in numerous ways: in the more enhanced role played by victims in some settings; as sentencers in the magistrates and youth courts; as volunteers or community representatives in developing bodies such as youth offender panels (Crawford and Newburn 2003); and, of course, in less formal ways, through involvement in community crime prevention activities (Crawford 2001). In relation to policing, responsibilisation and citizen involvement are played out in a number of ways. The first, already referred to, concerns the emergent realisation of the crime control limitations of the public police. The now visible extended police family is both cause and consequence. More particularly, so far as the police are concerned, there is the continuing emphasis on voluntary participation, the growing emphasis on public consultation (Jones and Newburn 2001), together with the relatively new development of 'independent lay oversight'. As Neyroud (2001: 19) notes:

> For all the difficulties around how they are selected, by whom and what their role is, greater lay participation does offer the police a further avenue to articulate and test their judgements . . . bringing lay involvement in close to the decision-makers . . . enhances the personal responsibility for decisions.

What does the future hold in this regard? The mixed economy of policing is a contemporary reality. It is one in which citizen involvement is likely to play an increasing role. Recent years have seen debates about police accountability shift, crudely, from issues of politics to questions of performance and finance (see Chapter 24). A number of 'crises' – the aftermath of the Stephen Lawrence Inquiry in particular – have begun a process in which the governance of public policing may once again begin to pay greater attention to citizen involvement in strategic decision-making. Independent advisory groups (IAGs), often involving the staunchest critics of local police services, were created to attempt to rebuild some trust and confidence in the police among minority ethnic communities (see Chapter 21). Though police–minority community relationships as an issue is likely to remain close to the top of the political agenda for the foreseeable future, there is a more general sense that contemporary policing needs to find ways of becoming more responsive to local communities and localised needs. Under these circumstances – pressure to be responsive and accountable to local communities – the emphasis on citizen involvement, via consultation and oversight, seems set to increase. The nature, effectiveness and impact of different forms of citizen involvement will undoubtedly remain a significant issue. Nevertheless, it seems likely that pressures to increase citizen involvement will increase, stemming primarily from the increasing recognition that many of the problems of contemporary policing flow from the distance that all too often exists between local policing services and local communities, rather than from any particular democratic impulse. Issues of democratic control, however, are likely to be a continuing issue of concern.

Pressures towards centralisation and regionalisation

The whole apparatus of criminal justice in the past 20 years has been subject to twin pressures of centralisation and managerialism (see Chapters 5, 24 and 25). Processes of responsibilisation and pluralisation could be interpreted as meaning that the state was of declining significance in the field of crime control. In practice, this appears not to have been the case. Rather, within what is now a more complex field of relations, the state has become more heavily involved in the steering of the criminal justice system and its individual components. The state has adapted to the increased visibility of its own limitations, in part, by increasing its attempts to control various parts of the system of justice. In the case of policing, this can be seen in a number of ways. First, the general trend in the past 40 years has been away from local democratic control of policing and towards increasing central influence of publicly provided policing services. Though there have been some counter-trends – not least in the enhanced fiscal powers of local police authorities – it is hard to deny that the overall consequence of the changes made to local governance of policing has been the enhancement of the power of government – and to a degree chief constables – at the expense of local authorities. There is little sign that this process is likely to be reversed. Indeed, the fact that policing under New Labour is even more acutely 'micro-managed' than was the case under the Conservative managerialist political culture of the early 1990s suggests that pressures in this direction may increase, though in June 2003 David Blunkett talked up the need to think about the possibility of reinvigorating local police authorities (Blunkett 2003). However, there appears already to be a barely concealed tension between government and police representatives – particularly ACPO – over the nature of contemporary police governance and it seems only a matter of time before this becomes much more explicitly contested terrain.

The focus of conflict is difficult to predict. One distinct possibility, however, concerns pressures towards regionalisation or amalgamation. Looking back, the history of policing in the UK has involved the progressive amalgamation of forces and rationalisation of force sizes. Recent years have seen government powers in this area extended, though as yet not used. However, the current performance culture, with its apparently ever-present desire to increase economy and efficiency, is bound, in time, to lead politicians once again to question the rationale of current force sizes and structures. Depending on the nature of any recommendations that may be made in this connection and, equally as importantly, the way in which they are made, proposals for the amalgamation of forces, particularly if radical in nature – involving the regionalisation of policing, for example – are likely to be highly controversial. This, it seems to me, is one area that may become an important symbolic battleground for police and government in the none-too-distant future.

Hand in hand with amalgamation and pressures toward centralising the police are likely to be concomitant pressures towards increased localisation. The last 20 years have seen the progressive empowerment of the managers of local police areas, now generally referred to as 'basic command units' (BCUs). Though there has been considerable resistance within the police to full devolution of powers, particularly financial responsibilities, to BCU level, pressure on performance is likely to lead to the progressive withering of some of the barriers. We have recently seen for the first time the publication of comparative performance indicators at BCU level and it is surely certain that government micro-management will focus more and more at that level of policing – especially as information about local variations in crime levels increases. What impact this will have on command structures within police forces is hard to gauge, but in theory such changes should lead to considerable internal restructuring of the police. They may even enhance the case for amalgamation and regionalisation.

Transnationalisation and democratic governance

Recent decades have seen a very significant expansion in international and, increasingly, transnational policing bodies. There is every likelihood that the role of transnational police organisations will increase. There are a number of reasons for this. Partly, this process has been set in train and is now difficult to stop. The nature of 'late modernity' means that an increasing amount of business – licit and illicit – is carried on in the transnational arena and therefore needs to be policed by organisations capable of occupying the same 'space'. Thirdly, we are seeing the emergence of what may be new threats – associated with terrorism and weapons of mass destruction – and, irrespective of whether one agrees with Bobbitt's (2002) thesis about the emergence of market societies (see Chapters 5 and 23), it seems undeniable that these new threats are unlikely to be dealt with exclusively by agents or agencies of nation-states.

The governance and oversight of transnational policing bodies are set to become a key area of political debate – all the more so given the powers that may accrue to them if some of the anticipated terrorist threats come to pass. Again, this may take a number of forms. In part, the issues that arise may well very be, as McLaughlin pointed out some years ago (1992), a result of potential for the emergent multi-tiered policing system to be independent of the political process – or at least a political process which is perceived by citizens to have any immediate bearing on their everyday concerns. In this regard the EU is the 'limiting case' of transnational police co-operation and the most likely site for such debate and controversy that may arise in this regard. However, once again we should not get too carried away focusing on new developments. As Walker (see Chapter 6) goes on to note, since 11 September there has been something of a re-emergence of a classical internationalist logic, with the USA being an especially important source of influence, and the reach of 'international' policing – and therefore how it is governed – may be just as important a consideration in our immediate future as the issues associated with 'transnationalisation'.

Localisation and managerialism

As a number of commentators have noted, processes of 'transnationalisation'/ 'globalisation' and 'localisation' tend in some respects to develop mutually. Thus, a further development that can reasonably safely be anticipated is that local policing will be continued to be stretched in these two, potentially contradictory, directions. For local police managers the future is likely to be a particularly problematic one. First, we can anticipate that localising pressures will continue to increase the focus on the policing of relatively small geographical areas and, at least at a rhetorical level, to stimulate further the devolution of responsibility to local commanders. Secondly, the international-ising and transnationalising developments that are likely to continue apace will put ever-greater pressures on localised policing resources – through the increased demands that they make for information and other resources. The greatest tension, however, is likely to be between centralisation and localisa-tion, specifically as a result of the managerialist logic that continues to inform and stimulate increased central control.

How best to monitor, manage and govern policing in ways that ensure that the public money devoted to these activities is spent wisely and efficiently will continue to be a central focus of political attention. We currently live in times in which an increasingly crude form of managerialism has taken hold. Indeed, government attempts in this regard appear to be characterised, at least in part, by a form of cognitive dissonance. The evidence that the imposition of ever-greater numbers of statistical performance targets is not only not having the intended benefits but also, in some cases, is stimulating almost the reverse of what was desired, is met not by the search for alternative ways of governing performance but by ever-more frantic attempts to make the existing, somewhat discredited methods, work. There is little sign of any 'solution' to this problem in sight. Far from backing off, government shows a desire to micro-manage policing at a local level in the belief that this will bring better results than other forms of governance. At the heart of this is a failure to understand policing. It is not that performance measurement is always a negative thing. Far from it. However, as a means of management it has a number of very obvious limits. This is particularly true when applied to policing, for policing is not a service like any other for much of it involves, in Hughes' (1961) terms, 'dirty work'. Peter Manning (1999: 95) has expressed this well:

> Policing is seen as a service, a distributional activity that reallocates collective goods. Yet police services are not fully elastic, and citizen demand, although elastic, is not permitted to expand beyond the limits set privately and backstage by the police. The police continue to pattern the rationing of service as before and to dramatize the ostensible efficacy of their actions. The police do not serve lawbreakers or those who cause disorder; they constrain them regardless of their market preferences and choices. They arrest people, keep a jail, and send people to court regardless of their status as customers of the service side of policing – the side that includes paperwork, insurance forms, burglary and stolen car reports, assistance in emergencies, traffic regulation and parking, and what might be called 'miscellaneous dirty work' such as chasing wild or escaped animals, disposing of bodies, delivering death notices to families, cleaning up streets of glass and metal after road accidents, and modula-ting disputes.

Much of this 'dirty work', of course, is not easily captured by performance indicators and league tables. Indeed, some of this work may simply not get done – or not get done by the police – under the imperatives of the new managerialist culture. There are challenges, therefore, for both government and the police service in the near future in finding and embracing methods of delivering and monitoring policing services that are both responsive to local needs and concerns and simultaneously cognisant of the need to account for the resources that are expended.

Though issues of efficiency and economy will no doubt continue to form a very significant element of police governance, one should anticipate (and, arguably, hope for) continuing debate, possibly heated, around appropriate forms of local service delivery of policing services. As attention, in part, becomes increasingly localised, the public police service will come under pressure to be seen to be willing and able to deliver appropriate services to communities according to their need. In particular, the challenge of policing diverse communities is likely to re-emerge (having once again disappeared somewhat from the political agenda) within and outside the police service.

Policing and diversity

The final years of the twentieth century saw considerable criticism of the policing of plural communities (HMIC 1997, 1999b; Macpherson 1999). In particular, the Macpherson Inquiry highlighted the gulf between the police service and some ethnic minority communities. In a report on police integrity, HMIC (1999a) concluded that 'all forces are trying hard to consult their communities and to understand their needs and concerns but each is failing to a greater or lesser extent in providing a better service to the disadvantaged groups in society, as well as ethnic minority groups'. Perhaps one of the safest predictions about the future of policing is that improving the understanding of, and responses to, the needs of minority communities will continue to be a core issue, and most likely a significant problem. Though the central focus of attention is likely to continue to be on the nature of police service delivery, the nature of police culture is also likely to be a source of continuing concern and a focus for reform efforts.

In recent decades the nature of recruitment to the police service, particularly to ACPO ranks, has changed markedly. Educational levels have risen significantly. Though the process has been slow, and far from easy, it is now also the case that women are far more prominent in the police service. This, I would hazard, is likely to be one of the most significant areas of change in the next two decades. There is every reason to expect that there will be a very substantial increase in the number of women in senior positions within the police service in the not too distant future. From the situation a decade ago where there had never been a woman chief constable, now six of the 53 forces in the UK are led by women (still a small number but a significant shift nevertheless). Outside issues of numbers and representation, one key issue is what qualitative differences will changes to the workforce of constabularies bring? As Heidensohn (see Chapter 22) explains, pioneer policewomen had primarily a 'protective mission' in mind. Their central concern was in protecting women, juveniles and children, with law enforcement originally being somewhat secondary. More recently, issues of equality and opportunity have become more prominent, though there has also been a renewed emphasis on protection issues, particularly around child protection. The big question in the 'post-Lawrence' environment is what difference will the increasing prominence and influence of women (and ethnic minorities should numbers and prominence increase) in policing make to the police and to the service that is delivered? Will the increasing influence of women officers, for example, change the culture – a culture that remains highly masculine – of the police? In Bourdieu's terms, what impact will the changing make-up of the service have on the 'doxa' of policing (see Chan 2003)? Relatedly, will this have a marked impact on how the police relate to local communities and to how local police services are delivered? There is much evidence to suggest that the police service – and the nature of the culture of police organisations – has remained relatively untouched by reform efforts in recent times. Yet there is also good evidence to suggest that the culture of such organisations can be changed (see Chapter 9). Indeed, the more progressive police managers have sought to bring about such changes and, more particularly, to reform the art of policing.

Techniques and technology?

As the chapter by Hoyle and Young (see Chapter 27) outlines in detail, one experiment which has attempted to bring about a significant change to the way in which police services are delivered is that concerning the importation of restorative justice-influenced practices into such areas as cautioning and police complaints system. In the UK Thames Valley police have begun to argue the case for a fairly radical reorientation of policing which has as its aim a shift in priorities away from 'minor street offending' towards a greater emphasis on serious white-collar crime. At least as importantly, it puts centre-stage the assumption that enlightened forms of policing practice require the explicit development of ethical codes of practice and an increased emphasis on ethical decision-making at all levels of the police service (see Chapter 23). The insertion of restorative practices into policing is, of course, highly problematic for until there is some form of radical reorientation of policing the reality is that police officers will remain 'responsible for enforcing the law through procedures that often stigmatise, and they frequently engage in practices which infringe the rights of suspects or inflict social discipline upon them' (Young and Hoyle 2003: 290). One of the implications of the shift towards an emphasis on taking responsibility for harms is the reform of police complaints and disciplinary procedures, and increasing interest is being shown in the potential of restorative justice in this area. This links back to the previous issue of diversity, however, for it is important to safeguard the 'rights' of the less powerful. As McLaughlin and Johansen (2002: 651) note, the more disen-franchised may perceive restorative approaches to be lacking in procedural legitimacy and 'for the sake of community relations and indeed the legitimacy of the new police complaints system . . . certain forms of seemingly "minor" police misconduct rather than being diverted into restorative justice will have to be subject to full rigour of independent investigation'.

Just as new 'techniques' may be introduced in an effort to reorient policing, so the emerging new technologies are beginning to offer policing agencies considerable opportunities. We are beginning now to see the potential of technological advances such as those associated with the use of DNA identification. How far reaching the impact of this will be is not at all clear. We can safely assume, however, that the impact will be noticeable. From 2000 DNA samples were collected routinely from offenders, along with fingerprints and photographs. More recently, the Home Office has established the national DNA database and announced a desire to have the DNA profiles of the 'known active criminal population' on the database by April 2004. Great changes are anticipated as a result of the spread of this new technology – government ministers hoping that it will lead to reductions in bureaucracy, increased detections and the speeding up communications as well as, on a more general level, the inculcation of a more problem-oriented approach to policing (http://www.cjsonline.gov.uk/access/news/2003/january/crimnaL dna_databse.html).

However, it is perhaps best not to overestimate the speed at which such change will take place. The extent to which technology has had an impact on public policing thus far is an indication of this. Computer technology has had a radical impact on our social, cultural and economic existence. And yet it is not clear that it has had a particularly dramatic impact on the police. Yes, it is true that data capture and retrieval are now much better than was the case 20, even 10, years ago. The ability to store vast amounts of data is grown exponentially. Nevertheless, the bulk of day-to-day policing is not that dramatically different now from 20 years ago. The daily activities of the average PC continue to be reactive rather than proactive. The main source of the information that influences daily activity continues to be the public, and generally provided via the telephone. We are some considerable distance, for example, from seeing anything like 'problem-oriented policing' as a daily reality. It remains the exception rather than the rule. Recent work by HMIC confirms both the potential of new technologies such as DNA profiling, but also illustrates the continued existence of organisational and cultural barriers to the full exploitation of the technology (HMIC 2002).

Policing futures

Against a backdrop of uncertainty, one thing we can say with some confidence is the era in which the public police in England somehow came to symbolise nationhood has passed and will not return (Loader and Mulcahy 2003). Policing has changed, as has the society being policed. The increasing visibility of a plurality of providers of security will mean, one way or another, that we will be forced to consider once again what it is we want policing in general, and the police service in particular, to achieve, and in what way we feel that it is appropriate to achieve these things.

Earlier in this chapter I outlined Bayley and Shearing's suggestion that we are currently experiencing a paradigmatic shift in the system of policing, and then noted that, as with all historical change, it is possible to emphasise *change* or *continuity*. Where some see radical restructuring, others see evolutionary change. The dominant academic discourse appears currently to privilege change over continuity. As Trevor Jones and I have argued elsewhere (Jones and Newburn 1999: 241; see also Jones and Newburn 2002), there is 'a tendency to exaggerate the degree of novelty in the new arrangements that are emerging, and to overstate the extent to which all developed economies are similarly subject to transnational or global pressures'. Wherever one sits in these debates, it is clear that important shifts have been taking place, and that the policing arrangements associated with Dixon of Dock Green are long gone (including from our imaginations, which may be the only place they ever truly existed). New ways of organising and understanding policing are emerging. Johnston (2000b: 76) suggests that:

> Late modern policing combines diversity and risk. The former leads to increased fragmentation of policing. The latter leads to similarity of thought and action between different security organisations. It may also lead to the proliferation of security, since risk-orientation fuels the demand for 'more policing'.

This apparent fragmentation of policing, and in particular the increased marketisation of crime control characteristic of our late modern times, raises some important issues. Three appear to be key. First are the dangers associated with inequalities in the provision of protection and the problem of 'majoritariansim'. One of the greatest dangers in the marketisation of protection is that the already existing material and social polarisation that exists will be exacerbated by the addition of further 'security differentials'. This may occur in a number of ways, including the simple purchasing of security and policing services by those who can afford them, as illustrated, for example, by the spread of defended or gated communities in the USA (Blakely and Snyder 1997) and, because of differences in the ability to articulate needs, the drawing away of public policing services from areas of greatest need to areas of least need. There is thus an obvious need for the principles of democracy, especially equity, to be reasserted in the context of the provision and organisation of security (Jones *et al.* 1994).

The second major issue for us therefore is governance. The question immediately arises as to how the public police are to be held accountable in an environment in which pluralism is encouraged. Related to this is the question of how the private security industry, and all its component parts, is to be regulated or otherwise controlled. Crucially in the context of the pluralisation of policing, there is the issue of the governance of security networks. With the recognition that plural policing is already with us, a number of commentators have begun to pay attention to this question (Blair 1998; Jones and Newburn 1998; Johnston 2000; Loader 2000). Though we may assume that police accountability will continue to be an important concern, it seems clear that questions of governance have begun to shift away from 'the police' towards 'policing', 'security' and 'social order'.

The third and final issue concerns the consequences of increasing fear and insecurity and how these are responded to and exploited politically. Garland argues that despite the encouragement of new 'preventive strategies' associated with crime prevention and community policing, governments are actually ambivalent about such strategies and frequently retreat from their implications:

> Under certain circumstances, or with respect to certain kinds of offences and offenders, they respond to the predicament by denying it; by reactivating the old myth of the sovereign state; and by engaging in a more expressive and more intensive mode of punishment that purports to convey public sentiment and the full force of state authority (2000: 349).

The symbolic reassertion of state sovereignty tends to involve, as Young (1999) has pointed out, two fallacies: a 'cosmetic fallacy' (crime is a superficial problem rather than a chronic problem) and the idea of the 'social as simple' (where problems have a small number of readily identifiable causes). The most visible manifestation of these fallacies in recent times has been the continual reassertion, in face of almost overwhelming evidence to the contrary, of the efficacy of the criminal justice state. More particularly, this has found voice, time and again, in exaggerated claims on the part of the police service in relation to crime control. There are considerable dangers in this, not least for a public continually seduced by the chimera of 'law and order' solutions to social problems. The reality of course is that the 'solutions' to the problems of security and order in our late modern urban environments do not lie with providers of policing services – be they public and/or private. The solution to our ills is not to be found in the marketplace: in the purchase of security or policing – whether provided 'publicly' or by other means. That this is, or at least should be, becoming increasingly clear means that, by any measure, policing in the near future faces some fairly dramatic challenges.

References

Bayley, D. and Shearing, C. (1996) 'The future of policing', *Law and Society Review*, 30(3): 585–606.

Blair, I. (1998) 'Where do the police fit into policing?', Speech to the ACPO conference, 16 July, unpublished.

Blakely, E. and Snyder, M. (1997) *Fortress America: Gated Communities in the United States*. Washington, DC: The Brookings Institute.

Blunkett, D. (2003) *Civil Renewal: A New Agenda*. London: Home Office.

Bobbitt, P. (2002) *The Shield of Achilles: War, Peace and the Course of History*. London: Penguin Books.

Chan, J. (2003) *Fair Cop: Learning the Art of Policing*. Toronto: University of Toronto Press.

Crawford, A. (2001) *Public Matters: Reviving Public Participation in Criminal Justice*. London: IPPR.

Crawford, A. and Newburn, T. (2003) *Youth Offending and Restorative Justice: Implementing Reform in Youth Justice*. Cullompton: Willan.

Garland, D. (1995) 'Penal modernism and postmodernism', in S. Cohen and T.G. Blomberg (eds) *Punishment and Social Control: Essays in Honor of Sheldon L. Messinger.* New York, NY: Aldine de Gruyter.

Garland, D. (2000) 'The culture of high crime societies: some preconditions of recent "law and order" policies', *British Journal of Criminology*, 40(3): 347–75.

Garland, D. (2001) *A Culture of Control.* Oxford: Oxford University Press.

HM Inspectorate of Constabulary (1997) *Winning the Race: Policing Plural Communities.* London: Home Office.

HM Inspectorate of Constabulary (1999a) *Police Integrity: Securing and Maintaining Public Confidence.* London: Home Office.

HM Inspectorate of Constabulary (1999b) *Winning the Race: Revisited.* London: Home Office.

HM Inspectorate of Constabulary (2002) *Under the Microscope – Refocused: A Revisit to the Investigative Use of DNA and Fingerprints.* London: Home Office.

Hughes, E. (1961) 'Good people and dirty work', *Social Problems*, 10: 1.

Johnston, L. (2000a) *Policing Britain: Risk, Security and Governance.* Harlow: Longman.

Johnston, L. (2000b) 'Private policing, problems and prospects', in F. Leishman *et al.* (eds) *Core Issues in Policing* (2nd edn). Harlow: Longman.

Johnston, L. and Shearing, C. (2003) *The Governance of Security.* London: Routledge.

Jones, T. and Newburn, T. (1998) *Private Security and Public Policing.* Oxford: Clarendon Press.

Jones, T. and Newburn, T. (1999) 'Urban change and policing, mass private property reconsidered', *European Journal on Criminal Policy and Research*, 7: 225–44.

Jones, T. and Newburn, T. (2001) *Widening Access: Improving Police Relations with Hard to Reach Groups.* London: Home Office.

Jones, T. and Newburn, T. (2002) 'The transformation of policing? Understanding current trends in policing systems', *British Journal of Criminology*, 42(1): 129–46.

Jones, T., Newburn, T. and Smith, D.J. (1994) *Democracy and Policing.* London: Policy Studies Institute.

Loader, I. (1997) 'Private security and the demand for protection in contemporary Britain', *Policing and Society*, 7: 143–62.

Loader, I. (1999) 'Consumer culture and the commodification of policing and security', *Sociology*, 33(2): 373–92.

Loader, I. (2000) 'Plural policing and democratic governance', *Social and Legal Studies*, 9(3): 323–45.

Loader, I. and Mulcahy, A. (2003) *Policing and the Condition of England: Memory, Politics and Culture.* Oxford: Clarendon Press.

Macpherson, W. (1999) *Inquiry into the Matters Arising from the Death of Stephen Lawrence: Final Report.* London: HMSO.

Manning, P. (1999) 'A dramaturgical perspective', in B. Forst and P.K. Manning (eds) *The Privatization of Policing: Two Views.* Washington, DC: Georgetown University Press.

McLaughlin, E. (1992) 'The democratic deficit: European Union and the accountability of the British police', *British Journal of Criminology*, 32(4): 473–87.

McLaughlin, E. and Johansen, A. (2002) 'A force for change? The prospects for applying restorative justice to citizen complaints against the police in England and Wales', *British Journal of Criminology*, 42(3): 635–53.

Morgan, R. and Newburn, T. (1997) *The Future of Policing.* Oxford: Oxford University Press.

Neyroud, P. (2001) *Public Participation in Policing.* London: IPPR.

O'Malley, P. (1996) 'Post-Keynesian policing', *Economy and Society*, 25(2): 137–55.

Shearing, C. (1996) 'Public and private policing', in W. Saulsbury *et al.* (eds) *Themes in Contemporary Policing.* London: Police Foundation/Policy Studies Institute.

Young, J. (1999) *The Exclusive Society*. London: Sage.

Young, R. and Hoyle, C. (2003) 'New, improved police-led restorative justice? Action research and the Thames Valley Police initiative', in A. von Hirsch *et al.* (eds) *Restorative Justice and Criminal Justice: Competing or Reconcilable Paradigms?* Oxford: Hart Publishing.

Glossary

Accountability
Generally, though somewhat crudely, thought of as a system for controlling agencies and individuals. In relation to policing a distinction is often drawn between individual forms of accountability ('controlling the constable') and organisational accountability (oversight of the policies and processes of constabularies). In relation to the latter an important distinction was drawn by Geoffrey Marshall between what he termed an 'explanatory and co-operative' form of accountability and a 'subordinate and obedient' form:

> *Explanatory and co-operative* – whereby chief constables may be required to give account of their decisions to the relevant authorities but are not required to take account of the response of those authorities.
> *Subordinate and obedient* – whereby chief constables are required both to give account of their decisions and to take account of any response.

(*See also* constabulary independence, governance, tripartite structure.)

Association of Chief Police Officers (ACPO)
The association representing all officers of assistant chief constable rank and above (and their equivalents in the Metropolitan Police). It is not a staff association (the separately constituted Chief Police Officers' Association fulfils that function). ACPO's work is on behalf of the service, rather than its own members. ACPO has the status of a private company limited by guarantee and is funded by a combination of a Home Office grant, contributions from each of the 44 police authorities, membership subscriptions and by the proceeds of its annual exhibition. It now has a full-time president (http://www.acpo. police.uk).

Audit Commission
A non-departmental public body established in the 1980s to promote economy, efficiency and effectiveness in the public services. Beginning with studies of policing, and subsequently of community safety and of youth justice, the Audit Commission has become increasingly influential in criminal justice in recent years (http://www.audit-commission.gov.uk).

Basic command unit (BCU)
Now the fundamental policing unit of delivery. What would previously have been referred to as a police division or subdivision, the BCU is headed by a chief superintendent and generally has its own management team, mirroring the management team that operates at individual force headquarters.

Best Value
Introduced by the Local Government Act 1999, Best Value is a further method of encouraging efficiency and effectiveness in local public services. Under the Act local police authorities are responsible for securing Best Value in local policing services. In doing so, they must consult widely with the community, including local council tax and business ratepayers, and service users.

Bramshill
The name of the main site for national police training, located in a country house in Hampshire (*see also* Centrex, Senior Command Course) (http://www.centrex.police.uk).

British Association for Women in Policing (BAWP)
The association was founded in 1987 and is the only organisation in the UK to draw members from all ranks of the police service and support staff. It has representatives not only from the geographical forces throughout England, Scotland, Wales and Northern Ireland but also from many others – including British Transport Police, Isle of Man Constabulary, Guernsey Police, UK Atomic Energy Constabulary, RAF Police, Ministry of Defence Police and Royal Military Police (http://www.bawp.org).

Centrex
Centrex is the name for the Central Police Training and Development Authority. Its role is to define, develop and promote excellence in the police service and it does so by providing a centre of policing excellence and support, and by creating and implementing the means to develop competence through policing careers (*see also* National Centre for Policing Excellence) (http://www.centrex.police.uk).

CID (officer)
Criminal investigation department – CID was the successor to the Detective Branch in the Metropolitan Police and has become the normal term for plain-clothes police detectives in the UK.

Community policing
A police organisational strategy that decentralises policing, seeks to be responsive to local citizen demands and to incorporate a general problem-oriented approach to policing, and to helping communities solve crime problems collaboratively, often through partnership working (*see also* partnership, problem-oriented policing).

Compstat
A system of using police data to improve police performance by holding local police commanders to account. Pioneered in New York City in the 1990s, Compstat has now spread much more widely and, predictably, varies in style

and content. The New York model, as originally practised under Bill Bratton and Jack Maple, involved public interrogation of local precinct commanders about local crimes, crime trends and police performance.

Constable
A term that originated in Norman times. By the thirteenth and fourteenth centuries there were a variety of posts with this title, the majority of which were linked to manors or parishes. The medieval constable was responsible for maintaining the King's peace. The office of constable is held by some to have declined somewhat with the emergence of the office of justice of the peace in the fourteenth century up until the establishment of the new police in 1829. 'Police constable' is now the main entry grade for all police officers.

> *Special constable* – special constables are volunteers who receive training from their local force to work with and offer support to regular police officers. They have the same powers as a regular officer and wear a similar uniform. They work a minimum of four hours per week.

(http://www.specialconstables.gov.uk/output/Page2.asp)

Constabulary independence
The idea that policing policy should be free from political interference. According to a judgement by Lord Denning in 1968 the chief constable in all his or her duties 'is not the servant of anyone, save of the law itself ... The responsibility for law enforcement lies on him. He is answerable to law and to the law alone'. This has been challenged by constitutional lawyers and, most recently, by the Patten Inquiry in Northern Ireland, but remains a powerful influence in discussions of police governance.

Corruption
The term 'police corruption' has been used to describe many activities: bribery, violence and brutality; fabrication and destruction of evidence; racism; and favouritism and nepotism. Most typologies include a range of activities that can be analysed along five dimensions: the acts and actors involved; the norms violated; the degree of support from the peer group; the degree of organisation of deviant practices; and the reaction of the police department. Police corruption, it is generally accepted, necessarily involves an abuse of position; what is corrupted is the special 'trust' invested in the occupation.

Covert human intelligence source (CHIS)
The now preferred term for 'informant'.

Covert methods
Advances in technology and the need to combat serious crime have had a significant impact on British policing. Covert investigative methods, such as the use of surveillance devices, informers (CHISs) and undercover operations, backed by extensive databases of criminal intelligence information, are now widely employed. Increasingly, attention is being paid to the need to regulate and control covert policing and both the Human Rights Act 1998 and the Regulation of Investigatory Powers Act 2000 are relevant in this regard.

Crime analysis
The synthesis of police and other relevant data to identify and interpret patterns and trends in crime (among offenders, offences, victims, spaces and places) to inform police and judicial practice. A number of more specific terms may also be identified:

Analytical process – a series of stages including, inter alia, collection of data, representation of data, interpretation of data, recommendations, evaluation.
Tactical analysis – aims to maximise the impact of enforcement by reviewing current crime problems and prolific offenders to inform investigations and operations.
Strategic analysis – identifies longer-term crime problems and future trends to provide an understanding of the scope and dimension of criminal activity in order to assist with local policy development and planning.
Analytical techniques – these may include crime pattern analysis, network analysis, time series analysis and risk analysis.

Crime mapping
Crime is unevenly spatially and temporally distributed. It is possible, therefore, to 'map' crime according to where and when it occurred (and by type of offence). Such mapping can help in the targeting, deployment and allocation of crime prevention resources to areas of vulnerability. Maps showing patterns or hotspots of crime can present effective visual images that help people to understand their distribution and to explore possible reasons behind certain types of criminal activity (*see also* crime analysis, hotspots, repeat victimisation).

Dixon of Dock Green
A fictional police officer, PC George Dixon, who originally appeared in the film *The Blue Lamp*. Though PC Dixon died at the end of the film his character was later resurrected and became the eponymous hero of the famous television series *Dixon of Dock Green*. The character has become a symbol of a supposed 'golden age' in policing, capturing the essence of the image of the unarmed 'British Bobby' at the heart of local postwar community life.

Due process and crime control
An ideal typical formulation of contrasting models of criminal justice outlined by Herbert Packer (a distinguished American academic lawyer). The ideal types are designed to contrast differing emphases on procedure and outcome. Thus, the values inherent in 'due process' give greater prominence to civil liberties in order to maximise the likelihood that the innocent will be acquitted. By contrast, the values inherent in the 'crime control' model give much greater prominence to the goal of convicting the guilty.

Europol
Europol is the European Union Law Enforcement Organisation that handles criminal intelligence. Its mission is to assist the law enforcement authorities of member states in their fight against serious forms of organised crime. It was established in the Maastricht Treaty in 1992 and is based in The Hague (http://www.europol.eu.int).

Evidence-based policing

The idea that practice should be underpinned by evidence of 'what works'. Thus, just as the National Institute for Clinical Excellence was established in the Health Service in 1999, so similar developments are being encouraged in policing, including the establishment of the National Centre for Policing Excellence (*see also* Centrex, National Centre for Policing Excellence, National Competency Framework).

Governance

A term from political science and sociological literature that focuses on the systems of regulation and ordering (governing) contemporary societies. Where once this might have focused on the agencies/institutions of the state, the term is now generally taken to refer to strategies of governing both within and beyond the state (*see also* accountability, transnational policing).

Harm reduction

A drugs policy which emphasises the need to control or mitigate the medical and social costs of drug abuse rather than advocating abstinence or focusing on law enforcement (*see also* War on Drugs).

Her Majesty's Inspectorate of Constabulary (HMIC)

For well over a century HM Inspectors of Constabulary (HMIs) have been charged with examining and improving the efficiency of the police service in England and Wales, with the first HMIs appointed under the provisions of the County and Borough Police Act 1856. In 1962, the Royal Commission on the Police formally acknowledged their contribution to policing. The statutory duties of HMIs are described in the Police Act 1996 (http://www.homeoffice.gov.uk/hmic/hmic.htm).

Home Office

The government department responsible for internal affairs in England and Wales and therefore for the police and policing policy (http://www.homeoffice.gov.uk).

'Home Office' and other police forces

Home Office forces are those forces for which the Home Secretary has direct responsibility for maintaining; in England and Wales, the 43 constabularies. Non-Home Office forces therefore include those in Jersey, Guernsey, the Isle of Man, the Ministry of Defence Police, British Transport Police, the UK Atomic Energy Authority Constabulary and the Royal Parks Constabulary.

Hot products

So-called 'hot products' are those that are most likely to be taken by thieves. Following insights from research on hotspots and repeat victimisation, the theory is that a better understanding of which products are 'hot', and why, could help reduce certain forms of crime (*see also* hotspot, repeat victimisation) (http://www.crimereduction.gov.uk/stolengoods1.htm).

Hotspot

Arising from the finding that crime is highly concentrated geographically and socially. Some communities have crime rates ten, twenty times or higher than others and, in crime prevention terms, focusing resources where crime is highest – 'hot spots' – is likely to yield greatest results. To do this accurately, information and analysis of crime data are required, usually referred to as crime mapping (*see also* crime analysis, crime mapping, repeat victimisation) (http://www.crimereduction.gov.uk/toolkits/p031309.htm).

Human rights
The Universal Declaration of Human Rights states that:

> Everyone shall be subject only to such limitations as are determined by law solely for the purpose of securing due recognition and respect for the rights and freedoms of others and of meeting the just requirements of morality, public order and the general welfare in a democratic society.

The increasing attention paid to human rights principles – and their incorporation into UK criminal law – has led to a developing debate over the implications of this for the nature and delivery of policing (*see also* due process, crime control).

Independent advisory groups (IAGs)
The Stephen Lawrence Inquiry report, and the *Winning the Race* series of reports from HMIC, identified a lack of faith in policing among minority ethnic groups, whether as victims of crime, suspects, potential recruits or members of local communities wanting to work in partnership with their local police to tackle crime. In the aftermath of the Stephen Lawrence Inquiry the Metropolitan Police established an independent advisory group to advise their Racial and Violent Crime Task Force. The perceived success of this approach has led to the establishment of other IAGs both within the MPD and elsewhere (*see also* police community consultative groups, Scarman Inquiry, Stephen Lawrence Inquiry).

Intelligence
Information derived from informants (CHISs) and other sources (*see also* crime analysis, covert human intelligence sources, intelligence-led policing).

Intelligence-led policing
Essentially, a model which seeks to increase the effectiveness of policing through greater emphasis on the collection and analysis of intelligence and the development of targeted responses to that analysis (*see also* crime analysis, National Intelligence Model, problem-oriented policing).

Interpol
'Interpol' was officially adopted as the International Criminal Police Organisation (abbreviated to ICPO-Interpol) in 1956. Interpol was set up to enhance and facilitate cross-border criminal police co-operation. Today, it is the second biggest international organisation after the United Nations, with 181 members countries spread over five continents (http://www.interpol.int/Default.asp).

Joint standing committee
The growth of provincial police forces in the nineteenth century led to the emergence of two systems of accountability. County forces were overseen by joint standing committees, made up of two thirds elected councillors and one

third magistrates, whereas borough police forces were overseen by wholly elected watch committees. This system was reformed by the Police Act 1964 (*see also* accountability, police authority, watch committee).

Leadership
Though, historically, the police service may have paid relatively little attention to the nature of leadership, in recent years this has changed. A number of different 'ideal types' of leadership are often discussed, of which three of the most important are as follows:

> *Command leadership* – a traditional form, relying on hierarchy and authority – and sometimes charisma – as the basis for leadership.
> *Transactional leadership* – 'transactional' leadership is a form of contractual agreement or a type of management-based 'contingency reward' (or 'management by exception'); often contrasted to 'transformational' leadership.
> *Transformational leadership* – a more responsive and reciprocal form of leadership designed to include all staff in decision-making and to stimulate a shared belief in the importance of particular goals.

Lesbian and Gay Police Association (LAGPA)
The Lesbian and Gay Police Association was formed in 1990 and is the only national staff association that specifically represents the needs and interests of lesbian and gay police employees in the UK. Further, the LAGPA is the only national organisation working to educate the police service about issues connected with sexual orientation. These include the investigation of homophobic hate crime, victim care and family liaison (http:// www.gay.police.uk).

Managerialism
A term associated with the shift in government policy towards 'new public management' characterised by, inter alia: elements of privatisation; marketisation; the increased use of performance indicators; a growing emphasis on outputs and outcomes; partnership working; and the redesignation of clients as 'customers' (*see also* Best Value, marketisation, partnerships, privatisation).

Marketisation
A term referring to the process that has been taking place since the early 1980s which has had as its goal improving the cost efficiency and performance effectiveness of public constabularies via the imposition of 'market disciplines' on the police service. The process has included the increasing recourse to target-setting, the flattening of organisational hierarchies, the introduction of business plans, the imposition of the 'Best Value' regime and the contracting out of a few 'non-core' functions (*see also* Best Value, managerialism, privatisation).

Mass private property
Large 'public' spaces which are often privately owned but which are, to differing extents, open to access by the public. The prime examples are large shopping malls, privately owned 'gated communities', large enclosed residen-

tial blocks and large recreational and educational complexes. Their central significance for policing is that they are generally guarded by private security and, indeed, the growth of such spaces has been held to be a key factor in the growth of private policing.

National Black Police Association (NBPA)
The National Black Police Association, which was established in 1994, seeks to improve the working environment of black staff by protecting the rights of those employed within the police service and to enhance racial harmony and the quality of service to the black community of the UK – thereby assisting the police service in delivering a fair and equitable service to all sections of the community (http://www.nationalbpa.com).

The National Centre for Policing Excellence (NCPE)
The concept of the National Centre for Policing Excellence was introduced in the government 2001 white paper, *Policing a New Century: A Blueprint for Reform* (http://www.archive.official-documents.co.uk/document/cm53/5326/cm5326.htm). Currently being established, the work programme of the NCPE will reflect the requirements of the National Policing Plan and will be achieved primarily by enhancing the capabilities of those involved in tackling and reducing crime in order to reverse the fall in detection and conviction rates (http://www.centrex.police.uk).

National Competency Framework
The National Competency Framework (NCF) applies to staff of all ranks and grades in the police service and aims to measure and improve individual officer performance. It has formal support from ACPO, Home Office, APA, HMIC, Police Federation and Superintendents' Association and now informs the OSPRE process, the National Recruitment Strategy, the High Potential Development Scheme and a number of courses at Centrex (*see also* Centrex, leadership).

The National Crime Squad (NCS)
The National Crime Squad was established in April 1998 as a result of a 1995 report by the Home Affairs Select Committee on the threat of organised crime and its impact on the UK, which argued for the replacement of the existing structure of separate regional crime squads by a more nationally co-ordinated structure (http://www.nationalcrimesquad.police.uk).

National Criminal Intelligence Service (NCIS)
NCIS provides strategic and tactical intelligence on serious and organised crime, nationally and internationally. It is the gateway for UK law enforcement inquiries overseas via Interpol, Europol and the overseas liaison officers networks. It is also the co-ordinating authority on behalf of police forces in the UK for the tasking of the Security Service, in accordance with the Security Service Act 1996 (http://www.ncis.co.uk).

National Intelligence Model (NIM)
It has been argued that intelligence has lagged behind investigation in the codification of best practice, professional knowledge and in the identification of selection and training requirements of police service staff. As a consequence,

a model – the National Intelligence Model – containing best practice in intelligence-led policing and law enforcement has been developed by NCIS (*see also* intelligence-led policing) (http://www.ncis.co.uk/nim.asp).

National Policing Plan

The National Policing Plan for England and Wales 2003–6 was published on 20 November 2002 and sets out for the first time the government's strategic priorities for the police service for the next three years (http://www.policereform.co.uk/natpoliceplan/index.html).

Neighbourhood Watch (NW)

Undoubtedly the best known and most widely adopted crime prevention programme in the UK (in which local residents take responsibility for watching each other's property and generally remaining alert to local crime opportunities and problems). NW first appeared in the early 1980s, was promoted initially by the Metropolitan Police and has now spread nationwide.

Offender profiling

Offender profiling is a set of techniques used by law enforcement agencies to try to identify perpetrators of serious crime. There has been a rapidly growing interest in this subject over recent years both within the police service and in the media through films like *Silence of the Lambs* and television programmes such as *Cracker*.

OSPRE

Prior to 1991 the police service in England and Wales assessed police officers' potential for promotion to the ranks of sergeant and inspector by one exam. The questions in the exam required an essay style of answer and only tested the legal knowledge of the candidate. With a view to testing management and supervisory skills as well as legal knowledge, the two-part Objective Structured Performance Related Examination (OSPRE) was introduced (Part 1 tests the candidates' knowledge of the law; Part 2 tests their management and supervisory potential).

Partnerships

The police are increasingly expected to work jointly with other organisations and agencies in preventing and reducing crime. In particular, the Crime and Disorder Act 1998 established crime and disorder partnerships comprising representatives of the police, police authorities, and health and probation services, who are responsible for the production of an audit of local crime and disorder, for consulting locally on its contents, and for formulating, implementing and monitoring a strategy based on problems highlighted in the audit (*see also* managerialism, marketisation, responsibilisation).

Performance indicators

A target against which 'performance' can be gauged. The police are subject to an increasing array of performance indicators, including those contained in the National Policing Plan, local policing plans and as part of Best Value (*see also* Best Value, managerialism, National Policing Plan).

Plural policing
Policing has become increasingly complex and the set of activities we understand as 'policing' is clearly delivered by a broad, and increasing, array of providers. These include the commercial security sector; new public sector provision such as local authority patrol, municipal police forces and wardens (as well as informal policing such as vigilantism); the range of regulatory agencies within local and national government; together with those transnational policing agencies that operate beyond individual states (*see also* policing, transnational policing).

Police authority
Police authorities are independent bodies responsible for the oversight of local policing. Their consultations with local people, which they are statutorily required to perform, are intended to provide an important link between the police and the public they serve. Police authorities are normally made up of 17 members: three magistrates, nine local councillors and five independent members (*see also* accountability, governance, tripartite structure).

Police community consultative groups
In the aftermath of the Brixton riots in 1981, the report of the Scarman Inquiry recommended the introduction of statutory liaison committees to increase police–public consultation. Subsequently, s. 106 of the Police and Criminal Evidence Act (now consolidated as s. 96 of the Police Act 1996) provided the statutory basis for such police–community consultative groups (sometimes referred to as s. 106 or s. 96 committees) (*see also* Scarman Inquiry, independent advisory groups).

Police Federation
The body that represents officers below the rank of superintendent. Each force has a branch and the federation represents members in matters of welfare, discipline and promotion (*see also* ACPO, Police Superintendents' Association).

The Police Information Technology Organisation (PITO)
The organisation responsible for the development and commissioning of information technology for the police service and other agencies in the criminal justice system. PITO's board contains representatives of the Home Office/Scottish Office, ACPO and the police authorities, and PITO's work falls under six main headings: communications; identification; police national computer; criminal justice; intelligence and investigation; and police support services (http://www.pito.org.uk).

Police reform
A programme of change instituted during the second term of the Labour government after the 2001 general election. Signalled by a white paper, *Policing a New Century: A Blueprint for Reform,* the programme so far has included the establishment of the Police Standards Unit, the passage of legislation, the Police Reform Act 2002 and the release of the first National Policing Plan (*see also* National Policing Plan, Police Standards Unit) (http://www.policere-form.co.uk).

The Police Skills and Standards Organisation (PSSO)

Since March 2001, the PSSO has been recognised as the national training organisation for the police. The PSSO is the standard-setting body for the UK police service. The core roles of the PSSO are to develop national occupational standards, increase skills levels and provide the recognised voice of the police service – addressing their needs across the whole spectrum of learning, skills, training and development issues (http://www.psso.co.uk).

Police Standards Unit (PSU)

The Police Standards Unit (PSU) was set up by the Home Secretary in July 2001 and is a central part of the government's police reform agenda. The focus of the unit's activities is to measure and compare basic command unit (BCU) and local partnership performance, understand the underlying causes of performance variations, identify and disseminate good practice and support those who need assistance (*see also* basic command unit, police reform) (http://www.policereform.gov.uk/psu/index.html).

Police Superintendents' Association (PSA)

The staff association for all officers of superintendent and chief superintendent rank (*see also* ACPO, Police Federation) (http://www.policesupers.com).

Policing

Much policing literature has traditionally focused on the activities of state policing bodies: 'the police'. The apparent increasing complexity of policing arrangements has led writers to focus more broadly on the array of 'providers' now involved in what broadly might be thought of as policing activities. Defining 'policing' is problematic. However, Jones and Newburn (*Private Security and Public Policing.* Oxford: Clarendon Press (1998) 18–19) defined it as:

> those organized forms of order maintenance, peacekeeping, rule or law enforcement, crime investigation and prevention and other forms of investigation and associated information-brokering – which may involve a conscious exercise of coercive power – undertaken by individuals or organizations, where such activities are viewed by them and/or others as a central or key defining part of their purpose.

Privatisation

At its simplest, the shift of ownership and control from the public to the private sector. In practice, privatisation can cover a range of policies including civilianisation, 'contracting out', the increasing use of sponsorship and private finance and the establishment of public–private partnerships.

Problem analysis triangle (PAT)

Linked to routine activities theory, the problem analysis triangle suggests that the 'solution' to any particular problem is to be found by looking at, and responding to, one or more of its three central features: an offender, class of offenders or other source of difficulty; a victim or class of victims; and a location or characteristic of particular locations (*see also* problem-oriented policing, prolific offenders, SARA).

Problem-oriented policing (POP)

The brainchild of US academic lawyer and police scientist, Herman Goldstein, POP begins from a critique of incident-driven policing and suggests that policing at heart should be about solving the underlying problems within communities. At its most radical it involves the empowerment of the local beat officer who is given responsibility for imaginative local problem-solving (*see also* crime analysis, problem analysis triangle, hot products, hotspots, repeat victimisation).

Prolific offender

Considerable criminological evidence points to the uneven distribution of offending. Put crudely, there is a small number of offenders who are responsible for a disproportionate amount of crime and who are variously referred to as 'prolific', 'persistent' or 'volume' offenders. These offenders have been the subject of considerable legislative attention – such as through the introduction of secure training centres for persistent juvenile offenders and mandatory minimum sentences for repeat offenders – and are also often a particular focus of police intelligence gathering and enforcement (*see also* problem-analysis triangle, SARA).

Repeat victimisation

Arising from the finding that crime is highly concentrated geographically and socially. Indeed, it is concentrated not only on particular places but also on particular people. This concentration at the level of the individual person, household or business is known as 'repeat victimisation' (*see also* crime analysis, crime mapping, hot products, hotspots) (http://www.crimereduction.gov.uk/toolkits/p031606.htm).

Responsibilisation

A term referring to a set of strategies in which governments have sought to redistribute the task of crime control among a plethora of actors beyond the state. It is associated with terms such as partnership, multi- and interagency co-operation, active citizenship and active communities.

Restorative justice (RJ)

One of the most significant social movements in criminal justice reform in recent times. Often viewed simply in opposition to formal justice, the most commonly used definition is of a 'process whereby the parties with a stake in a particular offence come together to resolve collectively how to deal with the aftermath of the offence and its implications for the future' (Marshall, T. (1996)'The evolution of restorative justice in Britain', *European Journal on Criminal Policy and Research*, 4(4): 37). In relation to policing, RJ is most associated with the reformed cautioning practices adopted by Thames Valley Police and is increasingly being used in areas such as police complaints.

Right of silence

The right of suspects to refuse to answer questions in a police interview, to refuse to testify and the privilege against self-incrimination. Amended by the Criminal Justice and Public Order Act 1994 to allow the judge under certain circumstances to tell the jury that it is permissible for them to draw inferences from the defendant's silence.

SARA
'Scanning', 'analysis', 'response' and 'assessment'. A set of procedures associated with problem-oriented policing. Put at its simplest, the idea assumes that problems are identified through scanning and are then analysed. The analysis results in the development of an appropriate policing response, the effectiveness of which is later assessed and the results fed back to inform future activity (*see also* crime analysis, problem analysis triangle, problem-oriented policing).

Scarman Inquiry
Established in the aftermath of the urban unrest in Brixton in 1981 the inquiry, chaired by Lord Scarman, was highly critical of the intensive police operation that had preceded the disorder. The inquiry's recommendations were wide ranging and covered recruitment of ethnic minorities to the police, increased consultation with local communities, the introduction of lay visitors and the introduction of an independent review of complaints against the police (*see also* police community consultative groups).

Senior Command Course
A course, now run by Centrex, based at Bramshill, which is mandatory for officers (generally chief superintendents) aspiring to chief officer rank (*see also* Bramshill, Centrex).

Situational crime prevention
According to Ron Clarke (*Situational Crime Prevention*. New York, NY: Harrow & Heston (1992): 4) this refers to:

> a pre-emptive approach that relies, not on improving society or its institutions, but simply on reducing opportunities for crime . . . Situational prevention comprises opportunity-reducing measures that are (1) directed at highly specific forms of crime, (2) that involve the management, design or manipulation of the immediate environment in as specific and permanent way as possible (3) so as to increase the effort and risks of crime and reduce the rewards as perceived by a wide range of offenders.

Special Branch
With origins in the Metropolitan Police's 'Irish Branch' in the nineteenth century, Special Branch became the policing body with primary responsibility initially for espionage and, in more recent times, terrorism. The Metropolitan Police's Special Branch remains the largest, but other forces have now all established their own special branches. Special Branch officers are involved in risk assessment in relation to terrorist threats and provide armed personal protection for people judged to be at risk. Because of their anti-terrorist role, Special Branch officers are permanently stationed at ports and airports to gather intelligence, identify suspects and to provide support to other anti-terrorist activity.

Stephen Lawrence Inquiry
Established to inquire into the murder in April 1993 of Stephen Lawrence in Eltham, southeast London, and the police investigation that followed. The inquiry, chaired by Sir William Macpherson, was set up by Jack Straw in 1997 and reported in February 1999. It made 70 recommendations, and famously concluded that 'the [police] investigation was marred by a combination of professional incompetence, institutional racism and a failure of leadership by senior officers' (*see also* independent advisory groups, Scarman Inquiry).

Terrorism
Another term that is highly problematic to define but, in shorthand, is often referred to simply as 'political violence'. The definition of terrorism in s. 1 of the Terrorism Act 2000 includes actual or threatened acts of violence against people and/or property designed to influence the government, to intimidate the public or a section of the public, or to advance a political, religious or ideological cause.

Transnational policing
Broadly speaking, this concerns policing other than that authorised and practised within the territorial boundaries and institutions of the state. However, and in contrast with certain forms of 'international policing', transnational policing refers to the activities of individuals and organisations that draw their authority from outside individual nation-states – i.e. non-state communities, such as the EU.

Tripartite structure
A reference to the system of governance established originally by the Police Act 1964; 'tripartite' because it has three pillars: chief constables, local police authorities and the Home Secretary. The system has subsequently been reformed, in particular by the Police and Magistrates' Courts Act 1994, but remains the basis for the governance of the police (*see also* accountability, constabulary independence, governance).

War on Drugs
'War' as a metaphor has been used with some frequency in the criminal justice arena since the early 1980s. Initially associated with the Reagan administration in the USA, the War on Drugs has seen very significant increases in the resources devoted to interdiction and policing compared with the financing of prevention and harm reduction initiatives (*see also* harm reduction).

Watch committee
The growth of provincial police forces in the nineteenth century led to the emergence of two systems of accountability. Borough police forces were overseen by wholly elected watch committees, whereas joint standing committees, made up of two thirds elected councillors and one third magistrates, oversaw the county forces. This system was reformed by the Police Act 1964 (*see also* accountability, joint standing committee, police authority).

Index

Added to the page number, 'b' denotes a box, 'f' denotes a figure, 'g' denotes the glossary and 't' denotes a table.

CCTV schemes 294
  anticipatory effects 303
  in police stations 240
  and the prevention of terrorism 486
CDA *see* Crime and Disorder Act (1998)
CDRPs (Crime and Disorder Reduction
      partnerships) 19, 177, 293, 616
cellular phones 662
censorship pressures on the media 265, 270
Central Drugs and Illegal Immigration Unit
      (CDIIU) 427
Central Drugs Intelligence Unit 427
central Europe, police systems 25–7
central government
  accretion of power 18, 94–6, 613–14
  control of the crime reduction agenda 294–5
  historical context on crime control 57–8
centralisation
  in the nineteenth-century 71–2, 74–5
  postwar years 91–6
  pressures towards 711–12
Centrex (Central Police Training and
      Development Authority) 180, 191, 192,
      642, 723g
charge
  decision to 238, 247
  and ethnic minority communities 538
cheka 23
chief constables
  professional autonomy 612
  responsibilities 94–5, 185t, 608, 610
  types of 637–8
Chief Constables' Association of England and
      Wales 93
chief pledge 43
Chief Police Officers' Staff Association
      (CPOSA) 186
child abuse
  policing response 569–71
    specialist policing units 510–11
    use of information technology 521
child pornography 501–2, 505, 513
  see also Operation Ore
Child Protection Operational Command Unit
      (SO5) 511
child protection teams *see* CPTs
China
  comparisons with Japan 33
  comparisons with the USSR 23–5
CHISs (covert human intelligence sources) *see*
      informants
Christopher Commission 559
CID 183
  establishment 365
  problems 376–7
  generalist offices 371–2, 378t
    pressure to perform 377, 379

reforms 383, 384–5
CID (officers) 365, 723g
cinema and police image 264–5, 270, 273–4
circle of crime theory 349
Citizen's Charter 19
citizenship
  forms 148
  importance 407–8
  see also active citizenship
city centres, security in 153–4
City of London Police 170
  and fraud investigation 451, 455
  rank structure 178t
city police in the USA 31
  development 28–9
civil actions against the police 250–51
  by the ethnic minority communities 545–6
Civil Aviation Authority (CAA) 458b
Civil Contingencies Committee (CCC) 491
civil liberties
  and covert policing 381
  and drugs law enforcement 428
  of ethnic minority communities 531
  protection 384
Civil Rights Movement 401, 402, 403, 404
civil sanctions in drugs policing 435
civilian policing 143b, 147–8
  see also Neighbourhood Watch; Special
      Constabulary
civilian staff 96–7, 149t, 157–8, 180–82
  effect of information technology 662
  research on 212
classification systems in offender profiling 348
climate-setting leadership 306–7
Climbié Inquiry 569–71
co-operation
  across boundaries 75, 92–3
    and cybercrime 511–13
  within continental Europe 19–20, 21
  see also partnership working; transnational
      policing
*Code of Practice for the Detention, Treatment and
      Questioning of Persons by Police Officers*
      239–40
*Code of Practice on Reporting and Recording Racist
      Incidents* 540
coercion in interrogations 240–41
collection of data 342
Colonial Police Service 22
colonial societies
  police systems 21–2
  see also Canada; USA
Combat 18 (C18) 469, 487–8
command leadership 728g
Command Team Programme *see* Senior
      Leadership Development Programme
commercial policing 148–51

Customs and Excise
  and financial investigation 449, 454, 456
  and rule-bending 437
Customs and Excise Investigations Division
  447
cyber-trespass 508–9
'cybercops' 503
cybercrime 501–22
  types 504–10
  policing 285, 502–4
    problems 511–19
    specialist units 510–11
    future 519–22
cyberspace *see* Internet
cyberstalking 513

Dangerous Drugs Acts (1965) and (1967) 425
DARE 298
data
  collection 342
  representation 342–3
  interpretation 343–4
  financial 428
  problems of 329–30, 355, 357
Data Protection Act (1998) 428
DEA (Drug Enforcement Administration) 31
Deadly Silence: Black Deaths in Custody 534
deaths in custody 534
deceptive methods of investigation 381–2
decision-making
  by offenders 353
  internal 184–5
  and 'working rules' 235–6
  see also discretion
Dedicated Cheque and Plastic Crime Unit 449,
  453, 457
deduction in crime analysis 344
Defence of the Realm Act (DORA) 424
'defensible space' theory 154
democratic framework of police governance
  606–7
  in England and Wales 620–24
  and the policing of terrorist activities 489–92
demographic and social trend analysis 346t
denial-of-service viruses 508
'The Department' 484
Department of Trade and Industry (DTI) 454,
  456, 457
Department of Work and Pensions (DWP) 454,
  456
Desborough Committee 77–8, 80
descriptive data 343
detection technologies 655, 658
detective services 69
  development 78–9
  see also CID
detention 237–9

coercive nature 240
  regulation 242–4
diffusion of benefits 300
'digital piracy' 506–7
Diplock courts 482, 483
Diplock Report (1972) 482
discretion 228–9, 233, 357, 583
  and bias 233–5
  effect of information technology 665
  and professionalism 588
discrimination 213–19, 528–30
  against policewomen 565–7
  and police governance 544
  working rules and patterns of 233–6
  see also racism
displacement 300, 354, 356t
  of the drugs problem 436
distal causes of crime 351–2
'distributed leadership' 643
distribution of power 607
  and police governance in England and
    Wales 621–2
  see also centralisation; localisation;
    nationalisation; regionalisation
Ditchley Circular (211/78) 87
diversity, policing and 715–16
'divided societies' 411–13
division of labour in policing *see* pluralisation
  of policing
Dixon of Dock Green 3, 81, 100–101, 265, 725g
Dixon of Dock Green 81
DNA identification 717
documentary stories about crime and policing
  268–9
'domestic terrorism' 469
domestic violence 236, 569, 573
door supervisors *see* bouncers
DORA (Defence of the Realm Act) 424
Drug Enforcement Administration (DEA) 31
drug referral schemes 436
Drug Trafficking Offences Act (DTOA) (1986)
  428
drugs policing 284–5, 422–39
  early history 423–5
  organisation and specialisation 426–7
  financial detection 427–8
  as a global issue 430–1
  national and local 431–36
  police misconduct 437–8
  transnationalisation 429–30
Drugs (Prevention of Misuse) Act (1964) 425
DTI (Department of Trade and Industry) 454,
  456, 457
due process 229–31, 725g
DWP (Department of Work and Pensions) 454,
  456

National Reporting Centre (NRC) 18, 92–3
'national security' 489, 493
National Strategy for Police Information
  Systems (NSPIS) 192
National Terrorist Financial Investigation Unit
  488
National Union of Police and Prison Officers
  (NUPPO) 76, 77, 78
nationalisation of policing 69, 91–2, 613–16
  and the Desborough Committee's report 77
  and the miners' strike 92–3
  and the Police and Magistrates' Courts Act
    (1994) 95
NBPA (National Black Police Association) 187,
  542, 729g
NCF (National Competency Framework) 191,
  647–8, 729g
NCIS 91, 92, 189, 190, 427, 448, 457, 472, 615–16,
  730g
NCPE (National Centre for Policing
  Excellence) 191, 192, 581, 586, 729g
NCS 91, 92, 189–90, 427, 447–8, 457, 472,
  615–16, 730g
NDIU (National Drugs Intelligence Unit) 190,
  427
negative labeling 207
'negotiated management' 408–10
neighbourhood disputes 698
neighbourhood policing see community
  policing
neighbourhood warden programme 146, 149t
Neighbourhood Watch (NW) 147, 331, 332, 591,
  730g
Netherlands 20, 21
  Stadswacht schemes 146
network analysis 346t
networked model of plural policing 157,
  159–60
'New Police' see Metropolitan Police
new public management
  definition 631–2
  and crime analysis 341
  and fraud policing 451–2
  and information technology 670
  and partnership working 641
  and problem-oriented policing 330
  shortcomings 638–9
  see also performance management
new social movements 413–14
  involvement of private security 414–15
news stories about crime and policing 268–9
  corruption in 269
  production of 270–71
newspapers and police image 269, 271
NFA (no further action) rates 247
NHTCU (National Hi-tech Crime Unit) 449,
  501–2, 520

Nigeria 22
night-time economy 154–6
NIM (National Intelligence Model) 184, 313,
  321, 322, 333, 340, 387–8, 730g
'noble cause corruption' 86, 306, 379, 582
  portrayal in the media 269
Nolan report (1995) 584, 588
'non-Home Office' police forces 170
'non-lethal' weapons 407, 408, 596, 598
non-police fraud investigations 446, 453
  agencies for 456
non-territorial terrorism 468
normalisation of emergency powers 476, 479
normalisation phase of the Troubles 481, 482–4
North America
  police systems 27–32
  see also USA
North-West Mounted Police 28
  see also Royal Canadian Mounted Police
    (RCMP)
Northern Ireland
  Ombudsman's Office 491
  paramilitaries 147
  police service 170
  use of internment 480
  use of negotiated settlements 410
  use of plastic baton rounds 407, 408
  see also Patten Inquiry; the Troubles
Northern Ireland (Emergency Provisions) Act
  (1973) 477b
Northern Ireland (Emergency Provisions) Act
  (1998) 478b
NOS (National Occupational Standards) 191
notifiable offences see recorded crime
NPM see new public management
NPT (National Police Training) 191
NRC (National Reporting Centre) 18, 92–3
NSPIS (National Strategy for Police
  Information Systems) 192
numbers
  plural policing 149t
  of police officers 2, 172–3t, 174
  of private security personnel 148–9
NUPPO (National Union of Police and Prison
  Officers) 76, 77, 78

Oaksey Committee 80–81
Oath of Attestation 586
Objective Structured Performance Related
  Police Promotion Exam (OSPRE) 180,
  730–31g
offender profiling 347–50, 730g
  approaches 348–9
  critiques 349–50
offenders
  decision-making process 353
  identification in the eighteenth century 55